《境外资本市场重要法律文献译丛》

编 委 会

《英国 2000 年金融服务与市场法》

总　编：张　凡

副总编：郭晓利　杨淑琴　巫克力

编　委：袁　涛　张　雷　汪琛德　王学勤
　　　　郑文博　赵　蓉　周鹏举

致　谢

郑州商品交易所对本书的出版给予了大力支持!

译者说明

英国《2000年金融服务与市场法》(Financial Services and Markets Act 2000)于2001年12月1日正式生效,取代了此前制定的一系列用于监管金融业的法律、法规。该法堪称英国金融业的一部"基本法",明确了新成立的金融服务管理局(Financial Services Authority)和被监管人的权力、义务及责任。统一了监管标准,规范了金融市场的运作。

《2000年金融服务与市场法》的颁布,标志着英国金融监管体制的重大变革,即从《1986年金融服务法》确立的"制定法框架下的行业自律"体制转变为"制定法规范的单一监管机构"体制(Statutory Single Regulator),并且确立了金融服务管理局的单一监管机构地位。金融服务管理局承继了前证券与投资局(SIB)对证券投资业务、英格兰银行对银行金融机构、财政部对保险机构的监管职能,其监管范围涵盖了全部金融领域,包括证券、银行、保险以及各类互助会。

《2000年金融服务与市场法》主要规定内容是:(1)规定金融业的单一监管机构,即金融服务管理局的法定监管权力。金融服务管理局的监管目标:一是保持公众对英国金融系统和金融市场的信心;二是向公众宣传,让公众了解金融系统以及同特殊金融产品相关的利益与风险;三是确保为消费者提供必要的保护;四是为发现和阻止金融犯罪提供协助。金融服务管理局除具有原有9个金融监管机构的监管权力以外,还负有对过去某些不受监管的领域,如金融机构与客户合同中的不公平条款、金融市场行业准则、为金融业提供服务的律师与会计师事务所等的规范与监管的职责。同时,它还规定了金融服务管理局的监管原则:必须有效并经济地使用其资源;负有监督金融机构高级管理层的职责;监管措施的成本,无论放松还是限制,必须与预期所能达到的监管效果相适应;促进监管手段的创新;注重金融服务市场的国际化特点,并保持英国金融业的竞争力;尽可能地减少因金融服务管理局为履行其职能而采取必要行动可能对竞争带来的副作用;促进金融服务管理局监管的金融机构之间的竞争。

(2)规定英国财政部的职权范围及其根据《2000年金融服务与市场法》所承担的职能,一般性禁止原则、获得许可的要件及对金融投资宣传的限制。规定任何人未经核准或豁免,不得在英国从事被监管的业务,若违反规定将受到处罚。规范了金融推介与诱导行为。

(3)授权金融服务管理局对从业人的申请及变更被监管业务的许可条件作出规

定,金融服务管理局对变更许可或撤销许可享有自由裁量权。

(4)金融业从业人员担任特定职务如需经金融服务管理局核准,上述人员应符合金融服务管理局作出的规定,金融服务管理局对违反规定者有处罚权。金融服务管理局有权发布命令,禁止上述人员从事部分或全部被监管的业务。

(5)授权金融服务管理局负责审核拟在伦敦证券交易所上市的申请,并有权制定相关的规则。

(6)授权金融服务管理局对各类不当行为(如内幕交易、操纵市场等)予以规范,规定具体处罚。

(7)设立专业金融裁判所,受理针对金融服务管理局依据本法作出处罚的申诉。

(8)授权金融服务管理局对被核准者从事受监管业务制定行为准则。

(9)规定金融服务管理局和财政部有调查权,可要求被调查者提供信息和文件资料,并可以向法院申请搜查特定场所进行取证。

(10)凡持有上市公司10%以上股权者,如拟取得控制性权益应报告金融服务管理局并取得其核准。

(11)授权金融服务管理局监管来自其他欧盟成员国的业者在英国从事受监管的业务。

(12)授权金融服务管理局可对违反本法规定的任何人进行公开谴责及作出处罚。

(13)设立独立的金融服务赔偿公司,在消费者因获授权人无力偿还时作出赔偿时,金融服务赔偿公司有权对有问题的被核准者进行检查。

(14)规定交易所及结算公司均由金融服务管理局监管。

(15)规定金融服务管理局应编撰并保存获授权人的公开资料,以及制定有关保密资料在特定情形下予以公开的规定。

(16)授权金融服务管理局可请求法院对获授权人启动清算和破产程序;对第三方启动的破产程序有权介入。

(17)规定金融服务管理局对未经核准从事受监管业务或违反本法规定事项的人可采取的处罚措施。

(18)规定金融服务管理局依法发出各种通知时应遵循的法律程序。

(19)规定金融服务管理局有权对误导性陈述、内幕交易、洗钱等进行起诉。

《2010年金融服务法》对《2000年金融服务与市场法》进行了修改,包括修改金融服务管理局的目标、惩戒权、金融教育相关规定以及金融服务和市场的其他相关规定。

《2010年金融服务法》的通过,为长期以来关于行业自律与立法监管两种模式之间的争论画上了句号:尽管行业自律的重要性不容忽视,但其作为主要的监管模式,已经不再适应当前金融领域的发展。金融服务管理局作为单一的监管机构,适应了金融全球化背景下混业经营的发展趋势,代表了今后金融监管模式的重要发展方向。由于英国在世界金融业的地位,金融服务管理局的影响不仅局限于英国国内,至少还影响了所有需要通过英国金融市场进行交易的金融机构或企业。鉴于英国金融监管机构的国际声誉，其监管模式无疑将对其他国家的监管者提供重要的借鉴意义。

目前，我国还严格坚持“分业经营，分业监管”的模式，这与英国的“混业经营，单一监管”模式具有质的差别。但是，英国《2010年金融服务法》与金融服务管理局的诸多监管技术与规范方面，如确定明晰的监管目标和原则，有效分配监管资源，提高监管者自身的可信度，与被监管对象建立起良好的沟通渠道等方面的内容无疑会为我国金融监管机构提供些许镜鉴。

北京思必锐翻译有限责任公司　宋金莹

总译校：

焦津洪：原对外经贸大学法学院副院长，教授、博士研究生导师，美国纽约哥伦比亚大学法学院、美国洛杉矶洛约拉大学法学院、加拿大不列颠哥伦比亚大学访问学者。中国法学会法学教育研究会理事、中国法学会世界贸易组织法研究会理事、中国国际经济贸易仲裁委员会仲裁员资格审查考核委员会委员、中国国际贸易促进会调解员、北京市仲裁委员会仲裁员、韩国商事仲裁院仲裁员、国际商会（中国）国际仲裁委员会委员、中国国际经济贸易仲裁委员会仲裁员、中国国际经济法学会理事，曾任中国证监会行政处罚委员会主任，现任深圳证监局局长。

审校人员：

程合红：中国政法大学法学博士，主要著作有《商事人格权论》、《国有股权研究》等，在《中国法学》、《政法论坛》、《法学》及《法制日报》等报刊发表多篇学术论文，现任中国证监会法律部副主任。

苏彦新：郑州大学法学院教授、博士研究生导师，华东政法大学法学博士，英国Dunee University访问学者。主要研究领域：民商法、比较法以及外国法律史。主译并总校有《美国法律史》等，在《环球法律评论》、《法学家》、《清华法治论衡》及《华东政法大学学报》等报刊发表多篇学术论文。

王丽：中国人民大学法学博士、英国伦敦大学国王学院法学硕士，现任中国证监会市场部交易监管处副调研员、公职律师。

王保民：西安交通大学法学院副院长，教授、博士研究生导师，丝绸之路国际法研究所副所长，北京大学法学博士，中美富布赖特高级研究学者（美国加州大学伯克利分校法学院）、布鲁塞尔自由大学访问学者。

周浩：中国政法大学法律硕士、伦敦大学学院（University College London）法学硕士（银行与金融法专业），现任国联安基金管理有限公司督察长，曾任中国证监会基金部监管三处副调研员、公职律师。

杨光：英国华威大学金融与会计专业学士、剑桥大学房地产金融学硕士，曾任美林银行投资银行部分析员。

翻译机构：

本书由北京思必锐翻译有限责任公司承担全部译校工作。思必锐成立于1996年，专注于金融、法律、文化等领域的多语种口笔译服务，是北京市高级人民法院指定翻译机构、中国译协会员、中国国际公关协会会员。

译者：

王强，北京思必锐翻译有限责任公司翻译质量总监，外交学院国际法硕士，国家人事部全国翻译专业资格英语一级笔译。

宋金莹，北京思必锐翻译有限责任公司译审，北京外国语大学高级翻译学院翻译硕士，南开大学英语专业、中国人民大学法学专业双学士，国家人事部全国翻译专业资格英语一级笔译，曾任司法部高级翻译。

总　　序

中国资本市场是适应我国经济体制改革和对外开放的形势要求逐步建立发展起来的。为了有效借鉴境外成熟市场的制度经验,中国资本市场从成立伊始,就特别注重按照"立足国情,为我所用"的原则,不断学习、消化和吸收境外成熟市场的运行规则和监管制度。目前,中国资本市场现行有效的法律、法规、规章、规范性文件共521件,加上大量的交易所和协会的自律规则,基本形成了我国资本市场的法律制度规范体系。这些制度规范构建起一整套与国际通行原则基本相符的法律框架、交易规则和监管体系,有效维护了市场秩序,保证了市场功能和作用的发挥,保护了投资者的合法权益。

经过20余年的改革发展,我国资本市场进入了创新发展的新阶段。立足于服务实体经济发展的大局需要,重点解决资本市场自身结构不平衡、服务实体经济能力不足、为居民提供投资理财产品相对匮乏等突出现实问题,资本市场现有的以股票公开发行并在交易所上市交易为主的境内市场体系,将逐步发展成为一个公募与私募并重、股票与债券平衡、场内与场外协调发展的资本市场体系。与此相适应,需要进一步发展壮大财富管理行业,立足于功能监管的制度定位,统一资产管理行为规则,放松行政管制,增强创新活力。实现这样的改革目标,需要我们更加重视学习境外成熟市场的制度经验,充分借鉴境外市场有关私募发行、债权融资、资产管理、期货及衍生品等方面的法律制度,在尊重市场规律的前提下,大胆进行制度和机制创新,确保我们的各项制度适应和满足市场改革的实际需要。

坚持对外开放是中国资本市场改革和发展的一贯方针。在经济全球化深入发展的时代背景下,适应我国经济结构调整和经济方式转变和"逐步实现人民币资本项目可兑换"的金融对外开放的总体要求,中国资本市场必须以更加积极的态度参与全球经济竞争,提高在全球范围内配置资源,服务实体经济发展的能力。不论是支持境内企业到境外发行融资,鼓励境内机构和个人到境外进行证券投资,还是畅通境外企业到境内发行融资渠道,平等保护境外机构和个人到境内进行证券投资,都需要在立足国情的前提下,实现制度衔接互通,消除制度壁垒。特别重要的是,市场竞争首先是制度规则的竞争,增强我国资本市场的国际竞争力,一方面要确保我国市场通过制度规则体现法治环境吸引力,另一方面还要增强我国在涉及资本市场对外开放的国际规则的制定中的话语权，增强我国在国际监管合作和跨境执法合作中的主动权。

同时，我们也注意到，2008年国际金融危机发生后，境外资本市场对监管体制、机制做了较为重大的调整，提出了不少新的监管要求，出台了不少新的法律文件。例如，美国制定了具有金融综合监管性质的《多德—弗兰克法案》，英国则将原来集证券、银行、保险于一身的《2000年金融服务与市场法》修改成《金融服务法》。对于境外相关法律制度的动态发展，需要及时掌握情况，借鉴有益经验，为进一步完善我国资本市场的基础性制度建设提供参考。

经过长期的努力，中国资本市场的制度借鉴和引进已经越过了概念化、碎片状的发展阶段，进入全面、系统、精细化的更高阶段。由于种种原因，对境外资本市场法律制度的介绍，无论是在法学界、法律界，还是在证券期货行业内，一直以来都存在及时性不够、系统性不足、权威性不强的情况。特别是翻译介绍的质量不高、精品不多，这在客观上影响了对境外经验的学习和借鉴。

为了适应资本市场学习借鉴境外制度经验的形势要求，中国证监会精选了境外资本市场国家和地区的重要法律文献，包括境外主要资本市场的重要法律、监管部门的监管规则、经典的司法判例、最新的资本市场立法成果以及相关法学理论权威著作等，组织翻译出版了这套《境外资本市场重要法律文献译丛》。译丛的翻译出版工作，在系统单位、部门和关心市场发展的专家学者的共同努力下，紧紧抓住保质量、出精品的关键环节，建立了“竞标择优确定翻译人员、知名专家评审保证翻译质量、适当报酬和学术声誉结合激励”的工作机制，落实“精选译题、精细翻译、精心审校、精致出版”的工作要求，是中国证监会打造国人了解国际资本市场法律制度权威平台的有益尝试。为此，愿以本文向参与丛书翻译、审校的国际金融、法律方面的专家和学者表示感谢，并与大家共勉，共同为建设起一个权力公平、机会公平、规则公平的资本市场而努力。

中国证监会

2013年2月

序

当今世界，属于英美法系的国家大概有30%，而属于大陆法系的则占70%左右。20世纪90年代以来，美国经济学家施莱佛(Andrei Shleifer)等人通过实证方法研究发现，金融市场发达，特别是证券市场比较发达的国家绝大部分属于英美法系国家，其原因主要是英美法比大陆法更能保护外部投资者免受公司内部人的掠夺和欺骗，因而有利于金融市场的发展。还有研究对102个国家从1960~1992年人均GDP平均年度增长率进行实证分析，发现具有英美法传统的国家要比非英美法国家每年高0.71个百分点。这一发现在经济学和法学界引起了强烈反响和激烈争论。有学者反驳说，是由于这些国家经济和金融发达才推动了英美法体系，特别是保护投资者的法律制度的完善和成熟。还有学者提出，这些国家金融市场的发达更多的是其他原因，如政治环境、公共执法、股份公司股权结构等。尽管存在争议，但对于英美法系与金融发展之间存在较强的关联关系这一点在学术上已经达成共识。

一般认为，证券市场最为发达、证券监管最为成熟的国家是美国。但是美国在20世纪30年代建立现代意义上的证券监管制度时，在很大程度上借鉴了英国的经验。1933年3月，罗斯福总统刚上任数天，就提出要起草证券法。哈佛大学法学院教授法兰克福特(Felix Frankfurter)带领三个哈佛法学院的毕业生仅在一个周末就起草出美国第一部专门的联邦证券法律——《1933年证券法》，确立了以强制信息披露为原则的监管理念，没有采纳当时很多人主张的"实质监管"（Merits Regulation)，其所依据的基础就是英国当时的《公司法》。因此可以说，就证券监管而言，英国和美国是有着共同的出发点的。然而，在美国制定《1934年证券交易法》并设立了专门监管证券市场的联邦独立监管机构——证券交易委员会（SEC）之后，英国和美国走向了不同模式的金融监管道路。美国更加依赖政府的监管和执法，辅之以行业协会、证券交易所等自律监管；而英国则主要依靠行业和证券交易所的自律，直到1997年，英国才真正建立专门的行政监管机构，即金融服务监管局(FSA)。

直到20世纪初，英国伦敦一直是全球第一金融中心，英国《经济学人》杂志主编白芝浩（Walter Bagehot）1873年在《隆巴特街》（*Lombard Street*）一书中曾把英国金融体系誉为"大英帝国王冠上的一颗宝石"。长期以来，英国证券市场上商人银行（即投资银行）、经纪商及交易商（做市商）三类机构之间有明确业务分工，各自采取"单一业务"

制度(Single Capacity)。商人银行负责公司融资,包括IPO、配股、公司并购、项目融资等;交易商通过为自营账户买卖证券维持市场的流动性;经纪商则作为连接证券发行人、商人银行、交易商的纽带,代理证券买卖。在单一业务制度下,各类证券机构分业经营,经纪商的佣金是固定的,交易商的风险控制也非常简单,因此英国证券公司以合伙制为主,规模较小,主要依靠行业封闭和垄断维持着较高利润。1976年,由于受到1975年5月美国证券行业取消固定佣金制改革的影响,英国工党政府推动通过一部新法案,将有关"反限制性商业惯例"的法律扩大适用于服务业。英国公平交易局要求伦敦交易所清理其交易规则并接受审查。英国公平交易局在审查后认为其中有150条规则违反"反限制性商业惯例"法,并于1979年对伦敦交易所提起诉讼。撒切尔作为保守党领袖当选首相后,大力推动国有企业私有化,而她认识到大规模私有化需要有强大的资本市场和具有国际竞争力证券行业给予支持,因此必须对英国证券行业进行改革。她派了副首相到伦敦交易所进行谈判,最终于1983年伦敦交易所与公平交易局达成协议,规定交易佣金可以自由协商确定;交易所会员可以同时兼任经纪商和交易商;交易所会员对任何符合条件的机构开放。该协议给了证券行业3年准备期,于1986年10月27日正式实施。这一次看起来并不是很大的改革其影响是却极为重大的,被称为英国金融史上的第一次"大爆炸"(Big Bang)。它彻底地改变了英国金融市场的面貌。英国本土证券公司几乎不再存在,伦敦交易所仍然是世界上最重要的证券交易所之一,实际上却已经不再属于英国。但是,英国金融市场因此重新恢复了活力,更为重要的是,为撒切尔政府的国有企业私有化改革的顺利实施提供了保障。而且,其影响更进一步辐射欧洲、美国以至日本等亚洲国家,成为推动金融市场全球化进程的重要动力。这一次金融变革被英国《金融时报》称为"最深得撒切尔时代精髓的改革","为伦敦金融城不可阻挡的崛起奠定了基础"。

第一次金融"大爆炸"后,以美国为代表的国际金融机构开始主导英国金融市场,市场竞争日益激烈,金融业混业经营越来越普遍,银行、保险及证券行业之间的界限日益模糊。而当时英国的金融监管体系非常复杂,有包括英格兰银行在内的9家监管机构对银行、证券、保险和住房协会等金融机构分别进行监管。传统的分立监管框架已经不适应新的形势,阻碍了金融业效率的进一步提高和创新发展。因此,英国政府于1997年将英格兰银行的金融监管职能分离出来,使其专注于货币政策,同时成立英国"金融服务监管局",逐步将分散的金融监管职能集中到"金融服务监管局"。这一以金融监管机构整合为核心的重大改革被称为英国第二次金融"大爆炸"。《2000年金融服务与市场法》即英国议会对金融监管机构整合成果的立法确认,因而也可以说是英国第二次金融"大爆炸"的产物。金融服务监管局的成立,标志着英国传统的以行业自律监管为主的模式的重要转变,英国由此转变成为以更加正式化行政监管为特点的"新型监管国家"。当然,可以想象,这种监管机构的整合以及监管模式的转变并不是一件轻而易举的事。在这一过程中,首任金融服务监管局主席戴维斯(Howard Davies)以其个人特有的能力和魅力发挥了关键作用。戴维斯在1997年10月28日就职讲演中信心满满地表示:"金融服务监管局的目标是要以其专业性和公正性成为在世界领先的金融监管者。”对于单一监管机构把审慎监管和市场行为监管混同在一起存在内在冲突，会使监管系统更加官僚化，从而降低监管对市场的反应效率，给市场增加不必要的监管成本等担忧，他认为无须担心。在此后的几年里，金融服务监管局的工作确实卓有成效。例如，在1999~2000年，外国企业在美国进行IPO的规模超过800亿美元，10倍于伦敦。而在2005年，在伦敦进行IPO的外国企业筹集了103亿美元，远远超过美国的60亿美元。此外，2002年，伦敦的投资基金管理着6100万美元的资产，而到2005年，管理资产规模达到了2.25亿美元，在全球资产中所占的比例从10%升至20%。一份调查表明，国际金融机构对金融服务监管局的表现给予了很高的评价，认为伦敦金融市场的强大与英国监管机构的监管能力直接相关。

然而，2008年国际金融危机的发生，使英国第二次金融“大爆炸”，甚至是1986年第一次金融“大爆炸”以来的所有改革开始受到严厉的质疑。《金融时报》2009年4月30日的一篇文章宣称，此次金融危机之后，“撒切尔时代的所有标志性政策和成就正在被逐一粉碎”，其中就包括1986年以来的以“放松管制”(Deregulation)为核心的金融改革。2011年6月，英国政府在正式发布《金融监管新方法：改革蓝图》白皮书，宣布将对英国金融监管体制进行全面改革，原有的“金融服务监管局”将被撤销，其职能分别由新成立的审慎监管局(PRA)和金融行为监管局(FCA)承担。新的《2012年金融服务法》(草案)也于2012年1月26日正式提交议会，争取在2012年年底前获得最终批准，新的监管体制于2013年年初开始运作。与英国相对应，在此次金融危机之后，美国国会于2010年通过了《多德—弗兰克华尔街改革与消费者保护法》，对华尔街的金融活动重新加强监管。可以说，以英美为代表的“盎格鲁—萨克逊”金融模式今天正面临前所未有的质疑和反思。

回顾金融服务监管局从1997年成立、辉煌，再到今天最终被撤销的历程，令人不免有“十年一觉扬州梦”的感慨。而以确立金融服务监管局为主要内容的《2000年金融服务与市场法》即将被全面修订，今天将其翻译成中文并在国内出版，从某种意义上说，更多具有类似于“标本”的意义，它可以使我们更好地了解英国金融服务监管局的这段历史，并为我国未来金融监管体制改革是提供启示和参照。

我国的金融监管体制改革和金融法制建设，离不开对市场经济发达国家有益经验的参考、借鉴乃至“移植”，“关门主义”是不可取的。但是，在学习国外先进经验的过程中，也不能采取“浪漫主义”态度，不顾中国的实际而简单照抄、照搬。更要避免的是“插花式移植”，就是把各国成功的各种制度、做法都移植过来，像日本“插花”艺术一样集合在一起，看上去非常美观、漂亮，但实际上却没有任何生命力，难以在中国的土壤中扎下根，更不可能结出丰硕果实。

英国《2000年金融服务与市场法》以及金融服务监管局的兴衰历史，再一次告诉我们，世界上并没有“放之四海而皆准”的“最佳”金融监管模式，只有把外国的经验与中国的实际、中国的问题结合起来，才能找到真正适合中国的“最佳”模式。

焦津洪

2013年11月

CONTENTS

目　录

PART VI OFFICIAL LISTING 118

第六部分　正式上市　119

PART VIII PENALTIES FOR MARKET ABUSE 186

PART IX HEARINGS AND APPEALS 202

PART XXI MUTUAL SOCIETIES 548

PART XXII AUDITORS AND ACTUARIES 558

PART XXIII PUBLIC RECORD, DISCLOSURE OF INFORMATION AND CO-OPERATION 568

第二十四部分　破产　589

第二十七部分　犯罪　663

第二十八部分　其他条款　679

SCHEDULES 731

Financial Services Act 2010 940

附录

Financial Services and Markets Act 2000

2000 年金融服务与市场法

An Act to make provision about the regulation of financial services and markets; torovide for the transfer of certain statutory functions relating to building societies, friendly societies, industrial and provident societies and certain other mutual societies; and for connected purposes. [14th June 2000]

Be it enacted by the Queen's most Excellent Majesty, by and with the advice and consent of the Lords Spiritual and Temporal, and Commons, in this resent Parliament assembled, and by the authority of the same, as follows:—

Annotations:

Modifications etc. (not altering text)

C1 Act modified (18.7.2002 for certain purposes and 21.8.2002 otherwise) by The Electronic Commerce Directive (Financial Services and Markets) Regulations 2002 (S.I. 2002/1775), regs. 1, 17

Act: power to modify, exclude or apply conferred (prosp.) by Open-Ended Investment Companies Act (Northern Ireland) 2002 (c. 13), ss. 1, 4

C2 Act extended (E.W.S.) (1.1.2003 subject to transitional provisions in arts. 3–5 of the commencing S.I.) by 2000 c. 39, s. 15(2); S.I. 2002/2711, art. 2

Act excluded (1.12.2001) by S.I. 2001/2617, arts. 2(b), 10(9); S.I. 2001/3538, art. 2(1)

Act: specified provisions excluded (1.12.2001) by S.I. 2001/2957, arts. 1, 13(8)(b); S.I. 2001/3538, art. 2(1)

Act restricted (1.12.2001) by S.I. 2001/3646, arts. 2(7)(b), 4(6)(b), 6(4)(b), 7(4)(c), 8(4)(b), 9(4)(b)

Act applied (with modifications) (1.12.2001) by S.I. 1994/188, reg. 4 (as amended (1.12.2001) by S.I. 2001/3649, arts. 1, 454)

Act restricted (11.8.2001) by S.I. 2001/2659, art. 2(4)(c)

为规范金融服务和市场监管;规定住房互助会、互相保险协会、行业节俭互助会及其他互助协会的具体相关法定职能的转变;并为实现其他相关目的,作出规定。[2000年6月14日]

本法以最杰出的女王陛下的权威为依据,经上议院神职议员和世俗议员以及下议院提出建议并同意,经议会批准,于本届议会召开之际颁布如下:

注释:

修改等(不涉及条文内容):

C1 本法为特定目的于2002年7月18日,否则于2002年8月21日依照《2002年电子商务指令条例》(金融服务与市场)(制定法文件S.I.2002/1775)第1条、第17条修订;

本法:依照《2002年开放式投资公司法》(北爱尔兰)(c.13)第1条、第4条授予其修改、排除及适用实施的权力(预期)。

C2 本法(E.W.S.)于2003年1月1日符合制定法文件S.I.伊始颁布第3条至第5条的过渡性条款的规定,依照2000年第39章第15条第(2)款;制定法文件S.I.2002/2711第2条扩大适用范围;

本法于2001年12月1日依照制定法文件S.I.2001/2617第2条第(b)款、第10条第(9)款;制定法文件S.I.2001/3538第2条第(1)款排除;

本法:特定法规于2001年12月1日依照制定法文件S.I.2001/2957第1条、第13条第(8)款第(b)项;制定法文件S.I.2001/3538第2条第(1)款排除;

本法于2001年12月1日受制定法文件S.I.2001/3646第2条第(7)款第(b)项、第4条第(6)款第(b)项、第6条第(4)款第(b)项、第7条第(4)款第(c)项、第8条第(4)款第(b)项、第9条第(4)款第(b)项限制;

本法(已修订)于2001年12月1日依照制定法文件S.I.1994/188第4条(于2001年12月1日依照制定法文件S.I.2001/3649第1条、第454条修正适用;

本法于2001年8月11日受制定法文件S.I.2001/2659第2条第(4)款第(c)项的限制。

PART I THE REGULATOR

1 The Financial Services Authority.

(1) The body corporate known as the Financial Services Authority ("the Authority") is to have the functions conferred on it by or under this Act.

(2) The Authority must comply with the requirements as to its constitution set out in Schedule 1.

(3) Schedule 1 also makes provision about the status of the Authority and the exercise of certain of its functions.

Annotations:

Modifications etc. (not altering text)

C3 S. 1(3) extended (17.8.2001) by S.I. 2001/2617, arts. 2(a), 4(3), 8, Sch. 2 para. 2

The Authority's general duties

2 The Authority's general duties.

(1) In discharging its general functions the Authority must, so far as is reasonably possible, act in a way—

(a) which is compatible with the regulatory objectives; and

(b) which the Authority considers most appropriate for the purpose of meeting those objectives.

(2) The regulatory objectives are—

(a) market confidence;

(b) public awareness;

(c) the protection of consumers; and

(d) the reduction of financial crime.

第一部分 监管机关

第1条 金融服务管理局

(1)被称为金融服务管理局的法人(以下简称管理局)享有本法或依照本法赋予的职能。

(2)管理局必须遵守附录1所列的关于其组织制度。

(3)附录1还规定了管理局的地位及其具体职能的履行。

注释:

修改等(不涉及条文内容)

C3 第1条第(3)款于2001年8月17日依照制定法文件S.I.2001/2617第2条第(a)款、第4条第(3)款、第8条,附录2第2条扩大适用范围。

管理局的基本职责

第2条 管理局的基本职责

(1)管理局履行其基本职能时,必须尽其合理可能,以下列方式活动:

(a)符合监管目标的方式;且

(b)管理局认为最适当的监管目标实现方式。

(2)监管目标为:

(a)市场信心[1];

(b)公众意识[2];

(c)保护消费者;以及

(d)减少金融犯罪。

1 本项依照《2010年金融服务法》第1条第(2)款修订。——译者注

2 本项依照《2010年金融服务法》第2条第(2)款第(a)项修订。——译者注

(3) In discharging its general functions the Authority must have regard to—

(a) the need to use its resources in the most efficient and economic way;

(b) the responsibilities of those who manage the affairs of authorised persons;

(c) the principle that a burden or restriction which is imposed on a person, or on the carrying on of an activity, should be proportionate to the benefits, considered in general terms, which are expected to result from the imposition of that burden or restriction;

(d) the desirability of facilitating innovation in connection with regulated activities;

(e) the international character of financial services and markets and the desirability of maintaining the competitive position of the United Kingdom;

(f) the need to minimise the adverse effects on competition that may arise from anything done in the discharge of those functions;

(g) the desirability of facilitating competition between those who are subject to any form of regulation by the Authority.

(4) The Authority's general functions are—

(a) its function of making rules under this Act (considered as a whole);

(b) its function of preparing and issuing codes under this Act (considered as a whole);

(c) its functions in relation to the giving of general guidance (considered as a whole); and

(d) its function of determining the general policy and principles by reference to which it performs particular functions.

(5) "General guidance" has the meaning given in section 158(5).

Annotations:

Modifications etc. (not altering text)

C4 S. 2(4)(a) restricted (17.8.2001) by S.I. 2001/2617, arts. 2(a), 4(3), Sch. 2 paras. 9, 11

C5 S. 2(4)(c) restricted (17.8.2001) by S.I. 2001/2617, arts. 2(a), 4(3), Sch. 2 paras. 13–16

The regulatory objectives

3 Market confidence.

(1) The market confidence objective is: maintaining confidence in the financial system.

(2) "The financial system" means the financial system operating in the United Kingdom and includes—

(a) financial markets and exchanges;

(3)管理局履行其基本职能时,必须考虑

(a)需要以最经济高效的方式利用其资源;

(b)管理获授权人事务的相关职责;

(c)对个人或从事活动所规定的责任或限制应当与通常预期由该责任或限制所产生的收益成比例的原则;

(d)有利于促进受监管活动的创新;

(e)金融服务和市场的国际性及有利于维持联合王国竞争地位;

(f)在履行这些职能时,需要尽量降低任何行为可能对竞争造成的不利影响;

(g)有利于促进受管理局任何形式监管的受监管人之间的竞争。[1]

(4)管理局的基本职能为:

(a)依照本法制定规则(被视为一个整体)的职能;

(b)依照本法制定并颁布准则(被视为一个整体)的职能;

(c)公布一般性指引(被视为一个整体)的职能;以及

(d)制定履行特定职能时参照的基本政策和原则的职能。

(5)"一般性指引"具有第158条第(5)款中的含义。

注释:

修改等(不涉及条文内容)

C4 第2条第(4)款第(a)项于2001年8月17日受制定法文件S.I.2001/2617第2条第(a)款、第4条第(3)款,附录2第9条和第11条限制。

C5 第2条第(4)款第(c)项于2001年8月17日受制定法文件S.I.2001/2617第2条第(a)款、第4条第(3)款,附录2第13条至第16条限制。

监 管 目 标

第3条 市场信心[2]

(1)市场信心方面目标为:维持对金融系统的信心。

(2)"金融系统",系指在联合王国运行的金融系统,包括:

(a)金融市场和交易所;

1 本项依照《2010年金融服务法》第2条第(2)款第(b)项修订。——译者注

2 本条依照《2010年金融服务法》附录2第一部分第2条修订。——译者注

(b) regulated activities; and

(c) other activities connected with financial markets and exchanges.

4 Public awareness.

(1) The public awareness objective is: promoting public understanding of the financial system.

(2) It includes, in particular—

(a) promoting awareness of the benefits and risks associated with different kinds of investment or other financial dealing; and

(b) the provision of appropriate information and advice.

(3) "The financial system" has the same meaning as in section 3.

5 The protection of consumers.

(1) The protection of consumers objective is: securing the appropriate degree of protection for consumers.

(2) In considering what degree of protection may be appropriate, the Authority must have regard to—

(a) the differing degrees of risk involved in different kinds of investment or other transaction;

(b) the differing degrees of experience and expertise that different consumers may have in relation to different kinds of regulated activity;

(c) the needs that consumers may have for advice and accurate information; and

(d) the general principle that consumers should take responsibility for their decisions.

(3) "Consumers" means persons—

(a) who are consumers for the purposes of section 138; or

(b) who, in relation to regulated activities carried on otherwise than by authorised persons, would be consumers for those purposes if the activities were carried on by authorised persons.

Annotations:

Modifications etc. (not altering text)

C6 S. 5(3) modified (18.6.2001) by S.I. 2001/1821, arts. 1(1), 3(4)

6 The reduction of financial crime.

(1) The reduction of financial crime objective is: reducing the extent to which it is

(b)受监管的活动;以及

(c)与金融市场和交易所相关的其他活动。

第4条　公众意识[1]

(1)公众意识方面目标为:促进公众对于金融系统的理解。

(2)该目标特别包括:

(a)促进了解与各类投资或其他金融交易相关的收益和风险;以及

(b)提供适当的信息和建议。

(3)"金融系统"含义与第3条中的含义相同。

第5条　保护消费者

(1)保护消费者方面目标为:确保对消费者给予适当程度的保护。

(2)考虑何种保护程度为适当时,管理局必须考虑

(a)各类不同的投资或其他交易涉及的不同风险程度;

(b)不同消费者对各类不同的受监管活动拥有不同程度的经验和专业知识;[2]

(c)消费者可能对咨询建议和准确信息的需求;以及

(d)消费者应当对其决定负责的基本原则。

(3)"消费者",系指符合下列条件的人:

(a)属于第138条所规定的消费者范围;或

(b)与获授权人从事活动有关的、从事受监管活动的非获授权人。[3]

注释:

修改等(不涉及条文内容)

C6　第5条第(3)款于2001年6月18日依照制定法文件S.I.2001/1821第1条第(1)款、第3条第(4)款修订。

第6条　减少金融犯罪[4]

(1)减少金融犯罪方面目标为:尽可能减少下列业务可能被用于金融犯罪相关目

1 本条依照《2010年金融服务法》第1条第(3)款、附录2第一部分第3条修订。——译者注

2 本项依照《2010年金融服务法》第2条第(4)款修订。——译者注

3 本款依照《2010年金融服务法》附录2第一部分第4条修订。——译者注

4 本条依照《2010年金融服务法》第2条第(5)款修订。——译者注

possible for a business carried on—

(a) by a regulated person, or

(b) in contravention of the general prohibition, to be used for a purpose connected with financial crime.

(2) In considering that objective the Authority must, in particular, have regard to the desirability of—

(a) regulated persons being aware of the risk of their businesses being used in connection with the commission of financial crime;

(b) regulated persons taking appropriate measures (in relation to their administration and employment practices, the conduct of transactions by them and otherwise) to prevent financial crime, facilitate its detection and monitor its incidence;

(c) regulated persons devoting adequate resources to the matters mentioned in paragraph (b).

(3) "Financial crime" includes any offence involving—

(a) fraud or dishonesty;

(b) misconduct in, or misuse of information relating to, a financial market; or

(c) handling the proceeds of crime.

(4) "Offence" includes an act or omission which would be an offence if it had taken place in the United Kingdom.

(5) "Regulated person" means an authorised person, a recognised investment exchange or a recognised clearing house.

Corporate governance

7 Duty of Authority to follow principles of good governance.

In managing its affairs, the Authority must have regard to such generally accepted principles of good corporate governance as it is reasonable to regard as applicable to it.

Arrangements for consulting practitioners and consumers

8 The Authority's general duty to consult.

The Authority must make and maintain effective arrangements for consulting practitioners and consumers on the extent to which its general policies and practices are consistent with its general duties under section 2.

Annotations:

Modifications etc. (not altering text)

C7 S. 8 excluded (17.8.2001) by S.I. 2001/2617, arts. 2(a), 4(3), 8, Sch. 2 para. 5

的的情况：

(a)受监管人从事的业务；或

(b)违反一般禁止性规定的业务。

(2)在考虑本目标时，管理局必须特别考虑有利于下列各项事项：

(a)受监管人了解其业务被用于实施金融犯罪的风险；

(b)受监管人采取适当措施(与受监管人的行政和雇佣惯例、其交易行为等相关)，防范金融犯罪，便于金融犯罪的侦破并监控其发生率；

(c)受监管人为第(b)项所述事项投入充足资源。

(3)“金融犯罪”包括涉及下列行为的任何犯罪行为：

(a)欺诈或不诚实的行为；

(b)在金融市场中的不端行为或滥用金融市场信息；或

(c)处理犯罪所得。

(4)“犯罪”包括发生在联合王国即构成犯罪的作为或不作为。

(5)“受监管人”，系指获授权人、获认可的投资交易所或获认可的结算所。

公司治理

第7条　管理局遵循良好治理原则的职责

管理局在管理其事务时，必须考虑普遍认可并被认为可适用于该局的公司良好治理原则。

征求从业人员和消费者意见的安排

第8条　管理局征求意见的基本职责

在管理局基本政策和做法符合第2条规定的其基本职责范围内，管理局必须进行并保持征求从业人员和消费者意见的有效安排。

注释：

修改等(不涉及条文内容)

C7　第8条于2001年8月17日依照制定法文件S.I.2001/2617第2条第(a)款、第4条第(3)款、第8条，附录2第5条排除。

9 The Practitioner Panel.

(1) Arrangements under section 8 must include the establishment and maintenance of a panel of persons (to be known as "the Practitioner Panel") to represent the interests of practitioners.

(2) The Authority must appoint one of the members of the Practitioner Panel to be its chairman.

(3) The Treasury's approval is required for the appointment or dismissal of the chairman.

(4) The Authority must have regard to any representations made to it by the Practitioner Panel.

(5) The Authority must appoint to the Practitioner Panel such—

(a) individuals who are authorised persons,

(b) persons representing authorised persons,

(c) persons representing recognised investment exchanges, and

(d) persons representing recognised clearing houses, as it considers appropriate.

10 The Consumer Panel.

(1) Arrangements under section 8 must include the establishment and maintenance of a panel of persons (to be known as "the Consumer Panel") to represent the interests of consumers.

(2) The Authority must appoint one of the members of the Consumer Panel to be its chairman.

(3) The Treasury's approval is required for the appointment or dismissal of the chairman.

(4) The Authority must have regard to any representations made to it by the Consumer Panel.

(5) The Authority must appoint to the Consumer Panel such consumers, or persons representing the interests of consumers, as it considers appropriate.

(6) The Authority must secure that the membership of the Consumer Panel is such as to give a fair degree of representation to those who are using, or are or may be contemplating using, services otherwise than in connection with businesses carried on by them.

(7) "Consumers" means persons, other than authorised persons—

(a) who are consumers for the purposes of section 138; or

(b) who, in relation to regulated activities carried on otherwise than by authorised persons, would be consumers for those purposes if the activities were carried on by authorised persons.

第9条　从业人员小组

(1)第8条规定的安排必须包括建立并维持一个由代表从业人员利益的人组成的小组(称为从业人员小组)。

(2)管理局必须任命从业人员小组的一名成员担任主席。

(3)任免主席须经财政部批准。

(4)管理局必须对从业人员小组向其提出的任何意见予以考虑。

(5)管理局必须任命其认为适当的下列人员进入从业人员小组:

(a)担任获授权人的个人,

(b)代表获授权人的人,

(c)代表获认可的投资交易所的人,以及

(d)代表获认可的结算所的人。

第10条　消费者小组

(1)第8条规定的安排必须包括建立并维持一个由代表消费者利益的人组成的小组(称为消费者小组)。

(2)管理局必须任命消费者小组的一名成员担任主席。

(3)任免主席须经财政部批准。

(4)管理局必须对消费者小组向其提出的任何意见予以考虑。

(5)管理局必须任命其认为适当的消费者或代表消费者利益的人进入消费者小组。

(6)管理局必须确保消费者小组的成员构成能公平地代表正在使用、考虑使用或可能考虑使用服务的人,而该服务与其从事的业务无关。

(7)“消费者”,系指除获授权人以外符合下列条件的人:

(a)属于第138条所规定的消费者范围;或

(b)与获授权人从事活动有关的、从事受监管活动的非获授权人,属于消费者范围。[1]

1 本款依照《2010年金融服务法》附录2第一部分第5条修订。——译者注

Annotations:

Modifications etc. (not altering text)

C8 S. 10(7) modified (18.6.2001) by S.I. 2001/1821, arts. 1(1), 3(4)

11 Duty to consider representations by the Panels.

(1) This section applies to a representation made, in accordance with arrangements made under section 8, by the Practitioner Panel or by the Consumer Panel.

(2) The Authority must consider the representation.

(3) If the Authority disagrees with a view expressed, or proposal made, in the representation, it must give the Panel a statement in writing of its reasons for disagreeing.

Reviews

12 Reviews.

(1) The Treasury may appoint an independent person to conduct a review of the economy, efficiency and effectiveness with which the Authority has used its resources in discharging its functions.

(2) A review may be limited by the Treasury to such functions of the Authority (however described) as the Treasury may specify in appointing the person to conduct it.

(3) A review is not to be concerned with the merits of the Authority's general policy or principles in pursuing regulatory objectives or in exercising functions under Part VI.

(4) On completion of a review, the person conducting it must make a written report to the Treasury—

(a) setting out the result of the review; and

(b) making such recommendations (if any) as he considers appropriate.

(5) A copy of the report must be—

(a) laid before each House of Parliament; and

(b) published in such manner as the Treasury consider appropriate.

(6) Any expenses reasonably incurred in the conduct of a review are to be met by the Treasury out of money provided by Parliament.

(7) "Independent" means appearing to the Treasury to be independent of the Authority.

Annotations:

Modifications etc. (not altering text)

C9 S. 12 modified (17.8.2001) by S.I. 2001/2617, arts. 2(a), 4(3), 8, Sch. 2 para. 6

注释：

修改等(不涉及条文内容) C8　第10条第(7)款于2001年6月18日依照制定法文件S.I.2001/1821第1条第(1)款、第3条第(4)款修订。

第11条　考虑小组意见的职责

(1)本条规定适用于从业人员小组或者消费者小组依照第8条规定的安排所提出的意见。

(2)管理局必须对该意见予以考虑。

(3)如管理局不同意该意见中表达的观点或提出的建议，则必须向小组提出书面说明，告知不同意的理由。

审　查

第12条　审查

(1)财政部可以任命一名独立人员，审查管理局在履行其职能的过程中使用其资源的经济性、效率和有效性。

(2)财政部任命审查人进行审查时，可将审查限定在财政部规定的管理局职能范围内(不管如何说明)。

(3) 审查不涉及管理局实现监管目标或履行第六部分规定职能的基本政策或原则依据。

(4)审查完成时，审查人必须向财政部提交一份书面报告

(a)说明审查结果；并

(b)提出其认为适当的建议(如有)。

(5)报告副本必须

(a)呈送议会上下两院；并

(b)以财政部认为适当的方式公布。

(6)因审查行为所发生的各项合理费用由财政部从议会拨款中列支。

(7)“独立”系指财政部认为独立于管理局。

注释：

修改等(不涉及条文内容) C9　第12条于2001年8月17日依照制定法文件S.I.2001/2617第2条第(a)款、第4条第(3)款、第8条，附录2第6条修订。

13 Right to obtain documents and information.

(1) A person conducting a review under section 12—

(a) has a right of access at any reasonable time to all such documents as he may reasonably require for purposes of the review; and

(b) may require any person holding or accountable for any such document to provide such information and explanation as are reasonably necessary for that purpose.

(2) Subsection (1) applies only to documents in the custody or under the control of the Authority.

(3) An obligation imposed on a person as a result of the exercise of powers conferred by subsection (1) is enforceable by injunction or, in Scotland, by an order for specific performance under section 45 of the [M1]Court of Session Act 1988.

Annotations:

Marginal Citations

M1 1988 c. 36.

Inquiries

14 Cases in which the Treasury may arrange independent inquiries.

(1) This section applies in two cases.

(2) The first is where it appears to the Treasury that—

(a) events have occurred in relation to—

(i) a collective investment scheme, or

(ii) a person who is, or was at the time of the events, carrying on a regulated activity (whether or not as an authorised person), which posed or could have posed a grave risk to the financial system or caused or risked causing significant damage to the interests of consumers; and

(b) those events might not have occurred, or the risk or damage might have been reduced, but for a serious failure in—

(i) the system established by this Act for the regulation of such schemes or of such persons and their activities; or

(ii) the operation of that system.

(3) The second is where it appears to the Treasury that—

(a) events have occurred in relation to listed securities or an issuer of listed securities

第13条 获得文件和信息的权利

(1)依照第12条进行审查的人

(a)有权在任何合理时间获得其为审查之目的而合理需要的所有文件;且

(b)可以要求任何掌握或对该等文件负有责任的人提供针对审查合理必要的信息和解释。

(2)第(1)款只适用于管理局保管或掌控的文件。

(3)因行使第(1)款赋予的权力而使个人承担的义务,可通过强制令强制执行,在苏格兰可通过[M1]《1988年高等民事法院法》第45条规定的实际履行令强制执行。

注释:

附注引文

M1 1988年第36章。

调 查

第14条 财政部可以安排独立调查的情况[1]

(1)本条规定适用于两种情况。

(2)第一种情况为,财政部认为

(a)发生了与下列计划或人相关的事件:

(i)集合投资计划[2],或

(ii)正在从事或事件发生时正在从事受监管活动的人(无论是否为获授权人),且该事件为金融系统带来或可能带来重大风险,或对消费者利益造成或可能造成严重损害;且

(b)如非下列情况,上述事件可能避免,或风险或损害可能减少

(i)本法为监管上述计划或人员及其活动而建立的系统严重失灵;或

(ii)该系统的运行严重失灵。

(3)第二种情况为,财政部认为

(a)发生了与上市证券或其发行人相关的事件,且该事件导致或可能导致上市证

---

1 本条依照《2010年金融服务法》附录2第一部分第6条修订。——译者注

2 集合投资计划(CollectiveInvestmentScheme)是国际上通行的资产管理业务形式。它通过设立集合投资计划,接受多个投资者的委托,以“专业管理、组合投资”的方式,将委托资金进行共同运作,发挥专业机构的优势,有效地对风险和收益进行匹配,克服了个人投资者在专业知识和资金等方面的局限。——译者注

which caused or could have caused significant damage to holders of listed securities; and

(b) those events might not have occurred but for a serious failure in the regulatory system established by Part Ⅵ or in its operation.

(4) If the Treasury consider that it is in the public interest that there should be an independent inquiry into the events and the circumstances surrounding them, they may arrange for an inquiry to be held under section 15.

(5) "Consumers" means persons—

(a) who are consumers for the purposes of section 138; or

(b) who, in relation to regulated activities carried on otherwise than by authorised persons, would be consumers for those purposes if the activities were carried on by authorised persons.

(6) "The financial system" has the same meaning as in section 3.

(7) "Listed securities" means anything which has been admitted to the official list under Part Ⅵ.

Annotations:

Modifications etc. (not altering text)

C10 S. 14(5) modified (18.6.2001) by S.I. 2001/1821, arts. 1(1), 3(4)

15 Power to appoint person to hold an inquiry.

(1) If the Treasury decide to arrange for an inquiry to be held under this section, they may appoint such person as they consider appropriate to hold the inquiry.

(2) The Treasury may, by a direction to the appointed person, control—

(a) the scope of the inquiry;

(b) the period during which the inquiry is to be held;

(c) the conduct of the inquiry; and

(d) the making of reports.

(3) A direction may, in particular—

(a) confine the inquiry to particular matters;

(b) extend the inquiry to additional matters;

(c) require the appointed person to discontinue the inquiry or to take only such steps as are specified in the direction;

(d) require the appointed person to make such interim reports as are so specified.

16 Powers of appointed person and procedure.

(1) The person appointed to hold an inquiry under section 15 may—

(a) obtain such information from such persons and in such manner as he thinks fit;

(b) make such inquiries as he thinks fit; and

券持有人遭受严重损害；且

(b)如非第六部分规定建立的监管系统或其运行严重失灵，则上述事件可能不会发生。

(4)如财政部认为出于公共利益应当对事件及其相关情况进行独立调查，则可以依照第15条规定安排调查。

(5)“消费者，”系指符合下列条件的人：

(a)属于第138条所规定的消费者范围；或

(b)与获授权人从事活动有关的、从事受监管活动的非获授权人，属于消费者范围。

(6)“金融系统”含义同第3条。

(7)“上市证券”，系指依照第六部分规定已获认可正式上市的任何证券。

注释：

修改等(不涉及条文内容)

C10 第14条第（5）款于2001年6月18日依照制定法文件S.I.2001/1821第1条第(1)款、第3条第(4)款修订。

第15条 任命调查人的权力

(1)如财政部决定依照本条规定安排调查，则可任命其认为适当的人进行调查。

(2)财政部可向被任命人发出指示，掌控下列事项：

(a)调查的范围；

(b)进行调查的期间；

(c)方式调查；以及

(d)形成调查报告。

(3)指示可以特别

(a)规定调查限于特定事项；

(b)规定调查扩大到额外事项；

(c)要求被任命人中止调查或只采取指示中规定的措施；

(d)要求被任命人根据规定的要求提交临时报告。

第16条 被任命人的权力和权力行使程序

(1)依照第15条规定任命的调查人可以

(a)以其认为适当的方式从其认为相关的人处获取其认为适当的信息；

(b)进行其认为适当的调查；并

(c) determine the procedure to be followed in connection with the inquiry.

(2) The appointed person may require any person who, in his opinion, is able to provide any information, or produce any document, which is relevant to the inquiry to provide any such information or produce any such document.

(3) For the purposes of an inquiry, the appointed person has the same powers as the court in respect of the attendance and examination of witnesses (including the examination of witnesses abroad) and in respect of the production of documents.

(4) "Court" means—

(a) the High Court; or

(b) in Scotland, the Court of Session.

17 Conclusion of inquiry.

(1) On completion of an inquiry under section 15, the person holding the inquiry must make a written report to the Treasury—

(a) setting out the result of the inquiry; and

(b) making such recommendations (if any) as he considers appropriate.

(2) The Treasury may publish the whole, or any part, of the report and may do so in such manner as they consider appropriate.

(3) Subsection (4) applies if the Treasury propose to publish a report but consider that it contains material—

(a) which relates to the affairs of a particular person whose interests would, in the opinion of the Treasury, be seriously prejudiced by publication of the material; or

(b) the disclosure of which would be incompatible with an international obligation of the United Kingdom.

(4) The Treasury must ensure that the material is removed before publication.

(5) The Treasury must lay before each House of Parliament a copy of any report or part of a report published under subsection (2).

(6) Any expenses reasonably incurred in holding an inquiry are to be met by the Treasury out of money provided by Parliament.

18 Obstruction and contempt.

(1) If a person ("A")—

(a) fails to comply with a requirement imposed on him by a person holding an inquiry under section 15, or

(b) otherwise obstructs such an inquiry,

the person holding the inquiry may certify the matter to the High Court (or, in Scotland, the Court of Session).

(2) The court may enquire into the matter.

(3) If, after hearing—

(c)确定调查所遵循的程序。

(2)被任命人对其认定能够提供任何与调查相关的信息或文件的人员,可要求其提供有关调查的信息或文件。

(3)为调查的目的,被任命人在传唤和询问证人(包括询问境外证人)以及提供文件时,享有与法院同等的权力。

(4)"法院"系指

(a)高等法院;或

(b)(苏格兰)高等民事法院。

第17条　调查的结论

(1)依照第15条规定进行的调查终结时,调查人必须向财政部提交一份书面报告

(a)说明审查结果;并

(b)提出其认为适当的建议(如有)。

(2)财政部可以通过其认为适当的方式公布报告全文或报告任何部分。

(3)如财政部拟公布报告,但考虑到其中包含有下列情况的材料,则适用第(4)款规定:

(a)涉及特定人的事务,且财政部认为公布该材料会严重损害特定人的利益;或

(b)披露该材料与联合王国的国际义务不符。

(4)财政部必须确保在公布前删除该材料。

(5)财政部必须将依照第(2)款规定公布的任何报告或报告部分内容呈送议会上下两院。

(6)因调查行为所合理发生的任何费用由财政部从议会拨款中列支。

第18条　妨碍和藐视

(1)如有人(以下简称A)

(a)未能满足依照第15条进行调查的人对其提出的要求,或

(b)以其他方式妨碍相关调查,

则调查人可向高等法院[或(苏格兰)高等民事法院]提交该问题。

(2)法院可调查此事。

(3)如法院经听审下列事项后确信,若该调查按进入法院审理的程序进行则A构

(a) any witnesses who may be produced against or on behalf of A, and

(b) any statement made by or on behalf of A, the court is satisfied that A would have been in contempt of court if the inquiry had been proceedings before the court, it may deal with him as if he were in contempt.

成藐视法庭,则法院可将其按藐视法庭处理:

(a)针对或代表A可提供的任何证词,以及

(b)由A或者其代表所作的任何供述。

PART Ⅱ REGULATED AND PROHIBITED ACTIVITIES

The general prohibition

19 The general prohibition.

(1) No person may carry on a regulated activity in the United Kingdom, or purport to do so, unless he is—

(a) an authorised person; or

(b) an exempt person.

(2) The prohibition is referred to in this Act as the general prohibition.

Requirement for permission

20 Authorised persons acting without permission.

(1) If an authorised person carries on a regulated activity in the United Kingdom, or purports to do so, otherwise than in accordance with permission—

(a) given to him by the Authority under Part Ⅳ, or

(b) resulting from any other provision of this Act,

he is to be taken to have contravened a requirement imposed on him by the Authority under this Act.

(2) The contravention does not—

(a) make a person guilty of an offence;

(b) make any transaction void or unenforceable; or

(c) (subject to subsection (3)) give rise to any right of action for breach of statutory duty.

(3) In prescribed cases the contravention is actionable at the suit of a person who suffers loss as a result of the contravention, subject to the defences and other incidents applying to actions for breach of statutory duty.

第二部分　受监管活动与禁止的活动

一般禁止性规定

第19条　一般禁止性规定

(1)任何人在联合王国不得从事或企图从事受监管活动,除非该人为

(a)获授权人;或

(b)享有豁免权的人。

(2)本法所述禁止性规定系指一般禁止性规定。

取得许可的要求

第20条　获授权人未经许可的行为

(1)如获授权人在联合王国从事或企图从事受监管活动,但未经以下许可:

(a)由管理局依照第四部分规定授予的许可;或

(b)依照本法任何其他规定授予的许可,

则认为获授权人违反了管理局依照本法对其作出的规定。

(2)该违反规定的行为不会

(a)导致构成犯罪;

(b)导致任何交易无效或无法履行;或

(c)[依照第(3)款规定]因违反法定职责而产生任何诉讼权利。

(3)在规定的情况下,因该违反规定的行为而遭受损失的人可以针对该行为提起诉讼,但须依照适用违反法定职责诉讼的抗辩理由和其他事由。

Annotations:

Modifications etc. (not altering text)

C11 S. 20 excluded (1.12.2001) by S.I. 2001/2636, arts. 1(2)(b), 62(1)-(4); S.I. 2001/3538, art. 2(1)

S. 20 applied (1.12.2001) by S.I. 2001/2636, arts. 1(2)(b), 62(5); S.I. 2001/3538, art. 2(1)

S. 20 modified (31.10.2001) by S.I. 2001/3374, art. 1,Sch. para. 2

Commencement Information

I1 S. 20 wholly in force at 1.12.2001; s. 20 not in force at Royal Assent see s. 431(2); s. 20(3) in force for certain purposes at 25.2.2001 by S.I. 2001/516, art. 2(b), Sch. Pt. 2; s. 20 in force in so far as not already in force at 1.12.2001 by S.I. 2001/3538, art. 2(1)

Financial promotion

21 Restrictions on financial promotion.

(1) A person ("A") must not, in the course of business, communicate an invitation or inducement to engage in investment activity.

(2) But subsection (1) does not apply if—

(a) A is an authorised person; or

(b) the content of the communication is approved for the purposes of this section by an authorised person.

(3) In the case of a communication originating outside the United Kingdom, subsection (1) applies only if the communication is capable of having an effect in the United Kingdom.

(4) The Treasury may by order specify circumstances in which a person is to be regarded for the purposes of subsection (1) as—

(a) acting in the course of business;

(b) not acting in the course of business.

(5) The Treasury may by order specify circumstances (which may include compliance with financial promotion rules) in which subsection (1) does not apply.

(6) An order under subsection (5) may, in particular, provide that subsection (1) does not apply in relation to communications—

(a) of a specified description;

(b) originating in a specified country or territory outside the United Kingdom;

(c) originating in a country or territory which falls within a specified description of country or territory outside the United Kingdom; or

(d) originating outside the United Kingdom.

注释：

修改等(不涉及条文内容)

C11 第20条于2001年12月1日依照制定法文件S.I.2001/2636第1条第(2)款第(b)项、第62条第(1)款至第(4)款；制定法文件S.I.2001/3538第2条第(1)款排除；

第20条于2001年12月1日依照制定法文件S.I.2001/2636第1条第(2)款第(b)项、第62条第(5)款；制定法文件S.I.2001/3538第2条第(1)款适用；

第20条于2001年10月31日依照制定法文件S.I.2001/3374第1条、附录第2条修订。

实施日期

I1 第20条于2001年12月1日全部生效；第20条在副署时尚未生效，见第431条第(2)款；第20条第(3)款为特定目的于2001年2月25日依照制定法文件S.I.2001/516第2条第(b)款、附录第二部分生效；第20条如于2001年12月1日尚未生效，则依照制定法文件S.I.2001/3538第2条第(1)款生效。

金 融 推 介

第21条 金融推介的限制

(1)任何人(以下简称A)在经营过程中不得传播关于从事投资活动的邀请或引诱。

(2)但如有下列情况，则不适用第(1)款规定：

(a)A是获授权人；或

(b)获授权人为本条规定的目的批准了传播的内容。

(3)如传播源自联合王国境外，则只有该传播能够影响联合王国时，才适用第(1)款规定。

(4)财政部可颁布法令，规定为第(1)款的目的将某人视为下列情况的情形：

(a)在经营过程中从事活动；

(b)不是在经营过程中从事活动。

(5)财政部可颁布法令，规定第(1)款不适用的情形(可包括遵守金融推介规则)。

(6)依照第(5)款颁布的法令可以特别规定第(1)款不适用于以下传播：

(a)特定说明书的传播；

(b)源自联合王国境外特定国家或地区的传播；

(c)源自属于联合王国境外指定类别的国家或地区的传播；或

(d)源自联合王国境外的传播。

(7) The Treasury may by order repeal subsection (3).

(8) "Engaging in investment activity" means—

(a) entering or offering to enter into an agreement the making or performance of which by either party constitutes a controlled activity; or

(b) exercising any rights conferred by a controlled investment to acquire, dispose of, underwrite or convert a controlled investment.

(9) An activity is a controlled activity if—

(a) it is an activity of a specified kind or one which falls within a specified class of activity; and

(b) it relates to an investment of a specified kind, or to one which falls within a specified class of investment.

(10) An investment is a controlled investment if it is an investment of a specified kind or one which falls within a specified class of investment.

(11) Schedule 2 (except paragraph 26) applies for the purposes of subsections (9) and (10) with references to section 22 being read as references to each of those subsections.

(12) Nothing in Schedule 2, as applied by subsection (11), limits the powers conferred by subsection (9) or (10).

(13) "Communicate" includes causing a communication to be made.

(14) "Investment" includes any asset, right or interest.

(15) "Specified" means specified in an order made by the Treasury.

Annotations:

Modifications etc. (not altering text)

C12 S. 21(1) modified (31.10.2001) by S.I. 2001/3374, art. 1, Sch. para. 6

Commencement Information

I2 S. 21 wholly in force at 1.12.2001; s. 21 not in force at Royal Assent see s. 431(2); s. 21 in force for certain purposes at 25.2.2001 by S.I. 2001/516, art. 2(b), Sch. Pt. 2; s. 21 in force in so far as not already in force at 1.12.2001 by S.I. 2001/3538, art. 2(1)

Regulated activities

22 The classes of activity and categories of investment.

(1) An activity is a regulated activity for the purposes of this Act if it is an activity of a specified kind which is carried on by way of business and—

(a) relates to an investment of a specified kind; or

(b) in the case of an activity of a kind which is also specified for the purposes of this

(7)财政部可颁布法令,废止第(3)款规定。

(8)"从事投资活动",系指

(a)订立或要约订立协议,且该协议任何一方订立或履行该协议均构成受控活动;或

(b)行使受控投资赋予的任何权利从而取得、处置、承销或转换受控投资。

(9)属于下列情况的活动为受控活动:

(a)属于规定种类或规定类别的活动;且

(b)与规定种类的投资或属于规定类别的投资相关。

(10)规定种类的投资或属于规定类别的投资为受控投资。

(11)附录2(除第26条外)为第(9)款和第(10)款的施行而适用时,其中述及第22条视为述及上述两款规定。

(12)依照第(11)款适用附录2时,其中的任何内容均不限制第(9)款和第(10)款所赋予的各项权力。

(13)"传播"包括致使他人传播。

(14)"投资"包括任何资产、权利或利益。

(15)"规定"系指财政部颁布法令中的规定。

注释:

修改等(不涉及条文内容)

C12　第21条第(1)款于2001年10月31日依照制定法文件S.I.2001/3374第1条,附录第6条修订。

实施日期

I2　第21条于2001年12月1日全部生效;第21条在副署时尚未生效,见第431条第(2)款;第21条为特定目的于2001年2月25日依照制定法文件S.I.2001/516第2条第(b)款、附录第二部分生效;第21条如于2001年12月1日尚未生效,则依照制定法文件S.I.2001/3538第2条第(1)款生效。

受监管活动

第22条　活动类别和投资种类

(1)以经营方式开展并属于下列情况的活动,是本法所称之受监管活动:

(a)与某种规定种类投资相关;或

(b)如该活动就本项而言属于规定种类,其实施与任何种类的财产相关。

paragraph, is carried on in relation to property of any kind.

(2) Schedule 2 makes provision supplementing this section.

(3) Nothing in Schedule 2 limits the powers conferred by subsection (1).

(4) "Investment" includes any asset, right or interest.

(5) "Specified" means specified in an order made by the Treasury.

Annotations:

Modifications etc. (not altering text)

C13 S. 22 applied (1.9.2002) by 1974 c. 39, s. 16(6E)(a) (as inserted (1.9.2002) by 2001/544, arts. 2(2)(b), 90(2))

Offences

23 Contravention of the general prohibition.

(1) A person who contravenes the general prohibition is guilty of an offence and liable—

(a) on summary conviction, to imprisonment for a term not exceeding six months or a fine not exceeding the statutory maximum, or both;

(b) on conviction on indictment, to imprisonment for a term not exceeding two years or a fine, or both.

(2) In this Act "an authorisation offence" means an offence under this section.

(3) In proceedings for an authorisation offence it is a defence for the accused to show that he took all reasonable precautions and exercised all due diligence to avoid committing the offence.

24 False claims to be authorised or exempt.

(1) A person who is neither an authorised person nor, in relation to the regulated activity in question, an exempt person is guilty of an offence if he—

(a) describes himself (in whatever terms) as an authorised person;

(b) describes himself (in whatever terms) as an exempt person in relation to the regulated activity; or

(2)附录2对本条作出了补充规定。

(3)附录2中的任何内容均不限制第(1)款所赋予的各项权力。

(4)“投资”包括任何资产、权利或利益。

(5)“规定”系指财政部颁布法令中的规定。

注释:

修改等(不涉及条文内容)

C13 第22条于2002年9月1日依照1974年第39章第16条第(6E)款第(a)项[于2002年9月1日依照制定法文件2001/544第2条第(2)款第(b)项、第90条第(2)款插入]适用。

犯 罪

第23条 违反一般禁止性规定

(1)违反一般禁止性规定者构成犯罪,并应承担下列责任:

(a)经简易程序定罪的[1],处以不超过6个月有期徒刑,或不超过法定最高限额的罚金,或两罚并处;

(b)经公诉程序定罪的,处以不超过2年有期徒刑,或罚金,或两罚并处。

(2)本法中“授权类犯罪”系指本条中规定的犯罪。

(3)在授权类犯罪诉讼程序中,被告人如能证明其已采取了一切合理预防措施并已尽应有谨慎防止犯罪,则可据此进行抗辩。

第24条 关于获授权或豁免的虚假陈述

(1)任何人如既不是获授权人,又不是对相关受监管活动享有豁免权的人,有下列情形的,则构成犯罪:

(a)(无论以何种措辞)宣称本人为获授权人;

(b)(无论以何种措辞)宣称本人为对受监管活动享有豁免权的人;或

1 简易程序定罪(on summary conviction)和公诉程序定罪(on conviction on indictment):在英国,刑事审判采取两种方式:简易程序审判和公诉程序审判。案件在两种审判方式之间的分配,多取决于犯罪的种类。在英格兰和威尔士,犯罪被分为三类:只能按公诉程序审判的犯罪、只能按简易程序审判的犯罪和按两种方式审判均可的犯罪。只能按公诉程序审判的犯罪主要是一些严重的犯罪如谋杀、非预谋杀人、抢劫、强奸、乱伦和故意伤害。只能按简易程序审判的犯罪主要是简单、轻微的犯罪。按两种方式审判均可的犯罪主要包括一般犯罪如偷窃、接受被偷物品、猥亵和较轻微的人身暴力。依简易程序审理的案件,检察官向治安法院起诉时只提交起诉书,不附带与案件有关的其他证据材料。依公诉程序审理的案件,检察官向刑事法院起诉前必须将案件提交治安法院预审。经过预审法庭的审查,如果预审法官认为检察官的起诉具有足够的证据,即作出向刑事法院移送起诉的决定。之后检察长必须任命大律师出庭支持公诉,起诉时大律师向刑事法院移送一份起诉书,不附带任何证据材料。——译者注

(c) behaves, or otherwise holds himself out, in a manner which indicates (or which is reasonably likely to be understood as indicating) that he is—

(i) an authorised person; or

(ii) an exempt person in relation to the regulated activity.

(2) In proceedings for an offence under this section it is a defence for the accused to show that he took all reasonable precautions and exercised all due diligence to avoid committing the offence.

(3) A person guilty of an offence under this section is liable on summary conviction to imprisonment for a term not exceeding six months or a fine not exceeding level 5 on the standard scale, or both.

(4) But where the conduct constituting the offence involved or included the public display of any material, the maximum fine for the offence is level 5 on the standard scale multiplied by the number of days for which the display continued.

25 Contravention of section 21.

(1) A person who contravenes section 21(1) is guilty of an offence and liable—

(a) on summary conviction, to imprisonment for a term not exceeding six months or a fine not exceeding the statutory maximum, or both;

(b) on conviction on indictment, to imprisonment for a term not exceeding two years or a fine, or both.

(2) In proceedings for an offence under this section it is a defence for the accused to show—

(a) that he believed on reasonable grounds that the content of the communication was prepared, or approved for the purposes of section 21, by an authorized person; or

(b) that he took all reasonable precautions and exercised all due diligence to avoid committing the offence.

Annotations:

Modifications etc. (not altering text)

C14 S. 25(2)(a) modified (31.10.2001) by S.I. 2001/3374, art. 1, Sch. para. 6

Enforceability of agreements

26 Agreements made by unauthorised persons.

(1) An agreement made by a person in the course of carrying on a regulated activity in contravention of the general prohibition is unenforceable against the other party.

(2) The other party is entitled to recover—

(a) any money or other property paid or transferred by him under the agreement; and (c)以行为或其他方式表明(或合理地有可能被理解为表明)本人为

(i)获授权人;或

(ii)对受监管活动享有豁免权的人。

(2)在针对本条规定的犯罪提起的诉讼程序中,被告人如能证明其已采取了一切合理预防措施并已尽应有谨慎防止犯罪,则可据此进行抗辩。

(3)犯有本条规定之罪的,经简易程序定罪,处以不超过6个月有期徒刑或不超过标准等级第5级的罚金,或两罚并处。

(4)但如构成犯罪的行为涉及或包括公开展示任何材料,则该犯罪的最高罚金为标准等级第5级的罚金乘以该展示持续的天数。

第25条　违反第21条规定

(1)违反第21条第(1)款构成犯罪的,并科以下列责任:

(a)经简易程序定罪的,处以不超过6个月有期徒刑,或不超过法定最高限额的罚金,或两罚并处;

(b)经公诉程序定罪的,处以不超过2年有期徒刑,或罚金,或两罚并处。

(2)在针对本条规定的犯罪提起的诉讼程序中,被告人如能证明下列情况,则可据此提出抗辩:

(a)被告人当时基于合理理由相信被传播的内容已由获授权人依照第21条准备或批准;或

(b)被告人已采取一切合理预防措施并已尽应有谨慎防止犯罪。

注释:

修改等(不涉及条文内容)

C14　第25条第(2)款第(a)项于2001年10月31日依照制定法文件S.I.2001/3374第1条,附录第6条修订。

协议的强制执行力

第26条　未获授权人签订的协议

(1)违反一般禁止性规定从事受监管活动的,从事受监管活动过程中签订的协议对另一方当事人不具有强制执行力。

(2)另一方当事人有权追偿

(a)其根据协议交付或转让的任何金钱或其他财产;及

(b) compensation for any loss sustained by him as a result of having parted with it.

(3) "Agreement" means an agreement—

(a) made after this section comes into force; and

(b) the making or performance of which constitutes, or is part of, the regulated activity in question.

(4) This section does not apply if the regulated activity is accepting deposits.

Annotations:

Modifications etc. (not altering text)

C15 S. 26(1)(2) applied (1.12.2001) by S.I. 2001/2657, arts. 1(1), 5(1)(4) (which was revoked (8.10.2001) by S.I. 2001/3083, arts. 1(2), 23); S.I. 2001/3538, art. 2(1)

S. 26(1)(2) applied (1.12.2001) by S.I. 2001/3083, arts. 1(2), 5(1); S.I. 2001/3538, art. 2(1)

27 Agreements made through unauthorised persons.

(1) An agreement made by an authorised person ("the provider")—

(a) in the course of carrying on a regulated activity (not in contravention of the general prohibition), but

(b) in consequence of something said or done by another person ("the third party") in the course of a regulated activity carried on by the third party in contravention of the general prohibition,is unenforceable against the other party.

(2) The other party is entitled to recover—

(a) any money or other property paid or transferred by him under the agreement; and

(b) compensation for any loss sustained by him as a result of having parted with it.

(3) "Agreement" means an agreement—

(a) made after this section comes into force; and

(b) the making or performance of which constitutes, or is part of, the regulated activity in question carried on by the provider.

(4) This section does not apply if the regulated activity is accepting deposits.

(b)其因交付或转让上述金钱或财产而遭受的任何损失。

(3)“协议”系指下列协议:

(a)本条规定生效后签订;且

(b)协议的签订或履行构成相关受监管活动,或构成该活动的一部分。

(4)如受监管活动为吸收存款,则本条规定不适用。

注释:

修改等(不涉及条文内容)

C15 第26条第(1)款、第(2)款于2001年12月1日依照制定法文件S.I.2001/2657第1条第(1)款,第5条第(1)款、第(4)款[于2001年10月8日依照制定法文件S.I.2001/3083第1条第(2)款、第23条废除];制定法文件S.I.2001/3538第2条第(1)款适用;

第26条第(1)款、第(2)款于2001年12月1日依照制定法文件S.I.2001/3083第1条第(2)款、第5条第(1)款;制定法文件S.I.2001/3538第2条第(1)款适用。

第27条 通过未获授权人签订的协议

(1)如获授权人(以下简称签订人)签订的协议有下列情况,则对另一方当事人不具有强制执行力:

(a)在从事受监管活动(未违反一般禁止性规定)的过程中签订,但

(b)该协议的签订是另一人(以下简称第三人)违反一般性禁止性规定从事受监管活动过程中的语言或行为所导致的结果。

(2)另一方当事人有权追偿

(a)其根据协议交付或转让的任何金钱或其他财产;及

(b)其因交付或转让上述金钱或财产而遭受的任何损失。

(3)“协议”系指下列协议:

(a)在本条规定生效后签订;且

(b)协议的签订或履行构成签订人所从事的相关受监管活动,或构成该活动的一部分。

(4)如受监管活动为吸收存款,则本条规定不适用。

Annotations:

Modifications etc. (not altering text)

C16 S. 27(1)(2) applied (1.12.2001) by S.I. 2001/2657, arts. 1(1), 5(2)(5) (which was revoked (8.10.2001) by S.I. 2001/3083, arts. 1(2), 23); S.I. 2001/3538, art. 2(1)

S. 27(1)(2) applied (1.12.2001) by S.I. 2001/3083, arts. 1(2), 5(2); S.I. 2001/3538, art. 2(1)

28 Agreements made unenforceable by section 26 or 27.

(1) This section applies to an agreement which is unenforceable because of section 26 or 27.

(2) The amount of compensation recoverable as a result of that section is—

(a) the amount agreed by the parties; or

(b) on the application of either party, the amount determined by the court.

(3) If the court is satisfied that it is just and equitable in the circumstances of the case, it may allow—

(a) the agreement to be enforced; or

(b) money and property paid or transferred under the agreement to be retained.

(4) In considering whether to allow the agreement to be enforced or (as the case may be) the money or property paid or transferred under the agreement to be retained the court must—

(a) if the case arises as a result of section 26, have regard to the issue mentioned in subsection (5); or

(b) if the case arises as a result of section 27, have regard to the issue mentioned in subsection (6).

(5) The issue is whether the person carrying on the regulated activity concerned reasonably believed that he was not contravening the general prohibition by making the agreement.

(6) The issue is whether the provider knew that the third party was (in carrying on the regulated activity) contravening the general prohibition.

(7) If the person against whom the agreement is unenforceable—

(a) elects not to perform the agreement, or

(b) as a result of this section, recovers money paid or other property transferred by him under the agreement,

he must repay any money and return any other property received by him under the agreement.

注释：

修改等(不涉及条文内容)

C16　第27条第(1)款、第(2)款于2001年12月1日依照制定法文件S.I.2001/2657第1条第(1)款,第5条第(2)款、第(5)款[于2001年10月8日依照制定法文件S.I.2001/3083第1条第(2)款、第23条废除];制定法文件S.I.2001/3538第2条第(1)款适用;

第27条第(1)款、第(2)款于2001年12月1日依照制定法文件S.I.2001/3083第1条第(2)款、第5条第(2)款;制定法文件S.I.2001/3538第2条第(1)款适用。

第28条　依照第26条或第27条规定不可强制执行的协议

(1)本条适用于依照第26条和第27条规定不可强制执行的协议。

(2)依照该条规定可请求赔偿的金额为:

(a)当事人协商同意的金额;或

(b)法院依一方当事人请求确定的金额。

(3)如法院根据案情确信符合公正公平原则,则可以允许

(a)履行协议;或

(b)保留根据协议交付或转让的金钱和财产。

(4)在考虑是否允许执行协议或保留根据协议交付或转让的金钱和财产(视情况而定)时,法院必须

(a)如案件因第26条而产生,则考虑第(5)款所述争议点;或

(b)如案件因第27条而产生,则考虑第(6)款所述争议点。

(5)前款所述争议点为,从事相关受监管活动的人当时是否合理地认为自己未因签订该协议而违反一般禁止性规定。

(6)前款所述争议点为,签订人当时是否明知第三方(在从事受监管活动时)违反一般禁止性规定。

(7)如协议对协议另一方不具有强制执行力,而另一方

(a)选择不履行该协议;或

(b)因本条规定追偿根据协议支付的金钱或转移的其他财产,

则该协议另一方必须返还其根据协议收到的任何金钱和任何其他财产。

(8) If property transferred under the agreement has passed to a third party, a reference in section 26 or 27 or this section to that property is to be read as a reference to its value at the time of its transfer under the agreement.

(9) The commission of an authorisation offence does not make the agreement concerned illegal or invalid to any greater extent than is provided by section 26 or 27.

Annotations:

Modifications etc. (not altering text)

C17 S. 28 applied (with modifications) (1.12.2001) by S.I. 2001/2657, arts. 1(1), 5(6) (which was revoked (8.10.2001) by S.I. 2001/3083, arts. 1(2), 23); S.I. 2001/3538, art. 2(1)

S. 28 applied (with modifications) (1.12.2001) by S.I. 2001/3083, arts. 1(2), 5(6); S.I. 2001/3538, art. 2(1)

29 Accepting deposits in breach of general prohibition.

(1) This section applies to an agreement between a person ("the depositor") and another person ("the deposit-taker") made in the course of the carrying on by the deposit-taker of accepting deposits in contravention of the general prohibition.

(2) If the depositor is not entitled under the agreement to recover without delay any money deposited by him, he may apply to the court for an order directing the deposit-taker to return the money to him.

(3) The court need not make such an order if it is satisfied that it would not be just and equitable for the money deposited to be returned, having regard to the issue mentioned in subsection (4).

(4) The issue is whether the deposit-taker reasonably believed that he was not contravening the general prohibition by making the agreement.

(5) "Agreement" means an agreement—

(a) made after this section comes into force; and

(b) the making or performance of which constitutes, or is part of, accepting deposits.

30 Enforceability of agreements resulting from unlawful communications.

(1) In this section—

"unlawful communication" means a communication in relation to which there has been a contravention of section 21(1);

"controlled agreement" means an agreement the making or performance of which by either party constitutes a controlled activity for the purposes of that section; and

"controlled investment" has the same meaning as in section 21.

(2) If in consequence of an unlawful communication a person enters as a customer into a controlled agreement, it is unenforceable against him and he is entitled to recover—

(8)如根据协议转移的财产已经交付第三人,则第26条、第27条或本条述及该财产时,该财产价值应视为其根据该协议转移时的价值。

(9) 涉及实施授权类犯罪并不导致协议的违法或无效超出第26条或第27条规定的范围。

注释:

修改等(不涉及条文内容)

C17 第28条(已修订)于2001年12月1日依照制定法文件S.I.2001/2657第1条第(1)款、第5条第(6)款[于2001年10月8日依照制定法文件S.I.2001/3083第1条第(2)款、第23条废除];制定法文件S.I.2001/3538第2条第(1)款适用;

第28条(已修订)于2001年12月1日依照制定法文件S.I.2001/3083第1条第(2)款、第5条第(6)款;制定法文件S.I.2001/3538第2条第(1)款适用。

第29条 违反一般禁止性规定吸收存款

(1)本条适用于一方当事人(以下简称存款人)与另一方当事人(以下简称吸收存款人)之间,在吸收存款人违反一般禁止性规定吸收存款时签订的协议。

(2)如存款人根据该协议无权立即收回其存款,则可以向法院申请执行令,要求吸收存款人向存款人返还存款。

(3)法院如在考虑第(4)款所述争议点后,认为返还存款不公正、不公平,则无须发布该执行令。

(4)前款所述争议点为,吸收存款人是否合理认为其签订协议并不违反一般禁止性规定。

(5)"协议"系指下列协议:

(a)在本条规定生效后签订;且

(b)协议的签订或履行构成吸收存款,或构成部分吸收存款。

第30条 非法传播导致的协议强制执行力

(1)本条中

"非法传播",系指违反第21条第(1)款的传播;

"受监管协议", 系指任何一方当事人对该协议的签订或履行依照第21条规定构成受监管活动的协议;

"受监管投资"含义同第21条。

(2)如因非法传播,一方当事人作为消费者签订了受监管协议,则该协议对其不具有强制执行力,且作为消费者的当事人有权追偿

(a) any money or other property paid or transferred by him under the agreement; and

(b) compensation for any loss sustained by him as a result of having parted with it.

(3) If in consequence of an unlawful communication a person exercises any rights conferred by a controlled investment, no obligation to which he is subject as a result of exercising them is enforceable against him and he is entitled to recover—

(a) any money or other property paid or transferred by him under the obligation; and

(b) compensation for any loss sustained by him as a result of having parted with it.

(4) But the court may allow—

(a) the agreement or obligation to be enforced, or

(b) money or property paid or transferred under the agreement or obligation to be retained, if it is satisfied that it is just and equitable in the circumstances of the case.

(5) In considering whether to allow the agreement or obligation to be enforced or (as the case may be) the money or property paid or transferred under the agreement to be retained the court must have regard to the issues mentioned in subsections (6) and (7).

(6) If the applicant made the unlawful communication, the issue is whether he reasonably believed that he was not making such a communication.

(7) If the applicant did not make the unlawful communication, the issue is whether he knew that the agreement was entered into in consequence of such a communication.

(8) "Applicant" means the person seeking to enforce the agreement or obligation or retain the money or property paid or transferred.

(9) Any reference to making a communication includes causing a communication to be made.

(10) The amount of compensation recoverable as a result of subsection (2) or (3) is—

(a) the amount agreed between the parties; or

(b) on the application of either party, the amount determined by the court.

(11) If a person elects not to perform an agreement or an obligation which (by virtue of subsection (2) or (3)) is unenforceable against him, he must repay any money and return any other property received by him under the agreement.

(12) If (by virtue of subsection (2) or (3)) a person recovers money paid or property transferred by him under an agreement or obligation, he must repay any money and return any other property received by him as a result of exercising the rights in question.

(13) If any property required to be returned under this section has passed to a third party, references to that property are to be read as references to its value at the time of its receipt by the person required to return it.

(a)其根据协议交付或转让的任何金钱或其他财产;及

(b)其因支付或上述金钱或财产而遭受的任何损失。

(3)如因非法传播,当事人行使了受监管投资赋予的任何权利,其因行使该权利而承担的任何义务均不具有强制执行力,且该人有权追偿

(a)其根据协议交付或转让的任何金钱或其他财产;及

(b)其因交付或转让上述金钱或财产而遭受的任何损失。

(4)但如法院根据案情确信符合公正公平原则,则可以允许

(a)履行该协议或义务,或

(b)保留依照协议或义务交付或转让的金钱或财产。

(5)在考虑是否允许履行协议或义务或是否保留根据协议交付或转让的金钱和财产时(视情况而定),法院必须考虑第(6)款和第(7)款所述争议点。

(6)如申请人进行了非法传播,则前款所述争议点为申请人是否合理认为其本人并未进行非法传播。

(7)如申请人未进行非法传播,则前款所述争议点为申请人是否明知协议是因非法传播而签订的。

(8)“申请人”,系指请求履行协议或义务或请求保留被交付或转让的金钱或财产的人。

(9)述及任何传播均包括述及致使他人进行传播。

(10)依照第(2)款或第(3)款规定可请求赔偿的金额为

(a)当事人协商同意的金额;或

(b)法院依一方当事人请求确定的金额。

(11)如协议或义务[依照第(2)款或第(3)款规定]对一方当事人不具有强制执行力,而该当事人选择不履行该协议或义务,则必须返还其根据协议受让的任何金钱和任何其他财产。

(12)如一方当事人[依照第(2)款或第(3)款规定]追偿其根据协议或义务交付的金钱或转让的其他财产,则必须返还其因行使相关权利而受让的任何金钱和任何其他财产。

(13)如依照本条规定应返还的财产已转让给第三人,则述及该财产的内容视为述及返还人在收到该财产时的价值。

PART Ⅲ AUTHORISATION AND EXEMPTION

Authorisation

31 Authorised persons.

(1) The following persons are authorised for the purposes of this Act—

(a) a person who has a Part Ⅳ permission to carry on one or more regulated activities;

(b) an EEA firm qualifying for authorisation under Schedule 3;

(c) a Treaty firm qualifying for authorisation under Schedule 4;

(d) a person who is otherwise authorised by a provision of, or made under, this Act.

(2) In this Act "authorised person" means a person who is authorised for the purposes of this Act.

Annotations:

Commencement Information

I3 S. 31 wholly in force at 1.12.2001; s. 31 not in force at Royal Assent see s. 431(2); s. 31(1)(b) in force for specified purposes at 25.2.2001 by S.I. 2001/516, art. 2(c), Sch. Pt. 3; s. 31(1)(b) in force for specified purposes at 18.6.2001 by S.I. 2001/1820, art. 2, Sch.; s. 31(1)(c) in force for specified purposes at 3.9.2001 by S.I. 2001/2632, art. 2(2), Sch. Pt. 2; s. 31 in force in so far as not already in force at 1.12.2001 by S.I. 2001/3538, art. 2(1)

32 Partnerships and unincorporated associations.

(1) If a firm is authorised—

(a) it is authorised to carry on the regulated activities concerned in the name of the firm; and

(b) its authorisation is not affected by any change in its membership.

(2) If an authorised firm is dissolved, its authorisation continues to have effect in relation to any firm which succeeds to the business of the dissolved firm.

(3) For the purposes of this section, a firm is to be regarded as succeeding to the

第三部分 授权与豁免

授 权

第31条 获授权人

(1)本法所称获授权人为下列人员:

(a)获得第四部分之许可从事一项或多项受监管活动的人;

(b)有资格依照附录3获得授权的欧洲经济区企业;

(c)有资格依照附录4获得授权的条约企业;

(d)其他根据本法或依照本法所制定的条款获得授权的人。

(2)本法中"获授权人",系指依照本法获得授权的人。

注释:

实施日期

I3 第31条于2001年12月1日全部生效;第31条在副署时尚未生效,见第431条第(2)款;第31条第(1)款第(b)项为特定目的于2001年2月25日依照制定法文件S.I. 2001/516第2条第(c)款、附录第三部分生效;第31条第(1)款第(b)项为特定目的于2001年6月18日依照制定法文件S.I.2001/1820第2条、附录生效;第31条第(1)款第(c)项为特定目的于2001年9月3日依照制定法文件S.I.2001/2632第2条第(2)款、附录第二部分生效;第31条于2001年12月1日尚未生效,则依照制定法文件S.I.2001/3538第2条第(1)款生效。

第32条 合伙和非法人

(1)如企业获得授权

(a)则该企业获准以本其自身名义从事受监管活动;且

(b)该合伙或非法人成员发生任何变动,该授权不受影响。

(2)如被授权企业解散,则其所获授权对承继被解散或非法人经营业务的任何企业继续有效。

(3)依照本条之规定,只有存在下列情况时,才能认为一家企业承继了另一家企

business of another firm only if—

(a) the members of the resulting firm are substantially the same as those of the former firm; and

(b) succession is to the whole or substantially the whole of the business of the former firm.

(4) "Firm" means

(a) a partnership; or

(b) an unincorporated association of persons.

(5) "Partnership" does not include a partnership which is constituted under the law of any place outside the United Kingdom and is a body corporate.

Ending of authorisation

33 Withdrawal of authorisation by the Authority.

(1) This section applies if—

(a) an authorised person's Part Ⅳ permission is cancelled; and

(b) as a result, there is no regulated activity for which he has permission.

(2) The Authority must give a direction withdrawing that person's status as an authorized person.

34 EEA firms.

(1) An EEA firm ceases to qualify for authorisation under Part Ⅱ of Schedule 3 if it ceases to be an EEA firm as a result of—

(a) having its EEA authorisation withdrawn; or

(b) ceasing to have an EEA right in circumstances in which EEA authorisation is not required.

(2) At the request of an EEA firm, the Authority may give a direction cancelling its authorisation under Part Ⅱ of Schedule 3.

(3) If an EEA firm has a Part Ⅳ permission, it does not cease to be an authorised person merely because it ceases to qualify for authorisation under Part Ⅱ of Schedule 3.

Annotations:

Modifications etc. (not altering text)

C18 S. 34(2) modified (1.12.2001) by S.I. 2001/2511, regs. 1(1), 8; S.I. 2001/3538, art. 2(1)

35 Treaty firms.

(1) A Treaty firm ceases to qualify for authorisation under Schedule 4 if its home State authorisation is withdrawn.

(2) At the request of a Treaty firm, the Authority may give a direction cancelling its

业的业务：

(a)新设立的企业的成员与原企业基本相同；且

(b)承继了原企业的全部或者主要业务。

(4)"企业"系指

(a)合伙；或

(b)非法人。

(5)"合伙"不包括依照联合王国境外任何其他国家或地区的法律设立且为法人的合伙。

授权的终止

第33条　管理局撤销授权

(1)如有下列情况，则适用本条规定：

(a)获授权人依照第四部分取得的许可被撤销；且

(b)获授权人因此不得再从事许可撤销前获准从事的受监管活动。

(2)管理局必须发出撤销该获授权人地位的指令。

第34条　欧洲经济区企业

(1)如一家欧洲经济区企业因下列原因不再是欧洲经济区企业，则将不再有资格获得附录3第二部分规定的授权：

(a)欧洲经济区授权被撤销；或

(b)在无须欧洲经济区授权的情况下，不再享有欧洲经济区权利。

(2)应欧洲经济区企业的请求，管理局可发出指令，撤销该企业附录3第二部分规定的授权。

(3)如欧洲经济区企业具有第四部分许可，则不得仅因不再有资格取得附录3第二部分规定的授权而不再是获授权人。

注释：

修改等(不涉及条文内容)

C18　第34条第(2)款于2001年12月1日依照制定法文件S.I.2001/2511第1条第(1)款、第8条；制定法文件S.I.2001/3538第2条第(1)款修订。

第35条　条约企业

(1)条约企业如在其本国所获授权被撤销，则不再有资格获得附录4规定的授权。

(2)应条约企业的请求，管理局可发出指令，撤销该企业依照附录4规定取得

Schedule 4 authorisation.

(3) If a Treaty firm has a Part Ⅳ permission, it does not cease to be an authorised person merely because it ceases to qualify for authorisation under Schedule 4.

36 Persons authorised as a result of paragraph 1(1) of Schedule 5.

(1) At the request of a person authorised as a result of paragraph 1(1) of Schedule 5, the Authority may give a direction cancelling his authorisation as such a person.

(2) If a person authorised as a result of paragraph 1(1) of Schedule 5 has a Part Ⅳ permission, he does not cease to be an authorised person merely because he ceases to be a person so authorised.

Exercise of EEA rights by UK firms

37 Exercise of EEA rights by UK firms.

Part Ⅲ of Schedule 3 makes provision in relation to the exercise outside the United Kingdom of EEA rights by UK firms.

Annotations:

Commencement Information

I4 S. 37 wholly in force at 1.12.2001; s. 37 not in force at Royal Assent see s. 431(2); s. 37 in force for specified purposes at 25.2.2001 by S.I. 2001/516, art. 2(c), Sch. Pt. 3; s. 37 in force for specified purposes at 18.6.2001 by S.I. 2001/1820, art. 2, Sch.; s. 37 in force for specified purposes at 3.9.2001 by S.I. 2001/2632, art. 2, Sch. Pt. 2; s. 37 in force in so far as not already in force at 1.12.2001 by S.I. 2001/3538, art. 2(1)

Exemption

38 Exemption orders.

(1) The Treasury may by order ("an exemption order") provide for—

(a) specified persons, or

(b) persons falling within a specified class,

to be exempt from the general prohibition.

(2) But a person cannot be an exempt person as a result of an exemption order if he has a Part Ⅳ permission.

(3) An exemption order may provide for an exemption to have effect—

(a) in respect of all regulated activities;

(b) in respect of one or more specified regulated activities;

(c) only in specified circumstances;

(d) only in relation to specified functions;

的授权。

(3)如条约企业具有第四部分许可,则不得仅因不再有资格取得附录4规定的授权而不再是获授权人。

第36条　因附录5第1条第(1)款获得授权的人

(1)应因附录5第1条第(1)款规定获得授权的人提出的请求,管理局可发出指令,撤销其因该款规定获得的授权。

(2)如因附录5第1条第(1)款获得授权的人具有第四部分许可,则不得仅因不再获得附录5第1条第(1)款规定的授权而不再是获授权人。

联合王国企业行使欧洲经济区权利

第37条　联合王国企业行使欧洲经济区权利

附录3第三部分规定了有关联合王国企业在联合王国境外行使的欧洲经济区权利。

注释:

实施日期

I4　第37条于2001年12月1日全部生效;第37条在副署时尚未生效,见第431条第(2)款;第37条为特定目的于2001年2月25日依照制定法文件S.I.2001/516第2条第(c)款、附录第三部分生效;第37条为特定目的于2001年6月18日依照制定法文件2001/1820附录第2条生效;第37条为特定目的于2001年9月3日依照制定法文件S.I.2001/2632第2条、附录第二部分生效;第37条如于2001年12月1日尚未生效,则依照制定法文件S.I.2001/3538第2条第(1)款生效。

豁　免　权

第38条　豁免令

(1)财政部可颁布法令(以下简称豁免令)规定

(a)特定的人,或

(b)属于特定类别的人,

不受一般禁止性规定限制。

(2)但具有第四部分许可的人,不得因豁免令而成为享有豁免权的人。

(3)豁免令可以规定豁免效力及于

(a)所有受监管活动;

(b)某种或某些受监管活动;

(c)仅限规定情形;

(d)仅限相关的规定职能;

(e) subject to conditions.

(4) "Specified" means specified by the exemption order.

Annotations:

Modifications etc. (not altering text)

C19 S. 38(2) modified (31.10.2001) by S.I. 2001/3374, art. 1, Sch. para. 3

39 Exemption of appointed representatives.

(1) If a person (other than an authorised person)—

(a) is a party to a contract with an authorised person ("his principal") which—

(i) permits or requires him to carry on business of a prescribed description, and

(ii) complies with such requirements as may be prescribed, and

(b) is someone for whose activities in carrying on the whole or part of that business his principal has accepted responsibility in writing,

he is exempt from the general prohibition in relation to any regulated activity comprised in the carrying on of that business for which his principal has accepted responsibility.

(2) A person who is exempt as a result of subsection (1) is referred to in this Act as an appointed representative.

(3) The principal of an appointed representative is responsible, to the same extent as if he had expressly permitted it, for anything done or omitted by the representative in carrying on the business for which he has accepted responsibility.

(4) In determining whether an authorised person has complied with a provision contained in or made under this Act, anything which a relevant person has done or omitted as respects business for which the authorised person has accepted responsibility is to be treated as having been done or omitted by the authorised person.

(5) "Relevant person" means a person who at the material time is or was an appointed representative by virtue of being a party to a contract with the authorised person.

(6) Nothing in subsection (4) is to cause the knowledge or intentions of an appointed representative to be attributed to his principal for the purpose of determining whether the principal has committed an offence, unless in all the circumstances it is reasonable for them to be attributed to him.

Annotations:

Modifications etc. (not altering text)

C20 S. 39(2) modified (31.10.2001) by S.I. 2001/3374, art. 1, Sch. para. 7

(e)附加条件。

(4)“规定”系指豁免令规定。

注释:

修改等(不涉及条文内容)

C19 第38条第(2)款于2001年10月31日依照制定法文件S.I.2001/3374第1条,附录第3条修订。

第39条 被任命代表的豁免

(1)如一方当事人(非获授权人)

(a)在与获授权人(“委托人”)订立的合同中为合同一方当事人,且该合同

(i)允许或者要求其从事合同约定的业务;且

(ii)符合所规定的要求;且

(b)委托人以书面形式对委托代表所从事的全部或部分业务承担责任,

则从事委托人已承担责任的业务时,被任命代表就该业务中所包含的任何受监管活动豁免于相关一般禁止性规定。

(2)依照本条第(1)款获得豁免的人在本法中称为被任命代表。

(3)对委托代表从事委托人承担责任的业务中的任何作为和不作为,被任命代表的委托人应予负责,等同于委托人已经明示允许了该作为或不作为。

(4)在确定获授权人是否遵守了本法中或依照本法制定的规定时,相关人的任何作为或不作为如与获授权人所承担责任的业务有关,则应视为获授权人的作为或不作为。

(5)“相关人”,系指因在与获授权人签订的合同中为合同一方当事人而在重要期担任或曾经担任被任命代表的人。

(6)在确定委托人是否构成犯罪时,不得依照本条第(4)款中任何规定将被任命代表的知悉内容或主观意图归属于其委托人,除非在特定情况下归属于该委托人是合理的。

注释:

修改等(不涉及条文内容)

C20 第39条第(2)款于2001年10月31日依照制定法文件S.I.2001/3374第1条,附录第7条修订。

Commencement Information

I5 S. 39 wholly in force at 1.12.2001; s. 39 not in force at Royal Assent see s. 431(2); s. 39(1) in force for certain purposes at 25.2.2001 by S.I. 2001/516, art. 2(b), Sch. Pt. 2; s. 39 in force in so far as not already in force at 1.12.2001 by S.I. 2001/3538, art. 2(1)

实施日期

I5 第39条于2001年12月1日全部生效;第39条在副署时尚未生效,见第431条第(2)款;第39条第(1)款为特定目的于2001年2月25日依照制定法文件S.I.2001/516第2条第(b)款、附录第二部分生效;第39条如于2001年12月1日尚未生效,则依照制定法文件S.I.2001/3538第2条第(1)款生效。

PART Ⅳ PERMISSION TO CARRY ON REGULATED ACTIVITIES

Annotations:

Modifications etc. (not altering text)

C21 Pt. IV (ss. 40–55) extended (1.12.2001) by S.I. 2001/2636, arts. 1(2)(b), 3–24; S.I. 2001/3538, art. 2(1)

Pt. IV (ss. 40–55) extended (with modifications) (1.12.2001) by S.I. 2001/2636, arts. 1(2)(b), 35(5)(a); S.I. 2001/3538, art. 2(1)

Pt. IV (ss. 40–50) excluded (1.12.2001) by S.I. 2001/3592, arts. 1(2), 107(2) (with art. 23(2))

Pt. IV (ss. 40–55) modified (1.12.2001) by S.I. 2001/3592, arts. 1(2), 114(3)(a), 121(3), 128(3)(a) (with art. 23(2))

Application for permission

40 Application for permission.

(1) An application for permission to carry on one or more regulated activities may be made to the Authority by—

(a) an individual;

(b) a body corporate;

(c) a partnership; or

(d) an unincorporated association.

(2) An authorised person may not apply for permission under this section if he has a permission—

(a) given to him by the Authority under this Part, or

第四部分　从事受监管活动的许可

注释：

修改等（不涉及条文内容）

C21　第四部分（第40条至第55条）于2001年12月1日依照制定法文件S.I.2001/2636第1条第（2）款第（b）项、第3条至第24条；制定法文件S.I.2001/3538第2条第（1）款扩大适用范围；

第四部分（第40条至第55条）（已修订）于2001年12月1日依照制定法文件S.I.2001/2636第1条第（2）款第（b）项、第35条第（5）款第（a）项；制定法文件S.I.2001/3538第2条第（1）款扩大适用范围；

第四部分（第40条至第50条）于2001年12月1日依照制定法文件S.I.2001/3592第1条第（2）款、第107条第（2）款[与第23条第（2）款]排除；

第四部分（第40条至第55条）于2001年12月1日依照制定法文件S.I.2001/3592第1条第（2）款、第114条第（3）款第（a）项、第121条第（3）款、第128条第（3）款第（a）项[与第23条第（2）款]修订。

许可的申请

第40条　许可的申请

（1）下列主体可以就从事一项或多项受监管活动向管理局提出许可申请：

（a）个人；

（b）法人；

（c）合伙；或

（d）非法人。

（2）获授权人如有下列有效许可，则不得申请本条规定的许可：

（a）管理局依照本部分规定给予的许可；或

(b) having effect as if so given,which is in force.

(3) An EEA firm may not apply for permission under this section to carry on a regulated activity which it is, or would be, entitled to carry on in exercise of an EEA right, whether through a United Kingdom branch or by providing services in the United Kingdom.

(4) A permission given by the Authority under this Part or having effect as if so given is referred to in this Act as "a Part Ⅳ permission".

Annotations:

Modifications etc. (not altering text)

C22 S. 40 extended (1.12.2001) by S.I. 2001/3592, arts. 1(2), 3, 98 [with art. 23(2)]

C23 S. 40 applied (with modifications) (8.4.2002) by The Financial Services and Markets Act 2000 (Permission and Applications) (Credit Unions etc.) Order 2002 (S.I. 2002/704), arts. 3, 4

C24 S. 40(2) excluded (10.8.2001) by S.I. 2001/2636, arts. 1(2)(a), 63(3)

S. 40(2) modified (31.10.2001) by S.I. 2001/3374, art. 1, Sch. para. 3

C25 S. 40 (3) excluded (1.12.2001) by S.I. 2001/2511, regs. 1 (1), 9 (5); S.I. 2001/3538, art. 2(1)

41 The threshold conditions.

(1) "The threshold conditions", in relation to a regulated activity, means the conditions set out in Schedule 6.

(2) In giving or varying permission, or imposing or varying any requirement, under this Part the Authority must ensure that the person concerned will satisfy, and continue to satisfy, the threshold conditions in relation to all of the regulated activities for which he has or will have permission.

(3) But the duty imposed by subsection (2) does not prevent the Authority, having due regard to that duty, from taking such steps as it considers are necessary, in relation to a particular authorised person, in order to secure its regulatory objective of the protection of consumers.

Annotations:

Modifications etc. (not altering text)

C26 S. 41 modified (3.9.2001) by S.I. 2001/2507, arts. 1(1), 3(1); S.I. 2001/2632, art. 2(2), Sch. Pt. 2

S. 41 applied (1.12.2001) by S.I. 2001/3592, arts. 1(2), 10(3)(b), 15(2), 18(4)(b), 29(4)(b) (with art. 23(2)) (b)已获得与第四部分许可效力相同的许可。

(3)如果欧洲经济区企业正在或者将要通过其设立在联合王国的分支机构或者在联合王国境内提供服务而享受欧洲经济区权利，并因此而实施受本部分监管的行为,则该企业不得再申请本部分项下的许可。

(4)管理局依照本部分规定授予的许可,或效力等同于依照本部分规定授予的许可,在本法中称为“第四部分许可”。

注释:

修改等(不涉及条文内容)

C22 第40条于2001年12月1日依照制定法文件S.I.2001/3592第1条(2)款、第3条、第98条[与第23条第(2)款]扩大适用范围。

C23 第40条(已修订)于2002年4月8日依照《2000年金融服务与市场法》(许可与申请)(信用合作社等)以及2002号令(制定法文件S.I.2002/704)第3条、第4条适用。

C24 第40条第(2)款于2001年8月10日依照制定法文件S.I.2001/2636第1条第(2)款(a)项、第63条第(3)款排除;

第40条第(2)款于2001年10月31日依照制定法文件S.I.2001/3374第1条,附录第3条修订。

C25 第40条第 (3) 款于2001年12月1日依照制定法文件S.I.2001/2511第1条第(1)款、第9条第(5)款;制定法文件S.I.2001/3538第2条第(1)款排除。

第41条 准入条件

(1)就受监管活动而言,“准入条件”系指附录6中规定的条件。

(2)依照本部分规定授予或修改许可,或提出或修改任何要求时,管理局必须确保利害关系人符合并将持续符合与其取得或将取得许可的所有受监管活动有关的准入条件。

(3)但第(2)款规定的职责并不妨碍管理局在适当考虑到该职责后为确保实现保护消费者之监管目标而对特定获授权人采取其认为需要的措施。

注释:

修改等(不涉及条文内容)

C26 第41条于2001年9月3日依照制定法文件S.I.2001/2507第1条第(1)款、第3条第(1)款及制定法文件S.I.2001/2632第2条第(2)款,附录第二部分修订;

第41条于2001年12月1日依照制定法文件S.I.2001/3592第1条第(2)款、第10条第(3)款第(b)项、第15条第(2)款、第18条第(4)款第(b)项、第29条第(4)款第(b)项[与第23条第(2)款]适用。

Commencement Information

I6 S. 41 wholly in force at 3.9.2001; s. 41 not in force at Royal Assent see s. 431(2); s. 40(1) in force at 25.2.2001 by S.I. 2001/516, art. 2(a), Sch. Pt. 1; s. 41(2)(3) in force at 3.9.2001 by S.I. 2001/2632, art. 2(2), Sch. Pt. 2

Permission

42 Giving permission.

(1) "The applicant" means an applicant for permission under section 40.

(2) The Authority may give permission for the applicant to carry on the regulated activity or activities to which his application relates or such of them as may be specified in the permission.

(3) If the applicant—

(a) in relation to a particular regulated activity, is exempt from the general prohibition as a result of section 39(1) or an order made under section 38(1), but

(b) has applied for permission in relation to another regulated activity,

the application is to be treated as relating to all the regulated activities which, if permission is given, he will carry on.

(4) If the applicant—

(a) in relation to a particular regulated activity, is exempt from the general prohibition as a result of section 285(2) or (3), but

(b) has applied for permission in relation to another regulated activity, the application is to be treated as relating only to that other regulated activity.

(5) If the applicant—

(a) is a person to whom, in relation to a particular regulated activity, the general prohibition does not apply as a result of Part XIX, but

(b) has applied for permission in relation to another regulated activity, the application is to be treated as relating only to that other regulated activity.

(6) If it gives permission, the Authority must specify the permitted regulated activity or activities, described in such manner as the Authority considers appropriate.

(7) The Authority may—

(a) incorporate in the description of a regulated activity such limitations (for example as to circumstances in which the activity may, or may not, be carried on) as it considers appropriate;

(b) specify a narrower or wider description of regulated activity than that to which the application relates;

(c) give permission for the carrying on of a regulated activity which is not included

实施日期

I6 第41条于2001年9月3日全部生效；第41条在副署时尚未生效，见第431条第（2）款；第40条第（1）款于2001年2月25日依照制定法文件S.I.2001/516第2条第（a）款、附录第一部分生效；第41条第（2）款、第（3）款于2001年9月3日依照制定法文件S.I.2001/2632第2条第（2）款、附录第二部分生效。

许　可

第42条　授予许可

（1）“申请人”，系指申请第40条所规定之许可的人。

（2）管理局可以向申请人授予许可，允许其从事受监管活动、与其申请相关的活动或许可中规定的一项或多项受监管活动。

（3）如申请人

（a）因第39条第（1）款规定或依照第38条第（1）款颁布的法令就特定受监管活动免受一般禁止性规定限制，但

（b）已就另一受监管活动申请许可，

则该申请应当视为与授予许可后申请人所从事的所有受监管活动相关。

（4）如申请人

（a）因第285条第（2）款或第（3）款规定就特定受监管活动免受一般禁止性规定限制，但

（b）已就另一受监管活动申请许可，则该申请应当视为只与该另一受监管活动相关。

（5）如申请人

（a）就特定受监管活动而言，为因第十九部分规定而不适用一般禁止性规定的人，但

（b）已就另一受监管活动申请许可，则该申请应当视为只与该另一受监管活动相关。

（6）如管理局授予许可，则必须以其认为适当的方式说明给予许可的一项或多项受监管活动。

（7）管理局可以

（a）在对受监管活动的说明中附加其认为适当的限制（如可以或不得从事该活动的情形）；

（b）规定宽于或窄于申请所列范围的受监管活动；

（c）给予许可从事申请范围外的受监管活动。

among those to which the application relates.

Annotations:

Modifications etc. (not altering text)

C27 S. 42 modified (31.10.2001) by S.I. 2001/3374, art. 1, Sch. para. 3

C28 S. 42(3)(4)(5) amended (temp. from 3.9.2001 to 1.12.2001) by S.I. 2001/2659, arts. 1(2), 3(4); S.I. 2001/3538, art. 2(1)

Commencement Information

I7 S. 42 wholly in force at 1.12.2001; s. 42 not in force at Royal Assent see s. 431(2); s. 42 in force for specified purposes at 3.9.2001 by S.I. 2001/2632, art. 2 (2), Sch. Pt. 2; s. 42 in force in so far as not already in force at 1.12.2001 by S.I. 2001/3538, art. 2(1)

43 Imposition of requirements.

(1) A Part Ⅳ permission may include such requirements as the Authority considers appropriate.

(2) A requirement may, in particular, be imposed—

(a) so as to require the person concerned to take specified action; or

(b) so as to require him to refrain from taking specified action.

(3) A requirement may extend to activities which are not regulated activities.

(4) A requirement may be imposed by reference to the person's relationship with—

(a) his group; or

(b) other members of his group.

(5) A requirement expires at the end of such period as the Authority may specify in the permission.

(6) But subsection (5) does not affect the Authority's powers under section 44 or 45.

Annotations:

Modifications etc. (not altering text)

C29 S. 43 modified (31.10.2001) by S.I. 2001/3374, art. 1, Sch. para. 3

S. 43 extended (1.12.2001) by S.I. 2001/2636, arts. 1(2)(b), 34–54; S.I. 2001/3538, art. 2(1)

S. 43 extended (1.12.2001) by S.I. 2001/3592, arts. 1(2), 4(2)(3) (with art. 23(2))

S. 43 extended (1.12.2001) by S.I. 2001/3647, art. 4, Sch. 2 para. 4(2)

注释：

修改等(不涉及条文内容)

C27　第42条于2001年10月31日依照制定法文件S.I.2001/3374第1条，附录第3条修订；

C28　第42条第(3)款、第(4)款、第(5)款暂时有效于2001年9月3日至2001年12月1日依照制定法文件S.I.2001/2659第1条第(2)款、第3条第(4)款；制定法文件S.I.2001/3538第2条第(1)款修正。

实施日期

I7　第42条于2001年12月1日全部生效；第42条在副署时尚未生效，见第431条第(2)款；第42条为特定目的于2001年9月3日依照制定法文件S.I.2001/2632第2条第(2)款、附录第二部分生效；第42条于2001年12月1日尚未生效，则依照制定法文件S.I.2001/3538第2条第(1)款生效。

第43条　提出要求

(1)第四部分许可可以包含管理局认为适当的要求。

(2)可以特别

(a)要求相关人作出规定的行为；或

(b)要求相关人不得作出规定的行为。

(3)要求可以扩展到不属于受监管活动的活动。

(4)要求可以参考相关人与下列各项的关系而提出：

(a)其所在的集团；或者

(b)其所在集团中的其他成员。

(5)要求于管理局在许可中规定的期限届满时失效。

(6)但第(5)款规定不影响第44条或第45条规定管理局的权力。

注释：

修改等(不涉及条文内容)

C29　第43条于2001年10月31日依照制定法文件S.I.2001/3374第1条，附录第3条修订；

第43条于2001年12月1日依照制定法文件S.I.2001/2636第1条第(2)款第(b)项、第34条至第54条；制定法文件S.I.2001/3538第2条第(1)款扩大适用范围；

第43条于2001年12月1日依照制定法文件S.I.2001/3592第1条第(2)款、第4条第(2)款、第(3)款[与第23条第(2)款]扩大适用范围；

第43条于2001年12月1日依照制定法文件S.I.2001/3647第4条，附录2第4条第(2)款扩大适用范围。

C30 S. 43(5)(6) excluded (1.12.2001) by S.I. 2001/2636, arts. 1(2)(b), 54(1); S.I. 2001/3538, art. 2(1)

Commencement Information

I8 S. 43 wholly in force at 1.12.2001; s. 43 not in force at Royal Assent see s. 431(2); s. 43 in force for specified purposes at 3.9.2001 by S.I. 2001/2632, art. 2 (2), Sch. Pt. 2; s. 43 in force in so far as not already in force at 1.12.2001 by S.I. 2001/3538, art. 2(1)

Variation and cancellation of Part IV permission

44 Variation etc. at request of authorised person.

(1) The Authority may, on the application of an authorised person with a Part IV permission, vary the permission by—

(a) adding a regulated activity to those for which it gives permission;

(b) removing a regulated activity from those for which it gives permission;

(c) varying the description of a regulated activity for which it gives permission;

(d) cancelling a requirement imposed under section 43; or

(e) varying such a requirement.

(2) The Authority may, on the application of an authorised person with a Part IV permission, cancel the permission.

(3) The Authority may refuse an application under this section if it appears to it—

(a) that the interests of consumers, or potential consumers, would be adversely affected if the application were to be granted; and

(b) that it is desirable in the interests of consumers, or potential consumers, for the application to be refused.

(4) If, as a result of a variation of a Part IV permission under this section, there are no longer any regulated activities for which the authorised person concerned has permission, the Authority must, once it is satisfied that it is no longer necessary to keep the permission in force, cancel it.

(5) The Authority's power to vary a Part IV permission under this section extends to including any provision in the permission as varied that could be included if a fresh permission were being given in response to an application under section 40.

Annotations:

Modifications etc. (not altering text)

C31 S. 44 modified (31.10.2001) by S.I. 2001/3374, art. 1, Sch. para. 3

C30　第43条第(5)款、第(6)款于2001年12月1日依照制定法文件S.I.2001/2636第1条第(2)款第(b)项、第54条第(1)款;制定法文件S.I.2001/3538第2条第(1)款排除。

实施日期

I8　第43条于2001年12月1日全部生效;第43条在副署时尚未生效,见第431条第(2)款;第43条为特定目的于2001年9月3日依照制定法文件S.I.2001/2632第2条第(2)款、附录第二部分生效;第43条如于2001年12月1日尚未生效,则依照制定法文件S.I.2001/3538第2条第(1)款生效。

第四部分许可的变更和撤销

第44条　应获授权人请求的变更等

(1)应已取得第四部分许可的获授权人的申请,管理局可以通过下列方式变更许可:

(a)增加授予许可的受监管活动;

(b)取消授予许可的受监管活动;

(c)变更对授予许可的受监管活动的说明;

(d)取消依照第43条规定提出的要求;或者

(e)变更该项要求。

(2)应已取得第四部分许可的获授权人的申请,管理局可以撤销许可。

(3)如管理局认为有下列情况,则可以驳回依照本条规定提出的申请:[1]

(a)如批准该申请,则消费者或潜在消费者的利益会受到不利影响;且

(b)驳回该申请有利于消费者或潜在消费者的利益。

(4)如因依照本条规定变更第四部分许可,相关获授权人不再就任何受监管活动持有许可,则管理局一经确信再无必要保留该许可,即必须撤销该许可。

(5)管理局依照本条规定变更第四部分许可的权力可扩展至,在变更许可时列入如依第40条的规定申请新授予许可应符合的规定。

注释:

C31　第44条于2001年10月31日依照制定法文件S.I.2001/3374第1条,附录第3条修订;

1 本款依照《2010年金融服务法》第3条第(2)款修订。——译者注

S. 44 extended (1.12.2001) by S.I. 2001/2636, arts. 1(2)(b), 46(3); S.I. 2001/3538, art. 2(1)

S. 44 extended (1.12.2001) by S.I. 2001/3592, arts. 1(2), 3, 4(1)(3), 8, 28(2) (with art. 23(2))

S. 44 amended (temp. from 3.9.2001 to 1.12.2001) by S.I. 2001/2659, arts. 1(2), 3(3); S.I. 2001/3538,art. 2(1)

C32 Ss. 44, 45 (except 45 (1) (b)) modified (temp.) (8.4.2002) by The Financial Services and Markets Act 2000 (Permission and Applications)(Credit Unions etc.) Order 2002 (S.I. 2002/704), art. 7

Commencement Information

I9 S. 44 wholly in force at 1.12.2001; s. 44 not in force at Royal Assent see s. 431(2); s. 44 in force for specified purposes at 3.9.2001 by S.I. 2001/2632, art. 2 (2), Sch. Pt. 2; s. 44 in force in so far as not already in force at 1.12.2001 by S.I. 2001/3538, art. 2(1)

45 Variation etc. on the Authority's own initiative.

(1) The Authority may exercise its power under this section in relation to anauthorized person if it appears to it that—

(a) he is failing, or is likely to fail, to satisfy the threshold conditions;

(b) he has failed, during a period of at least 12 months, to carry on a regulated activity for which he has a Part Ⅳ permission; or

(c) it is desirable to exercise that power in order to protect the interests of consumers or potential consumers.

(2) The Authority's power under this section is the power to vary a Part Ⅳ permission in any of the ways mentioned in section 44(1) or to cancel it.

(3) If, as a result of a variation of a Part Ⅳ permission under this section, there are no longer any regulated activities for which the authorised person concerned has permission, the Authority must, once it is satisfied that it is no longer necessary to keep the permission in force, cancel it.

(4) The Authority's power to vary a Part Ⅳ permission under this section extends to including any provision in the permission as varied that could be included if a fresh permission were being given in response to an application under section 40.

(5) The Authority's power under this section is referred to in this Part as its own–initiative power.

第44条于2001年12月1日依照制定法文件S.I.2001/2636第1条第(2)款第(b)项、第46条第(3)款;制定法文件S.I.2001/3538第2条第(1)款扩大适用范围;

第44条于2001年12月1日依照制定法文件S.I.2001/3592,第1条(2)款、第3条、第4条第(1)款第(3)项、第8条、第28条第(2)款[与第23条第(2)款]扩大适用范围;

第44条暂时有效,于2001年9月3日至2001年12月1日依照制定法文件S.I.2001/2659,第1条第(2)款,第3条第(3)款;制定法文件S.I.2001/3538第2条第(1)款修正;

C32 第44条、第45条[除第45条第(1)款第(b)项]暂时有效,于2002年4月8日依照《2000年金融服务与市场法》(许可与申请)(信用合作社等)2002号令(制定法文件S.I.2002/704)第7条修订。

实施日期

I9 第44条于2001年12月1日全部生效;第44条在副署时尚未生效,见第431条第(2)款;第44条为特定目的于2001年9月3日依照制定法文件S.I.2001/2632第2条第(2)款、附录第二部分生效;第44条如于2001年12月1日尚未生效,则依照制定法文件S.I.2001/3538第2条第(1)款生效。

第45条 管理局自行发起的变更等

(1)如管理局认为有下列情况,则可对获授权人行使本条规定的权力[1]:

(a)获授权人未满足或可能无法满足准入条件;

(b)获授权人已有至少12个月未从事其取得第四部分许可的受监管活动;或

(c)行使该项权力有利于保护消费者或潜在消费者的利益。

(2)本条规定的管理局权力,系指以第44条第(1)款所述任何方式变更或撤销第四部分许可的权力。

(3)如因依照本条规定变更第四部分许可,相关获授权人不再就任何受监管活动持有许可,则管理局一经确信该许可再无必要继续有效,即必须撤销该许可。

(4)管理局依照本条规定变更第四部分许可的权力可扩展至,在变更许可时列入如依第40条的规定申请新授予许可应符合的规定。

(5)管理局依照本条规定具有的权力在本部分中称为自行决定行使的权力。

1 本款依照《2010年金融服务法》第3条第(3)款修订。——译者注

Annotations:

Modifications etc. (not altering text)

C33 S. 45 amended (temp. from 3.9.2001 to 1.12.2001) by S.I. 2001/2659, arts. 1(2), 3(3); S.I. 2001/3538, art. 2(1)

S. 45 modified (temp. from 31.10.2001) by S.I. 2001/3374, arts. 1, 11

C34 Ss. 44, 45 (except 45(1)(b)) modified (temp.) (8.4.2002) by The Financial Services and Markets Act 2000 (Permission and Applications) (Credit Unions etc.) Order 2002 (S.I. 2002/704), art. 7

C35 S. 45(1)(b) excluded (temp. from 3.9.2001 to 1.12.2001) by S.I. 2001/2659, arts. 1(2), 3(3); S.I.2001/3538, art. 2(1)

Commencement Information

I10 S. 45 wholly in force at 1.12.2001; s. 45 not in force at Royal Assent see s. 431(2); s. 45 in force for specified purposes at 3.9.2001 by S.I. 2001/2632, art. 2(2), Sch. Pt. 2; s. 45 in force in so far as not already in force at 1.12.2001 by S.I. 2001/3538, art. 2(1)

46 Variation of permission on acquisition of control.

(1) This section applies if it appears to the Authority that—

(a) a person has acquired control over a UK authorised person who has a Part Ⅳ permission; but

(b) there are no grounds for exercising its own-initiative power.

(2) If it appears to the Authority that the likely effect of the acquisition of control on the authorised person, or on any of its activities, is uncertain the Authority may vary the authorised person's permission by—

(a) imposing a requirement of a kind that could be imposed under section 43 on giving permission; or

(b) varying a requirement included in the authorised person's permission under that section.

(3) Any reference to a person having acquired control is to be read in accordance with Part Ⅻ.

Annotations:

Modifications etc. (not altering text)

C36 S. 46 amended (temp. from 3.9.2001 to 1.12.2001) by S.I. 2001/2659, arts. 1(2), 3(3); S.I. 2001/3538, art. 2(1)

注释：

修改等（不涉及条文内容）

C33 第45条暂时有效，于2001年9月3日到2001年12月1日依照制定法文件S.I. 2001/2659第1条第（2）款、第3条第（3）款；制定法文件S.I.2001/3538第2条第（1）款修正；

第45条暂时有效，于2001年10月31日开始依照制定法文件S.I.2001/3374第1条、第11条修订；

C34 第44条、第45条［除第45条第（1）款第（b）项］（暂时有效于2002年4月8日）依照《2000年金融市场与服务法》（许可与申请）（信用合作社等）2002号令（制定法文件S.I. 2002/704）第7条修订；

C35 第45条第（1）款第（b）项暂时有效，于2001年9月3日到2001年12月1日依照制定法文件S.I.2001/2659第1条第（2）款、第3条第（3）款；制定法文件S.I.2001/3538，第2条第（1）款排除；

实施日期

I10 第45条于2001年12月1日全部生效；第45条在副署时尚未生效，见第431条第（2）款；第45条为特定目的于2001年9月3日依照制定法文件S.I.2001/2632第2条第（2）款、附录第二部分生效；如第45条于2001年12月1日尚未生效，则依照制定法文件S.I. 2001/3538第2条第（1）款生效。

第46条 取得控制权时许可的变更

（1）如管理局认为有下列情况，则适用本条规定：

（a）当事人已对持有第四部分许可的联合王国获授权人取得控制权；但

（b）管理局没有理由行使其自行决定行使的权力。

（2）如管理局认为取得控制权可能对获授权人或其任何活动产生的影响是不确定的，则可通过下列下方式变更获授权人的许可：

（a）提出依照第43条规定在授予通知时可提出的要求；或

（b）变更获授权人依照该条规定取得的许可中包含的要求。

（3）述及控制权取得人时，依照第十二部分规定解释。

注释：

修改等（不涉及条文内容）

C36 第46条暂时有效，于2001年9月3日至2001年12月1日依照制定法文件S.I. 2001/2659第1条第（2）款、第3条第（3）款；制定法文件S.I.2001/3538第2条第（1）款修正；

S. 46 modified (temp. from 31.10.2001) by S.I. 2001/3374, arts. 1, 11

C37 Ss. 46, 47, 48, 49, 50, 51(2) modified (temp.) (8.4.2002) by The Financial Services and Markets Act 2000 (Permission and Applications) (Credit Unions etc.) Order 2002 (S.I. 2002/704), art. 7

Commencement Information

I11 S. 46 wholly in force at 1.12.2001; s. 46 not in force at Royal Assent see s. 431(2); s. 46 in force for specified purposes at 3.9.2001 by S.I. 2001/2632, art. 2(2), Sch. Pt. 2; s. 46 in force in so far as not already in force at 1.12.2001 by S.I. 2001/3538, art. 2(1)

47 Exercise of power in support of overseas regulator.

(1) The Authority's own-initiative power may be exercised in respect of an authorized person at the request of, or for the purpose of assisting, a regulator who is—

(a) outside the United Kingdom; and

(b) of a prescribed kind.

(2) Subsection (1) applies whether or not the Authority has powers which are exercisable in relation to the authorised person by virtue of any provision of Part XIII.

(3) If a request to the Authority for the exercise of its own-initiative power has been made by a regulator who is—

(a) outside the United Kingdom,

(b) of a prescribed kind, and

(c) acting in pursuance of provisions of a prescribed kind,

the Authority must, in deciding whether or not to exercise that power in response to the request, consider whether it is necessary to do so in order to comply with a Community obligation.

(4) In deciding in any case in which the Authority does not consider that the exercise of its own-initiative power is necessary in order to comply with a Community obligation, it may take into account in particular—

(a) whether in the country or territory of the regulator concerned, corresponding assistance would be given to a United Kingdom regulatory authority;

(b) whether the case concerns the breach of a law, or other requirement, which has no close parallel in the United Kingdom or involves the assertion of a jurisdiction not recognised by the United Kingdom;

(c) the seriousness of the case and its importance to persons in the United Kingdom;

(d) whether it is otherwise appropriate in the public interest to give the assistance sought.

第46条暂时有效,于2001年10月开始依照制定法文件S.I.2001/3374第1条、第11条修订。

C37　第46条、第47条、第48条、第49条、第50条、第51条第(2)款暂时有效,于2002年4月8日依照《2000年金融服务与市场法》(许可与申请)(信用合作社等)2002号令(制定法文件S.I.2002/704)第7条修订。

实施日期

I11　第46条于2001年12月1日全部生效;第46条在副署时尚未生效,见第431条第(2)款;第46条为特定目的于2001年9月3日依照制定法文件S.I.2001/2632第2条第(2)款、附录第二部分生效;第46条如于2001年12月1日尚未生效,则依照制定法文件S.I.2001/3538第2条第(1)款生效。

第47条　支持境外监管机关的权利行使

(1)管理局可以应符合下列条件的监管机关请求,或为协助符合下列条件的监管机关,而对获授权人行使自行决定行使的权力:

(a)在联合王国境外;且

(b)属于规定种类。

(2)无论管理局依照第十三部分的任何规定是否具有可对获授权人行使的权力,第(1)款规定均适用。

(3)如符合下列条件的监管机关提出请求,请管理局行使其自行决定行使的权力:

(a)在联合王国境外,

(b)属于规定种类,且

(c)依照规定种类的条款而从事活动,

则在决定是否应此项请求而行使自行决定行使的权力时,管理局必须考虑,是否有必要为遵守共同体义务而行使该项权力。

(4)在任何情况下,如管理局认为没有必要为遵守共同体义务而行使其主动权力,则作出决定时可特别考虑

(a)相关监管机关所在的国家或地区是否会向联合王国的监管机关提供对等的协助;

(b)相关案件所涉及的违法行为,或违反其他要求的行为,在联合王国是否有相应的规定,或者是否涉及维护联合王国不予承认的管辖权主张;

(c)案件的重大程度以及对联合王国境内的人的重要性;

(d)给予所请求的协助是否在其他方面符合公共利益。

(5) The Authority may decide not to exercise its own-initiative power, in response to a request, unless the regulator concerned undertakes to make such contribution towards the cost of its exercise as the Authority considers appropriate.

(6) Subsection (5) does not apply if the Authority decides that it is necessary for it to exercise its own-initiative power in order to comply with a Community obligation.

(7) In subsections (4) and (5) "request" means a request of a kind mentioned in subsection (1).

Annotations:

Modifications etc. (not altering text)

C38 S. 47 amended (temp. from 3.9.2001 to 1.12.2001) by S.I. 2001/2659, arts. 1(2), 3(3); S.I. 2001/3538, art. 2(1)

S. 47 modified (temp. from 31.10.2001) by S.I. 2001/3374, arts. 1, 11

C39 Ss. 46, 47, 48, 49, 50, 51(2) modified (temp.) (8.4.2002) by The Financial Services and Markets Act 2000 (Permission and Applications) (Credit Unions etc.) Order 2002 (S.I. 2002/704), art. 7

Commencement Information

I12 S. 47 wholly in force at 1.12.2001; s. 47 not in force at Royal Assent see s. 431(2); s. 47(1)(3) in force for certain purposes at 25.2.2001 by S.I. 2001/516, art. 2(b), Sch. Pt. 2; s. 47 in force for specified purposes at 3.9.2001 by S.I. 2001/2632, art. 2(2), Sch. Pt. 2;s. 47 in force in so far as not already in force at 1.12.2001 by S.I. 2001/3538, art. 2(1)

48 Prohibitions and restrictions.

(1) This section applies if the Authority—

(a) on giving a person a Part Ⅳ permission, imposes an assets requirement on him; or

(b) varies an authorised person's Part Ⅳ permission so as to alter an assets requirement imposed on him or impose such a requirement on him.

(2) A person on whom an assets requirement is imposed is referred to in this section as "A".

(3) "Assets requirement" means a requirement under section 43—

(a) prohibiting the disposal of, or other dealing with, any of A's assets (whether in the United Kingdom or elsewhere) or restricting such disposals or dealings; or

(b) that all or any of A's assets, or all or any assets belonging to consumers but held by A or to his order, must be transferred to and held by a trustee approved by the Authority.

(5)管理局可决定不应请求行使其自行决定行使的权力,除非相关监管机关承诺分担管理局认为适当的权力行使费用。

(6)如管理局决定,为遵守共同体义务有必要行使自行决定行使的权力,则第(5)款规定不适用。

(7)第(4)款和第(5)款中“请求”系指第(1)款中所述请求。

注释:

修改等(不涉及条文内容)

C38　第47条暂时有效,于2001年9月3日至2001年12月1日依照制定法文件S.I.2001/2659第1条第(2)款、第3条第(3)款;制定法文件S.I.2001/3538第2条第(1)款修正;

第47条暂时有效,于2001年10月31日开始依照制定法文件S.I.2001/3374第1条、第11条修订。

C39　第46条、第47条、第48条、第49条、第50条、第51条第(2)款(暂时有效)于2002年4月8日依照《2000年金融服务与市场法》(许可和申请)(信用合作社等)2002号令(制定法文件S.I.2002/704)第7条修订。

实施日期

I12　第47条于2001年12月1日全部生效;第47条在副署时尚未生效,见第431条第(2)款;第47条第(1)款和第(3)款为特定目的于2001年2月25日依照制定法文件S.I.2001/516第2条第(b)款、附录第二部分生效;第47条为特定目的于2001年9月3日依照制定法文件S.I.2001/2632第2条第(2)款、附录第二部分生效;第47条如于2001年12月1日尚未生效,则依照制定法文件S.I.2001/3538第2条第(1)款生效。

第48条　禁止与限制

(1)如管理局有下列行为,则适用本条规定:

(a)在授予当事人第四部分许可时对其提出一项资产要求;或

(b)变更获授权人的第四部分许可,以改变对其提出的资产要求,或对其提出一项资产要求。

(2)本条中,如对当事人提出了资产要求,则该当事人称为“A”。

(3)“资产要求”系指第43条规定的下列要求:

(a)禁止或限制对A的资产(无论是否在联合王国境内)进行处置或其他交易;或

(b)A的全部或任何资产,或全部或任何属于客户但由A持有的资产,必须转交管理局批准的受托人持有。

(4) If the Authority—

(a) imposes a requirement of the kind mentioned in subsection (3)(a), and

(b) gives notice of the requirement to any institution with whom A keeps an account, the notice has the effects mentioned in subsection (5).

(5) Those effects are that—

(a) the institution does not act in breach of any contract with A if, having been instructed by A (or on his behalf) to transfer any sum or otherwise make any payment out of A's account, it refuses to do so in the reasonably held belief that complying with the instruction would be incompatible with the requirement; and

(b) if the institution complies with such an instruction, it is liable to pay to the Authority an amount equal to the amount transferred from, or otherwise paid out of, A's account in contravention of the requirement.

(6) If the Authority imposes a requirement of the kind mentioned in subsection (3)(b), no assets held by a person as trustee in accordance with the requirement may, while the requirement is in force, be released or dealt with except with the consent of the Authority.

(7) If, while a requirement of the kind mentioned in subsection (3)(b) is in force, A creates a charge over any assets of his held in accordance with the requirement, the charge is (to the extent that it confers security over the assets) void against the liquidator and any of A's creditors.

(8) Assets held by a person as trustee ("T") are to be taken to be held by T in accordance with a requirement mentioned in subsection (3)(b) only if—

(a) A has given T written notice that those assets are to be held by T in accordance with the requirement; or

(b) they are assets into which assets to which paragraph (a) applies have been transposed by T on the instructions of A.

(9) A person who contravenes subsection (6) is guilty of an offence and liable on summary conviction to a fine not exceeding level 5 on the standard scale.

(10) "Charge" includes a mortgage (or in Scotland a security over property).

(11) Subsections (6) and (8) do not affect any equitable interest or remedy in favour of a person who is a beneficiary of a trust as a result of a requirement of the kind mentioned in subsection (3)(b).

Annotations:

Modifications etc. (not altering text)

C40 S. 48 amended (temp. from 3.9.2001 to 1.12.2001) by S.I. 2001/2659, arts. 1(2), 3(3); S.I. 2001/3538, art. 2(1)

(4)如管理局

(a)提出了第(3)款第(a)项所述的要求,且

(b)向A设有账户的任何机构发出关于该要求的通知,则该通知具有第(5)款所述的效力。

(5)前款所述效力为

(a)如A(或代表A)作出的指示要求从A的账户划转任何金额或划出其他任何支付款项,而上述机构有合理理由相信遵从该指示将不合要求,则拒绝遵从该指示不构成违反与A的任何合同;且

(b)如上述机构遵从了上述指示,则有义务向管理局支付与违反要求从A的账户中划转或划出的金额相等的款项。

(6)如管理局提出了第(3)款第(b)项所述的要求,则除非经管理局同意,否则在该要求的有效期内,根据要求由受托人持有的任何资产均不得让与或交易。

(7)在第(3)款第(b)项中所述要求的有效期内,如A对任何其根据要求持有的资产设立了债务,则该等债务(在对资产设立抵押担保的范围内)对清算人或A的任何债权人无效。

(8)由受托人(以下简称T)持有的资产,只有在下列情况下可以视为受托人T依照第(3)款第(b)项所述的要求而持有:

(a)A曾书面通知T,该资产将由T根据要求而持有;或

(b)资产是第(a)项规定所适用的资产,且已经由T根据A的指示而改变。

(9)违反第(6)款规定的,构成犯罪,应当经简易程序定罪,处以不超过标准等级第5级的罚金。

(10)"债务"包括抵押(或者在苏格兰称为财产抵押担保)。

(11)对因第(3)款第(b)项所述要求而成为信托受益者的人,第(6)款和第(8)款规定不影响任何有利于该人的衡平法利益或救济。

注释:

修改等(不涉及条文内容)

C40　第48条暂时有效,于2001年9月3日至2001年12月1日依照制定法文件S.I. 2001/2659第1条第(2)款、第3条第(3)款;制定法文件S.I.2001/3538第2条第(1)款修正;

S. 48 modified (temp. from 31.10.2001) by S.I. 2001/3374, arts. 1, 11

C41 Ss. 46, 47, 48, 49, 50, 51(2) modified (temp.) (8.4.2002) by The Financial Services and Markets Act 2000 (Permission and Applications) (Credit Unions etc.) Order 2002 (S.I. 2002/704), art. 7

C42 S. 48(3)(a) extended (1.12.2001) by S.I. 2001/2636, arts. 1(2)(b), 48(2); S.I. 2001/3538, art. 2(1)

C43 S. 48(4)-(11) applied (1.12.2001) by S.I. 2001/2636, arts. 1(2)(b), 41(3); S.I. 2001/3538, art. 2(1)

C44 S. 48(4)-(7)(9)-(11) applied (1.12.2001) by S.I. 2001/2636, arts. 1(2)(b), 34(2), 35(4); S.I. 2001/3538, art. 2(1)

C45 S. 48(4)(5) applied (1.12.2001) by S.I. 2001/2636, arts. 1(2)(b), 48(2); S.I. 2001/3538, art. 2(1)

C46 S. 48(4)(b) extended (1.12.2001) by S.I. 2001/2636, arts. 1(2)(b), 42(4), 48(4); S.I. 2001/3538, art. 2(1)

C47 S. 48 (6) extended (1.12.2001) by S.I. 2001/2636, arts. 1 (2)(b), 36 (5); S.I. 2001/3538, art. 2(1)

C48 S. 48(8) excluded (1.12.2001) by S.I. 2001/2636, arts. 1(2)(b), 34(2), 35(4); S.I. 2001/3538, art. 2(1)

S. 48(8) modified (1.12.2001) by S.I. 2001/2636, arts. 1(2)(b), 41(5); S.I. 2001/3538, art. 2(1)

Connected persons

49 Persons connected with an applicant.

(1) In considering—

(a) an application for a Part Ⅳ permission, or

(b) whether to vary or cancel a Part IV permission, the Authority may have regard to any person appearing to it to be, or likely to be, in a relationship with the applicant or person given permission which is relevant.

(2) Before—

(a) giving permission in response to an application made by a person who is connected with an EEA firm, or

(b) cancelling or varying any permission given by the Authority to such a person, the

第48条暂时有效，于2001年10月31日开始依照制定法文件S.I.2001/3374第1条、第11条修订。

C41 第46条、第47条、第48条、第49条、第50条、第51条第（2）款（暂时有效）于2002年4月8日依照《2000年金融服务与市场法》（许可和申请）（信用合作社等）命令（制定法文件S.I.2002/704）第7条修订。

C42 第48条第（3）款第（a）项于2001年12月1日依照制定法文件S.I.2001/2636第1条第（2）款第（b）项、第48条第（2）款；制定法文件S.I.2001/3538第2条第（1）款扩大适用范围。

C43 第48条第（4）款至第（11）款于2001年12月1日依照制定法文件S.I.2001/2636第1条第（2）款第（b）项、第41条第（3）款；制定法文件S.I.2001/3538第1条第（2）款第（b）项适用。

C44 第48条第（4）款至第（7）款、第（9）款至第（11）款于2001年12月1日依照制定法文件S.I.2001/2636第1条第（2）款第（b）项、第34条第（2）款、第35条第（4）款；制定法文件S.I.2001/3538第2条第（1）款适用。

C45 第48条第（4）、第（5）款于2001年12月1日依照制定法文件S.I.2001/2636第1条第（2）款第（b）项、第48条第（2）款；制定法文件S.I.2001/3538第2条第（1）款适用。

C46 第48条第（4）款第（b）项于2001年12月1日依照制定法文件S.I.2001/2636第1条第（2）款第（b）项、第42条第（4）款、第48条第（4）款；制定法文件S.I.2001/3538第2条第（1）款扩大适用范围。

C47 第48条第（6）款于2001年12月1日依照制定法文件S.I.2001/2636第1条第（2）款第（b）项、第36条第（5）款；制定法文件S.I.2001/3538第2条第（1）款扩大适用范围。

C48 第48条第（8）款于2001年12月1日依照制定法文件S.I.2001/2636第1条第（2）款第（b）项、第34条第（2）款、第35条第（4）款；制定法文件S.I.2001/3538第2条第（1）款排除。

第48条第（8）款于2001年12月1日依照制定法文件S.I.2001/2636第1条第（2）款第（b）项、第41条第（5）款；制定法文件S.I.2001/3538第2条第（1）款修订。

关　联　人

第49条　申请人的关联人

（1）涉及下列情况：

（a）第四部分许可的申请，或

（b）是否变更或取消第四部分许可，管理局可以考虑其认为与申请人或被许可人是有关联或可能是有关联关系的任何人。

（2）在下述事项进行之前

（a）应当与欧洲经济区企业有关联的申请人提出的申请作出许可，或

（b）取消或变更任何管理局授予上述申请人的许可，

Authority must consult the firm's home state regulator.

(3) A person ("A") is connected with an EEA firm if—

(a) A is a subsidiary undertaking of the firm; or

(b) A is a subsidiary undertaking of a parent undertaking of the firm.

Annotations:

Modifications etc. (not altering text)

C49 Ss. 46, 47, 48, 49, 50, 51(2) modified (temp.) (8.4.2002) by The Financial Services and Markets Act 2000 (Permission and Applications) (Credit Unions etc.) Order 2002 (S.I. 2002/704), art. 7

Additional permissions

50 Authority's duty to consider other permissions etc.

(1) "Additional Part Ⅳ permission" means a Part Ⅳ permission which is in force in relation to an EEA firm, a Treaty firm or a person authorised as a result of paragraph 1 (1) of Schedule 5.

(2) If the Authority is considering whether, and if so how, to exercise its own-initiative power under this Part in relation to an additional Part Ⅳ permission, it must take into account—

(a) the home State authorisation of the authorised person concerned;

(b) any relevant directive; and

(c) relevant provisions of the Treaty.

Annotations:

Modifications etc. (not altering text)

C50 S. 50 amended (temp. from 3.9.2001 to 1.12.2001) by S.I. 2001/2659, arts. 1(2), 3(3); S.I. 2001/3538, art. 2(1)

S. 50 modified (temp. from 31.10.2001) by S.I. 2001/3374, arts. 1, 11

C51 Ss. 46, 47, 48, 49, 50, 51(2) modified (temp.) (8.4.2002) by The Financial Services and Markets Act 2000 (Permission and Applications) (Credit Unions etc.) Order 2002 (S.I. 2002/704), art. 7

Procedure

51 Applications under this Part.

(1) An application for a Part Ⅳ permission must—

管理局必须向该企业的本国监管机关征求意见。

(3)满足下列条件的人(以下简称A)为与欧洲经济区企业有关联:

(a)A是该企业的子企业;或

(b)A是该企业母企业的子企业。

注释:

修改等(不涉及条文内容)

C49　第46条、第47条、第48条、第49条、第50条、第51条第(2)款暂时有效,于2002年4月8日依照《2000年金融服务与市场法》(许可和申请)(信用合作社等)2002号令(制定法文件S.I.2002/704)第7条修订。

附加许可

第50条　管理局考虑其他许可的职责等

(1)"附加第四部分许可",系指与欧洲经济区企业、条约企业或根据附录5第1条第(1)款获得授权的人相关的有效许可。

(2)如管理局正在考虑是否以及如何依照本部分规定行使与附加第四部分许可相关的自行决定行使的权力,则必须考虑

(a)相关获授权人的本国授权;

(b)任何相关的指令;以及

(c)条约相关规定。

注释:

修改等(不涉及条文内容)

C50　第50条暂时有效,于2001年9月3日至2001年12月1日依照制定法文件S.I.2001/2659第1条第(2)款、第3条第(3)款;制定法文件S.I.2001/3538第2条第(1)款修正;

第50条暂时有效于2001年10月31日开始依照制定法文件S.I.2001/3374第1条、第11条修订。

C51　第46条、第47条、第48条、第49条、第50条、第51条第(2)款暂时有效,于2002年4月8日依照《2000年金融服务与市场法》(许可和申请)(信用合作社等)2002号令(制定法文件S.I.2002/704)第7条修订。

程　序

第51条　本部分规定的申请

(1)第四部分许可的申请

(a) contain a statement of the regulated activity or regulated activities which the applicant proposes to carry on and for which he wishes to have permission; and

(b) give the address of a place in the United Kingdom for service on the applicant of any notice or other document which is required or authorised to be served on him under this Act.

(2) An application for the variation of a Part Ⅳ permission must contain a statement—

(a) of the desired variation; and

(b) of the regulated activity or regulated activities which the applicant proposes to carry on if his permission is varied.

(3) Any application under this Part must—

(a) be made in such manner as the Authority may direct; and

(b) contain, or be accompanied by, such other information as the Authority may reasonably require.

(4) At any time after receiving an application and before determining it, the Authority may require the applicant to provide it with such further information as it reasonably considers necessary to enable it to determine the application.

(5) Different directions may be given, and different requirements imposed, in relation to different applications or categories of application.

(6) The Authority may require an applicant to provide information which he is required to provide under this section in such form, or to verify it in such a way, as the Authority may direct.

Annotations:

Modifications etc. (not altering text)

C52 S. 51(1)(b) applied (27.4.2002) by The Financial Services and Markets Act 2000 (Regulated Activities) Order 2001 (S.I. 2001/544), art. 9D(a) (as inserted by The Financial Services and Markets Act 2000 (Regulated Activities) (Amendment) Order 2002 (S.I. 2002/682), arts. 1(2), 4)

C53 Ss. 46, 47, 48, 49, 50, 51(2) modified (temp.) (8.4.2002) by The Financial Services and Markets Act 2000 (Permission and Applications) (Credit Unions etc.) Order 2002 (S.I. 2002/704), art. 7

C54 S. 51(3)-(6) applied (27.4.2002) by The Financial Services and Markets Act 2000 (Regulated Activities) Order 2001 (S.I. 2001/544), art. 9D(a) (as inserted by The Financial Services and Markets Act 2000 (Regulated Activities) (Amendment) Order 2002 (S.I. 2002/682), arts. 1(2), 4)

C55 S. 51(4) extended (1.12.2001) by S.I. 2001/3592, arts. 1(2), 26(6) (with art. 23(2))

(a)必须包含一份声明,说明申请人拟开展并希望获得许可的一项或多项被监管活动;且

(b)必须提供一处联合王国地址,以向申请人送达任何通知或本法规定要求或授权向其送达的其他文件。

(2)变更第四部分许可的申请必须包含一份声明

(a)说明希望进行的变更;且

(b)说明假设许可变更后申请人拟从事的一项或多项受监管活动。

(3)本部分规定的申请

(a)必须以管理局指示的方式作出;且

(b)必须载有或附有管理局合理要求提供的其他信息。

(4)管理局在收到申请后作出决定前,可随时要求申请人提供管理局合理认为对该申请作出决定所需的补充信息。

(5)针对不同的申请或申请种类,可发出不同的指示或提出不同的要求。

(6)管理局可以要求申请人以管理局指示的形式提供本条规定要求申请人提供的信息,或以管理局指示的方式验证其提供的信息。

注释:

修改等(不涉及条文内容)

C52 第51条第(1)款第(b)项于2002年4月27日依照《2000年金融服务与市场法》(受监管活动)2001号令(制定法文件S.I.2001/544)第9D条第(a)款[依照《2000年金融服务与市场法》(受监管活动)(修正案)2002号令(依照制定法文件S.I.2002/682)第1条第(2)款、第4条插入]适用。

C53 第46条、第47条、第48条、第49条、第50条、第51条第(2)款(暂时有效)于2002年4月8日依照《2000年金融服务与市场法》(许可和申请)(信用合作社等)2002号令(制定法文件S.I.2002/704)第7条修订。

C54 第51条第(3)款至第(6)款于2002年4月27日依照《2000年金融服务与市场法》(受监管活动)2001号令(制定法文件S.I.2001/544)第9D条第(a)款[依照《2000年金融服务与市场法》(受监管活动)(修正案)2002号令(制定法文件S.I.2002/682)第1条第(2)款、第4条插入]适用。

C55 第51条第(4)款于2001年12月1日依照制定法文件S.I.2001/3592第1条第(2)款、第26条第(6)款[与第23条第(2)款]扩大适用范围。

C56 S. 51(3)-(6) applied (27.4.2002) by The Financial Services and Markets Act 2000 (Regulated Activities) Order 2001 (S.I. 2001/544), art. 9D(a) (as inserted by The Financial Services and Markets Act 2000 (Regulated Activities) (Amendment) Order 2002 (S.I. 2002/682), arts. 1(2), 4)

C57 S. 51(3)-(6) applied (27.4.2002) by The Financial Services and Markets Act 2000 (Regulated Activities) Order 2001 (S.I. 2001/544), art. 9D(a) (as inserted by The Financial Services and Markets Act 2000 (Regulated Activities) (Amendment) Order 2002 (S.I. 2002/682), arts. 1(2), 4)

C58 S. 51(3)-(6) applied (27.4.2002) by The Financial Services and Markets Act 2000 (Regulated Activities) Order 2001 (S.I. 2001/544), art. 9D(a) (as inserted by The Financial Services and Markets Act 2000 (Regulated Activities) (Amendment) Order 2002 (S.I. 2002/682), arts. 1(2), 4)

Commencement Information

I13 S. 51 wholly in force at 3.9.2001; s. 51 not in force at Royal Assent see s. 431(2); s. 51(3) in force for specified purposes at 18.6.2001 by S.I. 2001/1820, art. 2, Sch.; s. 51 in force at 3.9.2001 by S.I. 2001/2632, art. 2(2), Sch. Pt. 2

52 Determination of applications

(1) An application under this Part must be determined by the Authority before the end of the period of six months beginning with the date on which it received the completed application.

(2) The Authority may determine an incomplete application if it considers it appropriate to do so; and it must in any event determine such an application within twelve months beginning with the date on which it received the application.

(3) The applicant may withdraw his application, by giving the Authority written notice, at any time before the Authority determines it.

(4) If the Authority grants an application for, or for variation of, a Part Ⅳ permission, it must give the applicant written notice.

(5) The notice must state the date from which the permission, or the variation, has effect.

(6) If the Authority proposes—

(a) to give a Part Ⅳ permission but to exercise its power under section 42(7)(a) or (b) or 43(1), or

(b) to vary a Part Ⅳ permission on the application of an authorised person but to exercise its power under any of those provisions (as a result of section 44(5)),

it must give the applicant a warning notice.

C56　第51条第(3)款至第(6)款于2002年4月27日依照《2000年金融服务与市场法》(受监管活动)2001号令(制定法文件S.I.2001/544)第9D条第(a)款[依照《2000年金融服务与市场法》(受监管活动)(修正案)2002号令(依照制定法文件S.I.2002/682)第1条第(2)款、第4条插入]适用。

C57　第51条第(3)款至第(6)款于2002年4月27日依照《2000年金融服务与市场法》(受监管活动)2001号令(制定法文件S.I.2001/544)第9D条第(a)款[依照《2000年金融服务与市场法》(受监管活动)(修正案)2002号令(依照制定法文件S.I.2002/682)第1条第(2)款、第4条插入]适用。

C58　第51条第(3)款至第(6)款于2002年4月27日依照《2000年金融服务与市场法》(受监管活动)2001号令(制定法文件S.I.2001/544)第9D条第(a)款[依照《2000年金融服务与市场法》(受监管活动)(修正案)2002号令(依照制定法文件S.I.2002/682)第1条第(2)款、第4条插入]适用。

实施日期

I13　第51条于2001年9月3日全部生效;第51条在副署时尚未生效,见第431条第(2)款;第51条第(3)款为特定目的于2001年6月18日依照制定法文件S.I.2001/1820第2条、附录生效;第51条于2001年9月3日依照制定法文件S.I.2001/2632,第2条第(2)款、附录第二部分生效。

第52条　申请的决定

(1)对本部分规定的申请,管理局必须于收到完整申请之日起6个月期间届满前作出决定。

(2)管理局如认为适当,则可对不完整的申请作出决定;且在任何情况下必须在首次收到该申请之日起12个月内作出决定。

(3)管理局对申请作出决定前,申请人可随时向管理局发出书面通知撤回申请。

(4)如管理局批准第四部分许可申请,或批准变更第四部分许可的申请,则必须书面通知申请人。

(5)前款所述通知必须说明获批准许可或变更的生效日期。

(6)如管理局拟

(a)授予第四部分许可,但依照第42条第(7)款第(a)项或第(b)项规定或第43条第(1)款规定行使权力,或;

(b)根据获授权人的申请变更第四部分许可,但[因第44条第(5)款]依照任何上述规定行使权力,

则必须向申请人发出预告通知。

(7) If the Authority proposes to refuse an application made under this Part, it must (unless subsection (8) applies) give the applicant a warning notice.

(8) This subsection applies if it appears to the Authority that—

(a) the applicant is an EEA firm; and

(b) the application is made with a view to carrying on a regulated activity in a manner in which the applicant is, or would be, entitled to carry on that activity in the exercise of an EEA right whether through a United Kingdom branch or by providing services in the United Kingdom.

(9) If the Authority decides—

(a) to give a Part Ⅳ permission but to exercise its power under section 42(7)(a) or (b) or 43(1),

(b) to vary a Part Ⅳ permission on the application of an authorised person but to exercise its power under any of those provisions (as a result of section 44(5)), or

(c) to refuse an application under this Part,

it must give the applicant a decision notice.

Annotations:

Modifications etc. (not altering text)

C59 S. 52 amended (temp. from 3.9.2001 to 1.12.2001) by S.I. 2001/2659, arts. 1(2), 3 (3); S.I. 2001/3538, art. 2(1);S. 52 modified (temp. from 31.10.2001) by S.I. 2001/3374, arts. 1, 11S. 52 extended (1.12.2001) by S.I. 2001/3592, arts. 1(2), 9 (with art. 23(2))

C60 Ss. 52, 53, 54, 55 modified (temp.) (8.4.2002) by The Financial Services and Markets Act 2000 (Permission and Applications) (Credit Unions etc.) Order 2002 (S.I. 2002/704), art. 7

C61 S. 52 (except subsections (6) (8) (9) (a) (b)) applied (27.4.2002) by The Financial Services and Markets Act 2000 (Regulated Activities) Order 2001 (S.I. 2001/544), art. 9D (b) (as inserted by The Financial Services and Markets Act 2000 (Regulated Activities) (Amendment) Order 2002 (S.I. 2002/682), arts. 1(2), 4)

C62 S. 52(1)(2) modified (1.12.2001) by S.I. 2001/3592, arts. 1(2), 26(6) (with art. 23(2))

C63 S. 52(2) restricted (1.12.2001) by S.I. 2001/3592, arts. 1(2), 26(4)(5) (with art. 23(2))

C64 S. 52(9) excluded (1.12.2001) by S.I. 2001/3592, arts. 1(2), 110(2), 115(2), 122(2), 129 (with art. 23(2))

C65 S. 52(9)(c) extended (1.12.2001) by S.I. 2001/3592, arts. 1(2), 5(3)(4) (with art. 23(2))

(7)如管理局拟驳回依照本部分规定提出的申请,则必须向申请人发出预告通知[除非第(8)款规定适用]。

(8)如管理局认为有下列情况,则适用本款规定:

(a)申请人是欧洲经济区企业;且

(b)提出申请旨在,以申请人在行使欧洲经济区企业权利时有权或将会有权从事受监管活动的方式从事该活动,无论申请人通过联合王国分支机构或通过在联合王国提供服务而行使该项权利。

(9)如管理局决定

(a)授予第四部分许可,但依照第42条第(7)款第(a)项或第(b)项规定或第43条第(1)款规定行使权力,

(b)根据获授权人的申请变更第四部分许可,但[因第44条第(5)款]依照任何上述规定行使权力,或

(c)驳回本部分规定的申请,

则必须向申请人发出决定通知。

注释:

修改等(不涉及条文内容)

C59 第52条暂时有效,于2001年9月3日至2001年12月1日依照制定法文件S.I. 2001/2659第1条第(2)款、第3条第(3)款;制定法文件S.I.2001/3538第2条第(1)款修正;第52条暂时有效于2001年10月31日开始依照制定法文件S.I.2001/3374第1条、第11条修订;第52条于2001年12月1日依照制定法文件S.I.2001/3592,第1条第(2)款、第9条[与第23条第(2)款]扩大适用范围。

C60 第52条、第53、第54条、第55条暂时有效,于2002年4月8日依照《2000年金融服务与市场法》(许可和申请)(信用合作社等)2002号令(制定法文件S.I.2002/704)第7条修订。

C61 第52条[第(6)款、第(8)款、第(9)款、第(a)款、第(b)款除外]于2002年4月27日依照《2000年金融服务与市场法》(受监管活动)2001号令(制定法文件S.I.2001/544)第9D条第(b)款[如《2000年金融服务与市场法》(受监管活动)(修正案)命令2002[依照制定法文件S.I.2002/682第1条第(2)款、第4条插入]适用。

C62 第52条第(1)款、第(2)款于2001年12月1日依照制定法文件S.I.2001/3592第1条第(2)款、第26条第(6)款[与第23条第(2)款]修订。

C63 第52条第(2)款于2001年12月1日受制定法文件S.I.2001/3592第1条第(2)款,第26条第(4)款、第(5)款[与第23条第(2)款]限制。

C64 第52条第(9)款于2001年12月1日依照制定法文件S.I.2001/3592第1条第(2)款、第110条第(2)款、第115条第(2)款、第122条第(2)款、第129条[与第23条第(2)款]排除。

C65 第52条第(9)款第(c)项于2001年12月1日依照制定法文件S.I.2001/3592第1条第(2)款,第5条第(3)款、第(4)款[与第23条第(2)款]扩大适用范围。

53 Exercise of own-initiative power: procedure.

(1) This section applies to an exercise of the Authority's own-initiative power to vary an authorised person's Part Ⅳ permission.

(2) A variation takes effect—

(a) immediately, if the notice given under subsection (4) states that that is the case;

(b) on such date as may be specified in the notice; or

(c) if no date is specified in the notice, when the matter to which the notice relates is no longer open to review.

(3) A variation may be expressed to take effect immediately (or on a specified date) only if the Authority, having regard to the ground on which it is exercising its owninitiative power, reasonably considers that it is necessary for the variation to take effect immediately (or on that date).

(4) If the Authority proposes to vary the Part Ⅳ permission, or varies it with immediate effect, it must give the authorised person written notice.

(5) The notice must—

(a) give details of the variation;

(b) state the Authority's reasons for the variation and for its determination as to when the variation takes effect;

(c) inform the authorised person that he may make representations to the Authority within such period as may be specified in the notice (whether or not he has referred the matter to the Tribunal);

(d) inform him of when the variation takes effect; and

(e) inform him of his right to refer the matter to the Tribunal.

(6) The Authority may extend the period allowed under the notice for making representations.

(7) If, having considered any representations made by the authorised person, the Authority decides—

(a) to vary the permission in the way proposed, or

(b) if the permission has been varied, not to rescind the variation,

it must give him written notice.

(8) If, having considered any representations made by the authorised person, the Authority decides—

(a) not to vary the permission in the way proposed,

第53条 行使自行决定行使的权力:程序

(1)管理局行使变更获授权人第四部分许可的自行决定行使的权力时,适用本条规定。

(2)变更在下列时间生效:

(a)如依照第(4)款规定情况发出通知,则立即生效;

(b)于通知规定之日生效;或

(c)如通知未规定日期,则于通知相关事项不再开放供审议时生效。

(3)只有管理局在考虑其行使自行决定行使的权力的理由后,合理地认为有必要使变更立即生效(或在指定日期生效),才可以明示该变更立即生效(或在指定日期生效)。

(4)如管理局拟变更第四部分许可,或使变更许可的决定立即生效,则必须向获授权人发出书面通知。

(5)前款所述通知必须

(a)详细说明变更情况;

(b)说明管理局作出变更及决定变更生效时间的理由;

(c)告知获授权人可在通知规定的期限内向管理局提出陈述(无论其是否已将该事项诉至裁判所;[1]

(d)告知获授权人变更生效时间;且

(e)告知获授权人有权将该事项诉至裁判所。

(6)管理局可以延长通知规定允许陈述的期限。

(7)如管理局在考虑获授权人作出的任何陈述后决定

(a)以其计划的方式变更许可;或

(b)如已变更许可,决定不废除该变更,

则必须向获授权人发出书面通知。

(8)如管理局在考虑获授权人作出的任何陈述后决定

(a)不以其计划的方式变更许可,

---

1 裁判所(the Tribunal),指金融服务与市场裁判所(The Financial Services and Markets Tribunal),依照本法第123条设立,其职能为裁判企业和个人对金融服务管理局(FSA)的申诉。当被监管的企业或个人对FSA的监管产生不服时可向该裁判所提出申诉。出于对企业和个人应有权利的保护,金融服务与市场裁判所完全独立于FSA。——译者注

(b) to vary the permission in a different way, or

(c) to rescind a variation which has effect,

it must give him written notice.

(9) A notice given under subsection (7) must inform the authorised person of his right to refer the matter to the Tribunal.

(10) A notice under subsection (8)(b) must comply with subsection (5).

(11) If a notice informs a person of his right to refer a matter to the Tribunal, it must give an indication of the procedure on such a reference.

(12) For the purposes of subsection (2)(c), whether a matter is open to review is to be determined in accordance with section 391(8).

Annotations:

Modifications etc. (not altering text)

C66 S. 53 amended (temp. from 3.9.2001 to 1.12.2001) by S.I. 2001/2659, arts. 1(2), 3(3); S.I. 2001/3538, art. 2(1)

S. 53 modified (temp. from 31.10.2001) by S.I. 2001/3374, arts. 1, 11

S. 53 excluded (1.12.2001) by S.I. 2001/3592, arts. 1(2), 61(1), 110(1), 115(1), 122(1), 129 (with art. 23(2))

C67 Ss. 52, 53, 54, 55 modified (temp.) (8.4.2002) by The Financial Services and Markets Act 2000 (Permission and Applications) (Credit Unions etc.) Order 2002 (S.I. 2002/704), art. 7

C68 S. 53(2)(c) excluded (1.12.2001) by S.I. 2001/3592, arts. 1(2), 15(3), 18(5), 29(5) (with art. 23(2))

C69 S. 53(4) extended (1.12.2001) by S.I. 2001/3592, arts. 1(2), 10, 14, 18(1)(a), 29, 30–34 (with art. 23(2))S. 53(4) modified (1.12.2001) by S.I. 2001/3592, arts. 1(2), 72(2) (with art. 23(2))

C70 S. 53(8) extended (1.12.2001) by S.I. 2001/3592, arts. 1(2), 16(1) (with art. 23(2))

Commencement Information

I14 S. 53 wholly in force at 1.12.2001; s. 53 not in force at Royal Assent see s. 431(2); s. 53 in force for specified purposes at 3.9.2001 by S.I. 2001/2632, art. 2(2), Sch. Pt. 2; s. 53 in force in so far as not already in force at 1.12.2001 by S.I. 2001/3538, art. 2(1) (b)以其他方式变更许可,或

(c)废除已经生效的许可,

则必须向获授权人发出书面通知。

(9)依照第(7)款规定发出的通知必须告知获授权人其有权将该事项诉至裁判所。

(10)依照第(8)款第(b)项规定发出的通知必须符合第(5)款的规定。

(11)如通知告知被通知人其有权将事项诉至裁判所,则必须说明诉至裁判所的程序。

(12)为实施第(2)款第(c)项规定,某事项是否开放供审议应当依照第391条第(8)款规定确定。

注释:

修改等(不涉及条文内容)

C66 第53条暂时有效,于2001年9月3日至2001年12月1日依照制定法文件S.I.2001/2659第1条第(2)款、第3条第(3)款;制定法文件S.I.2001/3538第2条第(1)款修正;

第53条暂时有效,于2001年10月31日开始依照制定法文件S.I.2001/3374第1条、第11条修订;

第53条于2001年12月1日依照制定法文件S.I.2001/3592,第1条第(2)款、第61条第(1)款、第110条第(1)款、第115条第(1)款、第122条第(1)款、第129条[与第23条第(2)款]排除。

C67 第52条、第53条、第54条、第55条于2002年4月8日依照《2000年金融服务与市场法》(许可和申请)(信用合作社等)2002号令(制定法文件S.I.2002/704)第7条修订。

C68 第53条第(2)款第(c)项于2001年12月1日依照制定法文件S.I.2001/3592第1条第(2)款、第15条第(3)款、第18条第(5)款、第29条第(5)款[与第23条第(2)款]排除。

C69 第53条第(4)款于2001年12月1日依照制定法文件S.I.2001/3592第1条第(2)款、第10条、第14条、第18条第(1)款(a)项、第29条、第30条至第34条[与第23条第(2)款]扩大适用范围;第53条第(4)款于2001年12月1日依照制定法文件S.I.2001/3592第1条第(2)款、第72条第(2)款[与第23条第(2)款]修订。

C70 第53条第(8)款于2001年12月1日依照制定法文件S.I.2001/35922第1条第(2)款、第16条第(1)款[与第23条第(2)款]扩大适用范围。

实施日期

I14 第53条于2001年12月1日全部生效;第53条在副署时尚未生效,见第431条第(2)款;第53条为特定目的于2001年9月3日依照制定法文件S.I.2001/2632第2条第(2)款、附录第二部分生效;第53条如在2001年12月1日尚未生效,则依照制定法文件S.I.2001/3538第2条第(1)款生效。

54 Cancellation of Part IV permission: procedure.

(1) If the Authority proposes to cancel an authorised person's Part Ⅳ permission otherwise than at his request, it must give him a warning notice.

(2) If the Authority decides to cancel an authorised person's Part Ⅳ permission otherwise than at his request, it must give him a decision notice.

Annotations:

Modifications etc. (not altering text)

C71 S. 54 amended (temp. from 3.9.2001 to 1.12.2001) by S.I. 2001/2659, arts. 1(2), 3(3); S.I. 2001/3538, art. 2(1)

S. 54 modified (temp. from 31.10.2001) by S.I. 2001/3374, arts. 1, 11

S. 54 excluded (1.12.2001) by S.I. 2001/3592, arts. 1(2), 61(1), 110(1), 115(1), 122(1), 129 (with art. 23(2))

C72 Ss. 52, 53, 54, 55 modified (temp.) (8.4.2002) by The Financial Services and Markets Act 2000 (Permission and Applications) (Credit Unions etc.) Order 2002 (S.I. 2002/704), art. 7

C73 S. 54 applied (with modifications) (27.4.2002) by The Financial Services and Markets Act 2000 (Regulated Activities) Order 2001 (S.I. 2001/544), art. 9E(3) (as inserted by The Financial Services and Markets Act 2000 (Regulated Activities) (Amendment) Order 2002 (S.I. 2002/682), arts. 1(2), 4)

C74 S. 54(2) modified (1.12.2001) by S.I. 2001/3592, arts. 1(2), 71(2) (with art. 23(2))

Commencement Information

I15 S. 54 wholly in force at 1.12.2001; s. 54 not in force at Royal Assent see s. 431(2); s. 54 in force for specified purposes at 3.9.2001 by S.I. 2001/2632, art. 2(2), Sch. Pt. 2; s. 54 in force in so far as not already in force at 1.12.2001 by S.I. 2001/3538, art. 2(1)

References to the Tribunal

55 Right to refer matters to the Tribunal.

(1) An applicant who is aggrieved by the determination of an application made under this Part may refer the matter to the Tribunal.

(2) An authorised person who is aggrieved by the exercise of the Authority's own-initiative power may refer the matter to the Tribunal.

第54条　第四部分许可的撤销:程序

(1)如管理局非应获授权人请求而拟撤销获授权人的第四部分许可,则必须向获授权人发出预告通知。

(2)如管理局非应获授权人请求而决定撤销获授权人的第四部分许可,则必须向获授权人发出决定通知。

注释:

修改等(不涉及条文内容)

C71　第54条暂时有效,于2001年9月3日至2001年12月1日依照制定法文件S.I. 2001/2659第1条第(2)款、第3条第(3)款、制定法文件S.I.2001/3538第2条第(1)款修正;

第54条暂时有效,于2001年10月31日开始依照制定法文件S.I.2001/3374第1条、第11条修订;

第54条于2001年12月1日依照制定法文件S.I.2001/3592第1条第(2)款、第61条第(1)款、第110条第(1)款、第115条第(1)款、第122条第(1)款、第129条[与第23条第(2)款]排除。

C72　第52条、第53条、第54条、第55条暂时有效,于2002年4月8日依照《2000年金融服务与市场法》(许可和申请)(信用合作社等)2002号令(制定法文件S.I.2002/704)第7条修订。

C73　第54条(已修订)于2002年4月27日依照《2000年金融服务与市场法》(受监管活动)2001号令(制定法文件S.I.2001/544)第9E条第(3)款[如《2000年金融服务与市场法》(受监管活动)(修正案)命令2002(制定法文件S.I.2002/682)第1条第(2)款、第4条所插入]适用。

C74　第54条第(2)款于2001年12月1日依照制定法文件S.I.2001/3592第1条第(2)款、第71条第(2)款[与第23条第(2)款]修订。

实施日期

I15　第54条于2001年12月1日全部生效;第54条在副署时尚未生效,见第431条第(2)款;第54条为特定目的于2001年9月3日依照制定法文件S.I.2001/516第2条第(2)款、附录第二部分生效;如于2001年12月1日尚未生效,则依照制定法文件S.I.2001/3538第2条第(1)款生效。

诉至裁判所

第55条　将事项诉至裁判所的权利

(1)对依照本部分规定提出的申请,申请人如不服对该申请作出的决定,可将该事项诉至裁判所。

(2)获授权人如不服管理局行使自行决定行使的权力,可将该事项诉至裁判所。

Annotations:

Modifications etc. (not altering text)

C75 S. 55 amended (temp. from 3.9.2001 to 1.12.2001) by S.I. 2001/2659, arts. 1(2), 3(3); S.I. 2001/3538, art. 2(1)

S. 55 modified (17.8.2001 for certain purposes otherwise 1.12.2001) by 1992 c. 40, s. 85(4C) (as inserted (17.8.2001 for certain purposes otherwise 1.12.2001) by S.I. 2001/2617, arts. 2(b), 13(1), Sch. 5 Pt. I para. 95 (with art. 13(3), Sch. 5)); S.I. 2001/3538, art. 2(1)

S. 55 modified (17.8.2001 for certain purposes otherwise 1.12.2001) by 1986 c. 53, s. 93(6B) (as substituted (17.8.2001 for certain purposes otherwise 1.12.2001) by S.I. 2001/2617, arts. 2(b), 13(1), Sch. 5 Pt. II para. 177(d) (with art. 13(3), Sch. 5)); S.I. 2001/3538, art. 2(1)

S. 55 modified (temp. from 31.10.2001) by S.I. 2001/3374, arts. 1, 11

S. 55 excluded (1.12.2001) by S.I. 2001/3592, arts. 1(2), 61(1), 110(1), 115(1), 122(1), 129 (with art. 23(2))

C76 Ss. 52, 53, 54, 55 modified (temp.) (8.4.2002) by The Financial Services and Markets Act 2000 (Permission and Applications) (Credit Unions etc.) Order 2002 (S.I. 2002/704), art. 7

C77 S. 55(1) applied (27.4.2002) by The Financial Services and Markets Act 2000 (Regulated Activities) Order 2001 (S.I. 2001/544), art. 9D(c) (as inserted by The Financial Services and Markets Act 2000 (Regulated Activities) (Amendment) Order 2002 (S.I. 2002/682), arts. 1(2), 4)

C78 S. 55(2) applied (with modifications) (27.4.2002) by The Financial Services and Markets Act 2000 (Regulated Activities) Order 2001 (S.I. 2001/544), art. 9E(3) (as inserted by The Financial Services and Markets Act 2000 (Regulated Activities) (Amendment) Order 2002 (S.I. 2002/682), arts. 1(2), 4)

注释：

修改等(不涉及条文内容)

C75　第55条暂时有效，于2001年9月3日至2001年12月1日依照制定法文件S.I. 2001/2659第1条第(2)款、第3条第(3)款；制定法文件S.I.2001/3538第2条第(1)款修正。

第55条为特定目的于2001年8月17日，否则于2001年12月1日依照1992年第40章第85条第(4C)款{为特定目的于2001年8月17日，否则于2001年12月1日插入}依照制定法文件S.I.2001/2617第2条第(b)款、第13条第(1)款，附录5第一部分第95条[与附录5第13条第(3)款]；制定法文件S.I.2001/3538第2条第(1)款修订；

第55条为特定目的于2001年8月17日，否则于2001年12月1日依照1986年本法第53条、第93条第(6B)款{为特定目的于2001年8月17日，否则于2001年12月1日依照制定法文件S.I.2001/2617第2条第(b)款、第13条第(1)款，附录5第二部分第177条第(d)款[与附录5第13条第(3)款]替换}；制定法文件S.I.2001/3538第2条第(1)款修订；

第55条暂时有效，于2001年10月31日开始依照制定法文件S.I.2001/3374第1条、第11条修订；

第55条于2001年12月1日依照制定法文件S.I.2001/3592，第1条第(2)款、第61条第(1)款、第110条第(1)款、第115条第(1)款、第122条第(1)款、第129条[与第23条第(2)款]排除。

C76　第52条、第53条、第54条、第55条暂时有效，于2002年4月8日依照《2000年金融服务与市场法》(许可和申请)(信用合作社等)2002号令(制定法文件S.I.2002/704)第7条修订。

C77　第55条第(1)款于2002年4月27日依照《2000年金融服务与市场法》(受监管活动)2001号令(制定法文件S.I.2001/544)第9D条第(c)款[依照《2000年金融服务与市场法》(受监管活动)(修正案)2002号令(制定法文件S.I.2002/682)第1条第(2)款、第4条插入]适用。

C78　第55条第(2)款(已修订)于2002年4月27日依照《2000年金融服务与市场法》(受监管活动)2001号令(制定法文件S.I.2001/544)第9E条第(3)款[依照《2000年金融服务与市场法》(受监管活动)(修正案)2002号令(制定法文件S.I.2002/682)第1条第(2)款、第4条插入]适用。

PART V PERFORMANCE OF REGULATED ACTIVITIES

Annotations:

Modifications etc. (not altering text)

C79 Pt. V (ss. 56–71) modified (1.12.2001) by S.I. 2001/3592, arts. 1(2), 114(3)(a), 128(3)(a) (with art. 23(2))

Prohibition orders

56 Prohibition orders.

(1) Subsection (2) applies if it appears to the Authority that an individual is not a fit and proper person to perform functions in relation to a regulated activity carried on by an authorised person.

(2) The Authority may make an order ("a prohibition order") prohibiting the individual from performing a specified function, any function falling within a specified description or any function.

(3) A prohibition order may relate to—

(a) a specified regulated activity, any regulated activity falling within a specified description or all regulated activities;

(b) authorised persons generally or any person within a specified class of authorised person.

(4) An individual who performs or agrees to perform a function in breach of a prohibition order is guilty of an offence and liable on summary conviction to a fine not exceeding level 5 on the standard scale.

(5) In proceedings for an offence under subsection (4) it is a defence for the accused to show that he took all reasonable precautions and exercised all due diligence to avoid committing the offence.

第五部分　受监管活动的履行

注释：

修改等(不涉及条文内容)

C79　第五部分(第56条至第71条)于2001年12月1日依照制定法文件S.I.2001/3592第1条第(2)款、第114条第(3)款第(a)项、第128条第(3)款第(a)项[与第23条第(2)款]修订。

禁　令

第56条　禁令

(1)如管理局认为,在获授权人从事的受监管活动中,个人不是行使该活动相关职能的适当人选,则适用第(2)款规定。

(2)管理局可以颁布法令(以下简称禁令)禁止个人行使某项规定职能、任何属于某种规定类别的职能或任何职能。

(3)禁令可以涉及

(a)某项规定的受监管活动、任何属于规定类别的受监管活动或全部受监管活动;

(b)一般获授权人或属于规定种类的任何获授权人。

(4)违反禁令履行或同意履行职能的个人构成犯罪,应当经简易程序定罪,处以不超过标准等级第5级的罚金。

(5)在针对第(4)款中规定的违法行为所进行的程序中,被告人如能证明其已采取了一切合理预防措施并已尽应有谨慎防止犯罪,则可以据此进行抗辩。

(6) An authorised person must take reasonable care to ensure that no function of his, in relation to the carrying on of a regulated activity, is performed by a person who is prohibited from performing that function by a prohibition order.

(7) The Authority may, on the application of the individual named in a prohibition order, vary or revoke it.

(8) This section applies to the performance of functions in relation to a regulated activity carried on by—

(a) a person who is an exempt person in relation to that activity, and

(b) a person to whom, as a result of Part XX, the general prohibition does not apply in relation to that activity,

as it applies to the performance of functions in relation to a regulated activity carried on by an authorised person.

(9) "Specified" means specified in the prohibition order.

Annotations:

Modifications etc. (not altering text)

C80 S. 56 amended (temp. from 3.9.2001 to 1.12.2001) by S.I. 2001/2659, arts. 1(2), 3(3); S.I. 2001/3538, art. 2(1)

S. 56 modified (temp. from 31.10.2001) by S.I. 2001/3374, arts. 1, 11

S. 56 extended (1.12.2001) by S.I. 2001/2636, arts. 1(2)(b), 79(1); S.I. 2001/3538, art. 2(1)

C81 Ss. 56, 60 modified (temp.) (8.4.2002) by The Financial Services and Markets Act 2000 (Permission and Applications) (Credit Unions etc.) Order 2002 (S.I. 2002/704), art. 7

C82 S. 56(7) extended (1.12.2001) by S.I. 2001/3592, arts. 1(2), 55(5) (with art. 23(2))

C83 S. 56 (8) amended (temp. from 3.9.2001 to 1.12.2001) by S.I. 2001/2659, arts. 1(2), 3(4); S.I. 2001/3538, art. 2(1)

Commencement Information

I16 S. 56 wholly in force at 1.12.2001; s. 56 not in force at Royal Assent see s. 431(2); s. 56 in force for specified purposes at 3.9.2001 by S.I. 2001/2632, art. 2(2), Sch. Pt. 2; s. 56 in force in so far as not already in force at 1.12.2001 by S.I. 2001/3538, art. 2(1)

(6)获授权人必须尽到合理的注意义务,以确保其与从事受监管活动有关的任何职能均未由禁令禁止履行该职能的人履行。

(7)管理局可以应禁令中所列个人的申请,变更或撤销该禁令。

(8)履行与下列人员从事的受监管活动相关的职能时,适用本条规定:

(a)与该活动相关的享有豁免权的人,以及
(b)由于第二十部分的规定,不适用与该活动相关的一般禁止性规定的人员,

等同于适用于行使与获授权人从事的受监管活动相关的职能。

(9)"规定的"系指禁令中规定的。

注释:

修改等(不涉及条文内容)

C80 第56条暂时有效,于2001年9月3日至2001年12月1日依照制定法文件S.I.2001/2659第1条第(2)款、第3条第(3)款;制定法文件S.I.2001/3538第2条第(1)款修正;

第56条暂时有效,于2001年10月31日开始依照制定法文件S.I.2001/3374第1条、第11条修订;

第56条于2001年12月1日依照制定法文件S.I.2001/2636第1条第(2)款第(b)项、第79条第(1)款、制定法文件S.I.2001/3538第2条第(1)款扩大适用范围。

C81 第56条、第60条暂时有效,于2002年4月8日依照《2000年金融服务与市场法》(许可和申请)(信用合作社等)2002号令(制定法文件S.I.2002/704)第7条修订。

C82 第56条第(7)款于2001年12月1日依照制定法文件S.I.2001/3592第1条第(2)款、第55条第(5)款[与第23条第(2)款]扩大适用范围。

C83 第56条第(8)款暂时有效,于2001年9月3日至2001年12月1日依照制定法文件S.I.2001/2659第1条第(2)款、第3条第(4)款;制定法文件S.I.2001/3538第2条第(1)款修正。

实施日期

I16 第56条于2001年12月1日全部生效;第56条在副署时尚未生效,见第431条第(2)款;第56条为特定目的于2001年9月3日依照制定法文件S.I.2001/2632第2条第(2)款、附录第二部分生效;第56条如于2001年12月1日尚未生效,则依照制定法文件S.I.2001/3538第2条第(1)款生效。

57 Prohibition orders: procedure and right to refer to Tribunal.

(1) If the Authority proposes to make a prohibition order it must give the individual concerned a warning notice.

(2) The warning notice must set out the terms of the prohibition.

(3) If the Authoritydecides to make a prohibition order it must give the individual concerned a decision notice.

(4) The decision notice must—

(a) name the individual to whom the prohibition order applies;

(b) set out the terms of the order; and

(c) be given to the individual named in the order.

(5) A person against whom a decision to make a prohibition order is made may refer the matter to the Tribunal.

Annotations:

Modifications etc. (not altering text)

C84 S. 57 excluded (1.12.2001) by S.I. 2001/3592, arts. 1(2), 110(3) (with art. 23 (2))

C85 S. 57(1) extended (1.12.2001) by S.I. 2001/3592, arts. 1(2), 55(1) (with art. 23 (2))

Commencement Information

I17 S. 57 wholly in force at 1.12.2001; s. 57 not in force at Royal Assent see s. 431(2); s. 57 in force for specified purposes at 3.9.2001 by S.I. 2001/2632, art. 2(2), Sch. Pt. 2; s. 57 in force in so far as not already in force at 1.12.2001 by S.I. 2001/3538, art. 2(1)

58 Applications relating to prohibitions: procedure and right to refer to Tribunal.

(1) This section applies to an application for the variation or revocation of a prohibition order.

(2) If the Authority decides to grant the application, it must give the applicant written notice of its decision.

(3) If the Authority proposes to refuse the application, it must give the applicant a warning notice.

(4) If the Authority decides to refuse the application, it must give the applicant a decision notice.

(5) If the Authority gives the applicant a decision notice, he may refer the matter to the Tribunal.

第57条　禁令:程序和诉至裁判所的权利

(1)如管理局拟发布禁令,则必须向相关个人发出预告通知。

(2)预告通知必须列明禁止的条款。

(3)如管理局决定发布禁令,则必须向相关个人发出决定通知。

(4)决定通知必须

(a)指明该禁令适用的个人;

(b)列明该禁令的事项;且

(c)送达该命令中指明的个人。

(5)作出禁令的决定针对的人可以将该事项诉至裁判所。

注释:

修改等(不涉及条文内容)

C84　第57条于2001年12月1日依照制定法文件S.I.2001/3592第1条第(2)款、第110条第(3)款[与第23条第(2)款]排除。

C85　第57条第(1)款于2001年12月1日依照制定法文件S.I.2001/3592第1条第(2)款、第55条第(1)款[与第23条第(2)款]扩大适用范围。

实施日期

I17　第57条于2001年12月1日全部生效;第57条在副署时尚未生效,见第431条第(2)款;第57条为特定目的于2001年9月3日依照制定法文件S.I.2001/2632第2条第(2)款、附录第二部分生效;第57条如于2001年12月1日尚未生效,则依照制定法文件S.I.2001/3538第2条第(1)款生效。

第58条　与禁止相关的申请:程序和诉至裁判所的权利

(1)为变更或废除禁令而提出申请的,适用本条规定。

(2)如管理局决定批准该申请,则必须就其决定向申请人发出书面通知。

(3)如管理局拟驳回该申请,则必须向申请人发出预告通知。

(4)如管理局决定驳回该申请,则必须向申请人发出决定通知。

(5)如管理局向申请人发出了决定通知,则申请人可将该事项诉至裁判所。

Annotations:

Modifications etc. (not altering text)

C86 S. 58 excluded (1.12.2001) by S.I. 2001/3592, arts. 1(2), 110(3) (with art. 23 (2))

Commencement Information

I18 S. 58 wholly in force at 1.12.2001; s. 58 not in force at Royal Assent see s. 431(2); s. 58 in force for specified purposes at 3.9.2001 by S.I. 2001/2632, art. 2(2), Sch. Pt. 2; s. 58 in force in so far as notalready in force at 1.12.2001 by S.I. 2001/3538, art. 2(1)

Approval

59 Approval for particular arrangements.

(1) An authorised person ("A") must take reasonable care to ensure that no person performs a controlled function under an arrangement entered into by A in relation to the carrying on by A of a regulated activity, unless the Authority approves the performance by that person of the controlled function to which the arrangement relates.

(2) An authorised person ("A") must take reasonable care to ensure that no person performs a controlled function under an arrangement entered into by a contractor of A in relation to the carrying on by A of a regulated activity, unless the Authority approves the performance by that person of the controlled function to which the arrangement relates.

(3) "Controlled function" means a function of a description specified in rules.

(4) The Authority may specify a description of function under subsection (3) only if, in relation to the carrying on of a regulated activity by an authorised person, it is satisfied that the first, second or third condition is met.

(5) The first condition is that the function is likely to enable the person responsible for its performance to exercise a significant influence on the conduct of the authorised person's affairs, so far as relating to the regulated activity.

(6) The second condition is that the function will involve the person performing it in dealing with customers of the authorised person in a manner substantially connected with the carrying on of the regulated activity.

(7) The third condition is that the function will involve the person performing it in dealing with property of customers of the authorised person in a manner substantially connected with the carrying on of the regulated activity.

(8) Neither subsection (1) nor subsection (2) applies to an arrangement which allows a person to perform a function if the question of whether he is a fit and proper person to perform the function is reserved under any of the single market directives to an authority in a country

注释:

修改等(不涉及条文内容)

C86 第58条于2001年12月1日依照制定法文件S.I.2001/359第1条第(2)款、第110条第(3)款[与第23条第(2)款]排除。

实施日期

I18 第58条于2001年12月1日全部生效;第58条在副署时尚未生效,见第431条第(2)款;第58条为特定目的于2001年9月3日依照制定法文件S.I.2001/2632第2条第(2)款、附录第二部分生效;第58条如于2001年12月1日尚未生效,则依照制定法文件S.I.2001/3538第2条第(1)款生效。

批　准

第59条　对特别安排的批准

(1)获授权人(以下简称A)必须尽到合理的注意义务,确保对于A从事的受监管活动,任何人未根据A所订立的相关安排行使受监管职能,除非管理局批准该人行使该项安排涉及的受监管职能。

(2)获授权人(以下简称A)必须尽到合理的注意,确保对于A从事的受监管活动,任何人未根据A的承包人所订立的相关安排行使受监管职能,除非管理局批准该人行使该项安排涉及的受监管职能。

(3)"受监管职能"系指规则中规定类别的职能。

(4)管理局只有确信就获授权人从事受监管活动而言,符合第一项、第二项或第三项条件,才可以依照第(3)款规定职能类别。

(5)第一项条件为,该职能可能使负责履行该职能者能够对获授权人从事与被监管活动相关的事务施加重大影响。

(6)第二项条件为,该职能将涉及该职能履行人以实质上与从事受监管活动相关的方式与获授权人的客户交往。

(7)第三项条件为,该职能将涉及该职能履行人以实质上与从事受监管活动相关的方式处理获授权人客户的财产。

(8)如依照任何单一市场指令,联合王国以外的国家或地区的机关对当事人是否为履行职能的适当人选尚存有疑问,则第(1)款和第(2)款规定均不适用于允许该人履行职能的安排。

or territory outside the United Kingdom.

(9) In determining whether the first condition is met, the Authority may take into account the likely consequences of a failure to discharge that function properly.

(10) "Arrangement"—

(a) means any kind of arrangement for the performance of a function of A which is entered into by A or any contractor of his with another person; and

(b) includes, in particular, that other person's appointment to an office, his becoming a partner or his employment (whether under a contract of service or otherwise).

(11) "Customer", in relation to an authorised person, means a person who is using, or who is or may be contemplating using, any of the services provided by the authorised person.

Annotations:

Modifications etc. (not altering text)

C87 S. 59 extended (1.12.2001) by S.I. 2001/2636, arts. 1(2)(b), 74(2), 76(2); S.I. 2001/3538, art. 2(1)

S. 59 extended (1.12.2001) by S.I. 2001/3592, arts. 1(2), 49(1) (with art. 23(2))

C88 S. 59 (1) extended (1.12.2001) by S.I. 2001/2636, arts. 1 (2)(b), 75 (2); S.I. 2001/3538, art. 2(1)

Commencement Information

I19 S. 59 wholly in force at 1.12.2001; s. 59 not in force at Royal Assent see s. 431(2); s. 59 in force for specified purposes at 18.6.2001 by S.I. 2001/1820, art. 2, Sch.; s. 59 in force for specified purposes at 3.9.2001 by S.I. 2001/2632, art. 2(2), Sch. Pt. 2; s. 59 in force in so far as not already in force at 1.12.2001 by S.I. 2001/3538, art. 2(1)

60 Applications for approval.

(1) An application for the Authority's approval under section 59 may be made by the authorised person concerned.

(2) The application must—

(a) be made in such manner as the Authority may direct; and

(b) contain, or be accompanied by, such information as the Authority may reasonably require.

(3) At any time after receiving the application and before determining it, the Authority may require the applicant to provide it with such further information as it reasonably considers necessary to enable it to determine the application.

(4) The Authority may require an applicant to present information which he is required

(9)在决定是否符合第一项条件时,管理局可以考虑无法适当履行该职能可能造成的后果。

(10)"安排"

(a)系指获授权人或获授权人的任何承包人为了行使获授权人的职能而与其他人订立的安排;且

(b)特别包含任命其他人担任某项职务、该人成为合伙人或受雇用(无论是否根据服务合同)。

(11)就获授权人而言,"客户"系指正在使用、正在考虑使用或可能正在考虑使用任何由获授权人提供的服务的人。

注释:

修改等(不涉及条文内容)

C87　第59条于2001年12月1日依照制定法文件S.I.2001/2636第1条第(2)款第(b)项、第74条第(2)款、第76条第(2)款;制定法文件S.I.2001/3538第2条第(1)款扩大适用范围。

第59条于2001年12月1日依照制定法文件S.I.2001/3592第1条第(2)款、第49条第(1)款[与第23条第(2)款]扩大适用范围。

C88　第59条第(1)款于2001年12月1日依照制定法文件S.I.2001/2636第1条第(2)款第(b)项、第75条第(2)款;制定法文件S.I.2001/3538第2条第(1)款扩大适用范围。

实施日期

I19　第59条于2001年12月1日全部生效;第59条在副署时尚未生效,见第431条第(2)款;第59条为特定目的于2001年6月18日依照制定法文件S.I.2001/1820第2条、附录生效;第59条为特定目的于2001年9月3日依照制定法文件S.I.2001/2632第2条第(2)款、附录第二部分生效;第59条如于2001年12月1日尚未生效,则依照制定法文件S.I.2001/3538第2条第(1)款生效。

第60条　批准申请

(1)相关获授权人可以申请管理局给予第59条规定的批准。

(2)该申请必须

(a)以管理局指示的方式提出;且

(b)载有或附有管理局合理要求提供的其他信息。

(3)管理局在收到申请后作出决定前,可以随时要求申请人提供管理局合理认为对该申请作出决定所需的补充信息。

(4)管理局可以要求申请人以管理局指示的形式提供本条规定要求申请人提供

to give under this section in such form, or to verify it in such a way, as the Authority may direct.

(5) Different directions may be given, and different requirements imposed, in relation to different applications or categories of application.

(6) "The authorised person concerned" includes a person who has applied for permission under Part Ⅳ and will be the authorised person concerned if permission is given.

Annotations:

Modifications etc. (not altering text)

C89 S. 60 amended (temp. from 3.9.2001 to 1.12.2001) by S.I. 2001/2659, arts. 1(2), 3(3); S.I. 2001/3538, art. 2(1)

S. 60 modified (temp. from 31.10.2001) by S.I. 2001/3374, arts. 1, 11

S. 60:"the authorised person concerned" extended (1.12.2001) by S.I. 2001/2511, regs. 1(1), 10; S.I. 2001/3538, art. 2(1)

S. 60 extended (1.12.2001) by S.I. 2001/3592, arts. 1(2), 50(1), 51(1), 53(1) (with art. 23(2))

C90 Ss. 56, 60 modified (temp.) (8.4.2002) by The Financial Services and Markets Act 2000 (Permission and Applications) (Credit Unions etc.) Order 2002 (S.I. 2002/704), art. 7

C91 S. 60(3) extended (1.12.2001) by S.I. 2001/3592, arts. 1(2), 50(5) (with art. 23(2))

Commencement Information

I20 S. 60 wholly in force at 1.12.2001; s. 60 not in force at Royal Assent see s. 431(2); s. 60(2)(4) in force for specified purposes at 18.6.2001 by S.I. 2001/1820, art. 2, Sch.; s. 60 in force for specified purposes at 3.9.2001 by S.I. 2001/2632, art. 2(2), Sch. Pt. 2; s. 60 in force in so far as not already in force at 1.12.2001 by S.I. 2001/3538, art. 2(1)

61 Determination of applications.

(1) The Authority may grant an application made under section 60 only if it is satisfied that the person in respect of whom the application is made ("the candidate") is a fit and proper person to perform the function to which the application relates.

(2) In deciding that question, the Authority may have regard (among other things) to whether the candidate, or any person who may perform a function on his behalf—

(a) has obtained a qualification,

(b) has undergone, or is undergoing, training, or

的信息,或以管理局指示的方式验证所提供的信息。

(5)针对不同的申请或申请种类,可以发出不同的指示或提出不同的要求。

(6)“相关获授权人”包括已申请第四部分许可且如授予许可则将成为相关获授权人的人。

注释:

修改等(不涉及条文内容)

C89　第60条暂时有效,于2001年9月3日至2001年12月1日依照制定法文件S.I.2001/2659第1条第(2)款、第3条第(3)款;制定法文件S.I.2001/3538第2条第(1)款修正;

第60条暂时有效,于2001年10月31日开始依照制定法文件S.I.2001/3374第1条、第11条修订;

第60条:“相关获授权人”于2001年12月1日依照制定法文件S.I.2001/2511第1条第(1)款、第10条;制定法文件S.I.2001/3538第2条第(1)款扩大适用范围;

第60条于2001年12月1日依照制定法文件S.I.2001/3592第1条第(2)款、第50条第(1)款、第51条第(1)款、第53条第(1)款[与第23条第(2)款]扩大适用范围。

C90　第56条、第60条(暂时有效)于2002年4月8日依照《2000年金融服务与市场法》(许可和申请)(信用合作社等)2002号令(制定法文件S.I.2002/704)第7条修订。

C91　第60条第(3)款于2001年12月1日依照制定法文件S.I.2001/3592第1条第(2)款、第50条第(5)款[与第23条第(2)款]扩大适用范围。

实施日期

I20　第60条于2001年12月1日全部生效;第60条在副署时尚未生效,见第431条第(2)款;第60条第(2)款、第(4)款为特定目的于2001年6月18日依照制定法文件S.I.2001/1820第2条第(2)款、附录第二部分生效;第60条为特定目的于2001年9月3日依照制定法文件S.I.2001/2632第2条第(2)款、附录第二部分生效;第60条如于2001年12月1日尚未生效,则依照制定法文件S.I.2001/3538第2条第(1)款生效。

第61条　申请的决定

(1)对依照第60条规定提出的申请,管理局只有确信该申请相关人(以下简称候选人)是履行申请所涉职能的适当人选,才可以批准该申请。

(2)在决定上述问题时,管理局可以考虑候选人,或任何可能代其履行职能的人,是否符合一般规则对该申请所涉职能履行人规定的下列要求(并考虑其他事项):

(a)已取得资格,

(b)已接受或正在接受培训,或

(c) possesses a level of competence,

required by general rules in relation to persons performing functions of the kind to which the application relates.

(3) The Authority must, before the end of the period of three months beginning with the date on which it receives an application made under section 60 ("the period for consideration"), determine whether—

(a) to grant the application; or

(b) to give a warning notice under section 62(2).

(4) If the Authority imposes a requirement under section 60 (3), the period for consideration stops running on the day on which the requirement is imposed but starts running again—

(a) on the day on which the required information is received by the Authority; or

(b) if the information is not provided on a single day, on the last of the days on which it is received by the Authority.

(5) A person who makes an application under section 60 may withdraw his application by giving written notice to the Authority at any time before the Authority determines it, but only with the consent of—

(a) the candidate; and

(b) the person by whom the candidate is to be retained to perform the function concerned, if not the applicant.

Annotations:

Modifications etc. (not altering text)

C92 S. 61(3) modified (1.12.2001) by S.I. 2001/3592, arts. 1(2), 49(3), 53(2) (with art. 23(2))

Commencement Information

I21 S. 61 wholly in force at 1.12.2001; s. 61 not in force at Royal Assent see s. 431(2); s. 61 in force for specified purposes at 3.9.2001 by S.I. 2001/2632, art. 2(2), Sch. Pt. 2; s. 61 in force in so far as not already in force at 1.12.2001 by S.I. 2001/3538, art. 2(1)

62 Applications for approval: procedure and right to refer to Tribunal.

(1) If the Authority decides to grant an application made under section 60 ("an application"), it must give written notice of its decision to each of the interested parties.

(2) If the Authority proposes to refuse an application, it must give a warning notice to each of the interested parties.

(3) If the Authority decides to refuse an application, it must give a decision notice to each of the interested parties.

(c)具备一定水平的能力。

(3)自接到依照第60条规定提出的申请之日起3个月期间届满前,管理局必须(以下简称审核期间)决定是否

(a)批准该申请;或

(b)依照第62条第(2)款规定发出预告通知。

(4)如管理局依照第60条第(3)款规定提出要求,则自该要求提出之日起,停止计算审核期间,但在下述时间再次开始计算

(a)自管理局收到所要求的信息之日起;或

(b)如上述信息不是在同一天提供的,则自管理局最后收到信息的日期起。

(5)依照第60条规定提出申请的人,在管理局对该申请作出决定前,可以随时向管理局发出书面通知,撤回申请,但须经下列人员同意

(a)候选人;和

(b)聘请候选人履行相关职能的人,如非申请人。

注释:

修改等(不涉及条文内容)

C92 第61条第(3)款于2001年12月1日依照制定法文件S.I.2001/3592第1条第(2)款、第49条第(3)款、第53条第(2)款[与第23条第(2)款]修订。

实施日期

I21 第61条于2001年12月1日全部生效;第61条在副署时尚未生效,见第431条第(2)款;第61条为特定目的于2001年9月3日依照制定法文件S.I.2001/2632第2条第(2)款、附录第二部分生效;第61条如在2001年12月1日尚未生效,则依照制定法文件S.I.2001/3538第2条第(1)款生效。

第62条 批准申请:程序和诉至裁判所的权利

(1)如管理局决定批准依照第60条提出的申请(以下简称申请),则必须将其决定书面通知利害关系人。

(2)如管理局拟驳回申请,则必须向利害关系人发出预告通知。

(3)如管理局决定驳回申请,则必须向利害关系人发出决定通知。

(4) If the Authority decides to refuse an application, each of the interested parties may refer the matter to the Tribunal.

(5) "The interested parties", in relation to an application, are—

(a) the applicant;

(b) the person in respect of whom the application is made ("A"); and

(c) the person by whom A's services are to be retained, if not the applicant.

Annotations:

Commencement Information

I22 S. 62 wholly in force at 1.12.2001; s. 62 not in force at Royal Assent see s. 431(2); s. 62 in force for specified purposes at 3.9.2001 by S.I. 2001/2632, art. 2(2), Sch. Pt. 2; s. 62 in force in so far as not already in force at 1.12.2001 by S.I. 2001/3538, art. 2(1)

63 Withdrawal of approval.

(1) The Authority may withdraw an approval given under section 59 if it considers that the person in respect of whom it was given is not a fit and proper person to perform the function to which the approval relates.

(2) When considering whether to withdraw its approval, the Authority may take into account any matter which it could take into account if it were considering an application made under section 60 in respect of the performance of the function to which the approval relates.

(3) If the Authority proposes to withdraw its approval, it must give each of the interested parties a warning notice.

(4) If the Authority decides to withdraw its approval, it must give each of the interested parties a decision notice.

(5) If the Authority decides to withdraw its approval, each of the interested parties may refer the matter to the Tribunal.

(6) "The interested parties", in relation to an approval, are—

(a) the person on whose application it was given ("A");

(b) the person in respect of whom it was given ("B"); and

(c) the person by whom B's services are retained, if not A.

Annotations:

Modifications etc. (not altering text)

C93 S. 63(1)(3)-(6) excluded (1.12.2001) by S.I. 2001/3592, arts. 1(2), 61(2) (with art. 23(2))

C94 S. 63(3) extended (1.12.2001) by S.I. 2001/3592, arts. 1(2), 52(2) (with art. 23(2))

(4)如管理局决定驳回申请,则利害关系人均可将该事项诉至裁判所。

(5)申请涉及的“利害关系人”系指

(a)申请人;

(b)申请针对其提出的人(以下简称A);且

(c)聘请A提供服务的人,如非申请人。

注释:

实施日期

I22 第62条于2001年12月1日全部生效;第62条在副署时尚未生效,见第431条第(2)款;第62条为特定目的于2001年9月3日依照制定法文件S.I.2001/2632第2条第(2)款、附录第二部分生效;第62条如在2001年12月1日尚未生效,则依照制定法文件S.I. 2001/3538第2条第(1)款生效。

第63条 批准的撤销[1]

(1)如管理局认为申请针对其提出的人不是履行批准所涉职能的适当人选,则可以撤销依照第59条给予的批准。

(2)管理局在考虑是否撤销批准时,可以考虑的事项包括对与该批准相关、依照第60条规定提出的申请进行考虑时可考虑的任何事项。

(3)如管理局拟撤销批准,则必须向利害关系人发出预告通知。

(4)如管理局决定撤销批准,则必须向利害关系人发出决定通知。

(5)如管理局决定撤销批准,则利害关系人均可以将该事项诉至裁判所裁决。

(6)申请涉及的“利害关系人”系指

(a)批准应其申请作出的人(以下简称A);

(b)批准针对其作出的人(以下简称B);以及

(c)聘请B提供服务的人,如非A。

注释:

修改等(不涉及条文内容)

C93 第63条第(1)款、第(3)款至第(6)款于2001年12月1日依照制定法文件S.I. 2001/3592第1条第(2)款、第61条第(2)款[与第23条第(2)款]排除。

C94 第63条第(3)款于2001年12月1日依照制定法文件S.I.2001/3592第1条第(2)款、第52条第(2)款[与第23条第(2)款]扩大适用范围。

1 本条依照《2010年金融服务法》第11条修订。——译者注

C95 S. 63(4) modified (1.12.2001) by S.I. 2001/3592, arts. 1(2), 75(2) (with art. 23(2))

Commencement Information

I23 S. 63 wholly in force at 1.12.2001; s. 63 not in force at Royal Assent see s. 431(2); s. 63 in force for specified purposes at 3.9.2001 by S.I. 2001/2632, art. 2(2), Sch. Pt. 2; s. 63 in force in so far as not already in force at 1.12.2001 by S.I. 2001/3538, art. 2(1)

Conduct

64 Conduct: statements and codes.

(1) The Authority may issue statements of principle with respect to the conduct expected of approved persons.

(2) If the Authority issues a statement of principle under subsection (1), it must also issue a code of practice for the purpose of helping to determine whether or not a person's conduct complies with the statement of principle.

(3) A code issued under subsection (2) may specify—

(a) descriptions of conduct which, in the opinion of the Authority, comply with a statement of principle;

(b) descriptions of conduct which, in the opinion of the Authority, do not comply with a statement of principle;

(c) factors which, in the opinion of the Authority, are to be taken into account in determining whether or not a person's conduct complies with a statement of principle.

(4) The Authority may at any time alter or replace a statement or code issued under this section.

(5) If a statement or code is altered or replaced, the altered or replacement statement or code must be issued by the Authority.

(6) A statement or code issued under this section must be published by the Authority in the way appearing to the Authority to be best calculated to bring it to the attention of the public.

(7) A code published under this section and in force at the time when any particular conduct takes place may be relied on so far as it tends to establish whether or not that conduct complies with a statement of principle.

(8) Failure to comply with a statement of principle under this section does not of itself give rise to any right of action by persons affected or affect the validity of any transaction.

(9) A person is not to be taken to have failed to comply with a statement of principle if he shows that, at the time of the alleged failure, it or its associated code of practice had not been published.

C95 第63条第(4)款于2001年12月1日依照制定法文件S.I.2001/3592第1条第(2)款、第75条第(2)款[与第23条第(2)款]修订。

实施日期

I23 第63条于2001年12月1日全部生效;第63条在副署时尚未生效,见第431条第(2)款;第63条为特定目的于2001年9月3日依照制定法文件S.I.2001/2632第2条第(2)款、附录第二部分生效;第63条如在2001年12月1日尚未生效,则依照制定法文件S.I.2001/3538第2条第(1)款生效。

经 营 行 为[1]

第64条 经营行为:声明和准则

(1)管理局可发布原则声明,规定对被批准人经营行为的要求。

(2)如管理局依照第(1)款规定发布原则声明,则还必须发布行为准则,以帮助决定行为人的经营行为是否符合原则声明。

(3)依照第(2)款规定发布的准则可规定

(a)管理局认为符合原则声明的经营行为类别;

(b)管理局认为不符合原则声明的经营行为类别;

(c)在决定当事人的经营行为是否符合原则声明时,管理局认为应纳入考虑范围的因素。

(4)管理局可随时变更或替换根据本条发布的声明或准则。

(5)如变更或替换声明或准则,管理局必须公布变更或替换后的声明或准则。

(6)管理局必须以其认为最便于公众了解的方式公布依照本条发布的声明或准则。

(7)依照本条规定公布,且在任何特定经营行为发生之时有效的准则,只要有助于判断该行为是否符合原则声明,即可作为依据。

(8)未遵守本条规定的声明或准则本身并不使受影响的人享有任何起诉权,亦不影响任何交易的有效性。

(9)如能证明在被指控的未遵守原则声明的经营行为发生时,该原则声明或其相关行为准则尚未公布,则不认为行为人未遵守原则声明。

1 依照《2010年金融服务法》附录2第一部分第7条修订。——译者注

(10) The Authority must, without delay, give the Treasury a copy of any statement or code which it publishes under this section.

(11) The power under this section to issue statements of principle and codes of practice—

(a) includes power to make different provision in relation to persons, cases or circumstances of different descriptions; and

(b) is to be treated for the purposes of section 2(4)(a) as part of the Authority's rule-making functions.

(12) The Authority may charge a reasonable fee for providing a person with a copy of a statement or code published under this section.

(13) "Approved person" means a person in relation to whom the Authority has given its approval under section 59.

65 Statements and codes: procedure.

(1) Before issuing a statement or code under section 64, the Authority must publish a draft of it in the way appearing to the Authority to be best calculated to bring it to the attention of the public.

(2) The draft must be accompanied by—

(a) a cost benefit analysis; and

(b) notice that representations about the proposal may be made to the Authority within a specified time.

(3) Before issuing the proposed statement or code, the Authority must have regard to any representations made to it in accordance with subsection (2)(b).

(4) If the Authority issues the proposed statement or code it must publish an account, in general terms, of—

(a) the representations made to it in accordance with subsection (2)(b); and

(b) its response to them.

(5) If the statement or code differs from the draft published under subsection (1) in a way which is, in the opinion of the Authority, significant—

(a) the Authority must (in addition to complying with subsection (4)) publish details of the difference; and

(b) those details must be accompanied by a cost benefit analysis.

(6) Neither subsection (2)(a) nor subsection (5)(b) applies if the Authority considers—

(a) that, making the appropriate comparison, there will be no increase in costs; or

(b) that, making that comparison, there will be an increase in costs but the increase will be of minimal significance.

(7) Subsections (1) to (6) do not apply if the Authority considers that the delay

(10)管理局必须不加迟延地向财政部提供一份依照本条规定公布的任何声明或准则。

(11)依照本条规定发布原则声明和行为准则的权力

(a)包括对不同类别的人、事件或情形作出不同规定的权力;且

(b)就第2条第(4)款第(a)项而言视为管理局规则制定职能的一项内容。

(12)管理局可以为向他人提供依照本条公布的声明或准则的副本收取合理费用。

(13)"被批准人"系指管理局依照第59条针对其作出批准的人。

第65条　声明和准则:程序

(1)在依照第64条规定发布声明和准则前,管理局必须以其认为最便于公众了解的方式公布该声明或准则的草案。

(2)该草案必须附有

(a)成本效益分析;和

(b)可在指定时间内就提案向管理局陈述的通知。

(3)在发布拟发布的声明或准则之前,管理局必须考虑依照第(2)款第(b)项规定向其作出的任何陈述。

(4)如管理局发布拟发布的声明或准则,则必须公布概括说明下列事项的报告:

(a)依照第(2)款第(b)项规定向其提出的陈述;

(b)管理局对上述陈述的答复。

(5)如管理局认为声明或准则与依照第(1)款公布的草案有明显差异,则

(a)管理局必须[除遵守第(4)款规定外]公布差异的详细情况;且

(b)该详细情况必须附有成本效益分析。

(6)如管理局认为有下列情况,则第(2)款第(a)项和第(5)款第(b)项规定不适用:

(a)进行适当比较后认为无成本增长;或

(b)进行适当比较后认为成本将增长,但该增长影响极小。

(7)如管理局认为延迟遵守声明或准则将损害消费者利益,则第(1)款至第(6)款

involved in complying with them would prejudice the interests of consumers.

(8) A statement or code must state that it is issued under section 64.

(9) The Authority may charge a reasonable fee for providing a copy of a draft published under subsection (1).

(10) This section also applies to a proposal to alter or replace a statement or code.

(11) "Cost benefit analysis" means an estimate of the costs together with an analysis of the benefits that will arise—

(a) if the proposed statement or code is issued; or

(b) if subsection (5)(b) applies, from the statement or code that has been issued.

(12) "The appropriate comparison" means

(a) in relation to subsection (2)(a), a comparison between the overall position if the statement or code is issued and the overall position if it is not issued;

(b) in relation to subsection (5)(b), a comparison between the overall position after the issuing of the statement or code and the overall position before it was issued.

66 Disciplinary powers.

(1) The Authority may take action against a person under this section if—

(a) it appears to the Authority that he is guilty of misconduct; and

(b) the Authority is satisfied that it is appropriate in all the circumstances to take action against him.

(2) A person is guilty of misconduct if, while an approved person—

(a) he has failed to comply with a statement of principle issued under section 64; or

(b) he has been knowingly concerned in a contravention by the relevant authorized person of a requirement imposed on that authorised person by or under this Act.

(3) If the Authority is entitled to take action under this section against a person, it may—

(a) impose a penalty on him of such amount as it considers appropriate; or

(b) publish a statement of his misconduct.

(4) The Authority may not take action under this section after the end of the period of two years beginning with the first day on which the Authority knew of the misconduct, unless proceedings in respect of it against the person concerned were begun before the end of that period.

(5) For the purposes of subsection (4)—

(a) the Authority is to be treated as knowing of misconduct if it has information from which the misconduct can reasonably be inferred; and

(b) proceedings against a person in respect of misconduct are to be treated as begun

规定不适用。

(8)声明或准则必须说明其为依照第64条规定发布。

(9)管理局可为提供依照第(1)款规定公布的草案收取合理费用。

(10)本条规定还适用于变更或替换声明或准则的提案。

(11)"成本效益分析",系指对下列情况成本的估计以及对所产生效益的分析:

(a)如发布拟发布的声明或准则;或

(b)如因已发布的声明或准则而适用第(5)款第(b)项规定。

(12)"适当比较"系指

(a)就第(2)款(a)项而言,系指比较假设声明或准则发布后的整体状况和假设不发布声明或准则的整体状况;

(b)就第(5)款(b)项而言,系指比较发布声明或准则后的整体状况和声明或准则发布前的整体状况之间的比较。

第66条 惩戒权[1]

(1)如有下列情况,则管理局可依照本条规定对某人采取行动:

(a)管理局认为该人因行为不端而构成犯罪;且

(b)管理局确信,在任何情况下针对该人采取行动均为适当。

(2)被批准人有下列情况的,因行为不端而构成犯罪:

(a)未能遵守依照第64条规定发布的原则声明;或

(b)明知相关获授权人违反本法或依照本法对其提出的要求而参与其中。

(3)如管理局有权依照本条规定对行为人采取行动,则可

(a)对行为人处以管理局认为适当的罚款;或

(b)公布关于其不端行为的声明。

(4)管理局在自其知悉该不当行为的第一天起2年期间届满后,不得依照本条规定采取行动,除非就该不端行为针对行为人的程序在该期间届满前开始。

(5)就第(4)款而言

(a)如管理局掌握可从中合理推断出不端行为的信息,则视为知悉该不端行为;且

(b)就不端行为针对行为人的程序,视为自依照第67条第(1)款规定向行为人发

1 本条依照《2010年金融服务法》第12条、附录2第一部分第8条修订。——译者注

when a warning notice is given to him under section 67(1).

(6) "Approved person" has the same meaning as in section 64.

(7) "Relevant authorised person", in relation to an approved person, means the person on whose application approval under section 59 was given.

Annotations:

Modifications etc. (not altering text)

C96 S. 66 modified (1.12.2001) by S.I. 2001/2657, arts. 1(1), 9 (which was revoked (8.10.2001) by S.I. 2001/3083, arts. 1(2), 23); S.I. 2001/3538, art. 2(1)

S. 66 modified (1.12.2001) by S.I. 2001/3083, arts. 1(2), 9; S.I. 2001/3538, art. 2(1)

C97 S. 66(3)(a) restricted (1.12.2001) by S.I. 2001/3592, arts. 1(2), 60(2) (with art. 23(2))

67 Disciplinary measures: procedure and right to refer to Tribunal.

(1) If the Authority proposes to take action against a person under section 66, it must give him a warning notice.

(2) A warning notice about a proposal to impose a penalty must state the amount of the penalty.

(3) A warning notice about a proposal to publish a statement must set out the terms of the statement.

(4) If the Authority decides to take action against a person under section 66, it must give him a decision notice.

(5) A decision notice about the imposition of a penalty must state the amount of the penalty.

(6) A decision notice about the publication of a statement must set out the terms of the statement.

(7) If the Authority decides to take action against a person under section 66, he may refer the matter to the Tribunal.

Annotations:

Modifications etc. (not altering text)

C98 S. 67 excluded (1.12.2001) by S.I. 2001/3592, arts. 1(2), 61(3), 85(5) (with art. 23(2))

C99 S. 67(4) modified (1.12.2001) by S.I. 2001/3592, arts. 1(2), 73(2), 74(2) (with art. 23(2))

出预告通知之时起开始。

(6)"被批准人"含义同第64条。

(7)"相关获授权人"与被批准人相关时,系指基于其申请而给予第59条规定的批准的人。

注释:

修改等(不涉及条文内容)

C96　第66条于2001年12月1日依照制定法文件S.I.2001/2657第1条第(1)款、第9条[于2001年10月8日依照制定法文件S.I.2001/3083第1条第(2)款、第23条废除];制定法文件S.I.2001/3538第2条第(1)款修订;

第66条于2001年12月1日依照制定法文件S.I.2001/3083第1条第(2)款、第9条;制定法文件S.I.2001/3538第2条第(1)款修订。

C97　第66条第(3)款第(a)项于2001年12月1日依照制定法文件S.I.2001/3592第1条第(2)款、第60条第(2)款[与第23条第(2)款]限制。

第67条　惩戒措施:程序和诉至裁判所的权利[1]

(1)如管理局拟依照第66条规定对行为人采取行动,则必须发出预告通知。

(2)关于拟处以罚款的预告通知必须说明罚款数额。

(3)关于拟公布声明的预告通知必须说明该声明的条款。

(4)如管理局决定依照第66条规定对行为人采取行动,则必须向该人发出决定通知。

(5)如为处以罚款,则决定通知中必须说明罚款数额。

(6)如为公布声明,则决定通知必须说明该声明的条款。

(7)如管理局决定依照第66条规定对行为人采取行动,则行为人可以将该事项诉至裁判所。

注释:

修改等(不涉及条文内容)

C98　第67条于2001年12月1日依照制定法文件S.I.2001/3592第1条第(2)款、第61条第(3)款、第85条第(5)款[与第23条第(2)款]排除。

C99　第67条第(4)款于2001年12月1日依照制定法文件S.I.2001/3592第1条第(2)款、第73条第(2)款、第74条第(2)款[与第23条第(2)款]修订。

1 本条依照《2010年金融服务法》附录2第一部分第9条修订。——译者注

68 Publication.

After a statement under section 66 is published, the Authority must send a copy of it to the person concerned and to any person to whom a copy of the decision notice was given.

69 Statement of policy.

(1) The Authority must prepare and issue a statement of its policy with respect to—

(a) the imposition of penalties under section 66; and

(b) the amount of penalties under that section.

(2) The Authority's policy in determining what the amount of a penalty should be must include having regard to—

(a) the seriousness of the misconduct in question in relation to the nature of the principle or requirement concerned;

(b) the extent to which that misconduct was deliberate or reckless; and

(c) whether the person on whom the penalty is to be imposed is an individual.

(3) The Authority may at any time alter or replace a statement issued under this section.

(4) If a statement issued under this section is altered or replaced, the Authority must issue the altered or replacement statement.

(5) The Authority must, without delay, give the Treasury a copy of any statement which it publishes under this section.

(6) A statement issued under this section must be published by the Authority in the way appearing to the Authority to be best calculated to bring it to the attention of the public.

(7) The Authority may charge a reasonable fee for providing a person with a copy of the statement.

(8) In exercising, or deciding whether to exercise, its power under section 66 in the case of any particular misconduct, the Authority must have regard to any statement of policy published under this section and in force at the time when the misconduct in question occurred.

70 Statements of policy: procedure.

(1) Before issuing a statement under section 69, the Authority must publish a draft of the proposed statement in the way appearing to the Authority to be best calculated to bring it to the attention of the public.

(2) The draft must be accompanied by notice that representations about the proposal may be made to the Authority within a specified time.

(3) Before issuing the proposed statement, the Authority must have regard to any representations made to it in accordance with subsection (2).

(4) If the Authority issues the proposed statement it must publish an account, in general terms, of—

第68条　公布

依照第66条规定公布声明后，管理局必须将该声明的副本送交声明所涉之人以及任何其他收到决定通知副本的人。

第69条　政策声明[1]

(1)管理局必须就关于下列事项的政策制定并发布声明：

(a)依照第66条规定处以罚款；

(b)依照第66条规定处以罚款的数额。

(2)管理局确定罚款数额的政策必须包括对下列事项的考虑：

(a)就相关原则或要求的性质而言，相关不端行为的严重性；

(b)该不端行为在何种程度上为故意实施或不计后果地实施；以及

(c)接受罚款的是否为个人。

(3)管理局可以随时变更或替换依照本条规定发布的声明。

(4)如对依照本条规定发布的声明进行变更或替换，则管理局必须发布变更或替换后的声明。

(5)管理局必须毫不延迟地向财政部提供根据本条规定公布的任何声明的副本。

(6)管理局必须以其认为最便于公众了解的方式公布依照本条规定发布的声明。

(7)管理局可以为向他人提供声明副本收取合理费用。

(8)对任何特定不端行为，管理局在行使或决定是否行使第66条规定的权力时，必须考虑依照本条规定公布、在该不端行为发生时有效的任何政策声明。

第70条　政策声明：程序

(1)管理局在依照第69条规定发布声明前，必须以其认为最便于公众了解的方式公布拟发布声明的草案。

(2)该草案必须附有可在规定时间内就该提案向管理局作出陈述的通知。

(3)管理局在发布拟发布的声明前必须考虑依照第(2)款规定向其作出的任何陈述。

(4)如管理局发布拟发布的声明，则必须公布概括说明下列事项的报告：

1 本条依照《2010年金融服务法》附录2第一部分第10条修订。——译者注

(a) the representations made to it in accordance with subsection (2); and

(b) its response to them.

(5) If the statement differs from the draft published under subsection (1) in a way which is, in the opinion of the Authority, significant, the Authority must (in addition to complying with subsection (4)) publish details of the difference.

(6) The Authority may charge a reasonable fee for providing a person with a copy of a draft published under subsection (1).

(7) This section also applies to a proposal to alter or replace a statement.

Breach of statutory duty

71 Actions for damages.

(1) A contravention of section 56(6) or 59(1) or (2) is actionable at the suit of a private person who suffers loss as a result of the contravention, subject to the defences and other incidents applying to actions for breach of statutory duty.

(2) In prescribed cases, a contravention of that kind which would be actionable at the suit of a private person is actionable at the suit of a person who is not a private person, subject to the defences and other incidents applying to actions for breach of statutory duty.

(3) "Private person" has such meaning as may be prescribed.

Annotations:

Commencement Information

I24 S. 71 wholly in force at 1.12.2001; s. 71 not in force at Royal Assent see s. 431(2); s. 71(2)(3) in force for certain purposes at 25.2.2001 by S.I. 2001/516, art. 2(b), Sch. Pt. 2; s. 71 in force in so far as not already in force at 1.12.2001 by S.I. 2001/3538, art. 2(1) (a)依照第(2)款规定向其作出的陈述;以及

(b)管理局对上述陈述的答复。

(5)如管理局认为该声明与依照第(1)款规定公布的草案有重大差异,则[除遵守第(4)款规定外]必须公布该差异的详细情况。

(6)管理局可以为向他人提供依照第(1)款公布的草案副本收取合理费用。

(7)本条规定也适用于变更或替换声明的提案。

违反法定职责

第71条　赔偿诉讼

(1)对违反第56条第(6)款规定或第59条第(1)款或第(2)款规定的行为,因该行为而遭受损失的个人可以提起诉讼,但须依照适用违反法定职责诉讼的抗辩理由和其他事由。

(2)在规定情况下,可以由因该行为而遭受损失的个人提起诉讼的违法行为,也可以由非个人提起诉讼,但须依照适用违反法定职责诉讼的抗辩理由和其他事由。

(3)"个人"具有规定含义。

注释:

实施日期

I24　第71条于2001年12月1日全部生效;第71条在副署时尚未生效,见第431条第(2)款;第71条第(2)款、第(3)款为特定目的于2001年2月25日依照制定法文件S.I. 2001/516第2条第(b)款、附录第二部分生效;第71条如于2001年12月1日尚未生效,则依照制定法文件S.I.2001/3538第2条第(1)款生效。

PART Ⅵ OFFICIAL LISTING

Annotations:

Modifications etc. (not altering text)

C100 Pt. VI (ss. 72–103) applied (with modifications) (1.12.2001) by S.I. 1995/1537, Sch. 4 (as amended (1.12.2001) by S.I. 2001/3649, arts. 1, 511)

The competent authority

72 The competent authority.

(1) On the coming into force of this section, the functions conferred on the competent authority by this Part are to be exercised by the Authority.

(2) Schedule 7 modifies this Act in its application to the Authority when it acts as the competent authority.

(3) But provision is made by Schedule 8 allowing some or all of those functions to be transferred by the Treasury so as to be exercisable by another person.

73 General duty of the competent authority.

(1) In discharging its general functions the competent authority must have regard to—

(a) the need to use its resources in the most efficient and economic way;

(b) the principle that a burden or restriction which is imposed on a person should be proportionate to the benefits, considered in general terms, which are expected to arise from the imposition of that burden or restriction;

(c) the desirability of facilitating innovation in respect of listed securities;

(d) the international character of capital markets and the desirability of maintaining the competitive position of the United Kingdom;

(e) the need to minimise the adverse effects on competition of anything done in the discharge of those functions;

(f) the desirability of facilitating competition in relation to listed securities.

第六部分　正式上市

注释：

修改等(不涉及条文内容)

C100　第六部分(第72条至第103条)(已修订)于2001年12月1日依照制定法文件1995/1537附录4(于2001年12月1日依照制定法文件S.I.2001/3649第1条、第511条修正)适用。

主管机关

第72条　主管机关

(1)本条规定一经生效,本部分赋予主管机关的职能即由管理局履行。

(2)附录7修改了管理局在作为主管机关行事时本法对其的适用。

(3)但附录8作出了规定,允许财政部转移部分或全部职能,使这些职能可由他人履行。

第73条　主管机关的基本职责

(1)主管机关行使基本职能时必须考虑下列事项:

(a)需要以最经济高效的方式使用其资源;

(b)对行为人规定的负担或限制应当与一般情况下预期由该负担或限制所产生的收益成比例的原则;

(c)有利于推动与上市证券有关的创新;

(d)资本市场的国际性及有利于维持联合王国的竞争地位;

(e)需要尽力减少行使这些职能的任何行为对竞争可能造成的不利影响;

(f)有利于促进与上市证券有关的竞争。

(2) The competent authority's general functions are—

(a) its function of making rules under this Part (considered as a whole);

(b) its functions in relation to the giving of general guidance in relation to this Part (considered as a whole);

(c) its function of determining the general policy and principles by reference to which it performs particular functions under this Part.

The official list

74 The official list.

(1) The competent authority must maintain the official list.

(2) The competent authority may admit to the official list such securities and other things as it considers appropriate.

(3) But—

(a) nothing may be admitted to the official list except in accordance with this Part; and

(b) the Treasury may by order provide that anything which falls within a description or category specified in the order may not be admitted to the official list.

(4) The competent authority may make rules ("listing rules") for the purposes of this Part.

(5) In the following provisions of this Part—

"security" means anything which has been, or may be, admitted to the official list; and

"listing" means being included in the official list in accordance with this Part.

Annotations:

Modifications etc. (not altering text)

C101 S. 74(5) applied (1.12.2001) by S.I. 2001/2957, arts. 1, 8(4); S.I. 2001/3538, art. 2(1)

Commencement Information

I25 S. 74 wholly in force at 1.12.2001; s. 74 not in force at Royal Assent see s. 431(2); s. 74(4)(5) in force at 18.6.2001 by S.I. 2001/1820, art. 2, Sch.; s. 74 in force in so far as not already in force at 1.12.2001 by S.I. 2001/3538, art. 2(1)

Listing

75 Applications for listing.

(1) Admission to the official list may be granted only on an application made to the competent authority in such manner as may be required by listing rules.

(2) No application for listing may be entertained by the competent authority unless it is

(2)主管机关的基本职能为

(a)依照本部分(被视为一个整体)制定规则的职能;

(b)作出与本部分(被视为一个整体)有关的一般性指引的相关职能;

(c)对据以依照本部分规定行使特定职能的一般政策和原则作出决定的职能。

正式上市名单

第74条 正式上市名单

(1)主管机关必须保存正式上市名单。

(2)主管机关可将其认为适当的证券等列入正式上市名单。

(3)但是

(a)如不符合本部分要求,则任何事物均不得列入正式上市名单;且

(b)财政部可颁布法令,要求不得将命令规定类别或种类的事物列入上市名单。

(4)主管机关可以为施行本部分规定制定规则(以下简称上市规则)。

(5)在本部分的后续条款中

"证券",系指任何已经或可能列入正式上市名单的;

"上市",系指依照本部分规定列入上市名单。

注释:

修改等(不涉及条文内容)

C101 第74条第(5)款于2001年12月1日依照制定法文件S.I.2001/2957第1条、第8条第(4)款;制定法文件S.I.2001/3538,第2条第(1)款适用。

实施日期

I25 第74条于2001年12月1日全部生效;第74条在副署时尚未生效,见第431条第(2)款;第74条第(4)款、第(5)款于2001年6月18日依照制定法文件S.I.2001/1820第2条、附录生效;第74条如于2001年12月1日尚未生效,则依照制定法文件S.I.2001/3538第2条第(1)款生效。

上 市

第75条 上市申请

(1)只有以上市规则要求的方式向主管机关提出上市申请,才可以获准列入正式上市名单。

(2)上市申请必须由相关证券的发行人提出,或经该发行人同意而提出,否则主

made by, or with the consent of, the issuer of the securities concerned.

(3) No application for listing may be entertained by the competent authority in respect of securities which are to be issued by a body of a prescribed kind.

(4) The competent authority may not grant an application for listing unless it is satisfied that—

(a) the requirements of listing rules (so far as they apply to the application), and

(b) any other requirements imposed by the authority in relation to the application, are complied with.

(5) An application for listing may be refused if, for a reason relating to the issuer, the competent authority considers that granting it would be detrimental to the interests of investors.

(6) An application for listing securities which are already officially listed in another EEA State may be refused if the issuer has failed to comply with any obligations to which he is subject as a result of that listing.

Annotations:

Modifications etc. (not altering text)

C102 S. 75(1) extended (1.12.2001) by S.I. 2001/2957, arts. 1, 4(2); S.I. 2001/3538, art. 2(1)

Commencement Information

I26 S. 75 wholly in force at 1.12.2001; s. 75 not in force at Royal Assent see s. 431(2); s. 75(3) in force for specified purposes at 25.2.2001 by S.I. 2001/516, art. 2(b), Sch. Pt. 2; s. 75(1) in force for specified purposes at 18.6.2001 by S.I. 2001/1820, art. 2, Sch.; s. 75 in force in so far as not already in force at 1.12.2001 by S.I. 2001/3538, art. 2(1)

76 Decision on application.

(1) The competent authority must notify the applicant of its decision on an application for listing—

(a) before the end of the period of six months beginning with the date on which the application is received; or

(b) if within that period the authority has required the applicant to provide further information in connection with the application, before the end of the period of six months beginning with the date on which that information is provided.

(2) If the competent authority fails to comply with subsection (1), it is to be taken to have decided to refuse the application.

(3) If the competent authority decides to grant an application for listing, it must give the applicant written notice.

管机关不得受理。

(3)对于规定种类的主体发行的证券,主管机关不得受理其上市申请。

(4)除非主管机关确信符合下列要求,否则不得批准上市申请:

(a)上市规则的要求(在适用于该申请的范围内),以及
(b)管理局就该申请提出的任何其他要求。

(5)如主管机关认为,因与发行人有关的原因,批准上市申请将有损投资者的利益,则可驳回申请。

(6)对在另一欧洲经济区国家已正式上市的证券,如发行人未能遵守该次上市应遵守的任何义务,则对为该证券提出的上市申请可予以驳回。

注释:

修改等(不涉及条文内容)

C102　第75条第(1)款于2001年12月1日依照制定法文件S.I.2001/2957第1条、第4条第(2)款;制定法文件S.I.2001/3538第2条第(1)款扩大适用范围。

实施日期

I26　第75条于2001年12月1日全部生效;第75条在副署时尚未生效,见第431条第(2)款;第75条第(3)款为特定目的于2001年2月25日依照制定法文件S.I.2001/516第2条第(b)款、附录第二部分生效;第75条第(1)款为特定目的于2001年6月18日依照制定法文件S.I.2001/1820第2条、附录生效;第75条如于2001年12月1日尚未生效,则依照制定法文件S.I.2001/3538第2条第(1)款生效。

第76条　申请的决定

(1)主管机关必须将其对上市申请的决定在下列时间通知申请人:

(a)在接到申请之日起 6 个月期间届满前;或

(b)如主管机关在该期间内要求申请人提供与申请相关的补充信息,则在该补充信息提供之日起 6 个月期间届满前。

(2)如主管机关未能遵守第(1)款规定,将视为其决定驳回该申请。

(3)如主管机关决定批准上市申请,则必须向申请人发出书面通知。

(4) If the competent authority proposes to refuse an application for listing, it must give the applicant a warning notice.

(5) If the competent authority decides to refuse an application for listing, it must give the applicant a decision notice.

(6) If the competent authority decides to refuse an application for listing, the applicant may refer the matter to the Tribunal.

(7) If securities are admitted to the official list, their admission may not be called in question on the ground that any requirement or condition for their admission has not been complied with.

Annotations:

Modifications etc. (not altering text)

C103 S. 76(1) modified (1.12.2001) by S.I. 2001/2957, arts. 1, 4(3); S.I. 2001/3538, art. 2(1)

77 Discontinuance and suspension of listing.

(1) The competent authority may, in accordance with listing rules, discontinue the listing of any securities if satisfied that there are special circumstances which preclude normal regular dealings in them.

(2) The competent authority may, in accordance with listing rules, suspend the listing of any securities.

(3) If securities are suspended under subsection (2) they are to be treated, for the purposes of sections 96 and 99, as still being listed.

(4) This section applies to securities whenever they were admitted to the official list.

(5) If the competent authority discontinues or suspends the listing of any securities, the issuer may refer the matter to the Tribunal.

Annotations:

Modifications etc. (not altering text)

C104 S. 77(2) extended (1.12.2001) by S.I. 2001/2957, arts. 1, 8(3); S.I. 2001/3538, art. 2(1)

Commencement Information

I27 S. 77 wholly in force at 1.12.2001; s. 77 not in force at Royal Assent see s. 431(2); s. 77 (1)(2)(4) in force for specified purposes at 18.6.2001 by S.I. 2001/1820, art. 2, Sch.; s. 77 in force in so far as not already in force at 1.12.2001 by S.I. 2001/3538, art. 2(1)

(4)如主管机关拟驳回上市申请,则必须向申请人发出预告通知。

(5)如主管机关决定驳回上市申请,则必须向申请人发出决定通知。

(6)如主管机关决定驳回上市申请,则申请人可将该事项诉至裁判所。

(7)对列入正式上市名单的证券,不得以不符合任何列入要求或条件为由对其提出质疑。

注释:

修改等(不涉及条文内容)

C103　第76条第(1)款于2001年12月1日依照制定法文件S.I.2001/2957第1条、第4条第(3)款;制定法文件S.I.2001/3538第2条第(1)款修订。

第77条　中止上市和暂停上市

(1)如主管机关确信有特殊情形妨碍任何证券正常交易,则可以依照上市规则对该证券中止上市。

(2)主管机关可以依照上市规则对任何证券暂停上市。

(3)依照第(2)款规定暂停上市的证券,与第96条和第99条相关时仍按上市证券对待。

(4)证券一经列入上市名单,即适用本条规定。

(5)如主管机关对任何证券中止上市或暂停上市,则发行人可以将该事项诉至仲裁庭。

注释:

修改等(不涉及条文内容)

C104　第77条第(2)款于2001年12月1日依照制定法文件S.I.2001/2957第1条、第8条第(3)款;制定法文件S.I.2001/3538第2条第(1)款扩大适用范围。

实施日期

I27　第77条于2001年12月1日全部生效;第77条在副署时尚未生效,见第431条第(2)款;第77条第(1)款、第(2)款、第(4)款为指定目的于2001年6月18日依照制定法文件S.I.2001/1820第2条、附录生效;第77条如于2001年12月1日尚未生效,则依照制定法文件S.I.2001/3538第2条第(1)款生效。

78 Discontinuance or suspension: procedure.

(1) A discontinuance or suspension takes effect—

(a) immediately, if the notice under subsection (2) states that that is the case;

(b) in any other case, on such date as may be specified in that notice.

(2) If the competent authority—

(a) proposes to discontinue or suspend the listing of securities, or

(b) discontinues or suspends the listing of securities with immediate effect,

it must give the issuer of the securities written notice.

(3) The notice must—

(a) give details of the discontinuance or suspension;

(b) state the competent authority's reasons for the discontinuance or suspension and for choosing the date on which it took effect or takes effect;

(c) inform the issuer of the securities that he may make representations to the competent authority within such period as may be specified in the notice (whether or not he has referred the matter to the Tribunal);

(d) inform him of the date on which the discontinuance or suspension took effect or will take effect; and

(e) inform him of his right to refer the matter to the Tribunal.

(4) The competent authority may extend the period within which representations may be made to it.

(5) If, having considered any representations made by the issuer of the securities, the competent authority decides—

(a) to discontinue or suspend the listing of the securities, or

(b) if the discontinuance or suspension has taken effect, not to cancel it,

the competent authority must give the issuer of the securities written notice.

(6) A notice given under subsection (5) must inform the issuer of the securities of his right to refer the matter to the Tribunal.

(7) If a notice informs a person of his right to refer a matter to the Tribunal, it must give an indication of the procedure on such a reference.

(8) If the competent authority decides—

(a) not to discontinue or suspend the listing of the securities, or

(b) if the discontinuance or suspension has taken effect, to cancel it,

the competent authority must give the issuer of the securities written notice.

(9) The effect of cancelling a discontinuance is that the securities concerned are to be readmitted, without more, to the official list.

(10) If the competent authority has suspended the listing of securities and proposes to refuse an application by the issuer of the securities for the cancellation of the suspension, it

第78条 中止上市或暂停上市:程序

(1)中止上市或暂停上市

(a)如依照第(2)款规定情况发出通知,则立即生效;

(b)在任何其他情况下,于通知规定之日生效。

(2)如主管机关

(a)拟中止或暂停证券上市;或

(b)中止或暂停证券上市且立即生效,

则必须向证券发行人发出书面通知。

(3)前款所述通知必须

(a)详细说明该中止或暂停;

(b)说明主管机关中止上市或暂停上市及选择其生效日期的理由;

(c)告知证券发行人可以在通知规定的期限内向主管机关作出陈述(无论是否已将该事项提交仲裁庭裁决);

(d)告知发行人该中止或暂停的生效或即将生效日期;且

(e)告知发行人其有权将该事项诉至裁判所。

(4)主管机关可以延长向其作出陈述的期限。

(5)如主管机关在考虑证券发行人向其作出的任何陈述后决定

(a)中止或暂停证券的上市,或

(b)如中止或暂停上市已生效,不将其撤销,

则主管机关必须向证券发行人发出书面通知。

(6)依照第(5)款规定发出的通知必须告知证券发行人有权将该事项诉至裁判所。

(7)如通知告知被通知人有权将相关事项诉至裁判所,则必须说明诉至裁判所的程序。

(8)如主管机关决定

(a)不中止或暂停证券上市,或

(b)如中止或暂停已生效,则将其撤销

则主管机关必须向证券发行人发出书面通知。

(9)撤销中止的效力为相关证券立即重新列入正式上市名单。

(10)如主管机关已暂停证券上市,且拟驳回证券发行人关于撤销暂停的申请,则必须向发行人发出预告通知。

must give him a warning notice.

(11) The competent authority must, having considered any representations made in response to the warning notice—

(a) if it decides to refuse the application, give the issuer of the securities a decision notice;

(b) if it grants the application, give him written notice of its decision.

(12) If the competent authority decides to refuse an application for the cancellation of the suspension of listed securities, the applicant may refer the matter to the Tribunal.

(13) "Discontinuance" means a discontinuance of listing under section 77(1).

(14) "Suspension" means a suspension of listing under section 77(2).

Listing particulars

79 Listing particulars and other documents.

(1) Listing rules may provide that securities (other than new securities) of a kind specified in the rules may not be admitted to the official list unless—

(a) listing particulars have been submitted to, and approved by, the competent authority and published; or

(b) in such cases as may be specified by listing rules, such document (other than listing particulars or a prospectus of a kind required by listing rules) as may be so specified has been published.

(2) "Listing particulars" means a document in such form and containing such information as may be specified in listing rules.

(3) For the purposes of this Part, the persons responsible for listing particulars are to be determined in accordance with regulations made by the Treasury.

(4) Nothing in this section affects the competent authority's general power to make listing rules.

Annotations:

Modifications etc. (not altering text)

C105 S. 79 extended (1.12.2001) by S.I. 2001/2957, arts. 1, 6(1)(3); S.I. 2001/3538, art. 2(1)

Commencement Information

I28 S. 79 wholly in force at 18.6.2001; s. 79 not in force at Royal Assent see s. 431(2); s. 79(3) in force at 25.2.2001 by S.I. 2001/516, art. 2(a), Sch. Pt. 1; s. 79 in force so far as not already in force at 18.6.2001 by S.I. 2001/1820, art. 2, Sch.

(11)主管机关在考虑任何就预告通知作出的陈述后

(a)如决定驳回该申请,则必须向证券发行人发出决定通知;

(b)如批准该申请,则必须书面向发行人通知其决定。

(12)如主管机关决定驳回撤销暂停证券上市的申请,则申请人可以将该事项诉至裁判所。

(13)"中止",系指依照第77条第(1)款规定中止上市。

(14)"暂停",系指依照第77条第(2)款规定暂停上市。

上市公告书

第79条 上市公告书及其他文件

(1)上市规则可以规定何种证券(新发行证券除外)不得列入正式上市名单,除非

(a)上市公告书已提交主管机关,获主管机关批准并已公布;或

(b)在上市规则可能规定的情况下,指定的文件(上市公告书或上市公告书中规定种类的招股说明书除外)已公布。

(2)"上市公告书",系指上市规则规定形式且包含上市规则要求信息的文件。

(3)本部分所称上市公告书负责人依照财政部制定的规则确定。

(4)本条中任何规定不影响主管机关制定上市规则的一般权力。

注释:

修改等(不涉及条文内容)

C105 第79条于2001年12月1日依照制定法文件S.I.2001/2957第1条、第6条第(1)款、第(3)款;制定法文件S.I.2001/3538第2条第(1)款扩大适用范围。

实施日期

I28 第79条于2001年6月18日全部生效;第79条在副署时尚未生效,见第431条第(2)款;第79条第(3)款于2001年2月25日依照制定法文件S.I.2001/516第2条第(a)款、附录第一部分生效;第79条如于2001年6月18日尚未生效,则依照制定法文件S.I.2001/1820第2条、附录生效。

80 General duty of disclosure in listing particulars.

(1) Listing particulars submitted to the competent authority under section 79 must contain all such information as investors and their professional advisers would reasonably require, and reasonably expect to find there, for the purpose of making an informed assessment of—

(a) the assets and liabilities, financial position, profits and losses, and prospects of the issuer of the securities; and

(b) the rights attaching to the securities.

(2) That information is required in addition to any information required by

(a) listing rules, or

(b) the competent authority,

as a condition of the admission of the securities to the official list.

(3) Subsection (1) applies only to information

(a) within the knowledge of any person responsible for the listing particulars; or

(b) which it would be reasonable for him to obtain by making enquiries.

(4) In determining what information subsection (1) requires to be included in listing particulars, regard must be had (in particular) to—

(a) the nature of the securities and their issuer;

(b) the nature of the persons likely to consider acquiring them;

(c) the fact that certain matters may reasonably be expected to be within the knowledge of professional advisers of a kind which persons likely to acquire the securities may reasonably be expected to consult; and

(d) any information available to investors or their professional advisers as a result of requirements imposed on the issuer of the securities by a recognized investment exchange, by listing rules or by or under any other enactment.

81 Supplementary listing particulars.

(1) If at any time after the preparation of listing particulars which have been submitted to the competent authority under section 79 and before the commencement of dealings in the securities concerned following their admission to the official list—

(a) there is a significant change affecting any matter contained in those particulars the inclusion of which was required by—

(i) section 80,

(ii) listing rules, or

(iii) the competent authority, or

(b) a significant new matter arises, the inclusion of information in respect of which would have been so required if it had arisen when the particulars were prepared,the issuer must, in accordance with listing rules, submit supplementary listing particulars of the change

第80条　上市公告书的基本披露职责

(1)依照第79条规定向主管机关提交的上市公告书,必须载有投资人及其职业顾问合理要求并合理预期在其中发现的全部信息,以对下列事项作出有信息根据的评估:

(a)证券发行人的资产和负债、财务状况、利润与亏损和前景展望;以及

(b)证券所附的权利。

(2)上述信息为除下列信息外另行要求提供的信息:

(a)上市规则要求提供的信息,或

(b)主管机关要求提供的信息

是列入正式上市名单的条件。

(3)第(1)款规定仅适用于下列信息:

(a)任何上市公告书负责人所知的信息;或

(b)上市公告书负责人通过进行询问可合理获得的信息。

(4)决定上市公告书中载有第(1)款要求的何种信息时,必须(特别)考虑

(a)证券及其发行人的性质;

(b)可能考虑购买证券的人的性质;

(c)对可能取得证券的人可能合理预期向其进行咨询的职业顾问,合理预期其所知的特定事项;及

(d)由获认可的投资交易所、上市规则或任何其他成文法对证券发行人提出的要求,而使任何投资人或其职业顾问可获得的信息。

第81条　补充上市公告书

(1)在制定上市公告书并依照第79条规定提交主管机关后、相关证券列入正式上市名单后开始进行交易前的任何时间,如有下列情况:

(a)发生重大变化,对上市公告书依照下列要求载有的任何事项有影响:

(i)第80条,

(ii)上市规则,或

(iii)主管机关,或

(b)新出现重大事项,且该事项若在制定上市公告书时出现,则要求其相关信息将列入上市公告书中,则发行人必须依照上市规则,就该变化或新事项制定补充上市公告书,提交主管机关批准,如获得批准,则予以公布。

or new matter to the competent authority, for its approval and, if they are approved, publish them.

(2) "Significant" means significant for the purpose of making an informed assessment of the kind mentioned in section 80(1).

(3) If the issuer of the securities is not aware of the change or new matter in question, he is not under a duty to comply with subsection (1) unless he is notified of the change or new matter by a person responsible for the listing particulars.

(4) But it is the duty of any person responsible for those particulars who is aware of such a change or new matter to give notice of it to the issuer.

(5) Subsection (1) applies also as respects matters contained in any supplementary listing particulars previously published under this section in respect of the securities in question.

Annotations:

Modifications etc. (not altering text)

C106 S. 81 modified (1.12.2001) by S.I. 2001/2957, arts. 1, 6 (1) (3) (4); S.I. 2001/3538, art. 2(1)

C107 S. 81(1) extended (1.12.2001) by S.I. 2001/2957, arts. 1, 6(1)(3)(4); S.I. 2001/3538, art. 2(1)

Commencement Information

I29 S. 81 wholly in force at 1.12.2001; s. 81 not in force at Royal Assent see s. 431(2); s. 81(1)(5) in force for specified purposes at 18.6.2001 by S.I. 2001/1820, art. 2, Sch.; s. 81 in force in so far as not already in force at 1.12.2001 by S.I. 2001/3538, art. 2(1)

82 Exemptions from disclosure.

(1) The competent authority may authorise the omission from listing particulars of any information, the inclusion of which would otherwise be required by section 80 or 81, on the ground—

(a) that its disclosure would be contrary to the public interest;

(b) that its disclosure would be seriously detrimental to the issuer; or

(c) in the case of securities of a kind specified in listing rules, that its disclosure is unnecessary for persons of the kind who may be expected normally to buy or deal in securities of that kind.

(2) But—

(a) no authority may be granted under subsection (1)(b) in respect of essential information; and

(2)“重大”,系指对进行第80条第(1)款所述有信息根据的评估影响重大。

(3)如证券发行人不知悉相关变化或新事项,则没有义务遵守第(1)款规定,除非上市公告书负责人已将该变化或新事项告知该人。

(4)但任何知悉上述变化或新事项的上市公告书负责人均有将该变化或新事项告知发行人的职责。

(5)先前依照本条规定公布的任何补充上市公告书所载事项,也适用第(1)款规定。

注释:

修改等(不涉及条文内容)

C106 第81条于2001年12月1日依照制定法文件S.I.2001/2957第1条、第6条第(1)款、第(3)款、第(4)款;制定法文件S.I.2001/3538第2条第(1)款修订。

C107 第81条第(1)款于2001年12月1日依照制定法文件S.I.2001/2957第1条、第6条第(1)款、第(3)款、第(4)款;制定法文件S.I.2001/3538第2条第(1)款扩大适用范围。

实施日期

I29 第81条于2001年12月1日全部生效;第81条在副署时尚未生效,见第431条第(2)款;第81条第(1)款、第(5)款为特定目的于2001年6月18日依照制定法文件S.I. 2001/1820第2条、附录生效;第81条如于2001年12月1日尚未生效,则依照制定法文件S.I. 2001/3538第2条第(1)款生效。

第82条 披露豁免

(1)基于下列理由,主管机关可以授权在上市公告书中排除任何第80条或第81条规定要求包含的信息:

(a)披露该信息违反公共利益;

(b)披露该信息对发行人严重不利;或

(c)对于上市规则中规定种类的证券,对通常预期会购买这种证券或对其进行交易的人没有必要披露该信息。

(2)但是

(a)对于重要信息,不得依照第(1)款第(b)项规定给予任何授权;且

(b) no authority granted under subsection (1)(b) extends to any such information.

(3) The Secretary of State or the Treasury may issue a certificate to the effect that the disclosure of any information (including information that would otherwise have to be included in listing particulars for which they are themselves responsible) would be contrary to the public interest.

(4) The competent authority is entitled to act on any such certificate in exercising its powers under subsection (1)(a).

(5) This section does not affect any powers of the competent authority under listing rules made as a result of section 101(2).

(6) "Essential information" means information which a person considering acquiring securities of the kind in question would be likely to need in order not to be misled about any facts which it is essential for him to know in order to make an informed assessment.

(7) "Listing particulars" includes supplementary listing particulars.

Annotations:

Commencement Information

I130 S. 82 wholly in force at 1.12.2001; s. 82 not in force at Royal Assent see s. 431(2); s. 82(1)(5)(7) in force for specified purposes at 18.6.2001 by S.I. 2001/1820, art. 2, Sch.; s. 82 in force in so far as not already in force at 1.12.2001 by S.I. 2001/3538, art. 2(1)

83 Registration of listing particulars.

(1) On or before the date on which listing particulars are published as required by listing rules, a copy of the particulars must be delivered for registration to the registrar of companies.

(2) A statement that a copy has been delivered to the registrar must be included in the listing particulars when they are published.

(3) If there has been a failure to comply with subsection (1) in relation to listing particulars which have been published

(a) the issuer of the securities in question, and

(b) any person who is a party to the publication and aware of the failure,

is guilty of an offence.

(4) A person guilty of an offence under subsection (3) is liable—

(a) on summary conviction, to a fine not exceeding the statutory maximum;

(b) on conviction on indictment, to a fine.

(5) "Listing particulars" includes supplementary listing particulars.

(6) "The registrar of companies" means—

(a) if the securities are, or are to be, issued by a company incorporated in Great Britain (b)依照第(1)款第(b)项给予的任何授权均不延伸至任何重要信息。

(3)国务大臣或财政部可以颁发证明书,说明披露任何信息(包括否则必须列入其负责的上市公告书的信息)违反公共利益。

(4)主管机关有权在行使第(1)款第(a)项规定的权力时根据上述任何证明书行动。

(5)本条规定不影响主管机关依照第101条第(2)款而制定的上市规则而拥有的权力。

(6)"重要信息"系指考虑购买相关证券的人,为了在其为作出有信息根据的评估而必须知悉的任何事实上不被误导,而可能需要的信息。

(7)"上市公告书"包括补充上市公告书。

注释:

实施日期

I30　第82条于2001年12月1日全部生效;第82条在副署时尚未生效,见第431条第(2)款;第82条第(1)款、第(5)款、第(7)款为特定目的于2001年6月18日依照制定法文件S.I.2001/1820第2条、附录生效;第82条如于2001年12月1日尚未生效,则依照制定法文件S.I.2001/3538第2条第(1)款生效。

第83条　上市公告书的登记

(1)在依照上市规则的要求公布上市公告书之日或之前,必须向公司注册署送交一份上市公告书副本用于登记。

(2)上市公告书公布时,其中必须包括一份表明上市公告书已送达注册人的声明。

(3)对于已公布的上市公告书,如未能遵守第(1)款规定,则

(a)相关证券发行人,和

(b)参与了公布行为且明知未能遵守规定的任何人,

构成犯罪。

(4)违反第(3)款规定而构成犯罪的,应当承担下列责任:

(a)经简易程序定罪的,处以不超过最高法定金额的罚金;

(b)经公诉程序定罪的,处以罚金。

(5)"上市公告书"包括补充上市公告书。

(6)"公司注册署"系指

(a)如证券由或将由在大不列颠设立且注册营业地在英格兰和威尔士的公司发

whose registered office is in England and Wales, the registrar of companies in England and Wales;

(b) if the securities are, or are to be, issued by a company incorporated in Great Britain whose registered office is in Scotland, the registrar of companies in Scotland;

(c) if the securities are, or are to be, issued by a company incorporated in Northern Ireland, the registrar of companies for Northern Ireland; and

(d) in any other case, any of those registrars.

Prospectuses

84 Prospectuses.

(1) Listing rules must provide that no new securities for which an application for listing has been made may be admitted to the official list unless a prospectus has been submitted to, and approved by, the competent authority and published.

(2) "New securities" means securities which are to be offered to the public in the United Kingdom for the first time before admission to the official list.

(3) "Prospectus" means a prospectus in such form and containing such information as may be specified in listing rules.

(4) Nothing in this section affects the competent authority's general power to make listing rules.

85 Publication of prospectus.

(1) If listing rules made under section 84 require a prospectus to be published before particular new securities are admitted to the official list, it is unlawful for any of those securities to be offered to the public in the United Kingdom before the required prospectus is published.

(2) A person who contravenes subsection (1) is guilty of an offence and liable—

(a) on summary conviction, to imprisonment for a term not exceeding three months or a fine not exceeding level 5 on the standard scale;

(b) on conviction on indictment, to imprisonment for a term not exceeding two years or a fine, or both.

(3) A person is not to be regarded as contravening subsection (1) merely because a prospectus does not fully comply with the requirements of listing rules as to its form or content.

(4) But subsection (3) does not affect the question whether any person is liable to pay compensation under section 90.

(5) Any contravention of subsection (1) is actionable, at the suit of a person who suffers loss as a result of the contravention, subject to the defences and other incidents applying to actions for breach of statutory duty.

行，指英格兰和威尔士公司注册署；

(b)如证券由或将由在大不列颠设立且注册营业地在苏格兰的公司发行，指在苏格兰公司注册署；

(c)如证券由或将由在北爱尔兰设立的公司发行，指北爱尔兰公司注册署；及

(d)在任何其他情况下，任何当地注册署。

招股说明书

第84条 招股说明书

(1)上市规则必须规定，除非招股说明书已提交主管机关并获批准，且予以公布，否则任何申请上市的新证券不得列入上市名单。

(2)"新证券"，系指列入上市名单前首次在联合王国公开发售的证券。

(3)"招股说明书"，系指上市规则规定形式、包含上市规则规定信息的招股说明书。

(4)本条任何规定均不影响主管机关制定上市规则的一般权力。

第85条 招股说明书的公布

(1)如依照第84条制定的上市规则要求特定新证券在列入上市名单之前公布招股说明书，则在要求的招股说明书公布前，该证券在联合王国公开发售为非法发售。

(2)违反第(1)款规定的，构成犯罪，且应承担下列责任：

(a)经简易程序定罪的，处以不超过3个月的有期徒刑或不超过标准等级第5级的罚金。

(b)经公诉程序定罪的，处以不超过2年的有期徒刑或罚金，或两罚并处。

(3)仅因招股说明书的形式或内容不完全满足上市规则的要求，不视为违反第(1)款规定。

(4)但第(3)款对于判断当事人是否应当依照第90条承担支付损害赔偿的责任不构成影响。

(5)对任何违反第(1)款规定的行为，因该违法行为而遭受损失的个人均可提起诉讼，但须依照适用违反法定职责诉讼的抗辩理由和其他事由。

86 Application of this Part to prospectuses.

(1) The provisions of this Part apply in relation to a prospectus required by listing rules as they apply in relation to listing particulars.

(2) In this Part—

(a) any reference to listing particulars is to be read as including a reference to a prospectus; and

(b) any reference to supplementary listing particulars is to be read as including a reference to a supplementary prospectus.

87 Approval of prospectus where no application for listing.

(1) Listing rules may provide for a prospectus to be submitted to and approved by the competent authority if—

(a) securities are to be offered to the public in the United Kingdom for the first time;

(b) no application for listing of the securities has been made under this Part; and

(c) the prospectus is submitted by, or with the consent of, the issuer of the securities.

(2) "Non-listing prospectus" means a prospectus submitted to the competent authority as a result of any listing rules made under subsection (1).

(3) Listingrules made under subsection (1) may make provision—

(a) as to the information to be contained in, and the form of, a non-listing prospectus; and

(b) as to the timing and manner of publication of a non-listing prospectus.

(4)The power conferred by subsection (3)(b) is subject to such provision made by or under any other enactment as the Treasury may by order specify.

(5) Schedule 9 modifies provisions of this Part as they apply in relation to non-listing prospectuses.

Annotations:

Modifications etc. (not altering text)

C108 S. 87 extended (1.12.2001) by S.I. 2001/2957, arts. 1, 6(4); S.I. 2001/3538, art. 2(1)

Commencement Information

I31 S. 87 wholly in force at 18.6.2001; s. 87 not in force at Royal Assent see s. 431(2); s. 87(4)(5) in force at 25.2.2001 by S.I. 2001/516, art. 2(a), Sch. Pt. 1; s. 87 in force in so far as not already in force at 18.6.2001 by S.I. 2001/1820, art. 2, Sch.

第86条　本部分对招股说明书的适用

(1)本部分规定适用于上市规则要求的招股说明书,等同于适用于上市公告书。

(2)本部分中

(a)述及任何上市公告书,视为包括招股说明书;且

(b)述及任何补充上市公告书,视为包括补充招股说明书。

第87条　无上市申请时招股说明书的批准

(1)上市规则可以规定,如符合下列条件,则招股说明书将提交主管机关批准:

(a)证券将首次在联合王国公开发售;

(b)未依照本部分规定提出证券上市申请;且

(c)招股说明书由证券发行人提交或经发行人许可而提交。

(2)"非上市招股说明书",系指因任何依照第(1)款制定的上市规则而向主管机关提交的招股说明书。

(3)依照第(1)款制定的上市规则可以规定

(a)非上市招股说明书应包含的信息及其形式;和

(b)非上市招股说明书公布的时间和方式。

(4)第(3)款第(b)项授予的权力,受符合财政部颁布法令规定的任何其他成文法的条款限制。

(5)附录9修改了本部分中的规定对非上市招股说明书的相关适用。

注释:

修改等(不涉及条文内容)

C108　第87条于2001年12月1日依照制定法文件S.I.2001/2957第1条、第6条第(4)款;制定法文件S.I.2001/3538第2条第(1)款扩大适用范围。

实施日期

I31　第87条于2001年6月18日全部生效;第87条在副署时尚未生效,见第431条第(2)款;第87条第(4)款、第(5)款于2001年2月25日依照制定法文件S.I.2001/516第2条第(a)款、附录第一部分生效;第87条如于2001年6月18日尚未生效,则依照制定法文件S.I.2001/1820第2条、附录生效。

Sponsors

88 Sponsors.

(1) Listing rules may require a person to make arrangements with a sponsor for the performance by the sponsor of such services in relation to him as may be specified in the rules.

(2) "Sponsor" means a person approved by the competent authority for the purposes of the rules.

(3) Listing rules made by virtue of subsection (1) may—

(a) provide for the competent authority to maintain a list of sponsors;

(b) specify services which must be performed by a sponsor;

(c) impose requirements on a sponsor in relation to the provision of services or specified services;

(d) specify the circumstances in which a person is qualified for being approved as a sponsor.

(4) If the competent authority proposes—

(a) to refuse a person's application for approval as a sponsor, or

(b) to cancel a person's approval as a sponsor, it must give him a warning notice.

(5) If, after considering any representations made in response to the warning notice, the competent authority decides—

(a) to grant the application for approval, or

(b) not to cancel the approval,

it must give the person concerned, and any person to whom a copy of the warning notice was given, written notice of its decision.

(6) If, after considering any representations made in response to the warning notice, the competent authority decides—

(a) to refuse to grant the application for approval, or

(b) to cancel the approval,

it must give the person concerned a decision notice.

(7) A person to whom a decision notice is given under this section may refer the matter to the Tribunal.

Annotations:

Commencement Information

I32 S. 88 wholly in force at 1.12.2001; s. 88 not in force at Royal Assent see s. 431(2); s. 88(1)-(3) in force at 18.6.2001 by S.I. 2001/1820, art. 2, Sch.; s. 88 in force in so far as not already in force at 1.12.2001 by S.I. 2001/3538, art. 2(1)

保 荐 人

第88条 保荐人

(1)上市规则可以要求一方与保荐人订立安排,以使保荐人履行规则中规定与其相关的服务。

(2)“保荐人”,系指就上市规则而言主管机关批准的人。

(3)基于第(1)款制定的上市规则可以

(a)规定主管机关保存保荐人名单;

(b)列举必须由保荐人履行的服务;

(c)就提供服务或提供规定服务对保荐人提出要求;

(d)规定在何种情况下符合获得批准成为保荐人的条件。

(4)如主管机关拟

(a)驳回某人提出的成为保荐人的申请,或

(b)撤销批准某人为保荐人的决定,则必须向该人发出预告通知。

(5)如主管机关在考虑针对预告通知作出的任何陈述后决定

(a)批准申请,或

(b)不撤销批准,

则必须向相关人和收到预告通知副本的任何其他人发出书面决定通知。

(6)如主管机关考虑针对预告通知作出的任何陈述后决定

(a)拒绝批准申请,或

(b)撤销批准,

则必须向相关人发出决定通知。

(7)依照本条规定向其发出决定通知的被通知人可以将该事项诉至裁判所。

注释:

实施日期

I32 第88条于2001年12月1日全部生效;第88条在副署时尚未生效,见第431条第(2)款;第88条第(1)款至第(3)款于2001年6月18日依照制定法文件S.I.2001/1820第2条、附录生效;第88条如于2001年12月1日尚未生效,则依照制定法文件S.I.2001/3538第2条第(1)款生效。

89 Public censure of sponsor.

(1) Listing rules may make provision for the competent authority, if it considers that a sponsor has contravened a requirement imposed on him by rules made as a result of section 88(3)(c), to publish a statement to that effect.

(2) If the competent authority proposes to publish a statement it must give the sponsor a warning notice setting out the terms of the proposed statement.

(3) If, after considering any representations made in response to the warning notice, the competent authority decides to make the proposed statement, it must give the sponsor a decision notice setting out the terms of the statement.

(4) A sponsor to whom a decision to the Tribunal.

Annotations:

Modifications etc. (not altering text)

C109 S. 89(2)–(4) applied (with modifications) (1.12.2001) by S.I. 2001/2957, arts. 1, 10(3), 12, 13; S.I. 2001/3538, art. 2(1)

Commencement Information

I33 S. 89 wholly in force at 1.12.2001; s. 89 not in force at Royal Assent see s. 431(2); s. 89(1) in force at 18.6.2001 by S.I. 2001/1820, art. 2, Sch.; s. 89 in force in so far as not already in force at 1.12.2001 by S.I. 2001/3538, art. 2(1)

Compensation

90 Compensation for false or misleading particulars.

(1) Any person responsible for listing particulars is liable to pay compensation to a person who has

(a) acquired securities to which the particulars apply; and

(b) suffered loss in respect of them as a result of

(i) any untrue or misleading statement in the particulars; or

(ii) the omission from the particulars of any matter required to be included by section 80 or 81.

(2) Subsection (1) is subject to exemptions provided by Schedule 10.

(3) If listing particulars are required to include information about the absence of a particular matter, the omission from the particulars of that information is to be treated as a statement in the listing particulars that there is no such matter.

(4) Any person who fails to comply with section 81 is liable to pay compensation to any person who has—

第89条　对保荐人的公开谴责

(1)上市规则可以规定,如主管机关认为保荐人违反了依照第88条第(3)款第(c)项制定的规则对其提出的要求,则可以公布关于该违反要求情况的声明。

(2)如主管机关拟公布声明,则必须向保荐人发出预告通知,列出拟公布的声明中所述条款。

(3)如主管机关考虑针对预告通知而作出的任何陈述后,决定发布拟发布的声明,则必须向保荐人发出决定通知,列出声明中所述条款。

(4)依照本条规定向其发出警告声明的保荐人可将该事项诉至裁判所。

注释:

修改等(不涉及条文内容)

C109　第89条第(2)款至第(4)款(已修订)于2001年12月1日依照制定法文件S.I. 2001/2957第1条、第10条第(3)款、第12条、第13条;制定法文件S.I.2001/3538第2条第(1)款适用。

实施日期

I33　第89条于2001年12月1日全部生效;第89条在副署时尚未生效,见第431条第(2)款;第89条第(1)款于2001年6月18日依照制定法文件S.I.2001/1820第2条、附录生效;第89条如于2001年12月1日尚未生效,则依照制定法文件S.I.2001/3538第2条第(1)款生效。

赔　偿

第90条　虚假或误导性公告书的赔偿

(1)任何上市公告书负责人均有责任向下列人员支付赔偿:

(a)购买了公告书适用的证券;且

(b)所购买证券因下列原因而遭受损失:

(i)公告书中任何非真实或误导性陈述;或

(ii)公告书中遗漏了第80条或第81条规定要求包含的任何事项。

(2)第(1)款的适用须遵守附录10的豁免规定。

(3)如要求上市公告书包含关于缺少特定事项的信息,则公告书中遗漏该信息视为在上市公告书中声明不存在该事项。

(4)任何未能遵守第81条规定的人有责任向下列人员支付赔偿:

(a) acquired securities of the kind in question; and

(b) suffered loss in respect of them as a result of the failure.

(5) Subsection (4) is subject to exemptions provided by Schedule 10.

(6) This section does not affect any liability which may be incurred apart from this section.

(7) References in this section to the acquisition by a person of securities include references to his contracting to acquire them or any interest in them.

(8) No person shall, by reason of being a promoter of a company or otherwise, incur any liability for failing to disclose information which he would not be required to disclose in listing particulars in respect of a company's securities—

(a) if he were responsible for those particulars; or

(b) if he is responsible for them, which he is entitled to omit by virtue of section 82.

(9) The reference in subsection (8) to a person incurring liability includes a reference to any other person being entitled as against that person to be granted any civil remedy or to rescind or repudiate an agreement.

(10) "Listing particulars", in subsection (1) and Schedule 10, includes supplementary listing particulars.

Annotations:

Modifications etc. (not altering text)

C110 S. 90 restricted (1.12.2001) by S.I. 2001/2957, arts. 1, 7(3); S.I. 2001/3538, art. 2(1)

Penalties

91 Penalties for breach of listing rules.

(1) If the competent authority considers that—

(a) an issuer of listed securities, or

(b) an applicant for listing,

has contravened any provision of listing rules, it may impose on him a penalty of such amount as it considers appropriate.

(2) If, in such a case, the competent authority considers that a person who was at the material time a director of the issuer or applicant was knowingly concerned in the contravention, it may impose on him a penalty of such amount as it considers appropriate.

(3) If the competent authority is entitled to impose a penalty on a person under this section in respect of a particular matter it may, instead of imposing a penalty on him in respect of that matter, publish a statement censuring him.

(4) Nothing in this section prevents the competent authority from taking any other steps

(a)取得了所涉及种类证券的人；

(b)就所取得证券因未能遵守第81条规定而遭受损失。

(5)第(4)款的适用须遵守附录10的豁免规定。

(6)本条规定不影响任何非因本条规定而引发的责任。

(7)本条中述及购买证券包含述及签订购买证券或证券任何权益的合同。

(8)任何人如有下列情况，则不因担任公司推广人或其他原因，而因未披露不要求其在上市公告书中披露的公司证券相关信息而产生任何责任：

(a)负责该公告书；或

(b)负责该公告书，且依照第82条规定有权省略信息。

(9)第(8)款中述及产生责任的人，包含述及针对该人有权获得民事赔偿或有权解除或拒绝履行协议的任何他人。

(10)"上市公告书"在第(1)款和附录10中包含补充上市公告书。

注释：

修改等(不涉及条文内容)

C110　第90条于2001年12月1日受制定法文件S.I.2001/2957第1条、第7条第(3)款；制定法文件S.I.2001/3538第2条第(1)款限制。

处　罚

第91条　违反上市规则的处罚

(1)如主管机关认为

(a)上市证券的发行人，或

(b)上市申请人，

违反上市规则的任何规定，则可对该发行人或申请人处以其认为适当数额的罚款。

(2)如在此类案件中，主管机关认为在重要期间发行人或申请人的董事明知该违反规则的行为而参与其中，则可以对该董事处以主管机关认为适当数额的罚款。

(3)如主管机关有权依照本条规定就特定事项对当事人处以罚款，则可以不处以罚款，改为公布对该人的公开谴责。

(4)本条中任何规定不妨碍主管机关采取任何依照本部分规定有权采取的其他

which it has power to take under this Part.

(5) A penalty under this section is payable to the competent authority.

(6) The competent authority may not take action against a person under this section after the end of the period of two years beginning with the first day on which it knew of the contravention unless proceedings against that person, in respect of the contravention, were begun before the end of that period.

(7) For the purposes of subsection (6)—

(a) the competent authority is to be treated as knowing of a contravention if it has information from which the contravention can reasonably be inferred; and

(b) proceedings against a person in respect of a contravention are to be treated as begun when a warning notice is given to him under section 92.

Annotations:

Modifications etc. (not altering text)

C111 S. 91(6)(7) applied (with modifications) (1.12.2001) by S.I. 2001/2957, arts. 1, 11(4)-(6); S.I.2001/3538, art. 2(1)

92 Procedure.

(1) If the competent authority proposes to take action against a person under section 91, it must give him a warning notice.

(2) A warning notice about a proposal to impose a penalty must state the amount of the proposed penalty.

(3) A warning notice about a proposal to publish a statement must set out the terms of the proposed statement.

(4) If the competent authority decides to take action against a person under section 91, it must give him a decision notice.

(5) A decision notice about the imposition of a penalty must state the amount of the penalty.

(6) A decision notice about the publication of a statement must set out the terms of the statement.

(7) If the competent authority decides to take action against a person under section 91, he may refer the matter to the Tribunal.

Annotations:

Modifications etc. (not altering text)

C112 S. 92(1)(3)(4)(6)(7) applied (with modificatons) (1.12.2001) by S.I. 2001/2957, arts. 1, 11(3), 12, 13; S.I. 2001/3538, art. 2(1)

措施。

(5)本条规定的罚款应向主管机关缴付。

(6)主管机关在自其知悉该违反行为的第一日起2年期间届满后,不得依照本条规定采取行动,除非就该违反行为针对当事人提起的程序在该期间届满前开始。

(7)就第(6)款而言

(a)如主管机关掌握可从中合理推断出违反行为的信息,则视为自知悉该违反行为;且

(b)就违反行为针对当事人提起的程序,视为自依照第92条规定向该人发出预告通知之时开始。

注释:

修改等(不涉及条文内容)

C111 第91条第(6)款、第(7)款(已修订)于2001年12月1日依照制定法文件S.I.2001/2957第1条、第11条第(4)款至第(6)款;制定法文件S.I.2001/3538第2条第(1)款适用。

第92条 程序

(1)如主管机关拟依照第91条规定对当事人取行动,则必须向该人发出预告通知。

(2)关于拟处以罚款的预告通知必须说明罚款数额。

(3)关于拟公布声明的预告通知必须说明拟公布声明的条款。

(4)如主管机关决定依照第91条规定对当事人采取行动,则必须向该人发出决定通知。

(5)如为处以罚款,则决定通知中必须说明罚款数额。

(6)如为公布声明,则决定通知中必须列明该声明的条款。

(7)如主管机关决定依照第91条规定对当事人采取行动,则该人可将该事项诉至裁判所。

注释:

修改等(不涉及条文内容)

C112 第92条第(1)款、第(3)款、第(4)款、第(6)款、第(7)款(已修订),于2001年12月1日依照制定法文件S.I.2001/2957第1条、第11条第(3)款、第12条、第13条;制定法文件S.I.2001/3538第2条第(1)款适用。

93 Statement of policy.

(1) The competent authority must prepare and issue a statement ("its policy statement") of its policy with respect to—

(a) the imposition of penalties under section 91; and

(b) the amount of penalties under that section.

(2) The competent authority's policy in determining what the amount of a penalty should be must include having regard to—

(a) the seriousness of the contravention in question in relation to the nature of the requirement contravened;

(b) the extent to which that contravention was deliberate or reckless; and

(c) whether the person on whom the penalty is to be imposed is an individual.

(3) The competent authority may at any time alter or replace its policy statement.

(4) If its policy statement is altered or replaced, the competent authority must issue the altered or replacement statement.

(5) In exercising, or deciding whether to exercise, its power under section 91 in the case of any particular contravention, the competent authority must have regard to any policy statement published under this section and in force at the time when the contravention in question occurred.

(6) The competent authority must publish a statement issued under this section in the way appearing to the competent authority to be best calculated to bring it to the attention of the public.

(7) The competent authority may charge a reasonable fee for providing a person with a copy of the statement.

(8) The competent authority must, without delay, give the Treasury a copy of any policy statement which it publishes under this section.

94 Statements of policy: procedure.

(1) Before issuing a statement under section 93, the competent authority must publish a draft of the proposed statement in the way appearing to the competent authority to be best calculated to bring it to the attention of the public.

(2) The draft must be accompanied by notice that representations about the proposal may be made to the competent authority within a specified time.

(3) Before issuing the proposed statement, the competent authority must have regard to any representations made to it in accordance with subsection (2).

(4) If the competent authority issues the proposed statement it must publish an account, in general terms, of—

(a) the representations made to it in accordance with subsection (2); and

(b) its response to them.

第93条　政策声明

(1)主管机关必须就关于下列事项的政策制定并发布声明(以下简称其政策声明):

(a)依照第91条规定处以罚款;以及

(b)依照第91条规定处以罚款的数额。

(2)主管机关确定罚金数额的政策必须考虑下列事项:

(a)就被违反要求的性质而言,相关违反行为的严重性;

(b)违反行为在何种程度上为故意或因重大过失而实施;及

(c)接受罚款的人是否为个人。

(3)主管机关可以随时变更或替换其政策声明。

(4)如对其政策声明进行变更或替换,则主管机关必须发布变更或替换后的声明。

(5)对任何特定违反行为,主管机关在行使或决定是否行使第91条规定的权力时,必须考虑依照本条规定公布、在该违反行为发生时有效的任何政策声明。

(6)主管机关必须以其认为最便于公众了解的方式公布依照本条规定发布的声明。

(7)主管机关可以为向他人提供声明副本而收取合理费用。

(8)主管机关必须毫不延迟地向财政部提供依照本条规定发布的任何政策声明的副本。

第94条　政策声明:程序

(1)主管机关在依照第93条规定发布声明前,必须以其认为最便于公众了解的方式公布所提议声明的草案。

(2)该草案必须附有可在规定时间就该提案向主管机关作出陈述的通知。

(3)主管机关在发布拟发布的声明前必须考虑依照第(2)款规定向其作出的任何陈述。

(4)如主管机关发布拟发布的声明,则必须公布概括说明下列事项的报告:

(a)依照第(2)款向其作出的陈述;以及

(b)主管机关对上述陈述的答复。

(5) If the statement differs from the draft published under subsection (1) in a way which is, in the opinion of the competent authority, significant, the competent authority must (in addition to complying with subsection (4)) publish details of the difference.

(6) The competent authority may charge a reasonable fee for providing a person with a copy of a draft published under subsection (1).

(7) This section also applies to a proposal to alter or replace a statement.

Competition

95 Competition scrutiny.

(1) The Treasury may by order provide for—

(a) regulating provisions, and

(b) the practices of the competent authority in exercising its functions under this Part ("practices"),to be kept under review.

(2) Provision made as a result of subsection (1) must require the person responsible for keeping regulating provisions and practices under review to consider—

(a) whether any regulating provision or practice has a significantly adverse effect on competition; or

(b) whether two or more regulating provisions or practices taken together have, or a particular combination of regulating provisions and practices has, such an effect.

(3) An order under this section may include provision corresponding to that made by any provision of Chapter Ⅲ of Part Ⅹ.

(4) Subsection (3) is not to be read as in any way restricting the power conferred by subsection (1).

(5) Subsections (6) to (8) apply for the purposes of provision made by or under this section.

(6) Regulating provisions or practices have a significantly adverse effect on competition if—

(a) they have, or are intended or likely to have, that effect; or

(b) the effect that they have, or are intended or likely to have, is to require or encourage behaviour which has, or is intended or likely to have, a significantly adverse effect on competition.

(7) If regulating provisions or practices have, or are intended or likely to have, the effect of requiring or encouraging exploitation of the strength of a market position they are to be taken to have, or be intended or be likely to have, an adverse effect on competition.

(8) In determining whether any of the regulating provisions or practices have, or are intended or likely to have, a particular effect, it may be assumed that the persons to whom the provisions concerned are addressed will act in accordance with them.

(5)如管理局认为该声明与依照第(1)款规定公布的草案有重大差异,则[除遵守第(4)款规定外]必须公布该差异的详细情况。

(6)主管机关可以为向他人提供依照第(1)款公布的草案副本收取合理费用。

(7)本条规定也适用于变更或替换声明的提案。

竞　　争

第95条　竞争审查

(1)财政部可以颁布法令,规定对

(a)监管规定,以及

(b)主管机关行使本部分规定职能时的惯例(以下简称惯例),进行不断审核。

(2)根据第(1)款作出的规定必须要求监管规定和惯例审核负责人考虑

(a)任何监管规定或惯例是否对竞争具有明显不利影响;或

(b)两项或以上监管规定或惯例加在一起,或监管规定和惯例的特定结合,是否对竞争具有明显不利影响。

(3)依照本条规定颁布的法令可以包含与第十部分第三章的任何规定相应的规定。

(4)第(3)款不得理解为以任何方式限制第(1)款规定授予的权力。

(5)第(6)款至第(8)款为施行依照本条制定的规定而适用。

(6)监管规定或惯例如有下列情况,则为对竞争具有明显不利影响:

(a)具有或者预计或可能具有对竞争有明显不利影响的效力;或

(b)具有或者预计或可能具有的效力为要求实施或鼓励实施预计或可能对竞争产生明显不利影响的行为。

(7)如监管规定或做法具有或者预计或可能具有要求利用或鼓励利用市场地位优势的效力,则应当将其视为对竞争具有或者预计或可能具有不利影响。

(8)在依照本章规定确定任何监管规定是否具有或者预计或可能具有特定效力时,可以认为相关规定针对的人将依照该规定行事。

(9) "Regulating provisions" means—

(a) listing rules,

(b) general guidance given by the competent authority in connection with its functions under this Part.

Miscellaneous

96 Obligations of issuers of listed securities.

(1) Listing rules may—

(a) specify requirements to be complied with by issuers of listed securities; and

(b) make provision with respect to the action that may be taken by the competent authority in the event of non-compliance.

(2) If the rules require an issuer to publish information, they may include provision authorising the competent authority to publish it in the event of his failure to do so.

(3) This section applies whenever the listed securities were admitted to the official list.

97 Appointment by competent authority of persons to carry out investigations.

(1) Subsection (2) applies if it appears to the competent authority that there are circumstances suggesting that—

(a) there may have been a breach of listing rules;

(b) a person who was at the material time a director of an issuer of listed securities has been knowingly concerned in a breach of listing rules by that issuer;

(c) a person who was at the material time a director of a person applying for the admission of securities to the official list has been knowingly concerned in a breach of listing rules by that applicant;

(d) there may have been a contravention of section 83, 85 or 98.

(2) The competent authority may appoint one or more competent persons to conduct an investigation on its behalf.

(3) Part XI applies to an investigation under subsection (2) as if—

(a) the investigator were appointed under section 167(1);

(b) references to the investigating authority in relation to him were to the competent authority;

(c) references to the offences mentioned in section 168 were to those mentioned in subsection (1)(d);

(d) references to an authorised person were references to the person under investigation.

98 Advertisements etc. in connection with listing applications.

(1) If listing particulars are, or are to be, published in connection with an application for listing, no advertisement or other information of a kind specified by listing rules may be issued in the United Kingdom unless the contents of the advertisement or other information have

(9)“监管规定”系指

(a)上市规则，

(b)主管机关就其本部分项下的职能作出的一般性指引。

其他规定

第96条　上市证券发行人的义务

(1)上市规则可以

(a)规定上市证券发行人应遵守的要求；且

(b)规定主管机关在发行人未遵守要求时可采取的行动。

(2)如规则要求发行人公开信息，则可以包含授权主管机关在发行人未能公开该信息时予以处罚的规定。

(3)上市证券一经列入正式上市名单，即适用本条规定。

第97条　主管机关对调查人的任命

(1)如主管机关认为有下列情况，则适用第(2)款规定：

(a)可能存在违反上市规则的行为；

(b)在重要期间上市证券发行人的董事明知该发行人违反上市规则而参与其中；

(c)在重要期间证券列入上市名单申请人的董事明知该申请人违反上市规则而参与其中；

(d)可能存在违反第83条、第85条或第98条的行为。

(2)主管机关可以任命一个或多个适格人员，代表主管机关进行调查。

(3)第十一部分适用于第(2)款规定的调查，等同于

(a)调查人系依照第167条第(1)款规定任命；

(b)述及与调查人相关的调查机关即为述及主管机关；

(c)述及第168条中规定的犯罪行为即为述及第(1)款第(d)项中规定的犯罪行为；

(d)述及获授权人即为述及接受调查人。

第98条　与上市申请相关的广告等

(1)如公布或将公布与上市申请相关的上市公告书，则不得在联合王国发布任何广告或其他上市规则中规定种类的信息，除非广告或其他信息的内容已提交给主管机关且主管机关已经

been submitted to the competent authority and that authority has—

(a) approved those contents; or

(b) authorised the issue of the advertisement or information without such approval.

(2) A person who contravenes subsection (1) is guilty of an offence and liable—

(a) on summary conviction, to a fine not exceeding the statutory maximum;

(b) on conviction on indictment, to imprisonment for a term not exceeding two years or a fine, or both.

(3)A person who issues an advertisement or other information to the order of another person is not guilty of an offence under subsection (2) if he shows that he believed on reasonable grounds that the advertisement or information had been approved, or its issue authorised, by the competent authority.

(4) If information has been approved, or its issue has been authorised, under this section, neither the person issuing it nor any person responsible for, or for any part of, the listing particulars incurs any civil liability by reason of any statement in or omission from the information if that information and the listing particulars, taken together, would not be likely to mislead persons of the kind likely to consider acquiring the securities in question.

(5) The reference in subsection (4) to a person incurring civil liability includes a reference to any other person being entitled as against that person to be granted any civil remedy or to rescind or repudiate an agreement.

Annotations:

Commencement Information

I34 S. 98 wholly in force at 1.12.2001; s. 98 not in force at Royal Assent see s. 431(2); s. 98(1) in force for specified purposes at 18.6.2001 by S.I. 2001/1820, art. 2, Sch.; s. 98 in force in so far as not already in force at 1.12.2001 by S.I. 2001/3538, art. 2(1)

99 Fees.

(1) Listing rules may require the payment of fees to the competent authority in respect of—

(a) applications for listing;

(b) the continued inclusion of securities in the official list;

(c) applications under section 88 for approval as a sponsor; and

(d) continued inclusion of sponsors in the list of sponsors.

(2) In exercising its powers under subsection (1), the competent authority may set such fees as it considers will (taking account of the income it expects as the competent authority) enable it—

(a) to meet expenses incurred in carrying out its functions under this Part or for any (a)批准上述内容;或

(b)授权发布未经批准的广告或信息。

(2)违反第(1)款规定的,构成犯罪并应承担下列责任:

(a)经简易程序定罪的,处以不超过最高法定数额的罚金;

(b)经公诉程序定罪的,处以不超过 2 年的有期徒刑或罚金,或两罚并处。

(3)因他人的命令而发布广告或其他信息的,如能证明其有合理理由相信该广告或信息已经主管机关批准,或该广告或信息的发布已经主管机关授权,则不构成第(2)款规定的犯罪。

(4)如依照本条规定,信息获得批准,或其发布获得授权,则如该信息和上市公告书共同考虑时不可能误导可能考虑购买该证券的人,则信息发布人和任何其他对上市公告书或上市公告书任何部分负责的人不因信息中的任何陈述或遗漏而产生任何民事责任。

(5)第(4)款中述及某人产生民事责任,包括任何他人针对该人有权获得的民事赔偿或有权解除或拒绝履行协议。

注释:

实施日期

I34 第98条于2001年12月1日全部生效;第98条在副署时尚未生效,见第431条第(2)款;第98条第(1)款为特定目的于2001年6月18日依照制定法文件S.I.2001/1820第2条、附录生效;第98条如于2001年12月1日尚未生效,则依照制定法文件S.I.2001/3538第2条第(1)款生效。

第99条 费用

(1)上市规则可以要求就下列事项向主管机关支付费用:

(a)上市申请;

(b)证券被持续列入上市名单;

(c)依照第88条规定申请作为保荐人获得批准;以及

(d)保荐人被持续列入保荐人名单。

(2)主管机关在行使第(1)款规定的权力时,可规定收取(考虑到作为主管机关所预期的收入)其认为可使其实现下列目标的费用:

(a)满足行使本部分规定职能或实现任何附带目的所发生的费用;

incidental purpose;

(b) to maintain adequate reserves; and

(c) in the case of the Authority, to repay the principal of, and pay any interest on, any money which it has borrowed and which has been used for the purpose of meeting expenses incurred in relation to—

(i) its assumption of functions from the London Stock Exchange Limited in relation to the official list; and

(ii) its assumption of functions under this Part.

(3) In fixing the amount of any fee which is to be payable to the competent authority, no account is to be taken of any sums which it receives, or expects to receive, by way of penalties imposed by it under this Part.

(4) Subsection (2)(c) applies whether expenses were incurred before or after the coming into force of this Part.

(5) Any fee which is owed to the competent authority under any provision made by or under this Part may be recovered as a debt due to it.

Annotations:

Modifications etc. (not altering text)

C113 S. 99(2) modified (1.12.2001) by S.I. 2001/3650, arts. 1(a), 25(3)

100 Penalties.

(1) In determining its policy with respect to the amount of penalties to be imposed by it under this Part, the competent authority must take no account of the expenses which it incurs, or expects to incur, in discharging its functions under this Part.

(2) The competent authority must prepare and operate a scheme for ensuring that the amounts paid to it by way of penalties imposed under this Part are applied for the benefit of issuers of securities admitted to the official list.

(3) The scheme may, in particular, make different provision with respect to different classes of issuer.

(4) Up to date details of the scheme must be set out in a document ("the scheme details").

(5) The scheme details must be published by the competent authority in the way appearing to it to be best calculated to bring them to the attention of the public.

(6) Before making the scheme, the competent authority must publish a draft of the proposed scheme in the way appearing to it to be best calculated to bring it to the attention of the public.

(7) The draft must be accompanied by notice that representations about the proposals

(b)维持充足的储备;以及

(c)如主管机关为管理局,偿还任何为满足下列相关目的而发生的费用所借款项的本金并支付其利息:

(i)其从伦敦证券交易所有限公司承继的与正式上市名单有关的职能;以及

(ii)承担本部分规定的职能。

(3)对应向主管机关支付的任何费用,确定其数额时不得将任何主管机关依照本部分规定收取或预期收取的罚款考虑在内。

(4)无论费用发生于本部分规定生效之前还是之后,均适用第(2)款第(c)项规定。

(5)任何依照本部分或在本部分之下制定的规定要求向主管机关支付的费用,均可作为主管机关的应收债务予以追偿。

注释:

> **修改等(不涉及条文内容)**
>
> C113　第99条第(2)款于2001年12月1日依照制定法文件S.I.2001/3650第1条第(a)款、第25条第(3)款修订。

第100条　处罚

(1)主管机关确定依照本部分规定处以罚款的数额时,不得将行使本部分规定职能所发生或预期发生的费用考虑在内。

(2)主管机关必须制订并执行一套计划,以确保依照本部分规定收取的罚款用于列入上市名单的证券发行人的利益。

(3)该计划特别可以就不同类别的发行人作出不同的规定。

(4)计划的最新详情必须在一份文件中列明(以下简称计划详情)。

(5)计划详情必须由主管机关以其认为最便于公众了解的方式公布。

(6)在制订计划前,主管机关必须以其认为最便于公众了解的方式公布拟订计划的草案。

(7)该草案必须附有关于可在指定时间内向主管机关就提案作出陈述的通知。

may be made to the competent authority within a specified time.

(8) Before making the scheme, the competent authority must have regard to any representations made to it under subsection (7).

(9) If the competent authority makes the proposed scheme, it must publish an account, in general terms, of—

(a) the representations made to it in accordance with subsection (7); and

(b) its response to them.

(10) If the scheme differs from the draft published under subsection (6) in a way which is, in the opinion of the competent authority, significant the competent authority must (in addition to complying with subsection (9)) publish details of the difference.

(11) The competent authority must, without delay, give the Treasury a copy of any scheme details published by it.

(12) The competent authority may charge a reasonable fee for providing a person with a copy of—

(a) a draft published under subsection (6);

(b) scheme details.

(13) Subsections (6) to (10) and (12) apply also to a proposal to alter or replace the scheme.

101 Listing rules: general provisions.

(1) Listing rules may make different provision for different cases.

(2) Listing rules may authorise the competent authority to dispense with or modify the application of the rules in particular cases and by reference to any circumstances.

(3) Listing rules must be made by an instrument in writing.

(4) Immediately after an instrument containing listing rules is made, it must be printed and made available to the public with or without payment.

(5) A person is not to be taken to have contravened any listing rule if he shows that at the time of the alleged contravention the instrument containing the rule had not been made available as required by subsection (4).

(6) The production of a printed copy of an instrument purporting to be made by the competent authority on which is endorsed a certificate signed by an officer of the authority authorised by it for that purpose and stating—

(a) that the instrument was made by the authority,

(b) that the copy is a true copy of the instrument, and

(c) that on a specified date the instrument was made available to the public as required by subsection (4),

is evidence (or in Scotland sufficient evidence) of the facts stated in the certificate.

(7) A certificate purporting to be signed as mentioned in subsection (6) is to be treated

(8)在制订计划之前,主管机关必须考虑任何依照第(7)款规定向其作出的陈述。

(9)如主管机关制订拟制订的计划,则必须公布概括下列内容的报告:

(a)依照第(7)款规定向其作出的陈述;以及
(b)主管机关对上述陈述的答复。
(10)如主管机关认为计划与依照第(6)款规定公布的草案有明显差异,则主管机关[除遵守第(9)款规定外]必须公布该差异的详细情况。

(11)主管机关必须不加迟延地向财政部送交所公布的任何计划详情的副本。

(12)主管机关可以为向他人提供下列文件副本而收取合理费用:

(a)依照第(6)款规定公布的草案;
(b)计划重要时间。
(13)第(6)款至第(10)款和第(12)款规定也适用于变更或替换计划的提案。

第101条　上市规则:一般规定
(1)上市规则可以对不同情况作出不同规定。
(2)上市规则可以授权主管机关免除或修改规则在特定情况下的适用,及通过指引,适用于任何情况。
(3)上市规则必须通过书面文件制定。
(4)包含上市规则的文件制定后,必须立即印制,有偿或无偿提供给公众。

(5)如能证明在声称的违法行为发生时,包含上市规则的文件未依照第(4)款规定向公众提供,则行为人不视为违反任何上市规则。

(6)出示声称由主管机关作出的文件的印刷本,该印刷本有经主管机关授权的官员签署的证明书证明,并表明

(a)该文件是主管机关作出的,
(b)该印刷本是该文件的真实复制件,以及
(c)该文件已按照第(4)款的要求在指定日期向公众提供,

为该证明书中所陈述事实的证据(或者在苏格兰称为充分证据)。
(7)声称依照第(6)款规定签署的证明书应视为已适当签署,除非表明情况相反。

as having been properly signed unless the contrary is shown.

(8) A person who wishes in any legal proceedings to rely on a rule-making instrument may require the Authority to endorse a copy of the instrument with a certificate of the kind mentioned in subsection (6).

102 Exemption from liability in damages.

(1) Neither the competent authority nor any person who is, or is acting as, a member, officer or member of staff of the competent authority is to be liable in damages for anything done or omitted in the discharge, or purported discharge, of the authority's functions.

(2) Subsection (1) does not apply—

(a) if the act or omission is shown to have been in bad faith; or

(b) so as to prevent an award of damages made in respect of an act or omission on the ground that the act or omission was unlawful as a result of section 6(1) of the [M2] Human Rights Act 1998.

Annotations:

Marginal Citations

M2 1998 c. 42

103 Interpretation of this Part.

(1) In this Part—

"application" means an application made under section 75;

"issuer", in relation to anything which is or may be admitted to the official list, has such meaning as may be prescribed by the Treasury;

"listing" has the meaning given in section 74(5);

"listing particulars" has the meaning given in section 79(2);

"listing rules" has the meaning given in section 74(4);

"new securities" has the meaning given in section 84(2);

"the official list" means the list maintained as the official list by the Authority immediately before the coming into force of section 74, as that list has effect for the time being;

"security" (except in section 74(2)) has the meaning given in section 74(5).

(2) In relation to any function conferred on the competent authority by this Part, any reference in this Part to the competent authority is to be read as a reference to the person by whom that function is for the time being exercisable.

(3) If, as a result of an order under Schedule 8, different functions conferred on the competent authority by this Part are exercisable by different persons, the powers conferred by section 91 are exercisable by such person as may be determined in accordance with the provisions of the order.

(8)在任何法律程序中希望依靠规则制定文件的,可以要求主管机关以第(6)款所述证明书来认可该文件的复制件。

第102条　损害赔偿责任的免除

(1)主管机关和主管机关的成员、高级职员或工作人员,或以上述身份行事的任何人,对行使或意图行使主管机关职能时的任何作为或不作为,均不承担损害赔偿责任。

(2)第(1)款不适用于

(a)有证据证明该作为或不作为出于恶意;或

(b)用于防止因[M2]《1998年人权法》第(6)条第(1)款规定的不合法作为或不作为而作出损害赔偿判决。

注释:

附注引文
M2　1998年第42章。

第103条　本部分的解释

(1)在本部分中

"申请"系指依照第75条规定提出的申请;

"发行人",就已经或可能列入正式上市名单的任何事物而言,具有财政部规定的含义;

"上市"具有第74条第(5)款中的含义;

"上市公告书"具有第79条第(2)款中的含义;

"上市规则"具有第74条第(4)款中的含义;

"新证券"具有第84条第(2)款中的含义;

"正式上市名单",系指由主管机关在第74条生效后立即作为上市名单保存的目前有效的名单;

"证券"[除在第74条第(2)款中]具有第74条第(5)款中的含义。

(2)就本部分规定授予主管机关的任何职能而言,本部分中任何时候提及主管机关,应当视为目前可行使该职能的人。

(3)如由于附录8规定的命令,本部分授予主管机关的不同职能由不同的人行使,则第91条所授予的权力应当根据法令中的规定来确定行使的人选。

(4) For the purposes of this Part, a person offers securities if, and only if, as principal—

(a) he makes an offer which, if accepted, would give rise to a contract for their issue or sale by him or by another person with whom he has made arrangements for their issue or sale; or

(b) he invites a person to make such an offer.

(5) "Offer" and "offeror" are to be read accordingly.

(6) For the purposes of this Part, the question whether a person offers securities to the public in the United Kingdom is to be determined in accordance with Schedule 11.

(7) For the purposes of subsection (4) "sale" includes any disposal for valuable consideration.

(4)就本部分而言,行为人只有作为委托人有下列情况,方为发售证券:

(a)行为人发出了要约,且如该要约被接受,将产生该人发行或出售,或与该人订立发行或出售安排的任何他人发行或出售证券的合同;或

(b)行为人邀请他人发出该要约。

(5)对"要约"和"要约人"应当作出相应的理解。

(6)就本部分而言,行为人是否在联合王国公开发售证券将根据附录11决定。

(7)就第(4)款而言,"出售"包括任何为了有价值的对价进行的处置。

PART Ⅶ CONTROL OF BUSINESS TRANSFERS

104 Control of business transfers.

No insurance business transfer scheme or banking business transfer scheme is to have effect unless an order has been made in relation to it under section 111(1).

Annotations:

Modifications etc. (not altering text)

C114 S. 104 applied (1.12.2001) by S.I. 2001/3626, arts. 1, 3(a)

S. 104 modified (1.12.2001) by S.I. 2001/3639, arts. 1(1), 7 (with art. 2)

Commencement Information

I35 S. 104 partly in force; s. 104 not in force at Royal Assent see s. 431(2); s. 104 in force for specified purposes at 1.12.2001 by S.I. 2001/3538, art. 2(1)(2)

105 Insurance business transfer schemes.

(1) A scheme is an insurance business transfer scheme if it—

(a) satisfies one of the conditions set out in subsection (2);

(b) results in the business transferred being carried on from an establishment of the transferee in an EEA State; and

(c) is not an excluded scheme.

(2) The conditions are that—

(a) the whole or part of the business carried on in one or more member States by a UK authorised person who has permission to effect or carry out contracts of insurance ("the authorised person concerned") is to be transferred to another body ("the transferee");

(b) the whole or part of the business, so far as it consists of reinsurance, carried on in the United Kingdom through an establishment there by an EEA firm qualifying for

第七部分　业务转让控制

第104条　业务转让控制

任何保险业务转让计划或银行业务转让计划，除非就该计划已依照第111条第(1)款规定颁布法令，否则均不得生效。

注释：

修改等(不涉及条文内容)

C114　第104条于2001年12月1日依照制定法文件S.I.2001/3626第1条、第3条第(a)款适用。

第104条于2001年12月1日依照制定法文件S.I.2001/3639第1条第(1)款、第7条(与第2条)修订。

实施日期

I35　第104条部分生效；第104在副署时尚未生效，见第431条第(2)款；第104条为特定目的于2001年12月1日依照制定法文件S.I.2001/3538第2条第(1)款、第(2)款生效。

第105条　保险业务转让计划

(1)有下列情况的计划属于保险业务转让计划：

(a)符合本条第(2)款所规定的条件之一；

(b)导致被转让之业务经由设立于某一欧洲经济区国家的受让人继续经营；并且

(c)不属于被排除的计划。

(2)前款所述条件为

(a)业务由经许可实施保险合同的联合王国获授权人(以下简称相关获授权人)在一个或多个成员国从事，该业务之全部或部分将被转让给另一人(以下简称受让人)；

(b)业务构成再保险，且经由在联合王国设立、拥有附录3规定之资格获准实施保险合同的欧洲经济区企业(以下简称相关获授权人)在联合王国从事，该业务的全部

authorisation under Schedule 3 which has permission to effect or carry out contracts of insurance ("the authorised person concerned") is to be transferred to another body ("the transferee");

(c) the whole or part of the business carried on in the United Kingdom by an authorised person who is neither a UK authorised person nor an EEA firm but who has permission to effect or carry out contracts of insurance ("the authorised person concerned") is to be transferred to another body ("the transferee").

(3) A scheme is an excluded scheme for the purposes of this section if it falls within any of the following cases:

(Case 1)

Where the authorised person concerned is a friendly society.

(Case 2)

Where—

(a) the authorised person concerned is a UK authorised person;

(b) the business to be transferred under the scheme is business which consists of the effecting or carrying out of contracts of reinsurance in one or more EEA States other than the United Kingdom; and

(c) the scheme has been approved by a court in an EEA State other than the United Kingdom or by the host state regulator.

(Case 3)

Where—

(a) the authorised person concerned is a UK authorised person;

(b) the business to be transferred under the scheme is carried on in one or more countries or territories (none of which is an EEA State) and does not include policies of insurance (other than reinsurance) against risks arising in an EEA State; and

(c) the scheme has been approved by a court in a country or territory other than an EEA State or by the authority responsible for the supervision of that business in a country or territory in which it is carried on.

(Case 4)

Where the business to be transferred under the scheme is the whole of the business of the authorised person concerned and—

(a) consists solely of the effecting or carrying out of contracts of reinsurance, or

(b) all the policyholders are controllers of the firm or of firms within the same group as the firm which is the transferee,

and, in either case, all of the policyholders who will be affected by the transfer have consented to it.

(4) The parties to a scheme which falls within Case 2, 3 or 4 may apply to the court for

或部分将被转让给另一人(以下简称受让人);

(c)业务由既不是联合王国获授权人又不是欧洲经济区企业,但获许可签订或实施保险合同的获授权人(以下简称相关获授权人)在联合王国从事,该业务的全部或部分将被转让给另一人(以下简称受让人)。

(3)为本条规定之实施,符合下列情形的计划属于被排除计划:

(情形1)

相关获授权人为互相保险协会成员。

(情形2)

有下列情况:

(a)相关获授权人是联合王国获授权人;

(b)计划转让之业务是在联合王国之外的一个或多个欧洲经济区国家签订或实施保险合同;并且

(c)计划已获联合王国之外的某一欧洲经济区国家的法院或所在国监管机关批准。

(情形3)

有下列情况:

(a)相关获授权人是联合王国获授权人;

(b)计划转让之业务在一个或多个国家或地区(均不属于欧洲经济区国家或地区)从事并且不涉及针对欧洲经济区国家发生之风险的保单(不包括再保险);并且

(c)计划已获非欧洲经济区国家或地区的法院或业务经营之国家或地区负责监管该等业务的机关批准。

(情形4)

如计划转让之业务是相关获授权人的全部业务并且

(a)业务之全部均为订立或实施再保险合同,或

(b)所有保单持有人均为受让企业的控制者或者同一受让企业集团中企业的控制者,

并且,无论为上述两种情况的哪一种,所有将受到转让影响的保单持有人均同意转让。

(4)符合情形2、情形3或情形4的计划各方可以向法院提出申请,请求法院作出将

an order sanctioning the scheme as if it were an insurance business transfer scheme.

(5) Subsection (6) applies if the scheme involves a compromise or arrangement falling within section 427A of the [M3] Companies Act 1985 (or Article 420A of the Companies [M4] (Northern Ireland) Order 1986).

(6) Sections 425 to 427 of that Act (or Articles 418 to 420 of that Order) have effect as modified by section 427A of that Act (or Article 420A of that Order) in relation to that compromise or arrangement.

(7) But subsection (6) does not affect the operation of this Part in relation to the scheme.

(8) "UK authorised person" means a body which is an authorised person and which—

(a) is incorporated in the United Kingdom; or

(b) is an unincorporated association formed under the law of any part of the United Kingdom.

(9) "Establishment" means, in relation to a person, his head office or a branch of his.

Annotations:

Marginal Citations

M3 1985 c. 6.

M4 S.I. 1986/1032 (N.I. 6).

106 Banking business transfer schemes.

(1) A scheme is a banking business transfer scheme if it—

(a) satisfies one of the conditions set out in subsection (2);

(b) is one under which the whole or part of the business to be transferred includes the accepting of deposits; and

(c) is not an excluded scheme.

(2) The conditions are that—

(a) the whole or part of the business carried on by a UK authorised person who has permission to accept deposits ("the authorised person concerned") is to be transferred to another body ("the transferee");

(b) the whole or part of the business carried on in the United Kingdom by an authorised person who is not a UK authorised person but who has permission to accept deposits ("the authorised person concerned") is to be transferred to another body which will carry it on in the United Kingdom ("the transferee").

(3) A scheme is an excluded scheme for the purposes of this section if—

(a) the authorised person concerned is a building society or a credit union; or

(b) the scheme is a compromise or arrangement to which section 427A(1) of the [M5] Companies Act 1985 or Article 420A of the [M6] Companies (Northern Ireland) Order 1986

其计划按照保险业务转让计划批准的命令。

（5）本条第（6）款适用于[M3]《1985年公司法》第427A条［或[M4]《1986年公司法令》（北爱尔兰）第420A条］规定的和解协议或安排。

（6）关于此等和解或安排，《1985年公司法》第425条至第427条［或《1986年公司法令》（北爱尔兰）第418条至第420条］具有的效力按照《1985年公司法》第427A条［或《1986年公司法令》（北爱尔兰）第420A条］的规定进行修正。

（7）但本条第（6）款不影响本部分与计划相关之施行效力。

（8）"联合王国获授权人"系指符合下列条件的获授权人：

（a）在联合王国设立；或

（b）是依照联合王国任一地方之法律设立的非法人。

（9）"机构"，就一方当事人而言系指其总部或某一分支机构。

注释：

附注引文

M3 1985年第6章。

M4 制定法文件S.I.1986/1032（N.I.6）。

第106条 银行业务转让计划

（1）如某项计划有下列情况，则为银行业务转让计划：

（a）满足第（2）款中规定的条件之一；

（b）根据该计划，被转让的全部或部分业务包括吸收存款；且

（c）不是被排除计划。

（2）前款所述条件为

（a）由非联合王国获授权人（以下简称相关获授权人）但具有吸收存款许可的人从事的全部或部分业务将被转让给另一主体（以下简称受让人）；

（b）由具有吸收存款许可的非联合王国获授权人（以下简称相关获授权人）在联合王国进行的全部或部分业务将被转让给另一个将在联合王国继续对其进行经营的主体（以下简称受让人）。

（3）为本条规定之实施，有下列情况的计划为被排除计划：

（a）相关获授权人为住房互助会或信用合作社；或

（b）该计划为一项和解或安排，且[M5]《1985年公司法》第427A条第（1）款或[M6]《1986年公司法令》（北爱尔兰）第420A条（上市公司的合并和分立）对其适用。

(mergers and divisions of public companies) applies.

(4) For the purposes of subsection (2)(a) it is immaterial whether or not the business to be transferred is carried on in the United Kingdom.

(5) "UK authorised person" has the same meaning as in section 105.

(6) "Building society" has the meaning given in the M7Building Societies Act 1986.

(7) "Credit union" means a credit union within the meaning of—

(a) the [M8] Credit Unions Act 1979;

(b) the [M9] Credit Unions (Northern Ireland) Order 1985.

Annotations:

Marginal Citations

M5 1985 c. 6.

M6 S.I. 1986/1032 (N.I.6).

M7 1986 c. 53.

M8 1979 c. 34.

M9 S.I. 1985/1205 (N.I. 12).

107 Application for order sanctioning transfer scheme.

(1) An application may be made to the court for an order sanctioning an insurance business transfer scheme or a banking business transfer scheme.

(2) An application may be made by—

(a) the authorised person concerned;

(b) the transferee; or

(c) both.

(3) The application must be made—

(a) if the authorised person concerned and the transferee are registered or have their head offices in the same jurisdiction, to the court in that jurisdiction;

(b) if the authorised person concerned and the transferee are registered or have their head offices in different jurisdictions, to the court in either jurisdiction;

(c) if the transferee is not registered in the United Kingdom and does not have his head office there, to the court which has jurisdiction in relation to the authorised person concerned.

(4) "Court" means—

(a) the High Court; or

(b) in Scotland, the Court of Session.

(4)就第(2)款第(a)项而言,将被转让的业务是否在联合王国从事无重要影响。

(5)"联合王国获授权人"具有第105条中的含义。

(6)"住房互助会"具有[M7]《1986年住房互助会法》中的含义。

(7)"信用合作社"系指在下列含义范围之内的信用合作社:

(a)[M8]《1979年信用合作社法》;

(b)[M9]《1985年信用合作社法令》(北爱尔兰)。

注释:

附注引文

M5 1985年第6章。

M6 制定法文件S.I.1986/1032(N.I.6)。

M7 1986年第53章。

M8 1979年第34章。

M19 制定法文件S.I.1985/1205(N.I.12)。

第107条 批准转让计划的命令申请

(1)批准保险业务转让计划或银行业务转让计划的命令可以向法院申请。

(2)申请可由下列人员作出:

(a)相关获授权人;

(b)受让人;或

(c)以上两者。

(3)申请必须按下列方式作出:

(a)如相关获授权人和受让人的注册地或总部所在地在同一个司法管辖区,则向该司法管辖区的法院申请;

(b)如相关获授权人和受让人的注册地或总部所在地不在同一个司法管辖区,则向两个司法管辖区中任意一个司法管辖区的法院申请;

(c)如受让人的注册地和总部均不在联合王国,则向对相关获授权人有管辖权的法院申请;

(4)"法院"系指

(a)高等法院;或

(b)(苏格兰)高等民事法院。

Annotations:

Modifications etc. (not altering text)

C115 S. 107 applied (1.12.2001) by S.I. 2001/3626, arts. 1, 3(a)

108 Requirements on applicants.

(1) The Treasury may by regulations impose requirements on applicants under section 107.

(2) The court may not determine an application under that section if the applicant has failed to comply with a prescribed requirement.

(3) The regulations may, in particular, include provision—

(a) as to the persons to whom, and periods within which, notice of an application must be given;

(b) enabling the court to waive a requirement of the regulations in prescribed circumstances.

Annotations:

Modifications etc. (not altering text)

C116 S. 108 applied (1.12.2001) by S.I. 2001/3626, arts. 1, 3(a)(b)

Commencement Information

I36 S. 108 wholly in force at 1.12.2001; s. 108 not in force at Royal Assent see s. 431(2); s. 108 in force for certain purposes at 25.2.2001 by S.I. 2001/516, art. 2 Sch. Pt. 2; s. 108 in force in so far as not already in force at 1.12.2001 by S.I. 2001/3538, art. 2(1)

109 Scheme reports.

(1) An application under section 107 in respect of an insurance business transfer scheme must be accompanied by a report on the terms of the scheme ("a scheme report").

(2) A scheme report may be made only by a person—

(a) appearing to the Authority to have the skills necessary to enable him to make a proper report; and

(b) nominated or approved for the purpose by the Authority.

(3) A scheme report must be made in a form approved by the Authority.

Annotations:

Modifications etc. (not altering text)

C117 S. 109 applied (1.12.2001) by S.I. 2001/3626, arts. 1, 3(a)

注释:

修改等(不涉及条文内容)

C115 第107条于2001年12月1日依照制定法文件S.I.2001/3626第1条、第3条第(a)款适用。

第108条 对申请人的要求

(1)财政部可以制定法规,对第107条规定的申请人提出要求。

(2)如申请人未能遵守规定的要求,则法院不得对依照该条规定提出的申请作出决定。

(3)法规特别包含下列规定:

(a)申请通知必须送达的人,和申请通知必须发出的期限。

(b)授权法院在规定的情况下免除法规中的要求。

注释:

修改等(不涉及条文内容)

C116 第108条于2001年12月1日依照制定法文件S.I.2001/3626第1条第3条第(a)款、第(b)款适用。

实施日期

I36 第108条于2001年12月1日全部生效;第108条在副署时尚未生效,见第431条第(2)款;第108条为特定目的于2001年2月25日依照制定法文件S.I.2001/516第2条、附录第二部分生效;第108条如在2001年12月1日尚未生效,则依照制定法文件S.I.2001/3538第2条第(1)款生效。

第109条 计划报告

(1)依照第107条规定就保险业务转让计划提出的申请必须附有一份计划条款报告(以下简称计划报告)。

(2)计划报告只能由下列人员作出:

(a)管理局认为拥有能够作出正确报告的必要技能;且

(b)由管理局为了该目的任命或批准。

(3)计划报告必须以管理局批准的形式作出。

注释:

修改等(不涉及条文内容)

C117 第109条于2001年12月1日依照制定法文件S.I.2001/3626第1条、第3条第(a)款适用。

110 Right to participate in proceedings.

On an application under section 107, the following are also entitled to be heard—

(a) the Authority, and

(b) any person (including an employee of the authorised person concerned or of the transferee) who alleges that he would be adversely affected by the carrying out of the scheme.

Annotations:

Modifications etc. (not altering text)

C118 S. 110 applied (1.12.2001) by S.I. 2001/3626, arts. 1, 3(a)

111 Sanction of the court for business transfer schemes.

(1) This section sets out the conditions which must be satisfiedbefore the court may make an order under this section sanctioning an insurance business transfer scheme or a banking business transfer scheme.

(2) The court must be satisfied that—

(a) the appropriate certificates have been obtained (as to which see Parts I and Ⅱ of Schedule 12);

(b) the transferee has the authorisation required (if any) to enable the business, or part, which is to be transferred to be carried on in the place to which it is to be transferred (or will have it before the scheme takes effect).

(3) The court must consider that, in all the circumstances of the case, it is appropriate to sanction the scheme.

Annotations:

Modifications etc. (not altering text)

C119 S. 111 applied (1.12.2001) by S.I. 2001/3626, arts. 1, 3(a)

Commencement Information

I37 S. 111 wholly in force at 1.12.2001; s. 111 not in force at Royal Assent see s. 431 (2); s. 111(2) in force for specified purposes at 25.2.2001 by S.I. 2001/516, art. 2(c), Sch. Pt. 3; s.

112 Effect of order sanctioning business transfer scheme.

(1) If the court makes an order under section 111(1), it may by that or any subsequent order make such provision (if any) as it thinks fit—

(a) for the transfer to the transferee of the whole or any part of the undertaking concerned and of any property or liabilities of the authorised person concerned;

第110条　程序参与权

对于依照第107条规定提出的申请，下列人员有权陈述意见：

(a)管理局；以及

(b)任何声称其会因计划的执行而受到不利影响的人（包括相关获授权人或受让人的雇员）。

注释：

修改等(不涉及条文内容)

C118　第110条于2001年12月1日依照制定法文件S.I.2001/3626第1条、第3条第(a)款适用。

第111条　法院对业务转让计划的批准

(1) 本条规定了法院依照本条颁布法令批准保险业务转让计划或银行业务转让计划之前必须得以满足的条件。

(2)法院必须确信

(a)已经取得了适当的证书（参见附录12第一部分和第二部分）。

(b)受让人具有使被转让的业务，或被转让业务的一部分，在转让后可以继续从事所需的授权（如有，或在计划生效前将获得此种授权）。

(3)法院必须认为在所有情况下批准该计划均为适当。

注释：

修改等(不涉及条文内容)

C119　第111条于2001年12月1日依照制定法文件S.I.2001/3626第1条、第3条第(a)款适用。

实施日期

I37　第111条于2001年12月1日全部生效；第111条在副署时未生效，见第431条第(2)款；第111条第(2)款为特定目的于2001年2月25日依照制定法文件S.I.2001/516第2条第(c)款、附录第三部分生效；第111条如于2001年12月1日尚未生效，则依照制定法文件S.I.2001/3538第2条第(1)款生效。

第112条　批准业务转让计划命令的效力

(1)如法院依照第111条第(1)款颁布了法令，则可通过该法令或任何后续法令对下列事项作出其认为适当的规定（如有）：

(a)向受让人转让全部或部分相关业务以及相关获授权人的任何财产或债务；

(b)for the allotment or appropriation by the transferee of any shares, debentures,policies or other similar interests in the transferee which under the scheme are to be allotted or appropriated to or for any other person;

(c) for the continuation by (or against) the transferee of any pending legal proceedings by (or against) the authorised person concerned;

(d) with respect to such incidental, consequential and supplementary matters as are, in its opinion, necessary to secure that the scheme is fully and effectively carried out.

(2) An order under subsection (1)(a) may—

(a) transfer property or liabilities whether or not the authorised person concerned otherwise has the capacity to effect the transfer in question;

(b) make provision in relation to property which was held by the authorised person concerned as trustee;

(c) make provision as to future or contingent rights or liabilities of the authorised person concerned, including provision as to the construction of instruments (including wills) under which such rights or liabilities may arise;

(d) make provision as to the consequences of the transfer in relation to any retirement benefits scheme (within the meaning of section 611 of the [M10]Income and Corporation Taxes Act 1988) operated by or on behalf of the authorised person concerned.

(3) If an order under subsection (1) makes provision for the transfer of property or liabilities—

(a) the property is transferred to and vests in, and

(b) the liabilities are transferred to and become liabilities of, the transferee as a result of the order.

(4) But if any property or liability included in the order is governed by the law of any country or territory outside the United Kingdom, the order may require the authorised person concerned, if the transferee so requires, to take all necessary steps for securing that the transfer to the transferee of the property or liability is fully effective under the law of that country or territory.

(5) Property transferred as the result of an order under subsection (1) may, if the court so directs, vest in the transferee free from any charge which is (as a result of the scheme) to cease to have effect.

(6) An order under subsection (1) which makes provision for the transfer of property is to be treated as an instrument of transfer for the purposes of the provisions mentioned in subsection (7) and any other enactment requiring the delivery of an instrument of transfer for the registration of property.

(7) The provisions are—

(a) section 183(1) of the[M11]Companies Act 1985;

(b)由受让人进行分配或拨付根据该计划将被分配给或拨付给任何其他人的任何股份、债券、保单或其他类似利益。

(c)由受让人继续进行(或针对受让人继续进行)任何相关获授权人进行(或针对相关获授权人)的未决法律程序。

(d)法院认为有必要确保计划完全有效执行的附带、间接或补充事项。

(2)第(1)款第(a)项规定的法令可以

(a)转移财产或债务,无论相关获授权人是否另外有能力使相关转让生效;

(b)对由相关获授权人作为受托人持有的财产作出规定;

(c)对相关获授权人的未来权利或义务或者或有权利或义务作出规定,包括对可能导致权利或义务的文书(包括遗嘱)的解释;

(d)对由相关获授权人管理的或代表相关获授权人进行管理的与任何退休福利计划(在[M10]《1988年所得税和公司税法》第611条中的含义范围之内)相关的转让的后果作出规定。

(3)如第(1)款规定的法令对财产或债务的转移作出了规定,则根据该法令的规定

(a)财产转让给并归属于受让人,且

(b)债务转移并加之于受让人。

(4)但是,如果法令中包含的任何财产或债务由任何联合王国以外的国家或地区的法律所管辖,则命令可以要求相关获授权人(如受让人如此要求)采取一切必要措施,确保向受让人进行的财产或债务转移根据该国家或地区的法律完全有效。

(5)依照第(1)款规定的法令而转移的财产,如法院如此指示,则归属于受让人且免于任何(由于该计划导致)停止生效的押记。

(6)第(1)款规定的对财产转让作出规定的法令,就第(7)款以及任何其他要求递交转让文书以进行产权登记的成文法所述规定而言,视为转让文书。

(7)前款所述规定为

(a)[M11]《1985年公司法》第183条第(1)款;

(b) Article 193(1) and (2) of the [M12] Companies (Northern Ireland) Order 1986.

(8) If the court makes an order under section 111(1) in relation to an insurance business transfer scheme, it may by that or any subsequent order make such provision (if any) as it thinks fit

(a) for dealing with the interests of any person who, within such time and in such manner as the court may direct, objects to the scheme;

(b) for the dissolution, without winding up, of the authorised person concerned;

(c) for the reduction, on such terms and subject to suchconditions (if any) as it thinks fit, of the benefits payable under

(i) any description of policy, or

(ii) policies generally,

entered into by the authorised person concerned and transferred as a result of the scheme.

(9) If, in the case of an insurance business transfer scheme, the authorised person concerned is not an EEA firm, it is immaterial for the purposes of subsection (1)(a), (c) or (d) or subsection (2), (3) or (4) that the law applicable to any of the contracts of insurance included in the transfer is the law of an EEA State other than the United Kingdom.

(10) The transferee must, if an insurance or banking business transfer scheme is sanctioned by the court, deposit two office copies of the order made under subsection (1) with the Authority within 10 days of the making of the order.

(11) But the Authority may extend that period.

(12) "Property" includes property, rights and powers of any description.

(13) "Liabilities" includes duties.

(14) "Shares" and "debentures" have the same meaning as in

(a) the [M13] Companies Act 1985; or

(b) in Northern Ireland, the [M14] Companies (Northern Ireland) Order 1986.

(15) "Charge" includes a mortgage (or, in Scotland, a security over property).

Annotations:

Modifications etc. (not altering text)

C120 S. 112 applied (1.12.2001) by S.I. 2001/3626, arts. 1, 3(a)

C121 S. 112(1) modified (1.12.2001) by S.I. 2001/3639, arts. 1(1), 4 (with art. 2)

Marginal Citations

M10 1988 c. 1.

M11 1985 c. 6.

(b)[M12]《1986年公司法令》(北爱尔兰)第193条第(1)款和第(2)款。

(8)如法院依照第111条第(1)款对保险业务转让计划颁布法令,则可通过该法令以及任何后续法令对下列事项作出其认为适当的规定(如有):

(a)对于任何在法院指示的时间内以法院指示的方式反对该计划的人的利益进行交易;

(b)相关获授权人不清算的解散;

(c)基于法院认为适当的条款根据其认为适当的条件(如有),减少依照下列文件应支付的利益:

(i)依照任何类别的保单,或

(ii)依照一般保单,

且保单为相关获授权人和受让人由于该计划而订立。

(9)如在保险业务转让计划中,相关获授权人不是欧洲经济区企业,则就第(1)款第(a)项、第(c)项或第(d)项,或第(2)款、第(3)款或第(4)款而言,对任何交易范围内保险合同所适用的法律是否为联合王国以外的欧洲经济区国家法律无重要影响。

(10)如保险或银行业务转让计划获得法院批准,则受让人必须于颁布法令后10日内,将第(1)款规定法令的两份副本交存管理局。

(11)但管理局可以延长上述期限。

(12)"财产"包含任何种类的财产、权利和权力。

(13)"债务"包含职责。

(14)"股份"和"债券"含义同下列法律:

(a)[M13]《1985年公司法》;或

(b)在北爱尔兰,[M14]《1986年公司法令》(北爱尔兰)。

(15)"负担"包含抵押(或者在苏格兰称为财产担保)。

注释:

修改等(不涉及条文内容)

C120　第112条于2001年12月1日依照制定法文件S.I.2001/3626第1条、第3条第(a)款适用。

C121　第112条第(1)款于2001年12月1日依照制定法文件S.I.2001/3639第1条第(1)款、第4条(与第2条)修订。

附注引文

M10　1988年第1章。

M11　1985年第6章。

M12 S.I. 1986/1032 (N.I. 6).
M13 1985 c. 6.
M14 S.I. 1986/1032 (N.I. 6).

113 Appointment of actuary in relation to reduction of benefits.

(1) This section applies if an order has been made under section 111(1).

(2) The court making the order may, on the application of the Authority, appoint an independent actuary—

(a) to investigate the business transferred under the scheme; and

(b) to report to the Authority on any reduction in the benefits payable under policies entered into by the authorised person concerned that, in the opinion of the actuary, ought to be made.

Annotations:

Modifications etc. (not altering text)

C122 S. 113 applied (1.12.2001) by S.I. 2001/3626, arts. 1, 3(a)

114 Rights of certain policyholders.

(1) This section applies in relation to an insurance business transfer scheme if—

(a) the authorised person concerned is an authorised person other than an EEA firm qualifying for authorisation under Schedule 3;

(b) the court has made an order under section 111 in relation to the scheme; and

(c) an EEA State other than the United Kingdom is, as regards any policy included in the transfer which evidences a contract of insurance, the State of the commitment or the EEA State in which the risk is situated ("the EEA State concerned").

(2) The court must direct that notice of the making of the order, or the execution of any instrument, giving effect to the transfer must be published by the transferee in the EEA State concerned.

(3) A notice under subsection (2) must specify such period as the court may direct as the period during which the policyholder may exercise any right which he has to cancel the policy.

(4) The order or instrument mentioned in subsection (2) does not bind the policyholder if—

(a) the notice required under that subsection is not published; or

(b) the policyholder cancels the policy during the period specified in the notice given under that subsection.

(5) The law of the EEA State concerned governs—

M12 制定法文件S.I.1986/1032(N.I.6)。
M13 1985年第6章。
M14 制定法文件S.I.1986/1032(N.I.6)。

第113条 涉及利益减少时对保险精算师的任命

(1)如依照第111条第(1)款颁布了法令,则适用本条规定。

(2)颁布该法令的法院可应管理局申请,任命一位独立保险精算师

(a)审查根据该计划转让的业务;以及

(b)在该精算师认为应当作出报告时,向管理局报告任何由相关获授权人订立的保单中规定应付利益的任何减少。

注释:

修改等(不涉及条文内容)

C122 第113条于2001年12月1日依照制定法文件S.I.2001/3626第1条、第3条第(a)款适用。

第114条 特定保单持有人的权利

(1)如有下列情况,则本条适用于保险业务转让计划:

(a)相关获授权人不是根据附录3符合授权条件的欧洲经济区企业;

(b)法院已依照第111条规定就该计划颁布法令;且

(c)就任何转让所包括的作为保险合同证据的保单而言,联合王国以外的欧洲经济区国家是约定国或风险所在的欧洲经济区国家(以下简称相关欧洲经济区国家)。

(2)法院必须指示,受让人必须在相关欧洲经济区国家就颁布使转让生效的法令,或执行任何使转让生效的文书,公布通知。

(3)依照第(2)款规定公布的通知,必须说明法院指示保单持有人可行使其任何保单撤销权的期间。

(4)如有下列情况,则第(2)款所述法令或文书不约束保单持有人:

(a)该款要求公布的通知未予公布;或

(b)保单持有人在根据该款发布的通知中说明的期间内撤销了保单。

(5)相关欧洲经济区国家的法律管辖

(a) whether the policyholder has a right to cancel the policy; and

(b) the conditions, if any, subject to which any such right may be exercised.

(6) Paragraph 6 of Schedule 12 applies for the purposes of this section as it applies for the purposes of that Schedule.

Annotations:

Modifications etc. (not altering text)

C123 S. 114 applied (1.12.2001) by S.I. 2001/3626, arts. 1, 3(a)

Business transfers outside the United Kingdom

115 Certificates for purposes of insurance business transfers overseas.

Part Ⅲ of Schedule 12 makes provision about certificates which the Authority may issue in relation to insurance business transfers taking place outside the United Kingdom.

116 Effect of insurance business transfers authorised in other EEA States.

(1) This section applies if, as a result of an authorised transfer, an EEA firm falling within paragraph 5(d) of Schedule 3 transfers to another body all its rights and obligations under any UK policies.

(2) This section also applies if, as a result of an authorised transfer, a company authorised in an EEA State other than the United Kingdom under Article 27 of the first life insurance directive, or Article 23 of the first non-life insurance directive, transfers to another body all its rights and obligations under any UK policies.

(3) If appropriate notice of the execution of an instrument giving effect to the transfer is published, the instrument has the effect in law—

(a) of transferring to the transferee all the transferor's rights and obligations under the UK policies to which the instrument applies, and

(b) if the instrument so provides, of securing the continuation by or against the transferee of any legal proceedings by or against the transferor which relate to those rights and obligations.

(4) No agreement or consent is required before subsection (3) has the effects mentioned.

(5) "Authorised transfer" means—

(a) in subsection (1), a transfer authorised in the home State of the EEA firm in accordance with—

(i) Article 11 of the third life directive; or

(ii) Article 12 of the third non-life directive; and

(b) in subsection (2), a transfer authorised in an EEA State other than the United Kingdom in accordance with—

(i) Article 31a of the first life directive; or

(a)保单持有人是否有权撤销保单;以及

(b)行使任何保单撤销权需满足的条件(如有)。

(6)附录12第6条为本条施行而适用时,等同于为该附录的施行而适用。

注释:

修改等(不涉及条文内容)

C123 第114条于2001年12月1日依照制定法文件S.I.2001/3626第1条、第3条第(a)款适用。

联合王国境外的业务转让

第115条 关于境外保险业务转让的证明书

附录12第三部分相关条款,就管理局针对发生在联合王国境外的保险业务转让可以签发的证明书作出了规定。

第116条 其他欧洲经济区国家授权的保险业务转让之效力

(1)属于附录3第5条第(d)款规定范围的欧洲经济区企业,如通过经授权转让,向另一机构转让其依照任何联合王国保单所享有的一切权利和承担的一切义务,则适用本条规定。

(2)依照第一人寿保险指令第27条或第一非人寿保险指令第23条在联合王国之外的欧洲经济区国家获得授权的企业,如通过经授权转让,向另一机构转让其依照任何联合王国保单所享有的一切权利和承担的一切义务,则也适用本条规定。

(3)对于使转让生效的文书,如执行该文书的适当通知已公布,则该文书具备下列法律效力:

(a)适用该文书的联合王国保单之下的一起权利义务均由转让人转移到受让人,并且

(b)如文书中有规定,则任何由转让人发起或针对转让人发起、与转让之权利义务相关的法律程序,均应保证转由受让人继续进行或针对受让人继续进行。

(4)在第(3)款所述效力生效前,无须作出任何协议或同意。

(5)“经授权转让”系指

(a)在第(1)款规定中,系指依照下列条款在欧洲经济区企业母国经授权的转让:

(i)第三人寿保险指令第11条;或

(ii)第三非人寿指令第12条;以及

(b)在第(2)款规定中,系指依照下列条款在联合王国以外的欧洲经济区国家经授权的转让:

(i)第一人寿保险指令第31a条;或

(ii) Article 28a of the first non-life directive.

(6) "UK policy" means a policy evidencing a contract of insurance (other than a contract of reinsurance) to which the applicable law is the law of any part of the United Kingdom.

(7) "Appropriate notice" means—

(a) if the UK policy evidences a contract of insurance in relation to which an EEA State other than the United Kingdom is the State of the commitment, notice given in accordance with the law of that State;

(b) if the UK policy evidences a contract of insurance where the risk is situated in an EEA State other than the United Kingdom, notice given in accordance with the law of that EEA State;

(c) in any other case, notice given in accordance with the applicable law.

(8) Paragraph 6 of Schedule 12 applies for the purposes of this section as it applies for the purposes of that Schedule.

Modifications

117 Power to modify this Part.

The Treasury may by regulations—

(a) provide for prescribed provisions of this Part to have effect in relation to prescribed cases with such modifications as may be prescribed;

(b) make such amendments to any provision of this Part as they consider appropriate for the more effective operation of that or any other provision of this Part.

(ii)第一非人寿保险指令第28a条。

(6)"联合王国保单",系指证明适用联合王国任何地区法律的保险合同的保单(再保险合同除外)。

(7)"适当通知"系指

(a)如证明保险合同的联合王国保单所涉之约定国是联合王国之外的欧洲经济区国家,则指依照该欧洲经济区国家法律规定发出的通知;

(b)如证明保险合同的联合王国保单所涉风险处于联合王国之外的欧洲经济区国家,则指依照该欧洲经济区国家法律规定发出的通知;

(c)在任何其他情况下,指依照适用的法律发出的通知。

(8)附录12第6条为本条的施行而适用时,等同于为该附录的施行而适用。

修　改

第117条　修改本部分规定的权力

财政部可以制定法规

(a)规定本部分中条款经规定修改后对规定案件具有效力;

(b)对本部分的任何条款作出其认为适当的修正,从而更有效地施行该条款或本部分任何其他规定。

PART Ⅷ PENALTIES FOR MARKET ABUSE

Market abuse

118 Market abuse.

(1) For the purposes of this Act, market abuse is behaviour (whether by one person alone or by two or more persons jointly or in concert)

(a) which occurs in relation to qualifying investments traded on a market to which this section applies;

(b) which satisfies any one or more of the conditions set out in subsection (2); and

(c) which is likely to be regarded by a regular user of that market who is aware of the behaviour as a failure on the part of the person or persons concerned to observe the standard of behaviour reasonably expected of a person in his or their position in relation to the market.

(2) The conditions are that

(a) the behaviour is based on information which is not generally available to those using the market but which, if available to a regular user of the market, would or would be likely to be regarded by him as relevant when deciding the terms on which transactions in investments of the kind in question should be effected;

(b) the behaviour is likely to give a regular user of the market a false or misleading impression as to the supply of, or demand for, or as to the price or value of, investments of the kind in question;

(c) a regular user of the market would, or would be likely to, regard the behaviour as behaviour which would, or would be likely to, distort the market in investments of the kind in question.

(3) The Treasury may by order prescribe (whether by name or by description)

(a) the markets to which this section applies; and

(b) the investments which are qualifying investments in relation to those markets.

第八部分[1] 市场滥用的处罚

市场滥用

第118条 市场滥用

(1)本法所称市场滥用系指下列行为(无论由一人单独行动还是由两人或以上共同或一致行动):

(a)与在适用本条的市场上进行交易的合格投资相关;

(b)满足第(2)款中所列一项或多项条件;且

(c)该市场上知悉该行为的一般用户,可能将该行为视为一个或多个行为人未能遵守合理预期处于该行为人地位的人应遵守的与该市场相关的行为标准。

(2)前款所述条件为

(a)该行为以市场用户通常无法接触到的信息为基础,但上述信息如果能够被该市场的一般用户获得,则将被或可能将被该人视为对决定该类投资的交易条款有关;

(b)该行为可能就相关种类投资的供给、需求、价格或价值给市场的一般用户造成错误印象或误导印象;

(c)市场的一般用户将会或可能会将此行为视为将会或可能会扭曲该种投资市场的行为。

(3)财政部可颁布法令,规定(无论通过名称还是通过描述)

(a)本条所适用的市场;及

(b)与上述市场有关的合格投资。

---

1 本部分依照《2010年金融服务法》第8条修订。——译者注

(4) The order may prescribe different investments or descriptions of investment in relation to different markets or descriptions of market.

(5) Behaviour is to be disregarded for the purposes of subsection (1) unless it occurs—

(a) in the United Kingdom; or

(b) in relation to qualifying investments traded on a market to which this section applies which is situated in the United Kingdom or which is accessible electronically in the United Kingdom.

(6) For the purposes of this section, the behaviour which is to be regarded as occurring in relation to qualifying investments includes behaviour which—

(a) occurs in relation to anything which is the subject matter, or whose price or value is expressed by reference to the price or value, of those qualifying investments; or

(b) occurs in relation to investments (whether qualifying or not) whose subject matter is those qualifying investments.

(7) Information which can be obtained by research or analysis conducted by, or on behalf of, users of a market is to be regarded for the purposes of this section as being generally available to them.

(8) Behaviour does not amount to market abuse if it conforms with a rule which includes a provision to the effect that behaviour conforming with the rule does not amount to market abuse.

(9) Any reference in this Act to a person engaged in market abuse is a reference to a person engaged in market abuse whether alone or with one or more other persons.

(10) In this section—

"behaviour" includes action or inaction;

"investment" is to be read with section 22 and Schedule 2;

"regular user", in relation to a particular market, means a reasonable person who regularly deals on that market in investments of the kind in question.

Annotations:

Commencement Information

I38 S. 118 wholly in force at 1.12.2001; s. 118 not in force at Royal Assent see s.431(2); s. 118(3)(4)(10) in force at 25.2.2001 by S.I. 2001/516, art. 2(a), Sch. Pt. 1; s. 118 in force so far as not already in force at 1.12.2001 by S.I. 2001/3538, art. 2 (1)

The code

119 The code.

(1) The Authority must prepare and issue a code containing such provisions as the

(4)命令可规定不同的投资,或描述与不同市场相关的投资,或对市场进行描述。

(5)就第(1)款而言,除非行为的发生有下列情况,否则将被忽视:

(a)在联合王国发生;或

(b)与在联合王国境内或在联合王国可通过电子手段进入且适用本条规定的市场上进行交易的合格投资有关。

(6)就本条而言,视为与合格投资相关而发生的行为包括下列行为:

(a)与任何合格投资的主要内容相关,或与通过参考合格投资的价格或价值而表达自身价格或价值的任何事物相关,而发生的行为;或

(b)与主要内容为合格投资的投资(无论是否为合格投资)相关而发生的行为。

(7)可由市场用户或其代表通过研究或分析获得的信息,就本条而言视为他们通常可以获得的信息。

(8)如规则规定符合该规则的行为不构成市场滥用,则行为符合该规则时不构成市场滥用。

(9)本法中任何时候述及市场滥用参与人,系指单独或与一个或多个其他人共同参与市场滥用的人。

(10)本条中

"行为"包括作为或不作为;

"投资"应结合第22条和附录2理解;

"一般用户",涉及特定的市场时,系指经常在该市场上进行相关种类投资交易的合理人。

注释:

实施日期

I38 第118条于2001年12月1日全部生效;第118条在副署时尚未生效,见第431条第(2)款;第118条第(3)款、第(4)款、第(10)款于2001年2月25日依照制定法文件S.I. 2001/516第2条第(a)款、附录第一部分生效;第118条如于2001年12月1日尚未生效,则依照制定法文件S.I.2001/3538第2条第(1)款生效。

准　则

第119条　准则

(1)管理局必须制定并发布一部准则,其中包含管理局认为将为决定行为是否构

Authority considers will give appropriate guidance to those determining whether or not behavior amounts to market abuse.

(2) The code may among other things specify—

(a) descriptions of behaviour that, in the opinion of the Authority, amount to market abuse;

(b) descriptions of behaviour that, in the opinion of the Authority, do not amount to market abuse;

(c) factors that, in the opinion of the Authority, are to be taken into account in determining whether or not behaviour amounts to market abuse.

(3) The code may make different provision in relation to persons, cases or circumstances of different descriptions.

(4) The Authority may at any time alter or replace the code.

(5) If the code is altered or replaced, the altered or replacement code must be issued by the Authority.

(6) A code issued under this section must be published by the Authority in the way appearing to the Authority to be best calculated to bring it to the attention of the public.

(7) The Authority must, without delay, give the Treasury a copy of any code published under this section.

(8) The Authority may charge a reasonable fee for providing a person with a copy of the code.

120 Provisions included in the Authority's code by reference to the City Code.

(1) The Authority may include in a code issued by it under section 119 ("the Authority's code") provision to the effect that in its opinion behaviour conforming with the City Code—

(a) does not amount to market abuse;

(b) does not amount to market abuse in specified circumstances; or

(c) does not amount to market abuse if engaged in by a specified description of person.

(2) But the Treasury's approval is required before any such provision may be included in the Authority's code.

(3) If the Authority's code includes provision of a kind authorised by subsection (1), the Authority must keep itself informed of the way in which the Panel on Takeovers and Mergers interprets and administers the relevant provisions of the City Code.

(4) "City Code" means the City Code on Takeovers and Mergers issued by the Panel as it has effect at the time when the behaviour occurs.

成市场滥用的人以适当指导的规定。

(2)该准则可以(除其他事项外)规定

(a)管理局认为构成市场滥用的行为;

(b)管理局认为不构成市场滥用的行为;

(c)管理局认为在决定行为是否构成市场滥用时应当纳入考虑的因素。

(3)该准则可对不同类别的人、情形或状况作出不同的规定。

(4)管理局可随时变更或替换该准则。

(5)如变更或替换该准则,则管理局必须发布变更或替换后的准则。

(6)管理局必须以其认为最便于公众了解的方式公布依照本条规定发布的准则。

(7)管理局必须毫不延迟地将依照本条规定公布的准则副本送交财政部。

(8)管理局可以为向他人提供准则副本而收取合理费用。

第120条　参照金融城准则[1]而纳入管理局准则的规定

(1)管理局可以在其依照第119条发布的准则(以下简称管理局准则)中规定,其认为符合金融城准则的行为的效力

(a)不构成市场滥用;

(b)在规定情况下不构成市场滥用;或

(c)如由规定类别的人参与则不构成市场滥用。

(2)但上述任何规定纳入管理局准则需经财政部批准。

(3)如管理局准则包含第(1)款授权列入的规定,则管理局必须了解收购与合并委员会如何解释并管理相关金融城准则规定。

(4)"金融城准则",系指委员会发布的在行为发生时有效的《金融城购买与合并准则》。

1 金融城准则,原文为"the City Code",全称"London City Code on Takeovers and Mergers",又译为《城市法典》、《金融城收购和合并守则》、《伦敦守则》、《金融城守则》等,颁布于1968年,是处理公司收购的自律性规则,在法律上并不产生与法律一样的强制力,仅是证券交易所的一项建议,被用于推广、维持优良的商业标准。——译者注

(5) "Specified" means specified in the Authority's code.

121 Codes: procedure.

(1) Before issuing a code under section 119, the Authority must publish a draft of the proposed code in the way appearing to the Authority to be best calculated to bring it to the attention of the public.

(2) The draft must be accompanied by—

(a) a cost benefit analysis; and

(b) notice that representations about the proposal may be made to the Authority within a specified time.

(3) Before issuing the proposed code, the Authority must have regard to any representations made to it in accordance with subsection (2)(b).

(4) If the Authority issues the proposed code it must publish an account, in general terms, of—

(a) the representations made to it in accordance with subsection (2)(b); and

(b) its response to them.

(5) If the code differs from the draft published under subsection (1) in a way which is, in the opinion of the Authority, significant—

(a) the Authority must (in addition to complying with subsection (4)) publish details of the difference; and

(b) those details must be accompanied by a cost benefit analysis.

(6) Subsections (1) to (5) do not apply if the Authority considers that there is an urgent need to publish the code.

(7) Neither subsection (2)(a) nor subsection (5)(b) applies if the Authority considers—

(a) that, making the appropriate comparison, there will be no increase in costs; or

(b) that, making that comparison, there will be an increase in costs but the increase will be of minimal significance.

(8) The Authority may charge a reasonable fee for providing a person with a copy of a draft published under subsection (1).

(9) This section also applies to a proposal to alter or replace a code.

(10) "Cost benefit analysis" means an estimate of the costs together with an analysis of the benefits that will arise—

(a) if the proposed code is issued; or

(b) if subsection (5)(b) applies, from the code that has been issued.

(11) "The appropriate comparison" means—

(a) in relation to subsection (2)(a), a comparison between the overall position if the code is issued and the overall position if it is not issued;

(b) in relation to subsection (5)(b), a comparison between the overall position after the

(5)“指定”,系指在管理局准则中指定。

第121条 准则:程序

(1)在依照第119条发布准则之前,管理局必须以其认为最便于公众了解的方式公布拟公布准则的草案。

(2)该草案必须附有

(a)成本效益分析;以及

(b)关于在规定时间内可就该提案向管理局作出陈述的通知。

(3)在发布拟发布的准则前,管理局必须考虑依照第(2)款第(b)项向其作出的任何陈述。

(4)如管理局发布拟发布的准则,则必须公布概述下列内容的报告:

(a)依照第(2)款第(b)项向其作出的陈述;以及

(b)管理局对上述陈述的答复。

(5)如管理局认为准则与依照第(1)款公布的草案有明显差异,则

(a)管理局[除遵守第(4)款规定外]必须公布该差异的详细情况;且

(b)详细情况中必须附有成本效益分析。

(6)如管理局认为迫切需要公布准则,则第(1)款至第(5)款规定不适用。

(7)如管理局认为有下列情况,则第(2)款第(a)项和第(5)款第(b)项规定不适用:

(a)进行恰当比较后认为无成本增长;或

(b)进行适当比较后认为成本将增长,但该增长影响极小。

(8)管理局可以为向他人提供依照第(1)款公布的草案而收取合理费用。

(9)本条还适用于变更或替换准则的提案。

(10)“成本效益分析”,系指对下列情况成本的估计以及对所产生效益的分析:

(a)如发布拟发布的准则;或

(b)如因已发布的准则而适用第(5)款第(b)项规定。

(11)“适当比较”系指

(a)就第(2)款第(a)项而言,系指比较假设准则发布后的整体状况和假设不发布准则的整体状况;

(b)就第(5)款第(b)项而言,系指比较准则发布后的整体状况和发布前的整

issuing of the code and the overall position before it was issued.

122 Effect of the code.

(1) If a person behaves in a way which is described (in the code in force under section 119 at the time of the behaviour) as behaviour that, in the Authority's opinion, does not amount to market abuse that behaviour of his is to be taken, for the purposes of this Act, as not amounting to market abuse.

(2) Otherwise, the code in force under section 119 at the time when particularbehavior occurs may be relied on so far as it indicates whether or not that behaviour should be taken to amount to market abuse.

Power to impose penalties

123 Power to impose penalties in cases of market abuse.

(1) If the Authority is satisfied that a person ("A")—

(a) is or has engaged in market abuse, or

(b) by taking or refraining from taking any action has required or encouraged another person or persons to engage in behaviour which, if engaged in by A, would amount to market abuse, it may impose on him a penalty of such amount as it considers appropriate.

(2) But the Authority may not impose a penalty on a person if, having considered any representations made to it in response to a warning notice, there are reasonable grounds for it to be satisfied that—

(a) he believed, on reasonable grounds, that his behaviour did not fall within paragraph (a) or (b) of subsection (1), or

(b) he took all reasonable precautions and exercised all due diligence to avoid behaving in a way which fell within paragraph (a) or (b) of that subsection.

(3) If the Authority is entitled to impose a penalty on a person under this section it may, instead of imposing a penalty on him, publish a statement to the effect that he has engaged in market abuse.

Statement of policy

124 Statement of policy.

(1) The Authority must prepare and issue a statement of its policy with respect to—

(a) the imposition of penalties under section 123; and

(b) the amount of penalties under that section.

(2) The Authority's policy in determining what the amount of a penalty should be must include having regard to—

(a) whether the behaviour in respect of which the penalty is to be imposed had an adverse effect on the market in question and, if it did, how serious that effect was;

体状况。

第122条　准则的效力

(1)如行为人的行为方式根据规定(根据第119条发布、在行为发生时有效的准则中)是管理局认为不构成市场滥用的行为,则依照本法规定,行为人的该项行为不构成市场滥用。

(2)否则,可以依靠根据第119条发布、在特定行为发生时有效的准则决定该行为是否应当视为市场滥用。

处　罚　权

第123条　市场滥用的处罚权

(1)如管理局确信当事人(以下简称A)

(a)实施或曾经实施市场滥用,或

(b)通过采取或不采取任何行动,要求或鼓励其他一方或多方参与如由A实施则将构成市场滥用的行为,则管理局可以对A处以其认为适当金额的罚款。

(2)但管理局如考虑到任何回应预告通知而向其作出的陈述,有合理理由确信有下列情况,则不得对当事人处以罚款:

(a)当事人基于合理理由相信其行为不属于第(1)款第(a)项或第(b)项规定的范围,或

(b)当事人已采取一切合理预防措施并已尽应有谨慎防止其行为属于第(1)款第(a)项或第(b)项规定的范围。

(3)如管理局有权根据本条对当事人处以罚款,作为替代可不处以罚款,而公布该人曾经参与市场滥用的声明。

政 策 声 明

第124条　政策声明

(1)管理局必须就关于下列事项的政策制定并发布声明:

(a)依照第123条处以罚款;以及

(b)依照该条处以罚款的数额。

(2)管理局决定罚款数额的政策必须考虑下列事项:

(a)处罚的行为是否对相关市场有不利影响,如有,影响的严重程度如何;

(b) the extent to which that behaviour was deliberate or reckless; and

(c) whether the person on whom the penalty is to be imposed is an individual.

(3) A statement issued under this section must include an indication of the circumstances in which the Authority is to be expected to regard a person as—

(a) having a reasonable belief that his behaviour did not amount to market abuse; or

(b) having taken reasonable precautions and exercised due diligence to avoid engaging in market abuse.

(4) The Authority may at any time alter or replace a statement issued under this section.

(5) If a statement issued under this section is altered or replaced,the Authority must issue the altered or replacement statement.

(6) In exercising, or deciding whether to exercise, its power under section 123 in the case of any particular behaviour, the Authority must have regard to any statement published under this section and in force at the time when the behaviour concerned occurred.

(7) A statement issued under this section must be published by the Authority in the way appearing to the Authority to be best calculated to bring it to the attention of the public.

(8) The Authority may charge a reasonable fee for providing a person with a copy of a statement published under this section.

(9) The Authority must, without delay, give the Treasury a copy of any statement which it publishes under this section.

125 Statement of policy: procedure.

(1) Before issuing a statement of policy under section 124, the Authority must publish a draft of the proposed statement in the way appearing to the Authority to be best calculated to bring it to the attention of the public.

(2) The draft must be accompanied by notice that representations about the proposal may be made to the Authority within a specified time.

(3) Before issuing the proposed statement, the Authority must have regard to any representations made to it in accordance with subsection (2).

(4) If the Authority issues the proposed statement it must publish an account, in general terms, of—

(a) the representations made to it in accordance with subsection (2); and

(b) its response to them.

(5) If the statement differs from the draft published under subsection (1) in a way which is, in the opinion of the Authority, significant, the Authority must (in addition to complying with subsection (4)) publish details of the difference.

(6) The Authority may charge a reasonable fee for providing aperson with a copy of a draft published under subsection (1).

(7) This section also applies to a proposal to alter or replace a statement.

(b)该行为在何种程度上为故意或因重大过失而实施;及

(c)接受罚款的人是否为个人。

(3)依照本条发布的声明必须表明在何种情况下管理局应将当事人视为

(a)有合理理由相信其行为不构成市场滥用;或

(b)已采取合理预防措施并已尽应有谨慎以避免参与市场滥用。

(4)管理局可随时变更或替换依照本条规定发布的声明。

(5)如变更或替换依照本条发布的声明,则管理局必须发布变更或替换后的声明。

(6)对任何特定行为,在行使或决定是否行使第123条规定的权力时,管理局必须考虑依照本条公布且在相关行为发生时有效的任何声明。

(7)管理局必须以其认为最便于公众了解的方式公布依照本条发布的声明。

(8)管理局可以为向他人提供依照本条公布的声明而收取合理费用。

(9)管理局必须毫不延迟地将其根据本条所公布的声明副本送交财政部。

第125条　政策声明:程序

(1)在依照第124条发布政策声明前,管理局必须以其认为最能引起公众注意的方式公布拟发布声明的草案。

(2)该草案必须附有关于可在规定时间内就该提案向管理局作出陈述的通知。

(3)在发布拟发布的声明前,管理局必须考虑任何依照第(2)款向其作出的陈述。

(4)如管理局发布拟发布的声明,则必须公布概述下列内容的报告:

(a)依照第(2)款规定向其作出的陈述;及

(b)管理局对上述陈述的答复。

(5)如管理局认为声明与依照第(1)款公布的草案有明显差异,则[(除遵守第(4)款规定外]必须公布该差异的详细情况。

(6)管理局可以为向他人提供依照第(1)款公布的草案而收取合理费用。

(7)本条还适用于变更或替换声明的提案。

Procedure

126 Warning notices.

(1) If the Authority proposes to take action against a person under section 123, it must give him a warning notice.

(2) A warning notice about a proposal to impose a penalty must state the amount of the proposed penalty.

(3) A warning notice about a proposal to publish a statement must set out the terms of the proposed statement.

127 Decision notices and right to refer to Tribunal.

(1) If the Authority decides to take action against a person under section 123, it must give him a decision notice.

(2) A decision notice about the imposition of a penalty must state the amount of the penalty.

(3) A decision notice about the publication of a statement must set out the terms of the statement.

(4) If the Authority decides to take action against a person under section 123, that person may refer the matter to the Tribunal.

Miscellaneous

128 Suspension of investigations.

(1) If the Authority considers it desirable or expedient because of the exercise or possible exercise of a power relating to market abuse, it may direct a recognised investment exchange or recognised clearing house—

(a) to terminate, suspend or limit the scope of any inquiry which the exchange or clearing house is conducting under its rules; or

(b) not to conduct an inquiry which the exchange or clearing house proposes to conduct under its rules.

(2) A direction under this section—

(a) must be given to the exchange or clearing house concerned by notice in writing; and

(b) is enforceable, on the application of the Authority, by injunction or, in Scotland, by an order under section 45 of the [M15] Court of Session Act 1988.

(3) The Authority's powers relating to market abuse are its powers—

(a) to impose penalties under section 123; or

(b) to appoint a person to conduct an investigation under section 168 in a case falling within subsection (2)(d) of that section.

程　　序

第126条　预告通知

（1）如管理局拟依照第123条对某人采取行动，则必须向该人发出预告通知。

（2）关于拟处以罚款的预告通知必须说明拟处以罚款的数额。

（3）关于拟公布声明的预告通知必须列明拟公布声明的条款。

第127条　决定通知与诉至裁判所的权利

（1）如管理局决定依照第123条对当事人采取行动，则必须向该人发出决定通知。

（2）如为处以罚款，则决定通知必须表明罚款数额。

（3）如为公布声明，则决定通知必须列出声明的条款。

（4）如管理局决定依照第123条对当事人采取行动，则当事人可以将该事项诉至裁判所。

其他规定

第128条　暂停调查

（1）如管理局认为因行使或可能行使与市场滥用相关的权力而有必要或适宜，则可以指示获认可的投资交易所或获得认可的结算所

（a）终止、暂停任何交易所或结算所根据其规则正在进行的调查或限制任何该等调查的范围；或

（b）不进行交易所或结算所根据其规则计划进行的调查。

（2）根据本条作出的指示

（a）必须以书面形式通知相关交易所或结算所；且

（b）根据管理局的申请，可以通过禁令强制执行，或者在苏格兰可以通过[M15]《1988年高等民事法院法》第45条的命令强制执行。

（3）管理局与市场滥用相关的权力为

（a）依照第123条施加处罚；或

（b）在属于第168条第（2）款第（d）项规定范围的案件中，依照第168条任命调查人。

Annotations:

Marginal Citations

M15 1988 c. 36.

129 Power of court to impose penalty in cases of market abuse.

(1) The Authority may on an application to the court under section 381 or 383 request the court to consider whether the circumstances are such that a penalty should be imposed on the person to whom the application relates.

(2) The court may, if it considers it appropriate, make an order requiring the person concerned to pay to the Authority a penalty of such amount as it considers appropriate.

130 Guidance.

(1) The Treasury may from time to time issue written guidance for the purpose of helping relevant authorities to determine the action to be taken in cases where behaviour occurs which is behaviour—

(a) with respect to which the power in section 123 appears to be exercisable; and

(b) which appears to involve the commission of an offence under section 397 of this Act or Part V of the [M16] Criminal Justice Act 1993 (insider dealing).

(2) The Treasury must obtain the consent of the Attorney General and the Secretary of State before issuing any guidance under this section.

(3) In this section "relevant authorities"—

(a) in relation to England and Wales, means the Secretary of State, the Authority, the Director of the Serious Fraud Office and the Director of Public Prosecutions;

(b) in relation to Northern Ireland, means the Secretary of State, the Authority, the Director of the Serious Fraud Office and the Director of Public Prosecutions for Northern Ireland.

(4) Subsections (1) to (3) do not apply to Scotland.

(5) In relation to Scotland, the Lord Advocate may from time to time, after consultation with the Treasury, issue written guidance for the purpose of helping the Authority to determine the action to be taken in cases where behaviour mentioned in subsection (1) occurs.

Annotations:

Marginal Citations

M16 1993 c. 36.

131 Effect on transactions.

The imposition of a penalty under this Part does not make any transaction void or unenforceable.

注释：

附注引文

M15 1988年第36章。

第129条 法院在市场滥用案件中课以处罚的权力

(1)管理局可以依照第381条或第383条向法院提出申请，请求法院考虑该情况是否为应该对申请相关人处以罚款的情形。

(2)法院如认为适当，则可作出命令要求相关人向管理局支付其认为数额适当的罚款。

第130条 指导

(1)财政部可以不时发布书面指导，以帮助相关机关决定在发生下列行为的情况下采取行动：

(a)第123条规定的何种权力初步认定可行使；且

(b)涉嫌本法第397条或[M16]《1993年刑事司法法》第五部分(内幕交易)规定的犯罪。

(2)财政部在根据本条发布任何指导前，必须得到司法部长和国务大臣的同意。

(3)在本条中，“相关机关”

(a)涉及英格兰和威尔士时，系指国务大臣、管理局、严重欺诈行为办公室主任和检察长；

(b)涉及北爱尔兰时，系指国务大臣、管理局、严重欺诈行为办公室主任和北爱尔兰检察长。

(4)苏格兰不适用第(1)款至第(3)款规定。

(5)涉及苏格兰时，检查总长向财政部征求意见后可不时发布书面指导，以帮助管理局决定在第(1)款所述行为发生时采取何种行动。

注释：

附注引文

M16 1993年第36章。

第131条 对交易的影响

根据本部分处以的罚款不导致任何交易无效或无法履行。

PART IX HEARINGS AND APPEALS

Annotations:

Modifications etc. (not altering text)

C124 Pt. IX (ss. 132–137) applied (17.8.2001 for certain purposes otherwise 1.12.2001) by 1986 c. 53, s. 46A(7) (as substituted (17.8.2001 for certain purposes otherwise 1.12.2001) by S.I. 2001/2617, arts. 2, 8, 13(1), Sch. 3 Pt. II para. 148 (with art. 13(1) Sch. 5)); S.I. 2001/3538, art. 2(1)

Pt. IX (ss. 132–137) applied (17.8.2001 for certain purposes otherwise 1.12.2001) by 1992 c. 40, s. 58A(7) (as substituted (17.8.2001 for ceratin purposes otherwise 1.12.2001) by S.I. 2001/2617, arts. 2, 8, 13 (1), Sch. 3 Pt. I para. 75 (with art. 13 (3), Sch. 5)); S.I. 2001/3538, art. 2(1)

Pt. IX (ss. 132–137) applied (with modifications) (17.8.2001 for certain purposes otherwise 1.12.2001) by 1992 c. 40, s. 85 (4C) (4D) (as inserted (17.8.2001 for certain purposes otherwise 1.12.2001) by S.I. 2001/2617, arts. 2, 8, 13(1), Sch. 3 Pt. I para. 95 (with art. 13(3), Sch. 5)); S.I. 2001/3538, art. 2(1)

Pt. IX (ss. 132–137) applied (with modifications) (17.8.2001 for certain purposes otherwise 1.12.2001) by 1986 c. 53, s. 93 (6B) (6C) (as substituted (17.8.2001 for certain purposes otherwise 1.12.2001) by S.I. 2001/2617, arts. 2, 8, 13(1), Sch. 3 Pt. II para. 177(d) (with art. 13(3), Sch. 5)); S.I. 2001/3538, art. 2(1)

132 The Financial Services and Markets Tribunal.

(1) For the purposes of this Act, there is to be a tribunal known as the Financial Services and Markets Tribunal (but referred to in this Act as "the Tribunal").

(2) The Tribunal is to have the functions conferred on it by or under this Act.

(3) The Lord Chancellor may by rules make such provision as appears to him to be

第九部分　受理和上诉

注释：

修改等(不涉及条文内容)

C124　第九部分(第132条至第137条)为特定目的于2001年8月17日，否则于2001年12月1日依照1986年第53章第46A条第(7)款{为特定目的于2001年8月17日，否则于2001年12月1日依照制定法文件S.I.2001/2617第2条、第8条、第13条第(1)款，附录3第二部分第148条[与附录5第13条第(1)款]被替代}；制定法文件S.I.2001/3538第2条第(1)款适用；

第九部分(第132条至第137条)为特定目的于2001年8月17日，否则于2001年12月1日依照1992年第40章第58A条第(7)款{为特定目的于2001年8月17日，否则于2001年12月1日依照制定法文件S.I.2001/2617第2条、第8条、第13条第(1)款，附录3第一部分第75条[与附录5第13条第(3)款]被替代}；制定法文件S.I.2001/3538第2条第(1)款适用；

第九部分(第132条至第137条)(已修订)为特定目的于2001年8月17日，否则于2001年12月1日依照1992年第40章第85条第(4C)款、第(4D)款{为特定目的于2001年8月17日，否则于2001年12月1日依照制定法文件S.I.2001/2617附录3第一部分第95条[与附录5第13条第(3)款]第2条、第8条、第13条第(1)款插入}；制定法文件S.I.2001/3538第2条第(1)款适用；

第九部分(第132条至第137条)(已修订)为特定目的于2001年8月17日，否则于2001年12月1日依照1986年第53章第93条第(6B)款、第(6C)款{为特定目的于2001年8月17日，否则于2001年12月1日依照制定法文件S.I.2001/2617第2条、第8条、第13条第(1)款，附录3第二部分第177(d)条[与附录5第13条第(3)款]被替代}；制定法文件S.I.2001/3538第2条第(1)款适用。

第132条　金融服务与市场裁判所

(1)为实施本法，将成立称为金融服务与市场裁判所的裁判所(但在本法中称为裁判所)。

(2)裁判所享有本法或依照本法赋予的职能。

(3)司法大臣可以通过规则制定其认为对裁判所程序的进行必要或适宜的规定。

necessary or expedient in respect of the conduct of proceedings before the Tribunal.

(4) Schedule 13 is to have effect as respects the Tribunal and its proceedings (but does not limit the Lord Chancellor's powers under this section).

Annotations:

Modifications etc. (not altering text)

C125 S. 132 amended (18.7.2002 for certain purposes and 21.8.2002 otherwise) by The Electronic Commerce Directive (Financial Services and Markets) Regulations 2002 (S.I. 2002/1775), regs. 1, 12(4)

Commencement Information

I39 S. 132 wholly in force at 3.9.2001; s. 132 not in force at Royal Assent see s. 431(2); s. 132(1) in force for specifed purposes at 25.2.2001 by S.I. 2001/516, art. 2(c), Sch. Pt. 3; s. 132(3) in force at 25.2.2001 by S.I. 2001/516, art. 2(a), Sch. Pt. I; s. 132 in force in so far as not already in force at 3.9.2001 by S.I. 2001/2632, art. 2(2), Sch. Pt. 2

133 Proceedings: general provision.

(1) A reference to the Tribunal under this Act must be made before the end of—

(a) the period of 28 days beginning with the date on which the decision notice or supervisory notice in question is given; or

(b) such other period as may be specified in rules made under section 132.

(2) Subject to rules made under section 132, the Tribunal may allow a reference to be made after the end of that period.

(3) On a reference the Tribunal may consider any evidence relating to the subject-matter of the reference, whether or not it was available to the Authority at the material time.

(4) On a reference the Tribunal must determine what (if any) is the appropriate action for the Authority to take in relation to the matter referred to it.

(5) On determining a reference, the Tribunal must remit the matter to the Authority with such directions (if any) as the Tribunal considers appropriate for giving effect to its determination.

(6) In determining a reference made as a result of a decision notice, the Tribunal may not direct the Authority to take action which the Authority would not, as a result of section 388(2), have had power to take when giving the decision notice.

(7) In determining a reference made as a result of a supervisory notice, the Tribunal may not direct the Authority to take action which would have otherwise required the giving of a decision notice.

(8)The Tribunal may, on determining a reference, make recommendations as to the

(4)附录13将对裁判所及其程序有效(但不限制司法大臣在本条项下的权力)。

注释:

修改等(不涉及条文内容)

C125　第132条为特定目的于2002年7月18日,否则于2002年8月21日依照《2002年电子商务指令条例》(金融服务与市场)(制定法文件S.I.2002/1775)第1条、第12条第(4)款修正。

实施日期

I39　第132条于2001年9月3日全部生效;第132条在副署时未生效,见附录第431条第(2)款;第132条第(1)款为特定目的于2001年2月25日依照制定法文件S.I.2001/516第2条第(c)款、附录第三部分生效;第132条第(3)款于2001年2月25日依照制定法文件S.I.2001/516第2条第(a)款、附录第一部分生效;第132条如于2001年9月3日尚未生效,则依照制定法文件S.I.2001/2632第2条第(2)款、附录第二部分生效。

第133条　程序:一般规定

(1)依照本法规定诉至裁判所必须在下列期间结束前进行:

(a)相关决定通知或监督通知送达之日起28日内;或

(b)依照第132条制定的规则规定的其他期间。

(2)裁判所可允许在上述期间届满后提起诉讼,但须符合第132条制定的规则。

(3)对于所诉事项,裁判所可考虑任何关于主要内容的证据,无论其在重要期间是否能够由管理局获得。

(4)对于所诉事项,裁判所必须决定管理局对所提交的事项采取何种(如有)适当行动。

(5)对所诉事项作出裁决时,裁判所必须将该事项发回管理局,并附带裁判所认为适当的指示(如有),以使其裁决生效。

(6)对因决定通知而诉至裁判所的事项作出裁决时,裁判所不得指示管理局采取管理局在发出决定通知时因第388条第(2)款规定而无权采取的行动。

(7)对因监督通知而诉至裁判所的事项作出裁决时,裁判所不得指示管理局采取可能会要求发出决定通知的行动。

(8)裁判所对所诉事项作出裁决时,可以对管理局的监管规定或监管程序提出

Authority's regulating provisions or its procedures.

(9) The Authority must not take the action specified in a decision notice

(a) during the period within which the matter to which the decision notice relates may be referred to the Tribunal; and

(b) if the matter is so referred, until the reference, and any appeal against the Tribunal's determination, has been finally disposed of.

(10) The Authority must act in accordance with the determinationof, and any direction given by, the Tribunal.

(11) An order of the Tribunal may be enforced

(a) as if it were an order of a county court; or

(b) in Scotland, as if it were an order of the Court of Session.

(12) "Supervisory notice" has the same meaning as in section 395.

Annotations:

Modifications etc. (not altering text)

C126 S. 133 applied (1.12.2001) by S.I. 2001/1228, regs. 1(2)(c), 11 (with reg. 1(2)(3)); S.I. 2001/3538, art. 2(1)

S. 133 applied (with modifications) (10.8.2001) by S.I. 2001/2636, arts. 1(2)(a), 58(6)

S. 133 applied (with modifications) (1.12.2001) by S.I. 2001/2657, arts. 1(1), 10(6), 11(6) (which was revoked (8.10.2001) by 2001/3083, arts. (2), 23); S.I. 2001/3538, art. 2(1)

S. 133 applied (with modifications) (1.12.2001) by S.I. 2001/3083, arts. 1(2), 10(6), 11(6); S.I. 2001/3538, art. 2(1)

S. 133 applied (with modifications) (1.12.2001) by S.I. 2001/3592, arts. 1(2), 62(2), 79(2) (with art. 23(2))

S. 133 applied (1.12.2001) by S.I. 2001/3592, arts. 1(2), 83(3) (with art. 23(2))

C127 S. 133 amended (18.7.2002 for certain purposes and 21.8.2002 otherwise) by The Electronic Commerce Directive (Financial Services and Markets) Regulations 2002 (S.I. 2002/1775), regs. 1, 12(4)

C128 S. 133 (6) modified (1.12.2001) by S.I. 2001/2957, arts. 1, 12 (8); S.I. 2001/3538, art. 2(1)

建议。

(9)管理局在下列期间不得采取决定通知中规定的行动:

(a)在与决定通知相关的事项可诉至裁判所的期间内;以及

(b)如将该事项诉至裁判所,在诉至裁判所的事项及任何针对裁判所裁决的上诉最终审结前。

(10)管理局必须根据裁判所的裁决以及其作出的任何指示采取行动。

(11)裁判所的命令可强制执行

(a)效力等同于郡法院的命令;或

(b)在苏格兰,效力等同于(苏格兰)高等民事法院的命令。

(12)"监督通知"含义同第395条。

注释:

修改等(不涉及条文内容)

C126　第133条于2001年12月1日依照制定法文件S.I.2001/1228第1条第(2)款第(c)项、第11条[与第1条第(2)款、第(3)款];制定法文件S.I.2001/3538第2条第(1)款适用;

第133条(已修订)于2001年8月10日依照制定法文件S.I.2001/2636第1条第(2)款第(a)项、第58条第(6)款适用;

第133条(已修订)于2001年12月1日依照制定法文件S.I.2001/2657第1条第(1)款、第10条第(6)款、第11条第(6)款[于2001年10月8日依照制定法文件2001/3083第(2)条、第23条撤销];制定法文件S.I.2001/3538第2条第(1)款适用;

第133条(已修订)于2001年12月1日依照制定法文件S.I.2001/3083第1条第(2)款、第10条第(6)款、第11条第(6)款;制定法文件S.I.2001/3538第2条第(1)款适用;

第133条依照制定法文件S.I.2001/3592第1条第(2)款、第62条第(2)款、第79条第(2)款[与第23条第(2)款]适用;

第133条于2001年12月1日依照制定法文件S.I.2001/3592第1条第(2)款、第83条第(3)款[与第23条第(2)款]适用。

C127　第133条于2002年7月18日为特定目的,否则于2002年8月21日依照《2002年电子商务指令条例》(金融服务与市场)(制定法文件S.I.2002/1775)第1条、第12条第(4)款修正。

C128　第133条第(6)款于2001年12月1日依制定法文件S.I.2001/2957第1条、第12条第(8)款;制定法文件S.I.2001/3538第2条第(1)款修订。

Legal assistance before the Tribunal

134 Legal assistance scheme.

(1) The Lord Chancellor may by regulations establish a scheme governing the provision of legal assistance in connection with proceedings before the Tribunal.

(2) If the Lord Chancellor establishes a scheme under subsection (1), it must provide that a person is eligible for assistance only if—

(a) he falls within subsection (3); and

(b) he fulfils such other criteria (if any) as may be prescribed as a result of section 135 (1)(d).

(3) A person falls within this subsection if he is an individual who has referred a matter to the Tribunal under section 127(4).

(4) In this Part of this Act "the legal assistance scheme" means any scheme in force under subsection (1).

135 Provisions of the legal assistance scheme.

(1) The legal assistance scheme may, in particular, make provision as to—

(a) the kinds of legal assistance that may be provided;

(b) the persons by whom legal assistance may be provided;

(c) the manner in which applications for legal assistance are to be made;

(d) the criteria on which eligibility for legal assistance is to be determined;

(e) the persons or bodies by whom applications are to be determined;

(f) appeals against refusals of applications;

(g) the revocation or variation of decisions;

(h) its administration and the enforcement of its provisions.

(2) Legal assistance under the legal assistance scheme may be provided subject to conditions or restrictions, including conditions as to the making of contributions by the person to whom it is provided.

136 Funding of the legal assistance scheme.

(1) The Authority must pay to the Lord Chancellor such sums at such times as he may, from time to time, determine in respect of the anticipated or actual cost of legal assistance provided in connection with proceedings before the Tribunal under the legal assistance scheme.

(2) In order to enable it to pay any sum which it is obliged to pay under subsection (1), the Authority must make rules requiring the payment to it by authorised persons or any class of authorised person of specified amounts or amounts calculated in a specified way.

(3) Sums received by the Lord Chancellor under subsection (1) must be paid into the Consolidated Fund.

(4) The Lord Chancellor must, out of money provided by Parliament fund the cost of

裁判所诉讼前的法律协助

第134条 法律协助计划

(1)司法大臣可制定法规,就规范裁判所程序相关法律协助条款建立计划。

(2)如司法大臣依照第(1)款规定建立了法律协助计划,则其中必须规定只有在下列情况下才有资格获得协助:

(a)属于第(3)款规定的范围;且

(b)满足第135条第(1)款第(d)项可能规定的其他条件(如有)。

(3)依照第127条第(4)款将事项诉至裁判所的个人属于本款规定的范围。

(4)在本法的本部分中,"法律协助计划"系指任何依照第(1)款规定生效的计划。

第135条 法律协助计划的规定

(1)法律协助计划可特别就下列事项作出规定:

(a)可能提供的法律协助的种类;

(b)可能提供法律协助的人;

(c)法律协助申请的提出方式;

(d)判断可以获得法律协助资格的标准;

(e)对申请作出决定的人或机关;

(f)对申请被驳回的上诉;

(g)决定的撤销或变更;

(h)规定的管理和执行。

(2)法律协助计划规定的法律协助提供可附条件或限制,包括由协助受益人分担费用的条件。

第136条 法律协助计划经费

(1)管理局必须在司法大臣决定的时间向其支付司法大臣就裁判所审理的法律程序中根据法律协助计划提供法律协助的预期或实际费用而不时确定的金额。

(2)为了能够支付根据第(1)款应当支付的金额,管理局必须制定规则,要求获授权人或任何种类的获授权人向其支付规定的金额或以规定的方法计算的金额。

(3)司法大臣根据第(1)款收到的金额必须存入统一基金。

(4)司法大臣必须从议会拨款中为根据法律协助计划提供的与裁判所审理的程

legal assistance provided in connection with proceedings before the Tribunal under the legal assistance scheme.

(5) Subsection (6) applies if, as respects a period determined by the Lord Chancellor, the amount paid to him under subsection (1) as respects that period exceeds the amount he has expended in that period under subsection (4).

(6) The Lord Chancellor must—

(a) repay, out of money provided by Parliament, the excess to the Authority; or

(b) take the excess into account on the next occasion on which he makes a determination under subsection (1).

(7) The Authority must make provision for any sum repaid to it under subsection (6)(a)—

(a) to be distributed among—

(i) the authorised persons on whom a levy was imposed in the period in question as a result of rules made under subsection (2); or

(ii) such of those persons as it may determine;

(b) to be applied in order to reduce any amounts which those persons, or such of them as it may determine, are or will be liable to pay to the Authority, whether under rules made under subsection (2) or otherwise; or

(c) to be partly so distributed and partly so applied.

(8) If the Authority considers that it is not practicable to deal with any part of a sum repaid to it under subsection (6)(a) in accordance with provision made by it as a result of subsection (7), it may, with the consent the Lord Chancellor, apply or dispose of that part of that sum in such manner as it considers appropriate.

(9) "Specified" means specified in the rules.

Annotations:

Commencement Information

I40 S. 136 wholly in force at 3.9.2001; s. 136 not in force at Royal Assent see s. 431(2); s. 136 in force for specified purposes at 18.6.2001 by S.I. 2001/1820, art. 2, Sch.; s. 136 in force in so far as not already in force at 3.9.2001 by S.I. 2001/2632, art. 2(2), Sch. Pt. 2

Appeals

137 Appeal on a point of law.

(1) A party to a reference to the Tribunal may with permission appeal—

(a) to the Court of Appeal, or

(b) in Scotland, to the Court of Session,

序有关的法律协助提供费用。

(5)如在司法大臣决定的期间内,依照第(1)款向司法大臣支付的金额超过了依照第(4)款在该期间内花费的金额,则适用第(6)款规定。

(6)司法大臣必须

(a)从议会拨款中向管理局返还超出部分;或

(b)在下一次根据第(1)款作出决定时将超出部分考虑在内。

(7)管理局必须规定任何依照第(6)款第(a)项返还的金额

(a)在下列人员中分配:

(i)在相关期间内由于依照第(2)款而制定的规则而被征收款项的获授权人;或

(ii)管理局决定的其他人;

(b)用于为减少上述人或管理局确定的人应向管理局支付的金额,无论基于依照第(2)款制定的规则还是其他;或

(c)部分分配或部分使用。

(8)如管理局认为依照第(7)款制定的规则用于处理依照第(6)款第(a)项向其返还的金额不可行,则可经司法大臣同意,以其认为适当的方式使用或处理该金额中经同意的部分。

(9)"规定的"系指规则中规定的。

注释:

实施日期

I40　第136条于2001年9月3日全部生效;第136条在副署时尚未生效,见附录第431条第(2)款;第136条为特定目的于2001年6月18日依照制定法文件S.I.2001/1820第2条、附录生效;第136条如于2001年9月3日尚未生效,则依照制定法文件S.I.2001/2632第2条第(2)款、附录第二部分生效。

上　诉

第137条　基于法律问题上诉

(1)诉至裁判所事项中的一方当事人经许可

(a)可以上诉至上诉法院,或

(b)在苏格兰,可以上诉至(苏格兰)高等民事法院,

on a point of law arising from a decision of the Tribunal disposing of the reference.

(2) "Permission" means permission given by the Tribunal or by the Court of Appeal or (in Scotland) the Court of Session.

(3) If, on an appeal under subsection (1), the court considers that the decision of the Tribunal was wrong in law, it may—

(a) remit the matter to the Tribunal for rehearing and determination by it; or

(b) itself make a determination.

(4) An appeal may not be brought from a decision of the Court of Appeal under subsection (3) except with the leave of—

(a) the Court of Appeal; or

(b) the House of Lords.

(5) An appeal lies, with the leave of the Court of Session or the House of Lords, from any decision of the Court of Session under this section, and such leave may be given on such terms as to costs, expenses or otherwise as the Court of Session or the House of Lords may determine.

(6) Rules made under section 132 may make provision for regulating or prescribing any matters incidental to or consequential on an appeal under this section.

Annotations:

Modifications etc. (not altering text)

C129 S. 137 applied (with modifications) (10.8.2001) by S.I. 2001/2636, arts. 1(2)(a), 58(6)

Commencement Information

I41 S. 137 wholly in force at 3.9.2001; s. 137 not in force at Royal Assent see s. 431(2); s. 137(6) in force at 25.2.2001 by S.I. 2001/516, art. 2(a), Sch. Pt. 1; s. 137 in force in so far as not already in force at 3.9.2001 by S.I. 2001/2632, art. 2(2), Sch. Pt. 2

上诉基于裁判所处理所诉事项的判决中出现的法律问题。

(2)"许可"系指裁判所或上诉法院或(苏格兰)高等民事法院作出的许可。

(3)如对于依照第(1)款作出的上诉,法院认为裁判所的裁决在法律上有错误,则可以

(a)将该事项发回裁判所重新审理并由其作出裁决;或

(b)自行作出判决。

(4)对上诉法院依照第(3)款作出的判决不得提起上诉,除非获得

(a)上诉法院的许可;或

(b)上议院的许可。

(5)经(苏格兰)高等民事法院或上议院的许可,可针对(苏格兰)高等民事法院依照本条作出的任何判决提起上诉。这种许可可以基于成本、费用或(苏格兰)高等民事法院或上议院可能确定的其他因素等条件作出。

(6)根据第132条制定的规则可为规范或规定任何本条规定上诉的附带事项或相应事项而作出规定。

注释:

修改等(不涉及条文内容)

C129 第137条(已修订)于2001年8月10日依照制定法文件S.I.2001/2636第1条第(2)款第(a)项、第58条第(6)款适用。

实施日期

I41 第137条于2001年9月3日全部生效;第137条在副署时尚未生效,见附录第431条第(2)款;第137条第(6)款于2001年2月25日依照制定法文件S.I.2001/516第2条第(a)款、附录第一部分生效;第137条如于2001年9月3日尚未生效,则依照制定法文件S.I.2001/2632第2条第(2)款、附录第二部分生效。

PART X RULES AND GUIDANCE

CHAPTER I RULE-MAKING POWERS

138 General rule-making power.

(1) The Authority may make such rules applying to authorised persons—

(a) with respect to the carrying on by them of regulated activities, or

(b) with respect to the carrying on by them of activities which are not regulated activities,

as appear to it to be necessary or expedient for the purpose of protecting the interests of consumers.

(2) Rules made under this section are referred to in this Act as the Authority's general rules.

(3) The Authority's power to make general rules is not limited by any other power which it has to make regulating provisions.

(4) The Authority's general rules may make provision applying to authorised persons even though there is no relationship between the authorised persons to whom the rules will apply and the persons whose interests will be protected by the rules.

(5) General rules may contain requirements which take into account, in the case of an authorised person who is a member of a group, any activity of another member of the group.

(6) General rules may not—

(a) make provision prohibiting an EEA firm from carrying on, or holding itself out as carrying on, any activity which it has permission conferred by Part II of Schedule 3 to carry on in the United Kingdom;

(b) make provision, as respects an EEA firm, about any matter responsibility for which is, under any of the single market directives, reserved to the firm's home state regulator.

(7) "Consumers" means persons—

第十部分 规则与指导

第一章 规则制定权

第138条 一般规则制定权[1]

(1)管理局可就下列事项制定适用于获授权人的规则:

(a)获授权人从事受监管活动,或

(b)获授权人从事非受监管活动,

如管理局认为为了保护消费者的利益这样做是必要或适宜的。[2]

(2)依照本条制定的规则在本法中称为管理局的一般规则。

(3)管理局制定一般规则的权力不受其享有的任何其他监管规定制定权限制。

(4)管理局的一般规则可以作出适用于获授权人的规定,即使适用该规则的获授权人与利益受该规则保护的人之间没有关联。

(5)获授权人为集团成员时,一般规则中可以包括将该集团其他成员的任何活动考虑在内的要求。

(6)一般规则不得

(a)规定禁止欧洲经济区企业进行,或自称进行任何其具有依照附录3第二部分授予的许可,可以在联合王国从事的活动;

(b)对于欧洲经济区企业,对根据任何单一市场指令,其责任保留给该企业母国监管机关的任何事项作出规定。

(7)"消费者"系指下列人员:

---

1 本条依照《2010年金融服务法》附录2第一部分第11条修订。——译者注

2 本款依照《2010年金融服务法》第3条第4款修订。——译者注

(a) who use, have used, or are or may be contemplating using, any of the services provided by—

(i) authorised persons in carrying on regulated activities; or

(ii) persons acting as appointed representatives;

(b) who have rights or interests which are derived from, or are otherwise attributable to, the use of any such services by other persons; or

(c) who have rights or interests which may be adversely affected by the use of any such services by persons acting on their behalf or in a fiduciary capacity in relation to them.

(8) If an authorised person is carrying on a regulated activity in his capacity as a trustee, the persons who are, have been or may be beneficiaries of the trust are to be treated as persons who use, have used or are or may be contemplating using services provided by the authorised person in his carrying on of that activity.

(9) For the purposes of subsection (7) a person who deals with an authorised person in the course of the authorised person's carrying on of a regulated activity is to be treated as using services provided by the authorised person in carrying on those activities.

Annotations:

Modifications etc. (not altering text)

C130 S. 138 modified (18.6.2001) by S.I. 2001/1821, arts. 1(1), 3(1)-(3)

C131 S. 138: power to make rules amended (18.7.2002 for certain purposes and 21.8.2002 otherwise) by The Electronic Commerce Directive (Financial Services and Markets) Regulations 2002 (S.I. 2002/1775), regs. 1, 3(1)(4)

S. 138 extended (with modifications) (2.7.2002) by The Financial Services and Markets Act 2002 (Consequential Amendments and Transitional Provisions) (Credit Unions) Order 2002 (S.I. 2002/1501), art. 4

C132 S. 138(4)(5) amended (18.7.2002 for certain purposes and 21.8.2002 otherwise) by The Electronic Commerce Directive (Financial Services and Markets) Regulations 2002 (S.I. 2002/1775), regs. 1, 3(2)

C133 S. 138(4)(5) amended (18.7.2002 for certain purposes and 21.8.2002 otherwise) by The Electronic Commerce Directive (Financial Services and Markets) Regulations 2002 (S.I. 2002/1775), regs. 1, 3(2)

C134 S. 138 (7)- (9) amended (18.7.2002 for certain purposes and 21.8.2002 otherwise) by The Electronic Commerce Directive (Financial Services and Markets) Regulations 2002 (S.I. 2002/1775), regs. 1, 3(2) (a)使用,或曾经使用,或正在或可能计划使用任何下列服务的人:

(i)由获授权人在进行受监管活动时提供的服务;或

(ii)以被任命代表身份从事活动的人提供的服务;

(b)从使用其他人提供的任何上述服务中获得,或由该服务引起权利或利益的人;或

(c)代表其实施行为的人或与其有信托关系的人使用任何上述服务可能会使其权利或利益受到负面影响的人。

(8)如获授权人正在以受托人的身份实施受监管活动,则目前、曾经是或可能是该信托受益人的人视为使用,或曾经使用或正在或可能计划使用由获授权人在从事该活动的过程中提供的服务的人。

(9)就第(7)款而言,在获授权人进行受监管活动的过程中与获授权人进行交易的人,视为使用由获授权人在从事上述活动的过程中提供的服务的人。

注释:

修改等(不涉及条文内容)

C130　第138条于2001年6月18日依照制定法文件S.I.2001/1821第1条(1)款、第3条第(1)款至第(3)款修订。

C131　第138条:规则制定权为特定目的于2002年7月18日,否则于2002年8月21日依照《2002年电子商务指令条例》(金融服务与市场)(制定法文件S.I.2002/1775)第1条、第3条第(1)款、第(4)款修正;

第138条(已修订)于2002年7月2日依照《2002年金融服务与市场法》(间接修改和过渡性规定)(信用合作社)2002号令(制定法文件S.I.2002/1501)第4条扩大适用范围。

C132　第138条第(4)款、第(5)款为特定目的于2002年7月18日,否则于2002年8月21日《2002年电子商务指令条例》(金融服务与市场)(制定法文件S.I.2002/1775)第1条、第3条第(2)款修正。

C133　第138条第(4)款、第(5)款为特定目的于2002年7月18日,否则于2002年8月21日《2002年电子商务指令条例》(金融服务与市场)(制定法文件S.I.2002/1775)第1条、第3条第(2)款修正。

C134　第138条第(7)款至第(9)款为特定目的于2002年7月18日,否则于2002年8月21日依照《2002年电子商务指令条例》(金融服务与市场)(制定法文件S.I.2002/1775)第1条、第3条第(2)款修正。

C135 S. 138 (7)- (9) modified (18.7.2002 for certain purposes and 21.8.2002 otherwise) by The Electronic Commerce Directive (Financial Services and Markets) Regulations 2002 (S.I. 2002/1775), regs. 1, 3(3)

C136 S. 138 (7)- (9) amended (18.7.2002 for certain purposes and 21.8.2002 otherwise) by The Electronic Commerce Directive (Financial Services and Markets) Regulations 2002 (S.I. 2002/1775), regs. 1, 3(2)

C137 S. 138 (7)- (9) amended (18.7.2002 for certain purposes and 21.8.2002 otherwise) by The Electronic Commerce Directive (Financial Services and Markets) Regulations 2002 (S.I. 2002/1775), regs. 1, 3(2)

C138 S. 138 (7)- (9) modified (18.7.2002 for certain purposes and 21.8.2002 otherwise) by The Electronic Commerce Directive (Financial Services and Markets) Regulations 2002 (S.I. 2002/1775), regs. 1, 3(3)

139 Miscellaneous ancillary matters.

(1) Rules relating to the handling of money held by an authorised person in specified circumstances ("clients' money") may—

(a) make provision which results in that clients' money being held on trust in accordance with the rules;

(b) treat two or more accounts as a single account for specified purposes (which may include the distribution of money held in the accounts);

(c) authorise the retention by the authorised person of interest accruing on the clients' money; and

(d) make provision as to the distribution of such interest which is not to be retained by him.

(2) An institution with which an account is kept in pursuance of rules relating to the handling of clients' money does not incur any liability as constructive trustee if money is wrongfully paid from the account, unless the institution permits the payment—

(a) with knowledge that it is wrongful; or

(b) having deliberately failed to make enquiries in circumstances in which a reasonable and honest person would have done so.

(3) In the application of subsection (1) to Scotland, the referenceto money being held on trust is to be read as a reference to its being held as agent for the person who is entitled to call for it to be paid over to him or to be paid on his direction or to have it otherwise credited to him.

(4) Rules may—

(a) confer rights on persons to rescind agreements with, or withdraw offers to, authorised

C135　第138条第(7)款至第(9)款为特定目的于2002年7月18日，否则于2002年8月21日《2002年电子商务指令条例》(金融服务与市场)(制定法文件S.I.2002/1775)第1条、第3条第(3)款修订。

C136　第138条第(7)款至第(9)款为特定目的于2002年7月18日，否则于2002年8月21日依照《2002年电子商务指令条例》(制定法文件S.I.2002/1775)第1条、第3条第(2)款修正。

C137　第138条第(7)款至第(9)款为特定目的于2002年7月18日，否则于2002年8月21日依照《2002年电子商务指令条例》(金融服务与市场)(制定法文件S.I.2002/1775)第1条、第3条第(2)款修正。

C138　第138条第(7)款至第(9)款为特定目的于2002年7月18日，否则于2002年8月21日依照《2002年电子商务指令条例》(金融服务与市场)(制定法文件S.I.2002/1775)第1条、第3条第(3)款修订。

第139条　其他附带事项[1]

(1)关于处理获授权人在规定情况下所持有资金(以下简称客户资金)的规则可以

(a)作出使客户资金可以根据规则以信托形式持有的规定；

(b)为规定的目的(包括分配账户中的资金)，将两个或以上账户视为一个账户；

(c)授权获授权人保留因客户资金获得的利息；及

(d)对不由获授权人留存的利息的分配作出规定。

(2)如资金被错误地从账户中支出，根据与处理客户资金有关的规则维护账户的机构不产生任何作为法律推定受托人的责任，除非允许此项支付的机构

(a)明知该项支付是错误的；或

(b)在理智且诚实的人会询问的情况下，故意不询问。

(3)第(1)款适用于苏格兰时，述及以信托形式持有的资金，视为资金被有权要求向其进行支付、或按照其指示进行支付或以其他方式存入其银行账户的代理人所持有。

(4)规则可以

(a)授权当事人在规定的期间内解除与获授权人的协议或撤回发给获授权人的要

1 本条依照《2010年金融服务法》第6条、第7条修订。——译者注

persons within a specified period; and

(b) make provision, in respect of authorised persons and persons exercising those rights, for the restitution of property and the making or recovery of payments where those rights are exercised.

(5) "Rules" means general rules.

(6) "Specified" means specified in the rules.

140 Restriction on managers of authorised unit trust schemes.

(1) The Authority may make rules prohibiting an authorised person who has permission to act as the manager of an authorised unit trust scheme from carrying on a specified activity.

(2) Such rules may specify an activity which is not a regulated activity.

141 Insurance business rules.

(1) The Authority may make rules prohibiting an authorised person who has permission to effect or carry out contracts of insurance from carrying on a specified activity.

(2) Such rules may specify an activity which is not a regulated activity.

(3) The Authority may make rules in relation to contracts entered into by anauthorized person in the course of carrying on business which consists of the effecting or carrying out of contracts of long–term insurance.

(4) Such rules may, in particular—

(a) restrict the descriptions of property or indices of the value of property by reference to which the benefits under such contracts may be determined;

(b) make provision, in the interests of the protection of policyholders, for the substitution of one description of property, or index of value, by reference to which the benefits under a contract are to be determined for another such description of property or index.

(5) Rules made under this section are referred to in this Act as insurance business rules.

142 Insurance business: regulations supplementing Authority's rules.

(1) The Treasury may make regulations for the purpose of preventing a person who is not an authorised person but who—

(a) is a parent undertaking of an authorised person who has permission to effect or carry out contracts of insurance, and

(b) falls within a prescribed class,

from doing anything to lessen the effectiveness of asset identification rules.

(2) "Asset identification rules" means rules made by the Authority which require an authorised person who has permission to effect or carry out contracts of insurance to identify assets which belong to him and which are maintained in respect of a particular aspect of his business.

约;及

(b)对于获授权人和行使上述权利的人,对在行使上述权利时恢复财产及作出或追偿付款作出规定。

(5)“规则”系指一般规则。

(6)“规定的”系指一般规则中规定的。

第140条　对获授权单位信托计划管理人的限制

(1)管理局可以制定规则,规定具有以获授权单位信托计划管理人身份实施活动的获授权人不得实施规定的活动。

(2)上述规则可以规定何种活动不是受监管活动。

第141条　保险业务规则

(1)管理局可以制定规则,禁止具有订立或履行保险合同许可的获授权人从事规定的活动。

(2)这种规则可规定何种活动不是受监管活动。

(3)管理局可以对获授权人在进行包括订立或履行长期保险合同的业务活动过程中订立的合同制定规则。

(4)这些规则可以特别

(a)限制据以决定此种合同项下收益的财产或财产价值指数的类型;

(b)为了保护保单持有人的利益,规定将据以决定此种合同项下收益的一类财产或财产价值指数替换为另一类财产或财产价值指数。

(5)依照本条制定的规则在本法中称为保险业务规则。

第142条　保险业务:补充管理局规则的法规

(1)财政部可以制定法规,以防止不是获授权人,但有下列情况的人:

(a)是具有订立或履行保险合同的许可的获授权人的母企业,且

(b)属于规定的种类,

从事任何削弱资产识别规则效力的活动。

(2)“资产识别规则”,系指管理局制定的要求具有订立或履行保险合同许可的获授权人识别出属于该获授权人且该获授权人为其特定方面的业务而保有的财产的规则。

(3) The regulations may, in particular, include provision—

(a) prohibiting the payment of dividends;

(b) prohibiting the creation of charges;

(c) making charges created in contravention of the regulations void.

(4) The Treasury may by regulations provide that, in prescribed circumstances, charges created in contravention of asset identification rules are void.

(5) A person who contravenes regulations under subsection (1) is guilty of an offence and liable on summary conviction to a fine not exceeding level 5 on the standard scale.

(6) "Charges" includes mortgages (or in Scotland securities over property).

Annotations:

Commencement Information

I42 S. 142 wholly in force at 1.12.2001; s. 142 not in force at Royal Assent see s. 431 (2); s. 142(1)-(4)(6) in force at 25.2.2001 by S.I. 2001/516, art. 2(a), Sch. Pt. 1; s. 142 in force in so far as not already in force at 1.12.2001 by S.I. 2001/3538, art. 2(1)

143 Endorsement of codes etc.

(1) The Authority may make rules ("endorsing rules")—

(a) endorsing the City Code on Takeovers and Mergers issued by the Panel on Takeovers and Mergers;

(b) endorsing the Rules Governing Substantial Acquisitions of Shares issued by the Panel.

(2) Endorsement may be—

(a) as respects all authorised persons; or

(b) only as respects a specified kind of authorised person.

(3) At any time when endorsing rules are in force, and if asked to do so by the Panel, the Authority may exercise its powers under Part Ⅳ or section 66 as if failure to comply with an endorsed provision was a ground entitling the Authority to exercise those powers.

(4) At any time when endorsing rules are in force and if asked to do so by the Panel, the Authority may exercise its powers under Part ⅩⅢ, ⅩⅣ or XXV as if the endorsed provisions were rules applying to the persons in respect of whom they are endorsed.

(5) For the purposes of subsections (3) and (4), a failure to comply with a requirement imposed, or ruling given, under an endorsed provision is to be treated as a failure to comply with the endorsed provision under which that requirement was imposed or ruling was given.

(6) If endorsed provisions are altered, subsections (3) and (4) apply to them as altered, but only if before the alteration the Authority has notified the Panel (and has not withdrawn its notification) that it is satisfied with the Panel's consultation procedures.

(3)法规可以特别包含下列规定:

(a)禁止支付股利;

(b)禁止创设任何收费;

(c)使违反法规创设的收费无效。

(4)财政部可以通过法规规定,在特定情况下,违反资产识别规则而创设的收费是无效的。

(5)违反根据第(1)款制定的规则构成犯罪,应经简易程序定罪处以不超过标准等级第5级数额的罚金。

(6)“收费”包括抵押(或者在苏格兰称为财产担保)。

注释:

实施日期

I42 第142条于2001年12月1日全部生效;第142条在副署时尚未生效,见第431条第(2)款;第142条第(1)款至第(4)款、第(6)款于2001年2月25日依照制定法文件S.I. 2001/516第2条第(a)款、附录第一部分生效;第142条如在2001年12月1日尚未生效,则依照制定法文件S.I.2001/3538第2条第(1)款生效。

第143条 准则等的认可

(1)管理局可以制定规则(以下简称认可规则)

(a)认可由购买与合并委员会颁布的《金融城购买与合并准则》;

(b)认可委员会颁布的《大宗股份购买管理规定》。

(2)认可可以

(a)对所有获授权人作出;或

(b)仅对规定种类的获授权人作出。

(3)在认可规则有效的任何时间,如委员会有要求,则管理局可以行使第四部分或第66条规定的权力,等同于管理局以未遵守被认可的规定为理由行使上述权力。

(4)在认可规则有效的任何时间,如委员会有要求,则管理局可以行使第十三部分、第十四部分或第二十五部分规定的权力,等同于被认可的规定是对其进行认可的人适用的规则。

(5)就第(3)款和第(4)款而言,未能遵守根据被认可的规定而提出的要求或作出的裁定,视为未能遵守据以提出要求或作出裁定的被认可规定。

(6)如被认可的规定被变更,第(3)款和第(4)款适用于变更后的规定,但是只有管理局在变更之前通知委员会(并且没有撤回其通知),管理局对委员会的磋商程序感到满意时,方可适用。

(7) "Consultation procedures" means procedures designed to provide an opportunity for persons likely to be affected by alterations to those provisions to make representations about proposed alterations to any of those provisions.

(8) Subsections (1), (2)(d), (4), (5), (6)(a) and (12) of section 155 apply (with the necessary modifications) to a proposal to give notification of the kind mentioned in subsection (6) as they apply to a proposal to make endorsing rules.

(9) This section applies in relation to particular provisions of the code or rules mentioned in subsection (1) as it applies to the code or the rules.

Annotations:

Commencement Information

I43 S. 143 wholly in force at 1.12.2001; s. 143 not in force at Royal Assent see s. 431 (2); s. 143 in force for specified purposes at 18.6.2001 by S.I. 2001/1820, art. 2, Sch.; s. 143 in force in so far as not already in force at 1.12.2001 by S.I. 2001/3538, art. 2(1)

Specific rules

144 Price stabilising rules.

(1) The Authority may make rules ("price stabilising rules") as to—

(a) the circumstances and manner in which,

(b) the conditions subject to which, and

(c) the time when or the period during which,

action may be taken for the purpose of stabilising the price of investments of specified kinds.

(2) Price stabilising rules—

(a) are to be made so as to apply only to authorised persons;

(b) may make different provision in relation to different kinds of investment.

(3) The Authority may make rules which, for the purposes of section 397(5)(b), treat a person who acts or engages in conduct—

(a) for the purpose of stabilising the price of investments, and

(b) in conformity with such provisions corresponding to price stabilising rules and made by a body or authority outside the United Kingdom as may be specified in the rules under this subsection,

as acting, or engaging in that conduct, for that purpose and in conformity with price stabilising rules.

(4) The Treasury may by order impose limitations on the power to make rules under this section.

(7)"磋商程序",系指为给可能受到规定变更影响的人提供就拟进行的规定变更作出陈述的机会而设计的程序。

(8)第155条第(1)款、第(2)款第(d)项、第(4)款、第(5)款、第(6)款第(a)项和第(12)款(和必要的修改一起)对发出第(6)款所述通知的提议适用,效力等同于对制定认可规则的提议适用。

(9)本条对第(1)款所述准则或法规中的特定规定适用,效力等同于对该准则或法规适用。

注释:

实施日期

I43 第143条于2001年12月1日全部生效;第143条在副署时尚未生效,见第431条第(2)款;第143条为特定目的于2001年6月18日依照制定法文件S.I.2001/1820第2条、附录生效;第143条如于2001年12月1日尚未生效,则依照制定法文件S.I.2001/3538第2条第(1)款生效。

特殊规则

第144条 价格稳定规则

(1)管理局可制定规则(以下简称价格稳定规则),规定在一定的

(a)情况和方式,

(b)条件,及

(c)时间点或时间段

为稳定规定种类投资的价格可以采取的行动。

(2)价格稳定规则

(a)仅为适用于获授权人而制定;

(b)对不同种类的投资可以作出不同的规定。

(3)可以为实施第397条第(5)款第(b)项制定规则,将实施或参与下列行为的人:

(a)以稳定投资价格为目的,并

(b)符合依照本条制定的规则中规定的联合王国以外的主体或主管机关制定的与价格稳定规则对等的规则,

视为为了该目的实施或参与该行为且符合价格稳定规则的人。

(4)财政部可以颁布法令,对依照本条制定规则的权力进行限制。

(5) Such an order may, in particular—

(a) specify the kinds of investment in relation to which price stabilising rules may make provision;

(b) specify the kinds of investment in relation to which rules made under subsection (3) may make provision;

(c) provide for price stabilising rules to make provision for action to be taken for the purpose of stabilising the price of investments only in such circumstances as the order may specify;

(d) provide for price stabilising rules to make provision for action to be taken for that purpose only at such times or during such periods as the order may specify.

(6) If provisions specified in rules made under subsection (3) are altered, the rules continue to apply to those provisions as altered, but only if before the alteration the Authority has notified the body or authority concerned (and has not withdrawn its notification) that it is satisfied with its consultation procedures.

(7) "Consultation procedures" has the same meaning as in section 143.

Annotations:

Commencement Information

I44 S. 144 wholly in force at 18.6.2001; s. 144 not in force at Royal Assent see s. 431 (2); s. 144(4)(5) in force at 25.2.2001 by S.I. 2001/516, art. 2(a), Sch. Pt. 1; s. 144 in force in so far as not already in force at 18.6.2001 by S.I. 2001/1820, art. 2, Sch.

145 Financial promotion rules.

(1) The Authority may make rules applying to authorised persons about the communication by them, or their approval of the communication by others, of invitations or inducements—

(a) to engage in investment activity; or

(b) to participate in a collective investment scheme.

(2) Rules under this section may, in particular, make provision about the form and content of communications.

(3) Subsection (1) applies only to communications which—

(a) if made by a person other than an authorised person, without the approval of an authorised person, would contravene section 21 (1);

(b) may be made by an authorised person without contravening section 238 (1).

(4) "Engage in investment activity" has the same meaning as in section 21.

(5) The Treasury may by order impose limitations on the power to make rules under this section.

(5)上述法令可以特别

(a)规定价格稳定规则可以对何种投资作出规定;

(b)规定依照第(3)款制定的规则可以对何种投资作出规定;

(c)规定只有在法令规定的情况下,价格稳定规则才可以对为稳定投资价格而采取的行动作出规定;

(d)规定只有在命令规定的时刻或期间内,价格稳定规则才可以对为了维持投资的价格而采取的行动作出规定。

(6)如依照第(3)款制定的规则中规定有所变更,则规则对变更后的条款继续有效,但只有管理局在作出变更前通知相关主体或机关(并且没有撤回其通知)管理局对其磋商程序感到满意时才可以适用。

(7)"磋商程序"含义同第143条。

注释:

实施日期

I44 第144条于2001年6月18日全部生效;第144条在副署时尚未生效,见第431条第(2)款;第144条第(4)款、第(5)款于2001年2月25日依照制定法文件S.I.2001/516第2条第(a)款、附录第一部分生效;第144条如于2001年6月18日尚未生效,则依照制定法文件S.I.2001/1820第2条、附录生效。

第145条 金融推介规则

(1)对获授权人或获授权人批准的其他人进行的关于下列邀请或诱导的传播,管理局制定适用于获授权人的规则:

(a)参与投资活动;或

(b)参与集合投资计划。

(2)本条规定的规则可以特别对传播的形式和内容作出规定。

(3)第(1)款仅适用于下列传播:

(a)如由获授权人以外的其他人作出且未经获授权人的同意,则将违反第21条第(1)款;

(b)可以由获授权人不违反第238条第(1)款而作出。

(4)"参与投资活动"含义同第21条。

(5)财政部可以通过法令对根据本条制定规则的权力作出限制。

Annotations:

Commencement Information

I45 S. 145 wholly in force at 18.6.2001; s. 145 not in force at Royal Assent see s. 431 (2); s. 145(5) in force at 25.2.2001 by S.I. 2001/516, art. 2(a), Sch. Pt. 1; s. 145 in force in so far as not already in force at 18.6.2001 by S.I. 2001/1820, art. 2, Sch.

146 Money laundering rules.

The Authority may make rules in relation to the prevention and detection of money laundering in connection with the carrying on of regulated activities by authorized persons.

147 Control of information rules.

(1) The Authority may make rules ("control of information rules") about the disclosure and use of information held by an authorised person ("A").

(2) Control of information rules may—

(a) require the withholding of information which A wouldotherwise have to disclose to a person ("B") for or with whom A does business in the course of carrying on any regulated or other activity;

(b) specify circumstances in which A may withhold information which he would otherwise have to disclose to B;

(c) require A not to use for the benefit of B information A holds which A would otherwise have to use in that way;

(d) specify circumstances in which A may decide not to use for the benefit of B information A holds which A would otherwise have to use in that way.

Modification or waiver

148 Modification or waiver of rules.

(1) This section applies in relation to the following—

(a) auditors and actuaries rules;

(b) control of information rules;

(c) financial promotion rules;

(d) general rules;

(e) insurance business rules;

(f) money laundering rules; and

(g) price stabilising rules.

(2) The Authority may, on the application or with the consent of an authorised person, direct that all or any of the rules to which this section applies—

(a) are not to apply to the authorised person; or

注释：

实施日期

I45　第145条于2001年6月18日全部生效；第145条在副署时尚未生效，见第431条第(2)款；第145条第(5)款于2001年2月25日依照制定法文件S.I.2001/516第2条第(a)款、附录第一部分生效；第145条如2001年6月18日尚未生效，则依照制定法文件S.I.2001/1820第2条、附录生效。

第146条　反洗钱规则

管理局可以就防止和发现与获授权人进行受监管活动相关的洗钱行为制定规则。

第147条　信息控制规则

(1)管理局可以对披露和使用由获授权人(以下简称A)持有的信息制定规则(以下简称信息控制规则)。

(2)信息控制规则可以

(a)要求A隐瞒否则必须向在进行任何受监管活动或其他活动的过程中为A或与A进行交易的人(以下简称B)披露的信息；

(b)规定A在何种情况下可以隐瞒否则必须披露给B的信息；

(c)要求A不得为了B的利益使A所持有的否则必须以该方式使用的信息；

(d)规定A在何种情况下可以决定为了B的利益不使用其所持有的否则必须以该方式使用的信息。

修改或放弃

第148条　修改或放弃执行规则

(1)本条适用于

(a)审计师和精算师规则；

(b)信息控制规则；

(c)金融推介规则；

(d)一般规则；

(e)保险业务规则；

(f)反洗钱规则；以及

(g)价格稳定规则。

(2)管理局可根据获授权人的申请或经获授权人同意，指示本条对其适用的全部或任何规则

(a)不对获授权人适用；或

(b) are to apply to him with such modifications as may be specified in the direction.

(3) An application must be made in such manner as the Authority may direct.

(4) The Authority may not give a direction unless it is satisfied that—

(a) compliance by the authorised person with the rules, or with the rules as unmodified, would be unduly burdensome or would not achieve the purpose for which the rules were made; and

(b) the direction would not result in undue risk to persons whose interests the rules are intended to protect.

(5) A direction may be given subject to conditions.

(6) Unless it is satisfied that it is inappropriate or unnecessary to do so, a direction must be published by the Authority in such a way as it thinks most suitable for bringing the direction to the attention of—

(a) those likely to be affected by it; and

(b) others who may be likely to make an application for a similar direction.

(7) In deciding whether it is satisfied as mentioned in subsection (6), the Authority must—

(a) take into account whether the direction relates to a rule contravention of which is actionable in accordance with section 150;

(b) consider whether its publication would prejudice, to an unreasonable degree, the commercial interests of the authorised person concerned or any other member of his immediate group; and

(c) consider whether its publication would be contrary to an international obligation of the United Kingdom.

(8) For the purposes of paragraphs (b) and (c) of subsection (7), the Authority must consider whether it would be possible to publish the direction without either of the consequences mentioned in those paragraphs by publishing it without disclosing the identity of the authorised person concerned.

(9) The Authority may—

(a) revoke a direction; or

(b) vary it on the application, or with the consent, of the authorised person to whom it relates.

(10) "Direction" means a direction under subsection (2).

(11) "Immediate group", in relation to an authorised person ("A"), means—

(a) A;

(b) a parent undertaking of A;

(c) a subsidiary undertaking of A;

(d) a subsidiary undertaking of a parent undertaking of A;

(b)根据指示中可能规定的修改对其适用。

(3)申请必须根据管理局可能指示的方式作出。

(4)管理局除非确信有下列事项,否则不得作出指示:

(a)授权人遵守规定,或遵守未变更的规定,将造成不合理的负担或不能达到制定这些规则的目的;且

(b)指示不会给规则所要保护其利益的人带来不合理的风险。

(5)可以附条件发出指示。

(6)管理局必须以其认为最便于下列人员了解的方式公布指示,除非管理局认为这样做不适当或不必要:

(a)可能受指示影响的人;以及

(b)其他可能就类似指示作出申请的人。

(7)在决定是否确信第(6)项中的事项时,管理局必须

(a)考虑指示是否涉及如违反则可以依照第150条起诉的规则;

(b)考虑公布指示是否将损害相关获授权人或其任何其他关联团体的成员的商业利益,且损害达到不合理的程度;及

(c)考虑公布指示是否违反联合王国的国际义务。

(8)为实施第(7)款第(b)项和第(c)项,管理局必须考虑是否有可能通过在公布指示时不披露相关获授权人的身份,而不发生上述两项所述的任何后果。

(9)管理局可以

(a)撤销指示;或

(b)根据申请或经过相关获授权人的同意而对指示进行变更。

(10)"指示"系指第(2)款规定的指示。

(11)与获授权人(以下简称A)相关的"关联团体"系指

(a)A;

(b)A的母企业;

(c)A的子企业;

(d)A的母企业的子企业;

(e) a parent undertaking of a subsidiary undertaking of A.

Annotations:

Modifications etc. (not altering text)

C139 S. 148 amended (temp. from 3.9.2001 to 1.12.2001) by S.I. 2001/2659, arts. 1(2), 3(3); S.I. 2001/3538, art. 2(1)

S. 148 modified (temp. from 31.10.2001) by S.I. 2001/3374, arts. 1, 11

S. 148 restricted (6.8.2001) by S.I. 2001/2512, arts. 1(1), 5(4)

C140 S. 148 modified (temp.) (8.4.2002) by The Financial Services and Markets Act 2000 (Permission and Applications) (Credit Unions etc.) Order 2002 (S.I. 2002/704), art. 7

C141 S. 148 applied (with modifications) (11.4.2002 for certain purposes and 27.4.2002 otherwise) by The Financial Services and Markets Act 2000 (Regulated Activities) Order 2001 (S.I. 2001/544), art. 9G(2) (as inserted by The Financial Services and Markets Act 2000 (Regulated Activities) (Amendment) Order 2002 (S.I. 2002/682), arts. 1(2), 4)

C142 S. 148: power to make rules amended (18.7.2002 for certain purposes and 21.8.2002 otherwise) by The Electronic Commerce Directive (Financial Services and Markets) Regulations 2002 (S.I. 2002/1775), regs. 1, 3(2)(a)

C143 S. 148 applied (6.8.2001) by S.I. 2001/2512, arts. 1(1), 7(1)

S. 148 applied (11.4.2002 for certain purposes and 27.4.2002 otherwise) by The Financial Services and Markets Act 2000 (Regulated Activities) Order 2001 (S.I. 2001/544), art. 9H (2) (as inserted by The Financial Services and Markets Act 2000 (Regulated Activities) (Amendment) Order 2002 (S.I. 2002/682), arts. 1(2), 4)

C144 S. 148(2) extended (1.12.2001) by S.I. 2001/3647, arts. 1, 4, Sch. 2 paras. 1–3

C145 S. 148 (3)–(9) (11) applied (with modifications) (3.9.2001 for specified purposes otherwise 1.12.2001) by S.I. 2001/1228, regs. 1(2)(b)(c), 7(3)(4) (with reg. 1(2)(3)); S.I. 2001/2632, art. 2(2), Sch. Pt. 2; S.I. 2001/3538, art. 2(1)

Commencement Information

I46 S. 148 wholly in force at 3.9.2001; s. 148 not in force at Royal Assent see s. 431(2); s. 148 in force for specified purposes at 18.6.2001 by S.I. 2001/1820, art. 2, Sch. s. 148 in so far as not already in force at 3.9.2001 by S.I. 2001/2632, art. 2(2), Sch. Pt. 2

(e)A的子企业的母企业。

注释：

修改等(不涉及条文内容)

C139　第148条暂时有效，于2001年9月3日至2001年12月1日依照制定法文件S.I. 2001/2659第1条第(2)款、第3条第(3)款；制定法文件S.I.2001/3538第2条第(1)款修正；

第148条暂时有效，于2001年10月31日开始依照制定法文件S.I.2001/3374第1条、第11条修订；

第148条于2001年8月6日受制定法文件S.I.2001/2512第1条第(1)款、第5条第(4)款的限制。

C140　第148条暂时有效，于2002年4月8日开始依照《2000年金融服务与市场法》(许可和批准)(信用合作社等)2002号令(制定法文件S.I.2002/704)第7条修订。

C141　第148条(已修订)为特定目的于2002年4月11日，否则于2002年4月27日依照《2000年金融服务与市场法》(受监管活动)2001号令(制定法文件S.I.2001/544)第9G条第(2)款[依照《2000年金融服务与市场法》(受监管活动)(修正)2002号令(制定法文件S.I. 2002/682)，第1条第(2)款、第4条插入]适用。

C142　第148条：规则指定权为特定目的于2002年7月18日，否则于2002年8月21日依照《2002年电子商务指令条例》(金融服务与市场)(制定法文件S.I.2002/1775)第1条、第3条第(2)款第(a)项修正。

C143　第148条于2001年8月6日依照制定法文件S.I.2001/2512第1条第(1)款、第7条第(1)款适用。

第148条于为特定目的于2002年4月11日，否则于2002年4月27日依照《2000年金融服务与市场法》(受监管活动)2001号令(制定法文件S.I.2001/544)第9H条第(2)款[依照《2000年金融服务与市场法》(受监管活动)(修正)2002号令(制定法文S.I.2002/682)第1条第(2)款、第4条插入]适用。

C144　第148条第(2)款于2001年12月1日依照制定法文件S.I.2001/3647第1条、第4条，附录2第1条至第3条扩大适用范围。

C145　第148条第(3)款至第(9)款、第(11)款(已修订)为特定目的于2001年9月3日，否则于2001年12月1日依照制定法文件S.I.2001/1228第1条第(2)款第(b)项、第(c)项，第7条第(3)款、第(4)款[与第1条第(2)款、第(3)款]；制定法文件S.I.2001/2632第2条第(2)款、附录第二部分；制定法文件S.I.2001/3538第2条第(1)款适用。

实施日期

I46　第148条于2001年9月3日全部生效；第148条在副署时尚未生效，见第431条第(2)款；第148条为特定目的于2001年6月18日依照制定法文件S.I.2001/1820第2条、附录生效；第148条如在2001年9月3日尚未生效，则依照制定法文件S.I.2001/2632第2条第(2)款、附录第二部分生效。

Contravention of rules

149 Evidential provisions.

(1) If a particular rule so provides, contravention of the rule does not give rise to any of the consequences provided for by other provisions of this Act.

(2) A rule which so provides must also provide—

(a) that contravention may be relied on as tending to establish contravention of such other rule as may be specified; or

(b) that compliance may be relied on as tending to establish compliance with such other rule as may be specified.

(3) A rule may include the provision mentioned in subsection (1) only if the Authority considers that it is appropriate for it also to include the provision required by subsection (2).

Annotations:

Modifications etc. (not altering text)

C146 S. 149(1) applied (2.7.2002) by The Financial Services and Markets Act 2000 (Consequential Amendments and Transitional Provisions) (Credit Unions) Order 2002 (S.I. 2002/1501), art. 11(1) (with art. 13)

C147 S. 149(2)(3) applied (with modifications) (2.7.2002) by The Financial Services and Markets Act 2000 (Consequential Amendments and Transitional Provisions) (Credit Unions) Order 2002 (S.I. 2002/1501), art. 11(2) (with art. 13)

150 Actions for damages.

(1) A contravention by an authorised person of a rule is actionable at the suit of a private person who suffers loss as a result of the contravention, subject to the defences and other incidents applying to actions for breach of statutory duty.

(2) If rules so provide, subsection (1) does not apply to contravention of a specified provision of those rules.

(3) In prescribed cases, a contravention of a rule which would be actionable at the suit of a private person is actionable at the suit of a person who is not a private person, subject to the defences and other incidents applying to actions for breach of statutory duty.

(4) In subsections (1) and (3) "rule" does not include—

(a) listing rules; or

(b) a rule requiring an authorised person to have or maintain financial resources.

(5) "Private person" has such meaning as may be prescribed.

对规则的违反

第149条　证据规则

(1)如果特定规则作出规定，则违反该规则不产生任何本法其他条款中规定的后果。

(2)作出上述规定的规则中必须还规定

(a)该违反行为可为证明违反指定的其他规则提供依据；或

(b)该合规行为可为证明符合指定的其他规则提供依据。

(3)规则只有在管理局认为其中包括第(2)款要求的规定适当时，方可包括第(1)款所述规定。

注释：

修改等(不涉及条文内容)

C146　第149条第(1)款于2002年7月2日依照《2000年金融服务与市场法》(间接修正和过渡性规定)(信用合作社)2002号令(制定法文件S.I.2002/1501)、第11条第(1)款(与第13条)适用。

C147　第149条第(2)款、第(3)款(已修订)于2002年7月2日依照《2000年金融服务与市场法》(间接修正和过渡性规定)(信用合作社)2002号令(制定法文件S.I.2002/1501)第11条第(2)款(与第13条)适用。

第150条　损害赔偿诉讼

(1)获授权人违反规则时，因该违反行为遭受损失的个人可提起诉讼，但须依照适用违反法定职责诉讼的抗辩理由和其他事由。

(2)如规则中有规定，则第(1)款不适用于对规则中特定条款的违反。

(3)在规定情况下，可以由因该行为而遭受损失的个人提起诉讼的违反规则行为，也可由非个人提起诉讼，但须依照适用违反法定职责诉讼的抗辩理由和其他事由。

(4)在第(1)款和第(3)款中，“规则”不包括

(a)上市规则；或

(b)要求获授权人拥有或维持财务资源的规则。[1]

(5)“个人”具有规定含义。

1　本款依照《2010年金融服务法》附录2第一部分第12条修订。——译者注

Annotations:

Modifications etc. (not altering text)

C148 S. 150 applied (1.12.2001) by S.I. 2001/1228, regs. 1(2)(c), 25(6) (with reg. 1(2)(3)); S.I. 2001/3538, art. 2(1)

C149 S. 150: power to make rules amended (18.7.2002 for certain purposes and 21.8.2002 otherwise) by The Electronic Commerce Directive (Financial Services and Markets) Regulations 2002 (S.I. 2002/1775), reg. 1, 3(2)(a)

C150 S. 150 applied (with modifications) (11.4.2002 for certain purposes and 27.4.2002 otherwise) by The Financial Services and Markets Act 2000 (Regulated Activities) Order 2001 (S.I. 2001/544), art. 9G (as inserted by The Financial Services and Markets Act 2000 (Regulated Activities) (Amendment) Order 2002 (S.I. 2002/682), arts. 1(2), 4)

S. 150 applied (2.7.2002) by The Financial Services and Markets Act 2000 (Consequential Amendments and Transitional Provisions) (Credit Unions) Order 2002 (S.I. 2002/1501) {art. 11(3)} (with art. 13)

Commencement Information

I47 S. 150 wholly in force at 1.12.2001; s. 150 not in force at Royal Assent see s. 431(2); s. 150(3)-(5) in force for certain purposes at 25.2.2001 by S.I. 2001/516, art. 2(b), Sch. Pt. 2; s. 150 in force for specified purposes at 18.6.2001 by S.I. 2001/1820, art. 2, Sch.; s. 150 in force in so far as not already in force at 1.12.2001 by S.I. 2001/3538, art. 2(1)

151 Limits on effect of contravening rules.

(1) A person is not guilty of an offence by reason of a contravention of a rule made by the Authority.

(2) No such contravention makes any transaction void or unenforceable.

Procedural provisions

152 Notification of rules to the Treasury.

(1) If the Authority makes any rules, it must give a copy to the Treasury without delay.

(2) If the Authority alters or revokes any rules, it must give written notice to the Treasury without delay.

(3) Notice of an alteration must include details of the alteration.

注释：

修改等(不涉及条文内容)

C148　第150条于2001年12月1日依照制定法文件S.I.2001/1228第1条第(2)款第(c)项、第25条第(6)款[与第1条第(2)款、第(3)款]；制定法文件S.I.2001/3538第2条第(1)款适用。

C149　第150条：规则制定权为特定目的于2002年7月18日，否则于2002年8月21日依照《2002年电子商务指令条例》(金融服务与市场)(制定法文件S.I.2002/1775)第1条、第3条第(2)款第(a)项修正。

C150　第150条(已修正)为特定目的于2002年4月11日，否则于2002年4月27日依照《2000年金融服务与市场法》(受监管活动)2001号令(制定法文件S.I.2001/544)第9G条[如《2000年金融服务与市场法》(受监管活动)(修正)2002号令制定法文件S.I.2002/682第1条第(2)款、第4条]适用；

第150条于2002年7月2日依照《2000年金融服务与市场法》(间接修正和过渡性规定)(信用合作社)2002号令(制定法文件S.I.2002/1501)[第11条第(3)款](与第13条)适用。

实施日期

I47　第150条于2001年12月1日全部生效；第150条在副署时尚未生效见第431条第(2)款；第150条第(3)款至第(5)款为特定目的于2001年2月25日依照制定法文件S.I.2001/516第2条第(b)款、附录第二部分生效；第150条为特定目的于2001年6月18日依照制定法文件S.I.2001/1820第2条、附录生效；第150条如在2001年12月1日尚未生效，则依照制定法文件S.I.2001/3538第2条第(1)款生效。

第151条　对违反规则的后果的限制

(1)某人违反管理局制定的规则不构成犯罪。

(2)该等违反行为不会使任何交易无效或无法履行。

程序性规定

第152条　将规则通知财政部

(1)如管理局制定了任何规则，则必须毫不延迟地向财政部送交一份副本。

(2)如管理局变更或废除任何规则，则必须毫不延迟地向财政部发出书面通知。

(3)变更通知中必须包含变更的详细情况。

Annotations:

Modifications etc. (not altering text)

C151 S. 152 applied (6.8.2001) by S.I. 2001/2512, arts. 1(1), 7(2)

153 Rule-making instruments.

(1) Any power conferred on the Authority to make rules is exercisable in writing.

(2) An instrument by which rules are made by the Authority ("a rule-making instrument") must specify the provision under which the rules are made.

(3) To the extent to which a rule-making instrument does not comply with subsection (2), it is void.

(4) A rule-making instrument must be published by the Authority in the way appearing to the Authority to be best calculated to bring it to the attention of the public.

(5) The Authority may charge a reasonable fee for providing a person with a copy of a rulemaking instrument.

(6) A person is not to be taken to have contravened any rule made by the Authority if he shows that at the time of the alleged contravention the rule-making instrument concerned had not been made available in accordance with this section.

Annotations:

Modifications etc. (not altering text)

C152 S. 153 applied (6.8.2001) by S.I. 2001/2512, arts. 1(1), 7(2)

154 Verification of rules.

(1) The production of a printed copy of a rule-making instrument purporting to be made by the Authority—

(a) on which is endorsed a certificate signed by a member of the Authority's staff authorised by it for that purpose, and

(b) which contains the required statements,

is evidence (or in Scotland sufficient evidence) of the facts stated in the certificate.

(2) The required statements are—

(a) that the instrument was made by the Authority;

(b) that the copy is a true copy of the instrument; and

(c) that on a specified date the instrument was made available to the public in accordance with section 153(4).

(3) A certificate purporting to be signed as mentioned in subsection (1) is to be taken to have been properly signed unless the contrary is shown.

注释：

修改等(不涉及条文内容)

C151　第152条于2001年8月6日依照制定法文件S.I.2001/2512第1条第(1)款、第7条第(2)款适用。

第153条　规则制定文件

(1)授予管理局的任何规则制定权均可以书面形式行使。

(2)管理局据以制定规则的文件(以下简称规则制定文件)必须具体表明这些规则是根据哪些条款所制定的。

(3)规则制定文件不符合第(2)款规定时，该文件无效。

(4)管理局必须以其认为最便于公众了解的方式公布规则制定文件。

(5)管理局可以为向某人提供规则制定文件的副本而收取合理费用。

(6)如能证明在声称的违反行为发生时，尚未根据本条规定公布相关的规则制定文件，则不视为行为人违反管理局制定的任何规则。

注释：

修改等(不涉及条文内容)

C152　第153条于2001年8月6日依照制定法文件S.I.2001/2512第1条第(1)款、第7条第(2)款适用。

第154条　规则的认可

(1)声称由管理局制作的规则制定文件的印刷本

(a)其中附有由管理局授权的工作人员为该目的签名认可的证明书，及

(b)包含要求的陈述，

则为证明书中所述事实的证据(或者在苏格兰称为充分证据)。

(2)前款要求的陈述为

(a)该文件系由管理局制作；

(b)该印刷本是真实的文件副本；及

(c)该文件在指定日期根据第153条第(4)款提供给公众。

(3)意图根据第(1)款签署的证明书视为已适当签署，除非证明有相反情况。

(4) A person who wishes in any legal proceedings to rely on a rule-making instrument may require the Authority to endorse a copy of the instrument with a certificate of the kind mentioned in subsection (1).

Annotations:

Modifications etc. (not altering text)

C153 S. 154 applied (6.8.2001) by S.I. 2001/2512, arts. 1(1), 7(2)

S. 154 excluded (6.8.2001) by S.I. 2001/2512, arts. 1(1), 7(4)

S. 154 excluded(2.7.2002) by The Financial Services and Markets Act 2000 (Consequential Amendments and Transitional Provisions) (Credit Unions) Order 2002 (S.I. 2002/1501), art. 12(1) (with art. 13)

155 Consultation.

(1) If the Authority proposes to make any rules, it must publish a draft of the proposed rules in the way appearing to it to be best calculated to bring them to the attention of the public.

(2) The draft must be accompanied by—

(a) a cost benefit analysis;

(b) an explanation of the purpose of the proposed rules;

(c) an explanation of the Authority's reasons for believing that making the proposed rules is compatible with its general duties under section 2; and

(d) notice that representations about the proposals may be made to the Authority within a specified time.

(3) In the case of a proposal to make rules under a provision mentioned in subsection (9), the draft must also be accompanied by details of the expected expenditure by reference to which the proposal is made.

(4) Before making the proposed rules, the Authority must have regard to any representations made to it in accordance with subsection (2)(d).

(5) If the Authority makes the proposed rules, it must publish an account, in general terms, of—

(a) the representations made to it in accordance with subsection (2)(d); and

(b) its response to them.

(6) If the rules differ from the draft published under subsection (1) in a way which is, in the opinion of the Authority, significant—

(a) the Authority must (in addition to complying with subsection (5)) publish details of the difference; and

(4)在任何法律程序中希望依靠规则制定文件的,可要求管理局以第(1)款中述及的证明书来认可该文件的复制件。

注释:

修改等(不涉及条文内容)

C153 第154条于2001年8月6日依照制定法文件S.I.2001/2512第1条第(1)款、第7条第(2)款。

第154条于2001年8月6日依照制定法文件S.I.2001/2512第1条第(1)款、第7条第(4)款排除。

第154条于2002年7月2日依照《2000年金融服务与市场法》(间接性修正和过渡性规定)(信用合作社)2002号令(制定法文件S.I.2002/1501)第12条第(1)款(与第13条)排除。

第155条 征求意见

(1)如管理局拟制定任何规则,则必须以其认为最便于公众了解的方式公布拟制定规则的草案。

(2)该草案必须附有

(a)成本效益分析;

(b)对拟制定规则的目的说明;

(c)对管理局认为制定规则符合其第2条规定的基本职责的理由的说明;以及

(d)关于可以在指定时间内向管理局就拟制定的规则作出陈述的通知。

(3)在计划根据第(9)款所述规定制定规则时,草案还必须附有该提案参照的详细预计开支。

(4)在制定拟制定的规则前,管理局必须考虑根据第(2)款第(d)项向其作出的任何陈述。

(5)如管理局制定拟制定的规则,则必须公布概述下列情况的报告:

(a)根据第(2)款第(d)项向其作出的陈述;以及

(b)管理局对上述陈述的答复。

(6)如管理局认为规则与根据第(1)款公布的草案有明显差异,则

(a)管理局[除遵守第(5)款规定外]必须公布该差异的详细情况;且

(b) those details must be accompanied by a cost benefit analysis.

(7) Subsections (1) to (6) do not apply if the Authority considers that the delay involved in complying with them would be prejudicial to the interests of consumers.

(8) Neither subsection (2)(a) nor subsection (6)(b) applies if the Authority considers—

(a) that, making the appropriate comparison, there will be no increase in costs; or

(b) that, making that comparison, there will be an increase in costs but the increase will be of minimal significance.

(9) Neither subsection (2)(a) nor subsection (6)(b) requires a cost benefit analysis to be carried out in relation to rules made under—

(a) section 136(2);

(b) subsection (1) of section 213 as a result of subsection (4) of that section;

(c) section 234;

(d) paragraph 17 of Schedule 1.

(10) "Cost benefit analysis" means an estimate of the costs together with an analysis of the benefits that will arise—

(a) if the proposed rules are made; or

(b) if subsection (6) applies, from the rules that have been made.

(11) "The appropriate comparison" means—

(a) in relation to subsection (2)(a), a comparison between the overall position if the rules are made and the overall position if they are not made;

(b) in relation to subsection (6)(b), a comparison between the overall position after the making of the rules and the overall position before they were made.

(12) The Authority may charge a reasonable fee for providing a person with a copy of a draft published under subsection (1).

Annotations:

Modifications etc. (not altering text)

C154 S. 155 excluded (6.8.2001) by S.I. 2001/2512, arts. 1(1), 7(3)

S. 155 excluded (31.10.2001) by S.I. 2001/3374, arts. 1, 12(2)

C155 S. 155(2)(c) restricted (17.8.2001) by S.I. 2001/2617, arts. 2(a), 4(3), 8, Sch. 2 paras. 9, 11(b), 13, 14 (b)上述详细情况中必须附有成本效益分析。

(7)如管理局认为延迟遵守规则将会损害消费者的利益,则第(1)款至第(6)款规定不适用。

(8)如管理局认为有下列情况,则第(2)款第(a)项和第(6)款第(b)项规定不适用:

(a)进行适当比较后认为无成本增长;或

(b)进行适当比较后认为成本将增长,但该增长影响极小。

(9)第(2)款(a)项和第(6)款第(b)项对于根据以下条款制定的规则,不要求进行成本效益分析:

(a)第136条第(2)款;

(b)由于第213条第(4)款而适用该条第(4)款;

(c)第234条;

(d)附录1第17条。[1]

(10)"成本效益分析",系指对下列情况成本的估计以及对所产生效益的分析:

(a)如制定拟制定的规则;或

(b)因已制定的规则而适用第(6)款规定。

(11)"适当比较"系指

(a)就第(2)款第(a)项而言,系指比较假如规则制定后的整体状况和假如不制定规则的整体状况;

(b)就第(6)款第(b)项而言,系指比较规则制定后的整体状况和规则制定前的整体状况。

(12)管理局可为向他人提供依照第(1)款规定公布的草案副本收取合理费用。

注释:

修改等(不涉及条文内容)

C154 第155条于2001年8月6日依照制定法文件S.I.2001/2512第1条第(1)款、第7条第(3)款排除;

第155条于2001年10月31日依照制定法文件S.I.2001/3374第1条、第12条第(2)款排除。

C155 第155条第(2)款第(c)项于2001年8月17日受制定法文件S.I.2001/2617第2条第(a)款、第4条第(3)款、第8条,附录2第9条、第11条第(b)款、第13条、第14条限制。

1 本项依照《2010年金融服务法》附录2第一部分第13条修订。——译者注

156 General supplementary powers.

(1) Rules made by the Authority may make different provision for different cases and may, in particular, make different provision in respect of different descriptions of authorized person, activity or investment.

(2) Rules made by the Authority may contain such incidental, supplemental, consequential and transitional provision as the Authority considers appropriate.

Annotations:

Modifications etc. (not altering text)

C156 S. 156 applied (6.8.2001) by S.I. 2001/2512, arts. 1(1), 7(2)

C157 S. 156: power to make rules amended (18.7.2002 for certain purposes and 21.8.2002 otherwise) by The Electronic Commerce Directive (Financial Services and Markets) Regulations 2002 (S.I. 2002/1775), regs. 1, 3(2)(a)

CHAPTER II GUIDANCE

157 Guidance.

(1) The Authority may give guidance consisting of such information and advice as it considers appropriate—

(a) with respect to the operation of this Act and of any rules made under it;

(b) with respect to any matters relating to functions of the Authority;

(c) for the purpose of meeting the regulatory objectives;

(d) with respect to any other matters about which it appears to the Authority to be desirable to give information or advice.

(2) The Authority may give financial or other assistance to persons giving information or advice of a kind which the Authority could give under this section.

(3) If the Authority proposes to give guidance to regulated persons generally, or to a class of regulated person, in relation to rules to which those persons are subject, subsections (1), (2) and (4) to (10) of section 155 apply to the proposed guidance as they apply to proposed rules.

(4) The Authority may—

(a) publish its guidance;

(b) offer copies of its published guidance for sale at a reasonable price; and

(c) if it gives guidance in response to a request made by any person, make a reasonable charge for that guidance.

第156条　一般补充权利

（1）管理局制定的规则可以对不同情况作出不同的规定，可以特别对不同种类的获授权人、活动或投资作出不同的规定。

（2）管理局制定的规则可以包含其认为适当的附带、间接、补充或过渡性条款。

注释：

修改等（不涉及条文内容）

C156　第156条于2001年8月6日依照制定法文件S.I.2001/2512第1条第（1）款、第7条第（2）款适用。

C157　第156条：规则制定权为特定目的于2002年7月18日，否则于2002年8月21日依照《2002年电子商务指令条例》（金融服务与市场）（制定法文件S.I.2002/1775）第1条、第3条第（2）款第（a）项修正。

第二章　指　导

第157条　指导

（1）管理局可以就下列事项作出包含其认为适当的信息和建议的指导：

（a）本法及任何根据本法制定的规则的运行；

（b）与管理局的职能有关的任何事项；

（c）为达到监管目标；

（d）管理局认为需要给出信息或建议的任何其他事项。

（2）对提供管理局根据本条能够给出的信息或建议的人，管理局可给予财务上或其他方面的帮助。

（3）如管理局拟向一般受监管人或者某类受监管人就其应遵守的规则发出指导，则第155条第（1）款、第（2）款及第（4）款至第（10）款适用于拟发出的指导，效力等同于对拟制定的规则适用。[1]

（4）管理局可以

（a）公布其指导；

（b）以合理的价格提供其公布的指导的供出售的副本；以及

（c）如为应某人请求而作出指导，可以为作出该指导收取合理费用。

1　本款依照《2010年金融服务法》附录2第一部分第14条修订。——译者注

(5) In this Chapter, references to guidance given by the Authority include references to any recommendation made by the Authority to persons generally, to regulated persons generally or to any class of regulated person.

(6) "Regulated person" means any—

(a) authorised person;

(b) person who is otherwise subject to rules made by the Authority.

Annotations:

Modifications etc. (not altering text)

C158 S. 157(3) modified (17.8.2001) by S.I. 2001/2617, arts. 2(a), 4(3), 8, Sch. 2 para. 12

158 Notification of guidance to the Treasury.

(1) On giving any general guidance, the Authority must give the Treasury a copy of the guidance without delay.

(2) If the Authority alters any of its general guidance, it must give written notice to the Treasury without delay.

(3) The notice must include details of the alteration.

(4) If the Authority revokes any of its general guidance, it must give written notice to the Treasury without delay.

(5) "General guidance" means guidance given by the Authority under section 157 which is—

(a) given to persons generally, to regulated persons generally or to a class of regulated person;

(b) intended to have continuing effect; and

(c) given in writing or other legible form.

(6) "Regulated person" has the same meaning as in section 157.

Annotations:

Modifications etc. (not altering text)

C159 S. 158(5) modified (17.8.2001) by S.I. 2001/2617, arts. 2(a), 4(3), 8, Sch. 2 para. 12

CHAPTER Ⅲ COMPETITION SCRUTINY

159 Interpretation.

(1) In this Chapter—

"Director" means the Director General of Fair Trading;

"practices", in relation to the Authority, means practices adopted by the Authority in the

(5)在本章中,述及管理局作出的指导包含管理局向一般人、一般受监管人或某类受监管人提出的任何建议。

(6)"受监管人"系指任何

(a)获授权人;

(b)以其他方式受制于管理局制定的规则的人。

注释:

修改等(不涉及条文内容)

C158 第157条第(3)款于2001年8月17日依照制定法文件S.I.2001/2617第2条第(a)款、第4条第(3)款、第8条,附录2第12条修订。

第158条 就指导向财政部发出通知

(1) 管理局作出任何一般性指引, 均必须毫不延迟地向财政部送交一份指导副本。

(2)如管理局变更作出的任何一般性指引,则必须毫不延迟地以书面形式通知财政部。

(3)通知中必须包含变更的详细情况。

(4)如管理局撤销作出的任何一般性指引,则必须毫不延迟地以书面形式通知财政部。

(5)"一般性指引"系指管理局根据第157条作出的下列指导:

(a)向一般人、一般受监管人或某类受监管人作出的指导;

(b)意图使其持续有效;且

(c)以书面或其他可读形式作出的指导。

(6)"受监管人"含义同第157条。

注释:

修改等(不涉及条文内容)

C159 第158条第(5)款于2001年8月17日依照制定法文件S.I.2001/2617第2条第(a)款、第4条第(3)款、第8条,附录2第12条修订。

第三章 竞争审查

第159条 释义

(1)本章中

"总理事"系指公平交易总理事;

"惯例",就管理局而言,系指管理局在根据本法履行其职能时采取的惯例;

exercise of functions under this Act;

"regulating provisions" means any—

(a) rules;

(b) general guidance (as defined by section 158(5));

(c) statement issued by the Authority under section 64;

(d) code issued by the Authority under section 64 or 119.

(2) For the purposes of this Chapter, regulating provisions or practices have a significantly adverse effect on competition if—

(a) they have, or are intended or likely to have, that effect; or

(b) the effect that they have, or are intended or likely to have, is to require or encourage behaviour which has, or is intended or likely to have, a significantly adverse effect on competition.

(3) If regulating provisions or practices have, or are intended or likely to have, the effect of requiring or encouraging exploitation of the strength of a market position they are to be taken, for the purposes of this Chapter, to have an adverse effect on competition.

(4) In determining under this Chapter whether any of the regulating provisions have, or are likely to have, a particular effect, it may be assumed that the persons to whom the provisions concerned are addressed will act in accordance with them.

Annotations:

Modifications etc. (not altering text)

C160 S. 159(1) restricted (17.8.2001) by S.I. 2001/2617, arts. 2(a), 4(3), 8, Sch. 2 paras. 7, 9, 11(c), 13, 14, 15, 17

160 Reports by Director General of Fair Trading.

(1) The Director must keep the regulating provisions and the Authority's practices under review.

(2) If at any time the Director considers that—

(a) a regulating provision or practice has a significantly adverse effect on competition, or

(b) two or more regulating provisions or practices taken together, or a particular combination of regulating provisions and practices, have such an effect,

he must make a report to that effect.

(3) If at any time the Director considers that—

(a) a regulating provision or practice does not have a significantly adverse effect on competition, or

(b) two or more regulating provisions or practices taken together, or a particular combination of regulating provisions and practices, do not have any such effect,

"监管规定"系指任何

(a)规则;

(b)一般性指引[根据第158条第(5)款中的定义];

(c)管理局依照第64条发布的声明;

(d)管理局依照第64条或第119条发布的准则。

(2)就本章而言,如有下列情况,则为监管规定或惯例对竞争有明显不利影响:

(a)具有或者预计或可能具有对竞争具有明显不利影响的效力;或

(b)具有或者预计或可能具有的效力为要求实施或鼓励实施预计或可能对竞争产生明显不利影响的行为。

(3)如监管规定或惯例具有或者预计或可能具有要求或鼓励利用市场地位优势的效力,则就本章而言应将上述规定或惯例视为对竞争具有不利影响。

(4)在依照本章规定确定任何监管规定是否具有或者预计或可能具有特定效力时,可认为相关规定针对的人将依照该规定行事。

注释:

修改等(不涉及条文内容)

C160 第159条第(1)款于2001年8月17日受制定法文件S.I.2001/2617第2条第(a)款、第4条第(3)款、第8条,附录2第7条、第9条、第11条第(c)款、第13条、第14条、第15条、第17条限制。

第160条 公平交易总理事的报告

(1)总理事必须审查监管规定和管理局的惯例。

(2)如总理事在任何时候认为

(a)监管规定或惯例对竞争有明显不利影响,或

(b)两项或以上监管规定或惯例一起,或监管规定和惯例的特定组合有这样的影响,

则必须就此作出报告。

(3)如果总理事在任何时候认为

(a)监管规定或惯例对竞争没有明显的不利影响,或

(b)两项或以上监管规定或惯例一起,或监管规定和惯例的特定组合没有这样的影响,

he may make a report to that effect.

(4) A report under subsection (2) must include details of the adverse effect on competition.

(5) If the Director makes a report under subsection (2) he must—

(a) send a copy of it to the Treasury, the Competition Commission and the Authority; and

(b) publish it in the way appearing to him to be best calculated to bring it to the attention of the public.

(6) If the Director makes a report under subsection (3)—

(a) he must send a copy of it to the Treasury, the Competition Commission and the Authority; and

(b) he may publish it.

(7) Before publishing a report under this section the Director must, so far as practicable, exclude any matter which relates to the private affairs of a particular individual the publication of which, in the opinion of the Director, would or might seriously and prejudicially affect his interests.

(8) Before publishing such a report the Director must, so far as practicable, exclude any matter which relates to the affairs of a particular body the publication of which, in the opinion of the Director, would or might seriously and prejudicially affect its interests.

(9) Subsections (7) and (8) do not apply in relation to copies of a report which the Director is required to send under subsection (5)(a) or (6)(a).

(10) For the purposes of the law of defamation, absolute privilege attaches to any report of the Director under this section.

161 Power of Director to request information.

(1) For the purpose of investigating any matter with a view to its consideration under section 160, the Director may exercise the powers conferred on him by this section.

(2) The Director may by notice in writing require any person to produce to him or to a person appointed by him for the purpose, at a time and place specified in the notice, any document which—

(a) is specified or described in the notice; and

(b) is a document in that person's custody or under his control.

(3) The Director may by notice in writing—

(a) require any person carrying on any business to provide him with such information as may be specified or described in the notice; and

(b) specify the time within which, and the manner and form in which, any such information is to be provided.

(4) A requirement may be imposed under subsection (2) or (3)(a) only in respect of

则可以就此作出报告。

(4)根据第(2)款作出的报告必须包含对竞争产生不利影响的详细情况。

(5)如总理事依照第(2)款作出了报告,则必须

(a)向财政部、竞争委员会和管理局发送报告副本;并

(b)以其认为最便于公众了解的方式公布报告。

(6)如总理事依照第(3)款作出了报告,则

(a)必须向财政部、竞争委员会和管理局发送报告副本;且

(b)可以公布报告。

(7)依照本条规定发布报告前,总理事如认为公布特定个人的个人事务将会或可能严重损害该人利益,则必须在切实可行的范围内排除任何涉及该事务的事项。

(8)公布报告前,总理事如认为公布某一特定主体的事务将会或可能严重损害该主体利益,则必须在切实可行范围内排除任何涉及该事务的事项。

(9)第(7)款和第(8)款规定不适用于总理事按照第(5)款第(a)项或第(6)款第(a)项的要求发送的报告副本。

(10)总理事根据本条规定作出的任何报告均享有诽谤法所称专有特权。

第161条 总理事要求提供信息的权力

(1)为调查任何根据第160条应考虑的事项,总理事可以行使本条授予的权力。

(2)总理事可以发出书面通知,要求任何人在通知中指定的时间和地点向总理事或其委派的人出示下列任何文件:

(a)通知中指定或描述的文件;及

(b)此人保管或控制的文件。

(3)总理事可发出书面通知

(a)要求从事任何业务的任何人向其提供通知中规定或描述的信息;并

(b)指定上述信息的提供时限、提供方式和形式。

(4)第(2)款或第(3)款第(a)项规定的要求只可针对与任何调查相关事项有关的

documents or information which relate to any matter relevant to the investigation.

(5) If a person ("the defaulter") refuses, or otherwise fails, to comply with a notice under this section, the Director may certify that fact in writing to the court and the court may enquire into the case.

(6) If, after hearing any witness who may be produced against or on behalf of the defaulter and any statement which may be offered in defence, the court is satisfied that the defaulter did not have a reasonable excuse for refusing or otherwise failing to comply with the notice, the court may deal with the defaulter as if he were in contempt.

(7) "Court" means—

(a) the High Court; or

(b) in relation to Scotland, the Court of Session.

162 Consideration by Competition Commission.

(1) If the Director—

(a) makes a report under section 160(2), or

(b) asks the Commission to consider a report that he has made under section 160(3),

the Commission must investigate the matter.

(2) The Commission must then make its own report on the matter unless it considers that, as a result of a change of circumstances, no useful purpose would be served by a report.

(3) If the Commission decides in accordance with subsection (2) not to make a report, it must make a statement setting out the change of circumstances which resulted in that decision.

(4) A report made under this section must state the Commission's conclusion as to whether—

(a) the regulating provision or practice which is the subject of the report has a significantly adverse effect on competition; or

(b) the regulating provisions or practices, or combination of regulating provisions and practices, which are the subject of the report have such an effect.

(5) A report under this section stating the Commission's conclusion that there is a significantly adverse effect on competition must also—

(a) state whether the Commission considers that that effect is justified; and

(b) if it states that the Commission considers that it is not justified, state its conclusion as to what action, if any, ought to be taken by the Authority.

(6) Subsection (7) applies whenever the Commission is considering, for the purposes of this section, whether a particular adverse effect on competition is justified.

(7) The Commission must ensure, so far as that is reasonably possible, that the conclusion it reaches is compatible with the functions conferred, and obligations imposed, on the Authority by or under this Act.

文件或信息提出。

(5)如某人(以下简称违反人)拒绝遵从或以其他方式不遵从依照本条规定发出的通知,则总理事可向法院书面提交该事项,法庭可调查该案。

(6)如法院在听审任何针对违反人或代表违反人提供的证词及任何辩护陈述后,确信该违反人无合理理由而拒绝遵从或以其他方式不遵从该通知,则可将违反人按藐视法庭处理。

(7)"法院"系指

(a)高等法院;或

(b)(苏格兰)高等民事法院。

第162条　竞争委员会的审议

(1)如总理事

(a)根据第160条第(2)款作出了报告,或

(b)要求委员会审议其依照第160条第(3)款作出的报告,

则委员会必须调查该事项。

(2)委员会必须对该事项作出报告,除非委员会认为由于情况变化,作出报告不起任何作用。

(3)如委员会依照第(2)款规定决定不作出报告,则必须作出声明,列出导致作出该决定的情况变化。

(4)根据本条作出的报告必须说明委员会对下列事项的结论:

(a)作为报告主题的监管规定或惯例是否对竞争有明显的负面影响;或

(b)作为报告主题的监管规定或惯例,或监管规定和惯例的结合,是否对竞争有这样的影响。

(5)根据本条作出的报告如表明委员会的结论是对竞争有明显不利影响,则还必须

(a)说明委员会是否认为该影响有正当理由;及

(b)如果它说明委员会认为该影响没有正当理由,则说明委员会对于管理局应当采取何种行为(如有)的结论。

(6)在委员会为本条之实施正在考虑对竞争产生的不利影响是否有正当理由时,即适用第(7)款规定。

(7)委员会必须在合理可行的范围内确保其作出的结论与本法或依照本法授予管理局的职能和施加给管理局的责任相一致。

(8) A report under this section must contain such an account of the Commission's reasons for its conclusions as is expedient, in the opinion of the Commission, for facilitating proper understanding of them.

(9) Schedule 14 supplements this section.

(10) If the Commission makes a report under this section it must send a copy to the Treasury,the Authority and the Director.

163 Role of the Treasury.

(1) This section applies if the Competition Commission makes a report under section 162(2) which states its conclusion that there is a significantly adverse effect on competition.

(2) If the Commission's conclusion, as stated in the report, is that the adverse effect on competition is not justified, the Treasury must give a direction to the Authority requiring it to take such action as may be specified in the direction.

(3) But subsection (2) does not apply if the Treasury consider—

(a) that, as a result of action taken by the Authority in response to the Commission's report, it is unnecessary for them to give a direction; or

(b) that the exceptional circumstances of the case make it inappropriate or unnecessary for them to do so.

(4) In considering the action to be specified in a direction under subsection (2), the Treasury must have regard to any conclusion of the Commission included in the report because of section 162(5)(b).

(5) Subsection (6) applies if—

(a) the Commission's conclusion, as stated in its report, is that the adverse effect on competition is justified; but

(b) the Treasury consider that the exceptional circumstances of the case require them to act.

(6) The Treasury may give a direction to the Authority requiring it to take such action—

(a) as they consider to be necessary in the light of the exceptional circumstances of the case; and

(b) as may be specified in the direction.

(7) The Authority may not be required as a result of this section to take any action—

(a) that it would not have power to take in the absence of a direction under this section; or

(b) that would otherwise be incompatible with any of the functions conferred, or obligations imposed, on it by or under this Act.

(8) Subsection (9) applies if the Treasury are considering—

(a) whether subsection (2) applies and, if so, what action is to be specified in a direction under that subsection; or

（8）根据本条作出的报告必须说明委员会认为有利于正确理解其结论的结论理由。

（9）附录14是对本条的补充。

（10）如委员会根据本条作出报告，则必须向财政部、管理局和总理事发送该报告副本。

第163条　财政部的职责

（1）如竞争委员会根据第162条第（2）款作出报告，表明其结论为存在对竞争的明显不利影响，则适用本条规定。

（2）如委员会在报告中表明的结论为，对竞争的不利影响无正当理由，则财政部必须向管理局作出指示，要求管理局采取指示中规定的行动。

（3）但如财政部认为有下列情况，则第（2）款不适用：

（a）由于管理局为回应委员会的报告而采取了行动，财政部无须作出指示；或

（b）由于特殊情况不适于或不必要作出指示。

（4）财政部在考虑根据第（2）款作出的指示中规定的行动时，必须考虑委员会在作出的报告中根据第162条第（5）款第（b）项得出的任何结论。

（5）如有下列情况，则适用第（6）款规定：

（a）委员会在报告中说明的结论为对竞争产生的负面影响有正当理由；但

（b）财政部认为由于特殊情况需要财政部采取行动。

（6）财政部可以向管理局作出指示，要求其采取下列行动：

（a）财政部认为考虑到特殊情况而有必要采取的行动；及

（b）指示中规定的行动。

（7）不得根据本条规定要求管理局采取任何下列行动：

（a）如无根据本条作出的指示，管理局无权采取的行动；或

（b）与本法或根据本法授予管理局的任何职能或施加给管理局的任何责任不一致的行动。

（8）如财政部正在考虑下列事项，则适用第（9）款规定：

（a）第（2）款是否适用，以及如适用，依照该款作出的指示中应当规定何种行动；或

(b) whether to give a direction under subsection (6).

(9) The Treasury must—

(a) do what they consider appropriate to allow the Authority, and any other person appearing to the Treasury to be affected, an opportunity to make representations; and

(b) have regard to any such representations.

(10) If, in reliance on subsection (3)(a) or (b), the Treasury decline to act under subsection (2), they must make a statement to that effect, giving their reasons.

(11) If the Treasury give a direction under this section they must make a statement giving—

(a) details of the direction; and

(b) if the direction is given under subsection (6), their reasons for giving it.

(12) The Treasury must—

(a) publish any statement made under this section in the way appearing to them best calculated to bring it to the attention of the public; and

(b) lay a copy of it before Parliament.

164 The Competition Act 1998.

(1) The Chapter I prohibition does not apply to an agreement the parties to which consist of or include—

(a) an authorised person, or

(b) a person who is otherwise subject to the Authority's regulating provisions, to the extent to which the agreement consists of provisions the inclusion of which in the agreement is encouraged by any of the Authority's regulating provisions.

(2) The Chapter I prohibition does not apply to the practices of an authorised person or a person who is otherwise subject to the regulating provisions to the extent to which the practices are encouraged by any of the Authority's regulating provisions.

(3) The Chapter II prohibition does not apply to conduct of—

(a) an authorised person, or

(b) a person who is otherwise subject to the Authority's regulating provisions,

to the extent to which the conduct is encouraged by any of the Authority's regulating provisions.

(4) "The Chapter I prohibition" means the prohibition imposed by section 2(1) of the [M17] Competition Act 1998.

(5) "The Chapter II prohibition" means the prohibition imposed by section 18(1) of that Act.

Annotations:

Marginal Citations

M17 1998 c. 41.

(b)是否要根据第(6)款作出指示。

(9)财政部必须

(a)采取其认为适当的措施,允许管理局和财政部认为受到影响的任何其他人有作出陈述的机会;及

(b)考虑上述任何陈述。

(10)如财政部凭借第(3)款第(a)项或第(b)项拒绝根据第(2)款采取行动,则必须作出相关声明并说明理由。

(11)如财政部依照本条作出指示,则必须作出声明

(a)详细说明该指示;且

(b)如指示为依照第(6)款作出,则说明作出指示的理由。

(12)财政部必须

(a)以其认为最便于公众了解的方式公布依照本条规定发布的任何声明;并

(b)将声明副本呈交议会。

第164条 《1998年竞争法》

(1) 第一章的禁止性规定不适用于由下列人员组成或包含以下人员的协议方订立的协议:

(a)获授权人,或

(b)受管理局监管规定约束的其他人,但前提为协议中包含管理局任何监管规定鼓励列入该协议的条款。

(2)如管理局任何监管规定鼓励获授权人或受制于管理局其他监管规定的人的实践,则第一章的禁止性规定不适用于此类实践。

(3)第二章的禁止性规定不适用于下列行为:

(a)获授权人的行为,或

(b)受制于管理局其他监管规定的人的行为,

但前提为该行为是管理局任何监管规定所鼓励的行为。

(4)"第一章的禁止性规定"系指[M17]《1998年竞争法》第2条第(1)款所规定的禁止。

(5)"第二章的禁止性规定"系指《1998年竞争法》第18条第(1)款所规定的禁止。

注释:

附注引文

M17　1998年第41章。

PART XI INFORMATION GATHERING AND INVESTIGATIONS

Annotations:

Modifications etc. (not altering text)

C161 Pt. XI (ss. 165–177) modified (1.12.2001) by S.I. 2001/2657, arts. 1(1), 18(2) (which was revoked (8.10.2001) by S.I. 2001/3083, arts. 1(2), 23); S.I. 2001/3538, art. 2(1)

Pt. XI (165–177) modified (1.12.2001) by S.I. 2001/3083, arts. 1(2), 18(2)(4); S.I. 2001/3538, art. 2(1)

Pt. XI (ss. 165–177) extended (with modifications) (1.12.2001) by S.I. 2001/3646, arts. 1(1), 6–9

Powers to gather information

165 Authority's power to require information.

(1) The Authority may, by notice in writing given to an authorised person, require him—

(a) to provide specified information or information of a specified description; or

(b) to produce specified documents or documents of a specified description.

(2) The information or documents must be provided or produced—

(a) before the end of such reasonable period as may be specified; and

(b) at such place as may be specified.

(3) An officer who has written authorisation from the Authority to do so may require an authorised person without delay—

(a) to provide the officer with specified information or information of a specified

第十一部分 信息收集与调查

注释：

修改等(不涉及条文内容)

C161 第十一部分(第165条至177条)于2001年12月1日依照制定法文件S.I.2001/2657第1条第(1)款、第18条第(2)款[于2001年10月8日依照制定法文件S.I.2001/3083第1条第(2)款、第23条被撤销];制定法文件S.I.2001/3538第2条第(1)款修订;

第十一部分(第165条至第177条)于2001年12月1日依照制定法文件S.I.2001/3083第1条第(2)款,第18条第(2)款、第(4)款;制定法文件S.I.2001/3538第2条第(1)款修订;

第十一部分(第165条至第177条)(已修订)于2001年12月1日依照制定法文件S.I.2001/3646第1条第(1)款、第6条至第9条扩大适用范围。

信息收集权

第165条 管理局要求提供信息的权力[1]

(1)管理局可以向获授权人发出书面通知,要求其

(a)提供规定信息或规定种类的信息;或

(b)出示规定的文件或规定种类的文件。

(2)提供信息和出示文件必须

(a)在规定的合理期间结束之前进行;且

(b)在规定的地点进行。

(3)拥有管理局书面授权可作出下列行为的官员,可以要求获授权人不加迟延地:

(a)向其提供规定信息或规定种类的信息;或

1 本条依照《2010年金融服务法》第18条第(2)款,附录2第一部分第15条修订。——译者注

description; or

(b) to produce to him specified documents or documents of a specified description.

(4) This section applies only to information and documents reasonably required in connection with the exercise by the Authority of functions conferred on it by or under this Act.

(5) The Authority may require any information provided under this section to be provided in such form as it may reasonably require.

(6) The Authority may require—

(a) any information provided, whether in a document or otherwise, to be verified in such manner, or

(b) any document produced to be authenticated in such manner, as it may reasonably require.

(7) The powers conferred by subsections (1) and (3) may also be exercised to impose requirements on—

(a) a person who is connected with an authorised person;

(b) an operator, trustee or depositary of a scheme recognised under section 270 or 272 who is not an authorised person;

(c) a recognised investment exchange or recognised clearing house.

(8) "Authorised person" includes a person who was at any time an authorised person but who has ceased to be an authorised person.

(9) "Officer" means an officer of the Authority and includes a member of the Authority's staff or an agent of the Authority.

(10) "Specified" means—

(a) in subsections (1) and (2), specified in the notice; and

(b) in subsection (3), specified in the authorisation.

(11) For the purposes of this section, a person is connected with an authorised person ("A") if he is or has at any relevant time been—

(a) a member of A's group;

(b) a controller of A;

(c) any other member of a partnership of which A is a member; or

(d) in relation to A, a person mentioned in Part I of Schedule 15.

Annotations:

Modifications etc. (not altering text)

C162 S. 165 amended (1.12.2001) by S.I. 2001/2657, arts. 1(1), 15(1) (which was revoked (8.10.2001) by S.I. 2001/3083, arts. 1(2), 23); S.I. 2001/3538, art. 2(1) (b)向其出示规定文件或规定种类的文件。

(4)本条仅适用于与管理局行使本法授予或根据本法授予管理局的职能相关的合理要求提供的信息和文件。

(5)管理局可以要求根据本条所提供的任何信息以其合理要求的形式提供。

(6)管理局可以要求

(a)以其合理要求的方式对提供的任何信息进行验证,无论是包含在文件中还是以任何其他形式提供的信息,或

(b)以其合理要求的方式认证出示的任何文件。

(7)第(1)款和第(3)款授予的权力还可以为对下列人员提出要求而行使:

(a)与获授权人有关联的人;

(b)根据第270条或第272条认可的计划的执行人、受托人或托管人,且为非授权人;

(c)获认可的投资交易所或获认可的清算所。

(8)"获授权人"包括在任何时候曾经是获授权人,但已不再是获授权人的人。

(9)"官员"系指管理局的一名官员,且包括管理局的工作人员中的一员或管理局的代理人。

(10)"规定"系指

(a)在第(1)款和第(2)款中,指通知中规定;

(b)在第(3)款中,指授权中规定。

(11)就本条而言,在任何相关时间属于或曾经属于下列情况的人,为与获授权人(以下简称A)有关联:

(a)A集团的成员;

(b)A的控制人;

(c)A是其成员的合伙中的任何其他成员;或

(d)与A相关,附录15第一部分所述的人。

注释:

修改等(不涉及条文内容)

C162　第165条于2001年12月1日依照制定法文件S.I.2001/2657第1条第(1)款、第15条第(1)款[于2001年10月8日依照制定法文件S.I.2001/3083,第1条第(2)款、第23条撤销];制定法文件S.I.2001/3538第2条第(1)款修正;

S. 165 amended (temp. from 11.8.2001 to 1.12.2001) by S.I. 2001/2659, arts. 1(2), 2; S. I. 2001/3538, art. 2(1)

S. 165 amended (1.12.2001) by S.I. 2001/3083, arts. 1(2), 15(1); S.I. 2001/3538, art. 2 (1)

C163 S. 165 modified (temp.) (8.4.2002) by The Financial Services and Markets Act 2000 (Permission and Applications) (Credit Unions etc.) Order 2002 (S.I. 2002/704), art. 8 (1)(3)

C164 S. 165 amended (18.7.2002 for certain purposes and 21.8.2002 otherwise) by The Electronic Commerce Directive (Financial Services and Markets) Regulations 2002 (S.I. 2002/1775), regs. 1, 12(3)

C165 S. 165(1)(2) extended (1.12.2001) by S.I. 2001/3646, arts. 1(1), 2(1)(3)(a)

C166 S. 165(2) applied (with modifications) (11.4.2002 for certain purposes and 27.4.2002 otherwise) by The Financial Services and Markets Act 2000 (Regulated Activities) Order 2001 (S.I. 2001/544), art. 9G(6) (as inserted by The Financial Services and Markets Act 2000 (Regulated Activities) (Amendment) Order 2002 (S.I. 2002/682), arts. 1(2), 4)

C167 S. 165(5)(6) extended (1.12.2001) by S.I. 2001/3646, arts. 1(1), 2(3)(b)(c)

C168 S. 165(5) applied (with modifications) (11.4.2002 for certain purposes and 27.4.2002 otherwise) by The Financial Services and Markets Act 2000 (Regulated Activities) Order 2001 (S.I. 2001/544), art. 9G(6) (as inserted by The Financial Services and Markets Act 2000 (Regulated Activities) (Amendment) Order 2002 (S.I. 2002/682), arts. 1(2), 4)

C169 S. 165(6) applied (with modifications) (11.4.2002 for certain purposes and 27.4.2002 otherwise) by The Financial Services and Markets Act 2000 (Regulated Activities) Order 2001 (S.I. 2001/544), art. 9G(6) (as inserted by The Financial Services and Markets Act 2000 (Regulated Activities) (Amendment) Order 2002 (S.I. 2002/682), arts. 1(2), 4)

166 Reports by skilled persons.

(1) The Authority may, by notice in writing given to a person to whom subsection (2) applies, require him to provide the Authority with a report on any matter about which the Authority has required or could require the provision of information or production of documents under section 165.

(2) This subsection applies to—

(a) an authorised person ("A"),

(b) any other member of A's group,

(c) a partnership of which A is a member, or

第165条暂时有效，于2001年8月11日至2001年12月1日依照制定法文件S.I. 2001/2659第1条第(2)款、第2条；制定法文件S.I.2001/3538第2条第(1)款修正；

第165条于2001年12月1日依照制定法文件S.I.2001/3083第1条第(2)款、第15条第(1)款；制定法文件S.I.2001/3538第2条第(1)款修正。

C163 第165条暂时有效，于2002年4月8日开始依照《2000年金融服务与市场法》(许可与申请)(信用合作社等)2002号令(制定法文件S.I.2002/704)第8条第(1)款、第(3)款修订。

C164 第165条为特定目的于2002年7月18日，否则于2002年8月21日《2002年电子商务指令条例》(金融服务与市场)(制定法文件S.I.2002/1775)，第1条、第12条第(3)款修正。

C165 第165条第(1)款、第(2)款于2001年12月1日依照制定法文件S.I.2001/3646第1条第(1)款、第2条第(1)款、第(3)款第(a)项扩大适用范围。

C166 第165条第(2)款(已修订)为特定目的于2002年4月11日，否则于2002年4月27日依照《2000年金融服务与市场法》(受监管活动)2001号令(制定法文件S.I.2001/544)第9G条第(6)款[依照《2000年金融服务与市场法》(受监管活动)(修正)2002号令(制定法文件S.I.2002/682)第1条第(2)款、第4条插入]适用。

C167 第165条第(5)款、第(6)款于2002年4月11日依照制定法文件S.I.2001/3646第1条第(1)款、第2条第(3)款第(b)项、第(c)项扩大适用范围。

C168 第165条第(5)款(已修订)为特定目的于2002年4月11日，否则于2002年4月27日依照《2000年金融服务与市场法》(受监管活动)2001号令(制定法文件S.I. 2001/544)，第9G条第(6)款[依照《2000年金融服务与市场法》(受监管活动)(修正)2002号令(制定法文件S.I.2002/682)第1条第(2)款、第4条插入]适用。

C169 第165条第(6)款(已修订)为特定目的于2002年4月11日，否则于2002年4月27日依照《2000年金融服务与市场法》(受监管活动)2001号令(制定法文件S.I. 2001/544)，第9G条第(6)款[依照《2000年金融服务与市场法》(受监管活动)(修正)2002号令(制定法文件S.I.2002/682)第1条第(2)款、第4条插入]适用。

第166条 掌握技能的人员所作的报告

(1)管理局可以向适用第(2)款的人发出书面通知，要求其向管理局就管理局依照第165条已要求或可要求就其提供信息或出示文件的任何事项向管理局提供报告。

(2)本款适用于

(a)获授权人(以下简称A)，

(b)A集团的任何其他成员，

(c)A为成员的合伙，或

(d) a person who has at any relevant time been a person falling within paragraph (a), (b) or (c),

who is, or was at the relevant time, carrying on a business.

(3) The Authority may require the report to be in such form as may be specified in the notice.

(4) The person appointed to make a report required by subsection (1) must be a person

(a) nominated or approved by the Authority; and

(b) appearing to the Authority to have the skills necessary to make a report on the matter concerned.

(5) It is the duty of any person who is providing (or who at any time has provided) services to a person to whom subsection (2) applies in relation to a matter on which a report is required under subsection (1) to give a person appointed to provide such a report all such assistance as the appointed person may reasonably require.

(6) The obligation imposed by subsection (5) is enforceable, on the application of the Authority, by an injunction or, in Scotland, by an order for specific performance under section 45 of the [M18]Court of Session Act 1988.

Annotations:

Modifications etc. (not altering text)

C170 S. 166 modified (1.12.2001) by S.I. 2001/2657, arts. 1(1), 16 (which wasrevoked (8.10.2001) by S.I. 2001/3083, arts. 1(2), 23); S.I. 2001/3538, art. 2(1)S. 166 modified (1.12.2001) by S.I. 2001/3083, arts. 1(2), 16; S.I. 2001/3538, art. 2(1)

C171 S. 166 amended (18.7.2002 for certain purposes and 21.8.2002 otherwise) by The Electronic Commerce Directive (Financial Services and Markets) Regulations 2002 (S.I. 2002/1775), regs. 1, 12(3)

C172 S. 166 applied (with modifications) (11.4.2002 for certain purposes and 27.4.2002 otherwise) by The Financial Services and Markets Act 2000 (Regulated Activities) Order 2001 (S.I. 2001/544), art. 9G(7) (as inserted by The Financial Services and Markets Act 2000 (Regulated Activities) (Amendment) Order 2002 (S.I. 2002/682), arts. 1(2), 4)

C173 S. 166(1)(3)(4) extended (1.12.2001) by S.I. 2001/3646, arts. 1(1), 4(1)(3)(4)

Marginal Citations

M18 1988 c. 36.

(d)在任何相关时间曾经属于第(a)项、第(b)项或第(c)项规定的人，

并且在相关时间正在或者曾经从事经营活动的人。

(3)管理局可以要求报告以其在通知中可能规定的形式作出。

(4)依照第(1)款的要求委派的报告制作人必须是

(a)由管理局提名或批准；且

(b)管理局认为掌握就相关事项作出报告的必要技能的人。

(5)向适用第(2)款的人就第(1)款要求作出报告的事项提供(或在任何时候曾经提供)服务的人，有职责向被委派制作报告的人提供被任命人合理要求获得的所有协助。

(6)第(5)款提出的义务基于管理局的申请，可通过强制令，或者在苏格兰通过 M18《1988年高等民事法院法》第45条规定的履行令强制执行。

注释：

修改等(不涉及条文内容)

C170　第166条于2001年12月1日依照制定法文件S.I.2001/2657，第1条第(1)款、第16条[于2001年10月8日依照制定法文件S.I.2001/3083，第1条第(2)款、第23条撤销]；制定法文件S.I.2001/3538第2条第(1)款修订。

C171　第166条为特定目的于2002年7月18日，否则于2002年8月21日依照《2002年电子商务指令条例》(金融服务与市场)(制定法文S.I.2002/1775)第1条、第12条第(3)款修正。

C172　第166条(已修订)为特定目的于2002年4月11日，否则于2002年4月27日依照《2000年金融服务与市场法》(受监管活动)2001号令(制定法文件S.I.2001/544)第9G条第(7)款(依照《2000年金融服务与市场法》(受监管活动)(修正)2002号令(制定法文件S.I.2002/682)第1条第(2)款、第4条插入]适用。

C173　第166条第(1)款、第(3)款、第(4)款于2001年12月1日依照制定法文件S.I.2001/3646第1条第(1)款，第4条第(1)款、第(3)款、第(4)款扩大适用范围。

附注引文

M18　1988年第36章。

Appointment of investigators

167 Appointment of persons to carry out general investigations.

(1) If it appears to the Authority or the Secretary of State ("the investigating authority") that there is good reason for doing so, the investigating authority may appoint one or more competent persons to conduct an investigation on its behalf into—

(a) the nature, conduct or state of the business of an authorised person or of an appointed representative;

(b) a particular aspect of that business; or

(c) the ownership or control of an authorised person.

(2) If a person appointed under subsection (1) thinks it necessary for the purposes of his investigation, he may also investigate the business of a person who is or has at any relevant time been—

(a) a member of the group of which the person under investigation ("A") is part; or

(b) a partnership of which A is a member.

(3) If a person appointed under subsection (1) decides to investigate the business of any person under subsection (2) he must give that person written notice of his decision.

(4) The power conferred by this section may be exercised in relation to a former authorized person (or appointed representative) but only in relation to—

(a) business carried on at any time when he was an authorised person (or appointed representative); or

(b) the ownership or control of a former authorised person at any time when he was an authorised person.

(5) "Business" includes any part of a business even if it does not consist of carrying on regulated activities.

Annotations:

Modifications etc. (not altering text)

C174 S. 167 modified (1.12.2001) by S.I. 2001/2657, arts. 1(1), 17 (which was revoked (8.10.2001) by S.I. 2001/3083, arts. 1(2), 23); S.I. 2001/3538, art. 2(1)

S. 167 modified (1.12.2001) by S.I. 2001/3083, arts. 1(2), 17; S.I. 2001/3538, art. 2(1)

C175 S. 167 amended (18.7.2002 for certain purposes and 21.8.2002 otherwise) by The Electronic Commerce Directive (Financial Services and Markets) Regulations 2002 (S.I. 2002/1775), regs. 1, 12(3)

168 Appointment of persons to carry out investigations in particular cases.

(1) Subsection (3) applies if it appears to an investigating authority that there are

调查人的任命

第167条　任命进行一般调查的人

(1)如管理局或国务大臣(以下简称调查机关)认为有理由进行调查,则调查机关可以任命一名或多名适格人员代表调查机关就下列事项展开调查:

(a)获授权人或被任命代表的业务性质、行为或状态;

(b)其业务的某一特定方面;或

(c)对获授权人的所有权或控制情况。

(2)如依照第(1)款被任命的调查人员认为对其调查有必要,也可对下列人员的业务进行调查:

(a)在任何相关时间内是或一直是被调查人(以下简称A)所属集团的成员;或

(b)在任何相关时间内是或一直是A所属的合伙。

(3)如依照本条第(1)款任命的调查人决定对本条第(2)款规定的人员的业务进行调查,则必须就其调查决定向被调查人发出书面通知。

(4)仅在与下列事项相关时,本条所授予的权力可以对以前的获授权人(或被任命代表)行使:

(a)被调查人作为获授权人(或被任命代表)时所从事的业务;或

(b)在被调查人仍是获授权人期间,对其享有的所有权或控制权。

(5)"业务"包括某一业务经营的所有部分,即使其中不包含从事任何受监管活动。

注释:

修改等(不涉及条文内容)

C174　第167条于2001年12月1日依照制定法文件S.I.2001/2657第1条第(1)款、第17条[于2001年10月8日依照制定法文件S.I.2001/3083第1条第(2)款、第23条被撤销];制定法文件S.I.2001/3538第2条第(1)款修订;

第167条于2001年12月1日依照制定法文件S.I.2001/3083第1条第(2)款、第17条;制定法文件S.I.2001/3538第2条第(1)款修订;

C175　为特定目的于2002年7月18日,否则于2002年8月21日第167条依《2002年电子商务指令条例》(金融服务与市场)(制定法文件S.I.2002/1775)第1条、第12条第(3)款修正。

第168条　任命对特定案件进行调查的人

(1)如调查机关认为有证据表明下列情况,则适用本条第(3)款规定:

circumstances suggesting that—

(a) a person may have contravened any regulation made under section 142; or

(b) a person may be guilty of an offence under section 177, 191, 346 or 398 (1) or under Schedule 4.

(2) Subsection (3) also applies if it appears to an investigating authority that there are circumstances suggesting that—

(a) an offence under section 24(1) or 397 or under Part V of the[M19]Criminal Justice Act 1993 may have been committed;

(b) there may have been a breach of the general prohibition;

(c) there may have been a contravention of section 21 or 238; or

(d) market abuse may have taken place.

(3) The investigating authority may appoint one or more competent persons to conduct an investigation on its behalf.

(4) Subsection (5) applies if it appears to the Authority that there are circumstances suggesting that—

(a) a person may have contravened section 20;

(b) a person may be guilty of an offence under prescribed regulations relating to money laundering;

(c) an authorised person may have contravened a rule made by the Authority;

(d) an individual may not be a fit and proper person to perform functions in relation to a regulated activity carried on by an authorised or exempt person;

(e) an individual may have performed or agreed to perform a function in breach of a prohibition order;

(f) an authorised or exempt person may have failed to comply with section 56(6);

(g) an authorised person may have failed to comply with section 59(1) or (2);

(h) a person in relation to whom the Authority has given its approval under section 59 may not be a fit and proper person to perform the function to which that approval relates; or

(i) a person may be guilty of misconduct for the purposes of section 66.

(5) The Authority may appoint one or more competent persons to conduct an investigation on its behalf.

(6) "Investigating authority" means the Authority or the Secretary of State.

(a)当事人可能违反了根据第142条制定的相关规定;或

(b)根据第177条、第191条、第346条或者第398条第(1)款或者附录4,当事人的行为可能构成犯罪。

(2)如调查机关认为有相关证据表明下列情况,则本条第(3)款仍然适用:

(a)可能存在实施了第24条第(1)款或第397条或[M19]《1993年刑事司法法》第五部分规定的犯罪的行为;

(b)可能存在违反了一般禁止性规定的行为;

(c)可能存在违反了第21条或第238条规定的行为;或

(d)可能发生了市场滥用行为。

(3)调查机关有权任命一名或多名适格人员代表其进行调查。

(4)如调查机关认为有证据表明下列情况,则适用本条第(5)款规定:[1]

(a)当事人可能违反了第20条的规定;

(b)当事人可能实施了洗钱犯罪相关法规的犯罪行为;

(c)获授权人可能违反了管理局制定的规则;

(d)对履行与由获授权人或享有豁免权的人进行的受监管活动有关的职能,某人可能不是适当人选。

(e)当事人可能已经实施或者同意实施违反禁令的行为;

(f)获授权人或享有豁免权的人未能遵守第56条第(6)款的规定;

(g)获授权人未能遵守第59条第(1)款或第(2)款的规定;

(h)管理局依照第59条给予许可的人可能不是履行与批准相关职能的适当人选;或

(i)为了第66条的目的,当事人可能因不当行为而犯罪。

(5)管理局可任命一名或多名适格人员代表其进行调查。

(6)“调查机关”系指管理局或国务大臣。

1 本款依照《2010年金融服务法》附录2第一部分第16条修订。——译者注

Annotations:

Modifications etc. (not altering text)

C176 S. 168 amended (18.7.2002 for certain purposes and 21.8.2002 otherwise) by The Electronic Commerce Directive (Financial Services and Markets) Regulations 2002 (S.I. 2002/1775), regs. 1, 12(3)

C177 S. 168(3)(5) applied (1.12.2001) by S.I. 2001/2657, arts. 1(1), 18(1)(3)(which was revoked 8.10.2001) by S.I. 2001/3083, arts. 1(2), 23); S.I. 2001/3538, art. 2(1)

S. 168(3)(5) applied (1.12.2001) by S.I. 2001/3083, arts. 1(2), 18(1)(3); S.I.2001/3538, art. 2(1)

C178 S. 168(4) applied (with modifications) (11.4.2002 for certain purposes and 27.4.2002 otherwise) by The Financial Services and Markets Act 2000 (Regulated Activities) Order 2001 (S.I. 2001/544), art. 9G(8) (as inserted by The Financial Services and Markets Act 2000 (Regulated Activities) (Amendment) Order 2002 (S.I. 2002/682), arts. 1(2), 4)

C179 S. 168(4)(c) amended (18.7.2002 for certain purposes and 21.8.2002 otherwise) by The Electronic Commerce Directive (Financial Services and Markets) Regulations 2002 (S. I. 2002/1775), regs. 1, 12(5)

Commencement Information

I48 S. 168 wholly in force at 3.9.2001; s. 168 not in force at Royal Assent see s. 431(2); s. 168(4)(b) in force for certain purposes at 25.2.2001 by S.I. 2001/516, art. 2(b), Sch. Pt. 2; s. 168 in force in so far as not already in force at 3.9.2001 by S.I. 2001/2632, art. 2(2), Sch. Pt. 2

Marginal Citations

M19 1993 c. 36.

Assistance to overseas regulators

169 Investigations etc. in support of overseas regulator.

(1) At the request of an overseas regulator, the Authority may

(a) exercise the power conferred by section 165; or

(b) appoint one or more competent persons to investigate any matter.

(2) An investigator has the same powers as an investigator appointed under section 168

注释：

修改等(不涉及条文内容)

C176　第168条为特定目的于2002年7月18日，否则于2002年8月21日依照《2002年电子商务指令条例》(金融服务与市场)(制定法文件S.I.2002/1775)第1条、第12条第(3)款修正。

C177　第168条第(3)款、第(5)款于2001年12月1日依照制定法文件S.I.2001/2657第1条第(1)款、第18条第(1)款、第(3)款(于2001年10月8日依照制定法文件S.I.2001/3083第1条第(2)款、第23条撤销)；制定法文件S.I.2001/3538第2条第(1)款适用；

第168条第(3)款、第(5)款于2001年12月1日依照制定法文件S.I.2001/3083第1条第(2)款，第18条第(1)款、第(3)款；制定法文件S.I.2001/3538第2条第(1)款适用；

C178　第168条第(4)款(已修订)为特定目的于2002年4月11日，否则于2002年4月27日依照《2000年金融服务与市场法》(受监管活动)2001号令(制定法文件S.I.2001/544)第9G条第(8)款[依照《2000年金融服务与市场法》(受监管活动)(修正)2002号令(制定法文件S.I.2002/682)第1条第(2)款、第4条插入]适用。

C179　第168条第(4)款第(c)项为特定目的于2002年7月18日，否则于2002年8月21日依照《2002年电子商务指令条例》(金融服务与市场)(制定法文件S.I.2002/1775)第1条、第12条第(5)款修正。

实施日期

I48　第168条于2001年9月3日全部生效；第168条在副署时尚未生效，见第431条第(2)款；第168条第(4)款第(b)项为特定目的于2001年2月25日依照制定法文件S.I.2001/516第2条第(b)款、附录第二部分生效；第168条如于2001年9月3日尚未生效，则依照制定法文件S.I.2001/2632第2条第(2)款、附录第二部分生效。

附注引文

M19　1993年第36章。

对境外监管机关的协助

第169条　支持境外监管机关的调查等活动[1]

(1)根据境外监管机关请求，管理局可以

(a)行使第165条授予的权力；或

(b)任命一名或多名适格人员就任何事项展开调查。

(2)本条所规定之调查人享有与依照第168条第(3)款[由于该条第(1)款的规定]

1 本条依照《2010年金融服务法》第18条第(3)款修订。——译者注

(3) (as a result of subsection (1) of that section).

(3) If the request has been made by a competent authority in pursuance of any Community obligation the Authority must, in deciding whether or not to exercise its investigative power, consider whether its exercise is necessary to comply with any such obligation.

(4) In deciding whether or not to exercise its investigative power, the Authority may take into account in particular—

(a) whether in the country or territory of the overseas regulator concerned, corresponding assistance would be given to a United Kingdom regulatory authority;

(b) whether the case concerns the breach of a law, or other requirement, which has no close parallel in the United Kingdom or involves the assertion of a jurisdiction not recognised by the United Kingdom;

(c) the seriousness of the case and its importance to persons in the United Kingdom;

(d) whether it is otherwise appropriate in the public interest to give the assistance sought.

(5) The Authority may decide that it will not exercise its investigative power unless the overseas regulator undertakes to make such contribution towards the cost of its exercise as the Authority considers appropriate.

(6) Subsections (4) and (5) do not apply if the Authority considers that the exercise of its investigative power is necessary to comply with a Community obligation.

(7) If the Authority has appointed an investigator in response to a request from an overseas regulator, it may direct the investigator to permit a representative of that regulator to attend, and take part in, any interview conducted for the purposes of the investigation.

(8) A direction under subsection (7) is not to be given unless the Authority is satisfied that any information obtained by an overseas regulator as a result of the interview will be subject to safeguards equivalent to those contained in Part XXIII.

(9) The Authority must prepare a statement of its policy with respect to the conduct of interviews in relation to which a direction under subsection (7) has been given.

(10) The statement requires the approval of the Treasury.

(11) If the Treasury approve the statement, the Authority must publish it.

(12) No direction may be given under subsection (7) before the statement has been published.

(13) "Overseas regulator" has the same meaning as in section 195.

(14) "Investigative power" means one of the powers mentioned in subsection (1).

(15) "Investigator" means a person appointed under subsection (1)(b).

任命的调查人相同的权力。

(3)如相应有权机关提出的请求乃是出于履行共同体义务之目的,则管理局在决定是否行使调查权时,必须考虑该等调查权的行使对于履行此等共同体义务是否必要。

(4)在决定是否行使其调查权时,管理局可以特别考虑

(a)相关境外监管机关的国家或地区是否向联合王国监管机关提供对等的协助;

(b)相关案件所涉及的违法行为,或违反其他要求的行为,在联合王国是否有相对应的规定,或者是否涉及联合王国不予承认的管辖权的主张;

(c)案件的严重性以及案件对在联合王国的人的重要性;

(d)给予所请求之协助是否在其他方面对公共利益是适当的。

(5)管理局可以决定不行使调查权,除非境外监管机关承诺分担管理局认为适当的调查权行使费用。

(6)如管理局认为行使其调查权对于遵守共同体义务是有必要的,则不适用第(4)款和第(5)款规定。

(7)如根据境外监管机关的请求,管理局任命了调查人,则管理局可以指示该调查人允许该监管机关的代表出席并参与该调查人为调查之目的进行的任何会谈。

(8)除非管理局认为境外监管机关在其所参与的会谈中所获取的信息能够处于与在第二十三部分中获得的保护相同的保护之下,否则本条第(7)款规定之指示不得作出。

(9)管理局必须就与依照第(7)款已经作出的指示有关的会谈行为制定一份政策声明。

(10)该声明需经财政部批准。

(11)如财政部批准了该声明,则管理局必须公开该声明。

(12)在上述声明公开前,不得依照第(7)款的规定作出指令。

(13)"境外监管机关"含义同第195条。

(14)"调查权"系指本条第(1)款所提及的任何一项权力。

(15)"调查人"系指依据本条第(1)款第(b)项所任命的人员。

Annotations:

Commencement Information

I49 S. 169 wholly in force at 3.9.2001; s. 169 not in force at Royal Assent see s. 431(2); s. 169 in force for specified purposes at 18.6.2001 by S.I. 2001/1820, art. 2, Sch.; s. 169 in force in so far as not already in force at 3.9.2001 by S.I. 2001/2632, art. 2(2), Sch. Pt. 2

Conduct of investigations

170 Investigations: general.

(1) This section applies if an investigating authority appoints one or more competent persons ("investigators") under section 167 or 168(3) or (5) to conduct an investigation on its behalf.

(2) The investigating authority must give written notice of the appointment of an investigator to the person who is the subject of the investigation ("the person under investigation").

(3) Subsections (2) and (9) do not apply if—

(a) the investigator is appointed as a result of section 168 (1) or (4) and the investigating authority believes that the notice required by subsection (2) or (9) would be likely to result in the investigation being frustrated; or

(b) the investigator is appointed as a result of subsection (2) of section 168.

(4) A notice under subsection (2) must—

(a) specify the provisions under which, and as a result of which, the investigator was appointed; and

(b) state the reason for his appointment.

(5) Nothing prevents the investigating authority from appointing a person who is a member of its staff as an investigator.

(6) An investigator must make a report of his investigation to the investigating authority.

(7) The investigating authority may, by a direction to an investigator, control—

(a) the scope of the investigation;

(b) the period during which the investigation is to be conducted;

(c) the conduct of the investigation; and

(d) the reporting of the investigation.

(8) A direction may, in particular—

(a) confine the investigation to particular matters;

(b) extend the investigation to additional matters;

(c) require the investigator to discontinue the investigation or to take only such steps as

注释：

实施日期

I49 第169条于2001年9月3日全部生效；第169条在副署时尚未生效，见第431条第(2)款；第169条为特定目的于2001年6月18日依照制定法文件S.I.2001/1820第2条、附录生效；第169条如于2001年9月3日尚未生效，则依照制定法文件S.I.2001/2632第2条第(2)款、附录第二部分生效。

调查的实施

第170条 调查：一般规定

(1)如调查机关依照第167条或第168条第(3)款或第168条第(5)款的规定任命了一名或多名适格人员(以下简称调查人)代表其进行调查，则适用本条规定。

(2)调查机关必须就调查人的任命向接受调查之人(以下简称被调查人)出具书面通知。

(3)如有下列情况，则本条第(2)款及第(9)款不适用：

(a)调查人的任命是依据第168条第(1)款或第(4)款的规定，并且管理局相信本条第(2)款及第(9)款所要求的通知很可能对调查产生破坏性影响；或

(b)调查人的任命是依照第168条第(2)款作出的。

(4)本条第(2)款规定的通知必须

(a)指明调查人的任命所依据和因由的条款；以及

(b)说明作出任命的理由。

(5)没有任何事项可以阻止调查机关任命其职员中的一员作为调查人。

(6)调查人必须向调查机关就其调查作出报告。

(7)调查机关可向调查人发出指示，控制

(a)调查范围；

(b)调查进行的期间；

(c)调查的具体实施；以及

(d)调查情况的汇报。

(8)指示可以特别

(a)将调查限定于特定事项；

(b)将调查范围拓宽至附加事项；

(c)要求调查人中止调查，或只能采取指令中所规定的行动；

are specified in the direction;

(d) require the investigator to make such interim reports as are so specified.

(9) If there is a change in the scope or conduct of the investigation and, in the opinion of the investigating authority, the person subject to investigation is likely to be significantly prejudiced by not being made aware of it, that person must be given written notice of the change.

(10) "Investigating authority", in relation to an investigator, means—

(a) the Authority, if the Authority appointed him;

(b) the Secretary of State, if the Secretary of State appointed him.

Annotations:

Modifications etc. (not altering text)

C180 S. 170(5)-(9) applied (1.12.2001) by S.I. 2001/1228, regs. 1(2)(c), 30(4) (with 1(2)(3)); S.I. 2001/3538, art. 2(1)

171 Powers of persons appointed under section 167.

(1) An investigator may require the person who is the subject of the investigation ("the person under investigation") or any person connected with the person under investigation—

(a) to attend before the investigator at a specified time and place and answer questions; or

(b) otherwise to provide such information as the investigator may require.

(2) An investigator may also require any person to produce at a specified time and place any specified documents or documents of a specified description.

(3) A requirement under subsection (1) or (2) may be imposed only so far as the investigator concerned reasonably considers the question, provision of information or production of the document to be relevant to the purposes of the investigation.

(4) For the purposes of this section and section 172, a person is connected with the person under investigation ("A") if he is or has at any relevant time been—

(a) a member of A's group;

(b) a controller of A;

(c) a partnership of which A is a member; or

(d) in relation to A, a person mentioned in Part I or II of Schedule 15.

(5) "Investigator" means a person conducting an investigation under section 167.

(6) "Specified" means specified in a notice in writing.

172 Additional power of persons appointed as a result of section 168(1) or (4).

(1) An investigator has the powers conferred by section 171.

(2) An investigator may also require a person who is neither the subject of the

(d)要求调查人根据规定就其调查作出中期报告。

(9)如调查的范围或实施发生变化,调查机关认为如果不向被调查人披露该等变化将会对被调查人造成严重的不公平,则必须就该等变化向被调查人发出书面通知。

(10)涉及调查人之时,"调查机关"

(a)如果是管理局任命了调查人,系指管理局;

(b)如果是国务大臣任命了调查人,系指国务大臣。

注释:

修改等(不涉及条文内容)

C180 第170条第(5)款至第(9)款于2001年12月1日依照制定法文件S.I.2001/1228第1条第(2)款第(c)项、第30条第(4)款[与第1条第(2)款、第(3)款];制定法文件S.I.2001/3538第2条第(1)款适用。

第171条 根据第167条被任命的人的权力

(1)调查人有权要求接受调查的人(以下简称被调查人)或与被调查人相关的人

(a)在具体的时间和地点会见调查人并回答问题;或

(b)以其他方式提供调查员要求的信息。

(2)调查人也有权要求任何人在规定的时间和地点出示规定文件或规定种类的文件。

(3)本条第(1)款和第(2)款规定之要求,仅在相关调查人合理相信其所要求回答的问题、要求提供的信息或要求出示的文件均与调查之目的相关之时,方可提出。

(4)就本条和第172条而言,属于下列范围或在相关时期内曾经属于下列范围的人,是与被调查人(以下简称A)相关的人:

(a)A所属集团的成员;

(b)A的控制人;

(c)A是其成员的合伙;或

(d)与A相关,附录15第一部分或第二部分提及的人员。

(5)"调查人"系指依照第167条规定实施调查的人。

(6)"规定"系指在书面通知中规定。

第172条 依据第168条第(1)款或第(4)款被任命的人的附加权力

(1)调查人享有第171条授予的权力。

(2)对于既不是接受调查的人(以下简称被调查人)也不是与被调查人相关之人,

investigation ("the person under investigation") nor a person connected with the person under investigation—

(a) to attend before the investigator at a specified time and place and answer questions; or

(b) otherwise to provide such information as the investigator may require for the purposes of the investigation.

(3) A requirement may only be imposed under subsection (2) if the investigator is satisfied that the requirement is necessary or expedient for the purposes of the investigation.

(4) "Investigator" means a person appointed as a result of subsection (1) or (4) of section 168.

(5) "Specified" means specified in a notice in writing.

173 Powers of persons appointed as a result of section 168(2).

(1) Subsections (2) to (4) apply if an investigator considers that any person ("A") is or may be able to give information which is or may be relevant to the investigation.

(2) The investigator may require A—

(a) to attend before him at a specified time and place and answer questions; or

(b) otherwise to provide such information as he may require for the purposes of the investigation.

(3) The investigator may also require A to produce at a specified time and place any specified documents or documents of a specified description which appear to the investigator to relate to any matter relevant to the investigation.

(4) The investigator may also otherwise require A to give him all assistance in connection with the investigation which A is reasonably able to give.

(5) "Investigator" means a person appointed under subsection (3) of section 168 (as a result of subsection (2) of that section).

174 Admissibility of statements made to investigators.

(1) A statement made to an investigator by a person in compliance with an information requirement is admissible in evidence in any proceedings, so long as it also complies with any requirements governing the admissibility of evidence in the circumstances in question.

(2) But in criminal proceedings in which that person is charged with an offence to whichthis subsection applies or in proceedings in relation to action to be taken against thatperson under section 123—

(a) no evidence relating to the statement may be adduced, and

(b) no question relating to it may be asked,

by or on behalf of the prosecution or (as the case may be) the Authority, unless evidence relating to it is adduced, or a question relating to it is asked, in the proceedings by or on behalf of that person.

调查人也有权要求其

(a)在规定的时间或地点与调查人会见并回答问题;或

(b)以其他方式向调查人提供因调查所需而要求其提供的信息。

(3)本条第(2)款规定的要求,只有在调查人认为为调查之目的,该相关要求有必要或适宜时,才可以提出。

(4)"调查人"系指依照第168条第(1)款或第(4)款任命的人。

(5)"规定"系指在书面通知中规定。

第173条　依据第168条第(2)款被任命的人的权力

(1)如调查员认为任何人(以下简称A)可能能够提供与调查相关或可能相关之信息,则本条第(2)款至第(4)款适用。

(2)调查人有权要求A

(a)在指定的时间和地点与调查人会见并回答问题;或

(b)以其他方式向调查人提供因调查所需而要求其提供的信息。

(3)调查人有权要求A在规定的时间地点出示调查人认为与调查涉及的任何事项有关的规定文件或规定种类的文件。

(4)调查人还有权要求A在其能够合理提供的范围内向调查人提供与调查相关的其他协助。

(5)"调查人"系指依照第168条第(3)款[由于该条第(2)款的规定]任命的人。

第174条　对调查人陈述的可采性

(1)对于某人依照信息要求而向调查人作出的陈述,只要该等陈述在也符合相关情形下管辖法律对证据采信规则的要求,则该等陈述可以在任何程序中作为证据予以采信。

(2)但是,如果某人被指控某项刑事罪名,且对于该罪名本条规定应予适用,则在该等刑事程序中,或者在依照第123条规定针对该人采取措施的相关程序中,检方或检方代表或者(视案件情况而定)管理局或管理局的代表应遵守下列规定:

(a)不得引用任何与该人作出之陈述相关的证据,并且

(b)不得提出与上述陈述相关的任何问题,

除非在由此人或代表此人发起的程序中,与其相关的证据被引出,或相关的问题被提出。

(3) Subsection (2) applies to any offence other than one—

(a) under section 177(4) or 398;

(b) under section 5 of the[M20]Perjury Act 1911 (false statements made otherwise than on oath);

(c) under section 44(2) of the[M21]Criminal Law (Consolidation)(Scotland) Act 1995 (false statements made otherwise than on oath); or

(d) under Article 10 of the[M22]Perjury (Northern Ireland) Order 1979.

(4) "Investigator" means a person appointed under section 167 or 168(3) or (5).

(5) "Information requirement" means a requirement imposed by an investigator under section 171, 172, 173 or 175.

Annotations:

Modifications etc. (not altering text)

C181 S. 174 applied (1.12.2001) by S.I. 2001/1228, regs. 1(2)(c), 30(5) (with reg. 1 (2)(3)); S.I. 2001/3538, art. 2(1)

S. 174 applied (with modifications) (1.12.2001) by S.I. 2001/3646, arts. 1(1), 2(4), 4 (5)

Marginal Citations

M20 1911 c. 6.

M21 1995 c. 39.

M22 S.I. 1979/1714 (N.I. 19).

175 Information and documents: supplemental provisions.

(1) If the Authority or an investigator has power under this Part to require a person to produce a document but it appears that the document is in the possession of a third person, that power may be exercised in relation to the third person.

(2) If a document is produced in response to a requirement imposed under this Part, the person to whom it is produced may—

(a) take copies or extracts from the document; or

(b) require the person producing the document, or any relevant person, to provide an explanation of the document.

(3) If a person who is required under this Part to produce a document fails to do so, the Authority or an investigator may require him to state, to the best of his knowledge and belief, where the document is.

(4) A lawyer may be required under this Part to furnish the name and address of his client.

(3)本条第(2)款适用于所有犯罪,但下列各项除外——

(a)第177条第(4)款或第398条规定的犯罪;

(b)[M20]《1911年伪证法》第5条规定的犯罪(以宣誓之外的其他方式作出的虚假陈述);

(c)[M21]《1995年刑法》(统一)(苏格兰)第44条第(2)款规定的犯罪(以宣誓之外的其他方式作出的虚假陈述);或

(d)[M22]《1979年伪证法令》(北爱尔兰)第10条规定的犯罪;

(4)"调查人",系指依照第167条、第168条第(3)款或第168条第(5)款规定任命的人。

(5)"信息要求",系指调查人依照第171条、第172条、第173条或第175条提出的要求。

注释:

修改等(不涉及条文内容)

C181 第174条于2001年12月1日依照制定法文件S.I.2001/1228第1条第(2)款第(c)项、第30条第(5)款[与第1条第(2)款、第(3)款];制定法文件S.I.2001/3538第2条第(1)款适用;

第174条(已修订)于2001年12月1日依照制定法文件S.I.2001/3646第1条第(1)款、第2条第(4)款、第4条第(5)款适用。

附注引文

M20 1911年第6章。

M21 1995年第39章。

M22 制定法文件S.I.1979/1714(N.I.19)。

第175条 信息与文件:补充规定

(1)如果依照本部分之规定,管理局或调查人有权要求某人出具文件,但该文件处于第三方控制之下,则管理局及调查人可对该第三方行使要求出示该等文件的权力。

(2)如依照本部分的要求出示了某一文件,则该等文件的接收方可以

(a)复制或摘录该文件;或

(b)要求文件的出示人或其他相关人就文件作出解释。

(3)如果依据本部分之规定被要求出示文件的人未能出示文件,则管理局或调查人有权要求此人根据其所知的所有信息说明该等文件位于何处。

(4)依据本部分之规定,可以要求律师提供其客户的名字和地址。

(5) No person may be required under this Part to disclose information or produce a document in respect of which he owes an obligation of confidence by virtue of carrying on the business of banking unless—

(a) he is the person under investigation or a member of that person's group;

(b) the person to whom the obligation of confidence is owed is the person under investigation or a member of that person's group;

(c) the person to whom the obligation of confidence is owed consents to the disclosure or production; or

(d) the imposing on him of a requirement with respect to such information or document has been specifically authorised by the investigating authority.

(6) If a person claims a lien on a document, its production under this Part does not affect the lien.

(7) "Relevant person", in relation to a person who is required to produce a document, means a person who—

(a) has been or is or is proposed to be a director or controller of that person;

(b) has been or is an auditor of that person;

(c) has been or is an actuary, accountant or lawyer appointed or instructed by that person; or

(d) has been or is an employee of that person.

(8) "Investigator" means a person appointed under section 167 or 168(3) or (5).

Annotations:

Modifications etc. (not altering text)

C182 S. 175 applied (with modifications) (11.4.2002 for certain purposes and 27.4.2002 otherwise) by The Financial Services and Markets Act 2000 (Regulated Activities) Order 2001 (S.I. 2001/544), art. 9G(9) (as inserted by The Financial Services and Markets Act 2000 (Regulated Activities) (Amendment) Order 2002 (S.I. 2002/682), arts. 1(2), 4)

C183 S. 175(2)-(4)(6) amended (1.12.2001) by S.I. 2001/1228, regs. 1(2)(c), 30 (6) (with reg. 1(2)(3)); S.I. 2001/3538, art. 2(1)

176 Entry of premises under warrant.

(1) A justice of the peace may issue a warrant under this section if satisfied on information on oath given by or on behalf of the Secretary of State, the Authority or an investigator that there are reasonable grounds for believing that the first, second or third set of conditions is satisfied.

(5)不得依照本部分之规定,要求任何人披露或出示该人因经营银行业务而负有保密义务的任何信息或文件,除非

(a)其是被调查人或被调查人的集团的成员;
(b)其负有保密义务的人是被调查人或是被调查人的集团的成员;

(c)其负有保密义务的人同意披露或出具信息或文件;或

(d)调查机关已经就要求其出示该等信息或文件作出了特别授权。

(6)如某人对某一文件主张留置权,本部分要求的文件出示不影响该留置权。

(7)"相关人",对于被要求出具文件之人而言,系指

(a)曾经是、目前是或计划成为此人的董事或控制者的人;
(b)曾经是或目前是此人的审计人员;
(c)曾经是或目前是此人任命的精算师、会计师或律师;或

(d)曾经是或目前是此人的雇员。
(8)"调查人"系指依照第167条、第168条第(3)款或第168条第(5)款规定任命的人员。

注释:

修改等(不涉及条文内容)

C182 第175条(已修订)为特定目的于2002年4月11日,否则于2002年4月27日依照《2000年金融服务与市场法》(受监管活动)2001号令(制定法文件S.I.2001/544)第9G条第(9)款[依照《2000年金融服务与市场法》(受监管活动)(修正)2002号令插入][制定法文件S.I.2002/682)第1条第(2)款、第4条]适用。

C183 第175条第(2)款至第(4)款、第(6)款于2001年12月1日依照制定法文件S.I.2001/1228第1条第(2)款第(c)项、第30条第(6)款[与第1条第(2)款、第(3)款];制定法文件S.I.2001/3538第2条第(1)款修正。

第176条 持核准令进入现场

(1)如基于国务大臣或其代表、管理局或其代表或调查人宣誓出具的信息,治安法官认为有合理的理由相信第一、第二或第三组条件已满足,则治安法官可以依照本条规定签发核准令。

(2) The first set of conditions is—

(a) that a person on whom an information requirement has been imposed has failed (wholly or in part) to comply with it; and

(b) that on the premises specified in the warrant

(i) there are documents which have been required; or

(ii) there is information which has been required.

(3) The second set of conditions is—

(a) that the premises specified in the warrant are premises of an authorised person or an appointed representative;

(b) that there are on the premises documents or information in relation to which an information requirement could be imposed; and

(c) that if such a requirement were to be imposed—

(i) it would not be complied with; or

(ii) the documents or information to which it related would be removed, tampered with or destroyed.

(4) The third set of conditions is—

(a) that an offence mentioned in section 168 for which the maximum sentence on conviction on indictment is two years or more has been (or is being) committed by any person;

(b) that there are on the premises specified in the warrant documents or information relevant to whether that offence has been (or is being) committed;

(c) that an information requirement could be imposed in relation to those documents or information; and

(d) that if such a requirement were to be imposed—

(i) it would not be complied with; or

(ii) the documents or information to which it related would be removed, tampered with or destroyed.

(5) A warrant under this section shall authorise a constable—

(a) to enter the premises specified in the warrant;

(b) to search the premises and take possession of any documents or information appearing to be documents or information of a kind in respect of which a warrant under this section was issued ("the relevant kind") or to take, in relation to any such documents or information, any other steps which may appear to be necessary for preserving them or preventing interference with them;

(c) to take copies of, or extracts from, any documents or information appearing to be of the relevant kind;

(d) to require any person on the premises to provide an explanation of any document or

(2)第一组条件是

(a)被要求提供信息的人未能满足(全部或部分)要求;

(b)在核准令中规定的场所

(i)存有所要求的文件;或

(ii)存在所要求的信息。

(3)第二组条件是

(a)核准令中规定的场所是获授权人或其被任命代表的营业场所;

(b)在该场所中存有可要求提供之文件或信息;并且

(c)如果提出该等要求

(i)该等要求不能得到满足;或

(ii)该等要求所涉及的文件或信息将被转移、损毁或销毁。

(4)第三组条件是

(a)任何人已经实施或正在实施第168条规定的经公诉程序定罪最高可处以2年或以上有期徒刑的犯罪;

(b)在核准令中规定的场所存在能够证明行为人是否已经实施或正在实施该等犯罪的文件或信息;

(c)可以针对该等文件或信息提出信息要求;并且

(d)如提出该等要求

(i)该等要求不能得到满足;或

(ii)该等要求所涉及的文件或信息将被转移、损毁或销毁。

(5)本条所规定之核准令,可以授权

(a)进入核准令中规定的场所;

(b)搜查该等场所,并提取任何可能与依照本条规定发出的核准令相关的文件或信息(以下简称相关文件或信息),或对任何该等信息或文件采取其他必要措施予以保存或防止该等信息或文件遭到破坏。

(c)对任何可能的相关文件或信息进行复制、摘录;

(d)要求场所内任何人就可能的相关文件或信息给出解释,或说明该等文件或信

information appearing to be of the relevant kind or to state where it may be found; and

(e) to use such force as may be reasonably necessary.

(6) In England and Wales, sections 15(5) to (8) and section 16 of the[M23]Police and Criminal Evidence Act 1984 (execution of search warrants and safeguards) apply to warrants issued under this section.

(7) In Northern Ireland, Articles 17(5) to (8) and 18 of the[M24]Police and Criminal Evidence (Northern Ireland) Order 1989 apply to warrants issued under this section.

(8) Any document of which possession is taken under this section may be retained—

(a) for a period of three months; or

(b) if within that period proceedings to which the document is relevant are commenced against any person for any criminal offence, until the conclusion of those proceedings.

(9) In the application of this section to Scotland—

(a) for the references to a justice of the peace substitute references to a justice of the peace or a sheriff; and

(b) for the references to information on oath substitute references to evidence on oath.

(10) "Investigator" means a person appointed under section 167 or 168(3) or (5).

(11) "Information requirement" means a requirement imposed—

(a) by the Authority under section 165 or 175; or

(b) by an investigator under section 171, 172, 173 or 175.

Annotations:

Modifications etc. (not altering text)

C184 S. 176 extended (17.8.2001 for certain purposes otherwise 1.12.2001) by 1992 c. 40, s. 62A (as inserted (17.8.2001 for certain purposes otherwise 1.12.2001) by S.I. 2001/2617, arts. 2, 8, 13(1), Sch. 3 Pt. I para. 77 (with art. 13(3), Sch. 5)); S.I. 2001/3538, art. 2(1)

S. 176 modified (17.8.2001 for certain purposes otherwise 1.12.2001) by 1986 c. 53, s. 52B (as substituted (17.8.2001 for certain purposes otherwise 1.12.2001) by S.I. 2001/2617, arts. 2, 8, 13(1), Sch. 3 Pt. I para. 151 (with art. 13(3), Sch. 5)); S.I. 2001/3538, art. 2(1)

S. 176 modified (1.12.2001) by S.I. 1995/1537, reg. 23(4) (as amended (1.12.2001) by S.I. 2001/3649, arts. 1, 509(e))

C185 S. 176 amended (18.7.2002 for certain purposes and 21.8.2002 otherwise) by The Electronic Commerce Directive (Financial Services and Markets) Regulations 2002 (S.I. 2002/1775), regs. 1, 12(3)

息的处所;并且

(e)动用合理且必要的强制力。

(6)在英格兰和威尔士,第15条第(5)款至第(8)款以及M23 1984年《警察及刑事证据法》第16条(搜查令的执行及保护措施)适用于依据本条发出的核准令。

(7)在北爱尔兰,第17条第(5)款至第(8)款以及M24《1989年警察及刑事证据法令》(北爱尔兰)第18条适用于依照本条规定签发的核准令。

(8)依照本条所取得的文件可以

(a)保留3个月;或

(b)如果在此3个月期间内,针对任何人的刑事犯罪提起了与此文件有关的刑事程序,则该等文件可保留至此等程序结束时为止。

(9)本条对苏格兰的适用

(a)述及治安法官时,替换为治安法官或司法长官;以及

(b)述及宣誓信息时,替换为宣誓证据。

(10)"调查人"系指依照第167条、第168条第(3)款或第168条第(5)款规定任命的人。

(11)"信息要求"系指提出的下列要求:

(a)由管理局依照第165条或第175条规定提出的要求;或[1]

(b)调查人依照第171条、第172条、第173条或第175条提出的要求。

注释:

修改等(不涉及条文内容)

C184 第176条为特定目的于2001年8月17日,否则于2001年12月1日依照1992年第40章第62A条{为特定目的于2001年8月17日,否则于2001年12月1日依照制定法文件S.I. 2001/2617第2条、第8条、第13条第(1)款、附录3第一部分第77条[与第13条第(3)款、附录5]插入};制定法文件S.I.2001/3538第2条第(1)款扩大适用范围;

第176条为特定目的于2001年8月17日,否则于2001年12月1日依照1986年第53章第52B条{为特定目的于2001年8月17日,否则于2001年12月1日依照制定法文件S.I. 2001/2617第2条、第8条、第13条第(1)款、附录3第一部分第151条[与第13条第(3)款、附录5]被替代};制定法文件S.I.2001/3538第2条第(1)款修订;

第176条于2001年12月1日依照制定法文件S.I.1995/1537第23条第(4)款[于2001年12月1日依照制定法文件S.I.2001/3649第1条、第509条第(e)款修正]修订。

C185 第176条为特定目的于2002年7月18日,否则于2002年8月21日依照《2002年电子商务指令条例》(金融服务与市场)(制定法文件S.I.2002/1775)第1条、第12条第(3)款修正;

1 本项依照《2010年金融服务法》附录2第一部分第17条修订。——译者注

S. 176 applied (with modifications) (11.4.2002 for certain purposes and 27.4.2002 otherwise) by The Financial Services and Markets Act 2000 (Regulated Activities) Order 2001 (S.I. 2001/544), art. 9G(9) (as inserted by The Financial Services and Markets Act 2000 (Regulated Activities) (Amendment) Order 2002 (S.I. 2002/682), arts. 1(2), 4)

C186 S. 176(1)-(9) applied (1.12.2001) by S.I. 2001/1228, regs. 1(2)(c), 30(7) (with reg. 1(2)(3)); S.I. 2001/3538, art. 2(1)

C187 S. 176(2) extended (1.12.2001) by S.I. 2001/3646, arts. 1(1), 13(2)

C188 S. 176(5) powers of seizure extended (prosp.) by 2001 c. 16, ss. 50, 52–54, 68, 138(2), Sch. 1 Pt. I para. 69

C189 S. 176(11) restricted (temp. from 11.8.2001 to 1.12.2001) by S.I. 2001/2659, arts. 1(3), 2(3); S.I. 2001/3538, art. 2(1)

C190 S. 176(8) applied (with modifications) (prosp.) by 2001 c. 16, ss. 57(1)(o)(4), 138(2)

C191 S. 176(11) restricted (temp.) (8.4.2002) by The Financial Services and Markets Act 2000 (Permission and Applications) (Credit Unions etc.) Order 2002 (S.I. 2002/704), art. 8(3)

Marginal Citations

M23 1984 c. 60.

M24 S.I. 1989/1341 (N.I. 12).

Offences

177 Offences.

(1) If a person other than the investigator ("the defaulter") fails to comply with a requirement imposed on him under this Part the person imposing the requirement may certify that fact in writing to the court.

(2) If the court is satisfied that the defaulter failed without reasonable excuse to comply with the requirement, it may deal with the defaulter (and in the case of a body corporate, any director or officer) as if he were in contempt .[F1; and "officer", in relation to a limited liability partnership, means a member of the limited liability partnership.].

(3) A person who knows or suspects that an investigation is being or is likely to be conducted under this Part is guilty of an offence if—

(a) he falsifies, conceals, destroys or otherwise disposes of a document which he knows or suspects is or would be relevant to such an investigation, or

(b) he causes or permits the falsification, concealment, destruction or disposal of such a

第176条(已修订)为特定目的于2002年4月11日,否则于2002年4月27日依照《2000年金融服务与市场法》(受监管活动)2001号令(制定法文件S.I.2001/544)第9G条第(9)款[依照《2000年金融服务与市场法》(受监管活动)(修正)2002号令(制定法文件S.I.2002/682)第1条第(2)款、第4条插入]适用。

C186 第176条第(1)款至第(9)款于2001年12月1日依照制定法文件S.I.2001/1228第1条第(2)款第(c)项、第30条第(7)款[与第1条第(2)款、第(3)款];S.I2001/3538第2条第(1)款适用。

C187 第176条第(2)款于2001年12月1日依照制定法文件S.I.2001/3646第1条第(1)款、第13条第(2)款扩大适用范围。

C188 第176条第(5)款没收权提议依照2001年第16章第50条、第52条至第54条、第68条、第138条第(2)款,附录1第一部分第69条扩大适用范围。

C189 第176条第(11)款暂时有效,于2001年8月11日到2001年12月1日受制定法文件S.I.2001/2659第1条第(3)款、第2条第(3)款;制定法文件S.I.2001/3538第2条第(1)款限制。

C190 第176条第(8)款(已修改)(提议)依照制定法文件2001年第16章第57条第(1)款第(o)项第(4)目、第138条第(2)款适用。

C191 第176条第(11)款暂时有效,于2002年4月8日受《2000年金融服务与市场法》(许可与申请)(信用合作社等)2002号令(制定法文件S.I.2002/704)第8条第(3)款限制。

附注引文

M23 1984年第60章。

M24 制定法文件S.I.1989/1341(N.I.12)。

犯 罪

第177条 犯罪

(1)如果调查人以外的人(以下简称违反人)未能遵守本部分对其提出的要求,则提出要求的人可以书面形式向法院提出该事项。

(2)如果法院认为违反人无合理理由而未能遵守要求,则可将违反人(如违反人为法人,任何董事或高级职员)按藐视法庭处理。[F1;"高级职员",对于有限责任合伙,系指有限责任合伙的合伙人。]

(3)知悉或猜测一项调查正在或可能将要依照本部分规定进行的人,如有下列情况,则构成犯罪:

(a)伪造、隐藏、破坏或以其他方式处理其知悉或怀疑与该调查有关或可能有关的文件,或

(b)引起或允许对该等文件的伪造、隐藏、破坏或处理,

document,unless he shows that he had no intention of concealing facts disclosed by the documents from the investigator.

(4) A person who, in purported compliance with a requirement imposed on him under this Part—

(a) provides information which he knows to be false or misleading in a material particular, or

(b) recklessly provides information which is false or misleading in a material particular,

is guilty of an offence.

(5) A person guilty of an offence under subsection (3) or (4) is liable—

(a) on summary conviction, to imprisonment for a term not exceeding six months or a fine not exceeding the statutory maximum, or both;

(b) on conviction on indictment, to imprisonment for a term not exceeding two years or a fine, or both.

(6) Any person who intentionally obstructs the exercise of any rights conferred by a warrant under section 176 is guilty of an offence and liable on summary conviction to imprisonment for a term not exceeding three months or a fine not exceeding level 5 on the standard scale, or both.

(7) "Court" means—

(a) the High Court;

(b) in Scotland, the Court of Session.

Annotations:

Amendments (Textual)

F1 Words in s. 177(2) inserted (6.4.2001) by S.I. 2001/1090, regs. 1, 9, Sch. 5 para. 21

Modifications etc. (not altering text)

C192 S. 177 applied (1.12.2001) by S.I. 2001/1228, regs. 1(2)(c), 30(6) (with reg. 1 (2)(3)); S.I. 2001/3538, art. 2(1)

S. 177 excluded (1.12.2001) by S.I. 2001/3646, arts. 1(1), 2(5)

S. 177 restricted (1.12.2001) by S.I. 2001/3646, arts. 1(1), 2(7)(a), 4(6)(a), 6(4)(a), 7(4)(a), 8(4)(a), 9(4) (a)

C193 S. 177 applied (with modifications) (11.4.2002 for certain purposes and 27.4.2002 otherwise) by The Financial Services and Markets Act 2000 (Regulated Activities) Order 2001 (S.I. 2001/544), art. 9G(9) (as inserted by The Financial Services and Markets Act 2000 (Regulated Activities) (Amendment) Order 2002 (S.I. 2002/682), arts. 1(2), 4)

除非证明自己没有意图对调查员隐藏文件中所披露的事实。

(4)如果声称遵守了根据本部分对其提出的要求的人

(a)就重要事项提供其明知为错误或误导的信息，或

(b)就重要事项因重大过失提供错误或误导信息，
则构成犯罪。

(5)依照第(3)款或第(4)款规定构成犯罪的人应承担下列责任：

(a)经简易程序定罪的，处以不超过6个月的有期徒刑或不超过法定最高额度的罚金，或两罚并处；

(b)经公诉程序定罪的，处以不超过2年的有期徒刑或罚金，或两罚并处。

(6)任何人故意妨碍行使第176条项下的核准令所授予的权利，构成犯罪，并应经简易程序定罪，处以不超过3个月的有期徒刑或不超过标准等级第5级的罚金，或两罚并处。

(7)“法院”系指

(a)高等法院；或

(b)(苏格兰)高等民事法院。

注释：

修正(文本)

F1　第177条第(2)款于2001年4月6日依照制定法文件S.I.2001/1090第1条、第9条、附录5第21条插入。

修改等(不涉及条文内容)

C192　第177条于2001年12月1日依照制定法文件S.I.2001/1228第1条第(2)款第(c)项、第30条第(6)款[与第1条第(2)款、第(3)款]；制定法文件S.I.2001/3538第2条(1)款适用；

第177条于2001年12月1日被制定法文件S.I.2001/3646第1条第(1)款、第2条第(5)款排除；

第177条于2001年12月1日受制定法文件S.I.2001/3646第1条第(1)款、第2条第(7)款第(a)项、第4条第(6)款第(a)项、第6条第(4)款第(a)项、第7条第(4)款第(a)项、第8条第(4)款第(a)项、第9条第(4)款第(a)项限制。

C193　第177条(已修订)为特定目的于2002年4月11日，否则于2002年4月7日依照《2000年金融服务与市场法》(受监管活动)2001号令(制定法文件S.I.2001/544)第9G条第(9)款[依照《2000年金融服务与市场法》(受监管活动)(修正)2002号令(制定法文件S.I.2002/682)第1条第(2)款、第4条插入]适用。

PART XII CONTROL OVER AUTHORISED PERSONS

Annotations:

Modifications etc. (not altering text)

C194 Pt. XII (ss. 178–192) modified (1.12.2001) by S.I. 2001/3592, arts. 1(2), 114(3)(a) (with art. 23(2))

Notice of control

178 Obligation to notify the Authority.

(1) If a step which a person proposes to take would result in his acquiring—

(a) control over a UK authorised person,

(b) an additional kind of control over a UK authorised person, or

(c) an increase in a relevant kind of control which he already has over a UK authorised person,

he must notify the Authority of his proposal.

(2) A person who, without himself taking any such step, acquires any such control or additional or increased control must notify the Authority before the end of the period of 14 days beginning with the day on which he first becomes aware that he has acquired it.

(3) A person who is under the duty to notify the Authority imposed by subsection (1) must also give notice to the Authority on acquiring, or increasing, the control in question.

(4) In this Part "UK authorised person" means an authorised person who—

(a) is a body incorporated in, or an unincorporated association formed under the law of, any part of the United Kingdom; and

(b) is not a person authorised as a result of paragraph 1 of Schedule 5.

(5) A notice under subsection (1) or (2) is referred to in this Part as "a notice of control".

第十二部分 对获授权人的控制

注释:

修改等(不涉及条文内容)

C194 第十二部分(第178条至第192条)于2001年12月1日依照制定法文件S.I. 2001/3592第1条第(2)款、第114条第(3)款第(a)项[与第23条第(2)款]修订。

控制权通知

第178条 通知管理局的义务

(1)如当事人拟采取的步骤将导致其

(a)取得联合王国获授权人的控制权;

(b)对联合王国获授权人增加新种类的控制权;或者

(c)对联合王国获授权人已取得的某类控制权程度增加,

则必须将其计划通知管理局。

(2)如当事人本人未采取上述任何措施而取得任何上述控制权、增加种类或增加程度的控制权,则须于其首次得知取得该控制权之日起14日期间届满前通知管理局。

(3)依照第(1)款承担通知职责的人还必须就取得或增加相关控制权通知管理局。

(4)本部分中"联合王国获授权人"系指符合下列条件的获授权人

(a)属于依照联合王国任何地区法律设立的法人或非法人;且

(b)非因附录5第1条获得授权。

(5)第(1)款或第(2)款规定的通知在本部分中称为"控制权通知"。

Annotations:

Modifications etc. (not altering text)

C195 S. 178 excluded (1.12.2001) by S.I. 2001/2638, arts. 1, 2(1)(b); S.I. 2001/3538, art. 2(1)

S. 178 excluded (1.12.2001) by S.I. 2001/3338, arts. 1, 2(1)(4); S.I. 2001/3538, art. 2(1)

S. 178 extended (1.12.2001) by S.I. 2001/2637, arts. 1, 5(2); S.I. 2001/3538, art. 2(1)

C196 S. 178(1) extended (1.12.2001) by S.I. 2001/2637, arts. 1, 3(1)(d); S.I. 2001/3538,. art. 2(1)

Acquiring, increasing and reducing control

179 Acquiring control.

(1) For the purposes of this Part, a person ("the acquirer") acquires control over a UK authorised person ("A") on first falling within any of the cases in subsection (2).

(2) The cases are where the acquirer—

(a) holds 10% or more of the shares in A;

(b) is able to exercise significant influence over the management of A by virtue of his shareholding in A;

(c) holds 10% or more of the shares in a parent undertaking ("P") of A;

(d) is able to exercise significant influence over the management of P by virtue of his shareholding in P;

(e) is entitled to exercise, or control the exercise of, 10% or more of the voting power in A;

(f) is able to exercise significant influence over the management of A by virtue of his voting power in A;

(g) is entitled to exercise, or control the exercise of, 10% or more of the voting power in P; or

(h) is able to exercise significant influence over the management of P by virtue of his voting power in P.

(3) In subsection (2)"the acquirer" means—

(a) the acquirer;

(b) any of the acquirer's associates; or

(c) the acquirer and any of his associates.

(4) For the purposes of this Part, each of the following is to be regarded as a kind of control—

(a) control arising as a result of the holding of shares in A;

注释：

修改等(不涉及条文内容)

C195 第178条于2001年12月1日依照制定法文件S.I.2001/2638第1条、第2条第(1)款第(b)项;制定法文件S.I.2001/3538第2条第(1)款排除;

第178条于2001年12月1日依照制定法文件S.I.2001/3338第1条、第2条第(1)款和第(4)款;制定法文件S.I.2001/3538第2条第(1)款排除;

第178条于2001年12月1日依照制定法文件S.I.2001/2637第1条、第5条第(2)款;制定法文件S.I.2001/3538第2条第(1)款扩大适用范围。

C196 第178条第1款于2001年12月1日依照制定法文件S.I.2001/2637第1条、第3条第(1)款第(d)项;制定法文件S.I.2001/3538第2条第(1)款扩大适用范围。

取得、增加和减少控制权

第179条 取得控制权

(1)就本部分而言,首次出现第(2)款所列情况的人(以下简称取得人)即为取得联合王国获授权人(以下简称A)控制权。

(2)前款所称情况为,取得人

(a)持有A的10%或以上股份;

(b)通过持有A股份能够对A的管理施加重要影响;

(c)持有A的母企业(以下简称P)10%或以上股份;

(d)通过持有P股份能够对P的管理施加重要影响;

(e)有权行使或控制行使A的10%或以上的表决权;

(f)通过行使A的表决权能够对A的管理施加重要影响;

(g)有权行使或控制行使P的10%或以上的表决权;或

(h)通过行使P的表决权能够对P的管理施加重要影响。

(3)第(2)款中"取得人"系指

(a)取得人;

(b)取得人的任何关联方;或

(c)取得人和取得人的任何关联方。

(4)就本部分而言,下列各项均视为一种控制权:

(a)因持有A股份而发生的控制权;

(b) control arising as a result of the holding of shares in P;

(c) control arising as a result of the entitlement to exercise, or control the exercise of, voting power in A;

(d) control arising as a result of the entitlement to exercise, or control the exercise of, voting power in P.

(5) For the purposes of this section and sections 180 and 181, "associate", "shares" and "voting power" have the same meaning as in section 422.

180 Increasing control.

(1) For the purposes of this Part, a controller of a person ("A") who is a UK authorized person increases his control over A if—

(a) the percentage of shares held by the controller in A increases by any of the steps mentioned in subsection (2);

(b) the percentage of shares held by the controller in a parent undertaking ("P") of A increases by any of the steps mentioned in subsection (2);

(c) the percentage of voting power which the controller is entitled to exercise, or control the exercise of, in A increases by any of the steps mentioned in subsection (2);

(d) the percentage of voting power which the controller is entitled to exercise, or control the exercise of, in P increases by any of the steps mentioned in subsection (2); or

(e) the controller becomes a parent undertaking of A.

(2) The steps are—

(a) from below 10% to 10% or more but less than 20%;

(b) from below 20% to 20% or more but less than 33%;

(c) from below 33% to 33% or more but less than 50%;

(d) from below 50% to 50% or more.

(3) In paragraphs (a) to (d) of subsection (1) "the controller" means—

(a) the controller;

(b) any of the controller's associates; or

(c) the controller and any of his associates.

(4) In the rest of this Part "acquiring control" or "having control" includes—

(a) acquiring or having an additional kind of control; or

(b) acquiring an increase in a relevant kind of control, or having increased control of a relevant kind.

181 Reducing control.

(1) For the purposes of this Part, a controller of a person ("A") who is a UK authorized person reduces his control over A if—

(a) the percentage of shares held by the controller in A decreases by any of the steps mentioned in subsection (2),

(b)因持有P股份而发生的控制权;
(c)因有权行使或控制行使A的表决权而发生的控制权;

(d)因有权行使或控制行使P的表决权而发生的控制权。

(5)本条及第180条、第181条所称之"关联方"、"股份"和"表决权"含义同第422条。

第180条 增加控制权

(1)就本部分而言,联合王国获授权人(以下简称A)的控制人如有下列情况即为增加对A的控制权:

(a)控制人所持A股份百分比按第(2)款所列任何等级增加;

(b)控制人所持A母企业(以下称P)股份百分比按第(2)款所列任何等级增加;

(c)控制人有权行使或控制行使的A表决权百分比按第(2)款所列任何等级增加;

(d)控制人有权行使或控制行使的P表决权百分比按第(2)款所列任何等级增加;或

(e)控制人成为A的母企业。

(2)前款所述等级为

(a)从10%以下增加至10%或10%以上、20%以下;
(b)从20%以下增加至20%或20%以上、33%以下;
(c)从33%以下增加至33%或33%以上、50%以下;
(d)从50%以下增加至50%或以上。

(3)第(1)款第(a)项至第(d)项中"控制人"系指

(a)控制人;
(b)控制人的任何关联方;或
(c)控制人及其任何关联方。

(4)本部分其余条款中"取得控制权"或"持有控制权"系指

(a)取得或持有更多种类的控制权;或
(b)取得的相关种类控制权增加,或增加相关种类的控制权。

第181条 减少控制权

(1)就本部分而言,联合王国获授权人(以下简称A)的控制人如有下列情况即为减少对A的控制权:

(a)控制人所持获授权人股份百分比按第(2)款所列任何等级减少;

(b) the percentage of shares held by the controller in a parent undertaking ("P") of A decreases by any of the steps mentioned in subsection (2),

(c) the percentage of voting power which the controller is entitled to exercise, or control the exercise of, in A decreases by any of the steps mentioned in subsection (2),

(d) the percentage of voting power which the controller is entitled to exercise, or control the exercise of, in P decreases by any of the steps mentioned in subsection (2), or

(e) the controller ceases to be a parent undertaking of A, unless the controller ceases to have the kind of control concerned over A as a result.

(2) The steps are—

(a) from 50% or more to 33% or more but less than 50%;

(b) from 33% or more to 20% or more but less than 33%;

(c) from 20% or more to 10% or more but less than 20%;

(d) from 10% or more to less than 10%.

(3) In paragraphs (a) to (d) of subsection (1) "the controller" means—

(a) the controller;

(b) any of the controller's associates; or

(c) the controller and any of his associates.

Acquiring or increasing control: procedure

182 Notification.

(1) A notice of control must—

(a) be given to the Authority in writing; and

(b) include such information and be accompanied by such documents as the Authority may reasonably require.

(2) The Authority may require the person giving a notice of control to provide such additional information or documents as it reasonably considers necessary in order to enable it to determine what action it is to take in response to the notice.

(3) Different requirements may be imposed in different circumstances.

Annotations:

Modifications etc. (not altering text)

C197 S. 182(2) extended (1.12.2001) by S.I. 2001/2637, arts. 1, 4(1); S.I. 2001/3538, art. 2(1)

Commencement Information

I50 S. 182 wholly in force at 1.12.2001; s. 182 not in force at Royal Assent see s. 431 (2); s. 182 in force for specified purposes at 18.6.2001 by S.I. 2001/1820, art. 2, Sch.; s. 182 in force in so far as not already in force at 1.12.2001 by S.I. 2001/3538, art. 2(1) (b)控制人所持获授权人母企业(以下简称P)股份百分比按第(2)款所列任何等级减少;

(c)控制人有权行使或控制行使的A表决权百分比按第(2)款所列任何等级减少;

(d)控制人有权行使或控制行使的P表决权百分比按第(2)款所列任何等级减少;或

(e)控制人成为A的母企业,除非导致控制人不再具有对A的相关种类控制权。

(2)前款所述等级为

(a)从50%或以上降至33%或33%以上、50%以下;

(b)从33%或以上降至20%或20%以上、33%以下;

(c)从20%或以上降至10%或10%以上、20%以下;

(d)从10%或以上降至10%以下。

(3)第(1)款第(a)项至第(d)项中"控制人"系指

(a)控制人;

(b)控制人的任何关联方;或

(c)控制人及其任何关联方。

取得或增加控制权的程序

第182条 通知

(1)控制权通知必须

(a)以书面形式提交管理局;且

(b)包含管理局合理要求提供的信息并附有管理局合理要求提供的文件。

(2)管理局可以要求控制权通知人提供管理局合理认为确定针对该通知采取何种行动所需的其他信息或文件。

(3)根据不同情况可以提出不同要求。

注释:

修改等(不涉及条文内容)

C197 第182条第(2)款于2001年12月1日依照制定法文件S.I.2001/2637第1条、第4条第(1)款;制定法文件S.I.2001/3538第2条第(1)款扩大适用范围。

实施日期

I50 第182条于2001年12月1日全部生效;第182条在副署时尚未生效,见第431条第(2)款;第182条为特定目的于2001年6月18日依照制定法文件S.I.2001/1820第2条、附录生效;第182条如于2001年12月1日尚未生效,则依照制定法文件S.I.2001/3538第2条第(1)款生效。

183 Duty of Authority in relation to notice of control.

(1) The Authority must, before the end of the period of three months beginning with the date on which it receives a notice of control ("the period for consideration"), determine whether—

(a) to approve of the person concerned having the control to which the notice relates; or

(b) to serve a warning notice under subsection (3) or section 185(3).

(2) Before doing so, the Authority must comply with such requirements as to consultation with competent authorities outside the United Kingdom as may be prescribed.

(3) If the Authority proposes to give the person concerned a notice of objection under section 186(1), it must give him a warning notice.

Annotations:

Modifications etc. (not altering text)

C198 S. 183 modified (1.12.2001) by S.I. 2001/2637, arts. 1, 4(2); S.I. 2001/3538, art. 2(1)

S. 183 modified (1.12.2001) by S.I. 2001/3592, arts. 1(2), 50(2), 51(2) (with art. 23 (2))

C199 S. 183(3) excluded (1.12.2001) by S.I. 2001/3592, arts. 1(2), 110(4), 115(3) (With art. 23(2))

Commencement Information

I51 S. 183 wholly in force at 1.12.2001; s. 183 not in force at Royal Assent see s. 431 (2); s. 183(2) in force for certain purposes at 25.2.2001 by S.I. 2001/516, art. 2(b), Sch. Pt. 2; s. 183 in force in so far as not already in force at 1.12.2001 by S.I. 2001/3538, art. 2(1)

184 Approval of acquisition of control.

(1) If the Authority decides to approve of the person concerned having the control to which the notice relates it must notify that person of its approval in writing without delay.

(2) If the Authority fails to comply with subsection (1) of section 183 it is to be treated as having given its approval and notified the person concerned at the end of the period fixed by that subsection.

(3) The Authority's approval remains effective only if the person to whom it relates acquires the control in question—

(a) before the end of such period as may be specified in the notice; or

(b) if no period is specified, before the end of the period of one year beginning with the date—

(i) of the notice of approval;

(ii) on which the Authority is treated as having given approval under subsection (2); or

第183条　管理局与控制权通知相关的职责

(1)管理局必须在收到控制权通知之日起3个月期间届满前(以下简称审核期间)决定

(a)批准相关通知人持有通知相关控制权;或

(b)依照第(3)款或第185条第(3)款送达预告通知。

(2)如有规定,则管理局作出上述决定前必须遵守与联合王国境外的主管机关协商的要求。

(3)如管理局拟依照186条第(1)款向相关通知人发出反对通知,则必须向其发出预告通知。

注释:

修改等(不涉及条文内容)

C198　第183条于2001年12月1日依照制定法文件S.I.2001/2637第1条、第4条第(2)款;制定法文件S.I.2001/3538第2条第(1)款修订;

第183条于2001年12月1日依照制定法文件S.I.2001/3592第1条第(2)款、第50条第(2)款、第51条第(2)款[与第23条(2)款]修订。

C199　第183条第(3)款依照制定法文件S.I.2001/3592第1条第(2)款、第110条第(4)款、第115条第(3)款[与第23条第(2)款]排除。

实施日期

I51　第183条于2001年12月1日全部生效;第183条在副署时尚未生效,见第431条第(2)款;第183条第(2)款为特定目的于2001年2月25日依照制定法文件S.I.2001/516第2条第(b)款、附录部分2生效;第183条如于2001年12月1日尚未生效,则依照制定法文件S.I.2001/3538第2条第(1)款生效。

第184条　取得控制权的批准

(1)如管理局决定批准相关通知人持有通知相关的控制权,则必须立即书面通知该人。

(2)如管理局未遵守第183条第(1)款规定,则在该款规定的期限届满时视为其已授予批准并已通知相关通知人。

(3)如有下列情况,则管理局的批准继续有效:

(a)该批准相关人在通知规定的期限届满前取得相关控制权;或

(b)如未规定期限,于下列日期起 1 年期间届满前取得相关控制权:

(i)批准通知发出之日;

(ii)依照第(2)款视为管理局已授予批准之日;或

(iii) of a decision on a reference to the Tribunal which results in the person concerned receiving approval.

Annotations:

Modifications etc. (not altering text)

C200 S. 184(1) extended (1.12.2001) by S.I. 2001/2637, arts. 1, 5(2); S.I. 2001/3538, art. 2(1)

C201 S. 184(2) extended (1.12.2001) by S.I. 2001/2637, arts. 1, 5(3); S.I. 2001/3538, art. 2(1)

C202 S. 184(3) applied (with modifications) (1.12.2001) by S.I. 2001/2637, arts. 1, 5(4)(5); S.I. 2001/3538, art. 2(1)

185 Conditions attached to approval.

(1) The Authority's approval under section 184 may be given unconditionally or subject to such conditions as the Authority considers appropriate.

(2) In imposing any conditions, the Authority must have regard to its duty under section 41.

(3) If the Authority proposes to impose conditions on a person it must give him a warning notice.

(4) If the Authority decides to impose conditions on a person it must give him a decision notice.

(5) A person who is subject to a condition imposed under this section may apply to the Authority—

(a) for the condition to be varied; or

(b) for the condition to be cancelled.

(6) The Authority may, on its own initiative, cancel a condition imposed under this section.

(7) If the Authority has given its approval to a person subject to a condition, he may refer to the Tribunal—

(a) the imposition of the condition; or

(b) the Authority's decision to refuse an application made by him under subsection (5).

Annotations:

Modifications etc. (not altering text)

C203 S. 185 (1) extended (1.12.2001) by S.I. 2001/2637, arts. 1, 10 (1); S.I. 2001/3538, art. 2(1)

C204 S. 185 (3) extended (1.12.2001) by S.I. 2001/2637, arts. 1, 9 (1) (3); S.I. 2001/3538, art. 2(1) (iii)使该相关人获得批准的裁判所裁决作出之日。

注释:

修改等(不涉及条文内容)

C200 第184条第(1)款于2001年12月1日依照制定法文件S.I.2001/2637第1条、第5条第(2)款;制定法文件S.I.2001/3538第2条第(1)款扩大适用范围。

C201 第184条第(2)款于2001年12月1日依照制定法文件S.I.2001/2637第1条、第5条第(3)款;制定法文件S.I.2001/3538第2条第(1)款扩大适用范围。

C202 第184条第(3)款(已修订)于2001年12月1日依照制定法文件S.I.2001/2637第1条、第5条第(4)款、第(5)款;制定法文件S.I.2001/3538第2条第(1)款适用。

第185条 批准附加条件

(1)管理局可以无条件授予第184条规定的批准,或附加该局认为适当的条件。

(2)管理局规定任何条件时必须考虑其依照第41条规定承担的职责。

(3)如管理局拟对当事人规定条件,则必须向该人发出预告通知。

(4)如管理局决定对当事人规定条件,则必须向该人发出决定通知。

(5)受本条规定条件约束的人可向管理局提出申请

(a)变更条件;或
(b)取消条件。
(6)管理局可以自行取消依照本条规定附加的条件。

(7)如管理局已授予当事人附条件批准,则该人可以将下列事项诉至裁判所:

(a)附加条件;或
(b)管理局驳回其依照第(5)款提出的申请。

注释:

修改等(不涉及条文内容)

C203 第185条第(1)款于2001年12月1日依照制定法文件S.I.2001/2637第1条、第10条第(1)款;制定法文件S.I.2001/3538第2条第(1)款扩大适用范围。

C204 第185条第(3)款于2001年12月1日依照制定法文件S.I.2001/2637第1条、第9条第(1)款、第9条第(3)款;制定法文件S.I.2001/3538第2条第(1)款扩大适用范围。

S. 185(3) excluded (1.12.2001) by S.I. 2001/3592, arts. 1(2); 110(4), 115(3) (with art. 23)

186 Objection to acquisition of control.

(1) On considering a notice of control, the Authority may give a decision notice under this section to the person acquiring control ("the acquirer") unless it is satisfied that the approval requirements are met.

(2) The approval requirements are that—

(a) the acquirer is a fit and proper person to have the control over theauthorized person that he has or would have if he acquired the control in question; and

(b) the interests of consumers would not be threatened by the acquirer's control or by his acquiring that control.

(3) In deciding whether the approval requirements are met, the Authority must have regard, in relation to the control that the acquirer—

(a) has over the authorised person concerned ("A"), or

(b) will have over A if the proposal to which the notice of control relates is carried into effect,

to its duty under section 41 in relation to each regulated activity carried on by A.

(4) If the Authority gives a notice under this section but considers that the approval requirements would be met if the person to whom a notice is given were to take, or refrain from taking, a particular step, the notice must identify that step.

(5) A person to whom a notice under this section is given may refer the matter to the Tribunal.

(6) "Consumers" means persons who are consumers for the purposes of section 138.

Annotations:

Modifications etc. (not altering text)

C205 S. 186(6) modified (18.6.2001) by S.I. 2001/1821, arts. 1(1), 3(5)

187 Objection to existing control.

(1) If the Authority is not satisfied that the approval requirements are met, it may give a decision notice under this section to a person if he has failed to comply with a duty to notify imposed by section 178.

(2) If the failure relates to subsection (1) or (2) of that section, the Authority may (instead of giving a notice under subsection (1)) approve the acquisition of the control in question by the person concerned as if he had given it a notice of control.

(3) The Authority may also give a decision notice under this section to a person who is a

第185条第(3)款于2001年12月1日依照制定法文件S.I.2001/3592第1条第(2)款、第110条第(4)款、第115条第(3)款(与第23条)排除。

第186条　反对取得控制权

(1)管理局考虑一项控制权通知时可以向控制权取得人(以下简称取得人)发出本条规定的决定通知,除非该局确信符合以下批准要求。

(2)前款所述批准要求为

(a)取得人如取得该相关控制权则就其对获授权人所持有或将持有的控制权而言为适当持有人;且

(b)取得人的控制权或取得人取得控制权不会对消费者的利益构成威胁。

(3)管理局在决定是否符合批准要求时,必须结合取得人的下列控制权

(a)取得人对相关获授权人(以下简称A)持有的控制权,或

(b)如与该控制权通知相关的计划生效,取得人将对A持有的控制权,

考虑管理局依照第41条所承担的与A实施的每项受监管活动相关的职责。

(4)如管理局发出本条规定的通知,但考虑到如通知接收人采取特定措施或不采取特定措施即可符合批准要求,则必须在该通知中指明该项措施。

(5)如收到依照本条规定发出的通知,则通知接收人可将该事项诉至裁判所。

(6)"消费者"系指第138条意义上的消费者。

注释:

修改等(不涉及条文内容)

C205　第186条第(6)款于2001年6月18日依照制定法文件S.I.2001/1821第1条第(1)款、第3条第(5)款修订。

第187条　反对现有控制权

(1)如当事人未遵守第178条规定的通知职责,管理局不确信该人符合批准要求,则可向该人发出本条规定的决定通知。

(2)如上述未遵守规定的情况与第178条第(1)款或第(2)款有关,则管理局可以批准该相关控制权的取得[而不依照第(1)款发出通知],等同于该人已提交控制权通知。

(3)如管理局得知导致其确信下列情况的事项,则可以向联合王国获授权人的控

controller of a UK authorised person if the Authority becomes aware of matters as a result of which it is satisfied that—

(a) the approval requirements are not met with respect to the controller; or

(b) a condition imposed under section 185 required that person to do (or refrain from doing) a particular thing and the condition has been breached as a result of his failing to do (or doing) that thing.

(4) A person to whom a notice under this section is given may refer the matter to the Tribunal.

(5) "Approval requirements" has the same meaning as in section 186.

Annotations:

Modifications etc. (not altering text)

C206 S. 187(1)(2) extended (1.12.2001) by S.I. 2001/2637, arts. 1, 7(1)(d); S.I. 2001/3538, art. 2(1)

C207 S. 187(3) explained and modified (1.12.2001) by S.I. 2001/2637, arts. 1, 12; S.I. 2001/3538, art. 2(1)

188 Notices of objection under section 187: procedure.

(1) If the Authority proposes to give a notice of objection to a person under section 187, it must give him a warning notice.

(2) Before doing so, the Authority must comply with such requirements as to consultation with competent authorities outside the United Kingdom as may be prescribed.

(3) If the Authority decides to give a warning notice under this section, it must do so before the end of the period of three months beginning—

(a) in the case of a notice to be given under section 187(1), with the date on which it became aware of the failure to comply with the duty in question;

(b) in the case of a notice to be given under section 187(3), with the date on which it became aware of the matters in question.

(4) The Authority may require the person concerned to provide such additional information or documents as it considers reasonable.

(5) Different requirements may be imposed in different circumstances.

(6) In this Part "notice of objection" means a notice under section 186 or 187.

Annotations:

Modifications etc. (not altering text)

C208 S. 188 excluded (1.12.2001) by S.I. 2001/3592, arts. 1 (2), 110 (4), 115(3) (with art. 23(2))

制人发出本条规定的决定通知：

(a)该控制人不符合相关批准要求；或

(b)依照第185条附加的条件要求该人实施(或不实施)某项行为，而该人未实施(或实施了)该行为，从而违反该条件。

(4)如收到依照本条规定发出的通知，则通知接收人可将该事项诉至裁判所。

(5)"批准要求"与第186条中的含义相同。

注释：

修改等(不涉及条文内容)

C206 第187条第(1)款和第(2)款于2001年12月1日依照制定法文件S.I.2001/2637第1条、第7条第(1)款第(d)项；制定法文件S.I.2001/3538第2条第(1)款扩大适用范围。

C207 第187条第(3)款于2001年12月1日依照制定法文件S.I.2001/2637第1条、第12条；制定法文件S.I.2001/3538第2条第(1)款解释并修订。

第188条 依照第187条发出反对通知的程序

(1)如管理局拟依照第187条向当事人发出反对通知，则必须向其发出预告通知。

(2)如有规定，管理局发出上述通知前必须遵守与联合王国境外的主管机关协商的要求。

(3)如管理局决定依照本条规定发出预告通知，则必须在自下列日期起3个月期间届满前发出该通知：

(a)如依照第187条第(1)款发出通知，则自管理局得知相关人未遵守职责之日起；

(b)如依照第187条第(3)款发出通知，则自管理局得知相关事项之日起。

(4)管理局可以要求该相关人提供该局认为合理的其他信息或文件。

(5)根据不同情况可提出不同要求。

(6)本部分中"反对通知"系指第186条或第187条规定的通知。

注释：

修改等(不涉及条文内容)

C208 第188条于2001年12月1日制定法文件S.I.2001/3592第1条第(2)款、第110条第(4)款、第115条第(3)款[与第23条第(2)款]排除。

C209 S. 188(1) extended (1.12.2001) by S.I. 2001/2637, arts. 1, 8(1), 11(1); S.I. 2001/3538, art. 2(1)

C210 S. 188(3) applied (with modifications) (1.12.2001) by S.I. 2001/2637, arts. 1, 7(2); S.I. 2001/3538, art. 2(1)

Commencement Information

I52 S. 188 wholly in force at 1.12.2001; s. 188 not in force at Royal Assent see s. 431(2); s. 188(2) in force for certain purposes at 25.2.2001 by S.I. 2001/516, art. 2(b), Sch. Pt. 2; s. 188 in force in so far as not already in force at 1.12.2001 by S.I. 2001/3538, art. 2(1)

Improperly acquired shares

189 Improperly acquired shares.

(1) The powers conferred by this section are exercisable if a person has acquired, or has continued to hold, any shares in contravention of—

(a) a notice of objection; or

(b) a condition imposed on the Authority's approval.

(2) The Authority may by notice in writing served on the person concerned ("a restriction notice") direct that any such shares which are specified in the notice are, until further notice, subject to one or more of the following restrictions—

(a) a transfer of (or agreement to transfer) those shares, or in the case of unissued shares any transfer of (or agreement to transfer) the right to be issued with them, is void;

(b) no voting rights are to be exercisable in respect of the shares;

(c) no further shares are to be issued in right of them or in pursuance of any offer made to their holder;

(d) except in a liquidation, no payment is to be made of any sums due from the body corporate on the shares, whether in respect of capital or otherwise.

(3) The court may, on the application of the Authority, order the sale of any shares to which this section applies and, if they are for the time being subject to any restriction under subsection (2), that they are to cease to be subject to that restriction.

(4) No order may be made under subsection (3)—

(a) until the end of the period within which a reference may be made to the Tribunal in respect of the notice of objection; and

(b) if a reference is made, until the matter has been determined or the reference withdrawn.

(5) If an order has been made under subsection (3), the court may, on the application of the Authority, make such further order relating to the sale or transfer of the shares as it thinks fit.

C209　第188条第(1)款于2001年12月1日制定法文件S.I.2001/2637第1条、第8条第(1)款、第11条第(1)款;制定法文件S.I.2001/3538第2条第(1)款扩大适用范围。

C210　第188条第(3)款于2001年12月1日(已修订)依照制定法文件S.I.2001/2637第1条、第7条第(2)款;制定法文件S.I.2001/3538第2条第(1)款适用。

实施日期

I52　第188条于2001年12月1日全部生效;第188条在副署时尚未生效,见第431条第(2)款;第188条第(2)款为特定目的于2001年2月25日依照制定法文件S.I.2001/516第2条第(b)款、附录第二部分而生效;第188条如于2001年12月1日尚未生效,则依照制定法文件S.I.2001/3538第2条第(1)款生效。

以不正当方式取得的股份

第189条　以不正当方式取得的股份

(1)如当事人违反下列规定取得或继续持有任何股份,则有关机构可行使本条赋予的权力:

(a)违反反对通知;或

(b)违反管理局的批准条件。

(2)管理局可以向相关人送达书面通知(以下简称限制通知),指示该通知中所列任何股份在另行通知前受下列一项或多项限制制约:

(a)上述股份的转让(或转让协议),或者未发行股份发行时所附权利的转让(或转让协议)无效;

(b)不得行使与上述股份相关的任何表决权;

(c)不得根据上述股份赋予的权利或依照向其持有人发出的任何要约发行新股;

(d)除清算外,不得就上述股份支付该法人应支付的任何款项,无论为资本或其他形式。

(3)法院可以应管理局申请命令出售适用本条规定的任何股份,如命令出售的股份其时受第(2)款所列任何限制的约束,则命上述股份不再受该限制约束。

(4)实现下列条件前不得作出第(3)款规定的命令:

(a)可以就反对通知提交裁判所裁决的期限届满;且

(b)如提交审判庭裁决,则至事项已裁决或诉请被驳回。

(5)如已依照第(3)款作出命令,则法院可以应管理局申请,就该股份的出售或转让进一步作出其认为适当的命令。

(6) If shares are sold in pursuance of an order under this section, the proceeds of sale, less the costs of the sale, must be paid into court for the benefit of the persons beneficially interested in them; and any such person may apply to the court for the whole or part of the proceeds to be paid to him.

(7) This section applies—

(a) in the case of an acquirer falling within section 178(1), to all the shares—

(i) in the authorised person which the acquirer has acquired;

(ii) which are held by him or an associate of his; and

(iii) which were not so held immediately before he became a person with control over the authorised person;

(b) in the case of an acquirer falling within section 178(2), to all the shares held by him or an associate of his at the time when he first became aware that he had acquired control over the authorised person; and

(c) to all the shares in an undertaking ("C")—

(i) which are held by the acquirer or an associate of his, and

(ii) which were not so held before he became a person withcontrol in relation to the authorised person,

where C is the undertaking in which shares were acquired by the acquirer (or an associate of his) and, as a result, he became a person with control in relation to that authorised person.

(8) A copy of the restriction notice must be served on—

(a) the authorised person to whose shares it relates; and

(b) if it relates to shares held by an associate of that authorised person, on that associate.

(9) The jurisdiction conferred by this section may be exercised by the High Court and the Court of Session.

Annotations:

Modifications etc. (not altering text)

C211 S. 189(2) power extended (1.12.2001) by S.I. 2001/2637, arts. 1, 13(4)(5); S.I. 2001/3538, art. 2(1)

S. 189(2) extended (1.12.2001) by S.I. 2001/2637, arts. 1, 13(2)(5); S.I. 2001/3538, art. 2(1)

C212 S. 189(2)(b) extended (1.12.2001) by S.I. 2001/2637, arts. 1, 13(1); S.I. 2001/3538, art. 2(1)

C213 S. 189(3) applied (with modifications) by S.I. 2001/2637, arts. 1, 13(2)(5); S.I. 2001/3538, art. 2(1)

(6)如依照本条规定的命令出售股份,则出售收入除去出售成本外必须上缴法院,用于该股份实益享有人的利益;任何上述实益享有人有权申请法院将该收入全部或部分向其支付。

(7)本条适用于

(a)就属于第178条第(1)款规定的取得人,适用于下列所有股份:

(i)取得人取得的获授权人股份;

(ii)取得人或其关联方持有的股份;以及

(iii)取得人成为获授权人的控制权人前未直接持有的股份。

(b)就属于第178条第(2)款规定的取得人,适用于该人或其关联方在该人首次得知已取得获授权人控制权时持有的所有股份;以及

(c)适用于一个企业(以下简称C)中的下列全部股份:

(i)取得人或其关联方持有的股份;以及

(ii)取得人成为与获授权人相关的控制权人前未持有的股份,

且C中的股份由取得人(或其关联方)取得,并且取得人由于取得股份而成为与获授权人相关的控制权人。

(8)限制通知必须抄送

(a)股份与该通知相关的获授权人;以及

(b)如与该获授权人的关联方所持股份相关,则抄送该关联方。

(9)本条规定授予的管辖权可由高等法院和(苏格兰)高等民事法院行使。

注释:

修改等(不涉及条文内容)

C211　第189条第(2)款于2001年12月1日依照制定法文件S.I.2001/2637第1条、第13条第(4)款和第(5)款;制定法文件S.I.2001/3538第2条第(1)款扩大适用范围;

第189条第(2)款于2001年12月1日依照制定法文件S.I.2001/2637第1条、第13条第(2)款和第(5)款;制定法文件S.I.2001/3538第2条第(1)款扩大适用范围。

C212　第189条第(2)款第(b)项于2001年12月1日依照制定法文件S.I.2001/2637第1条、第13条第(1)款;制定法文件S.I.2001/3538第2条第(1)款扩大适用范围。

C213　第189条第(3)款(已修订)依照制定法文件S.I.2001/2637第1条、第13条第(2)款和第(5)款;制定法文件S.I.2001/3538第2条第(1)款适用。

Reducing control: procedure

190 Notification.

(1) If a step which a controller of a UK authorised person proposes to take would result in his—

(a) ceasing to have control of a relevant kind over the authorised person, or

(b) reducing a relevant kind of control over that person,

he must notify the Authority of his proposal.

(2) A controller of a UK authorised person who, without himself taking any such step, ceases to have that control or reduces that control must notify the Authority before the end of the period of 14 days beginning with the day on which he first becomes aware that—

(a) he has ceased to have the control in question; or

(b) he has reduced that control.

(3) A person who is under the duty to notify the Authority imposed by subsection (1) must also give a notice to the Authority—

(a) on ceasing to have the control in question; or

(b) on reducing that control.

(4) A notice under this section must—

(a) be given to the Authority in writing; and

(b) include details of the extent of the control (if any) which the person concerned will retain (or still retains) over the authorised person concerned.

Annotations:

Modifications etc. (not altering text)

C214 S. 190 excluded (1.12.2001) by S.I. 2001/2638, arts. 1, 2(2)(b); S.I. 2001/3538, art. 2(1)

S. 190 excluded (1.12.2001) by S.I. 2001/3338, arts. 1(1), 3; S.I. 2001/3538, art. 2(1)

C215 S. 190(1) applied (1.12.2001) by S.I. 2001/2637, arts. 1, 15(1); S.I. 2001/3538, art. 2(1)

C216 S. 190(2) applied (with modifications) (1.12.2001) by S.I. 2001/2637, arts. 1, 15(2)-(4); S.I. 2001/3538, art. 2(1)

Offences

191 Offences under this Part.

(1) A person who fails to comply with the duty to notify the Authority imposed on him by section 178(1) or 190(1) is guilty of an offence.

(2) A person who fails to comply with the duty to notify the Authority imposed on him

减少控制权的程序

第190条　通知

(1)如联合王国获授权人的控制人拟采取的步骤将导致其

(a)不再对联合王国获授权人持有相关种类的控制权；或者

(b)对该获授权人持有的相关种类控制权减少，

则必须将其计划通知管理局。

(2)如联合王国获授权人的控制人本人未采取上述任何措施而不再持有或减少该控制权，则比须于其首次得知下列情况之日起14日期间届满前通知管理局：

(a)其不再持有相关控制权；或

(b)其所持有的该控制权减少。

(3)依照第(1)款承担通知管理局职责的人还必须就下列事项通知管理局：

(a)其不再持有相关控制权；或

(b)其所持有的该控制权减少。

(4)本条规定的通知必须

(a)以书面形式提交管理局；且

(b)详细说明相关人将继续持有(或仍继续持有)相关获授权人控制权(如有)的程度。

注释：

修改等(不涉及条文内容)

C214　第190条第(1)款于2001年12月1日依照制定法文件S.I.2001/2638第1条、第2条第(2)款第(b)项；制定法文件S.I.2001/3538第2条第(1)款排除；

第190条于2001年12月1日依照制定法文件S.I.2001/3338第1条第(1)款、第3条；制定法文件S.I.2001/3538第2条第(1)款排除。

C215　第190条第(1)款于2001年12月1日依照制定法文件S.I.2001/2637第1条、第15条第(1)款；制定法文件S.I.2001/3538第2条第(1)款适用。

C216　第190条第(2)款(已修订)于2001年12月1日依照制定法文件S.I.2001/2637第1条、第15条第(2)款至第(4)款；制定法文件S.I.2001/3538第2条第(1)款适用。

犯　罪

第191条　本部分规定的犯罪

(1)未遵守第178条第(1)款或第190条第(1)款规定的通知管理局职责的，构成犯罪。

(2)未遵守第178条第(2)款或第190条第(2)款规定的通知管理局职责的，构成

by section 178(2) or 190(2) is guilty of an offence.

(3) If a person who has given a notice of control to the Authority carries out the proposal to which the notice relates, he is guilty of an offence if—

(a) the period of three months beginning with the date on which the Authority received the notice is still running; and

(b) the Authority has not responded to the notice by either giving its approval or giving him a warning notice under section 183(3) or 185(3).

(4) A person to whom the Authority has given a warning notice under section 183(3) is guilty of an offence if he carries out the proposal to which the notice relates before the Authority has decided whether to give him a notice of objection.

(5) A person to whom a notice of objection has been given is guilty of an offence if he acquires the control to which the notice applies at a time when the notice is still in force.

(6) A person guilty of an offence under subsection (1), (2), (3) or (4) is liable on summary conviction to a fine not exceeding level 5 on the standard scale.

(7) A person guilty of an offence under subsection (5) is liable—

(a) on summary conviction, to a fine not exceeding the statutory maximum; and

(b) on conviction on indictment, to imprisonment for a term not exceeding two years or a fine, or both.

(8) A person guilty of an offence under subsection (5) is also liable on summary conviction to a fine not exceeding one tenth of the statutory maximum for each day on which the offence has continued.

(9) It is a defence for a person charged with an offence under subsection (1) to show that he had, at the time of the alleged offence, no knowledge of the act or circumstances by virtue of which the duty to notify the Authority arose.

(10) If a person—

(a) was under the duty to notify the Authority imposed by section 178(1) or 190(1) but had no knowledge of the act or circumstances by virtue of which that duty arose, but

(b) subsequently becomes aware of that act or those circumstances,

he must notify the Authority before the end of the period of 14 days beginning with the day on which he first became so aware.

(11) A person who fails to comply with the duty to notify the Authority imposed by subsection (10) is guilty of an offence and liable, on summary conviction, to a fine not exceeding level 5 on the standard scale.

犯罪。

(3)已向管理局提交控制权通知的,如有下列情况则构成犯罪:

(a)管理局收到该通知之日起的3个月期间尚未届满时实施该通知相关计划;以及

(b)管理局尚未依照第183条第(3)款或第185条第(3)款就该通知相应授予批准或发出预告通知时实施该通知相关计划。

(4)管理局依照第183条第(3)款发出预告通知的,通知接收人如在管理局决定是否对其发出反对通知前实施该通知相关计划,则构成犯罪。

(5)已发出反对通知的,通知接收人如在该通知有效期内取得该通知适用的控制权,则构成犯罪。

(6)依照第(1)款、第(2)款、第(3)款或第(4)款规定构成犯罪的,应经简易程序定罪处以不超过标准等级第5级的罚金。

(7)依照第(5)款规定构成犯罪的,应承担下列责任:

(a)经简易程序定罪的,处以不超过最高法定金额的罚金;

(b)经公诉程序定罪的,处以不超过2年的有期徒刑或罚金,或两罚并处。

(8)依照第(5)款构成犯罪的,还应经简易程序定罪,按犯罪持续期间每日不超过最高法定金额的1/10处以罚金。

(9)依照第(1)款被控有罪的,如可证明其在被控有罪时不知到产生通知管理局职责的行为或情况,则可据此进行抗辩。

(10)有下列情况的:

(a)依照第178条第(1)款或第190条第(1)款承担通知管理局的职责,但不知道产生该职责的行为或情况;但

(b)后来知悉了该行为或情况,

则该人必须在首次知悉之日起14日期间届满前通知管理局。

(11)如未遵守第(10)款规定的通知管理局职责,则构成犯罪,应经简易程序定罪处以不超过标准等级第5级的罚金。

Annotations:

Modifications etc. (not altering text)

C217 S. 191(10) applied (with modifications) (1.12.2001) by S.I. 2001/2637, arts. 1, 14; S.I. 2001/3538, art.2(1)

Miscellaneous

192 Power to change definitions of control etc.

The Treasury may by order—

(a) provide for exemptions from the obligations to notify imposed by sections 178 and 190;

(b) amend section 179 by varying, or removing, any of the cases in which a person is treated as having control over a UK authorised person or by adding a case;

(c) amend section 180 by varying, or removing, any of the cases in which a person is treated as increasing control over a UK authorised person or by adding a case;

(d) amend section 181 by varying, or removing, any of the cases in which a person is treated as reducing his control over a UK authorised person or by adding a case;

(e) amend section 422 by varying, or removing, any of the cases in which a person is treated as being a controller of a person or by adding a case.

Annotations:

Commencement Information

I53 S. 192 wholly in force at 1.12.2001; s. 192 not in force at Royal Assent see s. 431(2); s. 192(a) in force at 25.2.2001 by S.I. 2001/516, art. 2(a), Sch. Pt. 1; s. 192 in force in so far as not already in force at 1.12.2001 by S.I. 2001/3538, art. 2(1)

注释：

修改等（不涉及条文内容） C217　第191条第（10）款（已修订）于2001年12月1日依照制定法文件S.I.2001/2637第1条、第14条；制定法文件S.I.2001/3538第2条第（1）款适用。

其他条款

第192条　变更控制权定义的权力等

财政部可作出命令

（a）规定免除第178条和第190条规定的通知义务；

（b）修改第179条，变更或取消任何将某人视为对联合王国获授权人持有控制权的情形，或者增加一项情形；

（c）修改第180条，变更或取消任何将某人视为对联合王国获授权人增加控制权的情形，或者增加一项情形；

（d）修改第181条，变更或取消任何将某人视为对联合王国获授权人减少控制权的情形，或者增加一项情形；

（e）修改第422条，变更或取消任何将某人视为某人的控制权人的情形，或者增加一项情形。

注释：

实施日期 I53　第192条于2001年12月1日全部生效；第192条在副署时尚未生效，见第431条第（2）款；第192条（a）款于2001年2月25日依照制定法文件S.I.2001/516第2条第（a）项、附录第一部分生效；第192条如于2001年12月1日尚未生效，则依照制定法文件S.I.2001/3538第2条第（1）款生效。

PART XIII INCOMING FIRMS: INTERVENTION BY AUTHORITY

Annotations:

Modifications etc. (not altering text)

C218 Pt. XIII (ss. 193–204) modified (1.12.2001) by S.I. 2001/3592, arts. 1(2), 114(3)(a) (with art. 23(2))

Pt. XIII (ss. 193–204) extended (1.12.2001) by S.I. 2001/2636, arts. 1(2)(b), 32; S.I. 2001/3538, art. 2(1)

Pt. XIII(ss. 193–204) extended (5.10.2001 for specified purposes otherwise 1.12.2001) by S.I. 2001/3084, art. 2(7); S.I. 2001/3538, art. 2(1)

Pt XIII (ss. 193–204) excluded (1.12.2001) by S.I. 2001/3592, art. 107(2) (with art. 23(2))

Interpretation

193 Interpretation of this Part.

(1) In this Part—

"additional procedure" means the procedure described in section 199; "incoming firm" means—

(a) an EEA firm which is exercising, or has exercised, its right to carry on a regulated activity in the United Kingdom in accordance with Schedule 3; or

(b) a Treaty firm which is exercising, or has exercised, its right to carry on a regulated activity in the United Kingdom in accordance with Schedule 4; and

"power of intervention" means the power conferred on the Authority by section 196.

(2) In relation to an incoming firm which is an EEA firm, expressions used in this Part and in Schedule 3 have the same meaning in this Part as they have in that Schedule.

第十三部分　进入联合王国的企业：管理局的干预

注释：

修改等(不涉及条文内容)

C218　第十三部分(第193条至第204条)于2001年12月1日依照制定法文件S.I.第1条第(2)款、第114条第(3)款第(a)项[与第23条第(2)款]修订；

第十三部分(第193条至第204条)于2001年12月1日依照制定法文件S.I.第1条第(2)款第(b)项；制定法文件S.I.2001/3538第2条第(1)款扩大适用范围；

第十三部分(第193条至第204条)为特定目的于2001年10月5日，否则于2001年12月1日依照制定法文件S.I.2001/3084第2条第(7)款；制定法文件S.I.2001/3538第2条第(1)款扩大适用范围；

第十三部分(第193条至第204条)于2001年12月1日依照制定法文件S.I.2001/3592第107条第(2)款[与第23条第(2)款]排除。

释　义

第193条　本部分释义

(1)本部分中

"补充程序"系指第199条规定的程序；"进入联合王国的企业"系指

(a) 正在行使或已行使依照附录3在联合王国实施受监管活动权利的欧洲经济区企业；或

(b)正在行使或已行使依照附录4在联合王国实施受监管活动权利的条约企业；

"干预权"系指第196条赋予管理局的权力。

(2)进入联合王国的企业属于欧洲经济区企业的，本部分和附录3中使用的表达方式在本部分中含义与附录3中相同。

194 General grounds on which power of intervention is exercisable.

(1) The Authority may exercise its power of intervention in respect of an incoming firm if it appears to it that—

(a) the firm has contravened, or is likely to contravene, a requirement which is imposed on it by or under this Act (in a case where the Authority is responsible for enforcing compliance in the United Kingdom);

(b) the firm has, in purported compliance with any requirement imposed by or under this Act, knowingly or recklessly given the Authority information which is false or misleading in a material particular; or

(c) it is desirable to exercise the power in order to protect the interests of actual or potential customers.

(2) Subsection (3) applies to an incoming EEA firm falling within sub-paragraph (a) or (b) of paragraph 5 of Schedule 3 which is exercising an EEA right to carry on any Consumer Credit Act business in the United Kingdom.

(3) The Authority may exercise its power of intervention in respect of the firm if the Director General of Fair Trading has informed the Authority that—

(a) the firm,

(b) any of the firm's employees, agents or associates (whether past or present), or

(c) if the firm is a body corporate, a controller of the firm or an associate of such a controller,

has done any of the things specified in paragraphs (a) to (d) of section 25(2) of the [M25] Consumer Credit Act 1974.

(4) "Associate", "Consumer Credit Act business" and "controller" have the same meaning as in section 203.

Annotations:

Modifications etc. (not altering text)

C219 S. 194 applied (1.12.2001) by S.I. 2001/3592, arts. 1(2), 12(3)(b), 18(4)(b), 21(3) (with art. 23(2))

S. 194 amended (temp. from 3.9.2001 to 1.12.2001) by S.I. 2001/2659, arts. 1(2), 3(5); S.I. 2001/3538, art. 2(1)

Commencement Information

I54 S. 194 wholly in force at 1.12.2001; s. 194 not in force at Royal Assent see s. 431 (2); s. 194 in force for specified purposes at 3.9.2001 by S.I. 2001/2632, art. 2(2), Sch. Pt. 2; s. 194 in force in so far as not already in force at 1.12.2001 by S.I. 2001/3538, art. 2(1)

第194条　可行使干预权的一般依据

(1)管理局如认为有下列情况,则可以对进入联合王国的企业行使干预权:

(a)该企业违反或可能违反本法对其规定的要求(如由管理局负责联合王国的合规执行);

(b)企业在遵守本法规定或依据本法规定的要求时,就重要事项向管理局提供明知为虚假或误导的信息,或因重大过失而提供虚假或误导信息;或

(c)鼓励为保护实际或潜在消费者利益而行使该项权力。[1]

(2)第(3)款适用于属于附录3第5条第(a)款或第(b)款规定范围,并行使欧洲经济区在联合王国开展《消费信贷法》业务权利的进入联合王国的欧洲经济区企业。

(3)如公平交易总理事通知管理局下列事项,则管理局可对相关企业行使干预权:

(a)该企业;

(b)企业(过去或目前)的任何雇员、代理人或关联人;或

(c)企业为法人的,该企业控制者或该控制者的关联人,

实施了[M25]《1974年消费信贷法》第25条第(2)款第(a)项至第(d)项规定的任何行为。

(4)"关联人"、"《消费信贷法》业务"和"控制者"含义同第203条。

注释:

修改等(不涉及条文内容)

C219　第194条于2001年12月1日依照制定法文件S.I.2001/3592第1条第(2)款、第12条第(3)款第(b)项、第18条第(4)款第(b)项、第21条第(3)款[与第23条第(2)款]。

第194条暂从2001年9月3日至2001年12月1日依照制定法文件S.I.2001/2659第1条第(2)款、第3条第(5)款;制定法文件S.I.2001/3538第2条第(1)款修正。

实施日期

I54　第194条于2001年12月1日全部生效;第194条在副署时尚未生效,见第431条第(2)款;第194条为特定目的于2001年9月3日依照制定法文件S.I.2001/2632第2条第(2)款、附录第二部分生效;第194条如于2001年12月1日尚未生效,则依照制定法文件S.I.2001/3538第2条第(1)款生效。

1　本款依照《2010年金融服务法》第3条第5款修订。——译者注

Marginal Citations

M25 1974 c. 39.

195 Exercise of power in support of overseas regulator.

(1) The Authority may exercise its power of intervention in respect of an incoming firm at the request of, or for the purpose of assisting, an overseas regulator.

(2) Subsection (1) applies whether or not the Authority's power of intervention is also exercisable as a result of section 194.

(3) "An overseas regulator" means an authority in a country or territory outside the United Kingdom—

(a) which is a home state regulator; or

(b) which exercises any function of a kind mentioned in subsection (4).

(4) The functions are—

(a) a function corresponding to any function of the Authority under this Act;

(b) a function corresponding to any function exercised by the competent authority under Part VI in relation to the listing of shares;

(c) a function corresponding to any function exercised by the Secretary of State under the [M26]Companies Act 1985;

(d) a function in connection with—

(i) the investigation of conduct of the kind prohibited by Part V of the [M27]Criminal Justice Act 1993 (insider dealing); or

(ii) the enforcement of rules (whether or not having the force of law) relating to such conduct;

(e) a function prescribed by regulations made for the purposes of this subsection which, in the opinion of the Treasury, relates to companies or financial services.

(5) If—

(a) a request to the Authority for the exercise of its power of intervention has been made by a home state regulator in pursuance of a Community obligation, or

(b) a home state regulator has notified the Authority that an EEA firm's EEA authorisation has been withdrawn, the Authority must, in deciding whether or not to exercise its power of intervention, consider whether exercising it is necessary in order to comply with a Community obligation.

(6) In deciding in any case in which the Authority does not consider that the exercise of its power of intervention is necessary in order to comply with a Community obligation, it may take into account in particular—

(a) whether in the country or territory of the overseas regulator concerned, corresponding assistance would be given to a United Kingdom regulatory authority;

附注引文

M25　1974年第39章。

第195条　为支持境外监管机关而行使权力

(1)管理局可应境外监管机关请求或为支持境外监管机关目的对进入联合王国的企业行使干预权。

(2)无论管理局是否亦可依照第194条规定行使其干预权,第(1)款均适用。

(3)"境外监管机关"系指联合王国以外的国家或领土的下列机关:

(a)相关企业的母国监管机关;或

(b)行使第(4)款所列任何一类职能的机关。

(4)前款所述职能为

(a)与本法规定的任何管理局职能相应的职能;

(b)与主管机关依照第四部分行使的任何股票上市相关职能相应的职能;

(c)与国务大臣依照[M26]《1985年公司法》行使的任何职能相应的职能;

(d)与下列事项相关的职能:

(i)对[M27]《1993年刑事司法法》第五部分(内幕交易)禁止的行为展开调查;或

(ii)执行与上述行为相关的规则(无论是否具有法律效力)。

(e)为实施本款而制定、财政部认为与公司或金融服务相关的法规规定的职能。

(5)如有下列情况:

(a)相关企业的母国监管机关依照共同体义务请求管理局行使干预权;或

(b)相关企业的母国监管机关已通知管理局某欧洲经济区企业的欧洲经济区授权已取消,则管理局应在决定是否行使干预权时考虑为遵守共同体义务是否有必要行使该项权力。

(6)管理局在任何案件中决定其不认为有必要为遵守共同体义务而行使干预权时,可以特别考虑

(a)在相关境外监管机关的国家或地区联合王国监管机关是否会得到对等协助;

(b) whether the case concerns the breach of a law, or other requirement, which has no close parallel in the United Kingdom or involves the assertion of a jurisdiction not recognised by the United Kingdom;

(c) the seriousness of the case and its importance to persons in the United Kingdom;

(d) whether it is otherwise appropriate in the public interest to give the assistance sought.

(7) The Authority may decide not to exercise its power of intervention, in response to a request, unless the regulator concerned undertakes to make such contribution to the cost of its exercise as the Authority considers appropriate.

(8) Subsection (7) does not apply if the Authority decides that it is necessary for it to exercise its power of intervention in order to comply with a Community obligation.

Annotations:

Modifications etc. (not altering text)

C220 S. 195 amended (temp. from 3.9.2001 to 1.12.2001) by S.I. 2001/2659, arts. 1(2), 3(5); S.I. 2001/3538, art. 2(1)

Commencement Information

I55 S. 195 wholly in force at 1.12.2001; s. 195 not in force at Royal Assent see s. 431(2); s. 195 in force for specified purposes at 3.9.2001 by S.I. 2001/2632, art. 2(2), Sch. Pt. 2; s. 195 in force in so far as not already in force at 1.12.2001 by S.I. 2001/3538, art. 2(1)

Marginal Citations

M26 1985 c. 6.

M27 1993 c. 36.

196 The power of intervention.

If the Authority is entitled to exercise its power of intervention in respect of an incoming firm under this Part, it may impose any requirement in relation to the firm which it could impose if—

(a) the firm's permission was a Part Ⅳ permission; and

(b) the Authority was entitled to exercise its power under that Part to vary that permission.

Annotations:

Modifications etc. (not altering text)

C221 S. 196 amended (temp. from 3.9.2001 to 1.12.2001) by S.I. 2001/2659, arts. 1(2), 3(5); S.I. 2001/3538, art. 2(1)

S. 196 extended (1.12.2001) by S.I. 2001/2636, arts. 1(2)(b), 34–54; S.I. 2001/3538, art. 2(1) (b)案件涉及违反在联合王国无相似规定的法律或其他要求,或案件是否涉及行使联合王国不予承认的管辖权主张;

(c)案件的严重性以及案件对在联合王国的人的重要性;
(d)给予所请求之协助是否在其他方面对公共利益是适当的。

(7)管理局可以决定不应某项请求行使干预权,除非相关监管者承诺分担管理局认为适当的权力行使费用。

(8)如管理局认为有必要为遵守共同体义务而行使干预权时,则第(7)款不适用。

注释:

修改等(不涉及条文内容)

C220 第195条暂于2001年9月3日至2001年12月1日依照制定法文件S.I.2001/2659第1条第(2)款、第3条第(5)款;制定法文件S.I.2001/3538第2条第(1)款修正。

实施日期

I55 第195条于2001年12月1日全部生效;第195条在副署时尚未生效,见第431条第(2)款;第195条为特定目的于2001年9月3日依照制定法文件S.I.2001/2632第2条第(2)款、附录第二部分生效;第195条如于2001年12月1日尚未生效,则依制定法文件S.I.2001/3538第2条第(1)款生效。

附注引文

M26 1985年本法第6条。
M27 1993年本法第36条。

第196条 干预权

如管理局依照本部分有权就进入联合王国的企业行使干预权,则如有下列情况,管理局可对进入联合王国的企业提出管理局局可以提出的任何要求:

(a)企业许可为第四部分许可;且
(b)管理局可依照本部分规定行使变更该许可的权力。

注释:

修改等(不涉及条文内容)

C221 第196条暂从2001年9月3日至2001年12月1日依照制定法文件S.I.2001/2659第1条第(2)款、第3条第(5)款;制定法文件S.I.2001/3538第2条第(1)款修正;

第196条于2001年12月1日依照制定法文件S.I.2001/2636第1条第(2)款第(b)项、第34条至第54条;制定法文件S.I.2001/3538第2条第(1)款扩大适用范围;

S. 196 extended (1.12.2001) by S.I. 2001/3592, arts. 1(2), 4(2) (with art. 23(2))

Commencement Information

I56 S. 196 wholly in force at 1.12.2001; s. 196 not in force at Royal Assent see s. 431 (2); s. 196 in force for specified purposes at 3.9.2001 by S.I. 2001/2632, art. 2(2), Sch. Pt. 2; s. 196 in force in so far as not already in force at 1.12.2001 by S.I. 2001/3538, art. 2(1)

Exercise of power of intervention

197 Procedure on exercise of power of intervention.

(1) A requirement takes effect—

(a) immediately, if the notice given under subsection (3) states that that is the case;

(b) on such date as may be specified in the notice; or

(c) if no date is specified in the notice, when the matter to which it relates is no longer open to review.

(2) A requirement may be expressed to take effect immediately (or on a specified date) only if the Authority, having regard to the ground on which it is exercising its power of intervention, considers that it is necessary for the requirement to take effect immediately (or on that date).

(3) If the Authority proposes to impose a requirement under section 196 on an incoming firm, or imposes such a requirement with immediate effect, it must give the firm written notice.

(4) The notice must—

(a) give details of the requirement;

(b) inform the firm of when the requirement takes effect;

(c) state the Authority's reasons for imposing the requirement and for its determination as to when the requirement takes effect;

(d) inform the firm that it may make representations to the Authority within such period as may be specified in the notice (whether or not it has referred the matter to the Tribunal); and

(e) inform it of its right to refer the matter to the Tribunal.

(5) The Authority may extend the period allowed under the notice for making representations.

(6) If, having considered any representations made by the firm, the Authority decides—

(a) to impose the requirement proposed, or

(b) if it has been imposed, not to rescind the requirement,

it must give it written notice.

(7) If, having considered any representations made by the firm, the Authority decides—

第196条于2001年12月1日依照制定法文件S.I.2001/3592第1条第(2)款、第4条第(2)款[与第23条第(2)款]扩大适用范围。

实施日期

I56 第196条于2001年12月1日全部生效;第196条在副署时尚未生效,见第431条第(2)款;第196条为特定目的于2001年9月3日依照制定法文件S.I.2001/2632第2条第(2)款、附录第二部分生效;第196条如于2001年12月1日未生效,则依照制定法文件S.I.2001/3538第2条第(1)款生效。

行使干预权

第197条 行使干预权的程序

(1)提出的要求

(a)如依照第(3)款规定情况发出通知,则立即生效;

(b)于通知规定的日期生效;或

(c)如通知未规定日期,则于该要求相关事项不再开放共审议时生效。

(2)只有管理局在考虑其行使干预权的理由后认为某项要求有必要立即生效(或在指定日期生效),才可以明示该要求立即生效(或在指定日期生效)。

(3)如管理局拟依照第196条规定对进入联合王国的企业提出要求,或拟使上述要求立即生效,则必须向该企业发出书面通知。

(4)该通知必须

(a)详细说明该要求;

(b)告知该企业该要求何时生效;

(c)说明管理局提出该要求以及决定该要求生效时间的理由;

(d)告知该企业可以在通知规定的期限内向管理局作出陈述(无论该事项是否已诉至裁判所);且

(e)告知其有权将该事项诉至裁判所。

(5)管理局可以延长通知规定允许陈述的期限。

(6)如管理局在考虑企业作出的任何陈述后决定

(a)提出拟定的要求;或

(b)不撤销已提出的要求,

则必须向该企业发出书面通知。

(7)如管理局在考虑企业作出的任何陈述后决定

(a) not to impose the requirement proposed,

(b) to impose a different requirement from that proposed, or

(c) to rescind a requirement which has effect,

it must give it written notice.

(8) A notice given under subsection (6) must inform the firm of its right to refer the matter to the Tribunal.

(9) A notice under subsection (7)(b) must comply with subsection (4).

(10) If a notice informs a person of his right to refer a matter to the Tribunal, it must give an indication of the procedure on such a reference.

Annotations:

Modifications etc. (not altering text)

C222 S. 197 amended (temp. from 3.9.2001 to 1.12.2001) by S.I. 2001/2659, arts. 1(2), 3(5); S.I. 2001/3538, art. 2(1)

S. 197 excluded (1.12.2001) by S.I. 2001/3592, arts. 1(2), 61(4), 110(5), 115(4) (with art. 23(2))

C223 S. 197(1)(c) excluded (1.12.2001) by S.I. 2001/3592, arts. 1(2), 18(5), 21(4) (with art. 23(2))

C224 S. 197(3) extended (1.12.2001) by S.I. 2001/3592, arts. 1(2), 12(1), 18(1)(a), 20(1) (with art. 23(2))

S. 197(3) modified (1.12.2001) by S.I. 2001/3592, arts. 1(2), 72(2) (with art. 23(2))

C225 S. 197(7) extended (1.12.2001) by S.I. 2001/3592, arts. 1(2), 23(1) (with art. 23(2))

Commencement Information

I57 S. 197 wholly in force at 1.12.2001; s. 197 not in force at Royal Assent see s. 431(2); s. 197 in force for specified purposes at 3.9.2001 by S.I. 2001/2632, art. 2(2), Sch. Pt. 2; s. 197 in force in so far as not already in force at 1.12.2001 by S.I. 2001/3538, art. 2(1)

198 Power to apply to court for injunction in respect of certain overseas insurance companies.

(1) This section applies if the Authority has received a request made in respect of an incoming EEA firm in accordance with—

(a) Article 20.5 of the first non-life insurance directive; or

(b) Article 24.5 of the first life insurance directive.

(2) The court may, on an application made to it by the Authority with respect to the

(a)不提出拟定的要求；
(b)提出与拟定的要求不同的要求；或
(c)撤销已生效的要求，
则必须向该企业发出书面通知。
(8)依照第(6)款发出的通知必须告知企业其有权将该事项诉至裁判所。

(9)第(7)条第(b)项规定的通知必须符合第(4)款规定。
(10)如通知告知某人有权将相关事项诉至裁判所，则必须说明诉至裁判所的程序。

注释：

修改等(不涉及条文内容)

C222 第197条暂时有效，于2001年9月3日至2001年12月1日依照制定法文件S.I. 2001/2659第1条第(2)款、第3条第(5)款；制定法文件S.I.2001/3538第2条第(1)款修正；

第197条于2001年12月1日依照制定法文件S.I.2001/3592第1条第(2)款、第61条第(4)款、第110条第(5)款、第115条第(4)款[与第23条第(2)款]排除。

C223 第197条第(1)款第(c)项于2001年12月1日依照制定法文件S.I.2001/3592第1条第(2)款、第18条第(5)款、第21条第(4)款[与第23条第(2)款]排除。

C224 第197条第(3)款于2001年12月1日依照制定法文件S.I.2001/3592第1条第(2)款、第12条第(1)款、第18条第(1)款第(a)项、第20条第(1)款[与第23条第(2)款]扩大适用范围；

第197条第(3)款于2001年12月1日依照制定法文件S.I.2001/3592第1条第(2)款、第72条第(2)款[与第23条第(2)款]修订。

C225 第197条第(7)款于2001年12月1日依照制定法文件S.I.2001/3592第1条第(2)款、第23条第(1)款[与第23条第(2)款]扩大适用范围。

实施日期

I57 第197条于2001年12月1日全部生效；第197条在副署时尚未生效，见第431条第(2)款；第197条为特定目的于2001年9月3日依照制定法文件S.I.2001/2632第2条第(2)款、附录第二部分生效；第197条如于2001年12月1日尚未生效，则依照制定法文件S.I. 2001/3538第2条第(1)款生效。

第198条 申请法院对特定境外保险公司发出禁令的权力

(1)如管理局依照下列规定收到关于进入联合王国的欧洲经济区企业的请求：

(a)第一非寿险指令第20.5条；或
(b)第一寿险指令第24.5条。
(2)法院可以应管理局就该企业向其提出的申请，向该企业发出强制令(或在苏

firm, grant an injunction restraining (or in Scotland an interdict prohibiting) the firm disposing of or otherwise dealing with any of its assets.

(3) If the court grants an injunction, it may by subsequent orders make provision for such incidental, consequential and supplementary matters as it considers necessary to enable the Authority to perform any of its functions under this Act.

(4) "The court" means—

(a) the High Court; or

(b) in Scotland, the Court of Session.

199 Additional procedure for EEA firms in certain cases.

(1) This section applies if it appears to the Authority that its power of intervention is exercisable in relation to an EEA firm exercising EEA rights in the United Kingdom ("an incoming EEA firm") in respect of the contravention of a relevant requirement.

(2) A requirement is relevant if—

(a) it is imposed by the Authority under this Act; and

(b) as respects its contravention, any of the single market directives provides that a procedure of the kind set out in the following provisions of this section is to apply.

(3) The Authority must, in writing, require the firm to remedy the situation.

(4) If the firm fails to comply with the requirement under subsection (3) within a reasonable time, the Authority must give a notice to that effect to the firm's home state regulator requesting it—

(a) to take all appropriate measures for the purpose of ensuring that the firm remedies the situation which has given rise to the notice; and

(b) to inform the Authority of the measures it proposes to take or has taken or the reasons for not taking such measures.

(5) Except as mentioned in subsection (6), the Authority may not exercise its power of intervention unless satisfied—

(a) that the firm's home state regulator has failed or refused to take measures for the purpose mentioned in subsection (4)(a); or

(b) that the measures taken by the home state regulator have proved inadequate for that purpose.

(6) If the Authority decides that it should exercise its power of intervention in respect of the incoming EEA firm as a matter of urgency in order to protect the interests of consumers, it may exercise that power—

(a) before complying with subsections (3) and (4); or

(b) where it has complied with those subsections, before it is satisfied as mentioned in subsection (5).

(7) In such a case the Authority must at the earliest opportunity inform the firm's home

格兰为实际履行令),禁止该企业处置或以其他方式处理其任何资产。

(3)如法院发出强制令,则可通过后续命令对其认为管理局行使本法规定的任何职能所需的附带、相应及补充事项作出规定。

(4)“法院”系指

(a)高等法院;或

(b)(苏格兰)高等民事法院。

第199条 特定情况下欧洲经济区企业的附加程序

(1) 如管理局认为其可以针对在联合王国行使欧洲经济区权利的欧洲经济区企业(以下简称进入联合王国的欧洲经济区企业)就其违反相关要求的行为行使干预权,则适用本条规定。

(2)符合下列条件的要求为相关要求:

(a)由管理局依照本法提出;且

(b)就违反该要求,任何一项单一市场指令规定均适用于本条下文规定中所列种类的程序。

(3)管理局必须以书面形式要求该企业改正。

(4)如企业在合理时间内未遵守第(3)款规定的要求,则管理局必须将该结果通知该企业的母国监管机关

(a)采取一切适当措施,确保该企业对引起通知的情况加以改正;并

(b)告知管理局其拟采取的措施、已采取的措施或不采取措施的理由。

(5)除第(6)款规定外,管理局除非确信有下列情况,否则不得行使干预权:

(a)该企业的母国监管机关未能或拒绝为第(4)款第(a)项所述之目的采取措施;或

(b)有证据证明母国监管机关采取的措施不足以实现上述目的。

(6)如管理局决定,为保障消费者的利益,应对进入联合王国的欧洲经济区企业紧急行使干预权,则可以

(a)不经执行第(3)款和第(4)款规定的程序即行使该项权力;或

(b)已执行第(3)款和第(4)款规定程序的,可不经确信有第(5)款规定的情况而行使该项权力。

(7)在这种情况下,管理局必须尽早告知该企业的母国监管机关和委员会。

state regulator and the Commission.

(8) If—

(a) the Authority has (by virtue of subsection (6)) exercised its power of intervention before complying with subsections (3) and (4) or before it is satisfied as mentioned in subsection (5), and

(b) the Commission decides under any of the single market directives that the Authority must rescind or vary any requirement imposed in the exercise of its power of intervention, the Authority must in accordance with the decision rescind or vary the requirement.

Annotations:

Modifications etc. (not altering text)

C226 S. 199 extended (1.12.2001) by S.I. 2001/2636, arts. 1(2)(b), 37, 52(4); S.I. 2001/3538, art. 2(1)

S. 199 extended (1.12.2001) by S.I. 2001/3592, arts. 1(2), 22(6) (with art. 23(2))

C227 S. 199(7) modified (1.12.2001) by S.I. 2001/3084, arts. 1(1)(b), 2(7); S.I. 2001/3538, art. 2(1)

Commencement Information

I58 S. 199 wholly in force at 1.12.2001; s. 199 not in force at Royal Assent see s. 431(2); s. 199 in force for specified purposes at 3.9.2001 by S.I. 2001/2632, art. 2(2), Sch. Pt. 2; s. 199 in force in so far as not already in force at 1.12.2001 by S.I. 2001/3538, art. 2(1)

Supplemental

200 Rescission and variation of requirements.

(1) The Authority may rescind or vary a requirement imposed inexercise of its power of intervention on its own initiative or on the application of the person subject to the requirement.

(2) The power of the Authority on its own initiative to rescind a requirement is exercisable by written notice given by the Authority to the person concerned, which takes effect on the date specified in the notice.

(3) Section 197 applies to the exercise of the power of the Authority on its own initiative to vary a requirement as it applies to the imposition of a requirement.

(4) If the Authority proposes to refuse an application for the variation or rescission of a requirement, it must give the applicant a warning notice.

(5) If the Authority decides to refuse an application for the variation or rescission of a

(8)如有下列情况:

(a)管理局在执行第(3)款和第(4)款规定程序或确信有第(5)款规定情况前已[依照第(6)款]行使干预权,且

(b)委员会依照任何单一市场指令决定管理局必须撤销或变更其在行使干预权时提出的任何要求,则管理局必须根据该决定撤销或变更要求。

注释:

修改等(不涉及条文内容)

C226　第199条于2001年12月1日依照制定法文件S.I.2001/2636第1条第(2)款第(b)项、第37条、第52条第(4)款;制定法文件S.I.2001/3538第2条第(1)款扩大适用范围;

第199条于2001年12月1日依照制定法文件S.I.2001/3592第1条第(2)款、第22条第(6)款[与第23条第(2)款]扩大适用范围;

C227　第199条第(7)款于2001年12月1日依照制定法文件S.I.2001/3084第1条第(1)款第(b)项、第2条第(7)款;制定法文件S.I.2001/3538第2条第(1)款修订。

实施日期

I58　第199条于2001年12月1日全部生效;第199条在副署时尚未生效,见第431条第(2)款;第199条为特定目的于2001年9月3日依照制定法文件S.I.2001/2632第2条第(2)款、附录第二部分生效;第199条如于2001年12月1日尚未生效,则依照制定法文件S.I.2001/3538第2条第(1)款生效。

附　　则

第200条　要求的撤销和变更

(1)管理局可以主动或应要求接受人的申请撤销或变更行使干预权时提出的要求。

(2)管理局主动撤销要求的权力可通过管理局向相关人发出书面通知行使,该通知自其中指定的日期起生效。

(3)第197条适用于管理局行使主动变更要求的权力,效力等同于对提出要求适用。

(4)如管理局拟拒绝批准变更或撤销要求的申请,则必须向申请人发出预告通知。

(5)如管理局决定拒绝批准变更或撤销要求的申请,则

requirement—

(a) the Authority must give the applicant a decision notice; and

(b) that person may refer the matter to the Tribunal.

Annotations:

Modifications etc. (not altering text)

C228 S. 200 extended (1.12.2001) by S.I. 2001/3592, arts. 1(2), 4(2) (with art. 23 (2))

C229 S. 200(2)–(5) excluded (1.12.2001) by S.I. 2001/3592, arts. 1(2), 61(4), 110 (5), 115(4) (with art. 23(2))

C230 S. 200(5)(a) extended (1.12.2001) by S.I. 2001/3592, arts. 1(2), 7(3)(4) (with art. 23(2))

201 Effect of certain requirements on other persons.

If the Authority, in exercising its power of intervention, imposes on an incoming firm a requirement of a kind mentioned in subsection (3) of section 48, the requirement has the same effect in relation to the firm as it would have in relation to an authorised person if it had been imposed on the authorised person by the Authority acting under section 45.

202 Contravention of requirement imposed under this Part.

(1) Contravention of a requirement imposed by the Authorityunder this Part does not—

(a) make a person guilty of an offence;

(b) make any transaction void or unenforceable; or

(c) (subject to subsection (2)) give rise to any right of action for breach of statutory duty.

(2) In prescribed cases the contravention is actionable at the suit of a person who suffers loss as a result of the contravention, subject to the defences and other incidents applying to actions for breach of statutory duty.

Annotations:

Commencement Information

I59 S. 202 wholly in force at 3.9.2001; s. 202 not in force at Royal Assent see s. 431(2); s. 202(2) in force for certain purposes at 25.2.2001 by S.I. 2001/516, art. 2(b), Sch. Pt. 2; s. 202 in so far as not already in force at 3.9.2001 by S.I. 2001/2632, art. 2(2), Sch. Pt. 2

(a)管理局必须向申请人发出决定通知;且

(b)申请人可将该事项诉至裁判所。

注释:

修改等(不涉及条文内容)

C228　第200条于2001年12月1日依照制定法文件S.I.2001/3592第1条第(2)款、第4条第(2)款[与第23条第(2)款]扩大适用范围;

C229　第200条第(2)款至第(5)款于2001年12月1日依照制定法文件S.I.2001/3592第1条第(2)款、第61条第(4)款、第110条第(5)款、第115条第(4)款[与第23条第(2)款]排除。

C230　第200条第(5)款第(a)项于2001年12月1日依照制定法文件S.I.2001/3592,第1条第(2)款,第7条第(3)款、第(4)款[与第23条第(2)款]扩大适用范围。

第201条　特定要求对其他人的效力

如管理局在行使干预权时,对进入联合王国的企业提出第48条第(3)款规定种类的要求,则该要求对该企业的效力等同于管理局依照第45条对获授权人提出该要求时该要求对该获授权人的效力。

第202条　违反依照本部分规定提出的要求

(1)违反依照本部分规定提出的要求不会

(a)构成犯罪;

(b)造成任何交易无效或无法履行;或

(c)[在符合第(2)款规定的情况下]产生任何针对违反法定职责提起诉讼的权利。

(2)在规定情况下,对违反要求的行为,因违反要求而遭受损失的人可提起诉讼,但必须依照适用违反法定义务诉讼的抗辩理由和其他事由。

注释:

实施日期

I59　第202条于2001年9月3日全部生效;第202条在副署时尚未生效,见第431条第(2)款;第202条为特定目的于2001年2月25日依照制定法文件S.I.2001/516第2条第(b)款、附录第二部分生效;第202条如于2001年9月3日尚未生效,则依照制定法文件S.I.2001/2632第2条第(2)款、附录第二部分生效。

Powers of Director General of Fair Trading

203 Power to prohibit the carrying on of Consumer Credit Act business.

(1) If it appears to the Director General of Fair Trading ("the Director") that subsection (4) has been, or is likely to be, contravened as respects a consumer credit EEA firm, he may by written notice given to the firm impose on the firm a consumer credit prohibition.

(2) If it appears to the Director that a restriction imposed under section 204 on an EEA consumer credit firm has not been complied with, he may by written notice given to the firm impose a consumer credit prohibition.

(3) "Consumer credit prohibition" means a prohibition on carrying on, or purporting to carry on, in the United Kingdom any Consumer Credit Act business which consists of or includes carrying on one or more listed activities.

(4) This subsection is contravened as respects a firm if—

(a) the firm or any of its employees, agents or associates (whether past or present), or

(b) if the firm is a body corporate, any controller of the firm or an associate of any such controller, does any of the things specified in paragraphs (a) to (d) of section 25(2) of the [M28] Consumer Credit Act 1974.

(5) A consumer credit prohibition may be absolute or may be imposed—

(a) for such period,

(b) until the occurrence of such event, or

(c) until such conditions are complied with,

as may be specified in the notice given under subsection (1) or (2).

(6) Any period, event or condition so specified may be varied by the Director on the application of the firm concerned.

(7) A consumer credit prohibition may be withdrawn by written notice served by the Director on the firm concerned, and any such notice takes effect on such date as is specified in the notice.

(8) Schedule 16 has effect as respects consumer credit prohibitions and restrictions under section 204.

(9) A firm contravening a prohibition under this section is guilty of an offence and liable—

(a) on summary conviction, to a fine not exceeding the statutory maximum;

(b) on conviction on indictment, to a fine.

(10) In this section and section 204—

"a consumer credit EEA firm" means an EEA firm falling within any of paragraphs (a) to (c) of paragraph 5 of Schedule 3 whose EEA authorization covers any Consumer Credit

公平交易总理事的权力

第203条　禁止开展《消费信贷法》业务的权力

(1)如公平交易总理事(以下简称总理事)认为欧洲经济区消费信贷企业已经或可能违反第(4)款规定,则可以向该企业发出书面通知,对该企业提出消费信贷禁令。

(2)如总理事认为依照第204条规定对欧洲经济区消费信贷企业提出的限制未得到遵守,则可以向该企业发出书面通知,对该企业提出消费信贷禁令。

(3)"消费信贷禁令",系指禁止在联合王国开展或计划开展任何由一项或多项列出活动组成或包含一项或多项列出活动的《消费信贷法》业务。

(4)如企业有下列情况,则为违反本款规定:

(a)企业(过去或目前)的任何雇员、代理人或关联人;或

(b)企业为法人的,该企业控制者或该控制者的关联人,实施了[M28]《1974年消费信贷法》第25条第(2)款第(a)项至第(d)项规定的任何行为。

(5)消费信贷禁令可以为绝对禁令或可以附加下列条件:

(a)在通知规定的期间有效;

(b)至发生通知规定的事件发生为止;或

(c)至符合通知规定的条件为止,

或根据依照第(1)款或第(2)款规定发出的通知规定。

(6)总理事可以应相关企业申请变更上述通知规定的任何期间、事件或条件。

(7)总理事可以向相关企业送达书面通知,取消消费信贷禁令,任何此等通知自其中规定的日期起生效。

(8)附录16对第204条规定的消费信贷禁令和限制有效。

(9)企业违反本条禁令构成犯罪,应当承担下列责任:

(a)经简易程序定罪的,处以不超过最高法定金额的罚金;

(b)经公诉程序定罪的,处以罚金。

(10)本条及第204条中

"消费信贷欧洲经济区公司"系指属于附录3第5条第(a)项至第(c)项规定范围、其欧洲经济区授权涵盖任何《消费信贷法》业务的欧洲经济区公司;

Act business;

"Consumer Credit Act business" means consumer credit business, consumer hire business or ancillary credit business;

"consumer credit business", "consumer hire business" and "ancillary credit business" have the same meaning as in the [M29] Consumer Credit Act 1974;

"listed activity" means an activity listed in [[F2] Annex 1 to the banking consolidation directive] or the Annex to the investment services directive;

"associate" has the same meaning as in section 25(2) of the [M30]Consumer Credit Act 1974;

"controller" has the meaning given by section 189(1) of that Act.

Annotations:

Amendments (Textual)

F2 S. 203(10): words in definition of "listed activity" substituted (22.11.2000) by S.I. 2000/2952, reg. 8(2)

Modifications etc. (not altering text)

C231 S. 203(5) modified (1.12.2001) by S.I. 2001/2636, arts. 1(2)(b), 53(2); S.I. 2001/3538, art. 2(1)

Marginal Citations

M28 1974 c. 39.

M29 1974 c. 39.

M30 1974 c. 39.

204 Power to restrict the carrying on of Consumer Credit Act business.

(1) In this section "restriction" means a direction that a consumer credit EEA firm may not carry on in the United Kingdom, otherwise than in accordance with such condition or conditions as may be specified in the direction, any Consumer Credit Act business which—

(a) consists of or includes carrying on any listed activity; and

(b) is specified in the direction.

(2) If it appears to the Director that the situation as respects a consumer credit EEA firm is such that the powers conferred by section 203(1) are exercisable, the Director may, instead of imposing a prohibition, impose such restriction as appears to him desirable.

(3) A restriction—

(a) may be withdrawn, or

(b) may be varied with the agreement of the firm concerned,

by written notice served by the Director on the firm, and any such notice takes effect on such date as is specified in the notice.

《消费信贷法》业务系指消费信贷业务、消费租用业务或附属信贷业务；

“消费信贷业务”、“消费租用业务”和“附属信贷业务”含义与[M29]《1974年消费信贷法》中的含义相同；

“列出活动”系指[[F2]银行合并指令附录1]或投资服务指令附录列出的活动；

“关联人”含义与[M30]《1974年消费信贷法》第25条第(2)款规定含义相同；

“控制人”含义为该法第189条第(1)款中的含义。

注释：

修正(文本)

F2　第203条第(10)款:“列出活动”定义中的文字于2000年11月22日依照制定法文件S.I.2000/2952第8条第(2)款规定替换。

修改等(不涉及条文内容)

C231　第203条第(5)款于2001年12月1日依照制定法文件S.I.2001/2636第1条第(2)款第(b)项、第53条第(2)款、第2条第(1)款修订。

附注引文

M28　1974年第39章。

M29　1974年第39章。

M30　1974年第39章。

第204条　限制开展《消费信贷法》业务的权力

(1)本条中“限制”,系指以指令规定消费信贷欧洲经济区企业除依照该指令所列一项或多项条件外不得在联合王国开展下列任何《消费信贷法》业务

(a)由任何列出活动组成或包括任何列出活动的《消费信贷法》业务;以及

(b)指令中规定的《消费信贷法》业务。

(2)如总理事认为根据与消费信贷欧洲经济区企业相关的情况可行使第203条第(1)款赋予的权力,则可不提出禁令,而改为提出其认为必要的限制。

(3)限制

(a)撤销;或

(b)经相关企业同意后变更,

总理事可向相关企业送达书面通知,任何此等通知自其中规定的日期起生效。

(4) A firm contravening a restriction is guilty of an offence and liable

(a) on summary conviction, to a fine not exceeding the statutory maximum;

(b) on conviction on indictment, to a fine.

Annotations:

Modifications etc. (not altering text)

C232 S. 204 extended (1.12.2001) by S.I. 2001/2636, arts. 1(2)(b), 53(3); S.I. 2001/3538, art. 2(1)

(4)违反限制的企业构成犯罪,应承担下列责任:

(a)经简易程序定罪的,处以不超过最高法定金额的罚金;

(b)经公诉程序定罪的,处以罚金。

注释:

修改等(不涉及条文内容)

C232　第204条于2001年12月1日依照制定法文件S.I.2001/2636第1条第(2)款第(b)项、第53条第(3)款;制定法文件S.I.2001/3538第2条第(1)款扩大适用范围。

PART XIV DISCIPLINARY MEASURES

Annotations:

Modifications etc. (not altering text)

C233 Pt. XIV (ss. 205–211) applied (1.12.2001) by 1951 c. 65, s. 57(5) (as substituted (1.12.2001) by S.I. 2001/3647, art. 5, Sch. 3 Pt. I para. 5(3))

205 Public censure.

If the Authority considers that an authorised person has contravened a requirement imposed on him by or under this Act, the Authority may publish a statement to that effect.

Annotations:

Modifications etc. (not altering text)

C234 S. 205 modified (1.12.2001) by S.I. 2001/2657, arts. 1(1), 6, 7 (which was revoked (8.10.2001) by S.I. 2001/3083, arts. 1(2), 23); S.I. 2001/3538, art. 2(1)

S. 205 modified (1.12.2001) by S.I. 2001/3083, arts. 1(1), 6, 7; S.I. 2001/3538, art. 2(1)

S. 205 excluded (1.12.2001) by S.I. 2001/3592, arts. 1(2), 107(1) (with art. 23(2))

C235 S. 205 modified (18.7.2002 for certain purposes and 21.8.2002 otherwise) by The Electronic Commerce Directive (Financial Services and Markets) Regulations 2002 (S.I. 2002/1775), regs. 1, 12(1)

206 Financial penalties.

(1) If the Authority considers that an authorised person has contravened a requirement imposed on him by or under this Act, it may impose on him a penalty, in respect of the contravention, of such amount as it considers appropriate.

第十四部分 惩戒措施

注释：

修改等（不涉及条文内容）

C233 第十四部分（第205条至第211条）于2001年12月1日依照1951年第65章第57条第（5）款［于2001年12月1日依照制定法文件S.I.2001/3647第5条、附录3第一部分第5条第（3）款替换］适用。

第205条 公开谴责

如管理局认为获授权人违反了依照本法规定对其提出的要求，则可以针对此事公开发表声明。

注释：

修改等（不涉及条文内容）

C234 第205条于2001年12月1日依照制定法文件S.I.2001/2657第1条第（1）款、第6条、第7条（于2001年10月8日依照制定法文件S.I.2001/3083第1条第（2）款、第23条废除）；制定法文件S.I.2001/3538第2条第（1）款修订；

第205条于2001年12月1日依照制定法文件S.I.2001/3083第1条第（1）款、第6条、第7条；制定法文件S.I.2001/3538第2条第（1）款修订；

第205条于2001年12月1日依照制定法文件S.I.2001/3592第1条第（2）款、第107条第（1）款［与第23条第（2）款］排除。

C235 第205条为特定目的于2002年7月18日，否则于2002年8月21日依照《2002年电子商务指令条例》（金融服务和市场）（制定法文件S.I.2002/1775）第1条、第12条第（1）款修订。

第206条 经济处罚[1]

（1）如管理局认为获授权人违反了依照本法规定对其提出的要求，则可根据违反要求的情况对其处以适当数额的罚款。

1 本条依照《2010年金融服务法》第9条修订。——译者注

(2) The Authority may not in respect of any contravention both require a person to pay a penalty under this section and withdraw his authorisation under section 33.

(3) A penalty under this section is payable to the Authority.

Annotations:

Modifications etc. (not altering text)

C236 S. 206 excluded (1.12.2001) by S.I. 2001/3592, arts. 1(2), 107(1) (with art. 23(2))

S. 206 restricted (1.12.2001) by S.I. 2001/3592, arts. 1(2), 60(2) (with art. 23(2))

S. 206 modified (1.12.2001) by S.I. 2001/2657, arts. 1(1), 8 (which was revoked(8.10.2001) by S.I. 2001/3083, arts. 1(2), 23); S.I. 2001/3538, art. 2(1)

S. 206 modified (1.12.2001) by S.I. 2001/3083, arts. 1(2), 8; S.I. 2001/3538, art. 2(1)

C237 S. 206 modified (18.7.2002 for certain purposes and 21.8.2002 otherwise) by The Electronic Commerce Directive (Financial Services and Markets) Regulations 2002 (S.I. 2002/1775), regs. 1, 12(1)

207 Proposal to take disciplinary measures.

(1) If the Authority proposes—

(a) to publish a statement in respect of an authorised person (under section 205), or

(b) to impose a penalty on an authorised person (under section 206),

it must give the authorised person a warning notice.

(2) A warning notice about a proposal to publish a statement must set out the terms of the statement.

(3) A warning notice about a proposal to impose a penalty, must state the amount of the penalty.

Annotations:

Modifications etc. (not altering text)

C238 S. 207 excluded (1.12.2001) by S.I. 2001/3592, arts. 1(2), 61(5), 110(6) (with art.23(2))

C239 S. 207 modified (18.7.2002 for certain purposes and 21.8.2002 otherwise) by The Electronic Commerce Directive (Financial Services and Markets) Regulations 2002 (S.I. 2002/1775), regs. 1, 12(1)

（2）对任何违反要求的行为，管理局不得对行为人既依照本条规定处以罚款又依照第33条规定撤销授权。

（3）本条规定的罚款支付给管理局。

注释：

修改等（不涉及条文内容）

C236　第206条于2001年12月1日依照制定法文件S.I.2001/3592第1条第（2）款、第107条第（1）款［与第23条第（2）款］排除；

第206条于2001年12月1日受制定法文件S.I.2001/3592第1条第（2）款、第60条第（2）款［与第23条第（2）款］限制；

第206条于2001年12月1日依照制定法文件S.I.2001/2657第1条第（1）款、第8条［于2001年10月8日依制定法文件S.I.2001/3083第1条第（2）款、第23条废除］；制定法文件S.I.2001/3538第2条第（1）款修订；

第206条于2001年12月1日依照制定法文件S.I.2001/3083第1条第（2）款、第8条；制定法文件S.I.2001/3538第2条第（1）款修订。

C237　第206条为特定目的于2002年7月18日，否则于2002年8月21日依照《2002年电子商务指令条例》（金融服务和市场）（制定法文件S.I.2002/1775）第1条、第12条第（1）款修订。

第207条　采取惩戒措施的计划[1]

（1）如管理局拟

（a）（依照第205条规定）针对获授权人公开发表声明，或

（b）（依照第206条规定）对获授权人处以罚款，

则必须向获授权人发出预告通知。

（2）关于拟公开发表声明的预告通知必须说明该声明的条款。[2]

（3）关于拟处以罚款的预告通知必须说明罚款数额。

注释：

修改等（不涉及条文内容）

C238　第207条于2001年12月1日依照制定法文件S.I.2001/3592第1条第（2）款、第61条第（5）款、第110条第（6）款［与第23条第（2）款］排除。

C239　第207条为特定目的于2002年7月18日，否则于2002年8月21日依照《2002年电子商务指令条例》（金融服务和市场）（制定法文件S.I.2002/1775）第1条、第12条第（1）款修订。

1　本条依照《2010年金融服务法》附录2第一部分第18条修订。——译者注

2　本款依照《2010年金融服务法》第10条删除。——译者注

208 Decision notice.

(1) If the Authority decides—

(a) to publish a statement under section 205 (whether or not in the terms proposed), or

(b) to impose a penalty under section 206 (whether or not of the amount proposed), it must without delay give the authorised person concerned a decision notice.

(2) In the case of a statement, the decision notice must set out the terms of the statement.

(3) In the case of a penalty, the decision notice must state the amount of the penalty.

(4) If the Authority decides to—

(a) publish a statement in respect of an authorised person under section 205, or

(b) impose a penalty on an authorised person under section 206,

the authorised person may refer the matter to the Tribunal.

Annotations:

Modifications etc. (not altering text)

C240 S. 208 excluded (1.12.2001) by S.I. 2001/3592, arts. 1(2), 61(5), 110(6) (with art. 23(2))

C241 S. 208 modified (18.7.2002 for certain purposes and 21.8.2002 otherwise) by The Electronic Commerce Directive (Financial Services and Markets) Regulations 2002 (S.I. 2002/1775), regs. 1, 12(1)

C242 S. 208(1)(a)(b) modified (1.12.2001) by S.I. 2001/3592, arts. 1(2), 68(2), 69(2) (with art. 23(2))

209 Publication.

After a statement under section 205 is published, the Authority must send a copy of it to the authorised person and to any person on whom a copy of the decision notice was given under section 393(4).

Annotations:

Modifications etc. (not altering text)

C243 S. 209 modified (18.7.2002 for certain purposes and 21.8.2002 otherwise) by The Electronic Commerce Directive (Financial Services and Markets) Regulations 2002 (S.I. 2002/1775), regs. 1, 12(1)

第208条　决定通知[1]

(1)如管理局决定

(a)依照第205条规定公开发表声明(无论是否以计划的条款发表);或

(b)依照第206条规定处以罚金(无论是否为计划的金额),则必须毫不延迟地向相关获授权人发出决定通知。

(2)如为公开发表声明,则决定通知必须说明该声明的条款。

(3)如为处以罚款,则决定通知必须说明罚款数额。

(4)如管理局决定

(a)依照第205条规定针对获授权人公开发表声明;或

(b)依照第206条规定对获授权人处以罚款,

则获授权人可将该事项诉至裁判所。

注释:

修改等(不涉及条文内容)

C240　第208条于2001年12月1日依照制定法文件S.I.2001/3592第1条第(2)款、第61条第(5)款、第110条第(6)款[与第23条第(2)款]排除。

C241　第208条为特定目的于2002年7月18日,否则于2002年8月21日依照《2002年电子商务指令条例》(金融服务和市场)(制定法文件S.I.2002/1775)第1条、第12条第(1)款修订。

C242　第208条第(1)款第(a)项和第(b)项于2001年12月1日依照制定法文件S.I.2001/3592第1条第(2)款、第68条第(2)款、第69条第(2)款[与第23条第(2)款]修订。

第209条　公开发表

依照第205条规定公开发表声明后,管理局必须将该声明的副本送交获授权人以及依照第393条第(4)款规定向其发出决定通知副本的任何人。

注释:

修改等(不涉及条文内容)

C243　第209条为特定目的于2002年7月18日,否则于2002年8月21日依照《2002年电子商务指令条例》(金融服务和市场)(制定法文件S.I.2002/1775)第1条、第12条第(1)款修订。

1　本条依照《2010年金融服务法》附录2第一部分第19条修订。——译者注

210 Statements of policy.

(1) The Authority must prepare and issue a statement of its policy with respect to—

(a) the imposition of penalties under this Part; and

(b) the amount of penalties under this Part.

(2) The Authority's policy in determining what the amount of a penalty should be must include having regard to—

(a) the seriousness of the contravention in question in relation to the nature of the requirement contravened;

(b) the extent to which that contravention was deliberate or reckless; and

(c) whether the person on whom the penalty is to be imposed is an individual.

(3) The Authority may at any time alter or replace a statement issued under this section.

(4) If a statement issued under this section is altered or replaced, the Authority must issue the altered or replacement statement.

(5) The Authority must, without delay, give the Treasury a copy of any statement which it publishes under this section.

(6) A statement issued under this section must be published by the Authority in the way appearing to the Authority to be best calculated to bring it to the attention of the public.

(7) In exercising, or deciding whether to exercise, its power under section 206 in the case of any particular contravention, the Authority must have regard to any statement published under this section and in force at the time when the contravention in question occurred.

(8) The Authority may charge a reasonable fee for providing a person with a copy of the statement.

Annotations:

Modifications etc. (not altering text)

C244 S. 210(7) excluded (1.12.2001) by S.I. 2001/3592, arts. 1(2), 110(6) (with art. 23(2))

211 Statements of policy: procedure.

(1) Before issuing a statement under section 210, the Authority must publish a draft of the proposed statement in the way appearing to the Authority to be best calculated to bring it to the attention of the public.

(2) The draft must be accompanied by notice that representations about the proposal may be made to the Authority within a specified time.

(3) Before issuing the proposed statement, the Authority must have regard to any representations made to it in accordance with subsection (2).

第210条　政策声明[1]

(1)管理局必须就关于下列事项的政策制定并发布声明：

(a)依照本部分规定处以罚金的措施；以及

(b)依照本部分规定处以罚金的数额。

(2)管理局确定罚款数额的政策必须包括对下列事项的考虑：

(a)就被违反要求的性质而言，相关违反要求行为的严重性；

(b)违反要求的行为在何种程度上为故意或因重大过失而违反；以及

(c)接受罚款的是否为个人。

(3)管理局可以随时修改或更换依照本条规定发布的声明。

(4)如对依照本条规定发布的声明进行修改或更换，则管理局必须发布修改或更换的声明。

(5)管理局必须毫不延迟地向财政部送交依照本条规定所发布的任何声明的副本。

(6)管理局必须以其认为最便于公众了解的方式公布依照本条规定发布的声明。

(7)管理局对特定违反要求的行为行使或决定是否行使第206条规定的权力时，必须考虑依照本条规定公布的在该违反要求的行为发生时有效的任何声明。

(8)管理局可以为向他人提供声明副本收取合理费用。

注释：

修改等(不涉及条文内容)

C244　第210条第(7)款于2001年12月1日依照制定法文件S.I.2001/3592第1条第(2)款、第110条第(6)款[与第23条第(2)款]排除。

第211条　政策声明：程序

(1)管理局在依照第210条规定发布声明前必须以其认为最便于公众了解的方式公布拟发布声明的草案。

(2)草案必须附有关于可在规定时间就该提案向管理局作出陈述的通知。

(3)管理局在发布拟发布的声明前必须考虑依照第(2)款规定作出的任何陈述。

---

1 依照《2010年金融服务法》附录2第一部分第20条修订。——译者注

(4) If the Authority issues the proposed statement it must publish an account, in general terms, of—

(a) the representations made to it in accordance with subsection (2); and

(b) its response to them.

(5) If the statement differs from the draft published under subsection (1) in a way which is, in the opinion of the Authority, significant, the Authority must (in addition to complying with subsection (4)) publish details of the difference.

(6) The Authority may charge a reasonable fee for providing a person with a copy of a draft published under subsection (1).

(7) This section also applies to a proposal to alter or replace a statement.

(4)如管理局发布拟发布的声明,则必须公布概括说明下列事项的报告:

(a)依照第(2)款规定向其作出的陈述;以及
(b)管理局的答复。

(5)如管理局认为该声明与依照第(1)款公布的草案有重大差异,则[除遵守第(4)款规定外]必须公布差异的详细情况。

(6)管理局可以就向他人提供依照第(1)款公布的草案副本收取合理费用。

(7)本条也适用于修改或更换声明的计划。

PART XV THE FINANCIAL SERVICES COMPENSATION SCHEME

Annotations:

Modifications etc. (not altering text)

C245 Pt. XV(ss. 212–224) excluded (27.4.2002) by The Financial Services and Markets Act 2000 (Regulated Activities) Order 2001 (S.I. 2001/544), art. 9J (as inserted by The Financial Services and Markets Act 2000 (Regulated Activities) (Amendment) Order 2002 (S.I. 2002/682), arts. 1(2), 4)

Pt. XV (ss. 212–224) modified (2.7.2002) by The Financial Services and Markets Act 2000 (Consequential Amendments and Transitional Provisions) (Credit Unions) Order 2002 (S.I. 2002/1501), art. 5

The scheme manager

212 The scheme manager.

(1) The Authority must establish a body corporate ("the scheme manager") to exercise the functions conferred on the scheme manager by or under this Part.

(2) The Authority must take such steps as are necessary to ensure that the scheme manager is, at all times, capable of exercising those functions.

(3) The constitution of the scheme manager must provide for it to have—

(a) a chairman; and

(b) a board (which must include the chairman) whose members are the scheme manager's directors.

(4) The chairman and other members of the board must be persons appointed, and liable to removal from office, by the Authority (acting, in the case of the chairman, with the approval of the Treasury).

第十五部分[1] 金融服务补偿计划

注释：

修改等(不涉及条文内容)

C245 第十五部分(第212条至第224条)于2002年4月27日依照《2000年金融服务与市场法》(受监管活动)2001号令(制定法文件S.I.2001/544)第9J条[依照《2000年金融服务与市场法》(受监管活动)(修正案)2002号令(制定法文件S.I.2002/682)第1条第(2)款、第4条插入]排除；

第十五部分(第212条至第224条)依照于2002年7月2日《2000年金融服务与市场法》(相应修正案条例及过渡性规定)(信用合作社)2002号令(制定法文件S.I.2002/1501)第5条修订。

计划管理人

第212条 计划管理人

(1)管理局必须设立法人(以下简称计划管理人)，履行本部分规定授予或依照本部分规定授予计划管理人的职能。

(2)管理局必须采取必要的措施，以确保计划管理人在任何时间均能行使上述职能。[2]

(3)计划管理人的组织制度必须规定其设有

(a)主席一人；以及

(b)一个董事会(必须包括主席在内)，其成员为该计划管理人董事。

(4)主席和董事会其他成员必须由管理局任免(任免主席时须经财政部批准)。

1 本部分依照《2010年金融服务法》第17条修订。——译者注

2 本款依照《2010年金融服务法》附录2第一部分第21条修订。——译者注

(5) But the terms of their appointment (and in particular those governing removal from office) must be such as to secure their independence from the Authority in the operation of the compensation scheme.

(6) The scheme manager is not to be regarded as exercising functions on behalf of the Crown.

(7) The scheme manager's board members, officers and staff are not to be regarded as Crown servants.

The scheme

213 The compensation scheme.

(1) The Authority must by rules establish a scheme for compensating persons in cases where relevant persons are unable, or are likely to be unable, to satisfy claims against them.

(2) The rules are to be known as the Financial Services Compensation Scheme (but are referred to in this Act as "the compensation scheme").

(3) The compensation scheme must, in particular, provide for thescheme manager—

(a) to assess and pay compensation, in accordance with the scheme, to claimants in respect of claims made in connection with regulated activities carried on (whether or not with permission) by relevant persons; and

(b) to have power to impose levies on authorised persons, or any class ofauthorized person, for the purpose of meeting its expenses (including in particular expenses incurred, or expected to be incurred, in paying compensation, borrowing or insuring risks).

(4) The compensation scheme may provide for the scheme manager to have power to impose levies on authorised persons, or any class of authorised person, for the purpose of recovering the cost (whenever incurred) of establishing the scheme.

(5) In making any provision of the scheme by virtue of subsection (3)(b), the Authority must take account of the desirability of ensuring that the amount of the levies imposed on a particular class of authorised person reflects, so far as practicable, the amount of the claims made, or likely to be made, in respect of that class of person.

(6) An amount payable to the scheme manager as a result of any provision of the scheme made by virtue of subsection (3)(b) or (4) may be recovered as a debt due to the scheme manager.

(7) Sections 214 to 217 make further provision about the scheme but are not to be taken as limiting the power conferred on the Authority by subsection (1).

(8) In those sections"specified" means specified in the scheme.

(9) In this Part (except in sections 219, 220 or 224) "relevant person" means a person who was—

(a) an authorised person at the time the act or omission giving rise to the claim against

(5)但其聘用条款(特别是规定免职的条款)必须能够确保其运作补偿计划时独立于管理局。

(6)不得将计划管理人视为代表王国政府履行职能。

(7)不得将计划管理人的董事会成员、高级职员和工作人员视为王国政府雇员。

计　划

第213条　补偿计划

(1)管理局必须订立规则,建立补偿计划,在相关人无法或可能无法满足针对其提出的索赔要求时向索赔人提供补偿。

(2)该规则称为金融服务补偿计划(在本法中称"补偿计划")。

(3)补偿计划必须特别规定计划管理人

(a)就与相关人实施的受监管活动(无论是否取得许可)相关的索赔依照计划评估并向索赔人支付补偿;

(b)有权向获授权人或任何一类获授权人征收费用,以满足其开支(特别包括支付补偿、借贷或承保风险产生或可能产生的开支)。

(4)补偿计划可以规定计划管理人有权向被许可人或任何一类被许可人征收费用,以收回设立计划的成本(无论何时产生)。

(5)管理局在依照第(3)款第(b)项作出任何计划规定时,必须考虑到有必要确保对特定类别的获授权人征收的费用金额反映出与该类获授权人相关的索赔金额。

(6)因依照第(3)款第(b)项或第(4)款作出的计划规定而向计划管理人支付的金额可作为计划管理人的应收债务获得偿付。

(7)第214条至第217条对计划作出了进一步规定,但不得将其视为限制第(1)款赋予管理局的权力。

(8)上述各条中"规定"系指计划中规定。

(9)本部分中(第219条、第220条或第224条除外)"相关人"系指

(a)导致针对其提出索赔的作为或不作为发生时的获授权人;或

him took place; or

(b) an appointed representative at that time.

(10) But a person who, at that time—

(a) qualified for authorisation under Schedule 3, and

(b) fell within a prescribed category,

is not to be regarded as a relevant person in relation to any activities for which he had permission as a result of any provision of, or made under, that Schedule unless he had elected to participate in the scheme in relation to those activities at that time.

Annotations:

Modifications etc. (not altering text)

C246 S. 213(9) excluded (2.7.2002) by The Financial Services and Markets Act 2000 (Consequential Amendments and Transitional Provisions) (Credit Unions) Order 2002 (S.I. 2002/1501), art. 5(1)

Commencement Information

I60 S. 213 wholly in force at 18.6.2001; s. 213 not in force at Royal Assent see s. 431 (2); s. 213(10) in force for certain purposes at 25.2.2001 by S.I. 2001/516, art. 2(b), Sch. Pt. 2; s. 213 in force in so far as not already in force at 18.6.2001 by S.I. 2001/1820, art. 2, Sch.

Provisions of the scheme

214 General.

(1) The compensation scheme may, in particular, make provision—

(a) as to the circumstances in which a relevant person is to be taken (for the purposes of the scheme) to be unable, or likely to be unable, to satisfy claims made against him;

(b) for the establishment of different funds for meeting different kinds of claim;

(c) for the imposition of different levies in different cases;

(d) limiting the levy payable by a person in respect of a specified period;

(e) for repayment of the whole or part of a levy in specified circumstances;

(f) for a claim to be entertained only if it is made by a specified kind of claimant;

(g) for a claim to be entertained only if it falls within a specified kind of claim;

(h) as to the procedure to be followed in making a claim;

(i) for the making of interim payments before a claim is finally determined;

(j) limiting the amount payable on a claim to a specified maximum amount or a maximum amount calculated in a specified manner;

(k) for payment to be made, in specified circumstances, to a person other than the claimant.

(b)上述作为或不作为发生时的被任命代表。

(10)但有下列情况的人:

(a)依照附录3符合授权条件,且

(b)属于规定类别,

则不得将其视为与因该附录任何规定取得许可的任何活动或依照该附录实施的任何活动相关的相关人,除非该人当时已决定就上述活动参与该计划。

注释:

修改等(不涉及条文内容)

C246 第213条第(9)款于2002年7月2日依照《2000年金融服务与市场法》(相应修正案条例及过渡性规定)(信用合作社)2002号令(制定法文件S.I.2002/1501)第5条第(1)款排除。

实施日期

I60 第213条于2001年6月18日全部生效;第213条在副署时尚未生效,见第431条第(2)款;第213条第(10)款为特定目的于2001年2月25日依照制定法文件S.I.2001/516第2条第(b)项、附录第二部分生效;第213条如于2001年6月18日尚未生效,则依制定法文件S.I.2001/1820第2条、附录生效。

计划规定

第214条 一般规定

(1)补偿计划特别可以规定:

(a)在何种情况下(为该计划之目的)认为相关人无法或可能无法满足针对其提出的索赔要求;

(b)为满足不同类型的索赔要求设立不同的基金;

(c)在不同情况下征收不同的费用;

(d)限定某人在规定期间内缴纳应缴费用;

(e)在规定情况下全部或部分偿还征收的费用;

(f)仅受理规定类别的索赔人提出的索赔;

(g)仅受理规定类别的索赔;

(h)提出索赔要求应遵循的程序;

(i)索赔要求最终确定前临时支付补偿;

(j)将对索赔支付的金额限定在规定的最高金额或以规定方法计算的最高金额;

(k)在规定情况下向索赔人以外的人支付补偿。

(2) Different provision may be made with respect to different kinds of claim.

(3) The scheme may provide for the determination and regulation of matters relating to the scheme by the scheme manager.

(4) The scheme, or particular provisions of the scheme, may be made so as to apply only in relation to—

(a) activities carried on,

(b) claimants,

(c) matters arising, or

(d) events occurring, in specified territories, areas or localities.

(5) The scheme may provide for a person who—

(a) qualifies for authorisation under Schedule 3, and

(b) falls within a prescribed category,

to elect to participate in the scheme in relation to some or all of the activities for which he has permission as a result of any provision of, or made under, that Schedule.

(6) The scheme may provide for the scheme manager to have power—

(a) in specified circumstances,

(b) but only if the scheme manager is satisfied that the claimant is entitled to receive a payment in respect of his claim—

(i) under a scheme which is comparable to the compensation scheme, or

(ii) as the result of a guarantee given by a government or other authority,

to make a full payment of compensation to the claimant and recover the whole or part of the amount of that payment from the other scheme or under that guarantee.

Annotations:

Commencement Information

I61 S. 214 wholly in force at 18.6.2001; s. 214 not in force at Royal Assent see s. 431(2); s. 214(5) in force for certain purposes at 25.2.2001 by S.I. 2001/516, art. 2(b), Sch. Pt. 2; s. 214 in force in so far as not already in force at 18.6.2001 by S.I. 2001/1820, art. 2, Sch.

215 Rights of the scheme in relevant person's insolvency.

(1) The compensation scheme may, in particular, make provision—

(a) as to the effect of a payment of compensation under the scheme in relation to rights or obligations arising out of the claim against a relevant person in respect of which the payment was made;

(b) for conferring on the scheme manager a right of recovery against that person.

(2) Such a right of recovery conferred by the scheme does not, in the event of the relevant person's insolvency, exceed such right (if any) as the claimant would have had in

(2)就不同种类的索赔可作出不同规定。

(3)计划可规定由计划管理人决定并监管计划相关事项。

(4)可使计划或计划特定规定仅在规定领土、地区或地方适用于

(a)开展的活动,

(b)索赔人,

(c)产生的事项,或

(d)发生的事件。

(5)计划可以规定

(a)依照附录3符合授权条件,且

(b)属于规定类别的人,

选择就该人因该附录任何规定取得许可的全部或部分活动,或依照该附录实施的活动,参与计划。

(6)计划可以规定计划管理人

(a)在指定情况下,

(b)但仅在计划管理人确信索赔人

(i)根据与补偿计划同等的一项计划,或

(ii)因政府或其他机关作出的担保,

有权就其索赔获得偿付时,有权向索赔人全额支付补偿并向上述其他计划或担保追偿全部或部分支付款项。

注释:

实施日期

I61　第214条于2001年6月18日全部生效;第214条在副署时尚未生效,见第431条第(2)款;第214条第(5)款为特定目的于2001年2月25日依照制定法文件S.I.2001/516第2条第(b)款、附录第二部分生效;第214条如于2001年6月18日尚未生效,则依照制定法文件S.I.2001/1820第2条、附录生效。

第215条　相关人丧失清偿能力时计划的权利

(1)补偿计划可以特别规定:

(a)依照计划支付的补偿对因与针对相关人提出的与补偿支付相关的索赔要求而产生的权利或义务的效力。

(b)赋予计划管理人向该相关人追偿的权利。

(2)如相关人丧失清偿能力,则计划赋予的上述追偿权不超出索赔人在此等情况下享有的权利(如有)。

that event.

(3) If a person other than the scheme manager presents a petition under section 9 of the 1986 Act or Article 22 of the 1989 Order in relation to a company or partnership which is a relevant person, the scheme manager has the same rights as are conferred on the Authority by section 362.

(4) If a person other than the scheme manager presents a petition for the winding up of a body which is a relevant person, the scheme manager has the same rights as are conferred on the Authority by section 371.

(5) If a person other than the scheme manager presents a bankruptcy petition to the court in relation to an individual who, or an entity which, is a relevant person, the scheme manager has the same rights as are conferred on the Authority by section 374.

(6) Insolvency rules may be made for the purpose of integrating any procedure for which provision is made as a result of subsection (1) into the general procedure on the administration of a company or partnership or on a winding-up, bankruptcy or sequestration.

(7) "Bankruptcy petition" means a petition to the court

(a) under section 264 of the 1986 Act or Article 238 of the 1989 Order for a bankruptcy order to be made against an individual;

(b) under section 5 of the 1985 Act for the sequestration of the estate of an individual; or

(c) under section 6 of the 1985 Act for the sequestration of the estate belonging to or held for or jointly by the members of an entity mentioned in subsection (1) of that section.

(8) "Insolvency rules" are

(a) for England and Wales, rules made under sections 411 and 412 of the 1986 Act;

(b) for Scotland, rules made by order by the Treasury, after consultation with the Scottish Ministers, for the purposes of this section; and

(c) for Northern Ireland, rules made under Article 359 of the 1989 Order and section 55 of the [M31]Judicature (Northern Ireland) Act 1978.

(9) "The 1985 Act", "the 1986 Act", "the 1989 Order" and "court" have the same meaning as in Part XXIV.

Annotations:

Modifications etc. (not altering text)

C247 S. 215(3)(4)(6) applied (with modifications) (6.4.2001) by S.I. 2001/1090, regs. 1, 6

Commencement Information

I62 S. 215 wholly in force at 18.6.2001; s. 215 not in force at Royal Assent see s. 431(2); s. 215(6)(8)(9) in force at 25.2.2001 by S.I. 2001/516, art. 2(a), Sch. Pt. 1; s. 215 in force in so far as not already in force at 18.6.2001 by S.I. 2001/1820, art. 2, Sch.

(3)如计划管理人以外的人依照1986年法第9条或1989年法令第22条规定就为相关人的公司或合伙提交申请,则计划管理人具有与第362条所赋予权利同等的权利。

(4)如计划管理人以外的人提交相关人停业申请,则计划管理人具有与第371条所赋予权利同等的权利。

(5)如计划管理人以外的人就为相关人的个人或实体向法院提交破产申请,则计划管理人具有与第374条所赋予权利同等的权利。

(6)为将因第(1)款而规定的任何程序纳入公司或合伙破产管理一般程序或停业、破产或扣押一般程序,可制定破产规则。

(7)"破产申请"系指向法院提交的下列申请:

(a)依照1986年法第264条或1989年法令第238条申请针对个人发出破产令;

(b)依照1985年法第5条申请扣押个人财产;或

(c)依照1985年法第6条申请扣押属于该条第(1)款所列实体成员、为该成员持有或与该成员共同持有的财产。

(8)"破产规则"为

(a)在英格兰和威尔士为依照1986年法第411条、第412条制定的规则;

(b)在苏格兰为财政部经与苏格兰部长协商,为本条之目的通过颁布法令制定的规则;

(c)在北爱尔兰为依照1989年法令第359条和[M31]《1978年司法组织法》(北爱尔兰)第55条制定的规则。

(9)"1985年法"、"1986年法"、"1989年法令"和"法院"含义同第二十四部分。

注释:

修改等(不涉及条文内容)

C247 第215条第(3)款、第(4)款、第(6)款(已修订)于2001年4月6日依照制定法文件S.I.2001/1090第1条、第6条适用。

实施日期

I62 第215条于2001年6月18日全部生效;第215条副署时尚未生效,见第431条第(2)款;第215条第(6)款、第(8)款、第(9)款于2001年2月25日依照制定法文件S.I.2001/516第2条第(a)款、附录第一部分生效;第215条如于2001年6月18日尚未生效,则依照制定法文件S.I.2001/1820第2条、附录生效。

Marginal Citations

M31 1978 c. 23.

216 Continuity of long-term insurance policies.

(1) The compensation scheme may, in particular, include provision requiring the scheme manager to make arrangements for securing continuity of insurance for policyholders, or policyholders of a specified class, of relevant long-term insurers.

(2) "Relevant long-term insurers" means relevant persons who—

(a) have permission to effect or carry out contracts of long-term insurance; and

(b) are unable, or likely to be unable, to satisfy claims made against them.

(3) The scheme may provide for the scheme manager to take such measures as appear to him to be appropriate—

(a) for securing or facilitating the transfer of a relevant long-term insurer's business so far as it consists of the carrying out of contracts of long-term insurance, or of any part of that business, to another authorised person;

(b) for securing the issue by another authorised person to the policyholders concerned of policies in substitution for their existing policies.

(4) The scheme may also provide for the scheme manager to make payments to the policyholders concerned—

(a) during any period while he is seeking to make arrangements mentioned in subsection (1);

(b) if it appears to him that it is not reasonably practicable to make such arrangements.

(5) A provision of the scheme made by virtue of section 213(3)(b) may include power to impose levies for the purpose of meeting expenses of the scheme manager incurred in—

(a) taking measures as a result of any provision of the scheme made by virtue of subsection (3);

(b) making payments as a result of any such provision made by virtue of subsection (4).

217 Insurers in financial difficulties.

(1) The compensation scheme may, in particular, include provision for the scheme manager to have power to take measures for safeguarding policyholders, or policyholders of a specified class, of relevant insurers.

(2) "Relevant insurers" means relevant persons who—

(a) have permission to effect or carry out contracts of insurance; and

(b) are in financial difficulties.

(3) The measures may include such measures as the scheme manager considers appropriate for—

(a) securing or facilitating the transfer of a relevant insurer's business so far as it

附注引文

M31 1978年第23章。

第216条 长期保单的连续性

(1)补偿计划特别可以规定要求计划管理人作出安排,保障相关长期业务保险公司保单持有人或该等公司指定类别的保单持有人保险的连续性。

(2)"相关长期业务保险公司"系指有下列情况的相关人:

(a)经许可能够订立或实施长期保险合同;且

(b)无法或可能无法满足针对其提出的索赔要求。

(3)计划可以规定计划管理人为下列目的采取其认为适当的措施:

(a)确保或促使相关长期业务保险公司由实施长期保险合同组成的业务或该业务的任何部分转移到另一获授权人;

(b)确保另一获授权人向相关保单持有人发出替代其现有保单的保单。

(4)计划还可以规定,如符合下列条件,则计划管理人向相关保单持有人支付补偿:

(a)在计划管理人拟依照第(1)款规定作出安排的任何期间内;

(b)计划管理人认为作出上述安排并不合理可行。

(5)依照第213条第(3)款第(b)项作出的计划规定可包括为满足计划管理人在下列活动中产生的开支而征收费用的权力:

(a)因依照第(3)款规定作出的任何计划规定而采取措施;

(b)因依照第(4)款规定作出的任何计划规定而支付补偿。

第217条 发生财务困难的保险公司

(1)补偿计划可以特别规定,计划管理人有权采取措施,保障相关保险公司的保单持有人或该等公司指定类别的保单持有人。

(2)"相关保险公司"系指下列相关人:

(a)经许可能够订立或实施保险合同;且

(b)发生财务困难。

(3)上述措施可包括为下列目的计划管理人认为适当的措施:

(a)确保或促使相关保险公司由实施保险合同组成的业务,或该业务的任何部分,

consists of the carrying out of contracts of insurance, or of any part of that business, to another authorised person;

(b) giving assistance to the relevant insurer to enable it to continue to effect or carry out contracts of insurance.

(4) The scheme may provide—

(a) that if measures of a kind mentioned in subsection (3)(a) are to be taken, they should be on terms appearing to the scheme manager to be appropriate, including terms reducing, or deferring payment of, any of the things to which any of those who are eligible policyholders in relation to the relevant insurer are entitled in their capacity as such;

(b) that if measures of a kind mentioned in subsection (3)(b) are to be taken, they should be conditional on the reduction of, or the deferment of the payment of, the things to which any of those who are eligible policyholders in relation to the relevant insurer are entitled in their capacity as such;

(c) for ensuring that measures of a kind mentioned in subsection (3)(b) do not benefit to any material extent persons who were members of a relevant insurer when it began to be in financial difficulties or who had any responsibility for, or who may have profited from, the circumstances giving rise to its financial difficulties, except in specified circumstances;

(d) for requiring the scheme manager to be satisfied that any measures he proposes to take are likely to cost less than it would cost to pay compensation under the scheme if the relevant insurer became unable, or likely to be unable, to satisfy claims made against him.

(5) The scheme may provide for the Authority to have power—

(a) to give such assistance to the scheme manager as it considers appropriate for assisting the scheme manager to determine what measures are practicable or desirable in the case of a particular relevant insurer;

(b) to impose constraints on the taking of measures by the scheme manager in the case of a particular relevant insurer;

(c) to require the scheme manager to provide it with information about any particular measures which the scheme manager is proposing to take.

(6) The scheme may include provision for the scheme manager to have power—

(a) to make interim payments in respect of eligible policyholders of a relevant insurer;

(b) to indemnify any person making payments to eligible policyholders of a relevant insurer.

(7) A provision of the scheme made by virtue of section 213(3)(b) may include power to impose levies for the purpose of meeting expenses of the scheme manager incurred in—

(a) taking measures as a result of any provision of the scheme made by virtue of subsection (1);

(b) making payments or giving indemnities as a result of any such provision made by

转移到另一获授权人；

(b)向相关保险公司提供协助，使其能够继续订立或实施保险合同。

(4)计划可以规定

(a)如采取第(3)款第(a)项规定的一类措施，则该类措施必须以计划管理人认为适当的条款实施，条款中应当包括减少或延迟向符合条件的相关保险公司保单持有人支付其作为保单持有人有权取得的任何款项；

(b)如采取第(3)款第(b)项规定的一类措施，则该类措施必须以减少或延迟向符合条件的相关保险公司保单持有人支付其作为保单持有人有权取得的任何款项为条件；

(c)确保第(3)款第(b)项规定的一类措施不对相关保险公司开始出现财务困难时为其成员的人或者对导致该财务困难的情况负有责任或可能从中获利的人产生任何实质性收益；

(d)要求计划管理人确信，相对于相关保险公司无法或可能无法满足针对其提出的索赔要求时依照计划支付补偿，计划管理人拟采取的任何措施成本可能低于上述支付补偿的成本。

(5)计划可以规定管理局有权

(a)向计划管理人提供管理局认为适当的协助，以协助计划管理人确定就特定相关保险公司而言何种措施可行并且必要；

(b)对计划管理人就特定相关保险公司采取的措施提出限制；

(c)要求计划管理人向其提供计划管理人拟采取的任何特定措施的相关信息。

(6)计划可规定计划管理人有权

(a)对符合条件的相关保险公司保单持有人临时支付补偿；

(b)偿付任何对符合条件的相关保险公司保单持有人支付款项的人。

(7)依照第213条第(3)款第(b)项作出的计划规定可包括为满足计划管理人在下列活动中产生的开支而征收费用的权力：

(a)因依照第(1)款规定作出的计划规定而采取措施；

(b)因依照第(6)款规定作出的任何计划规定而支付补偿或给予偿付。

virtue of subsection (6).

(8) "Financial difficulties" and "eligible policyholders" have such meanings as may be specified.

Annual report

218 Annual report.

(1) At least once a year, the scheme manager must make a report to the Authority on the discharge of its functions.

(2) The report must—

(a) include a statement setting out the value of each of the funds established by the compensation scheme; and

(b) comply with any requirements specified in rules made by the Authority.

(3) The scheme manager must publish each report in the way it considers appropriate.

Information and documents

219 Scheme manager's power to require information.

(1) The scheme manager may, by notice in writing given to the relevant person in respect of whom a claim is made under the scheme or to a person otherwise involved, require that person—

(a) to provide specified information or information of a specified description; or

(b) to produce specified documents or documents of a specified description.

(2) The information or documents must be provided or produced—

(a) before the end of such reasonable period as may be specified; and

(b) in the case of information, in such manner or form as may be specified.

(3) This section applies only to information and documents the provision or production of which the scheme manager considers—

(a) to be necessary for the fair determination of the claim; or

(b) to be necessary (or likely to be necessary) for the fair determination of other claims made (or which it expects may be made) in respect of the relevant person concerned.

(4) If a document is produced in response to a requirement imposed under this section, the scheme manager may—

(a) take copies or extracts from the document; or

(b) require the person producing the document to provide an explanation of the document.

(5) If a person who is required under this section to produce a document fails to do so, the scheme manager may require the person to state, to the best of his knowledge and belief, where the document is.

(8)“财务困难”和“符合条件的保单持有人”具有指定含义。

年度报告

第218条　年度报告

(1)计划管理人必须至少每年1次就其职能履行情况向管理局提交报告。

(2)该报告必须

(a)包括一份声明,列出补偿计划设立的每项基金的价值;且

(b)符合管理局制定的规则规定的任何要求。

(3)计划管理人必须以其认为适当的方式公布每份报告。

信息与文件

第219条　计划管理人要求提供信息的权力

(1)计划管理人可以向依照计划受到索赔的相关人或以其他方式涉及之人发出书面通知,要求该人

(a)提供规定的信息或规定类别的信息;或

(b)出示规定的文件或规定类别的文件。

(2)信息或文件必须

(a)在规定的合理期限届满前提供或出示;且

(b)对信息而言以规定的方式或形式提供。

(3)本条仅适用于提供计划管理人认为符合下列条件的信息和文件:

(a)为公平裁决索赔而有必要提供;或

(b)为公平裁决对当事相关人提出(或预计可能提出)的其他索赔而有必要提供(或可能是必要提供)。

(4)如一份文件为应依照本条规定提出的要求而出示,则计划管理人可以

(a)对该文件制作副本或进行摘录;或

(b)要求文件出示人对文件进行解释。

(5)如依照本条规定被要求出示文件的人未能出示文件,则计划管理人可以要求该人就其所知所信说明文件的下落。

(6) If the relevant person is insolvent, no requirement may be imposed under this section on a person to whom section 220 or 224 applies.

(7) If a person claims a lien on a document, its production under this Part does not affect the lien.

(8) "Relevant person" has the same meaning as in section 224.

(9) "Specified" means specified in the notice given under subsection (1).

(10) A person is involved in a claim made under the scheme if he was knowingly involved in the act or omission giving rise to the claim.

Annotations:

Modifications etc. (not altering text)

C248 S. 219 extended (1.12.2001) by S.I. 2001/2967, arts. 1(2), 7(a), 12(4)(a); S.I. 2001/3538, art. 2(1)

220 Scheme manager's power to inspect information held by liquidator etc.

(1) For the purpose of assisting the scheme manager to discharge its functions in relation to a claim made in respect of an insolvent relevant person, a person to whom this section applies must permit a person authorised by the scheme manager to inspect relevant documents.

(2) A person inspecting a document under this section may take copies of, or extracts from, the document.

(3) This section applies to—

(a) the administrative receiver, administrator, liquidator or trustee in bankruptcy of an insolvent relevant person;

(b) the permanent trustee, within the meaning of the[M32] Bankruptcy (Scotland) Act 1985, on the estate of an insolvent relevant person.

(4) This section does not apply to a liquidator, administrator or trustee in bankruptcy who is—

(a) the Official Receiver;

(b) the Official Receiver for Northern Ireland; or

(c) the Accountant in Bankruptcy.

(5) "Relevant person" has the same meaning as in section 224.

Annotations:

Modifications etc. (not altering text)

C249 S. 220 extended (1.12.2001) by S.I. 2001/2967, arts. 1(2), 8, 12(4)(c); S.I. 2001/3538, art. 2(1)

(6)如相关人丧失清偿能力,则不得依照本条规定对第220条或第224条适用的人提出任何要求。

(7)如某人对文件主张留置权,则依照本部分规定出示该文件不影响该留置权。

(8)"相关人"含义同第224条。

(9)"规定"系指在依照第(1)款规定发出的通知中规定。

(10)如某人在知情的情况下参与作为或不作为,且该作为或不作为引起依照补偿计划提起的索赔,则该人即为依照补偿计划提起的索赔涉及之人。

注释:

修改等(不涉及条文内容)

C248　第219条于2001年12月1日依照制定法文件S.I.2001/2967第1条第(2)款、第7条第(a)款、第12条第(4)款第(a)项;制定法文件S.I.2001/3538第2条第(1)款扩大适用范围。

第220条　计划管理人检查清算人等所掌握信息的权力

(1)针对丧失清偿能力的相关人提出索赔要求的,为协助计划管理人履行其相关职能,本条规定适用之人必须允许计划管理人授权之人检查相关文件。

(2)依照本条规定检查文件之人可对该文件制作副本或进行摘录。

(3)本条规定适用于

(a)丧失清偿能力的相关人破产中的行政接管人、破产管理人、清算人或托管人;

(b)[M32]《1985年破产法》(苏格兰)规定含义的丧失清偿能力相关人财产永久托管人。

(4)本条规定不适用于下列清算人、破产管理人或托管人:

(a)破产管理署署长;

(b)北爱尔兰破产管理署署长;或

(c)破产核算员。

(5)"相关人"含义同第224条

注释:

修改等(不涉及条文内容)

C249　第202条于2001年12月1日依照制定法文件S.I.2001/2967第1条第(2)款、第8条、第12条第(4)款第(c)项;制定法文件S.I.2001/3538第2条第(1)款扩大适用范围。

Marginal Citations

M32 1985 c. 66.

221 Powers of court where information required.

(1) If a person ("the defaulter")—

(a) fails to comply with a requirement imposed under section 219, or

(b) fails to permit documents to be inspected under section 220, the scheme manager may certify that fact in writing to the court and the court may enquire into the case.

(2) If the court is satisfied that the defaulter failed without reasonable excuse to comply with the requirement (or to permit the documents to be inspected), it may deal with the defaulter (and, in the case of a body corporate, any director or officer) as if he were in contempt .[F3; and "officer", in relation to a limited liability partnership, means a member of the limited liability partnership.].

(3)"Court" means—

(a) the High Court;

(b) in Scotland, the Court of Session.

Annotations:

Amendments (Textual)

F3 Words in s. 221(2) inserted (6.4.2001) by S.I. 2001/1090, regs. 1, 9, Sch. 5 para. 21

Modifications etc. (not altering text)

C250 S. 221 extended (1.12.2001) by S.I. 2001/2967, arts. 1(2), 7(b), 8, 12(4)(b)(c); S.I. 2001/3538, art. 2(1)

Miscellaneous

222 Statutory immunity.

(1) Neither the scheme manager nor any person who is, or isacting as, its board member, officer or member of staff is to be liable in damages for anything done or omitted in the discharge, or purported discharge, of the scheme manager's functions.

(2) Subsection (1) does not apply—

(a) if the act or omission is shown to have been in bad faith; or

(b) so as to prevent an award of damages made in respect of an act or omission on the ground that the act or omission was unlawful as a result of section 6(1) of the M33 Human

附注引文

M32 1985年第66章。

第221条 要求提供信息时法院的权力

(1)如当事人(以下简称违反人)

(a)未遵守依照第219条规定提出的要求;或

(b)未依照第220条规定允许检查文件,则计划管理人可向法院书面提出该事项,法庭可调查该案。

(2)如法院确信该违反人无合理理由而未遵守要求(或允许检查文件),则可以将违反人(如违反人为法人,还包括任何董事或高级职员)按藐视法庭处理[F3;"高级职员",对于有限责任合伙,系指该有限责任合伙的合伙人]。

(3)"法院"系指

(a)高等法院;

(b)(苏格兰)高等民事法院。

注释:

修正(文本)

F3 第221条第(2)款的文字于2001年4月6日依照制定法文件S.I.2001/1090第1条、第9条,附录5第21条插入。

修改等(不涉及条文内容)

C250 第221条于2001年12月1日依照制定法文件S.I.2001/2967第1条第(2)款、第7条第(b)款、第8条、第12条第(4)款第(b)项和第(c)项;制定法文件S.I.2001/3538第2条第(1)款扩大适用范围。

其他条款

第222条 法定豁免权

(1)计划管理人或其董事会成员、高级职员或工作人员,或者代理上述职务的任何人,对行使或意图行使计划管理人职能时的任何作为或不作为不承担损害赔偿责任。

(2)如有下列情况,则第(1)款不适用:

(a)有证据证明该作为或不作为有恶意;或

(b)用于防止因[M33]《1998年人权法》第6条第(1)款规定的不合法作为或不作为而作出损害赔偿判决。

Rights Act 1998.

Annotations:

Marginal Citations

M33 1998 c. 42.

223 Management expenses.

(1) The amount which the scheme manager may recover, from the sums levied under the scheme, as management expenses attributable to a particular period may not exceed such amount as may be fixed by the scheme as the limit applicable to that period.

(2) In calculating the amount of any levy to be imposed by the scheme manager, no amount may be included to reflect management expenses unless the limit mentioned in subsection (1) has been fixed by the scheme.

(3) "Management expenses" means expenses incurred, or expected to be incurred, by the scheme manager in connection with its functions under this Act other than those incurred—

(a) in paying compensation;

(b) as a result of any provision of the scheme made by virtue of section 216 (3) or (4) or 217(1) or (6).

Annotations:

Commencement Information

I63 S. 223 wholly in force at 1.12.2001; s. 223 not in force at Royal Assent see s. 431 (2); s. 223 in force for specified purposes at 18.6.2001 by S.I. 2001/1820, art. 2, Sch.; s. 223 in force in so far as not already in force at 1.12.2001 by S.I. 2001/3538, art. 2(1)

224 Scheme manager's power to inspect documents held by Official Receiver etc.

(1) If, as a result of the insolvency or bankruptcy of a relevant person, any documents have come into the possession of a person to whom this section applies, he must permit any person authorised by the scheme manager to inspect the documents for the purpose of establishing—

(a) the identity of persons to whom the scheme manager may be liable to make a payment in accordance with the compensation scheme; or

(b) the amount of any payment which the scheme manager may be liable to make.

(2) A person inspecting a document under this section may take copies or extracts from

注释：

附注引文

M33　1998年第42章。

第223条　管理开支

（1）计划管理人可以从该计划征收款项中收回的特定期间管理开支，不得超过该计划设定的适用于该期间的限额。

（2）计划管理人计算任何征费金额时，除第（1）款所述计划设定的限额外，不得考虑反映管理开支。

（3）“管理开支”，系指计划管理人就本法规定的职权发生或预计发生的支出，但不包括[1]

（a）支付补偿时发生的开支；

（b）因依照第216条第（3）款或第（4）款或者第217条第（1）款或第（6）款作出的计划规定而发生的开支。

注释：

实施日期

I63　第223条于2001年12月1日全部生效；第223条在副署时尚未生效，见第431条第（2）款；第223条为特定目的于2001年6月18日依照制定法文件S.I.2001/1820第2条、附录生效；第223条如于2001年12月1日尚未生效，则依照制定法文件S.I.2001/3538第2条第（1）款生效。

第224条　计划管理人检查破产管理署署长等所掌握文件的权力

（1）如因相关人丧失清偿能力或破产，任何文件为本条规定适用之人所掌握，则该人必须允许计划管理人授权之人为下列目的检查相关文件：

（a）确定计划管理人可能有义务依照补偿计划支付补偿的受补偿人身份；或

（b）确定计划管理人可能有义务支付的任何补偿金额。

（2）依照本条规定检查文件之人可对该文件制作副本或进行摘录。

1 本款依照《2010年金融服务法》附录2第一部分第24条修订。——译者注

the document.

(3) In this section "relevant person" means a person who was—

(a) an authorised person at the time the act or omission which may give rise to the liability mentioned in subsection (1)(a) took place; or

(b) an appointed representative at that time.

(4) But a person who, at that time—

(a) qualified for authorisation under Schedule 3, and

(b) fell within a prescribed category,

is not to be regarded as a relevant person for the purposes of this section in relation to any activities for which he had permission as a result of any provision of, or made under, that Schedule unless he had elected to participate in the scheme in relation to those activities at that time.

(5) This section applies to—

(a) the Official Receiver;

(b) the Official Receiver for Northern Ireland; and

(c) the Accountant in Bankruptcy.

Annotations:

Modifications etc. (not altering text)

C251 S. 224 extended (1.12.2001) by S.I. 2001/2967, arts. 1(2), 8, 12(4)(c); S.I. 2001/3538, art. 2(1)

C252 S. 224(3) excluded (2.7.2002) by The Financial Services and Markets Act 2000 (Consequential Amendments and Transitional Provisions) (Credit Unions) Order 2002 (S.I. 2002/1501), art. 5(1)

Commencement Information

I64 S. 224 wholly in force at 1.12.2001; s. 224 not in force at Royal Assent see s. 431 (2); s. 224(4) in force for certain purposes at 25.2.2001 by S.I. 2001/516, art. 2(b), Sch. Pt. 2; s. 224 in force in so far as not already in force at 1.12.2001 by S.I. 2001/3538, art. 2(1)

(3)本条中"相关人"系指

(a)可能引起第(1)款第(a)项所列义务的作为或不作为发生时的获授权人;或

(b)上述作为或不作为发生时的被任命代表。

(4)但有下列情况的:

(a)依照附录3符合授权条件;且

(b)属于规定类别,

就本法而言不得视为与因该附录任何规定取得许可的任何活动或依照该附录实施的任何活动相关的相关人,除非该人当时已决定就上述活动参与该计划。

(5)本条规定适用于

(a)破产管理署署长;

(b)北爱尔兰破产管理署署长;或

(c)破产核算员。

注释:

修改等(不涉及条文内容)

C251 第224条于2001年12月1日依照制定法文件S.I.2001/2967第1条第(2)款、第8条、第12条第(4)款第(c)项、制定法文件S.I.2001/3538第2条第(1)款扩大适用范围。

C252 第224条第(3)款于2002年7月2日依照《2000年金融服务与市场法》(相应修正案条例及过渡性规定)(信用合作社)2002号令(制定法文件S.I.2002/1501)第5条第(1)款排除。

实施日期

I64 第224条于2001年12月1日全部生效;第224条在副署时尚未生效,见第431条第(2)款;第224条第(4)款为特定目的于2001年2月25日依照制定法文件S.I.2001/516第2条第(b)款、附录第二部分生效;第224条如于2001年12月1日尚未生效,则依照制定法文件S.I.2001/3538第2条第(1)款生效。

PART XVI THE OMBUDSMAN SCHEME

The scheme

225 The scheme and the scheme operator.

(1) This Part provides for a scheme under which certain disputes may be resolved quickly and with minimum formality by an independent person.

(2) The scheme is to be administered by a body corporate ("the scheme operator").

(3) The scheme is to be operated under a name chosen by the scheme operator but is referred to in this Act as "the ombudsman scheme".

(4) Schedule 17 makes provision in connection with the ombudsman scheme and the scheme operator.

226 Compulsory jurisdiction.

(1) A complaint which relates to an act or omission of a person ("the respondent") in carrying on an activity to which compulsory jurisdiction rules apply is to be dealt with under the ombudsman scheme if the conditions mentioned in subsection (2) are satisfied.

(2) The conditions are that—

(a) the complainant is eligible and wishes to have the complaintdealt with under the scheme;

(b) the respondent was an authorised person at the time of the act or omission to which the complaint relates; and

(c) the act or omission to which the complaint relates occurred at a time when compulsory jurisdiction rules were in force in relation to the activity in question.

(3) "Compulsory jurisdiction rules" means rules—

(a) made by the Authority for the purposes of this section; and

(b) specifying the activities to which they apply.

(4) Only activities which are regulated activities, or which could be made regulated activities by an order under section 22, may be specified.

(5) Activities may be specified by reference to specified categories (however described).

第十六部分　申诉专员计划

计　划

第225条　计划和计划执行人

(1)本部分规定可由独立人通过最简单的手续迅速解决某些争议的计划。

(2)该计划将由一个法人(以下简称计划执行人)执行。

(3)该计划以计划执行人选择的名称运作,但在本法中称为“申诉专员计划”。

(4)附录17就申诉专员计划及计划执行人作出了规定。

第226条　强制管辖权

(1)如与某人(以下简称被申诉人)在开展一项活动中的作为或不作为相关的申诉适用强制管辖权规则,且符合第(2)款所列条件,则该申诉依照申诉专员计划处理。

(2)前款所述条件为

(a)申诉人符合申诉依照该计划处理的条件并希望申诉依照该计划处理;

(b)被申诉人在申诉相关的作为或不作为发生时为获授权人;且

(c)该申诉相关的作为或不作为发生时强制管辖权规则对相关活动有效。

(3)“强制管辖权规则”系指

(a)管理局为本条规定的实施制定的;且

(b)规定上述规则适用于哪些活动的规则。

(4)只可规定受监管活动或通过依照第22条规定发布的命令成为受监管活动的活动。

(5)可以参照规定类别规定活动(不论如何描述)。

(6) A complainant is eligible, in relation to the compulsory jurisdiction of the ombudsman scheme, if he falls within a class of person specified in the rules as eligible.

(7) The rules—

(a) may include provision for persons other than individuals to be eligible; but

(b) may not provide for authorised persons to be eligible except in specified circumstances or in relation to complaints of a specified kind.

(8) The jurisdiction of the scheme which results from this section is referred to in this Act as the "compulsory jurisdiction".

Annotations:

Modifications etc. (not altering text)

C253 S. 226 extended (19.7.2001 for specified purposes otherwise 1.12.2001) by S.I. 2001/2326, arts. 1(1), 3(1); S.I. 2001/3538, art. 2(1)

C254 S. 226(2) excluded (19.7.2001 for specified purposes otherwise 1.12.2001) by S. I. 2001/2326, arts. 1(1), 2(4); S.I. 2001/3538, art. 2(1)

Commencement Information

I65 S. 226 wholly in force at 1.12.2001; s. 226 not in force at Royal Assent see s. 431 (2); s. 226 in force for specified purposes at 18.6.2001 by S.I. 2001/1820, art. 2, Sch.; s. 226 in force in so far as not already in force at 1.12.2001 by S.I. 2001/3538, art. 2(1)

227 Voluntary jurisdiction.

(1) A complaint which relates to an act or omission of a person ("the respondent") in carrying on an activity to which voluntary jurisdiction rules apply is to be dealt with under the ombudsman scheme if the conditions mentioned in subsection (2) are satisfied.

(2) The conditions are that—

(a) the complainant is eligible and wishes to have the complaint dealt with under the scheme;

(b) at the time of the act or omission to which the complaint relates, the respondent was participating in the scheme;

(c) at the time when the complaint is referred under the scheme, the respondent has not withdrawn from the scheme in accordance with its provisions;

(d) the act or omission to which the complaint relates occurred at a time when voluntary jurisdiction rules were in force in relation to the activity in question; and

(e) the complaint cannot be dealt with under the compulsory jurisdiction.

(3) "Voluntary jurisdiction rules" means rules—

(6)关于申诉专员计划强制管辖权,如申诉人属于规则中指定符合条件的类别,则为符合强制管辖权条件。

(7)规则

(a)可以规定个人以外的其他人符合条件,但

(b)除规定情况或与规定类别的申诉相关外,不得规定获授权人符合条件。

(8)申诉专员计划因本条规定而具有的管辖权在本法中称为"强制管辖权"。

注释:

修改等(不涉及条文内容)

C253　第226条为特定目的于2001年7月19日,否则于2001年12月1日依照制定法文件S.I.2001/2326第1条第(1)款、第3条第(1)款;制定法文件S.I.2001/3538第2条第(1)款扩大适用范围。

C254　第226条第(2)款为特定目的于2001年7月19日,否则于2001年12月1日依照制定法文件S.I.2001/2326第1条第(1)款、第2条第(4)款;制定法文件S.I.2001/3538第2条第(1)款排除。

实施日期

I65　第226条于2001年12月1日全部生效;第226条在副署时尚未生效,见第431条第(2)款;第226条为特定目的于2001年6月18日依照制定法文件S.I.2001/1820第2条、附录生效;第226条如于2001年12月1日尚未生效,则依照制定法文件S.I.2001/3538第2条第(1)款生效。

第227条　自愿管辖权

(1)如与某人(以下简称被申诉人)在开展一项活动中的作为或不作为相关的申诉适用自愿管辖权规则,且符合第(2)款所列条件,则该申诉依照申诉专员计划处理。

(2)前款所述条件为

(a)申诉人符合申诉依照该计划处理的条件并希望申诉依照该计划处理;

(b)被申诉人在申诉相关的作为或不作为发生时正在参与该计划;

(c)依照该计划提起申诉时,被申诉人未依照计划规定撤出计划;

(d)该申诉相关的作为或不作为发生时自愿管辖权规则对相关活动有效;

(e)该申诉不能在强制管辖权下处理。

(3)"自愿管辖权规则"系指

(a) made by the scheme operator for the purposes of this section; and

(b) specifying the activities to which they apply.

(4) The only activities which may be specified in the rules are activities which are, or could be, specified in compulsory jurisdiction rules.

(5) Activities may be specified by reference to specified categories (however described).

(6) The rules require the Authority's approval.

(7) A complainant is eligible, in relation to the voluntary jurisdiction of the ombudsman scheme, if he falls within a class of person specified in the rules as eligible.

(8) The rules may include provision for persons other than individuals to be eligible.

(9) A person qualifies for participation in the ombudsman scheme if he falls within a class of person specified in the rules in relation to the activity in question.

(10) Provision may be made in the rules for persons other than authorised persons to participate in the ombudsman scheme.

(11) The rules may make different provision in relation to complaints arising from different activities.

(12) The jurisdiction of the scheme which results from this section is referred to in this Act as the "voluntary jurisdiction".

(13) In such circumstances as may be specified in voluntary jurisdiction rules, a complaint—

(a) which relates to an act or omission occurring at a time before the rules came into force, and

(b) which could have been dealt with under a scheme which has to any extent been replaced by the voluntary jurisdiction,

is to be dealt with under the ombudsman scheme even though paragraph (b) or (d) of subsection (2) would otherwise prevent that.

(14) In such circumstances as may be specified in voluntary jurisdiction rules, a complaint is to be dealt with under the ombudsman scheme even though—

(a) paragraph (b) or (d) of subsection (2) would otherwise prevent that, and

(b) the complaint is not brought within the scheme as a result of subsection (13),

but only if the respondent has agreed that complaints of that kind were to be dealt with under the scheme.

(a)为本条之目的由计划执行人制定的规则;以及

(b)规定上述规则所适用活动的规则。

(4)规则中仅可规定强制管辖权规则中规定或可能规定的活动。

(5)可以参照规定类别规定活动(不论如何描述)。

(6)规则须经管理局批准。

(7)关于申诉专员计划自愿管辖权,如申诉人属于规则中规定符合条件的类别,则为符合自愿管辖权条件。

(8)规则可以规定个人以外的其他人符合条件。

(9)任何人如就相关活动属于规则规定类别,则为有资格参与申诉专员计划。

(10)规则可以规定获授权人以外的其他人参与申诉专员计划。

(11)规则可以对不同活动引起的申诉作出不同规定。

(12)申诉专员计划因本条规定而具有的管辖权在本法中称为"自愿管辖权"。

(13)在自愿管辖权规则规定的情况下,如申诉符合下列条件:

(a)涉及规则生效前发生的作为或不作为;以及

(b)可以依照在任何程度上为自愿管辖权所取代的计划处理,

则该申诉依照申诉专员计划处理,即使第(2)款第(b)项或第(d)项有相反规定。

(14)在自愿管辖权规则指定的情况下,即使有下列情况,申诉也依照申诉专员计划处理:

(a)第(2)款第(b)项或第(d)项有相反规定,且

(b)申诉并非因第(13)款规定而进入申诉专员计划,

但须经被申诉人同意该类申诉依照申诉专员计划处理。

Annotations:

Commencement Information

I66 S. 227 wholly in force at 1.12.2001; s. 227 not in force at Royal Assent see s. 431 (2); s. 227 in force for specified purposes at 18.6.2001 by S.I. 2001/1820, art. 2, Sch.; s. 227 in force in so far as not already in force at 1.12.2001 by S.I. 2001/3538, art. 2(1)

Determination of complaints

228 Determination under the compulsory jurisdiction.

(1) This section applies only in relation to the compulsory jurisdiction.

(2) A complaint is to be determined by reference to what is, in the opinion of the ombudsman, fair and reasonable in all the circumstances of the case.

(3) When the ombudsman has determined a complaint he must give a written statement of his determination to the respondent and to the complainant.

(4) The statement must—

(a) give the ombudsman's reasons for his determination;

(b) be signed by him; and

(c) require the complainant to notify him in writing, before a date specified in the statement, whether he accepts or rejects the determination.

(5) If the complainant notifies the ombudsman that he accepts the determination, it is binding on the respondent and the complainant and final.

(6) If, by the specified date, the complainant has not notified the ombudsman of his acceptance or rejection of the determination he is to be treated as having rejected it.

(7) The ombudsman must notify the respondent of the outcome.

(8) A copy of the determination on which appears a certificate signed by an ombudsman is evidence (or in Scotland sufficient evidence) that the determination was made under the scheme.

(9) Such a certificate purporting to be signed by an ombudsman is to be taken to have been duly signed unless the contrary is shown.

Annotations:

Modifications etc. (not altering text)

C255 S. 228 applied (1.12.2001) by S.I. 2001/2326, arts. 1(1)(b), 6(11), 7(1); S.I. 2001/3538, art. 2(1)

C256 S. 228(2) excluded (1.12.2001) by S.I. 2001/2326, arts. 1(1)(b), 6(1)(a); S.I. 2001/3538, art. 2(1)

注释:

实施日期

I66 第227条于2001年12月1日全部生效;第227条在副署时尚未生效,见第431条第(2)款;第227条为特定目的于2001年6月18日依照制定法文件S.I.2001/1820第2条、附录生效;第227条如于2001年12月1日尚未生效,则依照制定法文件S.I.2001/3538第2条第(1)款生效。

申 诉 裁 决

第228条 强制管辖权下的裁决

(1)本条规定仅在与强制管辖权相关时适用。

(2)申诉专员参考其认为在案件所有情况下公平合理的意见对申诉作出裁决。

(3)申诉专员对申诉作出裁决后,必须向被申诉人及申诉人发出书面裁决声明。

(4)裁决声明必须

(a)说明申诉专员裁决的理由;

(b)经申诉专员签字;且

(c)要求申诉人在声明中规定的日期前告知申诉专员是否接受该裁决。

(5)如申诉人通知申诉专员接受该裁决,则该裁决对被申诉人和申诉人具有约束力,且为终局裁决。

(6)如申诉人在规定日期前未通知申诉专员是否接受该裁决,则视为拒绝接受该裁决。

(7)申诉专员必须将有关结果通知被申诉人。

(8)附有经申诉专员签署的证书的裁决副本是该裁决依照申诉专员计划作出的证据(在苏格兰称为充分证据)。

(9)拟由申诉专员签署的证书视为已由申诉专员正式签署,除非证明情况相反。

注释:

修改等(不涉及条文内容)

C255 第228条于2001年12月1日依照制定法文件S.I.2001/2326第1条第(1)款第(b)项、第6条第(11)款、第(7)条第(1)款;制定法文件S.I.2001/3538第2条第(1)款适用。

C256 第228条于2001年12月1日依照制定法文件S.I.2001/2326第1条第(1)款第(b)项、第6条第(1)款第(a)项;制定法文件S.I.2001/3538第2条第(1)款排除;

C257 S. 228(4)(c)(5)-(7) excluded (1.12.2001) by S.I. 2001/2326, arts. 1(1)(b), 6(7)(8)(9); S.I. 2001/3538, art. 2(1)

229 Awards.

(1) This section applies only in relation to the compulsory jurisdiction.

(2) If a complaint which has been dealt with under the scheme is determined in favour of the complainant, the determination may include—

(a) an award against the respondent of such amount as the ombudsman considers fair compensation for loss or damage (of a kind falling within subsection (3)) suffered by the complainant ("a money award");

(b) a direction that the respondent take such steps in relation to the complainant as the ombudsman considers just and appropriate (whether or not a court could order those steps to be taken).

(3) A money award may compensate for—

(a) financial loss; or

(b) any other loss, or any damage, of a specified kind.

(4) The Authority may specify the maximum amount which may be regarded as fair compensation for a particular kind of loss or damage specified under subsection (3)(b).

(5) A money award may not exceed the monetary limit; but the ombudsman may, if he considers that fair compensation requires payment of a larger amount, recommend that the respondent pay the complainant the balance.

(6) The monetary limit is such amount as may be specified.

(7) Different amounts may be specified in relation to different kinds of complaint.

(8) A money award—

(a) may provide for the amount payable under the award to bear interest at a rate and as from a date specified in the award; and

(b) is enforceable by the complainant in accordance with Part Ⅲ of Schedule 17.

(9) Compliance with a direction under subsection (2)(b)—

(a) is enforceable by an injunction; or

(b) in Scotland, is enforceable by an order under section 45 of the[M34] Court of Session Act 1988.

(10) Only the complainant may bring proceedings for an injunction or proceedings for an order.

(11) "Specified" means specified in compulsory jurisdiction rules.

C257　第228条第(4)款第(c)项、第(5)款、第(6)款、第(7)款于2001年12月1日依照制定法文件S.I.2001/2326第1条第(1)款第(b)项,第6条第(7)款、第(8)款、第(9)款,制定法文件S.I.2001/3538第2条第(1)款排除。

第229条　判令支付

(1)本条规定只在与强制管辖权相关时适用。

(2)如依照申诉专员计划对申诉作出了有利于申诉人的裁决,则该裁决可包括:

(a)判令被申诉人支付申诉专员认为能够公平补偿申诉人损失或损害[第(3)款所列种类]的金额(以下简称判付赔偿金);

(b)指示被申请人对申诉人采取申诉专员认为公正适当的措施(不论法院是否可命令采取该措施)。

(3)判付赔偿金可以补偿

(a)经济损失;或

(b)规定种类的任何其他损失或损害。

(4)管理局可以就第(3)款第(b)项规定的特定种类损失或损害规定可视为公平补偿的最高金额。

(5)赔偿金不得超过金额限制;但申诉专员如认为公平补偿要求的金额更大,则可建议被申诉人向申诉人支付超出限制的差额。

(6)金额限制为规定金额。

(7)对不同种类的申诉可以规定不同金额。

(8)赔偿金的判付

(a)可以规定判付款项自判付裁决规定日期起按裁决规定的利率计算利息;且

(b)可以由申诉人依照附录17第三部分规定强制执行。

(9)依照第(2)款第(b)项作出的指示

(a)可以通过强制令强制执行;

(b)在苏格兰可以通过依照[M34]《1988年高等民事法院法》第45条规定发布的命令强制执行。

(10)只有申诉人才可以提起发出强制令或命令的法律程序。

(11)“规定”系指在强制管辖权规则中规定。

Annotations:

Modifications etc. (not altering text)

C258 S. 229 applied(1.12.2001) by S.I. 2001/2326, arts. 1(1)(b), 7(1); S.I. 2001/3538, art. 2(1)

S. 229 restricted(1.12.2001) by S.I. 2001/2326, arts. 1(1)(b), 6(1)(b)(4)(5); S.I. 2001/3538, art. 2(1)

C259 S. 229(8)(b) applied (1.12.2001) by S.I. 2001/2326, arts. 1(1)(b), 6(4); S.I. 2001/3538, art. 2(1)

C260 S. 229(9)(10) applied (1.12.2001) by S.I. 2001/2326, arts. 1(1)(b), 6(5); S.I. 2001/3538, art. 2(1)

Commencement Information

I67 S. 229 wholly in force at 1.12.2001; s. 229 not in force at Royal Assent see s. 431 (2); s. 229 in force for specified purposes at 18.6.2001 by S.I. 2001/1820, art. 2, Sch.; s. 229 in force in so far as not already in force at 1.12.2001 by S.I. 2001/3538, art. 2(1)

Marginal Citations

M34 1988 c. 36.

230 Costs.

(1) The scheme operator may by rules ("costs rules") provide for an ombudsman to have power, on determining a complaint under the compulsory jurisdiction, to award costs in accordance with the provisions of the rules.

(2) Costs rules require the approval of the Authority.

(3) Costs rules may not provide for the making of an award against the complainant in respect of the respondent's costs.

(4) But they may provide for the making of an award against thecomplainant in favour of the scheme operator, for the purpose of providing a contribution to resources deployed in dealing with the complaint, if in the opinion of the ombudsman—

(a) the complainant's conduct was improper or unreasonable; or

(b) the complainant was responsible for an unreasonable delay.

(5) Costs rules may authorise an ombudsman making an award in accordance with the rules to order that the amount payable under the award bears interest at a rate and as from a date specified in the order.

(6) An amount due under an award made in favour of the scheme operator is recoverable as a debt due to the scheme operator.

(7) Any other award made against the respondent is to be treated as a money award for

注释：

修改等(不涉及条文内容)

C258 第229条于2001年12月1日依照制定法文件S.I.2001/2326第1条第(1)款第(b)项、第7条第(1)款；制定法文件S.I.2001/3538第2条第(1)款适用；

第229条于2001年12月1日受制定法文件S.I.2001/2326第1条第(1)款第(b)项、第6条第(1)款第(b)项、第(4)条、第(5)条；制定法文件S.I.2001/3538第2条第(1)款限制。

C259 第229条第(8)款第(b)项于2001年12月1日依照制定法文件S.I.第1条第(1)款第(b)项、第6条第(4)款；制定法文件S.I.2001/3538第2条第(1)款适用。

C260 第229条第(9)款、第(10)款于2001年12月1日依照制定法文件S.I.第1条第(1)款第(b)项、第6条第(5)款；制定法文件S.I.2001/3538第2条第(1)款适用。

实施日期

I67 第229条于2001年12月1日全部生效；第229条在副署时尚未生效，见第431条第(2)款；第229条为特定目的于2001年6月18日依照制定法文件S.I.2001/1820第2条、附录而生效；第229条如在2001年12月1日尚未生效，则依照制定法文件S.I.2001/3538第2条第(1)款生效。

附注引文

M34 1988年第36章。

第230条 费用

(1)计划执行人可以通过规则(以下简称费用规则)规定申诉专员有权在强制管辖权申诉裁决中依照强制管辖权规则判付费用。

(2)费用规则须经管理局批准。

(3)费用规则不得规定判令申诉人支付被申诉人的费用。

(4)但可以规定，如申诉专员认为有下列情况，则判令申诉人向计划执行人支付费用，以分担为处理申诉而使用的资源：

(a)申诉人行为不当或不合理；或

(b)申诉人对不合理延迟负有责任。

(5)费用规则可以授权申诉专员依照该规则命令判付款项自该命令规定的日期起按命令规定的利率计算利息。

(6)对计划执行人有利的判付令规定的应付金额可作为计划执行人的应收债务追讨。

(7)为附录17第16条之目的，针对被申请人作出的任何其他判付视为判付赔

the purposes of paragraph 16 of Schedule 17.

Annotations:

Modifications etc. (not altering text)
C261 S. 230 applied (19.7.2001 for specified purposes otherwise 1.12.2001) by S.I. 2001/2326, arts. 1(1), 7(1); S.I. 2001/3538, art. 2(1)
S. 230 restricted(19.7.2001 for specified purposes otherwise 1.12.2001) by S.I. 2001/2326, arts. 1(1), 6(1)(c); S.I. 2001/3538, art. 2(1)
C262 S. 230(6)(7) applied (19.7.2001 for specified purposes otherwise 1.12.2001) by S.I. 2001/2326, arts. 1(1), 6(6); S.I. 2001/3538, art. 2(1)

Information

231 Ombudsman's power to require information.

(1) An ombudsman may, by notice in writing given to a party to a complaint, require that party—

(a) to provide specified information or information of a specified description; or

(b) to produce specified documents or documents of a specified description.

(2) The information or documents must be provided or produced—

(a) before the end of such reasonable period as may be specified; and

(b) in the case of information, in such manner or form as may be specified.

(3) This section applies only to information and documents the production of which the ombudsman considers necessary for the determination of the complaint.

(4) If a document is produced in response to a requirement imposed under this section, the ombudsman may—

(a) take copies or extracts from the document; or

(b) require the person producing the document to provide an explanation of the document.

(5) If a person who is required under this section to produce a document fails to do so, the ombudsman may require him to state, to the best of his knowledge and belief, where the document is.

(6) If a person claims a lien on a document, its production under this Part does not affect the lien.

(7) "Specified" means specified in the notice given under subsection (1).

偿金。

注释：

修改等(不涉及条文内容)

C261 第230条为特定目的于2001年7月19日，否则于2001年12月1日依照制定法文件S.I.2001/2326第1条第(1)款、第7条第(1)款；制定法文件S.I.2001/3538第2条第(1)款适用；

第230条为特定目的于2001年7月19日，否则于2001年12月1日依照制定法文件S.I. 2001/2326第1条第(1)款、第6条第(1)款第(c)项；制定法文件S.I.2001/3538第2条第(1)款限制。

C262 第230条第(6)款、第(7)款为特定目的于2001年7月19日，否则于2001年12月1日依照制定法文件 S.I.2001/2326第1条第（1）款、第6条第（6）款；制定法文件 S.I. 2001/3538第2条第(1)款适用。

信　息

第231条　申诉专员要求提供信息的权力

(1)申诉专员可书面通知申诉一方当事人，要求其

(a)提供规定的信息或规定类别的信息；或

(b)出示规定的文件或规定类别的文件。

(2)信息或文件必须

(a)在规定的合理期限届满前提供或出示；且

(b)对信息而言以规定的方式或形式提供。

(3)本条规定仅适用于申诉专员为作出申诉裁决认为有必要提供的信息和文件。

(4)如一份文件为根据依照本条规定提出的要求而出示，则申诉专员可以

(a)对该文件制作副本或进行摘录；或

(b)要求文件出示人对文件进行解释。

(5)如依照本条规定被要求出示文件的人未能出示文件，则申诉专员可要求该人就其所知所信说明文件的下落。

(6)如某人对文件主张留置权，则依照本部分规定出示该文件不影响该留置权。

(7)“指定”，系指在依照第(1)款规定发出的通知中指定。

Annotations:

Modifications etc. (not altering text)

C263 S. 231 applied(1.12.2001) by S.I. 2001/2326, arts. 1(1)(b), 11(5); S.I.2001/3538, art. 2(1)

232 Powers of court where information required.

(1) If a person ("the defaulter") fails to comply with a requirement imposed under section 231, the ombudsman may certify that fact in writing to the court and the court may enquire into the case.

(2) If the court is satisfied that the defaulter failed withoutreasonable excuse to comply with the requirement, it may deal with the defaulter (and, in the case of a body corporate, any director or officer) as if he were in contempt [F4; and "officer", in relation to a limited liability partnership, means a member of the limited liability partnership.].

(3) "Court" means—

(a) the High Court;

(b) in Scotland, the Court of Session.

Annotations:

Amendments (Textual)

F4 Words in s. 232(2) inserted(6.4.2001) by S.I. 2001/1090, regs. 1, 9, Sch. 5 para. 21

Modifications etc. (not altering text)

C264 S. 232 applied (1.12.2001) by S.I. 2001/2326, arts. 1(1)(b), 11(5); S.I. 2001/3538, art. 2(1)

233 Data protection.

In section 31 of the[M35] Data Protection Act 1998 (regulatory activity), after subsection (4), inser

"(4A)Personal data processed for the purpose of discharging any function which is conferred by or under Part XVI of the Financial Services and Markets Act 2000 on the body established by the Financial Services Authority for the purposes of that Part are exempt from the subject information provisions in any case to the extent to which the application of those provisions to the data would be likely to prejudice the proper discharge of the function."

Annotations:

Marginal Citations

M35 1998 c. 29.

注释：

修改等(不涉及条文内容)

C263　第231条于2001年12月1日依照制定法文件S.I.2001/2326第1条第(1)款第(b)项、第11条第(5)款；制定法文件S.I.2001/3538第2条第(1)款适用。

第232条　要求提供信息时法院的权力

(1)如当事人(以下简称违反人)未遵守依照第231条规定提出的要求，则申诉专员可向法院书面提出该事项，法庭可调查该案。

(2)如法院确信该违反人无合理理由而未遵守要求，则可将违反人(如违反人为法人，还包括任何董事或高级职员)按藐视法庭处理[F4；"高级职员"对于有限责任合伙，系指该有限责任合伙的合伙人]。

(3)"法院"系指

(a)高等法院；

(b)(苏格兰)高等民事法院。

注释：

修正(文本)

F4　第232条第(2)款的文字于2001年4月6日依照制定法文件S.I.2001/1090第1条、第9条，附录5第21条插入。

修改等(不涉及条文内容)

C264　第232条于2001年12月1日依照制定法文件S.I.2001/2326第1条第(1)款第(b)项、第11条第(5)款；制定法文件S.I.2001/3538第2条第(1)款适用。

第233条　数据保护

在[M35]《1998年数据保护法》(监管活动)第31条第(4)款后插入：

"(4A)对金融服务管理局为《2000年金融服务与市场法》第十六部分之目的设立的机构，为履行该部分规定赋予该机构的任何职能而处理的个人数据，如适用主题信息规定可能损害上述职能的正常履行，则在任何情况下可不遵守主题信息规定。"

注释：

附注引文

M35　1998年第29章。

Funding

234 Industry funding.

(1) For the purpose of funding—

(a) the establishment of the ombudsman scheme (whenever any relevant expense is incurred), and

(b) its operation in relation to the compulsory jurisdiction,

the Authority may make rules requiring the payment to it or to the scheme operator, by authorised persons or any class of authorised person of specified amounts (or amounts calculated in a specified way).

(2) "Specified" means specified in the rules.

Annotations:

Modifications etc. (not altering text)

C265 S. 234(1) amended (1.12.2001) by S.I. 2001/2326, arts. 1(1)(b), 12(1); S.I. 2001/3538, art. 2(1)

资　　助

第234条　行业资助

(1)为资助

(a)设立申诉专员计划(产生任何开支时);以及

(b)申诉专员计划与强制管辖权相关的运转,

管理局可制定规则,要求获授权人或任何一类获授权人向管理局或计划执行人支付规定金额(或以规定方式计算的金额)。

(2)"规定"系指在上述规则中规定。

注释:

修改等(不涉及条文内容)

C265　第234条第(1)款于2001年12月1日依照制定法文件S.I.2001/2326第1条第(1)款第(b)项、第12条第(1)款;制定法文件S.I.2001/3538第2条第(1)款修正。

PART XVII COLLECTIVE INVESTMENT SCHEMES

CHAPTER I INTERPRETATION

235 Collective investment schemes.

(1) In this Part "collective investment scheme" means any arrangements with respect to property of any description, including money, the purpose or effect of which is to enable persons taking part in the arrangements (whether by becoming owners of the property or any part of it or otherwise) to participate in or receive profits or income arising from the acquisition, holding, management or disposal of the property or sums paid out of such profits or income.

(2) The arrangements must be such that the persons who are to participate ("participants") do not have day-to-day control over the management of the property, whether or not they have the right to be consulted or to give directions.

(3) The arrangements must also have either or both of the following characteristics—

(a) the contributions of the participants and the profits or income out of which payments are to be made to them are pooled;

(b) the property is managed as a whole by or on behalf of the operator of the scheme.

(4) If arrangements provide for such pooling as is mentioned in subsection (3)(a) in relation to separate parts of the property, the arrangements are not to be regarded as constituting a single collective investment scheme unless the participants are entitled to exchange rights in one part for rights in another.

(5) The Treasury may by order provide that arrangements do not amount to a collective investment scheme—

(a) in specified circumstances; or

(b) if the arrangements fall within a specified category of arrangement.

第十七部分 集合投资计划

第一章 释 义

第235条 集合投资计划

（1）本部分中“集合投资计划”，系指与任何种类的财产，包括金钱在内的相关安排，其目的或效果在于使安排的参与者（不论通过成为财产持有人、成为财产任何部分的持有人或其他方式）能够分享或取得由购买、持有、管理或处置该财产而产生的利润或收入或者从该利润或收入中支付的款项。

（2）安排必须使参与者（以下简称参与者）对财产管理不具有日常控制权，无论其是否有权接受意见征询或发出指令。

（3）安排还必须具备下列任何一个或全部特点：

（a）参与者的投入以及向其支付的利润或收入被汇集在一起。

（b）财产由计划执行人或以计划执行人名义作为整体进行管理。

（4）如多项安排中规定依照第（3）款第（a）项规定财产汇集的独立部分，则除非参与者有权将对一部分财产的权利交换为对另一部分财产的权利，否则不得将上述安排视为构成单独的集合投资计划。

（5）财政部可颁布法令规定安排在下列情况下不得构成集合投资计划：

（a）在规定情况下；

（b）如安排属于规定类别。

236 Open-ended investment companies.

(1) In this Part "an open-ended investment company" means a collective investment scheme which satisfies both the property condition and the investment condition.

(2) The property condition is that the property belongs beneficially to, and is managed by or on behalf of, a body corporate ("BC") having as its purpose the investment of its funds with the aim of—

(a) spreading investment risk; and

(b) giving its members the benefit of the results of the management of those funds by or on behalf of that body.

(3) The investment condition is that, in relation to BC, a reasonable investor would, if he were to participate in the scheme—

(a) expect that he would be able to realize, within a period appearing to him to be reasonable, his investment in the scheme (represented, at any given time, by the value of shares in, or securities of, BC held by him as a participant in the scheme); and

(b) be satisfied that his investment would be realized on a basis calculated wholly or mainly by reference to the value of property in respect of which the scheme makes arrangements.

(4) In determining whether the investment condition is satisfied, no account is to be taken of any actual or potential redemption or repurchase of shares or securities under—

(a) Chapter VII of Part V of the[M36] Companies Act 1985;

(b) Chapter VII of Part VI of the[M37] Companies (Northern Ireland) Order 1986;

(c) corresponding provisions in force in another EEA State; or

(d) provisions in force in a country or territory other than an EEA state which the Treasury have, by order, designated as corresponding provisions.

(5) The Treasury may by order amend the definition of "an open-ended investment company" for the purposes of this Part.

Annotations:

Marginal Citations

M36 1985 c. 6.

M37 S.I. 1986/1032 (N.I. 6.)

237 Other definitions.

(1) In this Part "unit trust scheme" means a collective investment scheme under which the property is held on trust for the participants.

(2) In this Part—

第236条 开放式投资公司[1]

(1)本部分中"开放式投资公司"系指既符合财产条件又符合投资条件的集合投资计划。

(2)财产条件为财产由一个法人(以下简称BC)实益拥有管理,或以其名义管理,且该法人投资旨在

(a)分散投资风险;并

(b)给予其成员因该法人或代表该法人管理上述资金而产生的利益。

(3)投资条件为,就BC而言,理智投资者如参加该计划则会

(a)预计在其认为合理的期间内将能够实现对该计划的投资(以在任何给定时间其作为计划参与者持有的该BC股份或证券价值所代表);且

(b)确信其投资基于完全或主要参考该计划安排相关财产价值的计算实现。

(4)在确定是否满足投资条件时,不得考虑依照下列规定的任何实际或潜在股份或证券赎回或回购:

(a)[M36]《1985年公司法》第五部分第7章;

(b)[M37]《1986年公司法令》(北爱尔兰)第六部分第7章;

(c)在其他欧洲经济区国家有效的相应规定;或

(d)在欧洲经济区国家以外的国家或地区有效、经财政部颁布法令指定为相应规定的规定。

(5)财政部可颁布法令,为本部分之目的修订"开放式投资公司"的定义。

注释:

附注引文

M36 1985年第6章。

M37 制定法文件S.I.1986/1032(第6条)。

第237条 其他定义

(1)本部分中"单位信托计划",系指以信托形式为参与者持有财产的集合投资计划。

(2)本部分中

1 开放式投资公司是发行基金股份数量不固定,持股者有权退股,公司基金股份总额可以追加的投资公司。——译者注

"trustee", in relation to a unit trust scheme, means the person holding the property in question on trust for the participants;

"depositary", in relation to—

(a) a collective investment scheme which is constituted by a body incorporated by virtue of regulations under section 262, or

(b) any other collective investment scheme which is not a unit trust scheme,means any person to whom the property subject to the scheme is entrusted for safekeeping;

"the operator", in relation to a unit trust scheme with a separate trustee, means the manager and in relation to an open-ended investment company, means that company;

"units" means the rights or interests (however described) of the participants in a collective investment scheme.

(3) In this Part—

"an authorised unit trust scheme" means a unit trust scheme which is authorised for the purposes of this Act by an authorisation order in force under section 243;

"an authorised open-ended investment company" means a body incorporated by virtue of regulations under section 262 in respect of which an authorization order is in force under any provision made in such regulations by virtue of subsection (2)(l) of that section;

"a recognised scheme" means a scheme recognised under section 264, 270 or 272.

CHAPTER Ⅱ RESTRICTIONS ON PROMOTION

Annotations:

Modifications etc. (not altering text)

C266 Pt. XVII Ch. II (ss. 238–241) modified (31.10.2001) by S.I. 2001/3347, Sch. para. 8

238 Restrictions on promotion.

(1) An authorised person must not communicate an invitation or inducement to participate in a collective investment scheme.

(2) But that is subject to the following provisions of this section and to section 239.

(3) Subsection (1) applies in the case of a communication originating outside the United Kingdom only if the communication is capable of having an effect in the United Kingdom.

(4) Subsection (1) does not apply in relation to—

(a) an authorised unit trust scheme;

(b) a scheme constituted by an authorised open-ended investment company; or

(c) a recognised scheme.

(5) Subsection (1) does not apply to anything done in accordance with rules made by

“受托人”,就单位信托计划而言,系指以信托形式为参与者持有财产的人;

“托管人”与下列计划相关时:

(a)因依照第262条制定的法规而设立的机构组成的集合投资计划,或

(b)非单位信托计划的任何集合投资计划,系指受委托保管计划财产的任何人;

“执行人”,就具有独立受托人的单位信托计划而言,系指管理人,就开放式投资公司而言,系指该公司。

“单位”,系指集合投资计划参与者的权利或权益(无论如何描述)。

(3)本部分中

“获授权单位信托计划”,系指经依照第243条规定生效的授权令为本法之目的授权的单位信托计划;

“获授权开放式投资公司”,系指因依照第262条制定的法规而设立,且与其相关的授权令根据依照该条第(2)款第(l)项制定的法规生效的机构。

“获认可的计划”,系指依照第264条、第270条或第272条规定获认可的计划。

第二章　推介限制

注释:

修改等(不涉及条文内容)

C266　第十七部分第2章(第238条至第241条)于2001年10月31日依照制定法文件S.I.2001/3347附录第8条修订。

第238条　推介限制

(1)获授权人不得传播使他人参与集合投资计划的邀请或诱导。

(2)但上述规定受本条下列规定及第239条规定制约。

(3)如传播行为源于联合王国境外,则第(1)款仅在该传播行为可能在联合王国境内产生影响时适用。

(4)与下列计划相关时第(1)款不适用:

(a)获授权单位信托计划;

(b)由被授权开放式投资公司设立的计划;或

(c)获认可的计划。

(5)如管理局为使向非公众群体推广指定类别的计划豁免该款规定而制定规则,

the Authority for the purpose of exempting from that subsection the promotion otherwise than to the general public of schemes of specified descriptions.

(6) The Treasury may by order specify circumstances in which subsection (1) does not apply.

(7) An order under subsection (6) may, in particular, provide that subsection (1) does not apply in relation to communications—

(a) of a specified description;

(b) originating in a specified country or territory outside the United Kingdom;

(c) originating in a country or territory which falls within a specified description of country or territory outside the United Kingdom; or

(d) originating outside the United Kingdom.

(8) The Treasury may by order repeal subsection (3).

(9) "Communicate" includes causing a communication to be made.

(10) "Promotion otherwise than to the general public" includes promotion in a way designed to reduce, so far as possible, the risk of participation by persons for whom participation would be unsuitable.

(11) "Participate", in relation to a collective investment scheme, means become a participant (within the meaning given by section 235(2)) in the scheme.

Annotations:

Commencement Information

I68 S. 238 wholly in force at 1.12.2001; s. 238 not in force at Royal Assent see s. 431 (2); s. 238 in force for certain purposes at 25.2.2001 by S.I. 2001/516, art. 2(b), Sch. Pt. 2; s. 238 in force for specified purposes at 18.6.2001 by S.I. 2001/1820, art. 2, Sch.; s. 238 in force in so far as not already in force at 1.12.2001 by S.I. 2001/3538, art. 2(1)

239 Single property schemes.

(1) The Treasury may by regulations make provision for exempting single property schemes from section 238(1).

(2) For the purposes of subsection(1) a single property scheme is a scheme which has the characteristics mentioned in subsection(3) and satisfies such other requirements as are prescribed by the regulations conferring the exemption.

(3) The characteristics are—

(a) that the property subject to the scheme (apart from cash or other assets held for management purposes) consists of—

(i) a single building (or a single building with ancillary buildings) managed by or on behalf of the operator of the scheme, or

则第(1)款不适用于依照该规则实施的任何行为。

(6)财政部可颁布法令,规定第(1)款不适用的情况。

(7)第(6)款所述命令可以特别规定第(1)款在与下列传播行为相关时不适用:

(a)规定类别的传播行为;
(b)源于联合王国之外的规定国家或地区的传播行为;
(c)源于联合王国之外规定类别的国家或地区的传播行为;或

(d)源于联合王国之外的传播行为。
(8)财政部可命令废除第(3)款规定。
(9)"传播",包括造成他人实施传播行为。
(10)"向非公众群体推介",包括旨在尽可能降低不适合参与的人群参与计划的风险的推介。

(11)"参与",就集合投资计划而言,系指成为该计划的参与者[定义见第235条第(2)款]。

注释:

实施日期

I68 第238条于2001年12月1日全部生效;第238条在副署时未生效,见第431条第(2)款;第238条为特定目的于2001年2月25日依照制定法文件S.I.2001/516第2条第(b)款、附录第二部分生效;第238条为特定目的于2001年6月18日依照制定法文件S.I.2001/1820第2条、附录生效;第238条如于2001年12月1日尚未生效,则依照制定法文件S.I.2001/3538第2条第(1)款生效。

第239条 单一不动产计划

(1)财政部可制定法规,使单一不动产计划免受第238条第(1)款约束。

(2)就第(1)款而言,单一不动产计划是具有第(3)款所述特点并符合赋予豁免权的法规规定要求的计划。

(3)前款所述特点为
(a)该计划项下的财产(除现金或其他为管理目的而持有的资产)包括:

(i)计划管理人管理或以计划管理人名义管理的单体建筑(或带有附属建筑的单体建筑),或

(ii) a group of adjacent or contiguous buildings managed by him or on his behalf as a single enterprise,with or without ancillary land and with or without furniture, fittings or other contents of the building or buildings in question; and

(b) that the units of the participants in the scheme are either dealt in on arecognized investment exchange or offered on terms such that any agreement for their acquisition is conditional on their admission to dealings on such an exchange.

(4) If regulations are made under subsection(1), the Authority may make rules imposing duties or liabilities on the operator and (if any) the trustee or depositary of a scheme exempted by the regulations.

(5) The rules may include, to such extent as the Authority thinks appropriate, provision for purposes corresponding to those for which provision can be made under section 248 in relation to authorised unit trust schemes.

Annotations:

Commencement Information

I69 S. 239 wholly in force at 18.6.2001; s. 239 not in force at Royal Assent see s. 431 (2); s. 239(1)-(3) in force at 25.2.2001 by S.I. 2001/516, art. 2(a), Sch. Pt. 1; s. 239 in force in so far as not already in force at 18.6.2001 by S.I. 2001/1820, art. 2, Sch.

240 Restriction on approval of promotion.

(1) An authorised person may not approve for the purposes of section 21 the content of a communication relating to a collective investment scheme if he would be prohibited by section 238(1) from effecting the communication himself or from causing it to be communicated.

(2) For the purposes of determining in any case whether there has been a contravention of section 21(1), an approval given in contravention of subsection(1) is to be regarded as not having been given.

241 Actions for damages.

If an authorised person contravenes a requirement imposed on him by section 238 or 240, section 150 applies to the contravention as it applies to a contravention mentioned in that section.

CHAPTER Ⅲ AUTHORISED UNIT TRUST SCHEMES

Applications for authorisation

242 Applications for authorisation of unit trust schemes.

(1) Any application for an order declaring a unit trust scheme to be an authorised unit trust scheme must be made to the Authority by the manager and trustee, or proposed manager

(ii)作为单一企业由计划管理人管理的一组相邻或邻近的建筑,无论是否有配套土地、家具、配件或相关建筑物的其他内容;

(b)计划参与者的单位以承认的投资交换形式买卖,或在发售时规定任何购买协议以允许上述交换为条件。

(4)如依照第(1)款制定了法规,则管理局可制定规则,对免于遵守该法规的计划执行人或者受托人或托管人(如有)设定职责或义务。

(5)在管理局认为适当的范围内,前款所述规则可包括与依照第248条可作出的获授权单位信托计划相关规定目的一致的规定。

注释:

实施日期

I69 第239条于2001年6月18日全部生效;第239条在副署时尚未生效,见第431条第(2)款;第239条第(1)款至第(3)款于2001年2月25日依照制定法文件S.I.2001/516第2条第(a)款、附录第一部分生效;第239条如于2001年6月18日尚未生效,则通过制定法文件S.I.2001/1820第2条、附录生效。

第240条 推介批准限制

(1)对与集合投资计划相关的传播,如第238条第(1)款禁止获授权人本身传播或造成传播,则获授权人不得为第21条之目的批准传播内容。

(2)在任何情况下为确定是否发生了违反第21条第(1)款规定的情况,违反第(1)款规定给予的批准视为未给予批准。

第241条 损害赔偿诉讼

如获授权人违反第238条或第240条规定对其提出的要求,则第150条规定适用于该违反要求的行为,等同于适用于该条规定所述的违反行为。

第三章 获授权单位信托计划

授权申请

第242条 单位信托计划授权申请

(1)申请指令宣布单位信托计划为获授权单位信托计划的,须由该计划管理人和受托人或拟任管理人和受托人向管理局提出。

and trustee, of the scheme.

(2) The manager and trustee (or proposed manager and trustee) must be different persons.

(3) The application—

(a) must be made in such manner as the Authority may direct; and

(b) must contain or be accompanied by such information as the Authority may reasonably require for the purpose of determining the application.

(4) At any time after receiving an application and before determining it, the Authority may require the applicants to provide it with such further information as it reasonably considers necessary to enable it to determine the application.

(5) Different directions may be given, and different requirementsimposed, in relation to different applications.

(6) The Authority may require applicants to present information which they are required to give under this section in such form, or to verify it in such a way, as the Authority may direct.

Annotations:

Modifications etc. (not altering text)

C267 S. 242 extended (1.12.2001) by S.I. 2001/3592, arts. 1(2), 39(1) (with art. 23 (2))

Commencement Information

I70 S. 242 wholly in force at 1.12.2001; s. 242 not in force at Royal Assent see s. 431 (2); s. 242(3) in force for specified purposes at 18.6.2001 by S.I. 2001/1820, art. 2, Sch.; s. 242 in force for specified purposes at 3.9.2001 by S.I. 2001/2632, art. 2(2), Sch. Pt. 2; s. 242 in force in so far as not already in force at 1.12.2001 by S.I. 2001/3538, art. 2(1)

243 Authorisation orders.

(1) If, on an application under section 242 in respect of a unit trust scheme, the Authority—

(a) is satisfied that the scheme complies with the requirements set out in this section,

(b) is satisfied that the scheme complies with the requirements of the trust scheme rules, and

(c) has been provided with a copy of the trust deed and a certificate signed by a solicitor to the effect that it complies with such of the requirements of this section or those rules as relate to its contents,the Authority may make an order declaring the scheme to be an authorised unit trust scheme.

(2) If the Authority makes an order under subsection (1), it must give written notice of

(2)管理人和受托人(或拟任管理人和受托人)必须不同。

(3)申请必须

(a)以管理局指示的方式提出;且

(b)包含或附有管理局对申请作出决定所合理需要的信息。

(4)管理局在受理申请后、作出决定前,可以随时要求申请人进一步提供其认为作出决定所合理需要的信息。

(5)对不同申请可给予不同的指令,提出不同的要求。

(6)管理局可要求申请人以管理局指示的形式提交本条规定要求提供的信息,或以管理局指示的方式验证上述信息。

注释:

修改等(不涉及条文内容)

C267 第242条于2001年12月1日依照制定法文件S.I.2001/3592第1条第(2)款、第39条第(1)款[与第23条第(2)款]扩大适用范围。

实施日期

I70 第242条于2001年12月1日全部生效;第242条在副署时尚未生效,见第431条第(2)款;第242条第(3)款为特定目的于2001年6月18日依照制定法文件S.I.2001/1820第2条、附录生效;第242条为特定目的于2001年9月3日依照制定法文件S.I.2001/2632第2条第(2)款、附录第二部分生效;第242条如于2001年12月1日尚未生效,则依照制定法文件S.I.2001/3538第2条第(1)款生效。

第243条 授权令

(1)对依照第242条规定就单位信托计划提出的申请,如管理局

(a)确信该计划符合本条规定的要求,

(b)确信该计划符合信托计划规则规定的要求,且

(c)已提供信托契约副本并由事务律师签署证明书,证明该计划符合本条或信托计划规则中涉及该计划内容的要求,则管理局可以颁布法令,宣布该计划为获授权单位信托计划。

(2)如管理局依照第(1)款规定颁布法令,则必须向申请人发出该命令的书面

the order to the applicant.

(3) In this Chapter"authorisation order" means an order under subsection (1).

(4) The manager and the trustee must be persons who are independent of each other.

(5) The manager and the trustee must each—

(a) be a body corporate incorporated in the United Kingdom oranother EEA State, and

(b) have a place of business in the United Kingdom,and the affairs of each must be administered in the country in which it is incorporated.

(6) If the manager is incorporated in another EEA State, the scheme must not be one which satisfies the requirements prescribed for the purposes of section 264.

(7) The manager and the trustee must each be an authorised person and the manager must have permission to act as manager and the trustee must have permission to act as trustee.

(8) The name of the scheme must not be undesirable or misleading.

(9) The purposes of the scheme must be reasonably capable of being successfully carried into effect.

(10) The participants must be entitled to have their units redeemed in accordance with the scheme at a price—

(a) related to the net value of the property to which the units relate; and

(b) determined in accordance with the scheme.

(11) But a scheme is to be treated as complying with subsection(10) if it requires the manager to ensure that a participant is able to sell his units on an investment exchange at a price not significantly different from that mentioned in that subsection.

Annotations:

Modifications etc. (not altering text)

C268 S. 243(1) extended (1.12.2001) by S.I. 2001/2636, arts. 1(2)(b), 65(1); S.I. 2001/3538, art. 2(1)

Commencement Information

I71 S. 243 wholly in force at 1.12.2001; s. 243 not in force at Royal Assent see s. 431 (2); s. 243 in force for specified purposes at 3.9.2001 by S.I. 2001/2632, art. 2(2), Sch. Pt. 2; s. 243 in force in so far as not already in force at 1.12.2001 by S.I. 2001/3538, art. 2(1)

244 Determination of applications.

(1) An application under section 242 must be determined by the Authority before the end of the period of six months beginning with the date on which it receives the completed application.

(2) The Authority may determine an incomplete application if it considers it appropriate to do so; and it must in any event determine such an application within twelve months

通知。

(3)本章中“授权令”系指第(1)款规定的法令。

(4)管理人和受托人必须相互独立。

(5)管理人和受托人必须各自

(a)为在联合王国或其他欧洲经济区国家设立的法人,且

(b)在联合王国有营业场所,且必须在其设立的国家管理其事务。

(6)如管理人在另一个欧洲经济区国家设立,则该计划不得为符合为第264条之目的规定的要求的计划。

(7)管理人和受托人必须各自为获授权人,且管理人必须获得担任管理人的许可,受托人必须获得担任受托人的许可。

(8)计划名称不得为不良名称或产生误导。

(9)计划的目的在合理情况下必须能够成功实现

(10)参与者必须有权依照计划规定按下列价格赎回其单位:

(a)与单位相关财产净值有关;且

(b)依照计划规定确定。

(11)但如计划要求管理人确保参与者能够以投资交换形式,按照与第(10)款所述价格无明显差异的价格出售其单位,则视为该计划符合第(10)款规定。

注释:

修改等(不涉及条文内容)

C268　第243条第(1)款于2001年12月1日依照制定法文件S.I.2001/2636第1条第(2)款第(b)项、第65条第(1)款;制定法文件S.I.2001/3538第2条第(1)款扩大适用范围。

实施日期

I71　第243条于2001年12月1日全部生效;第243条在副署时尚未生效,见第431条第(2)款;第243条为特定目的于2001年9月3日依照制定法文件S.I.2001/2632第2条第(2)款、附录第二部分生效;第243条如于2001年12月1日尚未生效,则依照制定法文件S.I.2001/3538第2条第(1)款生效。

第244条　对申请作出的决定

(1)对依照第242条规定提出的申请,管理局必须在收到完整申请之日起6个月期间届满前作出决定。

(2)如管理局认为适当,则可以对不完整申请作出决定;且在任何情况下必须在首次收到该申请之日起12个月内作出决定。

beginning with the date on which it first receives the application.

(3) The applicant may withdraw his application, by giving the Authority written notice, at any time before the Authority determines it.

Annotations:

Modifications etc. (not altering text)

C269 S. 244 applied (1.12.2001) by S.I. 2001/3592, arts. 1(2), 39(1) (with art. 23(2))

Commencement Information

I72 S. 244 wholly in force at 1.12.2001; s. 244 not in force at Royal Assent see s. 431(2); s. 244 in force for specified purposes at 3.9.2001 by S.I. 2001/2632, art. 2(2), Sch. Pt. 2; s. 244 in force in so far as not already in force at 1.12.2001 by S.I. 2001/3538, art. 2(1)

Applications refused

245 Procedure when refusing an application.

(1) If the Authority proposes to refuse an application made under section 242 it must give each of the applicants a warning notice.

(2) If the Authority decides to refuse the application—

(a) it must give each of the applicants a decision notice; and

(b) either applicant may refer the matter to the Tribunal.

Annotations:

Commencement Information

I73 S. 245 wholly in force at 1.12.2001; s. 245 not in force at Royal Assent see s. 431(2); s. 245 in force for specified purposes at 3.9.2001 by S.I. 2001/2632, art. 2(2), Sch. Pt. 2; s. 245 in force in so far as not already in force at 1.12.2001 by S.I. 2001/3538, art. 2(1)

Certificates

246 Certificates.

(1) If the manager or trustee of a unit trust scheme which complies with the conditions necessary for it to enjoy the rights conferred by any relevant Community instrument so requests, the Authority may issue a certificate to the effect that the scheme complies with those conditions.

(2) Such a certificate may be issued on the making of an authorisation order in respect of the scheme or at any subsequent time.

（3）管理局对申请作出决定前，申请人可以向管理局发出书面通知撤回申请。

注释：

修改等（不涉及条文内容）

C269　第244条于2001年12月1日依照制定法文件S.I.2001/3592第1条第（2）款、第39条第（1）款[与第23条第（2）款]适用。

实施日期

I72　第244条于2001年12月1日全部生效；第244条在副署时尚未生效，见第431条第（2）款；第244条为特定目的于2001年9月3日依照制定法文件S.I.2001/2632第2条第（2）款、附录第二部分生效；第244条如于2001年12月1日尚未生效，则依照制定法文件S.I.2001/3538第2条第（1）款生效。

驳回申请

第245条　驳回申请的程序

（1）如管理局拟驳回依照第242条规定提出的申请，则必须向每个申请人发出预告通知。

（2）如管理局决定驳回申请，则

（a）必须向每个申请人发出决定通知；且

（b）各申请人均可将该事项诉至裁判所。

注释：

实施日期

I73　第245条于2001年12月1日全部生效；第245条在副署时尚未生效，见第431条第（2）款；第245条为特定目的于2001年9月3日依照制定法文件S.I.2001/2632第2条第（2）款、附录第二部分生效；第245条如于2001年12月1日尚未生效，则依照制定法文件S.I.2001/3538第2条第（1）款生效。

证明书

第246条　证明书

（1）如单位信托计划符合享有任何相关共同体法律文件赋予的权利所需要具备的条件，且该单位信托计划管理人或受托人提出请求，则管理局可签发证明书，证明该计划符合上述条件。

（2）上述证明书可在就该计划发布授权令时或其后任何时间签发。

Annotations:

Modifications etc. (not altering text)

C270 S. 246 extended (1.12.2001) by S.I. 2001/2636, arts. 1(2)(b), 65(3); S.I. 2001/3538, art. 2(1)

Commencement Information

I74 S. 246 wholly in force at 1.12.2001; s. 246 not in force at Royal Assent see s. 431 (2); s. 246 in force for specified purposes at 3.9.2001 by S.I. 2001/2632, art. 2(2), Sch. Pt. 2; s. 246 in force in so far as not already in force at 1.12.2001 by S.I. 2001/3538, art. 2(1)

Rules

247 Trust scheme rules.

(1) The Authority may make rules ("trust scheme rules") as to—

(a) the constitution, management and operation of authorised unit trust schemes;

(b) the powers, duties, rights and liabilities of the manager and trustee of any such scheme;

(c) the rights and duties of the participants in any such scheme; and

(d) the winding up of any such scheme.

(2) Trust scheme rules may, in particular, make provision—

(a) as to the issue and redemption of the units under the scheme;

(b) as to the expenses of the scheme and the means of meeting them;

(c) for the appointment, removal, powers and duties of an auditor for the scheme;

(d) for restricting or regulating the investment and borrowing powers exercisable in relation to the scheme;

(e) requiring the keeping of records with respect to the transactions and financial position of the scheme and for the inspection of those records;

(f) requiring the preparation of periodical reports with respect to the scheme and the provision of those reports to the participants and to the Authority; and

(g) with respect to the amendment of the scheme.

(3) Trust scheme rules may make provision as to the contents of the trust deed, including provision requiring any of the matters mentioned in subsection (2) to be dealt with in the deed.

(4) But trust scheme rules are binding on the manager, trustee and participants independently of the contents of the trust deed and, in the case of the participants, have effect as if contained in it.

(5) If—

注释：

修改等（不涉及条文内容）

C270　第246条于2001年12月1日依照制定法文件S.I.2001/2636第2条第（1）款第（b）项、第65条第（3）款；制定法文件S.I.2001/3538第2条第（1）款扩大适用范围。

实施日期

I74　第246条于2001年12月1日全部生效；第246条在副署时尚未生效，见第431条第（2）款；第246条为特定目的于2001年9月3日依照制定法文件S.I.2001/2632第2条第（2）款、附录第二部分生效；第246条如于2001年12月1日尚未生效，则依照制定法文件S.I.2001/3538第2条第（1）款生效。

规　则

第247条　信托计划规则

（1）管理局可就下列内容订立规则（以下简称信托计划规则）：

（a）获授权单位信托计划的组织制度、管理和运作；

（b）任何获授权单位信托计划管理人和受托人的权力、职责、权利和责任；

（c）任何获授权单位信托计划参与者的权利与职责；

（d）任何获授权单位信托计划的停业。

（2）信托计划规则特别规定：

（a）依照计划发售和赎回单位；

（b）该计划的开支以及满足开支的手段；

（c）计划审计人的任免、权力和职责；

（d）限制或监管与项目相关的投资权和借贷权；

（e）要求对计划交易和财务状况保留相关记录并对记录予以检查；

（f）要求编制并向参与者和管理局提供与计划相关的定期报告；以及

（g）计划的修改。

（3）信托计划规则可规定信托契约的内容，包括要求在契约中处理的第（2）款所列的任何事项。

（4）但信托计划规则独立于信托契约内容对管理人、受托人和参与者具有约束力，且对于参与者效力相当于该规则包含在信托契约内容中。

（5）如有下列情况：

(a) a modification is made of the statutory provisions in force in Great Britain or Northern Ireland relating to companies,

(b) the modification relates to the rights and duties of persons who hold the beneficial title to any shares in a company without also holding the legal title, and

(c) it appears to the Treasury that, for the purpose of assimilating the law relating to authorised unit trust schemes to the law relating to companies as so modified, it is expedient to modify the rule-making powers conferred on the Authority by this section,

the Treasury may by order make such modifications of thosepowers as they consider appropriate.

248 Scheme particulars rules.

(1) The Authority may make rules ("scheme particulars rules") requiring the manager of an authorised unit trust scheme—

(a) to submit scheme particulars to the Authority; and

(b) to publish scheme particulars or make them available to the public on request.

(2) "Scheme particulars" means particulars in such form, containing such information about the scheme and complying with such requirements, as are specified in scheme particulars rules.

(3) Scheme particulars rules may require the manager of an authorised unit trust scheme to submit, and to publish or make available, revised or further scheme particulars if there is a significant change affecting any matter—

(a) which is contained in scheme particulars previously published or made available; and

(b) whose inclusion in those particulars was required by the rules.

(4) Scheme particulars rules may require the manager of an authorised unit trust scheme to submit, and to publish or make available, revised or further scheme particulars if—

(a) a significant new matter arises; and

(b) the inclusion of information in respect of that matter would have been required in previous particulars if it had arisen when those particulars were prepared.

(5) Scheme particulars rules may provide for the payment, by the person or persons who in accordance with the rules are treated as responsible for any scheme particulars, of compensation to any qualifying person who has suffered loss as a result of—

(a) any untrue or misleading statement in the particulars; or

(b) the omission from them of any matter required by the rules to be included.

(6) "Qualifying person" means a person who—

(a) has become or agreed to become a participant in the scheme; or

(b) although not being a participant, has a beneficial interest in units in the scheme.

(7) Scheme particulars rules do not affect any liability which any person may incur

(a)对在联合王国或北爱尔兰有效的与公司相关成文法规定进行了修改;

(b)对持有公司股份享有收益权但无法定所有权的人的权利和职责进行了相关修改;以及

(c)为使获授权单位信托计划相关法律与经上述修改的公司相关法律相一致,财政部认为适宜修改本条规定赋予管理局的规则制定权,

则财政部可颁布法令,对上述权力作出其认为适当的修改。

第248条 计划细则规则

(1)管理局可以制定规则(以下简称计划细则规则),要求获授权单位信托计划管理人

(a)向管理局提交计划细则;并

(b)应当请求公布计划细则或将其提供给公众。

(2)“计划细则”,系指计划细则规则规定的形式、包含该规则指定内容并符合该规则规定要求的关于计划的细则。

(3)如发生影响下列事项的重大变化,则计划细则规则可要求获授权单位信托计划管理人提交、公布或提供修订或进一步的计划细则:

(a)先前公布或提供的计划细则中所载事项;以及

(b)计划细则规则要求列入细则的事项。

(4)如有下列情况,则计划细则规则可要求获授权单位信托计划管理人提交、公布或提供修订或进一步的计划细则:

(a)出现新的重大事项;且

(b)如该事项在制订先前的计划细则时出现,则该事项相关信息应列入先前的计划细则。

(5)计划细则规则可规定依照该规则视为对任何计划细则负责的人向任何因下列情况遭受损失的合资格人支付补偿:

(a)细则中所载任何不实陈述或误导性陈述;或

(b)细则中遗漏任何应包含的事项。

(6)“合资格人”系指

(a)已成为或同意成为该计划参与者的人;或

(b)尽管并非参与者,但在计划单位中拥有实益权益。

(7)计划细则规则不影响任何人在该规则之外可能招致的任何责任。

apart from the rules.

249 Disqualification of auditor for breach of trust scheme rules.

(1) If it appears to the Authority that an auditor has failed to comply with a duty imposed on him by trust scheme rules, it may disqualify him from being the auditor for any authorised unit trust scheme or authorised open-ended investment company.

(2) Subsections (2) to (5) of section 345 have effect in relation to disqualification under subsection (1) as they have effect in relation to disqualification under subsection (1) of that section.

250 Modification or waiver of rules.

(1) In this section "rules" means—

(a) trust scheme rules; or

(b) scheme particulars rules.

(2) The Authority may, on the application or with the consent of any person to whom any rules apply, direct that all or any of the rules—

(a) are not to apply to him as respects a particular scheme; or

(b) are to apply to him, as respects a particular scheme, with such modifications as may be specified in the direction.

(3) The Authority may, on the application or with the consent of the manager and trustee of a particular scheme acting jointly, direct that all or any of the rules—

(a) are not to apply to the scheme; or

(b) are to apply to the scheme with such modifications as may be specified in the direction.

(4) Subsections (3) to (9) and (11) of section 148 have effect in relation to a direction under subsection (2) as they have effect in relation to a direction under section 148(2) but with the following modifications—

(a) subsection (4)(a) is to be read as if the words "by the authorised person" were omitted;

(b) any reference to the authorised person (except in subsection (4)(a)) is to be read as a reference to the person mentioned in subsection (2); and

(c) subsection (7)(b) is to be read, in relation to a participant of the scheme, as if the word "commercial" were omitted.

(5) Subsections (3) to (9) and (11) of section 148 have effect in relation to a direction under subsection (3) as they have effect in relation to a direction under section 148(2) but with the following modifications—

(a) subsection (4)(a) is to be read as if the words "by the authorised person" were omitted;

(b) subsections(7)(b) and (11) are to be read as if references to the authorised person

第249条　因违反信托计划规则而取消审计人资格

（1）如管理局认为审计人未能遵守信托计划规则对其提出的职责要求，则可以取消其担任任何获授权单位信托计划或者获授权开放式投资公司审计人的资格。

（2）第345条第（2）款至第（5）款对本条第（1）款规定的取消资格所具有的效力，等同于对该条第（1）款规定的取消资格所具有的效力。

第250条　规则的修改或放弃

（1）本条中"规则"系指

（a）信托计划规则；或

（b）计划细则规则。

（2）应任何规则适用的任何人申请或经其同意，管理局可以指示全部或部分规则

（a）就特定计划不适用于该人；或

（b）就特定计划经依照指令进行指定修改后适用于该人。

（3）应某一特定计划的管理人和受托人共同申请或经其一致同意，管理局可以指示全部或部分规则

（a）不适用于该计划；或

（b）经依照指令进行指定修改后适用于该计划。

（4）第148条第（3）款至第（9）款以及第（11）款对本条第（2）款规定的指令所具有的效力，等同于对第148条第（2）款规定的指令所具有的效力，但须作下列修改：

（a）第（4）款第（a）项应当视为已删除"由获授权人"这一表述；

（b）述及任何获授权人［除第（4）条第（a）项外］均视为述及第（2）款所列之人；且

（c）第（7）款第（b）项与计划参与者相关时视为已删除"商业"一词。

（5）第148条第（3）款至第（9）款以及第（11）款对本条第（3）款规定的指示所具有的效力，等同于对第148条第（2）款规定的指示所具有的效力，但须作下列修改：

（a）第（4）款第（a）项应当视为已删除"由获授权人"这一表述；

（b）第（7）款第（b）项及第（11）款述及获授权人应视为述及计划管理人和受托人。

were references to each of the manager and the trustee of the scheme;

(c) subsection (7)(b) is to be read, in relation to a participant of the scheme, as if the word "commercial" were omitted;

(d) subsection (8) is to be read as if the reference to the authorised person concerned were a reference to the scheme concerned and to its manager and trustee; and

(e) subsection (9) is to be read as if the reference to the authorised person were a reference to the manager and trustee of the scheme acting jointly.

Annotations:

Modifications etc. (not altering text)

C271 S. 250(2) amended (temp. from 3.9.2001 to 1.12.2001) by S.I. 2001/2659, arts. 1(2), 3(6); S.I. 2001/3538, art. 2(1)

Alterations

251 Alteration of schemes and changes of manager or trustee.

(1) The manager of an authorised unit trust scheme must give written notice to the Authority of any proposal to alter the scheme or to replace its trustee.

(2) Any notice given in respect of a proposal to alter the scheme involving a change in the trust deed must be accompanied by a certificate signed by a solicitor to the effect that the change will not affect the compliance of the deed with the trust scheme rules.

(3) The trustee of an authorised unit trust scheme must give written notice to the Authority of any proposal to replace the manager of the scheme.

(4) Effect is not to be given to any proposal of which notice has been given under subsection (1) or (3) unless—

(a) the Authority, by written notice, has given its approval to the proposal; or

(b) one month, beginning with the date on which the notice was given, has expired without the manager or trustee having received from the Authority a warning notice under section 252 in respect of the proposal.

(5) The Authority must not approve a proposal to replace the manager or the trustee of an authorised unit trust scheme unless it is satisfied that, if the proposed replacement is made, the scheme will continue to comply with the requirements of section 243(4) to (7).

Annotations:

Modifications etc. (not altering text)

C272 S. 251 amended(temp. from 3.9.2001 to 1.12.2001) by S.I. 2001/2659, arts. 1(2), 3(7); S.I. 2001/3538, art. 2(1) (c)第(7)款第(b)项与计划参与者相关时视为已删除“商业”一词;

(d)第(8)款述及相关获授权人应视为述及相关计划及其管理人和受托人;

(e)第(9)款述及获授权人应视为述及共同行事的计划管理人和受托人。

注释:

修改等(不涉及条文内容)

C271　第250条第(2)款暂定于2001年9月3日至2001年12月1日依照制定法文件S.I.2001/2659第1条第(2)款、第3条第(6)款;制定法文件S.I.2001/3538第2条第(1)款修正。

变　更

第251条　计划变更与管理人或受托人改变

(1)获授权单位信托计划管理人提议变更计划或更换受托人的,必须向管理局发出书面通知。

(2)如变更计划涉及信托契约变更,则就提议变更计划发出的通知必须附有事务律师签署的证明书,证明该变更不影响契约对信托计划规则的合规性。

(3)获授权单位信托计划受托人提议变更计划或更换管理人的,必须向管理局发出书面通知。

(4)除非有下列情况,否则依照第(1)款或第(3)款发出通知的任何提议不得生效:

(a)管理局以书面通知形式对该拟行计划予以批准;或

(b)自发出通知之日起1个月期间届满,管理人或受托人未收到管理局依照第252条就该提议发出的预告通知。

(5)管理局必须确信,如实施提议的更换,该信托计划继续符合第24条第(4)款至第(7)款规定的要求,否则不得批准更换管理人或受托人的计划。

注释:

修改等(不涉及条文内容)

C272　第251条暂时有效,于2001年9月3日至2001年12月1日依照制定法文件S.I.2001/2659第1条第(2)款、第3条第(7)款;制定法文件S.I.2001/3538第2条第(1)款修正。

C273 S. 251(1) extended (1.12.2001) by S.I. 2001/3592, arts. 1(2), 40(1) (with art. 23(2))

C274 S. 251(3) extended (1.12.2001) by S.I. 2001/3592, arts. 1(2), 41(1) (with art. 23(2))

Commencement Information

I75 S. 251 wholly in force at 1.12.2001; s. 251 not in force at Royal Assent see s. 431 (2); s. 251(except subsection (4)(b)) in force for specified purposes at 3.9.2001 by S.I. 2001/2632, art. 2(2), Sch. Pt. 2; s. 251 in force in so far as not already in force at 1.12.2001 by S.I. 2001/3538, art. 2(1)

252 Procedure when refusing approval of change of manager or trustee.

(1) If the Authority proposes to refuse approval of a proposal to replace the trustee or manager of an authorised unit trust scheme, it must give a warning notice to the person by whom notice of the proposal was given under section 251(1) or (3).

(2) If the Authority proposes to refuse approval of a proposal to alter an authorised unit trust scheme it must give separate warning notices to the manager and the trustee of the scheme.

(3) To be valid the warning notice must be received by that person before the end of one month beginning with the date on which notice of the proposal was given.

(4) If, having given a warning notice to a person, the Authority decides to refuse approval—

(a) it must give him a decision notice; and

(b) he may refer the matter to the Tribunal.

Annotations:

Modifications etc. (not altering text)

C275 S. 252 amended (temp. from 3.9.2001 to 1.12.2001) by S.I. 2001/2659, arts. 1 (2),3(7); S.I. 2001/3538, art. 2(1)

C276 S. 252(3) modified (1.12.2001) by S.I. 2001/3592, arts. 1(2), 40(3), 41(2) (with art. 23(2))

Commencement Information

I76 S. 252 wholly in force at 1.12.2001; s. 252 not in force at Royal Assent see s. 431 (2); s. 252 in force for specified purposes at 3.9.2001 by S.I. 2001/2632, art. 2(2), Sch. Pt. 2; s. 252 in force in so far as not already in force at 1.12.2001 by S.I. 2001/3538, art. 2(1)

C273　第251条第(1)款于2001年12月1日依照制定法文件S.I.2001/3592第1条第(2)款、第40条第(1)款[与第23条第(2)款]扩大适用范围。

C274　第251条第(3)款于2001年12月1日依照制定法文件S.I.2001/3592第1条第(2)款、第41条第(1)款[与第23条第(2)款]扩大适用范围。

实施日期

I75　第251条于2001年12月1日全部生效;第251条在副署时尚未生效,见第431条第(2)款;第251条[除了第(4)款第(b)项]为特定目的于2001年9月3日依照制定法文件S.I.2001/2632第2条第(2)款、附录第二部分生效;第251条如于2001年12月1日尚未生效,则依照制定法文件S.I.2001/3538第2条第(1)款生效。

第252条　拒绝批准管理人或受托人变更的程序

(1)如管理局拟拒绝批准更换获授权单位信托计划受托人或管理人的提议,则必须向依照第251条第(1)款或第(3)款发出计划通知的通知人发出预告通知。

(2)如管理局拟拒绝批准拟变更获授权单位信托计划的提议,则必须向该信托计划的管理人和受托人发出预告通知。

(3)预告通知接收人必须于提议通知发出之日起1个月内收到预告通知方为有效。

(4)如管理局向某人发出预告通知后决定拒绝批准,则

(a)管理局必须向该人发出决定通知;且

(b)该人可将该事项诉至裁判所。

注释:

修改等(不涉及条文内容)

C275　第252条暂时有效,于2001年9月3日至2001年12月1日依照制定法文件S.I. 2001/2659第1条第(2)款、第3条第(7)款;制定法文件S.I. 2001/3538第2条第(1)款修正。

C276　第252条第(3)款于2001年12月1日依照制定法文件S.I.2001/3592第1条第(2)款、第40条第(3)款、第41条第(2)款[与第23条第(2)款]修订。

实施日期

I76　第252条于2001年12月1日全部生效;第252条在副署时尚未生效,见第431条第(2)款;第252条为特定目的于2001年9月3日依照制定法文件S.I.2001/2632第2条第(2)款、附录第二部分生效;第252条如于2001年12月1日尚未生效,则依照制定法文件S.I. 2001/3538第2条第(1)款生效。

Exclusion clauses

253 Avoidance of exclusion clauses.

Any provision of the trust deed of an authorised unit trust scheme is void in so far as it would have the effect of exempting the manager or trustee from liability for any failure to exercise due care and diligence in the discharge of his functions in respect of the scheme.

Ending of authorisation

254 Revocation of authorisation order otherwise than by consent.

(1) An authorisation order may be revoked by an order made by the Authority if it appears to the Authority that—

(a) one or more of the requirements for the making of the order are no longer satisfied;

(b) the manager or trustee of the scheme concerned has contravened a requirement imposed on him by or under this Act;

(c) the manager or trustee of the scheme has, in purported compliance with any such requirement, knowingly or recklessly given the Authority information which is false or misleading in a material particular;

(d) no regulated activity is being carried on in relation to the scheme and the period of that inactivity began at least twelve months earlier; or

(e) none of paragraphs (a) to (d) applies, but it is desirable to revoke the authorisation order in order to protect the interests of participants or potential participants in the scheme.

(2) For the purposes of subsection (1)(e), the Authority may take into account any matter relating to—

(a) the scheme;

(b) the manager or trustee;

(c) any person employed by or associated with the manager or trustee in connection with the scheme;

(d) any director of the manager or trustee;

(e) any person exercising influence over the manager or trustee;

(f) any body corporate in the same group as the manager or trustee;

(g) any director of any such body corporate;

(h) any person exercising influence over any such body corporate.

Annotations:

Modifications etc. (not altering text)

C277 S. 254 applied (with modifications) (1.12.2001) by S.I. 2001/3592, arts. 1(2), 46(4)(5) (with art. 23(2))

排除条款

第253条　避免排除条款

获授权单位信托计划信托契约的任何规定，如免除管理人或受托人在行使计划相关职能时因未尽应有的谨慎和勤勉义务而承担的责任，则该规定无效。

授权终止

第254条　无须同意的授权令撤销

(1)管理局如认为有下列情况，则可以颁布法令撤销授权令：

(a)发布授权令的要求中一项或多项已不再满足；

(b)相关计划的管理人或受托人违反本法对其规定的要求或依照本法对其提出的要求；

(c)计划管理人或受托人在遵守上述任何要求时，就重要事项向管理局提供明知为虚假或误导的信息，或因重大过失而提供虚假或误导信息。

(d)未开展与计划相关的受监管活动，且未开展活动的期间始于至少12个月前；

(e)第(a)项至第(d)项均不适用，但为保护计划参与者或潜在参与者的利益有必要撤销授权令。

(2)为了第(1)款第(e)项之目的，管理局可考虑与下列各项有关的任何事项：

(a)计划；

(b)管理人或受托人；

(c)管理人或受托人为计划聘用的任何人；

(d)管理人或受托人的任何董事；

(e)对管理人或受托人施加影响的任何人；

(f)与管理人或受托人属于同一集团的法人；

(g)上述任何法人的任何董事；

(h)对上述任何法人施加影响的任何人。

注释：

修改等(不涉及条文内容)

C277　第254条(已修订)于2001年12月1日制定法文件S.I.2001/3592第1条第(2)款，第46条第(4)款、第(5)款[与第23条第(2)款]适用。

C278 S. 254(1)(a) modified (1.12.2001) by S.I. 2001/2636, arts. 1(2)(b), 65(2); S.I. 2001/3538, art. 2(1)

C279 S. 254(1)(d) excluded (temp. from 3.9.2001 to 1.12.2001) by S.I. 2001/2659, arts. 1(2), 3(2); S.I. 2001/3538, art. 2(1)

255 Procedure.

(1) If the Authority proposes to make an order under section 254 revoking anauthorization order ("a revoking order"), it must give separate warning notices to the manager and the trustee of the scheme.

(2) If the Authority decides to make a revoking order, it must without delay give each of them a decision notice and either of them may refer the matter to the Tribunal.

Annotations:

Modifications etc. (not altering text)

C280 S. 255(1) extended (1.12.2001) by S.I. 2001/3592, arts. 1(2), 46(1) (with art. 23(2))

256 Requests for revocation of authorisation order.

(1) An authorisation order may be revoked by an order made by the Authority at the request of the manager or trustee of the scheme concerned.

(2) If the Authority makes an order under subsection (1), it must give written notice of the order to the manager and trustee of the scheme concerned.

(3) The Authority may refuse a request to make an order under this section if it considers that—

(a) the public interest requires that any matter concerning the scheme should be investigated before a decision is taken as to whether the authorisation order should be revoked; or

(b) revocation would not be in the interests of the participants or would be incompatible with a Community obligation.

(4) If the Authority proposes to refuse a request under this section, it must give separate warning notices to the manager and the trustee of the scheme.

(5) If the Authority decides to refuse the request, it must without delay give each of them a decision notice and either of them may refer the matter to the Tribunal.

Annotations:

Modifications etc. (not altering text)

C281 S. 256(1) extended (1.12.2001) by S.I. 2001/3592, arts. 1(2), 46(6) (with art. 23(2))

C278　第254条第(1)款第(a)项于2001年12月1日依照制定法文件S.I.2001/2636第1条第(2)款第(b)项、第65条第(2)款;制定法文件S.I.2001/3538第2条第(1)款修订。

C279　第254条第(1)款第(d)项暂时有效,于2001年9月3日至2001年12月1日依照制定法文件S.I.2001/2659第1条第(2)款、第3条第(2)款;制定法文件S.I.2001/3538第2条第(1)款排除。

第255条　程序

(1)管理局如拟依照第254条规定发布撤销授权令的命令(以下简称撤销令),则必须对计划管理人和受托人另行发出预告通知书。

(2)如管理局决定发布撤销令,则必须毫不延迟地向管理人和受托人分别发出决定通知。管理人和受托人均可将该事项诉至裁判所。

注释:

修改等(不涉及条文内容)

C280　第255条第(1)款于2001年12月1日依照制定法文件S.I.2001/3592第1条第(2)款、第46条第(1)款[与第23条第(2)款]扩大适用范围。

第256条　请求撤销授权令

(1)管理局可以应相关计划管理人或受托人的请求撤销授权令。

(2)如管理局依照第(1)款规定颁布法令,则必须向相关计划管理人和受托人发出该命令的书面通知。

(3)管理局如认为有下列情况,则可以驳回依照本条颁布法令的请求:

(a)公共利益要求在决定是否应撤销授权令前对计划相关的任何事项进行调查;或

(b)撤销不符合参与者利益或不符合共同体义务。

(4)如管理局拟驳回依照本条规定提出的请求,则必须向该计划的管理人和受托人另行发出预告通知。

(5)如管理局决定驳回请求,则必须毫不延迟地向管理人和受托人分别发出决定通知。管理人和受托人均可将该事项提交裁判所裁决。

注释:

修改等(不涉及条文内容)

C281　第256条第(1)款于2001年12月1日依照制定法文件S.I.2001/3592第1条第(2)款、第46条第(6)款[与第23条第(2)款]扩大适用范围。

Powers of intervention

257 Directions.

(1) The Authority may give a direction under this section if it appears to the Authority that—

(a) one or more of the requirements for the making of an authorisation order are no longer satisfied;

(b) the manager or trustee of an authorised unit trust scheme has contravened, or is likely to contravene, a requirement imposed on him by or under this Act;

(c) the manager or trustee of such a scheme has, in purported compliance with any such requirement, knowingly or recklessly given the Authority information which is false or misleading in a material particular; or

(d) none of paragraphs (a) to (c) applies, but it is desirable to give a direction in order to protect the interests of participants or potential participants in such a scheme.

(2) A direction under this section may—

(a) require the manager of the scheme to cease the issue or redemption, or both the issue and redemption, of units under the scheme;

(b) require the manager and trustee of the scheme to wind it up.

(3) If the authorisation order is revoked, the revocation does not affect any direction under this section which is then in force.

(4) A direction may be given under this section in relation to a scheme in the case of which the authorisation order has been revoked if a direction under this section was already in force at the time of revocation.

(5) If a person contravenes a direction under this section, section 150 applies to the contravention as it applies to a contravention mentioned in that section.

(6) The Authority may, either on its own initiative or on the application of the manager or trustee of the scheme concerned, revoke or vary a direction given under this section if it appears to the Authority—

(a) in the case of revocation, that it is no longer necessary for the direction to take effect or continue in force;

(b) in the case of variation, that the direction should take effect or continue in force in a different form.

Annotations:

Modifications etc. (not altering text)

C282 S. 257(1) extended (1.12.2001) by S.I. 2001/2636, arts. 1(2)(b), 69(1); S.I. 2001/3538, art. 2(1)

干 预 权

第257条 指示

(1)管理局如认为有下列情况,则可依照本条规定发布指示:

(a)发布授权令的要求中一项或多项已不再满足;

(b)获授权单位信托计划的管理人或受托人违反或可能违反本法对其规定或依照本法对其提出的要求;

(c)计划管理人或受托人在遵守上述任何要求时,就重要事项向管理局提供明知为虚假或误导信息,或因重大过失而提供虚假或误导信息;或

(d)第(a)项至第(c)项均不适用,但为保护计划参与者或潜在参与者的利益有必要发出指示。

(2)本条规定的指示可

(a)要求计划管理人停止发售或赎回,或停止发售和赎回计划项下的单位。

(b)要求计划管理人和受托人停止该计划。

(3)如授权令被撤销,则该撤销不影响依照本条规定发出、当时有效的指示。

(4)对授权令已被撤销的计划,如撤销时依照本条规定发出的指示已生效,则可就该计划依照本条规定发出指示。

(5)如某人违反依照本条规定发出的指示,则第150条规定适用于该违反要求的行为,等同于适用于该条规定所述违反行为。

(6)如管理局认为有下列情况,则可主动或应相关计划管理人或受托人申请,撤销或变更依照本条规定发出的指示:

(a)就撤销而言,指示不再有必要生效或继续有效;

(b)就变更而言,指示应以不同的形式生效或继续有效。

注释:

修改等(不涉及条文内容)

C282 第257条第(1)款于2001年12月1日依照制定法文件S.I.2001/2636第1条第(2)款第(b)项、第69条第(1)款;特立法文件2001/3538第2条第(1)款扩大适用范围。

C283 S. 257(1)(b) amended (temp. from 3.9.2001 to 1.12.2001) by S.I. 2001/2659, arts. 1(2), 3(7); S.I. 2001/3538, art. 2(1)

C284 S. 257(6) extended (1.12.2001) by S.I. 2001/2636, arts. 1(2)(b), 69(3); S.I. 2001/3538, art. 2(1)

Commencement Information

I77 S. 257 wholly in force at 1.12.2001; s. 257 not in force at Royal Assent see s. 431(2); s. 257 in force for specified purposes at 3.9.2001 by S.I. 2001/2632, art. 2(2), Sch. Pt. 2; s. 257 in force in so far as not already in force at 1.12.2001 by S.I. 2001/3538, art. 2(1)

258 Applications to the court.

(1) If the Authority could give a direction under section 257, it may also apply to the court for an order—

(a) removing the manager or the trustee, or both the manager and the trustee, of the scheme; and

(b) replacing the person or persons removed with a suitable person or persons nominated by the Authority.

(2) The Authority may nominate a person for the purposes of subsection (1)(b) only if it is satisfied that, if the order was made, the requirements of section 243(4) to (7) would be complied with.

(3) If it appears to the Authority that there is no person it can nominate for the purposes of subsection (1)(b), it may apply to the court for an orde—

(a) removing the manager or the trustee, or both the manager and the trustee, of the scheme; and

(b) appointing an authorised person to wind up the scheme.

(4) On an application under this section the court may make such order as it thinks fit.

(5) The court may, on the application of the Authority, rescind any such order as is mentioned in subsection (3) and substitute such an order as is mentioned in subsection (1).

(6) The Authority must give written notice of the making of an application under this section to the manager and trustee of the scheme concerned.

(7) The jurisdiction conferred by this section may be exercised by—

(a) the High Court;

(b) in Scotland, the Court of Session.

C283 第257条第(1)款第(b)项暂时有效,于2001年9月3日至2001年12月1日依照制定法文件S.I.2001/2659第1条第(2)款、第3条第(7)款;制定法文件S.I.2001/3538第2条第(1)款修正。

C284 第257条第(6)款于2001年12月1日依照制定法文件S.I.2001/2636第1条第(2)款第(b)项、第69条第(3)款;制定法文件S.I.2001/3538第2条第(1)款扩大适用范围。

实施日期

I77 第257条于2001年12月1日全部生效;第257条在副署时尚未生效,见第431条第(2)款;第257条为特定目的于2001年9月3日依照制定法文件S.I.2001/2632第2条第(2)款、附录第二部分生效;第257条如于2001年12月1日尚未生效,则依照制定法文件S.I.2001/3538第2条第(1)款生效。

第258条 向法院提出申请

(1)如管理局可以依照第257条发出指示,则亦可申请法院颁布法令

(a)罢免计划管理人或受托人职务,或罢免计划管理人和受托人;且

(b)将被罢免人更换为管理局提名的合适人选。

(2)为第(1)款第(b)项之目的,管理局仅在确信发出命令后第243条第(4)款至第(7)款的要求将得到遵守时,才可以提名人选。

(3)如管理局认为为第(1)款第(b)项之目的无人选提名,则可申请法院颁布法令

(a)罢免计划管理人或受托人,或罢免计划管理人和受托人;且

(b)指派获授权人终止计划。

(4)应当依照本条规定提出的申请,法院可以颁布其认为适当的命令。

(5)法院可以应管理局申请,撤销第(3)款所述任何命令,并以第(1)款所述命令代替。

(6)管理局必须将依照本条规定提出的申请书面通知相关计划的管理人和受托人。

(7)本条规定赋予的司法管辖权可由下列法院行使:

(a)高等法院;

(b)(苏格兰)高等民事法院。

259 Procedure on giving directions under section 257 and varying them on Authority's own initiative.

(1) A direction takes effect—

(a) immediately, if the notice given under subsection (3) states that that is the case;

(b) on such date as may be specified in the notice; or

(c) if no date is specified in the notice, when the matter to which it relates is no longer open to review.

(2) A direction may be expressed to take effect immediately (or on a specified date) only if the Authority, having regard to the ground on which it is exercising its power under section 257, considers that it is necessary for the direction to take effect immediately (or on that date).

(3) If the Authority proposes to give a direction under section 257, or gives such a direction with immediate effect, it must give separate written notice to the manager and the trustee of the scheme concerned.

(4) The notice must—

(a) give details of the direction;

(b) inform the person to whom it is given of when the direction takes effect;

(c) state the Authority's reasons for giving the direction and for its determination as to when the direction takes effect;

(d) inform the person to whom it is given that he may make representations to the Authority within such period as may be specified in it (whether or not he has referred the matter to the Tribunal); and

(e) inform him of his right to refer the matter to the Tribunal.

(5) If the direction imposes a requirement under section 257(2)(a), the notice must state that the requirement has effect until—

(a) a specified date; or

(b) a further direction.

(6) If the direction imposes a requirement under section 257(2)(b), the scheme must be wound up—

(a) by a date specified in the notice; or

(b) if no date is specified, as soon as practicable.

(7) The Authority may extend the period allowed under the notice for making representations.

(8) If, having considered any representations made by a person to whom the notice was given, the Authority decides—

(a) to give the direction in the way proposed, or

(b) if it has been given, not to revoke the direction,

第259条 依照第257条发出指令及管理局主动变更该指示的程序

(1)指示

(a)如依照第(3)款规定情况发出通知,则立即生效;

(b)于通知规定之日生效;或

(c)如通知未规定日期,则于该要求相关事项不再开放共审议时生效。

(2)只有管理局在考虑其依照第257条行使权力的理由后认为某项指示有必要立即生效(或在规定日期生效),才可以明示该指令立即生效(或在规定日期生效)。

(3)如管理局依照第257条规定发出指示,或使发出的指示立即生效,则必须向相关计划管理人和受托人另行发出书面通知。

(4)该通知必须

(a)详细说明该指示;

(b)告知被通知人该指示何时生效;

(c)说明管理局发出该指示以及决定其生效时间的理由;

(d)告知被通知人可在通知规定的期限内向管理局作出陈述(无论该事项是否已诉至裁判所);且

(e)告知被通知人有权将该事项诉至裁判所。

(5)如指示依照第257条第(2)款第(a)项规定提出要求,则该通知必须说明该要求有效期至

(a)规定日期;或

(b)发出进一步指示。

(6)如指示依照第257条第(2)款(b)项规定提出要求,则该计划必须

(a)于通知指定的日期前清算;或

(b)如未指定日期则尽早清算。

(7)管理局可以延长通知允许的陈述的期限。

(8)如管理局在考虑被通知人作出的任何陈述后决定

(a)以其计划的方式发出指示,或

(b)如已发出指示,决定不撤销该指示,

it must give separate written notice to the manager and the trustee of the scheme concerned.

(9) If, having considered any representations made by a person to whom the notice was given, the Authority decides—

(a) not to give the direction in the way proposed,

(b) to give the direction in a way other than that proposed, or

(c) to revoke a direction which has effect,

it must give separate written notice to the manager and the trustee of the scheme concerned.

(10) A notice given under subsection (8) must inform the person to whom it is given of his right to refer the matter to the Tribunal.

(11) A notice under subsection (9)(b) must comply with subsection (4).

(12) If a notice informs a person of his right to refer a matter to the Tribunal, it must give an indication of the procedure on such a reference.

(13) This section applies to the variation of a direction on the Authority's own initiative as it applies to the giving of a direction.

(14) For the purposes of subsection (1)(c), whether a matter is open to review is to be determined in accordance with section 391(8).

Annotations:

Commencement Information

I78 S. 259 wholly in force at 1.12.2001; s. 259 not in force at Royal Assent see s. 431 (2); s. 259 in force for specified purposes at 3.9.2001 by S.I. 2001/2632, art. 2(2), Sch. Pt. 2; s. 259 in force in so far as not already in force at 1.12.2001 by S.I. 2001/3538, art. 2(1)

260 Procedure: refusal to revoke or vary direction.

(1) If on an application under section 257(6) for a direction to be revoked or varied the Authority proposes—

(a) to vary the direction otherwise than in accordance with the application, or

(b) to refuse to revoke or vary the direction,

it must give the applicant a warning notice.

(2) If the Authority decides to refuse to revoke or vary the direction—

(a) it must give the applicant a decision notice; and

(b) the applicant may refer the matter to the Tribunal.

则必须向相关计划管理人和受托人另行发出书面通知。

(9)如管理局在考虑被通知人作出的任何陈述后决定

(a)不以其计划的方式发出指示,或
(b)以其他方式发出指示,或
(c)撤销生效的指示,
则必须向相关计划管理人和受托人另行发出书面通知。

(10)依照第(8)款发出的通知必须告知被通知人其有权将相关事项诉至裁判所。

(11)第(9)款第(b)项规定的通知必须符合第(4)款规定。

(12)如通知告知某人有权将相关事项诉至裁判所,则必须说明诉至裁判所的程序。

(13)本条规定适用于管理局主动变更指示,效力等同于对发出指示适用。

(14)为第(1)款第(c)项之目的,某一事项是否仍在审查中应当依照第391条第(8)款规定确定。

注释:

实施日期

I78 第259条于2001年12月1日全部生效;第259条在副署时尚未生效,见第431条第(2)款;第259条为特定目的于2001年9月3日依照制定法文件S.I.2001/2632第2条第(2)款、附录第二部分生效;第259条如于2001年12月1日尚未生效,则依照制定法文件S.I.2001/3538第2条第(1)款生效。

第260条 拒绝撤销或变更指令的程序

(1)如就依照第257条第(6)款规定提出的撤销或变更指示申请,管理局拟

(a)变更指示,但不根据申请进行变更,或
(b)拒绝撤销或变更指示,
则必须向申请人发出预告通知。
(2)如管理局决定拒绝撤销或变更指示,则
(a)必须向申请人发出决定通知;且
(b)申请人可将该事项诉至裁判所。

Annotations:

Commencement Information

I79 S. 260 wholly in force at 1.12.2001; s. 260 not in force at Royal Assent see s. 431(2); s. 260 in force for specified purposes at 3.9.2001 by S.I. 2001/2632, art. 2(2), Sch. Pt. 2; s. 260 in force in so far as not already in force at 1.12.2001 by S.I. 2001/3538, art. 2(1)

261 Procedure: revocation of direction and grant of request for variation.

(1) If the Authority decides on its own initiative to revoke a direction under section 257 it must give separate written notices of its decision to the manager and trustee of the scheme.

(2) If on an application under section 257(6) for a direction to be revoked or varied the Authority decides to revoke the direction or vary it in accordance with the application, it must give the applicant written notice of its decision.

(3) A notice under this section must specify the date on which the decision takes effect.

(4) The Authority may publish such information about the revocation or variation, in such way, as it considers appropriate.

Annotations:

Commencement Information

I80 S. 261 wholly in force at 1.12.2001; s. 261 not in force at Royal Assent see s. 431(2); s. 261 in force for specified purposes at 3.9.2001 by S.I. 2001/2632, art. 2 Sch. Pt. 2; s. 261 in force in so far as not already in force at 1.12.2001 by S.I. 2001/3538, art. 2(1)

CHAPTER Ⅳ OPEN-ENDED INVESTMENT COMPANIES

262 Open-ended investment companies.

(1) The Treasury may by regulations make provision for—

(a) facilitating the carrying on of collective investment by means of open-ended investment companies;

(b) regulating such companies.

(2) The regulations may, in particular, make provision—

(a) for the incorporation and registration in Great Britain of bodies corporate;

(b) for a body incorporated by virtue of the regulations to take such form as may be determined in accordance with the regulations;

(c) as to the purposes for which such a body may exist, the investments which it may issue and otherwise as to its constitution;

(d) as to the management and operation of such a body and the management of its

注释：

实施日期

I79　第260条于2001年12月1日全部生效；第260条在副署时尚未生效，见第431条第(2)款；第260条为特定目的于2001年9月3日依照制定法文件S.I.2001/2632第2条第(2)款、附录第二部分生效；第260条如于2001年12月1日尚未生效，则依照制定法文件S.I.2001/3538第2条第(1)款生效。

第261条　撤销指示和同意变更指示请求的程序

(1)如管理局拟依照第257条规定主动撤销指示，则必须向该计划的管理人和受托人另行发出书面通知。

(2)如应依照第257条第(6)款提出的撤销或变更指令申请，管理局决定撤销该指令或根据申请变更该指令，则管理局必须就其决定向申请人发出书面申请。

(3)依照本条规定发出的通知必须指定决定生效日期。

(4)管理局可以其认为适当的方式公布撤销或变更相关信息。

注释：

实施日期

I80　第261条于2001年12月1日全部生效；第261条在副署时尚未生效，见第431条第(2)款；第261条为特定目的于2001年9月3日依照制定法文件S.I.2001/2632第2条、附录第二部分生效；第261条如于2001年12月1日尚未生效，则依照制定法文件S.I.2001/3538第2条第(1)款生效。

第四章　开放式投资公司

第262条　开放式投资公司

(1)财政部可以为下列目的制定法规：

(a)促进以开放式投资公司方式进行集合投资；

(b)监管开放式投资公司。

(2)法规特别规定

(a)法人在联合王国的设立及登记；

(b)因该法规而设立的机构采取依照该法规确定的形式；

(c)该等机构存续的目的、可进行的投资及其组织制度；

(d)该等机构的管理和运营以及财产管理；

property;

(e) as to the powers, duties, rights and liabilities of such a body and of other persons, including—

(i) the directors or sole director of such a body;

(ii) its depositary (if any);

(iii) its shareholders, and persons who hold the beneficial title to shares in it without holding the legal title;

(iv) its auditor; and

(v) any persons who act or purport to act on its behalf;

(f) as to the merger of one or more such bodies and the division of such a body;

(g) for the appointment and removal of an auditor for such a body;

(h) as to the winding up and dissolution of such a body;

(i) for such a body, or any director or depositary of such a body, to be required to comply with directions given by the Authority;

(j) enabling the Authority to apply to a court for an order removing and replacing any director or depositary of such a body;

(k) for the carrying out of investigations by persons appointed by the Authority or the Secretary of State;

(l) corresponding to any provision made in relation to unit trust schemes by Chapter Ⅲ of this Part.

(3) Regulations under this section may—

(a) impose criminal liability;

(b) confer functions on the Authority;

(c) in the case of provision made by virtue of subsection (2)(l), authorise the making of rules by the Authority;

(d) confer jurisdiction on any court or on the Tribunal;

(e) provide for fees to be charged by the Authority in connection with the carrying out of any of its functions under the regulations (including fees payable on a periodical basis);

(f) modify, exclude or apply (with or without modifications) any primary or subordinate legislation (including any provision of, or made under, this Act);

(g) make consequential amendments, repeals and revocations of any such legislation;

(h) modify or exclude any rule of law.

(4) The provision that may be made by virtue of subsection (3)(f) includes provision extending or adapting any power to make subordinate legislation.

(5) Regulations under this section may, in particular—

(a) revoke the[M38] Open-Ended Investment Companies (Investment Companies with Variable Capital) Regulations 1996; and (e)该等机构和下列其他人的权力、职责、权利和责任：

(i)该等机构的董事或唯一董事；
(ii)其托管人(如有)；
(iii)其股东以及对其股份享有收益权但无法定所有权的持有人；

(iv)其审计人；以及
(v)代表或意图代表其行事的任何人。
(f)一个或多个该等机构的合并和分立；
(g)该等机构审计人的任免；
(h)该等机构的清算和解散；
(i)要求该等机构或其任何董事或托管人遵守管理局发出的指示；

(j)使管理局能够向法院申请撤换该等机构任何董事或托管人的命令；

(k)由管理局或国务大臣任命的人员进行调查；

(l)对应本部分第三章作出的任何有关单位信托计划的规定。

(3)依照本条制定的法规可以
(a)规定刑事责任；
(b)对管理局赋予职能；
(c)在依照第(2)款第(l)项制定规定的情况下，授权管理局制定规则；

(d)对任何法院或裁判所赋予管辖权；
(e)规定管理局就依照该法规履行的任何职能所收取的费用(包括应定期支付的费用)；
(f)修改、排除或适用(不论有否修订)任何主要或附属立法(包括本法任何规定或依照本法制定的任何规定)；
(g)对任何上述立法作出相应修订、废除和撤销；
(h)修改或排除任何法律规则。
(4)可以依照第(3)款第(f)项作出的规定包括规定延长或修改任何附属立法的制定权。
(5)依照本条制定的法规可以特别
(a)撤销[M38]《1996年开放式投资公司(可变资本投资公司)条例》；并

(b) provide for things done under or in accordance with those regulations to be treated as if they had been done under or in accordance with regulations under this section.

Annotations:

Marginal Citations

M38 S.I. 1996/2827.

263 Amendment of section 716 Companies Act 1985.

In section 716(1) of the [M39] Companies Act 1985 (prohibition on formation of companies with more than 20 members unless registered under the Act etc.), after "this Act," insert " is incorporated by virtue of regulations made under section 262 of the Financial Services and Markets Act 2000".

Annotations:

Marginal Citations

M39 1985 c. 6.

CHAPTER V RECOGNISED OVERSEAS SCHEMES

Schemes constituted in other EEA States

264 Schemes constituted in other EEA States.

(1) A collective investment scheme constituted in another EEA State is a recognized scheme if—

(a) it satisfies such requirements as are prescribed for the purposes of this section; and

(b) not less than two months before inviting persons in the United Kingdom to become participants in the scheme, the operator of the scheme gives notice to the Authority of his intention to do so, specifying the way in which the invitation is to be made.

(2) But this section does not make the scheme a recognised scheme if within two months of receiving the notice under subsection (1) the Authority notifies—

(a) the operator of the scheme, and

(b) the authorities of the State in question who are responsible for the authorization of collective investment schemes,

that the way in which the invitation is to be made does not comply with the law in force in the United Kingdom.

(3) The notice to be given to the Authority under subsection (1)—

(a) must be accompanied by a certificate from the authorities mentioned in subsection (2)(b) to the effect that the scheme complies with the conditions necessary for it to enjoy the rights conferred by any relevant Community instrument;

(b)规定依照上述条例实施的行为,视为依照本条规定的法规实施的行为。

注释:

附注引文

M38　制定法文件S.I.1996/2827。

第263条　修订《1985年公司法》第716条

[M39]《1985年公司法》第716条第(1)款(除依照本法登记外禁止成立成员超过20个的公司等)"本法"后插入"因依照《2000年金融服务与市场法》第262条规定制定的法规而设立"。

注释:

附注引文

M39　1985年本法第6条。

第五章　获认可的境外计划

欧洲经济区其他国家建立的计划

第264条　欧洲经济区其他国家建立的计划

(1) 欧洲经济区其他国家建立的集合投资计划如符合下列条件则为获认可的计划:

(a)符合为本条之目的而规定的要求;且

(b)计划管理人在邀请联合王国人参与该计划前至少2个月向管理局发出通知,告知该意图并说明邀请方式。

(2)但如管理局在收到第(1)款规定的通知后2个月内发出下列通知,则本条不能使该计划成为获认可的计划:

(a)通知计划管理人,并

(b)通知负责集合投资计划授权的相关国家机关,

邀请方式不符合联合王国现行法律规定。

(3)依照第(1)款规定向管理局发出的通知

(a)必须附有第(2)款第(b)项所述机关签发的证明书,足以证明该计划符合享有任何相关共同体法律文件赋予的权利所需要具备的条件。

(b) must contain the address of a place in the United Kingdom for the service on the operator of notices or other documents required or authorised to be served on him under this Act; and

(c) must contain or be accompanied by such other information and documents as may be prescribed.

(4) A notice given by the Authority under subsection (2) must—

(a) give the reasons for which the Authority considers that the law in force in the United Kingdom will not be complied with; and

(b) specify a reasonable period (which may not be less than 28 days) within which any person to whom it is given may make representations to the Authority.

(5) For the purposes of this section a collective investment scheme is constituted in another EEA State if—

(a) it is constituted under the law of that State by a contract or under a trust and is managed by a body corporate incorporated under that law; or

(b) it takes the form of an open-ended investment company incorporated under that law.

(6) The operator of a recognised scheme may give written notice to the Authority that he desires the scheme to be no longer recognised by virtue of this section.

(7) On the giving of notice under subsection (6), the scheme ceases to be arecognized scheme.

Annotations:

Modifications etc. (not altering text)

C285 S. 264 extended (1.12.2001) by S.I. 2001/2636, arts. 1(2)(b), 66(1); S.I. 2001/3538, art. 2(1)

C286 S. 264(1)(b) extended (1.12.2001) by S.I. 2001/3592, arts. 1(2), 42(1) (with art. 23(2))

C287 S. 264(2) modified (1.12.2001) by S.I. 2001/3592, arts. 1(2), 42(4) (with art. 23(2))

S. 264(2) amended (temp. from 3.9.2001 to 1.12.2001) by S.I. 2001/2659, arts. 1(2), 3(8); S.I. 2001/3538, art. 2(1)

Commencement Information

I81 S. 264 wholly in force at 1.12.2001; s. 264 not in force at Royal Assent see s. 431(2); s. 264(1)(3)(c) in force for certain purposes at 25.2.2001 by S.I. 2001/516, art. 2(b), Sch. Pt. 2; s. 264 in force for specified purposes at 3.9.2001 by S.I. 2001/2632, art. 2(2), Sch. Pt. 2; s. 264 in force in so far as not already in force at 1.12.2001 by S.I. 2001/3538, art. 2(1) (b)必须载有一处联合王国地址,作为向管理人送达通知或本法规定要求或授权送达的其他文件的地址;且

(c)必须包含或附有规定的其他信息和文件。

(4)管理局依照第(2)款规定发出的通知必须

(a)说明管理局认为不符合联合王国现行法律的理由;且

(b)规定任何被通知人可向管理局作出陈述的合理期限(不得少于28日)。

(5)就本条而言,符合下列条件的集合投资计划为欧洲经济区其他国家建立的集合投资计划:

(a)依照该国法律通过合同或信托建立,并由根据该法设立的法人管理;或

(b)采取依照该法设立的开放式投资公司形式。

(6)获认可的计划的管理人可向管理局发出书面通知,说明其希望该计划不再依照本条规定为获认可的计划。

(7)依照第(6)款规定发出通知时起,该计划不再为获认可的计划。

注释:

修改等(不涉及条文内容)

C285 第264条于2001年12月1日依照制定法文件S.I.2001/2636第1条第(2)款第(b)项、第66条第(1)款;制定法文件S.I.2001/3538第2条第(1)款扩大适用范围。

C286 第264条第(1)款第(b)项于2001年12月1日依照制定法文件S.I.2001/3592第1条第(2)款、第42条第(1)款[与第23条第(2)款]扩大适用范围。

C287 第264条第(2)款于2001年12月1日依照制定法文件S.I.2001/3592第1条第(2)款、第42条第(4)款[与第23条第(2)款]修订。

第264条第(2)款暂定于2001年9月3日至2001年12月1日依照制定法文件S.I.2001/2659第1条第(2)款、第3条第(8)款;制定法文件S.I.2001/3538第2条第(1)款修正。

实施日期

I81 第264条于2001年12月1日全部生效;第264条在副署时尚未生效,见第431条第(2)款;第264条第(1)款、第(3)款第(c)项为特定目的于2001年2月25日依照制定法文件S.I.2001/516第2条第(b)款、附录第二部分生效;第264条为特定目的于2001年9月3日依照制定法文件S.I.2001/1820第2条第(2)款、附录第二部分生效;第264条如于2001年12月1日尚未生效,则依照制定法文件S.I.2001/3538第2条第(1)款生效。

265 Representations and references to the Tribunal.

(1) This section applies if any representations are made to the Authority, before the period for making representations has ended, by a person to whom a notice was given by the Authority under section 264(2).

(2) The Authority must, within a reasonable period, decide in the light of those representations whether or not to withdraw its notice.

(3) If the Authority withdraws its notice the scheme is a recognised scheme from the date on which the notice is withdrawn.

(4) If the Authority decides not to withdraw its notice, it must give a decision notice to each person to whom the notice under section 264(2) was given.

(5) The operator of the scheme to whom the decision notice is given may refer the matter to the Tribunal.

Annotations:

Commencement Information

I82 S. 265 wholly in force at 1.12.2001; s. 265 not in force at Royal Assent see s. 431(2); s. 265 (except subsection (3)) in force at 3.9.2001 by S.I. 2001/2632, art. 2(2), Sch. Pt. 2; s. 265 in force in so far as not already in force at 1.12.2001 by S.I. 2001/3538, art. 2(1)

266 Disapplication of rules.

(1) Apart from—

(a) financial promotion rules, and

(b) rules under section 283(1),

rules made by the Authority under this Act do not apply to the operator, trustee or depositary of a scheme in relation to the carrying on by him of regulated activities for which he has permission in that capacity.

(2) "Scheme" means a scheme which is a recognised scheme by virtue of section 264.

267 Power of Authority to suspend promotion of scheme.

(1) Subsection (2) applies if it appears to the Authority that the operator of a scheme has communicated an invitation or inducement in relation to the scheme in a manner contrary to financial promotion rules.

(2) The Authority may direct that—

(a) the exemption from subsection (1) of section 238 provided bysubsection (4)(c) of that section is not to apply in relation to the scheme; and

(b) subsection (5) of that section does not apply with respect to things done in relation to the scheme.

(3) A direction under subsection (2) has effect—

第265条 陈述和诉至裁判所

(1)如管理局依照第264条第(2)款发出通知,被通知人在陈述期间届满前向管理局作出陈述,则适用本条规定。

(2)管理局必须在一段合理期间内根据陈述决定是否撤回通知。

(3)如管理局撤回通知,则该计划自通知撤回之日起为获认可的计划。

(4)如管理局决定不撤回通知,则必须向第264条第(2)款通知的每个被通知人发出决定通知。

(5)收到决定通知的计划管理人可将该事项诉至裁判所。

注释:

实施日期

I82 第265条于2001年12月1日全部生效;第265条在副署时尚未生效,见第431条第(2)款;第265条[除第(3)款外]于2001年9月3日依照制定法文件S.I.2001/2632第2条第(2)款、附录第二部分生效;第265条如于2001年12月1日尚未生效,则依照制定法文S.I. 2001/3538第2条第(1)款生效。

第266条 规则适用排除

(1)除下列规则外:

(a)金融推介规则,以及

(b)第283条第(1)款规定的规则,

管理局依照本法制定的规则不适用于计划执行人、受托人或托管人开展其以管理人、受托人或托管人身份获得许可的受监管活动。

(2)"获认可的计划"系指依照第264条规定获认可的计划。

第267条 管理局暂停计划推介的权力

(1) 如管理局认为计划管理人以违反金融推介规则的方式就该计划传播邀请或诱导,则适用第(2)款规定。

(2)管理局可以指示

(a)第(4)款第(c)项关于免于遵守第238条第(1)款的规定不适用于该计划;且

(b)该条第(5)款规定不适用于有关该计划的事项。

(3)第(2)款规定的指示

(a) for a specified period;

(b) until the occurrence of a specified event; or

(c) until specified conditions are complied with.

(4) The Authority may, either on its own initiative or on the application of the operator of the scheme concerned, vary a direction given under subsection (2) if it appears to the Authority that the direction should take effect or continue in force in a different form.

(5) The Authority may, either on its own initiative or on the application of the operator of the recognised scheme concerned, revoke a direction given under subsection (2) if it appears to the Authority—

(a) that the conditions specified in the direction have been complied with; or

(b) that it is no longer necessary for the direction to take effect or continue in force.

(6) If an event is specified, the direction ceases to have effect (unless revoked earlier) on the occurrence of that event.

(7) For the purposes of this section and sections 268 and 269—

(a) the scheme's home State is the EEA State in which the scheme is constituted (within the meaning given by section 264);

(b) the competent authorities in the scheme's home State are the authorities in that State who are responsible for the authorisation of collective investment schemes.

(8) "Scheme" means a scheme which is a recognised scheme by virtue of section 264.

(9) "Specified", in relation to a direction, means specified in it.

268 Procedure on giving directions under section 267 and varying them on Authority's own initiative.

(1) A direction under section 267 takes effect—

(a) immediately, if the notice given under subsection (3)(a) states that that is the case;

(b) on such date as may be specified in the notice; or

(c) if no date is specified in the notice, when the matter to which it relates is no longer open to review.

(2) A direction may be expressed to take effect immediately (or on a specified date) only if the Authority, having regard to its reasons for exercising its power under section 267, considers that it is necessary for the direction to take effect immediately (or on that date).

(3) If the Authority proposes to give a direction under section 267, or gives such a direction with immediate effect, it must—

(a) give the operator of the scheme concerned written notice; and

(b) inform the competent authorities in the scheme's home State of its proposal or (as the case may be) of the direction.

(4) The notice must—

(a) give details of the direction;

(a)在规定期间有效;
(b)效力至发生通知规定的事件为止;或
(c)效力至符合通知规定的条件为止。
(4)管理局如认为依照第(2)款规定发出的指示应以不同的方式生效或继续有效,则可主动或应相关计划管理人申请变更该指示。
(5)如管理局认为有下列情况,则可以主动或应相关获认可的计划的管理人申请撤销依照第(2)款规定发出的指示:
(a)指示中规定的条件已满足;或
(b)指示不再有必要生效或继续有效;
(6)如指示规定了事件,则该指示于该事件发生时不再具有效力(除非已提前撤销)。
(7)为本条及第268条、第269条之目的
(a)计划母国为建立该计划的欧洲经济区国家(定义见第264条);
(b)计划母国主管机关为该国负责集合投资计划授权的机关。
(8)"计划",系指依照第264规定获认可的计划。
(9)"规定",就指示而言,系指该指示中规定。

第268条　依照第267条发出指示及管理局主动变更该指示的程序

(1)第267条规定的指示
(a)如果依照第(3)款第(a)项规定情况发出通知,则立即生效;
(b)于通知规定之日生效;或
(c)如通知未规定日期,则于该通知相关事项不再开放供审议时生效。
(2)只有管理局在考虑其依照第267条行使权力的理由后认为某项指示有必要立即生效(或在规定日期生效),才可以明示该指示立即生效(或在指定日期生效)。
(3)如管理局拟依照第267条规定发出指示,或使该类指示立即生效,则必须
(a)向相关计划管理人发出书面通知;并
(b)将发出指令的计划或发出的指示(视情况而定)告知计划母国主管机关。
(4)该通知必须
(a)详细说明该指示;

(b) inform the operator of when the direction takes effect;

(c) state the Authority's reasons for giving the direction and for its determination as to when the direction takes effect;

(d) inform the operator that he may make representations to the Authority within such period as may be specified in it (whether or not he has referred the matter to the Tribunal); and

(e) inform him of his right to refer the matter to the Tribunal.

(5) The Authority may extend the period allowed under the notice for making representations.

(6) Subsection (7) applies if, having considered any representations made by the operator, the Authority decides—

(a) to give the direction in the way proposed, or

(b) if it has been given, not to revoke the direction.

(7) The Authority must—

(a) give the operator of the scheme concerned written notice; and

(b) inform the competent authorities in the scheme's home State of the direction.

(8) Subsection (9) applies if, having considered any representations made by a person to whom the notice was given, the Authority decides—

(a) not to give the direction in the way proposed,

(b) to give the direction in a way other than that proposed, or

(c) to revoke a direction which has effect.

(9) The Authority must—

(a) give the operator of the scheme concerned written notice; and

(b) inform the competent authorities in the scheme's home State of its decision.

(10) A notice given under subsection (7)(a) must inform the operator of his right to refer the matter to the Tribunal.

(11) A notice under subsection (9)(a) given as a result of subsection (8)(b) must comply with subsection (4).

(12) If a notice informs a person of his right to refer a matter to the Tribunal, it must give an indication of the procedure on such a reference.

(13) This section applies to the variation of a direction on the Authority's own initiative as it applies to the giving of a direction.

(14) For the purposes of subsection (1)(c), whether a matter is open to review is to be determined in accordance with section 391(8).

269 Procedure on application for variation or revocation of direction.

(1) If, on an application under subsection (4) or (5) of section 267, the Authority proposes—

(a) to vary a direction otherwise than in accordance with the application, or (b)告知管理人该指示何时生效;

(c)说明管理局发出该指示以及决定其何时生效的理由;

(d)告知管理人可在通知规定的期限内向管理局作出陈述(无论该事项是否已诉至裁判所);且

(e)告知管理人有权将该事项诉至裁判所。

(5)管理局可以延长通知规定允许陈述的期限。

(6)如管理局在考虑管理人作出的任何陈述后作出下列决定,则适用第(7)款规定:

(a)以其计划的方式发出指示,或

(b)如已发出指示,决定不撤销该指示。

(7)管理局必须

(a)向相关计划管理人发出书面通知;并

(b)将该指示告知计划母国主管机关。

(8)如管理局在考虑被通知人作出的任何陈述后作出下列决定,则适用第(9)款规定:

(a)不以其计划的方式发出指示,

(b)以其他方式发出指示,或

(c)撤销生效指示。

(9)管理局必须

(a)向相关计划管理人发出书面通知;并

(b)将该指示告知计划母国主管机关。

(10)依照第(7)款第(a)项发出的通知必须告知管理人其有权将该事项诉至裁判所。

(11)第(9)款第(a)项规定的因第(8)款第(b)项发出的通知必须符合第(4)款规定。

(12)如通知告知被通知人有权将相关事项诉至裁判所,则必须说明诉至裁判所的程序。

(13)本条规定适用于管理局主动变更指示,等同于适用于发出指示。

(14)为第(1)款第(c)项之目的,某一事项是否仍开放共审议应当依照第391条第(8)款规定确定。

第269条　应申请变更或撤销指示的程序

(1)如就依照第267条第(4)款或第(5)款规定提出的撤销或变更指示申请,管理局拟

(a)变更指示,但不根据申请进行变更,或

(b) to refuse the application,

it must give the operator of the scheme concerned a warning notice.

(2) If, on such an application, the Authority decides—

(a) to vary a direction otherwise than in accordance with the application, or

(b) to refuse the application,

it must give the operator of the scheme concerned a decision notice.

(3) If the application is refused, the operator of the scheme may refer the matter to the Tribunal.

(4) If, on such an application, the Authority decides to grant the application it must give the operator of the scheme concerned written notice.

(5) If the Authority decides on its own initiative to revoke a direction given under section 267 it must give the operator of the scheme concerned written notice.

(6) The Authority must inform the competent authorities in the scheme's home State of any notice given under this section.

Schemes authorised in designated countries or territories

270 Schemes authorised in designated countries or territories.

(1) A collective investment scheme which is not a recognised scheme by virtue of section 264 but is managed in, and authorised under the law of, a country or territory outside the United Kingdom is a recognised scheme if—

(a) that country or territory is designated for the purposes of this section by an order made by the Treasury;

(b) the scheme is of a class specified by the order;

(c) the operator of the scheme has given written notice to the Authority that he wishes it to be recognised; and

(d) either—

(i) the Authority, by written notice, has given its approval to the scheme's being recognised; or

(ii) two months, beginning with the date on which notice was given under paragraph (c), have expired without the operator receiving a warning notice from the Authority under section 271.

(2) The Treasury may not make an order designating any country or territory for the purposes of this section unless satisfied—

(a) that the law and practice under which relevant collective investment schemes are authorised and supervised in that country or territory affords to investors in the United Kingdom protection at least equivalent to that provided for them by or under this Part in the case of comparable authorised schemes; and (b)驳回该申请,

则必须向相关计划管理人发出预告通知。

(2)如管理局就该申请决定

(a)变更指示,但不根据申请进行变更,或

(b)驳回该申请,

则必须向相关计划管理人发出决定通知。

(3)如申请被驳回,则计划管理人可将该事项提交裁判所裁决。

(4)如管理局决定批准该申请,则必须向相关计划管理人发出书面通知。

(5)如管理局拟依照第267条规定主动撤销指令,则必须向该计划的管理人和受托人另行发出书面通知。

(6)管理局必须将依照本条发出的任何通知告知计划母国主管机关。

在规定国家或地区取得授权的计划

第270条　在规定国家或地区取得授权的计划

(1)集合投资计划不属于依照第264条规定获认可的计划,但依照联合王国以外的国家或地区法律管理并获授权的,如符合下列条件则为获认可的计划:

(a)该国家或地区为财政部为本条颁布法令之目的所规定的国家或地区;

(b)该计划属于该命令规定的类别;

(c)该计划管理人已向管理局发出书面通知,说明其希望计划获得认可;且

(d)下列任何一种情况:

(i)管理局以书面通知形式批准认可该计划;或

(ii)自依照第(c)项发出通知之日起2个月内,管理人未收到管理局依照第271条发出的预告通知。

(2)除非财政部确信有下列情况,否则不得为本条颁布法令之目的规定任何国家或地区:

(a)该国或该地区相关集合投资计划获授权和受监督依据的法律和惯例为联合王国投资者提供的保护,至少等同于本部分规定在类似获授权计划中为其提供的保护;且

(b) that adequate arrangements exist, or will exist, for co-operation between the authorities of the country or territory responsible for the authorisation and supervision of relevant collective investment schemes and the Authority.

(3) "Relevant collective investment schemes" means collective investment schemes of the class or classes to be specified by the order.

(4) "Comparable authorised schemes" means whichever of the following the Treasury consider to be the most appropriate, having regard to the class or classes of scheme to be specified by the order—

(a) authorised unit trust schemes;

(b) authorised open-ended investment companies;

(c) both such unit trust schemes and such companies.

(5) If the Treasury are considering whether to make an order designating a country or territory for the purposes of this section—

(a) the Treasury must ask the Authority for a report—

(i) on the law and practice of that country or territory in relation to the authorisation and supervision of relevant collective investment schemes,

(ii) on any existing or proposed arrangements for co-operation between it and the authorities responsible in that country or territory for the authorisation and supervision of relevant collective investment schemes,having regard to the Treasury's need to be satisfied as mentioned in subsection (2);

(b) the Authority must provide the Treasury with such a report; and

(c) the Treasury must have regard to it in deciding whether to make the order.

(6) The notice to be given by the operator under subsection (1)(c)—

(a) must contain the address of a place in the United Kingdom for the service on the operator of notices or other documents required or authorised to be served on him under this Act; and

(b) must contain or be accompanied by such information and documents as may be specified by the Authority.

Annotations:

Modifications etc. (not altering text)

C288 S. 270 extended (1.12.2001) by S.I. 2001/2636, arts. 1(2)(b), 67(2); S.I. 2001/3538, art. 2(1)

C289 S. 270(1) extended (1.12.2001) by S.I. 2001/2636, arts. 1(2)(b), 67(1); S.I. 2001/3538, art. 2(1)

C290 S. 270(1)(c) extended (1.12.2001) by S.I. 2001/3592, arts. 1(2), 43(1) (with art. 23(2)) (b)有或将有足够的安排,使该国或该地区负责相关集合投资计划授权和监督的机构能够与管理局合作。

(3)“相关集合投资计划”,系指属于法令规定种类的集合投资计划。

(4)“类似获授权计划”,系指下列各项中财政部考虑法令规定种类后认为最适当的一项:

(a)获授权单位信托计划;
(b)获授权开放式投资公司;
(c)上述单位信托计划和上述开放式投资公司。
(5)如财政部考虑是否为实施本条颁布法令规定任何国家或地区,则

(a)财政部必须要求管理局就下列事项提供报告:
(i)该国或该地区与相关集合投资计划授权和监督有关的法律和惯例,

(ii)使该国或该地区负责相关集合投资计划授权和监督的机构能够与管理局合作的任何现存或拟行安排。且应考虑到财政部确信第(2)款所述情况的需要;

(b)管理局必须向财政部提供上述报告;且
(c)财政部必须在决定是否颁布法令时对该报告予以考虑。
(6)管理人依照第(1)款第(c)项规定发出的通知
(a)必须包含一处联合王国地址,作为向管理人送达通知或本法要求或获准送达的其他文件的地址;且

(b)必须包含或附有管理局规定的其他信息和文件。

注释:

修改等(不涉及条文内容)

C288　第270条第(1)款于2001年12月1日依照制定法文件S.I.2001/2636第1条第(2)款第(b)项、第67条第(2)款;制定法文件S.I.2001/3538第2条第(1)款扩大适用范围。

C289　第270条第(1)款于2001年12月1日依照制定法文件S.I.2001/2636第1条第(2)款第(b)项、第67条第(1)款;制定法文件S.I.2001/3538第2条第(1)款扩大适用范围。

C290　第270条第(1)款第(c)项于2001年12月1日依照制定法文件S.I.2001/3592第1条第(2)款、第43条第(1)款[与第23条第(2)款]扩大适用范围。

Commencement Information

I83 S. 270 wholly in force at 1.12.2001; s. 270 not in force at Royal Assent see s. 431 (2); s. 270 in force for certain purposes at 25.2.2001 by S.I. 2001/516, art. 2(b), Sch. Pt. 2; s. 270 in force for specified purposes at 3.9.2001 by S.I. 2001/2632, art. 2(2), Sch. Pt. 2; s. 270 in force in so far as not already in force at 1.12.2001 by S.I. 2001/3538, art. 2(1)

271 Procedure.

(1) If the Authority proposes to refuse approval of a scheme's being a recognised scheme by virtue of section 270, it must give the operator of the scheme a warning notice.

(2) To be valid the warning notice must be received by the operator before the end of two months beginning with the date on which notice was given under section 270(1)(c).

(3) If, having given a warning notice, the Authority decides to refuse approval—

(a) it must give the operator of the scheme a decision notice; and

(b) the operator may refer the matter to the Tribunal.

Annotations:

Modifications etc. (not altering text)

C291 S. 271(2) modified (1.12.2001) by S.I. 2001/3592, arts. 1(2), 43(4) (with art. 23(2))

Commencement Information

I84 S. 271 wholly in force at 1.12.2001; s. 271 not in force at Royal Assent see s. 431 (2); s. 271(except subsection (2)) in force for specified purposes at 3.9.2001 by S.I. 2001/2632, art. 2 (2), Sch. Pt. 2; s. 271 in force in so far as not already in force at 1.12.2001 by S.I. 2001/3538, art. 2(1)

Individually recognised overseas schemes

272 Individually recognised overseas schemes.

(1) The Authority may, on the application of the operator of a collective investment scheme which—

(a) is managed in a country or territory outside the United Kingdom,

(b) does not satisfy the requirements prescribed for the purposes of section 264,

(c) is not managed in a country or territory designated for the purposes of section 270 or, if it is so managed, is of a class not specified by the designation order, and

(d) appears to the Authority to satisfy the requirements set out in the following provisions of this section,make an order declaring the scheme to be a recognised scheme.

(2) Adequate protection must be afforded to participants in the scheme.

实施日期

I83　第270条于2001年12月1日全部生效；第270条在副署时尚未生效，见第431条第(2)款；第270条为特定目的于2001年2月25日依照制定法文件S.I.2001/516第2条第(b)项、附录第二部分生效；第270条为特定目的于2001年9月3日依照制定法文件S.I.2001/2632第2条第(2)款、附录第二部分生效；第270条如于2001年12月1日尚未生效，则依照制定法文件S.I.2001/3538第2条第(1)款生效。

第271条　程序

(1)如管理局拟拒绝批准计划成为第270条规定的获认可计划，则必须对该计划管理人发出预告通知。

(2)管理人必须于拟依照第270条第(1)款第(c)项规定发出通知之日起2个月内收到预告通知，该通知方为有效。

(3)如管理局发出预告通知后决定拒绝批准，则

(a)管理局必须向计划管理人发出决定通知；且

(b)管理人可以将该事项诉至裁判所。

注释：

修改等(不涉及条文内容)

C291　第271条第(2)款于2001年12月1日依照制定法文件S.I.2001/3592第1条第(2)款、第43条第(4)款[与第23条第(2)款]修订。

实施日期

I84　第271条于2001年12月1日全部生效；第271条在副署时尚未生效，见第431条第(2)款；第271条[除第(2)款外]为规定目的于2001年9月3日依照制定法文件S.I.2001/2632第2条第(2)款、附录第二部分生效；第271条如于2001年12月1日尚未生效，则依照制定法文件S.I.2001/3538第2条第(1)款生效。

单独认可的境外计划

第272条　单独认可的境外计划

(1)管理局可以应符合下列条件的集合投资计划的管理人申请颁布法令，宣布该计划为获认可的计划：

(a)在联合王国以外的国家或地区管理，

(b)不符合为第264条之目的而规定的要求，

(c)不在为第270条之目的而指定的国家或地区管理，或者如在上述国家或地区管理，不属于指定命令中规定的种类，且

(d)管理局认为符合本条下列规定所提出的要求。

(2)必须给予计划参与者足够的保护。

(3) The arrangements for the scheme's constitution and management must be adequate.

(4) The powers and duties of the operator and, if the scheme hasa trustee or depositary, of the trustee or depositary must be adequate.

(5) In deciding whether the matters mentioned in subsection (3) or (4) are adequate, the Authority must have regard to—

(a) any rule of law, and

(b) any matters which are, or could be, the subject of rules,applicable in relation to comparable authorised schemes.

(6) "Comparable authorised schemes" means whichever of the following the Authority considers the most appropriate, having regard to the nature of scheme in respect of which the application is made—

(a) authorised unit trust schemes;

(b) authorised open-ended investment companies;

(c) both such unit trust schemes and such companies.

(7) The scheme must take the form of an open-ended investment company or (if it does not take that form) the operator must be a body corporate.

(8) The operator of the scheme must—

(a) if an authorised person, have permission to act as operator;

(b) if not an authorised person, be a fit and proper person to act as operator.

(9) The trustee or depositary (if any) of the scheme must—

(a) if an authorised person, have permission to act as trustee or depositary;

(b) if not an authorised person, be a fit and proper person to act as trustee or depositary.

(10) The operator and the trustee or depositary (if any) of the scheme must be able and willing to co-operate with the Authority by the sharing of information and in other ways.

(11) The name of the scheme must not be undesirable or misleading.

(12) The purposes of the scheme must be reasonably capable of being successfully carried into effect.

(13) The participants must be entitled to have their units redeemed in accordance with the scheme at a price related to the net value of the property to which the units relate and determined in accordance with the scheme.

(14) But a scheme is to be treated as complying with subsection (13) if it requires the operator to ensure that a participant is able to sell his units on an investment exchange at a price not significantly different from that mentioned in that subsection.

(15) Subsection (13) is not to be read as imposing a requirement that the participants must be entitled to have their units redeemed (or sold as mentioned in subsection (14)) immediately following a demand to that effect.

(3)有关计划组织制度和管理的安排必须充分。

(4)执行人的权力和职责必须充分，如该计划有受托人或托管人，则受托人或托管人的权力和职责也必须充分。

(5)管理局在决定第(3)款或第(4)款所述事项是否充分时必须考虑适用于相当于获授权计划的

(a)任何法律规则，以及

(b)是或可能是规则规范对象的任何事项，

(6)"相当于获授权计划"，系指下列各项中财政部在考虑申请相关计划的性质后认为最适当的一项：

(a)获授权单位信托计划；

(b)获授权开放式投资公司；

(c)上述单位信托计划和上述开放式投资公司。

(7)该计划必须采取开放式投资公司形式，或(如未采取该形式)其执行人必须为法人。

(8)计划执行人

(a)如为获授权人，则必须取得担任执行人的许可；

(b)如为非获授权人，则必须为担任执行人的适当人选；

(9)计划受托人或托管人(如有)

(a)如为获授权人，则必须取得担任受托人或托管人的许可；

(b)如为非获授权人，则为担任受托人或托管人的适当人选；

(10)计划执行人和受托人或托管人(如有)必须能够并愿意通过信息共享及其他方式与管理局合作。

(11)计划名称不得为不良名称或产生误导。

(12)计划的目的必须在合理情况下能够成功实现。

(13)参与者必须有权依照计划规定赎回其单位，赎回价格按与计划相关的并根据计划决定的单位财产相关净值确定。

(14)但如计划要求管理人确保参与者能够以投资交易形式按照与第(13)款所述价格无明显差异的价格出售其单位，则视为该计划符合第(13)款规定。

(15)第(13)款规定不视为要求参与者必须有权在作出赎回要求后立即能够赎回[或依照第(14)款所述出售]其单位。

Annotations:

Modifications etc. (not altering text)

C292 S. 272(1) extended (1.12.2001) by S.I. 2001/2636, arts. 1(2)(b), 68(1); S.I. 2001/3538, art. 2(1)

C293 S. 272(8)(9) modified (31.10.2001) by S.I. 2001/3374, art. 1, Sch. para. 9

Commencement Information

I85 S. 272 wholly in force at 1.12.2001; s. 272 not in force at Royal Assent see s. 431(2); s. 272 in force for specified purposes at 3.9.2001 by S.I. 2001/2632, art. 2(2), Sch. Pt. 2; s. 272 in force in so far as not already in force at 1.12.2001 by S.I. 2001/3538, art. 2(1)

273 Matters that may be taken into account.

For the purposes of subsections (8)(b) and (9)(b) of section 272, the Authority may take into account any matter relating to—

(a) any person who is or will be employed by or associated with the operator, trustee or depositary in connection with the scheme;

(b) any director of the operator, trustee or depositary;

(c) any person exercising influence over the operator, trustee or depositary;

(d) any body corporate in the same group as the operator, trustee or depositary;

(e) any director of any such body corporate;

(f) any person exercising influence over any such body corporate.

Annotations:

Commencement Information

I86 S. 273 wholly in force at 1.12.2001; s. 273 not in force at Royal Assent see s. 431(2); s. 273 in force for specified purposes at 3.9.2001 by S.I. 2001/2632, art. 2(2), Sch. Pt. 2; s. 273 in force in so far as not already in force at 1.12.2001 by S.I. 2001/3538, art. 2(1)

274 Applications for recognition of individual schemes.

(1) An application under section 272 for an order declaring a scheme to be arecognized scheme must be made to the Authority by the operator of the scheme.

(2) The application—

(a) must be made in such manner as the Authority may direct;

(b) must contain the address of a place in the United Kingdom for the service on the operator of notices or other documents required or authorised to be served on him under this Act;

注释：

修改等(不涉及条文内容)

C292　第272条第(1)款于2001年12月1日依照制定法文件S.I.2001/2636第1条第(2)款第(b)项、第68条第(1)款；制定法文件S.I.2001/3538第2条第(1)款扩大适用范围。

C293　第272条第(8)款和第(9)款于2001年10月31日依照制定法文件S.I.2001/3374第1条、附录第9条修订。

实施日期

I85　第272条于2001年12月1日全部生效；第272条在副署时尚未生效，见第431条第(2)款；第272条为特定目的于2001年9月3日依照制定法文件S.I.2001/2632第2条第(2)款、附录第二部分生效；第272条如于2001年12月1日尚未生效，则依照制定法文件S.I.2001/3538第2条第(1)款生效。

第273条　可考虑的事项

为第272条第(8)款第(b)项和第(9)款第(b)项之目的，管理局可以考虑与下列各项有关的任何事项：

(a)与该计划相关，执行人、受托人或托管人聘用或将聘用的任何人或与执行人、受托人或托管人相关联的任何人；

(b)执行人、受托人或托管人的任何董事；

(c)对执行人、受托人或托管人施加影响的任何人；

(d)与执行人、受托人或托管人属于同一集团的法人；

(e)上述任何法人的任何董事；

(f)对上述任何法人施加影响的任何人。

注释：

实施日期

I86　第273条于2001年12月1日全部生效；第273条在副署时尚未生效，见第431条第(2)款；第273条为特定目的于2001年9月3日依照制定法文件S.I.2001/2632第2条第(2)款、附录第二部分生效；第273条如于2001年12月1日尚未生效，则依照制定法文件S.I.2001/3538第2条第(1)款生效。

第274条　申请认可单独计划

(1)如依照第272条规定申请颁布法令宣布计划为获认可的计划，则该申请必须由该计划执行人向管理局提出。

(2)申请必须

(a)以管理局指示的方式提出；

(b)包含一处联合王国地址，作为向管理人送达通知或本法要求或授权送达的其他文件的地址；

(c) must contain or be accompanied by such information as the Authority may reasonably require for the purpose of determining the application.

(3) At any time after receiving an application and before determining it, the Authority may require the applicant to provide it with such further information as it reasonably considers necessary to enable it to determine the application.

(4) Different directions may be given, and different requirements imposed, in relation to different applications.

(5) The Authority may require an applicant to present information which he is required to give under this section in such form, or to verify it in such a way, as the Authority may direct.

Annotations:

Modifications etc. (not altering text)

C294 S. 274 extended (1.12.2001) by S.I. 2001/3592, arts. 1(2), 44(1) (with art. 23(2))

Commencement Information

I87 S. 274 wholly in force at 1.12.2001; s. 274 not in force at Royal Assent see s. 431(2); s. 274(2) in force for specified purposes at 18.6.2001 by S.I. 2001/1820, art. 2, Sch.; s. 274 in force for specified purposes at 3.9.2001 by S.I. 2001/2632, art. 2(2), Sch. Pt. 2; s. 274 in force in so far as not already in force at 1.12.2001 by S.I. 2001/3538, art. 2(1)

275 Determination of applications.

(1) An application under section 272 must be determined by theAuthority before the end of the period of six months beginning with the date on which it receives the completed application.

(2) The Authority may determine an incomplete application if it considers it appropriate to do so; and it must in any event determine such an application within twelve months beginning with the date on which it first receives the application.

(3) If the Authority makes an order under section 272 (1), it must give written notice of the order to the applicant.

Annotations:

Modifications etc. (not altering text)

C295 S. 275(1)(2) modified (1.12.2001) by S.I. 2001/3592, arts. 1(2), 44(2)(3) (with art. 23(2)) (c)载有或附有管理局对申请作出决定所合理需要的信息。

(3)管理局在收到申请后、作出决定前,可随时要求申请人进一步提供其认为作出决定所合理需要的信息。

(4)对不同申请可以给予不同的指示并提出不同的要求。

(5)管理局可以要求申请人以管理局指示的形式提交本条要求提供的信息,或以管理局指示的方式验证上述信息。

注释:

修改等(不涉及条文内容)

C294 第274条于2001年12月1日依照制定法文件S.I.2001/3592第1条第(2)款、第44条第(1)款[与第23条第(2)款]扩大适用范围。

实施日期

I87 第274条于2001年12月1日全部生效;第274条在副署时尚未生效,见第431条第(2)款;第274条第(2)款为特定目的于2001年6月18日依照制定法文件S.I.2001/1820第2条、附录生效;第274条为特定目的于2001年9月3日依照制定法文件S.I.2001/2632第2条第(2)款、附录第二部分生效;第274条如于2001年12月1日尚未生效,则依照制定法文件S.I.2001/3538第2条第(1)款生效。

第275条 对申请作出的决定

(1)对依照第272条规定提出的申请,管理局必须在收到完整申请之日起6个月期间届满前作出决定。

(2)如管理局认为适当,则可以对不完整申请作出决定;且在任何情况下必须在首次收到该申请之日起12个月内作出决定。

(3)如管理局依照第272条第(1)款规定颁布法令,则必须向申请人发出该法令的书面通知。

注释:

修改等(不涉及条文内容)

C295 第275条第(1)款和第(2)款于2001年12月1日依照制定法文件S.I.2001/3592第1条第(2)款、第44条第(2)款和第(3)款[与第23条第(2)款]修订。

Commencement Information

I88 S. 275 wholly in force at 1.12.2001; s. 275 not in force at Royal Assent see s. 431(2); s. 275 in force for specified purposes at 3.9.2001 by S.I. 2001/2632, art. 2(2), Sch. Pt. 2; s. 275 in force in so far as not already in force at 1.12.2001 by S.I. 2001/3538, art. 2(1)

276 Procedure when refusing an application.

(1) If the Authority proposes to refuse an application made under section 272 it must give the applicant a warning notice.

(2) If the Authority decides to refuse the application—

(a) it must give the applicant a decision notice; and

(b) the applicant may refer the matter to the Tribunal.

Annotations:

Commencement Information

I89 S. 276 wholly in force at 1.12.2001; s. 276 not in force at Royal Assent see s. 431(2); s. 276 in force for specified purposes at 3.9.2001 by S.I. 2001/2632, art. 2(2), Sch. Pt. 2; s. 276 in force in so far as not already in force at 1.12.2001 by S.I. 2001/3538, art. 2(1)

277 Alteration of schemes and changes of operator, trustee or depositary.

(1) The operator of a scheme recognised by virtue of section 272 must give written notice to the Authority of any proposed alteration to the scheme.

(2) Effect is not to be given to any such proposal unless—

(a) the Authority, by written notice, has given its approval to the proposal; or

(b) one month, beginning with the date on which notice was given under subsection (1), has expired without the Authority having given written notice to the operator that it has decided to refuse approval.

(3) At least one month before any replacement of the operator, trustee or depositary of such a scheme, notice of the proposed replacement must be given to the Authority—

(a) by the operator, trustee or depositary (as the case may be); or

(b) by the person who is to replace him.

Annotations:

Modifications etc. (not altering text)

C296 S. 277(1) amended (temp. from 3.9.2001 to 1.12.2001) by S.I. 2001/2659, arts. 1(2), 3(9); S.I. 2001/3538, art. 2(1)

S. 277(1) extended (1.12.2001) by S.I. 2001/3592, arts. 1(2), 45(1) (with art. 23(2))

实施日期

I88 第275条于2001年12月1日全部生效;第275条在副署时尚未生效,见第431条第(2)款;第275条为特定目的于2001年9月3日依照制定法文件S.I.2001/2632第2条第(2)款、附录第二部分生效;第275条如于2001年12月1日尚未生效,则依照制定法文件S.I.2001/3538第2条第(1)款生效。

第276条 驳回申请的程序

(1)如管理局拟驳回依照第272条规定提出的申请,则必须向申请人发出预告通知。

(2)如管理局决定驳回申请,则

(a)必须向申请人发出决定通知;且

(b)申请人可将该事项诉至裁判所。

注释:

实施日期

I89 第276条于2001年12月1日全部生效;第276条在副署时尚未生效,见第431条第(2)款;第276条为特定目的于2001年9月3日依照制定法文件S.I.2001/2632 附录第二部分生效;第276条如于2001年12月1日尚未生效,则依照制定法文件S.I.2001/3538 第2条第(1)款生效。

第277条 计划变更与执行人、受托人或托管人改变

(1)根据第272条获认可的计划,其执行人必须就任何对计划提议的变更向管理局发出书面通知。

(2)除非有下列情况,否则不得使该提议生效:

(a)管理局以书面通知形式对该提议予以批准;或

(b)自依照第(1)款规定发出通知之日起1个月期间届满,管理局未书面通知执行人其决定驳回申请。

(3)至少于更换计划执行人、受托人或托管人前1个月,必须由下列人员就所计划的更换向管理局发出通知:

(a)执行人、受托人或托管人(视情况而定);或

(b)执行人、受托人或托管人的接替人。

注释:

修改等(不涉及条文内容)

C296 第277条第(1)款暂定于2001年9月3日至2001年12月1日依照制定法文件S.I.2001/2659第1条第(2)款、第3条第(9)款、制定法文件S.I.2001/3538第2条第(1)款修正;

第277条第(1)款于2001年12月1日依照制定法文件S.I.2001/3592第1条第(2)款、第45条第(1)款[与第23条第(2)款]扩大适用范围。

C297 S. 277(2)(b) modified (1.12.2001) by S.I. 2001/3592, arts. 1(2), 45(2) (with art. 23(2))

C298 S. 277(3) extended (1.12.2001) by S.I. 2001/3592, arts. 1(2), 45(3) (with art. 23(2))

Commencement Information

I90 S. 277 wholly in force at 1.12.2001; s. 277 not in force at Royal Assent see s. 431 (2); s. 277 in force for specified purposes at 3.9.2001 by S.I. 2001/2632, art. 2(2), Sch. Pt. 2; s. 277 in force in so far as not already in force at 1.12.2001 by S.I. 2001/3538, art. 2(1) Schemes recognised under sections 270 and 272

Schemes recognised under sections 270 and 272

278 Rules as to scheme particulars.

The Authority may make rules imposing duties or liabilities on the operator of a scheme recognised under section 270 or 272 for purposes corresponding to those for which rules may be made under section 248 in relation to authorised unit trust schemes.

279 Revocation of recognition.

The Authority may direct that a scheme is to cease to berecognised by virtue of section 270 or revoke an order under section 272 if it appears to the Authority—

(a) that the operator, trustee or depositary of the scheme has contravened a requirement imposed on him by or under this Act;

(b) that the operator, trustee or depositary of the scheme has, in purported compliance with any such requirement, knowingly or recklessly given the Authority information which is false or misleading in a material particular;

(c) in the case of an order under section 272, that one or more of the requirements for the making of the order are no longer satisfied; or

(d) that none of paragraphs (a) to (c) applies, but it is undesirable in the interests of the participants or potential participants that the scheme should continue to be recognised.

Annotations:

Modifications etc. (not altering text)

C299 S. 279 applied (1.12.2001) by S.I. 2001/3592, arts. 1(2), 47(4)(b) (with art. 23 (2))

S. 279 applied (with modifications) (1.12.2001) by S.I. 2001/3592, arts. 1(2), 48(4)(5) (with art. 23(2))

C300 S. 279(c) modified (1.12.2001) by S.I. 2001/2636, arts. 1(2)(b), 68(2); S.I. 2001/3538, art. 2(1)

C297 第277条第(2)款第(b)项于2001年12月1日依制定法文件S.I.2001/3592第1条第(2)款、第45条第(2)款[与第23条第(2)款]修订。

C298 第277条第(3)款于2001年12月1日依照制定法文件S.I.2001/3592第1条第(2)款、第45条第(3)款[与第23条第(2)款]扩大适用范围。

实施日期

I90 第277条于2001年12月1日全部生效;第277条在副署时尚未生效,见第431条第(2)款;第277条为特定目的于2001年9月3日依照制定法文件S.I.2001/2632第2条第(2)款、附录第二部分生效;第277条如于2001年12月1日尚未生效,则依照制定法文件S.I.2001/3538第2条第(1)款生效。

依照第270条和第272条获认可的计划

第278条 计划公告书规则

管理局可以制定规则,规定依照第270条或第272条规定获认可的计划管理人承担的职责或责任。制定该规则的目的与依照第248条可作出的获授权单位信托计划相关规则的目的一致。

第279条 撤销认可

如管理局认为有下列情况,则可指示某项计划不再依照第270条规定为获认可的计划,或者依照第272条规定撤销一项命令:

(a)相关计划执行人、受托人或托管人违反本法对其规定的要求或依照本法对其提出的要求;

(b)计划执行人、受托人或托管人在遵守上述任何要求时,就重要事项向管理局提供明知为虚假或误导的信息,或因重大过失而提供虚假或误导信息;

(c)为第272条规定的法令之目的,发布该命令应满足的一项或多项要求不再满足;或

(d)第(a)项至第(c)项均不适用,但为保护计划参与者或潜在参与者的利益不宜使计划继续获得认可。

注释:

修改等(不涉及条文内容)

C299 第279条于2001年12月1日依照制定法文件S.I.2001/3592第1条第(2)款、第47条第(4)款第(b)项[与第23条第(2)款]适用;

第279条(已修订)于2001年12月1日依照制定法文件S.I.2001/3592第1条第(2)款、第48条第(4)款和第(5)款[与第23条第(2)款]适用。

C300 第279条第(c)项于2001年12月1日依照制定法文件S.I.2001/2636第1条第(2)款第(b)项、第68条第(2)款;制定法文件S.I.2001/3538第2条第(1)款修订。

280 Procedure.

(1) If the Authority proposes to give a direction under section 279 or to make an order under that section revoking a recognition order, it must give a warning notice to the operator and (if any) the trustee or depositary of the scheme.

(2) If the Authority decides to give a direction or make an order under that section—

(a) it must without delay give a decision notice to the operator and (if any) the trustee or depositary of the scheme; and

(b) the operator or the trustee or depositary may refer the matter to the Tribunal.

Annotations:

Modifications etc. (not altering text)

C301 S. 280(1) extended (1.12.2001) by S.I. 2001/3592, arts. 1(2), 47(1), 48(1) (with art. 23(2))

281 Directions.

(1) In this section a "relevant recognised scheme" means a scheme recognised under section 270 or 272.

(2) If it appears to the Authority that—

(a) the operator, trustee or depositary of a relevant recognised scheme has contravened, or is likely to contravene, a requirement imposed on him by or under this Act,

(b) the operator, trustee or depositary of such a scheme has, in purported compliance with any such requirement, knowingly or recklessly given the Authority information which is false or misleading in a material particular,

(c) one or more of the requirements for the recognition of a scheme under section 272 are no longer satisfied, or

(d) none of paragraphs (a) to (c) applies, but the exercise of the power conferred by this section is desirable in order to protect the interests of participants or potential participants in a relevant recognised scheme who are in the United Kingdom, it may direct that the scheme is not to be a recognised scheme for a specified period or until the occurrence of a specified event or until specified conditions are complied with.

Annotations:

Modifications etc. (not altering text)

C302 S. 281 extended (1.12.2001) by S.I. 2001/2636, arts. 1(2)(b), 70(b), 71(b); S.I. 2001/3538, art. 2(1)

S.281 amended (temp. from 3.9.2001 to 1.12.2001) by S.I. 2001/2659, arts. 1(2), 3(9); S.I. 2001/3538, art. 2(1)

第280条　程序

(1)如管理局拟依照第279条规定发出指示或依照该条规定撤销认可令,则必须向计划执行人和受托人或托管人(如有)发出预告通知。

(2)管理局如决定依照该条规定发布指令,则

(a)必须毫不迟延地向计划执行人和受托人或托管人(如有)发出决定通知;且

(b)执行人或者受托人或托管人可将该事项诉至裁判所。

注释:

修改等(不涉及条文内容)

C301　第280条第(1)款(已修订)于2001年12月1日依照制定法文件S.I.2001/3592第1条第(2)款、第47条第(1)款、第48条第(1)款[与第23条第(2)款]扩大适用范围。

第281条　指令

(1)本条中"相关获认可的计划"系指依照第270条或第272条规定获得认可的计划。

(2)如管理局认为

(a)获认可的计划的执行人、受托人或托管人违反或可能违反本法对其规定或依照本法对其提出的要求,

(b)该等计划的执行人、受托人或托管人在遵守上述任何要求时,就重要事项向管理局提供明知为虚假或误导的信息,或因重大过失而提供虚假或误导信息,

(c)依照第272条发布认可令所需满足的要求中一项或多项已不再满足,或

(d)第(a)项至第(c)项均不适用,但为保护相关获认可的计划在联合王国的参与者或潜在参与者的利益,有必要行使本条规定赋予的权力,则可以指示在指定期间内、直至指定事件发生或直至符合规定条件时止,该计划不是获认可的计划。

注释:

修改等(不涉及条文内容)

C302　第281条于2001年12月1日依照制定法文件S.I.2001/2636第1条第(2)款第(b)项、第70条第(b)项、第71条第(b)项;制定法文件S.I.2001/3538第2条第(1)款扩大适用范围;

第281条暂定于2001年9月3日至2001年12月1日依照制定法文件S.I.2001/2659第1条第(2)款、第3条第(9)款;制定法文件S.I.2001/3538第2条第(1)款修正。

282 Procedure on giving directions under section 281 and varying them otherwise than as requested.

(1) A direction takes effect—

(a) immediately, if the notice given under subsection (3) states that that is the case;

(b) on such date as may be specified in the notice; or

(c) if no date is specified in the notice, when the matter to which it relates is no longer open to review.

(2) A direction may be expressed to take effect immediately (or on a specified date) only if the Authority, having regard to the ground on which it is exercising its power under section 281, considers that it is necessary for the direction to take effect immediately (or on that date).

(3) If the Authority proposes to give a direction under section 281, or gives such a direction with immediate effect, it must give separate written notice to the operator and (if any) the trustee or depositary of the scheme concerned.

(4) The notice must—

(a) give details of the direction;

(b) inform the person to whom it is given of when the direction takes effect;

(c) state the Authority's reasons for giving the direction and for its determination as to when the direction takes effect;

(d) inform the person to whom it is given that he may make representations to the Authority within such period as may be specified in it (whether or not he has referred the matter to the Tribunal); and

(e) inform him of his right to refer the matter to the Tribunal.

(5) The Authority may extend the period allowed under the notice for making representations.

(6) If, having considered any representations made by a person to whom the notice was given, the Authority decides—

(a) to give the direction in the way proposed, or

(b) if it has been given, not to revoke the direction,

it must give separate written notice to the operator and (if any) the trustee or depositary of the scheme concerned.

(7) If, having considered any representations made by a person to whom the notice was given, the Authority decides—

(a) not to give the direction in the way proposed,

(b) to give the direction in a way other than that proposed, or

(c) to revoke a direction which has effect,

it must give separate written notice to the operator and (if any) the trustee or depositary

第282条 依照第281条发出指示及不应请求变更该指示的程序

(1)指示

(a)如依照第(3)款规定情况发出通知,则立即生效;

(b)于通知规定之日生效;或

(c)如通知未规定日期,则于该通知相关事项不再开放供审议时生效。

(2)只有管理局在考虑其依照第281条行使权力的理由后,认为某项指示有必要立即生效(或在规定日期生效),才可以明示该指示立即生效(或在规定日期生效)。

(3)如管理局依照第281条规定发出指示或使该指示立即生效,则必须向相关计划执行人和受托人或托管人(如有)另行发出书面通知。

(4)该通知必须

(a)详细说明该指示;

(b)告知被通知人该指示何时生效;

(c)说明管理局发出该指示以及决定其生效时间的理由;

(d)告知被通知人可在通知规定的期限内向管理局作出陈述(无论该事项是否已诉至裁判所);且

(e)告知其有权将该事项诉至裁判所。

(5)管理局可以延长通知规定允许陈述的期限。

(6)如管理局在考虑被通知人作出的任何陈述后决定

(a)以其计划的方式发出指示,或

(b)如已发出指示,决定不撤销该指示,

则必须向相关计划执行人和受托人或托管人(如有)另行发出书面通知。

(7)如管理局在考虑被通知人作出的任何陈述后决定

(a)不以其计划的方式发出指示,

(b)以其他方式发出指示,或

(c)撤销生效指示,

则必须向相关计划执行人和受托人或托管人(如有)另行发出书面通知。

of the scheme concerned.

(8) A notice given under subsection (6) must inform the person to whom it is given of his right to refer the matter to the Tribunal.

(9) A notice under subsection (7)(b) must comply with subsection (4).

(10) If a notice informs a person of his right to refer a matter to the Tribunal, it must give an indication of the procedure on such a reference.

(11) This section applies to the variation of a direction on the Authority's own initiative as it applies to the giving of a direction.

(12) For the purposes of subsection (1)(c), whether a matter is open to review is to be determined in accordance with section 391(8).

Facilities and information in UK

283 Facilities and information in UK.

(1) The Authority may make rules requiring operators of recognised schemes to maintain in the United Kingdom, or in such part or parts of it as may be specified, such facilities as the Authority thinks desirable in the interests of participants and as are specified in rules.

(2) The Authority may by notice in writing require the operator of any recognised scheme to include such explanatory information as is specified in the notice in any communication of his which—

(a) is a communication of an invitation or inducement of a kind mentioned in section 21 (1); and

(b) names the scheme.

(3) In the case of a communication originating outside the United Kingdom, subsection (2) only applies if the communication is capable of having an effect in the United Kingdom.

Annotations:

Commencement Information

I91 S. 283 wholly in force at 1.12.2001; s. 283 not in force at Royal Assent see s. 431 (2); s. 283(1) in force at 18.6.2001 by S.I. 2001/1820, art. 2, Sch.; s. 283 in force in so far as not already in force at 1.12.2001 by S.I. 2001/3538, art. 2(1)

CHAPTER Ⅵ INVESTIGATIONS

284 Power to investigate.

(1) An investigating authority may appoint one or more competent persons to investigate on its behalf—

(8)依照第(6)款发出的通知必须告知被通知人其有权将相关事项提交裁判所裁决。

(9)第(7)条第(b)项规定的通知必须符合第(4)款规定。

(10)如通知告知某人有权将相关事项诉至裁判所,则必须说明诉至裁判所的程序。

(11)本条适用于管理局主动变更指示,效力等同于对发出指示适用。

(12)为第(1)款第(c)项之目的,某一事项是否仍在开放供审议应当依照第391条第(8)款规定确定。

在联合王国的设施和信息

第283条　在联合王国的设施和信息

(1)管理局可以制定规则,要求获认可计划的执行人在联合王国或指定的地区保持管理局认为符合参与者利益的必要设施以及规则规定的设施。

(2)管理局可以书面通知形式,要求任何获认可计划的执行人在其下列任何传播活动中列入通知规定的解释性信息:

(a)第21条第(1)款所列传播邀请或诱导的活动;以及

(b)计划名称。

(3)如发出的邀请或诱导源于联合王国境外,则第(2)款仅在该邀请或诱导可以在联合王国境内产生影响时适用。

注释:

实施日期

I91　第283条于2001年12月1日全部生效;第283条在副署时尚未生效,见第431条第(2)款;第283条第(1)款于2001年6月18日依照制定法文件S.I.2001/1820第2条、附录生效;第283条如于2001年12月1日尚未生效,则依照制定法文件S.I.2001/3538第2条第(1)款生效。

第六章　调　　查

第284条　调查权

(1)调查机关可委派一名或多名适格人员代表其调查下列事项:

(a) the affairs of, or of the manager or trustee of, any authorised unit trust scheme,

(b) the affairs of, or of the operator, trustee or depositary of, any recognised scheme so far as relating to activities carried on in the United Kingdom, or

(c) the affairs of, or of the operator, trustee or depositary of, any other collective investment scheme except a body incorporated by virtue of regulations under section 262,

if it appears to the investigating authority that it is in the interests of the participants or potential participants to do so or that the matter is of public concern.

(2) A person appointed under subsection (1) to investigate the affairs of, or of the manager, trustee, operator or depositary of, any scheme (scheme "A"), may also, if he thinks it necessary for the purposes of that investigation, investigate—

(a) the affairs of, or of the manager, trustee, operator or depositary of, any other such scheme as is mentioned in subsection (1) whose manager, trustee, operator or depositary is the same person as the manager, trustee, operator or depositary of scheme A;

(b) the affairs of such other schemes and persons (including bodies incorporated by virtue of regulations under section 262 and the directors and depositaries of such bodies) as may be prescribed.

(3) If the person appointed to conduct an investigation under this section ("B") considers that a person ("C") is or may be able to give information which is relevant to the investigation, B may require C—

(a) to produce to B any documents in C's possession or under his control which appear to B to be relevant to the investigation,

(b) to attend before B, and

(c) otherwise to give B all assistance in connection with the investigation which C is reasonably able to give, and it is C's duty to comply with that requirement.

(4) Subsections (5) to (9) of section 170 apply if an investigating authority appoints a person under this section to conduct an investigation on its behalf as they apply in the case mentioned in subsection (1) of that section.

(5) Section 174 applies to a statement made by a person in compliance with a requirement imposed under this section as it applies to a statement mentioned in that section.

(6) Subsections (2) to (4) and (6) of section 175 and section 177 have effect as if this section were contained in Part XI.

(7) Subsections (1) to (9) of section 176 apply in relation to a person appointed under subsection (1) as if—

(a) references to an investigator were references to a person so appointed;

(b) references to an information requirement were references to a requirement imposed under section 175 or under subsection (3) by a person so appointed;

(c) the premises mentioned in subsection (3)(a) were the premises of a person whose (a)任何获授权单位信托计划的事务、其执行人或受托人的事务,

(b)任何获认可计划与在联合王国开展活动相关的事务,其执行人、受托人或托管人的事务,或

(c)除由依照第262条制定的法规设立的机构外,任何其他集合投资计划的事务,其执行人、受托人或托管人的事务,

如调查机关认为该项调查符合参与者或潜在参与者利益或者调查事项为公众关注事项。

(2)依照第(1)款规定接受委派调查任何计划(以下简称A计划)管理人、受托人或托管人的,如受委派人认为为实现调查目的有必要,则可调查下列事项:

(a)对属于第(1)款所列范围,与A计划管理人、受托人、执行人或托管人相同的任何其他计划,调查其事务或其管理人、受托人、执行人或托管人的事务;

(b)对规定的任何其他计划和人(包括依照第262条规定的法规设立的机构和该等机构的董事和托管人)调查其事务。

(3)如依照本条规定接受委派进行调查的人(以下简称B)认为某人(以下简称C)能够或可能能够提供与调查相关的信息,则B可要求C

(a)向B出示C持有或受其控制、B认为与调查相关的任何文件,

(b)到B面前,并

(c)就调查向B给予C能够合理给予的全部其他协助,且C有遵守此项要求的职责。

(4)如调查机关依照本条规定委任某人代表该机构开展调查,则适用第170条第(5)款至第(9)款规定,效力等同于对第170条第(1)款所列情况适用。

(5)第174条适用于某人遵守依照本条规定提出的要求而作出的陈述,效力等同于对第174条所列陈述适用。

(6)第175条第(2)款至第(4)款、第(6)款以及第177条对本条的效力等同于本条包含在第十一部分中。

(7)第176条第(1)款至第(9)款适用于第(1)款所列被委派人,效力等同于

(a)述及调查人即为述及被委派人;

(b)述及信息要求即为述及被委派人依照第175条或第(3)款规定提出的要求;

(c)第(3)款第(a)项所述所在地为,其事务应当依照本条规定接受调查的人或其

affairs are the subject of an investigation under this section or of an appointed representative of such a person.

(8) No person may be required under this section to disclose information or produce a document in respect of which he owes an obligation of confidence by virtue of carrying on the business of banking unless subsection (9) or (10) applies.

(9) This subsection applies if—

(a) the person to whom the obligation of confidence is owed consents to the disclosure or production; or

(b) the imposing on the person concerned of a requirement with respect to information or a document of a kind mentioned in subsection (8) has been specifically authorised by the investigating authority.

(10) This subsection applies if the person owing the obligation of confidence or the person to whom it is owed is—

(a) the manager, trustee, operator or depositary of any collective investment scheme which is under investigation;

(b) the director of a body incorporated by virtue of regulations under section 262 which is under investigation;

(c) any other person whose own affairs are under investigation.

(11) "Investigating authority" means the Authority or the Secretary of State.

Annotations:

Modifications etc. (not altering text)

C303 S. 284(1) extended (with modifications) (1.12.2001) by S.I. 2001/3646, arts. 1(2), 8

Commencement Information

I92 S. 284 wholly in force at 1.12.2001; s. 284 not in force at Royal Assent see s. 431(2); s. 284(2) in force for certain purposes at 25.2.2001 by S.I. 2001/516, art. 2(b), Sch. Pt. 2; s. 284 in force in so far as not already in force at 1.12.2001 by S.I. 2001/3538, art. 2(1)

被任命代表的所在地。

(8)除非第(9)款或第(10)款规定适用,否则不得依照本条规定要求任何负有保密义务的人披露其银行业务相关信息或出示相关文件。

(9)本款规定适用于下列情况:
(a)保密义务权利人同意披露或出示;或

(b)就第(8)款所述种类的信息或文件对向相关人提出的要求已经调查机关明确授权。

(10)如保密义务承担人或保密义务权利人为下列各项所列之人,则适用本款规定:
(a)受调查集合投资计划管理人、受托人、执行人或托管人;

(b)由依照第262条制定的法规设立、正在接受调查的机构的董事;

(c)自身事务正在接受调查的其他任何人。
(11)"调查机关",系指管理局或国务大臣。
注释:

修改等(不涉及条文内容)

C303　第284条第(1)款(已修订)于2001年12月1日依照制定法文件S.I.2001/3646第1条第(2)款、第8条扩大适用范围。

实施日期

I92　第284条于2001年12月1日全部生效;第284条在副署时尚未生效,见第431条第(2)款;第284条第(2)款为特定目的于2001年2月25日依照制定法文件S.I.2001/516第2条第(b)项、附录第二部分生效;第284条如于2001年12月1日尚未生效,则依照制定法文件S.I.2001/3538第2条第(1)款生效。

PART XVIII RECOGNISED INVESTMENT EXCHANGES AND CLEARING HOUSES

CHAPTER I EXEMPTION

General

285 Exemption for recognised investment exchanges and clearing houses.

(1) In this Act—

(a) "recognised investment exchange" means an investment exchange in relation to which a recognition order is in force; and

(b) "recognised clearing house" means a clearing house in relation to which a recognition order is in force.

(2) A recognised investment exchange is exempt from the general prohibition as respects any regulated activity—

(a) which is carried on as a part of the exchange's business as an investment exchange; or

(b) which is carried on for the purposes of, or in connection with, the provision of clearing services by the exchange.

(3) A recognised clearing house is exempt from the general prohibition as respects any regulated activity which is carried on for the purposes of, or in connection with, the provision of clearing services by the clearing house.

286 Qualification for recognition.

(1) The Treasury may make regulations setting out the requirements—

(a) which must be satisfied by an investment exchange or clearing house if it is to qualify as a body in respect of which the Authority may make a recognition order under this Part; and

(b) which, if a recognition order is made, it must continue to satisfy if it is to remain a recognised body.

第十八部分　获认可的投资交易所和结算所

第一章　豁　　免

一般规定

第285条　获认可的投资交易所和结算所的豁免

(1)本法中

(a)“获认可的投资交易所”,系指具有相关生效认可令的投资交易所;

(b)“获认可的结算所”,系指具有相关生效认可令的结算所。

(2)获认可的投资交易所豁免受与下列受监管活动相关的任何一般禁止性规定制约:

(a)作为投资交易所投资交易业务的一项内容开展的受监管活动;或

(b)为该交易所提供结算服务之目的或提供与结算服务相关的业务开展的被监管活动。

(3)获认可的结算所对为该所提供结算服务之目的或提供与结算服务相关的业务开展的受监管活动免受一般禁止性规定制约。

第286条　认可资格

(1)财政部可制定法规,规定下列要求:

(a)投资交易所或结算所获得管理局依照本部分规定发布认可令的资格所必须满足的要求;以及

(b)如认可令已发布,保有获认可的机构地位所必须满足的要求。

(2) But if regulations contain provision as to the default rules of an investment exchange or clearing house, or as to proceedings taken under such rules by such a body, they require the approval of the Secretary of State.

(3) "Default rules" means rules of an investment exchange or clearing house which provide for the taking of action in the event of a person's appearing to be unable, or likely to become unable, to meet his obligations in respect of one or more market contracts connected with the exchange or clearing house.

(4) "Market contract" means—

(a) a contract to which Part VII of the[M40] Companies Act 1989 applies as a result of section 155 of that Act or a contract to which Part V of the[M41] Companies (No. 2)(Northern Ireland) Order 1990 applies as a result of Article 80 of that Order; and

(b) such other kind of contract as may be prescribed.

(5) Requirements resulting from this section are referred to in this Part as "recognition requirements".

Annotations:

Marginal Citations

M40 1989 c. 40.

M41 S.I. 1990/1504 (N.I. 10).

Applications for recognition

287 Application by an investment exchange.

(1) Any body corporate or unincorporated association may apply to the Authority for an order declaring it to be a recognised investment exchange for the purposes of this Act.

(2) The application must be made in such manner as the Authority may direct and must be accompanied by—

(a) a copy of the applicant's rules;

(b) a copy of any guidance issued by the applicant;

(c) the required particulars; and

(d) such other information as the Authority may reasonably require for the purpose of determining the application.

(3) The required particulars are—

(a) particulars of any arrangements which the applicant has made, or proposes to make, for the provision of clearing services in respect of transactions effected on the exchange;

(b) if the applicant proposes to provide clearing services in respect of transactions other than those effected on the exchange, particulars of the criteria which the applicant will apply when determining to whom it will provide those services.

(2)但如法规包含关于投资交易所或结算所违规规则或者关于上述机构依照上述规则提起的法律程序的规定,则该法规需经国务大臣批准。

(3)“违规规则”,系指投资交易所或结算所规定在某人不能或有可能不再能履行与该交易所或结算所相关的一项或多项市场合同有关的义务时采取行动的规则。

(4)“市场合同”系指

(a)依照[M40]《1989年公司法》第155条适用该法第七部分或依照[M41]《1990年公司法令》(第2号)(北爱尔兰)第80条规定适用该法令第五部分的合同;以及

(b)规定的其他种类合同。

(5)因本条规定而提出的要求,在本部分中称为“认可要求”。

注释:

附注引文

M40 1989年第40章。

M41 制定法文件S.I.1990/1504(第10条)。

认 可 申 请

第287条 投资交易所的申请

(1)任何法人或非法团组织可以向管理局申请颁布法令,宣布其为本法所称之获认可的投资交易所。

(2)申请必须以管理局指示的方式提出,且必须附有

(a)申请人规章副本一份;

(b)申请人所发布的任何指引的副本一份;

(c)要求提供的详情;以及

(d)管理局为对申请作出决定可能合理要求其提供的其他信息。

(3)要求提供的详情为

(a)申请人为就本交易所实施的交易提供相关结算服务已作出或拟作出的任何安排的详情。

(b)如申请人拟就非本交易所实施的交易提供结算服务,则提供申请人在决定向何人提供上述服务时所采用标准的详情。

Annotations:

Commencement Information

I93 S. 287 wholly in force at 3.9.2001; s. 287 not in force at Royal Assent see s. 431(2); s. 287(2) in force for specified purposes at 18.6.2001 by S.I. 2001/1820, art. 2, Sch.; s. 287 in so far as not already in force at 3.9.2001 by S.I. 2001/2632, art. 2, Sch. Pt. 2

288 Application by a clearing house.

(1) Any body corporate or unincorporated association may apply to the Authority for an order declaring it to be a recognised clearing house for the purposes of this Act.

(2) The application must be made in such manner as the Authority may direct and must be accompanied by—

(a) a copy of the applicant's rules;

(b) a copy of any guidance issued by the applicant;

(c) the required particulars; and

(d) such other information as the Authority may reasonably require for the purpose of determining the application.

(3) The required particulars are—

(a) if the applicant makes, or proposes to make, clearing arrangements with a recognised investment exchange, particulars of those arrangements;

(b) if the applicant proposes to provide clearing services for persons other than recognised investment exchanges, particulars of the criteria which it will apply when determining to whom it will provide those services.

Annotations:

Commencement Information

I94 S. 288 wholly in force at 3.9.2001; s. 288 not in force at Royal Assent see s. 431(2); s. 288(2) in force for specified purposes at 18.6.2001 by S.I. 2001/1820, art. 2, Sch.; s. 288 in force in so far as not already in force at 3.9.2001 by S.I. 2001/2632, art. 2 Sch. Pt. 2

289 Applications: supplementary.

(1) At any time after receiving an application and before determining it, the Authority may require the applicant to provide such further information as it reasonably considers necessary to enable it to determine the application.

(2) Information which the Authority requires in connection with an application must be provided in such form, or verified in such manner, as the Authority may direct.

(3) Different directions may be given, or requirements imposed, by the Authority with

注释：

实施日期 I93　第287条于2001年9月3日全部生效；第287条在副署时尚未生效，见第431条第(2)款；第287条第(2)款为特定目的于2001年6月18日依照制定法文件S.I.2001/1820第2条、附录生效；第287条如于2001年9月3日尚未生效，则依照制定法文件S.I.2001/2632第2条、附录第二部分生效。

第288条　结算所的申请

(1)任何法人或非法团组织可向管理申请颁布法令，宣布其为本法所称之获得认可的结算所。

(2)申请必须以管理局指示的方式提出，且必须附有

(a)申请人规章副本一份；

(b)申请人所发布的任何指引的副本一份；

(c)要求提供的详情；以及

(d)管理局为对申请作出决定可能合理要求其提供的其他信息。

(3)要求提供的详情为

(a)如申请人与获认可的投资交易所作出或拟作出结算安排，则提供上述安排的详情；

(b)如申请人拟为除获认可的投资交易所以外的其他人提供结算服务，则提供申请人在决定向何人提供上述服务时所采用标准的详情。

注释：

实施日期 I94　第288条于2001年9月3日全部生效；第288条在副署时尚未生效，见第431条第(2)款；第288条第(2)款为特定目的于2001年6月18日依照制定法文件S.I.2001/1820第2条、附录生效；第288条如于2001年9月3日尚未生效，则依照制定法文件S.I.2001/2632第2条、附录第二部分生效。

第289条　申请：补充规定

(1)管理局在收到申请后、作出决定前，可以随时要求申请人进一步提供其认为对该申请作出决定所合理需要的信息。

(2)管理局要求提供的申请相关信息，必须以管理局指示的方式提供，或以管理局指示的方式验证。

(3)管理局对不同申请可给予不同的指示或提出不同的要求。

respect to different applications.

290 Recognition orders.

(1) If it appears to the Authority that the applicant satisfies the recognition requirements applicable in its case, the Authority may make a recognition order declaring the applicant to be—

(a) a recognised investment exchange, if the application is made under section 287;

(b) a recognised clearing house, if it is made under section 288.

(2) The Treasury's approval of the making of a recognition order is required under section 307.

(3) In considering an application, the Authority may have regard to any information which it considers is relevant to the application.

(4) A recognition order must specify a date on which it is to take effect.

(5) Section 298 has effect in relation to a decision to refuse to make a recognition order—

(a) as it has effect in relation to a decision to revoke such an order; and

(b) as if references to a recognised body were references to the applicant.

(6) Subsection (5) does not apply in a case in which the Treasury have failed to give their approval under section 307.

Annotations:

Commencement Information

I95 S. 290 wholly in force at 1.12.2001; s. 290 not in force at Royal Assent see s. 431 (2); s. 290 in force for specified purposes at 3.9.2001 by S.I. 2001/2632, art. 2(2), Sch. Pt. 2; s. 290 in force in so far as not already in force at 1.12.2001 by S.I. 2001/3538, art. 2(1)

291 Liability in relation to recognised body's regulatory functions.

(1) A recognised body and its officers and staff are not to be liable in damages for anything done or omitted in the discharge of the recognised body's regulatory functions unless it is shown that the act or omission was in bad faith.

(2) But subsection (1) does not prevent an award of damages made in respect of an act or omission on the ground that the act or omission was unlawful as a result of section 6(1) of the[M42] Human Rights Act 1998.

(3) "Regulatory functions" means the functions of the recognised body so far as relating to, or to matters arising out of, the obligations to which the body is subject under or by virtue of this Act.

第290条　认可令

(1)如管理局认为申请人满足可适用的认可要求,则可以发布认可令,宣布申请人为

(a)如申请依据第287条提出,则为获认可的投资交易所;

(b)如申请依照第288条提出,则为获认可的结算所。

(2)依照第307条规定,发布认可令需经财政部批准。

(3)管理局在考虑申请时,可以考虑其认为与申请相关的任何信息。

(4)认可令必须指定生效日期。

(5)第298条具有与拒绝发布认可令的决定相关的效力

(a)等同于与撤销该命令相关的效力;且

(b)述及获认可的机构等同于述及申请人。

(6)如财政部未依照第307条规定给予批准,则第(5)款规定不适用。

注释:

实施日期

I95　第290条于2001年12月1日全部生效;第290条在副署时尚未生效,见第431条第(2)款;第290条为特定目的于2001年9月3日依照制定法文件S.I.2001/2632第2条第(2)款、附录第2部分生效;第290条如于2001年12月1日尚未生效,则依照制定法文件S.I.2001/3538第2条第(1)款生效。

第291条　与获认可的机构监管职能相关的责任

(1)在行使获认可的机构的监管职能时,获认可的机构及其高级职员和工作人员对任何作为或不作为不承担损害赔偿责任,除非有证据证明该作为或不作为有恶意。

(2)但第(1)款规定不妨碍该作为或不作为因[M42]《1998年人权法》第6条第(1)款规定不合法而对该作为或不作为作出损害赔偿判决。

(3)"监管职能",系指获认可的机构与本法规定其承担或因本法而承担的义务相关的职能,或与因上述义务而产生的事项相关的职能。

Annotations:

Marginal Citations
M42 1998 c. 42.

292 Overseas investment exchanges and overseas clearing houses.

(1) An application under section 287 or 288 by an overseas applicant must contain the address of a place in the United Kingdom for the service on the applicant of notices or other documents required or authorised to be served on it under this Act.

(2) If it appears to the Authority that an overseas applicant satisfies the requirements of subsection (3) it may make a recognition order declaring the applicant to be—

(a) a recognised investment exchange;

(b) a recognised clearing house.

(3) The requirements are that—

(a) investors are afforded protection equivalent to that which they would be afforded if the body concerned were required to comply with recognition requirements;

(b) there are adequate procedures for dealing with a person who is unable, or likely to become unable, to meet his obligations in respect of one or more market contracts connected with the investment exchange or clearing house;

(c) the applicant is able and willing to co–operate with the Authority by the sharing of information and in other ways;

(d) adequate arrangements exist for co–operation between the Authority and those responsible for the supervision of the applicant in the country or territory in which the applicant's head office is situated.

(4) In considering whether it is satisfied as to the requirements mentioned in subsection (3) (a) and (b), the Authority is to have regard to—

(a) the relevant law and practice of the country or territory in which the applicant's head office is situated;

(b) the rules and practices of the applicant.

(5) In relation to an overseas applicant and a body or association declared to be arecognized investment exchange or recognised clearing house by a recognition order made by virtue of subsection (2)—

(a) the reference in section 313(2) to recognition requirements is to be read as a refer–ence to matters corresponding to the matters in respect of which provision is made in the recognition requirements;

(b) sections 296(1) and 297(2) have effect as if the requirements mentioned in section 296(1)(a) and section 297(2)(a) were those of subsection (3)(a), (b), and (c) of this section;

注释：

附注引文

M42 1998年第42章。

第292条 境外投资交易所和境外结算所

(1)由境外申请人依照第287条或第288条提出的申请必须载有一处联合王国地址，作为向该申请人送达通知或本法规定要求或授权送达的其他文件的地址。

(2)如管理局认为境外申请人满足第(3)款所列要求，则可发布认可令，宣布申请人为

(a)获认可的投资交易所；

(b)获认可的结算所。

(3)前款所述要求为

(a)为投资者提供的保护等同于要求该机构遵守认可要求时所提供的保护；

(b)如某人不能或有可能不再能够履行与该交易所或结算所相关的一项或多项市场合同有关的义务，则有足够的程序予以处理；

(c)申请人能够并愿意以信息共享和其他方式与管理局合作；

(d)有适当安排，使管理局与申请人总部所在国家或地区负责监管申请人的机关能够开展合作。

(4)管理局在考虑第(3)款第(a)项或第(b)项所列要求是否满足时应考虑

(a)申请人总部所在国家或地区的相关法律和惯例；

(b)申请人的规章和惯例。

(5)关于经依照第(2)款规定发布的认可令海外申请人或组织被宣布为获认可的境外投资交易所或获认可的结算所

(a)第313条第(2)款所述及的认可要求应视为述及与认可要求规定的事项相应的事项；

(b)第296条第(1)款和第297条第(2)款规定所具有的效力等同于第296条第(1)款第(a)项和第297条第(2)款第(a)项所述要求为本条第(3)款第(a)项、第(b)项和第(c)项规定的要求；

(c) section 297(2) has effect as if the grounds on which a recognition order may be revoked under that provision included the ground that in the opinion of the Authority arrangements of the kind mentioned in subsection (3)(d) no longer exist.

Annotations:

Commencement Information

I96 S. 292 wholly in force at 1.12.2001; s. 292 not in force at Royal Assent see s. 431 (2); s. 292(1) in force and s. 292(2)-(5) in force specified purposes at 3.9.2001 by S.I. 2001/2632, art. 2(2), Sch. Pt. 2; s. 292 in force in so far as not already in force at 1.12.2001 by S.I. 2001/3538, art. 2(1)

Supervision

293 Notification requirements.

(1) The Authority may make rules requiring a recognised body to give it—

(a) notice of such events relating to the body as may be specified; and

(b) such information in respect of those events as may bespecified.

(2) The rules may also require a recognised body to give the Authority, at such times or in respect of such periods as may be specified, such information relating to the body as may be specified.

(3) An obligation imposed by the rules extends only to a notice or information which the Authority may reasonably require for the exercise of its functions under this Act.

(4) The rules may require information to be given in a specified form and to be verified in a specified manner.

(5) If a recognised body—

(a) alters or revokes any of its rules or guidance, or

(b) makes new rules or issues new guidance,

it must give written notice to the Authority without delay.

(6) If a recognised investment exchange makes a change—

(a) in the arrangements it makes for the provision of clearing services in respect of transactions effected on the exchange, or

(b) in the criteria which it applies when determining to whom it will provide clearing services,

it must give written notice to the Authority without delay.

(7) If a recognised clearing house makes a change—

(a) in the recognised investment exchanges for whom it provides clearing services, or

(b) in the criteria which it applies when determining to whom (other than recognised (c)第297条第(2)款所具有的效力等同于可依照该款规定撤销认可令的理由包括管理局认为第(3)款第(d)项所述安排不再存在的理由。

注释:

实施日期

I96 第292条于2001年12月1日全部生效;第292条在副署时尚未生效,见第431条第(2)款;第292条第(1)款和第292条第(2)款至第(5)款为特定目的于2001年9月3日依照制定法文件S.I.2001/2632第2条第(2)款、附录第二部分生效;第292条如于2001年12月1日尚未生效,则依照制定法文件S.I.2001/3538第2条第(1)款生效。

监　　督

第293条　通知要求

(1)管理局可制定规则,要求获认可的机构

(a)就规定的该机构相关事件向管理局发出通知;并

(b)就上述事件向管理局提供规定的信息。

(2)该规则还可要求获认可的机构在规定的时间或规定的期间提供与该机构相关的规定信息。

(3)该规则规定的义务仅适用于管理局为行使本法规定的职能而合理要求提供的通知或信息。

(4)该规则可要求以规定的形式提供信息,并以规定的方式验证信息。

(5)如获认可的机构有下列情况:

(a)变更或撤销任何规章或指引,或

(b)制定新的章程或发布新的指引,

则必须毫不延迟地向管理局发出书面通知。

(6)如获认可的投资交易对下列事项进行变更:

(a)就本所实施的交易提供结算服务所做的安排,或

(b)在决定为何人提供结算服务时适用的标准,

则必须毫不延迟地向管理局发出书面通知。

(7)如获认可的结算所对下列事项进行变更:

(a)本所为那些获认可的投资交易所提供结算服务,或

(b)在决定为何人(除获认可的投资交易所外)提供结算服务时适用的标准,则必

investment exchanges) it will provide clearing services, it must give written notice to the Authority without delay.

(8) Subsections (5) to (7) do not apply to an overseas investment exchange or an overseas clearing house.

(9) "Specified" means specified in the Authority's rules.

Annotations:

Commencement Information

I97 S. 293 wholly in force at 1.12.2001; s. 293 not in force at Royal Assent see s. 431 (2); s. 293 in force for specified purposes at 18.6.2001 by S.I. 2001/1820, art. 2, Sch.; s. 293 in force in so far as not already in force at 1.12.2001 by S.I. 2001/3538, art. 2(1)

294 Modification or waiver of rules.

(1) The Authority may, on the application or with the consent of a recognised body, direct that rules made under section 293 or 295

(a) are not to apply to the body; or

(b) are to apply to the body with such modifications as may be specified in the direction.

(2) An application must be made in such manner as the Authority may direct.

(3) Subsections (4) to (6) apply to a direction given under subsection (1).

(4) The Authority may not give a direction unless it is satisfied that—

(a) compliance by the recognised body with the rules, or with the rules as unmodified, would be unduly burdensome or would not achieve the purpose for which the rules were made; and

(b) the direction would not result in undue risk to persons whose interests the rules are intended to protect.

(5) A direction may be given subject to conditions.

(6) The Authority may

(a) revoke a direction; or

(b) vary it on the application, or with the consent, of the recognised body to which it relates.

Annotations:

Modifications etc. (not altering text)

C304 S. 294 amended (temp. from 3.9.2001 to 1.12.2001) by S.I. 2001/2659, arts. 1 (2), 3(10); S.I. 2001/3538, art. 2(1)

须毫不延迟地向管理局发出书面通知。

(8)第(5)款和第(7)款规定不适用于境外投资交易所和境外结算所。

(9)“规定”系指在管理局的规则中规定。

注释:

实施日期

I97　第293条于2001年12月1日全部生效;第293条在副署时尚未生效,见第431条第(2)款;第293条为特定目的于2001年6月18日依照制定法文件S.I.2001/1820第2条、附录生效;第293条如于2001年12月1日尚未生效,则依照制定法文件S.I.2001/3538第2条第(1)款生效。

第294条　规则的修改或放弃

(1)应任何获得许可的机构申请或经其同意,管理局可以指示第293条或第295条规定的规则

(a)不适用于该机构;或

(b)经依照指示进行规定的修改后适用于该机构。

(2)申请必须以管理局指示的方式提出。

(3)第(4)款至第(6)款适用于依照第(1)款规定发出的指示。

(4)管理局除非确信有下列情况,否则不得发出指示:

(a)获认可的机构遵守该规则或修订的规则将过于烦琐或达不到制定该规则的目的;且

(b)指示不会对该规则意图保护权益的人造成不必要的风险。

(5)指示可附条件发出。

(6)管理局可以

(a)撤销指示,或

(b)针对与指示相关的获得许可机构的申请或经其同意变更指示。

注释:

修改等(不涉及条文内容)

C304　第294条暂时有效,于2001年9月3日至2001年12月1日依照制定法文件S.I.2001/2659第1条第(2)款、第3条第(10)款;制定法文件S.I.2001/3538第2条第(1)款修正。

Commencement Information

I98 S. 294 wholly in force at 3.9.2001; s. 294 not in force at Royal Assent see s. 431(2); s. 294(2) in force for specified purposes at 18.6.2001 by S.I. 2001/1820, art. 2, Sch.; s. 294 in force in so far as not already in force at 3.9.2001 by S.I. 2001/2632, art. 2 Sch. Pt. 2

295 Notification: overseas investment exchanges and overseas clearing houses.

(1) At least once a year, every overseas investment exchange and overseas clearing house must provide the Authority with a report.

(2) The report must contain a statement as to whether any events have occurred which are likely—

(a) to affect the Authority's assessment of whether it is satisfied as to the requirements set out in section 292(3); or

(b) to have any effect on competition.

(3) The report must also contain such information as may be specified in rules made by the Authority.

(4) The investment exchange or clearing house must provide the Treasury and the Director with a copy of the report.

Annotations:

Commencement Information

I99 S. 295 wholly in force at 1.12.2001; s. 295 not in force at Royal Assent see s. 431(2); s. 295 in force for specified purposes at 18.6.2001 by S.I. 2001/1820, art. 2, Sch.; s. 295 in force in so far as not already in force at 1.12.2001 by S.I. 2001/3538, art. 2(1)

296 Authority's power to give directions.

(1) This section applies if it appears to the Authority that a recognised body—

(a) has failed, or is likely to fail, to satisfy the recognition requirements; or

(b) has failed to comply with any other obligation imposed on it by or under this Act.

(2) The Authority may direct the body to take specified steps for the purpose of securing the body's compliance with—

(a) the recognition requirements; or

(b) any obligation of the kind in question.

(3) A direction under this section is enforceable, on the application of the Authority, by an injunction or, in Scotland, by an order for specific performance under section 45 of the[M43] Court of Session Act 1988.

实施日期

I98　第294条于2001年9月3日全部生效；第294条在副署时尚未生效，见第431条第(2)款；第294条第(2)款为特定目的于2001年6月18日依照制定法文件S.I.2001/1820第2条、附录生效；第294条如于2001年9月3日尚未生效，则依照制定法文件S.I.2001/2632第2条、附录第二部分生效。

第295条　通知：境外投资交易所和境外结算所

(1)各境外投资交易所和境外结算所必须至少每年1次向管理局提供一份报告。

(2)该报告必须包含针对是否发生了任何可能导致下列结果的事件所做的陈述：

(a)影响管理局评价第292条第(3)款规定的要求是否满足；或

(b)对竞争有任何影响。

(3)该报告还必须包含管理局制定的规则中指定的信息。

(4)投资交易所或结算所必须向财政部和总理事提供该报告的副本。

注释：

实施日期

I99　第295条于2001年12月1日全部生效；第295条在副署时尚未生效，见第431条第(2)款；第295条为特定目的于2001年6月18日依照制定法文件S.I.2001/1820第2条、附录生效；第295条如于2001年12月1日尚未生效，则依照制定法文件S.I.2001/3538第2条第(1)款生效。

第296条　管理局发出指示的权力

(1)如管理局认为获认可的机构有下列情况，则适用本条规定：

(a)未满足或可能未满足认可要求；或

(b)未遵守本法规定或依照本法应承担的任何其他义务。

(2)管理局可指示该机构采取指定措施，以确保该机构遵守

(a)认可要求；或

(b)任何相关种类的义务。

(3)本条规定的指令可经管理局申请，通过强制令强制执行，或在苏格兰可通过[M43]《1988年高等民事法院法》第45条规定的实际履行令强制执行。

(4) The fact that a rule made by a recognised body has been altered in response to a direction given by the Authority does not prevent it from being subsequently altered or revoked by the recognised body.

Annotations:

Modifications etc. (not altering text)

C305 S. 296 amended (temp. from 3.9.2001 to 1.12.2001) by S.I. 2001/2659, arts. 1(2), 3(11); S.I. 2001/3538, art. 2(1)

Marginal Citations

M43 1988 c. 36.

297 Revoking recognition.

(1) A recognition order may be revoked by an order made by the Authority at the request, or with the consent, of the recognised body concerned.

(2) If it appears to the Authority that a recognised body—

(a) is failing, or has failed, to satisfy the recognition requirements, or

(b) is failing, or has failed, to comply with any other obligation imposed on it by or under this Act,it may make an order revoking the recognition order for that body even though the body does not wish the order to be made.

(3) An order under this section ("a revocation order") must specify the date on which it is to take effect.

(4) In the case of a revocation order made under subsection (2), the specified date must not be earlier than the end of the period of three months beginning with the day on which the order is made.

(5) A revocation order may contain such transitional provisions as the Authority thinks necessary or expedient.

Annotations:

Modifications etc. (not altering text)

C306 S. 297 amended (temp. from 3.9.2001 to 1.12.2001) by S.I. 2001/2659, arts. 1(2), 3(11); S.I. 2001/3538, art. 2(1)

298 Directions and revocation: procedure.

(1) Before giving a direction under section 296, or making a revocation order under section 297(2), the Authority must

(a) give written notice of its intention to do so to the recognised body concerned;

(b) take such steps as it considers reasonably practicable to bring the notice to the attention of members (if any) of that body; and

(4)获认可的机构已根据管理局发出的指示对其指定的规则进行修改,并不妨碍该机构随后修改或撤销该规则。

注释:

修改等(不涉及条文内容)

C305 第296条暂时有效,于2001年9月3日至2001年12月1日依照制定法文件S.I. 2001/2659第1条第(2)款、第3条第(11)款;制定法文件S.I.2001/3538第2条第(1)款修正。

附注引文

M43 1988年第36章。

第297条 撤销认可

(1)管理局可以应相关获得许可的机构的请求或经其同意颁布法令撤销许可令。

(2)如管理局认为获认可的机构有下列情况:

(a)正不再满足或已经不再满足认可要求;或

(b)正在不遵守或已经不遵守本法规定或依照本法承担的任何其他义务,则可颁布法令,撤销该机构的认可令,即使该机构不希望发布该命令。

(3)依照本条规定发布的命令(以下简称撤销令)必须规定命令生效日期。

(4)依照第(2)款规定发布的命令,其规定的日期不得早于该命令发布之日起3个月。

(5)撤销令可载有管理局认为需要或适宜的过渡性规定。

注释:

修改等(不涉及条文内容)

C306 第297条暂时有效,于2001年9月3日至2001年12月1日依照制定法文件S.I. 2001/2659第1条第(2)款、第3条第(11)款;制定法文件S.I.2001/3538第2条第(1)款修正。

第298条 指示和撤销:程序

(1)管理局在依照第296条规定发出指示或依照297条第(2)款规定发布撤销令前必须

(a)向相关获得许可的机构发出书面通知,告知其意图发出指令或发布撤销令;

(b)采取其认为合理可行的措施,使该机构成员(如有)注意该通知;并

(c) publish the notice in such manner as it thinks appropriate for bringing it to the attention of other persons who are, in its opinion, likely to be affected.

(2) A notice under subsection (1) must—

(a) state why the Authority intends to give the direction or make the order; and

(b) draw attention to the right to make representations conferred by subsection (3).

(3) Before the end of the period for making representations—

(a) the recognised body,

(b) any member of that body, and

(c) any other person who is likely to be affected by the proposed direction or revocation order, may make representations to the Authority.

(4) The period for making representations is—

(a) two months beginning—

(i) with the date on which the notice is served on the recognised body; or

(ii) if later, with the date on which the notice is published; or

(b) such longer period as the Authority may allow in the particular case.

(5) In deciding whether to—

(a) give a direction, or

(b) make a revocation order,

the Authority must have regard to any representations made in accordance with subsection (3).

(6) When the Authority has decided whether to give a direction under section 296 or to make the proposed revocation order, it must—

(a) give the recognised body written notice of its decision; and

(b) if it has decided to give a direction or make an order, take such steps as it considers reasonably practicable for bringing its decision to the attention of members of the body or of other persons who are, in the Authority's opinion, likely to be affected.

(7) If the Authority considers it essential to do so, it may give a direction under section 296—

(a) without following the procedure set out in this section; or

(b) if the Authority has begun to follow that procedure, regardless of whether the period for making representations has expired.

(8) If the Authority has, in relation to a particular matter, followed the procedure set out in subsections (1) to (5), it need not follow it again if, in relation to that matter, it decides to take action other than that specified in its notice under subsection (1).

(c)以其认为适当的方式公布该通知,使其受到可能受影响的其他人注意。

(2)第(1)款规定的通知必须

(a)说明管理局为何有意发出指示或颁布法令;并

(b)提请注意第(3)款赋予的陈述权。

(3)在陈述期限届满前

(a)获得认可的机构,

(b)该机构的任何成员,以及

(c)可能受到拟发出的指示或撤销令影响的任何其他人,可以向管理局作出陈述。

(4)陈述期限为:

(a)从下列时间起2个月:

(i)通知送达获认可的机构之日;或

(ii)如较晚,则自通知公布之日起;或者

(b)管理局在特殊情况下允许的较长期限。

(5)在决定

(a)是否发出指示,或

(b)是否发布撤销令,

管理局必须考虑依照第(3)款规定向其作出的任何陈述。

(6)如管理局已决定依照第296条规定发出指示,或发布拟发布的撤销令,则必须

(a)向获得许可的机构发出书面通知,告知其决定;

(b)如已决定发出指示或颁布法令,则采取其认为合理可行的措施,使该决定受到该机构成员及管理局认为可能受影响的其他人注意。

(7)管理局如认为有必要,则可以依照第296条规定发出指示

(a)无须遵循本条规定的程序;或

(b)如管理局已开始遵循该程序,则无论陈述期限是否已届满均可发出指示。

(8)如管理局就某一特定事项相关问题已遵循了第(1)款至第(5)款规定的程序,则管理局就该事项决定不采取依照第(1)款规定发出的通知中指定的行动,而采取其他行动时,无须再次遵循上述程序。

Annotations:

Modifications etc. (not altering text)

C307 S. 298 amended(temp. from 3.9.2001 to 1.12.2001) by S.I. 2001/2659, arts. 1(2), 3(11); S.I. 2001/3538, art. 2(1)

Commencement Information

I100 S. 298 wholly in force at 1.12.2001; s. 298 not in force at Royal Assent see s. 431(2); s. 298 in force for specified purposes at 3.9.2001 by S.I. 2001/2632, art. 2 Sch. Pt. 2; s. 298 in force in so far as not already in force at 1.12.2001 by S.I. 2001/3538, art. 2(1)

299 Complaints about recognised bodies.

(1) The Authority must make arrangements for the investigation of any relevant complaint about a recognised body.

(2) "Relevant complaint" means a complaint which the Authority considers is relevant to the question of whether the body concerned should remain a recognised body.

300 Extension of functions of Tribunal.

(1) If the Treasury are satisfied that the condition mentioned in subsection (2) is satisfied, they may by order confer functions on the Tribunal with respect to disciplinary proceedings—

(a) of one or more investment exchanges in relation to which a recognition order under section 290 is in force or of such investment exchanges generally, or

(b) of one or more clearing houses in relation to which a recognition order under that section is in force or of such clearing houses generally.

(2) The condition is that it is desirable to exercise the power conferred under subsection (1) with a view to ensuring that—

(a) decisions taken in disciplinary proceedings with respect to which functions are to be conferred on the Tribunal are consistent with—

(i) decisions of the Tribunal in cases arising under Part Ⅷ; and

(ii) decisions taken in other disciplinary proceedings with respect to which the Tribunal has functions as a result of an order under this section; or

(b) the disciplinary proceedings are in accordance with the Convention rights.

(3) An order under this section may modify or exclude any provision made by or under this Act with respect to proceedings before the Tribunal.

(4) "Disciplinary proceedings" means proceedings under the rules of an investment exchange or clearing house in relation to market abuse by persons subject to the rules.

(5) "The Convention rights" has the meaning given in section 1 of the[M44] Human Rights Act 1998.

注释：

修改等(不涉及条文内容)

C307　第298条暂时有效，于2001年9月3日至2001年12月1日依照制定法文件S.I. 2001/2659第1条第(2)款、第3条第(11)款；制定法文件S.I.2001/3538第2条第(1)款修正。

实施日期

I100　第298条于2001年12月1日全部生效；第298条在副署时尚未生效，见第431条第(2)款；第298条为特定目的于2001年9月3日依照制定法文件S.I.2001/2632第2条第(2)款、附录第二部分生效；第298条如于2001年12月1日尚未生效，则依照制定法文件S.I. 2001/3538第2条第(1)款生效。

第299条　对获认可机构的投诉

(1)管理局必须作出安排，调查任何对获认可机构的相关投诉。

(2)“相关投诉”，系指管理局认为与相关机构是否应继续为获认可机构问题相关的投诉。

第300条　裁判所职能扩展

(1)如财政部确信满足第(2)款所述条件，则可以颁布法令，授予裁判所与针对下列各项的惩戒程序相关的职能：

(a)具有依照第290条规定发出的有效许可令所针对的一家或多家投资交易所，或普遍针对此类投资交易所；

(b)具有依照第290条规定发出的有效许可令所针对的一家或多家结算所，或普遍针对此类结算所。

(2)前款所述条件为，为确保实现下列目标有必要行使第(1)款赋予的权力：

(a)在赋予裁判所职能的相关惩戒程序中作出的裁决符合

(i)法院在第八部分规定的案件中作出的裁决；以及

(ii)在裁判所因依照本法发布的命令而具有职能的其他惩戒程序中作出的裁决；或

(b)惩戒程序与公约权利相一致。

(3)依照本条规定发布的命令可修改或排除依照本法制定、与裁判所审理的程序相关的任何规定。

(4)“惩戒程序”，系指投资交易所或结算所规章规定的、与受规章制约人员滥用市场有关的程序。

(5)“公约权利”具有[M44]《1998年人权法》第1条中的含义。

Annotations:

Marginal Citations

M44 1998 c. 42.

Other matters

301 Supervision of certain contracts.

(1) The Secretary of State and the Treasury, acting jointly, may by regulations provide for—

(a) Part VII of the[M45] Companies Act 1989 (financial markets and insolvency), and

(b) Part V of the[M46] Companies (No. 2)(Northern Ireland) Order 1990, to apply to relevant contracts as it applies

to contracts connected with a recognised body.

(2) "Relevant contracts" means contracts of a prescribed description in relation to which settlement arrangements are provided by a person for the time being included in a list ("the list") maintained by the Authority for the purposes of this section.

(3) Regulations may be made under this section only if the Secretary of State and the Treasury are satisfied, having regard to the extent to which the relevant contracts concerned are contracts of a kind dealt in by persons supervised by the Authority, that it is appropriate for the arrangements mentioned in subsection (2) to be supervised by the Authority.

(4) The approval of the Treasury is required for—

(a) the conditions set by the Authority for admission to the list; and

(b) the arrangements for admission to, and removal from, the list.

(5) If the Treasury withdraw an approval given by them under subsection (4), all regulations made under this section and then in force are to be treated as suspended.

(6) But if—

(a) the Authority changes the conditions or arrangements (or both), and

(b) the Treasury give a fresh approval under subsection (4),

the suspension of the regulations ends on such date as theTreasury may, in giving the fresh approval, specify.

(7) The Authority must—

(a) publish the list as for the time being in force; and

(b) provide a certified copy of it to any person who wishes to refer to it in legal proceedings.

(8) A certified copy of the list is evidence (or in Scotland sufficient evidence) of the contents of the list.

(9) A copy of the list which purports to be certified by or on behalf of the Authority is to

注释:

附注引文
M44 1998年第42章。

其他事项

第301条 特定合同的监督

(1)国务大臣和财政部可联合制定法规,规定

(a)[M45]《1989年公司法》(金融市场和破产)第七部分,以及
(b)[M46]《1990年公司法令》(第2号)(北爱尔兰)第五部分,

适用于相关合同等同于适用于与获得许可的机构相关的合同。

(2)“相关合同”,系指由管理局为本条之目的持有的名单(以下简称名单)中所列之人所提供的相关财产授予契约安排的规定种类合同。

(3)只有国务大臣和财政部经考虑相关合同在何种程度上为管理局的被监督人经营种类的合同,并适合于由管理局监督的第(2)款中涉及的安排,方可依照本条规定制定法规。

(4)下列事项须财政部批准:
(a)管理局设立的列入名单条件;以及
(b)列入名单和从名单中删除的安排。

(5)如财政部撤回依照第(4)款作出的批准,则依照本条规定制定并生效的所有法规视为终止。

(6)但如
(a)管理局变更上述条件或安排(或两者都变更),且
(b)财政部依照第(4)款规定重新作出批准,
法规的终止于财政部在重新作出的批准中指定的日期结束。

(7)管理局必须
(a)于名单生效之时公布该名单;且
(b)向希望在法律程序中引述该名单的任何人提供该名单经认证的副本。

(8)经认证的名单副本为该名单内容的证据(或在苏格兰为充分证据)。

(9)拟由管理局或以管理局名义认证的名单副本视为已经正式认证的副本,除非

be taken to have been duly certified unless the contrary is shown.

(10) Regulations under this section may, in relation to a person included in the list—

(a) apply (with such exceptions, additions and modifications as appear to the Secretary of State and the Treasury to be necessary or expedient) such provisions of, or made under, this Act as they consider appropriate;

(b) provide for the provisions of Part VII of the[M47] Companies Act 1989 and Part V of the[M48] Companies (No. 2)(Northern Ireland) Order 1990 to apply (with such exceptions, additions or modifications as appear to the Secretary of State and the Treasury to be necessary or expedient).

Annotations:

Marginal Citations

M45 1989 c. 40.

M46 S.I. 1990/1504 (N.I. 10).

M47 1989 c. 40.

M48 S.I. 1990/1504 (N.I. 10).

CHAPTER II COMPETITION SCRUTINY

302 Interpretation.

(1) In this Chapter and Chapter III—

"practices" means—

(a) in relation to a recognised investment exchange, the practices of the exchange in its capacity as such; and

(b) in relation to a recognised clearing house, the practices of the clearing house in respect of its clearing arrangements;

"regulatory provisions" means—

(a) the rules of an investment exchange or a clearing house;

(b) any guidance issued by an investment exchange or clearing house;

(c) in the case of an investment exchange, the arrangements and criteria mentioned in section 287(3);

(d) in the case of a clearing house, the arrangements and criteria mentioned in section 288(3).

(2) For the purposes of this Chapter, regulatory provisions or practices have a significantly adverse effect on competition if—

(a) they have, or are intended or likely to have, that effect; or

(b) the effect that they have, or are intended or likely to have, is to require or encourage behaviour which has, or is intended or likely to have, a significantly adverse effect on

证明情况相反。

(10)依照本条制定的法规,就名单所列之人

(a)可以适用其认为适当的依照本法制定的规定(包括国务大臣和财政部认为有必要或适宜的例外、补充和修改);

(b)可以规定适用[M47]《1989年公司法》第七部分和[M48]《1990年公司法令》(第2号)(北爱尔兰)(包括国务大臣和财政部认为有必要或适宜的例外、补充和修改)。

注释:

附注引文

M45 1989年第40章。

M46 制定法文件S.I.1990/1504(第10条)。

M47 1989年第40章。

M48 制定法文件S.I.1990/1504(第10条)。

第二章 竞争审查

第302条 释义

(1)本章和第三章中

"惯例"系指

(a)就获认可的投资交易所而言,系指该所以投资交易所身份进行活动中的惯例;

(b)就获认可的结算所而言,系指该所与其结算安排相关的惯例;

"监管规定"系指

(a)投资交易所或结算所的规章;

(b)投资交易所或结算所发布的任何指引;

(c)就投资交易所而言,第287条第(3)款所述安排和标准;

(d)就结算所而言,第288条第(3)款所述安排和标准。

(2)就本章而言,监管规定或惯例如有下列情况,则为对竞争具有明显不利影响:

(a)具有、预计或可能具有对竞争具有明显不利影响的效力;或

(b)具有、预计或可能具有的效力为,要求实施或鼓励实施预计或可能对竞争产生明显不利影响的行为。

competition.

(3) If regulatory provisions or practices have, or are intended or likely to have, the effect of requiring or encouraging exploitation of the strength of a market position they are to be taken, for the purposes of this Chapter, to have an adverse effect on competition.

(4) In determining under this Chapter whether any regulatory provisions have, or are intended or likely to have, a particular effect, it may be assumed that persons to whom the provisions concerned are addressed will act in accordance with them.

Role of Director General of Fair Trading

303 Initial report by Director.

(1) The Authority must send to the Treasury and to the Director a copy of any regulatory provisions with which it is provided on an application for recognition under section 287 or 288.

(2) The Authority must send to the Director such information in its possession as a result of the application for recognition as it considers will assist him in discharging his functions in connection with the application.

(3) The Director must issue a report as to whether—

(a) a regulatory provision of which a copy has been sent to him under subsection (1) has a significantly adverse effect on competition; or

(b) a combination of regulatory provisions so copied to him have such an effect.

(4) If the Director's conclusion is that one or more provisions have a significantly adverse effect on competition, he must state his reasons for that conclusion.

(5) When the Director issues a report under subsection (3), he must send a copy of it to the Authority, the Competition Commission and the Treasury.

304 Further reports by Director.

(1) The Director must keep under review the regulatory provisions and practices of recognised bodies.

(2) If at any time the Director considers that—

(a) a regulatory provision or practice has a significantly adverse effect on competition, or

(b) regulatory provisions or practices, or a combination of regulating provisions and practices have such an effect,

he must make a report.

(3) If at any time the Director considers that—

(a) a regulatory provision or practice does not have a significantly adverse effect on competition, or

(b) regulatory provisions or practices, or a combination of regulatory provisions and practices do not have any such effect,

(3)如监管规定或惯例具有、预计或可能具有要求或鼓励利用市场地位优势的效力,则就本章而言应将上述规定或惯例视为对竞争具有不利影响。

(4)在依照本章规定确定任何监管规定是否具有、预计或可能具有特定效力时,可以认为相关规定针对的人将依照该规定行事。

公平交易总理事的作用

第303条　总理事的初步报告

(1)管理局必须向财政部及总理事送交依照第287条或288条申请认可时向其提供的任何监管规定的副本。

(2)管理局必须向总理事送交其因申请认可而持有并认为有助于其行使申请相关职能的信息。

(3)总理事必须就下列事项发表一份报告:

(a)已依照第(1)款规定向其发送副本的监管规定是否对竞争具有明显不利影响;或

(b)向其发送副本的监管规定组合是否具有上述影响。

(4)如总理事的结论为一项或多项规定对竞争具有明显不利影响,则必须说明得出该结论的理由。

(5)总理事依照第(3)款规定发布报告时,必须向管理局、竞争委员会和财政部发送该报告副本。

第304条　总理事的进一步报告

(1)总理事必须不断审查获得认可机构的监管规定和惯例。

(2)如总理事在任何时间认为

(a)监管规定惯例对竞争具有明显不利影响,或

(b)监管规定或惯例或者一组监管规定或惯例具有上述影响。

则必须作出报告。

(3)如总理事在任何时间认为

(a)监管规定或惯例对竞争不具有明显不利影响,或

(b)监管规定或惯例或者一组监管规定或惯例不具有上述影响。

he may make a report to that effect.

(4) A report under subsection (2) must contain details of the adverse effect on competition.

(5) If the Director makes a report under subsection (2), he must—

(a) send a copy of it to the Treasury, to the Competition Commission and to the Authority; and

(b) publish it in the way appearing to him to be best calculated to bring it to the attention of the public.

(6) If the Director makes a report under subsection (3)—

(a) he must send a copy of it to the Treasury, to the Competition Commission and to the Authority; and

(b) he may publish it.

(7) Before publishing a report under this section, the Director must, so far as practicable, exclude any matter which relates to the private affairs of a particular individual the publication of which, in the opinion of the Director, would or might seriously and prejudicially affect his interests.

(8) Before publishing such a report, the Director must exclude any matter which relates to the affairs of a particular body the publication of which, in the opinion of the Director, would or might seriously and prejudicially affect its interests.

(9) Subsections (7) and (8) do not apply to the copy of a report which the Director is required to send to the Treasury, the Competition Commission and the Authority under subsection (5)(a) or (6)(a).

(10) For the purposes of the law of defamation, absolute privilege attaches to any report of the Director under this section.

305 Investigations by Director.

(1) For the purpose of investigating any matter with a view to its consideration under section 303 or 304, the Director may exercise the powers conferred on him by this section.

(2) The Director may by notice in writing require any person to produce to him or to a person appointed by him for the purpose, at a time and place specified in the notice, any document which—

(a) is specified or described in the notice; and

(b) is a document in that person's custody or under his control.

(3) The Director may by notice in writing—

(a) require any person carrying on any business to provide him with such information as may be specified or described in the notice; and

(b) specify the time within which, and the manner and form in which, any such information is to be provided.

则可作出报告说明该情况。

(4)第(2)款规定的报告必须载有对竞争不利影响的细节。

(5)如总理事依照第(2)款规定作出报告,则必须

(a)向财政部、竞争委员会和管理局发送该报告副本;并

(b)以其认为最便于公众了解的方式公布该报告。

(6)如总理事依照第(3)款规定作出报告,则

(a)必须向财政部、竞争委员会和管理局发送该报告副本;并

(b)可公布该报告。

(7)依照本条规定发布报告前,总理事如认为公布某一特定个人的私人事务将会或可能严重损害该人利益,则必须在切实可行的范围内排除任何涉及该事务的事项。

(8)公布报告前,总理事如认为公布某一特定组织的私人事务将会或可能严重损害该组织利益,则必须在切实可行范围内排除任何涉及该事务的事项。

(9)第(7)款和第(8)款规定不适用于依照第(5)款第(a)项或第(6)款第(a)项要求总理事向财政部、竞争委员会和管理局送交的报告副本。

(10)总理事依照本条规定作出的任何报告均享有诽谤法所称专有特权。

第305条　总理事的调查

(1)为调查依照第303条或第304条规定应考虑的任何事项,总理事可以行使本条赋予的权力。

(2)总理事可以发出书面通知,要求任何人在通知中指定的时间和地点向总理事或其委派的人出示下列任何文件:

(a)通知中规定或描述的文件;或

(b)该人保管或控制的文件。

(3)总理事可以发出书面通知

(a)要求从事任何业务的任何人向其提供通知中规定或描述的信息;并

(b)规定上述信息的提供时限、提供方式和形式。

(4) A requirement may be imposed under subsection (2) or (3)(a) only in respect of documents or information which relate to any matter relevant to the investigation.

(5) If a person ("the defaulter") refuses, or otherwise fails, to comply with a notice under this section, the Director may certify that fact in writing to the court and the court may enquire into the case.

(6) If, after hearing any witness who may be produced against or on behalf of the defaulter and any statement which may be offered in defence, the court is satisfied that the defaulter did not have a reasonable excuse for refusing or otherwise failing to comply with the notice, the court may deal with the defaulter as if he were in contempt.

(7) In this section, "the court" means—

(a) the High Court; or

(b) in Scotland, the Court of Session.

Annotations:

Commencement Information

I101 S. 305 wholly in force at 1.12.2001; s. 305 not in force at Royal Assent see s. 431 (2); s. 305 in force for specified purposes at 3.9.2001 by S.I. 2001/2632, art. 2(2), Sch. Pt. 2; s. 305 in force in so far as not already in force at 1.12.2001 by S.I. 2001/3538, art. 2(1)

Role of Competition Commission

306 Consideration by Competition Commission.

(1) If subsection (2) or (3) applies, the Commission must investigate the matter which is the subject of the Director's report.

(2) This subsection applies if the Director sends to theCompetition Commission a report—

(a) issued by him under section 303(3) which concludes that one or more regulatory provisions have a significantly adverse effect on competition, or

(b) made by him under section 304(2).

(3) This subsection applies if the Director asks the Commission to consider a report—

(a) issued by him under section 303(3) which concludes that one or more regulatory provisions do not have a significantly adverse effect on competition, or

(b) made by him under section 304(3).

(4) The Commission must then make its own report on the matter unless it considers that, as a result of a change of circumstances, no useful purpose would be served by a report.

(5) If the Commission decides in accordance with subsection (4) not to make a report, it must make a statement setting out the change of circumstances which resulted in that decision.

(4)第(2)款或第(3)款第(a)项规定的要求只可针对与任何调查相关事项有关的文件或信息提出。

(5)如某人(以下简称违反人)拒绝遵从或以其他方式不遵从依照第本条规定发出的通知,则总理事可以向法院书面提出该事项,法庭可调查该案。

(6)如法院在听取任何针对违反人或代表其提出的证人证言及任何辩护陈述后,确信该违反人无合理理由而未遵从该通知,则可将违反人按藐视法庭处理。

(7)本条中"法院"系指

(a)高等法院;或

(b)(苏格兰)高等民事法院。

注释:

实施日期

I101　第305条于2001年12月1日全部生效;第305条在副署时尚未生效,见第431条第(2)款;第305条为规定目的于2001年9月3日依照制定法文件S.I.2001/2632第2条第(2)款、附录第二部分生效;第305条如于2001年12月1日尚未生效,则依照制定法文件S.I. 2001/3538第2条第(1)款生效。

竞争委员会的作用

第306条　竞争委员会的审议

(1)如第(2)款或第(3)款规定适用,则委员会必须调查总理事报告中的主题事项。

(2)如总理事向竞争委员会送交下列报告,则适用本款规定:

(a)依照303条第(3)款规定由其发布,断定一项或多项监管规定对竞争具有明显不利影响的报告;或

(b)依照第304条第(2)款由其作出的报告。

(3)如总理事要求竞争委员会审议下列报告,则适用本款规定:

(a)依照303条第(3)款规定由其发布,断定一项或多项监管规定对竞争具有明显不利影响的报告;或

(b)依照第304条第(3)款由其作出的报告。

(4)委员会随后必须就该事项作出报告,除非委员会认为由于情况变化,作出报告不起任何作用。

(5)如委员会依照第(4)款规定决定不作出报告,则必须作出声明,说明导致作出该决定的情况变化。

(6) A report made under this section must state the Commission's conclusion as to whether—

(a) the regulatory provision or practice which is the subject of the report has a significantly adverse effect on competition, or

(b) the regulatory provisions or practices or combination of regulatory provisions and practices which are the subject of the report have such an effect.

(7) A report under this section stating the Commission's conclusion that there is a significantly adverse effect on competition must also—

(a) state whether the Commission considers that that effect is justified; and

(b) if it states that the Commission considers that it is notjustified, state its conclusion as to what action, if any, the Treasury ought to direct the Authority to take.

(8) Subsection (9) applies whenever the Commission is considering, for the purposes of this section, whether a particular adverse effect on competition is justified.

(9) The Commission must ensure, so far as that is reasonably possible, that the conclusion it reaches is compatible with the obligations imposed on the recognised body concerned by or under this Act.

(10) A report under this section must contain such an account of the Commission's reasons for its conclusions as is expedient, in the opinion of the Commission, for facilitating proper understanding of them.

(11) The provisions of Schedule 14 (except paragraph 2(b)) apply for the purposes of this section as they apply for the purposes of section 162.

(12) If the Commission makes a report under this section it must send a copy to the Treasury, the Authority and the Director.

Annotations:

Commencement Information

I102 S. 306 wholly in force at 1.12.2001; s. 306 not in force at Royal Assent see s. 431 (2); s. 306 in force for specified purposes at 3.9.2001 by S.I. 2001/2632, art. 2(2), Sch. Pt. 2; s. 306 in force in so far as not already in force at 1.12.2001 by S.I. 2001/3538, art. 2(1)

Role of the Treasury

307 Recognition orders: role of the Treasury.

(1) Subsection (2) applies if, on an application for a recognition order—

(a) the Director makes a report under section 303 but does not ask the Competition Commission to consider it under section 306;

(b) the Competition Commission concludes—

(6)依照本条规定作出的报告必须说明委员会就下列事项作出的结论：

(a)作为报告主题的监管规定或惯例是否对竞争具有明显不利影响，或

(b)作为报告主题的监管规定或惯例或者一组监管规定或惯例是否具有上述影响。

(7)依照本条规定作出的报告如声明委员会断定对竞争有明显不利影响，则该报告还必须

(a)说明委员会是否认为该影响有正当理由；且

(b)如说明委员会认为该影响没有正当理由，则说明其断定财政部应指示管理局采取何种行动。

(8)委员会为本条之目的而考虑对竞争产生的不利影响是否有正当理由时，应适用第(9)款规定。

(9)委员会必须在合理可行的范围内确保其作出的结论与本法或依照本法对获得认可的机构规定的义务相一致。

(10)依照本条规定作出的报告必须说明委员会认为有利于正确理解其结论的结论理由。

(11)附录14的规定[除第2款第(b)项外]适用于本条，效力等同于对第162条适用。

(12)如委员会依照本条规定作出报告，则必须向财政部、管理局和总理事发送该报告副本。

注释：

实施日期 I102　第306条于2001年12月1日全部生效；第306条在副署时尚未生效，见第431条第(2)款；第306条为特定目的于2001年9月3日依照制定法文件S.I.2001/2632第2条第(2)款、附录第二部分生效；第306条如于2001年12月1日尚未生效，则依照制定法文件S.I.2001/3538第2条第(1)款生效。

财政部的作用

第307条　认可令：财政部的作用

(1)如有下列情况则适用第(2)款规定：

(a)总理事应认可令申请依照第303条规定作出报告，但不要求竞争委员会依照第306条规定审议该报告；

(b)竞争委员会应认可令申请作出结论，认为

(i) that the applicant's regulatory provisions do not have a significantly adverse effect on competition; or

(ii) that if those provisions do have that effect, the effect is justified.

(2) The Treasury may refuse to approve the making of the recognition order only if they consider that the exceptional circumstances of the case make it inappropriate for them to give their approval.

(3) Subsection (4) applies if, on an application for a recognition order, the Competition Commission concludes—

(a) that the applicant's regulatory provisions have a significantly adverse effect on competition; and

(b) that that effect is not justified.

(4) The Treasury must refuse to approve the making of the recognition order unless they consider that the exceptional circumstances of the case make it inappropriate for them to refuse their approval.

308 Directions by the Treasury.

(1) This section applies if the Competition Commission makes a report under section 306(4) (other than a report on an application for a recognition order) which states the Commission's conclusion that there is a significantly adverse effect on competition.

(2) If the Commission's conclusion, as stated in the report, is that the adverse effect on competition is not justified, the Treasury must give a remedial direction to the Authority.

(3) But subsection (2) does not apply if the Treasury consider—

(a) that, as a result of action taken by the Authority or the recognised body concerned in response to the Commission's report, it is unnecessary for them to give a direction; or

(b) that the exceptional circumstances of the case make it inappropriate or unnecessary for them to do so.

(4) In considering the action to be specified in a remedial direction, the Treasury must have regard to any conclusion of the Commission included in the report because of section 306(7)(b).

(5) Subsection (6) applies if—

(a) the Commission's conclusion, as stated in its report, is that the adverse effect on competition is justified; but

(b) the Treasury consider that the exceptional circumstances of the case require them to act.

(6) The Treasury may give a direction to the Authority requiring it to take such action—

(a) as they consider to be necessary in the light of the exceptional circumstances of the case; and

(b) as may be specified in the direction.

(i)申请人的监管规定对竞争不具有明显不利影响;或

(ii)如上述规定对竞争具有明显不利影响,该影响有正当理由。

(2)财政部仅在其认为由于特殊情况不适于给予批准时,才可以拒绝批准发布认可令。

(3)如竞争委员会就认可令申请作出下列结论,则适用第(4)款规定:

(a)申请人的监管规定对竞争具有明显不利影响;且

(b)该影响无正当理由。

(4)除非认为由于特殊情况不适于拒绝批准,否则财政部必须拒绝批准发布认可令。

第308条　财政部发出的指示

(1)如竞争委员会依照第306条第(4)款作出报告(除就认可令申请作出的报告外),委员会断定对竞争具有明显不利影响,则适用本条规定。

(2)如报告中所述的委员会对竞争有不利影响的结论不合理,则财政部必须向管理局发出救济指示。

(3)如财政部认为有下列情况,则第(2)款规定不适用:

(a)由于管理局或获得认可的机构针对委员会的报告采取了行动,财政部无须作出指示;或

(b)由于特殊情况不适于或不必要作出指示。

(4)财政部在考虑救济指示中指定的行动时必须考虑委员会因第307条第(7)款第(b)项而作出的报告中所包含的任何结论。

(5)如有下列情况则适用第(6)款规定:

(a)委员会在其报告中声明对竞争产生不利影响的结论有正当理由;但

(b)财政部认为由于特殊情况需要财政部采取行动。

(6)财政部可向管理局发出指示,要求其采取下列行动:

(a)财政部认为因特殊情况而有必要采取的行动;以及

(b)指示中规定的行动。

(7) If the action specified in a remedial direction is the giving by the Authority of a direction —

(a) the direction to be given must be compatible with the recognition requirements applicable to the recognised body in relation to which it is given; and

(b) subsections (3) and (4) of section 296 apply to it as if it were a direction given under that section.

(8) "Remedial direction" means a direction requiring the Authority—

(a) to revoke the recognition order for the body concerned; or

(b) to give such directions to the body concerned as may be specified in it.

309 Statements by the Treasury.

(1) If, in reliance on subsection (3)(a) or (b) of section 308, the Treasury decline to act under subsection (2) of that section, they must make a statement to that effect, giving their reasons.

(2) If the Treasury give a direction under section 308 they must make a statement giving—

(a) details of the direction; and

(b) if the direction is given under subsection (6) of that section, their reasons for giving it.

(3) The Treasury must—

(a) publish any statement made under this section in the way appearing to them best calculated to bring it to the attention of the public; and

(b) lay a copy of it before Parliament.

310 Procedure on exercise of certain powers by the Treasury.

(1) Subsection (2) applies if the Treasury are considering—

(a) whether to refuse their approval under section 307;

(b) whether section 308(2) applies; or

(c) whether to give a direction under section 308(6).

(2) The Treasury must—

(a) take such steps as they consider appropriate to allow the exchange or clearing house concerned, and any other person appearing to the Treasury to be affected, an opportunity to make representations—

(i) about any report made by the Director under section 303 or 304 or by the Competition Commission under section 306;

(ii) as to whether, and if so how, the Treasury should exercise their powers under section 307 or 308; and

(b) have regard to any such representations.

(7)如救济指示中规定的行动为管理局发出指示,则

(a)发出的指示必须与适用于该指令相关获得认可机构的认可要求一致;且

(b)第296条第(3)款和第296条第(4)款适用该指示,等同于该指示为依照该条规定发出的指示。

(8)"救济指示"系指要求管理局采取下列行动的指示:

(a)撤销相关机构的认可令;或

(b)对相关机构发出救济指示中指定的指示。

第309条 财政部的声明

(1)如财政部凭借第308条第(3)款第(a)项或第(b)项拒绝依照该条第(2)款规定采取行动,则必须作出相应声明,说明其理由。

(2)如财政部依照第308条发出指令,则必须作出声明

(a)详细说明该指示;且

(b)如该指示为依照该条第(6)款发出,则说明发出指示的理由。

(3)财政部必须

(a)以其认为最便于公众了解的方式公布依照本条规定发布的任何声明;并

(b)将声明副本呈交议会。

第310条 财政部行使特定权力的程序

(1)如财政部在考虑下列情况,则适用第(2)款规定:

(a)是否依照第307条拒绝批准;

(b)第308条第(2)款规定是否适用;或

(c)是否依照第308条第(6)款规定发出指示。

(2)财政部必须

(a)采取其认为适当的措施,使相关交易所或结算所以及财政部认为受影响的其他任何人有机会就下列事项作出陈述:

(i)总理事依照第303条或第304条规定作出的任何报告,或竞争委员会依照第306条规定作出的任何报告;

(ii)财政部是否应当行使第307条或第308条规定的权力,如应行使该权力,如何行使;

(b)考虑上述任何陈述。

Annotations:

Commencement Information

I103 S. 310 wholly in force at 1.12.2001; s. 310 not in force at Royal Assent see s. 431 (2); s. 310 in force for specified purposes at 3.9.2001 by S.I. 2001/2632, art. 2(2), Sch. Pt. 2; s. 310 in force in so far as not already in force at 1.12.2001 by S.I. 2001/3538, art. 2(1)

CHAPTER Ⅲ EXCLUSION FROM THE COMPETITION ACT 1998

311 The Chapter I prohibition.

(1) The Chapter I prohibition does not apply to an agreement for the constitution of a recognised body to the extent to which the agreement relates to the regulatory provisions of that body.

(2) If the conditions set out in subsection (3) are satisfied, the Chapter I prohibition does not apply to an agreement for the constitution of—

(a) an investment exchange which is not a recognised investment exchange, or

(b) a clearing house which is not a recognised clearing house,

to the extent to which the agreement relates to the regulatory provisions of that body.

(3) The conditions are that—

(a) the body has applied for a recognition order in accordance with the provisions of this Act; and

(b) the application has not been determined.

(4) The Chapter I prohibition does not apply to a recognised body's regulatory provisions.

(5) The Chapter I prohibition does not apply to a decision made by a recognised body to the extent to which the decision relates to any of that body's regulatory provisions or practices.

(6) The Chapter I prohibition does not apply to practices of a recognised body.

(7) The Chapter I prohibition does not apply to an agreement the parties to which consist of or include—

(a) a recognised body, or

(b) a person who is subject to the rules of a recognised body,

to the extent to which the agreement consists of provisions the inclusion of which is required or encouraged by any of the body's regulatory provisions or practices.

(8) If a recognised body's recognition order is revoked, this section is to have effect as if that body had continued to be recognised until the end of the period of six months beginning

注释：

实施日期

I103　第310条于2001年12月1日全部生效；第310条在副署时尚未生效，见第431条第(2)款；第310条为规定目的于2001年9月3日依照制定法文件S.I.2001/2632第2条第(2)款、附录第二部分生效；第310条如于2001年12月1日尚未生效，则依照制定法文件S.I.2001/3538第2条第(1)款生效。

第三章　《1998年竞争法》的排除

第311条　第一章禁令

(1)如获认可机构的组织制度协议为与该机构监管规定相关的协议，则第一章禁令不适用于该协议。

(2)如符合第(3)款规定的条件，则第一章禁令不适用于下列机构的组织制度协议：

(a)不属于获认可投资交易所的投资交易所，或

(b)不属于获得认可结算所的结算所。

但该协议应与该机构的监管规定相关。

(3)前款所述条件为

(a)该机构已依照本法规定提出认可令申请；且

(b)针对该申请尚未作出决定。

(4)第一章禁令不适用于获得认可机构的监管规定。

(5)如获认可的机构作出决定与该机构任何监管规定或惯例相关，则第一章禁令不适用于该机构。

(6)第一章禁令不适用于获得认可机构的惯例。

(7)第一章禁令不适用于协议方由下列各项组成或包括下列各项的协议：

(a)获认可的机构，或

(b)受获认可的机构规章制约的人，

但该协议应由该机构任何监管规定或惯例要求或鼓励列入的规定组成。

(8)如获认可的机构认可令被撤销，则本条规定的效力等同于该机构仍获得认可，直至撤销生效之日起6个月期间届满之时。

with the day on which the revocation took effect.

(9) "The Chapter I prohibition" means the prohibition imposed by section 2(1) of the [M49] Competition Act 1998.

(10) Expressions used in this section which are also used in Part I of the Competition Act 1998 are to be interpreted in the same way as for the purposes of that Part of that Act.

Annotations:

Modifications etc. (not altering text)

C308 S. 311(1)(4)(5)(7)(8) amended (temp. from 3.9.2001 to 1.12.2001) by S.I. 2001/2659, arts. 1(2), 3(11); S.I. 2001/3538, art. 2(1)

Marginal Citations

M49 1998 c. 41.

312 The Chapter II prohibition.

(1) The Chapter II prohibition does not apply to

(a) practices of a recognised body;

(b) the adoption or enforcement of such a body's regulatory provisions;

(c) any conduct which is engaged in by such a body or by a person who is subject to the rules of such a body to the extent to which it is encouraged or required by the regulatory provisions of the body.

(2) "The Chapter II prohibition" means the prohibition imposed by section 18(1) of the [M50] Competition Act 1998.

Annotations:

Modifications etc. (not altering text)

C309 S. 312(1)(b) amended (temp. from 3.9.2001 to 1.12.2001) by S.I. 2001/2659, arts. 1(2), 3(11); S.I. 2001/3538, art. 2(1)

Marginal Citations

M50 1998 c. 41.

CHAPTER IV INTERPRETATION

313 Interpretation of Part XVIII.

(1) In this Part—

"application" means an application for a recognition order made under section 287 or 288;

(9)“第一章禁令”系指[M49]《1998年竞争法》第2条第(1)款规定的禁令。

(10)本条中的表述如在《1998年竞争法》第一部分亦有使用,则其解释与为该法之目的所作解释相同。

注释:

修改等(不涉及条文内容)

C308 第311条第(1)款、第(4)款、第(5)款、第(7)款、第(8)款暂时有效,于2001年9月3日至2001年12月1日依照制定法文件S.I.2001/2659第1条第(2)款、第3条第(11)款;制定法文件S.I.2001/3538第2条第(1)款修正。

附注引文

M49 1998年第41章。

第312条 第二章禁令

(1)第二章禁令不适用于

(a)获得认可机构的惯例;

(b)采纳或执行上述机构的监管规定;

(c)该机构或受该机构规章制约的人实施的任何行为,且该行为是该机构监管规定鼓励或要求实施的行为。

(2)“第二章禁令”系指[M50]《1998年竞争法》第18条第(1)款规定的禁令。

注释:

修改等(不涉及条文内容)

C309 第312条第(1)款第(b)项暂时有效,于2001年9月3日至2001年12月1日依照制定法文件S.I.2001/2659第1条第(2)款、第3条第(11)款;制定法文件S.I.2001/3538第2条第(1)款修正。

附注引文

M50 1998年第41章。

第四章 释 义

第313条 第十八部分释义

(1)本部分中

“申请”系指依照第287条或第288条规定提出的认可令申请;

"applicant" means a body corporate or unincorporated association which has applied for a recognition order;

"Director" means the Director General of Fair Trading;

"overseas applicant" means a body corporate or association which has neither its head office nor its registered office in the United Kingdom and which has applied for a recognition order;

"overseas investment exchange" means a body corporate or association which has neither its head office nor its registered office in the United Kingdom and in relation to which a recognition order is in force;

"overseas clearing house" means a body corporate or association which has neither its head office nor its registered office in the United Kingdom and in relation to which a recognition order is in force;

"recognised body" means a recognised investment exchange or a recognized clearing house;

"recognised clearing house" has the meaning given in section 285;

"recognised investment exchange" has the meaning given in section 285;

"recognition order" means an order made under section 290 or 292;

"recognition requirements" has the meaning given by section 286;

"remedial direction" has the meaning given in section 308(8);

"revocation order" has the meaning given in section 297.

(2) References in this Part to rules of an investment exchange (or a clearing house) are to rules made, or conditions imposed, by the investment exchange (or the clearing house) with respect to—

(a) recognition requirements;

(b) admission of persons to, or their exclusion from the use of, its facilities; or

(c) matters relating to its constitution.

(3) References in this Part to guidance issued by an investment exchange are references to guidance issued, or any recommendation made, in writing or other legible form and intended to have continuing effect, by the investment exchange to—

(a) all or any class of its members or users, or

(b) persons seeking to become members of the investment exchange or to use its facilities,

with respect to any of the matters mentioned in subsection (2)(a) to (c).

(4) References in this Part to guidance issued by a clearing house are to guidance issued, or any recommendation made, in writing or other legible form and intended to have continuing effect, by the clearing house to—

(a) all or any class of its members, or

(b) persons using or seeking to use its services,

with respect to the provision by it or its members of clearing services.

“申请人”系指已申请认可令的法人或非法人团体；

“总理事”系指公平交易总理事；

“境外申请人”系指总部和注册营业地均不在联合王国并已申请认可令的法人或组织；

“境外投资交易所”系指总部和注册营业地均不在联合王国并持有生效认可令的法人或组织；

“境外结算所”系指总部和注册营业地均不在联合王国并持有生效认可令的法人或组织；

“获认可的机构”系指获认可的投资交易所或者获认可的结算所；

“获认可的结算所”具有第285条中的含义；

“获认可的投资交易所”具有第285条中的含义；

“认可令”系指依照第290条或第292条规定发布的认可令；

“认可要求”具有第286条中的含义；

“救济指示”具有第308条第(8)款中的含义；

“撤销令”具有第297条中的含义。

(2)本部分中述及投资交易所(或结算所)规则即为述及该投资交易所(或结算所)就下列事项提出的条件：

(a)认可要求；

(b)允许或排除他人使用其设施；或

(c)与其组织制度相关的事项。

(3)本部分中述及投资交易所发布的指引即为述及投资交易所以书面形式或其他可阅读形式向下列人员作出并持续有效的任何建议：

(a)该交易所全部或任何种类的成员或用户，或

(b)谋求成为该投资交易所成员或使用其设施的人，

且该建议与第(2)款第(a)项至第(c)项所列事项相关。

(4)本部分中述及结算所发布的指引即为述及结算所以书面形式或其他可阅读形式向下列人员作出并持续有效的任何建议：

(a)该结算所全部或任何种类的成员，或

(b)正在使用或谋求使用其服务的人，

且该建议与该结算所或其成员提供的结算服务有关。

PART XIX LLOYD'S

General

314 Authority's general duty.

(1) The Authority must keep itself informed about—

(a) the way in which the Council supervises and regulates the market at Lloyd's; and

(b) the way in which regulated activities are being carried on in that market.

(2) The Authority must keep under review the desirability of exercising—

(a) any of its powers under this Part;

(b) any powers which it has in relation to the Society as a result of section 315.

The Society

315 The Society: authorisation and permission.

(1) The Society is an authorised person.

(2) The Society has permission to carry on a regulated activity of any of the following kinds—

(a) arranging deals in contracts of insurance written at Lloyd's ("the basic market activity");

(b) arranging deals in participation in Lloyd's syndicates ("the secondary market activity"); and

(c) an activity carried on in connection with, or for the purposes of, the basic or secondary market activity.

(3) For the purposes of Part Ⅳ, the Society's permission is to be treated as if it had been given on an application for permission under that Part.

(4) The power conferred on the Authority by section 45 may be exercised in anticipation of the coming into force of the Society's permission (or at any other time).

(5) The Society is not subject to any requirement of this Act concerning the registered office of a body corporate.

第十九部分 劳 合 社

一般规定

第314条 管理局的基本职责

(1)管理局必须持续了解

(a)理事会监督和监管劳合社市场的方式;以及

(b)该市场上受监管活动的开展方式。

(2)管理局必须不断审查是否有必要行使下列权力:

(a)本部分规定的任何管理局权力;

(b)因第315条规定与劳合社相关的任何权力。

劳 合 社

第315条 劳合社:授权与许可

(1)劳合社是获授权人。

(2)劳合社具有开展下列任何种类受监管活动的许可:

(a)安排在劳合社形成的书面保险合同的交易(以下简称基本市场活动);

(b)安排参与劳合社辛迪加(以下简称二级市场活动);以及

(c)与基本市场活动或二级市场活动相关或为其目的而开展的活动。

(3)为第四部分之目的,劳合社的许可应视为依照本部分规定提出的申请给予的许可。

(4)第45条赋予管理局的权力可在预期劳合社许可将生效时(或任何其他时间)行使。

(5)劳合社不受本法与法人注册营业地相关的任何要求制约。

Annotations:

Commencement Information

I104 S. 315 wholly in force at 1.12.2001; s. 315 not in force at Royal Assent see s. 431 (2); s. 315(3)-(5) in force for specified purposes at 3.9.2001 by S.I. 2001/2632, art. 2(2), Sch. Pt. 2; s. 315 in force in so far as not already in force at 1.12.2001 by S.I. 2001/3538, art. 2 (1)

Power to apply Act to Lloyd's underwriting

316 Direction by Authority.

(1) The general prohibition or (if the general prohibition is not applied under this section) a core provision applies to the carrying on of an insurance market activity by—

(a) a member of the Society, or

(b) the members of the Society taken together, only if the Authority so directs.

(2) A direction given under subsection (1) which applies a core provision is referred to in this Part as "an insurance market direction".

(3) In subsection (1)—"core provision" means a provision of this Act mentioned in section 317; and "insurance market activity" means a regulated activity relating to contracts of insurance written at Lloyd's.

(4) In deciding whether to give a direction under subsection (1), the Authority must have particular regard to—

(a) the interests of policyholders and potential policyholders;

(b) any failure by the Society to satisfy an obligation to which it is subject as a result of a provision of the law of another EEA State which—

(i) gives effect to any of the insurance directives; and

(ii) is applicable to an activity carried on in that State by a person to whom this section applies;

(c) the need to ensure the effective exercise of the functions which the Authority has in relation to the Society as a result of section 315.

(5) A direction under subsection (1) must be in writing.

(6) A direction under subsection (1) applying the general prohibition may apply it in relation to different classes of person.

(7) An insurance market direction—

(a) must specify each core provision, class of person and kind of activity to which it applies;

(b) may apply different provisions in relation to different classes of person and different kinds of activity.

注释：

实施日期

I104 第315条于2001年12月1日全部生效；第315条在副署时尚未生效，见第431条第（2）款；第315条第（3）款至第（5）款为特定目的于2001年9月3日依照制定法文件S.I. 2001/2632第2条第（2）款、附录第二部分生效；第315条如于2001年12月1日尚未生效，依照制定法文件S.I.2001/3538第2条第（1）款生效。

对劳合社的承保适用法律的权力

第316条 管理局指示

（1）只有管理局作出指示时，一般禁止性规定或（如一般禁止性规定依照本条规定不适用）核心规定，才可以适用于

（a）劳合社成员开展的保险市场活动，或

（b）劳合社成员共同开展的保险市场活动。

（2）依照第（1）款规定发出、适用于核心规定的指示在本部分中称为"保险市场指令"。

（3）第（1）款中，"核心规定"系指本法第317条所述规定；"保险市场活动"系指与在劳合社形成的书面保险合同相关的受监管活动。

（4）管理局在决定是否依照第（1）款规定发出指示时必须特别考虑

（a）保单持有人和潜在保单持有人的利益；

（b）劳合社任何未履行其因欧洲经济区另一国的下来法律规定而承担的义务

（i）使保险指示生效的规定；以及

（ii）适用于本条规定适用的人在该国开展的活动；

（c）需要确保管理局有效行使因第315条规定而与劳合社相关的职能。

（5）第（1）款规定的指示必须为书面形式。

（6）依照第（1）款发出、适用一般禁止性规定的指示可对不同类型的人适用一般性禁止性规定。

（7）保险市场指示

（a）必须指定其适用的每条核心规定、每一类人和每一类活动；

（b）可以对不同种类的人和活动适用不同规定。

(8) A direction under subsection (1) has effect from the date specified in it, which may not be earlier than the date on which it is made.

(9) A direction under subsection (1) must be published in the way appearing to the Authority to be best calculated to bring it to the attention of the public.

(10) The Authority may charge a reasonable fee for providing a person with a copy of the direction.

(11) The Authority must, without delay, give the Treasury a copy of any direction which it gives under this section.

Annotations:

Commencement Information

I105 S. 316 wholly in force at 1.12.2001; s. 316 not in force at Royal Assent see s. 431(2); s. 316(1) in force for specified purposes at 18.6.2001 by S.I. 2001/1820, art. 2, Sch.; s. 316 in force in so far as not already in force at 1.12.2001 by S.I. 2001/3538, art. 2(1)

317 The core provisions.

(1) The core provisions are Parts V, X, XI, XII, XIV, XV, XVI, XXII and XXIV, sections 384 to 386 and Part XXVI.

(2) References in an applied core provision to an authorised person are (where necessary) to be read as references to a person in the class to which the insurance market direction applies.

(3) An insurance market direction may provide that a core provision is to have effect, in relation to persons to whom the provision is applied by the direction, with modifications.

318 Exercise of powers through Council.

(1) The Authority may give a direction under this subsection to the Council or to the Society (acting through the Council) or to both.

(2) A direction under subsection (1) is one given to the body concerned—

(a) in relation to the exercise of its powers generally with a view to achieving, or in support of, a specified objective; or

(b) in relation to the exercise of a specified power which it has, whether in a specified manner or with a view to achieving, or in support of, a specified objective.

(3) "Specified" means specified in the direction.

(4) A direction under subsection (1) may be given—

(a) instead of giving a direction under section 316(1); or

(b) if the Authority considers it necessary or expedient to do so, at the same time as, or following, the giving of such a direction.

(8)依照第(1)款规定发出的指示自其中指定的日期起生效，该日期不得早于该指示发出的日期。

(9)依照第(1)款规定发出的指示必须以管理局认为最便于公众了解的方式公布。

(10)管理局可以为向他人提供该指令副本收取合理费用。

(11)管理局必须毫不延迟地向财政部送交依照本条规定发出的任何指示的副本。

注释:

实施日期

I105 第316条于2001年12月1日全部生效；第316条在副署时尚未生效，见第431条第(2)款；第316条第(1)款为特定目的于2001年6月18日依照制定法文件S.I.2001/1820第2条、附录生效；第316条如于2001年12月1日尚未生效，则依照制定法文件S.I.2001/3538第2条第(1)款生效。

第317条 核心规定

(1)核心规定为第五部分、第十部分、第十一部分、第十二部分、第十四部分、第十五部分、第十六部分、第二十二部分及第二十四部分、第384条至第386条和第二十六部分。

(2)在适用的核心规定中，述及获授权人(如有必要)视为述及保险市场指示适用类型的人。

(3)保险市场指令可规定核心规定经修改后对依照该指令适用该规定的人适用。

第318条 通过理事会行使权力

(1)管理局可以依照本条规定向理事会或劳合社(通过理事会行事)发出指令，或向两者同时发出指令。

(2)依照第(1)款规定发出的指示为就下列相关事项向相关人发出的指示：

(a)为实现或支持规定目标而行使一般权力；或

(b)以规定方式或者为实现或支持规定目标而行使指定权力。

(3)"规定"系指在上述指示中规定。

(4)第(1)款规定的命令

(a)代替第316条第(1)款规定的指示发出；或

(b)如管理局认为有必要或适宜，可以与上述指示同时发出或在其后发出。

(5) A direction may also be given under subsection (1) in respect of underwriting agents as if they were among the persons mentioned in section 316(1).

(6) A direction under this section—

(a) does not, at any time, prevent the exercise by the Authority of any of its powers;

(b) must be in writing.

(7) A direction under subsection (1) must be published in the way appearing to the Authority to be best calculated to bring it to the attention of the public.

(8) The Authority may charge a reasonable fee for providing a person with a copy of the direction.

(9) The Authority must, without delay, give the Treasury a copy of any direction which it gives under this section.

Annotations:

Commencement Information

I106 S. 318 wholly in force at 1.12.2001; s. 318 not in force at Royal Assent see s. 431 (2); s. 318(1) in force for specified purposes at 18.6.2001 by S.I. 2001/1820, art. 2, Sch.; s. 318 in force in so far as not already in force at 1.12.2001 by S.I. 2001/3538, art. 2(1)

319 Consultation.

(1) Before giving a direction under section 316 or 318, the Authority must publish a draft of the proposed direction.

(2) The draft must be accompanied by—

(a) a cost benefit analysis; and

(b) notice that representations about the proposed direction may be made to the Authority within a specified time.

(3) Before giving the proposed direction, the Authority must have regard to any representations made to it in accordance with subsection (2)(b).

(4) If the Authority gives the proposed direction it must publish an account, in general terms, of—

(a) the representations made to it in accordance with subsection (2)(b); and

(b) its response to them.

(5) If the direction differs from the draft published under subsection (1) in a way which is, in the opinion of the Authority, significant

(a) the Authority must (in addition to complying with subsection (4)) publish details of the difference; and

(b) those details must be accompanied by a cost benefit analysis.

(6) Subsections (1) to (5) do not apply if the Authority considers that the delay

(5)也可以对承保机构依照第(1)款规定发出指示,等同于该机构属于第316条第(1)款所列之人。

(6)本条规定的指示

(a)任何时间不阻止管理局行使其任何权力;

(b)必须为书面形式。

(7)依照第(1)款规定发出的指示必须以管理局认为最便于公众了解的方式公布。

(8)管理局可以为向他人提供该指示副本收取合理费用。

(9)管理局必须毫不延迟地向财政部送交依照本条规定发出的任何指示的副本。

注释:

实施日期

I106　第318条于2001年12月1日全部生效;第318条在副署时尚未生效,见第431条第(2)款;第318条第(1)款为特定目的于2001年6月18日依制定法文件S.I.2001/1820第2条、附录生效;第318条如于2001年12月1日尚未生效,则依照制定法文件S.I.2001/3538第2条第(1)款生效。

第319条　谘商

(1)管理局在依照第316条或第318条规定发出指令前必须公布拟发布指示的草案。

(2)该草案必须附有:

(a)成本效益分析;以及

(b)可在指定时间内就拟发出的指示向管理局陈述的通知。

(3)管理局在发出拟发出的指示前必须考虑依照第(2)款第(b)项规定作出的任何陈述。

(4)如管理局发出拟发出的指令,则必须公布概括说明下列事项的报告:

(a)依照第(2)款第(b)项规定向其提出的陈述;以及

(b)管理局对上述陈述的答复。

(5)如管理局认为指示与依照第(1)款规定公布的草案有明显差异,则

(a)管理局[除遵守第(4)款规定外]必须公布差异的详细情况;且

(b)这些详细情况必须附有成本效益分析。

(6)如管理局认为延迟遵守该指示将损害消费者利益,则第(1)款至第(5)款规定

involved in complying with them would be prejudicial to the interests of consumers.

(7) Neither subsection (2)(a) nor subsection (5)(b) applies if the Authority considers—

(a) that, making the appropriate comparison, there will be no increase in costs; or

(b) that, making that comparison, there will be an increase in costs but the increase will be of minimal significance.

(8) The Authority may charge a reasonable fee for providing a person with a copy of a draft published under subsection (1).

(9) When the Authority is required to publish a document under this section it must do so in the way appearing to it to be best calculated to bring it to the attention of the public.

(10) "Cost benefit analysis" means an estimate of the costs together with an analysis of the benefits that will arise—

(a) if the proposed direction is given; or

(b) if subsection (5)(b) applies, from the direction that has been given.

(11) "The appropriate comparison" means—

(a) in relation to subsection (2)(a), a comparison between the overall position if the direction is given and the overall position if it is not given;

(b) in relation to subsection (5)(b), a comparison between the overall position after the giving of the direction and the overall position before it was given.

Former underwriting members

320 Former underwriting members.

(1) A former underwriting member may carry out each contract of insurance that he has underwritten at Lloyd's whether or not he is an authorised person.

(2) If he is an authorised person, any Part Ⅳ permission that he has does not extend to his activities in carrying out any of those contracts.

(3) The Authority may impose on a former underwriting member such requirements as appear to it to be appropriate for the purpose of protecting policyholders against the risk that he may not be able to meet his liabilities.

(4) A person on whom a requirement is imposed may refer the matter to the Tribunal.

Annotations:

Commencement Information

I107 S. 320 wholly in force at 1.12.2001; s. 320 not in force at Royal Assent see s. 431 (2); s. 320(3)(4) in force for specified purposes at 3.9.2001 by S.I. 2001/2632, art. 2(2), Sch. Pt. 2; s. 320 in force in so far as not already in force at 1.12.2001 by S.I. 2001/3538, art. 2(1)

不适用。

(7)如管理局认为有下列情况,则第(2)款第(a)项或第(5)款第(b)项均不适用:

(a)进行适当比较后认为无成本增长;或

(b)进行适当比较后认为成本将增长,但该增长影响极小。

(8)管理局可以为向他人提供依照第(1)款公布的草案副本收取合理费用。

(9)如管理局依照本条规定须公布文件,则必须以其认为最便于公众了解的方式公布。

(10)"成本效益分析"系指对下列情况成本的估计以及对所产生效益的分析:

(a)如发出拟发出的指示;或

(b)如发出的指示适用第(5)款第(b)项。

(11)"适当比较"系指

(a)就第(2)款第(a)项而言,系指比较假设发出指示后的整体状况和假设不发出指令的整体状况。

(b)就第(5)款第(b)项而言,系指比较发出指示后的整体状况和发出指令前的整体状况。

先前承保成员

第320条 先前承保成员

(1)先前承保成员可执行其在劳合社承保的每份保险合同,无论该成员是否为获授权人。

(2)如该成员为获授权人,则其依照第四部分规定持有的许可不延伸至其执行上述任何合同的活动。

(3)为保护保单持有人免于承担先前承保成员可能无法履行责任的风险,管理局可对先前承保成员提出其认为适当的要求。

(4)该要求针对的人可将该事项诉至裁判所。

注释:

实施日期

I107 第320条于2001年12月1日全部生效;第320条在副署时尚未生效,见第431条第(2)款;第320条第(3)款和第(4)款为特定目的于2001年9月3日依制定法文件S.I. 2001/2632第2条第(2)款、附录第二部分生效;第320条如于2001年12月1日尚未生效,则依照制定法文件S.I.2001/3538第2条第(1)款生效。

321 Requirements imposed under section 320.

(1) A requirement imposed under section 320 takes effect—

(a) immediately, if the notice given under subsection (2) states that that is the case;

(b) in any other case, on such date as may be specified in that notice.

(2) If the Authority proposes to impose a requirement on a former underwriting member ("A") under section 320, or imposes such a requirement on him which takes effect immediately, it must give him written notice.

(3) The notice must—

(a) give details of the requirement;

(b) state the Authority's reasons for imposing it;

(c) inform A that he may make representations to the Authority within such period as may be specified in the notice (whether or not he has referred the matter to the Tribunal);

(d) inform him of the date on which the requirement took effect or will take effect; and

(e) inform him of his right to refer the matter to the Tribunal.

(4) The Authority may extend the period allowed under the notice for making representations.

(5) If, having considered any representations made by A, the Authority decides—

(a) to impose the proposed requirement, or

(b) if it has been imposed, not to revoke it,

it must give him written notice.

(6) If the Authority decides—

(a) not to impose a proposed requirement, or

(b) to revoke a requirement that has been imposed,

it must give A written notice.

(7) If the Authority decides to grant an application by A for the variation or revocation of a requirement, it must give him written notice of its decision.

(8) If the Authority proposes to refuse an application by A for the variation or revocation of a requirement it must give him a warning notice.

(9) If the Authority, having considered any representations made in response to the warning notice, decides to refuse the application, it must give A a decision notice.

(10) A notice given under—

(a) subsection (5), or

(b) subsection (9) in the case of a decision to refuse the application,

must inform A of his right to refer the matter to the Tribunal.

(11) If the Authority decides to refuse an application for a variation or revocation of the requirement, the applicant may refer the matter to the Tribunal.

(12) If a notice informs a person of his right to refer a matter to the Tribunal, it must

第321条　依照第320条规定提出的要求

(1)依照第320条规定提出的要求

(a)如依照第(2)条规定情况发出通知,则立即生效;

(b)在任何情况下于通知规定之日生效。

(2)如管理局拟依照第320条规定向先前承保成员(以下简称A)提出要求,或使提出的要求立即生效,则必须向其发出书面通知。

(3)该通知必须

(a)详细说明该要求;

(b)说明管理局提出该要求的理由;

(c)告知先前A可在通知指定的期限内向管理局陈述(无论该事项是否已诉至裁判所);

(d)告知通知生效或将生效的日期;并

(e)告知其有权将该事项诉至裁判所。

(4)管理局可延长通知规定允许陈述的期限。

(5)如管理局在考虑先前A作出的任何陈述后决定

(a)提出拟定的要求,或

(b)不撤销已提出的要求,

则必须向该前承保成员发出书面通知。

(6)如管理局决定

(a)不提出拟定的要求,或

(b)撤销已提出的要求,

则必须向该先前A发出书面通知。

(7)如管理局决定批准先前A变更或撤销要求的申请,则必须向其发出关于该决定的通知。

(8)如管理局拟拒绝批准前A变更或撤销要求的申请,则必须向其发出预告通知。

(9)如管理局考虑针对预告通知提出的任何陈述后决定驳回申请,则必须向先前A发出决定通知。

(10)依照下列规定发出的通知:

(a)第(5)款,或

(b)第(9)款(如决定驳回申请),

必须告知先前A有权将该事项提交裁判所裁决。

(11)如管理局决定拒绝批准变更或撤销要求的申请,则申请人可将该事项诉至裁判所。

(12)如通知告知某人有权将相关事项诉至裁判所,则必须说明诉至裁判所的

give an indication of the procedure on such a reference.

Annotations:

Commencement Information

I108 S. 321 wholly in force at 1.12.2001; s. 321 not in force at Royal Assent see s. 431(2); s. 321 in force for certain purposes at 3.9.2001 by S.I. 2001/2632, art. 2(2), Sch. Pt. 2; s. 321 in force in so far as not already in force at 1.12.2001 by S.I. 2001/3538, art. 2(1)

322 Rules applicable to former underwriting members.

(1) The Authority may make rules imposing such requirements on persons to whom the rules apply as appear to it to be appropriate for protecting policyholders against the risk that those persons may not be able to meet their liabilities.

(2) The rules may apply to—

(a) former underwriting members generally; or

(b) to a class of former underwriting member specified in them.

(3) Section 319 applies to the making of proposed rules under this section as it applies to the giving of a proposed direction under section 316.

(4) Part X (except sections 152 to 154) does not apply to rules made under this section.

Annotations:

Commencement Information

I109 S. 322 wholly in force at 1.12.2001; s. 322 not in force at Royal Assent see s. 431(2); s. 322 in force for specified purposes at 18.6.2001 by S.I. 2001/1820, art. 2, Sch.; s. 322 in force in so far as not already in force at 1.12.2001 by S.I. 2001/3538, art. 2(1)

Transfers of business done at Lloyd's

323 Transfer schemes.

The Treasury may by order provide for the application of any provision of Part VII (with or without modification) in relation to schemes for the transfer of the whole or any part of the business carried on by one or more members of the Society or former underwriting members.

Supplemental

324 Interpretation of this Part.

(1) In this Part—

"arranging deals", in relation to the investments to which this Part applies, has the same meaning as in paragraph 3 of Schedule 2;

程序。

注释:

实施日期

I108 第321条于2001年12月1日全部生效;第321条在副署时尚未生效,见第431条第(2)款;第321条为特定目的于2001年9月3日依照制定法文件S.I.2001/2632第2条第(2)款、附录第二部分生效;第321条如于2001年12月1日尚未生效,则依照制定法文件S.I.2001/3538第2条第(1)款生效。

第322条 适用于先前承保成员的规则

(1)管理局可制定规则,对适用该规则的人提出其认为适当的要求,以保护保单持有人免于承担该人可能无法偿还债务的风险。

(2)规则可适用于

(a)全体先前承保成员;或

(b)规则中指定类型的先前承保成员。

(3)第319条适用于依照本条规定拟制定的规则,等同于适用于依照第316条发出拟发出的指令。

(4)第十部分(除第152条至第154条外)不适用于依照本条规定制定的规则。

注释:

实施日期

I109 第322条于2001年12月1日全部生效;第322条在副署时尚未生效,见第431条第(2)款;第322条为特定目的于2001年6月18日依照制定法文件S.I.2001/1820第2条、附录生效;第322条如于2001年12月1日尚未生效,则依照制定法文件S.I.2001/3538第2条第(1)款生效。

转让在劳合社开展的业务

第323条 转让计划

对一个或多个劳合社成员或先前承保成员开展的业务,财政部可颁布法令,规定就全部或部分转让该业务的计划适用第七部分的任何规定(已修改或未修改)。

附 则

第324条 本部分释义

(1)本部分中

“安排交易”,就本部分适用的投资而言,与附录2第3条意义相同。

"former underwriting member" means a person ceasing to be an underwriting member of the Society on, or at any time after, 24 December 1996; and

"participation in Lloyd's syndicates", in relation to the secondary market activity, means the investment described in sub-paragraph (1) of paragraph 21 of Schedule 2.

(2) A term used in this Part which is defined in[M51] Lloyd's Act 1982 has the same meaning as in that Act.

Annotations:

Marginal Citations

M51 1982 c.xiv.

“先前承保成员”系指1996年12月24日或以后任何时间不再是劳合社承保成员的人；

“参与劳合社辛迪加”就二级市场活动而言，系指附录2第21条第(1)款所述的投资。

(2)本部分中如使用[M51]《1982年劳合社法》定义的词语，则该词语含义与该法中相同。

注释：

附注引文

M51　1982年第14章。

PART XX PROVISION OF FINANCIAL SERVICES BY MEMBERS OF THE PROFESSIONS

325 Authority's general duty.

(1) The Authority must keep itself informed about—

(a) the way in which designated professional bodies supervise and regulate the carrying on of exempt regulated activities by members of the professions in relation to which they are established;

(b) the way in which such members are carrying on exempt regulated activities.

(2) In this Part—

"exempt regulated activities" means regulated activities which may, as a result of this Part, be carried on by members of a profession which is supervised and regulated by a designated professional body without breaching the general prohibition; and

"members", in relation to a profession, means persons who are entitled to practise the profession in question and, in practising it, are subject to the rules of the body designated in relation to that profession, whether or not they are members of that body.

(3) The Authority must keep under review the desirability of exercising any of its powers under this Part.

(4) Each designated professional body must co-operate with the Authority, by the sharing of information and in other ways, in order to enable the Authority to perform its functions under this Part.

Annotations:

Commencement Information

I110 S. 325 wholly in force at 1.12.2001; s. 325 not in force at Royal Assent see s. 431(2); s. 325(4) in force at 3.9.2001 by S.I. 2001/2632, art. 2(2), Sch. Pt. 2; s. 325 in force in so far as not already in force at 1.12.2001 by S.I. 2001/3538, art. 2(1)

第二十部分　行业成员提供的金融服务

第325条　管理局的基本职责

(1)管理局必须了解

(a)规定的行业机构以何种方式监督和监管该相关机构行业成员开展获豁免的受监管活动;

(b)行业成员以何种方式开展获豁免的受监管活动。

(2)本部分中

"获豁免的受监管活动"系指因本部分规定,由指定行业机构监督和监管的专业人士开展且不违反一般禁止性规定的受监管活动;

"行业成员"系指有权在相关行业执业,且在执业时受该专业指定机构规则约束的人,无论其是否为该指定机构成员。

(3)管理局必须持续审查本部分规定的任何权力的行使是否可取。

(4)各指定行业机构必须通过信息共享或其他方式与管理局合作,以使管理局能够行使本部分规定的职能。

注释:

实施日期

I110　第325条于2001年12月1日全部生效;第325条在副署时尚未生效,见第431条第(2)款;第325条第(4)款为特定目的于2001年9月3日依照制定法文件S.I.第2条第(2)款、附录第二部分生效;第325条如于2001年12月1日尚未生效,则依照制定法文件S.I. 2001/3538第2条第(1)款生效。

326 Designation of professional bodies.

(1) The Treasury may by order designate bodies for the purposes of this Part.

(2) A body designated under subsection (1) is referred to in this Part as a designated professional body.

(3) The Treasury may designate a body under subsection (1) only if they are satisfied that—

(a) the basic condition, and

(b) one or more of the additional conditions, are met in relation to it.

(4) The basic condition is that the body has rules applicable to the carrying on by members of the profession in relation to which it is established of regulated activities which, if the body were to be designated, would be exempt regulated activities.

(5) The additional conditions are that—

(a) the body has power under any enactment to regulate the practice of the profession;

(b) being a member of the profession is a requirement under any enactment for the exercise of particular functions or the holding of a particular office;

(c) the body has been recognised for the purpose of any enactment other than this Act and the recognition has not been withdrawn;

(d) the body is established in an EEA State other than the United Kingdom and in that State—

(i) the body has power corresponding to that mentioned in paragraph (a);

(ii) there is a requirement in relation to the body corresponding to that mentioned in paragraph (b); or

(iii) the body is recognised in a manner corresponding to that mentioned in paragraph (c).

(6) "Enactment" includes an Act of the Scottish Parliament, Northern Ireland legislation and subordinate legislation (whether made under an Act, an Act of the Scottish Parliament or Northern Ireland legislation).

(7) "Recognised" means recognised by—

(a) a Minister of the Crown;

(b) the Scottish Ministers;

(c) a Northern Ireland Minister;

(d) a Northern Ireland department or its head.

327 Exemption from the general prohibition.

(1) The general prohibition does not apply to the carrying on of a regulated activity by a person ("P") if—

(a) the conditions set out in subsections (2) to (7) are satisfied; and

(b) there is not in force—

第326条　行业机构的指定

(1)财政部可以颁布法令,为本部分之目的指定机构。

(2)依照第(1)款规定指定的机构在本部分中称为指定行业机构。

(3)财政部只有确信符合下列条件,才可以依照第(1)款指定机构:

(a)相关基本条件,以及

(b)一项或多项相关附加条件。

(4)基本条件为,该机构具有适用于该机构相关专业领域执业人员开展受监管业务的规则,且开展的业务在该机构被指定时为获豁免的受监管活动。

(5)附加条件为

(a)该机构依照任何成文法有权监管该行业的执业活动;

(b)任何成文法要求行使特定职能或担任特定职务的人为行业成员;

(c)该机构为本法以外的任何其他成文法之目的获得认可且该认可未被撤销;

(d)该机构在联合王国以外的欧洲经济区国家设立,并且在该国

(i)该机构具有与第(a)项所述权力对等的权力;

(i)具有该机构相关的与第(b)项所述要求对等的要求;或

(iii)该机构以第(c)项所述方式获得认可。

(6)"成文法"包括苏格兰议会法、北爱尔兰立法以及(隶属于法律、苏格兰议会法或北爱尔兰立法的)附属立法。

(7)"获得认可"系指

(a)获得内阁阁员认可;

(b)获得苏格兰部长认可

(c)获得北爱尔兰部长认可;

(d)获得北爱尔兰部门或其负责人认可。

第327条　一般禁止性规定的豁免

(1)如有下列情况,则一般禁止性规定不适用于某人(以下简称P)开展的受监管活动:

(a)符合第(2)款至第(7)款规定的条件;且

(b)无下列生效指示或命令:

(i) a direction under section 328, or

(ii) an order under section 329,

which prevents this subsection from applying to the carrying on of that activity by him.

(2) P must be—

(a) a member of a profession; or

(b) controlled or managed by one or more such members.

(3) P must not receive from a person other than his client any pecuniary reward or other advantage, for which he does not account to his client, arising out of his carrying on of any of the activities.

(4) The manner of the provision by P of any service in the course of carrying on the activities must be incidental to the provision by him of professional services.

(5) P must not carry on, or hold himself out as carrying on, a regulated activity other than—

(a) one which rules made as a result of section 332(3) allow him to carry on; or

(b) one in relation to which he is an exempt person.

(6) The activities must not be of a description, or relate to an investment of a description, specified in an order made by the Treasury for the purposes of this subsection.

(7) The activities must be the only regulated activities carried on by P (other than regulated activities in relation to which he is an exempt person).

(8) "Professional services" means services—

(a) which do not constitute carrying on a regulated activity, and

(b) the provision of which is supervised and regulated by a designated professional body.

Annotations:

Modifications etc. (not altering text)

C310 S. 327(5)(7) restricted (1.12.2001) by S.I. 2001/544, arts. 2(1), 13(1); S.I. 2001/3538, art. 2(1)

Commencement Information

I111 S. 327 wholly in force at 1.12.2001; s. 327 not in force at Royal Assent see s. 431 (2); s. 327(6) in force for certain purposes at 25.2.2001 by S.I. 2001/516, art. 2(b), Sch. Pt. 2; s. 327 in force in so far as not already in force at 1.12.2001 by S.I. 2001/3538, art. 2(1)

328 Directions in relation to the general prohibition.

(1) The Authority may direct that section 327(1) is not to apply to the extent specified in the direction.

(2) A direction under subsection (1)—

(i)第328条规定的指示,或
(ii)第329条规定的命令,
阻止本款规定适用于该人开展该活动。
(2)P必须
(a)为行业成员;或
(b)受行业成员控制或管理。
(3)P不得因任何上述活动的开展而从其客户以外的任何人处收取任何未向其客户作出解释的金钱报酬或其他利益。
(4)P在开展上述活动时提供任何服务的方式必须与其提供的行业服务相关。
(5)除下列活动外,P不得开展或显示自己开展受监管活动:
(a)因第332条第(3)款规定制定的规则允许其开展的活动;或
(b)该人为享有豁免权的人的活动。
(6)上述活动不得属于财政部为本款规定之目的所发布的命令中指定的类别或与该命令指定类别的投资相关。
(7)上述活动必须仅为P开展的受监管活动(不包括其为享有豁免权的人的被监管活动)。
(8)"行业服务"系指符合下列条件的服务:
(a)不构成受监管活动,且
(b)该服务的提供不受指定行业机构的监督和监管。

注释:

修改等(不涉及条文内容)

C310 第327条第(5)款和第(7)款于2001年12月1日受制定法文件S.I.2001/544第2条第(1)款、第13条第(1)款;制定法文件S.I.2001/3538第2条第(1)款限制。

实施日期

I111 第327条于2001年12月1日全部生效;第327条在副署时尚未生效,见第431条第(2)款;第327条第(6)款为特定目的于2001年2月25日依照制定法文件S.I.2001/516第2条第(b)款、附录第二部分生效;第327条如于2001年12月1日尚未生效,则依照制定法文件S.I.2001/3538第2条第(1)款生效。

第328条 与一般禁止性规定相关的指示

(1)管理局可以指示第327条第(1)款不适用于指示规定的情况。
(2)第(1)款规定的指示

(a) must be in writing;

(b) may be given in relation to different classes of person or different descriptions of regulated activity.

(3) A direction under subsection (1) must be published in the way appearing to the Authority to be best calculated to bring it to the attention of the public.

(4) The Authority may charge a reasonable fee for providing a person with a copy of the direction.

(5) The Authority must, without delay, give the Treasury a copy of any direction which it gives under this section.

(6) The Authority may exercise the power conferred by subsection (1) only if it is satisfied that it is desirable in order to protect the interests of clients.

(7) In considering whether it is so satisfied, the Authority must have regard amongst other things to the effectiveness of any arrangements made by any designated professional body—

(a) for securing compliance with rules made under section 332(1);

(b) for dealing with complaints against its members in relation to the carrying on by them of exempt regulated activities;

(c) in order to offer redress to clients who suffer, or claim to have suffered, loss as a result of misconduct by its members in their carrying on of exempt regulated activities;

(d) for co-operating with the Authority under section 325(4).

(8) In this Part "clients" means—

(a) persons who use, have used or are or may be contemplating using, any of the services provided by a member of a profession in the course of carrying on exempt regulated activities;

(b) persons who have rights or interests which are derived from, or otherwise attributable to, the use of any such services by other persons; or

(c) persons who have rights or interests which may be adversely affected by the use of any such services by persons acting on their behalf or in a fiduciary capacity in relation to them.

(9) If a member of a profession is carrying on an exempt regulated activity in his capacity as a trustee, the persons who are, have been or may be beneficiaries of the trust are to be treated as persons who use, have used or are or may be contemplating using services provided by that person in his carrying on of that activity.

329 Orders in relation to the general prohibition.

(1) Subsection (2) applies if it appears to the Authority that a person to whom, as a result of section 327(1), the general prohibition does not apply is not a fit and proper person to carry on regulated activities in accordance with that section.

(a)必须为书面形式。

(b)可就不同种类的人或不同类别的受监管活动发出。

(3)依照第(1)款规定发出的指示必须以管理局认为最便于公众了解的方式公布。

(4)管理局可以为向他人提供该指令副本收取合理费用。

(5)管理局必须毫不延迟地向财政部送交依照本条规定发出的任何指令的副本。

(6)管理局只有确信为保护客户利益有必要,才可以行使第(1)款赋予的权力。

(7)管理局在考虑是否确信有上述情况时,除其他要素外还必须考虑任何行业机构所做的任何安排对实现下列目标的效果:

(a)确保遵守依照第332条第(1)款规定指定的规则;

(b)处理针对其成员开展获豁免的受监管活动提起的投诉;

(c)对因其成员在开展获豁免的受监管活动时实施的不当行为而遭受损失或声称因该行为遭受损失的客户予以补偿;

(d)依照第325条第(4)款与管理局合作。

(8)本部分中"客户"系指

(a)使用或已经使用,或者可能考虑使用行业成员在开展获豁免的被监管活动过程中提供的任何服务的人;

(b)享有来源于或归因于他人使用任何上述服务的权利或权益的人;或

(c)所享有的权利或利益可能因其代理人或具有与其相关的委托身份的人使用任何服务而受到不利影响的人。

(9)如行业成员以受托人身份开展获豁免的受监管活动,则该委托的受益人,或者曾经或可能为该委托受益人的人,视为使用、已使用或者正在考虑或可能正在考虑使用上述活动开展人所提供服务的人。

第329条　与一般禁止性规定相关的命令

(1)如管理局认为因第327条第(1)款规定不适用一般禁止性规定的人不是依照该条规定开展受监管活动的适当人选,则适用第(2)款规定。

(2) The Authority may make an order disapplying section 327(1) in relation to that person to the extent specified in the order.

(3) The Authority may, on the application of the person named in an order under subsection (1), vary or revoke it.

(4) "Specified" means specified in the order.

(5) If a partnership is named in an order under this section, the order is not affected by any change in its membership.

(6) If a partnership named in an order under this section is dissolved, the order continues to have effect in relation to any partnership which succeeds to the business of the dissolved partnership.

(7) For the purposes of subsection (6), a partnership is to be regarded as succeeding to the business of another partnership only if—

(a) the members of the resulting partnership are substantially the same as those of the former partnership; and

(b) succession is to the whole or substantially the whole of the business of the former partnership.

Annotations:

Modifications etc. (not altering text)

C311 S.329(1) amended (temp. from 3.9.2001 to 1.12.2001) by S.I. 2001/2659, arts. 1(2), 3(4); S.I. 2001/3538, art. 2(1)

330 Consultation.

(1) Before giving a direction under section 328(1), the Authority must publish a draft of the proposed direction.

(2) The draft must be accompanied by—

(a) a cost benefit analysis; and

(b) notice that representations about the proposed direction may be made to the Authority within a specified time.

(3) Before giving the proposed direction, the Authority must have regard to any representations made to it in accordance with subsection (2)(b).

(4) If the Authority gives the proposed direction it must publish an account, in general terms, of—

(a) the representations made to it in accordance with subsection (2)(b); and

(b) its response to them.

(5) If the direction differs from the draft published under subsection (1) in a way which is, in the opinion of the Authority, significant—

(2)管理局可以颁布法令,规定第327条第(1)款不适用于命令规定的情况。

(3)如法令中规定的人提出申请,则管理局可以变更或撤销该规定。

(4)"规定"系指在上述法令中规定。

(5)如依照本条颁布的法令中规定合伙,则该命令不受该合伙成员的任何变更影响。

(6)如依照本条规定颁布的法令规定的合伙解散,则该命令对继受其业务的任何合伙继续有效。

(7)为第(6)款之目的,合伙只有符合下列情况才视为承继另一合伙的业务:

(a)产生的合伙成员与前合伙大致相同;且

(b)承继的是前合伙的全部或几乎全部业务。

注释:

修改等(不涉及条文内容)

C311 第329条第(1)款暂时有效,于2001年9月3日至2001年12月1日依照制定法文件S.I.2001/2659第1条第(2)款、第3条第(4)款;制定法文件S.I.2001/3538第2条第(1)款修正。

第330条 谘商

(1)管理局在依照第328条第(1)款规定发出指示前必须公布拟发布指令的草案。

(2)该草案必须附有:

(a)成本效益分析;以及

(b)可在规定时间内就拟发出的指示向管理局作出陈述的通知。

(3)管理局在发出拟发出的指示前必须考虑依照第(2)款第(b)项规定作出的任何陈述。

(4)如管理局发出拟发出的指示,则必须公布概括说明下列事项的报告:

(a)依照第(2)款第(b)项规定向其提出的陈述;以及

(b)管理局的答复。

(5)如管理局认为指示与依照第(1)款规定公布的草案有明显差异,则

(a) the Authority must (in addition to complying with subsection (4)) publish details of the difference; and

(b) those details must be accompanied by a cost benefit analysis.

(6) Subsections (1) to (5) do not apply if the Authority considers that the delay involved in complying with them would prejudice the interests of consumers.

(7) Neither subsection (2)(a) nor subsection (5)(b) applies if the Authority considers—

(a) that, making the appropriate comparison, there will be no increase in costs; or

(b) that, making that comparison, there will be an increase in costs but the increase will be of minimal significance.

(8) The Authority may charge a reasonable fee for providing a person with a copy of a draft published under subsection (1).

(9) When the Authority is required to publish a document under this section it must do so in the way appearing to it to be best calculated to bring it to the attention of the public.

(10) "Cost benefit analysis" means an estimate of the costs together with an analysis of the benefits that will arise—

(a) if the proposed direction is given; or

(b) if subsection (5)(b) applies, from the direction that has been given.

(11) "The appropriate comparison" means—

(a) in relation to subsection (2)(a), a comparison between the overall position if the direction is given and the overall position if it is not given;

(b) in relation to subsection (5)(b), a comparison between the overall position after the giving of the direction and the overall position before it was given.

331 Procedure on making or varying orders under section 329.

(1) If the Authority proposes to make an order under section 329, it must give the person concerned a warning notice.

(2) The warning notice must set out the terms of the proposed order.

(3) If the Authority decides to make an order under section 329, it must give the person concerned a decision notice.

(4) The decision notice must—

(a) name the person to whom the order applies;

(b) set out the terms of the order; and

(c) be given to the person named in the order.

(5) Subsections (6) to (8) apply to an application for the variation or revocation of an order under section 329.

(6) If the Authority decides to grant the application, it must give the applicant written notice of its decision.

(a)管理局[除遵守第(4)款规定外]必须公布差异的详细情况;且

(b)这些详细情况必须附有成本效益分析。

(6)如管理局认为延迟遵守该指令将损害消费者利益,则第(1)款至第(5)款规定不适用。

(7)如管理局认为有下列情况,则第(2)款第(a)项或第(5)款第(b)项均不适用:

(a)进行适当比较后认为无成本增长;或

(b)进行适当比较后认为成本将增长,但该增长影响极小。

(8)管理局可以为向他人提供依照第(1)款公布的草案副本收取合理费用。

(9)如管理局依照本条规定须公布文件,则必须以其认为最便于公众了解的方式公布。

(10)"成本效益分析"系指对下列情况成本的估计以及对所产生效益的分析:

(a)如发出拟发出的指示;或

(b)如发出的指示适用第(5)款第(b)项。

(11)"适当比较"系指

(a)就第(2)款第(a)项而言,系指比较假设发出指示后的整体状况和假设不发出指令的整体状况;

(b)就第(5)款第(b)项而言,系指比较发出指示后的整体状况和发出指令前的整体状况。

第331条　依照第329条规定发布或变更命令的程序

(1)如管理局拟依照第329条颁布法令,则必须向相关人发出预告通知。

(2)预告通知必须列明拟颁布法令的条款。

(3)如管理局决定依照第329条颁布法令,则必须向相关人发出决定通知。

(4)决定通知必须

(a)规定法令适用于何人;

(b)列明法令的条款;并

(c)向法令中指定的人发出。

(5)第(6)款至第(8)款适用于依照第329条规定颁布的法令变更或撤销申请。

(6)如管理局决定批准申请,则必须就该决定向申请人发出书面通知。

(7) If the Authority proposes to refuse the application, it must give the applicant a warning notice.

(8) If the Authority decides to refuse the application, it must give the applicant a decision notice.

(9) A person—

(a) against whom the Authority have decided to make an order under section 329, or

(b) whose application for the variation or revocation of such an order the Authority had decided to refuse, may refer the matter to the Tribunal.

(10) The Authority may not make an order under section 329 unless—

(a) the period within which the decision to make to the order may be referred to the Tribunal has expired and no such reference has been made; or

(b) if such a reference has been made, the reference has been determined.

332 Rules in relation to persons to whom the general prohibition does not apply.

(1) The Authority may make rules applicable to persons to whom, as a result of section 327(1), the general prohibition does not apply.

(2) The power conferred by subsection (1) is to be exercised for the purpose of ensuring that clients are aware that such persons are not authorised persons.

(3) A designated professional body must make rules—

(a) applicable to members of the profession in relation to which it is established who are not authorised persons; and

(b) governing the carrying on by those members of regulated activities (other than regulated activities in relation to which they are exempt persons).

(4) Rules made in compliance with subsection (3) must be designed to secure that, in providing a particular professional service to a particular client, the member carries on only regulated activities which arise out of, or are complementary to, the provision by him of that service to that client.

(5) Rules made by a designated professional body under subsection (3) require the approval of the Authority.

Annotations:

Modifications etc. (not altering text)

C312 S. 332(3)(b) restricted (1.12.2001) by S.I. 2001/544, arts. 2(1), 13(1); S.I. 2001/3538, art. 2(1)

333 False claims to be a person to whom the general prohibition does not apply.

(1) A person who—

(7)如管理局拟驳回申请,则必须向申请人发出预告通知。

(8)如管理局决定驳回申请,则必须向申请人发出决定通知。

(9)如某人有下列情况:

(a)管理局已决定依照第329条发布针对该人的法令,或

(b)管理局已决定驳回其变更或撤销上述法令的申请,则该人可以将该事项诉至裁判所。

(10)除非有下列情况,否则管理局不得依照第329条规定颁布法令:

(a)可以将该命令诉至裁判所的期限届满而未提交裁判所;或

(b)如已提交审判庭裁决,则该事项已裁决。

第332条　与一般禁止性规定不适用的人相关的规则

(1)管理局可以制定规则,适用于因第327条第(1)款不适用一般禁止性规定的人。

(2)行使第(1)款赋予的权力,旨在确保客户知悉这些人不是获授权人。

(3)指定行业机构必须制定规则

(a)适用于属于行业机构相关行业成员的非获授权人;

(b)规制上述成员开展的受监管活动(不包括其为享有豁免权的人的被监管活动)。

(4)依照第(3)款制定的规则必须旨在确保在向特定客户提供特定行业服务时,成员只开展起因于其向该客户提供的该项服务或补充该项服务的受监管活动。

(5)指定行业机构依照第(3)款规定制定的规则必须经管理局批准。

注释:

修改等(不涉及条文内容)

C312　第332条第(3)款第(b)项于2001年12月1日受制定法文件S.I.2001/544第2条第(1)款、第13条第(1)款;制定法文件S.I.2001/3538第2条第(1)款限制。

第333条　虚假主张为一般禁止性规定不适用的人

(1)如某人有下列情况:

(a) describes himself (in whatever terms) as a person to whom the general prohibition does not apply, in relation to a particular regulated activity, as a result of this Part, or

(b) behaves, or otherwise holds himself out, in a manner which indicates (or which is reasonably likely to be understood as indicating) that he is such a person,

is guilty of an offence if he is not such a person.

(2) In proceedings for an offence under this section it is a defence for the accused to show that he took all reasonable precautions and exercised all due diligence to avoid committing the offence.

(3) A person guilty of an offence under this section is liable on summary conviction to imprisonment for a term not exceeding six months or a fine not exceeding level 5 on the standard scale, or both.

(4) But where the conduct constituting the offence involved or included the public display of any material, the maximum fine for the offence is level 5 on the standard scale multiplied by the number of days for which the display continued.

(a)(以任何措辞)将自己描述为因本部分规定就特定受监管活动不适用一般禁止性规定的人,或

(b)以行动或其他方式显示(或合理地有可能被理解为显示)自己为上述不适用一般禁止性规定的人,

如该人不是上述不适用一般禁止性规定的人,则构成犯罪。

(2)在与本条规定的犯罪相关的法律程序中,被告人如可证明其已采取一切合理的预防措施并已尽一切应有谨慎防止该项犯罪,则可据此进行抗辩。

(3)依照本条规定构成犯罪的人,应经简易程序定罪处以不超过6个月的有期徒刑或不超过标准等级第5级的罚金,或两罚并处。

(4)但如构成犯罪的行为涉及或包含向公众展示任何材料,则最高罚金为标准等级第5级乘以该展示持续的天数。

PART XXI MUTUAL SOCIETIES

Friendly societies

334 The Friendly Societies Commission.

(1) The Treasury may by order provide—

(a) for any functions of the Friendly Societies Commission to be transferred to the Authority;

(b) for any functions of the Friendly Societies Commission which have not been, or are not being, transferred to the Authority to be transferred to the Treasury.

(2) If the Treasury consider it appropriate to do so, they may by order provide for the Friendly Societies Commission to cease to exist on a day specified in or determined in accordance with the order.

(3) The enactments relating to friendly societies which are mentioned in Part I of Schedule 18 are amended as set out in that Part.

(4) Part Ⅱ of Schedule 18—

(a) removes certain restrictions on the ability of incorporated friendly societies to form subsidiaries and control corporate bodies; and

(b) makes connected amendments.

Annotations:

Commencement Information

I112 S. 334 wholly in force at 1.12.2001; s. 334 not in force at Royal Assent see s. 431(2); s. 334(1)(2) in force at 25.2.2001 by S.I. 2001/516, art. 2(a), Sch. Pt. 1; s. 334 in force in so far as not already in force at 1.12.2001 by S.I. 2001/3538, art. 2(1)

335 The Registry of Friendly Societies.

(1) The Treasury may by order provide—

(a) for any functions of the Chief Registrar of Friendly Societies, or of an assistant registrar of friendly societies for the central registration area, to be transferred to the Authority;

第二十一部分 互助协会

互相保险协会

第334条 互相保险协会委员会

(1)财政部可以颁布法令,规定

(a)将互相保险协会委员会的任何职能转移到管理局;

(b)将互相保险协会委员会尚未转移到管理局的任何职能转移给财政部。

(2)如果财政部认为适当,则可以颁布法令,规定互相保险协会委员会按照法令规定或决定的日期终止。

(3)附录18第一部分所述有关互相保险协会的成文法依据该部分之规定修订。

(4)附录18第二部分

(a)取消了对于注册为法人的互相保险协会在设立子企业和控制法人能力方面的某些限制;

(b)作出了相关的修订。

注释:

实施日期

I112 第334条于2001年12月1日全部生效;第334条在副署时尚未生效,见第431条第(2)款;第334条第(1)款和第(2)款于2001年2月25日依照制定法文件S.I.2001/516第2条第(a)款、附录第一部分生效;第334条如于2001年12月1日尚未生效,则依照制定法文件S.I.2001/3538第2条第(1)款生效。

第335条 互相保险协会的注册处

(1)财政部可颁布法令,规定

(a) 将负责中央注册区互相保险协会首席或助理注册官的任何职能转移到管理局;

(b) for any of their functions which have not been, or are not being, transferred to the Authority to be transferred to the Treasury.

(2) The Treasury may by order provide—

(a) for any functions of the central office of the registry of friendly societies to be transferred to the Authority;

(b) for any functions of that office which have not been, or are not being, transferred to the Authority to be transferred to the Treasury.

(3) The Treasury may by order provide—

(a) for any functions of the assistant registrar of friendly societies for Scotland to be transferred to the Authority;

(b) for any functions of the assistant registrar which have not been, or are not being, transferred to the Authority to be transferred to the Treasury.

(4) If the Treasury consider it appropriate to do so, they may by order provide for—

(a) the office of Chief Registrar of Friendly Societies,

(b) the office of assistant registrar of friendly societies for the central registration area,

(c) the central office, or

(d) the office of assistant registrar of friendly societies for Scotland, to cease to exist on a day specified in or determined in accordance with the order.

Building societies

336 The Building Societies Commission.

(1) The Treasury may by order provide—

(a) for any functions of the Building Societies Commission to be transferred to the Authority;

(b) for any functions of the Building Societies Commission which have not been, or are not being, transferred to the Authority to be transferred to the Treasury.

(2) If the Treasury consider it appropriate to do so, they may by order provide for the Building Societies Commission to cease to exist on a day specified in or determined in accordance with the order.

(3) The enactments relating to building societies which are mentioned in Part Ⅲ of Schedule 18 are amended as set out in that Part.

Annotations:

Commencement Information

I113 S. 336 wholly in force at 1.12.2001; s. 336 not in force at Royal Assent see s. 431(2); s. 336(1)(2) in force at 25.2.2001 by S.I. 2001/516, art. 2(a), Sch. Pt. 1; s. 336 in force in so far as not already in force at 1.12.2001 by S.I. 2001/3538, art. 2(1) (b)将首席或助理注册官尚未转移到管理局的任何职能转移到财政部。

(2)财政部可颁布法令,规定

(a)将互相保险协会注册处中央办公室的任何职能转移到管理局;

(b)将该办公室尚未转移到管理局的任何职能转移到财政部。

(3)财政部可以颁布法令,规定

(a)将负责苏格兰互相保险协会的助理注册官的职能转移到管理局;

(b)将该助理注册官尚未转移到管理局的任何职能转移到财政部。

(4)如果财政部认为适当,则可以颁布法令,规定将

(a)互相保险协会首席注册官的办公室,

(b)负责中央注册区互相保险协会的助理注册官的办公室,

(c)中心办公室,或

(d)负责苏格兰互相保险协会的助理注册官的办公室,按照法令规定的或决定的日期终止。

住房互助会

第336条　住房互助会委员会

(1)财政部可颁布法令,规定

(a)将住房互助会委员会的任何职能转移到管理局;

(b)将住房互助会委员会尚未转移到管理局的任何职能转移到财政部。

(2)如果财政部认为适当,则可以颁布法令,规定住房互助会委员会按照法令规定的或决定的日期终止。

(3)附录18第三部分提及的有关互相保险协会的成文法依据该部分之规定修订。

注释:

实施日期

I113　第336条于2001年12月1日全部生效;第336条在副署时尚未生效,见第431条第(2)款;第336条第(1)款和第(2)款于2001年2月25日依照制定法文件S.I.2001/516第2条第(a)款、附录第一部分生效;第336条如于2001年12月1日尚未生效,则依照制定法文件S.I.2001/3538第2条第(1)款生效。

337 The Building Societies Investor Protection Board.

The Treasury may by order provide for the Building Societies Investor Protection Board to cease to exist on a day specified in or determined in accordance with the order.

Industrial and provident societies and credit unions

338 Industrial and provident societies and credit unions.

(1) The Treasury may by order provide for the transfer to the Authority of any functions conferred by—

(a) the [M52] Industrial and Provident Societies Act 1965;

(b) the [M53] Industrial and Provident Societies Act 1967;

(c) the [M54] Friendly and Industrial and Provident Societies Act 1968;

(d) the [M55] Industrial and Provident Societies Act 1975;

(e) the [M56] Industrial and Provident Societies Act 1978;

(f) the [M57] Credit Unions Act 1979.

(2) The Treasury may by order provide for the transfer to the Treasury of any functions under those enactments which have not been, or are not being, transferred to the Authority.

(3) The enactments relating to industrial and provident societies which are mentioned in Part Ⅳ of Schedule 18 are amended as set out in that Part.

(4) The enactments relating to credit unions which are mentioned in Part V of Schedule 18 are amended as set out in that Part.

Annotations:

Commencement Information

I114 S. 388 wholly in force at 1.12.2001; s. 388 not in force at Royal Assent see s. 431 (2); s. 338(1)(2) in force at 25.2.2001 by S.I. 2001/516, art. 2(a), Sch. Pt. 1; s. 388 in force in so far as not already in force at 1.12.2001 by S.I. 2001/3538, art. 2(1)

Marginal Citations

M52 1965 c. 12.

M53 1967 c. 48.

M54 1968 c. 55.

M55 1975 c. 41.

M56 1978 c. 34.

M57 1979 c. 34.

第337条　住房互助会投资者保护委员会

财政部可颁布法令，规定住房互助会投资者保护委员会按照命令指定的或决定的日期终止。

行业节俭互助会及信用合作社

第338条　行业节俭互助会及信用合作社

(1)财政部可以颁布法令,规定将下列法规赋予的任何职能转移到管理局

(a)[M52]《1965年行业节俭互助会法》第52修正案;

(b)[M53]《1967年行业节俭互助会法》第53修正案;

(c)[M54]《1968年工业福利互济协会法》第54修正案;

(d)[M55]《1975年行业节俭互助会法》第55修正案;

(e)[M56]《1978年行业节俭互助会法》第56修正案;

(f)[M57]《1979年信用合作社法》第57修正案。

(2)财政部可以颁布法令,规定将上述成文法赋予但尚未或正在转移到管理局的任何职能转移到财政部。

(3)附录18第四部分所述有关行业节俭互助会的成文法依照该部分之规定修订。

(4)附录18第五部分所述有关信用合作社的成文法依据照该部分之规定修订。

注释:

实施日期

I114　第388条于2001年12月1日全部生效;第388条在副署时尚未生效,见第431条第(2)款;第338条第(1)款和第(2)款于2001年2月25日依照制定法文件S.I.2001/516第2条第(a)款、附录第一部分生效;第388条如于2001年12月1日尚未生效,则依照制定法文件S.I.2001/3538第2条第(1)款生效。

附注引文

M52　1965年第12章。

M53　1967年第48章。

M54　1968年第55章。

M55　1975年第41章。

M56　1978年第34章。

M57　1979年第34章。

Supplemental

339 Supplemental provisions.

(1) The additional powers conferred by section 428 on a person making an order under this Act include power for the Treasury, when making an order under section 334, 335, 336 or 338 which transfers functions, to include provision—

(a) for the transfer of any functions of a member of the body, or servant or agent of the body or person, whose functions are transferred by the order;

(b) for the transfer of any property, rights or liabilities held, enjoyed or incurred by any person in connection with transferred functions;

(c) for the carrying on and completion by or under the authority of the person to whom functions are transferred of any proceedings, investigations or other matters commenced, before the order takes effect, by or under the authority of the person from whom the functions are transferred;

(d) amending any enactment relating to transferred functions in connection with their exercise by, or under the authority of, the person to whom they are transferred;

(e) for the substitution of the person to whom functions are transferred for the person from whom they are transferred, in any instrument, contract or legal proceedings made or begun before the order takes effect.

(2) The additional powers conferred by section 428 on a person making an order under this Act include power for the Treasury, when making an order under section 334(2), 335(4), 336(2) or 337, to include provision—

(a) for the transfer of any property, rights or liabilities held, enjoyed or incurred by any person in connection with the office or body which ceases to have effect as a result of the order;

(b) for the carrying on and completion by or under the authority of such person as may be specified in the order of any proceedings, investigations or other matters commenced, before the order takes effect, by or under the authority of the person whose office, or the body which, ceases to exist as a result of the order;

(c) amending any enactment which makes provision with respect to that office or body;

(d) for the substitution of the Authority, the Treasury or such other body as may be specified in the order in any instrument, contract or legal proceedings made or begun before the order takes effect.

(3) On or after the making of an order under any of sections 334 to 338 ("the original order"), the Treasury may by order make any incidental, supplemental, consequential or transitional provision which they had power to include in the original order.

(4) A certificate issued by the Treasury that property vested in a person immediately

补　充

第339条　补充规定

(1)根据第428条赋予根据本法颁布法令者的额外权力,包括财政部根据第334条、第335条、第336条或第338条下达职能转移命令时作出下列规定的权力:

(a)将职能已根据命令转移的某个机构成员的任何职能,或者公务员或机构或个人之代理人的任何职能进行转移;

(b)将任何与已转移职能相关的任何人所拥有、享有或承担的任何财产权、权利或债务进行转移;

(c)由接受所转移之职能的人或根据其授权在法令生效之前继续并完成由职能被转移的人或根据其授权提起的任何法律程序、调查或其他事宜;

(d)就接受所转移之职能的人行使或根据其授权行使被转移之职能对与该职能有关的成文法进行修订;

(e)由接受所转移之职能的人在命令生效之前作出或提起任何文书、合同或法律程序中取代职能被转移的人。

(2)根据第428条赋予根据本法颁布法令者的额外权力,包括财政部根据第334条第(2)款、第335条第(4)款、第336条第(2)款或第337条下达职能转移命令时作出下列规定的权力:

(a)将任何与因为命令而不再有效之办公室或机构相关的任何人所拥有、享有或承担的任何财产权、权利或债务进行转移;

(b)由该人或根据其授权在命令生效之前根据命令的规定继续并完成由办公室因为命令而不再存在的人或因为命令而不再存在的机构或者根据其授权而开始的任何诉讼、调查或其他事宜;

(c)对就该办公室或机构作出规定的任何成文法进行修订;

(d)由管理局、财政部或命令规定的其他机构(在命令生效之前作出或开始的任何文书、合同或法律程序中)取代职能被转移的人或机构。

(3)在根据第334至338条颁布法令(以下简称原始法令)之时或之后,财政部可以根据其权力以命令形式在原始法令中作出附带、辅助、后续或过渡性的规定。

(4)财政部就在根据本部分规定下达命令之前某人名下的财产权因该命令转移

before an order under this Part takes effect has been transferred as a result of the order is conclusive evidence of the transfer.

(5) Subsections (1) and (2) are not to be read as affecting in any way the powers conferred by section 428.

而签发的证明书,是转移的确切证据。

(5)第(1)款和第(2)款不得解释为以任何方式影响第428条赋予的权力。

PART XXII AUDITORS AND ACTUARIES

Appointment

340 Appointment.

(1) Rules may require an authorised person, or an authorised person falling within a specified class—

(a) to appoint an auditor, or

(b) to appoint an actuary,

if he is not already under an obligation to do so imposed by another enactment.

(2) Rules may require an authorised person, or an authorised person falling within a specified class—

(a) to produce periodic financial reports; and

(b) to have them reported on by an auditor or an actuary.

(3) Rules may impose such other duties on auditors of, or actuaries acting for,authorized persons as may be specified.

(4) Rules under subsection (1) may make provision—

(a) specifying the manner in which and time within which an auditor or actuary is to be appointed;

(b) requiring the Authority to be notified of an appointment;

(c) enabling the Authority to make an appointment if no appointment has been made or notified;

(d) as to remuneration;

(e) as to the term of office, removal and resignation of an auditor or actuary.

(5) An auditor or actuary appointed as a result of rules under subsection (1), or on whom duties are imposed by rules under subsection (3)—

(a) must act in accordance with such provision as may be made by rules; and

(b) is to have such powers in connection with the discharge of his functions as may be provided by rules.

(6) In subsections (1) to (3) "auditor" or "actuary" means an auditor, or actuary, who

第二十二部分　审计人及精算师

任　命

第340条　任命

(1)规则可以要求获授权人或特定类别的获授权人

(a)任命审计人,或者

(b)任命精算师,

如该人尚未根据另一成文法承担此义务。

(2)规则可以要求获授权人或特定类别的获授权人

(a)定期提交财务报告;并且

(b)让审计人或精算师作出上述报告。

(3)规则可以对获授权人的审计人或代表获授权人行事的精算师设定其他职责。

(4)第(1)款项下的规则可以规定

(a)规定任命审计人或精算师的方式和时间

(b)要求向管理局通知任命情况;

(c)若未作出或通知任何任命,授权管理局进行任命;

(d)酬劳;

(e)审计人或精算师的任期、免职和辞职。

(5)根据第(1)款之规则被任命或者根据第(3)款之规则被设定职责的审计人或精算师

(a)必须根据规则的规定采取行动;并且

(b)就其职能的履行将拥有规则规定的权力。

(6)在第(1)款至第(3)款中,“审计人”或“精算师”系指在资格、经验及其他方面

satisfies such requirements as to qualifications, experience and other matters (if any) as may be specified.

(7) "Specified" means specified in rules.

Information

341 Access to books etc.

(1) An appointed auditor of, or an appointed actuary acting for, an authorised person—

(a) has a right of access at all times to the authorised person's books, accounts and vouchers; and

(b) is entitled to require from the authorised person's officers such information and explanations as he reasonably considers necessary for the performance of his duties as auditor or actuary.

(2) "Appointed" means appointed under or as a result of this Act.

342 Information given by auditor or actuary to the Authority.

(1) This section applies to a person who is, or has been, an auditor of an authorised person appointed under or as a result of a statutory provision.

(2) This section also applies to a person who is, or has been, an actuary acting for an authorised person and appointed under or as a result of a statutory provision.

(3) An auditor or actuary does not contravene any duty to which he is subject merely because he gives to the Authority—

(a) information on a matter of which he has, or had, become aware in his capacity as auditor of, or actuary acting for, the authorised person, or

(b) his opinion on such a matter,

if he is acting in good faith and he reasonably believes that the information or opinion is relevant to any functions of the Authority.

(4) Subsection (3) applies whether or not the auditor or actuary is responding to a request from the Authority.

(5) The Treasury may make regulations prescribing circumstances in which an auditor or actuary must communicate matters to the Authority as mentioned in subsection (3).

(6) It is the duty of an auditor or actuary to whom any such regulations apply to communicate a matter to the Authority in the circumstances prescribed by the regulations.

(7) The matters to be communicated to the Authority in accordance with the regulations may include matters relating to persons other than the authorised person concerned.

(如有)符合要求的审计人或精算师。

(7)“规定”系指规则规定。

信　息

第341条　查看账簿等

(1)被任命的审计人或被任命并代表获授权人的精算师

(a)有权随时查看获授权人的账簿、账目和凭单;

(b)有权要求获授权人的高级职员提供其合理认为对于其履行审计人或被精算师职责有必要知悉的信息和解释。

(2)“被任命的”系指根据或因为本法而被任命的。

第342条　审计人或精算师向管理局提供的信息

(1)本条适用于现在或已经是根据或因为某项法律规定而被任命的获授权人的审计人。

(2)本条也适用于现在或已经是根据或因为某项法律规定而被任命并代表获授权人行事的精算师。

(3)审计员或精算师不会仅仅因为向管理局提供下列信息而违反其任何职责:

(a)其担任代表获授权人行事的审计人或精算师而知悉之事项的信息,或

(b)其对该事项的观点,

只要其出于善意并合理地相信上述信息或观点与管理局的任何职能相关。

(4)无论审计人或精算师是否应管理局的要求作出回应,均适用第(3)款规定。

(5)财政部可以制定法规,规定审计人或精算师在何种情况下必须如第(3)款所述向管理局传送有关事项。

(6)该法规适用的审计人或精算师有在法规规定的情况下向管理局传送有关事项的职责。

(7)按法规向管理局传送的事项可包括与除有关获授权人外的人员有关的事项。

Annotations:

Commencement Information

I115 S. 342 wholly in force at 1.12.2001; s. 342 not in force at Royal Assent see s. 431 (2); s. 342(5) in force at 25.2.2001 by S.I. 2001/516, art. 2(a), Sch. Pt. 1; s. 342 in force in so far as not already in force at 1.12.2001 by S.I. 2001/3538, art. 2(1)

343 Information given by auditor or actuary to the Authority: persons with close links.

(1) This section applies to a person who—

(a) is, or has been, an auditor of an authorised person appointed under or as a result of a statutory provision; and

(b) is, or has been, an auditor of a person ("CL") who has close links with the authorised person.

(2) This section also applies to a person who—

(a) is, or has been, an actuary acting for an authorised person and appointed under or as a result of a statutory provision; and

(b) is, or has been, an actuary acting for a person ("CL") who has close links with the authorised person.

(3) An auditor or actuary does not contravene any duty to which he is subject merely because he gives to the Authority—

(a) information on a matter concerning the authorised person of which he has, or had, become aware in his capacity as auditor of, or actuary acting for, CL, or

(b) his opinion on such a matter,

if he is acting in good faith and he reasonably believes that the information or opinion is relevant to any functions of the Authority.

(4) Subsection (3) applies whether or not the auditor or actuary is responding to a request from the Authority.

(5) The Treasury may make regulations prescribing circumstances in which an auditor or actuary must communicate matters to the Authority as mentioned in subsection (3).

(6) It is the duty of an auditor or actuary to whom any such regulations apply to communicate a matter to the Authority in the circumstances prescribed by the regulations.

(7) The matters to be communicated to the Authority in accordance with the regulations may include matters relating to persons other than the authorised person concerned.

(8) CL has close links with the authorised person concerned ("A") if CL is—

(a) a parent undertaking of A;

(b) a subsidiary undertaking of A;

注释：

实施日期

I115　第342条于2001年12月1日全部生效；第342条在副署时尚未生效，见第431条第(2)款；第342条第(5)款于2001年2月25日依照制定法文件S.I.2001/516第2条第(a)款、附录第一部分生效；第342条如于2001年12月1日尚未生效，则依照制定法文件S.I.2001/3538第2条第(1)款生效。

第343条　审计人或精算师向管理局提供的信息：有密切关系的人员

(1)本条适用于

(a)现在或已经是根据或因为某项法律规定而被任命的获授权人的审计人；

(b)现在或已经是与获授权人关系密切者(以下简称CL)的审计人。

(2)本条也适用于

(a)现在或已经是根据或因为某项法律规定而被任命并代表获授权人行事的精算师；

(b)现在或已经是代表与获授权人关系密切者(以下简称CL)行事的精算师。

(3)审计人或精算师不会仅仅因为向管理局提供下列信息而违反其任何职责：

(a)其担任CL的审计人或代表其行事的精算师而知悉之事项的信息，或

(b)其对该事项的观点，

只要其出于善意并合理地相信上述信息或观点与管理局的任何职能相关。

(4)无论审计人或精算师是否应管理局的要求作出回应，均适用第(3)款规定。

(5)财政部可以制定法规，规定审计人或精算师在何种情况下必须如第3款所述向管理局传送有关事项的情况。

(6)该法规适用的审计人或精算师有在条例规定的情况下向管理局传送有关事项的职责。

(7)按法规向管理局传达的事项可包括与除有关获授权人外的人员有关的事项。

(8)在下列情况下，CL与相关获授权人(以下简称A)有密切关系：

(a)CL为A的母企业；

(b)CL为A的子企业；

(c) a parent undertaking of a subsidiary undertaking of A; or

(d) a subsidiary undertaking of a parent undertaking of A.

(9) "Subsidiary undertaking" includes all the instances mentioned in Article 1(1) and (2) of the Seventh Company Law Directive in which an entity may be a subsidiary of an undertaking.

Annotations:

Commencement Information

I116 S. 343 wholly in force at 1.12.2001; s. 343 not in force at Royal Assent see s. 431 (2); s. 343(5) in force at 25.2.2001 by S.I. 2001/516, art. 2(a), Sch. Pt. 1; s. 343 in force in so far as not already in force at 1.12.2001 by S.I. 2001/3538, art. 2(1)

344 Duty of auditor or actuary resigning etc. to give notice.

(1) This section applies to an auditor or actuary to whom section 342 applies.

(2) He must without delay notify the Authority if he—

(a) is removed from office by an authorised person;

(b) resigns before the expiry of his term of office with such a person; or

(c) is not re-appointed by such a person.

(3) If he ceases to be an auditor of, or actuary acting for, such a person, he must without delay notify the Authority—

(a) of any matter connected with his so ceasing which he thinks ought to be drawn to the Authority's attention; or

(b) that there is no such matter.

Disqualification

345 Disqualification.

(1) If it appears to the Authority that an auditor or actuary to whom section 342 applies has failed to comply with a duty imposed on him under this Act, it may disqualify him from being the auditor of, or (as the case may be) from acting as an actuary for, any authorised person or any particular class of authorised person.

(2) If the Authority proposes to disqualify a person under this section it must give him a warning notice.

(3) If it decides to disqualify him it must give him a decision notice.

(4) The Authority may remove any disqualification imposed under this section if satisfied that the disqualified person will in future comply with the duty in question.

(5) A person who has been disqualified under this section may refer the matter to the Tribunal.

(c)CL为A子企业的母企业;或者

(d)CL为A母企业的子企业。

(9)"子企业"包括《公司法第七号指令》第1条第(1)款和第(2)款所述有关某个实体可称为某企业之子企业的所有情形。

注释:

实施日期

I116 第343条于2001年12月1日全部生效;第343条在副署时尚未生效,见第431条第(2)款;第343条第(5)款于2001年2月25日依照制定法文件S.I.2001/516第2条第(a)款、附录第一部分生效;第343条如于2001年12月1日尚未生效,则依照制定法文件S.I.2001/3538第2条第(1)款生效。

第344条 审计人或精算师辞职时发出通知的职责

(1)本条适用于第342条所适用的审计人或精算师。

(2)如有下列情况,则应当毫不延误地通知管理局:

(a)被获授权人解职;

(b)在其受聘于获授权人的任期届满前辞职;或者

(c)未获获授权人再次任命。

(3)当其终止担任获授权人的审计人或代表获授权人行事的精算师时,必须毫不延迟地通知管理局

(a)其认为应该引起管理局注意并与其终止担任上述职务有关的任何事项;

(b)不存在上述事项。

剥 夺 资 格

第345条 剥夺资格

(1)如在管理局看来第342条适用的审计人或精算师未能遵守本法赋予其的职责,则管理局可以剥夺其担任任何获授权人或任何特定类别获授权人的审计人或(视情况而定)代表获授权人的精算师的资格。

(2)如管理局拟根据本条规定剥夺某人的资格,则必须向该人发出预告通知。

(3)如管理局决定剥夺该人的资格,则必须向其发出决定通知。

(4)如确信被剥夺资格者今后遵守本法赋予其的职责,则管理局可以撤销根据本条实施的剥夺资格行为。

(5)根据本条被剥夺资格的人可以将该事项诉至裁判所。

Annotations:

Modifications etc. (not altering text)

C313 S. 345 extended (1.12.2001) by S.I. 2001/2636, arts. 1 (2) (b), 78; S.I. 2001/3538, art. 2(1)

S. 345 amended (1.12.2001) by S.I. 2001/2657, arts. 1 (1), 19 (which was revoked (8.10.2001) by S.I. 2001/3083, arts. 1(2), 23); S.I. 2001/3538, art. 2(1)

S. 345 amended (1.12.2001) by S.I. 2001/3083, arts. 1(2), 19; S.I. 2001/3538, art. 2(1)

Offence

346 Provision of false or misleading information to auditor or actuary.

(1) An authorised person who knowingly or recklessly gives an appointed auditor or actuary information which is false or misleading in a material particular is guilty of an offence and liable—

(a) on summary conviction, to imprisonment for a term not exceeding six months or a fine not exceeding the statutory maximum, or both;

(b) on conviction on indictment, to imprisonment for a term not exceeding two years or a fine, or both.

(2) Subsection (1) applies equally to an officer, controller or manager of anauthorized person.

(3) "Appointed" means appointed under or as a result of this Act.

注释：

修改等(不涉及条文内容)

C313 第345条于2001年12月1日依照制定法文件S.I.2001/2636第1条第(2)款第(b)项、第78条；制定法文件S.I.2001/3538第2条第(1)款扩大适用范围。

第345条于2001年12月1日依照制定法文件S.I.2001/2657第1条第(1)款、第19条[于2001年10月8日依制定法文件S.I.2001/3083第1条第(2)款、第23条废除]；制定法文件S.I.2001/3538第2条第(1)款修正。

第345条于2001年12月1日依照制定法文件S.I.2001/3083第1条第(2)款、第19条；制定法文件S.I.2001/3538第2条第(1)款修正。

犯　罪

第346条　向审计人或精算师提供虚假或误导信息

(1)如获授权人在某个重要细节上向被任命的审计人或精算师提供明知为虚假或误导的信息，或因重大过失而提供虚假或误导信息，则构成犯罪，并应承担下列责任：

(a)经简易程序定罪的，处以不超过6个月的有期徒刑或不超过最高法定限额的罚金，或两罚并处；

(b)经公诉程序定罪的，处以不超过2年的有期徒刑或罚金，或两罚并处。

(2)第(1)款同样适用于获授权人的官员、控制者或管理人。

(3)“被任命的”系指根据或因为本法而被任命的。

PART XXIII PUBLIC RECORD, DISCLOSURE OF INFORMATION AND CO-OPERATION

The public record

347 The record of authorised persons etc.

(1) The Authority must maintain a record of every—

(a) person who appears to the Authority to be an authorised person;

(b) authorised unit trust scheme;

(c) authorised open-ended investment company;

(d) recognised scheme;

(e) recognised investment exchange;

(f) recognised clearing house;

(g) individual to whom a prohibition order relates;

(h) approved person; and

(i) person falling within such other class (if any) as the Authority may determine.

(2) The record must include such information as the Authority considers appropriate and at least the following information—

(a) in the case of a person appearing to the Authority to be an authorised person—

(i) information as to the services which he holds himself out as able to provide; and

(ii) any address of which the Authority is aware at which a notice or other document may be served on him;

(b) in the case of an authorised unit trust scheme, the name and address of the manager and trustee of the scheme;

(c) in the case of an authorised open-ended investment company, the name and address of—

(i) the company;

(ii) if it has only one director, the director; and

(iii) its depositary (if any);

第二十三部分　公共记录、信息披露及合作

公 共 记 录

第347条　获授权人的记录等

(1)管理局必须保存下列各项的记录：

(a)管理局认为是获授权人的人；

(b)被授权的单位信托计划；

(c)被授权的开放式投资公司；

(d)获认可的计划；

(e)获认可的投资交易所；

(f)获认可的结算所；

(g)禁令所及的个人；

(h)被批准人；以及

(i)属于管理局确定的其他类别(如有)的人。

(2)记录必须包括管理局认为适当的信息，并且至少应当包括下列信息：

(a)对管理局认为是获授权人的人而言

(i)关于其自称可以提供之服务的信息；以及

(ii)管理局知悉可以向其送达通知或其他文件的任何地址；

(b)对被授权的单位信托计划而言，计划的管理人和受托人的姓名和地址；

(c)对被授权的开放式投资公司而言

(i)公司的名称和地址；

(ii)董事(如果其仅有一个董事)的名称和地址；以及

(iii)其托管人(如有)的名称和地址；

(d) in the case of a recognised scheme, the name and address of—

(i) the operator of the scheme; and

(ii) any representative of the operator in the United Kingdom;

(e) in the case of a recognised investment exchange or recognised clearing house, the name and address of the exchange or clearing house;

(f) in the case of an individual to whom a prohibition order relates—

(i) his name; and

(ii) details of the effect of the order;

(g) in the case of a person who is an approved person—

(i) his name;

(ii) the name of the relevant authorised person;

(iii) if the approved person is performing a controlled function under an arrangement with a contractor of the relevant authorised person, the name of the contractor.

(3) If it appears to the Authority that a person in respect of whom there is an entry in the record as a result of one of the paragraphs of subsection (1) has ceased to be a person to whom that paragraph applies, the Authority may remove the entry from the record.

(4) But if the Authority decides not to remove the entry, it must—

(a) make a note to that effect in the record; and

(b) state why it considers that the person has ceased to be a person to whom that paragraph applies.

(5) The Authority must—

(a) make the record available for inspection by members of the public in a legible form at such times and in such place or places as the Authority may determine; and

(b) provide a certified copy of the record, or any part of it, to any person who asks for it—

(i) on payment of the fee (if any) fixed by the Authority; and

(ii) in a form (either written or electronic) in which it is legible to the person asking for it.

(6) The Authority may—

(a) publish the record, or any part of it;

(b) exploit commercially the information contained in the record, or any part of that information.

(7) "Authorised unit trust scheme", "authorised open-ended investment company" and "recognised scheme" have the same meaning as in Part XVII, and associated expressions are to be read accordingly.

(8) "Approved person" means a person in relation to whom the Authority has given its approval under section 59 and "controlled function" and "arrangement" have the same meaning as in that section.

(d)对获认可的计划而言

(i)计划管理人的名称和地址;

(ii)管理人在联合王国之任何代表的名称和地址;

(e)对获认可的投资交易所或获认可的结算所而言,交易所或结算所的名称和地址;

(f)对禁令所涉及的个人而言

(i)其姓名;以及

(ii)命令效力的详细情况;

(g)对被批准人而言

(i)其姓名;

(ii)相关获授权人的姓名;

(iii)如果被批准人正根据与相关获授权人的承包商达成的约定履行受监管职能,该承包商的名称。

(3)如在管理局看来第(1)款的某项规定对于因为该项规定而在记录中载有相关条目的人已不再适用,则管理局可以将该条目从记录中删除。

(4)但是如果管理局决定不删除该条目,则管理局必须

(a)在记录中作出具有上述效力的说明;以及

(b)说明管理局为何认为该项规定已不再适用于该人。

(5)管理局必须

(a)使记录以可读的形式在管理局确定的时间和地点供公众检查;以及

(b)对任何提出请求的人提供记录或记录任何部分的经认证副本,管理局应当

(i)收取其确定的费用(如有);并且

(ii)按照提出请求的人可读的形式(书面或电子)提供。

(6)管理局可以

(a)出版记录或其中任何一部分;

(b)商业性利用记录中所包含之信息或其任何部分。

(7)"被授权的单位信托计划"、"被授权的开放式投资公司"及"获认可的计划"具有与第十七部分中相同的含义,相关表述应作相应的解释。

(8)"被批准人"系指管理局已根据第59条给予批准的人,"受监管职能"及"安排"具有与该条中相同的含义。

(9)"Relevant authorised person" has the meaning given in section 66.

Annotations:

Commencement Information

I117 S. 347 partly in force; s. 347 not in force at Royal Assent see s. 431(2); s. 347(3)–(9) in force at 1.12.2001 by S.I. 2001/3538, art. 2(1); s. 347(1)(2) in force for specified purposes at 1.12.2001, 1.5.2002, 1.8.2002, 1.12.2002 by S.I. 2001/3528, art. 2(1)(3)

Disclosure of information

348 Restrictions on disclosure of confidential information by Authority etc.

(1) Confidential information must not be disclosed by a primary recipient, or by any person obtaining the information directly or indirectly from a primary recipient, without the consent of—

(a) the person from whom the primary recipient obtained the information; and

(b) if different, the person to whom it relates.

(2) In this Part"confidential information" means information which—

(a) relates to the business or other affairs of any person;

(b) was received by the primary recipient for the purposes of, or in the discharge of, any functions of the Authority, the competent authority for the purposes of Part Ⅵ or the Secretary of State under any provision made by or under this Act; and

(c) is not prevented from being confidential information by subsection (4).

(3) It is immaterial for the purposes of subsection (2) whether or not the information was received—

(a) by virtue of a requirement to provide it imposed by or under this Act;

(b) for other purposes as well as purposes mentioned in that subsection.

(4) Information is not confidential information if—

(a) it has been made available to the public by virtue of being disclosed in any circumstances in which, or for any purposes for which, disclosure is not precluded by this section; or

(b) it is in the form of a summary or collection of information so framed that it is not possible to ascertain from it information relating to any particular person.

(5) Each of the following is a primary recipient for the purposes of this Part—

(a) the Authority;

(b) any person exercising functions conferred by Part Ⅵ on the competent authority;

(c) the Secretary of State;

(9)"相关的获授权人"具有第66条中的含义。

注释:

实施日期

I117　第347条部分生效;第347条在副署时尚未生效,见第431条第(2)款;第347条第(3)款至第(9)款于2001年12月1日依照制定法文件S.I.2001/3538第2条第(1)款生效;第347条第(1)款、第(2)款为特定目的于2001年12月1日、2002年5月1日、2002年8月1日、2002年12月1日依照制定法文件S.I.2001/3528 第2条第(1)款和第(3)款生效。

信 息 披 露

第348条　对管理局披露保密信息的限制等

(1)保密信息未经下列人员同意不得由主接受者或者直接或间接从主接受者处得到该信息的任何人披露:

(a)向主接受者提供信息的人;以及

(b)如果不是同一人,则与信息相关的人。

(2)在本部分中,"保密信息"系指

(a)与任何人的业务或其他事务相关的信息;

(b)主接受者就管理局的任何职能而言或在履行上述职能时获得的信息、主管机关就第六部分而言获得的信息或者国务大臣根据本法的任何规定获得的信息;以及

(c)不受第(4)款限制的保密信息。

(3)就第(2)款而言,下列各项无关紧要:

(a)信息是否是由于本法要求提供该信息而获得;

(b)信息是否是为了第(2)款所述目的及其他目的而获得。

(4)信息在下列情况不属于保密信息:

(a)该信息由于在任何情况下被披露而为公众所知,而且在上述情况下的披露或披露的任何目的不受本条限制;或者

(b)信息采用了摘要或汇编的形式,以致无法根据其查明与任何特定个人有关的信息。

(5)就本部分而言,下列任何一项均为主接受者:

(a)管理局;

(b)履行第六部分赋予主管机关职能的人;

(c)国务大臣;

(d) a person appointed to make a report under section 166;

(e) any person who is or has been employed by a person mentioned in paragraphs (a) to (c);

(f) any auditor or expert instructed by a person mentioned in those paragraphs.

(6) In subsection (5)(f) "expert" includes—

(a) a competent person appointed by the competent authority under section 97;

(b) a competent person appointed by the Authority or the Secretary of State to conduct an investigation under Part XI;

(c) any body or person appointed under paragraph 6 of Schedule 1 to perform a function on behalf of the Authority.

Annotations:

Modifications etc. (not altering text)

C314 S. 348 extended (1.12.2001) by S.I. 2001/3648, arts. 1, 3(2), 4, 5(2), 7(2)

S. 348 modified (17.8.2001 for certain purposes otherwise 1.12.2001) by 1986 c. 53, s. 53A (as substituted (17.8.2001 for certain purposes otherwise 1.12.2001) by S.I. 2001/2617, arts. 2, 8, 13(1), Sch. 3 Pt. II para. 152); S.I. 2001/3538, art. 2(1)

S. 348 modified (17.8.2001 for certain purposes otherwise 1.12.2001) by 1992 c. 40, s. 63A(1)(as substituted(17.8.2001 for certain purposes otherwise 1.12.2001) by S.I. 2001/2617, arts. 2, 8, 13(1), Sch. 3 Pt. I para. 78); S.I. 2001/3538, art. 2(1)

349 Exceptions from section 348.

(1) Section 348 does not prevent a disclosure of confidential information which is—

(a) made for the purpose of facilitating the carrying out of a public function; and

(b) permitted by regulations made by the Treasury under this section.

(2) The regulations may, in particular, make provision permitting the disclosure of confidential information or of confidential information of a prescribed kind—

(a) by prescribed recipients, or recipients of a prescribed description, to any person for the purpose of enabling or assisting the recipient to discharge prescribed public functions;

(b) by prescribed recipients, or recipients of a prescribed description, to prescribed persons, or persons of prescribed descriptions, for the purpose of enabling or assisting those persons to discharge prescribed public functions;

(c) by the Authority to the Treasury or the Secretary of State for any purpose;

(d) by any recipient if the disclosure is with a view to or in connection with prescribed proceedings.

(3) The regulations may also include provision—

(d)根据第166条被指定的报告人;

(e)现在或已经受雇于第(a)项至第(c)项所述之人的人;

(f)接受上述各项所述之人指示的任何审计人或专家。

(6)在第(5)款第(f)项中,“专家”包括:

(a)主管部门根据第97条任命的适格人员;

(b)管理局或国务大臣任命的根据第十一部分规定进行调查的适格人员;

(c)根据附录1之第6条任命并代表管理局履行某项职能的机构或人。

注释:

修改等(不涉及条文内容)

C314　第348条于2001年12月1日依照制定法文件S.I.2001/3648第1条、第3条第(2)款、第4条、第5条第(2)款、第7条第(2)款扩大适用范围;

第348条为特定目的于2001年8月17日,否则于2001年12月1日依照1986年本法第53条、第53A条[为特定目的于2001年8月17日,否则于2001年12月1日依照制定法文件S.I.2001/2617第2条、第8条、第13条第(1)款、附录3第二部分第152条替换];制定法文件S.I.2001/3538第2条第(1)款修订;

第348条为特定目的于2001年8月17日,否则于2001年12月1日依照1992年本法第40条、第63A条第(1)款[为特定目的于2001年8月17日,否则于2001年12月1日依照制定法文件S.I.2001/2617第2条、第8条、第13条第(1)款、附录3第一部分第78条替换];制定法文件S.I.2001/3538第2条第(1)款修订。

第349条　第348条之例外

(1)第348条不妨碍

(a)为便利公共职能之履行而披露保密信息;

(b)因财政部根据本条制定之法规允许而披露保密信息。

(2)法规可以特别规定允许下列披露保密信息或规定类别保密信息的行为:

(a)由规定的接受者或规定类型的接受者向任何人披露,旨在许可或协助后者履行规定的公共职能;

(b)由规定的接受者或规定类型的接受者向规定之人或规定类型之人披露,旨在许可或协助后者履行规定的公共职能规定之人;

(c)由管理局向财政部或国务大臣披露,无论出于何种目的;

(d)由任何接受者出于对规定之法律程序的考虑或关系而披露。

(3)法规也可包括下列规定:

(a) making any permission to disclose confidential information subject to conditions (which may relate to the obtaining of consents or any other matter);

(b) restricting the uses to which confidential information disclosed under the regulations may be put.

(4) In relation to confidential information, each of the following is a "recipient"—

(a) a primary recipient;

(b) a person obtaining the information directly or indirectly from a primary recipient.

(5) "Public functions" includes—

(a) functions conferred by or in accordance with any provision contained in any enactment or subordinate legislation;

(b) functions conferred by or in accordance with any provision contained in the Community Treaties or any Community instrument;

(c) similar functions conferred on persons by or under provisions having effect as part of the law of a country or territory outside the United Kingdom;

(d) functions exercisable in relation to prescribed disciplinary proceedings.

(6) "Enactment" includes—

(a) an Act of the Scottish Parliament;

(b) Northern Ireland legislation.

(7) "Subordinate legislation" has the meaning given in the [M58]Interpretation Act 1978 and also includes an instrument made under an Act of the Scottish Parliament or under Northern Ireland legislation.

Annotations:

Modifications etc. (not altering text)

C315 S. 349 extended (1.12.2001) by S.I. 2001/3648, arts. 1, 3(2), 4, 5(2), 7(2)

S. 349 modified (17.8.2001 for certain purposes otherwise 1.12.2001) by 1986 c. 53, s. 53A as substituted (17.8.2001 for certain purposes otherwise 1.12.2001) by S.I. 2001/2617, arts. 2, 8, 13(1), Sch. 3 Pt. II para. 152; S.I. 2001/3538, art. 2(1)

S. 349 modified (17.8.2001 for certain purposes otherwise 1.12.2001) by 1992 c. 40 (as substituted (17.8.2001 for certain purposes otherwise 1.12.2001) by S.I. 2001/2617, arts. 2, 8, 13(1), Sch. 3 Pt. I para. 78; S.I. 2001/3538, art. 2(1) (a)在符合某些条件(可能涉及获得同意或任何其他事情)时允许披露保密信息;

(b)对按法规予以披露之保密信息的使用加以限制。

(4)下列人员为与保密信息相关的"接受者":

(a)主接受者;

(b)直接或间接从主接受者获得信息的人。

(5)"公共职能"包括:

(a)由或根据任何成文法或附属立法的任何规定所赋予的职能;

(b)由或根据共同体条约或文件的任何规定所赋予的职能;

(c)由或根据联合王国之外某国或地区法律中已生效的规定而赋予人们的类似职能;

(d)与规定的惩戒程序相关的可履行职能。

(6)"成文法"包括:

(a)苏格兰议会的法律;

(b)北爱尔兰的立法。

(7)"附属立法"具有M58《1978年解释本法》中的含义,还包括根据苏格兰议会的法律或者北爱尔兰的立法而制定的文书。

注释:

修改等(不涉及条文内容)

C315 第349条于2001年12月1日依照制定法文件S.I.2001/3648第1条、第3条第(2)款、第4条、第5条第(2)款、第7条第(2)款扩大适用范围;

第349条为特定目的于2001年8月17日,否则于2001年12月1日依照1986年本法第53条、第53A条[为特定目的于2001年8月17日,否则于2001年12月1日依照制定法文件S.I.2001/2617第2条、第8条、第13条第(1)款、附录3第二部分第152条替换];制定法文件S.I.2001/3538第2条第(1)款修订;

第349条为特定目的于2001年8月17日,否则于2001年12月1日依照1992年第40章[为特定目的于2001年8月17日,否则于2001年12月1日依照制定法文件S.I.2001/2617第2条、第8条、第13条第(1)款、附录第78条替换];制定法文件S.I.2001/3538第2条第(1)款修订。

Commencement Information

I118 S. 349 wholly in force at 18.6.2001; s. 349 not in force at Royal Assent see s. 431 (2); s. 349 in force for certain purposes at 25.2.2001 by S.I. 2001/516, art. 2(b), Sch. Pt. 2; s. 349 in force in so far as not already in force at 18.6.2001 by S.I. 2001/1820, art. 2, Sch.

Marginal Citations

M58 1978 c. 30.

350 Disclosure of information by the Inland Revenue.

(1) No obligation as to secrecy imposed by statute or otherwise prevents the disclosure of Revenue information to—

(a) the Authority, or

(b) the Secretary of State,

if the disclosure is made for the purpose of assisting in the investigation of a matter under section 168 or with a view to the appointment of an investigator under that section.

(2) A disclosure may only be made under subsection (1) by or under the authority of the Commissioners of Inland Revenue.

(3) Section 348 does not apply to Revenue information.

(4) Information obtained as a result of subsection (1) may not be used except—

(a) for the purpose of deciding whether to appoint an investigator under section 168;

(b) in the conduct of an investigation under section 168;

(c) in criminal proceedings brought against a person under this Act or the [M59] Criminal Justice Act 1993 as a result of an investigation under section 168;

(d) for the purpose of taking action under this Act against a person as a result of an investigation under section 168;

(e) in proceedings before the Tribunal as a result of action taken as mentioned in paragraph (d).

(5) Information obtained as a result of subsection (1) may not be disclosed except—

(a) by or under the authority of the Commissioners of Inland Revenue;

(b) in proceedings mentioned in subsection (4)(c) or (e) or with a view to their institution.

(6) Subsection (5) does not prevent the disclosure of information obtained as a result of subsection (1) to a person to whom it could have been disclosed under subsection (1).

(7) "Revenue information" means information held by a person which it would be an offence under section 182 of the [M60] Finance Act 1989 for him to disclose.

实施日期

I118　第349条于2001年6月18日全部生效;第349条在副署时尚未生效,见第431条第(2)款;第349条为特定目的于2001年2月25日依照制定法文件S.I.2001/516第2条第(b)款、附录第二部分生效;第349条如于2001年6月18日尚未生效,则依照制定法文件S.I.2001/1820第2条、附录生效。

附注引文

M58　1978年第30章。

第350条　由国内税务局披露信息

(1)法规或其他文件规定的保密义务不得妨碍向下列机关披露收入信息:

(a)管理局,或者

(b)国务大臣,

只要上述披露是为了协助根据168条对某事项的调查或者是着眼于根据该条任命调查人。

(2)第(1)款规定的披露只能由国内税务局特派员或根据其授权作出。

(3)第348条不适用于收入信息。

(4)由于第(1)款而获得的信息仅可用于

(a)决定是否根据168条任命调查者之目的;

(b)根据第168条进行调查;

(c)由于根据第168条所做之调查而根据本法或[M59]《1993年刑事司法法》对某人提起的刑事诉讼;

(d)由于根据第168条所作之调查而根据本法对某人采取行动之目的;

(e)由于第(d)项所述之行动而向裁判所提起的诉讼。

(5)由于第(1)款而获得的信息仅可以

(a)由国内税务局特派员或根据其授权披露;

(b)在第(4)款第(c)项或第(e)项所述的诉讼中或者着眼于这些诉讼的成立而披露。

(6)第(5)款不妨碍将由于第(1)款而获得的信息向根据第(1)款可披露之人披露。

(7)"收入信息"系指由某人所掌握的信息,并且该人对该信息的披露将构成[M60]《1989年金融法》第182条所规定的犯罪。

Annotations:

Modifications etc. (not altering text)

C316 S. 350 modified (17.8.2001 for certain purposes otherwise 1.12.2001) by 1986 c. 53, s. 53A (as substituted (17.8.2001 for certain purposes otherwise 1.12.2001) by S.I. 2001/2617, arts. 2, 8, 13(1), Sch. 3 Pt. II para. 152); S.I. 2001/3538, art. 2(1)

S. 350 modified (17.8.2001 for certain purposes otherwise 1.12.2001) by 1992 c. 40, s. 63A (as substituted (17.8.2001 for certain purposes otherwise 1.12.2001) by S.I. 2001/2617, arts. 2, 8, 13(1), Sch. 3 Pt. I para. 78); S.I. 2001/3538, art. 2(1)

Commencement Information

I119 S. 350 wholly in force 3.9.2001; s. 350 not in force at Royal Assent see s. 431(2); s. 350(3)(7) in force at 18.6.2001 by S.I. 2001/1820, art. 2, Sch.; s. 350 in force in so far as not already in force at 3.9.2001 by S.I. 2001/2632, art. 2(2), Sch. Pt. 2

Marginal Citations

M59 1993 c. 36.

M60 1989 c. 26.

351 Competition information.

(1) A person is guilty of an offence if he has competition information (whether or not it was obtained by him) and improperly discloses it—

(a) if it relates to the affairs of an individual, during that individual's lifetime;

(b) if it relates to any particular business of a body, while that business continues to be carried on.

(2) For the purposes of subsection (1) a disclosure is improper unless it is made—

(a) with the consent of the person from whom it was obtained and, if different—

(i) the individual to whose affairs the information relates, or

(ii) the person for the time being carrying on the business to which the information relates;

(b) to facilitate the performance by a person mentioned in the first column of the table set out in Part I of Schedule 19 of a function mentioned in the second column of that table;

(c) in pursuance of a Community obligation;

(d) for the purpose of criminal proceedings in any part of the United Kingdom;

(e) in connection with the investigation of any criminal offence triable in the United Kingdom or any part of the United Kingdom;

(f) with a view to the institution of, or otherwise for the purposes of, civil proceedings

注释：

修改等(不涉及条文内容)

C316　第350条为特定目的于2001年8月17日，否则于2001年12月1日依照1986年本法第53章第53A条[为特定目的于2001年8月17日，否则于2001年12月1日依照制定法文件S.I.2001/2617第2条、第8条、第13条第(1)款、附录3第二部分第152条替换]；制定法文件S.I.2001/3538第2条第(1)款修订；

第350条为特定目的于2001年8月17日，否则于2001年12月1日依照1992年本法第40条、第63A条[为特定目的于2001年8月17日，否则于2001年12月1日依照依制定法文件S.I.2001/2617第2条、第8条、第13条第(1)款、附录3第一部分第78条替换]；制定法文件S.I.2001/3538第2条第(1)款修订。

实施日期

I119　第350条于2001年9月3日全部生效；第350条在副署时尚未生效，见第431条第(2)款；第350条第(3)款和第(7)款于2001年6月18日依照制定法文件S.I.2001/1820第2条、附录生效；第350条如于2001年9月3日尚未生效，则依照制定法文件S.I.2001/2632第2条第(2)款、附录第二部分生效。

附注引文

M59　1993年第36章。

M60　1989年第26章。

第351条　竞争信息

(1)如果某人拥有竞争信息(无论该信息是否由该人获得)并将该信息不适当地披露，则在符合下列条件时该人构成犯罪：

(a)该信息与个人事务有关，且在该个人有生之年披露；

(b)该信息与机构的任何特定业务有关，且该业务仍在经营之中。

(2)就第(1)款而言，只有下列披露才是适当的：

(a)披露获得了提供信息者的同意，否则

(i)披露获得了信息相关人的同意，或者

(ii)披露获得了目前经营者信息相关业务之人的同意；

(b)披露是为了便利附录19第一部分所列表格第一栏所述之人履行该表格第二栏所提及的职能；

(c)依据共同体的某项义务而披露；

(d)为了在联合王国任何地区的刑事诉讼之目的而披露；

(e)披露与在联合王国或联合王国任何地区可裁判之刑事犯罪而进行之调查有关；

(f)着眼于民事诉讼程序的成立或者为该民事诉讼程序之目的而披露，上述民事

brought under or in connection with—

(i) a competition provision; or

(ii) a specified enactment.

(3) A person guilty of an offence under this section is liable—

(a) on summary conviction, to a fine not exceeding the statutory maximum;

(b) on conviction on indictment, to imprisonment for a term not exceeding two years or to a fine or to both.

(4) Section 348 does not apply to competition information.

(5) "Competition information" means information which—

(a) relates to the affairs of a particular individual or body;

(b) is not otherwise in the public domain; and

(c) was obtained under or by virtue of a competition provision.

(6) "Competition provision" means any provision of—

(a) an order made under section 95;

(b) Chapter Ⅲ of Part Ⅹ; or

(c) Chapter Ⅱ of Part ⅩⅧ.

(7) "Specified enactment" means an enactment specified in Part Ⅱ of Schedule 19.

Annotations:

Modifications etc. (not altering text)

C317 S. 351 modified (17.8.2001 for certain purposes otherwise 1.12.2001) by 1986 c. 53, s. 53A(as substituted(17.8.2001 for certain purposes otherwise 1.12.2001) by S.I. 2001/2617, arts. 2, 8, 13(1), Sch. 3 Pt. II para. 152); S.I. 2001/3538, art. 2(1)

S. 351 modified (17.8.2001 for certain purposes otherwise 1.12.2001) by 1992 c. 40, s. 63A (as substituted (17.8.2001 for certain purposes otherwise 1.12.2001) by S.I. 2001/2617, arts. 2, 8, 13(1), Sch. 3 Pt. I para. 78); S.I. 2001/3538, art. 2(1)

Commencement Information

I120 S. 351 wholly in force at 18.6.2001; s. 351 not in force at Royal Assent see s. 431 (2); s. 351(7) in force at 25.2.2001 by S.I. 2001/516, art. 2(a), Sch. Pt. 1; s. 351 in force in so far as not already in force at 18.6.2001 by S.I. 2001/1820, art. 2, Sch.

352 Offences.

(1) A person who discloses information in contravention of section 348 or 350(5) is guilty of an offence.

(2) A person guilty of an offence under subsection (1) is liable—

诉讼程序是根据下列各项而提起或与之有关：

(i)某项有关竞争的规定；或者

(ii)某个规定的成文法。

(3)根据本条规定行为构成犯罪之人，应承担下列责任：

(a)经简易程序定罪的，处以不超过最高法定限额的罚金；

(b)经公诉程序定罪的，处以不超过2年的有期徒刑或罚金，或两罚并处。

(4)第348条不适用于竞争信息。

(5)“竞争信息”系指

(a)与某一特定个人或机构之事务有关的信息；

(b)不处于公共领域的信息；以及

(c)根据或由于某项有关竞争的规定而获得的信息。

(6)“有关竞争的规定”系指

(a)根据第95条制定之法令的任何规定；

(b)第十部分第3章的任何规定；

(c)第十八部分第2章的任何规定。

(7)“规定的成文法”系指附录19第二部分规定的成文法。

注释：

修改等(不涉及条文内容)

C317　第351条为特定目的于2001年8月17日，否则于2001年12月1日依照1986年本法第53条、第53A条[依照为特定目的于2001年8月17日，否则于2001年12月1日制定法文件S.I.2001/2617第2条、第8条、第13条第(1)款、附录3第二部分第152条替换]；制定法文件S.I.2001/3538第2条第(1)款修订。

第351条为特定目的于2001年8月17日，否则于2001年12月1日依照1992年本法第40条、第63A条[为特定目的于2001年8月17日，否则于2001年12月1日依照制定法文件S.I. 2001/2617第2条、第8条、第13条第(1)款、附录3第一部分第78条替换]；制定法文件S.I. 2001/3538第2条第(1)款修订。

实施日期

I120　第351条于2001年6月18日全部生效；第351条在副署时尚未生效，见第431条第(2)款；第351条第(7)款于2001年2月25日依制定法文件S.I.2001/516第2条第(a)款、附录部分1生效；第351条如于2001年6月18日尚未生效，则依照制定法文件S.I.2001/1820第2条、附录生效。

第352条　犯罪

(1)违反第348条或第350条第(5)款披露信息的，构成犯罪。

(2)根据第(1)款构成犯罪之人

(a) on summary conviction, to imprisonment for a term not exceeding three months or a fine not exceeding the statutory maximum, or both;

(b) on conviction on indictment, to imprisonment for a term not exceeding two years or a fine, or both.

(3) A person is guilty of an offence if, in contravention of any provision of regulations made under section 349, he uses information which has been disclosed to him in accordance with the regulations.

(4) A person is guilty of an offence if, in contravention of subsection (4) of section 350, he uses information which has been disclosed to him in accordance with that section.

(5) A person guilty of an offence under subsection (3) or (4) is liable on summary conviction to imprisonment for a term not exceeding three months or a fine not exceeding level 5 on the standard scale, or both.

(6) In proceedings for an offence under this section it is a defence for the accused to prove—

(a) that he did not know and had no reason to suspect that the information was confidential information or that it had been disclosed in accordance with section 350;

(b) that he took all reasonable precautions and exercised all due diligence to avoid committing the offence.

Annotations:

Modifications etc. (not altering text)

C318 S. 352 modified (17.8.2001 for certain purposes otherwise 1.12.2001) by 1986 c. 53, s. 53A (as substituted (17.8.2001 for certain purposes otherwise 1.12.2001) by S.I. 2001/2617, arts. 2, 8, 13(1), Sch. 3 Pt. II para. 152); S.I. 2001/3538, art. 2(1)

S. 352 modified (17.8.2001 for certain purposes otherwise 1.12.2001) by 1992 c. 40, s. 63A (as substituted (17.8.2001 for certain purposes otherwise 1.12.2001) by S.I. 2001/2617, arts. 2, 8, 13(1), Sch. 3 Pt. I para. 78; S.I. 2001/3538, art. 2(1)

S. 352 extended (1.12.2001) by S.I. 2001/3648, arts. 1, 3(2)

Commencement Information

I121 S. 352 wholly in force at 3.9.2001; s. 352 not in force at Royal Assent see s. 431 (2); s. 352 in force for specified purposes at 18.6.2001 by S.I. 2001/1820, art. 2, Sch.; s. 352 in force in so far as not already in force at 3.9.2001 by S.I. 2001/2632, art. 2(2), Sch. Pt. 2

(a)经简易定罪的,处以不超过3个月的有期徒刑或最高法定限额的罚金,或两罚并处;

(b)经公诉程序定罪的,处以不超过2年的有期徒刑或罚金,或两罚并处。

(3)违反根据第349条所制定之法规的任何规定,使用根据该法规向他披露的信息,构成犯罪。

(4)违反第350条第(4)款的规定,使用根据该条向他披露的信息,构成犯罪。

(5)根据第(3)款或第(4)款构成犯罪的,应当经简易程序定罪,处以不超过3个月的有期徒刑或不超过标准等级第5级的罚金,或两罚并处。

(6)在有关本条项下罪行的诉讼程序中,被告人可证明下列事项为自己辩护:

(a)该人不知悉且没有理由怀疑信息为保密信息或该信息依照第350条披露;

(b)该人采取了所有合理的预防措施且已尽一切应尽勤勉防止犯罪。

注释:

修改等(不涉及条文内容)

C318 第352条为特定目的于2001年8月17日,否则于2001年12月1日依照1986年第53章第53A条[为特定目的于2001年8月17日,否则于2001年12月1日依照制定法文件S.I. 2001/2617第2条、第8条、第13条第(1)款、附录3第二部分第152条替换];制定法文件S.I. 2001/3538第2条第(1)款修订;

第352条为特定目的于2001年8月17日,否则于2001年12月1日依照1992年第40章第63A条 [为特定目的于2001年8月17日, 否则于2001年12月1日依照制定法文件S.I. 2001/2617第2条、第8条、第13条第(1)款、附录3第一部分第78条替换];制定法文件S.I. 2001/3538第2条第(1)款修订;

第352条于2001年12月1日依照制定法文件S.I.2001/3648第1条、第3条第(2)款扩大适用范围。

实施日期

I121 第352条于2001年9月3日全部生效;第352条在副署时尚未生效,见第431条第(2)款;第352条为特定目的于2001年6月18日依照制定法文件S.I.2001/1820第2条、附录生效;第352条如于2001年9月3日尚未生效,则依照制定法文件S.I.2001/1820第2条第(2)款、附录第二部分生效。

353 Removal of other restrictions on disclosure.

(1) The Treasury may make regulations permitting the disclosure of any information, or of information of a prescribed kind—

(a) by prescribed persons for the purpose of assisting or enabling them to discharge prescribed functions under this Act or any rules or regulations made under it;

(b) by prescribed persons, or persons of a prescribed description, to the Authority for the purpose of assisting or enabling the Authority to discharge prescribed functions.

(2) Regulations under this section may not make any provision in relation to the disclosure of confidential information by primary recipients or by any person obtaining confidential information directly or indirectly from a primary recipient.

(3) If a person discloses any information as permitted by regulations under this section the disclosure is not to be taken as a contravention of any duty to which he is subject.

Annotations:

Modifications etc. (not altering text)

C319 S. 353 modified (17.8.2001 for certain purposes otherwise 1.12.2001) by 1986 c. 53, s. 53A (as substituted (17.8.2001 for certain purposes otherwise 1.12.2001) by S.I. 2001/2617, arts. 2, 8, 13(1), Sch. 3 Pt. II para. 152); S.I. 2001/3538, art. 2(1)

S. 353 modified (17.8.2001 for certain purposes otherwise 1.12.2001) by 1992 c. 40, 63A (as substituted (17.8.2001 for certain purposes otherwise 1.12.2001) by S.I. 2001/2617, arts. 2, 8, 13(1), Sch. 3 Pt. I para. 78); S.I. 2001/3538, art. 2(1)

Co-operation

354 Authority's duty to co-operate with others.

(1) The Authority must take such steps as it considers appropriate to co-operate with other persons (whether in the United Kingdom or elsewhere) who have functions—

(a) similar to those of the Authority; or

(b) in relation to the prevention or detection of financial crime.

(2) Co-operation may include the sharing of information which the Authority is not prevented from disclosing.

(3) "Financial crime" has the same meaning as in section 6.

第353条　取消对信息披露的其他限制

(1)财政部可以制定法规,允许下列披露任何信息或规定类别信息的行为:

(a)由规定之人为了使自己能够履行或协助自己履行本法或根据本法制定之任何规则或法规所规定的职能而披露;

(b)由规定之人或规定类型之人向管理局披露,旨在使后者能够履行或协助后者履行规定的职能;

(2)根据本条制定的法规,不得就主接受者或任何直接或间接从主接受者获取保密信息之人披露保密信息的行为作出任何规定。

(3)如果某人披露根据本条制定之法规允许的任何信息,则其披露信息的行为不视为违反其任何职责。

注释:

修改等(不涉及条文内容)

C319　第353条为特定目的于2001年8月17日,否则于2001年12月1日依照1986年第53章第53A条[为特定目的于2001年8月17日,否则于2001年12月1日依照制定法文件S.I. 2001/2617第2条、第8条、第13条第(1)款、附录3第二部分第152条替换];制定法文件S.I. 2001/3538第2条第(1)款修订。

第353条为特定目的于2001年8月17日,否则于2001年12月1日依照1992年第40章第63A条[为特定目的于2001年8月17日,否则于2001年12月1日依照制定法文件S.I. 2001/2617第2条、第8条、第13条第(1)款、附录3第一部分第78条替换];制定法文件S.I. 2001/3538第2条第(1)款修订。

合　作

第354条　管理局与他人合作的职责

(1)管理局必须采取它所认为适当的措施与具有下列职能的其他人(无论该人在联合王国还是在其他地方)合作:

(a)与管理局之职能类似的职能;

(b)与防止或侦查金融犯罪相关的职能。

(2)合作可包括共享管理局不禁止披露的信息。

(3)"金融犯罪"含义同第6条。

PART XXIV INSOLVENCY

Interpretation

355 Interpretation of this Part.

(1) In this Part—

"the 1985 Act" means the [M61]Bankruptcy (Scotland) Act 1985;

"the 1986 Act" means the [M62]Insolvency Act 1986;

"the 1989 Order" means the [M63]Insolvency (Northern Ireland) Order 1989; "body" means a body of persons—

(a) over which the court has jurisdiction under any provision of, or made under, the 1986 Act (or the 1989 Order); but

(b) which is not a building society, a friendly society or an industrial and provident society; and "court" means—

(c) the court having jurisdiction for the purposes of the 1985 Act or the 1986 Act; or

(d) in Northern Ireland, the High Court.

(2) In this Part"insurer" has such meaning as may be specified in an order made by the Treasury.

Annotations:

Marginal Citations

M61 1985 c. 66.

M62 1986 c. 45.

M63 S.I. 1989/2405 (N.I. 19).

Voluntary arrangements

356 Authority's powers to participate in proceedings: company voluntary arrangements.

[[F5](1) Where a voluntary arrangement has effect under Part I of the 1986 Act in respect of a company or insolvent partnership which is an authorised person, the Authority may apply

第二十四部分 破　产

释　义

第355条　本部分释义

(1)在本部分中——

“1985年法”系指[M61]《1985年破产法》(苏格兰);

“1986年法”系指[M62]《1986年破产法》;

“1989年法令”系指[M63]《1989年破产法令》(北爱尔兰);“机构”系指下列人组成的机构:

(a)法院根据1986年法或1989年法令的任何规定对其拥有管辖权的人;但是

(b)该机构不是住房互助会、互相保险协会或行业节俭互助会;“法院”系指

(c)为了1985年法或1986年法的目的具有管辖权的法院;

(d)在北爱尔兰指高等法院。

(2)在本部分中,“保险人”具有财政部发布的命令中指定的含义。

注释:

附注引文

M61　1985年第66章。

M62　1986年第45章。

M63　制定法文件S.I.1989/2405(第19条)。

自愿安排

第356条　管理局参与法律程序的权力:公司自愿安排

[[F5](1)对于作为获授权人的公司或破产合伙而言,如自愿安排已根据1986年法第一部分生效,则管理局可以根据该法第6条或第7条向法院提出申请。]

to the court under section 6 or 7 of that Act.]

[F6 (2) Where a voluntary arrangement has been approved under Part II of the 1989 Order in respect of a company or insolvent partnership which is an authorised person, the Authority may apply to the court under Article 19 or 20 of that Order.]

(3) If a person other than the Authority makes an application to the court in relation to the company or insolvent partnership under [F7any] of those provisions, the Authority is entitled to be heard at any hearing relating to the application.

Annotations:

Amendments (Textual)

F5 S. 356(1) substituted (1.1.2003 subject to transitional provisions in arts. 3–5 of the commencing S.I.) by 2000 c. 39, s. 15(3)(a); S.I. 2002/2711, art. 2

F6 S. 356(2) substituted (1.1.2003 subject to transitional provisions in arts. 3–5 of the commencing S.I.) by 2000 c. 39, s. 15(3)(b); S.I. 2002/2711, art. 2

F7 Word in s. 356(3) substituted(1.1.2003 subject to transitional provisions in arts. 3–5 of the commencing S.I.) by 2000 c. 39, s. 15(3)(c); S.I. 2002/2711, art. 2

Modifications etc. (not altering text)

C320 S. 356 applied (with modifications) (6.4.2001) by S.I. 2001/1090, regs. 1, 6

357 Authority's powers to participate in proceedings: individual voluntary arrangements.

(1) The Authority is entitled to be heard on an application by an individual who is an authorised person under section 253 of the 1986 Act (or Article 227 of the 1989 Order).

(2) Subsections (3) to (6) apply if such an order is made on the application of such a person.

(3) A person appointed for the purpose by the Authority is entitled to attend any meeting of creditors of the debtor summoned under section 257 of the 1986 Act (or Article 231 of the 1989 Order).

(4) Notice of the result of a meeting so summoned is to be given to the Authority by the chairman of the meeting.

(5) The Authority may apply to the court—

(a) under section 262 of the 1986 Act (or Article 236 of the 1989 Order); or

(b) under section 263 of the 1986 Act (or Article 237 of the 1989 Order).

(6) If a person other than the Authority makes an application to the court under any provision mentioned in subsection (5), the Authority is entitled to be heard at any hearing relating to the application.

[F6(2)对于作为获授权人的公司或破产合伙而言,如自愿安排已根据1989年法令第二部分生效,则管理局可以根据该法令第19条或第20条向法院提出申请。]

(3)如管理局之外的人根据这些规定[F7的任何一条]向法院提出有关公司或破产合伙的申请,则管理局有权在与该申请有关的任何听证会上发表意见。

注释:

修正(文本)

F5 第356条第(1)款于2003年1月1日符合过渡条款有关的第3条至第5条规定,依照2000年第39章第15条第(3)款第(a)项;制定法文件S.I.2002/2711第2条替换。

F6 第356条第(2)款于2003年1月1日符合过渡条款有关的第3条至第5条规定,依照2000年第39章第15条第(3)款第(b)项;制定法文件S.I.2002/2711第2条替换。

F7 第356条第(3)款文字于2003年1月1日符合过渡条款有关的第3条至第5条规定,依照2000年第39章第15条第(3)款第(c)项;制定法文件S.I.2002/2711第2条替换。

修改等(不涉及条文内容)

C320 第356条(已修订)于2001年4月6日依照制定法文件S.I.2001/1090第1条、第6条适用。

第357条 管理局参与法律程序的权力:个人自愿安排

(1)管理局有权就作为获授权人的个人根据1986年法第253条(或1989年法令第227条)提出的申请发表意见。

(2)如对该人的申请发布任何命令,则适用第(3)款至第(6)款规定。

(3)管理局专门任命之人有权出席根据1986年法第257条(或1989年法令第231条)召集的任何债权人会议。

(4)会议主持人应当将此类会议的结果通知管理局。

(5)管理局可以根据下列规定向法院提出申请:

(a)1986年法第262条(或1989年法令第236条);

(b)1986年法第263条(或1989年法令第237条)。

(6)如果管理局之外的人根据第(5)款的任何规定向法院提出申请,则管理局有权在与该申请有关的任何听证会上发表意见。

358 Authority's powers to participate in proceedings: trust deeds for creditors in Scotland.

(1) This section applies where a trust deed has been granted by or on behalf of a debtor who is an authorised person.

(2) The trustee must, as soon as practicable after he becomes aware that the debtor is an authorised person, send to the Authority—

(a) in every case, a copy of the trust deed;

(b) where any other document or information is sent to every creditor known to the trustee in pursuance of paragraph 5(1)(c) of Schedule 5 to the 1985 Act, a copy of such document or information.

(3) Paragraph 7 of that Schedule applies to the Authority as if it were a qualified creditor who has not been sent a copy of the notice as mentioned in paragraph 5(1)(c) of the Schedule.

(4) The Authority must be given the same notice as the creditors of any meeting of creditors held in relation to the trust deed.

(5) A person appointed for the purpose by the Authority is entitled to attend and participate in (but not to vote at) any such meeting of creditors as if the Authority were a creditor under the deed.

(6) This section does not affect any right the Authority has as a creditor of a debtor who is an authorised person.

(7) Expressions used in this section and in the 1985 Act have the same meaning in this section as in that Act.

Administration orders

359 Petitions.

(1) The Authority may present a petition to the court under section 9 of the 1986 Act (or Article 22 of the 1989 Order) in relation to a company or insolvent partnership which—

(a) is, or has been, an authorised person;

(b) is, or has been, an appointed representative; or

(c) is carrying on, or has carried on, a regulated activity in contravention of the general prohibition.

(2) Subsection (3) applies in relation to a petition presented by the Authority by virtue of this section.

(3) If the company or partnership is in default on an obligation to pay a sum due and payable under an agreement, it is to be treated for the purpose of section 8(1)(a) of the 1986 Act (or Article 21(1)(a) of the 1989 Order) as unable to pay its debts.

(4) "Agreement" means an agreement the making or performance of which constitutes or

第358条　管理局参与法律程序的权力:苏格兰的债权人信托契约

(1)如果作为获授权人的债务人已亲自或由其代表签发信托契约,则适用本条规定。

(2)受托人必须在得知债务人为获授权人之后尽快向管理局发送

(a)在任何情况下发送信托契约的一份副本;

(b)如果已根据1985年法附录5第5条第(1)款第(c)项向信托人所知的每个债权人发送了任何其他文件或信息,则发送此等文件或信息的一份副本。

(3)该附录第7条适用于管理局,等同于管理局是有资格的债权人且未被发送附件第5条第(1)款第(c)项所述之通知的一份副本。

(4)管理局必须就信托契约有关之任何债权人会议得到与债权人相同的通知。

(5)管理局专门任命之人有权出席并参与任何此等会议(但不表决),等同于管理局是该契约项下的债权人。

(6)对于作为获授权人的某个债务人而言,本条不影响管理局作为该债务人的一个债权人而享有的任何权利。

(7)本条与1985年法中所使用的表述具有相同的含义。

接　管　令

第359条　申请

(1)管理局可根据1986年法第9条(或1989年法令第22条)针对有下列情形的公司或破产合伙向法院提交申请:

(a)该公司或破产合伙现在或已经是获授权人;

(b)该公司或破产合伙现在或已经是被任命的代表;或者

(c)该公司或破产合伙正在或曾经违反一般性禁止从事被监管的活动。

(2)第(3)款适用于管理局依据本条提交的申请。

(3)如果公司或合伙未履行某协议项下支付到期应付款项的义务,则就1986年法第8条第(1)款第(a)项[或1989年法令第21条第(1)款第(a)项]而言,该公司或合伙将被视同无力偿债。

(4)"协议",系指其签订或履行构成公司或合伙从事之受监管活动或其一部分的

is part of a regulated activity carried on by the company or partnership.

(5) "Company" means—

(a) a company to which section 8 of the 1986 Act applies; or

(b) in relation to Northern Ireland, a company to which Article 21 of the 1989 Order applies.

Annotations:

Modifications etc. (not altering text)

C321 S. 359(1)-(4) applied (with modifications) (6.4.2001) by S.I. 2001/1090, regs. 1, 6

360 Insurers.

(1) The Treasury may by order provide that such provisions of Part Ⅱ of the 1986 Act (or Part Ⅲ of the 1989 Order) as may be specified are to apply in relation to insurers with such modifications as may be specified.

(2) An order under this section—

(a) may provide that such provisions of this Part as may be specified are to apply in relation to the administration of insurers in accordance with the order with such modifications as may be specified; and

(b) requires the consent of the Secretary of State.

(3) "Specified" means specified in the order.

361 Administrator's duty to report to Authority.

(1) If—

(a) an administration order is in force in relation to a company or partnership by virtue of a petition presented by a person other than the Authority, and

(b) it appears to the administrator that the company or partnership is carrying on, or has carried on, a regulated activity in contravention of the general prohibition, the administrator must report the matter to the Authority without delay.

(2) "An administration order" means an administration order under Part Ⅱ of the 1986 Act (or Part Ⅲ of the 1989 Order).

Annotations:

Modifications etc. (not altering text)

C322 S. 361 applied (with modifications) (6.4.2001) by S.I. 2001/1090, regs. 1, 6

362 Authority's powers to participate in proceedings.

(1) This section applies if a person other than the Authority presents a petition to the court under section 9 of the 1986 Act (or Article 22 of the 1989 Order) in relation to a

协议。

(5)“公司”系指

(a)适用1986年法第8条的公司;

(b)在北爱尔兰则为适用1989年法令第21条的公司。

注释:

修改等(不涉及条文内容)

C321　第359条第(1)款至第(4)款(已修订)于2001年4月6日依照制定法文件S.I. 2001/1090第1条、第6条适用。

第360条　保险人

(1)财政部可以颁布法令,规定1986年本法第二部分(或1989年法令第三部分)可能指定的规定及其可能指定的修订适用于保险人。

(2)本条规定的命令

(a)可以规定本部分指定的规定及其指定的修订适用于根据该命令对保险人实施的管理;以及

(b)需要获得国务大臣的同意。

(3)“指定”系指命令中指定。

第361条　接管人向管理局报告的职责

(1)如果

(a)由于管理局之外的人提交申请,接管令对公司或合伙生效,并且

(b)在接管人看来该公司或合伙正在或已经违反一般性禁止从事被监管的活动,则接管人必须毫不延迟地向管理局报告该事项。

(2)“接管令”系指1986年法第二部分(或1989年法令第三部分)规定的接管令。

注释:

修改等(不涉及条文内容)

C322　第361条(已修订)于2001年4月6日依照制定法文件S.I.2001/1090第1条、第6条适用。

第362条　管理局参与法律程序的权力

(1)如管理局之外的人根据1986年法第9条(或1989年法令第22条)针对有下列情形的公司或合伙向法院提交申请,则适用本条规定:

company or partnership which—

(a) is, or has been, an authorised person;

(b) is, or has been, an appointed representative; or

(c) is carrying on, or has carried on, a regulated activity in contravention of the general prohibition.

(2) The Authority is entitled to be heard—

(a) at the hearing of the petition; and

(b) at any other hearing of the court in relation to the company or partnership under Part Ⅱ of the 1986 Act (or Part Ⅲ of the 1989 Order).

(3) Any notice or other document required to be sent to a creditor of the company or partnership must also be sent to the Authority.

(4) The Authority may apply to the court under section 27 of the 1986 Act (or Article 39 of the 1989 Order); and on such an application, section 27(1)(a) (or Article 39(1)(a)) has effect with the omission of the words "(including at least himself)".

(5) A person appointed for the purpose by the Authority is entitled—

(a) to attend any meeting of creditors of the company or partnership summoned under any enactment;

(b) to attend any meeting of a committee established under section 26 of the 1986 Act (or Article 38 of the 1989 Order); and

(c) to make representations as to any matter for decision at such a meeting.

(6) If, during the course of the administration of a company, a compromise or arrangement is proposed between the company and its creditors, or any class of them, the Authority may apply to the court under section 425 of the [M64]Companies Act 1985 (or Article 418 of the [M65]Companies (Northern Ireland) Order 1986).

Annotations:

Modifications etc. (not altering text)

C323 S. 362 applied (with modifications) (6.4.2001) by S.I. 2001/1090, regs. 1, 6

Marginal Citations

M64 1985 c. 6.

M65 S.I. 1986/1032 (N.I. 6).

Receivership

363 Authority's powers to participate in proceedings.

(1) This section applies if a receiver has been appointed in relation to a company which—

(a)现在或已经是获授权人;

(b)现在或已经是被任命代表;

(c)正在或已经违反一般性禁止从事被监管的活动。

(2)管理局有权出席下列场合并发表意见:

(a)有关申请的听证会;以及

(b)法院根据1986年法第二部分(或1989年法令第三部分)召集的有关该公司或合伙的任何其他听证会。

(3)被要求发送给该公司或合伙债权人的任何通知或其他文件,必须也发送给管理局。

(4)管理局可以根据1986年法第27条(或1989年法令第39条)向法院提出申请;第27条第(1)款第(a)项[或第39条第(1)款第(a)项]删除"(至少包括他自己)"后的内容对此等申请具有效力。

(5)管理局专门任命之人有权

(a)出席根据任何成文法召集的该公司或合伙债权人的任何会议;

(b)出席根据1986年法第26条(或1989年法令第38条)成立之委员会的任何会议;以及

(c)在此等会议上就需作出决议的任何事项发表陈述。

(6)如果在某公司的接管过程中,公司与其债权人或其中任何一类人提议达成妥协或安排,则管理局可以根据[M64]《1985年公司法》第425条[或[M65]《1986年公司法令》(北爱尔兰)第418条]向法院提出申请。

注释:

修改等(不涉及条文内容)

C323 第362条(已修订)于2001年4月6日依照制定法文件S.I.2001/1090第1条、第6条适用。

附注引文

M64 1985年第6章。

M65 制定法文件S.I.1986/1032(第6条)

破 产 清 算

第363条 管理局参与法律程序的权力

(1)如果针对有下列情形的公司已任命破产清算人,则适用本条规定:

(a) is, or has been, an authorised person;

(b) is, or has been, an appointed representative; or

(c) is carrying on, or has carried on, a regulated activity in contravention of the general prohibition.

(2) The Authority is entitled to be heard on an application made under section 35 or 63 of the 1986 Act (or Article 45 of the 1989 Order).

(3) The Authority is entitled to make an application under section 41(1)(a) or 69(1)(a) of the 1986 Act (or Article 51(1)(a) of the 1989 Order).

(4) A report under section 48(1) or 67(1) of the 1986 Act (or Article 58(1) of the 1989 Order) must be sent by the person making it to the Authority.

(5) A person appointed for the purpose by the Authority is entitled—

(a) to attend any meeting of creditors of the company summoned under any enactment;

(b) to attend any meeting of a committee established under section 49 or 68 of the 1986 Act (or Article 59 of the 1989 Order); and

(c) to make representations as to any matter for decision at such a meeting.

Annotations:

Modifications etc. (not altering text)

C324 S. 363 applied (with modifications) (6.4.2001) by S.I. 2001/1090, regs. 1, 6

364 Receiver's duty to report to Authority.

If—

(a) a receiver has been appointed in relation to a company, and

(b) it appears to the receiver that the company is carrying on, or has carried on, a regulated activity in contravention of the general prohibition,

the receiver must report the matter to the Authority without delay.

Annotations:

Modifications etc. (not altering text)

C325 S. 364 applied (with modifications) (6.4.2001) by S.I. 2001/1090, regs. 1, 6

Voluntary winding up

365 Authority's powers to participate in proceedings.

(1) This section applies in relation to a company which—

(a) is being wound up voluntarily;

(b) is an authorised person; and

(a)该公司现在或已经是获授权人；

(b)现在或已经是被任命代表；

(c)正在或已经违反一般禁止性规定从事被监管的活动。

(2)管理局有权就根据1986年法第35条或第63条(或1989年法第45条)提出的申请发表意见。

(3)管理局有权根据1986年法第41条第(1)款第(a)项或第69条第(1)款第(a)项[或1989年法令第51条第(1)款第(a)项]提出申请。

(4)1986年法第48条第(1)款或第67条第(1)款[或1989年法令第58条第(1)款]规定的报告必须由作出报告之人发送给管理局。

(5)管理局专门指定之人有权

(a)出席根据任何成文法召集的该公司债权人的任何会议；

(b)出席根据1986年法第49条或第68条(或1989年法令第59条)成立之委员会的任何会议；以及

(c)在此等会议上就需作出决议的任何事项发表陈述。

注释：

修改等(不涉及条文内容)

C324 第363条(已修订)于2001年4月6日依照制定法文件S.I.2001/1090第1条、第6条适用。

第364条 破产清算人向管理局报告的职责

如果

(a)针对某公司已任命一名破产清算人，并且

(b)在该破产清算人看来，该公司正在或已经违反一般性禁止从事被监管的活动，

则破产清算人必须毫不延迟地向管理局报告该事项。

注释：

更正修改等(不涉及条文内容)

C325 第364条(已修订)于2001年4月6日依照制定法文件S.I.2001/1090第1条、第6条适用。

自愿清算

第365条 管理局参与法律程序的权力

(1)本条适用于有下列情形的公司：

(a)正进行自愿清算；

(b)是获授权人；

(c) is not an insurer effecting or carrying out contracts of long-term insurance.

(2) The Authority may apply to the court under section 112 of the 1986 Act (or Article 98 of the 1989 Order) in respect of the company.

(3) The Authority is entitled to be heard at any hearing of the court in relation to the voluntary winding up of the company.

(4) Any notice or other document required to be sent to a creditor of the company must also be sent to the Authority.

(5) A person appointed for the purpose by the Authority is entitled—

(a) to attend any meeting of creditors of the company summoned under any enactment;

(b) to attend any meeting of a committee established under section 101 of the 1986 Act (or Article 87 of the 1989 Order); and

(c) to make representations as to any matter for decision at such a meeting.

(6) The voluntary winding up of the company does not bar the right of the Authority to have it wound up by the court.

(7) If, during the course of the winding up of the company, a compromise or arrangement is proposed between the company and its creditors, or any class of them, the Authority may apply to the court under section 425 of the[M66] Companies Act 1985 (or Article 418 of the[M67] Companies (Northern Ireland) Order 1986).

Annotations:

Modifications etc. (not altering text)

C326 S. 365 applied (with modifications) (6.4.2001) by S.I. 2001/1090, regs. 1, 6

Marginal Citations

M66 1985 c. 6.

M67 S.I. 1986/1032 (N.I. 6).

366 Insurers effecting or carrying out long-term contracts or insurance.

(1) An insurer effecting or carrying out contracts of long-term insurance may not be wound up voluntarily without the consent of the Authority.

(2) If notice of a general meeting of such an insurer is given, specifying the intention to propose a resolution for voluntary winding up of the insurer, a director of the insurer must notify the Authority as soon as practicable after he becomes aware of it.

(3) A person who fails to comply with subsection (2) is guilty of an offence and liable on summary conviction to a fine not exceeding level 5 on the standard scale.

(4) The following provisions do not apply in relation to a winding-up resolution—

(a) sections 378(3) and 381A of the [M68]Companies Act 1985 ("the 1985 Act"); and

(b) Articles 386(3) and 389A of the [M69]Companies (Northern Ireland) Order 1986 (c)不是签署或履行长期保险合同的保险人。

(2)针对该公司,管理局可以根据1986年法第112条(或1989年法令第98条)向法院提出申请。

(3)管理局有权在法院就该公司自愿清算举行的听证会上发表意见。

(4)要求发送给该公司或合伙债权人的任何通知或其他文件必须也发送给管理局。

(5)管理局专门任命之人有权

(a)出席根据任何成文法召集的该公司债权人的任何会议;

(b)出席根据1986年法第101条(或1989年法令第87条)成立之委员会的任何会议;以及

(c)在此等会议上就需作出决议的任何事项发表陈述。

(6)该公司自愿清算的行为不妨碍管理局要求法院对其进行清算的权利。

(7)如果在该公司清算的过程中,公司与其债权人或其中任何一类人提议达成妥协或安排,管理局可根据[M66]《1985年公司法》第425条[或[M67]《1986年公司法令》(北爱尔兰)第418条]向法院提出申请。

注释:

修改等(不涉及条文内容)

C326 第365条(已修订)于2001年4月6日依照制定法文件S.I.2001/1090第1条、第6条适用。

附注引文

M66 1985年第6章。

M67 制定法文件S.I.1986/1032(第6条)

第366条 订立或实施长期合同或保险的保险公司

(1)订立或实施长期保险合同的保险公司未经管理局同意不得自愿清算。

(2)如上述保险公司发出大会通知,说明有意提出该保险公司自愿清算的决议,则该保险公司董事在得知此事后必须尽快通知管理局。

(3)未遵守第(2)款规定的,构成犯罪,应当经简易程序定罪,处以不超过标准等级第5级的罚金。

(4)下列规定不适用于清算决议相关事项:

(a)[M68]《1985年公司法》(以下简称1985年法)第378条第(3)款和第381A条;以及

(b)[M69]《1986年公司法令》(北爱尔兰)(以下简称1986年令)第386条第(3)款和第

("the 1986 Order").

(5) A copy of a winding-up resolution forwarded to the registrar of companies in accordance with section 380 of the 1985 Act (or Article 388 of the 1986 Order) must be accompanied by a certificate issued by the Authority stating that it consents to the voluntary winding up of the insurer.

(6) If subsection (5) is complied with, the voluntary winding up is to be treated as having commenced at the time the resolution was passed.

(7) If subsection (5) is not complied with, the resolution has no effect.

(8) "Winding-up resolution" means a resolution for voluntary winding up of an insurer effecting or carrying out contracts of long-term insurance.

Annotations:

Marginal Citations

M68 1985 c. 6.

M69 S.I. 1986/1032 (N.I. 6).

Winding up by the court

367 Winding-up petitions.

(1) The Authority may present a petition to the court for the winding up of a body which—

(a) is, or has been, an authorised person;

(b) is, or has been, an appointed representative; or

(c) is carrying on, or has carried on, a regulated activity in contravention of the general prohibition.

(2) In subsection (1)"body" includes any partnership.

(3) On such a petition, the court may wind up the body if—

(a) the body is unable to pay its debts within the meaning of section 123 or 221 of the 1986 Act (or Article 103 or 185 of the 1989 Order); or

(b) the court is of the opinion that it is just and equitable that it should be wound up.

(4) If a body is in default on an obligation to pay a sum due and payable under an agreement, it is to be treated for the purpose of subsection (3)(a) as unable to pay its debts.

(5) "Agreement" means an agreement the making or performance of which constitutes or is part of a regulated activity carried on by the body concerned.

(6) Subsection (7) applies if a petition is presented under subsection (1) for the winding up of a partnership—

(a) on the ground mentioned in subsection (3)(b); or

389A条;

(5)依照1985年法第380条(或1986年令第388条)向公司注册署提交的清算决议副本必须附有管理局签发的证明书,说明该局同意该保险公司的自愿清算。

(6)如符合第(5)款规定,则视为该决议通过之时起开始自愿清算。

(7)如不符合第(5)款规定,则该决议无效。

(8)"清算决议",系指订立或实施长期保险合同的保险公司自愿清算的决议。

注释:

附注引文

M68　1985年第6章。

M69　制定法文件S.I.1986/1032(第6条)。

法院清算

第367条　清算申请

(1)管理局可以向法院提出清算下列机构的申请:

(a)是获授权人或已经是获授权人的机构;

(b)是被任命代表或已经是被任命代表的机构;或

(c)正在开展或已经开展违反一般禁止性规定的受监管活动的机构。

(2)第(1)款中"机构"包括任何合伙。

(3)如有下列情况,则法院可应该申请对该机构进行清算:

(a)该机构无力偿付1986年法第123条或第221条(或1989年法令第103条或第185条)规定含义的债务;或

(b)法院认为清算该机构是公正而且公平的。

(4)如该机构违反依照某项协议支付到期应付款项的义务,则为第(3)款第(a)项之目的视为无力偿付债务。

(5)"协议",系指其订立或履行构成相关机构开展受监管活动内容或是其一部分的协议。

(6)如依照第(1)款规定提出下列清算合伙的申请,则适用第(7)款规定:

(a)以第(3)款第(b)项所述理由提出的申请;或

(b) in Scotland, on a ground mentioned in subsection (3)(a) or (b).

(7) The court has jurisdiction, and the 1986 Act (or the 1989 Order) has effect, as if the partnership were an unregistered company as defined by section 220 of that Act (or Article 184 of that Order).

Annotations:

Modifications etc. (not altering text)

C327 S. 367 applied (with modifications) (6.4.2001) by S.I. 2001/1090, regs. 1, 6

S. 367 amended (1.12.2001) by S.I. 2001/2657, arts. 1(1), 12 (which was revoked(8.10.2001) by S.I. 2001/3083, arts. 1(2), 23); S.I. 2001/3538, art. 2(1)

S. 367 amended (1.12.2001) by S.I. 2001/3083, arts. 1(2), 12; S.I. 2001/3538, art. 2(1)

C328 S. 367(3)(a) modified (1.12.2001) by S.I. 2001/3650, arts. 1(a), 15

C329 S. 367(5) modified (1.12.2001) by S.I. 2001/3650, arts. 1(a), 14

368 Winding-up petitions: EEA and Treaty firms.

The Authority may not present a petition to the court under section 367 for the winding up of—

(a) an EEA firm which qualifies for authorisation under Schedule 3, or

(b) a Treaty firm which qualifies for authorisation under Schedule 4,

unless it has been asked to do so by the home state regulator of the firm concerned.

369 Insurers: service of petition etc. on Authority.

(1) If a person other than the Authority presents a petition for the winding up of an authorised person with permission to effect or carry out contracts of insurance, the petitioner must serve a copy of the petition on the Authority.

(2) If a person other than the Authority applies to have a provisional liquidator appointed under section 135 of the 1986 Act (or Article 115 of the 1989 Order) in respect of an authorised person with permission to effect or carry out contracts of insurance, the applicant must serve a copy of the application on the Authority.

370 Liquidator's duty to report to Authority.

If—

(a) a company is being wound up voluntarily or a body is being wound up on a petition presented by a person other than the Authority, and

(b) it appears to the liquidator that the company or body is carrying on, or has carried (b)在苏格兰以第(3)款第(a)项或第(b)项所述理由提出的请求。

(7)法院有管辖权,1986年法(或1989年法令)具有效力,等同于该合伙是该法第220条(或该法令第184条)所定义的未注册公司。

注释:

修改等(不涉及条文内容)

C327 第367条(已修订)于2001年4月6日制定法文件S.I.2001/1090第1条、第6条适用;

第367条于2001年12月1日依照制定法文件S.I.2001/2657第1条第(1)款、第12条(该条款已于2001年10月8日依制定法文件S.I.2001/3083第1条第(2)款、第23条废除);制定法文件S.I.2001/3538第2条第(1)款修正;

第367条于2001年12月1日依照制定法文件S.I.2001/3083第1条第(2)款、第12条、制定法文件S.I.2001/3538第2条第(1)款修正。

C328 第367条第(3)款第(a)项于2001年12月1日依照制定法文件S.I.2001/3650第1条第(a)款、第15条修订。

C329 第367条第(5)款于2001年12月1日依照制定法文件S.I.2001/3650第1条第(a)款、第14条修订。

第368条 清算申请:欧洲经济区和条约企业

管理局不得依照第367条规定向法院提起清算下列机构的申请:

(a)依照附录3符合授权条件的欧洲经济区企业,或

(b)依照附录4符合授权条件的条约企业,

除非相关企业的母国监管机关要求管理局提出请求。

第369条 保险公司:向管理局送达清算申请

(1) 如管理局以外的人针对经许可订立或实施保险合同的获授权人提出清算申请,则申请人必须向管理局送达申请副本。

(2)如管理局以外的人针对经许可订立或实施保险合同的获授权人申请依照1986年法第135条(或1989年法令第115条)指定清算人,则申请人必须向管理局送达申请书副本。

第370条 清算人向管理局报告的职责

如有下列情况:

(a)一家公司正在进行自愿清算或应管理局以外的其他人提出的申请而接受清算;且

(b)清算人认为该公司或机构正在开展或已经开展违反一般禁止性规定的被监

on, a regulated activity in contravention of the general prohibition, the liquidator must report the matter to the Authority without delay.

Annotations:

Modifications etc. (not altering text)

C330 S. 370 applied (with modifications) (6.4.2001) by S.I. 2001/1090, regs. 1, 6

371 Authority's powers to participate in proceedings.

(1) This section applies if a person other than the Authority presents a petition for the winding up of a body which—

(a) is, or has been, an authorised person;

(b) is, or has been, an appointed representative; or

(c) is carrying on, or has carried on, a regulated activity in contravention of the general prohibition.

(2) The Authority is entitled to be heard—

(a) at the hearing of the petition; and

(b) at any other hearing of the court in relation to the body under or by virtue of Part Ⅳ or Ⅴ of the 1986 Act (or Part Ⅴ or Ⅵ of the 1989 Order).

(3) Any notice or other document required to be sent to a creditor of the body must also be sent to the Authority.

(4) A person appointed for the purpose by the Authority is entitled—

(a) to attend any meeting of creditors of the body;

(b) to attend any meeting of a committee established for the purposes of Part Ⅳ or Ⅴ of the 1986 Act under section 101 of that Act or under section 141 or 142 of that Act;

(c) to attend any meeting of a committee established for the purposes of Part Ⅴ or Ⅵ of the 1989 Order under Article 87 of that Order or under Article 120 of that Order; and

(d) to make representations as to any matter for decision at such a meeting.

(5) If, during the course of the winding up of a company, a compromise or arrangement is proposed between the company and its creditors, or any class of them, the Authority may apply to the court under section 425 of the [M70] Companies Act 1985 (or Article 418 of the [M71] Companies (Northern Ireland) Order 1986).

Annotations:

Modifications etc. (not altering text)

C331 S. 371 applied (with modifications) (6.4.2001) by S.I. 2001/1090, regs. 1, 6

管活动,则清算人必须毫不延迟地向管理局报告。

注释:

修改等(不涉及条文内容)

C330 第370条(已修订)于2001年4月6日依照制定法文件S.I.2001/1090第1条、第6条适用。

第371条 管理局参与法定程序的权力

(1)如管理局以外的人向法院提起清算下列机构的申请,则适用本条规定:

(a)是获授权人或已经是获授权人的机构;

(b)是被任命代表或已经是被任命代表的机构;或

(c)正在开展或已经开展违反一般禁止性规定的受监管活动的机构。

(2)管理局有权在下列审理中陈述意见:

(a)在该申请审理中;以及

(b)在法院依照或因1986年法第四部分或第五部分(或1986年令第五部分或第六部分)规定就该机构进行的任何审理中。

(3)要求送交该机构债权人的任何通知或其他文件,也必须送交管理局。

(4)管理局为此目的而委派的人有权

(a)出席任何该机构债权人会议;

(b)出席依照1986年法第101条规定或者第141条或第142条规定、为该法第四部分或第五部分之目的设立的委员会召开的任何会议;

(c)出席依照1989年法令第87条规定或者第120条规定、为该法令第五部分或第六部分之目的设立的委员会召开的任何会议;

(d)就提交上述会议决定的任何事项作出陈述。

(5)如在公司清算期间,公司与其债权人或任何类别的债权人拟达成妥协或安排,则管理局可依照[M70]《1985年公司法》第425条[或[M71]《1986年公司法令》(北爱尔兰)第418条]向法院提出申请。

注释:

修改等(不涉及条文内容)

C331 第371条(已修订)于2001年4月6日依照制定法文件S.I.2001/1090第1条、第6条适用。

Marginal Citations

M70 1985 c. 6.

M71 S.I. 1986/1032 (N.I. 6).

Bankruptcy

372 Petitions.

(1) The Authority may present a petition to the court—

(a) under section 264 of the 1986 Act (or Article 238 of the 1989 Order) for a bankruptcy order to be made against an individual; or

(b) under section 5 of the 1985 Act for the sequestration of the estate of an individual.

(2) But such a petition may be presented only on the ground that—

(a) the individual appears to be unable to pay a regulated activity debt; or

(b) the individual appears to have no reasonable prospect of being able to pay a regulated activity debt.

(3) An individual appears to be unable to pay a regulated activity debt if he is in default on an obligation to pay a sum due and payable under an agreement.

(4) An individual appears to have no reasonable prospect of being able to pay a regulated activity debt if—

(a) the Authority has served on him a demand requiring him to establish to the satisfaction of the Authority that there is a reasonable prospect that he will be able to pay a sum payable under an agreement when it falls due;

(b) at least three weeks have elapsed since the demand was served; and

(c) the demand has been neither complied with nor set aside in accordance with rules.

(5) A demand made under subsection (4)(a) is to be treated for the purposes of the 1986 Act (or the 1989 Order) as if it were a statutory demand under section 268 of that Act (or Article 242 of that Order).

(6) For the purposes of a petition presented in accordance with subsection (1)(b)—

(a) the Authority is to be treated as a qualified creditor; and

(b) a ground mentioned in subsection (2) constitutes apparent insolvency.

(7) "Individual" means an individual—

(a) who is, or has been, an authorised person; or

(b) who is carrying on, or has carried on, a regulated activity in contravention of the general prohibition.

(8) "Agreement" means an agreement the making or performance of which constitutes or is part of a regulated activity carried on by the individual concerned.

(9) "Rules" means—

附注引文

M70　1985年第6章。

M71　制定法文件S.I.1986/1032(第6条)。

破　产

第372条　申请

(1)管理局可以向法院提出下列申请:

(a)依照1986年法第264条(或1989年法令第238条)规定请求针对个人发出破产令;或

(b)依照1985年法第5条请求扣押个人财产。

(2)但该申请只能基于下列理由提出:

(a)该个人似乎无力偿付受监管活动的债务;或

(b)该个人似乎无偿付受监管活动债务的合理预期。

(3)如个人违反依照某项协议支付到期应付款项的义务,则属于该人似乎无力偿付受监管活动的债务。

(4)如有下列情况,则属于该个人似乎无偿付受监管活动债务的合理预期:

(a)管理局已向其送达命令,要求其向管理局证明其有在某项协议规定的应付款项到期时予以支付的合理预期;

(b)该命令送达已至少3周;且

(c)该命令既未得到遵守,也未依照规则取消。

(5)依照第(4)款第(a)项作出的命令为1986年法(或1989年法令)之目的视为该法第268条(或该令第242条)规定的法定命令。

(6)为依照第(1)款第(b)项提出的申请之目的

(a)将管理局视为符合资格的债权人;

(b)以第(2)款所述理由构成明显丧失清偿能力。

(7)"个人"系指

(a)是获授权人或已经是获授权人的个人;或

(b)正在开展或已经开展违反一般禁止性规定的受监管活动的个人。

(8)"协议",系指其订立或履行构成相关个人开展受监管活动或其一部分的协议。

(9)"规则"系指

(a) in England and Wales, rules made under section 412 of the 1986 Act;

(b) in Scotland, rules made by order by the Treasury, after consultation with the Scottish Ministers, for the purposes of this section; and

(c) in Northern Ireland, rules made under Article 359 of the 1989 Order.

Annotations:

Commencement Information

I122 S. 372 wholly in force at 1.12.2001; s. 372 not in force at Royal Assent see s. 431 (2); s. 372 in force for certain purposes at 20.7.2001 by S.I. 2001/2632, art. 2(1), Sch. Pt. 1; s. 372 in force in so far as not already in force at 1.12.2001 by S.I. 2001/3538, art. 2(1)

373 Insolvency practitioner's duty to report to Authority.

(1) If—

(a) a bankruptcy order or sequestration award is in force in relation to an individual by virtue of a petition presented by a person other than the Authority, and

(b) it appears to the insolvency practitioner that the individual is carrying on, or has carried on, a regulated activity in contravention of the general prohibition, the insolvency practitioner must report the matter to the Authority without delay.

(2) "Bankruptcy order" means a bankruptcy order under Part Ⅸ of the 1986 Act (or Part Ⅸ of the 1989 Order).

(3) "Sequestration award" means an award of sequestration under section 12 of the 1985 Act.

(4) "Individual" includes an entity mentioned in section 374(1)(c).

374 Authority's powers to participate in proceedings.

(1) This section applies if a person other than the Authority presents a petition to the court—

(a) under section 264 of the 1986 Act (or Article 238 of the 1989 Order) for a bankruptcy order to be made against an individual;

(b) under section 5 of the 1985 Act for the sequestration of the estate of an individual; or

(c) under section 6 of the 1985 Act for the sequestration of the estate belonging to or held for or jointly by the members of an entity mentioned in subsection (1) of that section.

(2) The Authority is entitled to be heard—

(a) at the hearing of the petition; and

(b) at any other hearing in relation to the individual or entity under—

(i) Part Ⅸ of the 1986 Act;

(ii) Part Ⅸ of the 1989 Order; or

(a)在英格兰和威尔士为依照1986年法第412条制定的规则;

(b)在苏格兰为财政部经与苏格兰部长协商,为本条规定之目的通过发布命令制定的规则;且

(c)在北爱尔兰为依照1989年法令第359条制定的规则。

注释:

实施日期

I122　第372条于2001年12月1日全部生效;第372条在副署时尚未生效,见第431条第(2)款;第372条为特定目的于2001年7月20日依照制定法文件S.I.2001/2632第2条第(1)款、附录第一部分生效;第372条如于2001年12月1日尚未生效,则依照制定法文件S.I.2001/3538第2条第(1)款生效。

第373条　破产执行人向管理局报告的职责

(1)如有下列情况:

(a)因管理局以外的其他人提出的申请而使针对个人的破产令或扣押裁决生效,且

(b)破产执行人认为该个人正在开展或已经开展了违反一般禁止性规定的受监管活动,则破产执行人必须毫不延迟地向管理局报告。

(2)"破产令",系指1986年法第九部分(或第1989年法令第九部分)规定的破产令。

(3)"扣押裁决",系指1985年法第12条规定的扣押裁决。

(4)"个人"包括第374条第(1)款第(c)项所述实体。

第374条　管理局参与法律程序的权力

(1)如管理局以外的其他人向法院提起下列申请,则适用本条规定:

(a)依照1986年法第264条(或1989年法令第238条)规定请求针对个人发出破产令;

(b)依照1985年法第5条请求扣押个人财产;或

(c)依照1985年法第6条请求扣押属于该条第(1)款所列实体成员、为该成员持有或与该成员共同持有的财产。

(2)管理局有权在下列审理中陈述意见:

(a)在该申请审理中;以及

(b)在下列法律规定的任何与该个人或实体相关的审理中:

(i)1986年法第九部分;

(ii)1989年法令第九部分;或

(iii) the 1985 Act.

(3) A copy of the report prepared under section 274 of the 1986 Act (or Article 248 of the 1989 Order) must also be sent to the Authority.

(4) A person appointed for the purpose by the Authority is entitled—

(a) to attend any meeting of creditors of the individual or entity;

(b) to attend any meeting of a committee established under section 301 of the 1986 Act (or Article 274 of the 1989 Order);

(c) to attend any meeting of commissioners held under paragraph 17 or 18 of Schedule 6 to the 1985 Act; and

(d) to make representations as to any matter for decision at such a meeting.

(5) "Individual" means an individual who—

(a) is, or has been, an authorised person; or

(b) is carrying on, or has carried on, a regulated activity in contravention of the general prohibition.

(6) "Entity" means an entity which—

(a) is, or has been, an authorised person; or

(b) is carrying on, or has carried on, a regulated activity in contravention of the general prohibition.

Provisions against debt avoidance

375 Authority's right to apply for an order.

(1) The Authority may apply for an order under section 423 of the 1986 Act (or Article 367 of the 1989 Order) in relation to a debtor if—

(a) at the time the transaction at an undervalue was entered into, the debtor was carrying on a regulated activity (whether or not in contravention of the general prohibition); and

(b) a victim of the transaction is or was party to an agreement entered into with the debtor, the making or performance of which constituted or was part of a regulated activity carried on by the debtor.

(2) An application made under this section is to be treated as made on behalf of every victim of the transaction to whom subsection (1)(b) applies.

(3) Expressions which are given a meaning in Part XVI of the 1986 Act (or Article 367, 368 or 369 of the 1989 Order) have the same meaning when used in this section.

(iii)1985年法。

(3)依照1986年法第274条(或1989年法第248条)编写的报告副本亦须送交管理局。

(4)管理局为此目的而指定的人有权

(a)出席任何该个人或实体的债权人会议;

(b)出席依照1986年法第301条(或1989年法令第274条)成立的委员会召开的任何会议;

(c)出席依照1985年法附录6第17条或第18条规定召开的任何委员会议;并

(d)就提交上述会议决定的任何事项发表意见。

(5)“个人”系指

(a)是获授权人或已经是获授权人的个人;或

(b)正在开展或已经开展违反一般禁止性规定的受监管活动的个人。

(6)“实体”系指

(a)是获授权人或已经是获授权人的实体;或

(b)正在开展或已经开展违反一般禁止性规定的受监管活动的实体。

针对逃避债务的规定

第375条　管理局申请命令的权利

(1)如有下列情况,则管理局可以依照1986年法第423条(或1989年法令第367条)法规申请针对债务人的命令:

(a)在进行低价交易时,债务人正在开展受监管活动(不论是否违反一般性禁止性规定);且

(b)该交易的受害人是或曾经是与债务人订立协议的协议方,且该协议的订立或履行构成债务人开展的受监管活动或者是其部分内容。

(2)依照本条规定提出的申请视为代表适用第(1)款第(b)项的所有低价交易受害人提出的申请。

(3)1986年法第十六部分(或1989年法令第367条、第368条或第369条)定义的表述在本条规定中使用时具有相同含义。

Supplemental provisions concerning insurers

376 Continuation of contracts of long-term insurance where insurer in liquidation.

(1) This section applies in relation to the winding up of an insurer which effects or carries out contracts of long-term insurance.

(2) Unless the court otherwise orders, the liquidator must carry on the insurer's business so far as it consists of carrying out the insurer's contracts of long-term insurance with a view to its being transferred as a going concern to a person who may lawfully carry out those contracts.

(3) In carrying on the business, the liquidator—

(a) may agree to the variation of any contracts of insurance in existence when the winding up order is made; but

(b) must not effect any new contracts of insurance.

(4) If the liquidator is satisfied that the interests of the creditors in respect of liabilities of the insurer attributable to contracts of long-term insurance effected by it require the appointment of a special manager, he may apply to the court.

(5) On such an application, the court may appoint a special manager to act during such time as the court may direct.

(6) The special manager is to have such powers, including any of the powers of a receiver or manager, as the court may direct.

(7) Section 177(5) of the 1986 Act (or Article 151(5) of the 1989 Order) applies to a special manager appointed under subsection (5) as it applies to a special manager appointed under section 177 of the 1986 Act (or Article 151 of the 1989 Order).

(8) If the court thinks fit, it may reduce the value of one or more of the contracts of longterm insurance effected by the insurer.

(9) Any reduction is to be on such terms and subject to such conditions (if any) as the court thinks fit.

(10) The court may, on the application of an official, appoint an independent actuary to investigate the insurer's business so far as it consists of carrying out its contracts of long-term insurance and to report to the official—

(a) on the desirability or otherwise of that part of the insurer's business being continued; and

(b) on any reduction in the contracts of long-term insurance effected by the insurer that may be necessary for successful continuation of that part of the insurer's business.

(11) "Official" means—

(a) the liquidator;

关于保险公司的补充规定

第376条 保险公司清算时长期保险合同的延续

(1)本条规定适用于订立或实施长期保险合同的保险公司清算。

(2)除非法院另有命令,否则清算人必须继续保险公司由实施长期保险合同组成的业务,以使该业务作为持续经营的业务转移到可合法履行上述合同的人。

(3)在继续业务时,清算人

(a)在清算令发布时可同意对现有任何保险合同进行变更;但

(b)不得订立任何新的保险合同。

(4)如清算人确信,与保险公司就其订立的长期保险合同所承担的债务相关的债权人利益需要委派特别管理人,则可以向法院提出申请。

(5)法院可以应该申请委派一名特别管理人在法院指定的期间采取行动。

(6)特别管理人具有法院指定的权力,其中包括接管人或管理人的任何权力。

(7)1986年法第177条第(5)款[或1989年法令第151条第(5)款]对依照第(5)款规定委派的特别管理人适用,等同于对依照1986年法第177条(或1989年法令第151条)委派的特别管理人适用。

(8)如法院认为适当,则可以削减由该保险公司订立的一项或多项合同的价值。

(9)任何削减均以法院认为适当的条款进行并受法院认为适当的条件(如有)制约。

(10)法院可以应官员申请委派独立精算师调查保险公司由长期保险合同组成的业务并向官员报告

(a)保险公司该部分业务是否有必要继续;

(b)为继续保险公司该部分业务有必要对其订立的长期保险合同进行的任何削减。

(11)“官员”系指

(a)清算人;

(b) a special manager appointed under subsection (5); or

(c) the Authority.

(12) The liquidator may make an application in the name of the insurer and on its behalf under Part VII without obtaining the permission that would otherwise be required by section 167 of, and Schedule 4 to, the 1986 Act (or Article 142 of, and Schedule 2 to, the 1989 Order).

377 Reducing the value of contracts instead of winding up.

(1) This section applies in relation to an insurer which has been proved to be unable to pay its debts.

(2) If the court thinks fit, it may reduce the value of one or more of the insurer's contracts instead of making a winding up order.

(3) Any reduction is to be on such terms and subject to such conditions (if any) as the court thinks fit.

378 Treatment of assets on winding up.

(1) The Treasury may by regulations provide for the treatment of the assets of an insurer on its winding up.

(2) The regulations may, in particular, provide for—

(a) assets representing a particular part of the insurer's business to be available only for meeting liabilities attributable to that part of the insurer's business;

(b) separate general meetings of the creditors to be held in respect of liabilities attributable to a particular part of the insurer's business.

379 Winding-up rules.

(1) Winding-up rules may include provision—

(a) for determining the amount of the liabilities of an insurer to policyholders of any class or description for the purpose of proof in a winding up; and

(b) generally for carrying into effect the provisions of this Part with respect to the winding up of insurers.

(2) Winding-up rules may, in particular, make provision for all or any of the following matters—

(a) the identification of assets and liabilities;

(b) the apportionment, between assets of different classes or descriptions, of—

(i) the costs, charges and expenses of the winding up; and

(ii) any debts of the insurer of a specified class or description;

(c) the determination of the amount of liabilities of a specified description;

(d) the application of assets for meeting liabilities of a specified description;

(e) the application of assets representing any excess of a specified description.

(3) "Specified" means specified in winding-up rules.

(b)依照第(5)款规定委派的特别管理人;或

(c)管理局。

(12)清算人可以依照第七部分规定以保险人名义并代表其提出申请,无须取得1986年法第167条和附录4(或1989年法令第142条和附录2)要求取得的许可。

第377条 削减合同价值而不清算

(1)本条规定适用于经证明无力偿付债务的保险公司。

(2)如法院认为适当,则可以削减该保险公司的一项或多项合同的价值,而不发布清算令。

(3)任何削减均以法院认为适当的条款进行并受法院认为适当的条件(如有)制约。

第378条 清算时的资产处理

(1)财政部可以制定法规,规定保险公司清算时其资产的处理。

(2)法规可以特别规定:

(a)代表保险公司部分业务的资产只可用于偿付属于该部分业务的负债;

(b)就属于保险公司特定部分业务的负债单独召开债权人大会。

第379条 清算规则

(1)清算规则可以包括下列规定:

(a)在清算中为取证确定保险公司对任何类型的保单持有人的负债额;

(b)概括规定施行本部分与保险公司清算相关的规定。

(2)清算规则可以特别规定下列全部或任何事项:

(a)资产和负债鉴定;

(b)下列事项在不同类别或种类资产间的分摊:

(i)清算的成本、收费和开支;以及

(ii)保险公司任何指定类型或种类的债务;

(c)确定规定种类的负债额;

(d)偿付规定种类负债的资产用途;

(e)代表任何超出规定种类的资产用途。

(3)“规定”系指清算规则中规定。

(4) "Winding-up rules" means rules made under section 411 of the 1986 Act (or Article 359 of the 1989 Order).

(5) Nothing in this section affects the power to make winding-up rules under the 1986 Act or the 1989 Order.

（4）“清算规则”系指依照1986年法第411条（或1989年法令第359条）制定的规则。

（5）本条任何规定不影响依照1986年法或1989年法令制定清算规则的权力。

PART XXV INJUNCTIONS AND RESTITUTION

Annotations:

Modifications etc. (not altering text)

C332 Pt. XXV (ss. 380–386) amended (1.12.2001) by 2001/2657, arts. 1(1), 10(10), 11(10) (which was revoked (8.10.2001) by S.I. 2001/3083, arts. 1(2), 23); S.I. 2001/3538, art. 2(1)

Pt. XXV (ss. 380–386) amended (1.12.2001) by S.I. 2001/3083, arts. 1 (2), 10 (10), 11(10); S.I. 2001/3538, art. 2(1)

Pt. XXV (ss. 380–386) extended (1.12.2001) by S.I. 2001/3646, arts. 1(1), 3(1)(a)

Injunctions

380 Injunctions.

(1) If, on the application of the Authority or the Secretary of State, the court is satisfied—

(a) that there is a reasonable likelihood that any person will contravene a relevant requirement, or

(b) that any person has contravened a relevant requirement and that there is a reasonable likelihood that the contravention will continue or be repeated,

the court may make an order restraining (or in Scotland an interdict prohibiting) the contravention.

(2) If on the application of the Authority or the Secretary of State the court is satisfied—

(a) that any person has contravened a relevant requirement, and

(b) that there are steps which could be taken for remedying the contravention,

the court may make an order requiring that person, and any other person who appears to have been knowingly concerned in the contravention, to take such steps as the court may

第二十五部分　强制令和退赔

注释：

修改等(不涉及条文内容)

C332　第二十五部分(第380条至第386条)于2001年12月1日依照制定法文件S.I. 2001/2657第1条第(1)款、第10条第(10)款、第11条第(10)款(该条款已于2001年10月8日依制定法文件S.I.2001/3083第1条第(2)款、第23条废除);制定法文件S.I.2001/3538第2条第(1)款修正;

第二十五部分(第380条至第386条)于2001年12月1日依照制定法文件S.I.2001/3083第1条第(2)款、第10条第(10)款、第11条第(10)款;制定法文件S.I.2001/3538第2条第(1)款修正;

第二十五部分(第380条至第386条)于2001年12月1日依照制定法文件S.I.2001/3646第1条第(1)款、第3条第(1)款第(a)项扩大适用范围。

强　制　令

第380条　强制令

(1)如应管理局或国务大臣申请,法院确信有下列情况:

(a)有任何人将违反相关要求的合理可能,或

(b)任何人已违反相关要求且有继续或重复该违反行为的合理可能,

则法院可以发布强制令,制止(或在苏格兰发布禁令禁止)该违反行为。

(2)如应管理局或国务大臣申请,法院确信有下列情况:

(a)任何人违反了相关要求,且

(b)可采取措施补救该违反行为,

则法院可以颁布法令,要求该人以及任何似乎明知该违反行为而参与其中的其他人采取法院指定的措施进行补救。

direct to remedy it.

(3) If, on the application of the Authority or the Secretary of State, the court is satisfied that any person may have—

(a) contravened a relevant requirement, or

(b) been knowingly concerned in the contravention of such a requirement,

it may make an order restraining (or in Scotland an interdict prohibiting) him from disposing of, or otherwise dealing with, any assets of his which it is satisfied he is reasonably likely to dispose of or otherwise deal with.

(4) The jurisdiction conferred by this section is exercisable by the High Court and the Court of Session.

(5) In subsection (2), references to remedying a contravention include references to mitigating its effect.

(6) "Relevant requirement"—

(a) in relation to an application by the Authority, means a requirement—

(i) which is imposed by or under this Act; or

(ii) which is imposed by or under any other Act and whose contravention constitutes an offence which the Authority has power to prosecute under this Act;

(b) in relation to an application by the Secretary of State, means a requirement which is imposed by or under this Act and whose contravention constitutes an offence which the Secretary of State has power to prosecute under this Act.

(7) In the application of subsection (6) to Scotland—

(a) in paragraph (a)(ii) for "which the Authority has power to prosecute under this Act" substitute " mentioned in paragraph (a) or (b) of section 402(1)"; and

(b) in paragraph (b) omit "which the Secretary of State has power to prosecute under this Act".

Annotations:

Modifications etc. (not altering text)

C333 S. 380 modified (18.7.2002 for certain purposes and 21.8.2002 otherwise) by The Electronic Commerce Directive (Financial Services and Markets) Regulations 2002 (S.I. 2002/1775), regs. 1, 12(2)

C334 S. 380(1)(2) modified (1.12.2001) by S.I. 2001/2657, arts. 1(1), 20(3) (which was revoked (8.10.2001) by S.I. 2001/3083, arts. 1(2), 23); S.I. 2001/3538, art. 2(1)

S. 380(1)(2) modified (1.12.2001) by S.I. 2001/3083, arts. 1(2), 20(3); S.I. 2001/3538, art. 2(1)

C335 S. 380(2) extended (with modifications) (1.12.2001) by S.I. 2001/2657, arts. 1(1), 2 (which was revoked (8.10.2001) by S.I. 2001/3083, arts. 1(2), 23); S.I. 2001/3538, art. 2(1)

(3)如应管理局或国务大臣申请,法院确信任何人可能

(a)违反了相关要求,或

(b)明知违反要求而参与其中,

则可以发布强制令,制止(或在苏格兰发布禁令禁止)其处置或以其他方式处理法院合理认为其可能处置或以其他方式处理的任何资产。

(4)本条规定授予的管辖权可以由高等法院和(苏格兰)高等民事法院行使。

(5)第(2)款中述及的补救违反行为包括述及减轻其影响。

(6)"相关要求"

(a)就管理局提出的申请,系指

(i)本法规定或依照本法提出的要求;或

(ii)任何其他法律规定或依照其提出的要求,且违反该要求构成管理局依照本法规定有权起诉的犯罪;

(b)就国务大臣而言,系指本法规定或依照本法提出的任何要求,且违反该要求构成国务大臣依照本法规定有权起诉的犯罪;

(7)第(6)款规定在苏格兰适用时

(a)第(a)项第(ii)小项"管理局依照本法有权起诉"替换为"第402条第(1)款第(a)项或第(b)项所述";

(b)第(b)项删除"国务大臣依照本法有权起诉"。

注释:

修改等(不涉及条文内容)

C333 第380条为特定目的于2002年7月18日,否则于2002年8月21日依照《2002年电子商务指令条例》(金融服务和市场)(制定法文件S.I.2002/1775)第1条、第12条第(2)款修订。

C334 第380条第(1)款和第(2)款于2001年12月1日依照制定法文件S.I.2001/2657第1条第(1)款、第20条第(3)款[于2001年10月8日依制定法文件S.I.2001/3083第1条第(2)款、第23条废除];制定法文件S.I.2001/3538第2条第(1)款修订;

第380条第(1)款和第(2)款于2001年12月1日依照制定法文件S.I.2001/3083第1条第(2)款、第20条第(3)款;制定法文件S.I.2001/3538第2条第(1)款修订。

C335 第380条第(2)款(已修订)于2001年12月1日依照制定法文件S.I.2001/2657第1条第(1)款、第2条[该条已于2001年10月8日依制定法文件S.I.2001/3083第1条第(2)款、第23条废除];制定法文件S.I.2001/3538第2条第(1)款扩大适用范围;

S. 380(2) extended (with modifications) (1.12.2001) by S.I. 2001/3083, arts. 1(2), 2; S.I. 2001/3538, art. 2(1)

S. 380(2) extended (1.12.2001) by S.I. 2001/3646, arts. 1(2), 3(3)(a)

C336 S. 380(3)(a) extended (with modifications) (1.12.2001) by S.I. 2001/2657, arts. 1(1), 4 (which was revoked (8.10.2001) by S.I. 2001/3083, arts. 1(2), 23); S.I. 2001/3538, art. 2(1)

S. 380(3)(a) extended (with modifications) (1.12.2001) by S.I. 2001/3083, arts. 1(2), 4; S.I. 2001/3538, art. 2(1)

381 Injunctions in cases of market abuse.

(1) If, on the application of the Authority, the court is satisfied—

(a) that there is a reasonable likelihood that any person will engage in market abuse, or

(b) that any person is or has engaged in market abuse and that there is a reasonable likelihood that the market abuse will continue or be repeated,

the court may make an order restraining (or in Scotland an interdict prohibiting) the market abuse.

(2) If on the application of the Authority the court is satisfied—

(a) that any person is or has engaged in market abuse, and

(b) that there are steps which could be taken for remedying the market abuse, the court may make an order requiring him to take such steps as the court may direct to remedy it.

(3) Subsection (4) applies if, on the application of the Authority, the court is satisfied that any person—

(a) may be engaged in market abuse; or

(b) may have been engaged in market abuse.

(4) The court make an order restraining (or in Scotland an interdict prohibiting) the person concerned from disposing of, or otherwise dealing with, any assets of his which it is satisfied that he is reasonably likely to dispose of, or otherwise deal with.

(5) The jurisdiction conferred by this section is exercisable by the High Court and the Court of Session.

(6) In subsection (2), references to remedying any market abuse include references to mitigating its effect.

Restitution orders

382 Restitution orders.

(1) The court may, on the application of the Authority or the Secretary of State, make an

退 赔 令

> 第380条第(2)款(已修订)于2001年12月1日依照制定法文件S.I.2001/3083第1条第(2)款、第2条;制定法文件S.I.2001/3538第2条第(1)款扩大适用范围;
>
> 第380条第(2)款于2001年12月1日依照制定法文件S.I.2001/3646第1条第(2)款、第3条第(3)款第(a)项扩大适用范围。
>
> C336 第380条第(3)款第(a)项(已修订)于2001年12月1日依照制定法文件S.I.2001/2657第1条第(1)款、第4条[于2001年10月8日依制定法文件S.I.2001/3083第1条第(2)款、第23条废除];制定法文件S.I.2001/3538第2条第(1)款扩大适用范围;
>
> 第380条第(3)款第(a)项(已修订)于2001年12月1日依照制定法文件S.I.2001/3083第1条第(2)款、第4条;制定法文件S.I.2001/3538第2条第(1)款扩大适用范围。

第381条 市场滥用案件中的强制令

(1)如应管理局申请,法院确信有下列情况:

(a)有任何人将实施市场滥用行为的合理可能;

(b)任何人正在或已实施市场滥用行为且有继续或重复该行为的合理可能,

则法院可以发布强制令,制止(或在苏格兰发布禁令禁止)该市场滥用行为。

(2)如应管理局申请,法院确信有下列情况:

(a)任何人正在实施或已经实施市场滥用行为,且

(b)可采取措施补救该市场滥用行为,则法院可颁布法令,要求该人采取法院指定的措施补救该行为。

(3)如应管理局申请,法院确信有下列情况,则适用第(4)款规定:

(a)任何人可能实施市场滥用行为;或

(b)任何人可能已实施市场滥用行为。

(4)则法院可以发布强制令,制止(或在苏格兰发布禁令禁止)该人处置或以其他方式处理法院合理认为其可能处置或以其他方式处理的任何资产。

(5)本条规定授予的管辖权可由高等法院和(苏格兰)高等民事法院行使。

(6)第(2)款中述及的补救任何市场滥用行为包括述及减轻其影响。

退 赔 令

第382条 退赔令

(1)法院如确信某人违反了相关要求或明知违反要求而参与其中,且有下列情

order under subsection(2) if it is satisfied that a person has contravened a relevant requirement, or been knowingly concerned in the contravention of such a requirement, and—

(a) that profits have accrued to him as a result of the contravention; or

(b) that one or more persons have suffered loss or been otherwise adversely affected as a result of the contravention.

(2) The court may order the person concerned to pay to the Authority such sum as appears to the court to be just having regard—

(a) in a case within paragraph (a) of subsection (1), to the profits appearing to the court to have accrued;

(b) in a case within paragraph (b) of that subsection, to the extent of the loss or other adverse effect;

(c) in a case within both of those paragraphs, to the profits appearing to the court to have accrued and to the extent of the loss or other adverse effect.

(3) Any amount paid to the Authority in pursuance of an order under subsection (2) must be paid by it to such qualifying person or distributed by it among such qualifying persons as the court may direct.

(4) On an application under subsection (1) the court may require the person concerned to supply it with such accounts or other information as it may require for any one or more of the following purposes—

(a) establishing whether any and, if so, what profits have accrued to him as mentioned in paragraph (a) of that subsection;

(b) establishing whether any person or persons have suffered any loss or adverse effect as mentioned in paragraph (b) of that subsection and, if so, the extent of that loss or adverse effect; and

(c) determining how any amounts are to be paid or distributed under subsection (3).

(5) The court may require any accounts or other information supplied under subsection (4) to be verified in such manner as it may direct.

(6) The jurisdiction conferred by this section is exercisable by the High Court and the Court of Session.

(7) Nothing in this section affects the right of any person other than the Authority or the Secretary of State to bring proceedings in respect of the matters to which this section applies.

(8) "Qualifying person" means a person appearing to the court to be someone—

(a) to whom the profits mentioned in subsection (1)(a) are attributable; or

(b) who has suffered the loss or adverse effect mentioned in subsection (1)(b).

(9) "Relevant requirement"—

(a) in relation to an application by the Authority, means a requirement—

(i) which is imposed by or under this Act; or

况,则可以应管理局或国务大臣申请,依照第(2)款规定颁布法令,

(a)该人由于该违反要求的行为取得了利润;或

(b)一人或多人因该违反要求的行为遭受了损失或其他不利影响。

(2)法院可以在考虑下列情况后命令该人向管理局支付其认为公正的金额:

(a)就第(1)款第(a)项规定的情况而言,法院认为已产生的利润;

(b)就第(1)款第(b)项规定的情况而言,损失或其他不利影响的程度;

(c)就上述两项规定的情况而言,法院认为已产生的利润以及损失或其他不利影响的程度。

(3)依照第(2)款规定的命令向管理局支付的金额必须由该人向法院指定的合资格人支付或在多个合资格人间分配。

(4)应依照第(1)款规定提出的申请,法院可以要求有关人提供为实现下列一项或多项目的所需的账户或其他信息:

(a)确定该人是否取得了该款第(a)项所述利润,如取得了利润,取得了何种利润;

(b)确定是否有任何人遭受了第(b)项所述损失或不利影响,如遭受了损失或不利影响,遭受了何种损失或不利影响;

(c)确定如依照第(3)款规定支付或分配任何金额的款项。

(5)对依照第(4)款规定提供的任何账户或其他信息,法院可要求以其指定的方式予以核实。

(6)本条规定授予的管辖权可以由高等法院和(苏格兰)高等民事法院行使。

(7)本条任何规定不影响管理局或国务大臣以外的任何其他人就本条规定适用的事项提起诉讼。

(8)“合资格人”系指法院认为有下列情况的人:

(a)第(1)款第(a)项所述利润应归属于该人;或

(b)遭受了第(1)款第(b)项所述损失或不利影响。

(9)“相关要求”

(a)就管理局提出的申请,系指

(i)本法规定或依照本法提出的要求;或

(ii) which is imposed by or under any other Act and whose contravention constitutes an offence which the Authority has power to prosecute under this Act;

(b) in relation to an application by the Secretary of State, means a requirement which is imposed by or under this Act and whose contravention constitutes an offence which the Secretary of State has power to prosecute under this Act.

(10) In the application of subsection (9) to Scotland—

(a) in paragraph (a)(ii) for "which the Authority has power to prosecute under this Act" substitute "mentioned in paragraph (a) or (b) of section 402(1)"; and

(b) in paragraph (b) omit "which the Secretary of State has power to prosecute under this Act".

Annotations:

Modifications etc. (not altering text)

C337 S. 382 extended (with modifications) (1.12.2001) by S.I. 2001/2657, arts. 1(1), 2 (which was revoked (8.10.2001) by S.I. 2001/3083, arts. 1(2), 23); S.I. 2001/3538, art. 2 (1)

S. 382 extended (with modifications) (1.12.2001) by S.I. 2001/3083, arts. 1(2), 2; S.I. 2001/3538, art. 2(1)

C338 S. 382 modified (18.7.2002 for certain purposes and 21.8.2002 otherwise) by The Electronic Commerce Directive (Financial Services and Markets) Regulations 2002 (S.I. 2002/1775), regs. 1, 12(2)

C339 S. 382(3)-(5)(8) applied (with modifications) (26.11.2001) by S.I. 2001/3755, regs. 1, 9(7)(9) (with regs. 39, 45)

383 Restitution orders in cases of market abuse.

(1) The court may, on the application of the Authority, make an order under subsection (4) if it is satisfied that a person ("the person concerned")—

(a) has engaged in market abuse, or

(b) by taking or refraining from taking any action has required or encouraged another person or persons to engage in behaviour which, if engaged in by the person concerned, would amount to market abuse,

and the condition mentioned in subsection (2) is fulfilled.

(2) The condition is—

(a) that profits have accrued to the person concerned as a result; or

(b) that one or more persons have suffered loss or been otherwise adversely affected as a result.

(3) But the court may not make an order under subsection (4) if it is satisfied that—

(a) the person concerned believed, on reasonable grounds, that his behaviour did not (ii)任何其他法律规定或依照其提出的要求,且违反该要求构成管理局依照本法规定有权起诉的犯罪;

(b)就国务大臣而言,系指本法规定或依照本法提出的任何要求,且违反该要求构成国务大臣依照本法规定有权起诉的犯罪;

(10)第(9)款规定在苏格兰适用时

(a)第(a)项第(ii)小项"管理局依照本法有权起诉"替换为"第402条第(1)款(a)项或第(b)项所述";

(b)第(b)项删除"国务大臣依照本法有权起诉"。

注释:

修改等(不涉及条文内容)

C337 第382条(已修订)于2001年12月1日依照制定法文件S.I.2001/2657第1条第(1)款、第2条(该条已于2001年10月8日依制定法文件S.I.2001/3083第1条第(2)款、第23条废除);制定法文件S.I.2001/3538第2条第(1)款扩大适用范围;

第382条(已修订)于2001年12月1日依照制定法文件S.I.2001/3083第1条第(2)款、第2条;制定法文件S.I.2001/3538第2条第(1)款扩大适用范围。

C338 第382条为特定目的于2002年7月18日,否则于2002年8月21日依照《2002电子商务指令条例》(金融服务和市场)(制定法文件S.I.2002/1775)第1条、第12条第(2)款修订。

C339 第382条第(3)款至第(5)款、第(8)款(已修订)于2001年11月26日依照制定法文件S.I.2001/3755第1条、第9条第(7)款和第(9)款(与第39条和第45条)适用。

第383条 市场滥用案件中的退赔令

(1)法院如确信某人(以下简称该人)有下列情况,则可应管理局申请,依照第(4)款规定颁布法令:

(a)可能实施市场滥用行为,或

(b)通过采取或不采取任何行动,要求或鼓励他人实施如该人实施即构成市场滥用的行为,

并满足第(2)款所述条件。

(2)前款所述条件为

(a)该人由于该市场滥用行为取得了利润;或

(b)一人或多人因该市场滥用行为遭受了损失或其他不利影响。

(3)但法院如确信有下列情况,则不得依照第(4)款规定颁布法令:

(a)该人有合理理由相信其行为不属于第(1)款第(a)项或第(b)项规定的范围;或

fall within paragraph (a) or (b) of subsection (1); or

(b) he took all reasonable precautions and exercised all due diligence to avoid behaving in a way which fell within paragraph (a) or (b) of subsection (1).

(4) The court may order the person concerned to pay to the Authority such sum as appears to the court to be just having regard—

(a) in a case within paragraph (a) of subsection (2), to the profits appearing to the court to have accrued;

(b) in a case within paragraph (b) of that subsection, to the extent of the loss or other adverse effect;

(c) in a case within both of those paragraphs, to the profits appearing to the court to have accrued and to the extent of the loss or other adverse effect.

(5) Any amount paid to the Authority in pursuance of an order under subsection (4) must be paid by it to such qualifying person or distributed by it among such qualifying persons as the court may direct.

(6) On an application under subsection (1) the court may require the person concerned to supply it with such accounts or other information as it may require for any one or more of the following purposes—

(a) establishing whether any and, if so, what profits have accrued to him as mentioned in subsection (2)(a);

(b) establishing whether any person or persons have suffered any loss or adverse effect as mentioned in subsection (2)(b) and, if so, the extent of that loss or adverse effect; and

(c) determining how any amounts are to be paid or distributed under subsection (5).

(7) The court may require any accounts or other information supplied under subsection (6) to be verified in such manner as it may direct.

(8) The jurisdiction conferred by this section is exercisable by the High Court and the Court of Session.

(9) Nothing in this section affects the right of any person other than the Authority to bring proceedings in respect of the matters to which this section applies.

(10) "Qualifying person" means a person appearing to the court to be someone—

(a) to whom the profits mentioned in paragraph (a) of subsection (2) areattributable; or

(b) who has suffered the loss or adverse effect mentioned in paragraph (b) of that subsection.

Restitution required by Authority

384 Power of Authority to require restitution.

(1) The Authority may exercise the power in subsection (5) if it is satisfied that an authorised person ("the person concerned") has contravened a relevant requirement, or been

(b)该人已采取一切合理的预防措施并已尽一切应尽勤勉防止实施第(1)款第(a)项或第(b)项规定范围的行为。

(4)法院在考虑下列情况后可命令相关人向管理局支付其认为公正的金额:

(a)就第(2)款第(a)项而言,法院认为已产生的利润;

(b)就第(1)款第(b)项规定的情况而言,损失或其他不利影响的程度;

(c)就上述两项规定的情况而言,法院认为已产生的利润以及损失或其他不利影响的程度。

(5)依照第(4)款规定的命令向管理局支付的金额必须由该人向法院指定的合资格人支付或在多个合资格人间分配。

(6)应依照第(1)款规定提出的申请,法院可以要求有关人提供为实现下列一项或多项目的所需的账户或其他信息:

(a)确定该人是否取得了第(2)款第(a)项所述利润,如取得了利润,取得了何种利润;

(b)确定是否有任何人遭受了第(2)款第(b)项所述损失或不利影响,如遭受了损失或不利影响,遭受了何种损失或不利影响。

(c)确定如依照第(5)款规定支付或分配任何金额的款项。

(7)对依照第(6)款规定提供的任何账户或其他信息,法院可以要求以其指定的方式予以核实。

(8)本条规定授予的管辖权可以由高等法院和(苏格兰)高等民事法院行使。

(9)本条任何规定不影响管理局以外的任何其他人就本条规定适用的事项提起诉讼。

(10)"合资格人"系指法院认为有下列情况的人:

(a)第(2)款第(a)项所述利润应当归属于该人;或

(b)遭受了该款第(b)项所述损失或不利影响。

管理局要求的退赔

第384条　管理局要求的退赔

(1)如管理局确信获授权人(以下简称该人)违反了相关要求或明知违反要求而参与其中,且有下列情况,则可以行使第(5)款规定赋予的权力:

knowingly concerned in the contravention of such a requirement, and—

(a) that profits have accrued to him as a result of the contravention; or

(b) that one or more persons have suffered loss or been otherwise adversely affected as a result of the contravention.

(2) The Authority may exercise the power in subsection (5) if it is satisfied that a person ("the person concerned")—

(a) has engaged in market abuse, or

(b) by taking or refraining from taking any action has required or encouraged another person or persons to engage in behaviour which, if engaged in by the person concerned, would amount to market abuse,

and the condition mentioned in subsection (3) is fulfilled,

(3) The condition is—

(a) that profits have accrued to the person concerned as a result of the market abuse; or

(b) that one or more persons have suffered loss or been otherwise adversely affected as a result of the market abuse.

(4) But the Authority may not exercise that power as a result of subsection (2) if, having considered any representations made to it in response to a warning notice, there are reasonable grounds for it to be satisfied that—

(a) the person concerned believed, on reasonable grounds, that his behaviour did not fall within paragraph (a) or (b) of that subsection; or

(b) he took all reasonable precautions and exercised all due diligence to avoid behaving in a way which fell within paragraph (a) or (b) of that subsection.

(5) The power referred to in subsections (1) and (2) is a power to require the person concerned, in accordance with such arrangements as the Authority considers appropriate, to pay to the appropriate person or distribute among the appropriate persons such amount as appears to the Authority to be just having regard—

(a) in a case within paragraph (a) of subsection (1) or (3), to the profits appearing to the Authority to have accrued;

(b) in a case within paragraph (b) of subsection (1) or (3), to the extent of the loss or other adverse effect;

(c) in a case within paragraphs (a) and (b) of subsection (1) or (3), to the profits appearing to the Authority to have accrued and to the extent of the loss or other adverse effect.

(6) "Appropriate person" means a person appearing to the Authority to be someone—

(a) to whom the profits mentioned in paragraph (a) of subsection (1) or (3) are attributable; or

(b) who has suffered the loss or adverse effect mentioned in paragraph (b) of subsection (1) or (3).

(a)该人由于该违反要求的行为取得了利润;或

(b)一人或多人因该违反要求的行为遭受了损失或受到其他不利影响。

(2)如管理局确信某人(以下简称该人)有下列情况,则可以行使第(5)款规定的权力:

(a)可能实施市场滥用行为,或

(b)通过采取或不采取任何行动,要求或鼓励他人实施如该人实施即构成市场滥用的行为,

并满足第(3)款所述条件。

(3)前款所述条件为

(a)该人由于该市场滥用行为取得了利润;或

(b)一人或多人因该市场滥用行为遭受了损失或其他不利影响。

(4)但管理局如考虑针对预告通知提出的任何陈述后有合理理由确信下列情况,则不得因第(2)款规定行使权力:

(a)该人有合理理由相信其行为不属于该款第(a)项或第(b)项规定的范围;或

(b)该人已采取一切合理的预防措施并已尽一切应尽勤勉防止实施该款第(a)项或第(b)项规定范围的行为。

(5)第(1)款和第(2)款规定赋予的权力是要求该人依照管理局认为适当的安排向适当的人支付或分配管理局考虑下列情况后认为公正的金额:

(a)就第(1)款或第(3)款第(a)项规定的情况而言,管理局认为已产生的利润;

(b)就第(1)款或第(3)款第(b)项规定的情况而言,损失或其他不利影响的程度;

(c)就第(1)款或第(3)款第(a)项和第(b)项规定的情况而言,管理局认为已产生的利润以及损失或其他不利影响的程度。

(6)"适当的人"系指管理局认为有下列情况的人:

(a)第(1)款或第(3)款第(a)项所述利润应归属于该人;或

(b)遭受了第(1)款或第(3)款第(b)项所述损失或不利影响。

(7)"Relevant requirement" means—

(a) a requirement imposed by or under this Act; and

(b) a requirement which is imposed by or under any other Act and whose contravention constitutes an offence in relation to which this Act confers power to prosecute on the Authority.

(8) In the application of subsection (7) to Scotland, in paragraph (b) for"in relation to which this Act confers power to prosecute on the Authority" substitute " mentioned in paragraph (a) or (b) of section 402(1)".

Annotations:

385 Warning notices.

Modifications etc. (not altering text)

C340 S. 384 modified (18.7.2002 for certain purposes and 21.8.2002 otherwise) by The Electronic Commerce Directive (Financial Services and Markets) Regulations 2002 (S.I. 2002/1775), regs. 1, 12(1)

C341 S. 384(5) extended (with modifications) (1.12.2001) by S.I. 2001/2657, arts. 1 (1), 3 (which was revoked (8.10.2001) by S.I. 2001/3083, arts. 1(2), 23); S.I. 2001/3538, art. 2(1)

S. 384(5) extended (with modifications) (1.12.2001) by S.I. 2001/3083, arts. 1(2), 3; S. I. 2001/3538, art. 2(1)

(1) If the Authority proposes to exercise the power under section 384(5) in relation to a person, it must give him a warning notice.

(2) A warning notice under this section must specify the amount which the Authority proposes to require the person concerned to pay or distribute as mentioned in section 384(5).

Annotations:

386 Decision notices.

Modifications etc. (not altering text)

C342 S. 385 excluded (1.12.2001) by S.I. 2001/3592, arts. 1(2), 61(6) (with art. 23 (2))

(1) If the Authority decides to exercise the power under section 384(5), it must give a decision notice to the person in relation to whom the power is exercised.

(2) The decision notice must—

(a) state the amount that he is to pay or distribute as mentioned in section 384(5);

(b) identify the person or persons to whom that amount is to be paid or among whom that amount is to be distributed; and

(c) state the arrangements in accordance with which the payment or distribution is to be

(7)"相关要求"系指

(a)依照本法提出的要求;以及

(b)任何其他法律规定或依照其提出的要求,且违反该要求构成本法赋予管理局起诉权的犯罪;

(8)在苏格兰适用第(7)款时,第(b)项"本法赋予管理局起诉权"替换为"第402条第(1)款第(a)项或第(b)项所述"。

注释:

第385条 预告通知

修改等(不涉及条文内容)

C340 第384条为特定目的于2002年7月18日,否则于2002年8月21日依照《2002年电子商务指令条例》(金融服务和市场)(制定法文件S.I.2002/1775)第1条、第12条第(1)款修订。

C341 第384条第(5)款(已修订)于2001年12月1日依照制定法文件S.I.2001/2657第1条第(1)款、第3条[于2001年10月8日依照制定法文件S.I.2001/3083第1条第(2)款、第23条废除];制定法文件S.I.2001/3538第2条第(1)款扩大适用范围;

第384条第(5)款(已修订)于2001年12月1日依照制定法文件S.I.2001/3083第1条第(2)款、第3条;制定法文件S.I.2001/3538第2条第(1)款扩大适用范围。

(1)如管理局拟对某人行使384条第(5)款规定的权力,则必须向该人发出预告通知。

(2)本条规定的预告通知必须规定管理局拟依照第384条第(5)款要求该人支付或分配的金额。

注释:

第386条 决定通知

修改等(不涉及条文内容)

C342 第385条于2001年12月1日依照制定法文件S.I.2001/3592第(1)条第(2)款、第61条第(6)款[与第23条第(2)款]排除。

(1)如管理局决定行使384条第(5)款规定的权力,则必须向权力行使对象发出决定通知。

(2)决定通知必须

(a)说明该人依照第384条第(5)款应支付或分配的金额;

(b)指定接受支付或分配的一人或多人;并

(c)说明支付或分配依据的安排。

made.

(3) If the Authority decides to exercise the power under section 384(5), the person in relation to whom it is exercised may refer the matter to the Tribunal.

Annotations:

Modifications etc. (not altering text)

C343 S. 386 excluded (1.12.2001) by S.I. 2001/3592, arts. 1(2), 61(6) (with art. 23(2))

C344 S. 386(1) modified (1.12.2001) by S.I. 2001/3592, arts. 1(2), 70(2) (with art. 23(2))

(3)如管理局决定行使384条第(5)款规定的权力,则权力行使对象有权将该事项诉至裁判所。

注释:

修改等(不涉及条文内容)

C343　第386条于2001年12月1日依照制定法文件S.I.2001/3592第(1)条第(2)款、第61条第(6)款[与第23条第(2)款]排除。

C344　第386条第(1)款于2001年12月1日依照制定法文件S.I.2001/3592第1条第(2)款、第70条第(2)款[与第23条第(2)款]修订。

PART XXVI NOTICES

Annotations:

Modifications etc. (not altering text)

C345 Pt. XXVI (ss. 387–396) applied (with modifications) (17.8.2001 for certain purposes otherwise 1.12.2001) by 1992 c. 40, s. 58A(6)(8)(as substituted(17.8.2001 for certain purposes otherwise 1.12.2001) by 2001/2617, arts. 2, 8, 13(1), Sch. 3 Pt. I para. 75 (with art. 13(3), Sch.5)); S.I. 2001/3538, art. 2(1)

Pt. XXVI (ss. 387–396) applied (with modifications) (17.8.2001 for certain purposes otherwise 1.12.2001) by 1992 c. 40, s. 85(4B) (as inserted (17.8.2001 for certain purposes otherwise 1.12.2001) by S.I. 2001/2617, arts. 2, 8, 13(1), Sch. 3 Pt. I para. 95 (with art. 13 (3), Sch. 5)); S.I. 2001/3538, art. 2(1)

Pt. XXVI (ss. 387–396) applied (with modifications) (17.8.2001 for certain purposes otherwise 1.12.2001) by 1992 c. 40, s. 36A(5C)(5D) (as substituted (17.8.2001 for certain purposes otherwise 1.12.2001) by S.I. 2001/2617, arts. 2, 8, 13 (1), Sch. 3 Pt. II para. 142(c) (with art. 13(3), Sch. 5)); S.I. 2001/3538, art. 2(1)

Pt. XXVI (ss. 387–396) applied (with modifications) (17.8.2001 for certain purposes otherwise 1.12.2001) by 1986 c. 53, s. 46A (6) (8) (as substituted (17.8.2001 for certain purposes otherwise 1.12.2001) by S.I. 2001/2617, arts. 2, 8, 13(1), Sch. 3 Pt. II para. 148 (with art. 13(3), Sch. 5)); S.I. 2001/3538, art. 2(1)

Pt. XXVI (ss. 387–396) applied (with modifications) (17.8.2001 for certain purposes otherwise 1.12.2001) by 1986 c. 53, s. 93(6A) (as substituted (17.8.2001 for certain purposes otherwise 1.12.2001) by S.I. 2001/2617, arts. 2, 8, 13(1), Sch. 3 Pt. II para. 177(d) (with art. 13(3), Sch. 5)); S.I. 2001/3538, art. 2

第二十六部分　通　　知

注释：

修改等(不涉及条文内容)

C345　第二十六部分(第387条至第396条)(已修订)为特定目的于2001年8月17日,否则于2001年12月1日依照1992年第40章第58A条第(6)款、第(8)款{为特定目的于2001年8月17日,否则于2001年12月1日依照制定法文件S.I.2001/2617第2条、第8条、第13条第(1)款、附录3第一部分第75条[与第13条第(3)款、附录5]替换};制定法文件S.I.2001/3538第2条第(1)款适用;

第二十六部分(第387条至第396条)(已修订)为特定目的于2001年8月17日,否则于2001年12月1日依照1992年第40章第85条第(4B)款{为特定目的于2001年8月17日,否则于2001年12月1日依照制定法文件S.I.2001/2617第2条、第8条、第13条第(1)款、附录3第一部分第95条[与第13条第(3)款、附录5]插入};制定法文件S.I.2001/3538第2条第(1)款适用;

第二十六部分(第387条至第396条)(已修订)为特定目的于2001年8月17日,否则于2001年12月1日依照1992年第40章第36A条第(5C)款、第(5D)款{为特定目的于2001年8月17日,否则于2001年12月1日依照制定法文件S.I.2001/2617第2条、第8条、第13条第(1)款、附录3第二部分第142条第(c)项[与第13条第(3)款、附录5]替换};制定法文件S.I.2001/3538第2条第(1)款适用;

第二十六部分(第387条至第396条)(已修订)为特定目的于2001年8月17日,否则于2001年12月1日依照1986年第53章第46A条第(6)款、第(8)款{为特定目的于2001年8月17日,否则于2001年12月1日依照制定法文件S.I.2001/2617第2条、第8条、第13条第(1)款、附录3第二部分第148条[与第13条第(3)款、附录5]替换};制定法文件S.I.2001/3538第2条第(1)款适用;

第二十六部分(第387条至第396条)(已修订)为特定目的于2001年8月17日,否则于2001年12月1日依照1986年第53章第93条第(6A)款{为特定目的于2001年8月17日,否则于2001年12月1日依照制定法文件S.I.2001/2617第2条、第8条、第13条第(1)款、附录3第二部分第177条第(d)款[与第13条第(3)款、附录5]替换};制定法文件S.I.2001/3538第2条适用。

Warning notices

387 Warning notices.

(1) A warning notice must—

(a) state the action which the Authority proposes to take;

(b) be in writing;

(c) give reasons for the proposed action;

(d) state whether section 394 applies; and

(e) if that section applies, describe its effect and state whether any secondary material exists to which the person concerned must be allowed access under it.

(2) The warning notice must specify a reasonable period (which may not be less than 28 days) within which the person to whom it is given may make representations to the Authority.

(3) The Authority may extend the period specified in the notice.

(4) The Authority must then decide, within a reasonable period, whether to give the person concerned a decision notice.

Annotations:

Modifications etc. (not altering text)

C346 S. 387 applied (1.12.2001) by S.I. 2001/1228, regs. 1(2)(c), 8(a) (with reg. 1(2)(3)); S.I. 2001/3538, art. 2(1)

Decision notices

388 Decision notices.

(1) A decision notice must—

(a) be in writing;

(b) give the Authority's reasons for the decision to take the action to which the notice relates;

(c) state whether section 394 applies;

(d) if that section applies, describe its effect and state whether any secondary material exists to which the person concerned must be allowed access under it; and

(e) give an indication of—

(i) any right to have the matter referred to the Tribunal which is given by this Act; and

(ii) the procedure on such a reference.

(2) If the decision notice was preceded by a warning notice, the action to which the decision notice relates must be action under the same Part as the action proposed in the warning notice.

预告通知

第387条　预告通知

(1)预告通知必须

(a)说明管理局拟采取的行动;

(b)为书面形式;

(c)说明拟采取行动的理由;

(d)说明第394条规定是否适用;且

(e)如该条规定适用,则说明其效力,并说明是否存在必须允许该人查阅的二手资料。

(2)预告通知必须指定被通知人可向管理局提出陈述的合理期限(不得少于28日)。

(3)管理局可以延长该通知中指定的期限。

(4)管理局必须在合理期限内决定是否向该人发出决定通知。

注释:

修改等(不涉及条文内容)

C346　第387条于2001年12月1日依照制定法文件S.I.2001/1228第1条第(2)款第(c)项、第8条第(a)款[与第1条第(2)款和第(3)款];制定法文件S.I.2001/3538第2条第(1)款适用。

决定通知

第388条　决定通知

(1)决定通知必须

(a)为书面形式;

(b)说明管理局决定采取通知相关行动的理由;

(c)说明第394条规定是否适用;

(d)如该条规定适用,则说明其效力,并说明是否存在必须允许该人查阅的间接材料;且

(e)指明

(i)本法给予的将该事项诉至裁判所的权利;以及

(ii)诉至裁判所的程序。

(2)如发出决定通知前先发出了预告通知,则与决定通知相关的行动必须与预告通知书中拟采取的行动为同一部分规定的行动。

(3) The Authority may, before it takes the action to which a decision notice ("the original notice") relates, give the person concerned a further decision notice which relates to different action in respect of the same matter.

(4) The Authority may give a further decision notice as a result of subsection (3) only if the person to whom the original notice was given consents.

(5) If the person to whom a decision notice is given under subsection (3) had the right to refer the matter to which the original decision notice related to the Tribunal, he has that right as respects the decision notice under subsection (3).

Annotations:

Modifications etc. (not altering text)

C347 S. 388 applied (1.12.2001) by S.I. 2001/1228, regs. 1(2)(c), 8(b) (with reg. 1(2)(3)); S.I. 2001/3538, art. 2(1)

Conclusion of proceedings

389 Notices of discontinuance.

(1) If the Authority decides not to take—

(a) the action proposed in a warning notice, or

(b) the action to which a decision notice relates,

it must give a notice of discontinuance to the person to whom the warning notice or decision notice was given.

(2) But subsection (1) does not apply if the discontinuance of the proceedings concerned results in the granting of an application made by the person to whom the warning or decision notice was given.

(3) A notice of discontinuance must identify the proceedings which are being discontinued.

Annotations:

Modifications etc. (not altering text)

C348 S. 389 applied (1.12.2001) by S.I. 2001/1228, regs. 1(2)(c), 8(c) (with reg. 1(2)(3)); S.I. 2001/3538, art. 2(1)

390 Final notices.

(1) If the Authority has given a person a decision notice and the matter was not referred to the Tribunal within the period mentioned in section 133(1), the Authority must, on taking the action to which the decision notice relates, give the person concerned and any person to

(3)管理局在采取决定通知(以下简称原通知)相关的行动前,可以就针对相同事项的不同行动向相关人发出进一步决定通知。

(4)管理局只有经原通知被通知人同意,才可以依照第(3)款规定发出进一步决定通知。

(5)对依照第(3)款发出的决定通知,如被通知人有权将原通知相关事项诉至裁判所,则有权将该决定通知相关事项诉至裁判所。

注释:

修改等(不涉及条文内容) C347　第388条于2001年12月1日依照制定法文件S.I.2001/1228第1条第(2)款第(c)项、第8条第(b)款[与第1条第(2)款和第(3)款];制定法文件S.I.2001/3538第2条第(1)款适用。

法律程序的终结

第389条　中止通知

(1)如管理局决定

(a)不采取预告通知中提出的行动,或

(b)不采取与决定通知相关的行动,

则必须向预告通知或决定通知的被通知人发出中止通知。

(2)但如因相关法律程序中止,预告通知或决定通知的被通知人提出的申请获得批准,则第(1)款规定不适用。

(3)中止通知必须指明被中止的法律程序。

注释:

修改等(不涉及条文内容) C348　第389条于2001年12月1日依照制定法文件S.I.2001/1228第1条第(2)款第(c)项、第8条第(c)款[与第1条第(2)款和第(3)款];制定法文件S.I.2001/3538第2条第(1)款适用。

第390条　最后通知

(1)如管理局已发出决定通知,且在第133条第(1)款所述期限内该事项未诉至裁判所,则管理局在采取决定通知相关行动时必须向被通知人和接收决定通知副本的任何人发出最后通知。

whom the decision notice was copied a final notice.

(2) If the Authority has given a person a decision notice and the matter was referred to the Tribunal, the Authority must, on taking action in accordance with any directions given by—

(a) the Tribunal, or

(b) the court under section 137,

give that person and any person to whom the decision notice was copied a final notice.

(3) A final notice about a statement must—

(a) set out the terms of the statement;

(b) give details of the manner in which, and the date on which, the statement will be published.

(4) A final notice about an order must—

(a) set out the terms of the order;

(b) state the date from which the order has effect.

(5) A final notice about a penalty must—

(a) state the amount of the penalty;

(b) state the manner in which, and the period within which, the penalty is to be paid;

(c) give details of the way in which the penalty will be recovered if it is not paid by the date stated in the notice.

(6) A final notice about a requirement to make a payment or distribution in accordance with section 384(5) must state—

(a) the persons to whom,

(b) the manner in which, and

(c) the period within which,

it must be made.

(7) In any other case, the final notice must—

(a) give details of the action being taken;

(b) state the date on which the action is to be taken.

(8) The period stated under subsection (5)(b) or (6)(c) may not be less than 14 days beginning with the date on which the final notice is given.

(9) If all or any of the amount of a penalty payable under a final notice is outstanding at the end of the period stated under subsection (5)(b), the Authority may recover the outstanding amount as a debt due to it.

(10) If all or any of a required payment or distribution has not been made at the end of a period stated in a final notice under subsection (6)(c), the obligation to make the payment is enforceable, on the application of the Authority, by injunction or, in Scotland, by an order under section 45 of the[M72] Court of Session Act 1988.

(2)如管理局已向某人发出决定通知,且该事项已诉至裁判所,则管理局必须在依照下列指示采取行动时:

(a)裁判所发出的指示,或

(b)法院依照第137条发出的指示,

向通知相关人和接收决定通知副本的任何人发出最后通知。

(3)关于声明的最后通知必须

(a)说明声明条款;

(b)详细说明该声明公布的方式和日期。

(4)关于命令的最后通知必须

(a)列明命令的条款;

(b)说明该命令的生效日期。

(5)关于罚款的最后通知必须

(a)说明罚款金额;

(b)说明罚款支付的方式和期限;

(c)详细说明罚款未在通知指定日期支付时的追讨方式。

(6)关于要求依照第384条第(5)款规定支付或分配款项的最后通知必须说明

(a)向何人,

(b)以何种方式,以及

(c)在何期限内

支付或分配款项。

(7)在任何其他情况下,最后通知必须

(a)详细说明将采取的行动;

(b)说明采取行动的日期。

(8)依照第(5)款第(b)项或第(6)款第(c)项规定的期限自最后通知发出之日起不得少于14日。

(9)如依照最后通知应支付的款项在依照第(5)款第(b)项规定的期限届满时全部或部分未支付,则管理局可将其作为应收债务予以追讨。

(10)如要求支付或分配的款项在最后通知中依照第(6)款第(c)项规定的期限届满时全部或部分未支付或未分配,则管理局可申请通过强制令或在苏格兰依照《1988年高等民事法院法》第45条发布的命令强制执行该支付义务。M72

Annotations:

Modifications etc. (not altering text)

C349 S. 390 applied (1.12.2001) by S.I. 2001/1228, regs. 1(2)(c), 8(d) (with reg. 1(2)(3)); S.I. 2001/3538, art. 2(1)

C350 S. 390(3)(4)(7) applied (1.12.2001) by S.I. 2001/3592, arts. 1(2), 110(7) (with art. 23(2))

C351 S. 390(3)-(5)(8)(9) applied (1.12.2001) by S.I. 2001/3592, arts. 1(2), 85(5)(b) (with art. 23(2))

C352 S. 390(3)-(5)(7)-(9) applied (1.12.2001) by S.I. 2001/3592, arts. 1(2), 61(7) (with art. 23(2))

C353 S. 390(7) applied (1.12.2001) by S.I. 2001/3592, arts. 1(2), 115(5), 122(4), 129 (with art. 23(2))

Marginal Citations

M72 1988 c. 36.

Publication

391 Publication.

(1) Neither the Authority nor a person to whom a warning notice or decision notice is given or copied may publish the notice or any details concerning it.

(2) A notice of discontinuance must state that, if the person to whom the notice is given consents, the Authority may publish such information as it considers appropriate about the matter to which the discontinued proceedings related.

(3) A copy of a notice of discontinuance must be accompanied by a statement that, if the person to whom the notice is copied consents, the Authority may publish such information as it considers appropriate about the matter to which the discontinued proceedings related, so far as relevant to that person.

(4) The Authority must publish such information about the matter to which a final notice relates as it considers appropriate.

(5) When a supervisory notice takes effect, the Authority must publish such information about the matter to which the notice relates as it considers appropriate.

(6) But the Authority may not publish information under this section if publication of it

注释：

修改等(不涉及条文内容)

C349　第390条于2001年12月1日依照制定法文件S.I.2001/1228第1条第(2)款第(c)项、第8条第(d)款[与第1条第(2)款和第(3)款];制定法文件S.I.2001/3538第2条第(1)款适用。

C350　第390条第(3)款、第(4)款、第(7)款于2001年12月1日依照制定法文件S.I.2001/3592第1条第(2)款、第110条第(7)款[与第23条第(2)款]适用。

C351　第390条第(3)款至第(5)款、第(8)款、第(9)款于2001年12月1日依照制定法文件S.I.2001/3592第1条第(2)款、第85条第(5)款第(b)项[与第23条第(2)款]适用。

C352　第390条第(3)款至第(5)款、第(7)款至第(9)款于2001年12月1日依照制定法文件S.I.2001/3592第1条第(2)款、第61条第(7)款[与第23条第(2)款]适用。

C353　第390条第(7)款于2001年12月1日依照制定法文件S.I.2001/3592第1条第(2)款、第115条第(5)款、第122条第(4)款、第129条[与第23条第(2)款]适用。

附注引文

M72　1988年第36章。

公　　布

第391条　公布[1]

(1)管理局和预告通知或决定通知的被通知人或被抄送人均不得公布该通知或与该通知相关的任何细节。

(2)中止通知必须说明,经被通知人同意,管理局可以公布其认为适当的被中止程序相关事项。

(3)中止通知副本必须附有声明,说明经通知抄送人同意,管理局可以公布其认为适当且与该人相关的被中止程序相关的事项。

(4)管理局必须以其认为适当的方式公布与最后通知有关的信息。

(5)监督通知生效时,管理局必须公布其认为适当的通知相关事项信息。

(6)但如管理局认为公布信息对与采取的行动相关的人不公平或损害消费者利

1　本条依照《2010年金融服务法》第13条修订。——译者注

would, in its opinion, be unfair to the person with respect to whom the action was taken or prejudicial to the interests of consumers.

(7) Information is to be published under this section in such manner as the Authority considers appropriate.

(8) For the purposes of determining when a supervisory notice takes effect, a matter to which the notice relates is open to review if—

(a) the period during which any person may refer the matter to the Tribunal is still running;

(b) the matter has been referred to the Tribunal but has not been dealt with;

(c) the matter has been referred to the Tribunal and dealt with but the period during which an appeal may be brought against the Tribunal's decision is still running; or

(d) such an appeal has been brought but has not been determined.

(9) "Notice of discontinuance" means a notice given under section 389.

(10) "Supervisory notice" has the same meaning as in section 395.

(11) "Consumers" means persons who are consumers for the purposes of section 138.

Annotations:

Modifications etc. (not altering text)

C354 S. 391 applied (1.12.2001) by S.I. 2001/1228, regs. 1(2)(c), 9 (with reg. 1(2)(3)); S.I. 2001/3538, art. 2(1)

C355 S. 391(4)(6)(7) applied (1.12.2001) by S.I. 2001/2957, arts. 1, 13(8)(a), S.I. 2001/3538, art. 2(1)

C356 S. 391(4) applied (1.12.2001) by S.I. 2001/3592, arts. 1(2), 61(7), 85(5)(b), 110(7), 115(5), 122(4), 129 (with art. 23(2))

C357 S. 391(11) modified (18.6.2001) by S.I. 2001/1821, arts. 1(1), 3(5)

Third party rights and access to evidence

392 Application of sections 393 and 394.

Sections 393 and 394 apply to—

(a) a warning notice given in accordance with section 54(1), 57(1), 63(3), 67(1), 88(4)(b), 89(2), 92(1), 126(1), 207(1), 255(1), 280(1), 331(1), 345(2) (whether as a

益，则不得依照本条规定公布信息。

(7)管理局应当以其认为适当的方式依照本条规定公布信息。

(8)为确定监督通知何时生效之目的，如有下列情况，即为通知相关事项仍开放供审议：

(a)任何人可将该事项诉至裁判所的期限未届满；

(b)该事项已诉至裁判所但尚未审理；

(c)该事项已诉至裁判所并已审理，但针对裁决提起上诉的期限尚未届满；或

(d)已提起上诉但尚未判决。

(9)“中止通知”系指依照第389条规定发出的通知。

(10)“监督通知”与第395条中的含义相同。

(11)“消费者”系指第138条意义上的消费者。[1]

注释：

修改等(不涉及条文内容)

C354 第391条于2001年12月1日依照制定法文件S.I.2001/1228第1条第(2)款第(c)项、第9条[与第1条第(2)款、第(3)款]；制定法文件S.I.2001/3538第2条第(1)款适用。

C355 第391条第(4)款、第(6)款、第(7)款于2001年12月1日依照制定法文件S.I.2001/2957第1条、第13条第(8)款第(a)项；制定法文件S.I.2001/3538第2条第(1)款适用。

C356 第391条第(4)款于2001年12月1日依照制定法文件S.I.2001/3592第1条第(2)款、第61条第(7)款、第85条第(5)款第(b)项、第110条第(7)款、第115条第(5)款、第122条第(4)款、第129条[与第23条第(2)款]适用。

C357 第391条第（11）款于2001年6月18日依照制定法文件S.I.2001/1821第1条第(1)款、第3条第(5)款修订。

第三方的权利和获取证据

第392条 第393条和第394条的适用[2]

第393条和第394条规定适用于

(a)依照第54条第(1)款、第57条第(1)款、第63条第(3)款、第67条第(1)款、第88条第(4)款第(b)项、第89条第(2)款、第92条第(1)款、第126条第(1)款、第207条第(1)

1 本款依照《2010年金融服务法》附录2第一部分第28条修订。——译者注

2 本条依照《2010年金融服务法》附录2第一部分第29条修订。——译者注

result of subsection (1) of that section or section 249(1)) or 385(1);

(b) a decision notice given in accordance with section 54(2), 57(3), 63(4), 67(4), 88(6)(b), 89(3), 92(4), 127(1), 208(1), 255(2), 280(2), 331(3), 345(3) (whether as a result of subsection (1) of that section or section 249(1)) or 386(1).

Annotations:

Modifications etc. (not altering text)

C358 S. 392(a) excluded (1.12.2001) by S.I. 2001/3592, arts. 1(2), 46(2), 47(2), 48(2), 52(4), 55(2) (with art. 23(2))

393 Third party rights.

(1) If any of the reasons contained in a warning notice to which this section applies relates to a matter which—

(a) identifies a person ("the third party") other than the person to whom the notice is given, and

(b) in the opinion of the Authority, is prejudicial to the third party,a copy of the notice must be given to the third party.

(2) Subsection (1) does not require a copy to be given to the third party if the Authority—

(a) has given him a separate warning notice in relation to the same matter; or

(b) gives him such a notice at the same time as it gives the warning notice which identifies him.

(3) The notice copied to a third party under subsection (1) must specify a reasonable period (which may not be less than 28 days) within which he may make representations to the Authority.

(4) If any of the reasons contained in a decision notice to which this section applies relates to a matter which—

(a) identifies a person ("the third party") other than the person to whom the decision notice is given, and

(b) in the opinion of the Authority, is prejudicial to the third party,a copy of the notice must be given to the third party.

(5) If the decision notice was preceded by a warning notice, a copy of the decision notice must (unless it has been given under subsection (4)) be given to each person to whom the warning notice was copied.

(6) Subsection (4) does not require a copy to be given to the third party if the

款、第255条第(1)款、第280条第(1)款、第331条第(1)款、第345条第(2)款[无论因该条第(1)款或第249条第(1)款发出]或第385条第(1)款规定发出的预告通知;

(b)依照第54条第(2)款、第57条第(3)款、第63条第(4)款、第67条第(4)款、第88条第(6)款第(b)项、第89条第(3)款、第92条第(4)款、第127条第(1)款、第208条第(1)款、第255条第(2)款、第280条第(2)款、第331条第(3)款、第345条第(3)款[无论因该条第(1)款或第249条第(1)款发出]或第386条第(1)款规定发出的决定通知。

注释:

修改等(不涉及条文内容)

C358　第392条第(a)项于2001年12月1日依照制定法文件S.I.2001/3592第1条第(2)款、第46条第(2)款、第47条第(2)款、第48条第(2)款、第52条第(4)款、第55条第(2)款[与第23条第(2)款]排除。

第393条　第三方的权利

(1)适用本条规定的预告通知,如所载的任何理由与下列事项相关:

(a)对不是被通知人的人(以下简称第三方)确定其身份,且

(b)管理局认为对该第三方有损害,则必须向该第三方发出该通知副本。

(2)如管理局已实施下列行为,则无须依照第(1)款规定向该第三方发出副本:

(a)已就同一事项向其单独发出预告通知;或

(b)在发出确定其身份的预告通知的同时向其发出该通知。

(3)依照第(1)款抄送第三方的通知必须指定该人可向管理局提出陈述的合理期限(不得少于28日)。

(4)适用本条规定的决定通知,如所载的任何理由与下列事项相关:

(a)对不是被通知人的人(以下简称第三方)确定其身份,且

(b)管理局认为对该第三方有损害,则必须向该第三方发出该通知副本。

(5)如发出决定通知前发出了预告通知,则必须向各预告通知被抄送人发出该决定通知副本[不包括依照第(4)款规定发出的通知]。

(6)如管理局已实施下列行为,则无须依照第(4)款规定向该第三方发出副本:

Authority—

(a) has given him a separate decision notice in relation to the same matter; or

(b) gives him such a notice at the same time as it gives the decision notice which identifies him.

(7) Neither subsection (1) nor subsection (4) requires a copy of a notice to be given to a third party if the Authority considers it impracticable to do so.

(8) Subsections (9) to (11) apply if the person to whom a decision notice is given has a right to refer the matter to the Tribunal.

(9) A person to whom a copy of the notice is given under this section may refer to the Tribunal—

(a) the decision in question, so far as it is based on a reason of the kind mentioned in subsection (4); or

(b) any opinion expressed by the Authority in relation to him.

(10) The copy must be accompanied by an indication of the third party's right to make a reference under subsection (9) and of the procedure on such a reference.

(11) A person who alleges that a copy of the notice should have been given to him, but was not, may refer to the Tribunal the alleged failure and—

(a) the decision in question, so far as it is based on a reason of the kind mentioned in subsection (4); or

(b) any opinion expressed by the Authority in relation to him.

(12) Section 394 applies to a third party as it applies to the person to whom the notice to which this section applies was given, in so far as the material which the Authority must disclose under that section relates to the matter which identifies the third party.

(13) A copy of a notice given to a third party under this section must be accompanied by a description of the effect of section 394 as it applies to him.

(14) Any person to whom a warning notice or decision notice was copied under this section must be given a copy of a notice of discontinuance applicable to the proceedings to which the warning notice or decision notice related.

Annotations:

Modifications etc. (not altering text)

C359 S. 393 applied (1.12.2001) by S.I. 2001/1228, regs. 1(2)(c), 24(3) (with reg. 1(2)(3)); S.I. 2001/3538, art. 2(1)

S. 393 excluded (1.12.2001) by S.I. 2001/3592, arts. 1(2), 38(2), 46(2), 47(2), 48(2), 52(4), 55(2) (with art. 23(2))

C360 S. 393(1) extended (1.12.2001) by S.I. 2001/3592, arts. 1(2), 36(4) (with art. 23(2))

(a)已就同一事项向第三方单独发出决定通知;或

(b)同时向该第三方发出通知,告知管理局发出了确定其身份的决定通知。

(7)如管理局认为不可行,则第(1)款或第(4)款规定不要求向第三方发出通知副本。

(8)如被通知人有权将该事项诉至裁判所,则第(9)款至第(11)款适用。

(9)依照本条规定收到通知副本的人可将下列事项诉至裁判所:

(a)以第(4)款所述理由为依据的通知相关决定;或

(b)管理局表示的任何与其相关的意见。

(10)副本必须附有关于第三方有权依照第(9)款规定诉至裁判所以及诉至裁判所程序的说明。

(11)指控应向其发送通知副本但未发送的人可将其指控的未发送情况及下列事项诉至裁判所裁决:

(a)以第(4)款所述理由为依据的通知相关决定;或

(b)管理局表示的任何与其相关的意见。

(12)如管理局依照第394条规定必须披露的材料与确定第三方身份相关,则该条规定适用于该第三方,效力等同于对本条规定适用的通知所针对的被通知人适用。

(13)依照本条向第三方发出的通知副本必须附有对第394条适用于该第三方效力的说明。

(14)中止预告通知或决定通知相关程序的通知,其副本必须送达本条中该预告通知或决定通知的被抄送人。

注释:

修改等(不涉及条文内容)

C359 第393条于2001年12月1日依照制定法文件S.I.2001/1228第1条第(2)款第(c)项、第24条第(3)款[与第1条第(2)款和第(3)款];制定法文件S.I.2001/3538第2条第(1)款适用;

第393条于2001年12月1日依照制定法文件S.I.2001/3592第1条第(2)款、第38条第(2)款、第46条第(2)款、第47条第(2)款、第48条第(2)款、第52条第(4)款、第55条第(2)款[与第23条第(2)款]排除。

C360 第393条第(1)款于2001年12月1日依照制定法文件S.I.2001/3592第1条第(2)款、第36条第(4)款[与第23条第(2)款]扩大适用范围。

394 Access to Authority material.

(1) If the Authority gives a person ("A") a notice to which this section applies, it must—

(a) allow him access to the material on which it relied in taking the decision which gave rise to the obligation to give the notice;

(b) allow him access to any secondary material which, in the opinion of the Authority, might undermine that decision.

(2) But the Authority does not have to allow A access to material under subsection (1) if the material is excluded material or it—

(a) relates to a case involving a person other than A; and

(b) was taken into account by the Authority in A's case only for purposes of comparison with other cases.

(3) The Authority may refuse access A to particular material which it would otherwise have to allow him access to if, in its opinion, allowing him access to the material—

(a) would not be in the public interest; or

(b) would not be fair, having regard to—

(i) the likely significance of the material to A in relation to the matter in respect of which he has been given a notice to which this section applies; and

(ii) the potential prejudice to the commercial interests of a person other than A which would be caused by the material's disclosure.

(4) If the Authority does not allow A access to material because it is excluded material consisting of a protected item, it must give A written notice of—

(a) the existence of the protected item; and

(b) the Authority's decision not to allow him access to it.

(5) If the Authority refuses under subsection (3) to allow A access to material, it must give him written notice of—

(a) the refusal; and

(b) the reasons for it.

(6) "Secondary material" means material, other than material falling within paragraph (a) of subsection (1) which—

(a) was considered by the Authority in reaching the decision mentioned in that paragraph; or

(b) was obtained by the Authority in connection with the matter to which the notice to which this section applies relates but which was not considered by it in reaching that decision.

(7) "Excluded material" means material which—

[F8 (a) is material the disclosure of which for the purposes of or in connection with any legal proceedings is prohibited by section 17 of the Regulation of Investigatory Powers Act

第394条　获取管理局的材料

(1)管理局如向某人(以下简称A)发出适用本条规定的通知,则必须

(a)允许该人获取管理局作出产生通知义务的决定所依据的材料;

(b)允许该人获取管理局认为可能损害该决定的任何间接材料。

(2)但如该材料为被排除的材料或有下列情况,则管理局可不允许A依照第(1)款规定获取材料:

(a)与涉及A以外的其他人的案件相关;且

(b)管理局在A的案件中只为比较两起案件而考虑该材料。

(3)如管理局认为使A获取材料会导致下列结果,则可以拒绝该人获取否则可以获取的材料:

(a)违反公共利益;或

(b)考虑到下列情况不公平:

(i)就与向A发出且适用本条规定的通知相关的事项,该材料对A可能具有的重要性;以及

(ii)如披露该材料则可能对A以外的其他人造成的商业利益损害。

(4)管理局如因材料为含有受保护项目的被排除材料而不允许A获取材料,则必须向A就下列事项发出书面通知:

(a)存在受保护项目;以及

(b)管理局关于不允许其获取该材料的决定。

(5)如管理局依照第(3)款规定拒绝A获取材料,则必须就下列事项向其发出书面通知:

(a)拒绝其获取材料;以及

(b)拒绝的原因。

(6)"间接材料"系指不属于第(1)款第(a)项规定范围且有下列情况的材料:

(a)管理局在作出该项所述决定时考虑的材料;或

(b)管理局取得的与本条规定适用的通知相关的事项有关,但在作出决定时未予考虑的材料。

(7)"被排除的材料"系指

[F8(a)《2000年调查权法条例》第17条禁止为任何法律程序目的或与任何法律程序相关而披露的材料;或]

2000; or]

(b) is a protected item (as defined in section 413).

Annotations:

Amendments (Textual)

F8 S. 394(7)(a) substituted (2.10.2000) for s. 394(7)(a)(b) by 2000 c. 23, s. 82, Sch. 4 para. 11 (with s. 82(3)); S.I. 2000/2543, art. 3

Modifications etc. (not altering text)

C361 S. 394 applied (1.12.2001) by S.I. 2001/1228, regs. 1(2)(c), 24(3) (with reg. 1(2)(3)); S.I. 2001/3538, art. 2(1)

S. 394 excluded (1.12.2001) by S.I. 2001/3592, arts. 1(2), 36(3), 38(2), 46(2), 47(2), 48(2), 52(4), 55(2) (with art. 23(2))

The Authority's procedures

395 The Authority's procedures.

(1) The Authority must determine the procedure that it proposes to follow in relation to the giving of—

(a) supervisory notices; and

(b) warning notices and decision notices.

(2) That procedure must be designed to secure, among other things, that the decision which gives rise to the obligation to give any such notice is taken by a person not directly involved in establishing the evidence on which that decision is based.

(3) But the procedure may permit a decision which gives rise to an obligation to give a supervisory notice to be taken by a person other than a person mentioned in subsection (2) if—

(a) the Authority considers that, in the particular case, it is necessary in order to protect the interests of consumers; and

(b) the person taking the decision is of a level of seniority laid down by the procedure.

(4) A level of seniority laid down by the procedure for the purposes of subsection (3)(b) must be appropriate to the importance of the decision.

(5) The Authority must issue a statement of the procedure.

(6) The statement must be published in the way appearing to the Authority to be best calculated to bring it to the attention of the public.

(7) The Authority may charge a reasonable fee for providing a person with a copy of

(b)是受保护项目(定义见第413条)。

注释:

修正(文本)

F8　第394条第(7)款第(a)项于2000年10月2日依照2000年第23章第82条、附录4第11条[与第82条第(3)款];制定法文件S.I.2000/2543第3条替换为第394条第(7)款第(a)项、第(b)项替换。

修改等(不涉及条文内容)

C361　第394条于2001年12月1日依照制定法文件S.I.2001/1228第1条第(2)款第(c)项、第24条第(3)款[与第1条第(2)款和第(3)款];制定法文件S.I.2001/3538第2条第(1)款适用;

第394条于2001年12月1日依照制定法文件S.I.2001/3592第1条第(2)款、第36条第(3)款、第38条第(2)款、第46条第(2)款、第47条第(2)款、第48条第(2)款、第52条第(4)款、第55条第(2)款[与第23条第(2)款]排除。

管理局的程序

第395条　管理局的程序

(1)管理局必须确定发出下列通知时拟执行的相关程序:

(a)监督通知;以及

(b)预告通知及决定通知。

(2)该程序的设计,在满足其他要求之外,必须确保管理局有义务使发出上述通知的决定由未直接参与确定该决定依据的证据的人作出。

(3)但如有下列情况,则该程序可允许第(2)款所述人员以外的其他人作出使管理局有义务发出监督通知的决定:

(a)管理局认为在特定情况下为保护消费者的利益有必要如此;且

(b)作出决定的人符合该程序规定的资历水平要求。

(4)该程序为实施第(3)款第(b)项而规定的资历水平要求必须与决定的重要性相适应。

(5)管理局必须发布程序声明。

(6)该声明必须以管理局认为最便于公众了解的方式公布。

(7)管理局可以为向他人提供声明副本收取合理费用。

the statement.

(8) The Authority must, without delay, give the Treasury a copy of any statement which it issues under this section.

(9) When giving a supervisory notice, or a warning notice or decision notice, the Authority must follow its stated procedure.

(10) If the Authority changes the procedure in a material way, it must publish a revised statement.

(11) The Authority's failure in a particular case to follow its procedure as set out in the latest published statement does not affect the validity of a notice given in that case.

(12) But subsection (11) does not prevent the Tribunal from taking into account any such failure in considering a matter referred to it.

(13) "Supervisory notice" means a notice given in accordance with section—

(a) 53(4), (7) or (8)(b);

(b) 78(2) or (5);

(c) 197(3), (6) or (7)(b);

(d) 259(3), (8) or (9)(b);

(e) 268(3), (7)(a) or (9)(a) (as a result of subsection (8)(b));

(f) 282(3), (6) or (7)(b);

(g) 321(2) or (5).

Annotations:

Modifications etc. (not altering text)

C362 S. 395 applied (1.12.2001) by S.I. 2001/1228, regs. 1(2)(c), 10 (with reg. 1(2)(3)); S.I. 2001/3538, art. 2(1)

S. 395 amended (1.12.2001) by S.I. 2001/1228, regs. 1(2)(c), 27(15) (with reg. 1(2)(3)); S.I. 2001/3538, art. 2(1)

C363 S. 395 (1) (9) excluded (1.12.2001) by S.I. 2001/2957, arts. 1, 12 (9); S.I. 2001/3538, art. 2(1)

396 Statements under section 395: consultation.

(1) Before issuing a statement of procedure under section 395, the Authority must publish a draft of the proposed statement in the way appearing to the Authority to be best calculated to bring it to the attention of the public.

(2) The draft must be accompanied by notice that representations about the proposal may be made to the Authority within a specified time.

(8)管理局必须毫不延迟地向财政部送交依照本条规定所发布的任何声明的副本。

(9)管理局发出监督通知、预告通知或决定通知时必须遵循其声明的程序。

(10)如管理局对该程序进行重大变更,则必须公布经修订的声明。

(11)管理局在特定情况下未能遵守最新公布的声明中规定的程序,不影响在该情况下所发出通知的效力。

(12)但第(11)款不妨碍裁判所在审议向其提交的事项时考虑任何上述未遵守程序的情况。

(13)“监督通知”系指依照下列各条规定发出的通知:

(a)第53条第(4)款、第(7)款或第(8)款第(b)项;

(b)第78条第(2)款或第(5)款;

(c)第197条第(3)款、第(6)款或第(7)款第(b)项;

(d)第259条第(3)款、第(8)款或第(9)款第(b)项;

(e)第268条第(3)款、第(7)款第(a)项或第(9)款第(a)项[因第(8)款第(b)项发出];

(f)第282条第(3)款、第(6)款或第(7)款第(b)项;

(g)第321条第(2)款或第(5)款。

注释:

修改等(不涉及条文内容)

C362　第395条于2001年12月1日依照制定法文件S.I.2001/1228第1条第(2)款第(c)项、第10条[与第1条第(2)款和第(3)款];制定法文件S.I.2001/3538第2条第(1)款适用;

第395条于2001年12月1日依照制定法文件S.I.2001/1228第1条第(2)款第(c)项、第27条第(15)款[与第1条第(2)款和第(3)款];制定法文件S.I.2001/3538第2条第(1)款修正。

C363　第395条第(1)款、第(9)款于2001年12月1日依照制定法文件S.I.2001/2957第1条、第12条第(9)款;制定法文件S.I.2001/3538第2条第(1)款排除。

第396条　第395条规定的声明:谘商

(1)管理局在依照第395条规定的程序发布声明前必须以其认为最便于公众了解的方式公布拟发布声明的草案。

(2)草案必须附有可在规定时间就该提案向管理局陈述的通知。

(3) Before issuing the proposed statement of procedure, the Authority must have regard to any representations made to it in accordance with subsection (2).

(4) If the Authority issues the proposed statement of procedure it must publish an account, in general terms, of—

(a) the representations made to it in accordance with subsection (2); and

(b) its response to them.

(5) If the statement of procedure differs from the draft published under subsection (1) in a way which is, in the opinion of the Authority, significant, the Authority must (in addition to complying with subsection (4)) publish details of the difference.

(6) The Authority may charge a reasonable fee for providing a person with a copy of a draft published under subsection (1).

(7) This section also applies to a proposal to revise a statement of policy.

(3)管理局在发布拟发布的声明前必须考虑依照第(2)款规定向其作出的任何陈述。

(4)如管理局发布拟发布的声明,则必须公布概括说明下列事项的报告:

(a)依照第(2)款规定向其作出的陈述;以及

(b)管理局对上述陈述的答复。

(5)如管理局认为该声明与依照第(1)款公布的草案有重大差异,则[除遵守第(4)款规定外]必须公布差异的详细情况。

(6)管理局可以为向他人提供依照第(1)款公布的草案副本收取合理费用。

(7)本条规定也适用于修订政策声明的计划。

PART XXVII OFFENCES

Miscellaneous offences

397 Misleading statements and practices.

(1) This subsection applies to a person who—

(a) makes a statement, promise or forecast which he knows to be misleading, false or deceptive in a material particular;

(b) dishonestly conceals any material facts whether in connection with a statement, promise or forecast made by him or otherwise; or

(c) recklessly makes (dishonestly or otherwise) a statement, promise or forecast which is misleading, false or deceptive in a material particular.

(2) A person to whom subsection (1) applies is guilty of an offence if he makes the statement, promise or forecast or conceals the facts for the purpose of inducing, or is reckless as to whether it may induce, another person (whether or not the person to whom the statement, promise or forecast is made)—

(a) to enter or offer to enter into, or to refrain from entering or offering to enter into, a relevant agreement; or

(b) to exercise, or refrain from exercising, any rights conferred by a relevant investment.

(3) Any person who does any act or engages in any course of conduct which creates a false or misleading impression as to the market in or the price or value of any relevant investments is guilty of an offence if he does so for the purpose of creating that impression and of thereby inducing another person to acquire, dispose of, subscribe for or underwrite those investments or to refrain from doing so or to exercise, or refrain from exercising, any rights conferred by those investments.

(4) In proceedings for an offence under subsection (2) brought against a person to whom subsection (1) applies as a result of paragraph (a) of that subsection, it is a defence for him to show that the statement, promise or forecast was made in conformity with price stabilising rules or control of information rules.

(5) In proceedings brought against any person for an offence under subsection (3) it is

第二十七部分 犯 罪

各类犯罪

第397条 误导陈述和做法

(1)有下列行为的,适用本款规定:

(a)对重要事项作出其明知为误导、虚假或欺骗性的陈述、承诺或预测;

(b)不诚实地隐瞒重大事实,无论该事实是否与其作出的陈述、承诺或预测相关;或

(c)因重大过失(无论是否不诚实)对重要事项作出误导、虚假或欺骗性的陈述、承诺或预测。

(2)适用第(1)款规定的,如为诱导他人实施下列行为而作出该陈述、承诺或预测或隐瞒事实,或因重大过失而漠视该陈述、承诺或预测或隐瞒事实是否会诱导他人实施下列行为(无论他人是否为该陈述、承诺或预测作出的对象),则构成犯罪:

(a)订立或提议订立,或者不订立或不提议订立相关协议;或

(b)行使或不行使相关投资赋予的任何权利。

(3)任何人实施对任何投资市场或任何相关投资的价值制造虚假或误导性印象的任何行为,或从事造成上述结果的任何行为过程,如该人制造该印象目的在于诱导他人购买、处置、认购或承销上述投资或不从事上述活动,或者行使或不行使上述投资赋予的任何权利,则构成犯罪。

(4)在针对第(1)款规定适用的人就第(2)款规定的犯罪提起的诉讼程序中,该人如能证明作出该陈述、承诺或预测符合价格稳定规则或信息控制规则,则可以据此进行抗辩。

(5)在针对任何人就第(3)款规定的犯罪提起的诉讼程序中,该人如能证明下列

a defence for him to show—

(a) that he reasonably believed that his act or conduct would not create an impression that was false or misleading as to the matters mentioned in that subsection;

(b) that he acted or engaged in the conduct—

(i) for the purpose of stabilising the price of investments; and

(ii) in conformity with price stabilising rules; or

(c) that he acted or engaged in the conduct in conformity with control of information rules.

(6) Subsections (1) and (2) do not apply unless—

(a) the statement, promise or forecast is made in or from, or the facts are concealed in or from, the United Kingdom or arrangements are made in or from the United Kingdom for the statement, promise or forecast to be made or the facts to be concealed;

(b) the person on whom the inducement is intended to or may have effect is in the United Kingdom; or

(c) the agreement is or would be entered into or the rights are or would be exercised in the United Kingdom.

(7) Subsection (3) does not apply unless—

(a) the act is done, or the course of conduct is engaged in, in the United Kingdom; or

(b) the false or misleading impression is created there.

(8) A person guilty of an offence under this section is liable—

(a) on summary conviction, to imprisonment for a term not exceeding six months or a fine not exceeding the statutory maximum, or both;

(b) on conviction on indictment, to imprisonment for a term not exceeding seven years or a fine, or both.

(9) "Relevant agreement" means an agreement—

(a) the entering into or performance of which by either party constitutes an activity of a specified kind or one which falls within a specified class of activity; and

(b) which relates to a relevant investment.

(10) "Relevant investment" means an investment of a specified kind or one which falls within a prescribed class of investment.

(11) Schedule 2 (except paragraphs 25 and 26) applies for the purposes of subsections (9) and (10) with references to section 22 being read as references to each of those subsections.

(12) Nothing in Schedule 2, as applied by subsection (11), limits the power conferred by subsection (9) or (10).

(13) "Investment" includes any asset, right or interest.

(14) "Specified" means specified in an order made by the Treasury.

情况,则可据此进行抗辩:

(a)该人合理地相信自己的行为不会对该款规定所述事项造成虚假或误导性印象;

(b)该人实施或参与该活动

(i)目的在于稳定投资价格;且

(ii)符合价格稳定规则;或

(c)该人实施或参与该活动符合信息控制规则。

(6)除非有下列情况,否则第(1)款和第(2)款规定不适用:

(a)该陈述、承诺或预测是在联合王国或从联合王国作出,或者隐瞒事实的行为在联合王国发生或源自联合王国,或者该陈述、承诺或预测或隐瞒该事实的安排在联合王国作出或源自联合王国;

(b)意图诱导的对象或诱导可能产生效果的对象在联合王国;或

(c)协议在联合王国订立或将在联合王国订立,或者权利在联合王国行使或将在联合王国行使。

(7)除非有下列情况,否则第(3)款规定不适用:

(a)该行为或行为过程在联合王国实施或从事;或

(b)虚假或误导性印象在联合王国形成。

(8)依照本条规定构成犯罪的,应承担下列责任:

(a)经简易程序定罪的,处以不超过6个月的有期徒刑或不超过最高法定限额的罚金,或两罚并处;

(b)经公诉程序定罪的,处以不超过7年的有期徒刑或罚金,或两罚并处。

(9)"相关协议"系指符合下列条件的协议:

(a)任何一方订立或履行该协议构成规定种类的活动或属于规定类别的活动;且

(b)与相关投资有关。

(10)"相关投资"系指规定种类的投资或属于规定类别的投资。

(11)附录2(不包括第25条和第26条)为第(9)款和第(10)款之目的适用时,述及第22条视为述及该条每一款规定。

(12)附录2中依照第(11)款规定适用的任何规定不限制第(9)款或第(10)款规定赋予的权力。

(13)"投资"包括任何资产、权利或利益。

(14)"规定"系指在财政部颁布的法令中规定。

Annotations:

Commencement Information

I123 S. 397 wholly in force at 1.12.2001; s. 397 not in force at Royal Assent see s. 431 (2); s. 397(9)-(14) in force at 25.2.2001 by S.I. 2001/516, art. 2(a), Sch. Pt. 1; s. 397 in force in so far as not already in force at 1.12.2001 by S.I. 2001/3538, art. 2(1)

398 Misleading the Authority: residual cases.

(1) A person who, in purported compliance with any requirement imposed by or under this Act, knowingly or recklessly gives the Authority information which is false or misleading in a material particular is guilty of an offence.

(2) Subsection (1) applies only to a requirement in relation to which no other provision of this Act creates an offence in connection with the giving of information.

(3) A person guilty of an offence under this section is liable—

(a) on summary conviction, to a fine not exceeding the statutory maximum;

(b) on conviction on indictment, to a fine.

Annotations:

Modifications etc. (not altering text)

C364 S. 398 extended (1.12.2001) by S.I. 2001/3646, arts. 1(2), 3(3)(b)(4)

S. 398 excluded (1.12.2001) by S.I. 2001/3646, arts. 1(2), 2(6)

C365 S. 398 modified (18.7.2002 for certain purposes and 21.8.2002 otherwise) by The Electronic Commerce Directive (Financial Services and Markets) Regulations 2002 (S.I. 2002/1775), regs. 1, 12(2)

C366 S. 398(1)(3) applied (1.12.2001) by S.I. 1995/1537, reg. 23(5) (as amended (1.12.2001) by S.I. 2001/3649, arts. 1, 509(f))

399 Misleading the Director General of Fair Trading.

Section 44 of the[M73] Competition Act 1998 (offences connected with the provision of false or misleading information) applies in relation to any function of the Director General of Fair Trading under this Act as if it were a function under Part I of that Act.

Annotations:

Marginal Citations

M73 1998 c. 41.

注释:

实施日期

I123　第397条于2001年12月1日全部生效;第397条在副署时尚未生效,见第431条第(2)款;第397条第(9)款至第(14)款于2001年2月25日依照制定法文件S.I.2001/516第2条第(a)项、附录第一部分生效;第397条如于2001年12月1日尚未生效,则依照制定法文件S.I.2001/3538第2条第(1)款生效。

第398条　误导管理局:遗留案件

(1)在遵守本法规定或依据本法规定的要求时,如就重要事项向管理局提供明知为虚假或误导的信息或因重大过失而提供虚假或误导信息,则构成犯罪。

(2)只有针对某项要求本法任何其他条款未规定信息提供相关犯罪时,方适用第(1)款规定。

(3)依照本条规定构成犯罪的,应承担下列责任:

(a)经简易程序定罪的,处以不超过最高法定金额的罚金;

(b)经公诉程序定罪的,处以罚金。

注释:

修改等(不涉及条文内容)

C364　第398条于2001年12月1日依照制定法文件S.I.2001/3646第1条第(2)款、第3条第(3)款第(b)项、第(4)款扩大适用范围;

第398条于2001年12月1日依照制定法文件S.I.2001/3646第1条第(2)款、第2条第(6)款排除。

C365　第398条为特定目的于2002年7月18日,否则于2002年8月21日依照《2001年电子商务指令条例》(金融服务和市场)(制定法文件S.I.2002/1775)、第1条、第12条第(2)款修订。

C366　第398条第(1)款和第(3)款于2001年12月1日依照制定法文件S.I.1995/1537第23条第(5)款[于2001年12月1日依照制定法文件S.I.2001/3649第1条、第509条第(f)项修正]适用。

第399条　误导公平交易总理事

[M73]《1998年竞争法》第44条(与提供虚假或误导性信息有关的犯罪)适用于本法规定公平交易总理事行使的任何职能,效力等同于该职能为该法第一部分规定的职能。

注释:

附注引文

M73　1998本法第41条。

Bodies corporate and partnerships

400 Offences by bodies corporate etc.

(1) If an offence under this Act committed by a body corporate is shown

(a) to have been committed with the consent or connivance of an officer, or

(b) to be attributable to any neglect on his part,

the officer as well as the body corporate is guilty of the offence and liable to be proceeded against and punished accordingly.

(2) If the affairs of a body corporate are managed by its members, subsection (1) applies in relation to the acts and defaults of a member in connection with his functions of management as if he were a director of the body.

(3) If an offence under this Act committed by a partnership is shown—

(a) to have been committed with the consent or connivance of a partner, or

(b) to be attributable to any neglect on his part,

the partner as well as the partnership is guilty of the offence and liable to be proceeded against and punished accordingly.

(4) In subsection (3)"partner" includes a person purporting to act as a partner.

(5) "Officer", in relation to a body corporate, means—

(a) a director, member of the committee of management, chief executive, manager, secretary or other similar officer of the body, or a person purporting to act in any such capacity; and

(b) an individual who is a controller of the body.

(6) If an offence under this Act committed by an unincorporated association (other than a partnership) is shown—

(a) to have been committed with the consent or connivance of an officer of the association or a member of its governing body, or

(b) to be attributable to any neglect on the part of such an officer or member, that officer or member as well as the association is guilty of the offence and liable to be proceeded against and punished accordingly.

(7) Regulations may provide for the application of any provision of this section, with such modifications as the Treasury consider appropriate, to a body corporate or unincorporated association formed or recognised under the law of a territory outside the United Kingdom.

法人与合伙

第400条　法人犯罪等

(1)法人实施本法规定的犯罪,如证明

(a)系由高级职员同意或纵容实施,或

(b)可以归咎于该高级职员的任何过失,

则该高级职员及该法人构成犯罪,应当对其提起诉讼并处以相应刑罚。

(2)如法人的事务由其成员管理,则第(1)款规定适用于成员与其管理职能相关的行为和不履行,效力等同于该成员为该法人的董事。

(3)合伙实施本法规定的犯罪,如证明

(a)系由合伙人同意或纵容实施,或

(b)可以归咎于该合伙人的任何过失,

则该合伙人及该合伙构成犯罪,应当对其提起诉讼并处以相应刑罚。

(4)第(3)款中"合伙人"包括表明作为合伙人行事的人。

(5)就法人而言,"高级职员"系指

(a)董事、管理委员会成员、行政总裁、经理、秘书或该法人其他类似人员,或表明以该等身份行事的人;以及

(b)控制该法人的个人。

(6)非法人团体(不包括合伙)实施本法规定的犯罪,如证明

(a)系由该组织高级职员或管理组织成员同意或纵容实施,或

(b)可以归咎于该高级职员或成员的任何过失,则该高级职员或成员及该非法人团体构成犯罪,应当对其提起诉讼并处以相应刑罚。

(7)法规可规定本条任何规定连同财政部认为适当的修改适用于依照联合王国以外的地区法律设立或认可的法人或非法人团体。

Annotations:

Modifications etc. (not altering text)

C367 S. 400 applied (3.9.2001 for specified purposes otherwise 1.12.2001) by S.I. 2001/1228, regs. 1(2)(b)(c), 81 (with reg. 1(2)(3)); S.I. 2001/2632, art. 2(2), Sch. Pt. 2; S. I. 2001/3538, art. 2(1)

S. 400 applied (1.12.2001) by S.I. 1995/1537, reg. 23(6) (as amended (1.12.2001) by S.I. 2001/3649, arts. 1, 509(g))

S. 400 amended (1.12.2001) by S.I. 2001/2657, arts. 1(1), 10(8), 11(8) (which was revoked (8.10.2001) by S.I. 2001/3083, arts. 1(2), 23); S.I. 2001/3538, art. 2(1)

S. 400 amended(1.12.2001) by S.I. 2001/3083, arts. 1(2), 10(8), 11(8); S.I. 2001/3538, art. 2(1)

S. 400 modified (1.12.2001) by S.I. 2001/3646, arts. 1(1), 12(2), 13(3)

Institution of proceedings

401 Proceedings for offences.

(1) In this section "offence" means an offence under this Act or subordinate legislation made under this Act.

(2) Proceedings for an offence may be instituted in England and Wales only—

(a) by the Authority or the Secretary of State; or

(b) by or with the consent of the Director of Public Prosecutions.

(3) Proceedings for an offence may be instituted in Northern Ireland only—

(a) by the Authority or the Secretary of State; or

(b) by or with the consent of the Director of Public Prosecutions for Northern Ireland.

(4) Except in Scotland, proceedings for an offence under section 203 may also be instituted by the Director General of Fair Trading.

(5) In exercising its power to institute proceedings for an offence, the Authority must comply with any conditions or restrictions imposed in writing by the Treasury.

(6) Conditions or restrictions may be imposed under subsection (5) in relation to—

(a) proceedings generally; or

(b) such proceedings, or categories of proceedings, as the Treasury may direct.

注释:

修改等(不涉及条文内容)

C367　第400条为特定目的于2001年9月3日,否则于2001年12月1日依照制定法文件S.I.2001/1228第1条第(2)款第(b)项和第(c)项、第81条[与第1条第(2)款和第(3)款];制定法文件S.I.2001/2632第2条第(2)款、附录第二部分;制定法文件S.I.2001/3538第2条第(1)款适用;

第400条于2001年12月1日依照制定法文件S.I.1995/1537第23条第(6)款[于2001年12月1日依照制定法文件S.I.2001/3649第1条、第509条第(g)项修正]适用;

第400条于2001年12月1日依照制定法文件S.I.2001/2657第1条第(1)款、第10条第(8)款、第11条第(8)款[于2001年10月8日依照制定法文件S.I.2001/3083第1条第(2)款、第23条废除];制定法文件S.I.2001/3538第2条第(1)款修正;

第400条于2001年12月1日依照制定法文件S.I.2001/3083第1条第(2)款、第10条第(8)款、第11条第(8)款;制定法文件S.I.2001/3538第2条第(1)款修正;

第400条于2001年12月1日依照制定法文件S.I.2001/3646第1条第(1)款、第12条第(2)款、第13条第(3)款修订。

起　诉

第401条　针对犯罪的诉讼程序

(1)本条中"犯罪"系指本法或依照本法制定的附属立法规定的犯罪。

(2)在英格兰和威尔士针对犯罪的诉讼程序只能

(a)由管理局或国务大臣提起;或

(b)由检察长提起或经其同意提起。

(3)在北爱尔兰针对犯罪的诉讼程序只能

(a)由管理局或国务大臣提起;或

(b)由北爱尔兰检察长提起或经其同意提起。

(4)除苏格兰外,针对第203条规定的犯罪提起的诉讼程序亦可由公平交易总理事提起。

(5)在行使针对犯罪提起诉讼程序的权力时,管理局必须遵守财政部书面提出的任何条件或限制。

(6)可以就下列事项依照第(5)款规定提出条件或限制:

(a)一般诉讼程序;或

(b)财政部规定或规定类型的诉讼程序。

Annotations:

Modifications etc. (not altering text)

C368 S. 401 applied (1.12.2001) by S.I. 1995/1537, reg. 23(6) (as amended(1.12.2001) by S.I. 2001/3649, arts. 1, 509(g))

C369 S. 401 amended (1.12.2001) by S.I. 2001/2657, arts. 1(1), 10(8), 11(8), 13(1)(3) (which was revoked (8.10.2001) by S.I. 2001/3083, arts. 1(2), 23); S.I. 2001/3538, art. 2(1)

S. 401 amended (1.12.2001) by S.I. 2001/3083, arts. 1(2), 10(8), 11(8), 13(1); S.I. 2001/3538, art. 2(1)

S. 401 modified (1.12.2001) by S.I. 2001/3646, arts. 1(1), 12(2), 13(3)

402 Power of the Authority to institute proceedings for certain other offences.

(1) Except in Scotland, the Authority may institute proceedings for an offence under—

(a) Part V of the M74Criminal Justice Act 1993 (insider dealing); or

(b) prescribed regulations relating to money laundering.

(2) In exercising its power to institute proceedings for any such offence, the Authority must comply with any conditions or restrictions imposed in writing by the Treasury.

(3) Conditions or restrictions may be imposed under subsection (2) in relation to—

(a) proceedings generally; or

(b) such proceedings, or categories of proceedings, as the Treasury may direct.

Annotations:

Commencement Information

I124 S. 402 wholly in force at 1.12.2001; s. 402 not in force at Royal Assent see s. 431(2); s. 402(1)(b) in force for certain purposes at 25.2.2001 by S.I. 2001/516, art. 2(b), Sch. Pt. 2; s. 402 in force for specified purposes at 19.10.2001 by S.I. 2001/3436, art. 2; s. 402 in force in so far as not already in force at 1.12.2001 by S.I. 2001/3538, art. 2(1)

Marginal Citations

M74 1993 c. 36.

403 Jurisdiction and procedure in respect of offences.

(1) A fine imposed on an unincorporated association on its conviction of an offence is to

注释：

修改等(不涉及条文内容)

C368　第401条于2001年12月1日依照制定法文件S.I.1995/1537第23条第(6)款[于2001年12月1日依制定法文件S.I.2001/3649第1条、第509条第(g)项修正]适用。

C369　第401条于2001年12月1日依照制定法文件S.I.2001/2657第1条第(1)款、第10条第(8)款、第11条第(8)款、第13条第(1)款和第(3)款[于2001年10月8日依制定法文件S.I.2001/3083第1条第(2)款、第23条废除];制定法文件S.I.2001/3538第2条第(1)款修正;

第401条于2001年12月1日依照制定法文件S.I.2001/3083第1条第(2)款、第10条第(8)款、第11条第(8)款、第13条第(1)款;制定法文件S.I.2001/3538第2条第(1)款修正;

第401条于2001年12月1日依照制定法文件S.I.2001/3646第1条第(1)款、第12条第(2)款、第13条第(3)款修订。

第402条　管理局针对其他特定犯罪提起诉讼程序的权力

(1)除苏格兰外,管理局可依照下列规定针对一项犯罪提起诉讼程序:

(a)第五部分[M74]《1993年刑事司法法》第五部分(内幕交易);或

(b)与洗钱相关的规定法规。

(2)在行使针对任何上述犯罪提起诉讼程序的权力时,管理局必须遵守财政部书面提出的任何条件或限制。

(3)可以就下列事项依照第(2)款规定提出条件或限制:

(a)一般诉讼程序;或

(b)财政部规定或规定类型的诉讼程序。

注释：

实施日期

I124　第402条于2001年12月1日全部生效;第402条在副署时尚未生效,见第431条第(2)款;第402条第(1)款第(b)项为特定目的于2001年2月25日依照制定法文件S.I.2001/516第2条第(b)项、附录第二部分生效;第402条为特定目的于2001年10月19日依照制定法文件S.I.2001/3436第2条生效;第402条如于2001年12月1日尚未生效,则依照制定法文件S.I.2001/3538第2条第(1)款生效。

附注引文

M74　1993年第36章。

第403条　与犯罪相关的管辖和程序

(1)就针对非法人团体的有罪判决处以的罚金从该团体的资金中支付。

be paid out of the funds of the association.

(2) Proceedings for an offence alleged to have been committed by an unincorporated association must be brought in the name of the association (and not in that of any of its members).

(3) Rulesof court relating to the service of documents are to have effect as if the association were a body corporate.

(4) In proceedings for an offence brought against an unincorporated association—

(a) section 33 of the[M75] Criminal Justice Act 1925 and Schedule 3 to the[M76] Magistrates' Courts Act 1980 (procedure) apply as they do in relation to a body corporate;

(b) section 70 of the[M77] Criminal Procedure (Scotland) Act 1995 (procedure) applies as if the association were a body corporate;

(c) section 18 of the[M78] Criminal Justice (Northern Ireland) Act 1945 and Schedule 4 to the [M79]Magistrates' Courts (Northern Ireland) Order 1981 (procedure) apply as they do in relation to a body corporate.

(5) Summary proceedings for an offence may be taken—

(a) against a body corporate or unincorporated association at any place at which it has a place of business;

(b) against an individual at any place where he is for the time being.

(6) Subsection (5) does not affect any jurisdiction exercisable apart from this section.

(7) "Offence" means an offence under this Act.

Annotations:

Modifications etc. (not altering text)

C370 S. 403 applied (1.12.2001) by S.I. 1995/1537, reg. 23(6)(as amended(1.12.2001) by S.I. 2001/3649, arts. 1, 509(g))

C371 S. 403 amended (1.12.2001) by S.I. 2001/2657, arts. 1(1), 10(8), 11(8), 13(1)(3) (which was revoked (8.10.2001) by S.I. 2001/3083, arts. 1(2), 23); S.I. 2001/3538, art. 2(1)

S. 403 amended (1.12.2001) by S.I. 2001/3083, arts. 1(2), 10(8), 11(8), 13(1); S.I. 2001/3538, art. 2(1)

S. 403 modified (1.12.2001) by S.I. 2001/3646, arts. 1(1), 12(2), 13(3)

S. 403 applied (3.9.2001 for specified purposes otherwise 1.12.2001) by S.I. 2001/1228, regs.1(2)(b)(c), 82(with reg. 1(2)(3)); S.I. 2001/2632, art. 2(2), Sch. Pt. 2; S.I. 2001/3538, art. 2(1)

(2)就非法人涉嫌实施的犯罪提起的诉讼程序必须针对该团体(而非其任何成员)提起。

(3)与送达文件相关的法院裁决对非法人的效力等同于其为法人。

(4)在针对非法人犯罪提起的诉讼程序中

(a)[M75]《1925年刑事司法法》第33条和[M76]《1980年治安法院法》附录3(程序)适用于非法人等同于适用于法人组织;

(b)[M77]《1995年刑事程序法》(苏格兰)第70条(程序)适用于非法人效力等同于对法人适用;

(c)[M78]《1945年刑事司法法》(北爱尔兰)第18条和[M79]《1981年治安法院法令》(北爱尔兰)附录4(程序)适用于非法人,效力等同于对法人适用;

(5)就犯罪提起的简易诉讼程序

(a)可以在法人或非法人有营业场所的任何地点针对其提起;

(b)在个人当时所处的任何地点针对其提起。

(6)第(5)款规定不影响除本条规定外可行使的任何管辖权。

(7)"犯罪"系指本法规定的犯罪。

注释:

修改等(不涉及条文内容)

C370 第403条于2001年12月1日依照制定法文件S.I.1995/1537第23条第(6)款[于2001年12月1日依照制定法文件S.I.2001/3649第1条、第509条第(g)项修正]适用。

C371 第403条于2001年12月1日依照制定法文件S.I.2001/2657第1条第(1)款、第10条第(8)款、第11条第(8)款、第13条第(1)款和第(3)款[于2001年10月8日依照制定法文件S.I.2001/3083第1条第(2)款、第23条废除];制定法文件S.I.2001/3538第2条第(1)款修正;

第403条于2001年12月1日依照制定法文件S.I.第1条第(2)款、第10条第(8)款、第11条第(8)款、第13条第(1)款;制定法文件S.I.2001/3538第2条第(1)款修正;

第403条于2001年12月1日依照制定法文件S.I.2001/3646第1条第(1)款、第12条第(2)款、第13条第(3)款修订;

第403条为特定目的于2001年9月3日,否则于2001年12月1日依照制定法文件S.I.2001/1228第1条第(2)款第(b)项和第(c)项、第82条[与第1条第(2)款和第(3)款];制定法文件S.I.2001/2632第2条第(2)款、附录第二部分;制定法文件S.I.2001/3538第2条第(1)款适用。

Marginal Citations

M75 1925 c. 86.

M76 1980 c. 43.

M77 1995 c. 46.

M78 1945 c. 15 (N.I.).

M79 S.I. 1981/1675.

附注引文

M75　1925年第86章。

M76　1980年第43章。

M77　1995年第46章。

M78　1945年第15章(N.I.)。

M79　制定法文件S.I.1981/1675。

PART XXVIII MISCELLANEOUS

Schemes for reviewing past business

404 Schemes for reviewing past business.

(1) Subsection (2) applies if the Treasury are satisfied that there is evidence suggesting—

(a) that there has been a widespread or regular failure on the part ofauthorized persons to comply with rules relating to a particular kind of activity; and

(b) that, as a result, private persons have suffered (or will suffer) loss in respect of which authorised persons are (or will be) liable to make payments ("compensation payments").

(2) The Treasury may by order ("a scheme order") authorise the Authority to establish and operate a scheme for—

(a) determining the nature and extent of the failure;

(b) establishing the liability of authorised persons to make compensation payments; and

(c) determining the amounts payable by way of compensation payments.

(3) An authorised scheme must be made so as to comply with specified requirements.

(4) A scheme order may be made only if—

(a) the Authority has given the Treasury a report about the alleged failure and asked them to make a scheme order;

(b) the report contains details of the scheme which the Authority propose to make; and

(c) the Treasury are satisfied that the proposed scheme is an appropriate way of dealing with the failure.

(5) A scheme order may provide for specified provisions of or made under this Act to apply in relation to any provision of, or determination made under, the resulting authorized scheme subject to such modifications (if any) as may be specified.

(6) For the purposes of this Act, failure on the part of an authorised person to comply

第二十八部分　其他条款

过往业务审查计划

第404条　过往业务审查计划[1]

(1)如财政部确信有证据表明下列情况,则适用第(2)款规定:

(a)获授权人普遍或经常未遵守有关特定种类活动的规则;且

(b)个人因此遭受(或将遭受)损失,而获授权人有责任(或将有责任)就该损失支付款项(以下简称赔偿金)。

(2)财政部可以颁布法令(以下简称计划令),授权管理局为下列目的建立并执行一项计划:

(a)确定未遵守情况的性质和程度;

(b)确定获授权人支付赔偿金的责任;以及

(c)确定赔偿金的应付金额。

(3)授权的计划必须符合指定要求。

(4)只有在下列情况下方可发布计划令:

(a)管理局已就未遵守规则的情况报告财政部,请求财政部发布计划令;

(b)该报告详细说明了管理局拟实施的计划;且

(c)财政部确信拟实施的计划是处理该未遵守规则情况的适当方式。

(5)计划令可规定本法中或依照本法制定的规定经规定修改后(如有)适用于依照经该计划令授权的计划作出的规定或决定。

(6)为本法之目的,获授权人未遵守经授权计划的任何规定视为未遵守规则(受

1　本条依照《2010年金融服务法》第14条修订。——译者注

with any provision of an authorised scheme is to be treated (subject to any provision made by the scheme order concerned) as a failure on his part to comply with rules.

(7) The Treasury may prescribe circumstances in which loss suffered by a person ("A") acting in a fiduciary or other prescribed capacity is to be treated, for the purposes of an authorised scheme, as suffered by a private person in relation to whom A was acting in that capacity.

(8) This section applies whenever the failure in question occurred.

(9) "Authorised scheme" means a scheme authorised by a scheme order.

(10) "Private person" has such meaning as may be prescribed.

(11) "Specified" means specified in a scheme order.

Annotations:

Modifications etc. (not altering text)

C372 S. 404 modified (6.8.2001) by S.I. 2001/2512, arts. 1(1), 6(1)

Third countries

405 Directions.

(1) For the purpose of implementing a third country decision, the Treasury may direct the Authority to—

(a) refuse an application for permission under Part IV made by a body incorporated in, or formed under the law of, any part of the United Kingdom;

(b) defer its decision on such an application either indefinitely or for such period as may be specified in the direction;

(c) give a notice of objection to a person who has served a notice of control to the effect that he proposes to acquire a 50% stake in a UK authorised person; or

(d) give a notice of objection to a person who has acquired a 50% stake in a UK authorised person without having served the required notice of control.

(2) A direction may also be given in relation to—

(a) any person falling within a class specified in the direction;

(b) future applications, notices of control or acquisitions.

(3) The Treasury may revoke a direction at any time.

(4) But revocation does not affect anything done in accordance with the direction before it was revoked.

(5) "Third country decision" means a decision of the Council or the Commission under—

(a) Article 7(5) of the investment services directive;

相关计划令作出的任何规定制约)。

(7)财政部可以规定在何种情况下以受托人或其他规定身份行事的人(以下简称A)所遭受的损失为授权计划之目的视为与A以该身份行事相关的个人所遭受的损失。

(8)一旦发生相关未遵守规定情况即适用本条规定。

(9)“经授权计划”系指经计划令授权的计划。

(10)“个人”具有中的含义。

(11)“规定”系指在计划令中规定。

注释:

修改等(不涉及条文内容)

C372 第404条于2001年8月6日依照制定法文件S.I.2001/2512第1条第(1)款、第6条第(1)款修订。

第 三 国

第405条 指示

(1)为执行第三国决定,财政部可指示管理局

(a)驳回依照联合王国任何地区法律设立或成立的法人依照第四部分规定提出的许可申请;

(b)无限期推迟或依照指示中规定的期限推迟对上述申请作出决定;

(c)向送达控制通知、拟购买联合王国获授权人50%股份的人发出反对通知;或

(d)向未按要求发出控制通知而购买联合王国获授权人50%股份的人发出反对通知。

(2)也可以就下列事项发出指示

(a)属于指示中规定类别的任何人;

(b)未来的申请、控制通知或购买。

(3)财政部可以随时撤销指示。

(4)但撤销指示不影响撤销前依照该指示实施的任何行为。

(5)“第三国决定”系指理事会或委员会依照下列规定作出的决定:

(a)投资服务指令第7条第(5)款;

(b) [F9Article 23(5) of the banking consolidation directive];

(c) Article 29b(4) of the first non-life insurance directive; or

(d) Article 32b(4) of the first life insurance directive.

Annotations:

Amendments (Textual)

F9 Words in s. 405(5)(b) substituted (22.11.2000) by S.I. 2000/2952, reg. 8(3)

Commencement Information

I125 S. 405 wholly in force at 1.12.2001; s. 405 not in force at Royal Assent see s. 431 (2); s. 405 (except (1)(c)(d)) in force at 3.9.2001 by S.I. 2001/2632, art. 2(2), Sch. Pt. 2; s. 405 in force in so far as not already in force at 1.12.2001 by S.I. 2001/3538, art. 2(1)

406 Interpretation of section 405.

(1) For the purposes of section 405, a person ("the acquirer") acquires a 50% stake in a UK authorised person ("A") on first falling within any of the cases set out in subsection (2).

(2) The cases are where the acquirer—

(a) holds 50% or more of the shares in A;

(b) holds 50% or more of the shares in a parent undertaking ("P") of A;

(c) is entitled to exercise, or control the exercise of, 50% or more of the voting power in A; or

(d) is entitled to exercise, or control the exercise of, 50% or more of the voting power in P.

(3) In subsection (2)"the acquirer" means—

(a) the acquirer;

(b) any of the acquirer's associates; or

(c) the acquirer and any of his associates.

(4) "Associate", "shares" and "voting power" have the same meaning as in section 422.

407 Consequences of a direction under section 405.

(1) If the Authority refuses an application for permission as a result of a direction under section 405(1)(a)—

(a) subsections (7) to (9) of section 52 do not apply in relation to the refusal; but

(b) the Authority must notify the applicant of the refusal and the reasons for it.

(2) If the Authority defers its decision on an application for permission as a result of a direction under section 405(1)(b)—

(a) the time limit for determining the application mentioned in section 52 (1) or (2) (b)[F9银行合并指令第23条第(5)款];

(c)第一非人寿保险指令第29b条第(4)款;或

(d)第一人寿保险指令第32b条第(4)款。

注释:

修正(文本)

F9 第405条第(5)款第(b)项文字于2000年11月22日依照制定法文件S.I.2000/2952第8条第(3)款替换。

实施日期

I125 第405条于2001年12月1日全部生效;第405条在副署时尚未生效,见第431条第(2)款;第405条[除了第(1)款第(c)项第(d)项]于2001年9月3日依照制定法文件S.I.2001/2632第2条第(2)款、附录第二部分生效;第405条如于2001年12月1日尚未生效,则依照制定法文件S.I.2001/3538第2条第(1)款生效。

第406条 第405条释义

(1)为第405条之目的,首次出现第(2)款所列情况的人即为购买联合王国获授权人(以下简称A)50%股份的人(以下简称购买人)。

(2)前款所述情况为,购买人

(a)持有A的50%或以上股份;

(b)持有A的母企业(以下简称P)50%或以上股份;

(c)有权行使或控制行使A的50%或以上的投票权;或

(d)有权行使或控制行使P的50%或以上的投票权。

(3)第(2)款中购买人系指:

(a)购买人;

(b)购买人的任何关联人;或

(c)购买人及其任何关联人。

(4)关联人、股份和投票权含义同第422条。

第407条 第405条规定指示的结果

(1)如管理局因第405条第(1)款第(a)项规定驳回许可申请,则

(a)第52条第(7)款至第(9)款规定对该驳回不适用;但

(b)管理局必须通知申请人驳回其申请及驳回理由。

(2)如管理局因第405条第(1)款第(b)项规定推迟对许可申请作出决定,则

(a)第52条第(1)款或第(2)款规定的申请决定期限自推迟之日起终止,自指示指

stops running on the day of the deferral and starts running again (if at all) on the day the period specified in the direction (if any) ends or the day the direction is revoked; and

(b) the Authority must notify the applicant of the deferral and the reasons for it.

(3) If the Authority gives a notice of objection to a person as a result of a direction under section 405(1)(c) or (d)—

(a) sections 189 and 191 have effect as if the notice was a notice of objection within the meaning of Part XII; and

(b) the Authority must state in the notice the reasons for it.

Annotations:

Commencement Information

I126 S. 407 wholly in force at 1.12.2001; s. 407 not in force at Royal Assent see s. 431(2); s. 407(1)(2) in force at 3.9.2001 by S.I. 2001/2632, art. 2(2), Sch. Pt. 2; s. 407 in force in so far as not already in force at 1.12.2001 by S.I. 2001/3538, art. 2(1)

408 EFTA firms.

(1) If a third country decision has been taken, the Treasury may make a determination in relation to an EFTA firm which is a subsidiary undertaking of a parent undertaking which is governed by the law of the country to which the decision relates.

(2) "Determination" means a determination that the firm concerned does not qualify for authorisation under Schedule 3 even if it satisfies the conditions in paragraph 13 or 14 of that Schedule.

(3) A determination may also be made in relation to any firm falling within a class specified in the determination.

(4) The Treasury may withdraw a determination at any time.

(5) But withdrawal does not affect anything done in accordance with the determination before it was withdrawn.

(6) If the Treasury make a determination in respect of a particular firm, or withdraw such a determination, they must give written notice to that firm.

(7) The Treasury must publish notice of any determination (or the withdrawal of any determination)—

(a) in such a way as they think most suitable for bringing the determination (or withdrawal) to the attention of those likely to be affected by it; and

(b) on, or as soon as practicable after, the date of the determination (or withdrawal).

(8) "EFTA firm" means a firm, institution or undertaking which—

(a) is an EEA firm as a result of paragraph 5(a), (b) or (d) of Schedule 3; and

(b) is incorporated in, or formed under the law of, an EEA State which is not a

定的期间(如有)届满之日或指示撤销之日起继续执行;

(b)管理局必须通知申请人推迟决定及推迟决定的理由。

(3)如管理局因第405条第(1)款第(c)项或第(d)项规定向某人发出反对通知,则

(a)第189条和第191条对该通知的效力等同于该通知为第十二部分规定含义的反对通知;且

(b)管理局必须在该通知中说明理由。

注释:

实施日期

I126 第407条于2001年12月1日全部生效;第407条在副署时尚未生效,见第431条第(2)款;第407条第(1)款和第(2)款于2001年9月3日依照制定法文件S.I.2001/2632第2条第(2)款、附录第二部分生效;第407条如于2001年12月1日尚未生效,则依照制定法文件S.I.2001/3538第2条第(1)款生效。

第408条 欧洲自由贸易联盟企业

(1)如第三国作出决定,则财政部可以就受该决定相关国家法律管辖的母企业下属的欧洲自由贸易联盟企业作出决定。

(2)"决定"系指决定相关公司不符合附录3规定的授权条件,即使其满足该附录第13条或第14条规定的条件。

(3)也可以就属于决定中规定类别的任何公司作出决定。

(4)财政部可以随时撤销决定。

(5)但撤销决定不影响撤销前依照该决定实施的任何行为。

(6)如财政部就特定企业作出或撤销决定,则必须向该企业发出书面通知。

(7)财政部必须公布任何决定(或任何撤销决定)的通知,且

(a)以其认为引起可能受该决定(或撤销)影响的人注意的适当方式公布;

(b)在该决定(或撤销)之日或其后尽快公布。

(8)"欧洲自由贸易联盟企业"系指符合下列条件的公司、机构或企业:

(a)因附录3第5条第(a)项、第(b)项或第(d)项规定而为欧洲经济区企业;且

(b)依照欧洲经济区非成员国法律设立或成立。

member State.

(9) "Third country decision" has the same meaning as in section 405.

Annotations:

Commencement Information

I127 S. 408 wholly in force at 1.12.2001; s. 408 not in force at Royal Assent see s. 431 (2); s. 408 in force for specified purposes at 3.9.2001 by S.I. 2001/2632, art. 2 (2), Sch. Pt. 2; s. 408 in force in so far as not already in force at 1.12.2001 by S.I. 2001/3538, art. 2(1)

409 Gibraltar.

(1) The Treasury may by order—

(a) modify Schedule 3 so as to provide for Gibraltar firms of a specified description to qualify for authorisation under that Schedule in specified circumstances;

(b) modify Schedule 3 so as to make provision in relation to the exercise by UK firms of rights under the law of Gibraltar which correspond to EEA rights;

(c) modify Schedule 4 so as to provide for Gibraltar firms of a specified description to qualify for authorisation under that Schedule in specified circumstances;

(d) modify section 264 so as to make provision in relation to collective investment schemes constituted under the law of Gibraltar;

(e) provide for the Authority to be able to give notice under section 264 (2) on grounds relating to the law of Gibraltar;

(f) provide for this Act to apply to a Gibraltar recognised scheme as if the scheme were a scheme recognised under section 264.

(2) The fact that a firm may qualify for authorisation under Schedule 3 as a result of an order under subsection (1) does not prevent it from applying for a Part Ⅳ permission.

(3) "Gibraltar firm" means a firm which has its head office in Gibraltar or is otherwise connected with Gibraltar.

(4) "Gibraltar recognised scheme" means a collective investment scheme—

(a) constituted in an EEA State other than the United Kingdom, and

(b) recognised in Gibraltar under provisions which appear to the Treasury to give effect to the provisions of a relevant Community instrument.

(5) "Specified" means specified in the order.

(6) "UK firm" and "EEA right" have the same meaning as in Schedule 3.

International obligations

410 International obligations.

(1) If it appears to the Treasury that any action proposed to be taken by a relevant

(9)“第三国决定”与第405条中的含义相同。

注释：

实施日期

I127 第408条于2001年12月1日全部生效；第408条在副署时尚未生效，见第431条第(2)款；第408条为特定目的于2001年9月3日依照制定法文件S.I.2001/2632第2条第(2)款、附录第二部分生效；第408条如于2001年12月1日尚未生效，则依照制定法文件S.I.2001/3538第2条第(1)款生效。

第409条 直布罗陀

(1)财政部可以颁布法令

(a)修改附录3，使规定种类的直布罗陀企业在规定情况下依照该附录符合授权条件；

(b)修改附录3，就联合王国企业依照直布罗陀法律行使与欧洲经济区权利对应的权利作出规定；

(c)修改附录4，使规定种类的直布罗陀企业在规定情况下依照该附录符合授权条件；

(d)修改第264条，就依照直布罗陀法律建立的集合投资计划作出规定；

(e)规定管理局能够以直布罗陀法律相关理由依照第264条第(2)款规定发出通知；

(f)规定本法适用于直布罗陀获认可的计划，效力等同于对依照第264条规定获得认可的计划适用。

(2)企业可能依照第(1)款规定符合附录3的授权条件这一事实不妨碍申请第四部分许可。

(3)“直布罗陀企业” 系指公司总部位于直布罗陀或以其他方式与直布罗陀相关联。

(4)“直布罗陀获认可的计划”系指符合下列条件的集合投资计划：

(a)在联合王国以外的欧洲经济区国家建立；并

(b)在直布罗陀依照财政部认为使相关共同体法律文件生效的规定获得认可。

(5)规定系指在上述法令中规定。

(6)“联合王国企业”和“欧洲经济区权利”含义同附录3。

国际义务

第410条 国际义务

(1)如财政部认为相关人拟采取的任何行动与共同体义务或联合王国的任何其

person would be incompatible with Community obligations or any other international obligations of the United Kingdom, they may direct that person not to take that action.

(2) If it appears to the Treasury that any action which a relevant person has power to take is required for the purpose of implementing any such obligations, they may direct that person to take that action.

(3) A direction under this section—

(a) may include such supplemental or incidental requirements as the Treasury consider necessary or expedient; and

(b) is enforceable, on an application made by the Treasury, by injunction or, in Scotland, by an order for specific performance under section 45 of the [M80]Court of Session Act 1988.

(4) "Relevant person" means—

(a) the Authority;

(b) any person exercising functions conferred by Part Ⅵ on the competent authority;

(c) any recognised investment exchange (other than one which is an overseas investment exchange);

(d) any recognised clearing house (other than one which is an overseas clearing house);

(e) a person included in the list maintained under section 301; or

(f) the scheme operator of the ombudsman scheme.

Annotations:

Modifications etc. (not altering text)

C373 S. 410 applied (1.12.2001) by S.I. 1995/1537, reg. 23(3) (as amended (1.12.2001) by S.I. 2001/3649, arts. 1, 509(d))

Marginal Citations

M80 1988 c. 36.

Tax treatment of levies and repayments

411 Tax treatment of levies and repayments.

[F10] (1) ...

(2) After section 76 of the 1988 Act insert—

"76A Levies and repayments under the Financial Services and Markets Act 2000.

(1) In computing the amount of the profits to be charged under Case I of Schedule D arising from a trade carried on by an authorised person (other than an investment company)—

(a) to the extent that it would not be deductible apart from this section, any sum expended by the authorised person in paying a levy may be deducted as an allowable expense;

(b) any payment which is made to the authorised person as a result of a repayment

他国际义务不相容，则可以发出指令指示该人不采取该行动。

(2)如财政部认为为履行上述义务需要采取相关人有权采取的任何行动，则可以指示该人采取行动。

(3)本条规定的指示

(a)可以包括财政部认为必要或适宜的补充或附带要求；且

(b)可以应财政部申请，通过强制令强制执行，在苏格兰可通过[M80]《1988年高等民事法院法》第45条规定的实际履行令强制执行。

(4)"相关人"系指

(a)管理局；

(b)行使第六部分赋予主管机关的职能的任何人；

(c)任何获认可的投资交易所(不包括境外投资交易所)；

(d)任何获认可的结算所(不包括境外结算所)；

(e)依照第301条规定保有的名单中所列之人；或

(f)申诉专员计划的计划执行人。

注释：

修改等(不涉及条文内容)

C373 第410条于2001年12月1日依照制定法文件S.I.1995/1537第23条第(3)款[于2001年12月1日依照制定法文件S.I.2001/3649第1条、第509条第(d)项修正]适用。

附注引文

M80 1988年第36章。

费用征收及还款的税务处理

第411条 费用征收及还款的税务处理

[F10](1)……

(2)1988年法第76条后插入：

"第76A条 《2000年金融服务与市场法》规定的费用征收及还款

(1)在因获授权人(不包括投资公司)实施的交易而产生的附录D第一种情况下计算利润额时

(a)获授权人支付征收费用所支出的任何款项均可作为准予列支的费用扣除，但除依照本条规定外不得扣除；

(b)任何因还款规定而向获授权人支付的款项均视为营业收入。

provision is to be treated as a trading receipt.

(2) "Levy" has the meaning given in section 76(7A).

(3) "Repayment provision" means any provision made by virtue of—

(a) section 136(7) of the Financial Services and Markets Act 2000 ("the Act of 2000");

(b) section 214(1)(e) of the Act of 2000.

(4) "Authorised person" has the same meaning as in the Act of 2000.

76B Levies and repayments under the Financial Services and Markets Act 2000: investment companies.

(1) For the purposes of section 75 any sums paid by an investment company—

(a) by way of a levy, or

(b) as a result of an award of costs under costs rules, shall be treated as part of its expenses of management.

(2) If a payment is made to an investment company as a result of a repayment provision, the company shall be charged to tax under Case Ⅵ of Schedule D on the amount of that payment.

(3) "Levy" has the meaning given in section 76(7A).

(4) "Costs rules" means—

(a) rules made under section 230 of the Financial Services and Markets Act 2000;

(b) provision relating to costs contained in the standard terms fixed under paragraph 18 of Schedule 17 to that Act.

(5) "Repayment provision" has the meaning given in section 76A(3).

Annotations:

Amendments (Textual)

F10 S. 411(1) repealed (1.12.2001) by S.I. 2001/3629, arts. 1(2)(a), 109, Sch.

Gaming contracts

412 Gaming contracts.

(1) No contract to which this section applies is void or unenforceable because of—

(a) section 18 of the M81 Gaming Act 1845, section 1 of the M82 Gaming Act 1892 or Article 170 of the M83 Betting, Gaming, Lotteries and Amusements (Northern Ireland) Order 1985; or

(b) any rule of the law of Scotland under which a contract by way of gaming or wagering is not legally enforceable.

(2) This section applies to a contract if—

(a) it is entered into by either or each party by way of business;

(2)“费用征收”具有第76条第(7A)款中的含义。

(3)“还款规定”系指依照下列法律制定的规定:

(a)《2000年金融服务与市场法》(以下简称2000年法)第136条第(7)款。

(b)2000年法第214条第(1)款第(e)项。

(4)“获授权人”与2000年法中的含义相同。

第76B条 《2000年金融服务与市场法》规定的费用征收及还款:投资公司

(1)为本条及第75条之目的,投资公司

(a)以费用征收方式支付的款项,或

(b)依照法院裁决判付费用而支付的款项,应视为其管理支出。

(2)如依照还款规定向投资公司支付款项,则应当依照附录D第六种情况就支付金额收税。

(3)“费用征收”具有第76条第(7A)款中的含义。

(4)“费用规则”系指

(a)依照《2000年金融服务与市场法》第230条制定的规则。

(b)依照该法附录17第18条制定的标准条款所载费用相关规定。

(5)“还款规定”具有第76A条第(3)款中的含义。

注释:

修正(文本)

F10 第411条第(1)款于2001年12月1日依照制定法文件S.I.2001/3629第1条第(2)款第(a)项、第109条、附录废除。

博 彩 合 同

第412条 博彩合同

(1)本条规定适用的任何合同不因下列法律而无效或不可执行:

(a)[M81]《1845年博彩法》第18条、[M82]《1892年博彩法》第1条或[M83]《1985年赌博、彩票和娱乐法令》(北爱尔兰)第170条;或

(b)规定博彩或赌博合同无法定执行力的任何苏格兰法律。

(2)如有下列情况,则本条规定适用于合同:

(a)由营业中的合同各方订立;

(b) the entering into or performance of it by either party constitutes an activity of a specified kind or one which falls within a specified class of activity; and

(c) it relates to an investment of a specified kind or one which falls within a specified class of investment.

(3) Part II of Schedule 2 applies for the purposes of subsection (2)(c), with the references to section 22 being read as references to that subsection.

(4) Nothing in Part II of Schedule 2, as applied by subsection (3), limits the power conferred by subsection (2)(c).

(5) "Investment" includes any asset, right or interest.

(6) "Specified" means specified in an order made by the Treasury.

Annotations:

Commencement Information

I128 S. 412 wholly in force at 1.12.2001; s. 412 not in force at Royal Assent see s. 431 (2); s. 412 in force for certain purposes at 25.2.2001 by S.I. 2001/516, art. 2(b), Sch. Pt. 2; s. 412 in force in so far as not already in force at 1.12.2001 by S.I. 2001/3538, art. 2(1)

Marginal Citations

M81 1845 c. 109.

M82 1892 c. 9.

M83 S.I. 1985/1204 (N.I. 11).

Limitation on powers to require documents

413 Protected items.

(1) A person may not be required under this Act to produce, disclose or permit the inspection of protected items.

(2) "Protected items" means—

(a) communications between a professional legal adviser and his client or any person representing his client which fall within subsection (3);

(b) communications between a professional legal adviser, his client or any person representing his client and any other person which fall within subsection (3) (as a result of paragraph (b) of that subsection);

(c) items which—

(i) are enclosed with, or referred to in, such communications;

(ii) fall within subsection (3); and

(iii) are in the possession of a person entitled to possession of them.

(3) A communication or item falls within this subsection if it is made—

(b)任何一方订立或履行该协议构成规定种类的活动或属于规定类别的活动;且

(c)与规定种类的投资或属于规定类别的投资相关。

(3)附录2第二部分为实施第(2)款第(c)项而适用时,述及第22条视为述及该条每一款规定。

(4)依照第(3)款规定适用附录2第二部分任何规定,不限制第(2)款第(c)项规定赋予的权力。

(5)"投资"包括任何资产、权利或利益。

(6)"规定"系指在财政部发布的命令中规定。

注释:

实施日期

I128 第412条于2001年12月1日全部生效;第412条在副署时尚未生效,见第431条第(2)款;第412条为特定目的于2001年2月25日依照制定法文件S.I.2001/516,第2条第(b)款、附录第二部分生效;第412条如于2001年12月1日尚未生效,则依照制定法文件S.I.2001/3538第2条第(1)款生效。

附注引文

M81 1845年第109章。

M82 1892年第9章。

M83 制定法文件S.I.1985/1204(第11条)。

要求提供文件权的限制

第413条 受保护项目

(1)不得依照本法规定要求出示、披露或允许查阅受保护项目。

(2)"受保护项目"系指

(a)专业法律顾问与其客户或代表其客户的任何人之间属于第(3)款规定范围的通信;

(b)专业法律顾问与其客户或代表其客户的任何人及任何其他人之间属于第(3)款规定范围的通信[因该款第(b)项而进行];

(c)下列项目:

(i)在上述通信中附有或提及的项目;

(ii)属于第(3)款规定范围;且

(iii)为有权持有该项目的人所持有。

(3)如通信或项目有下列情况,则为属于本款规定范围:

(a) in connection with the giving of legal advice to the client; or

(b) in connection with, or in contemplation of, legal proceedings and for the purposes of those proceedings.

(4) A communication or item is not a protected item if it is held with the intention of furthering a criminal purpose.

Service of notices

414 Service of notices.

(1) The Treasury may by regulations make provision with respect to the procedure to be followed, or rules to be applied, when a provision of or made under this Act requires a notice, direction or document of any kind to be given or authorises the imposition of a requirement.

(2) The regulations may, in particular, make provision—

(a) as to the manner in which a document must be given;

(b) as to the address to which a document must be sent;

(c) requiring, or allowing, a document to be sent electronically;

(d) for treating a document as having been given, or as having been received, on a date or at a time determined in accordance with the regulations;

(e) as to what must, or may, be done if the person to whom a document is required to be given is not an individual;

(f) as to what must, or may, be done if the intended recipient of a document is outside the United Kingdom.

(3) Subsection (1) applies however the obligation to give a document is expressed (and so, in particular, includes a provision which requires a document to be served or sent).

(4) Section 7 of the [M84]Interpretation Act 1978 (service of notice by post) has effect in relation to provisions made by or under this Act subject to any provision made by regulations under this section.

Annotations:

Modifications etc. (not altering text)

C374 S. 414 amended (1.12.2001) by S.I. 2001/2657, arts. 1(1), 10(7), 11(7) (which was revoked (8.10.2001) by S.I. 2001/3083, arts. 1(2), 23); S.I. 2001/3538, art. 2(1)

S. 414 amended(1.12.2001) by S.I. 2001/3083, arts. 1(2), 10(7), 11(7); S.I.2001/3538, art. 2(1)

Commencement Information

I129 S. 414 wholly in force at 18.6.2001; s. 414 not in force at Royal Assent see s. 431 (2); s. 414(1)–(3) in force at 25.2.2001 by S.I. 2001/516, art. 2(a), Sch. Pt. 1; s. 414 in force in so far as not already in force at 18.6.2001 by S.I. 2001/1820, art. 2, Sch.

(a)与向客户提出法律建议相关;或

(b)与法律程序相关或为法律程序做准备并为该法律程序目的提出。

(4)如通信或项目为继续实现犯罪目的而持有,则不为受保护项目。

通知的送达

第414条 通知的送达

(1)财政部可以制定法规,就本法规定或依照本法制定的规定要求发出任何种类的通知、指令或文件时应遵循的程序或适用的规则作出规定或授权提出要求。

(2)法规可以特别规定

(a)发出文件的方式;

(b)文件必须发往的地址;

(c)规定或允许以电子方式发送文件;

(d)将依照该法规确定的日期或时间的文件处理视为已发出或已接收。

(e)如要求向其发出文件的对象不是个人,则必须或可以实施哪些活动;

(f)如文件接收人不在联合王国,则必须或可以实施哪些活动。

(3)无论发出文件的义务如何表述,均适用第(1)款规定(特别包括要求送达或发送文件的规定)。

(4)[M84]《1978年解释法》第7条(以邮递方式送达通知)对依照本法制定的规定或本法的规定有效,受依照本条规定制定的法规中任何规定的制约。

注释:

修改等(不涉及条文内容)

C374 第414条于2001年12月1日依照制定法文件S.I.2001/2657第1条第(1)款、第10条第(7)款、第11条第(7)款[于2001年10月8日依制定法文件S.I.2001/3083第1条第(2)款、第23条废除];制定法文件S.I.2001/3538第2条第(1)款修正;

第414条于2001年12月1日依照制定法文件S.I.2001/3083第1条第(2)款、第10条第(7)款、第11条第(7)款;制定法文件S.I.2001/3538第2条第(1)款修正。

实施日期

I129 第414条于2001年6月18日全部生效;第414条在副署时尚未生效,见第431条第(2)款;第414条第(1)款至第(3)款于2001年2月25日依照制定法文件S.I.2001/516第2条第(a)款、附录第一部分生效;第414条如于2001年6月18日尚未生效,则依照制定法文

Marginal Citations

M84 1978 c.30.

Jurisdiction

415 Jurisdiction in civil proceedings.

(1) Proceedings arising out of any act or omission (or proposed act or omission) of—

(a) the Authority,

(b) the competent authority for the purposes of Part VI,

(c) the scheme manager, or

(d) the scheme operator,

in the discharge or purported discharge of any of its functions under this Act may be brought before the High Court or the Court of Session.

(2) The jurisdiction conferred by subsection (1) is in addition to any other jurisdiction exercisable by those courts.

Annotations:

Modifications etc. (not altering text)

C375 S. 415 applied (1.12.2001) by S.I. 1995/1537, reg. 23(2) (as amended (1.12.2001) by S.I. 2001/3649, arts. 1, 509(c))

C376 S. 415 modified (17.8.2001) by S.I. 2001/2617, arts. 2(a), 4(3), 8, Sch. 2 para. 8

Removal of certain unnecessary provisions

416 Provisions relating to industrial assurance and certain other enactments.

(1) The following enactments are to cease to have effect—

(a) the[M85] Industrial Assurance Act 1923;

(b) the[M86] Industrial Assurance and Friendly Societies Act 1948;

(c) the[M87] Insurance Brokers (Registration) Act 1977.

(2) The[M88] Industrial Assurance (Northern Ireland) Order 1979 is revoked.

(3) The following bodies are to cease to exist—

(a) the Insurance Brokers Registration Council;

(b) the Policyholders Protection Board;

(c) the Deposit Protection Board;

件S.I.2001/1820第2条及附录生效。

附注引文

M84 1978年第30章。

管 辖

第415条 民事诉讼程序中的管辖[1]

(1)因下列各项:

(a)管理局,

(b)就第六部分而言的主管机关,

(c)计划管理人,或

(d)计划执行人,

在其行使或表明行使本法规定的任何职能时的任何行为或不作为(或计划中的作为或不作为)引起的诉讼程序可由高等法院或(苏格兰)高等民事法院审理。

(2)第(1)款规定授予的管辖权是上述法院行使的任何其他管辖权的增加。

注释:

修改等(不涉及条文内容)

C375 第415条于2001年12月1日依照制定法文件S.I.1995/1537第23条第(2)款[于2001年12月1日依照制定法文件S.I.2001/3649第1条、第509条第(c)项修正]适用。

C376 第415条于2001年8月17日依照制定法文件S.I.2001/2617第2条第(a)款、第4条第(3)款、第8条、附录2第8条修订。

去除某些不必要的规定

第416条 与工业保险和某些其他成文法相关的规定

(1)下列成文法停止生效:

(a)[M85]《1923年工业保险法》;

(b)[M86]《1948年工业保险与互相保险协会法》;

(c)[M87]《1977年保险经纪(登记)法》。

(2)撤销[M88]《1979年工业保险法令》(北爱尔兰)。

(3)下列机构停止存续:

(a)保险经纪人注册理事会;

(b)投保人保护委员会;

(c)存款保护委员会;

1 本条依照《2010年金融服务法》附录2第一部分第30条修订。——译者注

(d) the Board of Banking Supervision.

(4) If the Treasury consider that, as a consequence of any provision of this section, it is appropriate to do so, they may by order make any provision of a kind that they could make under this Act (and in particular any provision of a kind mentioned in section 339) with respect to anything done by or under any provision of Part XXI.

(5) Subsection (4) is not to be read as affecting in any way any other power conferred on the Treasury by this Act.

Annotations:

Commencement Information

I130 S. 416 wholly in force at 1.12.2001; s. 416 not in force at Royal Assent see s. 431 (2); s. 416(4)(5) in force at 25.2.2001 by S.I. 2001/516, art. 2(a), Sch. Pt. 1; s. 416(1)(c)(3)(a) in force at 30.4.2001 by S.I. 2001/1282, art. 2(a); s. 416 in force at 1.12.2001 so far as not already in force (except sub-section (3)(b)(c) which are in force at 2.3.2002) by S.I. 2001/3538, art. 2(1)(4)

Marginal Citations

M85 1923 c. 8.

M86 1948 c. 39.

M87 1977 c. 46.

M88 S.I. 1979/1574 (N.I. 13).

(d)银行业务监督委员会。

(4)如财政部因本条的任何规定而认为适当,则可以颁布法令,就依照第二十一部分任何规定实施的行为制定财政部依照本法规定可制定的任何规定(特别是第339条所述任何规定)。

(5)第(4)款不得视为以任何方式影响本法赋予财政部的任何其他权力。

注释:

实施日期

I130 第416条于2001年12月1日全部生效;第416条在副署时尚未生效,见第431条第(2)款;第416条第(4)款和第(5)款于2001年2月25日依照制定法文件S.I.2001/516第2条第(a)款、附录第一部分生效;第416条第(1)款第(c)项、第(3)款第(a)项于2001年4月30日依照制定法文件S.I.2001/1282第2条第(a)款生效;第416条如于2001年12月1日尚未生效[除了在2002年3月2日生效的第(3)款第(b)项和第(c)项外],则依照制定法文件S.I.2001/3538第2条第(1)款和第(4)款生效。

附注引文

M85 1923年第8章。

M86 1948年第39章。

M87 1977年第46章。

M88 制定法文件1979/1574(第13条)。

PART XXIX INTERPRETATION

417 Definitions.

(1) In this Act—

"appointed representative" has the meaning given in section 39(2);

"auditors and actuaries rules" means rules made under section 340;

"authorisation offence" has the meaning given in section 23(2);

"authorised open-ended investment company" has the meaning given in section 237(3);

"authorised person" has the meaning given in section 31(2);

"the Authority" means the Financial Services Authority;

"body corporate" includes a body corporate constituted under the law of a country or territory outside the United Kingdom;

"chief executive"—

(a) in relation to a body corporate whose principal place of business is within the United Kingdom, means an employee of that body who, alone or jointly with one or more others, is responsible under the immediate authority of the directors, for the conduct of the whole of the business of that body; and

(b) in relation to a body corporate whose principal place of business is outside the United Kingdom, means the person who, alone or jointly with one or more others, is responsible for the conduct of its business within the United Kingdom;

"collective investment scheme" has the meaning given in section 235;

"the Commission" means the European Commission (except in provisions relating to the Competition Commission);

"the compensation scheme" has the meaning given in section 213(2);

"control of information rules" has the meaning given in section 147(1);

"director", in relation to a body corporate, includes—

(a) a person occupying in relation to it the position of a director (by whatever name

第二十九部分 释 义

第417条 定义

(1)本法中[1]

“被任命代表”具有第39条第(2)款中的含义;

“审计师和精算师规则”系指依照第340条规定制定的规则;

“授权类犯罪”具有第23条第(2)款中的含义;

“获授权开放式投资公司”具有第237条第(3)款中的含义;

“获授权人”具有第31条第(2)款中的含义;

“管理局”系指金融服务管理局;

“法人”包括依照联合王国以外国家或地区法律成立的法人;

“行政总裁”

(a)就主要营业地在联合王国境内的法人而言,系指该法人中单独或与他人共同经董事直接授权负责开展该团体整体业务的雇员;

(b)就主要营业地在联合王国境外的法人而言,系指该法人中单独或与他人共同负责开展该团体联合王国境内业务的人;

“获认可的投资交易所”具有第235条中的含义;

“委员会”系指欧洲委员会(与竞争委员会相关的规定除外);

“补偿计划”具有第213条第(2)款中的含义;

“信息控制规则”具有第147条第(1)款中的含义。

“董事”就法人而言包括:

(a)担任与该法人相关的董事职务(无论名称为何)的人;以及

1 本款依照《2010年金融服务法》附录2第一部分第31条修订。——译者注

called); and

(b) a person in accordance with whose directions or instructions (not being advice given in a professional capacity) the directors of that body are accustomed to act;

"documents" includes information recorded in any form and, in relation to information recorded otherwise than in legible form, references to its production include references to producing a copy of the information in legible form;

[F11 "electronic commerce directive" means Directive 2000/31/EC of the European Parliament and the Council of 8 June 2000 on certain legal aspects of information society services, in particular electronic commerce, in the Internal Market (Directive on electronic commerce);]

"exempt person", in relation to a regulated activity, means a person who is exempt from the general prohibition in relation to that activity as a result of an exemption order made under section 38(1) or as a result of section 39(1) or 285(2) or (3);

"financial promotion rules" means rules made under section 145;

"friendly society" means an incorporated or registered friendly society;

"general prohibition" has the meaning given in section 19(2);

"general rules" has the meaning given in section 138(2);

"incorporated friendly society" means a society incorporated under the[M89] Friendly Societies Act 1992;

"industrial and provident society" means a society registered or deemed to be registered under the [M90]Industrial and Provident Societies Act 1965 or the[M91] Industrial and Provident Societies Act (Northern Ireland) 1969;

[F12 "information society service" means an information society service within the meaning of Article 2(a) of the electronic commerce directive;]

"market abuse" has the meaning given in section 118;

"Minister of the Crown" has the same meaning as in the Ministers of the[M92] Crown Act 1975;

"money laundering rules" means rules made under section 146;

"notice of control" has the meaning given in section 178(5);

"the ombudsman scheme" has the meaning given in section 225(3);

"open-ended investment company" has the meaning given in section 236;

"Part Ⅳ permission" has the meaning given in section 40(4);

"partnership" includes a partnership constituted under the law of a country or territory outside the United Kingdom;

"prescribed" (where not otherwise defined) means prescribed in regulations made by the Treasury;

"price stabilising rules" means rules made under section 144;

(b)该法人董事惯于依照其指令或指示(不是以专业人士身份提出的建议)行事的人;

“文件”包括以任何形式记录的信息,就以非可读形式记录的信息而言,述及提供该信息包含以可读形式提供该信息的副本;

[F11 “电子商务指令”系指欧洲议会和理事会2000年6月8日第2000/31/EC号指令,规定了国内市场上信息社会服务,特别是电子商务的某些法律层面(电子商务指令);]

“享有豁免权的人”就受监管活动而言系指因依照第38条第(1)款发布的命令或者因第39条第(1)款或第285条第(2)款或第(3)款而免于遵守与该行为相关的一般禁止性规定的人;

“金融推介规则”系指依照第145条规定制定的规则;

“互相保险协会”系指设立或注册的互相保险协会;

“一般禁止性规定”具有第19条第(2)款中的含义;

“一般规则”具有第138条第(2)款中的含义;

“作为法人设立的互相保险协会”系指依照M89《1992年互相保险协会法》设立的互相保险协会;

“行业节俭互助会”系指依照M90《1965年行业节俭互助会法》或M91《1969年行业节俭互助会法》(北爱尔兰)注册或视为注册的公会;

[F12 “信息社会服务”,系指电子商务指令第2条第(a)项规定含义的信息社会服务;]

“市场滥用”具有第118条中的含义;

“内阁阁员”定义与M92《1975年内阁阁员法》中规定的定义相同;

“反洗钱规则”系指依照第146条规定制定的规则;

“控制通知”具有第178条第(5)款中的含义;

“申诉专员计划”具有第225条第(3)款中的含义;

“开放式投资公司”具有第236条中的含义;

“第四部分许可”具有第40条第(4)款中的含义;

“合伙”包括依照联合王国以外国家或地区法律成立的合伙;

“规定的”(如无其他定义)系指在财政部制定的法规中规定;

“价格稳定规则”系指依照第144条规定制定的规则;

"private company" has the meaning given in section 1(3) of the[M93] Companies Act 1985 or in Article 12(3) of the[M94] Companies (Northern Ireland) Order 1986;

"prohibition order" has the meaning given in section 56(2);

"recognised clearing house" and "recognised investment exchange" have the meaning given in section 285;

"registered friendly society" means a society which is—

(a) a friendly society within the meaning of section 7(1)(a) of the[M95] Friendly Societies Act 1974; and

(b) registered within the meaning of that Act;

"regulated activity" has the meaning given in section 22;

"regulating provisions" has the meaning given in section 159(1);

"regulatory objectives" means the objectives mentioned in section 2;

"regulatory provisions" has the meaning given in section 302;

"rule" means a rule made by the Authority under this Act;

"rule-making instrument" has the meaning given in section 153;

"the scheme manager" has the meaning given in section 212(1);

"the scheme operator" has the meaning given in section 225(2);

"scheme particulars rules" has the meaning given in section 248(1);

"Seventh Company Law Directive" means the European Council Seventh Company Law Directive of 13 June 1983 on consolidated accounts (No. 83/349/EEC);

"threshold conditions", in relation to a regulated activity, has the meaning given in section 41;

"the Treaty" means the treaty establishing the European Community;

"trust scheme rules" has the meaning given in section 247(1);

"UK authorised person" has the meaning given in section 178(4); and

"unit trust scheme" has the meaning given in section 237.

(2) In the application of this Act to Scotland, references to a matter being actionable at the suit of a person are to be read as references to the matter being actionable at the instance of that person.

(3) For the purposes of any provision of this Act authorising or requiring a person to do anything within a specified number of days no account is to be taken of any day which is a public holiday in any part of the United Kingdom.

[[F13](4) For the purposes of this Act—

(a) an information society service is provided from an EEA State if it is provided from an establishment in that State;

(b) an establishment, in connection with an information society service, is the place at which the provider of the service (being a national of an EEA State or a company or firm as

"私营公司"具有[M93]《1985年公司法》第1条第(3)款或[M94]《1986年公司法令》(北爱尔兰)第12条第(3)款中的含义;

"禁令"具有第56条第(2)款中的含义;

"获认可的结算所"和"获认可的投资交易所"具有第285条规定的含义;

"注册互相保险协会"系指符合下列条件的互相保险协会:

(a)具有[M95]《1974年互相保险协会法》第7条第(1)款第(a)项规定含义;并

(b)在该法定义范围内经注册;

"受监管活动"具有第22条中的含义;

"监管规定"具有第159条第(1)款中的含义;

"监管目标"系指第2条所述目标;

"监管性规定"具有第302中的含义;

"规则"系指由管理局依照本法制定的规则;

"规则制定文书"具有第153条中的含义;

"计划管理人"具有第212条第(1)款中的含义;

"计划执行人"具有第225条第(2)款中的含义;

"计划详情规则"具有第248条第(1)款中的含义;

"第七公司法指令",系指欧洲理事会1983年6月13日关于综合账目的第七公司法指令(编号83/349/EEC);

"准入条件"就受监管活动而言具有第41条中的含义;

"条约"系指建立欧洲共同体的条约;

"信托计划规则"具有第247条第(1)款中的含义;

"联合王国获授权人"具有第178条第(4)款中的含义;

"单位信托计划"具有第237条中的含义。

(2)本法在苏格兰适用时,述及可针对某人提起诉讼的事项,视为述及可针对该人提起诉讼程序。

(3)就本法授权或要求在规定天数内实施任何行为的任何规定,不考虑任何在联合王国任何地区为公共假期的日期。

[[F13](4)就本法而言

(a)如信息社会服务由欧洲经济区国家中的机构提供,即为由该国提供;

(b)与信息社会服务相关的机构为服务提供者(为条约第48条所述欧洲经济区国民或公司或企业)在特定期间内有效从事经济活动的场所;

mentioned in Article 48 of the Treaty) effectively pursues an economic activity for an indefinite period;

(c) the presence or use in a particular place of equipment or other technical means of providing an information society service does not, of itself, constitute that place as an establishment of the kind mentioned in paragraph (b);

(d) where it cannot be determined from which of a number of establishments a given information society service is provided, that service is to be regarded as provided from the establishment where the provider has the centre of his activities relating to the service.]

Annotations:

Amendments (Textual)

F11 S. 417: definition of "electronic commerce directive" inserted(18.7.2002 for certain purposes and 21.8.2002 otherwise) by The Electronic Commerce Directive (Financial Services and Markets) Regulations 2002 (S.I. 2002/1775), regs. 1, 13(2)(a)

F12 S. 417: definition of "information society service" inserted (18.7.2002 for certain purposes and 21.8.2002 otherwise) by The Electronic Commerce Directive (Financial Services and Markets) Regulations 2002 (S.I. 2002/1775), regs. 1, 13(2)(b)

F13 S. 417(4) inserted(18.7.2002 for certain purposes and 21.8.2002 otherwise) by The Electronic Commerce Directive (Financial Services and Markets) Regulations 2002 (S.I. 2002/1775), regs. 1, 13(2) (c)

Marginal Citations

M89 1992 c. 40.

M90 1965 c. 12.

M91 1969 c. 24. (N.I.)

M92 1975 c. 26.

M93 1985 c. 6.

M94 S.I. 1986/1032 (N.I. 6).

M95 1992 c. 40.

418 Carrying on regulated activities in the United Kingdom.

(1) In the [F14 five] cases described in this section, a person who—

(a) is carrying on a regulated activity, but

(b) would not otherwise be regarded as carrying it on in the United Kingdom,

is, for the purposes of this Act, to be regarded as carrying it on in the United Kingdom.

(2) The first case is where—

(a) his registered office (or if he does not have a registered office his head office) is in the United Kingdom;

(b) he is entitled to exercise rights under a single market directive as a UK firm; and (c)在特定场所存在或使用提供信息社会服务的设备或其他技术手段本身不使该场所构成第(b)项所述种类的机构；

(d)如无法在众多机构中确定信息社会服务由哪家机构提供，则该服务视为由提供与该服务相关的核心活动的机构提供。]

注释：

修正(文本)

F11 第417条："电子商务指令"的定义为特定目的于2002年7月18日，否则于2002年8月21日依照《2002年电子商务指令条例》(金融服务和市场)(制定法文件S.I.2002/1775)第1条、第13条第(2)款第(a)项插入。

F12 第417条："信息社会服务"的定义为特定目的于2002年7月18日，否则于2002年8月21日依照《2002年电子商务指令条例》(金融服务和市场)(制定法文件S.I.2002/1775)第1条、第13条第(2)款第(b)项插入。

F13 第417条第(4)款为特定目的于2002年7月18日，否则于2002年8月21日依照《2002年电子商务指令条例》(金融服务和市场)(制定法文件S.I.2002/1775)第1条、第13条第(2)款第(c)项插入。

附注引文

M89 1992年第40章。

M90 1965年第12章。

M91 1969年第24章(N.I.)。

M92 1975年第26章。

M93 1985年第6章。

M94 制定法文件S.I.1986/1932(N.Z.第6条)。

M95 1992年第40章。

第418条 在联合王国开展受监管活动

(1)在本条描述的[F14 五]种情况下，有下列情况的人：

(a)正在开展受监管活动，但

(b)在其他情况下不视为在联合王国开展该活动，

为本法之目的视为在联合王国开展该活动。

(2)第一种情况为

(a)该人的注册营业地(如无注册营业地，则为总部)在联合王国；

(b)该人有权作为联合王国企业行使单一市场指令规定的权利；且

(c) he is carrying on in another EEA State a regulated activity to which that directive applies.

(3) The second case is where—

(a) his registered office (or if he does not have a registered office his head office) is in the United Kingdom;

(b) he is the manager of a scheme which is entitled to enjoy the rights conferred by an instrument which is a relevant Community instrument for the purposes of section 264; and

(c) persons in another EEA State are invited to become participants in the scheme.

(4) The third case is where—

(a) his registered office (or if he does not have a registered office his head office) is in the United Kingdom;

(b) the day-to-day management of the carrying on of the regulated activity is the responsibility of—

(i) his registered office (or head office); or

(ii) another establishment maintained by him in the United Kingdom.

(5) The fourth case is where—

(a) his head office is not in the United Kingdom; but

(b) the activity is carried on from an establishment maintained by him in the United Kingdom.

[F15 (5A) The fifth case is any other case where the activity—

(a) consists of the provision of an information society service to a person or persons in one or more EEA States; and

(b) is carried on from an establishment in the United Kingdom.]

(6) For the purposes of subsections (2) to [F16 (5A)] it is irrelevant where the person with whom the activity is carried on is situated.

Annotations:

Amendments (Textual)

F14 Word in s. 418(1) substituted (18.7.2002 for certain purposes and 21.8.2002 otherwise) by The Electronic Commerce Directive (Financial Services and Markets) Regulations 2002 (S.I. 2002/1775), regs. 1, 13(3)(a)

F15 S. 418(5A) inserted (18.7.2002 for certain purposes and 21.8.2002 otherwise) by The Electronic Commerce Directive (Financial Services and Markets) Regulations 2002 (S.I. 2002/1775), regs. 1, 13(3)(b)

F16 Word in s. 418(6) substituted (18.7.2002 for certain purposes and 21.8.2002 otherwise) by The Electronic Commerce Directive (Financial Services and Markets) Regulations 2002 (S.I. 2002/1775), regs. 1, 13(3)(c) (c)该人正在另一欧洲经济区国家开展该指令适用的受监管活动。

(3)第二种情况为

(a)该人的注册营业地(如无注册营业地,则为总部)在联合王国;

(b)该人为计划管理人且享有为第264条之目的作为相关共同体法律文件的法律文件赋予的权利;且

(c)另一欧洲经济区国家的人受到邀请参与该计划。

(4)第三种情况为

(a)该人的注册营业地(如无注册营业地,则为总部)在联合王国;

(b)开展受监管活动的日常管理

(i)由其注册营业地(或总部)负责;或

(ii)由其在联合王国保有的其他机构负责。

(5)第四种情况为

(a)该人总部不在联合王国;但

(b)该活动由其在联合王国保有的机构开展。

[F15(5A)第五种情况为该活动符合下列条件的任何其他情况:

(a)该活动包括向欧洲经济区一国或多国人提供信息社会服务;且

(b)由联合王国的机构开展。]

(6)就第(2)款至第[F16(5A)]款而言,活动开展对象所在地与上述规定不相关。

注释:

修正(文本)

F14 第418条第(1)款中的条文为特定目的于2002年7月18日,否则于2002年8月21日依照《2002年电子商务指令条例》(金融服务和市场)(制定法文件S.I.2002/1775) 第1条、第13条第(3)款第(a)项替换。

F15 第418条第(5A)款为特定目的于2002年7月18日,否则于2002年8月21日依照《2002年电子商务指令条例》(金融服务和市场)(制定法文件S.I.2002/1775)第1条、第13条第(3)款插入。

F16 第418条第(6)款为特定目的于2002年7月18日,否则于2002年8月21日依照《2002年电子商务指令条例》(金融服务和市场)(制定法文件S.I.2002/1775)第1条、第13条第(3)款第(c)项替换。

419 Carrying on regulated activities by way of business.

(1) The Treasury may by order make provision—

(a) as to the circumstances in which a person who would otherwise not be regarded as carrying on a regulated activity by way of business is to be regarded as doing so;

(b) as to the circumstances in which a person who would otherwise be regarded as carrying on a regulated activity by way of business is to be regarded as not doing so.

(2) An order under subsection (1) may be made so as to apply—

(a) generally in relation to all regulated activities;

(b) in relation to a specified category of regulated activity; or

(c) in relation to a particular regulated activity.

(3) An order under subsection (1) may be made so as to apply—

(a) for the purposes of all provisions;

(b) for a specified group of provisions; or

(c) for a specified provision.

(4) "Provision" means a provision of, or made under, this Act.

(5) Nothing in this section is to be read as affecting the provisions of section 428(3).

420 Parent and subsidiary undertaking.

(1) In this Act, except in relation to an incorporated friendly society, "parent undertaking" and "subsidiary undertaking" have the same meaning as in Part VII of the [M96]Companies Act 1985 (or Part VIII of the [M97]Companies (Northern Ireland) Order 1986).

(2) But—

(a) "parent undertaking" also includes an individual who would be a parent undertaking for the purposes of those provisions if he were taken to be an undertaking (and "subsidiary undertaking" is to be read accordingly);

(b) "subsidiary undertaking" also includes, in relation to a body incorporated in or formed under the law of an EEA State other than the United Kingdom, an undertaking which is a subsidiary undertaking within the meaning of any rule of law in force in that State for purposes connected with implementation of the Seventh Company Law Directive (and "parent undertaking" is to be read accordingly).

(3) In this Act "subsidiary undertaking", in relation to an incorporated friendly society, means a body corporate of which the society has control within the meaning of section 13(9) (a) or (aa) of the [M98]Friendly Societies Act 1992 (and "parent undertaking" is to be read accordingly).

第419条　营业中开展的受监管活动

(1)财政部可颁布法令

(a)规定在何种情况下将其他情况下不视为营业中开展受监管活动的行为视为开展该活动;

(b)规定在何种情况下将其他情况下视为营业中开展受监管活动的人视为未开展该活动。

(2)第(1)款规定的命令可以

(a)对所有受监管活动普遍适用;

(b)对指定类别的受监管活动适用;或

(c)对某项特定受监管活动适用。

(3)第(1)款规定的命令可以

(a)为所有规定之目的适用;

(b)为指定类别的规定之目的适用;或

(c)为指定的规定之目的适用。

(4)"规定"系指本法规定或依照本法制定的规定。

(5)本条中任何规定不得视为影响第428条第(3)款规定。

第420条　母企业和子企业

(1)本法中除与作为法人设立的互相保险协会相关外,"母企业"和"子企业"含义与[M96]《1985年公司法》第七部分[或[M97]《1986年公司法令》(北爱尔兰)第八部分]相同。

(2)但是

(a)"母企业"还包括为上述规定之目的,如视为企业则为母企业的个人("子企业"应作相应解释);

(b)就在联合王国以外的欧洲经济区国家设立或依照该国法律成立的法人而言,为实施第七公司法指令相关目的,"子企业" 还包括属于该国任何现行法律规定含义的子企业("母企业"应作相应解释)。

(3)本法中"子企业"就设立的互相保险协会而言系指该互相保险协会控制且属于[M98]《1992年互相保险协会》法第13条第(9)款第(a)项或第(aa)项定义范围的法人("母企业"应作相应解释)。

Annotations:

Marginal Citations

M96 1985 c. 6.

M97 S.I. 1986/1032 (N.I. 6).

M98 1992 c. 40.

421 Group.

(1) In this Act "group", in relation to a person ("A"), means A and any person who is—

(a) a parent undertaking of A;

(b) a subsidiary undertaking of A;

(c) a subsidiary undertaking of a parent undertaking of A;

(d) a parent undertaking of a subsidiary undertaking of A;

(e) an undertaking in which A or an undertaking mentioned in paragraph (a), (b), (c) or (d) has a participating interest;

(f) if A or an undertaking mentioned in paragraph (a) or (d) is a building society, an associated undertaking of the society; or

(g) if A or an undertaking mentioned in paragraph (a) or (d) is an incorporated friendly society, a body corporate of which the society has joint control (within the meaning of section 13(9)(c) or (cc) of the [M99]Friendly Societies Act 1992).

(2) "Participating interest" has the same meaning as in Part Ⅶ of the [M100]Companies Act 1985 or Part Ⅷ of the [M101]Companies (Northern Ireland) Order 1986; but also includes an interest held by an individual which would be a participating interest for the purposes of those provisions if he were taken to be an undertaking.

(3) "Associated undertaking" has the meaning given in section 119(1) of the [M102]Building Societies Act 1986.

Annotations:

Marginal Citations

M99 1992 c. 40.

M100 1985 c. 6.

M101 S.I. 1986/1032 (N.I. 6).

M102 1986 c. 53.

422 Controller.

(1) In this Act "controller", in relation to an undertaking ("A"), means a person who falls within any of the cases in subsection (2).

(2) The cases are where the person—

注释：

附注引文

M96 1985年第6章。

M97 制定法文件S.I.1986/1032(第6条)。

M98 1992年第40章。

第421条 集团

(1)本法中“集团”就某人(以下简称A)而言系指该人和下列任何人：

(a)A的母企业；

(b)A的子企业；

(c)A母企业的子企业；

(d)A子企业的母企业；

(e)A或第(a)项、第(b)项、第(c)项或第(d)项所述企业具有参与权益的企业；

(f)如A或第(a)项或第(d)项所述企业为建屋互相保险协会，该互相保险协会的关联企业；或

(g)如A或第(a)项或第(d)项所述企业为设立的互相保险协会，该互相保险协会共同控制的法人(在M99《1992年互相保险协会法》第13条第(9)款第(c)项或第(cc)项中的含义范围内)。

(2)“参与权益”含义与M100《1985年公司法》第七部分或M101《1986年公司法令》(北爱尔兰)第八部分中的含义相同；但还包括个人所持有、为上述规定目的如将该个人视为企业则为参与权益的权益。

(3)“关联企业”具有M102《1986年住房互助会法》第119条第(1)款中的含义。

注释：

附注引文

M99 1992年第40章。

M100 1985年第6章。

M101 制定法文件S.I.1986/1032(第6条)。

M102 1986年第53章。

第422条 控制人

(1)本法中“控制人”就企业(以下简称A)而言系指属于第(2)款的任何情况的人。

(2)前款所述情况为该人

(a) holds 10% or more of the shares in A;

(b) is able to exercise significant influence over the management of A by virtue of his shareholding in A;

(c) holds 10% or more of the shares in a parent undertaking ("P") of A;

(d) is able to exercise significant influence over the management of P by virtue of his shareholding in P;

(e) is entitled to exercise, or control the exercise of, 10% or more of the voting power in A;

(f) is able to exercise significant influence over the management of A by virtue of his voting power in A;

(g) is entitled to exercise, or control the exercise of, 10% or more of the voting power in P; or

(h) is able to exercise significant influence over the management of P by virtue of his voting power in P.

(3) In subsection (2)"the person" means—

(a) the person;

(b) any of the person's associates; or

(c) the person and any of his associates.

(4) "Associate", in relation to a person ("H") holding shares in an undertaking ("C") or entitled to exercise or control the exercise of voting power in relation to another undertaking ("D"), means—

(a) the spouse of H;

(b) a child or stepchild of H (if under 18);

(c) the trustee of any settlement under which H has a life interest in possession (or in Scotland a life interest);

(d) an undertaking of which H is a director;

(e) a person who is an employee or partner of H;

(f) if H is an undertaking—

(i) a director of H;

(ii) a subsidiary undertaking of H;

(iii) a director or employee of such a subsidiary undertaking; and

(g) if H has with any other person an agreement or arrangement with respect to the acquisition, holding or disposal of shares or other interests in C or D or under which they undertake to act together in exercising their voting power in relation to C or D, that other person.

(5) "Settlement", in subsection (4)(c), includes any disposition or arrangement under which property is held on trust (or subject to a comparable obligation).

(a)持有A的10%或以上股份；
(b)因在A持有的股份而能够对A的管理施加重要影响；

(c)持有A母企业(以下简称P)10%或以上股份；
(d)因在P持有的股份而能够对P的管理施加重要影响；

(e)有权行使或控制行使A的10%或以上的投票权；

(f)因在A的投票权而能够对A的管理施加重要影响；

(g)有权行使或控制行使P的10%或以上的投票权；或

(h)因在P的投票权而能够对P的管理施加重要影响。

(3)第(2)款中"该人"系指
(a)该人；
(b)该人的任何关联人；或
(c)该人及其任何关联人。
(4)"关联人"就持有某一企业(以下简称C)股份或有权行使或控制行使另一企业(以下简称D)投票权的人(以下简称H)而言，系指

(a)H的配偶；
(b)H的子女或继子女(如18岁以下)；
(c)H具有终身权益(在苏格兰为终身权益)的任何财产授予契约的受托人；

(d)H担任董事的企业；
(e)H的雇员或合伙人；
(f)如H为企业，则指
(i)H的董事；
(ii)H的子企业；
(iii)该子企业的董事或雇员；以及
(g)如H就购买、持有或处置C或D与其他任何人订有协议或安排，双方承诺共同行使与C或D相关的投票权，则指该其他人。

(5)第(4)款第(c)项中的"财产授予契约"包括任何财产信托持有(或受类似义务制约)的处置或安排。

(6) "Shares"—

(a) in relation to an undertaking with a share capital, means allotted shares;

(b) in relation to an undertaking with capital but no share capital, means rights to share in the capital of the undertaking;

(c) in relation to an undertaking without capital, means interests—

(i) conferring any right to share in the profits, or liability to contribute to the losses, of the undertaking; or

(ii) giving rise to an obligation to contribute to the debts or expenses of the undertaking in the event of a winding up.

(7) "Voting power", in relation to an undertaking which does not have general meetings at which matters are decided by the exercise of voting rights, means the right under the constitution of the undertaking to direct the overall policy of the undertaking or alter the terms of its constitution.

423 Manager.

(1) In this Act, except in relation to a unit trust scheme or a registered friendly society, "manager" means an employee who—

(a) under the immediate authority of his employer is responsible, either alone or jointly with one or more other persons, for the conduct of his employer's business; or

(b) under the immediate authority of his employer or of a person who is a manager by virtue of paragraph (a) exercises managerial functions or is responsible for maintaining accounts or other records of his employer.

(2) If the employer is not an individual, references in subsection (1) to the authority of the employer are references to the authority—

(a) in the case of a body corporate, of the directors;

(b) in the case of a partnership, of the partners; and

(c) in the case of an unincorporated association, of its officers or the members of its governing body.

(3) "Manager", in relation to a body corporate, means a person (other than an employee of the body) who is appointed by the body to manage any part of its business and includes an employee of the body corporate (other than the chief executive) who, under the immediate authority of a director or chief executive of the body corporate, exercises managerial functions or is responsible for maintaining accounts or other records of the body corporate.

424 Insurance.

(1) In this Act, references to—

(a) contracts of insurance,

(b) reinsurance,

(c) contracts of long-term insurance,

(6)“股份”

(a)就具有股份资本的企业而言,系指分配的股份;

(b)就具有资本但无股份资本的企业而言,系指分享该企业资本的权利;

(c)就无资本的企业而言,系指

(i)赋予分享企业利润权或分担企业损失义务的权益;或

(ii)产生在清算中分担企业债务或支出义务的权益。

(7)“投票权”就不召开大会行使表决权决定事项的企业而言,系指该企业组织制度规定的对该企业总体政策作出指示或变更组织制度条款的权利。

第423条　管理人

(1)在本法中,除非与单位信托计划或注册的互相保险协会相关,否则“管理人”系指有下列情况的雇员:

(a)根据雇主直接授权单独或与他人共同负责开展雇主的业务;或

(b)根据雇主或第(a)项规定的管理人直接授权行使管理职能或负责维护雇主的账面或其他记录。

(2)如雇主不是个人,则第(1)款中述及雇主的授权即为述及下列授权:

(a)就法人而言,为董事的授权;

(b)就合伙而言,为合伙人的授权;

(c)就非法人而言,为其高级职员或管理组织成员的授权。

(3)“管理人”就法人而言,系指该法人指定管理其任何部分业务的人(不包括该法人的雇员),并包括根据该法人董事或行政总裁直接授权行使管理职能或负责维护该法人账面或其他记录的雇员(不包括行政总裁)。

第424条　保险

(1)本法中述及下列事项:

(a)保险合同,

(b)再保险,

(c)长期保险合同,

(d) contracts of general insurance, are to be read with section 22 and Schedule 2.

(2) In this Act "policy" and "policyholder", in relation to a contract of insurance, have such meaning as the Treasury may by order specify.

(3) The law applicable to a contract of insurance, the effecting of which constitutes the carrying on of a regulated activity, is to be determined, if it is of a prescribed description, in accordance with regulations made by the Treasury.

Annotations:

Commencement Information

I131 S. 424 wholly in force at 1.12.2001; s. 424 not in force at Royal Assent see s. 431 (2); s. 424 (1)(2) in force and s. 424 (3) in force for certain purposes at 25.2.2001 by S.I. 2001/516, art. 2 (a)(b), Sch. Pts. 1, 2; s. 424 in force in so far as not already in force at 1.12.2001 by S.I. 2001/3538, art. 2(1)

425 Expressions relating to authorisation elsewhere in the single market.

(1) In this Act—

(a) "EEA authorisation", "EEA firm", "EEA right", "EEA State", "first life insurance directive", "first non-life insurance directive", "insurance directives", "investment services directive", "single market directives" and ("banking consolidation directive") have the meaning given in Schedule 3; and

(b) "home state regulator", in relation to an EEA firm, has the meaning given in Schedule 3.

(2) In this Act—

(a) "home state authorisation" has the meaning given in Schedule 4;

(b) "Treaty firm" has the meaning given in Schedule 4; and

(c) "home state regulator", in relation to a Treaty firm, has the meaning given in Schedule 4.

(d)一般保险合同,参照第22条和附录2解释。

(2)本法中"保单"和"投保人"就保险合同而言具有财政部颁布法令指定的含义。

(3)对于其订立构成开展受监管活动的保险合同,其适用的法律如属于规定类别,则应依照财政部制定的法规确定。

注释:

实施日期

I131　第424条于2001年12月1日全部生效;第424条在副署时尚未生效,见第431条第(2)款;第424条第(1)和第(2)款为特定目的于2001年2月25日依照制定法文件S.I. 2001/516第2条第(a)款、第(b)款,附录第一部分、第二部分生效;第424条如于2001年12月1日尚未生效,则依照制定法文件S.I.2001/3538第2条第(1)款生效。

第425条　与单一市场其他地方授权相关的表述[1]

(1)本法中

(a)"欧洲经济区授权"、"欧洲经济区企业"、"欧洲经济区权利"、"欧洲经济区国家"、"第一人寿保险指令"、"第一非人寿保险指令"、"保险指令"、"投资服务指令"、"单一市场指令"和("银行合并指令")具有附录3中的含义;

(b)"母国监管机关"就欧洲经济区企业而言,具有附录3中的含义。

(2)本法中

(a)"母国授权"具有附录4中的含义;

(b)"条约企业"具有附录4中的含义;

(c)"母国监管机关"就条约企业而言具有附录4中的含义。

1　本条依照《2010年金融服务法》附录2第一部分第32条修订。——译者注

PART XXX SUPPLEMENTAL

426 Consequential and supplementary provision.

(1) A Minister of the Crown may by order make such incidental, consequential, transitional or supplemental provision as he considers necessary or expedient for the general purposes, or any particular purpose, of this Act or in consequence of any provision made by or under this Act or for giving full effect to this Act or any such provision.

(2) An order under subsection (1) may, in particular, make provision—

(a) for enabling any person by whom any powers will become exercisable, on a date set by or under this Act, by virtue of any provision made by or under this Act to take before that date any steps which are necessary as a preliminary to the exercise of those powers;

(b) for applying (with or without modifications) or amending, repealing or revoking any provision of or made under an Act passed before this Act or in the same Session;

(c) dissolving any body corporate established by any Act passed, or instrument made, before the passing of this Act;

(d) for making savings, or additional savings, from the effect of any repeal or revocation made by or under this Act.

(3) Amendments made under this section are additional, and without prejudice, to those made by or under any other provision of this Act.

(4) No other provision of this Act restricts the powers conferred by this section.

Annotations:

Modifications etc. (not altering text)

C377 S. 426 modified (1.10.2001) by 2001 c. 16, s. 70, Sch. 2 Pt. 2 para. 26; S.I. 2001/3150, art. 2(d)

427 Transitional provisions.

(1) Subsections (2) and (3) apply to an order under section 426 which makes transitional provisions or savings.

(2) The order may, in particular—

(a) if it makes provision about the authorisation and permission of persons who before

第三十部分 补 充

第426条 后继规定和补充规定

(1)为了本法的一般性目的或任何特殊目的、由于本法或依照本法作出的规定，或者为了使本法或任何此等规定全部生效，内阁阁员可以颁布法令，作出其认为必需或适宜的附带规定、后继规定、过渡性规定或补充规定。

(2)第(1)款规定的法令可以特别规定

(a)使在本法设定或依照本法设定之日期可以行使根据本法或依照本法规定之任何权力的人能够在该日期之前为行使这些权力采取必要的准备步骤；

(b)适用(无论是否经过修订)或修改、废除或撤销在本法之前通过或与本法在同一次会议上通过之法律规定或依照该法制定的任何规定；

(c)撤销根据在本法通过之前通过之任何法律或签订之文书而设立的任何法人团体；

(d)在本法作出或依照本法作出之任何废除或撤销的效力中作出保留或附加保留。

(3)本条作出的修订是附加修订，不影响根据本法任何其他规定作出或其项下的规定。

(4)本法的任何其他规定不得限制本条所赋予的权力。

注释：

修改等(不涉及条文内容)
C377 第426条于2001年10月1日依照2001年本法第16条、第70条，附录2第二部分第26条；制定法文件S.I.2001/3150第2条第(d)项修订。

第427条 过渡性规定

(1)第(2)款和第(3)款适用于第426条规定的制定过渡性规定或保留的法令。

(2)该法令可以特别

(a)如果该法令对在生效之前有资格从事任何活动之人的授权和批准作出了规

commencement were entitled to carry on any activities, also include provision for such persons not to be treated as having any authorisation or permission (whether on an application to the Authority or otherwise);

(b) make provision enabling the Authority to require persons of such descriptions as it may direct to re-apply for permissions having effect by virtue of the order;

(c) make provision for the continuation as rules of such provisions (including primary and subordinate legislation) as may be designated in accordance with the order by the Authority, including provision for the modification by the Authority of provisions designated;

(d) make provision about the effect of requirements imposed, liabilities incurred and any other things done before commencement, including provision for and about investigations, penalties and the taking or continuing of any other action in respect of contraventions;

(e) make provision for the continuation of disciplinary and other proceedings begun before commencement, including provision about the decisions available to bodies before which such proceedings take place and the effect of their decisions;

(f) make provision as regards the Authority's obligation to maintain a record under section 347 as respects persons in relation to whom provision is made by the order.

(3) The order may—

(a) confer functions on the Treasury, the Secretary of State, the Authority, the scheme manager, the scheme operator, members of the panel established under paragraph 4 of Schedule 17, the Competition Commission or the Director General of Fair Trading;

(b) confer jurisdiction on the Tribunal;

(c) provide for fees to be charged in connection with the carrying out of functions conferred under the order;

(d) modify, exclude or apply (with or without modifications) any primary or subordinate legislation (including any provision of, or made under, this Act).

(4) In subsection (2) "commencement" means the commencement of such provisions of this Act as may be specified by the order.

428 Regulations and orders.

(1) Any power to make an order which is conferred on a Minister of the Crown by this Act and any power to make regulations which is conferred by this Act is exercisable by statutory instrument.

(2) The Lord Chancellor's power to make rules under section 132 is exercisable by statutory instrument.

(3) Any statutory instrument made under this Act may—

(a) contain such incidental, supplemental, consequential and transitional provision as the person making it considers appropriate; and

(b) make different provision for different cases.

定，则也包含不将此等人视为拥有任何授权或批准的规定（无论是向管理局提出申请的授权或批准还是其他授权或批准）；

（b）作出规定，使管理局能够要求该局指定类别的人重新申请因该法令而有效的批准；

（c）作出规定，使依照管理局发布的命令指定之规定（包括主体法和附属立法）延续成为规则，包括关于管理局对指定之规定进行修改的规定；

（d）对所提要求的效力、所产生的负债以及在生效之前所作之任何其他事项作出规定，包括针对或关于调查、罚款和针对违反行为采取或继续任何其他行动的规定；

（e）对在生效之前开始之惩戒程序和其他程序的延续作出规定，包括关于在这些程序开始后机构可以作出之决定及决定之效力的规定；

（f）关于管理局根据第347条针对与法令所作规定相关的人保存记录的义务作出规定。

（3）该法令可以

（a）赋予财政部、国务大臣、管理局、计划管理人、计划执行人、根据附录17第4条而设立的专家组成员、竞争委员会或公平交易总理事职能；

（b）赋予法院司法管辖权；

（c）规定与行使依照该法令赋予之职能将收取的费用；

（d）修改、排除或适用（无论是否经过修订）任何主立法或附属立法（包括本法规定或依照本法作出的任何规定）。

（4）第（2）款中的"生效"系指该法令中规定之本法条款的生效。

第428条　法规和法令

（1）本法赋予内阁阁员之颁布法令的任何权力以及本法赋予之制定法规的任何权力凭法定文书行使。

（2）司法大臣依照第132条制定规则的权力凭法定文书行使。

（3）依照本法制定的任何法定文书可以

（a）包含制定者认为适当的附带规定、补充规定、后继规定和过渡性规定；以及

（b）就不同的情况作出不同的规定。

429 Parliamentary control of statutory instruments.

(1) No order is to be made under—

(a) section 144(4), 192(b) or (e), 236(5), 404 or 419, or

(b) paragraph 1 of Schedule 8, unless a draft of the order has been laid before Parliament and approved by a resolution of each House.

(2) No regulations are to be made under section 262 unless a draft of the regulations has been laid before Parliament and approved by a resolution of each House.

(3) An order to which, if it is made, subsection (4) or (5) will apply is not to be made unless a draft of the order has been laid before Parliament and approved by a resolution of each House.

(4) This subsection applies to an order under section 21 if—

(a) it is the first order to be made, or to contain provisions made, under section 21(4);

(b) it varies an order made under section 21(4) so as to make section 21(1) apply in circumstances in which it did not previously apply;

(c) it is the first order to be made, or to contain provision made, under section 21(5);

(d) it varies a previous order made under section 21(5) so as to make section 21(1) apply in circumstances in which it did not, as a result of that previous order, apply;

(e) it is the first order to be made, or to contain provisions made, under section 21(9) or (10);

(f) it adds one or more activities to those that are controlled activities for the purposes of section 21; or

(g) it adds one or more investments to those which are controlled investments for the purposes of section 21.

(5) This subsection applies to an order under section 38 if—

(a) it is the first order to be made, or to contain provisions made, under that section; or

(b) it contains provisions restricting or removing an exemption provided by an earlier order made under that section.

(6) An order containing a provision to which, if the order is made, subsection (7) will apply is not to be made unless a draft of the order has been laid before Parliament and approved by a resolution of each House.

(7) This subsection applies to a provision contained in an order if—

(a) it is the first to be made in the exercise of the power conferred by subsection (1) of section 326 or it removes a body from those for the time being designated under that subsection; or

第429条　议会对法定文书的控制[1]

(1)不得依照下列条款发布任何命令：

(a)第144条第(4)款、第192条第(b)项或第(e)项、第236条第(5)款、第404条或第419条，或者

(b)附录8第1条，除非该命令草案已提交议会并经两议院决议批准。

(2)不得依照第262条制定法规，除非法规草案已提交议会并经两议院决议批准。

(3)如发布某项命令适用第(4)款或第(5)款规定，则除非该法令草案已提交议会并经两议院决议批准，否则不得发布。

(4)如有下列情况，则依照第21条颁布的法令适用本款规定：

(a)该法令是依照第21条第(4)款制定的或者包含该款项下规定的首个法令；

(b)该命令改变了依照第21条第(4)款制定的命令，以使第21条第(1)款在以前不适用的情况下适用；

(c)该命令是依照第21条第(5)款发布或者包含该款项下规定的首个命令；

(d)该命令改变了先前依照第21条第(5)款制定的法令，以使第21条第(1)款在以前不适用的情况下适用；

(e)该法令是依照第21条第(9)款或第(10)款制定的或者包含该款项下规定的首个法令；

(f)该法令向就第21条而言的受控活动中增添了一个或多个活动；或者

(g)该法令向就第21条而言的受控投资中增添了一项或多项投资。

(5)如有下列情况，则第38条规定的法令适用本款规定：

(a)该法令是依照该条制定的或者包含该条项下规定的首个法令；

(b)该法令包含限制或去除先前依照该条制定的法令所规定的豁免。

(6)如一项命令的发布适用第(7)款，则除非该命令草案已提交议会并经两议院决议批准，否则不得发布该命令。

(7)如有下列情况，则一项命令中包含的规定适用本款规定：

(a)该规定是在行使第326条第(1)款所赋予之权力时作出的首个规定，或者该规定暂时使某个机构被排除在依照该款所指定的机构之外；或

1　本条依照《2010年金融服务法》附录2第一部分第33条修订。——译者注

(b) it is the first to be made in the exercise of the power conferred by subsection (6) of section 327 or it adds a description of regulated activity or investment to those for the time being specified for the purposes of that subsection.

(8) Any other statutory instrument made under this Act, apart from one made under section 431(2) or to which paragraph 26 of Schedule 2 applies, shall be subject to annulment in pursuance of a resolution of either House of Parliament.

430 Extent.

(1) This Act, except Chapter Ⅳ of Part ⅩⅦ, extends to Northern Ireland.

(2) Except where Her Majesty by Order in Council provides otherwise, the extent of any amendment or repeal made by or under this Act is the same as the extent of the provision amended or repealed.

(3) Her Majesty may by Order in Council provide for any provision of or made under this Act relating to a matter which is the subject of other legislation which extends to any of the Channel Islands or the Isle of Man to extend there with such modifications (if any) as may be specified in the Order.

431 Commencement.

(1) The following provisions come into force on the passing of this Act—

(a) this section;

(b) sections 428, 430 and 433;

(c) paragraphs 1 and 2 of Schedule 21.

(2) The other provisions of this Act come into force on such day as the Treasury may by order appoint; and different days may be appointed for different purposes.

Annotations:

Subordinate Legislation Made

P1 S. 431(2) power partly exercised: 25.2.2001 appointed for specified provisions by S. I. 2001/516, art. 2 Sch.

S. 431 (2) power partly exercised: 30.4.2001 appointed for specified provisions by S.I. 2001/1282, art. 2

S. 431 (2) power partly exercised: 18.6.2001 appointed for specified provisions by S.I. 2001/1820, art. 2 Sch.

S. 431 (2) power partly exercised: 20.7.2001 and 3.9.2001 appointed for specified provisions by S.I. 2001/2632, art. 2 Sch.

S. 431(2) power partly exercised: 19.10.2001 appointed for specified provisions by S.I. 2001/3436, art. 2

S. 431(2) power partly exercised: different dates appointed for specified provisions by S.I. 2001/3538, art. 2

(b)该规定是在行使第327条第(6)款所赋予的权力时作出的首个规定,或者该规定暂时向就该款而言之指定类别的监管活动或投资增加了一项类别。

(8)除依照第431条第(2)款制定或适用附录2第26条外,依照本法制定的任何其他法定文书应可根据议会两院的决议废除。

第430条　适用范围

(1)本法除第四章第十七部分外适用范围扩及北爱尔兰。

(2)除非女王陛下的枢密院令另有规定,本法规定或者依照本法进行的任何修订或废除的适用范围与被修订或废除之规定的适用范围相同。

(3)如本法规定或依照本法制定的规定涉及的事项是适用范围扩及英属海峡群岛任何岛屿或马恩岛之其他法规的主题事项,则女王陛下可通过枢密院令规定该规定及其修订(如有)适用于上述岛屿。

第431条　生效日期

(1)下列规定在本法通过时生效:

(a)本条;

(b)第428条、第430条和第433条;

(c)附录21第1条、第2条。

(2)本法其他规定自财政部颁布法令指定之日起生效;且可以为了不同的目的指定不同的日期。

注释:

附属立法制定

P1　第431条第(2)款部分行使规定的权利:依照制定法文件S.I.2001/516第2条、附录指定2001年2月25日为特定条款生效日;

第431条第(2)款部分行使规定的权利:依照制定法文件S.I.2001/1282第2条指定2001年4月30日为特定条款生效日;

第431条第(2)款部分行使规定的权利:依照制定法文件S.I.2001/1820第2条、附录指定2001年6月18日为特定条款生效日;

第431条第(2)款部分行使规定的权利:依照制定法文件S.I.2001/2632第2条、附录指定2001年7月20日和2001年9月3日为特定条款生效日;

第431条第(2)款部分行使规定的权利:依照制定法文件S.I.2001/3436第2条指定2001年10月19日为特定条款生效日;

第431条第(2)款部分行使规定的权利:依照制定法文件S.I.2001/3538第2条指定不同日期为特定条款生效日。

432 Minor and consequential amendments, transitional provisions and repeals.

(1) Schedule 20 makes minor and consequential amendments.

(2) Schedule 21 makes transitional provisions.

(3) The enactments set out in Schedule 22 are repealed.

Annotations:

Commencement Information

I132 S. 432 wholly in force at 1.12.2001; s. 432 not in force at Royal Assent see s. 431(2); s. 432(3) in force for specified purposes at 30.4.2001 by S.I. 2001/1282, art. 2; s. 432(1) in force for specified purposes at 2.7.2001 by S.I. 2001/2364, art. 2(1)(b); s. 432(1) in force for specified purposes at 3.9.2001 by S.I. 2001/2632, art. 2 (2), Sch. Pt. 2; s. 432 in force in so far as not already in force at 1.12.2001 by S.I. 2001/3538, art. 2(1)

433 Short title.

This Act may be cited as the Financial Services and Markets Act 2000.

第432条　细微及后续修订、过渡性规定和废除

（1）附录20作出了细微和后续修订。
（2）附录21作出了过渡性规定。
（3）附录22中列出的成文法废除。

注释：

实施日期

I132　第432条于2001年12月1日全部生效；第432条在副署时尚未生效，见第431条第（2）款；第432条第（3）款为特定目的于2001年4月30日依照制定法文件S.I.2001/1282第2条生效；第432条第（1）款为特定目的于2001年7月2日依照制定法文件S.I.2001/2364第2条第（1）款第（b）项生效；第432条第（1）款为特定目的于2001年9月3日依照制定法文件S.I.2001/2632第2条第（2）款、附录第二部分生效；第432条如于2001年12月1日尚未生效，则依照制定法文件S.I.2001/3538第2条第（1）款生效。

第433条　简称

引用本法时可以简称为《2000年金融服务与市场法》。

SCHEDULES

SCHEDULE 1
THE FINANCIAL SERVICES AUTHORITY

Section 1

Annotations:

Modifications etc. (not altering text)

C378 Sch. 1 extended (17.8.2001) by S.I. 2001/2617, arts. 2(a), 4(3), 8, Sch. 2 para. 2

PART I GENERAL

Interpretation

1 (1) In this Schedule—

"the 1985 Act" means the [M103]Companies Act 1985;

"non-executive committee" means the committee maintained under paragraph 3;

"functions", in relation to the Authority, means functions conferred on the Authority by or under any provision of this Act.

(2) For the purposes of this Schedule, the following are the Authority's legislative functions—

(a) making rules;

(b) issuing codes under section 64 or 119;

(c) issuing statements under section 64, 69, 124 or 210;

(d) giving directions under section 316, 318 or 328;

(e) issuing general guidance (as defined by section 158(5)).

附 录

附录1[1] 管 理 局

第1条

注释：

修改等（不涉及条文内容）

C378 附录1于2001年8月17日依照制定法文件S.I. 2001/2617第2条第(a)款、第4条第(3)款、第8条，附录2第二部分扩大适用范围。

第一部分 总 则

释 义

第1条 (1)本附录中

“1985年法”系指[M103]《1985年公司法》；

“非执行委员会”系指依照本附录第3条保有的委员会；

与管理局相关的“职能”，系指由本法任何规定赋予或依照本法任何规定赋予的职能。

(2)就本附录而言，管理局的立法职能如下：

(a)制定规则；

(b)根据第64条或119条之规定颁布准则；

(c)根据第64条、第69条、第124条或第210条之规定发布声明；

(d)根据第316条、第318条或第328条之规定给予指示；

(e)颁布一般性指引(具有第158条第5款规定含义)。

1 本附录依照《2010年金融服务法》第2条第(6)款、附录2第一部分第34条修订。——译者注

Annotations:

Marginal Citations

M103 1985 c. 6.

Constitution

2 (1) The constitution of the Authority must continue to provide for the Authority to have—

(a) a chairman; and

(b) a governing body.

(2) The governing body must include the chairman.

(3) The chairman and other members of the governing body must be appointed, and be liable to removal from office, by the Treasury.

(4) The validity of any act of the Authority is not affected—

(a) by a vacancy in the office of chairman; or

(b) by a defect in the appointment of a person as a member of the governing body or as chairman.

Annotations:

Modifications etc. (not altering text)

C379 Sch. 1 Pt. I para. 2(3) modified (18.6.2001) by S.I. 2001/1821, arts. 1(1), 2(2)

Non-executive members of the governing body

3 (1) The Authority must secure—

(a) that the majority of the members of its governing body are non-executive members; and

(b) that a committee of its governing body, consisting solely of the nonexecutive members, is set up and maintained for the purposes of discharging the functions conferred on the committee by this Schedule.

(2) The members of the non-executive committee are to be appointed by the Authority.

(3) The non-executive committee is to have a chairman appointed by the Treasury from among its members.

Functions of the non-executive committee

4 (1) In this paragraph "the committee" means the non-executive committee.

(2) The non-executive functions are functions of the Authority but must be discharged

注释：

附注引文

M103 1985年第6章。

组 织 制 度

第2条 (1)管理局的机构设置必须为管理局持续委任

(a)一名主席；以及

(b)一个管理组织。

(2)主席必须为管理组织成员。

(3)主席和其他管理组织成员必须由财政部任命，并可被财政部免职。

(4)管理局任何行为的有效性不受下列情况影响：

(a)主席职位空缺；或

(b)对管理组织某成员或主席的委任有瑕疵。

注释：

修改等(不涉及条文内容)

C379 附录1第一部分第2条第(3)款于2001年6月18日依照制定法文件S.I. 2001/1821第1条第(1)款修订。

管理组织非执行成员

第3条 (1)管理局必须保证

(a)管理组织的大多数成员为非执行成员；且

(b)在管理组织中设立和保持一个仅由非执行成员组成的委员会，以履行本附录赋予该委员会的职能。

(2)非执行委员会成员由管理局任命。

(3)非执行委员会设一主席，由财政部在该委员会成员中委任。

非执行委员会职能

第4条 (1)本项中“委员会”系指非执行委员会。

(2)非执行职能为管理局的职能，但必须由委员会履行。

by the committee.

(3) The non-executive functions are—

(a) keeping under review the question whether the Authority is, in discharging its functions in accordance with decisions of its governing body, using its resources in the most efficient and economic way;

(b) keeping under review the question whether the Authority's internal financial controls secure the proper conduct of its financial affairs; and

(c) determining the remuneration of—

(i) the chairman of the Authority's governing body; and

(ii) the executive members of that body.

(4) The function mentioned in sub-paragraph(3)(b)and those mentioned in subparagraph (3)(c) may be discharged on behalf of the committee by a sub-committee.

(5) Any sub-committee of the committee—

(a) must have as its chairman the chairman of the committee; but

(b) may include persons other than members of the committee.

(6) The committee must prepare a report on the discharge of its functions for inclusion in the Authority's annual report to the Treasury under paragraph 10.

(7) The committee's report must relate to the same period as that covered by the Authority's report.

Arrangements for discharging functions

5 (1) The Authority may make arrangements for any of its functions to be discharged by a committee, sub-committee, officer or member of staff of the Authority.

(2) But in exercising its legislative functions, the Authority must act through its governing body.

(3) Sub-paragraph (1) does not apply to the non-executive functions.

Annotations:

Modifications etc. (not altering text)

C380 Sch. 1 Pt. I para. 5 extended (18.6.2001) by S.I. 2001/1821, arts. 1(1), 2(1)(b)(c)

Monitoring and enforcement

6 (1) The Authority must maintain arrangements designed to enable it to determine whether persons on whom requirements are imposed by or under this Act are complying with them.

(3)非执行职能为:

(a)随时考察管理局是否根据其管理组织的决定,以最有效和经济的方式运用其资源,履行其职能;

(b)随时考察管理局的内部资金管理是否能够确保其金融事务正常进行;且

(c)决定下列人员薪酬:

(i)管理局管理组织主席;及

(ii)管理组织执行成员。

(4)第(3)款第(b)项以及第(3)款第(c)项所述职能可由一个下属委员会代表委员会履行。

(5)委员会的任何下属委员会:

(a)其主席必须由委员会主席兼任;但

(b)可以包括委员会成员之外的人员。

(6)委员会必须制作一份关于履行职能情况的报告,列入根据本附录第10条管理局向财政部递交的年度报告中。

(7)委员会的报告在时间跨度上须与管理局的报告相一致。

履行职能的安排

第5条 (1)管理局可以制定安排,使其任何职能由委员会、下属委员会、高级职员或管理局工作人员履行。

(2)但管理局必须通过其管理组织履行立法职能。

(3)第(1)款不适用于非执行职能。

注释:

修改等(不涉及条文内容)

C380 附录1第一部分第5条于2001年6月18日依照制定法文件S.I. 2001/1821第1条第(1)款、第2条第(1)款第(b)项、第(c)项扩大适用范围。

监督和执法

第6条 (1)管理局必须保持某些安排,使该局能够确认是否应当依照本法履行某些要求的人正在遵守这些要求。

(2) Those arrangements may provide for functions to be performed on behalf of the Authority by any body or person who, in its opinion, is competent to perform them.

(3) The Authority must also maintain arrangements for enforcing the provisions of, or made under, this Act.

(4) Sub-paragraph (2) does not affect the Authority's duty under sub-paragraph (1).

Annotations:

Modifications etc. (not altering text)

C381 Sch. 1 para. 6 modified (18.7.2002 for certain purposes and 21.8.2002 otherwise) by The Electronic Commerce Directive (Financial Services and Markets) Regulations 2002 (S.I. 2002/1775), regs. 1, 12(2)

C382 Sch. 1 Pt. I para.6(2)applied(with modifications)(17.8.2001) by S.I. 2001/2617, arts. 2(a), 4(3), 8, Sch. 2 para. 3

Arrangements for the investigation of complaints

7 (1) The Authority must—

(a) make arrangements ("the complaints scheme") for the investigation of complaints arising in connection with the exercise of, or failure to exercise, any of its functions (other than its legislative functions); and

(b)appoint an independent person("the investigator") to be responsible for the conduct of investigations in accordance with the complaints scheme.

(2) The complaints scheme must be designed so that, as far as reasonably practicable, complaints are investigated quickly.

(3) The Treasury's approval is required for the appointment or dismissal of the investigator.

(4) The terms and conditions on which the investigator is appointed must be such as, in the opinion of the Authority, are reasonably designed to secure—

(a) that he will be free at all times to act independently of the Authority; and

(b) that complaints will be investigated under the complaints scheme without favouring the Authority.

(5) Before making the complaints scheme, the Authority must publish a draft of the proposed scheme in the way appearing to the Authority best calculated to bring it to the attention of the public.

(6) The draft must be accompanied by notice that representations about it may be made to the Authority within a specified time.

(7) Before making the proposed complaints scheme, the Authority must have regard to any representations made to it in accordance with sub-paragraph (6).

(2)上述安排可以规定职能由管理局认为有能力执行这些职能的任何团体和个人代表管理局执行。

(3)管理局也必须保持某些安排,使本法或依照本法制定的规定获得强制执行。

(4)第(2)款不影响第(1)款中规定的管理局职责。

注释:

修改等(不涉及条文内容)

C381　附录1第6条为特定目的于2002年7月18日,否则于2002年8月21日依照制定法文件《2002年电子商务指令条例》(金融服务与市场)(制定法文件S.I. 2002/1775)第1条、第12条第(2)款修订。

C382　附录1第一部分第6条第(2)款(已修订)2001年8月17日依照制定法文件S.I. 2001/2617第2条第(a)款、第4条第(3)款、第8条、附录2第3条适用。

申诉调查安排

第7条　(1)管理局必须

(a)为调查同履行、或未能履行其任何职能(非立法职能)相关而引发的申诉制定安排(以下简称申诉计划);且

(b)任命一个独立行为人(以下简称调查人)依照申诉计划负责执行相关调查。

(2)应当制定申诉计划,使申诉在合理可行的范围内尽快地获得调查。

(3)调查人的任免须经财政部批准。

(4)任命调查人的条款必须是管理局认为合理设计,确保下列各项的条款:

(a)调查人可随时独立于管理局行动;且

(b)依据申诉计划调查投诉事件,不倾向于管理局。

(5)在制定申诉计划前,管理局应当以其认为最能吸引公众注意的方式公布拟制定计划的草案。

(6)草案必须附有指定的时限内可就草案的制定向管理局进行陈述的通知。

(7)在制定拟制定的申诉计划前,管理局应当考虑任何依据第(6)款向管理局进行的陈述。

(8) If the Authority makes the proposed complaints scheme, it must publish an account, in general terms, of—

(a) the representations made to it in accordance with sub-paragraph (6); and

(b) its response to them.

(9) If the complaints scheme differs from the draft published under sub-paragraph (5) in a way which is, in the opinion of the Authority, significant the Authority must (in addition to complying with sub-paragraph (8)) publish details of the difference.

(10) The Authority must publish up-to-date details of the complaints scheme including, in particular, details of—

(a) the provision made under paragraph 8(5); and

(b) the powers which the investigator has to investigate a complaint.

(11) Those details must be published in the way appearing to the Authority to be best calculated to bring them to the attention of the public.

(12) The Authority must, without delay, give the Treasury a copy of any details published by it under this paragraph.

(13) The Authority may charge a reasonable fee for providing a person with a copy of—

(a) a draft published under sub-paragraph (5);

(b) details published under sub-paragraph (10).

(14) Sub-paragraphs(5) to(9) and(13)(a) also apply to a proposal to alter or replace the complaints scheme.

Annotations:

Modifications etc. (not altering text)

C383 Sch. 1 Pt. I para. 7(1)(a) restricted(19.7.2001) by S.I.2001/2326, arts. 1(1)(a), 18(3)

C384 Sch. 1 Pt. I para.7(2)-(14) applied (19.7.2001) by S.I. 2001/2326, arts. 1(1)(a), 18(2)(a)

Commencement Information

I133 Sch. 1 Pt. I para. 7 wholly in force at 3.9.2001; Sch. 1 Pt. I para. 7 not in force at Royal Assent see s. 431(2); Sch. 1 Pt. I para. 7 in force for specified purposes at 19.7.2001 by S.I. 2001/2364, art.2(2)(with art. 3); Sch. 1 Pt. I para.7 in force in so far as not already in force at 3.9.2001 by S.I. 2001/2632, art. 2(2), Sch. Pt. 2

Investigation of complaints

8 (1) The Authority is not obliged to investigate a complaint in accordance with the

(8)如管理局已制定拟制定的申诉计划,则必须公布概述下列事项的报告:

(a)依据第(6)款向管理局作出的陈述;及

(b)管理局对上述陈述的答复。

(9)如管理局认为,申诉计划与依据本附录第(5)款公布的草案之间存在明显差异,则管理局[除遵守第(8)款规定之外]应当公布差异的详情。

(10)管理局应当公布最新申诉计划的详情,特别是包括下列内容:

(a)依照第8条第(5)款制定的规定;及

(b)调查人为对申诉进行调查所具有的权力。

(11)管理局应当以其认为最便于公众了解的方式公布申诉计划的详情。

(12)管理局应当毫不延迟地就其依据本条公布的计划的详情向财政部送交一份副本。

(13)管理局可以因向某人提供下列文件而收取合理费用:

(a)依照第(5)款公布的草案;

(b)依照第(10)款公布的申诉计划详情。

(14)第(5)款至第(9)款及第(13)款第(a)项也适用于关于变更和替代申诉计划的提案。

注释:

修改等(不涉及条文内容)

C383 附录1第一部分第7条第(1)款第(a)项于2001年7月19日受制定法文件 S.I. 2001/2326第1条第(1)款第(a)项、第18条第(3)款限制。

C384 附录1第一部分第7条第(2)款至第(14)款于2001年7月19日依照制定法文件 S.I. 2001/2326,第1条第(1)款第(a)项、第18条第(2)款第(a)项适用。

实施日期

I133 附录1第一部分第7条于2001年9月3日全部生效;附录1第一部分第7条在副署时尚未生效,见第431条第(2)款;附录1第一部分第7条为特定目的于2001年7月19日依照制定法文件 S.I. 2001/2364第2条第(2)款(与第3条)生效;附录1第一部分第7条如于2001年9月3日尚未生效,则依照制定法文件 S.I. 2001/2632第2条第(2)款,附录第二部分生效。

投诉调查

第8条 (1)对包含在申诉计划之中,但管理局合理地认为以其他方式解决(如将

complaints scheme which it reasonably considers would be more appropriately dealt with in another way (for example by referring the matter to the Tribunal or by the institution of other legal proceedings).

(2) The complaints scheme must provide—

(a)for reference to the investigator of any complaint which the Authority is investigating; and

(b) for him—

(i) to have the means to conduct a full investigation of the complaint;

(ii) to report on the result of his investigation to the Authority and the complainant; and

(iii) to be able to publish his report (or any part of it) if he considers that it (or the part) ought to be brought to the attention of the public.

(3) If the Authority has decided not to investigate a complaint, it must notify the investigator.

(4) If the investigator considers that a complaint of which he has been notified under sub-paragraph (3) ought to be investigated,he may proceed as if the complaint had been referred to him under the complaints scheme.

(5) The complaints scheme must confer on the investigator the power to recommend, if he thinks it appropriate, that the Authority—

(a) makes a compensatory payment to the complainant,

(b) remedies the matter complained of, or takes both of those steps.

(6) The complaints scheme must require the Authority, in a casewhere the investigator—

(a) has reported that a complaint is well-founded, or

(b) has criticised the Authority in his report,

to inform the investigator and the complainant of the steps which it proposes to take in response to the report.

(7) The investigator may require the Authority to publish the whole or a specified part of the response.

(8) The investigator may appoint a person to conduct the investigation on his behalf but subject to his direction.

(9) Neither an officer nor an employee of the Authority may be appointed under subparagraph (8).

(10) Sub-paragraph (2) is not to be taken as preventing the Authority from making arrangements for the initial investigation of a complaint to be conducted by the Authority.

该事项诉至裁判所或依照其他法律程序惯例)更为适当的投诉,管理局无义务调查。

(2)申诉计划应当

(a)向调查人提供管理局正在进行的任何申诉调查作为参考;且

(b)对调查人

(i)规定其拥有执行完整调查的手段;

(ii)规定其向管理局和申诉人报告调查结果;以及

(iii)规定如调查人认为调查结果(或部分调查结果)应受到公众的关注,则可以公布调查结果(或部分调查结果)。

(3)如管理局已决定不调查某项申诉,则应当通知调查人。

(4)如调查人认为依据第(3)款通知其知悉的某项申诉应被调查,则可以继续调查,等同于该申诉已依据申诉计划指定其调查。

(5)申诉计划应当赋予调查人在其认为适当时向管理局提出下列建议的权力:

(a)向申诉人支付补偿金,

(b)申诉事项的救济办法,

或同时采取以上措施。

(6)调查人有下列情况时:

(a)报告申诉有充分根据,或

(b)在报告中指责管理局,

则申诉计划必须要求管理局向调查人及申诉人通告管理局对于调查报告将采取的应对措施。

(7)调查人可以要求管理局发布完整的或特定部分的应对措施。

(8)调查人可以指定某人代表其执行调查,但必须服从调查人的指示。

(9)任何管理局官员或工作人员不得接受依据第(8)款的指定。

(10)第(2)款不得视为防止管理局制定安排,使管理局对申诉进行初始阶段的调查。

Annotations:

Modifications etc. (not altering text)

C385 Sch. 1 Pt. I para. 8 power to apply conferred (19.7.2001) by S.I. 2001/2326, arts. 1(1)(a), 18(2)(b)

Commencement Information

I134 Sch. 1 Pt. I para. 8 wholly in force at 3.9.2001; Sch. 1 Pt. I para. 8 not in force at Royal Assent see s. 431(2); Sch. 1 Pt. I para. 8 in force for specified purposes at 19.7.2001 by S.I. 2001/2364, art. 2(2)(with art. 3); Sch. 1 Pt. I para. 8 in force in so far as not already in force at 3.9.2001 by S.I. 2001/2632, art. 2(2), Sch. Pt. 2

Records

9 The Authority must maintain satisfactory arrangements for—

(a) recording decisions made in the exercise of its functions; and

(b) the safe-keeping of those records which it considers ought to be preserved.

Annual report

10 (1) At least once a year the Authority must make a report to the Treasury on—

(a) the discharge of its functions;

(b) the extent to which, in its opinion, the regulatory objectives have been met;

(c) its consideration of the matters mentioned in section 2(3); and

(d) such other matters as the Treasury may from time to time direct.

(2) The report must be accompanied by—

(a) the report prepared by the non-executive committee under paragraph 4(6); and

(b) such other reports or information, prepared by such persons, as the Treasury may from time to time direct.

(3) The Treasury must lay before Parliament a copy of each report received by them under this paragraph.

(4) The Treasury may—

(a) require the Authority to comply with any provisions of the 1985 Act about accounts and their audit which would not otherwise apply to it; or

(b) direct that any such provision of that Act is to apply to the Authority with such modifications as are specified in the direction.

(5) Compliance with any requirement imposed under sub-paragraph (4)(a) or (b) is enforceable by injunction or, in Scotland, an order under section 45(b) of the [M104] Court of

注释：

修改等(不涉及条文内容)

C385　附录1第一部分第8项于2001年7月19日依照制定法文件S.I. 2001/2326，第1条第(1)款第(a)项、第18条第(2)款第(b)项被授予适用权利。

实施日期

I134　附录1第一部分第8条于2001年9月3日全部生效；附录1第一部分第8条在副署时尚未生效，见第431条第(2)款；附录1第一部分第8条为特定目的于2001年7月19日依照制定法文件S.I. 2001/2364第2条第(2)款(与第3条)生效；附录1第一部分第8条如于2001年9月3日尚未生效，则依照制定法文件S.I. 2001/2632第2条第(2)款、附录第二部分生效。

记　录

第9条　管理局应当为下列目的保留完备的安排：

(a)记录其在履行职能的过程中出台的决定；及

(b)妥善保管其认为需要保留的记录。

年度报告

第10条　(1)每年管理局至少应当就下列事项向财政部报告一次：

(a)其职能的履行；

(b)其认为监管目标的实现程度；

(c)第2条第(3)款所述事项的审议；及

(d)财政部不时指示的其他事项。

(2)报告应当附有：

(a)非执行委员会依据第4条第(6)款规定提交的报告；及

(b)由上述相关人员提交的经财政部不时指示的其他报告或信息。

(3)财政部必须将其依照本条规定收到的每份报告的副本提交至议会。

(4)财政部可以

(a)要求管理局遵守1985年法中任何原本不适用于管理局的账目及审计相关规定；

(b)指示该法中的任何条款经该指示中指定的修改后适用于管理局。

(5)第(4)款第(a)项或第(b)项提及的任何规定可通过强制令，或在苏格兰根据

M104《1988年高等民事法院法》第45条第(b)款发布的法令，强制执行。

Session Act 1988.

(6) Proceedings under sub-paragraph (5) may be brought only by the Treasury.

Annotations:

Marginal Citations

M104 1988 c. 36.

Annual public meeting

11 (1) Not later than three months after making a report under paragraph 10, the Authority must hold a public meeting ("the annual meeting") for the purposes of enabling that report to be considered.

(2) The Authority must organise the annual meeting so as to allow—

(a) a general discussion of the contents of the report which is being considered; and

(b) a reasonable opportunity for those attending the meeting to put questions to the Authority about the way in which it discharged, or failed to discharge, its functions during the period to which the report relates.

(3) But otherwise the annual meeting is to be organised and conducted in such a way as the Authority considers appropriate.

(4) The Authority must give reasonable notice of its annual meeting.

(5) That notice must—

(a) give details of the time and place at which the meeting is to be held;

(b) set out the proposed agenda for the meeting;

(c) indicate the proposed duration of the meeting;

(d) give details of the Authority's arrangements for enabling persons to attend; and

(e) be published by the Authority in the way appearing to it to be most suitable for bringing the notice to the attention of the public.

(6) If the Authority proposes to alter any of the arrangements which have been included in the notice given under sub-paragraph (4) it must—

(a) give reasonable notice of the alteration; and

(b) publish that notice in the way appearing to the Authority to be best calculated to bring it to the attention of the public.

Report of annual meeting

12 Not later than one month after its annual meeting, the Authority must publish a report of the proceedings of the meeting.

(6)只能由财政部依据第(5)款提出诉讼。

注释:

附注引文

M104　1988年第36章。

年度公开会议

第11条　(1)依照第10条发布报告之后的3个月内,管理局应举行公开会议(以下简称年会)审议年报。

(2)管理局应组织年会,允许

(a)对即将审议的年报内容进行一般性讨论;及

(b)为会议参加者提供一次合理的机会,查问报告期内管理局履行其职能,或未履行其职能的方式。

(3)但除此之外,年会应当按管理局认为适当的方式组织和实施。

(4)管理局应当对年会事项给予合理的通知。

(5)通知应当

(a)公布年会召开的具体时间和地点;

(b)提交会议日程预案;

(c)指明预计的会期;

(d)发布管理局对与会人员所做安排的详情;及

(e)以管理局认为最适于吸引公众注意的方式发布。

(6)如果当局拟对依照第(4)款发出的通知中包含的安排作出任何更改,则必须

(a)发出合理的更改通知;且

(b)以管理局认为最适于吸引公众注意的方式公布。

年会报告

第12条　管理局必须在年会结束后1个月内公布会议记录报告。

PART Ⅱ STATUS

13 In relation to any of its functions—

(a) the Authority is not to be regarded as acting on behalf of the Crown; and

(b) its members, officers and staff are not to be regarded as Crown servants.

Exemption from requirement of "limited" in Authority's name

14 The Authority is to continue to be exempt from the requirements of the 1985 Act relating to the use of "limited" as part of its name.

15 If the Secretary of State is satisfied that any action taken by the Authority makes it inappropriate for the exemption given by paragraph 14 to continue he may, after consulting the Treasury, give a direction removing it.

PART Ⅲ PENALTIES AND FEES

Penalties

16 (1) In determining its policy with respect to the amounts of penalties to be imposed by it under this Act, the Authority must take no account of the expenses which it incurs, or expects to incur, in discharging its functions.

(2) The Authority must prepare and operate a scheme for ensuring that the amounts paid to the Authority by way of penalties imposed under this Act are applied for the benefit of authorised persons.

(3) The scheme may, in particular, make different provision with respect to different classes of authorised person.

(4) Up to date details of the scheme must be set out in a document ("the scheme details").

(5) The scheme details must be published by the Authority in the way appearing to it to be best calculated to bring them to the attention of the public.

(6) Before making the scheme, the Authority must publish a draft of theproposed scheme in the way appearing to the Authority to be best calculated to bring it to the attention of the public.

(7) The draft must be accompanied by notice that representations about the proposals may be made to the Authority within a specified time.

(8) Before making the scheme, the Authority must have regard to any representations made to it in accordance with sub-paragraph (7).

(9) If the Authority makes the proposed scheme, it must publish an account, in general

第二部分 地 位

第13条 关于其任何职能

(a)管理局不代表内阁;

(b)其成员、高级职员、工作人员不视为内阁服务人员。

管理局称谓免于遵守使用“有限”的要求

第14条 管理局对1985年法关于在其称谓中使用“有限”字样的要求享有豁免。

第15条 如国务大臣确信管理局的任何行为使其不适合继续享有第14条赋予的豁免,则同财政部协商后,可以命令取消豁免。

第三部分 罚款及收费

罚 款

第16条 (1)就依照本法执行罚款的金额制定政策时,管理局不得将其履行职能过程中产生的,或可能产生的费用计算在内。

(2)管理局应当制定并执行一项计划,确保依据本法上缴给管理局的罚款被用于获授权人的权益。

(3)计划可以特别根据不同类型的获授权人分别制定不同条款。

(4)计划的最新详情应制成一个文件(以下简称计划详情)。

(5)管理局应当以其认为最能吸引公众注意的方式公布该计划详情。

(6)在制定计划之前,管理局应当以其认为最能吸引公众注意的方式公布计划草案。

(7)草案应当附有指定时限内可就草案的制定向管理局进行陈述的通知。

(8)在制定计划之前,管理局应当考虑任何依据第(7)款向管理局进行的陈述。

(9)如管理局已制定拟制定的计划,则应当公布概述下列内容的报告:

terms, of—

(a) the representations made to it in accordance with sub-paragraph (7); and

(b) its response to them.

(10) If the scheme differs from the draft published under sub-paragraph(6) in a way which is, in the opinion of the Authority, significant the Authority must (in addition to complying with sub-paragraph (9)) publish details of the difference.

(11) The Authority must, without delay, give the Treasury a copy of any scheme details published by it.

(12) The Authority may charge a reasonable fee for providing a person with a copy of—

(a) a draft published under sub-paragraph (6);

(b) scheme details.

(13) Sub-paragraphs (6) to (10) and (12)(a) also apply to a proposal to alter or replace the complaints scheme.

Fees

17 (1) The Authority may make rules providing for the payment to it of such fees, in connection with the discharge of any of its functions under or as a result of this Act, as it considers will (taking account of its expected income from fees and charges provided for by any other provision of this Act) enable it—

(a) to meet expenses incurred in carrying out its functions or for any incidental purpose;

(b) to repay the principal of, and pay any interest on, any money which it has borrowed and which has been used for the purpose of meeting expenses incurred in relation to its assumption of functions under this Act or the [M105] Bank of England Act 1998; and

(c) to maintain adequate reserves.

(2) In fixing the amount of any fee which is to be payable to the Authority, no account is to be taken of any sums which the Authority receives, or expects to receive, by way of penalties imposed by it under this Act.

(3) Sub-paragraph(1)(b) applies whether expenses were incurred before or after the coming into force of this Act or the [M106]Bank of England Act 1998.

(4) Any fee which is owed to the Authority under any provision made by or under this Act may be recovered as a debt due to the Authority.

Annotations:

Modifications etc. (not altering text)

C386 Sch. 1 Pt. Ⅲ para. 17 modified (1.12.2001) by S.I. 2001/3650, arts. 1(a), 25(1)(2) (a)依据第(6)款向管理局进行的陈述;及

(b)管理局对上述陈述的反应。

(10)如管理局认为,计划与依据第(6)款公布的草案之间存在明显差异,则管理局[除遵守第(9)款规定之外]应当公布差异的详情。

(11)管理局应当毫不延迟地就其公布的任何计划详情向财政部备案。

(12)管理局可以为向某人提供下列文件而收取合理的费用:

(a)依据第(6)款发布的草案;

(b)计划详情。

(13)第(6)款至第(10)款及第(12)款第(a)项的内容也适用于关于变更和替代申诉计划的提案。

费　用

第17条　(1)管理局可以针对其依据本法或由于本法的原因履行职能导致收取的费用制定相关规则,只要其认为该规则可(考虑到其预期的,由本法任何其他条款导致的费用和收费带来的收入)使其

(a)支付由其履行职能或任何附带目的的需要产生的开支;

(b)偿还其借贷的任何款项的本金或利息,该款项用于支付与管理局依照本法或[M105]《1998年联合王国银行法》承担的职能相关而产生的开支;及

(c)保持足够的储备。

(2)在修正管理局应收账款数量时,管理局依据本法收取的、或预计收取的罚款不应计入该总量。

(3)第(1)款第(b)项适用于本法或[M106]《1998年联合王国银行法》开始生效前或生效后产生的开支。

(4)依照本法任何条款欠管理局的费用可以作为管理局的应收债务加以追偿。

注释:

修改等(不涉及条文内容)

C386　附录1第三部分第17条于2001年12月1日依照制定法文件S.I. 2001/3650第1条第(a)款、第25条第(1)款、第(2)款修订。

C387 Sch. 1 Pt. Ⅲ para. 17(1) modified (17.8.2001) by S.I. 2001/2617, arts. 2(a), 4(3), 8, Sch. 2 paras. 9, 10

Marginal Citations

M105 1998 c. 11.

M106 1998 c. 11.

Services for which fees may not be charged

18 The power conferred by paragraph 17 may not be used to require—

(a) a fee to be paid in respect of the discharge of any of the Authority's functions under paragraphs 13, 14, 19 or 20 of Schedule 3; or

(b) a fee to be paid by any person whose application for approval under section 59 has been granted.

PART Ⅳ MISCELLANEOUS

Exemption from liability in damages

19 (1) Neither the Authority nor any person who is, or is acting as, a member, officer or member of staff of the Authority is to be liable in damages for anything done or omitted in the discharge, or purported discharge, of the Authority's functions.

(2) Neither the investigator appointed under paragraph 7 nor a person appointed to conduct an investigation on his behalf under paragraph 8(8) is to be liable in damages for anything done or omitted in the discharge, or purported discharge, of his functions in relation to the investigation of a complaint.

(3) Neither sub-paragraph (1) nor sub-paragraph (2) applies—

(a) if the act or omission is shown to have been in bad faith; or

(b) so as to prevent an award of damages made in respect of an act or omission on the ground that the act or omission was unlawful as a result of section 6(1) of the [M107] Human Rights Act 1998.

Annotations:

Modifications etc. (not altering text)

C388 Sch. 1 Pt. Ⅳ para. 19 extended (1.12.2001) by S.I. 2001/3650, arts. 1(a), 24(6)

C389 Sch.1 para.19(1) applied(1.12.2001) by S.I.1995/1537,reg. 23(1) (as amended (1.12.2001) by S.I. 2001/3649, arts. 1, 509(b)(i))

C387 附录1第三部分第17条第(1)款于2001年8月17日依照制定法文件S.I.2001/2617第2条第(a)款、第4条第(3)款、第8条,附录2第9条、第10条修订。

附注引文

M105 1998年第11章。

M106 1998年第11章。

不应收取费用的服务

第18条 第17条赋予的权力不可用于要求

(a)就管理局依照附录三第13条、第14条、第19条或第20条履行的职能收费;或

(b)向其依据第59条提交的认可申请被批准的人收费。

第四部分 其 他

损害赔偿的豁免

第19条 (1)管理局或任何其成员、高级职员或工作人员,或充当上述角色的人,履行或视为履行管理局职能时,对其任何作为或不作为不承担损害赔偿责任。

(2)任何依据第7条委任的调查人或依据第8条第(8)款委任的代表调查人执行调查的人,履行或视为履行申诉调查相关的职能时,对其任何作为或不作为不承担损害赔偿责任。

(3)如有下列情况,则不适用第(1)款和第(2)款规定:

(a)当其作为或不作为被视为不诚信时;

(b)为了防止因[M107]《1998年人权法》第6条第(1)款规定的不合法作为或不作为而作出损害赔偿判决。

注释:

修改等(不涉及条文内容)

C388 附录1第四部分第19条于2001年12月1日依照制定法文件S.I. 2001/3650第1条第(a)款、第24条第(6)款扩大适用范围。

C389 附录1第19条第(1)款于2001年12月1日依照制定法文件S.I. 1995/1537第23条第(1)款[于2001年12月1日依照制定法文件S.I.2001/3649第1条、第509条第(b)款第(i)项修订]适用。

Marginal Citations

M107 1998 c. 42.

Disqualification for membership of House of Commons

20 In Part Ⅲ of Schedule 1 to the [M108]House of Commons Disqualification Act 1975 (disqualifying offices), insert at the appropriate place—

"Member of the governing body of the Financial Services Authority".

Annotations:

Marginal Citations

M108 1975 c. 24.

Disqualification for membership of Northern Ireland Assembly

21 In Part Ⅲ of Schedule 1 to the [M109]Northern Ireland Assembly Disqualification Act 1975 (disqualifying offices), insert at the appropriate place—

"Member of the governing body of the Financial Services Authority".

Annotations:

Marginal Citations

M109 1975 c. 25.

SCHEDULE 2 REGULATED ACTIVITIES

Section 22(2)

Annotations:

Modifications etc. (not altering text)

C390 Sch. 2 applied (1.9.2002) by 1974 c. 39, s. 16(6E)(c) (as inserted (1.9.2002) by S.I. 2001/544, arts. 2(1)(2)(b), 90(2)); S.I. 2001/3538, art. 2(1)

附注引文

M107　1998年第42 章。

下议院成员身份的剥夺

第20条　在[M108]《1975年下议院身份剥夺法》附录1第三部分适当的位置，插入：

"金融服务管理局管理组织成员"。

注释：

附注引文

M108　1975年第24章。

北爱尔兰议会成员身份的剥夺

第21条　[M109]《1975年议会法》(北爱尔兰)附录1第三部分(官员免职)适当的位置，插入：

"金融服务管理局管理组织成员"。

注释：

附注引文

M109　1975年第25章。

附录2　受监管活动

第22条第(2)款

注释：

修改等(不涉及条文内容)

C390　附录2于2002年9月1日依照1974 年第39章第16条第(6E)款第(c)项[于2002年9月1日依照制定法文件 S.I. 2001/544第2条第(1)款、第(2)款第(b)项、第90条第(2)款插入]；制定法文件S.I. 2001/3538 第2条第(1)款适用。

PART I REGULATED ACTIVITIES

General

1 The matters with respect to which provision may be made under section 22(1) in respect of activities include, in particular, those described in general terms in this Part of this Schedule.

Dealing in investments

2 (1) Buying, selling, subscribing for or underwriting investments or offering or agreeing to do so, either as a principal or as an agent.

(2) In the case of an investment which is a contract of insurance, that includes carrying out the contract.

Arranging deals in investments

3 Making, or offering or agreeing to make—

(a) arrangements with a view to another person buying, selling, subscribing for or underwriting a particular investment;

(b) arrangements with a view to a person who participates in the arrangements buying, selling, subscribing for or underwriting investments.

Deposit taking

4 Accepting deposits.

Safekeeping and administration of assets

5 (1) Safeguarding and administering assets belonging to another which consist of or include investments or offering or agreeing to do so.

(2) Arranging for the safeguarding and administration of assets belonging to another, or offering or agreeing to do so.

Managing investments

6 Managing, or offering or agreeing to manage, assets belonging to another person where—

(a) the assets consist of or include investments; or

(b) the arrangements for their management are such that the assets may consist of or include investments at the discretion of the person managing or offering or agreeing to manage

第一部分　受监管活动

总　　则

第1条　第22条第(1)款涉及行为的规定所调整的事项特别包含本附录本部分规定的事项。

投资中的交易

第2条　(1)作为委托人或代理人进行买入、卖出、认购、包销、出价或达成协议。

(2)投资为保险合同时,包括该合同的执行。

投资中的安排交易

第3条　作出、提供或同意作出

(a)关于同他人进行买入、卖出、认购或包销某一特定投资的安排;

(b)关于同该项安排的参与者进行买入、卖出、认购获包销某一投资的安排。

提取保证金

第4条　接受保证金。

资产的保护和管理

第5条　(1)保护和管理、提供保护和管理或同意保护和管理属于他人的资产,且该资产由投资组成或包含投资。

(2)安排保护和管理、提供安排保护和管理或同意安排保护和管理他人的资产。

管理投资

第6条　管理、提供或同意管理他人的资产,当

(a)资产由投资组成或包含投资;或

(b)管理、提供或同意管理资产方应当在谨慎的原则下安排管理那些可能由投资组成或包含投资的资产。

them.

Investment advice

7 Giving or offering or agreeing to give advice to persons on—

(a) buying, selling, subscribing for or underwriting an investment; or

(b) exercising any right conferred by an investment to acquire, dispose of, underwrite or convert an investment.

Establishing collective investment schemes

8 Establishing, operating or winding up a collective investment scheme, including acting as—

(a) trustee of a unit trust scheme;

(b) depositary of a collective investment scheme other than a unit trust scheme; or

(c) sole director of a body incorporated by virtue of regulations under section 262.

Using computer-based systems for giving investment instructions

9 (1) Sending on behalf of another person instructions relating to an investment by means of a computer-based system which enables investments to be transferred without a written instrument.

(2) Offering or agreeing to send such instructions by such means on behalf of another person.

(3) Causing such instructions to be sent by such means on behalf of another person.

(4) Offering or agreeing to cause such instructions to be sent by such means on behalf of another person.

PART II INVESTMENTS

General

10 The matters with respect to which provision may be made under section 22(1) in respect of investments include, in particular, those described in general terms in this Part of this Schedule.

Securities

11 (1) Shares or stock in the share capital of a company.

(2) "Company" includes—

(a) any body corporate (wherever incorporated), and

(b) any unincorporated body constituted under the law of a country or territory outside

投资建议

第7条 给予、提供或同意就下列事项给予某人建议:

(a)买入、卖出、认购或包销一项投资;或

(b)行使由某项投资赋予的任何权利,用以获得、处置、包销或变更该投资。

建立集合投资计划

第8条 建立、执行或清算一个集合投资计划,包括作为:

(a)单位信托计划的受托人;

(b)单位信托计划受托人以外的集合投资计划的受托人;或

(c)依照第262条制定的法规规定的法人独立董事。

运用计算机系统发出投资指令

第9条 (1)代表某人凭借计算机系统发送关于某项投资的指令,该系统可以使交易在无纸质指令文件的情况下进行。

(2)提供或同意代表某人以这种方式发送指令。

(3)导致代表某人以这种方式发送指令。

(4)提供或同意造成代表某人以这种方式发送指令。

第二部分 投 资

总 则

第10条 第22条第(1)款涉及投资的规定所调整的事项特别包含本附录本部分规定的事项。

证 券

第11条 (1)股份或公司股本凭证。

(2)"公司"包括:

(a)任何法人(无论何处的有限责任公司),及

(b)联合王国本土外依据某国家或地区法律组成的非法人,

the United Kingdom,

other than an open-ended investment company.

Instruments creating or acknowledging indebtedness

12 Any of the following—

(a) debentures;

(b) debenture stock;

(c) loan stock;

(d) bonds;

(e) certificates of deposit;

(f) any other instruments creating or acknowledging a present or future indebtedness.

Government and public securities

13 (1) Loan stock, bonds and other instruments—

(a) creating or acknowledging indebtedness; and

(b) issued by or on behalf of a government, local authority or public authority.

(2) "Government, local authority or public authority" means—

(a) the government of the United Kingdom, of Northern Ireland, or of any country or territory outside the United Kingdom;

(b) a local authority in the United Kingdom or elsewhere;

(c) any international organisation the members of which include the United Kingdom or another member State.

Instruments giving entitlement to investments

14 (1) Warrants or other instruments entitling the holder to subscribe for any investment.

(2) It is immaterial whether the investment is in existence or identifiable.

Certificates representing securities

15 Certificates or other instruments which confer contractual or property rights—

(a) in respect of any investment held by someone other than the person on whom the rights are conferred by the certificate or other instrument; and

(b) the transfer of which may be effected without requiring the consent of that person.

Units in collective investment schemes

16 (1) Shares in or securities of an open-ended investment company.

(2) Any right to participate in a collective investment scheme.

开放式投资公司除外。

创设和承认债务的工具

第12条 任何下列工具：

(a)公司债券；

(b)债券凭证；

(c)借贷凭证；

(d)债券；

(e)存单；

(f)任何其他可以创设和承认现在或未来债务的工具。

政府或公共证券

第13条 (1)贷款凭证、债券及其他工具

(a)创设或承认债务；及

(b)由政府、地方当局或公共机关发行或委托发行。

(2)"政府、地方当局或公共机关"系指

(a)联合王国、北爱尔兰或其他国家和地区的政府；

(b)联合王国或其他地方的地方机关；

(c)任何包括联合王国或其他成员国的国际组织。

赋予投资权的文书

第14条 (1)许可证或其他可以使持有者拥有投资权的文书；

(2)该投资是否已发生或可确认并不重要。

代表证券的证书

第15条 赋予契约或财产权的证书或其他文书

(a)涉及任何投资的证书或文书由他人持有而不是权利人本人(权利由这些证书或文书赋予)。

(b)(证书和其他文书)转让的发生无须经权利人同意。

集合投资计划中的单位

第16条 (1)开放式投资公司的股份或证券。

(2)参与集合投资计划的任何权利。

Options

17 Options to acquire or dispose of property.

Futures

18 Rights under a contract for the sale of a commodity or property of any other description under which delivery is to be made at a future date.

Contracts for differences

19 Rights under—

(a) a contract for differences; or

(b) any other contract the purpose or pretended purpose of which is to secure a profit or avoid a loss by reference to fluctuations in—

(i) the value or price of property of any description; or

(ii) an index or other factor designated for that purpose in the contract.

Contracts of insurance

20 Rights under a contract of insurance, including rights under contracts falling within head C of Schedule 2 to the [M110]Friendly Societies Act 1992.

Annotations:

Marginal Citations

M110 1992 c. 40.

Participation in Lloyd's syndicates

21 (1) The underwriting capacity of a Lloyd's syndicate.

(2) A person's membership (or prospective membership) of a Lloyd's syndicate.

Deposits

22 Rights under any contract under which a sum of money (whether or not denominated in a currency) is paid on terms under which it will be repaid, with or without interest or a premium, and either on demand or at a time or in circumstances agreed by or on behalf of the person making the payment and the person receiving it.

Loans secured on land

23 (1) Rights under any contract under which—

(a) one person provides another with credit; and

选 择 权

第17条 获得或处置资产的选择权。

期 货

第18条 依据合同在未来某一时间交割的出售某种商品或其他形式的资产的权利。

差价合同

第19条 下列合同规定的权利：

(a)差价合同;或

(b)任何其他意图或试图参考下列波动确保盈利或避免损失的合同：

(i)任何形式资产的价值或价格的波动；

(ii)合同中为上述目的设计的指数或要素的波动。

保险合同

第20条 保险合同规定的权利，包括属于[M110]《1992年互相保险协会法》附录2标题c范围内的合同规定的权利。

注释：

附注引文
M110 1992年第40章。

参与劳合社辛迪加

第21条 (1)劳合社辛迪加的承销能力。

(2)劳合社辛迪加的成员身份(或预期的成员身份)。

保 证 金

第22条 在规定支付一定数额货币(无论是否以某一货币为面值)的合同中规定的权利，且该合同规定该支付以附加或不附加利息或额外费用的返还为条件，并规定应要求或在支付方和收款方商定或代表其商定的时间或情形中支付。

土地抵押贷款

第23条 (1)下列任何合同规定的权利：

(a)一人向他人提供贷款;且

(b) the obligation of the borrower to repay is secured on land.

(2) "Credit" includes any cash loan or other financial accommodation.

(3) "Cash" includes money in any form.

Rights in investments

24 Any right or interest in anything which is an investment as a result of any other provision made under section 22(1).

PART Ⅲ SUPPLEMENTAL PROVISIONS

The order-making power

25 (1) An order under section 22(1) may—

(a) provide for exemptions;

(b) confer powers on the Treasury or the Authority;

(c) authorise the making of regulations or other instruments by the Treasury for purposes of, or connected with, any relevant provision;

(d) authorise the making of rules or other instruments by the Authority for purposes of, or connected with, any relevant provision;

(e) make provision in respect of any information or document which, in the opinion of the Treasury or the Authority, is relevant for purposes of, or connected with, any relevant provision;

(f) make such consequential, transitional or supplemental provision as the Treasury consider appropriate for purposes of, or connected with, any relevant provision.

(2) Provision made as a result of sub-paragraph (1)(f) may amend any primary or subordinate legislation, including any provision of, or made under, this Act.

(3) "Relevant provision" means any provision—

(a) of section 22 or this Schedule; or

(b) made under that section or this Schedule.

Parliamentary control

26 (1) This paragraph applies to the first order made under section 22(1).

(2) This paragraph also applies to any subsequent order made under section 22(1) which contains a statement by the Treasury that, in their opinion, the effect (or one of the effects) of the proposed order would be that an activity which is not a regulated activity would become a regulated activity.

(3) An order to which this paragraph applies—

(a) must be laid before Parliament after being made; and

(b)借款人的还款义务用土地抵押的合同。

(2)"贷款"包括现金或其他财务融通。

(3)"现金"包括任何形式的货币。

投资中的权利

第24条 依照第22条第(1)款制定的任何规则调整的投资事项所产生的权利和利益。

第三部分 补充规定

颁布法令的权力

第25条 (1)第22条第(1)款规定的法令可以

(a)规定豁免;

(b)赋予财政部或管理局权力;

(c)批准财政部依据或围绕相关条款制定各种规则或其他文书;

(d)批准管理局依据或围绕相关条款制定各种规则或其他文书;

(e)就财政部或管理局认为与任何相关条款有关的信息或文件制定规则。

(f)制定财政部认为对于相关条款的目标或(条款)本身合理的最终条款、过渡性条款,或附加条款。

(2)依据第(1)款第(f)项制定的条款可以修正任何主要立法或附属立法,包括本法任何规定或依照本法制定的任何规定。

(3)"相关条款"系指

(a)第22条或本附录中的条款;或

(b)依据上述法规或附录制定的条款。

议会控制

第26条 (1)本条适用于依照第22条第(1)款颁布的第一项法令。

(2)本条也适用于依据第22条第(1)款制定的任何后续法令,内容包含财政部的声明,说明其认为该后续法令的效果(或部分效果)使非受控行为成为受控行为。

(3)适用本条规定的法令

(a)在制定后应当提交议会;且

(b) ceases to have effect at the end of the relevant period unless before the end of that period the order is approved by a resolution of each House of Parliament (but without that affecting anything done under the order or the power to make a new order).

(4) "Relevant period"means a period of twenty-eight days beginning with the day on which the order is made.

(5) In calculating the relevant period no account is to be taken of any time during which Parliament is dissolved or prorogued or during which both Houses are adjourned for more than four days.

Interpretation

27 (1) In this Schedule—

"buying" includes acquiring for valuable consideration;

"offering" includes inviting to treat;

"property" includes currency of the United Kingdom or anyother country or territory; and

"selling" includes disposing for valuable consideration.

(2) In sub-paragraph (1)"disposing" includes—

(a) in the case of an investment consisting of rights under a contract—

(i) surrendering, assigning or converting those rights; or

(ii) assuming the corresponding liabilities under the contract;

(b) in the case of an investment consisting of rights under other arrangements, assuming the corresponding liabilities under the contract or arrangements;

(c) in the case of any other investment, issuing or creating the investment or granting the rights or interests of which it consists.

(3) In this Schedule references to an instrument include references to any record (whether or not in the form of a document).

SCHEDULE 3 EEA PASSPORT RIGHTS

Sections 31(1)(b) and 37

Annotations:

Modifications etc. (not altering text)

C391 Sch. 3 extended (with modifications) (1.12.2001) by S.I. 2001/2636, arts. 1(2)(b), 25-27; S.I. 2001/3538, art. 2(1) (b)除非在相关期限届满前，获得议会两院决议的批准，否则该法令在期限届满后失去效力(但不影响依据命令已经发生的事项或制定新命令的权力)。

(4)“相关期限”系指法令制定之日起28日之内。

(5)议会解散或休会期间或议会各院休会超过4日以上时，不计入相关期限。

释　　义

第27条　(1)本附录中

(a)“买入”包括取得有值对价；

(b)“提供”包括邀请协商；

(c)“资产”包括联合王国或其他国家和地区的货币；且

(d)“卖出”包括处置有值对价。

(2)第(1)款中“处置”包括：

(a)投资合同中存在权力

(i)放弃、分配或转移这些权力；

(ii)根据合同承担相应义务。

(b)投资中依据其他安排存在权力，根据合同或安排承担相应义务。

(c)任何其他投资中，发起或创设投资或赋予投资中存在的权利或利益。

(3)本附录中，文书的参考目录包括任何记录的参考目录(无论是否为文件形式)。

附录3　欧洲经济区护照持有人的权利

第31条第(1)款第(b)项和第37条

注释：

修改等(不涉及条文内容)

C391　附录3(已修订)于2001年12月1日依照制定法文件S.I. 2001/2636第1条第(2)款第(b)项、第25条至第27条；制定法文件S.I.2001/3538第2条第(1)款扩大适用范围。

Sch. 3 extended(with modifications)(Gibraltar)(5.10.2001 for specified purposes otherwise 1.12.2001) by S.I. 2001/3084, arts. 1(1), 2–4; S.I. 2001/3538, art. 2(1)

Sch. 3 modified (1.12.2001) by S.I. 2001/3592, arts. 1(2), 114(3)(b), 128(3)(b) (with art. 23(2))

PART I DEFINED TERMS

The single market directives

1 "The single market directives" means—

[F17 (a) the banking consolidation directive;]

(c) the insurance directives; and

(d) the investment services directive.

Annotations:

Amendments (Textual)

F17 Sch. 3 Pt. I para.1(a) substituted(22.11.2000) for para.1(a)(b) by S.I. 2000/2952, Reg. 8(5)(a)

Commencement Information

I135 Sch. 3 Pt. I para. 1 wholly in force at 1.12.2001; Sch. 3 Pt. I para. 1 not in force at Royal Assent see s. 431(2); Sch. 3 Pt. I para. 1 in force for certain purposes at 25.2.2001 by S. I.2001/516,art.2(b)(c),Sch.Pts.2,3;Sch. 3 Pt. I para.1 in force for specified purposes at 18.6. 2001 by S.I. 2001/1820, art. 2, Sch.;

Sch. 3 Pt. I para. 1 in force in so far as not already in force at 1.12.2001 by S.I. 2001/3538, art. 2(1)

The banking co-ordination directives

[F18 2 "The banking consolidation directive" means Directive 2000/12/EC of the European Parliament and of the Council of 20 March 2000 relating to the taking up and pursuit of the business of credit institutions;]

Annotations:

Amendments (Textual)

F18 Sch. 3 Pt. I para. 2 substituted (22.11.2000) by S.I. 2000/2952, reg. 8(5)(b)

附录3(已修订)(直布罗陀)于2001年12月1日依照制定法文件S.I.2001/3084，第1条第(1)款、第2条至第4条；制定法文件S.I. 2001/3538第2条第(1)款扩大适用范围；

附录3于2001年12月1日依照制定法文件S.I. 2001/3592第1条第(2)款、第114条第(3)款第(b)项、第128条第(3)款第(b)项[与第23条第(2)款]修订。

第一部分 概念定义

单一市场指令

第1条 “单一市场指令”系指

[F17(a)银行合并指令]；

(c)保险业指令；及

(d)投资服务指令。

注释：

修正(文本)

F17 附录3第一部分第1条第(a)款于2000年11月22日依照制定法文件S.I. 2000/2952第8条第(5)款第(a)项代替第1条第(a)款、第(b)款。

实施日期

I135 附录3第一部分第1条于2001年12月1日全部生效；附录3第一部分第1条在副署时尚未生效，见第431条第(2)款；附录3第一部分第1条为特定目的于2001年2月25日依照制定法文件S.I.2001/516第2条第(b)款、第(c)款，附录第二部分、第三部分生效；附录3第一部分第1条为特定目的于2001年6月18日依照制定法文件S.I. 2001/1820第2条、附录生效；附录3第一部分第1条如于2001年12月1日尚未生效，则依照制定法文件S.I. 2001/3538 第2条第(1)款生效。

银行协调指令

[F18第2条“银行合并指令”，系指关于信用机构从事和追求商业机会的欧洲议会2000/12/EC号指令及欧洲理事会2000年3月20日指令。]

注释：

修正(文本)

F18 附录3第一部分第2条于2000年11月22日依照制定法文件S.I. 2000/2952第8条第(5)款第(b)项替代。

Commencement Information

I136 Sch. 3 Pt. I para. 2 wholly in force at 1.12.2001; Sch. 3 Pt. I para. 2 not in force at Royal Assent see s. 431(2); Sch. 3 Pt. I para. 2 in force for certain purposes at 25.2.2001 by S. I. 2001/516, art. 2 (b)(c), Sch. Pts. 2, 3; Sch. 3 Pt. I para. 2 in force for specified purposes at 18.6.2001 by S.I. 2001/1820, art. 2, Sch.; Sch. 3 Pt. I para. 2 in force in so far as not already in force at 1.12.2001 by S.I. 2001/3538, art. 2(1)

The insurance directives

3 (1) "The insurance directives" means the first, second and third non-life insurance directives and the first, second and third life insurance directives.

(2) "First non-life insurance directive" means the Council Directive of 24 July 1973 on the co-ordination of laws, regulations and administrative provisions relating to the taking up and pursuit of the business of direct insurance other than life assurance (No. 73/239/EEC).

(3) "Second non-life insurance directive" means the Council Directive of 22 June 1988 on the co-ordination of laws, etc, and laying down provisions to facilitate the effective exercise of freedom to provide services and amending Directive 73/239/ EEC (No. 88/357/EEC).

(4) "Third non-life insurance directive" means the Council Directive of 18 June 1992 on the co-ordination of laws, etc, and amending Directives 73/239/EEC and 88/357/ EEC (No. 92/49/EEC).

(5) "First life insurance directive" means the Council Directive of 5 March 1979 on the co-ordination of laws, regulations and administrative provisions relating to the taking up and pursuit of the business of direct life assurance (No. 79/267/EEC).

(6) "Second life insurance directive" means the Council Directive of 8 November 1990 on the co-ordination of laws, etc, and laying down provisions to facilitate the effective exercise of freedom to provide services and amending Directive 79/267/ EEC (No. 90/619/EEC).

(7) "Third life insurance directive" means the Council Directive of 10 November 1992 on the co-ordination of laws, etc, and amending Directives 79/267/EEC and 90/619/ EEC (No. 92/96/EEC).

Annotations:

Commencement Information

I137 Sch. 3 Pt. I para. 3 wholly in force at 1.12.2001; Sch. 3 Pt. I para. 3 not in force at Royal Assent see s. 431(2); Sch. 3 Pt. I para. 3 in force for certain purposes at 25.2.2001 by S. I. 2001/516, art. 2(b)(c), Sch. Pts.2,3; Sch.3 Pt.I para. 3 in force for specified purposes at 18.6.2001 by S.I. 2001/1820, art. 2, Sch.; Sch. 3 Pt. I para. 3 in force in so far as not already in force at 1.12.2001 by S.I. 2001/3538, art. 2(1)

实施日期

I136 附录3第一部分第2条于2001年12月1日全部生效；附录3第一部分第2条在副署时尚未生效，见第431条第(2)款；附录3第一部分第2条为特定目的于2001年2月25日依照制定法文件S.I. 2001/516第2条第(b)款、第(c)款，附录第二部分、第三部分生效；附录3第一部分第2条为特定目的于2001年6月18日依照制定法文件 S.I. 2001/1820第2条、附录生效；附录3第一部分第2条如于2001年12月1日尚未生效，则依照制定法文件S.I. 2001/3538，第2条第(1)款生效。

保险业指令

第3条 (1)“保险业指令”，系指第一、第二、第三非人寿保险指令及第一、第二、第三人寿保险指令。

(2)“第一非人寿保险指令”，系指理事会1973年7月24日令(No. 73/239/EEC)，协调关于从事直接保险而非人寿保险业务方面的法律、法规及行政条例。

(3)“第二非人寿保险指令”，系指理事会1988年6月22日令(No. 88/357/EEC)，协调法律文献等，并制定便于有效自由提供服务的规定，并修订1973年令。

(4)“第三非人寿保险指令”，系指理事会1992年6月18日令(No. 92/49/EEC)，协调法律文献等，并修订1973年令、1988年令。

(5)“第一人寿保险指令”，系指理事会1979年3月5日令(No. 79/267/EEC)，协调关于从事的直接人寿保险业务方面的法律、法规及行政条例。

(6)“第二人寿保险指令”，系指理事会1990年11月8日令(No. 90/619/EEC)，协调法律文献等、制定便于有效地自由提供服务方面的规定，并修订1979年令。

(7)“第三人寿保险指令”，系指1992年11月10日关于协调各项法律等修订79/267/EEC另指令和第90/619/EEC指令的理事会指令(No.92/96/EEC)。

注释：

实施日期

I137 附录3第一部分第3条于2001年12月1日全部生效；附录3第一部分第3条在副署时尚未生效，见第431条第(2)款；附录3第一部分第3条为特定目的于2001年2月25日依照制定法文件S.I. 2001/516第2条第(b)款、第(c)款，附录第二部分、第三部分生效；附录3第一部分第3条为特定目的于2001年6月18日依照制定法文件S.I. 2001/1820第2条、附录生效；附录3第一部分第3条如于2001年12月1日尚未生效，则依照制定法文件S.I. 2001/3538第2条第(1)款生效。

The investment services directive

4 "The investment services directive" means the Council Directive of 10 May 1993 on investment services in the securities field (No. 93/22/EEC).

Annotations:

Commencement Information

I138 Sch. 3 Pt. I para. 4 wholly in force at 1.12.2001; Sch. 3 Pt. I para. 4 not in force at Royal Assent see s. 431(2); Sch. 3 Pt. I para. 4 in force for certain purposes at 25.2.2001 by S. I. 2001/516, art. 2(b)(c), Sch. Pts. 2, 3; Sch. 3 Pt. I para. 4 in force for specified purposes at 18.6.2001 by S.I. 2001/1820, art. 2, Sch.; Sch. 3 Pt. I para. 4 in force in so far as not already in force at 1.12.2001 by S.I. 2001/3538, art. 2(1)

EEA firm

5 "EEA firm" means any of the following if it does not have its head office in the United Kingdom—

(a) an investment firm (as defined in Article 1.2 of the investment services directive) which is authorised (within the meaning of Article 3) by its home state regulator;

[F19 (b) a credit institution (as defined in Article 1 of the banking consolidation directive) which is authorised (within the meaning of Article 1) by its home state regulator;]

[F20 (c) a financial institution (as defined in Article 1 of the banking consolidation directive) which is a subsidiary of the kind mentioned in Article 19 and which fulfils the conditions in Articles 18 and 19; or]

(d) an undertaking pursuing the activity of direct insurance (within the meaning of Article 1 of the first life insurance directive or of the first non-life insurance directive) which has received authorisation under Article 6 from its home state regulator.

Annotations:

Amendments (Textual)

F19 Sch. 3 Pt. I para. 5(b) substituted (22.11.2000) by S.I. 2000/2952, reg. 8(5)(c)(i)

F20 Sch. 3 Pt. I para. 5(c) substituted (22.11.2000) by S.I. 2000/2952, reg. 8(5)(c)(ii)

投资服务指令

第4条 “投资服务指令”，系指理事会1993年5月10日令，调整有价证券领域的投资服务。

注释：

实施日期

I138 附录3 第一部分第4条于2001年12月1日全部生效；附录3 第一部分第4条在副署时尚未生效，见第431条第(2)款；附录3第一部分第4条为特定目的于2001年2月25日依照制定法文件S.I.2001/516第2条第(b)款、第(c)款，附录第二部分、第三部分生效；附录3第一部分第4条为特定目的于2001年6月18日通过制定法文件 S.I.2001/1820第2条、附录生效；附录3第一部分第4条如于2001年12月1日尚未生效，则依照制定法文件S.I. 2001/3538 第2条第(1)款生效。

欧洲经济区企业

第5条 “欧洲经济区企业”，系指下列总部不在联合王国境内的公司：

(a)由其所在国国管理者批准(如投资服务指令第3条之解释)的投资公司(如投资服务指令第1条、第2条之规定)。

[F19(b)由其所在国监管机关批准(如银行合并指令第1条之解释)的信用机构(如银行合并指令第1条之规定)。]

[F20(c)金融机构(如银行合并指令第1条之规定)，其系第19条所述机构的附属机构且满足第18条、第19条规定的条件；或]

(d)依据第6条已由其所在国监管机关批准的，从事直接保险(如第一人寿保险指令或第一非人寿保险指令第1条之解释)方面业务的企业。

注释：

修正(文本)

F19 附录3第一部分第5条第(b)项于2000年11月22日依照制定法文件S.I. 2000/2952，第8条第(5)款第(c)项(i)目代替。

F20 附录3第一部分第5条第(c)项于2000年11月22日制定法文件S.I. 2000/2952第8条第(5)款第(c)项(ii)目代替。

Commencement Information

I139 Sch. 3 Pt. I para. 5 wholly in force at 1.12.2001; Sch. 3 Pt. I para. 5 not in force at Royal Assent see s. 431(2); Sch. 3 Pt. I para. 5 in force for certain purposes at 25.2.2001 by S. I. 2001/516, art. 2(b)(c), Sch. Pts. 2, 3; Sch. 3 Pt. I para. 5 in force for specified purposes at 18.6.2001 by S.I. 2001/1820, art. 2 Sch.; Sch. 3 Pt. I para. 5 in force in so far as not already in force at 1.12.2001 by S.I. 2001/3538, art. 2(1)

EEA authorisation

6 "EEA authorisation" means authorisation granted to an EEA firm by its home state regulator for the purpose of the relevant single market directive.

Annotations:

Commencement Information

I140 Sch. 3 Pt. I para. 6 wholly in force at 1.12.2001; Sch. 3 Pt. I para. 6 not in force at Royal Assent see s. 431(2); Sch. 3 Pt. I para. 6 in force for certain purposes at 25.2.2001 by S. I. 2001/516, art. 2(b)(c), Sch. Pts. 2, 3; Sch. 3 Pt. I para. 6 in force for specified purposes at 18.6.2001 by S.I. 2001/1820, art. 2, Sch.;Sch. 3 Pt. I para. 6 in force in so far as not already in force at 1.12.2001 by S.I. 2001/3538, art. 2(1)

EEA right

7 "EEA right" means the entitlement of a person to establish a branch, or provide services, in an EEA State other than that in which he has his head office—

(a) in accordance with the Treaty as applied in the EEA; and

(b) subject to the conditions of the relevant single market directive.

Annotations:

Commencement Information

I141 Sch. 3 Pt. I para. 7 wholly in force at 1.12.2001; Sch. 3 Pt. I para. 7 not in force at Royal Assent see s. 431(2); Sch. 3 Pt. I para. 7 in force for certain purposes at 25.2.2001 by S. I. 2001/516, art. 2(b)(c), Sch. Pts. 2, 3; Sch. 3 Pt. I para. 7 in force for specified purposes at 18.6.2001 by S.I. 2001/1820, art. 2, Sch.; Sch. 3 Pt. I para. 7 in force in so far as not already in force at 1.12.2001 by S.I. 2001/3538, art. 2(1)

实施日期

I139　附录3第一部分第5条于2001年12月1日全部生效；附录3第一部分第5条在副署时尚未生效，见第431条第(2)款；附录3第一部分第5条为特定目的于2001年2月25日依照制定法文件S.I. 2001/516第2条第(b)款、第(c)款，附录第二部分、第三部分生效；附录3第一部分第5条为特定目的于2001年6月18日依照制定法文件 S.I. 2001/1820第2条、附录生效；附录3第一部分第5条如于2001年12月1日尚未生效，则依照制定法文件S.I. 2001/3538第2条第(1)款生效。

欧洲经济区的授权

第6条　“欧洲经济区授权”，系指因相关的单一市场指令起见，欧洲经济区公司母国监管机关给予该公司的授权。

注释：

实施日期

I140　附录3第一部分第6条于2001年12月1日全部生效；附录3第一部分第6条在副署时尚未生效，见第431条第(2)款；附录3第一部分第6条为特定目的于2001年2月25日依照制定法文件 S.I. 2001/516第2条第(b)款、第(c)款,附录第二部分、第三部分生效；附录3第一部分第6条为特定目的于2001年6月18日依照制定法文件S.I. 2001/1820第2条、附录生效；附录3第一部分第6条如于2001年12月1日尚未生效，则依照制定法文件 S.I. 2001/3538第2条第(1)款生效。

欧洲经济区权利

第7条　“欧洲经济区权利”，系指某人在其总部所在国以外的欧洲经济区国家内建立分支机构或提供服务的权利

(a)依照欧洲经济区已施行的协议；且

(b)受相关单一市场指令的条款制约。

注释：

实施日期

I141　附录3第一部分第7条于2001年12月1日全部生效；附录3第一部分第7条在副署时尚未生效，见第431条第(2)款；附录3第一部分第7条为特定目的于2001年2月25日依照制定法文件S.I. 2001/516第2条第(b)款、第(c)款，附录第二部分、第三部分生效；附录3第一部分第7条为特定目的于2001年6月18日依照制定法文件 S.I. 2001/1820第2条、附录生效；附录3第一部分第7条如于2001年12月1日尚未生效，则依照制定法文件 S.I. 2001/3538第2条第(1)款生效。

EEA State

8 "EEA State" means a State which is a contracting party to the agreement on the European Economic Area signed at Oporto on 2 May 1992 as it has effect for the time being.

Annotations:

Commencement Information

I142 Sch. 3 Pt. I para. 8 wholly in force at 1.12.2001; Sch. 3 Pt. I para. 8 not in force at Royal Assent see s. 431(2); Sch. 3 Pt. I para. 8 in force for certain purposes at 25.2.2001 by S. I. 2001/516, art. 2(b)(c), Sch. Pts. 2, 3; Sch. 3 Pt. I para. 8 in force for specified purposes at 18.6.2001 by S.I. 2001/1820, art. 2, Sch.; Sch. 3 Pt. I para. 8 in force in so far as not already in force at 1.12.2001 by S.I. 2001/3538, art. 2(1)

Home state regulator

9 "Home state regulator" means the competent authority (within the meaning of the relevant single market directive) of an EEA State (other than the United Kingdom) in relation to the EEA firm concerned.

Annotations:

Commencement Information

I143 Sch. 3 Pt. I para. 9 wholly in force at 1.12.2001; Sch. 3 Pt. I para. 9 not in force at Royal Assent see s. 431(2); Sch. 3 Pt. I para. 9 in force for certain purposes at 25.2.2001 by S. I. 2001/516, art. 2(b)(c), Sch. Pts. 2, 3; Sch. 3 Pt. I para. 9 in force for specified purposes at 18.6.2001 by S.I. 2001/1820, art. 2, Sch.; Sch. 3 Pt. I para. 9 in force in so far as not already in force at 1.12.2001 by S.I. 2001/3538, art. 2(1)

UK firm

10 "UK firm" means a person whose head office is in the UK and who has an EEA right to carry on activity in an EEA State other than the United Kingdom.

Annotations:

Commencement Information

I144 Sch. 3 Pt. I para. 10 wholly in force at 1.12.2001; Sch. 3 Pt. I para. 10 not in force at Royal Assent see s. 431(2); Sch. 3 Pt. I para. 10 in force for certain purposes at 25.2.2001 by S.I. 2001/516, art. 2(b)(c), Sch. Pts. 2, 3 Sch. 3 Pt. I para. 10 in force for specified purposes at 18.6.2001 by S.I. 2001/1820, art. 2 Sch.; Sch. 3 para. 10 in force in so far as not

欧洲经济区国家

第8条 “欧洲经济区国家”,系指目前具有效力的1992年5月2日波尔图欧洲经济区协定的缔约国。

注释:

实施日期

I142 附录3第一部分第8条于2001年12月1日全部生效;附录3第一部分第8条在副署时尚未生效,见第431条第(2)款;附录3第一部分第8条为特定目的于2001年2月25日依照制定法文件S.I. 2001/516第2条第(b)项、第(c)项,附录第二部分、第三部分生效;附录3第一部分第8条为特定目的于2001年6月18日 依照制定法文件 S.I. 2001/1820 第2条、附录生效;附录3第一部分第8条如于2001年12月1日尚未生效,则依照制定法文件S.I. 2001/3538第2条第(1)款生效。

母国监管机关

第9条 “母国监管机关”,系指与欧洲经济区企业相关的欧洲经济区国家(除联合王国外)的主管机关(如单一市场指令的相关解释)。

注释:

实施日期

I143 附录3第一部分第9条于2001年12月1日全部生效;附录3第一部分第9条在副署时尚未生效,见第431条第(2)款;附录3第一部分第9条为特定目的于2001年2月25日通过制定法文件S.I. 2001/516第2条第(b)款、第(c)款,附录第二部分、第三部分生效;附录3第一部分第9条为特定目的于2001年6月18日 通过制定法文件S.I. 2001/1820第2条、附录生效;附录3第一部分第9条如于2001年12月1日尚未生效,则通过制定法文件 S.I. 2001/3538第2条第(1)款生效。

联合王国企业

第10条 “联合王国企业”,系指总部在联合王国境内,并具有在联合王国以外的欧洲经济区国家开展活动的欧洲经济区权利的企业。

注释:

实施日期

I144 附录3第一部分第10条于2001年12月1日全部生效;附录3第一部分第10条在副署时尚未生效,见第431条(2)款;附录3第一部分第10条为特定目的于2001年2月25日通过制定法文件 S.I. 2001/516第2条第(b)款、第(c)款,附录第二部分、第三部分生效;附录3第一部分第10条为特定目的于2001年6月18日通过制定法文件S.I.

already in force at 1.12.2001 by S.I. 2001/3538, art. 2(1)

Host state regulator

11 "Host state regulator" means the competent authority (within the meaning of the relevant single market directive) of an EEA State (other than the United Kingdom) in relation to a UK firm's exercise of EEA rights there.

Annotations:

Commencement Information

I145 Sch. 3 Pt. I para. 11 wholly in force at 1.12.2001; Sch. 3 Pt. I para. 11 not in force at Royal Assent see s. 431(2); Sch. 3 Pt. I para. 11 in force for certain purposes (25.2.2001) by S.I. 2001/516, art. 2 Sch. Pts. 2, 3; Sch. 3 Pt. I para. 11 in force for specified purposes (18.6.2001) by S.I. 2001/1820, art. 2 Sch.; Sch. 3 Pt. I para. 11 in force in so far as not already in force at 1.12.2001 by S.I. 2001/3538, art. 2(1)

PART II EXERCISE OF PASSPORT RIGHTS BY EEA FIRMS

Firms qualifying for authorisation

12 (1) Once an EEA firm which is seeking to establish a branch in the United Kingdom in exercise of an EEA right satisfies the establishment conditions, it qualifies for authorisation.

(2) Once an EEA firm which is seeking to provide services in the United Kingdom in exercise of an EEA right satisfies the service conditions, it qualifies for authorisation.

Annotations:

Commencement Information

I146 Sch. 3 Pt. II para. 12 wholly in force at 1.12.2001; Sch. 3 Pt. II para. 12 not in force at Royal Assent see s. 431(2); Sch. 3 Pt. II para. 12 in force for certain purposes at 25.2.2001 by S.I. 2001/516, art. 2(b)(c), Sch. Pts. 2, 3; Sch. 3 Pt. II para. 12 in force for specified purposes at 18.6.2001 by S.I. 2001/1820, art. 2, Sch.; Sch. 3 Pt. II para. 12 in force in so far as not already in force at 1.12.2001 by S.I. 2001/3538, art. 2(1)

2001/1820第2条、附录生效;附录3第10条如于2001年12月1日尚未生效,则依照制定法文件S.I. 2001/3538,第2条第(1)款生效。

所在国监管机关

第11条 “所在国监管机关”,系指联合王国企业行使欧洲经济区权利的欧洲经济区国家(除联合王国外)的主管机关(如单一市场指令的相关解释)。

注释:

实施日期

I145 附录3第一部分第11条于2001年12月1日全部生效;附录3第一部分第11条在副署时尚未生效,见第431条第(2)款;附录3第一部分第11条为特定目的于2001年2月25日依照制定法文件S.I. 2001/516 第2条,附录第二部分、第三部分生效;附录3第一部分第11条为特定目的于2001年6月18日依照制定法文件S.I. 2001/1820第2条、附录生效;附录3第一部分第11条如于2001年12月1日尚未生效,则依照制定法文件S.I. 2001/3538第2条第(1)款生效。

第二部分 欧洲经济区企业行使护照持有人权利

具有授权资格的企业

第12条 (1)如果要行使欧洲经济区权利在联合王国设立分支机构的欧洲经济区企业满足设立条件,则该企业具有授权资格。

(2)如果要行使欧洲经济区权利在联合王国提供服务的欧洲经济区企业满足服务条件,则该企业具有授权资格。

注释:

实施日期

I146 附录3第二部分第12条于2001年12月1日全部生效;附录3第二部分第12条在副署时尚未生效,见第431条第(2)款;附录3第二部分第12条于2001年2月25日依照制定法文件S.I.2001/516第2条第(b)款、第(c)款,附录第二部分、第三部分生效;附录3第二部分第12条于2001年6月18日依照制定法文件S.I.2001/1820第2条、附录生效;附录3第二部分第12条如于2001年12月1日未尚生效,则依照制定法文件S.I. 2001/3538 第2条第(1)款生效。

Establishment

13 (1) The establishment conditions are that—

(a) the Authority has received notice ("a consent notice") from the firm's homestate regulator that it has given the firm consent to establish a branch in the United Kingdom;

(b) the consent notice—

(i) is given in accordance with the relevant single market directive;

(ii) identifies the activities to which consent relates; and

(iii) includes such other information as may be prescribed; and

(c) the firm has been informed of the applicable provisions or two months have elapsed beginning with the date when the Authority received the consent notice.

(2) If the Authority has received a consent notice, it must—

(a) prepare for the firm's supervision;

(b) notify the firm of the applicable provisions (if any); and

(c) if the firm falls within paragraph 5(d), notify its home state regulator of the applicable provisions (if any).

(3) A notice under sub-paragraph (2)(b) or (c) must be given before the end of the period of two months beginning with the day on which the Authority received the consent notice.

(4) For the purposes of this paragraph—

"applicable provisions" means the host state rules with which the firm is required to comply when carrying on a permitted activity through a branch in the United Kingdom;

"host state rules" means rules—

(a) made in accordance with the relevant single market directive; and

(b) which are the responsibility of the United Kingdom (both as to implementation and as to supervision of compliance) in accordance with that directive; and

"permitted activity" means an activity identified in the consent notice.

Annotations:

Modifications etc. (not altering text)

C392 Sch. 3 Pt. Ⅱ para. 13 extended (1.12.2001) by S.I. 2001/3592, arts. 1(2), 96 (with art. 23(2))

Commencement Information

I147 Sch. 3 Pt. Ⅱ para. 13 wholly in force at 1.12.2001; Sch. 3 Pt. II para. 13 not in force at Royal Assent see s. 431(2); Sch. 3 Pt. Ⅱ para. 13 in force for certain purposes at 25.2.2001 by S.I. 2001/516, art. 2(b)(c), Sch. Pts. 2, 3; Sch. 3 Pt. II para. 13 in force for specified purposes at 18.6.2001 by S.I. 2001/1820, art. 2, Sch.; Sch. 3 Pt. Ⅱ para. 13 in force in

设　立

第13条　(1)设立条件是:

(a)管理局从企业的母国监管机关收到通知(以下简称同意通知),同意企业在联合王国设立分支机构;

(b)同意通知

(i)按照相关单一市场指令发出;

(ii)确认与同意有关的活动;并且

(iii)包括其他规定的信息;和

(c)企业已经被告知适用的规定,或者从管理局收到同意通知之日起已经过了2个月。

(2)如果管理局收到了同意通知,则必须

(a)准备对企业进行监管;

(b)通知企业适用的规定(如有);并且

(c)如企业属于第5条第(d)款规定的情况,则通知其母国监管机关适用的规定(如有)。

(3)第(2)款第(b)项或第(c)项的通知必须在从管理局收到同意通知之日开始的2个月之内发出。

(4)就本条而言

"适用的规定",系指企业通过联合王国分支机构开展许可活动时需要遵守的所在国规则;

"所在国规则"系指下列规则:

(a)按照相关单一市场指令制定的;并且

(b)按照该指令由联合王国负责(实施与合规监管)的;

"许可活动"系指同意通知中确定的活动。

注释:

修改等(不涉及条文内容)

C392　附录3第二部分第13条于2001年12月1日依照制定法文件S.I.2001/3592第1条第(2)款、第96条[和第23条第(2)款]修改。

实施日期

I147　附录3第二部分第13条于2001年12月1日全部生效;附录3第二部分第13条在副署时尚未生效,见第431条第(2)款;附录3第二部分第13条为特定目的于2001年2月25日依照制定法文件S.I.2001/516第2条第(b)款、第(c)款,附录第二部分、第三部分生效;附录3第二部分第13条为特定目的于2001年6月18日依照制定法文件S.I.2001/1820第

so far as not already in force at 1.12.2001 by S.I. 2001/3538, art. 2(1)

Services

14 (1) The service conditions are that—

(a) the firm has given its home state regulator notice of its intention to provide services in the United Kingdom ("a notice of intention");

(b) if the firm falls within paragraph 5(a) or (d), the Authority has received notice ("a regulator's notice") from the firm's home state regulator containing such information as may be prescribed; and

(c) if the firm falls within paragraph 5(d), its home state regulator has informed it that the regulator's notice has been sent to the Authority.

(2) If the Authority has received a regulator's notice or, where none is required by subparagraph (1), has been informed of the firm's intention to provide services in the United Kingdom, it must—

(a) prepare for the firm's supervision; and

(b) notify the firm of the applicable provisions (if any).

(3) A notice under sub-paragraph (2)(b) must be given before the end of the period of two months beginning on the day on which the Authority received the regulator's notice, or was informed of the firm's intention.

(4) For the purposes of this paragraph—

"applicable provisions" means the host state rules with which the firm is required to comply when carrying on a permitted activity by providing services in the United Kingdom;

"host state rules" means rules—

(a) made in accordance with the relevant single market directive; and

(b) which are the responsibility of the United Kingdom (both as to implementation and as to supervision of compliance) in accordance with that directive; and

"permitted activity" means an activity identified in—

(a) the regulator's notice; or

(b) where none is required by sub-paragraph (1), the notice of intention.

Annotations:

Modifications etc. (not altering text)

C393 Sch. 3 Pt. II para. 14(1) extended (1.12.2001) by S.I. 2001/3592, arts. 1(2), 97 (with art. 23(2))

2条、附录生效；附录3第二部分第13条如于2001年12月1日尚未生效，则依照制定法文件S.I.2001/3538第2条第(1)款生效。

服　务

第14条　(1)服务条件为：

(a)企业已经通知其母国监管机关，其有意在联合王国提供服务(以下简称意向通知)；

(b)如企业属于第5条第(a)款或第(d)款的情况，管理局已经从企业的母国监管机关收到包含规定信息的通知(以下简称监管机关通知)；且

(c)如企业属于第5条第(d)款的情况，企业的母国监管机关已告知该企业，监管机关通知已经发给管理局。

(2)如管理局已经收到监管机关通知，或者如第(1)款不要求提供监管机关通知，已经被告知，企业有意在联合王国提供服务，则管理局必须

(a)准备对企业进行监管；并且

(b)通知企业适用的规定(如有)。

(3)第(2)款第(b)项规定的通知必须在从管理局收到监管机关通知或被告知企业的意向之日起2个月内发出。

(4)就本条而言

"适用的规定"，系指企业通过在联合王国提供服务开展许可活动时需要遵守的所在国规则；

"所在国规则"系指下列规则：

(a)按照相关单一市场指令制定的；并且

(b)按照该指令是联合王国的责任的(实施与合规监管)；

"许可活动"系指下列各项中确定的活动：

(a)监管机关通知；或者

(b)意向通知，若第(1)款不要求提供监管机关通知。

注释：

修改等(不涉及条文内容)

C393 附录3第二部分第14条第(1)款于2001年12月1日依照制定法文件S.I. 2001/3592第1条第(2)款、第97条[与第23条第(2)款]扩大适用范围。

Commencement Information

I148 Sch. 3 Pt. II para. 14 wholly in force at 1.12.2001; Sch. 3 Pt. II para. 14 not in force at Royal Assent see s. 431(2); Sch. 3 Pt. II para. 14 in force for certain purposes at 25.2.2001 by S.I. 2001/516, art. 2(b)(c), Sch. Pts. 2, 3; Sch. 3 Pt. II para. 14 in force for specified purposes at 18.6.2001 by S.I. 2001/1820, art. 2, Sch.;Sch. 3 Pt. II para. 14 in force in so far as not already in force at 1.12.2001 by S.I. 2001/3538, art. 2(1)

Grant of permission

15 (1) On qualifying for authorisation as a result of paragraph 12, a firm has, in respect of each permitted activity which is a regulated activity, permission to carry it on through its United Kingdom branch (if it satisfies the establishment conditions) or by providing services in the United Kingdom (if it satisfies the service conditions).

(2) The permission is to be treated as being on terms equivalent to those appearing from the consent notice, regulator's notice or notice of intention.

(3) Sections 21, 39(1) and 147(1) of the [M111]Consumer Credit Act 1974 (business requiring a licence under that Act) do not apply in relation to the carrying on of a permitted activity which is Consumer Credit Act business by a firm which qualifies for authorisation as a result of paragraph 12, unless the Director General of Fair Trading has exercised the power conferred on him by section 203 in relation to the firm.

(4) "Consumer Credit Act business" has the same meaning as in section 203.

Annotations:

Commencement Information

I149 Sch. 3 Pt. II para. 15 wholly in force at 1.12.2001; Sch. 3 Pt. II para. 15 not in force at Royal Assent see s. 431(2); Sch. 3 Pt. II para. 15 in force for certain purposes at 25.2.2001 by S.I. 2001/516, art. 2(b)(c), Sch. Pts. 2, 3; Sch. 3 Pt. II para. 15 in force for specified purposes at 18.6.2001 by S.I. 2001/1820, art. 2, Sch.;Sch. 3 Pt. II para. 15 in force in so far as not already in force at 1.12.2001 by S.I. 2001/3538, art. 2(1)

Marginal Citations

M111 1974 c. 39.

Effect of carrying on regulated activity when not qualified for authorisation

16 (1) This paragraph applies to an EEA firm which is not qualified for authorisation under paragraph 12.

实施日期

I148 附录3第二部分第14条于2001年12月1日全部生效；附录3第二部分第14条在副署时尚未生效，见附录第431条第(2)款；附录3第二部分第14条为特定目的于2001年2月25日依照制定法文件S.I. 2001/516第2条第(b)款、第(c)款，附录第二部分、第三部分生效；附录3第二部分第14条为特定目的于2001年6月18日通过制定法文件 S.I. 2001/1820第2条、附录生效；附录3第二部分第14条如于2001年12月1日尚未生效，则依照制定法文件 S.I. 2001/3538第2条第(1)款生效。

给予许可

第15条 (1)由于第12条而具有授权资格的企业，在每个属于受监管活动的许可活动方面具有通过其联合王国分支机构(如果它满足建立条件)或者通过在联合王国提供服务(如果它满足服务条件)开展该项活动的许可。

(2)许可的条件将被视为与同意通知、监管机关通知或意向通知的条件相当。

(3) [M111]《1974年消费信贷法》第21条、第39条第(1)款和第147条第(1)款(依照该法规定需要许可的业务)不适用于由于第12条而具有授权资格的企业开展属于消费信贷法业务的被许可活动，除非公平交易总理事对企业行使第203条赋予他的权力。

(4)“消费者信贷法业务”的意义与第203条中的意义相同。

注释：

实施日期

I149 附录3第二部分第15条于2001年12月1日全部生效；附录3第二部分第15条在副署时尚未生效，见附录第431条第(2)款；附录3第二部分第15条为特定目的于2001年2月25日通过制定法文件 S.I. 2001/51第2条第(b)款、第(c)款，附录第二部分、第三部分生效；附录3第二部分第15条为指定目的于2001年6月18日通过制定法文件 S.I. 2001/1820第2条、附录生效；附录3第二部分第15条如于2001年12月1日尚未生效，则依照制定法文件S.I. 2001/3538第2条第(1)款生效。

附注引文

M111 1974年第39章。

第16条 在无授权资格时开展受监管活动的效力

(1)本条适用于依照本附录第12条规定无授权资格的欧洲经济区企业。

(2) Section 26 does not apply to an agreement entered into by the firm.

(3) Section 27 does not apply to an agreement in relation to which the firm is a third party for the purposes of that section.

(4) Section 29 does not apply to an agreement in relation to which the firm is the deposittaker.

Annotations:

Commencement Information

I150 Sch. 3 Pt. Ⅱ para. 16 wholly in force at 1.12.2001; Sch. 3 Pt. Ⅱ para. 16 not in force at Royal Assent see s. 431(2); Sch. 3 Pt. Ⅱ para. 16 in force for certain purposes at 25.2.2001 by S.I. 2001/516, art. 2(b)(c), Sch. Pts. 2, 3; Sch. 3 Pt. Ⅱ para. 16 in force for specified purposes at 18.6.2001 by S.I. 2001/1820, art. 2, Sch.;Sch. 3 Pt. Ⅱ para. 16 in force in so far as not already in force at 1.12.2001 by S.I. 2001/3538, art. 2(1)

Continuing regulation of EEA firms

17 Regulations may—

(a) modify any provision of this Act which is an applicable provision (within the meaning of paragraph 13 or 14) in its application to an EEA firm qualifying for authorisation;

(b) make provision as to any change (or proposed change) of a prescribed kind relating to an EEA firm or to an activity that it carries on in the United Kingdom and as to the procedure to be followed in relation to such cases;

(c) provide that the Authority may treat an EEA firm's notification that it is to cease to carry on regulated activity in the United Kingdom as a request for cancellation of its qualification for authorisation under this Schedule.

Annotations:

Commencement Information

I151 Sch. 3 Pt. Ⅱ para. 17 wholly in force at 1.12.2001; Sch. 3 Pt. Ⅱ para. 17 not in force at Royal Assent see s. 431(2); Sch. 3 Pt. Ⅱ para. 17 in force for certain purposes at 25.2.2001 by S.I. 2001/516, art. 2(b)(c), Sch. Pts. 2, 3; Sch. 3 Pt. Ⅱ para. 17 in force for specified purposes at 18.6.2001 by S.I. 2001/1820, art. 2, Sch.; Sch. 3 Pt. Ⅱ para. 17 in force in so far as not already in force at 1.12.2001 by S.I. 2001/3538, art. 2(1)

(2)本法第26条不适用于该企业订立的协议。

(3)本法第27条不适用于该企业就该条而言为第三方的协议。

(4)本法第29条不适用于该企业作为存款吸收人的协议。

注释:

实施日期

I150 附录3第二部分第16条于2001年12月1日全部生效;附录3第二部分第16条在副署时尚未生效,见第431条第(2)款;附录3第二部分第16条为特定目的于2001年2月25日依照制定法文件S.I. 2001/5162条第(b)款、第(c)款,附录第二部分、第三部分生效;附录3第二部分第16条为特定目的于2001年6月18日依照制定法文件S.I. 2001/1820第2条、附录生效;附录3第二部分第16条如于2001年12月1日尚未生效,则依照制定法文件S.I. 2001/3538第2条第(1)款生效。

对欧洲经济区企业的继续管理

第17条 法规可以

(a)在适用于具有授权资格的欧洲经济区企业时修改本法属于适用规定的任何规定(在本附录第13或14条的意义之内);

(b)对与欧洲经济区企业有关的规定类别的任何变更(或所提出的变更),或者对欧洲经济区企业在联合王国开展的活动,以及对应遵守的与此等情况有关的程序作出规定;

(c)规定管理局可以将欧洲经济区企业关于停止在联合王国开展受监管活动的通知视为取消其在本附录项下的授权资格的请求。

注释:

实施日期

I151 附录3第二部分第17条于2001年12月1日全部生效;附录3第二部分第17条在副署时尚未生效,见第431条第(2)款;附录3第二部分第17条为特定目的于2001年2月25日依照制定法文件S.I. 2001/516附录2第三 部分第2条第(b)款、第(c)款,附录第二部分、第三部分生效;附录3第二部分第17条为特定目的于2001年6月18日依照制定法文件S.I. 2001/1820第2条、附录生效;附录3第二部分第17条如于2001年12月1日尚未生效,则依照制定法文件S.I. 2001/3538 第2条(1)款生效。

Giving up right to authorisation

18 Regulations may provide that in prescribed circumstances an EEA firm falling within paragraph 5(c) may, on following the prescribed procedure—

(a) have its qualification for authorisation under this Schedule cancelled; and

(b) seek to become an authorised person by applying for a Part Ⅳ permission.

Annotations:

Commencement Information

I152 Sch. 3 Pt. Ⅱ para. 18 wholly in force at 1.12.2001; Sch. 3 Pt. Ⅱ para. 18 not in force at Royal Assent see s. 431(2); Sch. 3 Pt. Ⅱ para. 18 in force for specified purposes at 25.2.2001 by S.I. 2001/516, art. 2(b)(c), Sch. Pts. 2, 3; Sch. 3 Pt. I para. 18 in force for specified purposes at 18.6.2001 by S.I. 2001/1820, art. 2 Sch.; Sch. 3 Pt. Ⅱ para. 18 in force in so far as not already in force at 1.12.2001 by S.I. 2001/3538, art. 2(1)

PART Ⅲ
EXERCISE OF PASSPORT RIGHTS BY UK FIRMS

Establishment

19 (1) A UK firm may not exercise an EEA right to establish a branch unless three conditions are satisfied.

(2) The first is that the firm has given the Authority, in the specified way, notice of its intention to establish a branch ("a notice of intention") which—

(a) identifies the activities which it seeks to carry on through the branch; and

(b) includes such other information as may be specified.

(3) The activities identified in a notice of intention may include activities which are not regulated activities.

(4) The second is that the Authority has given notice in specified terms ("a consent notice") to the host state regulator.

(5) The third is that—

(a) the host state regulator has notified the firm (or, where the EEA right in question derives from any of the insurance directives, the Authority) of the applicable provisions; or

(b) two months have elapsed beginning with the date on which the Authority gave the consent notice.

(6) If the firm's EEA right derives from the investment services directive or the [F21banking consolidation directive] and the first condition is satisfied, the Authority must give

放弃授权权利

第18条 法规可以规定,在规定的情况下,属于本附录第5条第(c)款情况的欧洲经济区企业可以按照规定的程序

(a)取消其在本附录项下的授权资格;和

(b)通过申请第四部分许可成为获授权人。

注释:

实施日期

I152 附录3第二部分第18条于2001年12月1日全部生效;附录3第二部分第18条在副署时尚未生效,见第431条第(2)款;附录3第二部分第18条为特定目的于2001年2月25日依照制定法文件S.I. 2001/516第2条第(b)款、第(c)款,附录第二部分、第三部分生效;附录3第二部分第18条为特定目的于2001年6月18日依照制定法文件S.I. 2001/1820第2条、附录生效;附录3第二部分第18条如于2001年12月1日尚未生效,则依照制定法文件S.I. 2001/3538第2条第(1)款生效。

第三部分 联合王国企业行使护照持有人权利

设 立

第19条 (1)除非满足三个条件,否则联合王国企业不得行使欧洲经济区权利建立分支机构。

(2)第一个条件为,企业以特定的方式通知管理局,该企业有意设立分支机构(以下简称意向通知),该通知

(a)确定该企业寻求通过分支机构开展的活动;并且

(b)包括其他规定信息。

(3)在意向通知中指明的活动可以包括不属于受监管活动的活动。

(4)第二个条件为,管理局已经通知所在国监管机关特定条件(以下简称同意通知)。

(5)第三个条件为:

(a)所在国监管机关已经通知企业(或者管理局,如果特定的欧洲经济区权利源自任何保险指令)适用的规定;或者

(b)从管理局发出同意通知之日起已经过了2个月。

(6)如企业的欧洲经济区权利源自投资服务指令或者[F2]银行合并指令]并且满足第一个条件,则管理局必须向所在国监管机关发出同意通知,除非管理局有理由怀疑

a consent notice to the host state regulator unless it has reason to doubt the adequacy of the firm's resources or its administrative structure.

(7) If the firm's EEA right derives from any of the insurance directives and the first condition is satisfied, the Authority must give a consent notice unless it has reason—

(a) to doubt the adequacy of the firm's resources or its administrative structure, or

(b) to question the reputation, qualifications or experience of the directors or managers of the firm or the person proposed as the branch's authorised agent for the purposes of those directives,

in relation to the business to be conducted through the proposed branch.

(8) If the Authority proposes to refuse to give a consent notice it must give the firm concerned a warning notice.

(9) If the firm's EEA right derives from any of the insurance directives and the host state regulator has notified it of the applicable provisions, the Authority must inform the firm of those provisions.

(10) Rules may specify the procedure to be followed by the Authority in exercising its functions under this paragraph.

(11) If the Authority gives a consent notice it must give written notice that it has done so to the firm concerned.

(12) If the Authority decides to refuse to give a consent notice—

(a) it must, within three months beginning with the date when it received the notice of intention, give the person who gave that notice a decision notice to that effect; and

(b) that person may refer the matter to the Tribunal.

(13) In this paragraph, "applicable provisions" means the host state rules with which the firm will be required to comply when conducting business through the proposed branch in the EEA State concerned.

(14) In sub-paragraph (13), "host state rules" means rules—

(a) made in accordance with the relevant single market directive; and

(b) which are the responsibility of the EEA State concerned (both as to implementation and as to supervision of compliance) in accordance with that directive.

(15) "Specified" means specified in rules.

Annotations:

Amendments (Textual)

F21 Words in Sch. 3 Pt. Ⅲ para. 19(6) substituted (22.11.2000) by S.I. 2000/2952, reg. 8(5)(d)

企业资源的充足性或其行政结构。

(7)如企业的欧洲经济区权利源自任何保险指令并且满足第一个条件,则管理局必须发出同意通知,除非关于将通过拟设立的分支机构开展的业务,管理局有理由

(a)怀疑企业资源或其行政结构不足以开展上述业务;或者
(b)为上述指令之目的,针对拟担任该分支机构被授权代理人的公司董事或经理,或拟担任该分支机构被授权代理人的人,就其名誉、资格或经验提出质疑。

(8)如管理局拟拒绝发出同意通知,则必须向相关企业发出预告通知。

(9)如企业的欧洲经济区权利源自任何保险指令并且所在国监管机关已经通知该企业适用的规定,则管理局必须告知企业这些规定。

(10)规则可以规定管理局在履行本项规定的职能时须遵守的程序。

(11)如管理局发出同意通知,则必须书面通知相关企业。

(12)如管理局决定拒绝发出同意通知,则
(a)必须在自该局收到意向通知之日起的3个月之内向发出该通知的人发出表达该意思的决定通知;并且
(b)此人可以将事项诉至裁判所。
(13)在本条中,"适用的规定"系指企业通过拟在相关欧洲经济区国家设立的分支机构开展业务时需要遵守的所在国规则。

(14)在第(13)款中,"所在国规则"系指下列规则:
(a)按照相关单一市场指令制定;并且
(b)按照该指令由相关欧洲经济区国家负责(实施与合规监管)。

(15)"规定"系指在规则中规定。

注释:

修正(文本)

F21 附录3第三部分第19条第(6)款之内容于2000年11月22日依照制定法文件S.I. 2000/2952第8条第(5)款第(d)项代替。

Modifications etc. (not altering text)

C394 Sch. 3 Pt. Ⅲ para. 19 applied (1.12.2001) by S.I. 2001/3592, arts. 1(2), 104(3)(a) (with art. 23(2))

Sch. 3 Pt. Ⅲ para. 19 modified(1.12.2001) by S.I. 2001/2636, arts. 1(2)(b), 77(1)-(3)(7); S.I. 2001/3538, art. 2(1)

C395 Sch. 3 Pt. Ⅲ para. 19(2)(4)(6)(7) extended (1.12.2001) by S.I. 2001/3592, arts. 1(2), 100 (with art. 23(2))

Commencement Information

I153 Sch. 3 Pt. Ⅲ para. 19 wholly in force at 1.12.2001; Sch. 3 Pt. Ⅲ para. 19 not in force at Royal Assent see s. 431(2); Sch. 3 Pt. Ⅲ para. 19 in force for certain purposes at 25.2.2001 by S.I. 2001/516, art. 2(b)(c), Sch. Pts. 2, 3; Sch. 3 Pt. Ⅲ para. 19 in force for specified purposes at 18.6.2001 by S.I. 2001/1820, art. 2, Sch.;

Sch. 3 Pt. Ⅲ para. 19 in force for specified purposes at 3.9.2001 by S.I. 2001/2632, art. 2(2), Sch. Pt. 2;

Sch. 3 Pt. Ⅲ para. 19 in force in so far as not already in force at 1.12.2001 by S.I. 2001/3538, art. 2(1)

Services

20 (1) A UK firm may not exercise an EEA right to provide services unless the firm has given the Authority, in the specified way, notice of its intention to provide services ("a notice of intention") which—

(a) identifies the activities which it seeks to carry out by way of provision of services; and

(b) includes such other information as may be specified.

(2) The activities identified in a notice of intention may include activities which are not regulated activities.

(3) If the firm's EEA right derives from the investment services directive or [F22 the banking consolidation directive], the Authority must, within one month of receiving a notice of intention, send a copy of it to the host state regulator.

[F23 (3A) If the firm's EEA right derives from any of the insurance directives, the Authority must, within one month of receiving the notice of intention—

(a) give notice in specified terms ("a consent notice") to the host state regulator; or

(b) give written notice to the firm of—

(i) its refusal to give a consent notice; and

(ii) its reasons for that refusal.]

修改等(不涉及条文内容)

C394　附录3第三部分第19条于2001年12月1日依照制定法文件S.I. 2001/3592第1条第(2)款、第104条第(3)款第(a)项[第23条第(2)款]适用;

附录3第三部分第19条于2001年12月1日依照制定法文件S.I. 2001/2636第1条第(2)款第(b)项,第77条第(1)款至第(3)款和第(7)款;制定法文件S.I. 2001/3538第2条第(1)款修订。

C395　附录3第三部分第19条第(2)款、第(4)款、第(6)款、第(7)款于2001年12月1日依照制定法文件S.I. 2001/3592 第1条第(2)款、第100条[(与第23条第(2)款]扩大适用范围。

实施日期

I153　附录3第三部分第19条于2001年12月1日全部生效;附录3第三部分第19条在副署时尚未生效,见第431条第(2)款;附录3第三部分第19项为特定目的于2001年2月25日依照制定法文件S.I. 2001/516第2条第(b)款、第(c)款,附录第二部分、第三部分生效;附录3第三部分第19条为特定目的于2001年6月18日依照制定法文件S.I.2001/1820第2条、附录生效;附录3第三部分第19条为指定目的于2001年9月3日依照制定法文件S.I. 2001/2632第2条第(2)款、附录第二部分生效;附录3第三部分第19条如于2001年12月1日尚未生效,则依照制定法文件S.I. 2001/3538第2条第(1)款生效。

服　务

第20条　(1)联合王国企业不得行使欧洲经济区权利提供服务,除非企业已经以特定的方式通知管理局其有意提供服务(以下简称意向通知),该通知

(a)确定该企业要通过提供服务开展的活动;并且

(b)包括其他规定的信息。

(2)意向通知中确定的活动可以包含不属于受监管活动的活动。

(3)如企业的欧洲经济区权利源自投资服务指令或者[F22银行合并指令],则管理局必须在收到意向通知后的1个月之内向所在国监管机关发送通知的一份副本。

[F23(3A)如企业的欧洲经济区权利源自任何保险指令,则管理局必须在收到意向通知后的1个月之内

(a)将指定条件通知所在国监管机关(以下简称同意通知);或者

(b)书面通知企业

(i)管理局拒绝发出同意通知;以及

(ii)拒绝发出同意通知的理由。]

(4) When the Authority sends the copy under sub-paragraph (3) [F24 or gives a consent notice], it must give written notice to the firm concerned.

[F25 (4A) If the firm is given notice under sub-paragraph (3A)(b), it may refer the matter to the Tribunal.

(4B) If the firm's EEA right derives from any of the insurance directives, it must not provide the services to which its notice of intention relates until it has received written notice under sub-paragraph (4).

(4C) Rules may specify the procedure to be followed by the Authority under this paragraph.]

F26 (5) ...

(6) "Specified" means specified in rules.

Annotations:

Amendments (Textual)

F22 Words in Sch. 3 Pt. Ⅲ para. 20(3) substituted (22.11.2000) by S.I. 2000/2952, reg. 8(5)(e)

F23 Sch. 3 Pt. Ⅲ para. 20(3A) inserted (30.4.2001) by S.I. 2001/1376, regs. 1, 2(2)

F24 Words in Sch. 3 Pt. Ⅲ para. 20(4) inserted (30.4.2001) by S.I. 2001/1376, regs. 1, 2(3)

F25 Sch. 3 Pt. Ⅲ para. 20(4A)-(4C) inserted (30.4.2001) by S.I. 2001/1376, regs. 1, 2(4)

F26 Sch. 3 Pt. Ⅲ para. 20(5) omitted (30.4.2001) by virtue of S.I. 2001/1376, regs. 1, 2(5)

Modifications etc. (not altering text)

C396 Sch. 3 Pt. Ⅲ para. 20(1) modified (1.12.2001) by S.I. 2001/2636, arts. 1(2)(b), 77(1)(4)-(7); S.I. 2001/3538, art. 2(1)

C397 Sch. 3 Pt. Ⅲ para. 20(1)(3A)(a) extended (1.12.2001) by S.I. 2001/3592, arts. 1(2), 101 (with art. 23(2))

Commencement Information

I154 Sch. 3 Pt. Ⅲ para. 20 wholly in force at 1.12.2001; Sch. 3 Pt. Ⅲ para. 20 not in force at Royal Assent see s. 431(2); Sch. 3 Pt. Ⅲ para. 20 in force for certain purposes at 25.2.2001 by S.I. 2001/516, art. 2(b)(c), Sch. Pts. 2, 3; Sch. 3 Pt. Ⅲ para. 20 in force for specified purposes at 18.6.2001 by S.I. 2001/1820, art. 2, Sch.; Sch. 3 Pt. Ⅲ para. 20 in force for specified purposes at 3.9.2001 by S.I. 2001/2632, art. 2(2), Sch. Pt. 2;Sch. 3 Pt. Ⅲ para. 20

(4)管理局发送第(3)款规定的副本[F24或发出同意通知]时,必须书面通知相关企业。

[F25(4A)如向企业发出第(3A)条第(b)款规定的通知,则该企业可以将事项诉至裁判所。

(4B)如企业的欧洲经济区权利源自任何保险指令,则该企业在收到第(4)款规定的书面通知以前不得提供与其意向通知有关的服务。

(4C)规则可以规定管理局依照本条须遵守的程序。]

F26(5)……

(6)"规定"系指在规则中规定。

注释:

修正(文本)

F22 附录3第三部分第20条第(3)款下内容于2000年11月2日依照制定法文件S.I. 2000/2952第8条第(5)款第(e)项替代。

F23 附录3第三部分第20条第(3A)款于2001年4月30日依照制定法文件S.I. 2001/1376第1条、第2条第(2)款插入。

F24 附录3第三部分第20条第(4)款下内容于2001年4月30日依照制定法文件S.I. 2001/1376第1条、第2条第(3)款插入。

F25 附录3第三部分第20条第(4A)款至第(4C)款于2001年4月30日依照制定法文件S.I. 2001/1376第1条、第2条第(4)款插入。

F26 附录3第三部分第20条第(5)款于2001年4月30日依照制定法文件S.I. 2001/1376第1条、第2条第(5)款被省略。

修改等(不涉及条文内容)

C396 附录3第三部分第20条第(1)款于2001年12月1日依照制定法文件S.I. 2001/2636第1条第(2)款第(b)项、第77条第(1)款、第(4)款至第(7)款;制定法文件S.I. 2001/3538第2条第(1)款修订。

C397 附录3第三部分第20条第(1)款、第(3A)款第(a)项于2001年12月1日依照制定法文件S.I. 2001/3592第1条第(2)款、第101条[与第23条第(2)款]扩大适用范围。

实施日期

I154 附录3第三部分第20条于2001年12月1日全部生效;附录3第三部分第20条在副署时尚未生效,见第431条第(2)款;附录3第三部分第20条为特定目的于2001年2月25日依照制定法文件S.I. 2001/516附录2第三部分第2条第(b)款、第(c)款,附录第二部分、第三部分生效;附录3第三部分第20条为特定目的于2001年6月18日依照制定法文件S.I. 2001/1820附录第2条、附录生效;附录3第三部分第20条为特定目的于2001年9月3日依

in force in so far as not already in force at 1.12.2001 by S.I. 2001/3538, art. 2(1)

Offence relating to exercise of passport rights

21 (1) If a UK firm which is not an authorised person contravenes the prohibition imposed by—

(a) sub-paragraph (1) of paragraph 19, or

(b) sub-paragraph (1) or [F27 (4B)] of paragraph 20,

it is guilty of an offence.

(2) A firm guilty of an offence under sub-paragraph (1) is liable—

(a) on summary conviction, to a fine not exceeding the statutory maximum; or

(b) on conviction on indictment, to a fine.

(3) In proceedings for an offence under sub-paragraph(1), it is a defence for the firm to show that it took all reasonable precautions and exercised all due diligence to avoid committing the offence.

Annotations:

Amendments (Textual)

F27 Word in Sch. 3 Pt. Ⅲ para. 21(1)(b) substituted (30.4.2001) by S.I. 2001/1376, regs. 1, 2(6)

Commencement Information

I155 Sch. 3 Pt. Ⅲ para. 21 wholly in force at 1.12.2001; Sch. 3 Pt. Ⅲ para. 21 not in force at Royal Assent see s. 431(2); Sch. 3 Pt. Ⅲ para. 21 in force for certain purposes at 25.2.2001 by S.I. 2001/516, art. 2(b)(c), Sch. Pts. 2, 3; Sch. 3 Pt. Ⅲ para. 21 in force for specified purposes at 18.6.2001 by S.I. 2001/1820, art. 2, Sch.; Sch. 3 Pt. Ⅲ para. 21 in force in so far as not already in force at 1.12.2001 by S.I. 2001/3538, art. 2(1)

Continuing regulation of UK firms

22 (1) Regulations may make such provision as the Treasury consider appropriate in relation to a UK firm's exercise of EEA rights, and may in particular provide for the application (with or without modification) of any provision of, or made under, this Act in relation to an activity of a UK firm.

照制定法文件S.I. 2001/2632第2条第(2)款、附录第二部分生效;附录3第三部分第20条如于2001年12月1日尚未生效,则依照制定法文件 S.I. 2001/3538第2条第(1)款生效。

与行使护照持有人权利有关的犯罪

第21条 (1)不是获授权人的联合王国企业,如违反下列各项提出的禁止性规定:

(a)本附录第19条第(1)款,或者

(b)本附录第20条第(1)款或[F27(4B)]款,

则构成犯罪。

(2)依照第(1)款构成犯罪的企业,应当承担下列责任:

(a)经简易程序定罪的,处以不超过最高法定限额的罚金;或者

(b)经公诉程序定罪的,处以罚金。

(3)在针对第(1)款规定的犯罪的诉讼中,企业如能证明采取了所有合理的预防措施并已尽一切应尽勤勉来避免实施该犯罪,则可以据此进行抗辩。

注释:

修正(文本)

F27 附录3第三部分第21条第(1)款第(b)项的内容于2001年4月30日依照制定法文件S.I. 2001/1376第1条、第2条第(6)款替代。

实施日期

I155 附录3第三部分第21条于2001年12月1日全部生效;附录3第三部分第21条在副署时尚未生效,见第431条第(2)款;附录3第三部分第21条为特定目的于2001年2月25日依照制定法文件 S.I. 2001/516第2条第(b)款、第(c)款,附录第二部分、第三部分生效;附录3第三部分第21条为特定目的于2001年6月18日依照制定法文件S.I.2001/1820第2条、附录生效;附录3第三部分第21条如于2001年12月1日尚未生效,则依照制定法文件S.I. 2001/3538第2条第(1)款生效。

对联合王国企业的继续管理

第22条 (1)法规可以对联合王国企业行使欧洲经济区权利作出财政部认为适当的规定,并且可以特别规定本法任何规定或依照本法作出的任何规定适用于联合王国企业的活动(经修改或不经修改)。

(2) Regulations may—

(a) make provision as to any change (or proposed change) of a prescribed kind relating to a UK firm or to an activity that it carries on and as to the procedure to be followed in relation to such cases;

(b) make provision with respect to the consequences of the firm's failure to comply with a provision of the regulations.

(3) Where a provision of the kind mentioned in sub-paragraph (2) requires the Authority's consent to a change (or proposed change)—

(a) consent may be refused only on prescribed grounds; and

(b) if the Authority decides to refuse consent, the firm concerned may refer the matter to the Tribunal.

Annotations:

Commencement Information

I156 Sch. 3 Pt. Ⅲ para. 22 wholly in force at 1.12.2001; Sch. 3 Pt. Ⅲ para. 22 not in force at Royal Assent see s. 431(2); Sch. 3 Pt. Ⅲ para. 22 in force for certain purposes at 25.2.2001 by S.I. 2001/516, art. 2(b)(c), Sch.Pts. 2, 3; Sch. 3 Pt. Ⅲ para. 22 in force for specified purposes at 18.6.2001 by S.I. 2001/1820, art. 2, Sch.;Sch. 3 Pt. Ⅲ para. 22 in force in so far as not already in force at 1.12.2001 by S.I. 2001/3538, art. 2(1)

23 (1) Sub-paragraph (2) applies if a UK firm—

(a) has a Part Ⅳ permission; and

(b) is exercising an EEA right to carry on any Consumer Credit Act business in an EEA State other than the United Kingdom.

(2) The Authority may exercise its power under section 45 in respect of the firm if the Director of Fair Trading has informed the Authority that—

(a) the firm,

(b) any of the firm's employees, agents or associates (whether past or present), or

(c) if the firm is a body corporate, a controller of the firm or an associate of such a controller,

has done any of the things specified in paragraphs (a) to (d) of section 25(2) of the [M112] Consumer Credit Act 1974.

(3) "Associate", "Consumer Credit Act business" and "controller" have the same meaning as in section 203.

(2)法规可以

(a)对与联合王国企业有关的规定类别的任何变更(或所提出的变更)或者对联合王国企业开展的活动以及对应遵守的与此等情况有关的程序作出规定;

(b)对企业不遵守法规规定的后果作出规定。

(3)如第(2)款中所述类别的规定,其变更(或拟作出的变更)需经管理局同意

(a)只可以规定的理由不予同意;并且

(b)如果管理局不予同意,则相关企业可以将事项诉至裁判所。

注释:

实施日期

I156 附录3第三部分第22条于2001年12月1日全部生效;附录3第三部分第22条在副署时尚未生效,见第431条第(2)款;附录3第三部分第22条为特定目的于2001年2月25日依照制定法文件 S.I. 2001/516第2条第(b)款、第(c)款,附录第二部分、第三部分生效;附录3第三部分第22条为特定目的于2001年6月18日依照制定法文件S.I. 2001/1820第2条,附录生效;附录3第三部分第22条如于2001年12月1日尚未生效,则依照制定法文件 S.I. 2001/3538第2条第(1)款生效。

第23条 (1)如联合王国企业有下列情况,则适用第(2)款规定:

(a)获得了第四部分许可;并且

(b)正在行使欧洲经济区权利,在联合王国以外的欧洲经济区国家开展消费信贷法业务。

(2)如公平交易总理事已经告知管理局有下列情况,则管理局可以对企业行使本法第45条规定的权力:

(a)企业,

(b)企业的任何雇员、代理人或关联人(不论是过去的还是现在的),或者

(c)如企业是法人,该企业的控制人或该控制人的关联人,

作出[M112]《1974年消费信贷法》第25条第(2)款第(a)项至第(d)项列举的任何事情。

(3)"关联人"、"消费信贷法业务"和"控制人"含义同第203条。

Annotations:

Commencement Information

I157 Sch. 3 Pt. Ⅲ para. 23 wholly in force at 1.12.2001; Sch. 3 Pt. Ⅲ para. 23 not in force at Royal Assent see s. 431(2); Sch. 3 Pt. Ⅲ para. 23 in force for certain purposes at 25.2.2001 by S.I. 2001/516, art. 2(b)(c) Sch. Pts. 2, 3; Sch. 3 Pt. Ⅲ para. 23 in force for specified purposes at 18.6.2001 by S.I. 2001/1820, art. 2, Sch.; Sch. 3 Pt. Ⅲ para. 23 in force in so far as not already in force at 1.12.2001 by S.I. 2001/3538, art. 2(1)

Marginal Citations

M112 1974 c. 39.

24 (1) Sub-paragraph (2) applies if a UK firm—

(a) is not required to have a Part Ⅳ permission in relation to the business which it is carrying on; and

(b) is exercising the right conferred by [F28Article 19 of the banking consolidation directive] to carry on that business in an EEA State other than the United Kingdom.

(2) If requested to do so by the host state regulator in the EEA State in which the UK firm's business is being carried on, the Authority may impose any requirement in relation to the firm which it could impose if—

(a) the firm had a Part Ⅳ permission in relation to the business which it is carrying on; and

(b) the Authority was entitled to exercise its power under that Part to vary that permission.

Annotations:

Amendments (Textual)

F28 Words in Sch. 3 Pt. Ⅲ para. 24(1)(b) substituted (22.11.2000) by S.I. 2000/2952, reg. 8(5)(f)

Commencement Information

I158 Sch. 3 Pt. Ⅲ para. 24 wholly in force at 1.12.2001; Sch. 3 Pt. Ⅲ para. 24 not in force at Royal Assent see s. 431(2); Sch. 3 Pt. Ⅲ para. 24 in force for certain purposes at 25.2.2001 by S.I. 2001/516, art. 2(b)(c), Sch. Pts. 2, 3; Sch. 3 Pt. Ⅲ para. 24 in force for specified purposes at 18.6.2001 by S.I. 2001/1820, art. 2, Sch.;Sch. 3 Pt. Ⅲ para. 24 in force in so far as not already in force at 1.12.2001 by S.I. 2001/3538, art. 2(1)

注释:

实施日期

I157　附录3第三部分第23条于2001年12月1日全部生效;附录3第三部分第23条在副署时尚未生效,见第431条第(2)款;附录3第三部分第23条为特定目的于2001年2月25日依照制定法文件S.I. 2001/516 第2条第(b)款、第(c)款,附录第二部分、第三部分生效;附录3第三部分第23条为特定目的于2001年6月18日依照制定法文件S.I. 2001/1820第2条、附录生效;附录3第三部分第23条如于2001年12月1日尚未生效,则依照制定法文件S.I. 2001/3538第2条第(1)款生效。

附注引文

M112　1974年第39章。

第24条　(1)如联合王国企业有下列情况,则适用第(2)款规定:

(a)无须就其开展的业务获得第四部分许可;并且

(b)正在行使[F28 银行合并指令第19条]赋予的权利,在联合王国以外的欧洲经济区国家开展该业务。

(2)如开展联合王国企业业务的欧洲经济区国家的所在国监管机关向管理局提出请求,且有下列情况,则管理局可以向企业提出其可以提出的任何要求:

(a)企业就其开展的业务获得了第四部分许可;并且

(b)管理局有权依照该部分规定行使变更该许可的权力。

注释:

修正(文本)

F28　附录3第三部分第24条第(1)款第(b)项的内容于2000年11月22日依照制定法文件S.I. 2000/2952第8条第(5)款第(f)项替代。

实施日期

I158　附录3第三部分第24条于2001年12月1日全部生效;附录3第三部分第24条在副署时尚未生效,见第431条第(2)款;附录3第三部分第24条为特定目的于2001年2月25日依照制定法文件S.I. 2001/516第2条第(b)款、第(c)款,附录第二部分、第三部分生效;附录3第三部分第24条为规定目的于2001年6月18日依照制定法文件S.I. 2001/1820第2条、附录生效;附录3第三部分第24条如于2001年12月1日尚未生效,则依照制定法文件S.I. 2001/3538 2条第(1)款生效。

SCHEDULE 4 TREATY RIGHTS

Section 31(1)(c)

Annotations:

Modifications etc. (not altering text)

C398 Sch. 4 extended(1.12.2001) by S.I. 2001/2636, arts.1(2)(b), 28–32; S.I.2001/3538, art. 2(1)

Definitions

1 In this Schedule—

"consumers" means persons who are consumers for the purposes of section 138;

"Treaty firm" means a person—

(a) whose head office is situated in an EEA State (its "home state") other than the United Kingdom; and

(b) which is recognised under the law of that State as its national; and

"home state regulator", in relation to a Treaty firm, means the competent authority of the firm's home state for the purpose of its home state authorization (as to which see paragraph 3(1)(a)).

Firms qualifying for authorisation

2 Once a Treaty firm which is seeking to carry on a regulated activity satisfies the conditions set out in paragraph 3(1), it qualifies for authorisation.

Exercise of Treaty rights

3 (1) The conditions are that—

(a) the firm has received authorisation ("home state authorisation") under the law of its home state to carry on the regulated activity in question ("the permitted activity");

(b) the relevant provisions of the law of the firm's home state—

(i) afford equivalent protection; or

(ii) satisfy the conditions laid down by a Community instrument for the co-ordination or

附录4 条约权利

第31条第(1)款第(c)项

注释:

修改等(不涉及条文内容) C398 附录4于2001年12月1日依照制定法文件S.I. 2001/2636第1条第(2)款第(b)项、第28条至第32条;制定法文件S.I. 2001/3538第2条第(1)款扩大适用范围。

定 义

第1条 在本附录中[1]

"消费者"系指就第138条而言是消费者的人;

"条约企业"系指符合下列情况的人:

(a)其总部位于联合王国以外的欧洲经济区国家(以下简称母国);并且

(b)依照该国法律被认定为该国国民;

对于条约企业而言,为其母国授权之目的[见第3条第(1)款第(a)项],"母国监管机关"系指企业母国的主管机关。

具有授权资格的企业

第2条 如果要开展受监管活动的条约企业满足第3条第(1)款中规定的条件,则具有授权资格。

行使条约权利

第3条 行使条约权利

(1)条件为:

(a)企业已获得其本国法律规定的授权(以下简称母国授权)开展特定的被监管活动(以下简称许可活动);

(b)企业的母国法律的相关规定

(i)给予同等的保护;或者

(ii)满足共同体文件为协调或统一与开展该项活动有关的成员国的法律、法规和

1 本条依照《2010年金融服务法》附录2第一部分第35条修订。——译者注

approximation of laws, regulations or administrative provisions of member States relating to the carrying on of that activity; and

(c) the firm has no EEA right to carry on that activity in the manner in which it is seeking to carry it on.

(2) A firm is not to be regarded as having home state authorisation unless its home state regulator has so informed the Authority in writing.

(3) Provisions afford equivalent protection if, in relation to the firm's carrying on of the permitted activity, they afford consumers protection which is at least equivalent to that afforded by or under this Act in relation to that activity.

(4) A certificate issued by the Treasury that the provisions of the law of a particular EEA State afford equivalent protection in relation to the activities specified in the certificate is conclusive evidence of that fact.

Annotations:

Commencement Information

I159 Sch. 4 para. 3 wholly in force at 1.12.2001; Sch. 4 para. 3 not in force at Royal Assent see s. 431(2); Sch. 4 para. 3 force for specified purposes at 3.9.2001 by S.I. 2001/2632, art. 2(2), Sch. Pt. 2; Sch. 4 para. 3 in force in so far as not already in force at 1.12.2001 by S.I. 2001/3538, art. 2(1)

Permission

4 (1) On qualifying for authorisation under this Schedule, a Treaty firm has permission to carry on each permitted activity through its United Kingdom branch or by providing services in the United Kingdom.

(2) The permission is to be treated as being on terms equivalent to those to which the firm's home state authorisation is subject.

(3) If, on qualifying for authorisation under this Schedule, a firm has a Part IV permission which includes permission to carry on a permitted activity, the Authority must give a direction cancelling the permission so far as it relates to that activity.

(4) The Authority need not give a direction under sub-paragraph (3) if it considers that there are good reasons for not doing so.

Notice to Authority

5 (1) Sub-paragraph (2) applies to a Treaty firm which—

(a) qualifies for authorisation under this Schedule, but

(b) is not carrying on in the United Kingdom the regulated activity, or any of the regulated activities, which it has permission to carry on there.

管理规定所设定的条件；并且

(c)企业没有以其要开展该项活动的方式开展该项活动的欧洲经济区权利。

(2)除非其母国监管机关以书面形式告知管理局，否则企业不被视为具有母国授权。

(3) 如果规定就企业开展许可活动给予的消费者保护至少相当于本法或依照本法对该项活动给予的保护，则为给予同等的保护。

(4)财务部出具的特定欧洲经济区国家的法律规定对其中列举的活动给予同等保护的证明书，是该项事实的结论性证据。

注释：

实施日期

I159 附录4第3条于2001年12月1日全部生效；附录4第3条在副署时尚未生效，见第431条第(2)款；附录4第3条为特定目的于2001年9月3日依照制定法文件S.I.2001/2632第2条第(2)款、附录第二部分生效；附录4第3条如于2001年12月1日尚未生效，则依照制定法文件S.I. 2001/3538第2条第(1)款生效。

许　可

第4条 (1)依照本附录获得授权资格以后，条约企业即持有许可，可通过其联合王国分支机构或者通过在联合王国提供服务开展每项许可活动。

(2)许可的条件被视为与企业母国授权的条件相当。

(3)如依照本附录规定获得授权资格以后，企业具有第四部分许可，其中包括开展经许可的活动，则管理局必须发出指示，取消该许可，只要该许可与该项活动有关。

(4)管理局如认为有充分理由不依照第(3)款规定发出指示，则无须发出该指示。

通知管理局

第5条 (1)第(2)款适用于下列条约企业：

(a)依照本附录规定具有授权资格，但是

(b)不在联合王国开展该受监管活动或许可其开展的任何受监管活动。

(2) At least seven days before it begins to carry on such a regulated activity, the firm must give the Authority written notice of its intention to do so.

(3) If a Treaty firm to which sub-paragraph (2) applies has given notice under that subparagraph, it need not give such a notice if it again becomes a firm to which that sub-paragraph applies.

(4) Subsections (1), (3) and (6) of section 51 apply to a notice under sub-paragraph (2) as they apply to an application for a Part Ⅳ permission.

Annotations:

Modifications etc. (not altering text)

C399 Sch. 4 para. 5(1) amended (temp. from 3.9.2001 to 1.12.2001) by S.I. 2001/2659, arts. 1(2), 3(12); S.I. 2001/3538, art. 2(1)

Commencement Information

I160 Sch. 4 para. 5 wholly in force at 1.12.2001; Sch. 4 para. 5 not in force at Royal Assent see s. 431(2); Sch. 4 para. 5 force for specified purposes at 3.9.2001 by S.I. 2001/2632, art. 2(2), Sch. Pt. 2; Sch. 4 para. 5 in force in so far as not already in force at 1.12.2001 by S.I. 2001/3538, art. 2(1)

Offences

6 (1) A person who contravenes paragraph 5(2) is guilty of an offence.

(2) In proceedings against a person for an offence under sub-paragraph (1) it is a defence for him to show that he took all reasonable precautions and exercised all due diligence to avoid committing the offence.

(3) A person is guilty of an offence if in, or in connection with, a notice given by him under paragraph 5(2) he—

(a) provides information which he knows to be false or misleading in a material particular; or

(b) recklessly provides information which is false or misleading in a material particular.

(4) A person guilty of an offence under this paragraph is liable—

(a) on summary conviction, to a fine not exceeding the statutory maximum;

(b) on conviction on indictment, to a fine.

(2)企业必须在其开始开展此等受监管活动前至少7日书面通知管理局该企业有意这样做。

(3)如果适用第(2)款的条约企业已经发出该款规定的书面通知,则该企业再次成为适用该款规定的企业时无须发出该通知。

(4)第51条第(1)款、第(3)款和第(6)款适用于第(2)款规定的通知,也适用于申请第四部分许可。

注释:

修改等(不涉及条文内容)

C399 附录4第5条第(1)款暂时有效于2001年9月3日至2001年12月1日依照制定法文件S.I. 2001/2659第1条第(2)款、第3条第(12)款;制定法文件S.I.2001/3538第2条第(1)款修正。

实施日期

I160 附录4第5条于2001年12月1日全部生效;附录4第5条在副署时尚未生效,见第431条第(2)款;附录4第5条为特定目的于2001年9月3日依照制定法文件S.I. 2001/2632第2条第(2)款、附录第二部分生效;附录4第5条如于2001年12月1日尚未生效,则依照制定法文件S.I. 2001/3538第2条第(1)款生效。

犯　罪

第6条 (1)违反第5条第(2)款的人构成犯罪。

(2)在就第(1)款规定的犯罪针对某人提起的诉讼中,如该人证明其采取了所有合理的预防措施并尽一切应尽勤勉来避免实施该项犯罪,则可据此进行抗辩。

(3)某人如在其依照第5条第(2)款规定发出的通知中或者与其依照第5条第(2)款发出的通知相关,实施下列行为,则构成犯罪:

(a)就重大事项提供明知为虚假或误导的信息;或者

(b)就重大事项因重大过失而提供虚假或误导的信息。

(4)依照本条规定构成犯罪的,应承担下列责任:

(a)经简易程序定罪的,处以不超过最高法定限额的罚金;或者

(b)经公诉程序定罪的,处以罚金。

SCHEDULE 5 PERSONS CONCERNED IN COLLECTIVE INVESTMENT SCHEMES

Section 36

Authorisation

1 (1) A person who for the time being is an operator, trustee or depositary of a recognized collective investment scheme is an authorised person.

(2)"Recognised" means recognised by virtue of section 264.

(3) An authorised open-ended investment company is an authorised person. Permission.

2 (1) A person authorised as a result of paragraph 1(1) has permission to carry on, so far as it is a regulated activity—

(a) any activity, appropriate to the capacity in which he acts in relation to the scheme, of the kind described in paragraph 8 of Schedule 2;

(b) any activity in connection with, or for the purposes of, the scheme.

(2) A person authorised as a result of paragraph 1(3) has permission to carry on, so far as it is a regulated activity—

(a) the operation of the scheme;

(b) any activity in connection with, or for the purposes of, the operation of the scheme.

SCHEDULE 6 THRESHOLD CONDITIONS

Section 41

Annotations:

Modifications etc. (not altering text)

C400 Sch. 6 modified (3.9.2001) by S.I. 2001/2507, arts. 1(1), 3(1); S.I. 2001/2632, art. 2(2), Sch. Pt. 2

附录5　集合投资计划中的相关人

第36条

授　权

第1条　(1)暂时担任获认可的集合投资计划的执行人、受托人或托管人的人，是获授权人。

(2)“获认可的”系指因第264条获得认可。

(3)获授权开放式投资公司是获授权人。

第2条　许可(1)由于第1条第(1)款而获授权的人具有开展下列各项活动的许可，只要该活动是受监管活动：

(a)属于附录2第8条中所述的类别，且适合该人就计划行事的身份的任何活动；

(b)与计划有关或为计划施行开展的任何活动。

(2)由于第1条第(3)款而获授权的人具有开展下列各项活动的许可，只要该活动是受监管活动：

(a)计划的执行；

(b)与计划的执行有关或为计划执行之目的开展的任何活动。

附录6　准入条件

第41条

注释：

修改等(不涉及条文内容)

C400　附录6于2001年9月3日依照制定法文件S.I. 2001/2507第1条第(1)款、第3条第(1)款；制定法文件S.I. 2001/2632第2条第(2)款、附录第二部分修订。

PART I PART IV PERMISSION

Legal status

1 (1) If the regulated activity concerned is the effecting or carrying out of contracts of insurance the authorised person must be a body corporate [F29 (other than a limited liability partnership)], a registered friendly society or a member of Lloyd's.

(2) If the person concerned appears to the Authority to be seeking to carry on, or to be carrying on, a regulated activity constituting accepting deposits [F30 or issuing electronic money], it must be—

(a) a body corporate; or

(b) a partnership.

Annotations:

Amendments (Textual)

F29 Words in Sch. 6 para. 1(1) inserted (3.9.2001) by S.I. 2001/2507, arts. 1(1), 2; S.I. 2001/2632, art. 2(2), Sch. Pt. 2

F30 Words in Sch. 6 para. 1(2) inserted (11.4.2002) by The Financial Services and Markets Act 2000 (Regulated Activities) (Amendment) Order 2002 (S.I. 2002/682), art. 8

Location of offices

2 (1) If the person concerned is a body corporate constituted under the law of any part of the United Kingdom—

(a) its head office, and

(b) if it has a registered office, that office,

must be in the United Kingdom.

(2) If the person concerned has its head office in the United Kingdom but is not a body corporate, it must carry on business in the United Kingdom.

[F31 2A Appointment of claims representatives

(1) If it appears to the Authority that—

(a) the regulated activity that the person concerned is carrying on, or is seeking to carry on, is the effecting or carrying out of contracts of insurance, and

(b) contracts of insurance against damage arising out of or in connection with the use of motor vehicles on land (other than carrier's liability) are being, or will be, effected or carried out by the person concerned,

that person must have a claims representative in each EEA State other than the United

第一部分　第四部分许可

法　律

第1条　(1)如相关受监管活动是订立或实施保险合同,则获授权人必须是法人[[F29] 有限责任合伙除外]、注册的互相保险协会或劳合社成员。

(2)如该人在管理局看来要开展或者正在开展构成吸收存款吸收存款[[F30] 或发行电子货币]的受监管活动,则该人必须是

(a)法人;或者

(b)合伙。

注释:

修正(文本)

F29　附录6第1条第(1)款的内容于2001年9月3日依照制定法文件S.I. 2001/2507第1条第(1)款;第2条、制定法文件S.I. 2001/2632第2条第(2)款、附录第二部分插入。

F30　附录6第1条第(2)项的内容于2002年4月11日依照《2000年金融服务与市场法》(受监管活动)(修正)2002号令(制定法文件S.I. 2002/682)第8条插入。

营 业 住 所

第2条　(1)如果相关人是依照联合王国任何地区的法律设立的法人

(a)其总部,和

(b)注册营业地(如有),

必须位于联合王国。

(2)如果相关人的总部在联合王国但不是法人,则该人必须在联合王国开展业务。

[[F31] **第2A条**　索赔代表的任命

(1)如管理局认为

(a)相关的人在开展或者准备开展的受监管活动是实行或实施保险合同,并且

(b) 相关的人在或将要订立或实施针对使用陆地机动车辆引起的或与之有关的损害的保险合同(承运人责任除外),

则此人必须在联合王国以外的每个欧洲经济区国家有一位索赔代表。

Kingdom.

(2) For the purposes of sub-paragraph (1)(b), contracts of reinsurance are to be disregarded.

(3) A claims representative is a person with responsibility for handling and settling claims arising from accidents of the kind mentioned in Article 1 (2) of the fourth motor insurance directive.

(4) In this paragraph "fourth motor insurance directive" means Directive 2000/26/EC of the European Parliament and of the Council of 16th May 2000 on the approximation of the laws of the Member States relating to insurance against civil liability in respect of the use of motor vehicles and amending Council Directives 73/239/EEC and 88/357/EEC.]

Annotations:

Amendments (Textual)

F31 Sch. 6 para. 2A inserted (19.1.2003) by The Financial Services and Markets Act 2000 (Variation of Threshold Conditions) Order 2002 (S.I. 2002/2707), art. 2

Close links

3 (1) If the person concerned ("A") has close links with another person ("CL") the Authority must be satisfied—

(a) that those links are not likely to prevent the Authority's effective supervision of A; and

(b) if it appears to the Authority that CL is subject to the laws, regulations or administrative provisions of a territory which is not an EEA State ("the foreign provisions"), that neither the foreign provisions, nor any deficiency in their enforcement, would prevent the Authority's effective supervision of A.

(2) A has close links with CL if—

(a) CL is a parent undertaking of A;

(b) CL is a subsidiary undertaking of A;

(c) CL is a parent undertaking of a subsidiary undertaking of A;

(d) CL is a subsidiary undertaking of a parent undertaking of A;

(e) CL owns or controls 20% or more of the voting rights or capital of A; or

(f) A owns or controls 20% or more of the voting rights or capital of CL.

(3) "Subsidiary undertaking" includes all the instances mentioned in Article 1(1) and (2) of the Seventh Company Law Directive in which an entity may be a subsidiary of an undertaking.

(2)就第(1)款第(b)项而言,不考虑再保险合同。

(3)索赔代表负责处理和解决第四机动车辆保险指令第1条第(2)款中所述类别的事故引起的索赔。

(4)在本条中,“第四机动车辆保险指令”系指2000年5月16日关于统一各成员国机动车辆使用民事责任保险相关法律的欧洲议会和理事会指令2000/26/EC,修正欧洲议会指令73/239/EEC和88/357/EEC。]

注释:

修正(文本)

F31 附录6第2A条于2003年1月19日依照《2000年金融服务与市场法》(准入条件的多样性)2002号令(制定法文件S.I. 2002/2707)第2条插入。

密切联系

第3条 (1)如相关人(以下简称A)和另一个人(以下简称CL)有密切联系,则管理局必须确信

(a)这些密切联系不会妨碍管理局对A的有效监管;并且

(b)如管理局认为CL须遵守不是欧洲经济区国家的地区的法律、法规或管理规定(以下简称外国规定),则外国规定或其执行中的任何不足不会妨碍管理局对该相关人的有效监管。

(2)如有下列情况,则A和CL有密切联系:

(a)CL是A的母企业;

(b)CL是A的子企业;

(c)CL是A子企业的母企业;

(d)CL是A母企业的子企业;

(e)CL拥有或控制A20%或以上的投票权或资本;或者

(f)A拥有或控制CL20%或以上的投票权或资本。

(3)“子企业”包含第七公司法指令第1条第(1)款和第(2)款中所述实体可以是企业子企业的所有情况。

Annotations:

> **Modifications etc. (not altering text)**
>
> C401 Sch. 6 para. 3 restricted (3.9.2001) by S.I. 2001/2507, arts. 1(1), 3(3); S.I. 2001/2632, art. 2(2), Sch. Pt. 2

Adequate resources

4 (1) The resources of the person concerned must, in the opinion of the Authority, be adequate in relation to the regulated activities that he seeks to carry on, or carries on.

(2) In reaching that opinion, the Authority may—

(a) take into account the person's membership of a group and any effect which that membership may have; and

(b) have regard to—

(i) the provision he makes and, if he is a member of a group, which other members of the group make in respect of liabilities (including contingent and future liabilities); and

(ii) the means by which he manages and, if he is a member of a group, which other members of the group manage the incidence of risk in connection with his business.

Annotations:

> **Modifications etc. (not altering text)**
>
> C402 Sch. 6 para. 4 restricted (3.9.2001) by S.I. 2001/2507, arts. 1(1), 3(3); S.I. 2001/2632, art. 2(2), Sch. Pt. 2

Suitability

5 The person concerned must satisfy the Authority that he is a fit and proper person having regard to all the circumstances, including—

(a) his connection with any person;

(b) the nature of any regulated activity that he carries on or seeks to carry on; and

(c) the need to ensure that his affairs are conducted soundly and prudently.

Annotations:

> **Modifications etc. (not altering text)**
>
> C403 Sch. 6 para. 5 restricted (3.9.2001) by S.I. 2001/2507, arts. 1(1), 3(3); S.I. 2001/2632, art. 2(2), Sch. Pt. 2

注释：

修改等（不涉及条文内容）

C401 附录6第3条于2001年9月3日受制定法文件S.I. 2001/2507第1条第（1）款、第3条第（3）款；制定法文件S.I. 2001/2632第2条第（2）款、附录第二部分限制。

适当的资源

第4条 （1）相关人具有的资源必须在管理局看来，适于开展其要开展或正在开展的受监管活动。

（2）在形成上述观点的过程中，管理局可以

（a）考虑此人是一个集团的成员以及该成员资格的任何可能的效力；和

（b）考虑

（i）该人作出的，以及如果该人是一个集团的成员，该集团的其他成员作出的关于责任（包括或有和未来责任）的规定；和

（ii）该人管理与其业务有关的风险发生率的方式，以及如果该人为一个集团的成员，该集团的其他成员管理与其业务有关的风险发生率的方式。

注释：

修改等（不涉及条文内容）

C402 附录6第4条于2001年9月3日受制定法文件S.I. 2001/2507，第1条第（1）款、第3条第（3）款；制定法文件S.I. 2001/2632第2条第（2）款、附录第二部分限制。

适 合 性

第5条 相关人必须使管理局确信他是考虑所有情况的适当的人，包括：

（a）该人和任何人的关系；

（b）该人开展或准备开展的任何受监管活动的性质；和

（c）确保充分和审慎地进行其事务的需要。

注释：

修改等（不涉及条文内容）

C403 附录6第5条于2001年9月3日受制定法文件 S.I. 2001/2507第1条第（1）款、第3条第（3）款；制定法文件S.I. 2001/2632第2条第（2）款、附录第二部分限制。

PART Ⅱ AUTHORISATION

Authorisation under Schedule 3

6 In relation to an EEA firm qualifying for authorisation under Schedule 3, the conditions set out in paragraphs 1 and 3 to 5 apply, so far as relevant, to—

(a) an application for permission under Part Ⅳ;

(b) exercise of the Authority's own-initiative power under section 45 in relation to a Part Ⅳ permission.

Authorisation under Schedule 4

7 In relation to a person who qualifies for authorisation under Schedule 4, the conditions set out in paragraphs 1 and 3 to 5 apply, so far as relevant, to—

(a) an application for an additional permission;

(b) the exercise of the Authority's own-initiative power under section 45 in relation to additional permission.

PART Ⅲ ADDITIONAL CONDITIONS

8 (1) If this paragraph applies to the person concerned, he must, for the purposes of such provisions of this Act as may be specified, satisfy specified additional conditions.

(2) This paragraph applies to a person who—

(a) has his head office outside the EEA; and

(b) appears to the Authority to be seeking to carry on a regulated activity relating to insurance business.

(3) "Specified" means specified in, or in accordance with, an order made by the Treasury.

Annotations:

Commencement Information

I161 Sch. 6 Pt. Ⅲ para. 8 wholly in force at 3.9.2001; Sch. 6 Pt. Ⅲ para. 8 not in force at Royal Assent see s. 431(2); Sch. 6 Pt. Ⅲ para. 8 in force for certain purposes at 25.2.2001 by S.I. 2001/516, art. 2(b), Sch. Pt. 2; Sch. 6 Pt. Ⅲ para. 8 in force in so far as not already in force at 3.9.2001 by S.I. 2001/2632, art. 2(2), Sch. Pt. 2

9 The Treasury may by order—

(a) vary or remove any of the conditions set out in Parts I and Ⅱ;

(b) add to those conditions.

第二部分　授　权

附录3　规定的授权

第6条　对于依照附录3规定具有授权资格的欧洲经济区企业，第1条和第3条至第5条中规定的条件，只要相关，则适用于下列各项：

(a)依照第四部分规定申请许可；

(b)依照第45条规定对第四部分许可行使管理局的自行决定行使的权力。

附录4　规定的许可

第7条　对于依照附录4具有授权资格的人，第1条和第3条至第5条中规定的条件，只要相关，则适用于下列各项：

(a)申请附加许可；

(b)依照第45条对附加许可行使管理局的自行决定行使的权力。

第三部分　附 加 条 件

第8条　(1)如本条适用于相关人，则该人必须为指定的本法规定之目的满足特定的附加条件。

(2)本法适用于下列人：

(a)其总部位于欧洲经济区以外；并且

(b)管理局认为该人在准备开展与保险业务有关的受监管活动。

(3)"规定"，系指在财政部作出的命令中或按照财政部颁布的法令中规定。

注释：

实施日期

I161　附录6第三部分第8条于2001年9月3日全部生效；附录6第三部分第8条副署时尚未生效，见第431条第(2)款；附录6第三部分第8条为特定目的于2001年2月25日通过制定法文件S.I. 2001/516第2条第(b)项、附录第二部分生效；附录6第三部分第8条如于2001年9月3日尚未生效，则依照制定法文件 S.I. 2001/2632第2条第(2)款、附录第二部分生效。

第9条　财政部可以颁布法令

(a)变更或取消第一部分和第二部分中规定的任何条件；

(b)增加其他条件。

Annotations:

Commencement Information

I162 Sch. 6 Pt. Ⅲ para. 9 wholly in force at 3.9.2001; Sch. 6 Pt. Ⅲ para. 9 not in force at Royal Assent sees. 431(2); Sch. 6 Pt. Ⅲ para. 9 in force for certain purposes at 25.2.2001 by S.I. 2001/516, art. 2(b), Sch. Pt. 2; Sch. 6 Pt. Ⅲ para. 9 in force in so far as not already in force at 3.9.2001 by S.I. 2001/2632, art. 2(2), Sch. Pt. 2

SCHEDULE 7 THE AUTHORITY AS COMPETENT AUTHORITY FOR PART Ⅵ

Section 72(2)

General

1 This Act applies in relation to the Authority when it is exercising functions under Part Ⅵ as the competent authority subject to the following modifications.

The Authority's general functions

2 In section 2—

(a) subsection (4)(a) does not apply to listing rules;

(b) subsection (4)(c) does not apply to general guidance given in relation to Part Ⅵ; and

(c) subsection (4)(d) does not apply to functions under Part Ⅵ.

Duty to consult

3 Section 8 does not apply.

Rules

4 (1) Sections 149, 153, 154 and 156 do not apply.

(2) Section 155 has effect as if—

(a) the reference in subsection (2)(c) to the general duties of the Authority under section 2 were a reference to its duty under section 73; and

(b) section 99 were included in the provisions referred to in subsection (9).

注释：

实施日期
I162　附录6第三部分第9条于2001年9月3日全部生效；附录6第三部分第9条在副署时尚未生效，见第431条第(2)款；附录6第三部分第9条为特定目的于2001年2月25日依照制定法文件S.I. 2001/516第2条第(b)项、附录第二部分生效；附录6第三部分第9条如于2001年9月3日尚未生效，则依照制定法文件S.I. 2001/2632第2条第(2)款、附录第二部分生效。

附录7　管理局作为第六部分的主管机关

第72条第(2)款

总　　则

第1条　管理局按照下列修改作为主管机关行使第六部分规定的职能时，本法适用于管理局。

管理局的基本职能

第2条　在本法第2条中

(a)第(4)款第(a)项不适用于上市规则；

(b)第(4)款第(c)项不适用于与第六部分有关的一般性指引；并且

(c)第(4)款第(d)项不适用于第六部分规定的职能。

咨 询 职 责

第3条　本法第8条不适用。

规　　则

第4条　(1)第149条、第153条、第154条和第156条不适用。

(2)第155条有效，等同于

(a)在第(2)款第(c)项中述及本法第2条规定的管理局基本职责为述及第73条规定的管理局职责；并且

(b)第99条包括在第(9)款中述及的规定中。

Statements of policy

5 (1) Paragraph 5 of Schedule 1 has effect as if the requirement to act through the Authority's governing body applied also to the exercise of its functions of publishing statements under section 93.

(2) Paragraph 1 of Schedule 1 has effect as if section 93 were included in the provisions referred to in sub-paragraph (2)(d).

Penalties

6 Paragraph 16 of Schedule 1 does not apply in relation to penalties under Part VI (for which separate provision is made by section 100).

Fees

7 Paragraph 17 of Schedule 1 does not apply in relation to fees payable under Part VI (for which separate provision is made by section 99).

Exemption from liability in damages

8 Schedule 1 has effect as if—

(a) sub-paragraph (1) of paragraph 19 were omitted (similar provision being made in relation to the competent authority by section 102); and

(b) for the words from the beginning to "(a)" in sub-paragraph (3) of that paragraph, there were substituted " Sub-paragraph (2) does not apply".

SCHEDULE 8
TRANSFER OF FUNCTIONS UNDER PART VI

Section 72(3)

The power to transfer

1 (1) The Treasury may by order provide for any function conferred on the competent authority which is exercisable for the time being by a particular person to be transferred so as to be exercisable by another person.

(2) An order may be made under this paragraph only if—

(a) the person from whom the relevant functions are to be transferred has agreed in writing that the order should be made;

(b) the Treasury are satisfied that the manner in which, or efficiency with which, the

政 策 声 明

第5条 (1)附录1第5条效力等同于通过管理局的管理组织行动的要求也适用于管理局依照第93条规定行使其公布声明的职能。

(2)附录1第1条效力等同于本法第93条包含在第(2)款第(d)项述及的规定中。

罚 款

第6条 附录1第16条不适用于第六部分规定的处罚(本法第100条对此作出了单独规定)。

费 用

第7条 附录1第17条不适用于第六部分规定的费用(本法第99条对此作出了单独规定)。

损害赔偿责任的豁免

第8条 附录1有效,等同于

(a)该附录第19条第(1)款被删除(本法第102条对主管机关作出了类似规定);并且

(b)从开头到该条第(3)款中的"(a)"的文字被替换为"第(2)款不适用"。

附录8 第六部分规定的职能转让

第72条第(3)款

转 让 权

第1条 (1)财政部可以颁布法令,规定将已授予主管机关,目前由特定的人履行的任何职能,转让于另一人履行。

(2)只有在下列情况下,才可以发布本条规定的法令:

(a)相关职能转让后将履行该职能的人书面同意应该颁布该法令;

(b)财政部确信如果将职能转让给受让人,则履行职能的方式或效率将显著改

functions are discharged would be significantly improved if they were transferred to the transferee; or

(c) the Treasury are satisfied that it is otherwise in the public interest that the order should be made.

Supplemental

2 (1) An order under this Schedule does not affect anything previously done by any person ("the previous authority") in the exercise of functions which are transferred by the order to another person ("the new authority").

(2) Such an order may, in particular, include provision—

(a) modifying or excluding any provision of Part VI, IX or XXVI in its application to any such functions;

(b) for reviews similar to that made, in relation to the Authority, by section 12;

(c) imposing on the new authority requirements similar to those imposed, in relation to the Authority, by sections 152, 155 and 354;

(d) as to the giving of guidance by the new authority;

(e) for the delegation by the new authority of the exercise of functions under Part VI and as to the consequences of delegation;

(f) for the transfer of any property, rights or liabilities relating to any such functions from the previous authority to the new authority;

(g) for the carrying on and completion by the new authority of anything in the process of being done by the previous authority when the order takes effect;

(h) for the substitution of the new authority for the previous authority in any instrument, contract or legal proceedings;

(i) for the transfer of persons employed by the previous authority to the new authority and as to the terms on which they are to transfer;

(j) making such amendments to any primary or subordinate legislation (including any provision of, or made under, this Act) as the Treasury consider appropriate in consequence of the transfer of functions effected by the order.

(3) Nothing in this paragraph is to be taken as restricting the powers conferred by section 428.

3 If the Treasury have made an order under paragraph 1 ("the transfer order") they may, by a separate order made under this paragraph, make any provision of a kind that could have been included in the transfer order.

善;或者

(c)财政部确信作出命令在其他方面有利于公共利益。

补　充

第2条　(1)本附录规定的命令不影响任何人(以下简称先前的机关)先前在行使通过命令被转让给另一人(以下简称新的机关)的职能时作出的任何事。

(2)此等命令可以特别包括下列规定:

(a)在其适用于任何此等职能时修改或排除第六部分、第九部分或第二十六部分的任何规定;

(b)与第12条对管理局作出的规定类似的审查规定;

(c)对新的机关提出与第152条、第155条和第354条对管理局提出的要求类似的要求;

(d)关于新的机关提供指导的规定;

(e)关于新的机关委托行使第六部分规定的职能和委托结果的规定;

(f)将与先前的机关的任何此等职能有关的任何财产、权利或负债转让给新的机关;

(g)新的机关开展和完成在命令生效时先前的机关正在做的任何事;

(h)在任何文件、合同或法律程序中将先前的机关替换为新的机关;

(i)关于将先前的机关雇用的人转让给新的机关和转让条件的规定;

(j)作出财政部由于通过命令实现的职能转让而认为适当的对任何主体立法或附属立法(包括本法或依照本法作出的任何规定)的任何修正。

(3)本条中的任何内容不得视为限制本法第428条授予的权力。

第3条　如财政部已经发布本附录第1条规定的命令(以下简称转让令),则可以依照该条就可以包含于转让令中的任何规定单独颁布法令。

SCHEDULE 9
NON–LISTING PROSPECTUSES

Section 87(5)

General application of Part Ⅵ

1 The provisions of Part Ⅳ apply in relation to a non–listing prospectus as they apply in relation to listing particulars but with the modifications made by this Schedule.

References to listing particulars

2 (1) Any reference to listing particulars is to be read as a reference to a prospectus.

(2) Any reference to supplementary listing particulars is to be read as a reference to a supplementary prospectus.

General duty of disclosure

3 (1) In section 80(1), for "section 79" substitute "section 87".

(2) In section 80(2), omit "as a condition of the admission of the securities to the official list".

Supplementary prospectuses

4 In section 81(1), for "section 79 and before the commencement of dealings in the securities concerned following their admission to the official list" substitute "section 87 and before the end of the period during which the offer to which the prospectus relates remains open".

Exemption from liability for compensation

5 (1) In paragraphs 1(3) and 2(3) of Schedule 10, for paragraph (d) substitute—

"(d) the securities were acquired after such a lapse of time that he ought in the circumstances to be reasonably excused and, if the securities are dealt in on an approved exchange, he continued in that belief until after the commencement of dealings in the securities on that exchange."

(2) After paragraph 8 of that Schedule, insert—

附录9 非上市招股说明书

第87条第(5)款

第六部分的普遍适用

第1条 第六部分的规定适用于非上市招股说明书以及上市公告书,但必须于本附录作出的修改后适用。

对上市公告书的引述

第2条 (1)对上市公告书的任何引述视为引述招股说明书。
(2)对补充上市公告书的任何引述视为引述补充招股说明书。

基本披露职责

第3条 (1)在第80条第(1)款中,将"第79条"替换为"第87条"。
(2)在第80条第(2)款中,删除"作为允许证券正式上市的条件"。

补充招股说明书

第4条 在第81条第(1)款中,将"第79条以及在被允许正式上市后、开始交易相关证券前"替换为"第87条以及与招股说明书有关的发行公告期结束前"。

赔偿责任的豁免

第5条 (1)在附录10第1条第(3)款和第2条第(3)款中,将第(d)项替换为:
"(d)在情有可原的情况下在正当购买证券的期间结束后购买证券,并且如果证券在被批准的交易所交易,他一直相信如此,直到证券在该交易所开始交易。"

(2)在该附录第8条之后加入:

“*Meaning of ‘approved exchange’*

9 ‘Approved exchange’ has such meaning as may be prescribed.”

Advertisements

6 In section 98(1), for “If listing particulars are, or are to be, published in connection with an application for listing,” substitute “If a prospectus is, or is to be, published in connection with an application for approval, then, until the end of the period during which the offer to which the prospectus relates remains open,”.

Fees

7 Listing rules made under section 99 may require the payment of fees to the competent authority in respect of a prospectus submitted for approval under section 87.

SCHEDULE 10
COMPENSATION: EXEMPTIONS

Section 90(2) and (5)

Annotations:

Modifications etc. (not altering text)

C404 Sch. 10 restricted (1.12.2001) by S.I. 2001/2957, arts. 1, 7(3); S.I. 2001/3538, art. 2(1)

Statements believed to be true

1 (1) In this paragraph “statement” means—

(a) any untrue or misleading statement in listing particulars; or

(b) the omission from listing particulars of any matter required to be included by section 80 or 81.

(2) A person does not incur any liability under section 90(1) for loss caused by a statement if he satisfies the court that, at the time when the listing particulars were submitted to the competent authority, he reasonably believed (having made such enquiries, if any, as were reasonable) that—

"'被批准的交易所'的含义

第9条 '被批准的交易所'具有规定的含义。"

广　告

第6条 在第98条第(1)款中，将"如果上市公告书和上市申请一同公布，或将和上市申请一同公布"替换为"如果招股说明书和批准申请一同公布，或将和批准申请一同公布，则直到与招股说明书有关的发行公告期结束"。

费　用

第7条 依照第99条制定的上市规则可以规定向主管机关支付与依照第87条提交招股说明书请求批准相关的费用。

附录10　损害赔偿：豁免

第90条第(2)款和第(5)款

注释：

修改等(不涉及条文内容)

C404　附录10于2001年12月1日受制定法文件S.I. 2001/2957第1条、第7条第(3)款；制定法文件S.I. 2001/3538第2条第(1)款限制。

被认为真实的声明

第1条 (1)在本条中，"声明"系指

(a)上市公告书中的任何不真实或误导性的声明；或者

(b)上市公告书遗漏第80条或第81条要求列入的任何事项。

(2)如果当事人使法院确信在上市公告书提交给主管机关之时，他合理相信下列情况(已经进行了合理的询问，如有)，则该人对声明造成的损失不承担任何第90条第(1)款规定的责任：

(a) the statement was true and not misleading, or

(b) the matter whose omission caused the loss was properly omitted, and that one or more of the conditions set out in sub-paragraph (3) are satisfied.

(3) The conditions are that—

(a) he continued in his belief until the time when the securities in question were acquired;

(b) they were acquired before it was reasonably practicable to bring a correction to the attention of persons likely to acquire them;

(c) before the securities were acquired, he had taken all such steps as it was reasonable for him to have taken to secure that a correction was brought to the attention of those persons;

(d) he continued in his belief until after the commencement of dealings in the securities following their admission to the official list and they were acquired after such a lapse of time that he ought in the circumstances to be reasonably excused.

Statements by experts

2 (1) In this paragraph "statement" means a statement included in listing particulars which—

(a) purports to be made by, or on the authority of, another person as an expert; and

(b) is stated to be included in the listing particulars with that other person's consent.

(2) A person does not incur any liability under section 90(1) for loss in respect of any securities caused by a statement if he satisfies the court that, at the time when the listing particulars were submitted to the competent authority, he reasonably believed that the other person—

(a) was competent to make or authorise the statement, and

(b) had consented to its inclusion in the form and context in which it was included,

and that one or more of the conditions set out in sub-paragraph (3) are satisfied.

(3) The conditions are that—

(a) he continued in his belief until the time when the securities were acquired;

(b) they were acquired before it was reasonably practicable to bring the fact that the expert was not competent, or had not consented, to the attention of persons likely to acquire the securities in question;

(c) before the securities were acquired he had taken all such steps as it was reasonable for him to have taken to secure that that fact was brought to the attention of those persons;

(d) he continued in his belief until after the commencement of dealings in the securities following their admission to the official list and they were acquired after such a lapse of time that he ought in the circumstances to be reasonably excused.

(a)声明是真实的并且没有误导性;或者

(b)造成损失的遗漏为正当遗漏,

且满足本条第(3)款中规定的一项或多项条件。

(3)前款所述条件为:

(a)当事人在相关证券被购买时一直相信;

(b)在合理可行地使可能购买相关证券的人注意到改正以前,相关证券即被购买;

(c)在证券被购买以前,当事人采取了所有对其而言合理的措施,以确保可能购买证券的人会注意到改正;

(d)当事人一直相信如此,直到证券在被列入正式上市名单并开始交易以后,并且在情有可原的情况下在正当购买证券的期间结束后购买证券。

专家声明

第2条 (1)在本条中,"声明"系指包括在上市公告书中的下列声明:

(a)声称由另一人作为专家作出或授权作出;并且

(b)表明经该人同意列入上市公告书中。

(2)如果当事人使法院确信在上市公告书提交给主管机关时,他合理相信前款所述另一人属于下列情况,则对声明造成的任何证券方面的损失不承担任何第90条第(1)款规定的责任:

(a)该另一人有能力作出或授权作出声明,并且

(b)已经同意将声明列入包含该声明的形式和上下文,

且满足本条第(3)款中规定的一项或多项条件。

(3)前款所述条件为:

(a)该另一人在证券被购买时一直相信;

(b)在合理可行地让可能购买相关证券的人注意到专家没有能力或没有同意以前,证券即被购买;

(c)在证券被购买以前,该另一人采取了所有对其而言合理的措施,以确保可能购买证券的人会注意到该事实;

(d)当事人一直相信如此,直到证券在列入正式上市名单并开始交易以后,并且在情有可原的情况下在其正当购买证券的期间结束后购买证券。

Corrections of statements

3 (1) In this paragraph "statement" has the same meaning as in paragraph 1.

(2) A person does not incur liability under section 90(1) for loss caused by a statement if he satisfies the court—

(a) that before the securities in question were acquired, a correction had been published in a manner calculated to bring it to the attention of persons likely to acquire the securities; or

(b) that he took all such steps as it was reasonable for him to take to secure such publication and reasonably believed that it had taken place before the securities were acquired.

(3) Nothing in this paragraph is to be taken as affecting paragraph 1.

Corrections of statements by experts

4 (1) In this paragraph "statement" has the same meaning as in paragraph 2.

(2) A person does not incur liability under section 90(1) for loss caused by a statement if he satisfies the court—

(a) that before the securities in question were acquired, the fact that the expert was not competent or had not consented had been published in a manner calculated to bring it to the attention of persons likely to acquire the securities; or

(b) that he took all such steps as it was reasonable for him to take to secure such publication and reasonably believed that it had taken place before the securities were acquired.

(3) Nothing in this paragraph is to be taken as affecting paragraph 2.

Official statements

5 A person does not incur any liability under section 90(1) for loss resulting from—

(a) a statement made by an official person which is included in the listing particulars, or

(b) a statement contained in a public official document which is included in the listing particulars, if he satisfies the court that the statement is accurately and fairly reproduced.

False or misleading information known about

6 A person does not incur any liability under section 90(1) or (4) if he satisfies the court that the person suffering the loss acquired the securities in question with knowledge—

(a) that the statement was false or misleading,

(b) of the omitted matter, or

(c) of the change or new matter,

改 正 声 明

第3条 (1)在本条中,“声明”的含义与本附录第1条中的含义相同。

(2)当事人如使法院确信有下列情况,则对声明造成的损失不承担第90条第(1)款规定的责任:

(a)在相关证券被购买以前,已经以旨在使可能购买证券的人引起注意的方式对改正予以公布;或者

(b)在证券被购买以前,当事人采取了所有对其而言合理的措施,以确保对改正予以公布并且合理相信已经公布。

(3)本条中的任何内容不得视为影响本附录第1条规定。

改正专家声明

第4条 (1)在本条中,“声明”的含义与本附录第2条中的含义相同。

(2)当事人如使法院确信有下列情况,则对声明造成的损失不承担第90条第(1)款规定的责任:

(a)在相关证券被购买以前,已经以旨在使可能购买证券的人引起注意的方式公布专家没有能力或没有同意这个事实;或者

(b)在证券被购买以前,当事人采取了所有对其而言合理的措施,以确保对该事实予以公布,并且合理相信已经公布。

(3)本条中的任何内容不得视为影响本附录第2条规定。

官 方 声 明

第5条 当事人对下列声明造成的损失,不承担任何第90条第(1)款规定的责任:

(a)包含在上市公告书中的官方人士作出的声明,或者

(b)包含在上市公告书中的公共官方文件中包含的声明,如当事人使法院确信该声明被准确和适当地复制。

已经知悉的虚假或误导信息

第6条 当事人如使法院确信遭受损失的人在购买相关证券时知悉下列情况,则不承担任何第90条第(1)款或第(4)款规定的责任:

(a)知悉声明是虚假或误导声明,

(b)知悉遗漏的事项,或者

(c)知悉变更或新的事项,视情况而定。

as the case may be.

Belief that supplementary listing particulars not called for

7 A person does not incur any liability under section 90(4) if he satisfies the court that he reasonably believed that the change or new matter in question was not such as to call for supplementary listing particulars.

Meaning of "expert"

8 "Expert" includes any engineer, valuer, accountant or other person whose profession, qualifications or experience give authority to a statement made by him.

SCHEDULE 11 OFFERS OF SECURITIES

Section 103(6)

The general rule

1 (1) A person offers securities to the public in the United Kingdom if—

(a) to the extent that the offer is made to persons in the United Kingdom, it is made to the public; and

(b) the offer is not an exempt offer.

(2) For this purpose, an offer which is made to any section of the public, whether selected—

(a) as members or debenture holders of a body corporate,

(b) as clients of the person making the offer, or

(c) in any other manner,

is to be regarded as made to the public.

Exempt offers

2 (1) For the purposes of this Schedule, an offer of securities is an "exempt offer" if, to the extent that the offer is made to persons in the United Kingdom—

(a) the condition specified in any of paragraphs 3 to[F32 24A] is satisfied in relation to the offer, or

(b) the condition specified in one relevant paragraph is satisfied in relation to part, but not the whole, of the offer and, in relation to each other part of the offer, the condition specified in a different relevant paragraph is satisfied.

相信不需要补充上市公告书

第7条 当事人如果使法院确信他合理相信相关变更或新的事项不需要补充上市公告书，则不承担任何第90条第(4)款规定的责任。

“专家”的含义

第8条 “专家”包括其职业、资格或经验使他作出的声明具有权威性的任何工程师、估价人、会计师或其他人。

附录11 证券的发行

第103条第(6)款

一般规则

第1条 (1)如有下列情况，则为在联合王国公开发行证券：

(a)发行为面向联合王国境内的人的公开发行；并且

(b)发行不是豁免发行。

(2)为该目的，对任何部分的公开发行，不论

(a)对选定法人的成员或债券持有人，

(b)对选定发行人的客户，或者

(c)以任何其他方式选定，均视为公开发行。

豁免发行

第2条 (1)就本附录而言，如果在向联合王国的人发行的情况下，有下列情形，则发行为“豁免发行”：

(a)发行满足第3条到[F32 第24A条]中的任何一项规定的条件；或者

(b)发行的一部分，而不是全部，满足相关条款规定的条件，并且发行的任何其他部分满足另一相关条款规定的条件。

(2) The relevant paragraphs are 3 to 8, 12 to 18 and 21.

Annotations:

Amendments (Textual)

F32 Word in Sch. 11 para. 2(1)(a) substituted (14.9.2001) by S.I. 2001/2955, regs. 1, 2(a)

Offers for business purposes

3 The securities are offered to persons—

(a) whose ordinary activities involve them in acquiring, holding, managing or disposing of investments (as principal or agent) for the purposes of their businesses, or

(b) who it is reasonable to expect will acquire, hold, manage or dispose of investments (as principal or agent) for the purposes of their businesses,

or are otherwise offered to persons in the context of their trades, professions or occupations.

Offers to limited numbers

4 (1) The securities are offered to no more than fifty persons.

(2) In determining whether this condition is satisfied, the offer is to be taken together with any other offer of the same securities which was—

(a) made by the same person;

(b) open at any time within the period of 12 months ending with the date on which the offer is first made; and

(c) not an offer to the public in the United Kingdom by virtue of this condition being satisfied.

(3) For the purposes of this paragraph—

(a) the making of an offer of securities to trustees or members of a partnership in their capacity as such, or

(b) the making of such an offer to any other two or more persons jointly,

is to be treated as the making of an offer to a single person.

Clubs and associations

5 The securities are offered to the members of a club or association (whether or not incorporated) and the members can reasonably be regarded as having a common interest with each other and with the club or association in the affairs of the club or association and in what is to be done with the proceeds of the offer.

(2)相关条款为本附录第3条至第8条、第12条至第18条和第21条。

注释:

修正(文本) F32　附录11第2条第(1)款第(a)项的内容于2001年9月14日依照制定法文件S.I. 2001/2955第1条、第2条第(a)项被代替 。

为业务目的的发行

第3条　证券向符合下列条件的人发行:

(a)其普通活动涉及为其业务之目的购买、持有、管理或处置投资(作为委托人或代理人),或者

(b)可以合理预期他们将为其业务之目的购买、持有、管理或处置投资(作为委托人或代理人),或者按照行业、专业或职业向其他人发行。

向少数人发行

第4条　(1)证券向不多于50人发行。

(2)在确定是否满足此项条件时,发行将与下列任何其他相同证券的发行同时考虑:

(a)由相同的人进行;

(b)在截至第一次发行之日的12个月期间内的任何时间开放;并且

(c)由于满足此项条件而不属于在联合王国的公开发行。

(3)就本条而言

(a)向受托人或担任受托人的合伙成员发行证券,或者

(b)同时向任何其他两个或更多人发行证券,视为向一个人发行。

俱乐部和协会

第5条　证券向俱乐部或协会(不论是否为法人)的成员发行,并且成员可以合理地视为在俱乐部或协会的事务和发行收益的使用中与其他成员和俱乐部或协会拥有共同利益。

Restricted circles

6 (1) The securities are offered to a restricted circle of persons whom the offeror reasonably believes to be sufficiently knowledgeable to understand the risks involved in accepting the offer.

(2) In determining whether a person is sufficiently knowledgeable to understand the risks involved in accepting an offer of securities, any information supplied by the person making the offer is to be disregarded, apart from information about—

(a) the issuer of the securities; or

(b) if the securities confer the right to acquire other securities, the issuer of those other securities.

Underwriting agreements

7 The securities are offered in connection with a genuine invitation to enter into an underwriting agreement with respect to them.

Offers to public authorities

8 (1) The securities are offered to a public authority.

(2) "Public authority" means—

(a) the government of the United Kingdom;

(b) the government of any country or territory outside the United Kingdom;

(c) a local authority in the United Kingdom or elsewhere;

(d) any international organisation the members of which include the United Kingdom or another EEA State; and

(e) such other bodies, if any, as may be specified.

Maximum consideration

9 (1) The total consideration payable for the securities cannot exceed 40, 000 euros (or an equivalent amount).

(2) In determining whether this condition is satisfied, the offer is to be taken together with any other offer of the same securities which was—

(a) made by the same person;

(b) open at any time within the period of 12 months ending with the date on which the offer is first made; and

(c) not an offer to the public in the United Kingdom by virtue of this condition being satisfied.

有限人群

第6条 (1)向要约人合理相信具有足够的知识,能够理解接受要约涉及的风险的有限人群发行证券。

(2)在确定一个人是否具有足够的知识能够理解接受证券要约涉及的风险时,对要约人提供的任何信息将不予考虑,但关于下列各项的信息除外:

(a)证券的发行人;或者
(b)如果证券授予购买其他证券的权利,这些其他证券的发行人。

承销协议

第7条 按照签订与关于证券的承销协议的真实邀请发行证券。

向公共机关发行

第8条 向公共机关发行
(1)证券向公共机关发行。
(2)"公共机关"系指
(a)联合王国的政府;
(b)联合王国以外的任何国家或地区的政府;
(c)联合王国或其他地方的地方机关;
(d)成员包括联合王国或其他欧洲经济区国家的任何国际组织;和
(e)规定的其他机构(如有)。

最高对价

第9条 (1)证券的应付总对价不得超过4万欧元(或者同等金额)。

(2)在确定是否满足此项条件时,发行将与下列任何其他相同证券的发行同时考虑:
(a)由相同的人进行;
(b)在截至首次发行之日的12个月期间中的任何时间开放;并且

(c)由于满足此项条件而不属于在联合王国公开发行。

(3) An amount (in relation to an amount denominated in euros) is an "equivalent amount" if it is an amount of equal value, calculated at the latest practicable date before (but in any event not more than 3 days before) the date on which the offer is first made, denominated wholly or partly in another currency or unit of account.

Minimum consideration

10 (1) The minimum consideration which may be paid by any person for securities acquired by him pursuant to the offer is at least 40,000 euros (or an equivalent amount).

(2) Paragraph 9(3) also applies for the purposes of this paragraph.

Securities denominated in euros

11 (1) The securities are denominated in amounts of at least 40, 000 euros (or an equivalent amount).

(2) Paragraph 9(3) also applies for the purposes of this paragraph.

Takeovers

12 (1) The securities are offered in connection with a takeover offer.

(2) "Takeover offer" means—

(a) an offer to acquire shares in a body incorporated in the United Kingdom which is a takeover offer within the meaning of the takeover provisions (or would be such an offer if those provisions applied in relation to any body corporate);

(b) an offer to acquire all or substantially all of the shares, or of the shares of a particular class, in a body incorporated outside the United Kingdom; or

(c) an offer made to all the holders of shares, or of shares of a particular class, in a body corporate to acquire a specified proportion of those shares.

(3) "The takeover provisions" means—

(a) Part XIII A of the [M113] Companies Act 1985; or

(b) in relation to Northern Ireland, Part XIV A of the [M114] Companies (Northern Ireland) Order 1986.

(4) For the purposes of sub-paragraph (2)(b), any shares which the offeror or any associate of his holds or has contracted to acquire are to be disregarded.

(5) For the purposes of sub-paragraph (2)(c), the following are not to be regarded as holders of the shares in question—

(a) the offeror;

(3)如果金额(相对于以欧元计价的金额)全部或部分以另一种货币或计算单位计价,在首次发行日之前的最晚可行日期(但在任何情况下不得早于首次发行日之前3日)计算时价值相同,则为"同等金额"。

最低对价

第10条 (1)任何人可以为他按照要约购买的证券支付的最低对价为最少4万欧元(或者同等金额)。

(2)本附录第9条第(3)款也适用于本条之目的。

以欧元计价的证券

第11条 (1)证券以至少4万欧元(或者同等金额)计价。

(2)本附录第9条第(3)款也适用于本条之目的。

购　买

第12条 (1)证券根据购买要约发行。

(2)"购买要约"系指

(a)关于取得在联合王国设立的法人股份,且属于在购买中的含义范围内的购买要约(或者如果这些规定适用于任何法人机构则将属于该范围的要约);

(b)取得联合王国以外的法人机构的全部或绝大部分股份或者全部或绝大部分特定类别的股份的要约;或者

(c)向法人机构的股份或特定类别的股份的全部持有人发出的取得这些股份的特定比例的要约。

(3)"购买规定"系指

(a)[M113]《1985年公司法》第十三A部分;或者

(b)对于北爱尔兰,[M114]《1986年公司法令》(北爱尔兰)第十四A部分。

(4)就第(2)款第(b)项而言,要约人或其任何关联人持有或已经签约购买的股份不予考虑。

(5)就第(2)款第(c)项而言,下列各项不视为相关股份的持有人:

(a)要约人;

(b) any associate of the offeror; and

(c) any person whose shares the offeror or any associate of the offeror has contracted to acquire.

(6) "Associate" has the same meaning as in—

(a) section 430E of the [M115]Companies Act 1985; or

(b) in relation to Northern Ireland, Article 423E of the [M116]Companies (Northern Ireland) Order 1986.

Annotations:

Marginal Citations

M113 1985 c. 6.

M114 S.I. 1986/1032 (N.I. 6).

M115 1985 c. 6.

M116 S.I. 1986/1032 (N.I. 6).

Mergers

13 The securities are offered in connection with a merger (within the meaning of Council Directive No. 78/855/EEC).

Free shares

14 (1) The securities are shares and are offered free of charge to any or all of the holders of shares in the issuer.

(2) "Holders of shares" means the persons who at the close of business on a date—

(a) specified in the offer, and

(b) falling within the period of 60 days ending with the date on which the offer is first made, were holders of such shares.

Exchange of shares

15 The securities—

(a) are shares, or investments of a specified kind relating to shares, in a body corporate, and

(b) are offered in exchange for shares in the same body corporate, and the offer cannot result in any increase in the issued share capital of the body corporate.

Qualifying persons

16 (1) The securities are issued by a body corporate and are offered—

(a) by the issuer, by a body corporate connected with the issuer or by a relevant trustee;

(b)要约人的任何关联人;和

(c)要约人或要约人的任何关联人已经签约购买其股份的任何人。

(6)“关联人”的含义和下列各项中的含义相同:

(a)[M115]《1985年公司法》第430E条;或者

(b)对于北爱尔兰,[M116]《1986年公司法令》(北爱尔兰)第423E条。

注释:

附注引文

M113　1985年第6章。

M114　制定法文件S.I. 1986/1032(N.I. 6)。

M115　1985年第6章。

M116　制定法文件S.I. 1986/1032(N.I. 6)。

合　并

第13条　证券根据合并(理事会指令第78/855/EEC号的意义范围内)发行。

无偿股份

第14条　(1)证券是股份并且向发行人的任何或所有股份持有人免费发行。

(2)“股份持有人”系指在下列日期营业结束时是此等股份持有人的人:

(a)要约中指定的日期,以及

(b)截至首次发行日的60日期间内的日期。

股份交换

第15条　证券

(a)是法人的股份或对法人股份的特定类别投资,并且

(b)为交换相同的法人机构的股份而发行,并且发行不会造成该法人已发行股本的任何增加。

合资格人

第16条　(1)证券由法人机构发行,并且

(a)由发行人、与发行人有关联的法人或相关的受托人发行;

(b) only to qualifying persons; and

(c) on terms that a contract to acquire any such securities may be entered into only by the qualifying person to whom they were offered or, if the terms of the offer so permit, any qualifying person.

(2) A person is a "qualifying person", in relation to an issuer, if he is a genuine employee or former employee of the issuer or of another body corporate in the same group or the wife, husband, widow, widower or child or stepchild under the age of eighteen of such an employee or former employee.

(3) In relation to an issuer of securities, "connected with" has such meaning as may be prescribed.

(4) "Group" and "relevant trustee" have such meaning as may be prescribed.

Convertible securities

17 (1) The securities result from the conversion of convertible securities and listing particulars (or a prospectus) relating to the convertible securities were (or was) published in the United Kingdom under or by virtue of Part VI or such other provisions applying in the United Kingdom as may be specified.

(2) "Convertible securities" means securities of a specified kind which can be converted into, or exchanged for, or which confer rights to acquire, other securities.

(3) "Conversion" means conversion into or exchange for, or the exercise of rights conferred by the securities to acquire, other securities.

Charities

18 The securities are issued by—

(a) a charity within the meaning of—

(i) section 96(1) of the [M117] Charities Act 1993, or

(ii) section 35 of the [M118] Charities Act (Northern Ireland) 1964,

(b) a recognised body within the meaning of section 1(7) of the [M119] Law Reform (Miscellaneous Provisions) (Scotland) Act 1990,

(c) a housing association within the meaning of—

(i) section 5(1) of the [M120] Housing Act 1985,

(ii) section 1 of the [M121] Housing Associations Act 1985, or

(iii) Article 3 of the [M122] Housing (Northern Ireland) Order 1992,

(d) an industrial or provident society registered in accordance with—

(i) section 1(2)(b) of the [M123] Industrial and Provident Societies Act 1965, or (b)向合资格发行;并且

(c)购买任何此等证券的合同只能由向其发行证券的合资格人签订,或者如果要约的条件允许,由任何合资格人签订。

(2)对于发行人而言,如果一个人是发行人或相同集团中另一个法人的实际雇员或前雇员,或者雇员或前雇员的妻子、丈夫、孀妇、鳏夫或18岁以下的子女或继子女,则为"合资格人"。

(3)对于证券的发行人而言,"关联"具有规定的含义。

(4)"集团"和"相关受托人"具有规定的含义。

可转换证券

第17条 (1)证券通过转换可转换证券产生,并且与可转换证券有关的上市公告书(或者招股说明书)依照第六部分或规定在联合王国适用的其他规定,或由于第六部分或规定在联合王国适用的其他规定,在联合王国公布。

(2)"可转换证券",系指可以转换为其他证券、与其他证券交换或者授予购买其他证券的权利的特定类别的证券。

(3)"转换",系指转换为其他证券、与其他证券交换或者行使证券授予的购买其他证券的权利。

慈善机构

第18条 证券的发行人为:

(a)在下列各项的含义范围内的慈善机构:

(i)[M117]《1993年慈善机构法》第96条第(1)款,或者

(ii)[M118]《1964年慈善机构法》(北爱尔兰)第35条,

(b)在[M119]《1990年法律改革法》(其他规定)(苏格兰)第1条第(7)款的含义范围内的获认可的机构,

(c)在下列各项的含义范围内的住房互助会:

(i)[M120]《1985年住房法》第5条第(1)款,

(ii)[M121]《1985年住房协会法》第1条,或者

(iii)[M122]《1992年住房法令》(北爱尔兰)第3条,

(d)按照下列各项注册的行业节俭互助会:

(i)[M123]《1965年行业节俭互助会法》第1条第(2)款第(b)项,或者

(ii) section 1(2)(b) of the M124Industrial and Provident Societies Act 1969, or

(e) a non-profit making association or body, recognised by the country or territory in which it is established, with objectives similar to those of a body falling within any of paragraphs (a) to (c),

and the proceeds of the offer will be used for the purposes of the issuer's objectives.

Annotations:

Marginal Citations

M117 1993 c. 10.

M118 1964 c. 33 (N.I.)

M119 1990 c. 40.

M120 1985 c. 68.

M121 1985 c. 69

M122 S.I. 1992/1725 (N.I. 10).

M123 1965 c. 12.

M124 1969 c. 24 (N.I.).

Building societies etc.

19 The securities offered are shares which are issued by, or ownership of which entitles the holder to membership of or to obtain the benefit of services provided by—

(a) a building society incorporated under the law of, or of any part of, the United Kingdom;

(b) any body incorporated under the law of, or of any part of, the United Kingdom relating to industrial and provident societies or credit unions; or

(c) a body of a similar nature established in another EEA State.

Euro-securities

20 (1) The securities offered are Euro-securities and no advertisement relating to the offer is issued in the United Kingdom, or is caused to be so issued—

(a) by the issuer of the Euro-securities;

(b) by any credit institution or other financial institution through which the Eurosecurities may be acquired pursuant to the offer; or

(c) by any body corporate which is a member of the same group as the issuer or any of those institutions.

(2) But sub-paragraph (1) does not apply to an advertisement of a prescribed kind.

(3) "Euro-securities" means investments which—

(ii)[M124]《1969年行业节俭互助会法》第1条第(2)款第(b)项,或者

(e)在其建立的国家或地区获认可的非营利协会或机构,其目标与属于第(a)项到第(c)项中的任何一项的机构的目标相似,

并且发行的收益将用于实现发行人的目标。

注释:

附注引文

M117 1993年第10章。
M118 1964年第33章(N.I.)。
M119 1990年第40章。
M120 1985年第68章。
M121 1985年第69章。
M122 制定法文件S.I. 1992/1725 (N.I. 10)。
M123 1965第12章。
M124 1969第24章 (N.I.)。

住房互助会等

第19条 发行的证券是由下列机构发行的股份,或者持有该证券使持有人有权获得下列机构的会员资格或获得其提供的服务的利益:

(a)按照联合王国或者联合王国任何部分的法律设立的住房互助会;

(b)按照联合王国或者联合王国任何部分的法律设立的与行业节俭互助会或信用合作社有关的任何机构;或者

(c)在另一个欧洲经济区国家设立的性质类似的机构。

欧元证券

第20条 (1)发行的证券是欧元证券,并且下列主体不在联合王国发布或导致发布与发行有关的广告:

(a)欧元证券的发行人;

(b)可以按照要约通过其购买欧元证券的任何信用机构或其他金融机构;或者

(c)与发行人同为相同集团成员的任何法人机构或任何上述机构。

(2)但第(1)款对规定类别的广告不适用。

(3)"欧元证券"系指下列投资:

(a) are to be underwritten and distributed by a syndicate at least two of the members of which have their registered offices in different countries or territories;

(b) are to be offered on a significant scale in one or more countries or territories, other than the country or territory in which the issuer has its registered office; and

(c) may be acquired pursuant to the offer only through a credit institution or other financial institution.

(4) "Credit institution" means a credit institution as defined in [F33 Article 1(1)(a)] of [F34 the banking consolidation directive].

(5) "Financial institution" means a financial institution as defined in Article 1 of [F34 the banking consolidation directive].

(6) "Underwritten" means underwritten by whatever means, including by acquisition or subscription, with a view to resale.

Annotations:

Amendments (Textual)

F33 Words in Sch. 11 para. 20(4) substituted (27.4.2002) by The Electronic Money (Miscellaneous Amendments) Regulations 2002 (S.I. 2002/765), reg. 4

F34 Words in Sch. 11 para. 20(4)(5) substituted (22.11.2000) by S.I. 2000/2952, reg. 8(6)(a)(b)

Same class securities

21 The securities are of the same class, and were issued at the same time, as securities in respect of which a prospectus has been published under or by virtue of—

(a) Part VI;

(b) Part III of the M125 Companies Act 1985; or

(c) such other provisions applying in the United Kingdom as may be specified.

Annotations:

Marginal Citations

M125 1985 c. 6.

Short date securities

22 The securities are investments of a specified kind with a maturity of less than one year from their date of issue.

(a)由至少两个成员在不同的国家或地区有注册办事处的辛迪加认购和分销;

(b)在发行人有注册营业地的国家或地区以外的一个或多个国家或地区大规模发行;且

(c)只能通过信用机构或其他金融机构按照要约购买。

(4)"信用机构"系指在[F34银行合并指令]的[F33 第1条第(1)款第(a)项]中定义的信用机构。

(5)"金融机构",系指在[F34银行合并指令]第1条中定义的金融机构。

(6)"认购",系指以转售为目的的通过任何方式认购,包括购买或认缴。

注释:

修正(文本)

F33 附录11第20条第(4)款的内容于2002年4月27日依照《2002年电子货币(杂项修订)条例》(制定法文件S.I. 2002/765)第4条被替代。

F34 附录11第20条第(4)款、第(5)款的内容于2000年11月22日依照制定法文件S.I. 2000/2952第8条第(6)款第(a)项、第(b)项被替代。

同类别证券

第21条 证券属于相同的类别,同时作为证券发行,关于它们的招股说明书已经依照或者通过下列各项规定公布:

(a)本法第六部分;

(b)[M125]《1985年公司法》第三部分;或者

(c)指定的在联合王国适用的其他规定。

注释:

附注引文

M125 1985年第6章。

短期证券

第22条 证券是特定类别的投资,到期日距离其发行日期少于1年。

Government and public securities

23 (1) The securities are investments of a specified kind creating or acknowledging indebtedness issued by or on behalf of a public authority.

(2) "Public authority" means—

(a) the government of the United Kingdom;

(b) the government of any country or territory outside the United Kingdom;

(c) a local authority in the United Kingdom or elsewhere;

(d) any international organisation the members of which include the United Kingdom or another EEA State; and

(e) such other bodies, if any, as may be specified.

Non-transferable securities

24 The securities are not transferable.

[F35 24A Units in a collective investment scheme

The securities are units (as defined by section 237 (2)) in a collective investment scheme.]

Annotations:

Amendments (Textual)

F35 Sch. 11 para. 24A and cross-heading inserted (14.9.2001) by S.I. 2001/2955, regs. 1, 2(b)

General definitions

25 For the purposes of this Schedule—

"shares" has such meaning as may be specified; and

"specified" means specified in an order made by the Treasury.

政府和公共证券

第23条　(1)证券是特定类别的投资,创设或承认由或代表公共机关发行的债务。

(2)"公共机关"系指

(a)联合王国的政府;

(b)联合王国以外的任何国家或地区的政府;

(c)联合王国或其他地方的地方机关;

(d)成员包括联合王国或其他欧洲经济区国家的任何国际组织;和

(e)规定的其他机构(如有)。

不可转让证券

第24条　证券不可转让。

{[F35]24A集合投资计划中的单位

证券是集合投资计划中的单位[见本法第237条第(2)款的定义]。}

注释:

修正(文本)

F35　附录11第24A条和文内小标题于2001年9月14日依照制定法文件S.I. 2001/2955第1条、第2条第(b)款插入。

一般定义

第25条　为本附录之目的

"股份"具有规定的含义;并且

"规定"系指财政部通过法令予以规定。

SCHEDULE 12
TRANSFER SCHEMES: CERTIFICATES

Sections 111(2) and 115

PART I INSURANCE BUSINESS TRANSFER SCHEMES

Annotations:

Modifications etc. (not altering text)

C405 Sch. 12 Pt. I (paras. 1–6) applied (1.12.2001) by S.I. 2001/3626, arts. 1, 3(c)

1 (1) For the purposes of section 111(2) the appropriate certificates, in relation to an insurance business transfer scheme, are—

(a) a certificate under paragraph 2;

(b) if sub-paragraph (2) applies, a certificate under paragraph 3;

(c) if sub-paragraph (3) applies, a certificate under paragraph 4;

(d) if sub-paragraph (4) applies, a certificate under paragraph 5.

(2) This sub-paragraph applies if—

(a) the authorised person concerned is a UK authorised person which has received authorisation under Article 6 of the first life insurance directive or of the first non-life insurance directive from the Authority; and

(b) the establishment from which the business is to be transferred under the proposed insurance business transfer scheme is in an EEA State other than the United Kingdom.

(3) This sub-paragraph applies if—

(a) the authorised person concerned has received authorisation under Article 6 of the first life insurance directive from the Authority;

(b) the proposed transfer relates to business which consists of the effecting or carrying out of contracts of long-term insurance; and

(c) as regards any policy which is included in the proposed transfer and which evidences a contract of insurance (other than reinsurance), an EEA State other than the United Kingdom is the State of the commitment.

(4) This sub-paragraph applies if—

(a) the authorised person concerned has received authorisation under Article 6 of the first non-life insurance directive from the Authority;

附录12　转让计划:证书

第111条第(2)款和第115条

第一部分　保险业务转让计划

注释:

修改等(不涉及条文内容)

C405　附录12第一部分(第1条至第6条)于2001年12月1日依照制定法文件S.I. 2001/3626第1条、第3条第(c)款适用。

第1条　(1)就本法第111条第(2)款而言,关于保险业务转让计划的适当证书是

(a)本附录第2条规定的证书;

(b)本附录第3条规定的证书,如果第(2)款适用;

(c)本附录第4条规定的证书,如果第(3)款适用;

(d)本附录第5条规定的证书,如果第(4)款适用。

(2)如有下列规定,则适用本款规定:

(a)相关的获授权人是已经从管理局获得第一人寿保险指令或第一非人寿保险指令第6条规定授权的联合王国获授权人;并且

(b)将依照所提出的保险业务转让计划转让业务的机构位于联合王国以外的欧洲经济区国家。

(3)如有下列规定,则适用本款规定:

(a)相关的获授权人已经从当局获得第一人寿保险指令第6条规定的授权;

(b)所提出的转让与包括实行或实施长期保险合同的业务有关;并且

(c)对于包括在所提出的转让中并且证明保险合同(再保险除外)的任何保险单,联合王国以外的欧洲经济区国家是约定国。

(4)如有下列规定,则适用本款规定:

(a)相关获授权人已经从当局获得第一非人寿保险指令第6条规定的授权;

(b) the business to which the proposed insurance business transfer scheme relates is business which consists of the effecting or carrying out of contracts of general insurance; and

(c) as regards any policy which is included in the proposed transfer and which evidences a contract of insurance (other than reinsurance), the risk is situated in an EEA State other than the United Kingdom.

Annotations:

Modifications etc. (not altering text)

C406 Sch. 12 Pt. I para. 1(2)(a)(3)(a)(4)(a) modified (1.12.2001) by S.I. 2001/3626, arts. 1, 5(2)

Certificates as to margin of solvency

2 (1) A certificate under this paragraph is to be given—

(a) by the relevant authority; or

(b) in a case in which there is no relevant authority, by the Authority.

(2) A certificate given under sub-paragraph (1)(a) is one certifying that, taking the proposed transfer into account—

(a) the transferee possesses, or will possess before the scheme takes effect, the necessary margin of solvency; or

(b) there is no necessary margin of solvency applicable to the transferee.

(3) A certificate under sub-paragraph (1)(b) is one certifying that the Authority has received from the authority which it considers to be the authority responsible for supervising persons who effect or carry out contracts of insurance in the place to which the business is to be transferred that, taking the proposed transfer into account —

(a) the transferee possesses or will possess before the scheme takes effect the margin of solvency required under the law applicable in that place; or

(b) there is no such margin of solvency applicable to the transferee .

(4) "Necessary margin of solvency" means the margin of solvency required in relation to the transferee, taking the proposed transfer into account, under the law which it is the responsibility of the relevant authority to apply.

(5) "Margin of solvency" means the excess of the value of the assets of the transferee over the amount of its liabilities.

(6) "Relevant authority" means—

(a) if the transferee is an EEA firm falling within paragraph 5 (d) of Schedule 3, its home state regulator;

(b) if the transferee is a Swiss general insurer, the authority responsible in Switzerland for supervising persons who effect or carry out contracts of insurance;

(b)与所提出的保险业务转让计划相关的业务是包括订立实施普通保险合同的业务;并且

(c)就包含在所提出的转让中作为保险合同证据的任何保单(不包括再保险)而言,所涉风险处于联合王国之外的欧洲经济区国家。

注释:

修改等(不涉及条文内容)

C406 附录12第一部分第1条第(2)款第(a)项、第(3)款第(a)项、第(4)款第(a)项于2001年12月1日依照制定法文件S.I.2001/3626第1条、第5条第(2)款修改。

关于清偿能力限度的证书

第2条 (1)本条规定的证书发出者是

(a)有关机关;或者

(b)如无有关机关,则为管理局。

(2)依照第(1)款第(a)项发出的证书证明,考虑到拟作出的转让

(a)受让人具有或者将在计划生效之前具有必要清偿能力限度;或者

(b)没有适用于受让人的必要清偿能力限度。

(3)第(1)款第(b)项规定的证书证明,管理局已经从其认为负责对在业务受让地点实行或实施保险合同的人进行监督的机关处知悉,考虑到拟作出的转让

(a)受让人具有或者将在计划生效之前具有在该地点的适用法律项下所要求清偿能力限度;或者

(b)没有适用于受让人的此等清偿能力限度。

(4)"必要清偿能力限度",系指考虑到拟作出的转让,依照有关机关负责实施的法律要求受让人具有的清偿能力限度。

(5)"清偿能力限度",系指受让人的资产价值超出其负债金额的部分。

(6)"有关机关"系指

(a)如受让人为欧洲经济区企业,属于附录3第5条第(d)款规定的情况,则为受让人的母国监管机关,

(b)如受让人为瑞士的一般承保人,则为在瑞士负责监督订立或实施保险合同的人的机关,

(c) if the transferee is an authorised person not falling within paragraph (a) or (b), the Authority.

(7) In sub-paragraph (6), any reference to a transferee of a particular description includes a reference to a transferee who will be of that description if the proposed scheme takes effect.

(8) "Swiss general insurer" means a body—

(a) whose head office is in Switzerland;

(b) which has permission to carry on regulated activities consisting of the effecting and carrying out of contracts of general insurance; and

(c) whose permission is not restricted to the effecting or carrying out of contracts of reinsurance.

Certificates as to consent

3 A certificate under this paragraph is one given by the Authority and certifying that the host State regulator has been notified of the proposed scheme and that—

(a) that regulator has responded to the notification; or

(b) that it has not responded but the period of three months beginning with the notification has elapsed.

Certificates as to long-term business

4 A certificate under this paragraph is one given by the Authority and certifying that the authority responsible for supervising persons who effect or carry out contracts of insurance in the State of the commitment has been notified of the proposed scheme and that—

(a) that authority has consented to the proposed scheme; or

(b) the period of three months beginning with the notification has elapsed and that authority has not refused its consent.

Certificates as to general business

5 A certificate under this paragraph is one given by the Authority and certifying that the authority responsible for supervising persons who effect or carry out contracts of insurance in the EEA State in which the risk is situated has been notified of the proposed scheme and that—

(a) that authority has consented to the proposed scheme; or

(b) the period of three months beginning with the notification has elapsed and that authority has not refused its consent.

Interpretation of Part I

6 (1) "State of the commitment", in relation to a commitment entered into at any date,

(c)如受让人为获授权人,不属于第(a)项或第(b)项规定的情况,则为管理局。

(7)在第(6)款中,对特定种类的受让人的任何述及包括如果所提出的计划生效将属于该种类的受让人。

(8)“瑞士的一般承保人”系指有下列情况的机构:
(a)总部在瑞士;
(b)取得批准进行包括订立和实施普通保险合同的受监管活动;并且

(c)其批准不只限于订立或实施再保险合同。

关于同意的证书

第3条 本条规定的证书由管理局发出,证明已通知所在国监管机关拟实施的计划并且
(a)该监管机关已经对通知作出回应;或者
(b)该监管机关未作出回应,但通知之后的3个月期限已届满。

关于长期业务的证书

第4条 本条规定的证书由管理局发出,证明已通知在约定国负责监督订立或实施保险合同的人的机关所提出的计划并且

(a)该机关已经同意所提出的计划;或者
(b)通知之后的3个月期限已过并且该机关未拒绝同意。

关于普通业务的证书

第5条 本条规定的证书由管理局发出,证明已通知在风险所在的欧洲经济区国家负责监督订立或实施保险合同的人的机关所提出的计划并且

(a)该机关已经同意所提出的计划;或者
(b)通知之后的3个月期限已过并且该机关未拒绝同意。

对第一部分的解释

第6条 (1)对于在任何日期订立的约定,“约定国”系指

means—

(a) if the policyholder is an individual, the State in which he had his habitual residence at that date;

(b) if the policyholder is not an individual, the State in which the establishment of the policyholder to which the commitment relates was situated at that date.

(2) "Commitment" means a commitment represented by contracts of insurance of a prescribed class.

(3) References to the EEA State in which a risk is situated are—

(a) if the insurance relates to a building or to a building and its contents (so far as the contents are covered by the same policy), to the EEA State in which the building is situated;

(b) if the insurance relates to a vehicle of any type, to the EEA State of registration;

(c) in the case of policies of a duration of four months or less covering travel or holiday risks (whatever the class concerned), to the EEA State in which the policyholder took out the policy;

(d) in a case not covered by paragraphs (a) to (c)—

(i) if the policyholder is an individual, to the EEA State in which he has his habitual residence at the date when the contract is entered into; and

(ii) otherwise, to the EEA State in which the establishment of the policyholder to which the policy relates is situated at that date.

Annotations:

Commencement Information

I163 Sch. 12 Pt I para. 6 wholly in force at 1.12.2001; Sch. 12 Pt. I para. 6 not in force at Royal Assent see s. 431(2); Sch. 12 para. 6(2) in force at 25.2.2001 by S.I. 2001/516, art. 2 (b), Sch. Pts. 1, 3; Sch. 12 Pt. I para. 6 in force in so far as not already in force at 1.12.2001 by S.I. 2001/3538, art. 2(1)

PART II BANKING BUSINESS TRANSFER SCHEMES

7 (1) For the purposes of section 111(2) the appropriate certificates, in relation to a banking business transfer scheme, are—

(a) a certificate under paragraph 8; and

(b) if sub-paragraph (2) applies, a certificate under paragraph 9.

(2) This sub-paragraph applies if the authorised person concerned or the transferee is an EEA firm falling within paragraph 5(b) of Schedule 3.

(a)如保单持有人为个人,则指在该日期保单持有人拥有的经常居所所在的国家;

(b)如保单持有人非个人,则指在该日期与约定有关的保单持有人的机构所在的国家。

(2)"约定"系指指定种类的保险合同所体现的约定。

(3)述及风险所在的欧洲经济区国家系指

(a)如保险与建筑或者建筑以及其容纳物(只要容纳物在相同保单的承保范围之内)有关,则指建筑所在的欧洲经济区国家;

(b)如保险与任何类型的车辆有关,则指进行注册的欧洲经济区国家;

(c)如承保旅行或假日风险(不论有关的种类如何)的保单期限为四个月或以下,则指保单持有人取得保险单的欧洲经济区国家;

(d)在第(a)项至第(c)项以外的情况下

(i)如保单持有人为个人,则指在签订合同之日保单持有人拥有的经常居所所在的欧洲经济区国家,

(ii)如保单持有人非个人,则指在该日期与保单有关的保单持有人的机构所在的欧洲经济区国家。

注释:

实施日期

I163 附录12第一部分第6条于2001年12月1日全部生效;附录12第一部分第6条在副署时尚未生效,见第431条第(2)款;附录12第6条第(2)款于2001年2月25日依照制定法文件S.I.2001/516第2条第(b)款,附录第一部分、第三部分生效;附录12第一部分第6条如于2001年12月1日尚未生效,则依照制定法文件S.I.2001/3538第2条第(1)款生效。

第二部分 银行业务转让计划

第7条 (1)就本法第111条第(2)款而言,关于银行业务转让计划的适当证书是

(a)本附录第8条规定的证书;和

(b)如果适用第(2)款,则指本附录第9条规定的证书。

(2)如果相关获授权人或受让人是欧洲经济区企业,属于附录3第5条第(b)款的情况,则适用本款。

Certificates as to financial resources

8 (1) A certificate under this paragraph is one given by the relevant authority and certifying that, taking the proposed transfer into account, the transferee possesses, or will possess before the scheme takes effect, adequate financial resources.

(2) "Relevant authority" means—

(a) if the transferee is a person with a Part IV permission or with permission under Schedule 4, the Authority;

(b) if the transferee is an EEA firm falling within paragraph 5(b) of Schedule 3, its home state regulator;

(c) if the transferee does not fall within paragraph (a) or (b), the authority responsible for the supervision of the transferee's business in the place in which the transferee has its head office.

(3) In sub-paragraph (2), any reference to a transferee of a particular description of person includes a reference to a transferee who will be of that description if the proposed banking business transfer scheme takes effect.

Certificates as to consent of home state regulator

9 A certificate under this paragraph is one given by the Authority and certifying that the home State regulator of the authorised person concerned or of the transferee has been notified of the proposed scheme and that—

(a) the home State regulator has responded to the notification; or

(b) the period of three months beginning with the notification has elapsed.

PART III INSURANCE BUSINESS TRANSFERS EFFECTED OUTSIDE THE UNITED KINGDOM

10 (1) This paragraph applies to a proposal to execute under provisions corresponding to Part VII in a country or territory other than the United Kingdom an instrument transferring all the rights and obligations of the transferor under general or long-term insurance policies, or under such descriptions of such policies as may be specified in the instrument, to the transferee if any of the conditions in sub-paragraphs (2), (3) or (4) is met in relation to it.

(2) The transferor is an EEA firm falling within paragraph 5(d) of Schedule 3 and the transferee is an authorised person whose margin of solvency is supervised by the Authority.

(3) The transferor is a company authorised in an EEA State other than the United Kingdom under Article 27 of the first life insurance directive, or Article 23 of the first non-life insurance directive and the transferee is a UK authorised person which has received authorisation under Article 6 of either of those directives.

关于财务资源的证书

第8条 (1)本条规定的证书由有关机关发出,证明对于所提出的转让,受让人具有或者将在计划生效之前具有足够财务资源。

(2)“有关机关”系指

(a)管理局,如受让人为获得第四部分许可或附录4规定许可的人;

(b)受让人的母国监管机关,如受让人为欧洲经济区企业,属于附录3第5条第(b)款的情况;

(c)在受让人的总部所在地负责监督受让人业务的机关,如受让人不属于第(a)项或第(b)项规定的情况。

(3)在第(2)款中,对特定种类受让人的任何述及包括如果所提出的银行业务转让计划生效则将属于这个种类的受让人。

关于母国监管机关同意的证书

第9条 本条规定的证书由管理局发出,证明已通知相关的获授权人或受让人的母国监管机关所提出的计划并且

(a)母国监管机关已经对通知作出答复;或者

(b)通知之后的3个月期限已过。

第三部分 在联合王国境外实行的保险业务转让

第10条 (1)本条适用于按照与第七部分对应的规定在联合王国以外的国家或地区执行将转让人在普通或长期保单项下或在文件中指定种类的此等保单的项下的所有权利和义务转让给受让人的文件的提议,如果满足第(2)款、第(3)款或第(4)款中的与之有关的任何条件。

(2)转让人是欧洲经济区企业,属于附录3第5条第(d)款的情况,而受让人是偿付能力受管理局监管的获授权人。

(3)转让人是第一人寿保险指令第27条或第一非人寿保险指令第23条规定的联合王国以外欧洲经济区国家的被授权公司,而受让人是依照第一人寿保险指令或第一非人寿保险指令第6条获得授权的联合王国获授权人。

(4) The transferor is a Swiss general insurer and the transferee is a UK authorised person which has received authorisation under Article 6 of the first life insurance directive or the first non–life insurance directive.

(5) In relation to a proposed transfer to which this paragraph applies, the Authority may, if it is satisfied that the transferee possesses the necessary margin of solvency, issue a certificate to that effect.

(6) "Necessary margin of solvency" means the margin of solvency which the transferee, taking the proposed transfer into account, is required by the Authority to maintain.

(7) "Swiss general insurer" has the same meaning as in paragraph 2.

(8) "General policy" means a policy evidencing a contract which, if it had been effected by the transferee, would have constituted the carrying on of a regulated activity consisting of the effecting of contracts of general insurance.

(9) "Long–term policy" means a policy evidencing a contract which, if it had been effected by the transferee, would have constituted the carrying on of a regulated activity consisting of the effecting of contracts of long–term insurance.

SCHEDULE 13 THE FINANCIAL SERVICES AND MARKETS TRIBUNAL

Section 132(4)

PART I GENERAL

Interpretation

1 In this Schedule—

"panel of chairmen" means the panel established under paragraph 3(1);

"lay panel" means the panel established under paragraph 3(4);

"rules" means rules made by the Lord Chancellor under section 132.

PART II THE TRIBUNAL

President

2 (1) The Lord Chancellor must appoint one of the members of the panel of chairmen to preside over the discharge of the Tribunal's functions.

(2) The member so appointed is to be known as the President of the Financial Services

(4)转让人是瑞士的一般承保人,而受让人是已经依照第一人寿保险指令或第一非人寿保险指令第6条获得授权的联合王国获授权人。

(5)对于适用本条规定拟进行的转让,管理局如果确信受让人具有必要的偿付能力,则可发出证书予以证明。

(6)“必要的清偿能力限度”系指考虑到拟进行的转让,管理局要求受让人维持的清偿能力限度。

(7)“瑞士的一般承保人”具有第2条中的含义。

(8)“一般保单”,系指证明如果被受让人订立则将构成开展包括订立一般保险合同的受监管活动的合同的保险单。

(9)“长期保单”,系指证明如由受让人订立则构成开展以订立长期保险合同为内容的受监管活动的保险单。

附录13 金融服务与市场裁判所

第132条第(4)款

第一部分 总 则

释 义

第1条 在本附录中

“委员小组”系指依照第3条第(1)款设立的小组;

“非专业人员小组”系指依照第3条第(4)款设立的小组;

“规则”系指司法大臣依照本法第132条制定的规则。

第二部分 裁 判 所

审 判 长

第2条 (1)司法大臣必须任命委员小组成员中的一位主持裁判所职能的履行。

(2)被任命的成员将称为金融服务和市场裁判所审判长(但是在本法中称为审判长)。

and Markets Tribunal (but is referred to in this Act as "the President").

(3) The Lord Chancellor may appoint one of the members of the panel of chairmen to be Deputy President.

(4) The Deputy President is to have such functions in relation to the Tribunal as the President may assign to him.

(5) The Lord Chancellor may not appoint a person to be the President or Deputy President unless that person—

(a) has a ten year general qualification within the meaning of section 71 of the [M126] Courts and Legal Services Act 1990;

(b) is an advocate or solicitor in Scotland of at least ten years' standing; or

(c) is—

(i) a member of the Bar of Northern Ireland of at least ten years' standing; or

(ii) a solicitor of the Supreme Court of Northern Ireland of at least ten years' standing.

(6) If the President (or Deputy President) ceases to be a member of the panel of chairmen, he also ceases to be the President (or Deputy President).

(7) The functions of the President may, if he is absent or is otherwise unable to act, be discharged—

(a) by the Deputy President; or

(b) if there is no Deputy President or he too is absent or otherwise unable to act, by a person appointed for that purpose from the panel of chairmen by the Lord Chancellor.

Annotations:

Marginal Citations

M126 1990 c. 41.

Panels

3 (1) The Lord Chancellor must appoint a panel of persons for the purposes of serving as chairmen of the Tribunal.

(2) A person is qualified for membership of the panel of chairmen if—

(a) he has a seven year general qualification within the meaning of section 71 of the [M127] Courts and Legal Services Act 1990;

(b) he is an advocate or solicitor in Scotland of at least seven years' standing; or

(c) he is—

(i) a member of the Bar of Northern Ireland of at least seven years' standing; or

(ii) a solicitor of the Supreme Court of Northern Ireland of at least seven years' standing.

(3) The panel of chairmen must include at least one member who is a person of the kind

(3)司法大臣可以任命委员小组成员中的一位为副审判长。

(4)副审判长具有审判长向其分派的与裁判所有关的职能。

(5)司法大臣只可以任命满足下列条件的人为审判长或副审判长：

(a)具有[M126]《1990年法院与法律服务法》第71条规定含义范围内的10年普通资格；

(b)是从业至少10年的苏格兰律师或事务律师；或者
(c)是
(i)从业至少10年的北爱尔兰律师会成员；或者
(ii)从业至少10年的北爱尔兰最高法院的事务律师。
(6)如审判长(或副审判长)不再是委员小组的成员，则也不再是审判长(或副审判长)。
(7)审判长如缺席或者由于其他原因无法采取行动，则其职能可以

(a)由副审判长履行；或者
(b)如无副审判长，或者副审判长也缺席或者由于其他原因无法行事，则由司法大臣为此目的在委员小组中指定的人履行。

注释：

附注引文

M126 1990年第41章。

小组

第3条 (1)司法大臣必须为担任裁判所委员之目的任命一个人员小组。

(2)满足下列条件的人有资格成为委员小组的成员：
(a)具有[M127]《1990年法院与法律服务法》第71条规定含义范围内的7年普通资格；

(b)是从业至少7年的苏格兰律师或事务律师；或者
(c)是
(i)从业至少7年的北爱尔兰律师会成员；或者
(ii)从业至少7年的北爱尔兰最高法院的事务律师。

(3)委员小组中必须至少有一位成员是第(2)款第(b)项中所述类别的人。

mentioned in sub-paragraph (2)(b).

(4) The Lord Chancellor must also appoint a panel of persons who appear to him to be qualified by experience or otherwise to deal with matters of the kind that may be referred to the Tribunal.

Annotations:

Marginal Citations

M127 1990 c. 41.

Terms of office etc

4 (1) Subject to the provisions of this Schedule, each member of the panel of chairmen and the lay panel is to hold and vacate office in accordance with the terms of his appointment.

(2) The Lord Chancellor may remove a member of either panel (including the President) on the ground of incapacity or misbehaviour.

(3) A member of either panel—

(a) may at any time resign office by notice in writing to the Lord Chancellor;

(b) is eligible for re-appointment if he ceases to hold office.

Remuneration and expenses

5 The Lord Chancellor may pay to any person, in respect of his service—

(a) as a member of the Tribunal (including service as the President or Deputy President), or

(b) as a person appointed under paragraph 7(4), such remuneration and allowances as he may determine.

Staff

6 (1) The Lord Chancellor may appoint such staff for the Tribunal as he may determine.

(2) The remuneration of the Tribunal's staff is to be defrayed by the Lord Chancellor.

(3) Such expenses of the Tribunal as the Lord Chancellor may determine are to be defrayed by the Lord Chancellor.

PART Ⅲ CONSTITUTION OF TRIBUNAL

7 (1) On a reference to the Tribunal, the persons to act as members of the Tribunal for the purposes of the reference are to be selected from the panel of chairmen or the lay panel in accordance with arrangements made by the President for the purposes of this paragraph ("the

(4)司法大臣还必须任命一个人员小组,其成员必须在司法大臣看来由于有经验或者其他原因而有资格处理可提交给裁判所裁决的事务。

注释:

附注引文
M127 1990年第41章。

任职规定等

第4条 (1)根据本附录的规定,委员小组和非专业人员小组的每个成员将根据其任命规定任职和离职。

(2)司法大臣可以以不胜任或行为不端为由开除任何小组的成员(包括审判长)。

(3)任何小组的成员

(a)可以随时通过书面通知司法大臣辞职;

(b)如不再任职,有资格获得再次任命。

报酬和费用

第5条 司法大臣可以向任何人支付其确定的担任下列职务的报酬和津贴:

(a)裁判所成员(包括担任审判长或者副审判长),或者

(b)依照第7条第(4)款任命的人。

工作人员

第6条 (1)司法大臣可以任命其确定的裁判所工作人员。

(2)裁判所工作人员的报酬由司法大臣支付。

(3)司法大臣确定的裁判所费用由司法大臣支付。

第三部分 裁判所的组织制度

第7条 (1)事项诉至裁判所后,将按照审判长为本条之目的作出的安排(以下简称常设安排),从委员小组或非专业人员小组中选择将为所诉事项之目的担任裁判所成员的人。

standing arrangements").

(2) The standing arrangements must provide for at least one member to be selected from the panel of chairmen.

(3) If while a reference is being dealt with, a person serving as member of the Tribunal in respect of the reference becomes unable to act, the reference may be dealt with by—

(a) the other members selected in respect of that reference; or

(b) if it is being dealt with by a single member, such other member of the panel of chairmen as may be selected in accordance with the standing arrangements for the purposes of the reference.

(4) If it appears to the Tribunal that a matter before it involves a question of fact of special difficulty, it may appoint one or more experts to provide assistance.

PART IV TRIBUNAL PROCEDURE

8 For the purpose of dealing with references, or any matter preliminary or incidental to a reference, the Tribunal must sit at such times and in such place or places as the Lord Chancellor may direct.

9 Rules made by the Lord Chancellor under section 132 may, in particular, include provision—

(a) as to the manner in which references are to be instituted;

(b) for the holding of hearings in private in such circumstances as may be specified in the rules;

(c) as to the persons who may appear on behalf of the parties;

(d) for a member of the panel of chairmen to hear and determine interlocutory matters arising on a reference;

(e) for the suspension of decisions of the Authority which have taken effect;

(f) as to the withdrawal of references;

(g) as to the registration, publication and proof of decisions and orders.

Practice directions

10 The President of the Tribunal may give directions as to the practice and procedure to be followed by the Tribunal in relation to references to it.

Evidence

11 (1) The Tribunal may by summons require any person to attend, at such time and place as is specified in the summons, to give evidence or to produce any document in his custody or under his control which the Tribunal considers it necessary to examine.

(2) The Tribunal may—

(2)常设安排必须规定至少一位成员从委员小组中选择。

(3)如在处理诉至裁判所的事项时,为所诉事项担任裁判所成员的人无法行事,则可以由下列人员处理所诉事项:

(a)为所诉事项选择的其他成员;或者

(b)为所诉之目的按照常设安排选择的委员小组的其他成员,如所诉事项由一位成员单独处理。

(4)如果裁判所认为诉至裁判所的事项涉及特别困难的事实问题,则可任命一位或多位专家提供援助。

第四部分 裁判所程序

第8条 为处理所诉事项或所诉事项的任何初步或附带事项,裁判所必须在司法大臣指定的时间和地点开庭。

第9条 司法大臣依照第132条制定的规则特别可以包括下列规定:

(a)与事项诉至裁判所的方式有关;

(b)在规则中规定的情况下秘密审理;

(c)与可以代表各方出席的人有关的;

(d)委员小组的一位成员审理和确定所述事项引起的中间事项;

(e)暂停已经生效的管理局决定;

(f)与撤回所诉事项有关;

(g)与决定和命令的注册、公布和证明有关。

做 法 指 示

第10条 裁判所审判长可以就裁判所须遵守的关于诉至裁判所事项的做法和程序发出指示。

证 据

第11条 (1)裁判所可以通过传票要求任何人在传票中指定的时间和地点出庭,提供裁判所认为有必要查证的证据或出具裁判所认为有必要查证且由该人保管或控制的任何文件。

(2)裁判所可以

(a) take evidence on oath and for that purpose administer oaths; or

(b) instead of administering an oath, require the person examined to make and subscribe a declaration of the truth of the matters in respect of which he is examined.

(3) A person who without reasonable excuse—

(a) refuses or fails—

(i) to attend following the issue of a summons by the Tribunal, or

(ii) to give evidence, or

(b) alters, suppresses, conceals or destroys, or refuses to produce a document which he may be required to produce for the purposes of proceedings before the Tribunal, is guilty of an offence.

(4) A person guilty of an offence under sub-paragraph (3)(a) is liable on summary conviction to a fine not exceeding the statutory maximum.

(5) A person guilty of an offence under sub-paragraph (3)(b) is liable—

(a) on summary conviction, to a fine not exceeding the statutory maximum;

(b) on conviction on indictment, to imprisonment for a term not exceeding two years or a fine or both.

Decisions of Tribunal

12 (1) A decision of the Tribunal may be taken by a majority.

(2) The decision must—

(a) state whether it was unanimous or taken by a majority;

(b) be recorded in a document which—

(i) contains a statement of the reasons for the decision; and

(ii) is signed and dated by the member of the panel of chairmen dealing with the reference.

(3) The Tribunal must—

(a) inform each party of its decision; and

(b) as soon as reasonably practicable, send to each party and, if different, to any authorised person concerned, a copy of the document mentioned in subparagraph (2).

(4) The Tribunal must send the Treasury a copy of its decision.

Costs

13 (1) If the Tribunal considers that a party to any proceedings on a reference has acted vexatiously, frivolously or unreasonably it may order that party to pay to another party to the proceedings the whole or part of the costs or expenses incurred by the other party in connection with the proceedings.

(2) If, in any proceedings on a reference, the Tribunal considers that a decision of the

(a)录取宣誓证据并为该目的主持宣誓仪式;或者

(b)不主持宣誓仪式,但要求受审查人就被审查事项的真实性作出并签署声明。

(3)如果当事人没有合理理由

(a)拒绝或未能

(i)在裁判所发出传票后出庭,或者

(ii)提供证据,或者

(b)变造、隐瞒、隐藏或毁灭或者拒绝出具他需要为裁判所程序之目的出具的文件,则构成犯罪。

(4)依照第(3)款第(a)项构成犯罪的,应当经简易程序定罪处以不超过法定最高限额的罚金。

(5)依照第(3)款第(b)项构成犯罪的,应当承担下列责任:

(a)经简易程序定罪的,处以不超过法定最高限额的罚金;

(b)经公诉程序定罪的,处以不超过2年的有期徒刑或罚金,或两罚并处。

裁判所的决定

第12条 (1)裁判所的决定可以由多数成员作出。

(2)决定必须

(a)说明其为一致决定还是多数决定;

(b)在下列文件中记录

(i)包含决定原因声明;并且

(ii)由处理所诉事项的委员小组的成员签名并标注日期。

(3)裁判所必须

(a)告知各方当事人其决定;并且

(b)在合理可行时尽快向各方当事人送达第(2)款所述文件的副本,并且向任何相关的获授权人(如与当事人不同)送达第(2)款所述文件的副本。

(4)裁判所必须向财政部送达其决定的副本。

成　本

第13条 (1)如果裁判所认为所诉事项的任何程序中一方当事人实施了旨在为难对方、轻佻或无理的行为,则可以命令该方当事人向程序的另一方当事人支付其发生的与程序有关的全部或部分成本或费用。

(2)如果在关于所诉事项的任何程序中裁判所认为作为所诉事项主体的管理局

Authority which is the subject of the reference was unreasonable it may order the Authority to pay to another party to the proceedings the whole or part of the costs or expenses incurred by the other party in connection with the proceedings.

SCHEDULE 14
ROLE OF THE COMPETITION COMMISSION

Section 162

Provision of information by Treasury

1 (1) The Treasury's powers under this paragraph are to be exercised only for the purpose of assisting the Commission in carrying out an investigation under section 162.

(2) The Treasury may give to the Commission—

(a) any information in their possession which relates to matters falling within the scope of the investigation; and

(b) other assistance in relation to any such matters.

(3) In carrying out an investigation under section 162, the Commission must have regard to any information given to it under this paragraph.

Consideration of matters arising on a report

2 In considering any matter arising from a report made by the Director under section 160, the Commission must have regard to—

(a) any representations made to it in connection with the matter by any person appearing to the Commission to have a substantial interest in the matter; and

(b) any cost benefit analysis prepared by the Authority (at any time) in connection with the regulatory provision or practice, or any of the regulatory provisions or practices, which are the subject of the report.

Applied provisions

3 (1) The provisions mentioned in sub-paragraph (2) are to apply in relation to the functions of the Commission under section 162 as they apply in relation to the functions of the Commission in relation to a reference to the Commission under the [M128] Fair Trading Act 1973.

(2) The provisions are—

(a) section 82(2), (3) and (4) of the Fair Trading Act 1973 (general provisions about reports);

决定不合理，则可以命令管理局向程序的另一方当事人支付其发生的与程序有关的全部或部分成本或费用。

附录14 竞争委员会的作用

第162条

财政部提供信息

第1条 (1)财政部依照本条拥有的权力只能为协助委员会进行本法第162条规定的调查之目的行使。

(2)财政部可以给予委员会

(a)其持有的与调查范围内的事项有关的任何信息;和

(b)与任何此等事项有关的其他协助。

(3)在进行第162条项下的调查时,委员会必须考虑在本项项下向其提供的任何信息。

对报告引起的事项的考虑

第2条 在考虑总理事依照第160条作出的报告引起的任何事项时，委员会必须考虑

(a)委员会认为在事项中有实质利害关系的任何人向其作出的与事项有关的任何陈述;以及

(b)管理局(在任何时间)就其所编制的报告涵盖的监管规定或行为或报告涵盖的监管规定或行为中的任何一项进行的任何成本效益分析。

适用规定

第3条 (1)第(2)款所述的规定适用于第162条规定的委员会职能,还适用于与《1973年公平交易法》规定的向委员会提交事项有关的委员会职能。M128

(2)前款所述规定如下:

(a)《1973年公平交易法》第82条第(2)款、第(3)款和第(4)款(关于报告的一般规定);

(b) section 85 of that Act (attendance of witnesses and production of documents);

(c) section 93B of that Act (false or misleading information);

(d) section 24 of the [M129] Competition Act 1980 (modifications of provisions about the performance of the Commission's functions);

(e) Part Ⅱ of Schedule 7 to the [M130] Competition Act 1998 (performance by the Commission of its general functions).

(3) But the reference in paragraph 15(7)(b) in Schedule 7 to the 1998 Act to section 75(5) of that Act is to be read as a reference to the power of the Commission to decide not to make a report in accordance with section 162(2).

Annotations:

Marginal Citations

M128 1973 c. 41.

M129 1980 c. 21.

M130 1998 c. 41.

Publication of reports

4 (1) If the Commission makes a report under section 162, it must publish it in such a way as appears to it to be best calculated to bring it to the attention of the public.

(2) Before publishing the report the Commission must, so far as practicable, exclude any matter which relates to the private affairs of a particular individual the publication of which, in the opinion of the Commission, would or might seriously and prejudicially affect his interests.

(3) Before publishing the report the Commission must, so far as practicable, also exclude any matter which relates to the affairs of a particular body the publication of which, in the opinion of the Commission, would or might seriously and prejudicially affect its interests.

(4) Sub-paragraphs (2) and (3) do not apply in relation to copies of a report which the Commission is required to send under section 162(10).

(b)该法第85条(证人的出庭和出示文件);

(c)该法第93B条(虚假或误导信息);

(d)[M129]《1980年竞争法》第24条(对关于履行委员会职能的规定的修改);

(e)[M130]《1988年竞争法》附录7第二部分(委员会基本职能的履行)。

(3)但是在1998年法附录7第15条第(7)款第(b)项中,述及该法第75条第(5)款视为述及委员会决定不按照第162条第(2)款作出报告的权力。

注释:

附注引文

M128 1973年第41章。

M129 1980年第21章。

M130 1998年第41章。

报告的公布

第4条 (1)如果委员会依照第162条作出报告,则必须以其认为最便于公众了解的方式公布该报告。

(2)在发布报告前,委员会如认为公布与某一特定个人的个人事务相关的事项将会或可能严重损害该人利益,则必须在切实可行的范围内排除任何涉及该事务的事项。

(3)在发布报告以前,委员会如认为公布与某一特定机构的事务相关的事项将会或可能严重损害该机构的利益,则必须在切实可行的范围内赔偿任何涉及该事务的事项。

(4)第(2)款和第(3)款不适用于本法第162条第(10)款要求委员会发送的报告副本。

SCHEDULE 15 INFORMATION AND INVESTIGATIONS: CONNECTED PERSONS

Sections 165(11) and 171(4)

PART I RULES FOR SPECIFIC BODIES

Annotations:

Modifications etc. (not altering text)

C407 Sch. 15 Pt. I (paras. 1–7) modified (1.12.2001) by S.I. 2001/2657, arts. 1(1), 15 (2) (which was revoked (8.10.2001) by S.I. 2001/3083, arts. 1(2), 23); S.I. 2001/3538, art. 2(1)

Sch. 15 Pt. I (paras. 1–7) modified (1.12.2001) by S.I. 2001/3083, arts. 1(2), 15(2); S. I. 2001/3538, art. 2(1)

Sch. 15 Pt. I (paras. 1–7) amended (temp. from 11.8.2001 to 1.12.2001) by S.I. 2001/2659, arts. 1(2), 2(2); S.I. 2001/3538, art. 2(1)

C408 Sch. 15 Pt. I modified (8.4.2002) by The Financial Services and Markets Act 2000 (Permission and Applications) (Credit Unions etc.) Order 2002 (S.I. 2002/704), art. 8 (2)

Corporate bodies

1 If the authorised person ("BC") is a body corporate, a person who is or has been—

(a) an officer or manager of BC or of a parent undertaking of BC;
(b) an employee of BC;
(c) an agent of BC or of a parent undertaking of BC.

Partnerships

2 If the authorised person ("PP") is a partnership, a person who is or has been a member, manager, employee or agent of PP.

Unincorporated associations

3 If the authorised person ("UA") is an unincorporated association of persons which

附录15 信息和调查:关联人

第165条第(11)款和第171条第(4)款

第一部分 特定机构的规则

注释:

修改等(不涉及条文内容)

C407 附录15第一部分(第1条至第7条)于2001年12月1日依照制定法文件S.I. 2001/2657第1条第(1)款、第15条第(2)款[于2001年10月8日依照制定法文件S.I.2001/3083第1条第(2)款、第23条废除];制定法文件S.I. 2001/3538第2条第(1)款修订;

附录15第一部分(第1条至第7条)于2001年12月1日依照过制定法文件S.I.2001/3083第1条第(2)款,第15条第(2)款;制定法文件S.I.2001/3538,第2条第(1)款修订;

附录15第一部分(第1条至第7条)暂定于2001年8月11日至2001年12月1日依照制定法文件S.I. 2001/2659第1条第(2)款;第2条第(2)款;制定法文件S.I. 2001/3538第2条第(1)款修正。

C408 附录15第一部分于2002年4月8日依照《2000年金融服务与市场法》(许可和申请)(信用合作社等)2002号令(制定法文件S.I. 2002/704)第8条第(2)款修订。

法 人

第1条 如获授权人(以下简称BC)为法人,则关联人系指现在或已经是下列人士的人:

(a)BC或者BC的母企业的高级职员或经理;

(b)BC的雇员;

(c)BC或者BC的母企业的代理人。

合 伙

第2条 如获授权人(以下简称PP)为合伙,则关联人系指现在或已经是PP的成员、经理、雇员或代理人的人。

非 法 人

第3条 如获授权人(以下简称UA)为非法人,且既不是合伙,也不是非法人互相

is neither a partnership nor an unincorporated friendly society, a person who is or has been an officer, manager, employee or agent of UA.

Friendly societies

4 (1) If the authorised person ("FS") is a friendly society, a person who is or has been an officer, manager or employee of FS.

(2) In relation to FS, "officer" and "manager" have the same meaning as in section 119 (1) of the [M131] Friendly Societies Act 1992.

Annotations:

Marginal Citations

M131 1992 c. 40.

Building societies

5 (1) If the authorised person ("BS") is a building society, a person who is or has been an officer or employee of BS.

(2) In relation to BS, "officer" has the same meaning as it has in section 119(1) of the [M132] Building Societies Act 1986.

Annotations:

Marginal Citations

M132 1986 c. 53.

Individuals

6 If the authorised person ("IP") is an individual, a person who is or has been an employee or agent of IP.

Application to sections 171 and 172

7 For the purposes of sections 171 and 172, if the person under investigation is not an authorised person the references in this Part of this Schedule to an authorised person are to be taken to be references to the person under investigation.

PART II ADDITIONAL RULES

8 A person who is, or at the relevant time was, the partner, manager, employee, agent, appointed representative, banker, auditor, actuary or solicitor of—

(a) the person under investigation ("A");

保险协会，则关联人系指现在或已经是UA的高级职员、经理、雇员或代理人的人。

互相保险协会

第4条 (1)如获授权人(以下简称FS)为互相保险协会，则关联人系指现在或已经是FS的高级职员、经理或雇员的人。

(2)对FS而言，"高级职员"和"经理"具有[M131]《1992年互相保险协会法》第119条第(1)款中的含义。

注释：

附注引文

M131 1992年第40章。

住房互助会

第5条 (1)如获授权人(以下简称BS)为住房互助会，则关联人系指现在或已经是BS的高级职员或雇员的人。

(2)就BS而言，"高级职员"具有[M132]《1986年住房互助会法》第119条第(1)款中的含义。

注释：

附注引文

M132 1986年第53章。

个 人

第6条 如获授权人(以下简称IP)为个人，则关联人系指现在或已经是IP的雇员或代理人的人。

适用第171条和第172条

第7条 就本法第171条和第172条而言，如被调查人不是获授权人，则在本附录本部分中述及被授权人视为述及被调查人。

第二部分 附 则

第8条 现在或者在相关时间是下列各项的合伙人、经理、雇员、代理人、被任命代表、银行家、审计员、保险统计员或事务律师的人：

(a)被调查人(以下简称A)；

(b) a parent undertaking of A;

(c) a subsidiary undertaking of A;

(d) a subsidiary undertaking of a parent undertaking of A; or

(e) a parent undertaking of a subsidiary undertaking of A.

SCHEDULE 16 PROHIBITIONS AND RESTRICTIONS IMPOSED BY DIRECTOR GENERAL OF FAIR TRADING

Section 203(8)

Preliminary

1 In this Schedule—

"appeal period" has the same meaning as in the [M133] Consumer Credit Act 1974;

"prohibition" means a consumer credit prohibition under section 203;

"restriction" means a restriction under section 204.

Annotations:

Marginal Citations

M133 1974 c. 39.

Notice of prohibition or restriction

2 (1) This paragraph applies if the Director proposes, in relation to a firm—

(a) to impose a prohibition;

(b) to impose a restriction; or

(c) to vary a restriction otherwise than with the agreement of the firm.

(2) The Director must by notice—

(a) inform the firm of his proposal, stating his reasons; and

(b) invite the firm to submit representations in accordance with paragraph 4.

(3) If he imposes the prohibition or restriction or varies the restriction, the Director may give directions authorising the firm to carry into effect agreements made before the coming into force of the prohibition, restriction or variation.

(4) A prohibition, restriction or variation is not to come into force before the end of the appeal period.

(5) If the Director imposes a prohibition or restriction or varies a restriction, he must serve a copy of the prohibition, restriction or variation—

(b)A的母企业；
(c)A的子企业；
(d)A母企业的子企业；或者
(e)A子企业的母企业。

附录16 公平交易总理事提出的禁止和限制

第203条第(8)款

初步规定

第1条 在本附录中

“复议期”具有[M133]《1974年消费信贷法》中的意义；
“禁止”系指本法第203条规定的消费信贷禁止；
“限制”系指本法第204条规定的限制。

注释：

附注引文
M133 1974年第39章。

禁止或限制通知

第2条 (1)如果总理事拟对一家企业采取下列行动，则适用本条规定：
(a)加以禁止；
(b)加以限制；或者
(c)未经企业同意变更限制。
(2)总理事必须通过通知
(a)告知该企业其拟采取的行动，陈述理由；并且
(b)请该企业按照第4条规定提交陈述。
(3)如果总理事加以禁止或限制或者变更限制，则可以发出指令，授权企业执行在禁止、限制或变更生效之前订立的协议。

(4)在复议期结束之前，禁止、限制或变更不生效。

(5)如果总理事加以禁止或限制或者变更限制，则必须将禁止、限制或变更的副本送达

(a) on the Authority; and

(b) on the firm's home state regulator.

Annotations:

Modifications etc. (not altering text)

C409 Sch. 16 para. 2(2) extended (1.12.2001) by S.I. 2001/3592, arts. 1(2), 24 (with art. 23(2))

C410 Sch. 16 para. 2(3) extended (1.12.2001) by S.I. 2001/2636, arts. 1(2)(b), 53 (4); S.I. 2001/3538, art. 2(1)

Application to revoke prohibition or restriction

3 (1) This paragraph applies if the Director proposes to refuse an application made by a firm for the revocation of a prohibition or restriction.

(2) The Director must by notice—

(a) inform the firm of the proposed refusal, stating his reasons; and

(b) invite the firm to submit representations in accordance with paragraph 4.

Representations to Director

4 (1) If this paragraph applies to an invitation to submit representations, the Director must invite the firm, within 21 days after the notice containing the invitation is given to it or such longer period as he may allow—

(a) to submit its representations in writing to him; and

(b) to give notice to him, if the firm thinks fit, that it wishes to make representations orally.

(2) If notice is given under sub-paragraph (1)(b), the Director must arrange for the oral representations to be heard.

(3) The Director must give the firm notice of his determination.

Appeals

5 Section 41 of the [M134] Consumer Credit Act 1974(appeals to the Secretary of State) has effect as if—

(a) the following determinations were mentioned in column 1 of the table set out at the end of that section—

(i) imposition of a prohibition or restriction or the variation of a restriction; and

(ii) refusal of an application for the revocation of a prohibition or restriction; and (a)管理局;和

(b)企业的母国监管机关。

注释:

修改等(不涉及条文内容)

C409 附录16第2条第(2)款于2001年12月1日依照制定法文件S.I. 2001/3592第1条第(2)款、第24条[与第23条第(2)款]扩大适用范围。

C410 附录16第2条第(3)款于2001年12月1日依照制定法文件S.I. 2001/2636第1条第(2)款第(b)项、第53条第(4)款;制定法文件S.I. 2001/3538第2条第(1)款扩大适用范围。

申请撤销禁止或限制

第3条 (1)如总理事拟驳回企业作出的撤销禁止或限制的申请,则适用本条规定。

(2)总理事必须通过通知

(a)告知企业拟驳回申请,陈述其理由;并且

(b)请企业依照第4条规定提交陈述。

提交给总理事的陈述

第4条 (1)如本条规定适用于提交陈述的请求,则总理事必须请企业在向该企业发出包含该请求的通知后21日内或者总理事允许的更长期限内

(a)向总理事提交其书面陈述;并且

(b)如企业认为适当,则通知总理事,该企业希望进行口头陈述。

(2)如依照第(1)款第(b)项发出通知,则总理事必须安排听取口头陈述。

(3)总理事必须将其决定通知企业。

复 议

第5条 [M134]《1974年消费信贷法》(向国务大臣申请复议)第41条有效,等同于

(a)下列决定在该条最后的表格第一栏中述及:

(i)加以禁止或限制,或变更限制;和

(ii)驳回撤销禁止或限制的申请;并且

(b) the firm concerned were mentioned in column 2 of that table in relation to those determinations.

Annotations:

Marginal Citations

M134 1974 c. 39.

SCHEDULE 17 THE OMBUDSMAN SCHEME

Section 225(4)

PART I GENERAL

Interpretation

1 In this Schedule—

"ombudsman" means a person who is a member of the panel; and

"the panel" means the panel established under paragraph 4.

PART II THE SCHEME OPERATOR

Establishment by the Authority

2 (1) The Authority must establish a body corporate to exercise the functions conferred on the scheme operator by or under this Act.

(2) The Authority must take such steps as are necessary to ensure that the scheme operator is, at all times, capable of exercising those functions.

Constitution

3 (1) The constitution of the scheme operator must provide for it to have—

(a) a chairman; and

(b) a board (which must include the chairman) whose members are the scheme operator's directors.

(2) The chairman and other members of the board must be persons appointed, and liable to removal from office, by the Authority (acting, in the case of the chairman, with the approval of the Treasury).

(3) But the terms of their appointment (and in particular those governing removal from

(b)相关企业就上述决定在该表格第二栏中述及。

注释：

附注引文
M134 1974年第39章。

附录17 申诉专员计划

第225条第(4)款

第一部分 总 则

释 义

第1条 在本附录中

"申诉专员"指的是小组的成员；

"小组"系指依照第4条建立的小组。

第二部分 计划执行人

由管理局建立

第2条 (1)管理局必须建立一个法人，履行本法或依照本法授予计划执行人的职能。

(2)管理局必须采取下列必要步骤以确保计划执行人在任何时候能够履行这些职能。

组织制度

第3条 (1)计划执行人的组织制度必须规定设有

(a)一位主席；和

(b)一个董事会(必须包括主席)，其成员是计划执行人的董事。

(2)主席和董事会的其他成员必须由管理局任命，并且可以被管理局免职(如果是主席，需要获得财政部的批准)。

(3)但主席和董事会其他成员的任命条款(特别是免职规定)必须确保其在计划

office) must be such as to secure their independence from the Authority in the operation of the scheme.

(4) The function of making voluntary jurisdiction rules under section 227 and the functions conferred by paragraphs 4, 5, 7, 9 or 14 may be exercised only by the board.

(5) The validity of any act of the scheme operator is unaffected by—

(a) a vacancy in the office of chairman; or

(b) a defect in the appointment of a person as chairman or as a member of the board.

The panel of ombudsmen

4 (1) The scheme operator must appoint and maintain a panel of persons, appearing to it to have appropriate qualifications and experience, to act as ombudsmen for the purposes of the scheme.

(2) A person's appointment to the panel is to be on such terms (including terms as to the duration and termination of his appointment and as to remuneration) as the scheme operator considers—

(a) consistent with the independence of the person appointed; and

(b) otherwise appropriate.

The Chief Ombudsman

5 (1) The scheme operator must appoint one member of the panel to act as Chief Ombudsman.

(2) The Chief Ombudsman is to be appointed on such terms (including terms as to the duration and termination of his appointment) as the scheme operator considers appropriate.

Status

6 (1) The scheme operator is not to be regarded as exercising functions on behalf of the Crown.

(2) The scheme operator's board members, officers and staff are not to be regarded as Crown servants.

(3) Appointment as Chief Ombudsman or to the panel or as a deputy ombudsman does not confer the status of Crown servant.

Annual reports

7 (1) At least once a year—

(a) the scheme operator must make a report to the Authority on the discharge of its functions; and

(b) the Chief Ombudsman must make a report to the Authority on the discharge of his

执行中独立于管理局。

（4）依照本法第227条制定自愿管辖权规则的职能和本附录第4条、第5条、第7条、第9条或第14条赋予的职能只可以由委员会行使。

（5）计划执行人的任何行为的效力不受下列各项的影响：

（a）主席职务空缺；或者

（b）任命一个人为主席或委员会成员存在瑕疵。

申诉专员小组

第4条 （1）计划执行人必须任命并维持其认为拥有适当资格和经验的人员小组，为计划的施行以申诉专员身份处理事务。

（2）对小组成员的任命将遵守计划执行人认为

（a）与被任命人的独立性相一致；且

（b）在其他方面适当的规定（包括关于任职期限和终止以及报酬的规定）。

首席申诉专员

第5条 （1）计划执行人必须任命小组的一位成员作为首席申诉专员行事。

（2）对首席申诉专员的任命将遵守计划执行人认为适当的规定（包括关于任命期限和终止以及报酬的规定）。

地　位

第6条 （1）计划执行人不视为代表内阁履行职能。

（2）计划执行人的董事会成员、高级职员和工作人员不视为内阁雇员。

（3）对首席申诉专员或小组成员或副申诉专员的任命不赋予内阁雇员的身份。

年度报告

第7条 （1）至少每年1次

（a）计划执行人必须向管理局作出关于履行其职能的报告；并且

（b）首席申诉专员必须向管理局作出关于履行其职能的报告。

functions.

(2) Each report must distinguish between functions in relation to the scheme's compulsory jurisdiction and functions in relation to its voluntary jurisdiction.

(3) Each report must also comply with any requirements specified in rules made by the Authority.

(4) The scheme operator must publish each report in the way it considers appropriate.

Guidance

8 The scheme operator may publish guidance consisting of such information and advice as it considers appropriate and may charge for it or distribute it free of charge.

Budget

9 (1) The scheme operator must, before the start of each of its financial years, adopt an annual budget which has been approved by the Authority.

(2) The scheme operator may, with the approval of the Authority, vary the budget for a financial year at any time after its adoption.

(3) The annual budget must include an indication of—

(a) the distribution of resources deployed in the operation of the scheme, and

(b) the amounts of income of the scheme operator arising or expected to arise from the operation of the scheme,

distinguishing between the scheme's compulsory and voluntary jurisdiction.

Annotations:

Modifications etc. (not altering text)

C411 Sch. 17 para. 9(3) excluded (18.6.2001) by S.I. 2001/1821, arts. 1(1), 4(1)

Exemption from liability in damages

10 (1) No person is to be liable in damages for anything done or omitted in the discharge, or purported discharge, of any functions under this Act in relation to the compulsory jurisdiction.

(2) Sub-paragraph (1) does not apply—

(a) if the act or omission is shown to have been in bad faith; or

(b) so as to prevent an award of damages made in respect of an act or omission on the ground that the act or omission was unlawful as a result of section 6(1) of the [M135] Human Rights Act 1998.

(2)每份报告必须区分与计划的强制管辖权有关的职能和与其自愿管辖权有关的职能。

(3)每份报告还必须符合在管理局制定的规则中规定的任何要求。

(4)计划执行人必须以其认为适当的方式公布每份报告。

指　　南

第8条　计划执行人可以公布包括其认为适当的信息和建议的指南,并且可以收费或免费发行该指南。

预　　算

第9条　(1)计划执行人必须在每个财政年度开始之前通过管理局已批准的年度预算。

(2)经管理局批准,计划执行人可以在通过财政年度预算后的任何时间变更财政年度预算。

(3)年度预算必须包括表明

(a)在计划执行中配置的资源的分配,和

(b)计划执行产生或预计产生的计划执行人的收入数额,

区分制度的强制管辖权和自愿管辖权。

注释:

修改等(不涉及条文内容)

C411　附录17第9条第(3)款于2001年6月18日依照制定法文件S.I. 2001/1821第1条第(1)款、第4条第(1)款排除。

损害赔偿责任的免除

第10条　(1)任何人履行或声称履行本法与强制管辖权有关的任何职能时,对任何行为或不作为不承担赔偿责任。

(2)如有下列情况,则第(1)款不适用

(a)有证据证明该作为或不作为出于不诚信;或

(b)用于防止因依照[M135]《1998年人权法》第6条第(1)款规定的违法作为或不作为而作出损害赔偿判决。

Annotations:

Modifications etc. (not altering text)

C412 Sch. 17 para. 10 (1) amended (19.7.2001 for specified purposes otherwise 1.12.2001) by S.I. 2001/2326, arts. 1(1), 13; S.I. 2001/3538, art. 2(1)

Marginal Citations

M135 1998 c. 42.

Privilege

11 For the purposes of the law relating to defamation, proceedings in relation to a complaint which is subject to the compulsory jurisdiction are to be treated as if they were proceedings before a court.

Annotations:

Modifications etc. (not altering text)

C413 Sch. 17 para. 11 amended (19.7.2001 for specified purposes otherwise 1.12.2001) by S.I. 2001/2326, arts. 1(1), 14; S.I. 2001/3538, art. 2(1)

PART III THE COMPULSORY JURISDICTION

Introduction

12 This Part of this Schedule applies only in relation to the compulsory jurisdiction.

Authority's procedural rules

13 (1) The Authority must make rules providing that a complaint is not to be entertained unless the complainant has referred it under the ombudsman scheme before the applicable time limit (determined in accordance with the rules) has expired.

(2) The rules may provide that an ombudsman may extend that time limit in specified circumstances.

(3) The Authority may make rules providing that a complaint is not to be entertained (except in specified circumstances) if the complainant has not previously communicated its substance to the respondent and given him a reasonable opportunity to deal with it.

(4) The Authority may make rules requiring an authorised person who may become subject to the compulsory jurisdiction as a respondent to establish such procedures as the Authority considers appropriate for the resolution of complaints which—

注释：

修改等(不涉及条文内容)

C412　附录17第10条第(1)款为特定目的于2001年7月19日,否则于2001年12月1日依照制定法文件S.I. 2001/2326第1条第(1)款、第13条;制定法文件S.I. 2001/3538第2条第(1)款修正。

附注引文

M135　1998年第42章。

特　　权

第11条　就诽谤相关法律而言,与适用强制管辖权的申诉有关的程序将被视为在法院审理的程序。

注释：

修改等(不涉及条文内容)

C413　附录17第11条为特定目的于2001年7月19日,否则于2001年12月1日依照制定法文件S.I. 2001/2326第1条第(1)款、第14条;制定法文件S.I. 2001/3538第2条第(1)款修正。

第三部分　强制管辖权

引　　言

第12条　本附录本部分只适用于强制管辖权。

管理局的程序规则

第13条　(1)管理局必须制定规则,规定除非申诉人在适用的期限(按照规则确定)届满以前依照申诉专员计划提交申诉,否则申诉不予受理。

(2)规则可以规定申诉专员可以在特定情况下延长期限。

(3)管理局可以制定规则,规定如申诉人先前未将其内容告知被申诉人并且未给予被申诉人合理的机会对该申诉进行处理,则该申诉不予受理(在特定情况下除外)。

(4)管理局可以制定规则,要求可能成为强制管辖权适用对象和被申诉人的获授权人建立管理局认为适当的程序,以解决下列申诉:

(a) may be referred to the scheme; and

(b) arise out of activity to which the Authority's powers under Part X do not apply.

Annotations:

Modifications etc. (not altering text)

C414 Sch. 17 para. 13 amended (19.7.2001 for specified purposes otherwise 1.12.2001) by S.I. 2001/2326, arts. 1(1), 4; S.I. 2001/3538, art. 2(1)

The scheme operator's rules

14 (1) The scheme operator must make rules, to be known as "scheme rules", which are to set out the procedure for reference of complaints and for their investigation, consideration and determination by an ombudsman.

(2) Scheme rules may, among other things—

(a) specify matters which are to be taken into account in determining whether an act or omission was fair and reasonable;

(b) provide that a complaint may, in specified circumstances, be dismissed without consideration of its merits;

(c) provide for the reference of a complaint, in specified circumstances and with the consent of the complainant, to another body with a view to its being determined by that body instead of by an ombudsman;

(d) make provision as to the evidence which may be required or admitted, the extent to which it should be oral or written and the consequences of a person's failure to produce any information or document which he has been required (under section 231 or otherwise) to produce;

(e) allow an ombudsman to fix time limits for any aspect of the proceedings and to extend a time limit;

(f) provide for certain things in relation to the reference, investigation or consideration (but not determination) of a complaint to be done by a member of the scheme operator's staff instead of by an ombudsman;

(g) make different provision in relation to different kinds of complaint.

(3) The circumstances specified under sub-paragraph (2)(b) may include the following—

(a) the ombudsman considers the complaint frivolous or vexatious;

(b) legal proceedings have been brought concerning the subject-matter of the complaint and the ombudsman considers that the complaint is best dealt with in those proceedings; or

(c) the ombudsman is satisfied that there are other compelling reasons why it is (a)可以向计划提交的申诉;和

(b)管理局依照第十部分拥有的权力不适用的越权行为引起的申诉。

注释:

修改等(不涉及条文内容)

C414 附录17第13条为特定目的于2001年7月19日,否则于2001年12月1日依照制定法文件S.I. 2001/2326第1条第(1)款、第4条;制定法文件S.I. 2001/3538第2条第(1)款修正。

计划执行人的规则

第14条 (1)计划执行人必须制定规则,称为“计划规则”,规定提交申诉和申诉专员调查、考虑和决定申诉的程序。

(2)除了其他方面,计划规则可以

(a)规定在确定作为或不作为是否公平合理时将考虑的事项;

(b)规定申诉在特定情况下可以不考虑其法律依据而被驳回;

(c)规定申诉在特定情况下经申诉人同意提交另一个机构,由该机构而不是申诉专员作出决定;

(d)规定可以要求提供或采纳的证据、该证据在何种程度应为口头或书面形式,并规定一个人未能出示(第231条或其他条款)要求其出示的任何信息或文件的后果;

(e)允许申诉专员为程序的任何方面确定期限并延长期限;

(f)规定与申诉的提交、调查或考虑(但不包括决定)有关的某些事项由计划执行人的工作人员而不是申诉专员实施;

(g)对不同种类的申诉作出不同的规定。

(3)第(2)款第(b)项所述特定情况可以包括以下各项:

(a)申诉专员认为申诉无足轻重或旨在为难对方;

(b)已经就申诉标的提起法律程序,并且申诉专员认为申诉最好在这些程序中处理;或者

(c)申诉专员确信有其他令人信服的原因表明申诉依照申诉专员计划处理是不适

inappropriate for the complaint to be dealt with under the ombudsman scheme.

(4) If the scheme operator proposes to make any scheme rules it must publish a draft of the proposed rules in the way appearing to it to be best calculated to bring them to the attention of persons appearing to it to be likely to be affected.

(5) The draft must be accompanied by a statement that representations about the proposals may be made to the scheme operator within a time specified in the statement.

(6) Before making the proposed scheme rules, the scheme operator must have regard to any representations made to it under sub-paragraph (5).

(7) The consent of the Authority is required before any scheme rules may be made.

Annotations:

Modifications etc. (not altering text)

C415 Sch. 17 para. 14 amended (19.7.2001 for specified purposes otherwise 1.12.2001) by S.I. 2001/2326, arts. 1(1), 5; S.I. 2001/3538, art. 2(1)

C416 Sch. 17 para. 14(4)(5) amended (19.7.2001) by S.I. 2001/2326, arts. 1(1)(a), 16(a); S.I. 2001/3538, art. 2(1)

Fees

15 (1) Scheme rules may require a respondent to pay to the scheme operator such fees as may be specified in the rules.

(2) The rules may, among other things—

(a) provide for the scheme operator to reduce or waive a fee in a particular case;

(b) set different fees for different stages of the proceedings on a complaint;

(c) provide for fees to be refunded in specified circumstances;

(d) make different provision for different kinds of complaint.

Annotations:

Modifications etc. (not altering text)

C417 Sch. 17 para. 15 amended (19.7.2001 for specified purposes otherwise 1.12.2001) by S.I. 2001/2326, arts. 1(1), 12(2)(3); S.I. 2001/3538, art. 2(1)

Enforcement of money awards

16 A money award, including interest, which has been registered in accordance with scheme rules may

当的。

(4)如果计划执行人拟制定任何计划规则,则必须以其认为最能引起其认为可能受影响的人注意的方式公布拟制定规则的草案。

(5)草案必须附有声明:关于提议的陈述可以在声明中的指定期限内向计划执行人作出。

(6)在制定拟制定的计划规则以前,计划执行人必须考虑依照第(5)款向其作出的任何陈述。

(7)在制定任何计划规则以前,必须获得管理局同意。

注释:

修改等(不涉及条文内容)

C415　附录17第14条为特定目的于2001年7月19日,否则于2001年12月1日依照制定法文件S.I. 2001/2326第1条第(1)款、第5条;制定法文件S.I. 2001/3538第2条第(1)款修正。

C416　附录17第14条第(4)款、第(5)款于2001年7月19日依照制定法文件S.I. 2001/2326第1条第(1)款第(a)项、第16条第(a)项;制定法文件S.I. 2001/3538第2条第(1)款修正。

费　用

第15条　(1)计划规则可以要求被申诉人向计划执行人支付规则中指定的费用。

(2)除了其他方面,规则可以

(a)规定计划执行人必须在特定情况下减少或免除费用;

(b)为申诉程序的不同阶段设定不同的费用;

(c)规定费用在特定情况下将退还;

(d)对不同种类的申诉作出不同的规定。

注释:

修改等(不涉及条文内容)

C417　附录17第15条为特定目的于2001年7月19日,否则于2001年12月1日依照制定法文件S.I. 2001/2326第1条第(1)款,第12条第(2)款、第(3)款;制定法文件S.I. 2001/3538第2条第(1)款修正。

赔偿金支付判决的执行

第16条　按照计划规则登记的赔偿金支付判决,包括利息,可以

(a) if a county court so orders in England and Wales, be recovered by execution issued from the county court (or otherwise) as if it were payable under an order of that court;

(b) be enforced in Northern Ireland as a money judgment under the [M136]Judgments Enforcement (Northern Ireland) Order 1981;

(c) be enforced in Scotland by the sheriff, as if it were a judgment or order of the sheriff and whether or not the sheriff could himself have granted such judgment or order.

Annotations:

Modifications etc. (not altering text)

C418 Sch.17para.16applied (19.7.2001 for specified purposes otherwise 1.12.2001) by S.I. 2001/2326, arts. 1(1), 16(4)(6); S.I. 2001/3538, art. 2(1)

Marginal Citations

M136 S.I. 1981/226 (N.I.6).

PART Ⅳ THE VOLUNTARY JURISDICTION

Introduction

17 This Part of this Schedule applies only in relation to the voluntary jurisdiction.

Terms of reference to the scheme

18 (1) Complaints are to be dealt with and determined under the voluntary jurisdiction on standard terms fixed by the scheme operator with the approval of the Authority.

(2) Different standard terms may be fixed with respect to different matters or in relation to different cases.

(3) The standard terms may, in particular—

(a) require the making of payments to the scheme operator by participants in the scheme of such amounts, and at such times, as may be determined by the scheme operator;

(b) make provision as to the award of costs on the determination of a complaint.

(4) The scheme operator may not vary any of the standard terms or add or remove terms without the approval of the Authority.

(5) The standard terms may include provision to the effect that (unless acting in bad faith) none of the following is to be liable in damages for anything done or omitted in the discharge or purported discharge of functions in connection with the voluntary jurisdiction—

(a) the scheme operator;

(b) any member of its governing body;

(c) any member of its staff;

(a)如英格兰和威尔士的郡法院这样命令,则通过郡法院(或以其他方式)强制执行而收回,效力等同于该赔偿金根据该法院的命令应当支付;

(b)在北爱尔兰作为[M136]《1981年判决执行法令》(北爱尔兰)规定的赔偿判决执行;

(c)在苏格兰由郡治安官执行,效力等同于郡治安官的判决或命令,不论郡治安官能否自行作出这样的判决或命令。

注释:

修改等(不涉及条文内容)

C418　附录17第16条为特定目的于2001年7月19日,否则于2001年12月1日依照制定法文件S.I. 2001/2326第1条第(1)款、第16条第(4)款、第(6)款;制定法文件S.I. 2001/3538第2条第(1)款适用。

附注引文

M136　制定法文件S.I. 1981/226(N.I.6)。

第四部分　自愿管辖权

引　言

第17条　本附录本部分只适用于自愿管辖权。

向计划提交的规定

第18条　(1)申诉将按照计划执行人经管理局批准确定的标准规定按照自愿管辖权处理和确定。

(2)可以对不同的事项或不同的情况确定不同的标准规定。

(3)具体而言,标准规定可以

(a)要求制度参与者在计划执行人确定的时间向计划执行人支付计划执行人确定的金额;

(b)作出关于在决定申诉后支付费用的规定。

(4)未经管理局批准,计划执行人不得变更任何标准规定或者增加或废除规定。

(5)标准规定可以包括下列规定(恶意行事除外):下列各项均不对在履行或声称履行与自愿管辖权有关的职能中的任何作为或不作为承担赔偿责任:

(a)计划执行人;

(b)其理事机构的任何成员;

(c)其工作人员中的任何成员;

(d) any person acting as an ombudsman for the purposes of the scheme.

Delegation by and to other schemes

19 (1) The scheme operator may make arrangements with a relevant body—

(a) for the exercise by that body of any part of the voluntary jurisdiction of the ombudsman scheme on behalf of the scheme; or

(b) for the exercise by the scheme of any function of that body as if it were part of the voluntary jurisdiction of the scheme.

(2) A "relevant body" is one which the scheme operator is satisfied—

(a) is responsible for the operation of a broadly comparable scheme (whether or not established by statute) for the resolution of disputes; and

(b) in the case of arrangements under sub-paragraph(1)(a), will exercise the jurisdiction in question in a way compatible with the requirements imposed by or under this Act in relation to complaints of the kind concerned.

(3) Such arrangements require the approval of the Authority.

Voluntary jurisdiction rules: procedure

20 (1) If the scheme operator makes voluntary jurisdiction rules, it must give a copy to the Authority without delay.

(2) If the scheme operator revokes any such rules, it must give written notice to the Authority without delay.

(3) The power to make voluntary jurisdiction rules is exercisable in writing.

(4) Immediately after making voluntary jurisdiction rules, the scheme operator must arrange for them to be printed and made available to the public.

(5) The scheme operator may charge a reasonable fee for providing a person with a copy of any voluntary jurisdiction rules.

Verification of the rules

21 (1) The production of a printed copy of voluntary jurisdiction rules purporting to be made by the scheme operator—

(a) on which is endorsed a certificate signed by a member of the scheme operator's staff authorised by the scheme operator for that purpose, and

(b) which contains the required statements, is evidence (or in Scotland sufficient evidence) of the facts stated in the certificate.

(2) The required statements are—

(a) that the rules were made by the scheme operator;

(b) that the copy is a true copy of the rules; and

(d)为施行计划作为申诉专员行事的任何人。

由或向其他计划委托

第19条 (1)计划执行人可以与相关机构进行安排

(a)由该机构代表该计划行使申诉专员计划自愿管辖权的任何部分;或者

(b)由该计划行使该机构的任何职能,等同于该职能属于该计划的自愿管辖权。

(2)"相关机构"是计划执行人确信符合下列情况的机构:

(a)负责具有广泛可比性的争议解决计划(不论是否通过法令建立)的管理;并且

(b)在有第(1)款第(a)项规定的安排的情况下,将以符合由本法或依照本法就相关种类的申诉要求的方式行使特定的管辖权。

(3)此等安排必须经管理局批准。

自愿管辖权规则:程序

第20条 (1)如计划执行人制定自愿管辖权规则,则必须立即将一份副本发给管理局。

(2)如计划执行人撤销任何此等规则,则必须立即书面通知管理局。

(3)制定自愿管辖权规则的权力只可以通过书面形式行使。

(4)在制定自愿管辖权规则以后,计划执行人必须立即安排印刷并将其提供给公众。

(5)计划执行人可以为向他人提供自愿管辖权规则副本收取合理费用。

规则的核实

第21条 (1)出示符合下列条件的据称由计划执行人制定的自愿管辖权规章的印刷副本:

(a)附有经计划执行人为该目的授权的计划执行人工作人员认证的证书,且

(b)其中包含要求作出的声明,是证书中所述的事实的证据(在苏格兰称为充分证据)。

(2)要求作出的声明是

(a)规则由计划执行人制定;

(b)副本是规则的真实副本;并且

(c) that on a specified date the rules were made available to the public in accordance with paragraph 20(4).

(3) A certificate purporting to be signed as mentioned in sub-paragraph(1) is to be taken to have been duly signed unless the contrary is shown.

Consultation

22 (1) If the scheme operator proposes to make voluntary jurisdiction rules, it must publish a draft of the proposed rules in the way appearing to it to be best calculated to bring them to the attention of the public.

(2) The draft must be accompanied by—

(a) an explanation of the proposed rules; and

(b) a statement that representations about the proposals may be made to the scheme operator within a specified time.

(3) Before making any voluntary jurisdiction rules, the scheme operator must have regard to any representations made to it in accordance with sub-paragraph (2)(b).

(4) If voluntary jurisdiction rules made by the scheme operator differ from the draft published under sub-paragraph (1) in a way which the scheme operator considers significant, the scheme operator must publish a statement of the difference.

Annotations:

Modifications etc. (not altering text)

C419 Sch. 17 para. 22(1)(2) amended (19.7.2001) by S.I. 2001/2326, arts. 1(1)(a), 16(b); S.I. 2001/3538, art. 2(1)

SCHEDULE 18 MUTUALS

Sections 334, 336 and 338

PART I FRIENDLY SOCIETIES

The Friendly Societies Act 1974 (c.46)

1 Omit sections 4 (provision for separate registration areas) and 10 (societies registered in one registration area carrying on business in another).

2 In section 7 (societies which may be registered), in subsection (2)(b), for "in the

(c)规则在指定日期按照本附录第20条第(4)款向公众提供。

(3)第(1)款中所述声称已签署的证书视为已正式签署，除非证明并非如此。

谘　商

第22条　(1)如果计划执行人拟制定自愿管辖权规则，则必须以其认为最便于公众了解的方式公布拟制定规则的草案。

(2)草案必须附有

(a)对拟制定规则的解释；和

(b)关于可以在指定期限内向计划执行人就拟制定的规则作出陈述的声明。

(3)在制定任何自愿管辖权规则以前，计划执行人必须考虑按照第(2)款第(b)项向其作出的任何陈述。

(4)如计划执行人认为其制定的自愿管辖权规则与依照第(1)款发布的草案具有重大差异，则计划执行人必须发布关于该差异的声明。

注释：

修改等(不涉及条文内容)

C419　附录17第22条第(1)款、第(2)款于2001年7月19日依照制定法文件S.I. 2001/2326第1条第(1)款第(a)项、第16条第(b)项；制定法文件S.I. 2001/3538第2条第(1)款修正。

附录18　互助协会

第334条、第336条和第338条

第一部分　互相保险协会

1974年互相保险协会法(c.46)

第1条　删除第4条(关于单独注册区域的规定)和第10条(在一个注册区域注册、在另一个注册区域开展业务的协会)。

第2条　在第7条(可以注册的协会)第(2)款第(b)项中，将“在中心注册区域或在

central registration area or in Scotland" substitute " in the United Kingdom, the Channel Islands or the Isle of Man".

3 In section 11 (additional registration requirements for societies with branches), omit "and where any such society has branches in more than one registration area, section 10 above shall apply to that society".

4 In section 99(4)(punishment of fraud etc and recovery of property misapplied), omit "in the central registration area".

The Friendly Societies Act 1992 (c.40)

5 Omit sections 31 to 36A (authorisation of friendly societies business).

6 In section 37 (restrictions on combinations of business), omit subsections (1), (1A) and (7A) to (9).

7 Omit sections 38 to 43 (restrictions on business of certain authorised societies).

8 Omit sections 44 to 50 (regulation of friendly societies business).

PART II FRIENDLY SOCIETIES: SUBSIDIARIES AND CONTROLLED BODIES

Interpretation

9 In this Part of this Schedule—

"the 1992 Act" means the [M137] Friendly Societies Act 1992; and

"section 13" means section 13 of that Act.

Annotations:

Marginal Citations

M137 1992 c. 40.

Qualifying bodies

10 (1) Subsections (2) to (5) of section 13 (incorporated friendly societies allowed to form or acquire control or joint control only of qualifying bodies) cease to have effect.

(2) As a result, omit—

(a) subsections (8) and (11) of that section, and

(b) Schedule 7 to the 1992 Act (activities which may be carried on by a subsidiary of, or body jointly controlled by, an incorporated friendly society).

Bodies controlled by societies

11 In section 13(9) (defined terms), after paragraph (a) insert—

苏格兰"替换为"在联合王国、海峡群岛或马恩岛"。

第3条 在第11条(对有分支机构的协会的额外注册要求)中,删除"并且如果任何此等协会在一个以上的注册区域有分支机构,则以上第10条应当适用于该协会"。

第4条 在第99条第(4)款(惩罚欺诈等和追回滥用的财产)中,删除"在中心注册区域"。

1992年互相保险协会法(c.40)

第5条 删除第31条至第36A条(互相保险协会业务授权)。

第6条 在第37条(业务合并限制)中,删除第(1)款、第(1A)款和第(7A)款至第(9)款。

第7条 删除第38条至第43条(某些被授权协会的业务限制)。

第8条 删除第44条至第50条(互相保险协会业务监管)。

第二部分 互相保险协会:附属机构和受控机构

释 义

第9条 在本附录本部分中

"1992年法"系指[M137]《1992年互相保险协会法》;

"第13条"系指该法第13条。

注释:

附注引文

M137 1992年第40章。

有资格的机构

第10条 (1)第13条第(2)款至第(5)款(可以对有资格的机构形成或获得控制或共同控制的法人互相保险协会)不再有效。

(2)因此,删除

(a)该条第(8)款和第(11)款,和

(b)1992年法律附录7(法人互相保险协会的附属机构或共同控制机构可以进行的活动)。

协会控制的机构

第11条 在第13条第(9)款中(词语定义),在第(a)项后插入:

"(aa) an incorporated friendly society also has control of a body corporate if the body corporate is itself a body controlled in one of the ways mentioned in paragraph (a)(i), (ii) or (iii) by a body corporate of which the society has control; ".

Joint control by societies

12 In section 13(9), after paragraph (c) insert—

"(cc) an incorporated friendly society also has joint control of a body corporate if—

(i) a subsidiary of the society has joint control of the body corporate in a way mentioned in paragraph (c)(i), (ii) or (iii);

(ii) a body corporate of which the society has joint control has joint control of the body corporate in such a way; or

(iii) the body corporate is controlled in a way mentioned in paragraph (a)(i), (ii) or (iii) by a body corporate of which the society has joint control; ".

Acquisition of joint control

13 In section 13(9),in the words following paragraph (d), after"paragraph (c)" insert " or (cc)".

Amendment of Schedule 8 to the 1992 Act

14 (1) Schedule 8 to the 1992 Act (provisions supplementing section 13) is amended as follows.

(2) Omit paragraph 3(2).

(3) After paragraph 3 insert—

"3A (1) A body is to be treated for the purposes of section 13(9) as having the right to appoint to a directorship if—

(a) a person's appointment to the directorship follows necessarily from his appointment as an officer of that body; or

(b) the directorship is held by the body itself.

(2)A body("B")and some other person("P")together are to be treated, for the purposes of section 13(9), as having the right to appoint to a directorship if—

(a) P is a body corporate which has directors and a person's appointment to the directorship follows necessarily from his appointment both as an officer of B and a director of P;

(b) P is a body corporate which does not have directors and a person's appointment to the directorship follows necessarily from his appointment both as an officer of B and as a member of P's managing body; or

(c) the directorship is held jointly by B and P.

"(aa)法人互相保险协会也控制该协会控制的法人以第(a)项第(i)子项,第(ii)子项或第(iii)子项中所述方式控制的法人"。

协会的共同控制

第12条 在第13条第(9)款中,在第(c)项后插入:

"(cc)法人互相保险协会还共同控制下列法人:

(i)协会的附属机构以第(c)项第(i)子项、第(ii)子项或第(iii)子项中所述方式共同控制的法人;

(ii)协会共同控制的法人以任何上述方式共同控制的法人;或

(iii)协会共同控制的法人以第(a)项第(i)子项、第(ii)子项或第(iii)子项中提及的方式控制的法人"。

获得共同控制

第13条 在第13条第(9)款中,在第(d)项后面的文字中的"第(c)项"后插入"或第(cc)项"。

1992年法附录8修正案

第14条 (1)1992年法附录8(第13条的补充规定)进行如下修正。

(2)删除第3条第(2)款。

(3)在第3条后插入:

"第3A条 (1)就第13条第(9)款而言,如有下列情况,则机构被视为拥有董事职务任命权:

(a)对一个人的董事职务任命是任命该人为该机构高级职员的必然结果;或者

(b)该机构本身拥有董事职务。

(2)就第13条第(9)款而言,如有下列情况,则机构(以下简称B)和某个其他人(以下简称P)共同被视为拥有董事职务任命权:

(a)P是有董事的法人机构,并且对一个人的董事职务任命是同时任命该人为B的高级职员和P的董事的必然结果;

(b)P是没有董事的法人机构,并且对一个人的董事职务任命是任命该人为B的高级职员和P的管理机构成员的必然结果;或者

(c)B和P共同拥有董事职务。

(3) For the purposes of section 13 (9), a right to appoint (or remove) which is exercisable only with the consent or agreement of another person must be left out of account unless no other person has a right to appoint (or remove) in relation to that directorship.

(4) Nothing in this paragraph is to be read as restricting the effect of section 13(9)."

(4) In paragraph 9 (exercise of certain rights under instruction by, or in the interests of, incorporated friendly society) insert at the end " or in the interests of any body over which the society has joint control".

Consequential amendments

15 (1) Section 52 of the 1992 Act is amended as follows.

(2) In subsection (2), omit paragraph (d).

(3) In subsection (3), for"(4) below" substitute " (2)".

(4) For subsection (4) substitute—

"(4) A court may not make an order under subsection (5) unless it is satisfied that one or more of the conditions mentioned in subsection (2) are satisfied."

(5) In subsection (5), omit the words from"or, where" to the end.

References in other enactments

16 References in any provision of, or made under, any enactment to subsidiaries of, or bodies jointly controlled by, an incorporated friendly society are to be read as including references to bodies which are such subsidiaries or bodies as a result of any provision of this Part of this Schedule.

PART Ⅲ BUILDING SOCIETIES

The Building Societies Act 1986 (c.53)

17 Omit section 9 (initial authorisation to raise funds and borrow money).

18 Omit Schedule 3 (supplementary provisions about authorisation).

PART Ⅳ INDUSTRIAL AND PROVIDENT SOCIETIES

The Industrial and Provident Societies Act 1965 (c.12)

19 Omit section 8 (provision for separate registration areas for Scotland and for England, Wales and the Channel Islands).

20 Omit section 70 (scale of fees to be paid in respect of transactions and inspection of documents).

(3)就第13条第(9)款而言,只能在另一个人同意或赞同时行使的任命(或免职)权必须不予考虑,除非没有其他人拥有该董事职务的任命(或免职)权。

(4)本条中的任何内容不得解释为限制第13条第(9)款的效力。"

(4)在第9条(在法人互相保险协会的指示下或为互相保险协会的利益行使某些权利)中,在结尾处加入"或为了该协会有共同控制权的任何机构的利益"。

后续修正

第15条 (1)1992年法第52条进行如下修正。

(2)在第(2)款中,删除第(d)项。

(3)在第(3)款中,将"下文第(4)款"替换为"第(2)款"。

(4)将第(4)款替换为:

"(4)法院除非确信满足第(2)款中所述一项或多项条件,否则不得发布第(5)款规定的命令。"

(5)在第(5)款中,删除从"或者,如果"到结尾的部分。

其他成文法中的引述

第16条 在任何成文法的任何规定中或依照任何法规作出的任何规定中述及法人互相保险协会的附属机构或共同控制机构,视为包含由于本附录本部分的任何规定而属于此类的附属机构或机构。

第三部分 住房互助会

1986年住房互助会法(c.53)

第17条 删除第9条(对募集资金和借款的初步授权)。

第18条 删除附录3(关于授权的补充规定)。

第四部分 行业节俭互助会

1965年行业节俭互助会法(c.12)

第19条 删除第8条(对苏格兰的单独注册区域以及英格兰、威尔士和海峡群岛的规定)。

第20条 删除第70条(支付交易和文件检查费的标准)。

PART V CREDIT UNIONS

The Credit Unions Act 1979 (c.34)

21 In section 6 (minimum and maximum number of members), omit subsections (2) to (6).

22 In section 11 (loans), omit subsections (2) and (6).

23 Omit sections 11B (loans approved by credit unions), 11C (grant of certificates of approval) and 11D (withdrawal of certificates of approval).

24 In section 12, omit subsections (4) and (5).

25 In section 14, omit subsections (2), (3), (5) and (6).

26 In section 28 (offences), omit subsection (2).

SCHEDULE 19
COMPETITION INFORMATION

Section 351

PART I PERSONS AND FUNCTIONS FOR THE PURPOSES OF SECTION 351

1 The Table set out after this paragraph has effect for the purposes of section 351(3)(b).

Table

Person	Function
1. The Commission.	Any function of the Commission under Community law relating to competition.
2. The Comptroller and Auditor General.	Any function of his.
3. A Minister of the Crown.	Any function of his under a specified enactment.
4. Director General of Telecommunications.	Any function of his under a specified enactment.
5. Director General of Gas Supply	Any function of his under a specified enactment
6. The Director General of Gas for Northern Ireland.	Any function of his under a specified enactment.
7. The Director General of Electricity Supply.	Any function of his under a specified enactment.
8. The Director General of Electricity Supply for Northern Ireland.	Any function of his under a specified enactment.
9. The Director General of Water Services.	Any function of his under a specified enactment.
10. The Civil Aviation Authority.	Any function of that authority under a specified enactment.
11. The Rail Regulator.	Any function of his under a specified enactment.
12. The Director General of Fair Trading.	Any function of his under a specified enactment.
13. The Competition Commission.	Any function of the Competition Commission under a specified enactment.
14. The Authority.	Any function of the Authority under a specified enactment.
15. A person of a description Specified in an order made by the Treasury.	Any function of his which is specified in the order.

第五部分　信用合作社

1979年信用合作社法（c.34）

第21条　在第6条（成员的最低和最高人数）中，删除第（2）款至第（6）款。

第22条　在第11条（贷款）中，删除第（2）款至第（6）款。

第23条　删除第11B条（信用合作社批准的贷款）、第11C条（给予批准证书）和第11D条（收回批准证书）。

第24条　在第12条中，删除第（4）款和第（5）款。

第25条　在第14条中，删除第（2）款、第（3）款、第（5）款和第（6）款。

第26条　在第28条（违法行为）中，删除第（2）款。

附录19　竞争信息

第351条

第一部分　为第351条之目的的人和职能

第1条　为本法第351条第（3）款第（b）项之目的，本条后所列表格有效。

表格

人	职能
1. 委员会	共同体法规定的与竞争有关的任何委员会职能
2. 主计审计长	其承担的任何职能
3. 内阁阁员	特定成文法规定其承担的任何职能
4. 电信总理事	特定成文法规定其承担的任何职能
5. 供气总理事	特定成文法规定其承担的任何职能
6. 北爱尔兰燃气总理事	特定成文法规定其承担的任何职能
7. 供电总理事	特定成文法规定其承担的任何职能
8. 北爱尔兰供电总理事	特定成文法规定其承担的任何职能
9. 水务总理事	特定成文法规定其承担的任何职能
10. 民航管理局	特定成文法规定的任何管理局职能
11. 铁路监管机关	特定成文法规定其承担的任何职能
12. 公平交易总理事	特定成文法规定其承担的任何职能
13. 竞争委员会	特定成文法规定的任何竞争委员会职能
14. 管理局	特定成文法规定的任何管理局职能
15. 财政部作出的命令中指定种类的人	该法令规定其承担的任何职能

PART Ⅱ THE ENACTMENTS

1 The [M138] Fair Trading Act 1973

Annotations:

Marginal Citations

M138 1973 c. 41.

2 The [M139] Consumer Credit Act 1974

Annotations:

Marginal Citations

M139 1974 c. 39.

3 The [M140] Estate Agents Act 1979

Annotations:

Marginal Citations

M140 1979 c. 38.

4 The [M141] Competition Act 1980

Annotations:

Marginal Citations

M141 1980 c. 21.

5 The [M142] Telecommunications Act 1984

Annotations:

Marginal Citations

M142 1984 c. 12.

6 The [M143] Airports Act 1986

Annotations:

Marginal Citations

M143 1986 c. 31.

第二部分 成 文 法

第1条 [M138]《1973年公平交易法》

注释：

附注引文

M138 1973年第41章。

第2条 [M139]《1974年消费信贷法》

注释：

附注引文

M139 1974年第39章。

第3条 [M140]《1979年房地产中介机构法》

注释：

附注引文

M140 1979年第38章。

第4条 [M141]《1980年竞争法》

注释：

附注引文

M140 1980年第21章。

第5条 [M142]《1984年电信法》

注释：

附注引文

M142 1984年第12章。

第6条 [M143]《1986年机场法》

注释：

附注引文

M143 1986年第31章。

7 The [M144] Gas Act 1986

Annotations:

Marginal Citations

M144 1986 c. 45.

8 The [M145] Control of Misleading Advertisements Regulations 1988

Annotations:

Marginal Citations

M145 S.I. 1988/915.

9 The [M146] Electricity Act 1989

Annotations:

Marginal Citations

M146 1989 c. 29.

10 The [M147] Broadcasting Act 1990

Annotations:

Marginal Citations

M147 1990 c. 42.

11 The [M148] Water Industry Act 1991

Annotations:

Marginal Citations

M148 1991 c. 56.

12 The [M149] Electricity (Northern Ireland) Order 1992

Annotations:

Marginal Citations

M149 S.I. 1992/231 (N.I. 1).

第7条 [M144]《1986年燃气法》

注释：

附注引文

M144 1986年本法第45条。

第8条 [M145]《1988年管制误导广告法规》

注释：

附注引文

M145 制定法文件S.I. 1988/915。

第9条 [M146]《1989年电力法》

注释：

附注引文

M146 1989年第29章。

第10条 [M147]《1990年广播法》

注释：

附注引文

M147 1990年第42章。

第11条 [M148]《1991年水产业法》

注释：

附注引文

M148 1991年第56章。

第12条 [M149]《1992年电力法令》(北爱尔兰)

注释：

附注引文

M149 制定法文件S.I.1992/231(N.I.1)。

13 The [M150] Railways Act 1993

Annotations:

Marginal Citations

M150 1993 c. 43.

14 Part IV of the [M151] Airports (Northern Ireland) Order 1994

Annotations:

Marginal Citations

M151 S.I. 1994/426 (N.I. 1).

15 The [M152] Gas (Northern Ireland) Order 1996

Annotations:

Marginal Citations

M152 S.I. 1996/275 (N.I. 2).

16 The [M153] EC Competition (Articles 88 and 89) Enforcement Regulations 1996

Annotations:

Marginal Citations

M153 S.I. 1996/2199.

17 The [M154] Unfair Terms in Consumer Contracts Regulations 1999

Annotations:

Marginal Citations

M154 S.I. 1999/2083.

18 This Act.

19 An enactment specified for the purposes of this paragraph in an order made by the Treasury.

Annotations:

Commencement Information

I164 Sch. 19 Pt. II para. 19 wholly in force at 1.12.2001; Sch. 19 Pt. II para. 19 not in force at Royal Assent see s. 431(2); Sch. 19 Pt. II para. 19 in force for certain purposes at 25.2.2001 by S.I. 2001/516, art. 2(b), Sch. Pt. 2; Sch. 19 Pt. II para. 19 in force for specified purposes at 18.6.2001 by S.I. 2001/1820, art. 2, Sch.; Sch. 19 Pt. II para. 19 in force in so far as not already in force at 1.12.2001 by S.I. 2001/3538, art. 2(1)

第13条 [M150]《1993年铁路法》

注释：

附注引文

M150 1993年第43章。

第14条 [M151]《1994年机场法令》(北爱尔兰)第四部分

注释：

附注引文

M151 制定法文件S.I. 1994/426（N.I. 1）。

第15条 [M152]《1996年燃气法令》(北爱尔兰)

注释：

附注引文

M152 制定法文件S.I. 1996/275（N.I. 2）。

第16条 [M153]《1996年欧洲共同体竞争实施法规》(第88条和第89条)

注释：

附注引文

M153 制定法文件S.I. 1996/2199。

第17条 [M154]《1999年消费者合同法规》中的不公平规定

注释：

附注引文

M154 制定法文件S.I. 1999/2083。

第18条 本法

第19条 为实施本条在财政部颁布的法令中规定的成文法

注释：

实施日期

I164 附录19第二部分第19条于2001年12月1日全部生效；附录19第二部分第19条在副署时尚未生效，见第431条第(2)款；附录19第二部分第19条为特定目的于2001年2月25日依照制定法文件S.I. 2001/516第2条第(b)款，附录第二部分生效；附录19第二部分第19条为特定目的于2001年6月18日依照制定法文件S.I. 2001/1820第2条，附录生效；附录19第二部分第 19条如于2001年12月1日尚未生效，则依照制定法文件S.I.2001/3538第2条第(1)款生效。

SCHEDULE 20 MINOR AND CONSEQUENTIAL AMENDMENTS

Section 432(1)

The House of Commons Disqualification Act 1975 (c. 24)

1 In Part III of Schedule 1 to the House of Commons Disqualification Act 1975 (disqualifying offices)—

(a) omit—

"Any member of the Financial Services Tribunal in receipt of remuneration"; and

(b) at the appropriate place, insert—

"Any member, in receipt of remuneration, of a panel of persons who may be selected to act as members of the Financial Services and Markets Tribunal".

Annotations:

Commencement Information

I165 Sch. 20 para. 1 wholly in force at 1.12.2001; Sch. 20 para. 1 not in force at Royal Assent see s. 431(2); Sch. 20 para. 1(b) in force at 3.9.2001 by S.I. 2001/2632, art. 2(2), Sch. Pt. 2; Sch. 20 para. 1 in force in so far as not already in force at 1.12.2001 by S.I. 2001/3538, art. 2(1)

The Northern Ireland Assembly Disqualification Act 1975 (c. 25)

2 In Part III of Schedule 1 to the Northern Ireland Assembly Disqualification Act 1975 (disqualifying offices)—

(a) omit—

"Any member of the Financial Services Tribunal in receipt of remuneration"; and

(b) at the appropriate place, insert—

"Any member, in receipt of remuneration, of a panel of persons who may be selected to act as members of the Financial Services and Markets Tribunal".

附录20 细微及后续修正

第432条第(1)款

《1975年下议院剥夺资格法》(c. 24)

第1条 在《1975年下议院剥夺资格法》附录1第三部分(剥夺任职资格)中

(a)删除:

"收取报酬的金融服务裁判所的任何成员";

(b)并且

在适当处加入:

"可以被选为金融服务与市场裁判所成员的人士组成的小组中收取报酬的任何成员。"

注释:

实施日期

I165 附录20第1条于2001年12月1日全部生效;附录20第1条在副署时尚未生效,见第431条第(2)款;附录20第1条第(b)款于2001年9月3日依照制定法文件S.I. 2001/2632第2条第(2)款,附录第二部分生效;附录20第1条如于2001年12月1日尚未生效,则依照制定法文件S.I.2001/3538第2条第(1)款生效。

《1975年北爱尔兰议会剥夺资格法》(c. 25)

第2条 在《1975年北爱尔兰议会剥夺资格法》附录1第三部分(剥夺任职资格)中

(a)删除:

"收取报酬的金融服务裁判所的任何成员";

(b)并且在适当处加入:

"可以被选为金融服务和市场裁判所成员的人士组成的小组中收取报酬的任何成员。"

Annotations:

Commencement Information

I166 Sch. 20 para. 2 wholly in force at 1.12.2001; Sch. 20 para. 2 not in force at Royal Assent see s. 431(2); Sch. 20 para. 2(b) in force at 3.9.2001 by S.I. 2001/2632, art. 2(2), Sch. Pt. 2; Sch. 20 para. 2 in force in so far as not already in force at 1.12.2001 by S.I. 2001/3538, art. 2(1)

The Civil Jurisdiction and Judgments Act 1982 (c. 27)

3 In paragraph 10 of Schedule 5 to the Civil Jurisdiction and Judgments Act 1982 (proceedings excluded from the operation of Schedule 4 to that Act), for "section 188 of the Financial Services Act 1986" substitute "section 415 of the Financial Services and Markets Act 2000".

The Income and Corporation Taxes Act 1988 (c. 1)

4 (1) The Income and Corporation Taxes Act 1988 is amended as follows.

(2) In section 76 (expenses of management: insurance companies), in subsection (8), omit the definitions of—

"the 1986 Act";

"authorised person";

"investment business";

"investor";

"investor protection scheme";

"prescribed"; and

"recognised self-regulating organisation".

(3) In section 468 (authorised unit trusts), in subsections (6) and (8), for "78 of the Financial Services Act 1986" substitute "243 of the Financial Services and Markets Act 2000".

(4) In section 469(7) (other unit trust schemes), for "Financial Services Act 1986" substitute "Financial Services and Markets Act 2000".

(5) In section 728(information in relation to transfers of securities), in subsection (7)(a), for "Financial Services Act 1986" substitute "Financial Services and Markets Act 2000".

(6) In section 841(3) (power to apply certain provisions of the Tax Acts to recognized investment exchange), for "Financial Services Act 1986" substitute "Financial Services and Markets Act 2000".

注释：

实施日期

I166 附录20第2条于2001年12月1日全部生效；附录20第2条在副署时尚未生效，见第431条第(2)款；附录20第2条第(b)款于2001年9月3日依照制定法文件S.I. 2001/2632第2条第(2)款，附录第二部分生效；附录20第2条如于2001年12月1日尚未生效，则依照制定法文件S.I.2001/3538第2条第(1)款生效。

1982年《民事管辖权和判决法》(c. 27)

第3条 在《1982年民事管辖权和判决法》附录5第10条(从该法附录4的操作中排除的程序)中，将"《1986年金融服务法》第188条"替换为"《2000年金融服务与市场法》第415条"。

《1988年收入及公司税务法》(c. 1)

第4条 (1)《1988年收入及公司税务法》进行如下修正。

(2)在第76条(管理费用：保险公司)第(8)款中，删除下列定义：

"1986年法"；
"获授权人"；
"投资业务"；
"投资者"；
"投资者保护计划"；
"规定的"；和
"获认可的自我监管组织"。

(3)在第468条(被授权单位信托)第(6)款和第(8)款中，将"《1986年金融服务法》第78条"替换为"《2000年金融服务与市场法》第243条"。

(4)在第469条第(7)款(其他单位信托计划)中，将"《1986年金融服务法》"替换为"《2000年金融服务与市场法》"。

(5)在第728条(关于证券转让的信息)第(7)款第(a)项中，将"《1986年金融服务法》"替换为"《2000年金融服务与市场法》"。

(6)在第841条第(3)款(将税务法的某些规定适用于获认可的投资交易所的权力)中，将"《1986年金融服务法》"替换为"《2000年金融服务与市场法》"。

The Finance Act 1991 (c. 31)

5 (1) The Finance Act 1991 is amended as follows.

(2) In section 47 (investor protection schemes), omit subsections (1), (2) and (4).

(3) In section 116 (investment exchanges and clearing houses: stamp duty), in subsection (4)(b), for "Financial Services Act 1986" substitute " Financial Services and Markets Act 2000".

The Tribunals and Inquiries Act 1992 (c. 53)

6 (1) The Tribunals and Inquiries Act 1992 is amended as follows.

(2) In Schedule 1 (tribunals under supervision of the Council on Tribunals), for the entry relating to financial services and paragraph 18, substitute—

"Financial services and markets

18.The Financial Services and Markets Tribunal."

Annotations:

Commencement Information

I167 Sch. 20 para. 6 in force at 3.7.2001; Sch. 20 para. 6 not in force at Royal Assent see s.431(2); Sch.20 para. 6 in force at 3.7.2001 by S.I. 2001/2364, art. 2(a) (with transitional savings in art. 3)

The Judicial Pensions and Retirement Act 1993 (c. 8)

7 (1) The Judicial Pensions and Retirement Act 1993 is amended as follows.

(2) In Schedule 1 (offices which may be qualifying offices), in Part II, after the entry relating to the President or chairman of the Transport Tribunal insert—

"President or Deputy President of the Financial Services and Markets Tribunal"

(3) In Schedule 5 (relevant offices in relation to retirement provisions)—

(a) omit the entry—

"Member of the Financial Services Tribunal appointed by the Lord Chancellor"; and

(b) at the end insert—

"Member of the Financial Services and Markets Tribunal".

Annotations:

Commencement Information

I168 Sch. 20 para. 7 wholly in force at 1.12.2001; Sch. 20 para. 7 not in force at Royal Assent see s. 431(2); Sch. 20 para. 7(except sub-para. (3)(a)) in force at 3.9.2001 by S.I. 2001/2632, art. 2(2), Sch. Pt. 2; Sch. 20 para. 7 in force in so far as not already in force at 1.12.2001 by S.I. 2001/3538, art. 2(1)

《1991年金融法》(c. 31)

第5条 (1)《1991年金融法》进行如下修正。

(2)在第47条(投资者保护计划)中,删除第(1)款、第(2)款和第(4)款。

(3)在第116条(投资交易所和清算所:印花税)第(4)款第(b)项中,将"《1986年金融服务法》"替换为"《2000年金融服务与市场法》"。

《1992年裁判所与调查法》(c. 53)

第6条 (1)《1992年裁判所与调查法》进行如下修正。

(2)在附录1(受裁判所理事会监管的裁判所)中,将关于金融服务的条目和第18条替换为:

"金融服务与市场

18.金融服务与市场裁判所。"

注释:

实施日期

I167 附录20第6条于2001年7月3日生效;附录20第6条在副署时尚未生效,见第431条第(2)款;附录20第6条于2001年7月3日依照制定法文件S.I.2001/2364第2条第(a)款(与第3条的过渡储蓄)生效。

《1993年司法人员退休金及退休法》(c. 8)

第7条 (1)《1993年司法人员退休金及退休法》进行如下修正。

(2)在附录1(可以成为合资格的办事处的办事处)第二部分中,在与运输裁判所审判长或委员有关的条目后加入:

"金融服务与市场裁判所审判长或副审判长"。

(3)在附录5(与退休规定有关的办事处)中

(a)删除:

"司法大臣任命的金融服务裁判所成员";并且

(b)在结尾处加入:

"金融服务与市场裁判所成员"。

注释:

实施日期

I168 附录20第7条于2001年12月1日全部生效;附录20第7条在副署时尚未生效,见第431条第(2)款;附录20第7条[除第(3)款第(a)项外]于2001年9月3日依照制定法文件S.I.2001/2632 第2条第(2)款,附录第二部分生效;附录20第7条如于2001年12月1日尚未生效,则依照制定法文件S.I. 2001/3538第2条第(1)款生效。

SCHEDULE 21
TRANSITIONAL PROVISIONS AND SAVINGS

Section 432(2)

Self-regulating organisations

1 (1) No new application under section 9 of the 1986 Act(application for recognition) may be entertained.

(2) No outstanding application made under that section before the passing of this Act may continue to be entertained.

(3) After the date which is the designated date for a recognised self-regulating organisation—

(a) the recognition order for that organisation may not be revoked under section 11 of the 1986 Act (revocation of recognition);

(b) no application may be made to the court under section 12 of the 1986 Act (compliance orders) with respect to that organisation.

(4) The powers conferred by section 13 of the 1986 Act(alteration of rules for protection of investors) may not be exercised.

(5) "Designated date" means such date as the Treasury may by order designate.

(6) Sub-paragraph (3)does not apply to a recognised self-regulating organisation in respect of which a notice of intention to revoke its recognition order was given under section 11(3) of the 1986 Act before the passing of this Act if that notice has not been withdrawn.

(7) Expenditure incurred by the Authority in connection with the winding up of any body which was, immediately before the passing of this Act, a recognised self-regulating organisation is to be treated as having been incurred in connection with the discharge by the Authority of functions under this Act.

(8) "Recognised self-regulating organisation" means an organisation which,immediately before the passing of this Act, was such an organisation for the purposes of the 1986 Act.

(9) "The 1986 Act" means the [M155] Financial Services Act 1986.

Annotations:

Marginal Citations

M155 1986 c. 60.

附录21 过渡性规定和保留

第432条第(2)款

自我监管组织

第1条 (1)不得受理依照1986年法第9条(认可申请)新提出的申请。

(2)在本法通过以前提出、未受理完毕的申请,不得继续受理。

(3)在获认可的自我监管组织的指定日期以后

(a)不得依照1986年法第11条(撤销认可)规定撤销对该组织的认可令;

(b)不得依照1986年法第12条(合规令)规定对该组织向法院作出申请。

(4)不得行使1986年法第13条(保护投资者规章变更)赋予的权力。

(5)“规定日期”系指财政部通过法令规定的日期。

(6)对本法通过以前依照1986年法第11条第(3)款向其发出撤销其认可令的意向通知的获认可的自我监管组织,如该通知未撤回,则第(3)款不适用。

(7)管理局发生的与任何本法通过前为获认可的自我监管组织的机构解散有关的支出,视为与管理局依照本法履行职能有关的支出。

(8)“获认可的自我监管组织”,系指在本法通过以前就1986年法而言是此等的组织的组织。

(9)“1986年法”系指[M155]《1986年金融服务法》。

注释:

附注引文

M155 1986年第60章。

Self-regulating organisations for friendly societies

2 (1) No new application under paragraph 2 of Schedule 11 to the 1986 Act (application for recognition) may be entertained.

(2) No outstanding application made under that paragraph before the passing of this Act may continue to be entertained.

(3) After the date which is the designated date for a recognised self-regulating organisation for friendly societies—

(a) the recognition order for that organisation may not be revoked under paragraph 5 of Schedule 11 to the 1986 Act (revocation of recognition);

(b) no application may be made to the court under paragraph 6 of that Schedule (compliance orders) with respect to that organisation.

(4) "Designated date" means such date as the Treasury may by order designate.

(5) Sub-paragraph (3) does not apply to a recognised self-regulating organisation for friendly societies in respect of which a notice of intention to revoke its recognition order was given under section 11(3) of the 1986 Act (as applied by paragraph 5(2) of that Schedule) before the passing of this Act if that notice has not been withdrawn.

(6) Expenditure incurred by the Authority in connection with the winding up of any body which was, immediately before the passing of this Act, a recognised selfregulating organisation for friendly societies is to be treated as having been incurred in connection with the discharge by the Authority of functions under this Act.

(7) "Recognised self-regulating organisation for friendly societies" means an organisation which, immediately before the passing of this Act, was such an organisation for the purposes of the 1986 Act.

(8) "The 1986 Act" means the [M156]Financial Services Act 1986.

Annotations:

Marginal Citations

M156 1986 c. 60.

互相保险协会的自我监管组织

第2条 (1)不得受理依照1986年法附录11第2条(认可申请)新提出的申请。

(2)在本法通过前提出、未受理完毕的申请,不得继续受理。

(3)在为获认可的互相保险协会自我监管组织规定的日期以后

(a)不得依照1986年法附录11第5条(撤销认可)撤销对该组织的认可令;

(b)不得依照该附录第6条(合规令)对该组织向法院作出申请。

(4)“规定的日期”系指财政部通过法令规定的日期。

(5)对本法通过前依照1986年法第11条第(3)款[通过该附录第5条第(2)款]规定收到撤销其认可令的意向通知的获认可的互相保险协会自我监管组织,如该通知未撤回,则第(3)款不适用。

(6)管理局发生的与任何本法通过前是获认可的互相保险协会自我监管组织的机构解散有关的支出,视为与管理局依照本法履行职能有关的支出。

(7)“获认可的互相保险协会自我监管组织”,系指本法通过前就1986年法而言是此等组织的组织。

(8)“1986年法律”系指[M156]《1986年金融服务法》。

注释:

附注引文

M156 1986年第60章。

SCHEDULE 22 REPEALS

Section 432(3)

Annotations:

Commencement Information

I169 Sch. 22 wholly in force at 2.7.2002; Sch. 22 not in force at Royal Assent see s. 431(2); Sch. 22 in force for specified purposes at 30.4.2001 by S.I. 2001/1282, art. 2(b); Sch. 22 in force 2.7.2002 in relation to the Credit Union Act 1979 by S.I. 2001/3538, art. 2(5)(b); Sch. 22 in force at in so far as not already in force at 1.12.2001 by S.I. 2001/3538, art. 2(1)

Chapter	Short title	Extent of repeal
1923 c. 8.	The Industrial Assurance Act 1923.	The whole Act.
1948 c. 39.	The Industrial Assurance and Friendly Societies Act 1948.	The whole Act.
1965 c. 12.	The Industrial and Provident Societies Act 1965.	Section 8. Section 70.
1974 c. 46.	The Friendly Societies Act 1974.	Section 4. Section 10. In section 11, from "and where" to "that society". In section 99(4), "in the central registration area".
1975 c. 24.	The House of Commons Disqualification Act 1975.	In Schedule 1, in Part III, "Any member of the Financial Services Tribunal in receipt of remuneration".
1975 c. 25.	The Northern Ireland Assembly Dis – qualification Act 1975.	In Schedule 1, in Part III, "Any member of the Financial Services Tribunal in receipt of remuneration".
1977 c. 46.	The Insurance Brokers (Registration) Act 1977.	The whole Act.
1979 c. 34.	The Credit Unions Act 1979.	Section 6(2) to (6). Section 11(2) and (6). Sections 11B, 11C and 11D. Section 12(4) and (5). In section 14, subsections (2), (3), (5) and (6). Section 28(2).
1986 c. 53.	The Building Societies Act 1986.	Section 9. Schedule 3.
1988 c. 1.	The Income and Corporation Taxes Act 1988.	In section 76, in subsection (8), the definitions of "the 1986 Act", "authorised person", "investment business", "investor", "investor protection scheme", "prescribed" and "recognised self – regulating organisation".

附录22 废止的规定

第432条第(3)款

注释:

实施日期

I169 附录22于2002年7月2日全部生效;附录22在副署时尚未生效,见第431条第(2)款;附录22为特定目的于2001年4月30日依照制定法文件S.I. 2001/1282第2条第(b)款生效;附录22于2002年7月2日依照制定法文件S.I. 2001/3538第2条第(5)款第(b)项涉及《1979年信用合作社法》生效;附录22如于2001年12月1日尚未生效,则依照制定法文件S.I.2001/3538第2条第(1)款生效。

章	简称	废止范围
1923 年第 8 章	《1923 年工业保险法》	整部法律
1984 年第 39 章	《1948 年行业节俭互助会法》	整部法律
1965 年第 12 章	《1965 年行业节俭互助会法》	第 8 条 第 70 条
1974 年第 46 章	《1974 年互相保险协会法》	第 4 条 第 10 条 在第 11 条中,从“并且如果”到“该协会” 在第 99 条第(4)款中,“在中心注册区域”
1975 年第 24 章	《1975 年下议院剥夺资格法》	在附录 1 第三部分中,“收取报酬的金融服务裁判所的任何成员”
1975 年第 25 章	《1975 年北爱尔兰议会剥夺资格法》	在附录 1 第三部分中,“收取报酬的金融服务裁判所的任何成员”
1977 年第 46 章	《1977 年保险经纪人(注册)法》	整部法律
1979 年第 34 章	《1979 年信用合作社法》	第 6 条第(2)款至第(6)款 第 11 条第(2)款和第(6)款 第 11B 条、第 11C 条和第 11D 条 第 12 条第(4)款和第(5)款 第 14 条第(2)款、第(3)款、第(5)款和第(6)款 第 28 条第(2)款
1986 年第 53 章	《1986 年住房互助会法》	第 9 条 附录 3
1988 年第 1 章	《1988 年收入及公司税务法》	在第 76 条第(8)款中,“1986 年法律”、“获授权人”、“投资业务”、“投资者”、“投资者保护计划”、“规定的”和“获认可的自我监管组织”

Chapter	Short title	Extent of repeal
1991 c. 31.	The Finance Act 1991.	In section 47, subsections (1), (2) and (4).
1992 c. 40.	The Friendly Societies Act 1992.	In section 13, subsections (2) to (5), (8) and (11). Sections 31 to 36. In section 37, subsections (1), (1A) and (7A) to (9). Sections 38 to 50. In section 52, subsection (2)(d) and, in subsection (5), the words from "or where" to the end. Schedule 7. In Schedule 8, paragraph3(2).
1993 c. 8.	The Judicial Pensions and Retirement Act 1993.	In Schedule 5, "Member of the Financial Services Tribunal appointed by the Lord Chancellor".

Changes to legislation:

There are outstanding changes not yet made by the legislation.gov.uk editorial team to Financial Services and Markets Act 2000. Any changes that have already been made by the team appear in the content and are referenced with annotations.

Changes and effects yet to be applied to the whole Act, associated Parts and Chapters:

—Act by 2002 c. 29

—Act by 2002 c. 40

—S.R. 2004/333 commences (2002 c. 13 (N.I.))

—S.R. 2006/21 commences (SI 2005/1455 (N.I. 10))

—S.R. 2006/22 transitional provisions for effects of SR 2006/21

—S.I. 2003/120 commences (2002 c. 29. This SI is amended by SI 2003/333)

—S.I. 2003/1397 commences (2002 c. 40)

—S.I. 2003/2093 commences (2002 c. 40. This SI is amended by SI 2003/2332)

—S.I. 2003/3142 commences (2002 c. 11 and 2003 c. 21. This SI is amended by SI 2004/545, SI 2004/697 and SI 2004/1492)

—S.I. 2003/708 commences (2001 c. 16)

—S.I. 2003/766 commences (2002 c. 40)

—S.I. 2004/827 commences (2003 c. 20)

—S.I. 2005/1432 commences (2005 c. 12)

—S.I. 2005/3175 commences (2004 c. 33)

—S.I. 2006/1014 commences (2005 c. 4)

—S.I. 2006/1508 commences (2006 c. 14)

章	简称	废止范围
1991 年第 31 章	《1991 年金融法》	第 47 条第(1)款、第(2)款和第(4)款 第 13 条第(2)款至第(5)款、第(8)款和第(11)款
1992 年第 40 章	《1992 年互相保险协会法》	第 31 条至第 36 条 第 37 条第(1)款、第(1A)款和第(7A)款至第(9)款 第 38 条至第 50 条 第 52 条第(2)款第(d)项,在第(5)款中从"或者如果"到结尾 附录 7 附录 8 第 3 条第(2)款
1993 年第 8 章	《1993 年司法人员退休金及退休法》	在附录 5 中,"司法大臣任命的金融服务裁判所成员"

立法修改：

Legislation.gov.uk编辑小组尚未在《2000年金融服务与市场法》中作出修改。该小组已作出的任何修改均出现在内容中并附有注释。[1]

尚未应用到整部法律、相关部分和章节的修改和效力：

依照第29章《2002年犯罪所得法》制定本法

依照第40章《2002年企业法》制定本法

法定规则2004/333 开始生效[2002年本法第13（N.I.)条]

法定规则2006/21开始生效[制定法文件S.I. 2005/1455（N.I. 10)]

法定规则2006/22 关于法定规则2006/21效力的过渡性规定

制定法文件S.I. 2003/120开始生效(2002年第29章。此行政立法性文件经制定法文件S.I. 2003/333修正)

制定法文件S.I. 2003/1397开始生效(2002年第40章)

制定法文件S.I. 2003/2093开始生效(2002年第40章。此行政立法性文件经制定法文件S.I. 2003/2332修正)

制定法文件S.I. 2003/3142开始生效(2002年第11章和2003年第21章。此行政立法性文件经制定法文件S.I.2004/545、制定法文件S.I. 2004/697与制定法文件S.I. 2004/1492修正)

制定法文件S.I. 2003/708开始生效(2001年第16章)

制定法文件S.I. 2003/766开始生效(2002年第40章)

制定法文件S.I. 2004/827开始生效(2003年第20章)

制定法文件S.I. 2005/1432开始生效(2005年第12章)

制定法文件S.I. 2005/3175开始生效(2004年第33章)

制定法文件S.I. 2006/1014开始生效(2005年第4章)

制定法文件S.I. 2006/1508开始生效(2006年第14章)

1 该部分为原文后附说明,并非法条内容,为保证文本完整性保留该部分内容。——译者注

—S.I. 2006/3272 commences （2005 c. 19. This SI is amended by SI 2006/3361, SI 2007/1157, SI 2007/1527 and SI 2007/2169）

—S.I. 2006/3428 commences（2006 c. 46. This SI is amended by SI 2007/3495 and SI 2008/2860）

—S.I. 2007/1093 commences（2006 c. 46. This SI is amended by SI 2008/2860）

—S.I. 2007/3300 commences（2006 c. 14）

—S.I. 2007/3546 commences（2007 c. 17）

—S.I. 2007/94 commences（2006 c. 29）

—S.I. 2008/1653 commences（2007 c. 15）

—S.I. 2008/1886 commences（2006 c. 46. This SI is amended by SI 2008/2860）

—S.I. 2009/1604 commences（2005 c. 4）

—S.I. 2009/296 commences（2009 c. 1）

—S.I. 2009/3000 commences（2009 c. 1）

—S.I. 2009/36 commences（2007 c. 26）

—S.I. 2009/490 commences（2008 c. 31）

—S.I. 2010/2480 commences（2010 c. 28）

—S.I. 2010/816 commences（2009 c. 25）

—Act Sch. 4 para. 1 renumbered as Sch. 4 para. 1(1) by 2010 c. 28

—Act added by 2009 c. 1

—Act added by S.I. 2005/1433

—Act added by S.I. 2007/2403

—Act amendment to earlier affecting provision SI 2003/1476 art. 20 by S.I. 2004/1610

—Act amendment to earlier affecting provision SI 2008/3249 Sch. para. 14–18 by S.I. 2010/22

—Act amendment to earlier affecting provision SI 2008/718 Sch. para. 15–19 by S.I. 2010/22

—Act applied by S.R. 2004/335

—Act applied by 2008 c. 28

—Act applied by S.I. 2003/1102

—Act applied by S.I. 2004/353

—Act applied by S.I. 2004/454

—Act applied by S.I. 2008/2546

—Act applied by S.I. 2008/2644

制定法文件S.I. 2006/3272开始生效(2005年第19章。此行政立法性文件经制定法文件S.I.2006/3361、制定法文件S.I.2007/1157、制定法文件S.I. 2007/1527与制定法文件S.I. 2007/2169修正)

制定法文件S.I. 2006/3428开始生效(2006年第46章。此行政立法性文件经制定法文件S.I. 2007/3495 和制定法文件S.I. 2008/2860修正)

制定法文件S.I. 2007/1093开始生效(2006年第46章。此行政立法性文件经制定法文件S.I. 2008/2860修正)

制定法文件S.I. 2007/3300开始生效(2006年第14章)

制定法文件S.I. 2007/3546开始生效(2007年第17章)

制定法文件S.I. 2007/94 开始生效(2006年第29章)

制定法文件S.I. 2008/1653开始生效(2007年第15章)

制定法文件S.I. 2008/1886开始生效(2006年第46章。此行政立法性文件经制定法文件S.I. 2008/2860修正)

制定法文件S.I. 2009/1604开始生效(2005年第4章)

制定法文件S.I. 2009/296开始生效(2009年第1章)

制定法文件S.I. 2009/3000开始生效(2009年第1章)

制定法文件S.I. 2009/36开始生效(2007年第26章)

制定法文件S.I. 2009/490开始生效(2008年第31章)

制定法文件S.I. 2010/2480开始生效(2010年第28章)

制定法文件S.I. 2010/816开始生效(2009年第25章)

附录4第1条依照2010年本法第28条重新编号为附录4第1条第(1)款

本法依照2009年第1章添加内容

本法依照制定法文件S.I. 2005/1433添加内容

本法依照制定法文件S.I. 2007/2403添加内容

本法依照制定法文件S.I. 2004/1610修正先前有影响的规定：制定法文件S.I. 2003/1476 第20条

本法依照制定法文件S.I. 2010/22修正先前有影响的规定：制定法文件S.I. 2008/3249附录第14~18条

本法依照制定法文件2010/22修正先前有影响的规定:制定法文件S.I. 2008/718附录第15~19条

本法适用法定规则2004/335

本法适用2008年第28章

本法适用制定法文件S.I. 2003/1102

本法适用制定法文件S.I. 2004/353

本法适用制定法文件S.I. 2004/454

本法适用制定法文件S.I. 2008/2546

本法适用制定法文件S.I. 2008/2644

—Act applied by S.I. 2008/2666
—Act applied by S.I. 2008/2674
—Act applied by S.I. 2008/346
—Act applied by S.I. 2009/209
—Act applied by S.I. 2009/3226
—Act applied by S.I. 2010/89
—Act applied by S.I. 2010/906
—Act applied (with modifications) by S.R. 2004/307
—Act applied (with modifications) by S.R. 2004/335
—Act applied (with modifications) by 2006 c. 29
—Act applied (with modifications) by 2009 c. 1
—Act applied (with modifications) by 2010 c. 28
—Act applied (with modifications) by S.I. 2004/1045
—Act applied (with modifications) by S.I. 2004/2737
—Act applied (with modifications) by S.I. 2004/353
—Act applied (with modifications) by S.I. 2007/2157
—Act applied (with modifications) by S.I. 2007/3298
—Act applied (with modifications) by S.I. 2008/3249
—Act applied (with modifications) by S.I. 2008/346
—Act applied (with modifications) by S.I. 2008/432
—Act applied (with modifications) by S.I. 2008/718
—Act applied (with modifications) by S.I. 2009/1810
—Act applied (with modifications) by S.I. 2009/209
—Act applied (with modifications) by S.I. 2010/89
—Act applied (with modifications) by S.I. 2010/906
—Act applied by 2004 c. 27 s. 15A(7) (as substituted) by S.I. 2008/948
—Act applied by SI 2001/544 art. 95(10) (as inserted) by S.I. 2003/1476

—Act disapplied by S.I. 2004/2615
—Act excluded by S.I. 2003/1102
—Act excluded by S.I. 2003/1475
—Act excluded by S.I. 2003/1476
—Act excluded by S.I. 2004/1862
—Act excluded by S.I. 2004/2615
—Act excluded by S.I. 2004/3351
—Act excluded by S.I. 2004/353
—Act excluded by S.I. 2005/1998

本法适用制定法文件S.I. 2008/2666
本法适用制定法文件S.I. 2008/2674
本法适用制定法文件S.I. 2008/346
本法适用制定法文件S.I. 2009/209
本法适用制定法文件S.I. 2009/3226
本法适用制定法文件S.I. 2010/89

本法适用(已修订)法定规则2004/307
本法适用(已修订)法定规则2004/335
本法适用(已修订)2006年第29章
本法适用(已修订)2009年第1章
本法适用(已修订)2010年第28章
本法适用(已修订)制定法文件S.I. 2004/1045
本法适用(已修订)制定法文件S.I. 2004/2737
本法适用(已修订)制定法文件S.I. 2004/353
本法适用(已修订)制定法文件S.I. 2007/2157
本法适用(已修订)制定法文件S.I. 2007/3298
本法适用(已修订)制定法文件S.I. 2008/3249
本法适用(已修订)制定法文件S.I. 2008/346
本法适用(已修订)制定法文件S.I. 2008/432
本法适用(已修订)制定法文件S.I. 2008/718
本法适用(已修订)制定法文件S.I. 2009/1810
本法适用(已修订)制定法文件S.I. 2009/209
本法适用(已修订)制定法文件S.I. 2010/89
本法适用(已修订)制定法文件S.I. 2010/906
依照2004年第27章第15A条第(7)款(依照制定法文件2008/948替换)适用
依照制定法文件S.I.2001/544第95条第(10)款(依照制定法文件S.I.2003/1476插入)适用
本法不适用制定法文件S.I. 2004/2615
依照制定法文件S.I. 2003/1102排除本法
依照制定法文件S.I. 2003/1475排除本法
依照制定法文件S.I. 2003/1476排除本法
依照制定法文件S.I. 2004/1862排除本法
依照制定法文件S.I. 2004/2615排除本法
依照制定法文件S.I. 2004/3351排除本法
依照制定法文件S.I. 2004/353排除本法
依照制定法文件S.I. 2005/1998排除本法

—Act excluded by S.I. 2006/1183
—Act excluded by S.I. 2006/3259
—Act excluded by S.I. 2007/3510
—Act excluded by 2005 c. 15 s. 71(6B) (as inserted) by 2009 c. 25
—Act excluded by SI 2002/1454 art. 12(1) (as inserted) by S.I. 2004/1609

—Act excluded by SI 2002/1454 art. 12(2) (as inserted) by S.I. 2004/1609

—Act extended by S.I. 2003/1633
—Act extended by S.I. 2004/1045
—Act extended by S.I. 2004/454
—Act extended by SI 2000/1119 Sch. 3 Pt. 1 (as amended) by S.I. 2004/1628

—Act inserted by 2005 c. 12
—Act inserted by 2005 c. 24
—Act inserted by 2005 c. 4
—Act inserted by 2006 c. 14
—Act inserted by 2006 c. 46
—Act inserted by 2006 c. 55
—Act inserted by 2007 c. 17
—Act inserted by 2008 c. 28
—Act inserted by 2008 c. 31
—Act inserted by 2009 c. 1
—Act inserted by 2010 c. 28
—Act inserted by S.I. 2003/1473
—Act inserted by S.I. 2003/1476
—Act inserted by S.I. 2003/2066
—Act inserted by S.I. 2005/1433
—Act inserted by S.I. 2005/381
—Act inserted by S.I. 2006/1183
—Act inserted by S.I. 2006/2975
—Act inserted by S.I. 2007/126
—Act inserted by S.I. 2007/1973
—Act inserted by S.I. 2007/3253
—Act inserted by S.I. 2008/1468
—Act inserted by S.I. 2008/948
—Act inserted by S.I. 2009/1342

依照制定法文件S.I. 2006/1183排除本法

依照制定法文件S.I. 2006/3259排除本法

依照制定法文件S.I. 2007/3510排除本法

依照2005年第15章第71条第(6B)款(依照2009年第25章插入)排除本法

依照制定法文件S.I.2002/1454第12条第(1)款(依照制定法文件2004/1609插入)排除本法

依照制定法文件S.I.2002/1454第12条第(2)款(依照制定法文件2004/1609插入)排除本法

依照制定法文件S.I.2003/1633扩大本法适用范围

依照制定法文件S.I.2004/1045扩大本法适用范围

依照制定法文件S.I.2004/454扩大本法适用范围

依照制定法文件S.I.2000/1119附录3第一部分(依照制定法文件2004/1682修订)延长本法有效期

依照 2005年第12章对本法插入内容

依照2005年第24章对本法插入内容

依照2005年第4章对本法插入内容

依照2006年第14章对本法插入内容

依照2006年第46章对本法插入内容

依照2006年第55章对本法插入内容

依照2007年第17章对本法插入内容

依照2008年第28章对本法插入内容

依照 2008年第31章对本法插入内容

依照 2009年第1章对本法插入内容

依照 2010年第28章对本法插入内容

依照制定法文件S.I. 2003/1473对本法插入内容

依照制定法文件S.I. 2003/1476对本法插入内容

依照制定法文件S.I. 2003/2066对本法插入内容

依照制定法文件S.I. 2005/1433对本法插入内容

依照制定法文件S.I. 2005/381对本法插入内容

依照制定法文件S.I. 2006/1183对本法插入内容

依照制定法文件S.I. 2006/2975对本法插入内容

依照制定法文件S.I. 2007/126对本法插入内容

依照制定法文件S.I. 2007/1973对本法插入内容

依照制定法文件S.I. 2008/1468对本法插入内容

依照制定法文件S.I. 2008/948对本法插入内容

依照制定法文件S.I. 2009/1342对本法插入内容

—Act inserted by S.I. 2009/2461

—Act inserted by S.I. 2009/534

—Act inserted by S.I. 2010/1192

—Act inserted by S.I. 2010/1193

—Act inserted by SI 2001/544 art. 97 (as inserted) by S.I. 2004/1610

—Act modified by S.R. 2004/335

—Act modified by 2007 c. 26

—Act modified by 2010 c. 28

—Act modified by S.I. 2003/1102

—Act modified by S.I. 2003/1475

—Act modified by S.I. 2003/1476

—Act modified by S.I. 2004/1862

—Act modified by S.I. 2004/2615

—Act modified by S.I. 2004/3219

—Act modified by S.I. 2004/353

—Act modified by S.I. 2004/454

—Act modified by S.I. 2006/1969

—Act modified by S.I. 2007/3298

—Act modified by S.I. 2007/3510

—Act modified by S.I. 2008/2546

—Act modified by S.I. 2008/2644

—Act modified by S.I. 2008/2666

—Act modified by S.I. 2008/2674

—Act modified by S.I. 2008/346

—Act modified by S.I. 2008/432

—Act modified by S.I. 2009/1342

—Act modified by S.I. 2009/209

—Act modified by S.I. 2009/317

—Act modified by S.I. 2009/3226

—Act modified by S.I. 2009/814

—Act modified by SI 2000/1119 Sch. 4 para. 11 (as substituted) by S.I. 2009/1587

—Act modified by SI 2009/209 Sch. 7 para. 3(1) (as inserted) by S.I. 2009/2475

—Act modified by SI 2009/209 Sch. 7 para. 3(2) (as inserted) by S.I. 2009/2475

依照制定法文件S.I. 2009/2461对本法插入内容

依照制定法文件S.I. 2009/534对本法插入内容

依照制定法文件S.I. 2010/1192对本法插入内容

依照制定法文件S.I. 2010/1193对本法插入内容

依照制定法文件S.I.2001/544第97条(依照制定法文件2004/1610插入)对本法插入内容

本法依照法定规则2004/335修订

本法依照2007年第26章修订

本法依照2010年第28章修订

本法依照制定法文件S.I. 2003/1102修订

本法依照制定法文件S.I. 2003/1475修订

本法依照制定法文件S.I. 2003/1476修订

本法依照制定法文件S.I. 2004/1862修订

本法依照制定法文件S.I. 2004/2615修订

本法依照制定法文件S.I. 2004/3219修订

本法依照制定法文件S.I. 2004/353修订

本法依照制定法文件S.I. 2004/454修订

本法依照制定法文件S.I. 2006/1969修订

本法依照制定法文件S.I. 2007/3298修订

本法依照制定法文件S.I. 2007/3510修订

本法依照制定法文件S.I. 2008/2546修订

本法依照制定法文件S.I. 2008/2644修订

本法依照制定法文件S.I. 2008/2666修订

本法依照制定法文件S.I. 2008/2674修订

本法依照制定法文件S.I. 2008/346修订

本法依照制定法文件S.I. 2008/432修订

本法依照制定法文件S.I. 2009/1342修订

本法依照制定法文件S.I. 2009/209修订

本法依照制定法文件S.I. 2009/317修订

本法依照制定法文件S.I. 2009/3226修订

本法依照制定法文件S.I. 2009/814修订

依照制定法文件S.I. 2000/1119附录4第11条(依照制定法文件S.I. 2009/1587替换)修订本法

依照制定法文件S.I. 2009/209 附录7第3条第(1)款(依照制定法文件S.I. 2009/2475插入)修订本法

依照制定法文件S.I. 2009/209 附录7第3条第(2)款(依照制定法文件S.I. 2009/2475插入)修订本法

—Act omitted by 2009 c. 1

—Act omitted by 2010 c. 28

—Act omitted by S.I. 2007/1973

—Act omitted by S.I. 2009/2035

—Act omitted by S.I. 2010/1193

—Act omitted by S.I. 2010/22

—Act repealed by 2005 c. 19

—Act repealed by 2006 c. 46

—Act repealed by 2007 c. 11

—Act repealed by 2007 c. 3

—Act repealed by 2009 c. 4

—Act repealed by 2010 c. 4

—Act repealed by S.I. 2005/1433

—Act repealed by S.I. 2006/3221

—Act repealed by S.I. 2007/1093

—Act repealed by S.I. 2007/126

—Act repealed by S.I. 2008/948

—Act repealed by S.I. 2010/22

—Act restricted by 2005 c. 11

—Act restricted by 2006 c. 41

—Act restricted by S.I. 2003/1102

—Act restricted by S.I. 2008/2546

—Act restricted by S.I. 2008/2644

—Act restricted by S.I. 2008/2666

—Act restricted by S.I. 2008/2674

—Act restricted by S.I. 2008/432

—Act s. 224A renumbered as s. 224A(1) by 2010 c. 28

—Act substituted by S.I. 2005/1455 (N.I.)

—Act substituted by 2005 c. 4

—Act substituted by 2006 c. 46

—Act substituted by 2007 c. 15

—Act substituted by 2008 c. 31

—Act substituted by 2009 c. 1

—Act substituted by 2010 c. 28

—Act substituted by S.I. 2003/1473

—Act substituted by S.I. 2003/2066

本法依照2009年第1章删除
本法依照 2010年第28章删除
本法依照制定法文件S.I. 2007/1973删除
本法依照制定法文件S.I. 2009/2035删除
本法依照制定法文件S.I. 2010/1193删除
本法依照制定法文件S.I. 2010/22删除
依照2005年第19章废止本法规定
依照2006年第46章废止本法规定
依照2007年第11章废止本法规定
依照2007年第3章废止本法规定
依照2009年第4章废止本法规定
依照2010年第4章废止本法规定
依照制定法文件S.I. 2005/1433废止本法规定
依照制定法文件S.I. 2005/381废止本法规定
依照制定法文件S.I. 2006/3221废止本法规定
依照制定法文件S.I. 2007/1093废止本法规定
依照制定法文件S.I. 2007/126废止本法规定
依照制定法文件S.I. 2008/948废止本法规定
依照制定法文件S.I. 2010/22废止本法规定
依照2005年第11章限制本法
依照 2006年第41章限制本法
依照制定法文件S.I. 2003/1102限制本法
依照制定法文件S.I. 2008/2546限制本法
依照制定法文件S.I. 2008/2644限制本法
依照制定法文件S.I. 2008/2666限制本法
依照制定法文件S.I. 2008/2674限制本法
依照制定法文件S.I. 2008/432限制本法
本法第 224A条依照2010年第28章重新编号为第 224A(1)条
依照制定法文件S.I. 2005/1455 (N.I.)替换本法
依照2005年第4章替换本法
依照 2006年第46章替换本法
依照 2007年第15章替换本法
依照2008年第31章替换本法
依照2009年第1章替换本法
依照2010年第28章替换本法
依照制定法文件S.I. 2003/1473替换本法
依照制定法文件S.I. 2003/2066替换本法

—Act substituted by S.I. 2004/3379
—Act substituted by S.I. 2005/1433
—Act substituted by S.I. 2005/381
—Act substituted by S.I. 2006/242
—Act substituted by S.I. 2006/3221
—Act substituted by S.I. 2007/108
—Act substituted by S.I. 2007/126
—Act substituted by S.I. 2007/1973
—Act substituted by S.I. 2007/2194
—Act substituted by S.I. 2007/3253
—Act substituted by S.I. 2008/948
—Act substituted by S.I. 2009/2461
—Act substituted by S.I. 2009/534
—Act substituted by S.I. 2010/1192
—Act substituted by S.I. 2010/1193
—Act substituted by S.I. 2010/22
—Act substituted for Sch. 3 para. 3(5)-(7) by S.I. 2004/3379
—Act substituted for s. 103 by S.I. 2005/1433
—Act substituted for s. 105(5)-(7) by S.I. 2008/948
—Act substituted for s. 118 by S.I. 2005/381
—Act substituted for s. 133 by S.I. 2010/22
—Act substituted for s. 178-191 by S.I. 2009/534
—Act substituted for s. 210(1)(a)(b) by 2010 c. 28
—Act substituted for s. 214B by 2010 c. 28
—Act substituted for s. 229(11) by 2006 c. 14
—Act substituted for s. 236(4)(a)(b) by S.I. 2009/1941
—Act substituted for s. 404C-H by 2010 c. 28
—Act substituted for s. 422 by S.I. 2009/534
—Act substituted for s. 69(a)(b) by 2010 c. 28
—Act substituted for s. 84-87 by S.I. 2005/1433
—Act text amended by S.I. 2005/1455 (N.I.)
—Act text amended by S.R. 2004/307
—Act text amended by 2003 c. 20
—Act text amended by 2003 c. 21
—Act text amended by 2003 c. 44
—Act text amended by 2004 c. 33
—Act text amended by 2005 c. 12

依照制定法文件S.I. 2004/3379替换本法
依照制定法文件S.I. 2005/1433替换本法
依照制定法文件S.I. 2005/381替换本法
依照制定法文件S.I. 2006/242替换本法
依照制定法文件S.I. 2006/3221替换本法
依照制定法文件S.I. 2007/108替换本法
依照制定法文件S.I. 2007/126替换本法
依照制定法文件S.I. 2007/1973替换本法
依照制定法文件S.I. 2007/2194替换本法
依照制定法文件S.I. 2007/3253替换本法
依照制定法文件S.I. 2008/948替换本法
依照制定法文件S.I. 2009/2461替换本法
依照制定法文件S.I. 2009/534替换本法
依照制定法文件S.I. 2010/1192替换本法
依照制定法文件S.I. 2010/1193替换本法
依照制定法文件S.I. 2010/22替换本法
本法附录3第3条第(5)款至第(7)款依照制定法文件S.I. 2004/3379替换
本法第103条依照制定法文件S.I. 2005/1433替换
本法第105条第(5)款至第(7)款依照制定法文件S.I. 2008/948替换
本法第118条依照制定法文件S.I. 2005/381替换
本法第133条依照制定法文件S.I. 2010/22替换
本法第178~191条依照制定法文件S.I. 2009/534替换
本法第210条第(1)款第(a)项、第(b)项依照2010年第28章替换
本法第214B条依照2010年本法第28条替换
本法第229条第(11)款依照2006年本法第14条替换
本法第236条第(4)款第(a)项、第(b)项依照制定法文件S.I. 2009/1941替换
本法第404C-H条依照2010年第28章替换
本法第422条依照制定法文件S.I. 2009/534替换
本法第69条第(a)项、第(b)项依照2010年第28条替换
本法第84~87条依照制定法文件S.I. 2005/1433替换
本法条文依照制定法文件S.I. 2005/1455 (N.I.) 修正
本法条文依照法定规则2004/307修正
本法条文依照2003年第20章修正
本法条文依照2003年第21章修正
本法条文依照 2003年第44章修正
本法条文依照2004年第33章修正
本法条文依照2005年第12章修正

—Act text amended by 2005 c. 19
—Act text amended by 2005 c. 4
—Act text amended by 2006 c. 14
—Act text amended by 2006 c. 46
—Act text amended by 2007 c. 15
—Act text amended by 2008 c. 28
—Act text amended by 2008 c. 31
—Act text amended by 2009 c. 1
—Act text amended by 2010 c. 28
—Act text amended by S.I. 2003/1473
—Act text amended by S.I. 2003/1476
—Act text amended by S.I. 2003/2066
—Act text amended by S.I. 2004/3379
—Act text amended by S.I. 2005/1433
—Act text amended by S.I. 2005/381
—Act text amended by S.I. 2006/2383
—Act text amended by S.I. 2006/2975
—Act text amended by S.I. 2006/3221
—Act text amended by S.I. 2006/745
—Act text amended by S.I. 2007/126
—Act text amended by S.I. 2007/1973
—Act text amended by S.I. 2007/2194
—Act text amended by S.I. 2007/3253
—Act text amended by S.I. 2008/1439
—Act text amended by S.I. 2008/1468
—Act text amended by S.I. 2008/3053
—Act text amended by S.I. 2008/948
—Act text amended by S.I. 2009/1342
—Act text amended by S.I. 2009/1941
—Act text amended by S.I. 2009/209
—Act text amended by S.I. 2009/3128
—Act text amended by S.I. 2009/534
—Act text amended by S.I. 2009/805
—Act text amended by S.I. 2010/1193
—Act text amended by S.I. 2010/22
—Act text amended by S.I. 2010/2628

本法条文依照2005年第19章修正
本法条文依照2005年第4章修正
本法条文依照2006年第14章修正
本法条文依照2006年第46章修正
本法条文依照2007年第15章修正
本法条文依照2008年第28章修正
本法条文依照2008年第31章修正
本法条文依照2009年第1章修正
本法条文依照2010年第28章修正
本法条文依照制定法文件S.I. 2003/1473修正
本法条文依照制定法文件S.I. 2003/1476修正
本法条文依照制定法文件S.I. 2003/2066修正
本法条文依照制定法文件S.I. 2004/3379修正
本法条文依照制定法文件S.I. 2005/1433修正
本法条文依照制定法文件S.I. 2005/381修正
本法条文依照制定法文件S.I. 2006/2383修正
本法条文依照制定法文件S.I. 2006/2975修正
本法条文依照制定法文件S.I. 2006/3221修正
本法条文依照制定法文件S.I. 2006/745修正
本法条文依照制定法文件S.I. 2007/126修正
本法条文依照制定法文件S.I. 2007/1973修正
本法条文依照制定法文件S.I. 2007/2194修正
本法条文依照制定法文件S.I. 2007/3253修正
本法条文依照制定法文件S.I. 2008/1439修正
本法条文依照制定法文件S.I. 2008/1468修正
本法条文依照制定法文件S.I. 2008/3053修正
本法条文依照制定法文件S.I. 2008/948修正
本法条文依照制定法文件S.I. 2009/1342修正
本法条文依照制定法文件S.I. 2009/1941修正
本法条文依照制定法文件S.I. 2009/209修正
本法条文依照制定法文件S.I. 2009/3128修正
本法条文依照制定法文件S.I. 2009/534修正
本法条文依照制定法文件S.I. 2009/805修正
本法条文依照制定法文件S.I. 2010/1193修正
本法条文依照制定法文件S.I. 2010/22修正
本法条文依照制定法文件S.I. 2010/2628修正

ELIZABETH II c.28

伊丽莎白二世

Financial Services Act 2010

2010年金融服务法

An Act to make provision amending the Financial Services and Markets Act 2000, including provision about financial education, and other provision about financial services and markets; and to make provision for the administration of court funds by the Director of Savings. [8th April 2010]

BE IT ENACTED by the Queen's most Excellent Majesty, by and with the advice and consent of the Lords Spiritual and Temporal, and Commons, in this present Parliament assembled, and by the authority of the same, as follows:—

Objectives of FSA etc

1 Financial stability objective

(1) The Financial Services and Markets Act 2000 is amended as follows.

(2) In section 2(2) (the FSA's regulatory objectives), after paragraph (a) insert—

"(ab) financial stability; ".

(3) After section 3 insert—

"3A Financial stability

(1)The financial stability objective is: contributing to the protection and enhancement of the stability of the UK financial system.

(2) In considering that objective the Authority must have regard to—

(a) the economic and fiscal consequences for the United Kingdom of instability of the UK financial system;

(b) the effects (if any) on the growth of the economy of the United Kingdom of anything done for the purpose of meeting that objective; and

(c) the impact(if any) on the stability of the UK financial system of events or circumstances outside the United Kingdom (as well as in the United Kingdom).

(3) The Authority must, consulting the Treasury, determine and review its strategy in relation to the financial stability objective."

2 Enhancing public understanding of financial matters etc

(1)The Financial Services and Markets Act 2000 is amended as follows.

(2) In section 2 (the FSA's general duties)—

(a) in subsection (2)(the FSA's regulatory objectives),omit paragraph (b)(which provides that public awareness is one of those objectives), and

为规定对《2000年金融服务与市场法》的修订，包括修订金融教育相关规定以及金融服务和市场的其他相关规定，并就储蓄理事的法院经费管理作出规定，制定本法。[2010年4月8日]

本法以最杰出的女王陛下的权威为依据，经上议院神职议员和世俗议员以及下议院提出建议并同意，经议会批准，于本届议会召开之际颁布如下：

金融服务法的目标等

第1条　金融稳定目标

(1)《2000年金融服务与市场法》修订如下。

(2)第2条第(2)款(金融服务管理局的监管目标)中，第(a)项后插入：

“(ab)金融稳定”。

(3)第3条后插入：

“**第3A条　金融稳定**

(1)金融稳定目标为：有助于保护和加强联合王国金融系统的稳定性。

(2)管理局在考虑该目标时必须

(a)考虑联合王国金融系统不稳定对联合王国的经济和财政造成的后果；

(b)为实现该目标实施的任何行为对联合王国经济增长的影响(如有)；以及

(c)联合王国境外(以及境内)的事件或情况对联合王国金融系统稳定的影响(如有)。

(3)管理局必须经征求财政部意见确定并审查其金融稳定目标相关战略。”

第2条　加强公众对金融事项的理解等

(1)《2000年金融服务与市场法》修订如下。

(2)第2条(金融服务管理局的一般性职责)

(a)第(2)款(金融服务管理局的监管目标)删除第(b)项(规定公众意识为一项目标)，以及

(b) in subsection (3)(matters to which FSA must have regard in discharging its general functions), after paragraph (g) insert—

"(h) the desirability of enhancing the understanding and knowledge of members of the public of financial matters(including the UK financial system)."

(3) Omit section 4 (public awareness).

(4) In section 5(2) (the protection of consumers), after paragraph (b) insert—

"(ba) any information which the consumer financial education body has provided to the Authority in the exercise of the consumer financial education function; ".

(5) After section 6 insert—

"*Enhancing public understanding of financial matters etc*

6A Enhancing public understanding of financial matters etc

(1) The Authority must establish a body corporate ("the consumer financial education body") whose function ("the consumer financial education function") is to enhance—

(a) the understanding and knowledge of members of the public of financial matters (including the UK financial system); and

(b) the ability of members of the public to manage their own financial affairs.

(2) The consumer financial education function includes, in articular—

(a) promoting awareness of the benefits of financial planning;

(b) promoting awareness of the financial advantages and disadvantages in relation to the supply of particular kinds of goods or services;

(c) promoting awareness of the benefits and risks associated with different kinds of financial dealing (which includes informing the Authority and other bodies of those benefits and risks);

(d) the publication of educational materials or the carrying out of other educational activities; and

(e) the provision of information and advice to members of the public.

(3) Schedule 1A makes further provision about the consumer financial education body."

(6) After Schedule 1 insert the Schedule 1A set out in Schedule 1 to this Act.

(7) If members of staff of the FSA are transferred to the consumer financial education body, the transfer is to be regarded for the purposes of TUPE as a relevant transfer, whether or not it would otherwise be so regarded.

(8) In subsection (7)—

"the consumer financial education body" has the same meaning as in section 6A of the Financial Services and Markets Act 2000,

"the FSA" means the Financial Services Authority, and

"TUPE"means the Transfer of Undertakings(Protection of Employment) Regulations (b)第(3)款(金融服务管理局在履行其一般性职能时必须考虑的事项)第(g)项后插入:

"(h)是否有必要加强公众对金融事项(包括联合王国金融系统)的理解和认识。"

(3)删除第4条(公众意识)。

(4)第5条第(2)款(保护消费者)第(b)项后插入:

"(ba)消费者金融教育机构在履行消费者金融教育职能时向管理局提供的任何信息。"

(5)第6条后插入:

"加强公众对金融事项的理解等

第6A条　加强公众对金融事项的认识等

(1)管理局必须成立一个法人(以下简称消费者金融教育机构),其职能(以下简称消费者金融教育职能)为加强

(a)公众对金融事项(包括联合王国金融系统)的理解和认识;以及

(b)公众管理自身金融事务的能力。

(2)消费者金融教育职能特别包括:

(a)促进了解理财规划的益处;

(b)促进认识与特定种类商品或服务的供应相关的金融优势和劣势;

(c)促进了解与不同类型的金融交易相关的收益和风险(包括将这些收益和风险通知管理局和其他机构);

(d)公布教育材料或开展其他教育活动;以及

(e)向公众提供信息和建议。

(3)附录1A对金融教育机构作出进一步规定。"

(6)附录1后插入本法附录1所述附录1A。

(7)如管理局工作人员调职至消费者教育机构,则该调职为营业转让法之目的视为相关调职,无论为其他目的是否将其视为相关调职。

(8)第(7)款中

"消费者金融教育机构"含义与《2000年金融服务与市场法》第6A条中的含义相同。

"管理局"系指金融服务管理局,及

"营业转让法"系指《2006年营业转让(保护就业)条例》。

2006.

3 Meeting FSA's regulatory objectives

(1) The Financial Services and Markets Act 2000 is amended as follows.

(2) In section 44(3)(refusal of application by authorised person to vary or cancel its Part Ⅳ permission), for the words from "to it—" to the end substitute "to it that it is desirable to refuse the application in order to meet any of its regulatory objectives."

(3) In section 45 (variation or cancellation of Part Ⅳ permissions:FSA's own initiative power)—

(a) in subsection (1), for paragraph (c) substitute—

"(c) it is desirable to exercise the power in order to meet any of its regulatory objectives.", and

(b) after that subsection insert—

"(1A) For the purposes of subsection (1)(c) it does not matter whether there is a relationship between the authorised person and the persons whose interests will be protected by the exercise of the power under this section."

(4) In section 138(1) and (1A)(general rule-making power), for "protecting the interests of consumers" substitute "meeting any of its regulatory objectives".

(5) In section 194 (general grounds on which power of intervention is exercisable)—

(a) in subsection (1), for paragraph (c) substitute—

"(c) it is desirable to exercise the power in order to meet any of its regulatory objectives.", and

(b) after that subsection insert—

"(1A) For the purposes of subsection (1)(c) it does not matter whether there is a relationship between the incoming firm and the persons whose interests will be protected by the exercise of the power of intervention."

Remuneration of executives of authorised persons

4 Executives' remuneration reports

(1) The Treasury may make provision by regulations about the preparation, approval and disclosure of executives' remuneration reports.

(2) An executives' remuneration report is a report containing information about—

(a) the remuneration of relevant executives of an authorised person, or

(b) anything connected with the remuneration of relevant executives of an authorised person.

第3条 实现管理局的监管目标

(1)《2000年金融服务与市场法》修订如下。

(2)第44条第(3)款(驳回获授权人关于变更或撤销第四部分许可的申请),自"如管理局认为"一词至结尾替换为"如管理局认为为实现其任何监管目标有必要驳回该申请"。

(3)第45条(第四部分许可的变更或撤销:管理局自行决定行使的权力)

(a)第(1)款第(c)项替换为:

"(c)行使该项权力有助于实现其任何监管目标",和

(b)第(1)款后插入:

"(1A)为第(1)款第(c)项之目的,对如依照本条行使权力则获授权人利益受保护的人,被核准人与该人之间是否有关系不妨碍该项规定的效力。"

(4)第138条第(1)款和第(1A)款[1](一般规定制定权)中"保护消费者的利益"替换为"实现其任何监管目标"。

(5)第194条(可行使干预权的一般依据)

(a)第(1)款第(c)项替换为:

"(c)行使该项权力有助于实现其任何监管目标。"

(b)第(1)款后插入:

"(1A)为第(1)款第(c)项之目的,对如依照本条行使权力则利益受保护的人,进入联合王国的企业与该人之间是否有关系不影响该项规定的效力。"

获授权人高层管理人员的薪酬

第4条 高层管理人员薪酬报告

(1)财政部可以制定法规,规定高层管理人员薪酬报告的编制、批准和披露。

(2)高层管理人员薪酬报告为包含下列相关信息的报告:

(a)获授权人相关高层管理人员的薪酬,或

(b)与相关获授权人高层管理人员的薪酬有关的任何信息。

---

1 《2000年金融服务与市场法》第138条第(1A)款至第(1C)款依照《2006年关于〈2000年金融服务与市场法〉的法规(金融工具市场、权力修改)》第3条插入,参见http://www.legislation.gov.uk/uksi/2006/2975/regulation/3/made. ——译者注

(3) The following are relevant executives of an authorised person—

(a) officers of the authorised person,

(b) employees of the authorised person who fall within a prescribed description, and

(c) other individuals who have a prescribed connection with the authorised person.

(4) The individuals who may fall within subsection (3)(c) include any description of—

(a) individuals who provide services, or whose services are provided (directly or indirectly), to the authorised person, or

(b) individuals who are officers or employees of a member of the same group as the authorised person.

(5) Regulations under this section may apply in relation to a prescribed description of authorised person.

(6) Regulations under this section are subject to affirmative resolution procedure.

5 Executives' remuneration reports: supplementary

(1) Regulations under section 4 may, in particular, make provision as to—

(a) the information that must be contained in an executives' remuneration report,

(b) how information is to be set out in the report, and

(c) what is to be the auditable part of the report.

(2) The information that may be required to be contained in an executives' remuneration report includes—

(a) information corresponding to information that could be required by regulations under section 421 of the Companies Act 2006 to be contained in a directors' remuneration report, and

(b) information comparing the remuneration of relevant executives of an authorised person with the remuneration of employees of the authorised person who fall within a prescribed description.

(3) Regulations under section 4 may, in particular, make provision —

(a) for the filing of executives' remuneration reports with the registrar of companies for any part of the United Kingdom or with the FSA, and

(b) for the publication by the FSA of reports filed with it.

(4) Regulations under section 4 may apply any provision made by or under the Companies Act 2006 relating to directors' remuneration reports, subject to such exceptions, adaptations and modifications as the Treasury consider appropriate.

(5) The provisions that may be applied include provisions creating offences; but the regulations may not impose a liability for an offence which is more onerous than the liability for the offence under the applied provision.

(6) Regulations under section 4 may provide that any requirement imposed on an authorised person by the regulations is to be treated for the purposes of prescribed provisions

(3)下列人员为获授权人相关高层管理人员：

(a)获授权人的高级职员；

(b)属于规定类别的获授权人雇员；以及

(c)与获授权人具有规定联系的其他个人。

(4)属于第(3)款第(c)项规定范围的个人包括下列任何类别：

(a)向获授权人提供服务或其服务(直接或间接)向获授权人提供的个人；或

(b)担任获授权人同一集团成员的高级职员或雇员的个人。

(5)本条规定的法规可以适用于规定类别的获授权人。

(6)本条规定的法规符合决议程序规定。

第5条　高层管理人员薪酬报告：补充规定

(1)第4条规定的法规可以特别就下列事项作出规定：

(a)高层管理人员薪酬报告必须包含的信息；

(b)如何在报告中列出信息；以及

(c)报告中哪些内容为可审计的部分。

(2)可以要求高层管理人员薪酬报告包含的信息有：

(a)与依照《2006年公司法》第421条规定的法规所要求包含在董事薪酬报告中的信息对应的信息；以及

(b)对获授权人相关高层管理人员薪酬与该获授权人规定类别的雇员薪酬进行比较的信息。

(3)第4条规定的法规可以特别规定

(a)向联合王国任何地区的公司注册署或管理局提交高层管理人员薪酬报告；以及

(b)管理局公布向其提交的报告。

(4)第4条规定的法规可以适用于依照《2006年公司法》制定或该法中包含的任何与董事薪酬报告相关的规定，符合财政部认为适当的例外、改编或修改规定。

(5)可适用的规定包括关于何种行为构成犯罪的规定，但法规规定的犯罪责任不得重于适用规定所列犯罪责任。

(6)第4条项下的法规可规定，该法规对获授权人提出的任何要求，为规定的《2000年金融服务和市场法》条款之目的，视为该法条款对该获授权人提出的要求。

of the Financial Services and Markets Act 2000 as if it had been imposed on the person by a provision of that Act.

(7) For the purposes of section 4 and this section—

"authorised person" has the same meaning as in the Financial Services and Markets Act 2000 (see section 31),

"the FSA" means the Financial Services Authority,

"group" has the same meaning as in the Financial Services and Markets Act 2000 (see section 421),

"officer"—

(a) in relation to a partnership, means a partner, and

(b) in relation to a body corporate whose affairs are managed by its members, means a member, and

"prescribed" means specified in, or determined in accordance with, regulations under section 4.

6 Rules made by FSA about remuneration

In the Financial Services and Markets Act 2000, after section 139 insert—

"139A General rules about remuneration

(1) The Authority must exercise its power to make general rules so as to make rules requiring each authorised person (or each authorized person of a specified description) to have, and act in accordance with, a remuneration policy.

(2) A "remuneration policy" is a policy about the remuneration by the authorised person of—

(a) officers,

(b) employees, and

(c) other persons,

of a specified description.

(3) The rules must secure that any remuneration policy that an authorized person is required by the rules to have is consistent with—

(a) the effective management of risks; and

(b) the Implementation Standards.

(4) When making rules about remuneration policies, the Authority must have regard to any other international standards about the remuneration of individuals working in the financial sector (or certain such individuals).

(5) The Treasury may direct the Authority to consider whether the remuneration policies of authorised persons specified in the direction (or of authorised persons of a description so specified) comply with requirements imposed by the rules as to the contents of the policies.

(6) Before giving a direction under subsection (5), the Treasury must consult the

(7)为第4条及本条之目的

“获授权人”含义与《2000年金融服务与市场法》中的含义相同(见第31条)。

“管理局”系指金融服务管理局,

“集团”含义与《2000年金融服务与市场法》中的含义相同(见第421条)。

“高级职员”

(a)就合伙而言系指合伙人,和

(b)就事务由其成员管理的法人而言系指其成员,

“规定的”系指第4条项下的法规中规定或依照该法规确定的。

第6条 管理局制定的薪酬相关规则

《2000年金融服务与市场法》第139条后插入:

“第139A条 关于薪酬的一般规则

(1)管理局必须行使其制定一般规则的权力,制定规则要求各获授权人(或规定类别的被授权人)均制定并执行薪酬政策。

(2)‘薪酬政策’系指获授权人向指定类别的下列人员支付薪酬的政策:

(a)高级职员;

(b)雇员;以及

(c)其他人。

(3)该规则必须确保要求获授权人制定的任何薪酬政策

(a)符合有效风险管理;并

(b)符合执行标准。

(4)管理局在制定薪酬政策相关规则时必须考虑任何其他与在金融行业工作的个人(或特定个人)薪酬有关的国际标准。

(5)财政部可以指示管理局考虑该指示中规定的获授权人(或规定类别的获授权人)的薪酬政策内容是否符合该规则提出的要求。

(6)依照第(5)款规定发出指示前,财政部必须征求管理局意见。

Authority.

(7) If the Authority considers that a remuneration policy fails to make provision which complies with the requirements mentioned in subsection (5), the Authority must take such steps as it considers appropriate to deal with the failure.

(8) The steps that the Authority may take include requiring the remuneration policy to be revised.

(9) General rules may—

(a) prohibit persons (or persons of a specified description) from being remunerated in a specified way;

(b) provide that any provision of an agreement that contravenes such a prohibition is void; and

(c) provide for the recovery of any payment made, or other property transferred, in pursuance of a provision that is void by virtue of paragraph (b).

(10) A prohibition may be imposed under subsection (9)(a) only for the purpose of ensuring that the provision of remuneration is consistent with—

(a) the effective management of risks; or

(b) the Implementation Standards.

(11) A provision that, at the time the rules are made, is contained in an agreement made before that time may not be rendered void under subsection (9)(b) unless it is subsequently amended so as to contravene a prohibition under subsection (9)(a).

(12) In this section—

"the Implementation Standards" means the Implementation Standards for Principles for Sound Compensation Practices, issued by the Financial Stability Board on 25 September 2009; and

"specified" (except in subsection (5)) means specified by the rules.

(13) References to the Implementation Standards or to international standards of a kind mentioned in subsection (4) are to standards that are for the time being in force."

Recovery and resolution plans

7 Rules made by FSA about recovery and resolution plans

(1) In the Financial Services and Markets Act 2000, after section 139A (which is inserted by section 6 above) insert—

"**139B Rules about recovery plans**

(1) The Authority must exercise its power to make general rules so as to make rules requiring each authorised person (or each authorized person of a specified description) to prepare, and keep up-to-date, a recovery plan.

(2) A "recovery plan" is a document containing information within subsection(3) or

(7)如管理局认为薪酬政策未作出符合第(5)款所述要求的规定,则必须采取其认为适当的措施,对不符合要求的情况作出处理。

(8)管理局可以采取的措施包括要求修订该薪酬政策。

(9)一般规则可以

(a)禁止(或禁止规定类别的人)以规定形式获得薪酬;

(b)规定违反上述禁止性要求的任何协议条款无效;并

(c)规定对依照第(b)项无效的条款支付的款项或转让的其他财产予以追回。

(10)只有为确保薪酬规定符合下列事项,才可以依照第(9)款第(a)项提出禁止性要求。

(a)符合有效风险管理;或

(b)符合执行标准。

(11)该规则制定前某项协议所含条款不得依照第(9)款第(b)项视为无效,除非该条款在该规则制定后进行修订,修订后违反第(9)款第(a)项规定的禁止性要求。

(12)本条中

'执行标准'系指2009年9月25日由金融稳定委员会发布的《良好薪酬实践原则执行标准》

'规定'[不包括第(5)款中规定]系指在上述规则中规定。

(13)述及执行标准或第(4)款规定种类的国际标准为当时有效的标准。"

恢复计划与解决计划

第7条　管理局制定的恢复计划与解决计划相关规则

(1)《2000年金融服务与市场法》第139A条(依照前文第6条插入)后插入:

"第139B条　关于恢复计划的规则

(1)管理局必须行使其制定一般规则的权力,制定规则要求各获授权人(或规定类别的被核准人)均制定并及时更新恢复计划。

(2)'恢复计划'为载有第(3)款或第(4)款规定类别信息的文件。

(4) of a specified description.

(3) Information is within this subsection if it relates to action to be taken to secure that, in the event of specified circumstances affecting the carrying on of the business (or any part of the business) of the authorised person—

(a) the business of the authorised person, or

(b) a specified part of the business of the authorised person,

is capable of being carried on (whether or not by the authorised person and whether or not in the same way as previously).

(4) Information is within this subsection if it would facilitate the carrying on of the business (or any part of the business) of the authorised person by any other person.

(5) The Authority must consider whether each recovery plan makes satisfactory provision in relation to the matters required by the rules to be covered by the plan.

(6) If the Authority considers that a recovery plan fails to make satisfactory provision in relation to any such matter, the Authority must take such steps as it considers appropriate to deal with the failure.

(7) The steps that the Authority may take include requiring the recovery plan to be revised.

(8) The authorised persons subject to general rules about recovery plans must include authorised persons in relation to whom any power under Part 1 of the Banking Act 2009 (special resolution regime) is exercisable.

(9) Before preparing a draft of general rules about recovery plans having effect in relation to those persons, the Authority must consult—

(a) the Treasury; and

(b) the Bank of England.

139C Rules about resolution plans

(1) The Authority must exercise its power to make general rules so as to make rules requiring each authorised person (or each authorized person of a specified description) to prepare, and keep up-to-date, a resolution plan.

(2) A "resolution plan" is a document containing information within subsection (3) or (4) of a specified description.

(3) Information is within this subsection if it relates to action to be taken in the event of—

(a) circumstances arising in which it is likely that the business (or any part of the business) of the authorised person will fail; or

(b) the failure of the business (or any part of the business) of the authorised person.

(4) Information is within this subsection if it would facilitate anything falling to be done by any person in consequence of that failure.

(3)在影响获授权人业务(或部分业务)开展的规定情况下,与为确保实现下列目标而采取的行动相关的信息,属于本款规定范围:

(a)获授权人业务;或
(b)获授权人业务中的规定部分,
能够继续开展(无论是否由该获授权人开展或是否以与先前相同的方式开展)。

(4)有利于任何他人继续开展获授权人业务(或任何部分业务)的信息属于本款规定范围。

(5)管理局必须考虑是否每项恢复计划均就规则规定其应包括的事项作出了符合要求的规定。

(6)如管理局认为恢复计划未就上述任何事项作出符合要求的规定,则必须采取其认为适当的措施对该不符合要求的情况作出处理。

(7)管理局可以采取的措施包括要求修订该恢复计划。

(8)符合恢复计划一般规则规定的获授权人必须包含可对其行使《2009年银行法》第一部分(特别决议制度)规定权力的获授权人。

(9)管理局在起草针对上述人有效的恢复计划相关一般规则前,必须向下列机构征求意见:
(a)财政部;以及
(b)英格兰银行。

第139C条 关于解决计划的规则

(1)管理局必须行使其制定一般规则的权力,制定规则要求各获授权人(或规定类别的被授权人)均制定并及时更新解决计划。

(2)'解决计划'为包含第(3)款或第(4)款规定类别信息的文件。

(3)与下列情况下采取的行动相关的信息属于本款规定范围:

(a)获授权人的业务(或任何部分业务)可能失败的情况;或

(b)获授权人业务(或任何部分业务)失败。

(4)如信息有利于任何人因上述失败而采取行动,则属于本款规定范围。

(5) An example of information within subsection (4) is information that, in the event of that failure, would facilitate —

(a) planning by the Treasury in relation to the possible exercise of any of their powers under Part 1 of the Banking Act 2009; or

(b) planning by the Bank of England in relation to the possible exercise of any of its powers under Part 1, 2 or 3 of that Act.

(6) The Authority must consider whether each resolution plan makes satisfactory provision in relation to the matters required by the rules to be covered by the plan.

(7) If the Authority considers that a resolution plan fails to make satisfactory provision in relation to any such matter, the Authority must take such steps as it considers appropriate to deal with the failure.

(8) The steps that the Authority may take include requiring the resolution plan to be revised.

(9) The authorised persons subject to general rules about resolution plans must include authorised persons in relation to whom any power under Part 1 of the Banking Act 2009 is exercisable.

(10) Before preparing a draft of general rules about resolution plans having effect in relation to those persons, the Authority must consult—

(a) the Treasury; and

(b) the Bank of England.

139D Sections 139B and 139C: interpretation

(1) In sections 139B and 139C any reference to the taking of action includes the taking of action by—

(a) the authorised person;

(b) any other person in the same group as the authorised person; or

(c) a partnership of which the authorised person is a member.

(2) In subsection (1)(b) the definition of "group" in section 421 applies with the omission of subsection (1)(e) and (f) of that section.

(3) For the purposes of section 139C the cases in which the business (or any part of the business) of the authorised person is to be regarded as having failed include—

(a) the insolvency or bankruptcy of the authorised person;

(b) the authorised person entering into administration; and

(c) a power under Part 1 of the Banking Act 2009 being exercised in relation to the authorised person.

(4) In sections 139B and 139C references to the business of an authorized person include the business of—

(a) any person in the same group as the authorised person; and

(5)第(4)款规定范围内的信息包括出现上述失败情况时有利于下列行动的信息:

(a)财政部就其可能依照《2009年银行法》第一部分规定行使的权力作出计划;或

(b)英格兰就其可能依照《2009年银行法》第一部分、第二部分或第三部分规定行使的权力作出计划。

(6)管理局必须考虑是否每项解决计划均就规则规定该计划应包括的事项作出了符合要求的规定。

(7)如管理局认为解决计划未就上述任何事项作出符合要求的规定,则必须采取其认为适当的措施,对该不符合要求的情况作出处理。

(8)管理局可采取的措施包括要求修订该解决计划。

(9)符合解决计划一般规则规定的获授权人,必须包含可对其行使《2009年银行法》第一部分规定权力的获授权人。

(10)管理局在起草针对上述人有效的解决计划相关一般规则前,必须向下列机构征求意见:

(a)财政部;以及

(b)英格兰银行。

第139D条　第139B条和第139C条:释义

(1)第139B条和第139C条中对采取行动的任何述及包括:

(a)获授权人采取的行动;

(b)与获授权人属于同一集团的任何他人采取的行动;或

(c)获授权人为成员的合伙采取的行动。

(2)第(1)款第(b)项中'集团'适用第421条规定的定义,但应删除该条第(1)款第(e)项和第(f)项的规定。

(3)就第139C条而言,视为失败的获授权人业务(或任何部分业务)包括:

(a)获授权人丧失清偿能力或破产;

(b)获授权人进入破产接管;以及

(c)针对该获授权人行使了《2009年银行法》第一部分规定的权力。

(4)第139B条和第139C条中述及获授权人的义务包括:

(a)与获授权人属于同一集团的任何他人采取的行动;以及

(b) a partnership of which the authorised person is a member;

and, accordingly, references in subsection (3)(a) to (c) of this section to the authorised person include any person within paragraph (a) or (b).

(5) In sections 139B and 139C "specified" means specified in general rules.

(6) In this section—

"administration" includes administration under Part 3 of the Banking Act 2009;

"insolvency" includes insolvency under Part 2 of that Act.

139E Rules about recovery and resolution plans: supplementary provision

(1) General rules about recovery or resolution plans may, in particular—

(a) impose a requirement on authorised persons to collect, and keep up-to-date, information of a description specified in the rules; and

(b) make provision as to the inclusion in the plans of information in respect of the steps to be taken to ensure compliance with that requirement.

(2) If the Authority considers that an authorised person has contravened that requirement, the Authority may require the authorised person to appoint a skilled person to collect or update the information in question.

(3) References in this section to a skilled person are to a person—

(a) nominated or approved by the Authority; and

(b) appearing to the Authority to have the skills necessary to collect or update the information in question.

(4) The skilled person may require any person to provide all such assistance as the skilled person may reasonably require to collect or update the information in question.

(5) A requirement imposed by subsection (4) is enforceable, on the application of the Authority, by an injunction or, in Scotland, by an order for specific performance under section 45 of the Court of Session Act 1988.

(6) A contractual or other requirement imposed on a person ("P") to keep any information in confidence does not apply if—

(a) the information is or may be relevant to anything required to be done as a result of section 139B or 139C or this section;

(b) an authorised person or a skilled person requests or requires P to provide the information for the purpose of securing that those things are done; and

(c) the Authority has approved the making of the request or the imposition of the requirement before it is made or imposed.

(7) An authorised person may provide information (whether received under subsection (6) or otherwise) that would otherwise be subject to a contractual or other requirement to keep in confidence if it is provided for the purposes of anything required to be done as a result of section 139B or 139C or this section.

(b)获授权人为成员的合伙采取的行动;

本条第(3)款第(a)项至第(c)项述及获授权人相应包括第(a)项或第(b)项规定范围内的任何人。

(5)第139B条或第139C条中‘规定’系指在一般规则中规定。

(6)本条中

‘破产接管’包含《2009年银行法》第三部分规定的破产接管;

‘丧失清偿能力’包含《2009年银行法》第二部分规定的丧失清偿能力。

第139E条 关于恢复计划与解决计划的规则:补充规定

(1)关于恢复计划或解决计划的一般规则可以特别

(a)要求获授权人收集规则指定类别的信息并随时更新;并

(b)规定在计划中列入与确保符合该要求而采取的措施相关的信息。

(2)如管理局认为获授权人已违反该规定,则可以要求获授权人委派具有技能的人收集或更新相关信息。

(3)本条中述及具有技能的人系指

(a)由管理局提名或批准的人;以及

(b)管理局认为具有收集或更新相关信息所需技能的人。

(4)具有技能的人可以要求任何人提供该人为收集或更新相关信息而合理要求提供的一切协助。

(5)依照第(4)款规定提出的要求可经管理局申请,通过强制令强制执行,在苏格兰可通过《1988年高等民事法院法》第45条规定的实际履行令执行。

(6)如有下列情况,则对当事人(以下简称P)提出的关于对任何信息保密的合同要求或其他要求不适用:

(a)信息与因第139B条、第139C条或本条规定采取的行动相关或可能相关;

(b)获授权人或具有技能的人为确保采取上述行动请求或要求P提供信息;且

(c)该请求或要求在提出前已获管理局批准。

(7)获授权人可以提供其他情况下符合合同要求或其他要求规定应保密的信息[无论是否为依照第(6)款规定获得],如该信息为采取第139B条、第139C条或本条要求采取的行动而提供。

(8) General rules about recovery or resolution plans may, in particular, make provision about the form of the plans.

(9) When making general rules about recovery or resolution plans, the Authority must have regard to any international standards about documents whose purpose corresponds to the purpose of recovery or resolution plans.

139F Special provision in relation to resolution plans

(1) In the case of resolution plans required to be prepared by general rules, the Authority must consult—

(a) the Treasury, and

(b) the Bank of England ("the Bank"),

about the adequacy of the plans so far as relating to any matter which may be relevant to the exercise by the Treasury or the Bank of any power under Part 1, 2 or 3 of the Banking Act 2009.

(2) After being consulted under subsection (1)—

(a) the Treasury or the Bank may notify the Authority that, in the opinion of the Treasury or the Bank, a resolution plan fails to make satisfactory provision in relation to any such matter; and

(b) if the Treasury or the Bank give a notification under paragraph (a), the Treasury or the Bank must give reasons for being of that opinion to the Authority.

(3) The Authority must have regard to any notification given under paragraph (a) of subsection (2) before considering whether any resolution plan makes satisfactory provision in relation to any such matter.

(4) If—

(a) a notification is given under that paragraph, but

(b) the Authority is nonetheless of the opinion that the resolution plan makes satisfactory provision in relation to any such matter, the Authority must give reasons for being of that opinion to the person who gave the notification."

(2) The Treasury may by order require the FSA to make, by a date specified in the order, recovery plan rules, or resolution plan rules, which impose requirements on authorised persons who are of a description specified in the order.

(3) Before making an order under subsection (2), the Treasury must consult the FSA.

(4) An order under subsection (2) is subject to negative resolution procedure.

(5) In this section—

"the FSA" means the Financial Services Authority,

"recovery plan rules" means general rules imposing requirements of a kind mentioned in section 139B(1) of the Financial Services and Markets Act 2000, and

"resolution plan rules" means general rules imposing requirements of a kind mentioned

(8)关于恢复计划或解决计划的一般规则可以特别就计划的形式作出规定。

(9)管理局在作出恢复或解决计划相关一般规定时,必须就任何目标与恢复计划或解决计划对等的文件考虑其国际标准。

第139F条　与解决计划相关的特别规定

(1)如一般规则要求制定解决计划,则管理局必须征求下列机构意见:

(a)财政部;以及

(b)英格兰银行(以下简称银行)。

征求意见的相关事项为,就与财政部或银行依照《2009年银行法》第一部分、第二部分或第三部分行使权力相关的任何事项而言,该计划是否充分。

(2)依照第(1)款收到征求意见请求后

(a)财政部或银行可通知管理局,财政部或银行认为某项解决计划未就上述任何事项作出符合要求的规定;且

(b)如财政部或银行依照第(a)项规定发出通知,则财政部或银行必须向管理局说明持有该意见的理由。

(3)管理局在考虑任何一项解决计划是否就上述任何事项作出了符合要求的规定前,必须考虑依照前款第(a)项规定发出的通知。

(4)如有下列情况:

(a)依照第(2)款第(a)项发出了通知,但

(b)管理局仍认为某项解决计划就上述任何事项作出了符合要求的规定,则管理局必须向通知发出人说明持有该意见的理由。”

(2)财政部可以颁布法令,要求管理局在该法令规定日期前制定恢复计划规则或解决计划规则,对该法令规定类型的获授权人提出要求。

(3)依照第(2)款规定颁布法令前,财政部必须征求管理局意见。

(4)依照第(2)款规定颁布的法令符合反对决议程序规定。

(5)本条中

‘管理局’系指金融服务管理局,

‘恢复计划规则’系指提出《2000年金融服务与市场法》第139B条第(1)款所述种类要求的一般规则

‘解决计划规则’系指提出《2000年金融服务与市场法》第139c条第(1)款所述种类

in section 139C(1) of that Act.

Short selling

8 Power of FSA to prohibit, or require disclosure of, short selling

In the Financial Services and Markets Act 2000, after Part 8 insert—

"PART 8A SHORT SELLING

Short selling rules

131B Short selling rules

(1) The Authority may make rules prohibiting in specified cases persons from engaging in short selling in relation to relevant financial instruments (or relevant financial instruments of a specified description).

(2) The Authority may make rules requiring—

(a) a person who has engaged in short selling in relation to relevant financial instruments (or relevant financial instruments of a specified description), or

(b) an authorised person of a specified description who has acted on behalf of such a person, to disclose in specified cases specified information, or information of a specified description, about the short selling.

(3) Rules under subsection (2) may specify the time by which, and the way in which, the disclosure must be made (and may in particular provide for the information to be disclosed to the Authority or published in a specified way).

(4) Rules under subsection (2) may apply in relation to short selling engaged in before the rules are made where the resulting short position is still open when the rules are made.

(5) The reference to a short position being open is to be read in accordance with provision made by the rules.

(6) Rules under this section may apply to short selling wholly outside the United Kingdom by persons outside the United Kingdom, but only in so far as the rules relate to UK financial instruments.

(7) The description of relevant financial instruments that may be specified by the rules includes relevant financial instruments issued by a specified person.

(8) Rules under this section are referred to in this Part as "short selling rules".

(9) The Authority must, when making short selling rules, have regard to any international agreement as to measures to be taken in respect of short selling.

131C Short selling rules: definitions etc.

(1) This section supplements section 131B.

(2) The cases in which a person ("S") engages in short selling in relation to a financial

要求的一般规则。”

卖　　空

第8条　管理局禁止或要求披露卖空交易的权力

《2000年金融服务与市场法》第八部分后插入：

“第八A部分　卖　　空

卖空规则

第131B条　卖空规则

(1)管理局可以制定规则,在指定情况下禁止从事相关金融工具(或规定类别的相关金融工具)的卖空交易。

(2)管理局可以制定规则,要求

(a)从事相关金融工具(或规定类别的相关金融工具)卖空交易的人;或

(b)代表上述人行事的规定类别获授权人,在指定情况下披露与该卖空交易相关的规定信息或规定类别信息。

(3)依照第(2)款规定制定的规则可以对必须作出的披露规定披露时间和方式(可以特别规定以规定方式向管理局披露或公布的信息)。

(4)依照第(2)款规定制定的规则可适用于在规则制定前从事、规则制定时仍空头持仓的卖空交易。

(5)述及空头持仓应当依照规则规定解释。

(6)依照本条规定制定的规则可适用于联合王国境外的人完全在联合王国境外从事的卖空交易,但必须在该规则与联合王国金融工具相关的范围内适用。

(7)规则可以规定类别的相关金融工具包括规定人发行的相关金融工具。

(8)根据本条制定的规则在本部分中称为‘卖空规则’。

(9)管理局在制定卖空规则时必须考虑与针对卖空采取措施有关的任何国际协议。

第131C条　卖空规则:定义等

(1)本条规定补充第131B条。

(2)某人(以下简称S)从事金融工具(以下简称卖空工具)卖空交易的情况包括下

instrument (a "shorted instrument") include any case where—

(a) S enters into a transaction which creates, or relates to, another financial instrument; and

(b) the effect (or one of the effects) of the transaction is to confer a financial advantage on S in the event of a decrease in the price or value of the shorted instrument.

(3) "Financial instrument" has the meaning given by Article 4.1(17) of the markets in financial instruments directive.

(4) "Relevant financial instrument" means a financial instrument that—

(a) is admitted to trading on a regulated market or on any other prescribed market in an EEA State; or

(b) has such other connection with a market in an EEA State as may be specified.

(5) "Specified" means specified by short selling rules.

(6) "UK financial instrument" means a financial instrument that is admitted to trading on a market in the United Kingdom.

(7) In the case of a financial instrument that is admitted to trading on—

(a) a market in the United Kingdom or another EEA State, and

(b) one or more markets in a country or territory, or countries or territories, anywhere else in the world, short selling rules may apply in relation to trading on both or all markets.

(8) In any case where—

(a) a financial instrument ("instrument A") is admitted to trading on a market in the United Kingdom or another EEA State,

(b) another financial instrument ("instrument B") is admitted to trading on one or more markets in a country or territory, or countries or territories, anywhere else in the world, and

(c) the price or value of instrument A depends on the price or value of instrument B (or vice versa), short selling rules may apply in relation to trading on both or all markets.

(9) In subsection (4)(a) "regulated market" has the meaning given by Article 4.1(14) of the markets in financial instruments directive.

(10) References in this section to a market in a country or territory are to a market situated or operating in the country or territory.

131D Short selling rules: procedure in urgent cases

(1) The Authority may make short selling rules (and may subsequently amend those rules) without complying with section 155 (consultation in relation to proposed rules) if it considers that it is necessary to do so, in order to—

(a) maintain confidence in the UK financial system; or

(b) protect the stability of the UK financial system.

(2) Any rules made by virtue of subsection (1) ("emergency rules") cease to have effect at the end of the period of three months beginning with the day on which the rules are made

列任何情况：

(a)S参与了创建其他金融工具或与其他金融工具相关的交易；且

(b)该交易的效力(或其中一项效力)为在卖空工具价格或价值下降时赋予S金融利益。

(3)‘金融工具’具有金融工具市场指令第4.1条第(17)款中的含义。

(4)‘相关金融工具’系指

(a)在欧洲经济区国家受监管市场或其他任何规定市场允许交易的金融工具；或

(b)与欧洲经济区国家市场具有指定的其他联系。

(5)‘规定’，系指在卖空规则中规定。

(6)‘联合王国金融工具’，系指在联合王国市场上允许交易的金融工具。

(7)就在下列市场允许交易的金融工具而言：

(a)联合王国或其他欧洲经济区国家的市场，以及

(b)世界其他国家或地区的一个或多个市场，卖空规则可适用于所有市场的交易。

(8)在下列任何情况下：

(a)联合王国或其他欧洲经济区国家市场上允许交易的金融工具(以下简称工具A)；

(b)世界其他国家或地区的一个或多个市场允许交易的金融工具(以下简称工具B)；以及

(c)工具A的价格或价值取决于工具B的价格或价值(或相反)，卖空规则可适用于所有市场的交易。

(9)第(4)款第(a)项中‘受监管市场’具有金融工具市场指令第4.1条第(14)款的含义。

(10)本条中述及一国或地区市场为述及位于该国或地区，或者在该国或地区运转的市场。

第131D条　卖空规则：紧急情况下的程序

(1)如管理局认为为实现下列目的有必要，则可以不遵守第155条规定(就拟制定的规则征求意见)而制定卖空规则(也可随后修改该规则)：

(a)维护对联合王国金融系统的信息；或

(b)保护联合王国金融系统的稳定性。

(2)依照第(1)款规定(以下简称紧急规则)制定的任何规则，在该规则制定之日(以下简称相关日)起3个月期间届满时失效；但受下列规定制约。

("the relevant day"); but this is subject as follows.

(3) The Authority may direct that emergency rules are to cease to have effect at the end of a period (not exceeding six months beginning with the relevant day) specified in the direction.

(4) A direction under subsection (3) may be made only if, immediately before the end of the period mentioned in subsection (2), the Authority considers that it is necessary to do so, in order to—

(a) maintain confidence in the UK financial system; or

(b) protect the stability of the UK financial system.

(5) Such a direction must be published by the Authority in the way appearing to the Authority to be best calculated to bring it to the attention of the public.

(6) Nothing in subsection (2) or (3) prevents the Authority from revoking emergency rules before the end of the periods referred to there.

Power to require information

131E Power to require information

(1) The Authority may, by notice in writing, require a person ("P")—

(a) to provide specified information or information of a specified description; or

(b) to produce specified documents or documents of a specified description.

(2) This section applies only to information and documents that the Authority reasonably requires for the purpose of determining whether P, or a person connected with P, has contravened any provision of short selling rules.

(3) Information or documents required under this section must be provided or produced—

(a) before the end of such reasonable period as may be specified; and

(b) at such place as may be specified.

(4) The Authority may require any information provided under this section to be provided in such form as it may reasonably require.

(5) The Authority may require—

(a) any information provided, whether in a document or otherwise, to be verified in such manner as it may reasonably require; or

(b) any document produced to be authenticated in such manner as it may reasonably require.

(6) In this section "specified" means specified in the notice.

(7) For the purposes of this section a person is connected with another person ("P") if the person is or has at any relevant time been—

(a) a member of P's group;

(3)管理局可以发布指令,规定紧急规则在该指令中规定的期间(自相关日起不超过6个月)届满时失效。

(4)只有管理局在第(2)款所述期间即将届满时认为为实现下列目的有必要时,才可以依照第(3)款发布指令:

(a)维护对联合王国金融系统的信息;或

(b)保护联合王国金融系统的稳定性。

(5)该指令必须由管理局以其认为最便于公众了解的方式公布。

(6)第(2)款或第(3)款规定不禁止管理局在该款述及的期间届满前撤销紧急规则。

要求提供信息的权力

第131E条　要求提供信息的权力

(1)管理局可发出书面通知,要求某人(以下简称P)

(a)提供规定的信息或规定类别的信息;或

(b)出示规定的文件或规定类别的文件。

(2)本条规定仅适用于管理局为确定P或与P相关联的人是否违反卖空规则的任何规定而合理要求提供的信息和文件。

(3)依照本条规定要求提供或出示的信息或文件必须

(a)在规定的合理期限届满前提供或出示;且

(b)在规定的地点提供。

(4)管理局可以要求依照本条规定提供的任何信息以管理局合理要求的形式提供。

(5)管理局可以要求

(a)对在文件中或以其他方式提供的任何信息以管理局合理要求的方式进行核实;或

(b)对出示的任何文件以管理局合理要求的方式进行验证。

(6)本条中'规定'系指在通知中规定。

(7)就本条而言,当事人如在任何时间有下列情况,则为与另一人(以下简称P)相关联:

(a)是P集团中的成员;

(b) a controller of P;

(c) any other member of a partnership of which P is a member; or

(d) in relation to P, a person mentioned in Part 1 of Schedule 15 (reading references in that Part to the authorised person as references to P).

131F Power to require information: supplementary

(1) If the Authority has power under section 131E to require a person to produce a document but it appears that the document is in the possession of a third person, that power may be exercised in relation to the third person.

(2) If a document is produced in response to a requirement imposed under section 131E, the Authority may—

(a) take copies of or extracts from the document; or

(b) require the person producing the document, or any relevant person, to provide an explanation of the document.

(3) In subsection (2)(b) "relevant person", in relation to a person who is required to produce a document, means a person who—

(a) has been or is or is proposed to be a director or controller of that person;

(b) has been or is an auditor of that person;

(c) has been or is an actuary, accountant or lawyer appointed or instructed by that person; or

(d) has been or is an employee of that person.

(4) If a person who is required under section 131E to produce a document fails to do so, the Authority may require the person to state, to the best of the person's knowledge and belief, where the document is.

(5) A lawyer may be required under section 131E to provide the name and address of the lawyer's client.

(6) A person ("P") may not be required under section 131E to disclose information or produce a document in respect of which P owes an obligation of confidence by virtue of carrying on the business of banking unless—

(a) P is the person under investigation or a member of that person's group;

(b) the person to whom the obligation of confidence is owed is the person under investigation or a member of that person's group; or

(c) the person to whom the obligation of confidence is owed consents to the disclosure or production.

(7) If a person claims a lien on a document, its production under section 131E does not affect the lien.

(b)是P的控制人;

(c)是P为成员的合伙中任何其他成员;或

(d)附录15第一部分所述与P有关的人(该部分述及获授权人视为述及P)。

第131F条　要求提供信息的权力:补充规定

(1)如管理局有权依照第131E条规定要求当事人出示文件,但有迹象表明该文件为第三人所持有,则可以针对该第三人行使该权力。

(2)如一份文件为应依照第131E条规定提出的要求而出示,则管理局可以

(a)对该文件制作副本或进行摘录;或

(b)要求文件出示人或任何相关人对文件进行解释。

(3)第(2)款第(b)项中“相关人”就被要求出示文件的人而言系指

(a)曾经、正在或拟担任该人董事或控制人;

(b)曾经或正在担任该人的审计人;

(c)曾经或正在担任该人指定或指示的精算师、会计或律师;或

(d)曾经或正在担任该人的雇员。

(4)如依照第131E条规定被要求出示文件的人未能出示文件,则管理局可以要求该人就其所知所信声明文件的下落。

(5)可以依照第131E条规定要求律师提供其委托人的姓名和地址。

(6)除非有下列情况,否则不得依照第131E条规定要求某人(以下简称P)披露其负有保密义务的银行业务相关信息或出示相关文件:

(a)P是被调查人或被调查人集团成员;

(b)保密义务权利人是被调查人或被调查人集团成员;或

(c)保密义务权利人同意披露或出示。

(7)如某人对文件主张留置权,则依照第131E条规定出示该文件不影响该留置权。

Breach of short selling rules etc

131G Power to impose penalty or issue censure

(1) This section applies if the Authority is satisfied that a person has contravened—

(a) any provision of short selling rules; or

(b) any requirement imposed on the person under section 131E or 131F.

(2) The Authority may impose a penalty of such amount as it considers appropriate on—

(a) the person who contravened the provision or requirement; or

(b) any person who was knowingly concerned in the contravention.

(3) It may, instead of imposing a penalty on a person, publish a statement censuring the person.

(4) The Authority may not take action against a person under this section after the end of the limitation period unless, before the end of that period, it has given a warning notice to the person under section 131H.

(5) "The limitation period" means the period of three years beginning with the first day on which the Authority knew of the contravention.

(6) For this purpose the Authority is to be treated as knowing of a contravention if it has information from which the contravention can reasonably be inferred.

131H Procedure and right to refer to Tribunal

(1) If the Authority proposes to take action against a person under section 131G, it must give the person a warning notice.

(2) A warning notice about a proposal to impose a penalty must state the amount of the penalty.

(3) A warning notice about a proposal to publish a statement must set out the terms of the statement.

(4) If the Authority decides to take action against a person under section 131G, it must give the person a decision notice.

(5) A decision notice about the imposition of a penalty must state the amount of the penalty.

(6) A decision notice about the publication of a statement must set out the terms of the statement.

(7) If the Authority decides to take action against a person under section 131G, the person may refer the matter to the Tribunal.

131 I Duty on publication of statement

After a statement under section 131G(3) is published, the Authority must send a copy of the statement to—

(a) the person in respect of whom it is made; and

违反卖空规则等

第131G条　罚款或发布谴责的权力

(1)如管理局确信某人违反下列规定,则本条规定适用:

(a)卖空规则的任何规定;或

(b)依照第131E条或第131F条对该人提出的任何要求。

(2)管理局可对下列人员按其认为适当的金额处以罚款:

(a)违反规定或要求的人;或

(b)明知行为违反规定或要求而参与其中的任何人。

(3)管理局可以不对当事人处以罚款,而改为公布谴责该人的声明。

(4)管理局在时效期限届满后不得依照本条规定对当事人采取行动,除非在该期限届满前管理局已依照第131H条规定向该人发出预告通知。

(5)'时效期限'系指自管理局知悉该违反规定或要求的情况之日起3年的期限。

(6)为此目的,管理局如获得可以从中合理推断出有违反规定或要求情况的信息,则视为管理局知悉该违反规定或要求的情况。

第131H条　提交裁判所裁决的程序和权利

(1)如管理局拟依照第131G条对当事人采取行动,则必须向该人发出预告通知。

(2)关于拟处以罚款的预告通知必须说明罚款数额。

(3)关于拟公布声明的预告通知必须列明该声明的措辞。

(4)如管理局决定依照第131G条对当事人采取行动,则必须向该人发出决定通知。

(5)关于处以罚款的决定通知必须说明罚款数额。

(6)关于公布声明的决定通知必须说明该声明的措辞。

(7)如管理局决定依照第131G条规定对当事人采取行动,则该人可以将该事项诉至裁判所。

第131I条　公布声明的职责

依照第131G条第(3)款公布声明后,管理局必须将该声明副本送交

(a)该声明针对的人;以及

(b) any person to whom a copy of the decision notice was given under section 393(4).

131J Imposition of penalties under section 131G: statement of policy

(1) The Authority must prepare and issue a statement of its policy with respect to—

(a) the imposition of penalties under section 131G; and

(b) the amount of penalties under that section.

(2) The Authority's policy in determining what the amount of a penalty should be must include having regard to—

(a) the seriousness of the contravention;

(b) the extent to which the contravention was deliberate or reckless; and

(c) whether the person on whom the penalty is to be imposed is an individual.

(3) The Authority may at any time alter or replace a statement issued under this section.

(4) If a statement issued under this section is altered or replaced, the Authority must issue the altered or replaced statement.

(5) The Authority must, without delay, give the Treasury a copy of any statement which it publishes under this section.

(6) A statement issued under this section must be published by the Authority in the way appearing to the Authority to be best calculated to bring it to the attention of the public.

(7) The Authority may charge a reasonable fee for providing a person with a copy of the statement.

(8) In exercising, or deciding whether to exercise, a power under section 131G in the case of any particular contravention, the Authority must have regard to any statement of policy published under this section and in force at a time when the contravention occurred.

131K Statement of policy: procedure

(1) Before issuing a statement under section 131J, the Authority must publish a draft of the proposed statement in the way appearing to the Authority to be best calculated to bring it to the attention of the public.

(2) The draft must be accompanied by notice that representations about the proposal may be made to the Authority within a specified time.

(3) Before issuing the proposed statement, the Authority must have regard to any representations made to it in accordance with subsection (2).

(4) If the Authority issues the proposed statement it must publish an account, in general terms, of—

(a) the representations made to it in accordance with subsection (2); and

(b) its response to them.

(5) If the statement differs from the draft published under subsection (1) in a way which is, in the opinion of the Authority, significant, the Authority must (in addition to complying with subsection (4)) publish details of the difference.

(b)依照第393条第(4)款规定向其发出决定副本的任何人。

第131J条　依照第131G条规定处以罚款:政策声明

(1)管理局必须制定并发布关于下列事项的政策声明:

(a)依照第131G条规定处以罚款;以及

(b)依照第131G条规定处以罚款的数额。

(2)管理局确定罚款数额的政策必须包括对下列事项的考虑:

(a)违反情况的严重程度;

(b)违反情况在何种程度上为故意或因重大过失而违反;以及

(c)接受罚款的是否为个人。

(3)管理局可以随时修改或更换依照本条规定发布的声明。

(4)如对依照本条规定发布的声明进行修改或更换,则管理局必须发布修改或更换的声明。

(5)管理局必须毫不延迟地向财政部送交依照本条规定所发布的任何声明的副本。

(6)管理局必须以其认为最便于公众了解的方式公布依照本条规定发布的声明。

(7)管理局可以就向他人提供声明副本收取合理费用。

(8)管理局对特定违反要求的行为行使或决定是否行使第131G条规定的权力时,必须考虑依照本条规定公布且在该违反要求的行为发生时有效的任何声明。

第131K条　政策声明:程序

(1)管理局在依照第131J条规定发布声明前,必须以其认为最便于公众了解的方式公布拟发布声明的草案。

(2)草案必须附有可在规定时间就该提案向管理局陈述的通知。

(3)管理局在发布拟发布的声明前必须考虑依照第(2)款规定提出的任何陈述。

(4)如管理局发布拟发布的声明,则必须公布概括说明下列事项的报告:

(a)依照第(2)款规定向其提出的陈述;以及

(b)管理局对上述陈述的回应。

(5)如管理局认为该声明与依照第(1)款公布的草案有重大差异,则[除遵守第(4)款规定外]必须公布差异的详细情况。

(6) The Authority may charge a reasonable fee for providing a person with a copy of a draft published under subsection (1).

(7) This section also applies to a proposal to alter or replace a statement."

FSA's disciplinary powers

9 Suspending permission to carry on regulated activities etc

In Part 14 of the Financial Services and Markets Act 2000 (disciplinary measures), after section 206 insert—

"206A Suspending permission to carry on regulated activities etc

(1) If the Authority considers that an authorised person has contravened a relevant requirement imposed on the person, it may—

(a) suspend, for such period as it considers appropriate, any permission which the person has to carry on a regulated activity; or

(b) impose, for such period as it considers appropriate, such limitations or other restrictions in relation to the carrying on of a regulated activity by the person as it considers appropriate.

(2) In subsection (1)—

"permission" means any permission that the authorised person has, whether given (or treated as given) by the Authority or conferred by any provision of this Act;

"relevant requirement" means a requirement imposed—

(a) by or under this Act; or

(b) by any directly applicable Community regulation made under the markets in financial instruments directive.

(3) The period for which a suspension or restriction is to have effect may not exceed 12 months.

(4) A suspension may relate only to the carrying on of an activity in specified circumstances.

(5) A restriction may, in particular, be imposed so as to require the person concerned to take, or refrain from taking, specified action.

(6) The Authority may—

(a) withdraw a suspension or restriction; or

(b) vary a suspension or restriction so as to reduce the period for which it has effect or otherwise to limit its effect.

(7) The power under this section may (but need not) be exercised so as to have effect in relation to all the regulated activities that the person concerned carries on.

(8) Any one or more of the powers under—

(a) subsection (1)(a) and (b) of this section, and

(6)管理局可以就向他人提供依照第(1)款公布的草案副本收取合理费用。

(7)本条规定也适用于修改或更换声明的计划。”

管理局的惩戒权

第9条　终止开展受监管活动的许可等

《2000年金融服务与市场法》第十四部分(惩戒措施)第206条后插入:

“第206A条　终止开展受监管活动的许可等

(1)如管理局认为获授权人违反了对该人提出的相关要求,则可以

(a)在其认为适当的期间内终止该人持有的开展受监管活动的许可;或

(b)在其认为适当的期间内对该人持有的开展受监管活动的许可提出其认为适当的限制范围或其他限制性规定。

(2)第(1)款中

‘许可’系指获授权人持有的任何许可,无论是否由管理局授予(或视为由管理局授予)或依照本法任何规定授予;

‘相关要求’系指依照下列规定提出的要求:

(a)本法提出或依照本法提出的要求;或

(b)任何依照金融工具市场指令制定并直接适用的共同体法规提出的要求。

(3)终止或限制有效期限不得超过12个月。

(4)终止只与在指定情况下从事的活动相关。

(5)可以特别规定就要求相关人采取或不采取指定行动提出限制。

(6)管理局可以

(a)撤销终止或限制;或

(b)变更终止或限制,缩短其有效期限或以其他方式限制其效力。

(7)行使本条规定的权力可以(但不必须)对相关人从事的全部受监管活动具有效力。

(8)下列条款规定的一项或多项权力

(a)第(1)款第(a)项和第(b)项;以及

(b) sections 205 and 206,

may be exercised in relation to the same contravention."

10 Removal of restriction on imposing a penalty and cancelling authorization

In section 206 of the Financial Services and Markets Act 2000 (financial penalties), omit subsection (2) (which prevents the FSA from imposing a penalty under that section as well as withdrawing a person's authorization under section 33).

11 Performance of controlled function without approval

In the Financial Services and Markets Act 2000, after section 63 insert—

"*Performance of controlled functions without approval*

63A Power to impose penalties

(1) If the Authority is satisfied that—

(a) a person ("P") has at any time performed a controlled function without approval, and

(b) at that time P knew, or could reasonably be expected to have known, that P was performing a controlled function without approval,

it may impose a penalty on P of such amount as it considers appropriate.

(2) For the purposes of this section P performs a controlled function without approval at any time if at that time—

(a) P performs a controlled function under an arrangement entered into by an authorised person ("A"), or by a contractor of A, in relation to the carrying on by A of a regulated activity; and

(b) the performance by P of the function was not approved under section 59.

(3) The Authority may not impose a penalty under this section after the end of the limitation period unless, before the end of that period, it has given a warning notice to the person concerned under section 63B(1).

(4) "The limitation period" means the period of three years beginning with the first day on which the Authority knew that the person concerned had performed a controlled function without approval.

(5) For this purpose the Authority is to be treated as knowing that a person has performed a controlled function without approval if it has information from which that can reasonably be inferred.

(6) Any expression which is used both in this section and section 59 has the same meaning in this section as in that section.

63B Procedure and right to refer to Tribunal

(1) If the Authority proposes to impose a penalty on a person under section 63A, it must give the person a warning notice.

(b)第205条和第206条。

可以针对同样的违反行为行使。”

第10条　去除对处以罚款和取消核准的限制

《2000年金融服务与市场法》第206条(经济处罚)删除第(2)款(禁止管理局依照该款规定处以罚款及依照第33条规定撤销当事人的核准)。

第11条　未经批准行使受监管职能

《2000年金融服务与市场法》第63条后插入:

“未经批准行使受监管职能

第63A条　处以罚款的权力

(1)如管理局确信

(a)当事人(以下简称P)在任何时间未经批准履行了受监管职能,且

(b)当时P明知,或可合理预期其明知,自己正在未经批准履行受监管职能,

则可以对该人按其认为适当的数额处以罚款。

(2)为本条之目的,如P在任何时间有下列情况,则为未经批准履行受监管职能:

(a)P依照获授权人(以下简称A)或A的承包商就获授权人从事受监管活动订立的安排行使受监管职能;且

(b)P行使该职能未依照第59条规定获得批准。

(3)管理局在时效期限届满后不得依照本条规定对当事人采取行动,除非在该期限届满前管理局已依照第63B条第(1)款规定向该人发出预告通知。

(4)‘时效期限’系指自管理局知悉相关人未经批准行使受监管职能之日起3年的期限。

(5)为此目的,管理局如获得可从中合理推断出某人未经批准行使受监管职能的信息,则视为管理局知悉该人未经批准行使受监管职能。

(6)本条中和第59条中均使用的表述,在本条中与第59条中含义相同。

第63B条　提交裁判所裁决的程序和权利

(1)如管理局拟依照第63A条对某人处以罚款,则必须向该人发出预告通知。

(2) A warning notice must state the amount of the penalty.

(3) If the Authority decides to impose a penalty on a person under section 63A, it must give the person a decision notice.

(4) A decision notice must state the amount of the penalty.

(5) If the Authority decides to impose a penalty on a person under section 63A, the person may refer the matter to the Tribunal.

63C Statement of policy

(1) The Authority must prepare and issue a statement of its policy with respect to—

(a) the imposition of penalties under section 63A; and

(b) the amount of penalties under that section.

(2) The Authority's policy in determining whether a penalty should be imposed, and what the amount of a penalty should be, must include having regard to—

(a) the conduct of the person on whom the penalty is to be imposed;

(b) the extent to which the person could reasonably be expected to have known that a controlled function was performed without approval;

(c) the length of the period during which the person performed a controlled function without approval; and

(d) whether the person on whom the penalty is to be imposed is an individual.

(3) The Authority's policy in determining whether a penalty should be imposed on a person must also include having regard to the appropriateness of taking action against the person instead of, or in addition to, taking action against an authorised person.

(4) A statement issued under this section must include an indication of the circumstances in which the Authority would expect to be satisfied that a person could reasonably be expected to have known that the person was performing a controlled function without approval.

(5) The Authority may at any time alter or replace a statement issued under this section.

(6) If a statement issued under this section is altered or replaced, the Authority must issue the altered or replaced statement.

(7) The Authority must, without delay, give the Treasury a copy of any statement which it publishes under this section.

(8) A statement issued under this section must be published by the Authority in the way appearing to the Authority to be best calculated to bring it to the attention of the public.

(9) The Authority may charge a reasonable fee for providing a person with a copy of the statement.

(10) In exercising, or deciding whether to exercise, its power under section 63A in the case of any particular person, the Authority must have regard to any statement of policy published under this section and in force at a time when the person concerned performed a

(2)预告通知必须说明罚款数额。

(3)如管理局决定依照第63A条对某人处以罚款,则必须向该人发出决定通知。

(4)决定通知必须说明罚款数额。

(5)如管理局决定依照第63A条规定对某人处以罚款,则该人可以将该事项诉至裁判所。

第63C条 政策声明

(1)管理局必须制定并发布关于下列事项的政策声明:

(a)依照第63A条规定处以罚款;以及

(b)依照第63A条规定处以罚款的数额。

(2)管理局确定罚款数额的政策必须包括对下列事项的考虑:

(a)被罚款人的行为;

(b)在何种程度上可合理预期该人明知在未经批准履行受监管职能;

(c)被罚款人未经批准履行受监管职能的时间长度;以及

(d)接受罚款的是否为个人。

(3)管理局确定罚款数额的政策必须考虑对被罚款人采取行动而不对获授权人采取行动是否适当。

(4)依照本条规定发布的声明,必须说明管理局在何种情况下确信可合理预期该人知悉在未经批准行使受监管职能。

(5)管理局可以随时修改或更换依照本条规定发布的声明。

(6)如对依照本条规定发布的声明进行修改或更换,则管理局必须发布修改或更换的声明。

(7)管理局必须毫不延迟地向财政部送交依照本条规定所发布的任何声明的副本。

(8)管理局必须以其认为最便于公众了解的方式公布依照本条规定发布的声明。

(9)管理局可以为向他人提供声明副本收取合理费用。

(10)管理局针对任何特定人行使或决定是否行使第63A条规定的权力时,必须考虑依照本条规定公布、在相关人未经批准行使受监管职能时有效的任何声明。

controlled function without approval.

63D Statement of policy: procedure

(1) Before issuing a statement under section 63C, the Authority must publish a draft of the proposed statement in the way appearing to the Authority to be best calculated to bring it to the attention of the public.

(2) The draft must be accompanied by notice that representations about the proposal may be made to the Authority within a specified time.

(3) Before issuing the proposed statement, the Authority must have regard to any representations made to it in accordance with subsection (2).

(4) If the Authority issues the proposed statement it must publish an account, in general terms, of—

(a) the representations made to it in accordance with subsection (2); and

(b) its response to them.

(5) If the statement differs from the draft published under subsection (1) in a way which is,in the opinion of the Authority,significant,the Authority must(in addition to complying with subsection (4)) publish details of the difference.

(6) The Authority may charge a reasonable fee for providing a person with a copy of a draft published under subsection (1).

(7) This section also applies to a proposal to alter or replace a statement."

12 Approved persons guilty of misconduct

(1) Section 66 of the Financial Services and Markets Act 2000 (performance of regulated activities: disciplinary powers) is amended as follows.

(2) In subsection (3)—

(a) in the opening words, for "it may—" substitute "it may do one or more of the following—", and

(b) after paragraph (a) (but before the "or" at the end of it) insert—

"(aa) suspend, for such period as it considers appropriate, any approval of the performance by him of any function to which the approval relates;

(ab) impose, for such period as it considers appropriate, such limitations or other restrictions in relation to the performance by him of any function to which any approval relates as it considers appropriate; ".

(3) After that subsection insert—

"(3A) The period for which a suspension or restriction is to have effect may not exceed two years.

(3B) A suspension or restriction may have effect in relation to part of a function.

第63D条　政策声明:程序

(1)管理局在依照第63C条规定发布声明前必须以其认为最便于公众了解的方式公布拟发布声明的草案。

(2)草案必须附有可在规定时间就该提案向管理局作出陈述的通知。

(3)管理局在发布拟发布的声明前必须考虑依照第(2)款规定作出的任何陈述。

(4)如管理局发布拟发布的声明,则必须公布概括说明下列事项的报告:

(a)依照第(2)款规定向其作出的陈述;以及

(b)管理局对上述陈述的答复。

(5)如管理局认为该声明与依照第(1)款公布的草案有重大差异,则[除遵守第(4)款规定外]必须公布差异的详细情况。

(6)管理局可以为向他人提供依照第(1)款公布的草案副本收取合理费用。

(7)本条也适用于修改或更换声明的计划。"

第12条　行为不端构成犯罪的被批准人[1]

(1)《2000年金融服务与市场法》第66条(开展受监管活动:惩戒权)修订如下。

(2)第(3)款中

(a)引言中"可以"替换为"可以采取下列一项或多项行动",

(b)第(a)项后(结尾"或"前)插入:

"(aa)在其认为适当的期间内终止批准其履行与该批准相关的任何职能;

(ab)在其认为适当的期间内对就该人履行与任何批准相关的任何职能提出其认为适当的限制。"

(3)第(3)款后插入:

"(3A)终止或限制有效期限不得超过2年。

(3B)终止或限制可对部分职能生效。

---

1 "被批准人"定义参见《2000年金融服务与市场法》第64条第(13)款。——译者注

(3C) A restriction may, in particular, be imposed so as to require any person to take, or refrain from taking, specified action.

(3D) The Authority may—

(a) withdraw a suspension or restriction; or

(b) vary a suspension or restriction so as to reduce the period for which it has effect or otherwise to limit its effect."

(4) In subsection (4), for "two years" substitute "three years".

13 Publication of decision notices

(1) Section 391 of the Financial Services and Markets Act 2000 (publication) is amended as follows.

(2) In subsection (1)(which prevents the FSA and the person to whom a warning or decision notice is given or copied from publishing the notice or any details concerning it), omit "or decision notice".

(3) After that subsection insert—

"(1A) A person to whom a decision notice is given or copied may not publish the notice or any details concerning it unless the Authority has published the notice or those details."

(4) In subsection (4) (duty of FSA to publish information about a final notice), before "final notice" insert "decision notice or".

Measures to protect consumers

14 Consumer redress schemes

(1) In the Financial Services and Markets Act 2000, for section 404 (and the italic cross–heading before it) substitute—

"*Consumer redress schemes*

404 Consumer redress schemes

(1) This section applies if—

(a) it appears to the Authority that there may have been a widespread or regular failure by relevant firms to comply with requirements applicable to the carrying on by them of any activity;

(b) it appears to it that, as a result, consumers have suffered (or may suffer) loss or damage in respect of which, if they brought legal proceedings, a remedy or relief would be available in the proceedings; and

(c) it considers that it is desirable to make rules for the purpose of securing that redress is made to the consumers in respect of the failure (having regard to other ways in which consumers may obtain redress).

(2) "Relevant firms" means—

(3C)可以特别为要求任何人采取或不采取规定行动而提出限制。

(3D)管理局可以:
(a)撤销终止或限制;或
(b)变更终止或限制,缩短其有效期限或以其他方式限制其效力。”

(4)第(4)款中“2年”替换为“3年”。

第13条　公布决定通知

(1)《2000年金融服务与市场法》第391条(公布)修订如下。

(2)第(1)款(禁止管理局和预告通知或决定通知的被通知人和被抄送人公布该通知或任何与该通知相关的细节)中,删除“或决定通知”。

(3)第(1)款后插入:
“(1A)预告通知或决定通知的被抄送人不得公布该通知或与该通知相关的任何细节,除非管理局已公布该通知或细节。”
(4)第(4)款(管理局公布最后通知相关信息的职责)中在“最后通知”前插入“决定通知或”。

消费者保护措施

第14条　消费者赔偿计划

(1)《2000年金融服务与市场法》第404条(及该条前的斜体小标题)替换为:

“消费者赔偿计划

第404条　消费者赔偿计划

(1)本条适用于下列情况:
(a)管理局认为相关企业可能普遍或经常未遵守开展任何活动适用的要求;

(b)管理局因此认为消费者已经遭受(或可能遭受)损失或损害,如提起法律程序,则在该程序中将给予救济或济助;且

(c)管理局(考虑到消费者可获得赔偿的其他途径)认为,为确保就该未遵守要求的情况对消费者予以赔偿,有必要制定规则。

(2)‘相关企业’系指

(a) authorised persons; or

(b) payment service providers.

(3) The Authority may make rules requiring each relevant firm (or each relevant firm of a specified description) which has carried on the activity on or after the specified date to establish and operate a consumer redress scheme.

(4) A "consumer redress scheme" is a scheme under which the firm is required to take one or more of the following steps in relation to the activity.

(5) The firm must first investigate whether, on or after the specified date, it has failed to comply with the requirements mentioned in subsection (1)(a) that are applicable to the carrying on by it of the activity.

(6) The next step is for the firm to determine whether the failure has caused (or may cause) loss or damage to consumers.

(7) If the firm determines that the failure has caused (or may cause) loss or damage to consumers, it must then—

(a) determine what the redress should be in respect of the failure; and

(b) make the redress to the consumers.

(8) A relevant firm is required to take the above steps in relation to any particular consumer even if, after the rules are made, a defence of limitation becomes available to the firm in respect of the loss or damage in question.

(9) Before making rules under this section, the Authority must consult the scheme operator of the ombudsman scheme.

(10) For the meaning of consumers, see section 404E.

404A Rules under s.404: supplementary

(1) Rules under section 404 may make provision—

(a) specifying the activities and requirements in relation to which relevant firms are to carry out investigations under consumer redress schemes;

(b) setting out, in relation to any specified description of case, examples of things done, or omitted to be done, that are to be regarded as constituting a failure to comply with a requirement;

(c) setting out, in relation to any specified description of case, matters to be taken into account, or steps to be taken, by relevant firms for the purpose of—

(i) assessing evidence as to a failure to comply with a requirement; or

(ii) determining whether such a failure has caused (or may cause) loss or damage to consumers;

(d) as to the kinds of redress that are, or are not, to be made to consumers in specified descriptions of case and the way in which redress is to be determined in specified descriptions of case;

(a)获授权人;或

(b)支付服务提供商。

(3)管理局可以制定规则,要求在规定日期或规定日期后开展活动的各相关企业(或规定类别的各相关企业)建立并实施消费者赔偿计划。

(4)‘消费者赔偿计划’系指要求企业就活动采取下列一项或多项措施的计划。

(5)企业必须首先调查在规定日期或规定日期后是否未遵守第(1)款第(a)项所述适用于其开展活动的要求。

(6)企业采取的第二步措施为,确定该未遵守要求的情况是否已经(或可能)使消费者遭受损失或损害。

(7)如企业确定该未遵守要求的情况已经(或可能)使消费者遭受损失或损害,则随后必须

(a)确定针对该未遵守要求的情况应给予哪种赔偿;以及

(b)向消费者作出赔偿。

(8)即使在规则制定后相关企业就相关损失或损害具有时效抗辩理由,也要求其对任何特定消费者采取上述措施。

(9)管理局在依照本条规定制定规则前必须征求申诉专员计划执行人的意见。

(10)消费者的定义见第404E条。

第404A条　第404条规定的规则:补充

(1)第404条规定的规则可以就下列事项作出规定:

(a)规定相关企业依照消费者赔偿计划开展调查的相关活动和要求;

(b)举例规定在任何规定类别的情况下视为未遵守要求的作为或不作为作为或不作为;

(c)规定在任何规定类别的情况下相关企业为下列目的考虑的事项或采取的措施:

(i)评估未遵守要求情况的证据;或

(ii)确定该未遵守要求的情况是否已经(或可能)使消费者遭受损失或损害;

(d)在规定情况下给予或不给予消费者的赔偿种类以及在规定情况下确定赔偿的方式;

(e) as to the things that relevant firms are, or are not, to do in establishing and operating consumer redress schemes;

(f) securing that relevant firms are not required to investigate anything occurring after a specified date;

(g) specifying the times by which anything required to be done under any consumer redress scheme is to be done;

(h) requiring relevant firms to provide information to the Authority;

(i) authorising one or more competent persons to do anything for the purposes of, or in connection with, the establishment or operation of any consumer redress scheme;

(j) for the nomination or approval by the Authority of persons authorised under paragraph (i);

(k) as to the circumstances in which, instead of a relevant firm, the Authority (or one or more competent persons acting on the Authority's behalf) may carry out the investigation and take the other relevant steps under any consumer redress scheme;

(l) as to the powers to be available to those carrying out an investigation by virtue of paragraph (k);

(m) as to the enforcement of any redress (for example, in the case of a money award, as a debt owed by a relevant firm).

(2) The only examples that may be set out in the rules as a result of subsection (1)(b) are examples of things done, or omitted to be done, that have been, or would be, held by a court or tribunal to constitute a failure to comply with a requirement.

(3) Matters may not be set out in the rules as a result of subsection (1)(c) if they have not been, or would not be, taken into account by a court or tribunal for the purpose mentioned there.

(4) The Authority must exercise the power conferred as a result of subsection (1)(d) so as to secure that, in relation to any description of case, the only kinds of redress to be made are those which it considers to be just in relation to that description of case.

(5) In acting under subsection(4),the Authority must have regard (among other things) to the nature and extent of the losses or damage in question.

(6) The provision that may be made under subsection (1)(h)includes provision applying (with or without modifications)—

(a) any provision of section 165; or

(b) any provision of Part 11 relating to that section.

(7) The reference in subsection (1)(k) to the other relevant steps under any consumer redress scheme is a reference to the Authority making the determinations mentioned in section 404(6) and (7) (with the firm still required to make the redress).

(8) If the rules include provision under subsection (1)(k),they must also include

(e)相关企业在建立和执行消费者赔偿计划时应采取或不应采取的行动;

(f)确保不要求相关企业调查规定日期后发生的任何事项;

(g)规定任何消费者赔偿计划要求实施的行动的实施时间;

(h)要求相关企业向管理局提供信息;

(i)授权一个或多个适格人员实施为建立或实施任何消费者赔偿计划目的或与之相关的行动;

(j)管理局提名并批准第(i)项规定的获授权人;

(k)在何种情况下管理局(或代表管理局行事的一个或多个适格人员)可以代替相关企业开展调查并依照任何消费者赔偿计划采取其他相关措施;

(l)依照第(k)项开展调查的调查人拥有的权力;

(m)任何赔偿的执行(如在判付赔偿金的情况下作为相关企业的应付债务执行)。

(2)因第(1)款第(b)项而制定的规则中可规定的举例,只可以对法院或裁判所已认定或会认定构成未遵守要求的作为或不作为举例。

(3)法院或裁判所为上述目的未考虑或不会考虑的事项,不得在依照第(1)款第(c)项制定的规则中规定。

(4)管理局必须行使因第(1)款第(d)项而赋予的权力,以确保在任何规定类别的情况下只作出其认为在该情况下公正的赔偿。

(5)管理局在依照第(4)款规定行事时必须考虑(除其他事项外)相关损失或损害的性质和程度。

(6)可以依照第(1)款第(h)项作出的规定包括(经修改或未经修改)适用下列各项的规定:

(a)第165条的任何规定;或

(b)第十一部分中与第165条规定相关的任何规定。

(7)第(1)款第(k)项中述及任何消费者赔偿计划规定的其他相关措施,即为述及管理局作出第404条第(6)款和第(7)款所述决定(仍然要求该企业作出赔偿)。

(8)如规则包含第(1)款第(k)项的规定,则同时必须包括下列规定:

provision for—

(a) giving warning and decision notices, and

(b) conferring rights on relevant firms to refer matters to the Tribunal,

in relation to any determination mentioned in section 404(6) and(7) made by the Authority.

(9) Nothing in this section is to be taken as limiting the power conferred by section 404.

404B Complaints to the ombudsman scheme

(1) If—

(a) a consumer makes a complaint under the ombudsman scheme in respect of an act or omission of a relevant firm, and

(b) at the time the complaint is made, the subject-matter of the complaint falls to be dealt with (or has been dealt with) under a consumer redress scheme, the way in which the complaint is to be determined by the ombudsman is to be as mentioned in subsection (4).

(2) If a consumer—

(a) is not satisfied with a determination made by a relevant firm under a consumer redress scheme, or

(b) considers that a relevant firm has failed to make a determination in accordance with a consumer redress scheme, the consumer may, in respect of that determination or failure, make a complaint under the ombudsman scheme.

(3) A complaint mentioned in subsection (1) or(2) is referred to in the following provisions of this section as a "relevant complaint".

(4) A relevant complaint is to be determined by reference to what, in the opinion of the ombudsman, the determination under the consumer redress scheme should be or should have been (subject to subsection (5)).

(5) If, in determining a relevant complaint, the ombudsman determines that the firm should make (or should have made) a payment of an amount to the consumer, the amount awarded by the ombudsman (a "money award") must not exceed the monetary limit (within the meaning of section 229).

(6) But the ombudsman may recommend that the firm pay a larger amount.

(7) A money award—

(a) may specify the date by which the amount awarded is to be paid;

(b) may provide for interest to be payable, at a rate specified in the award, on any amount which is not paid by that date; and

(c) is enforceable by the consumer in accordance with Part 3 or 3A of Schedule 17 (as the case may be).

(8) If, in determining a relevant complaint, the ombudsman determines that the firm should take(or should have taken) particular action in relation to the consumer, the ombudsman

(a)规定发出预告通知及决定通知;以及

(b)规定授予相关企业将事项诉至裁判所的权利,

且上述规定与依照第404条第(6)款和第(7)款作出的任何决定相关。

(9)本条任何规定不得视为限制第404条赋予的权力。

第404B条　向申诉专员计划提出的申诉

(1)如有下列情况:

(a)消费者依照申诉专员计划就相关企业的作为或不作为提出申诉;且

(b)提出申诉时,该申诉的标的事项属于消费者赔偿计划应当处理的范围(或已依照消费者赔偿计划处理),

则申诉专员以第(4)款所述方式对该申诉作出决定。

(2)如消费者

(a)对相关企业依照消费者赔偿计划作出的决定不满意;或

(b)认为相关企业未依照消费者赔偿计划作出决定,则可以就该决定或未作出决定的情况依照申诉专员计划提出申诉。

(3)第(1)款或第(2)款所述申诉在本条下列规定中称为'相关申诉'。

(4)对相关申诉作出的决定参照申诉专员认为依照消费者赔偿计划应当作出的决定[符合第(5)款规定]。

(5)如在对相关申诉作出决定时,申诉专员决定该企业应当向(或应已向)消费者支付某一数额的款项,则申诉专员判决支付的金额(以下简称赔偿金支付判决)不得超出金钱限额(第229条规定的含义范围内)。

(6)但申诉专员可以建议该企业支付更大数额。

(7)赔偿金支付判决

(a)可以规定判付金额在何日期前支付;

(b)可以规定以判付裁决中规定的利率对未于上述日期前支付的任何金额支付利息;且

(c)可以由消费者依照附录17第三部分或第三A部分(视情况而定)强制执行。

(8)如在对相关申诉作出决定时,申诉专员决定该企业应当采取(或应当已采取)与消费者相关的特定行动,则申诉专员可以指示该企业采取该行动。

may direct the firm to take that action.

(9) Compliance with a direction under subsection (8) is enforceable, on the application of the consumer, by an injunction or, in Scotland, by an order for specific performance under section 45 of the Court of Session Act 1988.

(10) In consequence of the provision made by this section, sections 228(2) and 229 do not apply in relation to relevant complaints; but all other provision made by or under Part 16 applies in relation to those complaints.

(11) The compulsory jurisdiction of the ombudsman scheme is to include the jurisdiction resulting from this section.

(12) Nothing in subsection (1) is to be taken as requiring the ombudsman to determine a complaint in any case where (apart from that subsection) the complaint would not fall to be determined (whether as a result of rules made under Schedule 17 or otherwise).

(13) Nothing in subsection (2) is to be taken as conferring an entitlement on a person who, for the purposes of the ombudsman scheme, is not an eligible complainant in relation to the subject-matter of the determination mentioned there.

404C Enforcement

The following provisions—

(a) Part 14 (disciplinary measures), and

(b) so much of this Act as relates to any provision of that Part,

(which apply only in relation to authorised persons) are also to apply in relation to relevant firms which are not (or are no longer) authorized persons.

404D Applications to Tribunal to quash rules or provision of rules

(1) Any person may apply to the Tribunal for a review of any rules made under section 404.

(2) The Tribunal may—

(a) dismiss the application; or

(b) make an order (a "quashing order") quashing any rules made under section 404 or any provision of those rules.

(3) An application may be made only if permission to make it has first been obtained from the Tribunal.

(4) The Tribunal may grant permission to make an application only if it considers that the applicant has a sufficient interest in the matter to which the application relates.

(5) The general rule is that, in determining an application, the Tribunal is to apply the principles applicable on an application for judicial review.

(6) If (or so far as) an application relates to an example set out in the rules as a result of section 404A(1)(b), the Tribunal may determine whether the example constitutes a failure to comply with the requirement in question.

(9)依照第(8)款规定发出的指示可经消费者申请,通过强制令强制执行,在苏格兰可通过《1988年高等民事法院法》第45条规定的实际履行令强制执行。

(10)因依照本条制定的规定,第228条第(2)款和第229条规定不适用于相关申诉;但第十六部分和依照第十六部分制定的规定适用于上述申诉。

(11)申诉专员计划的强制管辖权包括因本条规定而具有的管辖权。

(12)第(1)款中任何规定不得视为要求申诉专员在任何情况下对不属于决定范围的申诉作出决定(无论是否因依照附录17制定的规则)。

(13)第(2)款中任何规定不得视为向就申诉专员计划而言不符合条件的申诉人赋予与该款所述决定的标的事项相关的权力。

第404C条　强制执行

下列规定:

(a)第十四部分(惩戒措施);以及

(b)本法与该部分任何规定相关的规定,

(只对获授权人适用)同样适用于不是(或不再是)获授权人的相关企业。

第404D条　申请裁判所撤销规则或规则中的规定

(1)任何人可以申请裁判所复核依照第404条规定制定的任何规则。

(2)裁判所可以

(a)驳回申请;或

(b)颁布法令(以下简称撤销令),撤销依照第404条规定制定的任何规则或上述规则中的任何规定。

(3)只有事先获得裁判所许可,才可以提出申请。

(4)裁判所只有在认为申请人在申请相关的事项中有充分利益,才可以发出申请许可。

(5)一般规则为,在就一项申请作出决定时,裁判所适用司法复核申请适用的原则。

(6)如申请与因第404A条第(1)款第(b)项制定的规则所列举例相关(或在此范围内),则裁判所可以决定该举例是否构成未遵守相关要求的情况。

(7) If (or so far as) an application relates to a matter set out in the rules as a result of section 404A(1)(c),the Tribunal may determine whether the matter should be taken into account as mentioned in that provision.

(8) In the case of an application within subsection (6) or (7),the Tribunal's jurisdiction under that subsection is in addition to its jurisdiction under subsection (5).

(9) A quashing order may be enforced as if it were an order made, on an application for judicial review, by the High Court or, in Scotland, the Court of Session.

(10) The Tribunal may award damages to the applicant if—

(a) the application includes a claim for damages arising from any matter to which the application relates; and

(b) the Tribunal is satisfied that an award would have been made by the High Court or, in Scotland, the Court of Session if the claim had been made in an action begun in that court by the applicant when making the application.

(11) An award of damages under subsection(10) may be enforced as if it were an award made by the High Court or, in Scotland, the Court of Session.

(12) In the case of any proceedings under this section, the judge presiding at the proceedings must be—

(a) a judge of the High Court or the Court of Appeal or a judge of the Court of Session; or

(b) such other person as may be agreed from time to time by—

(i) the Lord Chief Justice, the Lord President or the Lord Chief Justice of Northern Ireland (as the case may be); and

(ii) the Senior President of Tribunals.

(13) Section 133 does not apply in the case of an application under this section, but—

(a) Tribunal Procedure Rules may make provision for the suspension of rules made under section 404 or of any provision of those rules, pending determination of the application; and

(b) in the case of an application within subsection (6) or (7), the Tribunal may consider any evidence relating to the application's subject-matter, whether or not it was available at the time the rules were made.

(14) If—

(a) the Tribunal refuses to grant permission to make an application under this section, and

(b) on an appeal by the applicant, the Court of Appeal grants the permission, the Court of Appeal may go on to decide the application under this section.

404E Meaning of "consumers"

(1) For the purposes of sections 404 to 404B "consumers" means persons who—

(7)如申请与因第404A条第(1)款第(c)项制定的规则所列事项相关(或在此范围内),则裁判所可以决定该事项是否应按该规定所述予以考虑。

(8)如有第(6)款或第(7)款规定范围内的申请,则该款规定的裁判所管辖权附加于第(5)款规定的管辖权。

(9)撤销令可以由高等法院或(苏格兰)高等民事法院强制执行,效力等同于该令为应司法复核申请而作出。

(10)如有下列情况,则裁判所可以判决对申请人支付损害赔偿:

(a)申请包含因任何该申请相关事项而提起的损害赔偿请求;且

(b)裁判所确信,如申请人提出申请时在向高等法院或(苏格兰)高等民事法院提起的诉讼中提出该请求,则该法院将作出损害赔偿判决。

(11)依照第(10)条规定判令支付的损害赔偿可强制执行,效力等同于高等法院或(苏格兰)最高民事法院判令支付。

(12)本条规定的任何诉讼程序中,主审法官必须为

(a)高等法院或上诉法院法官,或苏格兰高等民事法院法官;或

(b)经下列人员同意的任何其他人:

(i)首席大法官、枢密院议长或北爱尔兰首席大法官(视情况而定);以及

(ii)高级裁判所长官。

(13)第133条不适用于本条规定的申请,但

(a)《裁判所程序规则》可以规定在对申请作出决定前对依照第404条规定制定的规则或该规则中任何规定进行监督;且

(b)如有属于第(6)款或第(7)款规定范围内的申请,则裁判所可以考虑任何与该申请标的事项相关的证据,无论规则制定时该证据是否可用。

(14)如有下列情况:

(a)裁判所拒绝给予依照本条规定提出申请的许可;

(b)上诉法院应申请人上诉给予许可,

则上诉法院可以继续就本条规定的申请作出决定。

第404E条 ‘消费者’的含义

(1)就第404条至第404B条而言,‘消费者’系指

(a) have used, or may have contemplated using, any of the services within subsection (2); or

(b) have relevant rights or interests in relation to any of the services within that subsection.

(2) The services within this subsection are services provided by—

(a) authorised persons in carrying on regulated activities;

(b) authorised persons in carrying on a consumer credit business in connection with the accepting of deposits;

(c) authorised persons in communicating, or approving the communication by others of, invitations or inducements to engage in investment activity;

(d) authorised persons who are investment firms, or credit institutions, in providing relevant ancillary services;

(e) persons acting as appointed representatives; or

(f) payment service providers in providing payment services.

(3) A person ("P") has a "relevant right or interest" in relation to any services within subsection (2) if P has a right or interest—

(a) which is derived from, or is otherwise attributable to, the use of the services by others; or

(b) which may be adversely affected by the use of the services by persons acting on P's behalf or in a fiduciary capacity in relation to P.

(4) If a person is providing a service within subsection (2) as a trustee, the persons who have been, or may have been, beneficiaries of the trust are to be treated as persons who have used, or may have contemplated using, the service.

(5) A person who deals with another person("B") in the course of B providing a service within subsection (2) is to be treated as using the service.

(6) In this section—

"accepting", in relation to deposits, includes agreeing to accept;

"consumer credit business" has the same meaning as in the Consumer Credit Act 1974 (see section 189(1));

"credit institution" has the meaning given by section 138(1B);

"engage in investment activity" has the meaning given by section 21;

"payment services" has the same meaning as in the Payment Services Regulations 2009;

"payment service provider" means a person who is a payment service provider for the purposes of those regulations as a result of falling within any of paragraphs (a) to (e) of the definition in regulation 2(1);

"relevant ancillary services" has the meaning given by section 138(1C).

(a)使用或考虑使用第(2)款规定范围的任何服务的人;或

(b)具有与第(2)款规定范围内任何服务相关的权利或利益。

(2)本款规定范围内的服务为下列服务:

(a)获授权人在开展受监管活动时提供的服务;

(b)获授权人在开展与吸收存款相关的消费信贷业务时提供的服务;

(c)获授权人在传播或批准他人传播参与投资活动的邀请或诱导时提供的服务;

(d)投资企业或信贷机构获授权人提供相关附属服务时提供的服务;

(e)作为被任命代表的人提供的服务;或

(f)支付服务提供商在提供支付服务时提供的服务。

(3)某人(以下简称P)如具有下列权利或利益,即为就第(2)款规定范围内的任何服务具有'相关权利或利益':

(a)从使用他人服务中产生或以其他方式归因于使用他人服务的权利或利益;或

(b)可能因使用代表P行事或具有与P相关委托地位的人提供的服务而受到不利影响的权利或利益。

(4)如某人以受托人身份提供属于第(2)款规定范围内的服务,则该委托的受益人或者曾经或可能为该委托受益人的人视为已使用或者可能已考虑使用该项服务的人。

(5)在另一人提供第(2)款规定范围内的服务期间与其交易的人视为使用该服务。

(6)本条中

'吸收'就存款而言包括同意吸收;

'消费信贷业务'与《1974年消费信贷法》[见第189条第(1)款]中的含义相同。

'信贷机构'具有第138条第(1B)款规定的含义;

'参与投资活动'具有第21条规定的含义;

'支付服务'与《2009年支付服务条例》规定的含义相同;

'支付服务提供商'系指属于该条例第2条第(1)款第(a)项至第(e)项定义的支付服务提供商;

'相关附属服务'具有第138条第(1c)款规定的含义。

404F Other definitions etc

(1) For the purposes of sections 404 to 404B—

"redress" includes—

(a) interest; and

(b) a remedy or relief which could not be awarded in legal proceedings;

"specified" means specified in rules made under section 404.

(2) In determining for the purposes of those sections whether an authorised person has failed to comply with a requirement, anything which an appointed representative has done or omitted as respects business for which the authorised person has accepted responsibility is to be treated as having been done or omitted by the authorised person.

(3) References in those sections to the failure by a relevant firm to comply with a requirement applicable to the carrying on by it of any activity include anything done, or omitted to be done, by it in carrying on the activity—

(a) which is in breach of a duty or other obligation, prohibition or restriction; or

(b) which otherwise gives rise to the availability of a remedy or relief in legal proceedings.

(4) It does not matter whether—

(a) the duty or other obligation, prohibition or restriction, or

(b) the remedy or relief,

arises as a result of any provision made by or under this or any other Act, a rule of law or otherwise.

(5) References in sections 404 to 404B to a relevant firm include—

(a) a person who was at any time a relevant firm but has subsequently ceased to be one; and

(b) a person who has assumed a liability (including a contingent one) incurred by a relevant firm in respect of a failure by the firm to comply with a requirement applicable to the carrying on by it of any activity.

(6) References in those sections to the carrying on of an activity by a relevant firm are, accordingly, to be read in that case with the appropriate modifications.

(7) If the Authority varies a permission or authorisation of a person so as to impose requirements on the person to establish and operate a scheme which corresponds to, or is similar to, a consumer redress scheme, the provision that may be included in the permission or authorisation as varied includes—

(a) provision imposing requirements on the person corresponding to those that could be included in rules made under section 404; and

(b) provision corresponding to section 404B.

(8) In subsection (7) the reference to the variation of a permission or authorisation

第404F条　其他定义等

(1)就本条及第404条至第404B条而言

‘赔偿’包括：

(a)利息；以及

(b)法律诉讼程序中不能判决给予的救济或济助；

‘指定’，系指在依照第404条规定制定的规则中指定。

(2)为上述条款之目的决定获授权人是否未遵守要求时，如被任命代表的作为或不作为与相关业务有关并且由获授权人接受责任，则视为获授权人的作为或不作为。

(3)上述条款中，述及相关企业未遵守适用于其开展的任何活动的要求，包括该相关企业开展该活动时的下列任何作为或不作为：

(a)违反职责或其他义务、禁止性规定或限制性规定的作为或不作为；或

(b)在法律诉讼程序中可判决救济或济助的其他作为或不作为。

(4)无论

(a)违反职责或其他义务、禁止性规定或限制性规定；或

(b)救济或济助

是否因依照本法或任何其他法律、法规或以其他方式制定的任何规定而产生。

(5)第404条至第404B条述及相关企业包括：

(a)在任何时间为相关企业，但随后不再为相关企业的人；以及

(b)相关企业未遵守适用于其开展任何活动的要求时承担由此产生的责任(包括附带责任)的人。

(6)上述条款中述及相关企业开展活动，在该种情况下应经适当修改后作相应解释。

(7)如管理局变更对某人的许可或授权，以对该人提出建立并实施与消费者赔偿计划相应或类似的计划，则变更的许可或授权中可包含的规定包括：

(a)与依照第404条制定的规则中可包含的规定相应、对该人提出要求的规定；以及

(b)与第404B条相应的规定。

(8)第(7)款中述及管理局变更许可或核准即为述及

by the Authority is a reference to—

(a) the variation under section 44 or 45 of a Part Ⅵ permission; or

(b) the variation under regulation 8 or 11 of the Payment Services Regulations 2009 of an authorisation under those regulations.

404G Power to widen the scope of consumer redress schemes

(1) The Treasury may by order amend the definition of "relevant firms" in section 404 or the definition of "consumers" in section 404E (or both).

(2) An order under this section may make consequential amendments of any provision of sections 404 to 404F."

(2) This section has effect in relation to failures occurring before the commencement of this section (as well as in relation to failures occurring at or after the commencement of this section).

15 Restrictions on provision of credit card cheques

(1) The Consumer Credit Act 1974 ("the CCA 1974") is amended as follows.

(2) After section 51 insert—

"51A Restrictions on provision of credit card cheques

(1) A person who provides credit card cheques otherwise than in accordance with this section commits an offence.

(2) Credit card cheques may be provided only to a person who has asked for them.

(3) They may be provided only on a single occasion in respect of each request that is made.

(4) The number of cheques provided in respect of a request must not exceed three (or, if less, the number requested).

(5) Where a single request is made for the provision of credit card cheques in connection with more than one credit-token agreement, subsections (3) and (4) apply as if a separate request had been made in relation to each agreement.

(6) Where more than one request for the provision of cheques is made in the same document or at the same time—

(a) they may be provided in respect of only one of the requests, but

(b) if the requests relate to more than one credit-token agreement, in relation to each agreement they may be provided only in respect of one of the requests made in relation to that agreement.

(7) "Credit card cheque" means a cheque (whether or not drawn on a banker) which, whenever used, will result in the provision of credit under a credit-token agreement.

(8) Accordingly, "credit card cheque" does not include a cheque to be used only in connection with a current account.

(a)依照第44条或第45条规定变更第四部分规定的许可;或

(b)依照《2009年支付服务条例》第8条或第11条规定变更该条例规定的核准。

第404G条 扩大消费者赔偿计划范围的权力

(1)财政部可以颁布法令,修改第404条中'相关企业'的定义或第404E条中'消费者'的定义(或修改两项定义)。

(2)本条规定的命令可以对第404条或第404F条的任何规定作出相应修改。"

(2)本条规定对其生效前(以及生效时或生效后)发生的未遵守要求情况有效。

第15条 提供信用卡支票的限制

(1)《1974年消费信贷法》(以下简称1974年法)修订如下。

(2)第51条后插入:

"条51A条 提供信用卡支票的限制

(1)未依照本条规定提供信用卡支票的,构成犯罪。

(2)信用卡支票只可以向要求提供的人提供。

(3)只可以应每次请求一次性提供。

(4)应每次请求提供的支票数不得超过3张(或请求中低于3张的数量)。

(5)一次就一项以上信用代价券协议提出信用卡支票请求的,适用第(3)款和第(4)款规定,效力等同于就每项协议单独提出请求。

(6)在同一份文件中或同时提出多项提供支票请求的

(a)只可以应其中一项请求提供;但

(b)如请求与一项以上信用代价券协议相关,则针对每项协议只可以就与该协议相关的一项请求提供。

(7)'信用卡支票'系指一旦使用会导致依照信用代价券协议提供信用的支票(无论是否为银行开出)。

(8)'信用卡支票'相应不包括只与经常账户相联系而使用的支票。

51B Section 51A: exemption for business

(1) Section 51A does not apply to credit card cheques provided in connection with a credit-token agreement that is entered into by the debtor wholly or predominantly for the purposes of a business carried on, or intended to be carried on, by the debtor.

(2) If a credit-token agreement includes a declaration made by the debtor to the effect that the agreement is entered into as mentioned in subsection (1), the agreement is treated for the purposes of that subsection as having been so entered into.

(3) Subsection (2) does not apply if, when the agreement is entered into—

(a) the creditor, or

(b) any person who has acted on behalf of the creditor in connection with the entering into of the agreement, knows, or has reasonable cause to suspect, that the agreement is not entered into as mentioned in subsection (1).

(4) The Secretary of State may by order make provision about the form, content and signing of declarations for the purposes of subsection (2).

(5) Where an agreement has two or more creditors, references in subsection (3) to the creditor are to any one or more of them."

(3) In Schedule 1 (prosecution and punishment of offences), after the entry relating to section 51(1) insert—

"51A(1) Breach of restrictions on provision of credit card cheques.

(a) Summarily.The statutory maximum.

(b) On indictment.A fine."

(4) An offence under section 51A of the CCA 1974 is to be treated for the purposes of Part 3 of the Regulatory Enforcement and Sanctions Act 2008 (civil sanctions) as contained in the CCA 1974 immediately before the day on which that Act of 2008 was passed.

Financial Services Compensation Scheme

16 Contribution to costs of special resolution regime

(1) In the Financial Services and Markets Act 2000, for section 214B substitute—

"214B Contribution to costs of special resolution regime

(1) This section applies if—

(a) a stabilisation power under Part 1 of the Banking Act 2009 has been exercised in respect of a bank, building society or credit union within the meaning of that Part ("the institution"); and

(b) the Treasury think that the institution was or was likely to have been, or but for the exercise of the power would have become, unable to satisfy claims against it.

第51B条　第51A条:业务豁免

(1)对债务人完全或主要以其开展或意图开展的业务为目的订立的信用代价券协议,与该协议相关提供的信用卡支票不适用第51A条规定。

(2)如信用代价券协议包含债务人作出的声明,说明该协议为第(1)款所述订立的协议,则为该款之目的,该协议视为该款所述订立的协议。

(3)如协议订立时有下列情况,则第(2)款规定不适用:

(a)债权人;或

(b)就该协议的订立代表债权人行事的任何人,知悉或有合理理由怀疑该协议不是第(1)款所述订立的协议。

(4)国务大臣可以颁布法令,为施行第(2)款就声明的形式、内容和签署作出规定。

(5)如协议有两个或两个以上债权人,则第(3)款中述及债权人为述及任何一个或一个以上债权人。"

(3)附录1中(犯罪的起诉与处罚)与第51条第(1)款相关的条目后插入:

"**第51A条**　(1)违反提供信用卡支票的限制。

(a)经简易程序定罪。法定最高限额。

(b)经公诉程序定罪。罚金。"

(4)1974年法第51A条规定的犯罪,就《2008年监管执行与制裁法》第三部分(民事制裁)而言,视为在2008年法通过之日前夕包含在1974年法内。

金融服务补偿计划

第16条　分担特别决议制度的费用

(1)《2000年金融服务与市场法》第214B条[1]替换为:

"**第214B条　分担特别决议制度的费用**

(1)如有下列情况则适用本条规定:

(a)针对《2009年银行法》第一部分定义的银行、住房互助会或信用合作社(以下简称该机构)行使了该部分规定的稳定权;

(b)财政部认为该机构不能满足、可能不能满足或如不行使该权力即不能满足针对其提出的索赔要求。

1 《2000年金融服务与市场法》第214B条依照《2009年银行法》第171条第(1)款插入,参见http://www.legislation.gov.uk/ukpga/2009/1/section/171/prospective。——译者注

(2) The Treasury may require the scheme manager to make payments (to the Treasury or any other person) in respect of expenses of a prescribed description incurred (by the Treasury or that person) in connection with the exercise of the power.

(3) Subsection (2) is subject to section 214C (limit on amount of special resolution regime payments).

(4) In subsection (2) "expenses" includes interest at a specified rate on the difference, at any time, between—

(a) the total amount of expenses (including interest) incurred at or before that time; and

(b) the total amount recovered, or received from the scheme manager, in respect of the institution, at or before that time, by—

(i) the Treasury; and

(ii) any other person who has incurred expenses in connection with the exercise of the power that are of a description prescribed under subsection (2).

(5) Any payment made by the scheme manager under subsection (2) is to be treated for the purposes of this Part as an expense under the compensation scheme.

(6) In this section and section 214C "specified rate" means a rate specified by the Treasury.

(7) Different rates may be specified under different provisions or for different periods.

(8) A rate may be specified by reference to a rate set (from time to time) by any person.

214C Limit on amount of special resolution regime payments

(1) The total amount of special resolution regime payments required to be made in respect of a person ("the institution") may not exceed—

(a) notional net expenditure (see subsection (3)), minus

(b) actual net expenditure (see subsection (4)).

(2) A "special resolution regime payment" is—

(a) a payment under section 214B(2); or

(b) a payment required to be made by the scheme manager by virtue of section 61 of the Banking Act 2009 (special resolution regime: compensation).

(3) Notional net expenditure is—

(a) the total amount of expenses that would have been incurred under the compensation scheme in respect of the institution if the stabilisation power had not been exercised and the institution had been unable to satisfy claims against it, minus

(b) the total amount that would have been likely, at the time when the power was exercised, to be recovered by the scheme manager in respect of the institution in those circumstances.

(4) Actual net expenditure is—

(a) the total amount of expenses (other than special resolution regime payments)

(2)财政部可以要求计划管理人(向财政部或其他任何人)就(财政部或该人)行使该权力产生的规定类别的相关支出支付款项。

(3)第(2)款规定符合第214C条(特别决议制度支付限额)规定。

(4)第(2)款中‘支出’包括对下列金额的差额按指定利率计算的利息:

(a)行使该权力时或之前产生的支出总额(包括利息);以及

(b)行使该权力时或之前针对该机构从计划管理人处追回或获得的总金额,上述金额为

(i)财政部产生、追回或获得;以及

(ii)与行使该权力相关产生第(2)款规定类别支出的任何人。

(5)计划管理人依照第(2)款规定支付的任何款项,就本部分而言视为依照补偿计划进行的支出。

(6)本条和第214C条中‘规定利率’系指财政部规定的利率。

(7)依照不同规定或在不同期间可以规定不同利率。

(8)利率的规定可以参照任何人(不时)设定的利率。

第214C条　特别决议制度支付限额

(1)针对某人(以下简称该机构)要求作出的特别决议制度支付总额不得超过

(a)名义净支出[见第(3)款],减去

(b)实际净支出[见第(4)款]。

(2)‘特别决议制度支付’为

(a)第214B条第(2)款规定的支付;或

(b)计划管理人依照《2009年银行法》第61条规定(特别决议制度:补偿)要求作出的支付。

(3)名义净支出为

(a)如不行使稳定权且该机构不能满足针对其的索赔要求则依照补偿计划产生的与该机构相关的支出总额,减去

(b)行使该项权力时,在该种情况下可能由计划管理人针对该机构追回的总金额。

(4)实际净支出为

(a)计划管理人就该机构实际产生的支出总额(不包括特别决议制度支付),减去

actually incurred by the scheme manager in respect of the institution, minus

(b) the total amount actually recovered by the scheme manager in respect of the institution.

(5) In subsection(3)(a)"expenses"includes interest at a specified rate on the difference, at any time, between—

(a) the total amount of expenses (including interest) that would have been incurred as mentioned in subsection (3)(a) at or before that time; and

(b) the total amount that would have been likely to have been recovered as mentioned in subsection (3)(b) at or before that time.

(6) In subsection(4)(a)"expenses"includes interest at a specified rate on the difference, at any time, between—

(a) the total amount of expenses (including special resolution regime payments and interest) actually incurred by the scheme manager in respect of the institution at or before that time; and

(b) the total amount actually recovered by the scheme manager in respect of the institution at or before that time.

(7) In paragraph (b) of subsections (3) to (6) references to amounts recovered (or likely to have been recovered) by the scheme manager do not include any levy received (or likely to have been received) by it.

214D Contributions under section 214B: supplementary

(1) This section supplements sections 214B and 214C.

(2) The scheme manager must determine—

(a) the amounts of expenses (other than interest) that would have been incurred as mentioned in section 214C(3)(a); and

(b) the time or times at which those amounts would have been likely to have been incurred.

(3) The Treasury, or a person designated by the Treasury, must in accordance with regulations appoint a person ("the valuer") to determine—

(a) the amounts that would have been likely, at the time when the stabilisation power was exercised, to be recovered as mentioned in section 214C(3)(b); and

(b) the time or times at which those amounts would have been likely to be recovered.

The person appointed under this subsection may be the person appointed as valuer under section 54 of the Banking Act 2009 in respect of the exercise of the stabilisation power.

(4) Regulations may enable the Treasury to specify principles to be applied by—

(a) the scheme manager when exercising functions under subsection (2); or

(b) the valuer when exercising functions under subsection (3).

(5) The regulations may in particular enable the Treasury to require the scheme

(b)计划管理人针对该机构实际追回或收到的总金额。

(5)第(3)款第(a)项中‘支出’包括任何时间对下列金额之间的差额按规定利率计算的利息：

(a)行使该权力时或之前会依照第(3)款第(a)项所述产生的支出总额(包括利息)；以及

(b)行使该权力时或之前可能会依照第(3)款第(b)项所述追回的支出总额(包括利息)。

(6)第(4)款第(a)项中‘支出’包括任何时间对下列金额的差额按指定利率计算的利息：

(a)行使该权力时或之前计划管理人就该机构实际产生的支出总额(包括特别决议制度支付款项和利息)；以及

(b)计划管理人在行使该权力时或之前针对该机构实际追回的总金额。

(7)在第(3)款第(b)项至第(6)款述及计划管理人已追回(或可能已追回)的金额，不包括其获得(或可能获得的)任何征收费用。

第214D条　依照第214B条分担费用：补充

(1)本条规定补充第214B条和第214C条规定。

(2)计划管理人必须确定

(a)依照第214C条第(3)款第(a)项所述产生的支出额(不包括利息)；以及

(b)上述支出额可能发生的时间。

(3)财政部或由财政部指定的人必须依照法规委派一人(以下简称估价人)确定

(a)行使稳定权时可能会依照第214C条第(3)款第(b)项所述追回的金额；以及

(b)上述金额可能追回的时间。

依照本款规定委派的人可为依照《2009年银行法》第54条就行使稳定权委派为估价人的人。

(4)法规可以允许财政部规定下列情况下适用的原则：

(a)计划管理人依照第(2)款规定行使职能时；或

(b)估价人依照第(3)款规定行使职能时。

(5)法规可以特别允许财政部要求计划管理人或估价人

manager or valuer—

(a) to use, or not to use, specified methods;

(b) to take specified matters into account in a specified manner; or

(c) not to take specified matters into account.

(6) Regulations—

(a) must provide for independent verification of expenses within section 214B(2);

(b) may provide for the independent verification of other matters; and

(c) may contain provision about the appointment and payment of an auditor.

(7) Regulations—

(a) must contain provision enabling the valuer to reconsider a decision;

(b) must provide a right of appeal to a court or tribunal against any decision of the valuer;

(c) may provide for payment of the valuer; and

(d) may apply (with or without modifications) or make provision corresponding to—

(i) any provision of sections 54 to 56 of the Banking Act 2009; or

(ii) any provision made, or that could be made, by virtue of any of those sections.

(8) Regulations may make provision for payments under section 214B(2) to be made—

(a) before any verification required by the regulations is undertaken, and

(b) before the limit imposed by section 214C is calculated, subject to any necessary later adjustment.

(9) If they do so they must provide that the amount of any payment required by virtue of subsection (8) must not be such as to give rise to an expectation that an amount will be required to be repaid to the scheme manager (once any necessary verification has been undertaken and the limit imposed by section 214C has been calculated).

(10) Regulations may—

(a) make provision supplementing section 214B or 214C or this section;

(b) make further provision about the method by which amounts to be paid under section 214B(2) are to be determined;

(c) make provision about timing;

(d) make provision about procedures to be followed;

(e) provide for discretionary functions to be exercised by a specified body or by persons of a specified class; and

(f) make provision about the resolution of disputes (which may include provision conferring jurisdiction on a court or tribunal).

(11) "Regulations" means regulations made by the Treasury.

(12) Any payment made by the Treasury by virtue of this section is to be met out of money provided by Parliament.

(a)使用或不使用规定的方法;

(b)以规定方式考虑规定事项;或

(c)不考虑规定事项。

(6)法规

(a)必须规定对第214B条第(2)款规定范围内的支出进行独立验证;

(b)可以规定对其他事项进行独立验证;且

(c)可以包括审计人委派和报酬支付的相关规定。

(7)法规

(a)必须包括使估价人能够重新考虑决定的规定;

(b)必须规定针对估价人的决定向法院或裁判所提起上诉的权利;

(c)可以规定估价人的报酬支付;且

(d)可以适用于(不论是否经修改)下列规定或作出与之相应的规定:

(i)依照《2009年银行法》第54条至第56条的任何规定;或

(ii)依照上述各条规定制定或可制定的任何规定。

(8)法规可以规定第214B条第(2)款规定的支付

(a)在法规规定的任何验证实施前作出;且

(b)在计算第214C条规定的限额前作出,但以此后进行的任何必要调整为准。

(9)如法规作出上述规定,则必须规定第(8)款要求支付的任何款项金额(一旦实施任何必要的验证且已计算第214C条规定的限额)不得产生要求向计划管理人偿付款项的预期。

(10)法规可以

(a)作出补充第214B条、第214C条或本条的规定;

(b)就以何种方式决定依照第214B条第(2)款规定支付款项的金额作出进一步规定;

(c)就时间确定作出规定;

(d)就应遵循的程序作出规定;

(e)规定指定机构或指定类别的人应行使的自决职能;且

(f)就争议解决作出规定(可包括对法院或裁判所授予管辖权的规定)。

(11)'法规'系指财政部规定的法规。

(12)财政部依照本条规定支付的任何款项从议会提供的资金中支付。

(13) The compensation scheme may make provision about payments under section 214B(2) and levies in connection with such payments (except provision inconsistent with any provision made by or under section 214B or 214C or this section)."

(2) Sections 214B to 214D of the Financial Services and Markets Act 2000 (as substituted by subsection (1))apply to any case where a stabilisation power was exercised before the commencement of this section as if the references in sections 214B(4) and 214C (5) and (6) of that Act to any time were to any time on or after 19 November 2009.

17 Power to require FSCS manager to act in relation to other schemes

In the Financial Services and Markets Act 2000, after Part 15 insert—

"PART 15A POWER TO REQUIRE FSCS MANAGER TO ACT IN RELATION TO OTHER SCHEMES

Introduction

224B Meaning of "relevant scheme" etc

(1) The following provisions apply for the purposes of this Part.

(2) "Relevant scheme" means a scheme or arrangement (other than the FSCS) for the payment of compensation (in certain cases) to customers of persons who provide financial services or carry on a business connected with the provision of such services.

(3) References to the manager of a relevant scheme are to the person who administers it or (if there is no such person) the person responsible for making payments under it.

(4) "The FSCS" means the Financial Services Compensation Scheme (see section 213 (2)).

(5) "The FSCS manager" means the scheme manager as defined by section 212(1).

(6) "Expense" includes anything that, if incurred in relation to the FSCS, would amount to an expense for the purposes of the FSCS.

(7) "Notice" means a notice in writing.

(8) In subsection (2)—

(a) "customers" includes customers outside the United Kingdom;

(b) "persons" includes persons outside the United Kingdom;

(c) references to the provision of financial services include the provision outside the United Kingdom of such services.

(9) This Part applies to cases where the manager of the relevant scheme is the Treasury or any other Minister of the Crown as it applies to cases where that manager is any other person.

(13)补偿计划可就第214B条第(2)款规定的款项支付以及与该支付相关的费用征收作出规定（不包括与依照第214B条、第214C条或本条制定的规定不一致的规定）。"

(2)《2000年金融服务与市场法》第214B条至第214D条规定[依照第(1)款替换]适用于本条规定开始生效前行使稳定权的任何情况,如同该法第214B条第(4)款和第214C条第(5)款、第(6)款述及的任何时间为2009年11月19日或该日以后的任何时间。

第17条　要求金融服务补偿计划管理人采取与其他计划相关行动的权力

《2000年金融服务与市场法》第十五部分后插入:

"第十五A部分　要求金融服务补偿计划管理人采取与其他计划相关行动的权力

概　要

第224B条　'相关计划'的含义等

(1)下列规定适用于本部分。

(2)'相关计划',系指提供金融服务或开展金融服务提供相关业务的人(在特定情况下)向消费者支付补偿的计划或安排(不包括金融服务补偿计划)。

(3)述及相关计划管理人,即为述及管理该计划的人或(如无管理该计划的人)负责依照该计划规定支付款项的人。

(4)'金融服务补偿计划',系指金融服务补偿计划[见第213条第(2)款]。

(5)'金融服务补偿计划管理人',系指第212条第(1)款定义的计划管理人。

(6)'支出'如与金融服务补偿计划相关而产生,则包含构成该计划相关支出的任何款项。

(7)'通知'系指书面通知。

(8)第(2)款中

(a)'消费者'包括联合王国境外的消费者;

(b)'人'包括联合王国境外的人;

(c)述及金融服务规定包括联合王国境外提供金融服务的规定。

(9)本部分适用于相关计划管理人是财政部或任何其他内阁阁员的情况,效力等同于对管理人是任何其他人的情况适用。

Power to require FSCS manager to act

224C Power to require FSCS manager to act on behalf of manager of relevant scheme

(1) This section applies if compensation is payable under a relevant scheme.

(2) The Treasury may by notice require the FSCS manager to exercise (on behalf of the manager of the relevant scheme) specified functions in respect of specified claims for compensation under the relevant scheme.

(3) A notice may be given only with the consent of the manager of the relevant scheme.

(4) In subsection (2) "specified" means specified, or of a description specified, in the notice.

(5) Claims or descriptions of claims may be specified by reference to the persons or description of persons whose claims they are.

224D Cases where FSCS manager may decline to act

(1) This section applies where a notice under section 224C(2)(a "section 224C notice") has been given in respect of a relevant scheme.

(2) The FSCS manager is not under a duty to comply with the section 224C notice if, as soon as reasonably practicable after receiving it, the FSCS manager gives a notice to the Treasury stating that a ground set out in section 224E applies.

(3) Where a notice under subsection (2) is given, the FSCS manager may recover from the manager of the relevant scheme an amount equal to the total expenses incurred by the FSCS manager in connection with the relevant scheme in the period—

(a) beginning with the giving of the section 224C notice; and

(b) ending with the giving of the notice under subsection (2).

(4) The duty to comply with the section 224C notice ceases if, after starting to comply with it, the FSCS manager gives a notice to the Treasury and the manager of the relevant scheme stating that a ground set out in section 224E applies.

(5) Where a notice under subsection (4) is given, the FSCS manager must give the Treasury such information connected with the FSCS manager's exercise of functions in relation to the relevant scheme as the Treasury may reasonably require.

(6) Any notice under this section—

(a) may be given only if, before giving it, the FSCS manager has taken reasonable steps to deal with anything that is causing the ground or grounds in question to apply; and

(b) must contain details of those steps.

224E Grounds for declining to act

(1) This section sets out the grounds referred to in section 224D(2) and (4).

(2) The first ground is that the FSCS manager is not satisfied that it will be able to

要求金融服务补偿计划管理人采取行动的权力

第224C条　要求金融服务补偿计划管理人代表相关计划管理人采取行动的权力

(1)如依照相关计划应支付补偿,则适用本条规定。

(2)财政部可以发出通知,要求金融服务补偿计划管理人(代表相关计划管理人)就相关计划指定的补偿请求履行规定职能。

(3)只有经相关计划管理人同意才可以发出通知。

(4)第(2)款中"规定"系指通知中规定或规定类别。

(5)可以参照请求人或请求人的类别规定补偿请求或补偿请求的类别。

第224D条　金融服务补偿计划管理人可以拒绝采取行动的情况

(1)如就相关计划发出了第224C条第(2)款规定的通知,则适用本条规定。

(2)如金融服务补偿计划管理人在接到通知后在合理可行的范围内尽快向财政部发出通知,说明适用第224E条规定的理由,则无遵守第224C条规定通知的职责。

(3)如发出了第(2)款规定的通知,则对金融服务补偿计划管理人在下列期间产生的与相关计划有关的全部支出, 金融服务补偿计划管理人可以从相关计划管理人处追回与该支出相等的金额:

(a)自发出第224C条规定通知时起;

(b)至依照第(2)款规定发出通知时止。

(4)如金融服务补偿计划管理人在开始遵照第224C条规定的通知行事时向财政部和相关项目管理人发出通知,说明适用第224E条规定的理由,则不再承担遵守该通知的职责。

(5)如依照第(4)款规定发出了通知,则金融服务补偿计划管理人必须按照财政部的合理要求向财政部提供与该金融服务补偿计划管理人就相关计划行使职能相关的信息。

(6)本条规定的任何通知

(a)在使相关理由适用的任何情况下,只有金融服务补偿计划管理人在发出该通知前已采取合理措施处理该情况,方可发出该通知;且

(b)必须包含上述措施的详细信息。

第224E条　拒绝采取行动的理由

(1)本条规定了第224D条第(2)款和第(4)款所述理由。

(2)第一个理由为,金融服务补偿计划管理人不确信其能够获得遵守第224C条规

obtain any information required in order to comply with the section 224C notice.

(3) The second ground is that the FSCS manager is not satisfied that it will be able to obtain any advice or other assistance from the manager of the relevant scheme that is required in order to comply with the section 224C notice.

(4) The third ground is—

(a) that the FSCS manager has not received an amount at least equal to the total expenses it expects to incur in connection with its relevant scheme functions; and

(b) either—

(i) that there are no arrangements for the provision of funds to the FSCS manager to enable it to exercise those functions and meet those expenses; or

(ii) that the FSCS manager considers that any such arrangements are unsatisfactory.

(5) The fourth ground is that the FSCS manager considers that complying with the section 224C notice would detrimentally affect the exercise of its functions under the FSCS.

(6) The fifth ground is—

(a) that there is no undertaking from the manager of the relevant scheme not to bring proceedings against the FSCS manager; or

(b) that the FSCS manager considers that the terms of any such undertaking are unsatisfactory.

(7) The sixth ground is—

(a) that there are no arrangements for the reimbursement of any expenses incurred by the FSCS manager in connection with any proceedings brought against it in respect of its relevant scheme functions (including expenses incurred in meeting any award of damages made against it); or

(b) that the FSCS manager considers that any such arrangements are unsatisfactory.

(8) In subsection (6) references to an undertaking of the kind mentioned there are to an undertaking not to bring proceedings in respect of the FSCS manager's relevant scheme functions except proceedings in respect of an act or omission of the FSCS manager that is alleged to have been in bad faith.

(9) In this section "proceedings" includes proceedings outside the United Kingdom.

Rules

224F Rules about relevant schemes

(1) The Authority may by rules make provision in connection with the exercise by the FSCS manager of functions in respect of relevant schemes.

(2) The provision that may be made by the rules includes any provision corresponding to provision that could be contained in the FSCS; but this is subject to subsections (3) and (4).

定通知所需的任何信息。

(3)第二个理由为,金融服务补偿计划管理人不确信其能够为遵守第224C条规定通知从相关计划管理人处获得所需的任何建议或其他协助。

(4)第三个理由为,

(a)金融服务补偿计划管理人未收到与其预期就相关计划职能产生的总支出至少金额相等的款项;且

(b)下列任何一种情况:

(i)没有安排向金融服务补偿计划管理人提供资金,使其能够行使上述职能并支付上述支出;或

(ii)金融服务补偿计划管理人认为任何上述安排不符合要求。

(5)第四个理由为,金融服务补偿计划管理人认为遵守第224C条规定的通知会对其金融服务补偿计划规定的职能造成不利影响。

(6)第五个理由为,

(a)相关计划管理人未承诺不针对金融服务补偿计划管理人提起法律程序;或

(b)金融服务补偿计划管理人认为任何上述承诺不符合要求。

(7)第六个理由为,

(a)对金融服务补偿计划管理人就与其相关计划职能针对其提起的任何法律程序产生的任何支出(包括支付任何判令其支付的损害赔偿所产生的支出),未安排给予偿付。

(b)金融服务补偿计划管理人认为任何上述安排不符合要求。

(8)第(6)款所述承诺为,承诺不就金融服务补偿计划管理人的相关计划职能提起法律程序,但不包括就金融服务补偿计划管理人不真诚的作为或不作为提起的法律程序。

(9)本条中'法律程序'包括联合王国境外的法律程序。

规　　则

第224F条　相关计划的规则

(1)管理局可以制定规则,就金融服务补偿计划管理人行使与相关计划有关的职能作出规定。

(2)上述可由规则制定的规定包括任何与该金融服务补偿计划可包括的规定相应的规定;但符合第(3)款和第(4)款规定。

(3) The rules may confer on the FSCS manager a power to impose levies on authorised persons (or any class of authorised persons) for the purpose of meeting its management expenses incurred in connection with its functions in respect of relevant schemes.

(4) But if the rules confer such a power they must provide that the power may be exercised in relation to expenses incurred in connection with a relevant scheme only if the FSCS manager has tried its best to obtain reimbursement of the expenses from the manager of the relevant scheme.

(5) The rules may apply any provision of the FSCS, with or without modifications.

(6) An amount payable to the FSCS manager as a result of any provision of the rules made by virtue of subsection (3) may be recovered as a debt due to the FSCS manager.

(7) References to the FSCS manager's "management expenses" are to its expenses incurred otherwise than in paying compensation."

Powers to require information

18 Information relating to financial stability

(1) The Financial Services and Markets Act 2000 is amended as follows.

(2) After section 165 insert—

"165A Authority's power to require information: financial stability

(1) The Authority may, by notice in writing given to a person to whom this section applies, require the person—

(a) to provide specified information or information of a specified description; or

(b) to produce specified documents or documents of a specified description.

(2) This section applies to—

(a) a person who has a legal or beneficial interest in any of the assets of a relevant investment fund;

(b) a person who is responsible for the management of a relevant investment fund;

(c) a person (a "service provider") who provides any service to an authorised person;

(d) a person prescribed by an order made by the Treasury or any person of a description prescribed by such an order (and see also section 165C);

(e) a person who is connected with a person to whom this section applies as a result of any of the above paragraphs.

(3) This section applies only to information and documents that the Authority considers are, or might be, relevant to the stability of one or more aspects of the UK financial system.

(4) A notice may be given to a service provider, or to a person who is connected with a service provider, only if the Authority considers that—

(a) the service or the way in which it (or any part of it) is provided, or

(b) any failure to provide the service (or any part of it),

(3)规则可以规定金融服务补偿计划管理人有权向获授权人(或任何一类获授权人)征收费用,以支付其与相关计划有关的职能产生的相关管理支出。

(4)但如规则授予上述权力,则必须规定,对与相关计划有关而产生的支出,只有金融服务补偿计划管理人已尽最大努力从相关计划管理人处获得偿付,方可行使该项权力。

(5)规则可以经修改或不经修改适用于金融服务补偿计划的任何规定。

(6)因依照第(3)款制定的规则中的任何规定而应向金融服务补偿计划管理人支付的款项,可以作为应收债务予以追偿。

(7)述及金融服务补偿计划管理人的'管理支出',即为述及除支付补偿外产生的支出。"

要求提供信息的权力

第18条　与金融稳定相关的信息

(1)《2000年金融服务与市场法》修订如下。

(2)第165条后插入:

"第165A条　管理局要求提供相关信息的权力:金融稳定

(1)管理局可以向本条规定适用的人发出书面通知,要求该人

(a)提供规定的信息或规定类别的信息;或

(b)出示规定的文件或规定类别的文件。

(2)本条规定适用于

(a)在任何相关投资基金资产中具有法定权益或实益权益的人;

(b)负责管理相关投资基金的人;

(c)向获授权人提供任何服务的人(以下简称服务提供商);

(d)财政部发布的命令中规定的人或规定类别的人(并见第165C条);

(e)与因上述各项中的任何一项规定适用本条的人相关联的人。

(3)本条只适用于管理局认为与联合王国金融系统的一个或多个方面的稳定相关或可能与之相关的信息和文件。

(4)管理局只有认为有下列情况,才可以对服务提供商或与服务提供商有关联的人发出通知:

(a)服务或服务(或任何部分服务)提供的方式;或

(b)任何未能提供服务(或任何部分服务)的情况,

poses, or would be likely to pose, a serious threat to the stability of the UK financial system.

(5) Information or documents required under this section must be provided or produced—

(a) before the end of such reasonable period as may be specified; and

(b) at such place as may be specified.

(6) The Authority may require any information provided under this section to be provided in such form as it may reasonably require.

(7) The Authority may require—

(a) any information provided, whether in a document or otherwise, to be verified in such manner as it may reasonably require; or

(b) any document produced to be authenticated in such manner as it may reasonably require.

(8) In this section—

"management" includes any of the activities listed in Annex II to the UCITS directive;

"relevant investment fund" means an investment fund whose assets consist of or include financial instruments which—

(a) are traded in the United Kingdom; or

(b) were issued by a body incorporated in the United Kingdom;

"service" includes facility;

"specified" means specified in the notice.

(9) For the purposes of the definition of "relevant investment fund"—

(a) arrangements may constitute an investment fund even if there is only one person participating in the arrangements; and

(b) the reference to financial instruments has the meaning given by Article 4.1 (17) of the markets in financial instruments directive.

(10) For the purposes of this section a person is connected with another person ("A") if the person is or has at any relevant time been—

(a) a member of A's group;

(b) a controller of A;

(c) any other member of a partnership of which A is a member; or

(d) in relation to A, a person mentioned in Part 1 of Schedule 15 (reading references in that Part to the authorised person as references to A).

165B Safeguards etc in relation to exercise of power under section 165A

(1) If the Authority proposes to impose a requirement on a person under section 165A, it must give the person a notice in writing warning the person that the Authority is proposing to impose the requirement.

对联合王国金融系统的稳定造成或可能造成严重威胁。

(5)依照本条规定要求提供或出示的信息或文件必须

(a)在规定的合理期限届满前提供或出示;且

(b)在规定的地点提供。

(6)对依照本条规定要求提供的任何信息,管理局可以要求以其合理要求的形式提供。

(7)管理局可以要求

(a)对在文件中或以其他方式提供的任何信息以管理局合理要求的方式进行核实;或

(b)对出示的任何文件以管理局合理要求的方式进行验证。

(8)本条中

'管理'包括可转让证券集合投资计划附录2中所列任何活动;

'相关投资基金'系指资产由下列金融工具构成或包括下列金融工具的投资基金:

(a)在联合王国境内交易的金融工具;或

(b)由在联合王国境内设立的机构发行的金融工具;

'服务'包括设施;

'规定'系指在通知中规定。

(9)就'相关投资基金'而言

(a)即使只有一人参与安排,该安排亦可构成投资基金;且

(b)述及金融工具,具有金融工具市场指令第4.1条第(17)款规定的含义。

(10)就本条而言,一人如在任何时间有下列情况,则为与另一人(以下简称A)相关联:

(a)是A集团中的成员;

(b)是A的控制人;

(c)是A为成员的合伙中任何其他成员;或

(d)附录15第一部分所述与A有关的人(该部分述及获授权人视为述及A)。

第165B条 与依照第165A条行使权力相关的保障等

(1)如管理局拟依照第165A条规定对某人提出要求,则必须向该人发出书面通知,警告该人管理局拟提出该要求。

(2) The notice under subsection (1) must—

(a) give the Authority's reasons for proposing to impose the requirement; and

(b) specify a reasonable period within which the person may make representations to the Authority.

(3) The Authority must then decide, within a reasonable period, whether to impose the requirement.

(4) Subsections (1) to (3) do not apply in any case where the Authority is satisfied that it is necessary for the information or documents to be provided or produced without delay.

(5) If the Authority imposes a requirement on a person under section 165A, the notice under that section must give the Authority's reasons for imposing the requirement.

(6) The Authority must prepare a statement of its policy with respect to the exercise of the power conferred by section 165A.

(7) The statement requires the approval of the Treasury.

(8) If the Treasury approve the statement, the Authority must publish it.

(9) The power conferred by section 165A may not be exercised before the statement has been published.

165C Orders under section 165A(2)(d)

(1) The Treasury may make an order under section 165A(2)(d) only if they consider that—

(a) the activities carried on by the prescribed person or persons of the prescribed description, or the way in which those activities (or any part of them) are carried on, or

(b) any failure to carry on those activities (or any part of them), pose, or would be likely to pose, a serious threat to the stability of the UK financial system.

(2) Subject as follows, an order under section 165A(2)(d) may not be made unless a draft of the order has been laid before, and approved by a resolution of, each House of Parliament.

(3) Subsection (2) does not apply in any case where the Treasury are satisfied that it is necessary to make an order under section 165A(2)(d) without laying a draft for approval.

(4) In that case, the order—

(a) must be laid before Parliament after being made; and

(b) ceases to have effect at the end of the relevant period unless before the end of that period it is approved by a resolution of each House of Parliament.

(5) If an order ceases to have effect as a result of subsection (4)(b) that does not affect—

(a) anything done under it; or

(b) the power to make a new one.

(6) "Relevant period" means a period of 28 days beginning with the day on which the

(2)第(1)款规定的通知必须

(a)说明管理局拟提出该要求的理由;且

(b)指定该人可向管理局作出陈述的合理期限。

(3)管理局随后必须在合理期限内决定是否向该人发出决定通知。

(4)在任何情况下如管理局确信有必要毫不延迟地提供信息或文件,则第(1)款至第(3)款规定不适用。

(5)如管理局依照第165A条规定对当事人提出要求,则依照该条规定发出的通知必须说明管理局提出该要求的理由。

(6)管理局必须就行使第165A条赋予的权力制定政策声明。

(7)该声明须经财政部批准。

(8)如获得财政部批准,则管理局必须公布该声明。

(9)该声明公布前不得行使第165A条赋予的权力。

第165C条　第165A条第(2)款第(d)项规定的法令

(1)财政部只有认为有下列情况,方可依照第165A条第(2)款第(d)项规定颁布法令:

(a)规定的人或规定类别的人开展的活动或该活动(或其任何部分)开展的方式;或

(b)任何未能开展该活动(或其任何部分)的情况,对联合王国金融系统的稳定造成或可能造成严重威胁。

(2)受下列规定制约,第165A条第(2)款第(d)项规定的法令未经命令草案呈送议会并决议批准不得发布。

(3)在任何情况下,如财政部确信有必要不将草案呈送议会批准即依照第165A条第(2)款第(d)项颁布法令,则第(2)款规定不适用。

(4)在上述情况下,该法令

(a)必须在发布后呈送议会;且

(b)在相关期限届满之时停止生效,除非在该期限届满前得到议会决议批准。

(5)命令因第(4)款第(b)项规定停止生效不影响

(a)依照该法令实施的任何行为;或

(b)发布新法令的权力。

(6)'相关期限',系指自命令发出之日起28日的期限。

order is made.

(7) In calculating the relevant period no account is to be taken of any time during which Parliament is dissolved or prorogued or during which both Houses are adjourned for more than four days.

(8) If a statutory instrument containing an order under section 165A(2)(d) would, apart from this subsection, be treated as a hybrid instrument for the purposes of the Standing Orders of either House of Parliament, it is to proceed in that House as if it were not a hybrid instrument."

(3) After section 169 insert—

"169A Support of overseas regulator with respect to financial stability

(1) At the request of an overseas regulator, the Authority may exercise a corresponding section 165A power.

(2) An "overseas regulator" means an authority in a country or territory outside the United Kingdom which exercises functions with respect to the stability of the financial system operating in that country or territory.

(3) A "corresponding section 165A power" means a power corresponding to the one conferred by section 165A, but reading references in that section to the stability of the UK financial system as references to the stability of the financial system operating in the country or territory of the overseas regulator.

(4) The following provisions apply in relation to the exercise of the corresponding section 165A power—

(a) section 165B(1) to (5); and

(b) section 169(3), (4)(a) and (d), (5) and (6).

(5) In this section "the financial system" includes—

(a) financial markets and exchanges;

(b) activities that would be regulated activities if carried on in the United Kingdom; and

(c) other activities connected with financial markets and exchanges."

19 Asset protection scheme etc

(1) The Treasury may, by notice in writing, require a person who participates (or is proposing to participate) in the asset protection scheme or a qualifying scheme—

(a) to provide such information, or

(b) to produce such documents,

as they may reasonably require for the purposes of, or in connection with, the scheme or a relevant scheme agreement.

(2) "The asset protection scheme" means the scheme known as the Asset Protection Scheme that was the subject of a statement made by the Chancellor of the Exchequer on 26 February 2009.

(7)在计算相关期限时,议会解散或闭会期间的任何时间或议会上下两院均休会超过4天时的任何时间,不得考虑在内。

(8)如包含第165A条第(2)款第(d)项规定命令的行政性立法文件除本款规定外就议会任何议院议事规则而言被视为混合文件,则该文件在该议院处理时如同该文件不是混合文件。"

(3)第169条后插入:

"第169A条 向境外监管机关提供与金融稳定相关的支持

(1)应境外监管机关请求,管理局可以行使第165A条规定的相应权力。

(2)'境外监管机关',系指在联合王国以外的国家或地区就该国或该地区运行的金融系统稳定行使相关职能的机关。

(3)'第165A条相应权力',系指与第165A条赋予的权力相应的权力,但在该相应权力中,将该条中述及联合王国金融系统的稳定视为述及境外监管机关的国家或地区运行的金融系统稳定。

(4)下列规定就行使第165A条相应权力适用:

(a)第165B条第(1)款至第(5)款;以及

(b)第169条第(3)款、第(4)款第(a)项和第(d)项、第(5)款以及第(6)款。

(5)本条中'金融系统'包括:

(a)金融市场与交易所;

(b)如在联合王国开展即为受监管活动的活动;以及

(c)与金融市场和交易所相关联的其他活动。"

第19条 资产保护计划等

(1)财政部可以发出书面通知,要求参与(或拟参与)资产保护计划或相关计划的人

(a)提供信息;或

(b)出示文件,

该信息或文件是财政部为该计划或相关计划协议目的或与之相关合理要求提供的信息或文件。

(2)"资产保护计划",系指受财政大臣2009年2月26日发表声明的规范、称为"资产保护计划"的计划。

(3) "Qualifying scheme" means a scheme specified in an order made by the Treasury.

(4) "Relevant scheme agreement" means an agreement entered into (or proposed to be entered into) under the asset protection scheme or a qualifying scheme.

(5) The information or documents must be provided or produced at such times, and at such place, as the Treasury may specify in the notice.

(6) The Treasury may require the information to be provided in such form as they may reasonably require.

(7) A requirement imposed on a person as a result of this section is enforceable by an injunction or, in Scotland, by an order for specific performance under section 45 of the Court of Session Act 1988.

(8) The Treasury may specify a scheme in an order under subsection (3) only if it appears to them that the purpose of the scheme corresponds to, or is connected with, the purpose of the asset protection scheme.

(9) An order under subsection (3) is subject to negative resolution procedure.

Banking Act 2009

20 Services forming part of recognised inter-bank payment systems

In Part 5 of the Banking Act 2009 (inter-bank payment systems), after section 206 insert—

"206A Services forming part of recognised inter-bank payment systems

(1) The Treasury may by order make provision applying any provision of this Part to persons who are service providers in relation to a recognised inter-bank payment system.

(2) A person is a service provider in relation to a recognised inter-bank payment system if—

(a) the person provides services that form part of the arrangements constituting the system, and

(b) the person is specified as a person within paragraph (a) by the Treasury in the recognition order made in respect of the system.

(3) Telecommunication or information technology services are examples of the kind of services that may fall within subsection (2)(a).

(4) Before specifying persons under subsection (2)(b), the Treasury must—

(a) consult the Bank of England and the FSA,

(b) notify the operator of the system and the persons whom the Treasury proposes to specify, and

(c) consider any representations made.

(5) The Treasury may not specify the Bank of England under subsection (2)(b).

(6) Before making an order under subsection (1), the Treasury must consult—

(3)"相关计划",系指在财政部颁布的法令中规定的计划。

(4)"相关计划协议",系指依照资产保护计划或相关计划订立(或拟订立)的协议。

(5)信息或文件于财政部在通知中规定的时间和地点提供或出示。

(6)财政部可以要求以其合理要求的方式提供信息。

(7)因本条规定对当事人提出的要求可以通过强制令强制执行,在苏格兰可以通过《1988年最高民事法院法》第45条规定的实际履行令强制执行。

(8)对于第(3)款规定的计划,财政部只有认为该计划与财产保护计划的目的相应或相关联,才可以在法令中规定该计划。

(9)依照第(3)款规定颁布的法令符合反对决议程序规定。

《2009年银行法》

第20条　属于经认可的银行间支付系统的服务

《2009年银行法》第五部分(银行间支付系统)第206条后插入:

"第206A条　属于经认可的银行间支付系统的服务

(1)财政部可通过颁布法令制定规定,使本部分任何条款适用于为经认可的银行间支付系统担任服务提供商的人。

(2)如有下列情况,则为针对经认可的银行间支付系统担任服务提供商:

(a)为构成该系统的安排提供属于安排内容的服务;且

(b)在财政部就该系统发布的认可令中指定为属于第(a)项规定范围的人。

(3)电信和信息技术服务属于第(2)条第(a)项规定范围的服务。

(4)财政部在依照第(2)款第(b)项规定指定当事人前必须

(a)征求英格兰银行和管理局意见;

(b)通知该系统经营者和财政部拟指定之人;且

(c)考虑作出的任何陈述。

(5)财政部不得依照第(2)款第(b)项规定指定英格兰银行。

(6)依照第(1)款规定发出命令前,财政部必须向下列机构或人员征求意见:

(a) the Bank of England,

(b) the FSA, and

(c) such other persons as the Treasury consider appropriate.

(7) An order under subsection (1)—

(a) may modify any provision of this Part in its application to persons who are service providers in relation to a recognized inter-bank payment system;

(b) may (but need not) take the form of textual amendment.

(8) An order under subsection (1)—

(a) is to be made by statutory instrument, and

(b) may not be made unless a draft has been laid before and approved by resolution of each House of Parliament."

21 Minor amendments of provision made by Banking Act 2009

(1) The Banking Act 2009 is amended as follows.

(2) After section 48 insert—

"48A Creation of liabilities

(1) The provision that may be made by a property transfer instrument or order in reliance on section 33(1)(b), 42(3)(b), 43(3)(b), 44(4)(c), 45(3)(b) or 46(3)(b) includes provision for the creation of liabilities.

(2) The provision may be framed by reference to an agreement which has been or is to be entered into, or anything else which has been or is to be done, by any person (including a person other than the person making the instrument or order)."

(3) In section 55 (independent valuer: supplemental), at the end insert—

"(10) But subsection (9)(b)does not apply if the order is contained in a statutory instrument that contains an order to which section 62 applies."

(4) In section 56 (independent valuer: money)—

(a) in subsection (1), after paragraph (c) (but before the "and" at the end of it) insert—

"(ca) persons mentioned in section 54(4)(b), ", and

(b) at the end insert—

"(6) But subsection (5)(b)does not apply if the order is contained in a statutory instrument that contains an order to which section 62 applies."

(5) In section 84(application of Part 1 to building societies), in the entry in the table relating to sections 49 to 62, in paragraph (c) of the third column, at the end insert "but the Treasury may make a third party compensation order".

(6) In section 145(6) (bank administration: general powers, duties and effect), in table 1 of applied provisions (Schedule B1 to the Insolvency Act 1986), for the entry relating to paragraph 80 substitute—

(a)英格兰银行;

(b)管理局;以及

(c)财政部认为适当的其他人。

(7)第(1)款规定的命令

(a)在本部分任何规定适用于与经认可的银行间支付系统相关的服务提供商时,可进行修改;

(b)可以(但非必须)采取文本修正案形式。

(8)第(1)款规定的命令

(a)以行政性立法文件发布;且

(b)除非命令草案已呈送议会上下两院并经其批准,否则不得发布。”

第21条　对依照《2009年银行法》制定的规定进行的细微修订

(1)《2009年银行法》修订如下。

(2)第48条后插入:

“第48A条　责任创设

(1)财产转让文书或命令依照第33条第(1)款第(b)项、第42条第(3)款第(b)项、第43条第(3)款第(b)项、第44条第(4)款第(c)项、第45条第(3)款第(b)项或第46条第(3)款第(b)项可制定的规定包括创设责任的规定。

(2)规定的制定可以参照任何人(包括该文书或命令发出人以外的人)已签订或将签订的协议或已实施或将实施的任何行为。”

(3)第55条(独立估价人:补充规定)结尾处插入:

“(10)但如包含该命令的行政性立法文件包含适用第62条规定的命令,则第(9)款第(b)项规定不适用。”

(4)第56条(独立估价人:金钱)

(a)第(1)款第(c)项后(但在结尾处的“以及”前)插入:

“(ca)第54条第(4)款第(b)项所述之人,”

(b)结尾处插入:

“(6)但如包含该命令的行政性立法文件包含适用第62条规定的命令,则第(5)款第(b)项规定不适用。”

(5)第84条(第一部分规定适用于住房互助会),在与第49条至第62条相关的表格中,第三栏第(c)项结尾处插入“但财政部可发布第三方补偿令”。

(6)第145条第(6)款(银行管理:一般权力、职责和效力),适用规定表1(《1986年破产法》附录B1)中与第80条相关的条目替换为:

"Para. 79	Termination: successful rescue	(a) Ignore sub-para. (2). (b) See section 153."

(7) In section 153 (successful rescue), for subsections (2) and (3) substitute—

"(2) The bank administrator shall make an application under paragraph 79 of Schedule B1 to the Insolvency Act 1986 (court ending administration on achievement of objectives).

(3) A bank administrator who makes an application in accordance with subsection (2) must send a copy to the FSA."

(8) In section 219(3A) of the Financial Services and Markets Act 2000 (which was inserted by section 176(6) of the Banking Act 2009)—

(a) after "a bank," insert "building society or credit union,", and

(b) for "the bank or the Bank of England" substitute "the bank, building society or credit union, or the Bank of England,".

Director of Savings

22 Administration of court funds by Director of Savings

(1) In this section "relevant function" means a function of the Accountant General of the Senior Courts ("the Accountant General") under court funds rules.

(2) The Director of Savings ("the Director") may discharge a relevant function if appointed by the Accountant General under court funds rules to do so.

(3) The functions of the Director that are within section 69(1)(a) of the Deregulation and Contracting Out Act 1994 (contracting out of statutory functions) include any power of the Director, conferred under court funds rules, to discharge a relevant function.

(4) In this section "court funds rules" means rules under section 38(7) of the Administration of Justice Act 1982.

General

23 Orders or regulations

(1) This section applies to orders or regulations under this Act made by the Treasury or the Secretary of State.

(2) Orders or regulations—

(a) may contain incidental, supplementary, consequential, transitory, transitional or saving provision, and

(b) may make different provision for different cases or circumstances.

(3) Orders or regulations are to be made by statutory instrument.

(4) Where orders or regulations are subject to "affirmative resolution procedure" the orders or regulations may not be made unless a draft of the statutory instrument containing them has been laid before, and approved by a resolution of, each House of Parliament.

“第79项	终止:成功救援	(a)忽略第(2)款。 (b)见第153条。”

(7)第153条(成功救援)第(2)款、第(3)款替换为:

“(2)银行管理者应依照《1986年破产法》附录B1第79条(目标实现时法院结束管理)提出申请。

(3)依照第(2)款规定提出申请的银行管理者必须向管理局送交副本。”

(8)《2000年金融服务与市场法》第219条第(3A)款(依照《2009年银行法》第176条第(6)款插入):

(a)“银行”后插入“住房互助会或信用合作社”;以及

(b)“银行或英格兰银行”替换为“银行、住房互助会或信用合作社,或英格兰银行”。

储 蓄 理 事

第22条 储蓄理事管理法院经费

(1)本条中的“相关职能”,系指法院经费规则规定的高等法院总会计师(以下简称总会计师)职能。

(2)储蓄理事(以下简称理事)如经总会计师依照法院经费规则指派,则可履行相关职能。

(3)《1994年放松管制和外包法》第69条第(1)款第(a)项(法定职能外包)规定范围内的理事职能,包括法院经费规则赋予该理事的执行相关职能的任何权力。

(4)本条中“法院经费规则”,系指《1982年司法行政法》第38条第(7)款规定的规则。

一 般 规 定

第23条 命令或法规

(1)本条适用于依照本法由财政部或国务秘书制定的法令或法规。

(2)法令或法规

(a)可包含附带、补充、后继、暂时、过渡性或保留条款;且

(b)可以就不同案件或情况作出不同规定。

(3)法令或法规以行政性立法文件制定。

(4)如法令或法规符合“赞成决议程序制定”,则该法令或法规未经草案呈送议会两院并决议批准不得制定。

(5) Where orders or regulations are subject to "negative resolution procedure" the statutory instrument containing them is subject to annulment in pursuance of a resolution of either House of Parliament.

24 Minor and consequential amendments

(1) Schedule 2 contains minor and consequential amendments.

(2) In that Schedule—

(a) Part 1 contains amendments of the Financial Services and Markets Act 2000, and

(b) Part 2 contains amendments of other legislation.

(3) The Treasury or the Secretary of State may by order make such other provision amending, repealing or revoking any enactment as they consider necessary or expedient in consequence of any provision made by this Act.

(4) "Enactment" includes—

(a) an enactment contained in subordinate legislation within the meaning of the Interpretation Act 1978,

(b) an enactment contained in, or in an instrument made under, an Act of the Scottish Parliament,

(c) an enactment contained in, or in an instrument made under, Northern Ireland legislation, or

(d) an enactment contained in, or in an instrument made under, a Measure or Act of the National Assembly for Wales.

(5) An order under subsection (3) is subject to negative resolution procedure.

25 Extent

This Act extends to England and Wales, Scotland and Northern Ireland.

26 Commencement

(1) The following provisions of this Act come into force on the day on which this Act is passed—

(a) section 1,

(b) section 2(1) and(5) to (8) (subject, in the case of subsection (6),to the exception mentioned in paragraph (k)),

(c) section 3(1) and (4),

(d) sections 4 and 5,

(e) section 16,

(f) sections 19 to 23,

(g) in section 24—

(i) subsections(1) and (2) so far as relating to the paragraphs of Schedule 2 mentioned in paragraph (l), and

(ii) subsections (3) to (5),

(5)如法令或法规符合"反对决议程序制定",则包含该命令或条例的行政性立法文件可依照议会上院或下院决议废止。

第24条　细微及后续修订

(1)附录2包括细微及后续修订。

(2)此附录中

(a)第一部分包含对《2000年金融服务与市场法》的修订;以及

(b)第二部分包含对其他立法的修订。

(3)财政部或国务大臣,受本法制定的规定制约,在其认为必要或合宜的情况下,可颁布法令,规定修改、撤销或废止任何成文法。

(4)"成文法"包括:

(a)《1978年解释法》管辖下的附属立法中包含的成文法;

(b)包含于苏格兰议会法或根据该法制定的法律文书中的成文法;

(c)包含于北爱尔兰立法或根据该法制定的法律文书中的成文法;或

(d)包含于威尔士国民议会法或根据该法指定的法律文书中的成文法。

(5)依据第(3)款制定的命令受反对决议程序制约。

第25条　适用范围

本法管辖范围为英格兰、威尔士、苏格兰和北爱尔兰。

第26条　生效日期

(1)本法下列条款于本法获得通过之日生效:

(a)第1条,

(b)第2条第(1)款及第(5)款至第(8)款[第(6)款服从于本条第(k)项提及的例外],

(c)第3条第(1)款及第(4)款,

(d)第4条和第5条,

(e)第16条,

(f)第19条至第23条,

(g)第24条中

(i)第(1)款、第(2)款,只要与第(1)款所述附录2条款相关,以及

(ii)第(3)款至第(5)款,

(h) section 25,

(i) this section,

(j) section 27,

(k) Schedule 1 except so far as that Schedule relates to paragraph 13, 15 or 16 of Schedule 1A to the Financial Services and Markets Act 2000, and

(l) paragraphs 1 to 6, 11, 13, 16(1) and (2), 22, 24(1) and (2), 25, 27, 28, 30 to 32, 33(1) and (3), 34, 35, 37 to 45 and 48 of Schedule 2.

(2) The following provisions of this Act come into force at the end of the period of 2 months beginning with the day on which this Act is passed—

(a) section 3(2), (3) and (5),

(b) sections 6 to 12,

(c) section 18,

(d) section 24(1) and (2) so far as relating to the paragraphs of Schedule 2 mentioned in paragraph (e), and

(e) paragraphs 7 to 10,12,14,15,16(3),17 to 20,26,29,33(4),46 and 47 of Schedule 2.

(3) The other provisions of this Act come into force on such day as the Treasury or the Secretary of State may by order appoint (and different days may be appointed for different purposes).

(4) The Treasury or the Secretary of State may by order make such provision as they consider necessary or expedient for transitory, transitional or saving purposes in connection with the commencement of any provision made by this Act.

27 Short title

This Act may be cited as the Financial Services Act 2010.

(h)第25条,

(i)本条,

(j)第27条,

(k)附录一,但与《2000年金融服务与市场法》附录1A中第13条、第15条、第16条相关的条款除外,

(l)附录2第1条至第6条、第11条、第13条、第16条第(1)款和第(2)款、第22条、第24条第(1)款和第(2)款、第25条、第27条、第28条、第30条至第32条、第33条第(1)款和第(3)款、第34条、第35条、第37条至第45条以及第48条。

(2)本法下列条款于本法通过之日起2个月后生效:

(a)第3条第(2)款、第(3)款、第(5)款;

(b)第6条至第12条;

(c)第18条;

(d)第24条第(1)款、第(2)款,只要与第(e)项所述附录2条款相关;以及

(e)附录2第7条至第10条、第12条、第14条、第15条、第16条第(3)款、第17条至 第20条、第26条、第29条,第33条第(4)款,第46条、第47条。

(3)本法其他条款于财政部或国务大臣颁布的法令中规定的日期生效(根据不同意图指定不同日期)。

(4)财政部或国务大臣为了临时、过渡或保留的目的,在其认为必要或合宜的情况下,可发布命令,制定与本法任何条款生效时间相关的规定。

第27条　法律简称

本法可以简称为《2010年金融服务法》。

SCHEDULES

SCHEDULE 1 FURTHER PROVISION ABOUT THE CONSUMER FINANCIAL EDUCATION BODY

Section 2

1 This is the Schedule 1A to be inserted in the Financial Services and Markets Act 2000 after Schedule 1—

"SCHEDULE 1A FURTHER PROVISION ABOUT THE CONSUMER FINANCIAL EDUCATION BODY

Section 6A

PART 1 GENERAL

Ensuring exercise of consumer financial education function etc

1 (1) The Authority must take such steps as are necessary to ensure that the consumer financial education body is, at all times, capable of exercising the consumer financial education function.

(2) In complying with the duty under sub-paragraph (1) the Authority may,in

附　录

附录1　对金融教育机构作出进一步规定

第2条

第1条　本附录1A插入《2000年金融服务与市场法》附录1之后：

“附录1A　对金融教育机构作出进一步规定

第6A条

第一部分　总　则

确保履行消费者金融教育职能等

第1条　(1)金融管理局应采取必要措施，确保消费者金融教育机构可随时履行金融教育职能。

(2)为履行第(1)款所述职能，管理局可特别向其认可的有助于执行上述职能的

particular, provide services to that body which the Authority considers would facilitate the exercise of that function.

Constitution

2 (1) The constitution of the consumer financial education body must provide for it to have—

(a) a chair;

(b) a chief executive; and

(c) a board (which must include the chair and chief executive) whose members are the body's directors.

(2) The members of the board must be persons appointed, and liable to removal from office, by the Authority (acting, in the case of the chair or chief executive, with the approval of the Treasury).

(3) But the terms of appointment of members of the board (and in particular those governing removal from office) must be such as to secure their independence from the Authority in the exercise of the consumer financial education function.

(4) The Authority may appoint a person to be a member of the board only if it is satisfied that the person has knowledge or experience which is likely to be relevant to the exercise by the body of the consumer financial education function.

Status

3 (1) The consumer financial education body is not to be regarded as exercising functions on behalf of the Crown.

(2) The body's board members, officers and staff are not to be regarded as Crown servants.

Discharge of function by others

4 (1) The consumer financial education body may discharge the consumer financial education function by—

(a) supporting the doing by other persons of anything that it considers would enhance the understanding, knowledge or ability mentioned in section 6A(1); or

(b) arranging for other persons to do anything that it considers would enhance that understanding, knowledge or ability.

(2) The reference in sub-paragraph (1)(a) to support includes financial support.

(3) The reference in sub-paragraph (1)(b) to arrangements includes arrangements under which payments are made to the other persons.

(4) Nothing in this paragraph is to limit other ways in which the consumer financial

机构提供服务。

组织制度

第2条 (1)消费者金融教育机构组织制度应规定该机构设有:

(a)主席一名;
(b)首席执行官一名;及
(c)由机构董事组成的董事会(应当包括主席和首席执行官)。

(2)董事会董事应当由管理局(主席或首席执行官必须由财政部批准)任免。

(3)但任命董事会成员的条件(特别是关于免职的条件)应当保证他们在履行消费者金融教育的职能时独立于管理会。

(4)管理局只能任命满足具有相关执行消费者金融教育职能的知识和经验条件的人担任董事会成员。

地 位

第3条 (1)消费者金融教育机构不视为代表内阁履行职责。

(2)机构董事会成员、高级职员、工作人员不视为内阁公务人员。

其他履行职能者

第4条 (1)消费者金融教育机构可通过下列行为履行金融教育职能:

(a)支持第6A条第(1)款所述,其认为能增强理解、认知和能力的他人行为;或

(b)安排他人作出其认为能增强理解、认知和能力的任何行为。

(2)第1款第(a)项述及的支持包括财务支持。

(3)第1款第(b)项述及的安排包括向他人支付款项。

(4)本条规定不限制金融教育机构的其他履行金融教育职能的方式。

education body may discharge the consumer financial education function.

5 (1) This paragraph applies if the consumer financial education body arranges for any person (including one established by or under an enactment) to do anything that it considers would enhance the understanding, knowledge or ability mentioned in section 6A(1).

(2) The person may do that thing despite any limitation on its capacity (whether under a rule of law or otherwise) which, but for this paragraph, would have applied.

Market confidence and financial stability

6 In discharging the consumer financial education function, the consumer financial education body must have regard to the importance of—

(a) maintaining confidence in the UK financial system; and

(b) maintaining the stability of the UK financial system.

Budget

7 (1) The consumer financial education body must adopt an annual budget which has been approved by the Authority.

(2) The budget must be adopted—

(a) in the case of the body's first financial year, as soon as reasonably practicable after the body is established; and

(b) in the case of each subsequent financial year, before the start of the financial year.

(3) The consumer financial education body may, with the approval of the Authority, vary the budget for a financial year at any time after its adoption.

(4) Before adopting or varying a budget, the consumer financial education body must consult—

(a) the Treasury;

(b) the Secretary of State;

(c) the Office of Fair Trading; and

(d) such other persons (if any) as the body considers appropriate.

(5) The consumer financial education body must publish each budget, and each variation of a budget, in the way it considers appropriate.

Annual plan

8 (1) The consumer financial education body must in respect of each of its financial years prepare an annual plan which has been approved by the Authority.

(2) The plan must be prepared—

(a) in the case of the body's first financial year, as soon as reasonably practicable after the body is established; and

第5条 (1)如金融教育机构安排他人(包括成文法或依据现行法确定的人)从事其认为能增强第6A条第(1)款所述理解、认知和能力的行为,则适用本条规定。

(2)该人可从事这些行为,无论是否超出如无本条规定则对其适用的身份限制(无论是否为依照法规适用)。

市场信心和金融稳定

第6条 履行消费者金融教育职能时,金融教育机构应重视

(a)保持联合王国金融系统的信心;以及
(b)保持联合王国金融系统的稳定。

预 算

第7条 (1)金融教育机构应采用经管理局批准的年度预算;

(2)预算应在下列时间采用:
(a)在第一个财政年度,机构一经建立应尽快合理可行地采用预算;

(b)在后续的财政年度,在每个财政年度开始前采用预算。
(3)金融教育机构经管理局批准,在年度财政预算被采用后可随时变更。

(4)采用或变更预算前,金融教育机构应向下列机构或人员征求意见:

(a)财政部;
(b)国务大臣;
(c)公平交易办公室;以及
(d)其他金融教育机构认为适当的人员(如果有)。
(5)金融教育机构应以其认为适当的方式公布财政预算或预算的变更。

年 度 计 划

第8条 (1)金融教育机构应针对每一财政年度制定年度计划,并经管理局批准。

(2)计划的制定应符合下列规定:
(a)在机构第一个财政年度,机构一经建立应尽快合理可行地制定计划;且

(b) in the case of each subsequent financial year, before the start of the financial year.

(3) The consumer financial education body may, with the approval of the Authority, vary the plan in respect of a financial year at any time after its preparation.

(4) An annual plan in respect of a financial year must set out—

(a) the objectives of the consumer financial education body for the year;

(b) how the extent to which each of those objectives is met is to be determined;

(c) the relative priorities of each of those objectives; and

(d) how its resources are to be allocated among the activities to be carried on in connection with the discharge of the consumer financial education function.

(5) In sub-paragraph (4) references to objectives for a financial year include objectives for a longer period that includes that year.

(6) Before preparing or varying an annual plan, the consumer financial education body must consult—

(a) the Treasury;

(b) the Secretary of State;

(c) the Office of Fair Trading;

(d) the Practitioner Panel;

(e) the Consumer Panel; and

(f) such other persons (if any) as the body considers appropriate.

(7) The consumer financial education body must publish each annual plan, and each variation of an annual plan, in the way it considers appropriate.

Annual reports

9 (1) At least once a year, the consumer financial education body must make a report to the Authority in relation to the discharge of the consumer financial education function.

(2) The report must—

(a) set out the extent to which the body has met its objectives and priorities for the period covered by the report;

(b) include a copy of its latest accounts; and

(c) comply with any requirements specified in rules made by the Authority.

(3) The consumer financial education body must publish each report in the way it considers appropriate.

(4) Nothing in this paragraph requires the consumer financial education body to make a report at any time in the period of 12 months beginning with its establishment.

Exemption from consumer credit rules

10 (1) A licence is not required under Part 3 of the Consumer Credit Act 1974 in

(b)在机构后续财政年度,应在每个财政年度开始前制定计划。
(3)金融教育机构经管理局批准,在年度计划制定后可随时变更。

(4)每财政年度的年度计划应设定
(a)金融教育机构本年度的目标;
(b)决定每一目标须完成到何种程度;
(c)每一目标对应的优先权;以及
(d)如何为与履行金融教育机构职能相关的行动分配资源。

(5)第(4)款中,述及财政年度目标包括从该年度开始的长期目标。

(6)准备或变更年度计划前,金融教育机构应向下列机构或人员征求意见:

(a)财政部;
(b)国务大臣;
(c)公平交易办公室;
(d)从业人员小组;
(e)消费者小组;以及
(f)机构认为适当的其他人员(如有)。
(7)金融教育机构应以其认为适当的方式公布年度计划或计划的变更。

年度报告

第9条 (1)金融教育机构应当每年至少向管理局提交一次关于履行其职能方面的报告。
(2)报告应当
(a)设定机构完成其目标的程度及报告所涉时段的工作重点;

(b)包含最新账目副本;以及
(c)遵照管理局规定中明确的要求。
(3)金融教育机构应以其认为适当的方式公布每项报告。

(4)本条不要求金融教育机构在其成立之日起12个月之内的任何时间作出报告。

消费信贷原则的豁免

第10条 (1)依照《1974年消费信贷法》第三部分,下列行为不需要许可证:

respect of anything done by—

(a) the consumer financial education body in discharging the consumer financial education function; or

(b) a person acting on its behalf in accordance with arrangements made under paragraph 4(1)(b).

(2) Nothing in Part 4 or 10 of that Act (seeking business or ancillary credit business) is to apply in relation to anything done by—

(a) the consumer financial education body in discharging the consumer financial education function; or

(b) a person acting on its behalf in accordance with arrangements made under paragraph 4(1)(b).

PART 2 FUNDING

Meaning of "the relevant costs"

11 (1) In this Part of this Schedule "the relevant costs" means—

(a) the expenses incurred by the Authority in establishing the consumer financial education body; and

(b) the expenses incurred, or expected to be incurred, by the consumer financial education body in connection with the discharge of the consumer financial education function.

(2) For the purposes of sub-paragraph(1)(a)it does not matter when the expenses were incurred.

Funding of the relevant costs by authorised persons or payment service providers

12 (1) For the purpose of meeting a proportion of the relevant costs the Authority may makes rules requiring—

(a) authorised persons or payment service providers, or

(b) any specified class of authorised person or payment service provider,

to pay to the Authority specified amounts or amounts calculated in a specified way.

(2) Before making the rules the Authority must have regard to other anticipated sources of funding of the relevant costs.

(3) The amounts to be paid under the rules may include a component to cover the expenses of the Authority in collecting the payments ("collection costs").

(4) The Authority must pay to the consumer financial education body the amounts that it receives under the rules apart from amounts in respect of its collection costs (which it may keep).

(5) "Payment service provider" means a person who is a payment service provider for

(a)金融教育机构履行其金融教育职能;或

(b)当事人按照第4条第(1)款第(b)项制定的安排进行的个人行为。

(2)该法第四部分或第十部分(寻求交易或附属信贷交易)不适用于下列行为:

(a)金融教育机构履行其金融教育职能;或

(b)当事人按照第4条第(1)款第(b)项制定的安排进行的个人行为。

第二部分 资 金

‘相关费用’的定义

第11条 (1)在本附录中,‘相关费用’系指

(a)管理局因建立金融教育机构产生的费用;及

(b)金融教育机构因履行其金融教育职责产生的或预期产生的费用。

(2)为第(1)款第(a)项之目的产生的费用无时间限制。

获授权人或支付服务提供商对相关费用的筹集

第12条 (1)为筹集部分相关费用,管理局可制定规则,要求

(a)获授权人、支付服务提供商;或

(b)任何规定类型的获授权人或支付服务提供商,

向管理局支付一定费用或经特定方式计算的费用。

(2)制定规则前,管理局应参考其他预期的相关费用筹款来源。

(3)根据规则支付的费用可包括管理局收集筹款的成本(以下简称收款成本)。

(4)管理局应向金融教育机构支付依照规则收到的款项,但不包括与收款成本相关的费用(管理局可以保留)。

(5)‘支付服务提供商’,系指《2009年支付服务法》第2条第(1)款第(a)项至第(f)

the purposes of the Payment Services Regulations 2009 as a result of falling within any of paragraphs (a) to (f) of the definition in regulation 2(1).

(6) "Specified" means specified in the rules.

Funding of the relevant costs by consumer credit licensees etc

13 (1) For the purpose of meeting a proportion of the relevant costs the OFT may, with the approval of the Secretary of State and the Treasury, from time to time require—

(a) qualifying consumer credit licensees or applicants, or

(b) any specified class of qualifying consumer credit licensee or applicant, to pay to the OFT specified amounts or amounts calculated in a specified way.

(2) The requirements are to be imposed by general notice.

(3) "Qualifying consumer credit licensee or applicant" means—

(a) a licensee under a licence which covers to any extent the carrying on of a type of business specified in an order under section 226A(2)(e); or

(b) an applicant for a licence, or for the renewal of a licence, which (if granted or renewed) will fall within paragraph (a) above.

(4) Before giving a general notice the OFT must have regard to other anticipated sources of funding of the relevant costs.

(5) Before giving a general notice, the OFT must consult—

(a) the Authority;

(b) the consumer financial education body; and

(c) such other persons (if any) as the OFT considers appropriate.

(6) The amounts to be paid under a general notice may include a component to cover the expenses of the OFT in collecting the payments ("collection costs").

(7) The OFT must pay to the consumer financial education body the amounts that it receives under a general notice apart from amounts in respect of its collection costs (which it may keep).

(8) A general notice may—

(a) specify the time at or by which the payments are to be made;

(b) provide for exceptions from requirements imposed on a class of qualifying consumer credit licensee or applicant;

(c) impose different requirements on different classes of qualifying consumer credit licensee or applicant;

(d) make provision for refunds in specified circumstances.

(9) Expressions which are used in sub-paragraph (3) and in the Consumer Credit Act 1974 have the same meaning in that subparagraph as in that Act.

项定义的支付服务提供商。

(6)'规定'系指(管理局)规则中的规定。

消费信贷执照持有人对相关费用的筹集

第13条 (1)为筹集部分的相关费用,公平交易办公室可经国务大臣及财政部批准,不时要求

(a)有资格的消费信贷执照持有人或申请人;或

(b)任何特定类型的消费信贷执照持有者或申请人,向公平交易办公室支付一定费用或经特定方式计算的费用。

(2)要求通过常规通知的方式实施。

(3)'有资格的消费信贷执照持有人或申请人'系指

(a)许可依据第226A条第(2)款第(e)项发布的命令中指定交易的执照的持有人;或

(b)属于第(a)项规定范围的执照或更新执照申请人(如申请或更新成功)。

(4)在发出常规通知前,公平交易办公室应参考其他预期的相关费用筹款来源。

(5)在发出常规通知前,公平交易办公室应向下列机构或人员征求意见:

(a)管理局;

(b)金融教育机构;且

(c)公平交易办公室认为适当的人(如有)。

(6)根据常规通知支付的费用可包括公平交易办公室收集筹款的成本(以下简称收款成本)。

(7)公平交易办公室应向金融教育机构支付依照常规通知收到的款项,但不包括与收款成本相关的费用(公平交易办公室可保留)。

(8)常规通知可以

(a)规定费用支付的具体时间或截止日期;

(b)对某类型的消费者信用执照持有者或申请人的豁免;

(c)对不同类型的消费者信用执照持有者或申请人提出不同的要求;

(d)特殊情况下制定偿还条款。

(9)第(3)款中的表述与《1974年消费信贷法》中的表述在本法中含义相同。

(10) In this paragraph—

"general notice" means a notice published by the OFT at a time and in a manner appearing to it suitable for securing that the notice is seen within a reasonable time by persons likely to be affected by it;

"the OFT" means the Office of Fair Trading;

"specified" means specified in the general notice.

Funding by grants or loans etc made by Treasury or Secretary of State

14 (1) The Treasury or the Secretary of State may—

(a) make grants or loans, or

(b) provide any other form of financial assistance,

to the consumer financial education body for the purpose of meeting any expenses incurred by it in connection with the discharge of the consumer financial education function.

(2) Any grant or loan or other form of financial assistance under this paragraph may be made or provided subject to such terms as the Treasury or the Secretary of State consider appropriate.

(3) Any expenses incurred by the Treasury or the Secretary of State under this paragraph are to be met out of money provided by Parliament.

PART 3 REVIEWS

Reviews of economy etc of the consumer financial education body

15 (1) The Authority may appoint an independent person to conduct a review of the economy, efficiency and effectiveness with which the onsumer financial education body has used its resources in discharging the consumer financial education function.

(2) The Authority must consult the Treasury before acting under this paragraph.

(3) A review is not to be concerned with the merits of the body's general policy or principles in discharging the consumer financial education function.

(4) On completion of a review, the person conducting it must make a written report to the Authority—

(a) setting out the result of the review; and

(b) making such recommendations (if any) as the person considers appropriate.

(5) The Authority must publish a copy of the report in the way it considers appropriate.

(6) Any expenses reasonably incurred in the conduct of the review are to be met by the Authority.

(7) "Independent" means appearing to the Authority to be independent of the consumer financial education body.

(10)本条中

'常规通知',系指公平交易办公室在一段时间内以其认为适当的方式发布,并确保可能受该通知影响的人在合理的时间内看到的通知;

'OFT'系指公平交易办公室;

'规定'系指常规通知中规定。

财政部或国务大臣的划拨或借贷等其他方式的筹款

第14条 (1)财政部或国务大臣可以

(a)划拨或借贷;或

(b)提供其他形式的财政资助,

以抵消金融教育机构为履行其职能产生的花费。

(2)任何符合本条规定提供的划拨、贷款或其他形式的财政资助,服从财政部或国务大臣认为适当的原则。

(3)财政部或国务大臣依照本条产生的费用,从议会提供的经费中拨付。

第三部分 复 核

金融教育机构经济状况的复核

第15条 (1)管理局可任命独立的人复核金融教育机构在履行其金融教育职能过程中使用资源的节约情况、效率和效果。

(2)管理局在执行此项复核前应征求财政部意见。

(3)复核不考虑机构履行其金融教育职能的总政策和原则。

(4)复核完成时,复核人应当向管理局提交书面报告

(a)说明复核结果;以及

(b)提出复核人认为适当的建议(如有)。

(5)管理局应以其认为适当的方式发布报告的副本。

(6)执行复核过程中产生的合理费用由管理局支付。

(7)'独立'指管理局认定独立于金融教育机构。

Right to obtain documents and information

16 (1) A person conducting a review under paragraph 15—

(a) has a right of access at any reasonable time to all such documents as the person may reasonably require for the purposes of the review; and

(b) may require any person holding or accountable for any such document to provide such information and explanation as are reasonably required for those purposes.

(2) This paragraph applies only to documents in the custody or under the control of the consumer financial education body.

(3) An obligation imposed on a person as a result of this paragraph is enforceable by an injunction or, in Scotland, by an order for specific performance under section 45 of the Court of Session Act 1988."

2 (1) This paragraph applies to rules under paragraph 12 of Schedule 1A to FSMA 2000 (as inserted by this Schedule).

(2) The FSA may before commencement—

(a) propose to make rules under that paragraph, and

(b) publish a draft of the proposed rules in the way appearing to it to be best calculated to bring them to the attention of the public.

(3) The draft must be accompanied by—

(a) an explanation of the purpose of the proposed rules,

(b) an explanation of the FSA's reasons for believing that making the proposed rules is compatible with its general duties under section 2 of FSMA 2000,

(c) notice that representations about the proposals may be made to the FSA within a specified time, and

(d) details of the expected expenditure by reference to which the proposal is made.

(4) Before making the proposed rules after commencement, the FSA must have regard to any representations made to it in accordance with sub-paragraph (3)(c).

(5) If the FSA makes the proposed rules, it must publish an account, in general terms, of—

(a) the representations made to it in accordance with sub-paragraph (3)(c), and

(b) its response to them.

(6) If the rules differ from the draft published under sub-paragraph (2) in a way which is, in the FSA's opinion, significant, the FSA must (in addition to complying with sub-paragraph (5)) publish details of the difference.

(7) If the FSA acts in accordance with this paragraph, section 155 of FSMA 2000 (which contains corresponding provision) does not apply.

(8) The FSA may charge a reasonable fee for providing a person with a copy of a draft

文件和信息的获得权

第16条 (1)依据第15条执行复核的人

(a)有权为了复核目的合理要求在任何合理时间取得相应文件;并且

(b)可以要求相应文献的持有人或责任人提供为复核目的合理要求提供的信息和说明。

(2)本条适用于由金融教育机构保存或控制的文件。

(3)本条加于当事人的义务可通过强制令强制执行,或在苏格兰依据《1988年最高民事法院法》第45条发布的实际履行令强制执行。"

第2条 (1)本条适用于《2000年金融服务与市场法》附录1A第12条(依照本附录插入)规定的规则。

(2)管理局在本条生效前

(a)可以提议依照该条制定规则;且

(b)应当以其认为最便于公众了解的方式发布拟制定规则的草案。

(3)草案应附有下列内容:

(a)说明拟制定规则的目的;

(b)管理局以何种理由认为制定拟制定的规则不违背《2000年金融服务与市场法》第2条规定的一般职责;

(c)关于在规定时间内就拟制定的规则向管理局作出陈述的通知;以及

(d)详细说明制定拟制定规则预期的支出。

(4)成立后制定拟制定规则前,管理局应当已考虑任何依照第(3)款第(c)项向管理局作出的陈述。

(5)如管理局已制定拟制定的规则,则应当公布概述下列内容的报告:

(a)依照第(3)款第(c)项向管理局作出的陈述;及

(b)管理局对上述陈述的答复。

(6)如管理局认为,拟制定的规则与依照本条第(2)款公布的草案之间存在明显差异,则管理局[除遵守第(5)款规定外]应当公布差异的详情。

(7)如管理局依照本条采取行动,则《2000年金融服务与市场法》第155条(包括相应的条款)不适用。

(8)管理局可以为向他人提供依照第(2)款发布的草案副本收取合理费用。

published under sub-paragraph (2).

(9) In this paragraph—

"commencement" means the commencement of paragraph 12 of Schedule 1A to FSMA 2000;

"the FSA" means the Financial Services Authority;

"FSMA 2000" means the Financial Services and Markets Act 2000.

SCHEDULE 2
MINOR AND CONSEQUENTIAL AMENDMENTS

Section 24

PART 1 AMENDMENTS OF FINANCIAL SERVICES AND MARKETS ACT 2000

1 The Financial Services and Markets Act 2000 is amended as follows.

2 (1) Section 3 (market confidence) is amended as follows.

(2) In subsection (1), for "the financial system" substitute "the UK financial system".

(3) In subsection (2), for"The financial system"substitute"In this Act"the UK financial system"".

3 Until the commencement of the repeal of section 4 (public awareness) by section 2 (3) of this Act, section 4 has effect as if—

(a) the reference in subsection (1) to the financial system were to the UK financial system, and

(b) subsection (3) were omitted.

4 In section 5 (the protection of consumers), for subsection (3) substitute—

"(3) Sections 425A and 425B (meaning of "consumers") apply for the purposes of this section."

5 In section 10 (the Consumer Panel), for subsection (7) substitute—

"(7) Sections 425A and 425B (meaning of "consumers") apply for the purposes of this section, but the references to consumers in this section do not include consumers who are authorised persons."

6 (1) Section 14 (cases in which the Treasury may arrange independent inquiries) is amended as follows.

(2) In subsection (2)(a), for "the financial system" substitute "the UK financial system".

(9)本条中

“生效”系指《2000年金融服务与市场法》附录1A第12条生效；

“管理局”系指金融服务管理局；

“FSMA2000”系指《2000年金融服务与市场法》。

附录2　细微及后续修订

第24条

第一部分　《2000年金融服务与市场法》修订

第1条　《2000年金融服务与市场法》修订如下。

第2条　(1)第3条(市场信心)修订如下。

(2)第(1)款中“金融系统”替换为“联合王国金融系统”。

(3)第(2)款中“金融系统”替换为“本法中‘联合王国金融系统’”。

第3条　直至依照本法第2条第(3)款规定废除第4条(公众意识)为止,第4条具有效力,等同于

(a)第(1)款中述及金融系统为述及联合王国金融系统,且

(b)删除第(3)款规定。

第4条　第5条(保护消费者)第(3)款替换为:

“(3)为本条之目的适用第425A条和第425B条(‘消费者’的含义)。”

第5条　第10条(消费者协会)第(7)款替换为:

“(7)为本条之目的适用第425A条和第425B条(‘消费者’的含义),但本条中述及消费者不包括获授权人消费者。”

第6条　(1)第14条(财政部可安排独立调查的情况)修订如下。

(2)第(2)款第(a)项中“金融系统”替换为“联合王国金融系统”。

(3) For subsection (5) substitute—

"(5) Sections 425A and 425B (meaning of "consumers") apply for the purposes of this section."

(4) Omit subsection (6).

7 In the italic cross-heading before section 64, at the end insert "*of approved persons*".

8 (1) Section 66 (performance of regulated activities: disciplinary powers) is amended as follows.

(2) After subsection (5) insert—

"(5A) "Approval" means an approval given under section 59."

(3) In subsection (7), omit "under section 59".

(4) After that subsection insert—

"(8) In relation to any time while a suspension is in force under subsection (3)(aa) in relation to part of a function, any reference in section 59 or 63A to the performance of a function includes the performance of part of a function.

(9) If at any time a restriction imposed under subsection (3)(ab) is contravened, the approval in relation to the person concerned is to be treated for the purposes of sections 59 and 63A as if it had been withdrawn at that time."

9 (1) Section 67 (disciplinary measures: procedure and right to refer to Tribunal) is amended as follows.

(2) In subsection (1), at the end insert "; and if it proposes to take action under subsection (3)(aa) or (ab) of that section, it must also give each of the other interested parties a warning notice."

(3) After subsection (2) insert—

"(2A) A warning notice about a proposal—

(a) to suspend an approval, or

(b) to impose a restriction in relation to the performance of a function, must state the period for which the suspension or restriction is to have effect."

(4) In subsection(4), at the end insert"; and if it decides to take action under subsection (3)(aa) or(ab) of that section, it must also give each of the other interested parties a decision notice."

(5) After subsection (5) insert—

"(5A) A decision notice about—

(a) the suspension of an approval, or

(b) the imposition of a restriction in relation to the performance of a function,

must state the period for which the suspension or restriction is to have effect."

(6) In subsection(7), at the end insert"; and if the Authority decides to take action under

(3)第(5)款替换为:

"(5)为本条之目的适用第425A和425B条('消费者'的含义)。"

(4)删除第(6)款。

第7条 第64条前的斜体字小标题前插入"获批准人的"。

第8条 (1)第66条(开展受监管活动:惩戒权)修订如下。

(2)第(5)款后插入:

"(5A)'批准'系指依照第59条规定给予的批准。"

(3)第(7)款中删除"依照第59条规定"。

(4)该款后插入:

"(8)依照第(3)款第(aa)项对某项职能部分内容的终止有效期间内的任何时间,第59条或第63A条所述履行职能包括履行该项职能其部分内容。

(9)如在任何时间违反第(3)款第(ab)项规定的限制,则与相关人有关的批准就第59条及第63A条而言视为在违反限制时已撤销。"

第9条 (1)第67条(惩戒措施:程序和诉至裁判所的权利)修订如下。

(2)第(1)款中结尾处插入";如拟依照该条第(3)款第(aa)项或第(ab)项规定采取行动,则还必须向其他各利害关系人发出预告通知。"

(3)第(2)款后插入:

"(2A)关于下列拟采取行动的预告通知:

(a)终止批准;或

(b)就行使某项职能提出相关限制,

必须说明终止或限制有效的期限。"

(4)第(4)款中结尾处插入";如决定依照该条第(3)款第(aa)项或第(ab)项规定采取行动,则还必须向其他各利害关系人发出决定通知。"

(5)第(5)款后插入:

"(5A)关于下列行动的决定通知:

(a)终止批准;或

(b)就行使某项职能提出相关限制,

必须说明终止或限制有效的期限。"

(6)第(7)款结尾处插入";如管理局决定依照第66条第(3)款第(aa)项或第(ab)项

section 66(3)(aa) or(ab), each of the other interested parties may also refer the matter to the Tribunal."

(7) After that subsection insert—

"(8) "Approval" means an approval given under section 59.

(9) "Other interested parties", in relation to an approved person ("A"), are—

(a) the person on whose application the approval was given ("B"); and

(b) the person by whom A's services are retained, if not B.

The reference in this subsection to an approved person has the same meaning as in section 64."

10 (1) Section 69 (statement of policy) is amended as follows.

(2) In subsection (1), for paragraphs (a) and (b) substitute—

"(a) the imposition of penalties, suspensions or restrictions under section 66;

(b) the amount of penalties under that section; and

(c) the period for which suspensions or restrictions under that section are to have effect."

(3) In subsection (2)—

(a) in the opening words, after "should be" insert ", or what the period for which a suspension or restriction is to have effect should be, ", and

(b) in paragraph (c), for "the person on whom the penalty is to be imposed" substitute "the person against whom action is to be taken".

11 In section 138 (general rule-making power), omit subsections (3) and (7) to (9).

12 In section 150(4) (actions for damages), after paragraph (a) (but before the "or" at the end of it) insert—

"(aa) rules under section 131B (short selling rules); ".

13 In section 155(9)(consultation: exception to general rule that cost benefit analysis required), after paragraph (d) insert—

"(e) paragraph 12 of Schedule 1A."

14 In section 157 (guidance), after subsection (3) insert—

"(3A) Subsection (3) also applies in relation to guidance which the Authority proposes to give to persons generally, or to a class of person, in relation to rules under section 131B (short selling rules) to which those persons are subject."

15 In section 165(FSA's power to require information), in the heading, at the end insert ": authorised persons etc".

16 (1) Section 168(appointment of persons to carry out investigations in particular cases) is amended as follows.

(2) In subsection(4),in paragraph(c), for "an authorised person" substitute "a person".

规定采取行动,则各其他利害关系人也可将该事项诉至裁判所。”

(7)该款后插入:

“(8)‘批准’系指依照第59条规定给予的批准。

(9)‘其他利害关系人’就获批准人(以下简称A)而言,为

(a)应其申请给予批准的申请人(以下简称B);以及

(b)聘用A提供服务的人(如不是B)。

本款中述及获批准人含义与第64条中的含义相同。”

第10条 (1)第69条(政策声明)修订如下。

(2)第(1)款中第(a)项和第(b)项替换为:

“(a)依照第66条规定处以罚款、终止或限制;

(b)依照该条规定处以罚款的数额;以及

(c)依照该条规定提出的终止或限制有效的期限。”

(3)第(2)款中

(a)引言中“应”后插入“或终止或限制有效的期限应”,

(b)第(c)项中“被处以罚款之人”替换为“针对其采取行动的人”。

第11条 第138条(一般规则制定权),删除第(3)款及第(7)款至第(9)款。

第12条 第150条第(4)款(损害赔偿诉讼)第(a)项后(但在结尾处的“或”前)插入:

“(aa)第131B条(卖空规则)规定的规则。”

第13条 第155条第(9)款(征求意见:要求进行成本效益分析的一般规则的例外情况)第(d)项后插入:

“(e)附录1A第12项。”

第14条 第157条(指引)第(3)款后插入:

“(3A)管理局拟向受第131B条(卖空规则)项下规则制约的人或一类人就该规则发出通用指引的,亦适用第(3)款规定。”

第15条 第165条(管理局要求提供信息的权利),小标题结尾处插入“:获授权人等”。

第16条 (1)第168条(委派人员在特别情况下开展调查)修订如下。

(2)第(4)款第(c)项中“获授权人”替换为“人”。

(3) In that subsection, after paragraph (h) insert—

"(ha) a person may have performed a controlled function without approval for the purposes of section 63A; ".

17 In section 176(11)(a) (entry of premises under warrant), after "165" insert ", 165A, 169A".

18 (1) Section 207 (proposal to take disciplinary measures) is amended as follows.

(2) In subsection(1), omit the"or" before paragraph(b)and at the end of that paragraph insert "or

(c) to suspend a permission of an authorised person or impose a restriction in relation to the carrying on of a regulated activity by an authorised person (under section 206A), ".

(3) At the end insert—

"(4) A warning notice about a proposal to suspend a permission or impose a restriction must state the period for which the suspension or restriction is to have effect."

19 (1) Section 208 (decision notice) is amended as follows.

(2) In subsection (1), omit the "or" before paragraph (b)and at the end of that paragraph insert "or

(c) to suspend a permission or impose a restriction under section 206A (whether or not in the manner proposed), ".

(3) After subsection (3) insert—

"(3A) In the case of a suspension or restriction, the decision notice must state the period for which the suspension or restriction is to have effect."

(4) In subsection(4),omit the"or" before paragraph (b) and at the end of hat paragraph insert "or

(c) suspend a permission of an authorised person, or impose a restriction in relation to the carrying on of a regulated activity by an authorised person, under section 206A, ".

20 (1) Section 210 (statements of policy) is amended as follows.

(2) In subsection (1), for paragraphs (a) and (b) substitute—

"(a) the imposition of penalties, suspensions or restrictions under this Part;

(b) the amount of penalties under this Part; and

(c) the period for which suspensions or restrictions under this Part are to have effect."

(3) In subsection (2)—

(a) in the opening words, after "should be" insert ", or what the period for which a suspension or restriction is to have effect should be, ", and

(b) in paragraph (c), for "the person on whom the penalty is to be imposed" substitute "the person against whom action is to be taken".

(4) In subsection (7), after "206" insert "or 206A".

21 In section 212(2) (the scheme manager), after "those functions" insert "and the

(3)该款中第(h)项后插入:

"(ha)为第63A条之目的,某人可能已未经批准履行受监管职能"。

第17条 第176条第(11)款第(a)项(持授权令进入现场)中"第165条"后插入"、第165A条和第169A条"。

第18条 (1)第207条(采取惩戒措施的计划)修订如下。

(2)第(1)款中删除第(b)项前的"或",在该项结尾处插入"或

(c)对获授权人开展的受监管活动终止许可或提出限制(依照第206A条规定)。"

(3)结尾处插入:

"(4)关于拟终止许可或提出限制的预告通知,必须说明该终止或限制有效的期限。"

第19条 (1)第208条(决定通知)修订如下。

(2)第(1)款中删除第(b)项前的"或",在该项结尾处插入"或

(c)依照第206A条规定终止许可或提出限制(无论是否以拟采取的方式)。"

(3)第(3)款后插入:

"(3A)在终止许可或提出限制的情况下,决定通知必须说明终止或限制有效的期限。"

(4)第(4)款中删除第(b)项前的"或",在该项结尾处插入"或

(c) 针对获授权人依照第206A条开展的受监管活动终止获授权人的许可或提出限制。"

第20条 (1)第210条(政策声明)修订如下。

(2)第(1)款中第(a)项和第(b)项替换为:

"(a)依照本部分规定处以罚款、终止或限制;

(b)依照本部份规定处以罚款的数额;以及

(c)依照本部分规定提出的终止或限制有效的期限。"

(3)第(2)款中

(a)引言中"应"后插入"或终止或限制有效的期限应",

(b)第(c)项中"被处以罚款之人"替换为"针对其采取行动的人"。

(4)第(7)款"第206条"后插入"或第206A条"。

第21条 第212条第(2)款(计划管理人)中"上述职能"后插入"以及第十五A部分

functions conferred on it by or under Part 15A".

22 In section 219(3A)(scheme manager's power to require information), for "applying regulations under section 214B(3) above" substitute "determining the matters mentioned in section 214D(2)(a) and (b) above".

23 In section 221A(3)(delegation of functions of FSCS manager), after "management expenses of the scheme manager" insert "except where the function in question is one under Part 15A".

24 (1) Section 223 (FSCS manager's management expenses) is amended as follows.

(2) In subsection (3), in paragraph (c), after "214B" insert "or 214D".

(3) After that paragraph insert—

"(d) under Part 15A."

25 (1) Section 224A (functions under the Banking Act 2009) is amended as follows.

(2) The existing provision becomes subsection (1) of that section.

(3) After that subsection insert—

"(2) Any payment required to be made by the scheme manager by virtue of section 61 of that Act (special resolution regime: compensation) is to be treated for the purposes of this Part as an expense under the compensation scheme."

26 In section 348(5)(d)(restrictions on disclosure of confidential information by Authority etc), after "a person appointed" insert "to collect or update information under section 139E or".

27 In section 354(FSA's duty to co-operate with others), after subsection (1A) insert—

"(1B) In pursuing its financial stability objective, the Authority must take such steps as it considers appropriate to co-operate with other relevant bodies (including the Treasury and the Bank of England)."

28 In section 391 (publication), for subsection (11) substitute—

"(11) Section 425A(meaning of "consumers") applies for the purposes of this section."

29 (1) Section 392 (warning and decision notices: third party rights and access to evidence) is amended as follows.

(2) In paragraph (a)—

赋予其的职能”。

第22条 第219条第(3A)款(计划管理人要求提供信息的权力)[1]中“适用上述第214B条第(3)款规定的法规”替换为“决定上述第214D条第(2)款第(a)项和第(b)项所述事项”。

第23条 第221A条[2]第(3)款(委托金融服务补偿计划管理人职能)中“计划管理人管理支出”后插入“除第十五A部分规定的相关职能外”。

第24条 (1)第223条(金融服务补偿计划管理支出)修订如下。

(2)第(3)款第(c)项中“第214B条”后插入“或第214D条”。

(3)该款后插入:

“(d)第十五A部分规定。”

第25条 (1)第224A条(《2009年银行法》规定的职能)[3]修订如下。

(2)现有规定成为该条第(1)款。

(3)该款后插入:

“(2)计划管理人依照该法第61条规定(特别决议制度:补偿)要求支付的任何款项,就本部分规定而言,视为依照补偿计划进行的支出。”

第26条 第348条第(5)款第(d)项(对管理局披露保密信息的限制等)中“指定的”后插入“依照第139E条规定收集或更新信息或”。

第27条 第354条(管理局与他人合作的职责)第(1A)款[4]后插入:

“(1B)管理局在追求金融稳定目标时,必须采取其认为适当的措施与其他相关机构(包括财政部和英格兰银行)合作。”

第28条 第391条(公布)第(11)款替换为:

“(11)为施行本条规定适用第425A(‘消费者’的含义)规定。”

第29条 (1)第392条(预告通知和决定通知:第三方权利与证据取得)修订如下。

(2)第(a)项中

---

1 《2000年金融服务与市场法》第219条(3A)款为依照《2009年银行法》第176条第(6)款插入,参见http://www.legislation.gov.uk/ukpga/2009/1/section/176/prospective。——译者注

2 《2000年金融服务与市场法》第221A条依照《2009年银行法》第179条第(1)款插入,参见http://www.legislation.gov.uk/ukpga/2009/1/section/179/prospective。——译者注

3 《2000年金融服务与市场法》第224A条依照《2009年银行法》第180条插入,参见http://www.legislation.gov.uk/ukpga/2009/1/section/180/prospective。——译者注

4 《2000年金融服务与市场法》第354条第(1A)款为依照《2006年公司法》第964条第(5)款插入,参见http://www.legislation.gov.uk/ukpga/2006/46/section/964。——译者注

(a) after "63(3)," insert "63B(1),", and

(b) after "126(1)," insert "131H(1),".

(3) In paragraph (b)—

(a) after "63(4)," insert "63B(3),", and

(b) after "127(1)," insert "131H(4),".

30 After section 415 insert—

"*Powers of the Authority*

415A Powers of the Authority

Any power which the Authority has under any provision of this Act is not limited in any way by any other power which it has under any other provision of this Act."

31 In section 417(1)(definitions),after the definition of "UK authorised person" (but before the "and" at the end of it) insert—

""the UK financial system" has the meaning given in section 3;".

32 After section 425 insert—

"425A Consumers: regulated activities etc carried on by authorised persons

(1) This section has effect for the purposes of the provisions of this Act which apply this section.

(2) "Consumers" means persons who—

(a) use, have used or may use any of the services within subsection (3); or

(b) have relevant rights or interests in relation to any of those services.

(3) The services within this subsection are services provided by—

(a) authorised persons in carrying on regulated activities;

(b) authorised persons who are investment firms, or credit institutions, in providing relevant ancillary services; or

(c) persons acting as appointed representatives.

(4) A person ("P") has a "relevant right or interest" in relation to any services within subsection (3) if P has a right or interest—

(a) which is derived from, or is otherwise attributable to, the use of the services by others; or

(b) which may be adversely affected by the use of the services by persons acting on P's behalf or in a fiduciary capacity in relation to P.

(5) If a person is providing a service within subsection (3) as a trustee, the persons who are, have been or may be beneficiaries of the trust are to be treated as persons who use, have used or may use the service.

(6) A person who deals with another person ("A") in the course of A providing a service within subsection (3) is to be treated as using the service.

(a)"第63条第(3)款"后插入"第63B条第(1)款",

(b)"第126条第(1)款"后插入"第131H条第(1)款 "。

(3)(b)项中

(a)"第63条第(4)款"后插入"第63B条第(3)款",

(b)"第127条第(1)款"后插入"第131H条第(4)款"。

第30条 第415条后插入:

"管理局的权力

第415A条 管理局的权力

管理局依照本法任何规定享有的任何权力不以任何方式受到其依照本法任何其他规定享有的任何其他权力限制。"

第31条 第417条第(1)款(定义)中,"联合王国获授权人"定义后插入:

"'联合王国金融系统'具有第3条规定的含义"。

第32条 第425条后插入:

"**第425A条** 消费者:获授权人开展受监管活动等

(1)本条规定对本法中适用本条的规定有效。

(2)"消费者"系指

(a)使用、曾经使用或可能使用第(3)款规定范围的任何服务的人;或

(b)具有与第(3)款规定范围内任何服务相关的权利或利益。

(3)本款规定范围内的服务为由下列人提供的服务:

(a)获授权人在开展受监管活动时提供的服务;

(b)投资企业或信贷机构获授权人提供相关附属服务时提供的服务;或

(c)作为被任命代表行事的人提供的服务。

(4)当事人(以下简称P)如具有下列权利或利益,即为就第(3)款规定范围内的任何服务具有"相关权利或利益":

(a)从使用他人服务中产生或以其他方式归因于使用他人服务的权利或利益;或

(b)可能因使用代表P行事或具有与P相关委托地位的人提供的服务而受到不利影响的权利或利益。

(5)如当事人以受托人身份提供第(3)款规定范围内的服务,则该委托的受益人或者曾经或可能为该委托受益人的人视为使用、曾经使用或者可能使用该项服务的人。

(6)在另一人(以下简称A)提供第(3)款规定范围内的服务期间与A交易的人,视为使用该服务。

(7) In this section—

"credit institution" means—

(a) a credit institution authorised under the banking consolidation directive; or

(b) an institution which would satisfy the requirements for authorisation as a credit institution under that directive if it had its registered office (or if does not have one, its head office) in an EEA State;

"relevant ancillary service" means any service of a kind mentioned in Section B of Annex I to the markets in financial instruments directive the provision of which does not involve the carrying on of a regulated activity.

425B Consumers: regulated activities carried on by others

(1) This section has effect for the purposes of the provisions of this Act which apply this section.

(2) "Consumers" means persons who, in relation to regulated activities carried on otherwise than by authorised persons, would be consumers as defined by section 425A if the activities were carried on by authorised persons."

33 (1) Section 429 (Parliamentary control of statutory instruments) is amended as follows.

(2) In subsection (1)(a)—

(a) omit "404", and

(b) after "236(5), " insert "404G".

(3) In subsection (2), after "214B" insert ", 214D".

(4) In subsection (8), after "one made under section" insert "165A(2)(d) or".

34 (1) Schedule 1 (general provision about the FSA) is amended as follows.

(2) In paragraph 5(2)(a), after "paragraph 1(2)(a) to (d)" insert "or in determining or reviewing its strategy in relation to the financial stability objective".

(3) After paragraph 19A insert—

"Amounts required by rules to be paid to the Authority

19B Any amount (other than a fee) which is required by rules to be paid to the Authority may be recovered as a debt due to the Authority."

35 (1) In Schedule 4 (treaty rights), paragraph 1 is amended as follows.

(2) The existing provision becomes sub-paragraph (1) of that paragraph.

(3) In that sub-paragraph, omit the definition of "consumers".

(4) After that sub-paragraph insert—

"(2) Section 425A (meaning of "consumers") applies for the purposes of this Schedule."

(7)本条中

‘信贷机构’系指

(a)依照银行合并指令核准的信贷机构;或

(b)如其注册营业地在欧洲经济区国家(或总部,如无营业地)则复核依照该指令的信贷机构核准要求的机构。

‘相关附属服务’系指金融工具市场指令附录1第B条所述种类的任何服务,且提供服务不包括开展受监管活动。

第425B条　消费者:他人开展的受监管活动

(1)本条规定对本法中适用本条的规定有效。

(2)‘消费者’,系指就非获授权人开展的受监管活动而言,如该活动由获授权人开展则为第425A条定义的消费者的人。”

第33条　(1)第429条(行政性立法文件的议会控制)修订如下。

(2)第(1)款第(a)项

(a)删除“第404条”,

(b)“第236条第(5)款”后插入“第404G条”。

(3)第(2)款“第214B条”后插入“、第214D条”。

(4)第(8)款“依照”后插入“第165A条第(2)款第(d)项或”。

第34条　(1)附录一(金融服务法一般性条款)修订如下。

(2)第5条第(2)款第(a)项,在第1条第2款第(a)至第(d)项之后增加,“确定或复核其关于金融稳定目标的策略”。

(3)第19条之后增加

“依照规则向管理局支付的款项

19B　任何一会早规则应向管理局支付的款项(除了费用)可作为管理局的应收债务予以追偿。”

第35条　(1)附录4(条约权利)第1条修订如下。

(2)现有条文成为该条第(1)款。

(3)该款中删除“消费者”的定义。

(4)该款后插入:

“(2)为本附录之目的适用第425A条(‘消费者’的含义)。”

PART 2 AMENDMENTS OF OTHER LEGISLATION

Consumer Credit Act 1974

36 In section 25(2A)(b) of the Consumer Credit Act 1974 (evidence as to whether a licensee is a fit person), after sub-paragraph (i) insert—

"(ia) paragraph 13 of Schedule 1A to the Financial Services and Markets Act 2000; ".

Contracting Out (Functions Relating to National Savings) Order 1998

37 In article 3 of the Contracting Out (Functions Relating to National Savings) Order 1998 (contracting out of functions), after paragraph (2) insert—

"(3) Any function conferred on the Director under rules made under section 38 (7) of the Administration of Justice Act 1982 (court funds rules) may be exercised by, or by employees of, such person (if any) as may be authorised in that behalf by the Director."

Financial Services and Markets Act 2000 (Markets in Financial Instruments) (Modification of Powers) Regulations 2006

38 In the Financial Services and Markets Act 2000(Markets in Financial Instruments) (Modification of Powers)Regulations 2006, omit regulation 3 (b) (ii) (which made an amendment of the Financial Services and Markets Act 2000 superseded by this Act).

Banking Act 2009

39 The Banking Act 2009 is amended as follows.

40 In section 1(6)(table describing provisions of Part 1), in the entry relating to sections 33 to 48, for "48" substitute "48A".

41 In section 61(2)(b) (sources of compensation), for the words from "subject" to "below), " substitute "subject to section 214C of the Financial Services and Markets Act 2000 (limit on amount of special resolution regime payments), ".

42 In section 83(2)(h) (supplemental), omit "– inserted by section 171 below".

43 Omit section 171 (which made amendments of the Financial Services and Markets Act 2000 superseded by this Act).

44 In section 183(c)(interpretation of expressions for purposes of Part 5), omit "to "the financial system"".

45 In section 204(1)(a) (inter-bank payment systems : information), after "order" insert "or an order under section 206A".

46 Omit section 248 (which made an amendment of the Financial Services and Markets Act 2000 superseded by this Act).

第二部分　对其他立法的修订

《1974年消费信贷法》

第36条　《1974年消费信贷法》第25条第(2A)款第(b)项(许可证持有人是否为适当人选的证据)(i)小项后插入:

(ia)《2000年金融服务与市场法》附录1A第13条”。

《1998年外包法令(国民储蓄相关职能)》

第37条　《1998年外包法令(国民储蓄相关职能)》第3条(职能外包)第(2)款后插入:

“(3)依照《1982年司法行政法》第38条第(7)款规定(法院经费规则)制定的规则授予理事的任何职能可由理事就该事项授权的人(如有)或其雇员行使。”

《〈2000年金融服务与市场法〉(金融工具市场)(权力修改)2006年条例》

第38条　《〈2000年金融服务与市场法〉(金融工具市场)(权力修改)2006年条例》中删除第3条第(b)款第(ii)项(其对《2000年金融服务与市场法》的修订由本法取代)。

《2009年银行法》

第39条　《2009年银行法》修订如下。

第40条　第1条第(6)款(描述第一部分规定的表格)与第33条至第48条相关的条目中“48”替换为“48A”。

第41条　第61条第(2)款第(b)项(补偿来源)中自“受”至“下述”的词句替换为“符合《2000年金融服务与市场法》第214C条规定(对特别决议制度支付金额的限制),”

第42条　第83条第(2)款第(h)项(补充规定)中删除(依照下述第171条插入)。

第43条　删除第171条(其对《2000年金融服务与市场法》修订由本法取代)。

第44条　第183条第(c)款(为第五部分之目的进行的表述释义)中删除“向“金融系统””。

第45条　第204条第(1)款第(a)项(银行间支付系统:信息)中“命令”后插入“或第206A条规定的命令”。

第46条　删除第248条(其对《2000年金融服务与市场法》修订由本法取代)。

47 In section 250 (2) (collection of information by FSA relevant to financial stability)—

(a) after "section 165" insert "or 165A", and

(b) after "as qualified" insert ", in the case of the section 165 power, ".

48 (1) Section 259 (statutory instruments) is amended as follows.

(2) In the table in subsection (3), omit the entry relating to section 171.

(3) In that table, after the entry relating to section 204 insert—

(4) In subsection (5), omit paragraph (o) and the "and" before it.

"206A	Services forming part of recognised inter-bank payment systems	Draft affirmative esolution"

4/2010 445966 19585

第47条 第250条第(2)款(管理局收集与金融稳定相关的信息)

(a)"第165条"后插入"或第165A条 ",
(b)"合资格的"后插入",在第165条规定的权力情况下"。
第48条 (1)第259条(行政性立法文件)修订如下。
(2)第(3)款表格中删除与第171条相关的条目。
(3)该表格中与第204条相关的条目后插入:
(4)第(5)款中删除第(o)项和该项前的"以及"。

"第206A条	属于经认可的银行间支付系统的服务	草案赞成决议"

4/2010 445966 19585

Glossary 词汇表

absolute privilege	专有特权
Accountant in Bankruptcy	破产核算员
Actions for damages	损害赔偿诉讼
Additional Part Ⅳ permission	附加第四部分许可
administration	(破产)管理
administration orders	接管令
admissibility of statements made to investigators	对调查人陈述的可采性
affirmative resolution procedure	赞成决议程序
ancillary credit business	附属信贷业务
appeals	复议/上诉
applicant	申请人
appointed person	被任命人
approved person	被批准人
assets requirement	资产要求
associate	关联方
associated undertaking	关联企业
at the material time	在重要期间
Attorney General	司法部长
authorised persons	获授权人
authorised unit trust schemes	获授权单位信托计划
"banking consolidation directive"	银行合并指令
banking co-ordination directives	银行协调指令
bankruptcy petition	破产呈请
building society	住房互助会
cancel	取消
categories of investment	投资类别
Chief Registrar of Friendly Societies	互相保险协会首席注册官
class, kind	类别

续表

client, customer	客户
clients' money	客户资金
code of practice	行为准则
collective investment scheme	集合投资计划
Commencement Information	实施日期
commitment	约定
communicate	传播
community instrument	共同体法律文件
community obligation	共同体义务
compensation	损害赔偿/赔偿/补偿
competent authority	主管机关
competent persons	适格人员
competition scrutiny	竞争审查
compulsory jurisdiction	强制管辖权
confidential information	保密信息
connected person	关联人
Consolidated Fund	统一基金
constitution	组织制度
consultation procedures	磋商程序
Consumer Credit Act	《消费信贷法》
Consumer Credit Act business	《消费信贷法》业务
consumer hire business	消费租用业务
Consumer Panel	消费者小组
consumer redress scheme	消费者赔偿计划
contravention	违反
control of business transfers	业务转让控制
controller	控制人
controlled activity	受控活动
controlled function	受监管职能
cost benefit analysis	成本效益分析
county court	郡法院
conviction on indictment	经公诉程序定罪

续表

Court of Session	(苏格兰)高等民事法院
credit card cheques	信用卡支票
credit-token agreement	信用代价券协议
credit union	信用合作社
decide	决定
decision on application	申请的决定
defence	辩护/抗辩
desirability	有利于
determination	决定
direction	指示
directive	指令
Director General of Fair Trading(the Director)	公平交易总理事(总理事)
Director of Savings	储蓄理事
disciplinary powers	惩戒权
discontinuance and suspension of listing	中止上市和暂停上市
Disqualification	取消资格
dissolution	解散
EEA	欧洲经济区
EEA passport rights	欧洲经济区护照权利
effecting or carrying out (contracts of long-term insurance)	订立或实施(长期保险合同)
enactment	成文法
endorsement of codes	准则的认可
entry of premises under warrant	持核准令进入现场
essential information	重要信息
evidential provisions	证据规则
excluded material	被排除材料
excluded scheme	被排除计划
exclusion clauses	排除条款
executives of authorised persons	被授权人高层管理人员
exempt offers	豁免发行
exempt person	享有豁免权的人

续表

exemption order	豁免令
exemptions from disclosure	披露豁免
facilities and information in UK	在联合王国的设施和信息
final notice	最后通知
financial penalties	经济处罚
financial promotion rules	金融推介规则
Financial Services and Markets Tribunal	金融服务与市场裁判所
Financial Services Authority(the Authority)	金融服务管理局(管理局)
first life insurance directive	第一人寿保险指令
first non-life insurance directive	第一非人寿保险指令
former underwriting member	先前承保成员
friendly societies	互相保险协会
Friendly Societies Commission	互相保险协会委员会
funding of the legal assistance scheme	法律协助计划拨款
general guidance	一般性指引
general notice	常规通知
general prohibition	一般禁止性规定
grant the application	批准申请
group	集团
home state regulator	母国监管机关
host state regulator	所在国监管机关
immediate group	关联团体
Implementation Standards for Principles for Sound Compensation Practices	《良好薪酬实践原则执行标准》
imposition of requirements	提出要求
incident	事由
incoming firm	进入联合王国的企业
independent inquiries	独立调查
Individually recognised overseas schemes	单独认可的境外计划
industrial and provident societies	行业节俭互助会
initial report	初步报告

续表

Inland Revenue	国内税务局
injunction	强制令
insolvency practitioner	破产执行人
interdict	禁令
inquiry	调查
insolvency rules	破产规则
instruments creating or acknowledging indebtedness	创设或承认债务的工具
insurance business rules	保险业务规则
insurance business transfer scheme or banking business transfer scheme	保险、银行业务转让计划
lay panel	非专业人员小组
Legal assistance scheme	法律协助计划
liability in damages	损害赔偿责任
liquidator	清算人
listed activity	列出活动
listed securities	上市证券
listing particulars	上市公告书
listing rules	上市规则
Lloyd's syndicates	劳合社辛迪加
loans secured on land	土地抵押贷款
London Stock Exchange Limited	伦敦证券交易所有限公司
management expenses	管理费用
margin of solvency	清偿能力限度
market abuse	市场滥用
maximum consideration	最高对价
member of the governing body of the Financial Services Authority	金融服务管理局管理组织成员
members of the professions	行业成员
minor and consequential amendments	细微及后续修订
Minister of the Crown	内阁阁员
modification or waiver of rules	修改或放弃执行规则

续表

money award	判付赔偿金
monitoring and enforcement	监督和执法
negative resolution procedures	反对决议程序
non-executive committee	非执行委员会
non-listing prospectus	非上市招股说明书
notices of discontinuance	终止通知
negative resolution procedure	反对决议程序
offer	要约
offeror	要约人
officer	官员/高级职员
official listing	正式上市
official list	正式上市名单
Official Receiver	破产管理署署长
open-ended investment company	开放式投资公司
operator, trustee or depositary	执行人、受托人或托管人
order for specific performance	(苏格兰)实际履行令
overall position	整体状况
overseas regulator	境外监管机关
own-initiative power	自行决定行使的权力
Panel on Takeovers and Mergers	收购与合并委员会
parent undertaking	母公司
participating interest	参与权益
partnership	合伙
Part Ⅳ permission	第四部分许可
permanent trustee	永久托管人
petitions	申请
policy holder	保单持有人
policy of insurance	保单
pooling	汇集
power of intervention	干预权
practices	惯例

续表

practice of the profession	该行业的执业活动
practitioner panel	从业人员小组
price stabilising rules	价格稳定规则
private person	个人
proceedings	程序
professional body	行业机构
promoter	推广人
prospectus	招股说明书
protected item	受保护项目
protection of consumers	保护消费者
Provisions included in the Authority's code by reference to the City Code	参照金融城准则而纳入管理局准则的规定
public authority	公共机关
public censure	公开谴责
purport to	意图
qualification	资格
qualifying person	合资格人
qualifying office	合资格的办事处
qualifying scheme	相关计划
disqualifying office	官员免职
Receivership	破产清算
receiver	破产清算人
recipient	接受者
recognised clearing house	获认可的结算所
recognised investment exchange	获认可的投资交易所
recognized overseas scheme	获认可的境外计划
recovery plan	恢复计划
registrar of companies	公司注册署
registration of listing particulars	上市公告书的登记
regular user	一般用户
regulated activities	受监管活动

续表

regulating provision	监管规定
relevant authorities	相关机关
relevant long-term insurer	相关长期业务保险公司
relevant person	相关人
remedial direction	救济指示
remedy or relief	救济或济助
repayment provision	还款规定
repeals	废除
representation	陈述
request	请求
resolution plan	解决计划
restitution orders	退赔令
restricted circles	有限人群
restrictions on promotion	推介限制
retirement benefits scheme	退休福利计划
rule-making instruments	规则制定文件
rule-making power	规则制定权
scheme manager	计划管理人
scheme operator	计划执行人
secondary material	间接材料
Secretary of State	国务大臣
Sequestration award	扣押裁决
Senior President of Tribunals	高级裁判所长官
set of conditions	一组条件
settlement	财产授予契约
short position being open	空头持仓
single merket directive	单一市场指令
single property schemes	单一不动产计划
skilled person	掌握技能的人员
specified	规定的/特定的
sponsors	保荐人

续表

standard scale	标准等级
statement of policy	政策声明
statements and codes	声明和准则
subject information provisions	主题信息规定
subordinate legislation	附属立法
subsidiary undertaking	子公司
sufficient evidence	充分证据
summary conviction	经简易程序定罪
supervisory notice	监督通知
takeover offer	购买要约
territories, areas or localities	领土、地区或地方
the acquirer	购买人
the authorised person concerned	相关获授权人
the City Code on Takeovers and Mergers	《金融城购买与合并准则》
the Court of Session Act 1988	《1988 年高等民事法院法》
the defaulter	违反人
the depositor, the deposit-taker	存款人、吸收存款人
the deposit-taker	吸收存款人
the depositor	有款人
the Director of the Serious Fraud Office	严重欺诈行为办公室主任
the Financial Services Compensation Scheme	金融服务补偿计划
the interested parties	利害关系人
the investigating authority	调查机关
the Lord Advocate	(苏格兰)检察总长
the ombudsman scheme	申诉专员计划
the period for consideration	审核期间
the respondent	被申诉人
the scheme details	计划详情
the Treasury	财政部
threshold conditions	准入条件
transferee	受让人

续表

treaty firm	条约企业
Tribunal	裁判所
trust deeds for creditors	债权人信托契约
TUPE	营业转让法
UK policy	联合王国保单
unauthorised persons	未获授权人
unit trust scheme	单位信托计划
unlawful communication	非法传播
variation etc. on the Authority's own initiative	管理局自行发起的变更等
victim	受害人
voluntary arrangements	自愿安排
voluntary jurisdiction	自愿管辖权
winding up	清算

Postscript

China's capital market was established and has developed on the basis of learning from the experience of major foreign capital markets. As a result, China is constantly faced with issues for which it needs to acquire knowledge of, learn from and refer to examples set by foreign capital market systems. However, the current Chinese translations of foreign securities legislations are not sufficiently systematic, professional, authoritative and are often inaccurate. The acquisition of a comprehensive and precise knowledge of the operating systems and regulatory rules of major foreign capital markets is essential for China to benefit from the experience developed and lessons drawn by these markets, and thus is objectively necessary for China to further improve the construction of its capital market system, promote a stable and healthy development of the said system and enhance the participation of Chinese market entities in international competition. For the aforementioned purposes, the China Securities Regulatory Commission(CSRC) has hereby initiated the project to translate the most important foreign capital market legislations published as the Digest of Legislation Related to Foreign Capital Markets (hereinafter referred to as the "Digest"). The Digest is composed of such translations after editing, creating an authoritative platform through which the most significant laws and regulations for major foreign securities markets are to be introduced to China.

To facilitate the implementation of the project, at the CSRC we established a mechanism which consisted of entrusting the translation to a translation team through a bidding process and the translation review to relevant experts to ensure the quality of the translation. In the bidding process, the translation team was selected based on its competences in legal translation and the quality of its trial translation. On the other hand, the translation draft was reviewed and validated by individuals from relevant units and departments of the CSRC and prestigious universities deemed to be experts in the concerned foreign languages and the Chinese language, well versed in Chinese and relevant foreign laws and having an in-depth knowledge of both Chinese and foreign capital markets. In addition, the CSRC has designated those experts, whose work experience and educational background are the most relevant to the subject matters dealt with in specific sections of the translation draft, to revise the same. Every section was examined respectively by two experts in an

后 记

中国资本市场是在学习、借鉴境外主要资本市场经验的基础上建立并发展起来的。在此过程中,仍不断遇到需要了解、借鉴、参考境外市场制度的问题。但是,现有的境外证券法律的中文译本,存在着系统性、专业性、权威性、准确性不足等问题。全面、准确掌握境外主要资本市场运行制度、监管规则的信息,是科学借鉴发达市场经验教训的必要基础,是进一步完善市场制度建设、推进市场稳定健康发展、推动市场主体参与国际竞争的客观要求。为此,中国证监会启动了打造介绍境外市场法律制度权威平台的项目,即组织翻译主要资本市场重要法律规则,并将翻译成果编辑成《境外资本市场重要法律文献译丛》(以下简称《译丛》)公开出版发行。

为了做好此项工作,我们建立了"竞标择优确定翻译人员、专家评审保证翻译质量"的工作机制。一方面,以法律文献翻译实力和试译稿质量为标准,采用竞标择优方式选定翻译单位;另一方面,从证监会系统相关单位、部门和知名高校院所等推荐的"三通"专家(即精通中外语言、精通中外法律、精通中外资本市场)中,抽选工作学习经历与具体项目最相关的专家负责审校翻译初稿,每部分译稿由两位专家分别独立审校,再集体讨论定稿,并由一位权威专家负责统稿审校工作。

independent manner and finished after collective discussions. Their revised version was eventually submitted to an authoritative expert for final review and overall proofreading for the purpose of consistency.

As one volume of the Digest, *Financial Services and Markets Act 2000*, is about to come to the press, as the undertaker for its translation and publication we would like to express our earnest and profound gratitude to the many organizations and individuals as follows. First of all, we would like to thank the CSRC's Department of Legal Affairs and its members involved in the project, who provided us with comprehensive and detailed arrangement and guidance, with the *Markets in Financial Instruments Directive of the European Union (MiFID)* already published under their organization acting as a model for us. Secondly, our thanks are due to the translation team from Beijing Spirit Translation Co., Ltd. led by Xu Liqun and the panel of review composed of ten experts, including Su Yanxin; together they completed the translation and the review work conscientiously and rigorously. Our thanks go to Jiao Jinhong who, amid his heavy schedule, took up the overall and final review of the work and contributed a preface for this book. Thirdly, we owe our gratitude to relevant departments and units of the CSRC and their members involved in the project, as well as relevant experts, for the valuable support they gave to our endeavor. Finally, we thank the staff at Law Press·China, especially Ms. Shen Xiaoying and Ms. Wang Jinjing, who contributed enormously to the editing and publication of the book. Again, we address our most sincere thanks to all those who are mentioned above!

Due to time constraints pertaining to the translation and editing work, errors and inaccuracies in the book will be inevitable. Your comments, criticism and corrections will be welcome.

Zhengzhou Commodity Exchange

November 2013

在《译丛》之《英国 2000 年金融服务与市场法》即将付梓之际，作为本书翻译出版的承办单位，我们有许多发自肺腑的感谢之辞：首先，感谢中国证监会法律部及其相关工作人员，作为《译丛》的组织者，他们为本书的翻译和出版做了全面且细致的统筹和指导，其组织完成的《译丛》之《欧盟金融工具市场指令》为本书树立了榜样；其次，感谢许立群带领的北京思必锐翻译有限责任公司的翻译团队，以及苏彦新等 10 位评审专家，他们以认真负责的态度和严谨务实的作风，完成了翻译和审校工作；感谢焦津洪在百忙中拨冗亲自承担总译校工作，并欣然为本书作序；再次，感谢证监会其他相关部门及其工作人员和有关专家，对我们工作的支持；最后，感谢法律出版社及其相关工作人员，尤其是沈小英女士、王津京女士为本书的编辑、出版做了大量工作。我们在此一并致以诚挚的谢意！

由于编译时间有限，书中难免有疏漏、不足之处，欢迎读者批评指正。

郑州商品交易所

2013 年 11 月

图书在版编目(CIP)数据

英国2000年金融服务与市场法/中国证券监督管理委员会组织编译. —北京:法律出版社, 2014.2
(境外资本市场重要法律文献译丛)
ISBN 978-7-5118-5731-6

Ⅰ.①英… Ⅱ.①中… Ⅲ.①金融法—研究—英国
Ⅳ.①D956.122.8

中国版本图书馆CIP数据核字(2013)第286207号

责任编辑/王津京 **装帧设计**/贾丹丹

出版/法律出版社 **编辑统筹**/财税出版分社
总发行/中国法律图书有限公司 **经销**/新华书店
印刷/北京中科印刷有限公司 **责任印制**/吕亚莉

开本/787毫米×1092毫米 1/16 **印张**/71.25 **字数**/1460千
版本/2014年2月第1版 **印次**/2014年2月第1次印刷

法律出版社/北京市丰台区莲花池西里7号(100073)
电子邮件/info@lawpress.com.cn **销售热线**/010-63939792/9779
网址/www.lawpress.com.cn **咨询电话**/010-63939796

中国法律图书有限公司/北京市丰台区莲花池西里7号(100073)
全国各地中法图分、子公司电话:
第一法律书店/010-63939781/9782 **西安分公司**/029-85388843 **重庆公司**/023-65382816/2908
上海公司/021-62071010/1636 **北京分公司**/010-62534456 **深圳公司**/0755-83072995

书号:ISBN 978-7-5118-5731-6 **定价**:380.00元